2004

2004

The Kurdish Question in U.S. Foreign Policy

The Kurdish Question in U.S. Foreign Policy

A Documentary Sourcebook

Lokman I. Meho

Documentary Reference Collections

Westport, Connecticut
London

Library of Congress Cataloging-in-Publication Data

The Kurdish question in U.S. foreign policy : a documentary sourcebook / [compiled] by
  Lokman I. Meho.
      p.   cm.—(Documentary reference collections)
      Includes bibliographical references and index.
      ISBN 0–313–31435–7 (alk. paper)
      1. United States—Foreign relations—Iraq—Sources.   2. United States—Foreign
relations—Turkey—Sources.   3. United States—Foreign relations—Iran—Sources.   4.
Kurds—Government policy—United States—History—20th century—Sources.   5.
Kurds—Government policy—Middle East—History—20th century—Sources.   6. Iraq—Foreign
relations—United States—Sources.   7. Turkey—Foreign relations—United States—Sources.   8
Iran—Foreign relations—United States—Sources.   I. Meho, Lokman I., 1968–   II. Series.
E183.8.I57K87   2004
327.730566′7—dc22   2003057996

British Library Cataloguing in Publication Data is available.

Library of Congress Catalog Card Number: 2003057996
ISBN: 0–313–31435–7

First published in 2004

Praeger Publishers, 88 Post Road West, Westport, CT 06881
An imprint of Greenwood Publishing Group, Inc.
www.praeger.com

Printed in the United States of America

The paper used in this book complies with the
Permanent Paper Standard issued by the National
Information Standards Organization (Z39.48–1984).

10 9 8 7 6 5 4 3 2 1

To my parents

CONTENTS

PREFACE

The idea behind compiling this documentary sourcebook originated from several studies that examined the information-seeking behavior of social science faculty studying the Kurdish question.[1] In particular, Meho and Haas found that the majority of historians and political scientists who study the Kurds use U.S. government documents in at least half of their publications on the topic. These scholars have, on the other hand, identified several interrelated barriers to using these documents, which can be summarized as follows: (1) Their university libraries do not list all the acquired government materials in the online catalog, thus, making access to these materials very difficult; (2) The collection of government publications in their university libraries is very small; (3) Because of cataloging problems, they find it difficult to determine which publications their libraries have or do not have; and (4) The classification scheme of government materials is confusing to them.

The Kurdish Question in U.S. Foreign Policy: A Documentary Sourcebook assembles a comprehensive selection of documents that provides the ideological and political grounds for United States' policy towards the Kurds in the twentieth century. Students, educators, researchers, news agencies, and policy makers interested in the Kurdish question will find this sourcebook as an indispensable tool for any research or reading on the topic. Over 527 items are included in this sourcebook ranging from congressional documents and presidential documents to Department of State documents and those of the Central Intelligence Agency. Also included are books, monographs, scholarly journal articles, and chapters in books, both governmental and non-governmental. The publication date of the documents and items included or identified range from the 1920s through the year 2002.

The sourcebook is divided into three parts: (I) Essays; (II) Full-Text Documents; and (III) Non-Full-Text Items. The Essay part includes two chapters. In the first chapter, Gunter examines three temporal periods of U.S. foreign policy toward the Kurds: the World War I period (briefly), the Kissinger period during the 1970s (briefly), and the more recent stage in the 1990s. In particular, Gunter analyzes why U.S. foreign policy tends to treat the Iraqi Kurds as "good" Kurds, while it considers the Turkish Kurds to be "bad" Kurds. Support for the Iraqi Kurds is perceived as supportive of overall U.S. foreign policy against Saddam Hussein's Iraq. Turkey, however, is seen as a valuable geostrategic NATO ally necessary to support to maintain its continuing allegiance. In the second chapter, Meho and Nehme discuss the Kissinger period in detail and the 1991 episode in briefly. They analyze these two episodes within the context of U.S. foreign policy toward self-determination movements as well as U.S. intervention in Third World countries.

---

[1]See Lokman I. Meho and Helen R. Tibbo, "Modeling the Information-Seeking Behavior of Social Scientists: Ellis's Study Revisited," Journal of the American Society for Information Science and Technology 54, no. 6 (April 2003): 569-586; Lokman I. Meho and Stephanie W. Haas, "Information-Seeking Behavior and Use of Social Science Faculty Studying Stateless Nations: A Case Study." *Library & Information Science Research* 23, no. 1 (May 2001): 5-25; Lokman I. Meho and Diane H. Sonnenwald, "Citation Ranking Versus Peer Evaluation of Senior Faculty Research Performance: A Case Study of Kurdish Scholarship." *Journal of the American Society for Information Science* 51, no. 2 (January 2000): 123-138.

The Full-Text part provides a chronological list of documents subdivided into several sections according to the original source: *The Congressional Record, Foreign Relations of the United States, American Foreign Policy: Current Documents, U.S. Department of State Dispatch, Weekly Compilation of Presidential Documents*, and several other sources. Although the majority of full-text documents included in this sourcebook was available online free of charge, they were included in this sourcebook for several reasons, most importantly:

(1) Any search on the Kurds in an online source such as the *Congressional Record* or *FirstGov* (both described below) will result in thousands of records. The time required to sift through these records to determine which documents are relevant to a particular topic on the Kurds can be overwhelming if not impossible; and

(2) There are too many government sources to use to identify and locate relevant materials on the Kurds. This sourcebook both reduces the time needed on behalf of the scholars to identify relevant documents and provides them with a guide for identifying subsequently published documents.

The Non-Full-Text part includes governmental and non-governmental sources, primarily in the form of books, monographs, scholarly journal articles, and chapters in books that discuss U.S. foreign policy towards the Kurds. This part also includes CIA, Department of State, and Presidential or national security documents in the custody of the National Archives of the United States.

All items included in the Non-Full-Text part are accompanied by 50-300 words-long annotations written by the compiler himself or extracted from sources such as book reviews and periodical databases. Items in this part are divided into four sections: General, Iran, Iraq, and Turkey and then arranged alphabetically by author name. Because many titles in this and other parts of the *Sourcebook* cover more than one geographical area or topic, a comprehensive subject index is provided at the end of the book.

Documents and items included in this sourcebook were gleaned from many print and electronic sources. Before discussing these sources, it should be noted that over the last few years, the Internet, particularly the World Wide Web, has become one of the primary vehicles for the dissemination of U.S. government information. Virtually every government agency has a web site today and many provide the full-text of their publications free of charge. Moreover, while many government publications continue to be available in print or microfiche formats, others have been discontinued and are now published exclusively on the web. In some instances, information that was not available in print is now available on the web. Despite this, a major portion of U.S. government information is still not on the web, and what is available is selective and tend to focus on recently published materials.

Most of the sources listed below are published or disseminated by the Government Printing Office (GPO). The GPO (www.gpo.gov/) prints, binds, and distributes government publications, and through its Office of Superintendent of Documents, sells selected publications, manages *GPO Access* (see below) for distributing electronic media, administers the Federal Depository Library Program, and performs related services. The sources or tools used to create this sourcebook are divided into separate sections representing the different branches of the government.[2]

GENERAL TOOLS

FIRSTGOV. WEB. *FirstGov* (www.firstgov.gov/) describes itself as "the first-ever government website to provide the public with easy, one-stop access to all online U.S. Federal Government resources." Managed through the General Services Administration,

---

[2]Books used to identify and describe these sources include: Peter Hernon, *U.S. Government on the Web: Getting the Information You Need*, 2nd ed. (Englewood, CO: Libraries Unlimited, 2001); Joe Morehead, *Introduction to United States Government Information Sources*, 6th ed. (Englewood, CO: Libraries Unlimited, 1999); Greg R. Notess, *Government Information on the Internet*, 3rd ed. (Lanham, MD: Bernan Press, 2000); and Jean L. Sears and Marilyn K. Moody, *Using Government Information Sources: Electronic and Print*, 3rd ed. (Englewood, CO: Libraries Unlimited, 2001).

FirstGov attempts to provide access to over 50 million pages of government information, services, and online transactions through a powerful search engine. A major part of *FirstGov*'s opening screen offers a list of topics divided into broad subject categories; the most relevant to the Kurdish question is "Defense and Global Affairs." Clicking on this topic takes the information seeker to a page of more specific and direct links to Federal government web sites, such as U.S. Department of State (www.state. gov/) through "Foreign Policy" link, and to different publications, such as *Country Reports on Human Rights Practices* (see below). First-time users of this site should carefully read the "Search Tips" screen so that they can conduct searches as effectively as possible (accessible through the "Help" screen). *FirstGov* provides two search options: basic and advanced. Because *FirstGov* organizes searches through millions of records, and that the results often depend on how well a user knows the subject of the search and the kinds of words to choose in conducting that search, it is advisable to use the advanced search.

GPO Access. WEB. U.S. Government Printing Office. Superintendent of Documents (www.access.gpo.gov/). The *GPO Access* initiative provides free online access to many government databases and information sources. The site also provides access to many full-text materials, such as the full-text of *Congressional Record* (from 1995 on). *GPO Access* is continually expanding, and the fact that it is free of charge to users makes it, along with *FirstGov* one of the most important starting points for finding and using U.S. government resources in electronic formats.

U.S. Government Periodicals Index. PRINT, CD-ROM. Bethesda, MD: Congressional Information Service, Inc., 1988-. Quarterly. This is the most comprehensive index of U.S. government periodicals. It indexes over 170 journals issued by federal government agencies, such as the Army, Marines, Navy, and Air Force. Titles covered range from the popular to the research journal. A previous CD-ROM version titled *US Government Periodicals Index on CD-ROM* has been discontinued.

CONGRESS[3]

CIS/Index. PRINT, CD-ROM. Bethesda, MD: Congressional Information Service, 1970-. Monthly. *CIS/Index* is a comprehensive index to the publications of the U.S. Congress. Publications indexed include hearings, committee prints, House and Senate reports and documents, Senate executive reports, Senate treaty documents, and special publications of the House and Senate. Publications of joint committees and subcommittees, special commissions, special committees, and other congressionally affiliated agencies are also indexed. Coverage extends back to 1970. *CIS/Index* is available as a web version within *Congressional Universe* (see below).

Congressional Record Index: Proceedings and Debates of the ... Congress. PRINT, WEB. GPO, 1873-to-present. Semi-monthly. Also available through the web from the Government Printing Office's *GPO Access* web site (1983 on). Commercial online services, such as *Congressional Universe* and *Westlaw* also provide access to the index and full-text of documents published from 1985 on. *Congressional Record Index* is a subject and name index providing bi-weekly access to the contents of the daily *Congressional Record*. In the cumulated, bound, annual index, page numbers are changed to reflect the single numbering sequence of the bound volumes.

Congressional Universe. WEB. Bethesda, MD: Congressional Information Service, 1970-. *Congressional Universe* is a comprehensive information system covering all aspects of congressional activities. A major component of the system is an electronic version of the *CIS/Index*, providing coverage back to 1970. In addition, *Congressional Universe* includes the full-text of a great number of congressional publications (e.g., *Congressional Record*) that are indexed and abstracted in *CIS/Index*.

---

[3]Full-text of articles from such newspapers as *The Christian Science Monitor, The Herald Tribune, The New Republic, The New York Times*, and *The Washington Post* that are inserted in the *Congressional Record* are not included in this sourcebook due to copyright restrictions.

DEPARTMENT OF STATE

The Department of State's web site (www. state.gov/) is a rich source of information about other countries and is the single best source for understanding official foreign policy of the United States. Apart from information about the department and its services to U.S. citizens, the web site provides information, for example, about the different countries and regions of the world and international topics and issues. Under "Countries and Regions" (www.state.gov/countries/), a user can find the six principal bureaus that cover U.S. global relationships: African Affairs; East Asian and Pacific Affairs; European and Eurasian Affairs (includes New Independent States of the former U.S.S.R.); Near Eastern Affairs; South Asian Affairs; and Western Hemisphere Affairs. Each of these bureaus is the touchstone between the policy developed by the President and Secretary in Washington, D.C., and the immediate reporting and observations of America's hundreds of foreign missions around the globe. Through "International Topics and Issues" and its sub-topics, a user can access several important information sources that discuss the Kurds, including:

Annual Report on International Religious Freedom Report. PRINT, WEB. Washington, DC: Bureau of Democracy, Human Rights, and Labor, 1999-. Annual. (www.state.gov/g/drl/irf/rpt/). This report is issued by the Senate Committee on Foreign Relations and submitted annually to the Congress by the Department of State. The law provides that the Secretary of State shall transmit to Congress by September 1 of each year, or the first day thereafter on which the appropriate House of Congress is in session, "an Annual Report on International Religious Freedom supplementing the most recent Human Rights Reports by providing additional detailed information with respect to matters involving international religious freedom." This annual report includes 195 reports on countries worldwide. Full-text of reports for the years 1999-2002 on Iraq (the only country reportedly to persecute the Kurds on religious bases) are included in this source and can be found at the following addresses:

- 1999: www.state.gov/www/global/human_ rights/irf/irf_rpt/1999/irf_iraq99.html

- 2000: www.state.gov/www/global/human_ rights/irf/irf_rpt/irf_iraq.html

- 2001: www.state.gov/g/drl/rls/irf/2001/5693. htm

- 2002: www.state.gov/g/drl/rls/irf/2002/13996. htm

Background Notes. PRINT. WEB. Washington, DC: GPO, 1964-. Irregular. (www.state. gov/r/pa/ei/bgn/). Each issue of *Background Notes* provides basic information on an individual country. A profile of the country starts each *Note*, and provides brief statistical and factual information. The *Background Notes* include a broad overview of a country and its people, history, economy, geography, and government. *Notes* also includes a discussion of U.S. relations with the country and the country's relationships with other countries. They are updated and/or revised as they are received from regional bureaus and are added to the database of the Department of State web site.

Country Reports on Human Rights Practices. PRINT, WEB. Washington, DC: U.S. GPO, 1977-. Annual. (www.state.gov/g/drl/hr/ c1470.htm). This report is issued as a joint committee print (House Committee on International Relations and Senate Committee on Foreign Relations) and submitted annually to the Congress by the Department of State. The report covers internationally recognized individual, civil, political, and worker rights, as set forth in the Universal Declaration of Human Rights. The human rights reports reflect a year of effort by hundreds of State Department and other U.S. Government employees. The U.S. embassies around the world which prepare the initial drafts of the reports, gather information throughout the year from a variety of sources, including contacts across the political spectrum, government officials, jurists, military sources, journalists, human rights monitors, academics, and labor union members. The draft reports are then reviewed by the U.S. Bureau of Human Rights and Humanitarian Affairs, in cooperation with other relevant offices in the State Department. As they corroborate, analyze, and edit the reports, Department officers draw on their own additional sources of information. These include reports and consultations with U.S. and other human rights groups, foreign government officials, representatives from the U.N. and other international and regional organizations and institutions, and experts from academia and the media. The Report covers human rights violations around the world. It describes a world where people who by right are born free and with dignity too often suffer the cruelties of authorities who deprive them of their rights in order to perpetuate their own power. It mainly covers countries that are ruled by dictators or rent by armed conflict, where bullets, torture, arbitrary detention, rape, disappearances, and other abuses are used to silence those who struggle for political freedom; to crush those whose ethnicity, gender, race or religion mark them for discrimination; or to frighten and mistreat those who have no defenses. Documents violations and domestic and international reaction. Full-text of reports for the years 1996-2001 on Iran, Iraq, Syria, Turkey, and other countries can be found at the following addresses:

- 1996: www.state.gov/www/global/human_right s/1996_hrp_report/96hrp_report_toc.html

- 1997: www.state.gov/www/global/human_right s/1997_hrp_report/97hrp_report_toc.html

- 1998: www.state.gov/www/global/human_right s/1998_hrp_report/98hrp_report_toc.html

- 1999: www.state.gov/g/drl/rls/hrrpt/1999/

- 2000: www.state.gov/g/drl/rls/hrrpt/2000/

- 2001: www.state.gov/g/drl/rls/hrrpt/2001/

Foreign Relations of the United States. PRINT, WEB. U.S. Department of State. Bureau of Public Affairs. Office of the Historian, 1818-. Irregular. This series presents the official documentary historical record of major U.S. foreign policy decisions and significant diplomatic activity. The series, which is produced by the State Department's Office of the Historian, began in 1861 and now comprises more than 350 individual volumes. The volumes published over the last two decades increasingly contain declassified records from all the foreign affairs agencies. Foreign Relations volumes contain documents from Presidential libraries, Departments of State and Defense, National Security Council, Central Intelligence Agency, Agency for International Development, and other foreign affairs agencies, as well as the private papers of individuals involved in formulating U.S. foreign policy. In general, the editors choose documentation that illuminates policy formulation and major aspects and repercussions of its execution. Volumes published over the past few years have expanded the scope of the series in two important ways: first by including documents from a wider range of government agencies, particularly those involved with intelligence activity and covert actions, and second by including transcripts prepared from Presidential tape recordings. A staff of approximately 20 historians and editors at the Office of the Historian in the Department of State compile and prepare the volumes for publication. Agencies whose documents are included in a volume participate in a declassification review. The Office can appeal the results of these reviews in an effort to release as much material as possible. The Office receives guidance from the Advisory Committee on Historical Diplomatic Documentation, a group of distinguished scholars from outside the U.S. Government. The Committee meets four times a year to review progress and make recommendations concerning the Foreign Relations series. FRUS experiences a time lag of more than thirty years between date of publication and the period covered. Volumes on the Nixon administration are now being researched, annotated, and prepared for publication. Volumes in the series since 1952 are organized chronologically according to Presidential administrations, and geographically and topically within each subseries. Although selected volumes of the set are being made available online (www.state.gov/r/pa/ho/frus /), the full-text of all relevant documents from this series that relate to the Kurds are included in this book. The earliest document goes back to 1936.

Patterns of Global Terrorism. PRINT. WEB. Washington, DC: U.S. Department of State, 1976-. Annual. This report (www.state.gov/s/ ct/rls/pgtrpt/) is submitted to the Congress by the Department of State to provide a full and complete annual report on country-by-country review and analysis of terrorist attacks; statistics on terrorism attacks and casualties; description of and background information on organizations engaging in terrorism. This source is one of the best and most complete for looking at terrorism from a U.S. foreign policy perspective. Full-text of reports for the years 1996-2001 for Europe (the region reportedly witnessing PKK terrorist activities) can be found at the following addresses:

- 1996: www.state.gov/www/global/terrorism/ 1996 Report/europe.html

- 1997: www.state.gov/www/global/terrorism/ 1997Report/eurasia.html

- 1998: www.state.gov/www/global/terrorim/ 1998Report/europe.html

- 1999: www.state.gov/www/global/terrorim/ 1999report/europe.html

- 2000: www.state.gov/s/ct/rls/pgtrpt/2000/434. htm

- 2001: www.state.gov/s/ct/rls/pgtrpt/2001/html/ 10240.htm

U.S. Department of State Dispatch. PRINT, WEB. U.S. Department of State. Office of Public Communication. Bureau of Public Affairs, 1990-1999 (www.state.gov/www/publ ications/dispatch/). The *Dispatch* contains the text of treaties and agreements on a selective basis, the text of the speeches given by the president and high officials in the State Department, news conferences, and so forth. The *Dispatch* is indexed in *American Foreign Policy and Treaty Index*; on the *InfoTrac* database; *EBSCO, Expanded Academic ASAP*; and in the *Readers' Guide to Periodical Literature*. Full-text editions are available through LEXIS-NEXIS; the Department of State Foreign Affairs Network web site (http://dosfan. lib.uic.edu/ERC/index.html); and the Department of State web site (www.state.gov/). This

last Internet address requires knowledge of the specific issue.

Other sources that index materials from the Department of State include:

American Foreign Policy and Treaty Index. PRINT. Bethesda, MD: Congressional Information Service, 1993-. Quarterly. Began in 1993 as *American Foreign Policy Index* and is issued quarterly in abstracts and index volumes with an annual cumulation. There is an accompanying AFPTI Microfiche Collection containing the full-text of the documents indexed. Conceived as a comprehensive guide to foreign policy-related government publications, AFPTI covers a wide range of topics culled from the State Department, the Office of the President, executive branch departments and agencies, independent entities, and the Congress. Publications indexed include monographs, serials, series, and periodicals. Individual documents and articles announced in AFPTI are available on demand on microfiche or in paper.

American Foreign Policy: Current Documents. PRINT. U.S. Department of State. Bureau of Public Affairs. Office of the Historian, 1955-1967, 1981-1990. Annual. Unlike *Foreign Relations of the United States*, which experiences a 30-year time lag before publication, *American Foreign Policy: Current Documents* contains contemporary foreign policy materials, indexed and arranged by subject and geography. It was issued annually from 1955 to 1967 and resumed its annual schedule in 1981. It includes major official messages; addresses, statements, and interviews; press conference and briefing reports; congressional testimonies; and communications by the White House, the Department of State, and other federal agencies or officials involved in the conduct of foreign policy. It ceased publication in 1990. The full-text of all relevant documents from this series is included in this book.

U.S. Foreign Affairs on CD-ROM. GPO, 1993-. Quarterly. This irregularly issued database has not only the full-text of the *Department of State Dispatch* but also press briefings, speeches by the president and key Department of State officials, congressional testimony, *Background Notes*, and so forth.

PRESIDENCY

Many of the presidential documents relevant to the Kurds are indexed or made available in full-text by the sources listed in the section of "Department of State" above. The two titles listed below, however, exclusively include information issued by various U.S. presidents.

Public Papers of the Presidents of the United States. PRINT, WEB. U.S. National Archives and Records Administration. Office of the Federal Register, 1957- to present (www.gpo. gov/nara/pubpaps/srchpaps.html). This series includes the text of addresses and remarks; communications to Congress; letters, messages, telegrams, and news conferences of the president. Volumes published cover the period from 1789 to 1999. Current volumes in this series (1989-1999) arrange presidential materials in chronological order within each week. Text notes, footnotes, and cross-references are furnished by the editors for purposes of identification and clarity. The information is indexed by subject entries and by categories reflecting the type of presidential activity or document. The Internet edition of this work for the years 1993-1999 is made available through the Government Printing Office, National Archives and Records Administration's web site. This book includes all documents that relate to the Kurds until 1999.

Weekly Compilation of Presidential Documents. PRINT, WEB. U.S. National Archives and Records Administration. Office of the Federal Register, 1965-. Weekly. This is the single most accessible collection of presidential activities in the public record (www. access.gpo.gov/nara/nara003.html). It includes the text of proclamations and executive orders; addresses and remarks; communications to Congress; letters, messages, telegrams, and news conferences. Published each Monday, the WCPD contains the various presidential actions for the previous week. The Internet edition has been available on the *GPO Access*

web site since January 6, 1997. This *Sourcebook* includes full-text of all documents that relate to the Kurds until December 31, 2001.

ACKNOWLEDGEMENT

This book has been made possible thanks to the University of North Carolina at Chapel Hill (UNC-CH) and Duke University. Their excellent library collections provided all the information needed to complete this project. Thanks and appreciation are also due to the School of Information and Library Science at UNC-CH as well as to the School of Information Science and Policy at University at Albany, State University of New York (SUNY). This project started while I was a student at UNC and was completed during my first year as a professor at SUNY.

I very much thank Cynthia Harris, the editor of Greenwood General Reference, for her work over the years. I also very much like to thank Kristina Spurgin, my research assistant, for her help and incredible efficiency in working on this project.

Finally, I am certain that without the support of my family I would not be able to claim this accomplishment. This is the result of the love and prayers of my parents and the love and encouragement of my siblings. My parents, to whom this sourcebook is dedicated, are a continual source of love and sacrifice. They have always been there for me and have shown great love, help, and understanding.

Lokman I. Meho
Albany, NY

PART I

ESSAYS

UNITED STATES FOREIGN POLICY TOWARD THE KURDS*

Michael M. Gunter

American involvement in Kurdistan dates back to World War I and President Woodrow Wilson's famous Fourteen Points, the twelfth of which concerned a forlorn promise of "autonomy" for "the other nationalities [of the Ottoman Empire] which are now under Turkish rule."[1] Resurgent Kemalist Turkey's successful struggle to regain its territorial integrity,[2] and British Iraq's decision to maintain control over the oil-rich Kurdish region of northern Kurdistan, however, quashed nascent Kurdish hopes for independence or even some type of autonomy.[3] The first brief stage of U.S. foreign policy concern with the Kurds was over.

SECOND STAGE

More than a half century later, the United States again became involved with the Kurds. In foreign policy, because of the NATO alliance, the United States supported the Turkish government's position on the Kurdish issue. This was to deny the Kurds any minority rights as they might escalate into further demands that would threaten Turkish territorial integrity.[4] Thus, Kurds who came to support the Kurdistan Workers Party (PKK) in Turkey became "bad Kurds" from the point of view of U.S. foreign policy.[5]

In Iraq, however, the United States encouraged Mulla Mustafa Barzani's revolt in the early 1970s, and thus the Iraqi Kurds became "good Kurds" from the point of view of U.S. foreign policy.[6] The United States pursued this path for several reasons: (1) As a favor to its then-ally Iran, who hated Iraq; (2) As a gambit in the Cold War as Iraq was an ally of the Soviet Union; (3) As a means to relieve pressure on Israel so Iraq would not join some future Arab attack on the Jewish state; and (4) As a means to possibly satisfy its own need for Mid-

*This article was originally published in *Orient* 40, no. 3 (Spring 1999): 427-437.

[1] See Samuel Flagg Bemis, *A Diplomatic History of the United States* (5th ed.; New York: Holt, Rinehart and Winston, Inc., 1965), p. 626.

[2] On Ataturk and the Turkish War of Independence following World War I, see Stanford J. Shaw and Ezel Kural Shaw, *History of the Ottoman Empire and Modern Turkey*, Vol. II *Reform, Revolution and Republic: The Rise of Modern Turkey, 1808-1975* (Cambridge University Press, 1977), pp. 340-72; Bernard Lewis, *The Emergence of Modern Turkey* (2nd ed.; London: Oxford University Press, 1968), pp. 239-93; and Erik J. Zurcher, *Turkey: A Modern History* (London: I. B. Tauris, 1994), pp. 138-72.

[3] For background, see C.J. Edmonds, *Kurds, Turks and Arabs: Politics, Travel and Research in North- Eastern Iraq, 1919-1925* (London: Oxford University Press, 1957).

[4] For background, see Michael M. Gunter, *The Kurds and the Future of Turkey* (New York: St. Martin's Press, 1997); Henri J. Barkey and Graham E. Fuller, *Turkey's Kurdish Question* (New York: Rowman & Littlefield, 1998); and Kemal Kirisci and Gareth M. Winrow, *The Kurdish Question and Turkey: An Example of a Trans-state Ethnic Conflict* (London: Frank Cass, 1997).

[5] In U.S. domestic politics, however, the Greek and Armenian lobbies, plus a tradition of support for human rights, did create some sympathy for the plight of the Kurds in Turkey.

[6] For background, see Edmund Ghareeb, *The Kurdish Question in Iraq* (Syracuse, NY: Syracuse University Press, 1981). More recently, see Michael M. Gunter, *The Kurdish Predicament in Iraq: A Political Analysis* (New York: St. Martin's Press, 1999).

dle East oil since Barzani had promised that the United States could look to a friend in OPEC once oil-rich Kurdistan had achieved independence. Thus U.S. President Nixon and his National Security Advisor Henry Kissinger first encouraged the Iraqi Kurds to revolt against Baghdad, but then with their ally Iran double-crossed the Kurds when the Shah decided to cut a deal with Saddam Hussein. To rationalize American actions, Kissinger argued that "the benefit of Nixon's Kurdish decision was apparent in just over a year: Only one Iraqi division was available to participate in the October 1973 Middle East War."[7] Cynically, he also explained that "covert action should not be confused with missionary work."[8]

Mulla Mustafa Barzani himself died a broken man four years later in U.S. exile as an unwanted ward of the CIA.[9] Years later Jonathan Randal argued that Barzani's son and eventual successor, Massoud Barzani, had "never forgotten Kissinger's treachery in 1975, had never totally recovered from the humiliation of his years of enforced exile, which he blamed on the United States... [and] never stopped worrying about American constancy."[10] Massoud himself recently explained that "we have had bitter experience with the U.S. government. . . . In 1975... it changed its alliances purely in its own interest at the expense of our people's suffering and plight."[11]

More than a quarter of a century later, Kissinger revisited what the United States had done under his stewardship,[12] and argued that "those who afterward spoke so righteously about 'cynicism' and 'betrayal'—having remained silent, or worse, about the far vaster tragedy taking place in Indochina—never put forward an alternative course we could, in fact, have pursued." He maintained that "even from the perspectives of two decades, I like the alternates to the course we pursued even less," although he admitted that "for the Kurdish people, perennial victims of history, this is, of course, no consolation."

More specifically, Kissinger explained that "saving the Kurds would have required the opening of a new front in inhospitable mountains close to the Soviet border." Thus, "we did not have the option of overt support in a war so logistically difficult, so remote, and so incomprehensible to the American public." Moreover, "the Shah had made the decision, and we had neither the plausible arguments nor strategies to dissuade him." Kissinger concluded: "As a case study, the Kurdish tragedy provides material for a variety of conclusions: the need to clarify objectives at the outset; the importance of relating goals to available means; the need to review an operation periodically; and the importance of coherence among allies." In other words the Iraqi Kurds had played the role of dispensable pawns for U.S. foreign policy.

THE 1990s

The third and current stage of U.S. foreign policy involvement with the Iraqi Kurds, of course, began with the Gulf War in 1991 and the United States's continuing attempt to contain and remove Saddam from power. As the Iraqi military was being ousted from Kuwait, U.S. President George Bush encouraged "the Iraqi people to take matters into their own hands—to force Saddam Hussein, the dictator,

---

[7]Henry Kissinger, *White House Years* (Boston: Little, Brown and Co., 1979), p. 1265.

[8]Cited in the unauthorized publication of U.S. House of Representatives Pike Committee Report investigating the CIA published as "The CIA Report the President Doesn't Want You to Read," *Village Voice*, February 16, 1976, pp. 70-92. The part dealing with the Kurds is entitled "Case 2: Arms Support," and appears on pp. 85 and 87-88.

[9]See David A. Korn, "The Last Years of Mustafa Barzani," *Middle East Quarterly* 1 (June 1994), pp. 12-27.

[10]Jonathan C. Randal, *After Such Knowledge What Forgiveness?* (New York: Farrar, Straus and Giroux, 1997), p. 299.

[11]Cited in "Iraq: KDP's Barzani Urges Arab-Kurdish Dialogue," *Al-Majallah* (London), October 5-11, 1997, p. 29; as cited in *Foreign Broadcast Information Service—Near East & South Asia* (97-283), Oct.10, 1997, p. 2. Hereafter cited as

FBIS-NES.

[12]The following discussion and citations are taken from the chapter on the "Kurdish tragedy" in Henry Kissinger, *Years of Renewal* (New York: Simon and Schuster, 1999), pp. 576-96.

to step aside."[13] Despite initial successes, however, neither the Iraqi Shiites nor the Kurds proved able to cope with Saddam's stronger military. As Saddam began to put the Kurdish rebellion down, the two Iraqi Kurdish leaders— Massoud Barzani of the Kurdistan Democratic Party and Jalal Talabani of the Patriotic Union of Kurdistan—appealed to Bush for help by reminding him: "You personally called upon the Iraqi people to rise up against Saddam Hussein's brutal dictatorship."[14]

For a variety of reasons, however, the United States decided not to intervene in the internal Iraqi strife. Doing so could lead, it was feared, to an unwanted, protracted U.S. occupation that would be politically unpopular in the United States, to an unstable government in Iraq, or even "Lebanization" of the country and destabilization of the Middle East. Furthermore, the United States also concluded that Saddam could win. To support the Kurds against him might require an unwanted, permanent U.S. commitment. Possibly too, the memory of overstepping itself in the Korean War by trying to totally replace the North Korean regime after initially liberating South Korea, also influenced U.S. thinking. In addition, Kurdish success in Iraq might provoke Kurdish uprisings in Turkey, Syria, or Iran, states whose cooperation the United States felt it needed. A U.S. Senate Foreign Relations staff report written by Peter Galbraith and issued a month after Saddam had put down the rebellion confirmed that the United States "continued to see the opposition in caricature" and feared that the Kurds would seek a separate state and that the Shiites wanted an Iranian-style Islamic republic.[15]

Once it became clear the United States was

not going to intervene, the uneven struggle turned into a rout and some 1.5 million Kurdish refugees fled to the Iranian and Turkish frontiers where they faced death from the hostile climate and lack of provisions. This refugee dilemma quickly created a disastrous political problem for everyone involved, including the United States, Turkey, and Iran. After much soul searching, the United States reversed itself and took several steps to protect the Kurds. United Nations Security Council Resolution 688 of April 5, 1991, condemned "the repression of the Iraqi civilian population . . . in Kurdish populated areas" and demanded "that Iraq . . . immediately end this repression." Under the aegis of Operation Provide Comfort (OPC) and a no-fly zone imposed against Baghdad, the Kurds were able to return to their homes in northern Iraq where they began to build a fledgling de facto state and government.

Turkey's permission and logistical support for OPC (since January 1, 1997, Operation Northern Watch) and the no-fly zone to protect the Iraqi Kurds proved indispensable. Without them, it would have been almost impossible for the United States to maintain the no-fly zone because there was nowhere else to base it. Furthermore, given the double economic blockade placed on the Kurds by the United Nations—Iraqi Kurdistan was still legally part of Iraq which remained under U.N. sanctions—and Baghdad itself, the ground outlet to Turkey became the Kurds' lifeline to the outside world. As Hoshyar Zebari, the foreign policy spokesman for Barzani's KDP explained: "Turkey is our lifeline to the West and the whole world in our fight against Saddam Husayn. We are able to secure allied air protection and international aid through Turkey's cooperation. If Poised Hammer (OPC) is withdrawn, Saddam's units will again reign in this region and we will lose everything."[16]

The continuance of OPC became a major political issue in Turkey, however, because many Turks believed it was facilitating the vac-

---

[13]"Remarks to the American Association for the Advancement of Science," February 15, 1991; cited in *Public Papers of the Presidents of the United States: George Bush, 1991*, Vol. 1 (Washington: Government Printing Office, 1991), p. 145.

[14]Cited in "United States Turns Down Plea to Intervene as Kirkuk Falls," *International Herald Tribune*, March 30, 1991.

[15]See United States Congress, Senate, Committee on Foreign Relations, *Civil War in Iraq: A Staff Report to the Committee on Foreign Relations, United States Senate*, by Peter W. Galbraith, 102nd Congress, 1st Session, May 1991.

[16]Cited in "Iraqi Kurds Reportedly to Block Terrorist Attacks," Ankara TRT Television Network, 1600 GMT, April 8, 1992; as cited in *Foreign Broadcast Information Service—West Europe*, April 9, 1992, p. 43. Hereafter cited as *FBIS-WEU*.

uum of authority in northern Iraq that enabled the Kurdistan Workers Party (PKK) to enjoy sanctuaries there. Some even argued that OPC was the opening salvo of a new Treaty of Sevres (1920) that would lead to the creation of a Kurdish state in northern Iraq as almost happened after World War I. Thus, went the argument, Turkey was facilitating its own demise by housing OPC.

To abandon OPC, however, would alienate the United States and strip Ankara of important influence over the course of events. OPC, for example, enabled the Turks to launch military strikes into Iraqi Kurdistan against the PKK at almost any time. If the United States refused to allow such Turkish incursions, Turkey could threaten to withdraw its permission for OPC. Although it might have seemed ironic that an operation that was supposed to protect the Iraqi Kurds was allowing Turkey to attack the Turkish Kurds as well as inflict collateral damage on the host Iraqi Kurds, such was the logic of the Kurdish imbroglio and part of the dilemma for U.S. foreign policy.

In May 1994, the two main Iraqi Kurdish parties—Barzani's KDP and Talabani's PUK—fell into a civil war that immensely complicated U.S. policy toward them. How could the United States help and protect the Iraqi Kurds when they were busy killing themselves? In late January 1995, U.S President Bill Clinton sent a message to both Barzani and Talabani in which he warned: "We will no longer cooperate with the other countries to maintain security in the region if the clashes continue."[17]

Finally, the United States attempted to play a mediatory role similar to one carried out by the French a year earlier. Robert Deutsch, the director of the Office of Northern Gulf Affairs in the U.S. State Department, persuaded the warring parties to meet in Drogheda, a suburb of Dublin, Ireland, from August 9 to 11, 1995, in the presence of senior U.S. officials. Turkey sent observers. As in Paris the previous year, a solution initially seemed possible, capped once again by a proposal to have Barzani and Tala-

bani ratify the final settlement, this time by journeying to Washington at the end of September 1995.

At this point Turkey's security interests compounded the Kurdish divisions. When the U.S.-brokered Drogheda talks appeared to be leading to a settlement of the Iraqi Kurdish civil war, as well as to security guarantees for Turkey in the form of the KDP policing the border to prevent PKK raids into Turkey, the PKK struck out at the KDP. For their own reasons such regional powers as Syria and Iran, as well as the PUK, encouraged the PKK. Syria and Iran did so because they did not want to see their U.S. enemy successfully broker an end to the KDP-PUK strife and possibly go on from there to sponsor an Iraqi Kurdish state, while Talabani sought in effect to open a second front against Barzani.

Given these complications, the second round of the Drogheda talks in mid-September 1995 failed, as the KDP and PUK proved unable to reach agreement on such key issues as the demilitarization of Irbil—held then by the PUK—and the collection of customs revenues by the KDP. Talabani also blamed Turkey for giving arms to the KDP. For his part, Muhammad Baqir al-Hakim, the leader of the Iranian-supported Iraqi Shiite opposition party the Supreme Assembly of the Islamic Revolution in Iraq (SAIRI), explained: "the talks failed because they were conducted with the aims of the U.S. and Turkey behind them and were against the policies of Iran, Syria, and other neighboring countries."[18]

The situation was then allowed to drift with the United States declining to try harder to effect a cease-fire between the Iraqi Kurds or to contribute a mere $2 million to an international mediation force that might have forestalled the next round of fighting.[19] In August 1996, a sud-

[17]Cited in Selim Caglayan, "Clinton Reprimands Barzani and Talabani," *Hurriyet* (Istanbul), January 28, 1995, p. 18; as cited in *FBIS-WEU*, February 1, 1995, p. 27.

[18]Cited in "SAIRI Chief Interviewed on Internecine Strife," *Tehran Times*, October 11, 1995, p. 2; as cited in *FBIS-NES*, October 26, 1995, p. 46.

[19]Kevin McKierman, "The Kurdish Question and U.S. Policy," *Independent* (Santa Barbara, California), September 19, 1996, p. 16. Also see Katherine A. Williams, "How We Lost the Kurdish Game," *Washington Post*, September 15, 1996, p. C1.

den renewal of the intra-Kurdish struggle seemed likely to result in a PUK victory given arms it had received from Iran. Desperate, Barzani did the unthinkable and invited Saddam in to help him against Talabani.

How could the United States enforce the no-fly zone against Saddam when the very people it was supposed to protect had invited Saddam in? Halfheartedly, the United States responded by bombing a few meaningless targets south of Baghdad. Saddam used the few hours he had to capture and execute some 96 Iraqis who had defected to the U.S.-financed Iraqi opposition, Iraqi National Congress (INC). A senior INC official claimed, "in two hours, the Iraqi opposition [had] lost its entire infrastructure,"[20] while a U.S. official concluded, "our entire covert program has gone to hell."[21] But since the United States's ally Turkey was now supporting Barzani (to restrain the PKK), the United States was now partially on the same side as Saddam. Indeed, Iran—supporting Talabani—claimed that "Saddam's army moved into the Kurdish area with the U.S. green light."[22] Although the line separating the KDP and the PUK eventually returned to virtually the status quo before this latest round of fighting—with the exception that the KDP now held Irbil—the Kurdish issue was clearly becoming more and more difficult for U.S. foreign policy.

The so-called Ankara peace process initiated by the United States, Britain, and Turkey at the end of October 1996 sought to extend the tenuous cease-fire of exhaustion into a renewed search for peace through a new series of talks. The KDP's temporary alliance with Baghdad had put a strain on all of the Kurds' relations with the United States and made it more difficult to justify their military defense and continuing need for aid. The United States, for example, had closed down its small, but symbolically important Military Coordination Center in Zakho, Iraqi Kurdistan, and terminated most of

its relief operations. Furthermore, the following May 1997, some 50,000 Turkish troops entered Iraqi Kurdistan in an attempt to destroy the PKK units based there and to shore up the KDP forces Turkey hoped would help prevent future PKK attacks upon Turkey from the region. In contrast to earlier incursions, this time the Turks did not fully withdraw after completing their mission but maintained a military presence that amounted to an unofficial security zone. Talabani concluded, "Turkey has discarded its neutral role and is now an ally of Barzani."[23]

Given this situation and their continuing differences, the Ankara peace process failed to resolve the continuing impasse between the KDP and the PUK. In October 1997, the PUK attacked the KDP in a misguided attempt to break the deadlock and made initial gains. This caused the Turks to intervene heavily on the side of the KDP, charging that Talabani was now actively cooperating with the PKK. This accusation was apparently not without some merit.[24] Turkish tanks actually advanced to within a few miles of Irbil. By the middle of November 1997, the KDP had reasserted control over all the territory it had lost during the PUK offensive the previous month.

New peace initiatives early the following year, however, led to significant developments and renewed attempts by the United States to bring the Kurds together. In a letter to Congress on the "Status of Efforts to Obtain Iraq's Compliance with U.N. Resolutions," U.S. President Bill Clinton argued that since "both Barzani and Talabani have made positive, forward-looking statements on political reconciliation," the United States "will continue our efforts to reach a permanent reconciliation through mediation in order to help the people of northern Iraq find the permanent, stable settlement which they deserve."[25] The U.S. president also declared

---

[20]Cited in Tim Weiner, "Iraqi Offensive into Kurdish Zone Disrupts U.S. Plot to Oust Hussein," *New York Times*, September 7, 1996, p. 4.

[21]Cited in Kevin Fedarko, "Saddam's Coup," *Time*, September 23, 1996, p. 44.

[22]*Tehran Times*, September 3, 1996, p. 2; as cited in *FBIS-NES*, September 3, 1996, p.1.

[23]Cited in *Ittihad* (PUK), May 31, 1997; as cited in "Iraq: Talabani Interviewed on Turkish Operation, Other Issues," *FBIS-NES* (97-152), June 1, 1997, p. 2.

[24]"PUK-KDP Truce Ends, Turkish Jets Raid Region," *Turkish Daily News*, October 25, 1997, accessed over the Internet.

[25]Cited in Saadet Oruc, "Diplomatic Maneuvers in Iraqi Kurdistan," *Turkish Probe*, July

that he sought "to minimize the opportunities for Baghdad and Tehran to insert themselves into the conflict and threaten Iraqi citizens in this region."[26]

In mid July, David Welch, the U.S. principal deputy assistant secretary of state for Near Eastern affairs, led a delegation of U.S. state department officials and a Turkish foreign ministry official to Iraqi Kurdistan in an effort to galvanize these new initiatives. The Welch delegation met first with Barzani and then Talabani. Although no substantive agreement war reached, Welch invited both Kurdish leaders to Washington for talks.

Following a successful high-level meeting at the end of August between KDP officials and Talabani, in early September 1998 first Barzani and then Talabani actually journeyed to Washington. On the way both stopped off for talks in Ankara. After separate individual meetings with U.S. state department officials, the two Kurdish leaders finally met personally for the first time since the summer of 1994, when their fighting had first started. After two days of lengthy sessions, they reached a tentative agreement that came to be called the Washington Accord.

In announcing this achievement, U.S. Secretary of State Madeleine Alright also made general promises of U.S. support for the Kurds—contingent upon their continuing unity—by declaring, "the United States will decide how and when to respond to Baghdad's actions based on the threat they pose to Iraq's neighbors, to regional security, to vital U.S. interests and to the Iraqi people, including those in the north."[27] President Clinton repeated Albright's tepid assurances in letters to Congress on November 6, 1998, and again on May 19, 1999.[28] While announcing a halt to the four-day

bombing of Iraq on December 19, 1998, however, Clinton seemed to make a much stronger guarantee by declaring, "we will maintain a strong military presence in the area, and we will remain ready to use it if Saddam . . . moves against the Kurds. We also will continue to enforce no-fly zones in the North [and the South]."[29] In addition, on April 22, 1999, Martin Indyk, the assistant secretary of state for Near Eastern affairs, declared in a speech to the Council on Foreign Relations in New York, "we maintain a robust force in the region, which we have made clear we are prepared to use should Saddam cross our well-established red lines. Those red lines include: ... should he move against his own people, especially in the north; or, should he challenge us in the no fly zone."[30] Indyk repeated these promises of protection for the Iraqi Kurds in testimony before the House International Relations Committee on June 8, 1999.[31]

Although these pronouncements did not constitute an ironclad agreement of protection, they were—in contrast to Nixon's and Kissinger's covert and unkept promises of a quarter of a century earlier—public declarations. Thus, they could not be so cavalierly ignored. Yet at the best, these guarantees applied only against Saddam. They did not apply to Turkey or Iran, both of whom continued to militarily intervene at will in Iraqi Kurdistan, especially Turkey in pursuit of the PKK. Whenever this occurred, collateral damage to Iraqi Kurdish life and property inevitably occurred. As Jalal Talabani tellingly observed, "the [U.S.] international protection is . . . against alleged or possible Iraqi oppression and is not for protection against Turkish or Iranian interference . . . We believe that the Turkish military interference can sometimes be more dangerous than the Iraqi

---

26, 1998, accessed over the Internet.

[26]Cited in *ibid.*

[27]Cited in Harun Kazaz, "Ambiguity Surrounds N. Iraq Kurdish Agreement," *Turkish Probe*, October 11, 1998, accessed over the Internet.

[28]Both letters were entitled "Text of a Letter from the President to the Speaker of the House of Representatives and the President Pro Tempore of the Senate," and dated respectively November 6, 1998, and May 19, 1999. They both were accessed

over the Internet.

[29]Cited in "Remarks of the President on Iraq," December 19, 1998, accessed over the Internet.

[30]Cited in "Amb. Martin S. Indyk Assistant Secretary of State for Near Eastern Affairs Remarks to the Council on Foreign Relations, NYC April 22, 1999," accessed over the Internet.

[31]See "Martin Indyk Statement, House International Relations Committee, June 8," *Iraq News*, June 11, 1999, accessed over the Internet.

military interference."[32] Finally, the U.S. guarantees apparently would not apply against a post-Saddam Iraqi government hostile to the Iraqi Kurds. The U.S. concern for the Iraqi Kurds was largely motivated by its continuing animus toward Saddam. Once the Iraqi leader disappeared from the scene it seemed unlikely the United States would continue its support for the Kurds.[33]

Despite the initial hopes for the Washington Accord, all that could be said for it as of June 1999, was that the cease-fire had held. None of the Accord's deadlines for the KDP sharing its revenues with the PUK, creating an interim joint KDP-PUK government, resolving the status of Irbil, or holding new elections that would lead to a unified Kurdish administration or regional government had been met. Indeed, the KDP was now also accusing the PUK of allowing the PKK to maintain bases in its territory (contrary to the terms of the Washington Accord) and to use these bases to attack the KDP.

In an attempt to resolve some of these issues and revitalize the Accord, the U.S. State Department hosted representatives of the Higher Coordination Committee—tasked by the KDP and PUK to implement the Accord—in Washington in mid June 1999. It remained to be seen, however, if the United States would be any more successful than before. Previous experience suggested that it would not because the inherent struggle for power between the two parties—fueled by the hostility of the regional powers—prevented the actual implementation of a comprehensive settlement.

TURKISH KURDS

Unlike the situation in Iraq (Iran and Syria for that matter too) where the Kurds are geographically distinct and largely unassimilated,

many Kurds in Turkey have migrated out of their traditional homeland in the southeast and assimilated to one degree or another into the larger Turkish population. Accordingly, the PKK clearly does not represent as large a percentage of the Turkish Kurds as the KDP and PUK do the Iraqi Kurds.[34] This is a fact that objective Kurdish nationalists must come to grips with when analyzing the situation.

On the other hand, Turkish nationalists exaggerate this situation and claim that the PKK is simply a terrorist organization alienated from most of the ethnic Kurdish population in Turkey. To further illustrate their point, these Turkish nationalists point to the mere 4 per cent of the total vote HADEP (the legal Kurdish nationalist party) received in the parliamentary elections held in April 1999. This figure of 4 per cent, however, greatly underestimates the support and sympathy that exist for the PKK in Turkey for the following reasons. During the recent election campaign, the state used a variety of threats and coercive methods to discourage and prevent ethnic Kurds from supporting HADEP. The other parties participating in the election did not suffer from such disabilities. Indeed HADEP itself was under the threat of being closed down for its alleged support for the PKK as its predecessors DEP and HEP had been. In addition, many potential HADEP supporters had recently been forced by the Turkish military to abandon their homes and relocate as a means of drying up local support for the PKK. The result was that these migrants were not registered to vote. Finally, the state's heavy-handed tactics against even the mildest expression of support for any Kurdish cultural rights had led to the elimination of almost all moderate groups supporting Kurdish rights. The result was that the PKK had become practically the only representative of the Kurdish cause in Turkey. For these reasons then, the support for the PKK is clearly stronger than the mere 4 per cent that voted for HADEP.

In contrast to its support given the "good" KDP and PUK as the representatives of the

[32]Cited in Salah Awwad, "Interview with Jalal Talabani," *Al-Quds al-Arabi*, September 22, 1998, p. 3; as cited in *FBIS-NES* (98-266), September 23, 1998.

[33]For a recent elaboration of this point, see Christopher de Bellaigue, "Justice and the Kurds," *New York Review of Books*, June 24, 1999.

[34]See U.S. State Dept. Annual Human Rights Report on Turkey, issued February 26, 1999, accessed over the Internet: www.state.gov/www/global/human_rights/1998_hrp_report/turkey.html.

Iraqi Kurds, the United States, as noted above, has very strongly opposed the "bad" PKK. Turkey's longtime and continuing geostrategically important position as an U.S. NATO ally is clearly the main reason for this situation. Other explanations include the U.S. fear of Islamic fundamentalism and Turkey's developing alliance with Israel. As a constitutionally secular state, Turkey is seen as a bastion against Islamic fundamentalism, while support for Israel, of course, remains a given for U.S. foreign policy. Clearly, these constitute powerful reasons for the position U.S. foreign policy has maintained regarding the PKK.

As the twentieth century draws to a close, several developments illustrate this U.S. foreign policy support for Turkey against the "bad" PKK. Although it continues to criticize Turkey in its annual human rights report, the U.S. State Department maintains in the same report that the PKK are "terrorists" who "frequently kill noncombatants, and target village officials, village guards, teachers, and other perceived representatives of the state."[34] The State Department has also placed the PKK on its list of terrorist organizations. "The PKK are terrorists. Turkey is going after terrorists. The PKK are indiscriminately killing their own people. They are not supported by the majority of Kurds,"[35] explained one official from the State Department. Other U.S. officials claim that they have compiled a thick dossier on the PKK that includes murder, drug trafficking, extortion, robbery and trafficking in illegal immigrants.[36]

Abdullah (Apo) Ocalan, the longtime leader of the PKK, admits that "the PKK has made mistakes. This is true. But compared to what Turkey has done to the Kurds over the years, it should be obvious who is the real terrorist. Susurluk has the facts. Everything is said in the Susurluk report."[37] Indeed, many would

argue that Ocalan has done more to re-establish a sense of Kurdish self esteem and nationalism in Turkey than any other Kurdish leader in recent years. In the process he once again illustrates the old adage that one person's freedom fighter is another's terrorist.

For a short period in the early 1990s, Ocalan actually seemed close to achieving military success. In the end, however, he overextended himself, while the Turkish military spared no excesses in containing him. Slowly but steadily, the Turks marginalized the PKK's military threat. Ocalan's ill-advised decision in August 1995 to also attack Barzani's KDP because of its support for Turkey further sapped his strength. Another blow came when Turkey threatened to go to war against Syria in October 1998 unless Damascus expelled Ocalan from his longtime sanctuary in that country. The United States supported Turkey by sending a strongly worded letter to Syria regarding the situation.[38] After a short, surreptitious stay in Russia, Ocalan landed in Italy where for a brief period it looked like he might be able to turn his military defeat into a political victory by having the European Union try him and thus also try Turkey.

Although the Italians and other Europeans such as the Germans initially appeared sympathetic, at this point the United States weighed in heavily by denouncing Ocalan in the strongest of terms as a terrorist. The United States also pressured Italy—and any other state tempted to offer the PKK leader asylum and a platform from which to negotiate—to instead extradite him to Turkey for trial. An editorial from the U.S. State Department broadcast by the Voice of America (VOA) declared: "It is neither U.S. practice nor policy to provide an international platform from which terrorists can expound their views or try to justify their criminal ac-

---

[35]Cited in Toni Marshall, "Kurds Call Turkey Hypocritical," *Washington Times*, April 9, 1999, accessed over the Internet.

[36]Interview with the author, U.S. State Dept., Washington, D.C., April 4, 1997.

[37]Interview with the author, Damascus, Syria, March 14, 1998. The reference to Susurluk (October 1996) illustrated how the Turkish state by its own admission hired right-wing criminals on the

lam to extrajudicially murder thousands of Turkish citizens of Kurdish ethnic heritage in an attempt to silence their alleged support for Kurdish rights and the PKK. In exchange, the state turned a blind eye to their drug trafficking and other criminal activities. Three years after the scandal broke, virtually no one had been brought to justice.

[38]The following data were taken from *Briefing* (Ankara), November 30, 1998, p. 16.

tions. No one should doubt our views on Ocalan; the United States considers him a terrorist who should be brought to justice for his crimes."[39]

When Italy permitted Ocalan to leave in January 1999, James Foley, the acting spokesman of the U.S. State Department, angrily observed: "It is obvious that the road taken by Italy does not serve in the goal of Ocalan's being tried. We feel sorrow over this. Ocalan should be brought to justice on charges of terrorism."[40] U.S. Secretary of State Madeleine Albright also renewed her call for any states that might host the PKK leader to try him. Ocalan became not only a man without a country but one lacking even a place to land. As he flew from country to county, the U.S. State Department representative James Foley mocked him by joking, "I'd hate to be the pilot of that small plane."[41] During his final hours of freedom, Russia, the Netherlands, and Switzerland all rejected him. Rather pathetically, Ocalan had become like the "Flying Dutchman" of legend whose ship was condemned to sail the seas until Judgment Day.

Desperate, Ocalan finally allowed the Greeks to take him to their embassy in Nairobi, Kenya, where U.S. intelligence agents had inundated the country following the U.S. embassy bombing there the previous summer. Now American animus toward the Kurdish leader entered its final stage by providing Turkey with the technical intelligence to pinpoint his whereabouts and capture him. Ironically, at this very moment the United States especially needed Turkey as a runway for U.S. planes to bomb Iraq in support to the "good" Iraqi Kurds. The United States had to give its Turkish ally something tangible like Ocalan because at that very moment Iraq's deputy prime minister Tariq Aziz was in Turkey in a futile attempt to end Turkey's support for the United States. Given Ocalan's fate, the Iraqi Kurds must have won-

dered how much longer the United States would continue to support them once Saddam was eliminated. Mark Parris, the U.S. ambassador to Turkey, gleefully spoke of "Ocalan's rendition,"[42] an archaic term referring to the surrender of a fugitive slave. Ocalan's final hours illustrate again the old Kurdish maxim: "The Kurds have no friends."

Kosovo further illustrated the lengths to which the United States would support Turkey against the PKK. When NATO began its bombing campaign against Yugoslavia to force it to withdraw its forces from Kosovo so that the ethnic Albanians living there could obtain their minority rights, autonomy, and even possibly independence, the obvious precedent with the Kurdish situation in Turkey arose. Indeed, as members of NATO, both the United States and Turkey participated in the Kosovo operation. The United States, however, claimed to see no double standard here. The U.S. State Department spokesman squared the circle and claimed: "The comparison I just think is not accurate ... Turkey is a democratic country, committed to seeking a peaceful solution to the Kurdish issue ... A comparison is grossly unfair."[43] Some Turks, however, queried whether the Kosovo precedent might not be an opening salvo by the United States to begin effecting similar changes in Turkish policy toward the Kurds. Although this seemed doubtful, only time would tell.

CONCLUSION

The seeming U.S. inability to deal coherently with the Kurds is perhaps symbolized

---

[39]Cited in *Turkish Daily News*, December 25, 1998, accessed over the Internet.

[40]Cited in *Turkish Daily News*, January 19, 1999, accessed over the Internet.

[41]Cited in "U.S. Says Ocalan Should Be Brought to Justice," Reuters, February 1, 1999, accessed over the Internet.

[42]Cited in "Remarks by Ambassador Mark R. Parris to the American-Turkish Council's 18th Annual Conference on U.S.-Turkish Relations," May 6, 1999, accessed over the Internet. In the same speech the U.S. ambassador went on to note that five U.S. four-star generals had visited Ankara in a month, and an agreement for $517 million had just been signed for Turkey to purchase Sikorsky utility helicopter, among other items.

[43]Cited in "U.S. Department of State Daily Press Briefing Index," April 7, 1999, accessed over the Internet.

by the State Department's division of responsibility for these stateless people into separate Bureaus. Since Turkey is in the European Bureau, problems involving the Turkish Kurds fall under this bureaucracy. Iraq, however, is in the Near East Bureau, and therefore problems concerning the Iraqi Kurds fall under this bureaucracy. It makes sense for a state-centric model of foreign policy, but creates difficulties for such people as the Kurds.

The seeming double standard the United States applies to the Kurds, of course, is really explained by perceived U.S. national interests. In the case of Kosovo, the United States felt that it was necessary to stop ethnic violence in Europe before it escalated and expanded. The Kurds, in Turkey, however, do not present such an immediate threat. Therefore, the Kurdish problem can be left to fester. Moreover, as regards the "good" Kurds in Iraq and the "bad" ones in Turkey, this too can be explained in terms of perceived U.S. national interest. Turkey is seen as a valuable geostrategic NATO ally necessary to support for its continuing allegiance. Saddam's Iraq, on the other hand, has held the position as one of the main enemies of the United States since its ill-conceived invasion of Kuwait in 1990. Support for the Iraqi Kurds, therefore, is perceived as supportive of over-all U.S. policy against Iraq. Although a double standard for the Kurds, it seemingly makes perfect sense in terms of immediate U.S. national interest.

Long-term U.S. national interest as regards the Kurds, of course, may well be a different matter. As the Arab-Israeli dispute slowly winds down, the Kurdish issue will bid to replace it as the leading factor of instability in the geostrategically important Middle East. Furthermore, since the Kurds sit on a great deal of the Middle East's oil and possibly even more important water resources, the Kurdish issue will become even more important in the next century. Thus, it behooves U.S. foreign policy to look beyond the immediate and survey the broader landscape down the road.

When this is done, it will be found that most Kurds would probably still be satisfied with meaningful cultural rights and real democracy. If these legitimate demands were instituted, most Kurds would be willing to accept the current state boundaries. However, if the status quo of nothing for the Kurds continues to be the policy, the frustrated Kurds will continue to be alienated and increasingly radicalized. Eventually they will explode and jeopardize the security of all.

THE LEGACY OF U.S. SUPPORT TO KURDS: TWO MAJOR EPISODES

Lokman I. Meho and Michel G. Nehme

Kurdish unity has always been regarded as a threat to western interests in the Middle East. At the peak of support provided to Kurds after the Gulf war of 1991, the U.S. maintained humanitarian attention short of real political recognition of the pledged interests of the Kurdish population. The State Department called the Iraqi Kurds "good Kurds" and deliberately ignored the Kurds of Iran, Syria, and former Soviet Union. Notwithstanding, the Kurds of Turkey were branded "terrorists." The western allied forces protection flights over Northern Iraq were meant to undermine the authority of Saddam's regime but not to save the Kurds whenever Turkey launched an impending cross-border operation to pursue Kurdish rebels. The West headed by the U.S. gave Turkey a leading role in the affairs of northern Iraq and that was to substitute the Iraqi control, which was very much needed before the March 1991 but condemned afterwards.

Turkish west-blessed intervention in the Kurdish affairs was not different from that of the old and continuing Saddam's influence on stability among the different Kurdish factions and coalitions. Turkish policy towards Iraqi Kurds, in secret coordination with Saddam's regime, was one of the main causes of the fighting between the Kurdish Democratic Party (KDP) and the Patriotic Union of Kurdistan (PUK), which first came to head in April 1994. War among the Kurdish factions gave Turkey and the West an excuse to repeatedly strike in northern Iraq and to undermine Kurdish ambitions for full political authority in the area.

The apparent disunity manifested between the KDP and PUK, as well as by these two groups toward Kurdish political groups in Iran and Turkey, played still further into the hands of the neighboring countries as well as the Western alliance, all of whom work toward denying the Kurds self-rule. The West deliberately overlooks the fact that Kurdish internal politics has many similarities with that of most of third world communities that currently enjoy self-rule. It has comparable ingredients of conflict and lack of proper institutions, yet, the west continues to consider the Kurds as not fit for self-rule.

Politically, there are the two main bitter rivals in Iraqi Kurdistan, the KDP and PUK, in addition to right-wing nationalist parties, Islamic parties, and other small village oriented factions. Recent research and experience in Kurdistan showed that the vast majority of Kurds do not have a strict commitment and allegiance to any of the factions. The Kurdish populations are increasingly becoming more sophisticated politically to think in terms of peace, justice, economic well-being, and freedom. They no more trust the major regional and international powers. They have had a long history of trial and error. This experience shows that irrespective of the political factionalism and geographical dispersion of the Kurds, it is possible to establish a system with a considerable degree of harmony compared to their long history of domestic bloody confrontations.

Despite the absence of any real income or external support, and despite the double imposition of *de facto* sanctions on Kurdistan, the Kurdish population in Iraq has managed to survive and recently grow in strength. The vast majority of its current problems are due to lack of funds and political security. However, careful consideration clearly must be paid to the kind of support coming from the West because this support usually comes when the West wants to prepare the Kurds to be involved in bloody clashes against one of the regional powers that ultimately bare its tragic consequences.

Old and recent history has repeatedly proven that in their plight towards the establishment of self-determination, the Kurds, as one of the principal players in Middle Eastern politics, have had horrific results due to manipulation among themselves and with the regional and international powers. This manipulation was established as a trend and a precept in balancing the divergent powers in the Middle East. The 1991 international coalition, orchestrated by the United States to destroy the rising Iraqi military power in the region, openly encouraged the Kurds to participate in the fight against Saddam Hussein. After the destruction of half of Iraq's military and the re-establishment of the monarchy in Kuwait, President Bush decided it would be unwise to "interfere in the internal affairs" of Iraq. This American attitude encouraged Saddam to retaliate and vandalize the Kurds for their support of the Americans in the 1990-1991 Gulf War.

The American foreign policy towards self-determination of people in repressive regimes did not change with the New World Order. Apparently, the American Administration still believes in international system based entirely on the sovereignty of nation states. Verbal criticism is the limit for handling governments brutalizing people within their borders, even if these people do not identify themselves with the status quo. When Secretary of State, James Baker, was personally investigating, on the ground, the conditions of one million homeless Kurds, he said: "Today, we have witnessed the suffering and despair of the Iraqi people." The implication of avoiding the use of the word 'Kurds' is a clear indication of American stance towards the Kurds. This is not new in the American Iraqi-Kurds relations, especially if we recall the 1972-1975 episode. Henry Kissinger, the Secretary of State then, stated in his *White House Years*[1] volume:

Nixon agreed also to encourage the Shah in supporting the autonomy of the Kurds in Iraq. The Kurdish affair and its tragic outcome in the 1972-1975 period is, of course, outside the scope of this volume ... I shall explain these in a second volume. (Kissinger ignored the issue completely in his second volume).

As a reference note to this statement, Kissinger added:

The Shah's decision in 1975 to settle the Kurdish problem with Iraq was based on the judgment, almost certainly correct, that the Kurds were about to be overwhelmed ... The Shah was not willing to commit the former (his military forces) ... If we had sought this escalation of our covert intelligence operation (the emphasis here is on escalation) ... the Kurds' tragic fate would have probably led the charge against it.

Twenty years later Kissinger wrote a 21-page long chapter on the Kurds.[2] In it, he re-examines what the U.S. and its international tool, the CIA, had done with his acknowledgment to the Kurds. After indicating that "the Kurdish tragedy was imposed largely by history and geography, but it was also exacerbated by our own national divisions," Kissinger maintains that the United States, despite its pronouncements on self-determination, showed no interest at all in the case of the Kurds. The American priority, during the final months of the 1972-75 war and in its aftermath, was to reinforce central authority in Iran and block Soviet influence. The Kurds tried to obtain the sponsorship of the western powers but were rebuffed. However, it must still be admitted that in opting for the backing of the U.S. which had no inherent interest in their cause, and was merely engaged in a great power game, they made a historic mistake.

Kissinger goes on to say, "even from the perspectives of two decades, I like the alternatives to the course we pursued even less," although he admitted, "for the Kurdish people,

---

[1]Henry A. Kissinger, *White House Years* (Boston: Little Brown and Company, 1979), pp. 1265-66.

[2]Henry A. Kissinger, "Tragedy of the Kurds," in *Years of Renewal* (New York: Simon and Schuster, 1999), pp. 576-596.

perennial victims of history, this is, of course, no consolation."

Indirectly, Kissinger explained that saving the Kurds would have been too expensive for the U.S. because it would have required the opening of a new front in inhospitable mountains close to the Soviet border. Thus, we did not have the option of overt support in a war so logistically difficult, so remote, and so incomprehensible to the American taxpayer. Moreover, "the Shah had made the decision, and we had neither the plausible arguments nor strategies to dissuade him." Now that he is not in office, Kissinger feels at liberty to say: "As a case study, the Kurdish tragedy provides material for a variety of conclusions: the need to clarify objectives at the outset; the importance of relating goals to available means; the need to review an operation periodically; and the importance of coherence among allies." In short, the Iraqi Kurds had played the role of dispensable pawns for U.S. foreign policy.

The Americans have failed in two episodes to protect Iraqi Kurds from devastation after instigating them against the regime. In both cases intervention, whether covert as in the last years of the 1961-1975 Kurdish war or overt as in the 1991 war, took place only to preserve international stability and the *de facto* regional balance of power. This purpose undermines the fate of 30 million Kurds struggling for the last 75 years to have their own independent state.

KURDS' HISTORY IN BRIEF

The Kurds have had a long historical struggle to sustain an identity of their own. They are one of the oldest communities in the Middle East yet, still without their own state. Because of their intrinsic readiness to revolt against chastisement, they have been exploited habitually by regional and international powers to assume a militaristic role in destabilizing regional regimes. Their history jets back to the days of the ancient Gutis some four thousand years ago. Of an Aryan stock, their language is Indo-European of the Iranian group, with the majority being followers of Islam. Ever since their ancient days, the Kurds

have been trenching a historic and strategic triangle of 400,000 square km.

In 1516, the Kurdish inhabited regions were divided between the Sunni Ottoman Empire and the Shi'ite Safavid Empire of Persia. Being frontiers' protectors of two contending empires, the Kurds managed to preserve relative autonomy. The Sykes-Picot plan of 1916 and its implementation after World War I dispersed the Kurds. Population estimates in the late 1990's indicate a division of 30 million Kurds among Turkey (51%), Iran (24%), Iraq (16%), Syria (5%), Europe (3%), and former Soviet Union (1%).[3]

The Kurds were, in majority, tribal communities constrained by their ethnic origin. They reproduced themselves along an intrinsic agrarian mode of production. Their allegiance in large was to their petty principalities controlled by *Aghas* and/or religious leaders. At the end of the Nineteenth Century, Kurdish nationalism began to entertain the minds of the Kurdish elite after being a romantic endeavor among few urban intellectuals. Kurdish nationalism as a new political trend became an additional mobilizing force to perpetuate the authority of the established elite, and assist them in withstanding the assimilation attempts mainly by the modern governments of Turkey, Iran and Iraq. As an ethnic community, the Kurds were discriminated against for at least, two of their characteristics. To the Shiite Iranians the Kurds are Sunni. To the Arabs the Kurds are non-Arabs and to the Turks, the Kurds belong to a different racial and ethnic civilization. The Kurds felt alienated by the societies surrounding them. Their alienation bred in them a force to resist assimilation. Being disjunctioned in their region and marginal in the international system makes them a stump easy to manipulate especially by major powers. The Kurd's ongoing struggle towards some form of autonomy is a natural result of their cultural rehabilitation development in a hostile environment. Their endeavor of becoming autonomous has become the contrivance to all powers interested in the region to use, scheme and exploit. That is why they are often labeled as pawns of the

---

[3]Lokman I. Meho, *Kurdish Culture and Society: An Annotated Bibliography* (Westport, CT: Greenwood Press, 2001), p. 4.

Middle East political playhouse. In the 1920s the British enticed them to rebel against Turkey to balance Turkish-Iraqi account. The Americans insinuated flawed promises to instigate them against Iraq to bolster their ally the Shah during the 1970s Iran-Iraq disputes. Syria, Iraq and Iran have nonetheless manipulated the Kurds of one another as a mean to score points in their political contention. In all instances however, the Kurds were abandoned to their miserable fate to face the bloody retrieval of their own local authorities.[4]

KURDS IN IRAQ

The Iraqi-Kurdish predicament dates back to the creation of the state in 1920. Iraq was designed by the British to comprise three provinces, each contained different sectarian and ethnic group; the Baghdad province in the Middle mainly of Sunni Arabs and the Mosul province to the North dominant by Kurds. The incorporation of the resource affluent area of the Kurds in the North to Iraq served two essential British objectives: First, it was cardinal for a viable Iraq and, second, it partitioned the Kurdish people thus decreasing future possibility of constituting a Kurdish national state. This state-design, as the case in most newly independent countries, had neither respect nor a future vision for the well-being of minorities and the potential internal strife that could be generated from such inceptions. The Kurds rebelled against this measure demanding autonomy but they were brutally suppressed by the British.

The deposing of the monarchy on July 14, 1958 by General Qassim depicted a turning point in the fate of the Iraqi Kurds. It enticed the fortification of the Kurdish nationalist movement as manifested mainly in the Kurdish wars of 1961-1975 and 1991, both of which were intervened by the U.S. The Americans had two basic objectives behind their direct intervention in these two wars. In both wars, the U.S., first, wanted to preserve the balance of power in the region; and, second, to assist its friends the Shah in the former

war, and Turkey and Saudi Arabia in the later war. The United States in both times established contacts with the Kurdish leaders—covertly in the 1972-1975 period and overtly in 1991—promising military support and encouraging their plight for autonomy. These American promises of support boosted the moral of the Kurds to fight vigorously suffering in the processes tens of thousands of casualties and a total devastation of their pilot cities and villages. The American timing to use the stooges Kurds in both cases came at a point when the Iraqi government was militarily eager to destroy the Kurds. The enigmatic questions in this respect are the following:

What was the crux of the American-Kurdish connections? Did the Americans achieve their objectives in both times? How did the Iraqi Kurds serve the political interests of the United States? Were the Americans aware from the first beginning that their long term objectives are in conflict with those of the Kurds? Why the Kurds were abandoned and betrayed in 1975 and 1991? These questions could only be answered within a study framework of American foreign policy; its goals, formulation, tools and implementation.

U.S. FOREIGN POLICY AND SELF-DETERMINATION MOVEMENTS

There appear to be a number of aspects pertinent to American Foreign policy with respect to self-determination in the Third World and more broadly, with respect to separatists in their plight for independence or relative autonomy. These aspects are widely shared in both the policy-making and academic worlds. Hans Morgenthau, Henry Kissinger and the realists have asserted that, dominant American perspectives on Third World politics have displayed little sympathy for, and often considerable resistance to objectives basic to radical conceptions of the national liberation process. The overt policy of the United States has been that self-determination is a universal right of subject peoples. However, there is little clarity on whom this right pertains to. This policy has always been exploited not to further the aspiration of liberation movements but to promote American

---

[4]Graham E. Fuller, "The Fate of the Kurds," *Foreign Affairs* 72 (Spring 1993), p. 108.

national and vital interests. The contention prevailing between the USA and the USSR during the Cold War forced the former to pursue a covert policy with regard to all national movements in the Third World, and especially with regard to supporting the autonomy of the Kurds in Iraq. However, after the disintegration of the Soviet Union, the United States started to follow an overt policy with regard to such movements as the case with Iraqi Kurds in 1991.

Arnold Wolfers asserts that the United States has an ambiguous set of principles to guide their foreign policy.[5] This ambiguity combined with their enormous resources allows them to be flexible in their national goal poignant with the changing circumstances.[6] Realists argue that foreign policy of super powers is tested only by their ability to manipulate their national security interest which include; protecting and supporting friends and allies, preserving a benevolent balance of power among the different contenders and protecting citizens abroad.[7] Moralists, on the other hand, criticize the realists for giving moral norms secondary attention in their studies of how and why policy decisions are made. They argue that the term "national security interest" in itself implies a selfish and unprincipled approach the conduct of foreign relations. It implies a nation's concern with its geopolitical and economic advantage without regard for morality, law, or the welfare of others, except insofar as these serve as instruments for the nation's own advantage.[8] Moralists have often criticized the foreign policy adopted by the United States in pursuing its self-interest at the expense of principles. They

assert that this lead the U.S. to immoral political behavior.[9]

Morgenthau justifies the call for self-interest as being the ultimate goal of every nation and that "survival" is the highest moral principle of a state. The state has no right to risk its national interest for the sake of certain moral principles. National interest overpowers morality.[10] The fact that all governments pursue the same foreign policy goals implies that the desire for self-interest is ethically justifiable and the calling for ideals only leads to self destruction. The problem is that goals as such cannot be secured except at the expense of other nations' interests.[11] As Holsti puts it "regardless of reasons of conscience, prestige, and self-interest, governments in most cases conduct their relations with each other in accordance with the commonly accepted rules of the game."[12]

With the emerging of the new world order, many ethnic groups thought that the United States may have entered a new cycle of foreign policy assessment, however, American foreign policy remained "generally hard-headed, pragmatic and at times ruthless."[13] The United States' rhetoric of principles and aspirations are only a brood to its reality. Some of these principles are democracy and freedom for all peoples, eliminating hunger and poverty, maintaining friendship with all nations.[14]

A strenuous predicament has faced the American policy makers between the early 1960s and the mid 1970s. There has been a clash between the administration and Congress over the role of each in the formulation

---

[5]For further discussion on this issue, see Arnold Wolfers, "National, Security' as an Ambiguous Symbol," *Political Science Quarterly* 67 (December 1952): 481-502.

[6]Samuel C. Patterson, Roger H. Davidson, and Randall B. Ripley, *A More Perfect Union: Introduction to American Government*, revised edition (Homewood, IL: The Dorsey Press, 1982), pp. 593-595.

[7]Ibid, p. 595

[8]Seth P. Tillman, *The United States in the Middle East: Interests and Obstacles* (Bloomington, IN: Indiana University Press, 1982), p. 43.

[9]K. J. Holsti, *International Politics: A Framework for Analysis*, 5th ed. (Englewood Cliffs, NJ: Prentice- Hall International Inc., 1988), p. 381.

[10]Hans J. Morgenthau, "Another 'Great Debate': The National Interest of the United States," *The American Political Science Review* 46 (December 1952), p. 985. Cited in Thomas W. Robinson "National Interests," in *International Politics and Foreign Policy: A Reader in Research and Theory*, edited by James N. Rosenau (New York: The Free Press, 1969), p. 186.

[11]Holsti, pp. 381-392.

[12]Ibid, p. 393.

[13]Morgenthau, pp. 970-911.

[14]Patterson, p. 596.

of foreign policy.[15] Observers attested this clash as a result to "chronic tension" between the democratic political system and its snobbish national security system.[16] The President being in control of the Department of State, the National Security Council (NSC), and the Central Intelligence Agency (CIA) in addition to his constitutional powers playa dominant role in foreign policy and manipulates the congress. He is often tagged as the imperial president.[17] This has been the case at least until the mid-1970s 'when some of the presidential powers procured impediments by the Congress.[18] The Vietnam War, Watergate, and the illegal U.S. involvement in covert activities in Third World enticed the Congress to claim restrictions on the President's freedom of action.[19]

This procedure adopted by the Congress was crucial to avoid; first, "future Vietnams" by making debates on national security open rather than closed within the circle of presidents and their immediate staff. Second, to check on the excessive powers that characterized the national security bureaucratic elites headed by an "imperial president" who circumvented the authority of Congress and the courts. Presidents have perceived themselves as being above the law, particularly in foreign policy matters, and used secrecy and distor-

tion to deceive Congress and the public in order to score high in foreign policy.[20]

Some of the Third World regions were relegated to play the role of pawns in the East-West conflict. Mike Bowker argues that superpower relationship went through three stages since the end of World War II: The first is between 1945 and 1962, a period of high East-West tension with the possibility of direct superpower conflict. The second is between 1962 and 1989, a period of competitive coexistence in which the level of direct conflict between the two superpowers decreased, however, "found expression through the arms race and proxy wars in the Third World. The third is after 1989, a period of cooperative coexistence[21] in which U.S. policy toward self-determination claims remained skeptic[22] with a far easier atmosphere for intervention in the internal affairs of states as long as it serves the vital interests of the United States.

U.S. INTERVENTION IN THE THIRD WORLD

Schraeder defines interventions as "the purposeful and calculated use of political, economic, and military instruments by one country to influence the domestic politics or the foreign policy of another country."[23] Intervention could ensue two divergent temperaments; it is either covert or overt. Because U.S. intervention in the Iraqi-Kurdish war of

---

[15]Lec H. Hamilton, "America's Role in the World: A Congressional Perspective," in *U.S. Foreign Policy in the 1990s*, edited by Greg Schmergel (London: Macmillan, 1991), p. 60; and Peter J. Schraeder, "It's the Third World Stupid! Why the Third World Should be the Priority of the Clinton Administration," *Third World Quarterly* 14, no.2 (1993), p. 220.

[16]Kenneth E. Sharpe, "The Real Case of Iran-Gate," *Foreign Policy*, no, 68 (1987), p. 19. Cited in Schraeder, p. 220.

[17]Patterson, pp. 606- 620; James Q. Wilson *American Government: Institutions and Policies*, 5th ed. (Lexington, MA: D.C. Heath and Company, 1992), pp. 547-548; and Loch K. Johnson, *America's Secret Power: The CIA in a Democratic Society* (New York: Oxford University Press, 1989), p. 16.

[18]Wilson, p. 551.

[19]Schraeder, pp. 222- 223; and Wilson, p. 550. For further information, see Wilson, pp. 551-552.

[20]Morris J. Blachman and Kenneth E. Sharpe, "De-Democratising American Foreign Policy: Dismantling the Post-Vietnam Formula," *Third World Quarterly* 4 (1986), p. 1271. Cited in Schraeder, pp. 220-221.

[21]Mike Bowker, "Superpower Relations Since 1945," in *Encyclopedia of Government and Politics*, edited by Mary Hawkesworth and Maurice Kogan (London: Routledgc, 1992), p. 1083.

[22]Morton H. Halperin and David J. Scheffer, with Patricia L. Small. *Self-Determination in the New World Order* (Washington, DC: Carnegie Endowment for International Peace, 1992), pp. 10-11.

[23]Peter J. Schraeder, "Concepts, Relevance, Themes, and Overview," in *Intervention in the 1980s: U.S. Foreign Policy in the Third World*, edited by Peter J. Schraeder (Boulder, CO: Lynne Rienner Publishers, 1989), p. 2.

1961-1975 was of a covert paramilitary nature, we need first to delineate its distinctive characteristics. The CIA defines covert intervention as "special activity conducted abroad in support of the United States foreign policy objectives and executed so that the role of the United States government is not apparent or acknowledged publicly."[24] In matters of core national security the CIA reports directly to the president through the National Security Council (NSC). It has been given by the National Security Act of 1947 five specific authorities: first, advise the NSC on intelligence activities related to national security; second, make recommendations to the NSC for the coordination of such activities; third, correlate, evaluate and disseminate intelligence within the government; fourth, carry out services for existing agencies that the NSC decides might be best done centrally; and fifth, perform such other functions and duties related to intelligence affecting the national security as the NSC may from time to time direct.[25] The first four authorities are of a pure intelligence nature while the last is intended for a "wide range of covert actions around the world." Truman's Doctrine which was designed to contain the threat of communism towards areas of vital interests to the United States, namely, Greece, Turkey and other Middle Eastern newly emerging or established governments further enhanced this fifth authority.[26] But how would containment be achieved? Johnson argues that, in addition to traditional governmental instruments, containment could be achieved also through CIA covert action which is of four kinds: propaganda, political, economic, and paramilitary means.[27] Paramilitary covert action often involves large-scale secret wars in which the U.S. provides economic as well as military aid to rebels intending to overthrow or undermine an anti-American government. In such actions

the rebels are used as proxies to avoid counterproductive direct U.S. intervention.[28] This partly explains why a clash exists between the administration and Congress concerning the foreign policy making process in the field of covert actions. Two set of arguments result from this clash: one in favor of covert action and another against it. Advocates of covert action provide the following justifications: (1) The Soviet Union strongly supports the secret activities of the KGB; (2) The U.S. has an obligation of credibility to support its allies and friends, often this obligation requires covert actions to save a friend from regional or international embarrassment; (3) Speed and secrecy are of vital importance for success in critical situation, thus the CIA should be able to avoid informing the public ahead of time; and (4) Covert action is the best tool at the disposal of the administration to safeguard national security. Such actions are prospectively affective only if tagged as classified information.[29]

THE WAR OF 1961-1975

After Qassim's coup of July 14, 1958, the established leader of the Kurdish national movement, Mullah Mustapha Barzani, was permitted to return to Iraq after thirteen-years of exile in the Soviet Union. He supported Qassim against his foes. In return, the Kurds were to be given relative autonomy within the Iraqi state. Qassim declined his promise and eventually had to face a harsh Kurdish rebellion.[30] During the ongoing revolt that started in 1961, Barzani conducted on-and-off negotiations with the consequent Iraqi authorities proposing an end to the revolt in exchange for relative autonomy. His first approach was with Premier Abdul-Rahman al-Bazzaz in

---

[24]Harry Howe Ranson, "Covert Intervention," in *Intervention in the 1980s: U.S. Foreign Policy in the Third World*, edited by Peter J. Schraeder (Boulder, CO: Lynne Rienner Publishers, 1989), p. 101.
[25]Johnson, pp. 16-17.
[26]Philip L. Groisser and Seymour P. Lachman, *The United States and the Middle East* (Albany, NY: State University of New York Press, 1982).
[27]Johnson, p. 26.

---

[28]Ibid, pp. 26-27; and Peter J. Schraeder, "Paramilitary Intervention," in *Intervention in the 1980s: U.S. Foreign Policy in the Third World*, edited by Peter J. Schraeder (Boulder, CO: Lynne Rienner Publishers, 1989), p. 115.
[29]Ransom, pp. 112-113.
[30]Ismet Sheriff Vanly, "Kurdistan in Iraq," in *People Without a Country: The Kurds and Kurdistan*, edited by Gerard Chaliand and translated from French by Michael Pallis (London: Zed Press, 1980), pp. 165-167.

1965. The later declared that the government's intention is to establish a "centralized constitutional system" and to preserve Iraq's unity.[31] The revolt continued until the mid-1966. In the process, the Iraqi army was debilitated in attempting to curb the Kurdish rebels. This failure raised many questions concerning the wisdom of depleting the Iraqi's resources in a never ending Iraqi-Kurdish warfare.[32] Al-Bazzaz offered a peace settlement program composed of 12 points that met Barzani's demands for relative autonomy. The military elites within the Iraqi government accused al-Bazzaz of betrayal the constitution. Al-Bazzaz government was ousted right after the agreement with the Kurds. The revolt continued with the return of the al-Ba'th party to power in 1968.[33]

Al-Ba'th party, in principle, was committed to the unification of Iraq.[34] However, newly returning to power, they considered their own establishment and consolidation of strength as top priority. They decided to relax their relation with the Kurds, and endorse a mutual agreement conferred in March 1970. It attended to the following:

1. Recognition of Kurdish as the official language in those areas where Kurds constitute a majority. Kurdish and Arabic would be taught together in all schools;
2. Participation of Kurds in government, including the appointment of Kurds to Key posts in the state;
3. Furtherance of Kurdish education and culture;
4. Requirement that officials in the Kurdish areas speak Kurdish;
5. Right to establish Kurdish student, youth, women's, and teachers' organizations;
6. Economic development of the Kurdish area;
7. Return of Kurds to their villages or financial compensation;

8. Agrarian reform;
9. Amendment of the constitution to read 'the Iraqi people consist of two main nationalities: The Arab and Kurdish nationalities;
10. Return of the clandestine radio stations and heavy weapons to the government;
11. Appointment of a Kurdish vice-president;
12. Amendment of provincial laws in accordance with this declaration; and
13. Formations of a Kurdish area with self-government[35]

This Agreement promised Barzani that those regions in which the Kurds constituted a majority were to be granted self-governing status within four years from the date of its signature. Barzani went along with this solution, even though he was aware that it would not be totally implemented. His own forces were exhausted after nine years of non stop fighting, and there was no way he could convince his forces to fight after being exposed to the propaganda of the government crediting itself in the alleged Agreement.[36] The Ba'th party failed to carry out a census of the Kurdish inhabited regions, especially Kirkuk—the oil-rich region of Iraqi Kurdistan. No genuine representation was offered to the Kurds. The five ministerial posts given to the Kurds were symbolic. Barzani and some of his sons were targets of the regime's assassination plots. At the end of the four-year period, in March 1974, the al-Ba'th party, having generated military strength and supported by the Soviets, unilaterally promulgated its Law for Autonomy in 'the Area of Kurdistan. The Kurds being supported by the U.S. viewed the Autonomy Law as an insufficient implementation of the 1970 Agreement. Eventually, they rejected it proclaiming that not only the Ba'thists failed to implement their promises, but had also not granted the Autonomous Administration of Kurdistan any real power. In the wake of this rejection, the war intensified between the Kurdish forces and the Iraqi army.[37]

[31]Majid Khadduri, *Republican 'Iraq: A Study in 'Iraqi Politics Since the Revolution of 1958* (London: Oxford University Press, 1969), p. 253.

[32]Marioun Farouk-Sluglett and Peter Sluglett. *Iraq Since 1958: From Revolution to Dictatorship* (London: I. B. Tauris & Co. Ltd., 1990), pp. 103-104.

[33]David McDowall, *The Kurds: A Nation Denied* (London: Minority Rights Publications, 1992), pp. 88-89.

[34]Saddam Hussein, *On Current Events in Iraq* (London: Longman Group Ltd., 1977), p. 15.

[35]Edmund Ghareeb, *The Kurdish Question in Iraq* (Syracuse, NY: Syracuse University Press, 1981), p. 87.

[36]Ibid, pp. 88-89.

[37]McDowall, pp. 92-94; Vanly, pp. 170-173; Lee C. Buchheit, *Secession: The Legitimacy of self-Determination* (New Haven: Yale University Press,

AMERICAN INVOLVEMENT, 1972-1975

After the death of Nasser in 1970 and the British withdrawal from the Persian Gulf in 1971, Iran coveted to fill the power vacuum in the region. Their first objective was to weaken Iraq economically and militarily. They decided to instigate the Kurds to refuse the Iraqi concessions and to continue with their military struggle to attain a better deal. Nonetheless, The Ba'th party in Iraq was ambitious to assume Nasser's leadership of the Arab World and to deter Iran from exerting its hegemony on the Arabian Gulf. For the fulfillment of its ambitions, the Iraqi regime signed the Treaty of Friendship and Cooperation with the Soviet Union in 1972. In return the Soviets supplied Iraq with sophisticated military weapons.

The increased Soviet influence in Iraq and the increased Iraqi expenditure on military preparedness alarmed the Iranians, Israel and the United States. The Iranians intensified their contacts with the Kurds to encourage the aggravation of their revolt against the Iraqis. Barzani, being fearful of the Iraqi newly purchased sophisticated weapons, an afraid of future betrayal by the Iranians, requested an international guarantee that he will not be abandoned and left victim to the retribution of the Iraqis. When Nixon and Kissinger visited Tehran on May 30, 1972 on their way back from a summit conference with Brezhnev, the Shah displayed the Kurdish conditions: The Kurds have sublime confidence in the U.S. and wants to be armed by you. Nixon accepted the Kurdish demands.[38] "Anything for a friend and loyal ally said Nixon."[39]

The U.S., with Richard Nixon in office (his era was labeled as the "imperial presidency") and Henry Kissinger as adviser of the National Security Council, set up the American apparatus for the Kurdish secret war.[40] They assured Barzani of their goodwill. This attestation was classified and emanated from Nixon's own office, because he had no trust in the bureaucracy of the State Department. The American-Kurdish deal was a timely betrayal of the statement of principles that had already been signed in Moscow. In his news conference in Moscow, Kissinger had stated that both the United States and the Soviet Union were in agreement on the need to defuse tension in the Middle East and;

> to contribute what they can to bringing about a general settlement... such a settlement would also contribute to the relaxation of the armaments race in that area... Speaking for our side, I can say we will attempt to implement these principles in the spirit in which they were promulgated.

By accepting the Iranian-Kurdish deal, the American "spirit" lasted one day.[41] For Nixon and Kissinger the deal was extremely inducive to be refuted for the following reasons:

1. They were bewildered by the nationalization of the Iraqi Petroleum Company;
2. They viewed Iraq as a Soviet delinquent towards the encroachment of the Gulf region;
3. An internal Iraqi strife could enhance the bargaining positions of U.S. allies and friends; Iran's role as the policeman of the Gulf region, the Kuwaitis contrasting to any Iraqi territorial claims of their estate. Israel could be better off

---

1978), pp. 158-159; and Michael M. Gunter, *The Kurds of Iraq: Tragedy and Hope* (New York: St. Martin's Press, 1992), pp. 16-17.

[38]John Prados, *Presidents' Secret Wars: CIA and Pentagon Covert Operations Since World War II* (New York: William Morrow and Company, Inc., 1986), p. 298. It is debated that U.S. contacts with Iraqi Kurds started long before 1972, however, there are no reliable sources. The primary source of information for this secret war is the Staff Report of the Secret Committee on Intelligence; U.S. House of Representatives, based on hearings held during 1975. Publication of the report was suppressed by the full House until the White House could censor it. But portions of the uncensored report, which came to be known as The Pike Report after the Committee's chairman Representative Otis G. Pike,

---

were leaked to the press, in particular *The Village Voice* of New York which published much of it in its issues of 16th and 23rd of February 1976. Hence, The Village Voice will be referred to in following footnotes.

[39]William Blum, The CIA: A Forgotten History-U.S. Global Interventions Since World War 2 (London: Zed Books Ltd., 1986), p.1 275.

[40]Prados, pp. 297-314.

[41]Seymour M. Hersh, *The Price of Power: Kissinger in the Nixon White House* (New York: Summit Books, 1983), p. 542n.

in its military strategic balance with the Arab World;[42] and

4. This deal will undermine the leftist tendencies among some of the Kurdish factions.

American military and financial furtherance to the Kurds began in August 1972. The operation was entrusted to the CIA. The State Department was not involved. Barzani was unaware of this actuality. He thought that dealing with the President and his Secretary is dealing, with all of the USA.[43] In a short period of time, Barzani raised 100,000 fighters to engage against the Iraqi forces.[44] Over the next three years, $16 million in CIA funds were funneled to the Kurds.[45] A sum that is far less than how much the confrontation required to be successful ($300 million according to Kissinger). The Shah tried to make up for the shortage. By time, the American aid proved to be basically symbolic. Being trapped in the war and in order to induce more U.S. support, Barzani frequently stated that "he trusted no other major power" than the United States, "ready to become the 51st state of the USA[46] "to make the oil fields at the disposal of the U.S."[47] and that "the U.S. could rely on a friend in OPEC once the oil-rich Kurdistan achieve its independence."[48] The Kurds trusted the Americans' pledge that they will not. be abandoned neither by them nor by the Shah in their fierce war against Iraq. Later, it was discovered that "neither the Shah nor the President and Kissinger desired victory for the Kurds. They merely hoped to ensure that the insurgents would be capable of sustaining a level of hostility just high enough to sap the resources of Iraq.[49] A CIA report of March 22, 1974 depicted the Iranian and the U.S. foreign policy towards this issue:

We would think that Iran would not look with favor on the establishment of a formalized (Kurdish) autonomous government. Iran, like ourselves, has seen benefit in a stalemate situation... in which Iraq is intrinsically weakened by the Kurd's refusal to relinquish its semi-autonomy. Neither Iran nor ourselves wish to see the matter resolved one way or the other.[50]

This policy, as stated by the same report "was not imparted to our clients [Kurds], who were encouraged to continue fighting... Even in the context of covert action... this was a cynical enterprise."[51] The Pike report (Congressional Investigating Team Report) is supportive of this assessment at least in as much as it explains the "no win" policy of the United States and Iran.

In the heat of the October 1973 war between the Arabs and Israel, the Iraqis dispatched a battalion to take part in the confrontation. Induced by Israel, the Kurds were planning on propelling major attacks on the Iraqi forces. Kissinger, observed the drawback of American interests if the Kurds are to gain military improvement against the Iraqis. He ordered the CIA on October 16 of the same year to send this message to the Kurds: "We do not consider it advisable for you to undertake the offensive military actions that .Israel has suggested to you." Having faith in the Americans, the Kurds considered the content of this message in their best interest and complied.[52] The Kurds' faith in American foreign policy proved to be hazardous. The CIA had all along facts suggesting that the Shah would abandon the Kurds the minute he comes to an agreement with Iraq over border disputes.[53] The Shah viewed the Kurds as instruments and not as people in his dispute with Iraq. The. CIA was not any different. It characterized the Kurds as a "uniquely useful tool for weakening Iraq's potential for regional adventurism."[54]

---

[42]Jon Kimche, "Selling Out the Kurds," *The New Republic* 172 (April 19, 1975), p. 17.

[43]Vanly, p. 184.

[44]Prados, p. 314.

[45]Ibid; Blum, p. 276; and Vanly, p. 184.

[46]*The Village Voice* (February 11, 1976). Cited in Ghareeb, p. 140.

[47]Aharon Latham, "*What Kissinger was Afraid of*," p. 59. Cited in Ghareeb, p. 140.

[48]*New York Times*, March 13, 1975. Cited in Ghareeb, p. 140.

[49]Vanly, pp. 184-185.

---

[50]*The Village Voice*, p. 87. Cited in Blum, p. 276.

[51]Ibid.

[52]Ibid.

[53]Blum, p. 277.

[54]*The Village Voice*, p. 87. Cited in Blum, p. 277.

Being weakened by the Kurdish war and fearing its continuation, the Iraqis accepted an Iranian proposal to confer territorial concessions at their common borders in return for Iranian cessation of support to the Kurds. The agreement was concluded on March 6, 1975 during the OPEC Conference held in Algiers. Immediately after signing the Agreement, Iran sealed its borders to the Iraqi Kurds. In the following days the Iraqi army launched its enormous brutal offensive. The Kurds, being abandoned by the Shah and the Americans were unable to withstand the Iraqi killing-machine. Their military power was crushed for several years to come. During the Iraqi transgression, the bewildered Kurds sent a desperate message to the CIA: "There is confusion and dismay among our people and forces. Our people's fate is in unprecedented danger. Complete destruction hanging over our head. No explanation for all this. We appeal to you and to the United States government to intervene as you have promised...[55]

Another message was sent to Kissinger:

> Your Excellency, having always believed in the peaceful solution of disputes including those between Iran and Iraq, we are pleased to see that these two countries have come to some agreement... However, our hearts bleed to see that an immediate byproduct of their agreement is the destruction of our defenseless people... All are silent. Your Excellency, we feel that the United States has a commitment to defend us and has a moral and political responsibility towards our people.[56]

The Kurds did not receive any direct attention and nothing was done to salvage the over 200,000 displaced people. When Kissinger was interviewed by the staff of the Pike Committee about the United States involvement in the Kurdish misfortune, he responded: "Covert action should not be confused with missionary work."[57]

George Lenczowski, spoke volumes when he said that the Algiers Agreement blessed by the Americans is a sort of Yalta for the Kurd-

ish nationalists.[58] Arthur Turner's comments have taken this issue further when he implied that the Algiers Agreement was a textbook example of how underprivileged people would be sacrificed by larger states for the sake of their own interests.[59]

AMERICAN INVOLVEMENT, 1991

History is full of astonishments, some of them are tragic and treacherous. Immediately after the end of the military operations in February 1991, and following the defeat of the Iraqi forces, the U.S. president called on the Iraqi people to revolt and bring down Saddam's regime. This statement has trapped the U.S. in an international and regional political and security dilemma, caused a geopolitical shock and is still causing waves of instability in the balance of power of the region. Both the Shiite South and the Kurdish North were more than eager to respond to this call. While the Shiite did not fare well in the South, the Kurds with the help of the United Nations and the allied Poised Hammer forces stationed in Southeastern Turkey, were able to establish a chaotic independent Kurdish enclave.[60]

Stability in the region, as president Bush argued it, could only be achieved after the ousting of Saddam Hussein. He exerted much diplomatic effort on the United Nations Security Council to pass Resolution 678 on November 29, 1990. Article 2, of this Resolution was intentionally ambiguous to allow for different interpretations and actions. It authorizes the member-states cooperating with Kuwait to use "... all means necessary to restore international peace and security in the area..."

The consequences of Bush's unwise statement did not lead to the ousting of Saddam but to the dangerous prospect of frag-

---

[55]Ibid.

[56]Ibid.

[57]Blum, p. 278.

[58]George Lenczowski, *The Middle East in World Affairs* 4th ed. (Ithaca: Cornell University Press, 1980), p. 220.

[59]Arthur Campbell Turner, "Kurdish Nationalism," in *Ideology and Power in the Middle East: Studies in Honor of George Lenczowski*, edited by Peter J. Chelkowski and Robert J. Pranger, (Durham: Duke University Press, 1988), p. 408.

[60]Faleh Abd Al-Jabbar, "Why the Uprising Failed," *Middle East Report* 22 (May/June 1992), pp. 2-14.

menting the republic of Iraq into three separate entities; Shiite to the South, Sunni to the Center and Kurdish to the North. Potentially, this prospect disturbs the erstwhile shivering balance of power in the region. The same Kurdish-Iraqi experience of 1972- 75 was repeated. After being encouraged by the United States to rebel against Saddam, the Kurds were left to bear the bloody consequences alone with no help from the Americans. Facing accusations of irresponsibility, Bush responded with anger:

> Do I think that the United States should bear guilt because of suggesting that the Iraqi people take matters into their hands, with implication being given that the United States would be there to support them militarily? That was not true. We never implied that.[61]

The gradual withdrawal of American rhetorical support for the Iraqi opposition was first expressed by Colin Powel when he warned Saddam... to . be a little careful how he goes about suppressing the various insurrections that are taking place[62] (to be a little careful does not mean to stop). Then on March 26, it was made clear that the administration decided not to intervene in support of the rebels. By this time the American commander of the allied forces general Norman Schwartzkopf and his Iraqi counterpart were in agreement to allow the Iraqi military to use helicopter gunships and armored cars to crush the rebels.[63] A few days later a major offensive on Kurdish positions began. Major cities fell to government forces and thousands of fearful Kurds began fleeing to the mountains in .a desperate attempt to escape genocide. By the end of April, over 2 million refugees were driven along the Iranian and Turkish borders. Having resolved the Kuwaiti problem and restored the regional balance of power, the U.S. created a new dimensional problem of major security implications that was left hang-

ing for the contending powers of the region to struggle with.

Saddam surprised observers with his speedy brutal repressive ability to control the Iraqi heartland and sustain his authority. Brent Scowcroft replied "we did not expect the severity of the attacks on the Kurds."[64] This reaction of brutal force triggered the Security Council on April 5, 1991 to issue resolution 688 that condemned the repression of the Iraqi civilian population especially in the Kurdish populated areas and allow for the creation of a Safe Haven, which has now for all practical purposes become a separate Iraqi enclave altogether.

The Iranians were burdened with the one million Iraqi Kurds arriving along their border who joined the already 600,000 refugees stationed in Iran from previous expulsions. Turkey also received another million Kurd as refugees. However, having been a major participant in the Second Gulf War and having enough problems with its own Kurds, Turkey was allowed by the West to play the decisive role in handling the Kurdish enigma. It imposed from the first beginning its own logic of the longer-term policy of how to deal with the refugee crisis. Refugees as asserted by its leaders have to be moved out of Turkish soil as soon as possible. However, they should not return to a separate Kurdish state. They should be given safety within an integrated Iraqi state.[65] Further undermining of Iraq and the establishment of an independent Kurdish state will shift the balance of power in favor of the Iran-Syrian tacit coalition. On April 7, President Ozal said "We have to put those people (Kurds) in the Iraqi territory and take care of them"[66] (the emphasis is on the term Iraqi territories.) James Baker being sympathetic to

---

[61]Bush's News Conference, USIA, April 16, 1991.

[62]*The New York Times* (March 23, 1991).

[63]Laurie Mylroie, "How We Helped Saddam Survive," *The Washington Post* (April 14, 1991).

[64]The U.S. Administration was aware of the Consequences of leaving the Kurds to their fate. They have pr-positioned supplies in Turkey to cope with the anticipated refugee problem. They predicted a number of 20,000—one hundred times less than the actual number of refugees. See *International Herald Tribune* (April 15, 1991).

[65]Robert Olson, "The Kurdish Question in the Aftermath of the Gulf War: Geopolitical and Geostrategic Changes in the Middle East," *Third World Quarterly* 13, no.2 (1992), pp. 475–499.

[66]*The Independent* (April 14, 1991).

the Turkish interests and in order to convey to the Kurds American reluctance to support their fight against the government of Iraq, announced in Turkey "The United States would not go down the slippery slope of being sucked into a civil war."[67] The implication was that however brutal, the Saddam government is still the legal authority in Iraq. The setting of international relief centers on Iraqi soil without Iraq's consent is the maximum interference the U.S. could extend against the sovereignty of an internationally recognized state. The justification for respecting the integrity of Iraq is drawn from the same principle that the coalition had just fought a ferocious war in Kuwait.

CONCLUSION

In the words of Gur-Arieh: "No nation in the 20th century has been made the pawn of regional and global powers as often as the Kurds."[68] U.S. policy towards the Iraqi Kurds is a significant subject of various interpretations. Its involvement in the Iraqi internal affairs contains all the makings of Machiavellian literature. The encouragement to resort to war, that the Kurds had received from the Americans, has twice eliminated all possible opportunities for them to live peacefully within a united Iraqi state.

The U.S. Administration in both cases considered the Kurdish people as a tool defying by that all moral and humanistic principles that the USA have set up as a foundation for its foreign policy. In the 1972-1975 case, to make sure that the operation would succeed without any objection and criticism, the president suspended the normal 'watchdog' procedures for an intelligence operation. The level of secrecy associated with that venture was extremely high. The Congress, the Department of State, and even the U.S. Ambassador in Iraq had all denied allegations of being informed about the project. The President and his Secretary made sure that there will be no

official leak of information that would endanger the plan. A plan that was aware of its drastic end. A plan that could not have been approved had it been displayed for discussion through the established procedures of foreign policy decision-making process.

Also, in the 1991 case, the Americans failed to meet their implied promises of creating a state under circumstances that could hardly be more favorable: Bush's brace to the Kurds was limited to the degree of sustaining an opposition against Saddam but short of enabling them to be successful in breaking up Iraq. The overture of recent international events is reinforcing the U.S. realist foreign policy. Balance of power is its first thought and solid postulate. Bush was very concerned that, although Iraq had to be defeated, it should not be destroyed as a country. The destruction of Iraq will enduringly disrupt the Balance of power in the Middle East and the surrounding regions. Until a duplicate replacement of Saddam is accessible, someone who could hold down the always rebellious Kurds in the North and the Shiite Muslims in the South who prefer to be part of Iran, better Saddam Hussein in power than chaos in Iraq and the destabilization of the region. If the Kurds are to take chunks out of Iraq, or create an independent Kurdistan, the traditional balance of power will be transformed. The perplexity of how the Americans are dealing with the Iraqi and the Kurdish problems defies any assured line of human rights conception. One thing is for sure, in dealing with both problems, the internal situations and the intra-relations of the different regional powers in the Middle East are cautiously calculated. In short, the U.S. has a vital interest in the region that goes beyond assurances of minority and ethnic human rights.

Throughout its revolts, the Kurdish leadership had been hoping to achieve their national rights through foreign support; however, it did not realize that it was only fighting a proxy war on behalf of the United States and its allies. It is argued that the Kurdish leaders assume part of the blame for lacking international political insight. Their ignorance encouraged the CIA and the Administration to exploit the Kurds' enigma and to "toss them aside like broken toys." It is puzzling whom should we blame; the CIA, the Administration

---

[67]Judith Miller, "Iraq Accused: A Case of Genocide," *The New York Times Magazine* (January 3, 1993), p. 36.

[68]Danny Gur-Arieh, "Kurds: The Elusive Quest," *New Outlook* 34 (April/May 1991), p. 6.

or the American system as a whole for the unhappy chapter of U.S. intervention in the Kurdish-Iraqi conflicts. The surprising reality emanating from these disappointing episodes is that the Kurds never learned to restrain themselves from being pawns of interests for superpower manipulation. They repeatedly immolated themselves as forfeitures for the dictates of geopolitics, and twice the sacrifice of the U.S. and its allies.

PART II

FULL-TEXT DOCUMENTS

THE CONGRESSIONAL RECORD

1.

[November 6, 1973 (Extension of Remarks), p. 36047]

SOVIET UNION AND POISON GAS
HON. ROBERT J. HUBER
OF MICHIGAN
IN THE HOUSE OF REPRESENTA-TIVES

Tuesday, November 6, 1973

Mr. HUBER. Mr. Speaker, in recent days the role of the Soviet Union as a troublemaker in the Middle East has again been nakedly revealed. The United States was hard pressed to match the enormous amount of weaponry that the Soviet Union was pouring into Arab states. By now the lack of scruples of the Soviet Union in this regard should be evident to all.

In this connection, an article appeared in the *Detroit News* on September 4 to the effect that the Soviets have supplied poison gas to Iraq for possible use against Iraq's Kurdish minority. This would be tragic, but it would not be unprecedented. it can be recalled that in 1967, the Soviet Union furnished poison gas to Egypt to use against the Yemeni Royalists. The case was documented by the International Committee of the Red Cross. Therefore, I think this item that follows deserves the closest attention of my colleagues.

IRAQ KURDS FEAR POISON GAS ATTACK

WASHINGTON. Representatives of the Kurdish minority in Iraq charged yesterday that the Baghdad government had obtained poison gas from the Soviet Union in preparation for an extermination attempt against the Kurds.

Sources said the Baath regime in Baghdad had obtained 60,000 gas masks from the Soviet Union for Iraqi soldiers. The Soviets also have sent eight poison gas experts to train Baghdad's soldiers, said the sources.

The Kurds, who number about 100,000 in Iraq, are a non-Arab tribal people who occupy the mountains of Iraq and have been seeking an autonomous state of their own.

They have fought several civil wars in the past century with various Iraqi governments, the last ending in 1970.

Under terms reached at that time, Baghdad promised the Kurds a semiautonomous region to be established by March 1974, Kurdish representatives now say Iraq is reneging on that agreement and has started military attacks on Kurdish outposts.

The latest such attacks, Kurdish officials here say, took place in mid-August in the Sinjar region of Iraq. The fighting ended with 30 Iraqi soldiers killed and several Kurdish officials wounded.

The sources claim Iraq used artillery and MIG aircraft in the fighting. They said they had hoped the repulse of the Iraqi attack would have ended the Baghdad government's attempts to violate the 1970 agreement.

However, they now say the supply of gas from the Soviet Union indicates Baghdad is attempting a "final solution" similar to Hitler's extermination of Jews.

According to Kurdish spokesmen, the gas is stored at the Taji army camp west of Baghdad and at the headquarters of the 2nd Araqi Division at Kirkuk and the 4th Division headquarters Mosul.

The spokesman said only world opinion could head off the use of poison gas against I, the Kurds and called upon the public to urge the Soviet Union to withdraw the gas and its advisers.

2.

[July 11, 1974 (Extension of Remarks), pp. 23066-67]

THE KURDS IN IRAQ
HON. LEE H. HAMILTON
OF INDIANA
IN THE HOUSE OF REPRESENTA-
TIVES

Thursday, July 11, 1974

Mr. HAMILTON. Mr. Speaker, almost unnoticed in the newspapers these days is yet another armed conflict now raging in the Middle East. It is between Kurdish irregular forces and supporters of the Kurdish Democratic Party on the one hand and the Iraqi Armed Forces on the other side. At issue is what kind of regional autonomy the Kurds should have within an independent Iraq. This struggle is not a new one and open conflict has occurred intermittently for some 13 years.

Recently, Congressman FRASER and I met with representatives of the Kurdish Democratic Party—KDP—at their request to discuss the war and its implications for peace and stability in the Middle East. Without commenting on the merits of the Kurdish case, possible human rights violations in recent escalations of the fighting, and other essentially internal Iraqi matters, we do believe that the Kurdish viewpoint needs to be heard, and to that end, we asked the Department of State to meet informally at the policy level with these representatives of KDP. The Department of State declined.

While I believe that the question of any aid, overt or covert, to the Kurdish rebels is absolutely out of the question, I regret the unwillingness of senior State Department officials to meet informally with two former Iraqi ministers who are also members of the KDP. A useful opportunity to keep informed about one viewpoint of a war that has escalated considerably in the last two months was thereby lost.

Copies of the letter to the Department of State and its reply follow:

COMMITTEE ON FOREIGN AFFAIRS
HOUSE OF REPRESENTATIVES,
Washington, D.C., June 13, 1974.
Hon. HENRY A. KISSINGER,
Secretary of State, Washington, D.C.

DEAR MR. SECRETARY: We would like to request that a senior representative of the Department of State, Under Secretary of State Joseph J. Sisco, or Assistant Secretary of State Alfred Atherton, meet with Messrs. M. M. Abdul Rahman and M. Dizayee, two former Iraqi ministers, and Shafiq Qazzaz, all senior officials of the Kurdish Democratic Party who are currently in the United States making a presentation to the United Nations.

Without passing any judgment on the merits of their appeal, we believe that their case deserves a hearing by senior representatives of the Department of State. The civil war in Iraq, which has gone on intermittently for some thirteen years now, has recently degenerated in more serious and more bloody fighting with considerable loss of' life. We believe that because this fighting has the potential of affecting the delicate situation in the Middle East and of involving some of Iraq's neighbors, the United States must be informed directly on all facets of the continuing controversy.

We would appreciate your immediate attention to this matter.

Sincerely yours,
LEE H. HAMILTON,
Chairman, Subcommittee on the Near East and
South Asia
DONALD M. FRASER,
Chairman, Subcommittee on International Organizations and Movements.

DEPARTMENT OF STATE,
Washington, D.C., July 3,1974.
Hon. LEE H. HAMILTON,

Chairman, Subcommittee on the Near East and South Asia, House of Representatives, Washington, D.C.

DEAR MR. CHAIRMAN: The Secretary has asked me to reply to your letter of' June 13, also signed by Chairman Fraser, requesting that Under Secretary Sisco or Assistant Secretary Atherton meet with senior representatives of the Kurdish Democratic Party.

We have received several requests from Kurdish representatives for meetings. For the past year, contacts with the KDP have been limited to the Country Officer or Country Director level. To change this policy at this time could well be subject to misinterpretation by both the Kurds and the Government In Baghdad. We have noted as a result of our policy, a fall-off in Iraqi allegations that the United States is supporting the Kurdish insurrection.

While many Americans are sympathetic toward the Kurds the Department of State takes the position that the conflict is primarily an internal Iraqi problem We do not wish to encourage the Kurds to believe that we are prepared to support overtly or covertly, their insurrection in Iraq.

This being the case, we seek to afford Kurdish representatives every opportunity to state their case, but do not wish to hold out the prospect of support. Our contacts with the KDP are, of course, reported to Assistant Secretary Atherton and the Under Secretary.

If we were to break with precedent and receive KDP representatives at a higher level this fact would inevitably come to the attention of the Government of Iraq and other Arab states. it could be interpreted as meddling in Iraq's internal affairs and might militate against any possible improvement in U.S-Iraqi relations. Any encouragement we might offer to a minority in its battle for autonomy against an Arab state could raise suspicions of our intentions in the Arab world. Consequently, I do not think it would serve a useful purpose to raise the level of reception.

The above is not Intended to imply an endorsement of Iraqi policy vis-a-vis the Kurds or to disparage the national aspirations of the Kurdish people. Our position is essentially one of neutrality toward an internal dispute in which we do not feel we should become involved.

While we do not believe it would be in our best interests to change our policy toward the KDP at this time, I would be pleased to arrange a meeting between Mr. Abdul Rahman, Mr. Dizayee, and the appropriate Country Director at a mutually convenient time. Mr. Chafiq Qazzaz of the KDP was received in the Department of State on June 19 and three other Kurdish representatives called at our United Nations delegation on the same day.

Please let me know if you or Chairman Fraser would like an informal briefing on our policy regarding the Iraqi-Kurdish problem.

Cordially,
LINWOOD HOLTON,
Assistant Secretary for Congressional Relations.

3.

[April 17, 1975 (House), pp. 10519]

THE FATE OF THE KURDS

The SPEAKER pro tempore. Under a previous order of the House, the gentleman from New York (Mr. KOCH) is recognized for 5 minutes.

Mr. KOCH. Mr. Speaker, for the better part of the past year, the Kurds have been fighting a bloody battle against the Government of Iraq for their deserved right of self-determination. Denied a degree of political autonomy promised by Iraq, the Kurdish leader, Mustafa Barzani, called his people to fight the Russian-supplied Iraqi Army. Due in part to the arms and ammunition sent to the Kurds from the Shah of Iran, the Kurds fought bravely and with some success.

The Shah's motive should be understood for what it was: an attempt to cripple his bitter enemy, Iraq, by using the Kurds as cannon fodder. The recently concluded Pact of Algiers between Iran and Iraq reflects the Shah's callous attitude toward the Kurds. The Shah agreed to end all aid to the Kurds and to seal the borders to Kurdish refugees on April 1 of this year. In effect, the Shah signed the death warrants for those Kurds who did not flee their homelands.

The tragedy of the betrayal has been compounded by the inaction of the United Nations. While the U.N. showered plaudits on Yasir Arafat, it has treated the Kurds with indifference, brusquely rejecting Kurdish overtures because they came from "a nongovernmental agency." What hypocrisy!

The Kurds wanted simply to live in peace and in their own way. International expediency has doomed their efforts. We should do all we can to facilitate humanitarian efforts for the Kurds, both for those who are refugees in Iran and for those who remain under Iraqi control. The United States, always known as the haven for political exiles, should accept the Kurdish leader Barzani if he requests asylum.

The Kurds, a rugged mountain people, have inhabited their land for thousands of years. The land was theirs long before the oil underneath them assumed such importance. Indeed, how tragic it is that some nations consider the oil more important than these brave people and their right to live.

There is a final note in this story which troubles me greatly. Unique among movements for national liberation, Barzani's *pesh merga* has refused to resort to terrorism. In this war, Barzani published lists of Iraqi POW's and allowed Red Cross visits, despite the harsh treatment accorded Kurdish prisoners. The Kurds dared to defend their freedom without resort to such spectacular and gruesome tactics. How ominous for civilization if those who reject terrorism suffer disaster while those who embrace it gain recognition.

4.

[May 8, 1978 (Senate), pp. 12890-91]

KURDISH SITUATION PROVES NEED FOR GENOCIDE CONVENTION

Mr. PROXMIRE. Mr. President, there are many compelling reasons why the Genocide Convention should be ratified by the U.S. Senate. I have spoken many times of the geno-

cide which is today occurring in Cambodia and Uganda, and of course all of us are only too aware of the vicious extermination of 6 million Jews by the Nazis during World War II. The Genocide Convention represents an effort by many of the nations of the world to stamp out the atrocious crime of genocide, and the treaty itself would make the commission of genocide an international crime.

But surely one of the most compelling of all arguments for passage of the Genocide Convention is that genocide could reoccur in the future. Recently the *Washington Star* carried an article on the moving story of the Kurdish leader Gen. Mulla Mustafa Barzani . The Kurds number several million, and live in the mountains of Iraq, Iran, Syria, and Turkey. For years, the Kurds fought to establish their own homeland in Iraq, but their rebellion was quashed when U.S. support was cut off in 1975.

It is difficult for Americans to imagine what life would be like without a land to call our own. it is easy, though, for the Kurds and General Barzani to imagine such a life. General Barzani lived in the Iraqi mountains in a small town named Barzan. In 1931, Barzan was surrounded by Iraqi troops and destroyed. Since then the town of Barzan has been leveled 14 times. Today, General Barzani lives in the United States with the knowledge that his many relatives are scattered through Iran and Iraq in "relocation centers."

Iraqi authorities have attempted to disperse the Kurdish populations to the south of Iraq where they can be watched and gradually assimilated into the local society. In many cases families have been broken up. Former resistance fighters have been identified and killed. What is happening is no less than an attempt to extinguish a cultural identity.

Without on the spot information it is impossible to determine if the killings are isolated or systematic. We do not know if genocide, as defined by the Genocide Convention, is occurring. But we do know that an entire cultural and ethnic population is being persecuted and that the United States bears part of the responsibility.

I ask unanimous consent that the article from the *Washington Star*, which was written by Lynn Rosellini, be printed in full immediately following my remarks ["The Last Battles of Gen. Mulla Mustafa Barzani, Who Played by Different Bulks," Apr. 18, 1978].

The PRESIDING OFFICER (Mr. GRAVEL). Without objection, it is so ordered.

Mr. PROXMIRE. I would also like to take this opportunity to remind the Senate that the Kurdish situation is vivid evidence of the need for the Genocide Convention. This treaty has been before the Senate now for 30 years. For 30 years, ever since President Truman signed the treaty, every President has pleaded with the Senate to ratify the Genocide Convention. Eisenhower, Kennedy, Johnson, Nixon, Ford, and most recently President Carter have all given their support for the treaty. I urge the Senate to ratify the Genocide Convention as soon as possible . . .

5.

[March 7, 1979 (Senate), pp. 4133-34]

THE DEATH OF GEN. MUSTAFA BARZANI

Mr. PROXMIRE. Mr. President, I take a moment to take notice of the death of Gen. Mustafa Barzani who for 40 years fought for the freedom of his Kurdish people. On one occasion about 3 years ago General Barzani asked to come to my office. Through an interpreter he explained that he was present to thank me for a speech I had made dealing with the repressive measures taken against Kurdish tribesmen and women by the Iraqi and Iranian regimes. He spoke softly and directly. He indicated that one of the major disappointments of his life was the reversal in policy dictated by Secretary of State Kissinger hat led to the bloody suppression of his revolt against the Iraqi Government. He asked for assistance, where possible, for Kurdish refugees. And then he left. He had said what he came to say.

The story of the U.S. role in the Kurdish revolt is not a pleasant one. it is an example of the worst form of geopolitics, the political games played by individuals and nations.

When it served U.S. purposes, we supplied aid to the Kurdish cause. And when Secretary Kissinger felt it necessary to seal an alliance with the Shah of Iran, who was increasingly concerned about his western border, then the United States abruptly withdrew its assistance. The Kurdish people were the pawns in the chess game.

When Secretary Kissinger speaks of not allowing concern for human rights to dominate U.S. policy, perhaps he is thinking of the example of the Kurdish people—a four century struggle for independence that once looked promising but was snuffed out in a quick behind-the-scenes diplomatic agreement.

Mr. President, I ask unanimous consent that articles from the *Washington Post* [March 3, 1979] and *New York Times* [March 1, 1979] on General Barzani be printed in the RECORD.

There being no objection, the articles were ordered to be printed in the RECORD ...

6.

[September 14, 1979 (Extension of Remarks), pp. 24714-15]

THE KURDS—BEYOND THE MELTING POT
HON. ROBERT H. MICHEL
OF ILLINOIS
IN THE HOUSE OF REPRESENTATIVES

Friday, September 14, 1979

Mr. MICHEL. Mr. Speaker, one of the great myths that has not survived the last half of the 20th century is the "melting pot" theory of national and international affairs. We were told by experts that high-speed transportation and electronic communications media would erase differences between various nations and ethnic groups. We were told that everyone was eager to cast aside old ways and old beliefs and jump on the jolly bandwagon of progress as defined by Western intellectuals and experts.

Well, it has not quite turned out that way. Instead of the world becoming one great melting pot we have fierce tribal wars in Africa and rising nationalistic fervor among the Scottish and the Welsh, The Vietnamese, Cambodian, and Chinese are engaged in conflicts with each other that are as much ethnic as political in origin.

The Kurds, an ancient and proud people have also refused to be thrown into the melting pot. They deserve our attention.

At this point I wish to insert in the RECORD, "The Kurds and the PLO," an editorial in the *Peoria Journal Star*, September 7, 1979: . . .

mous Kurdistan for over 100 years. For centuries these people have been subject to invasion and suppression, first at the hands of the Greeks, then the Mongols, Turks, and Britons.

The best account of the recent and gloomy history of the Kurds was an article published in the *Washington Star* on September 16, by Smith Hempstone, a Washington-based syndicated columnist who spent the summer of 1974 with Mulla Mustafa Barzani's guerrillas in Iraq. Coincidentally, Barzani died in Washington this past spring. Unfortunately, his leadership and pro-Western attitude will be sorely missed . . .

7.

[November 29, 1979 (Extension of Remarks), pp. 34161-62]
THE KURDS, ORPHANS OF THE UNIVERSE
HON. THOMAS A. DASCHLE
OF SOUTH CAROLINA
IN THE HOUSE OF REPRESENTATIVES

Thursday, November 29, 1979

Mr. DASCHLE. Mr. Speaker, in light of the present crisis in Iran, where American diplomats are being held hostage, I believe it is important to acknowledge that Ayatollah Khomeini's venomous anti-Americanism is not shared by all the peoples of that country. I refer specifically to the Kurdish minority in northwest Iran.

In fact, at this very minute the Kurds are in their own life and death struggle against Khomeini and his band of bloodthirsty fanatics. The Kurds in years past have been pro-American. Though their enthusiasm was dampened by the end of American assistance a few years ago in their fight for an autonomous Kurdistan, the Kurds remain a significant force in Iran.

This would seem the proper time to rectify our past injustices and open a new chapter with the Kurds in Iran.

The Kurds, a much maligned, unfortunate people, have been struggling for an autono-

8.

[December 6, 1982 (Senate), p. 28794]

PLIGHT OF KURDS REMINDS US OF POTENTIAL FOR GENOCIDE

Mr. PROXMIRE. Mr. President, on October 24, 1982, the *New York Times* published a letter to the editor describing the terrible plight of the Kurdish people. The letter was written in response to Vincent Canby's October 6, 1982, review of "Yol," a movie which tells the story of a young Kurd who goes home on leave from prison to discover that his village is being terrorized by Turkish anti-Kurdish forces. The author of the letter, Vera Beaudin Saeedpour, commends the director, Yilmaz Guney, both for sharing a glimpse of Kurdish culture with the West, and for portraying the tools of oppression in Turkey today.

In her letter, the author also describes the efforts of the Turkish Government to eradicate the identity of the Kurdish people. She says that the Turks do not acknowledge the 8 to 10 million Kurdish people living in their country. The author includes a report from Amnesty International saying that a Turkish sociologist was imprisoned for 10 years for calling the Kurds a separate ethnic group.

In addition, the writer points out that Turkey is not the only country which oppresses Kurdish people living within its borders. She says: "Turkey is a terrible place to be Kurdish, but so is Iran, and so is Iraq, and so is Syria."

Even abroad, many Kurds live in silence because they fear retaliation against their families at home.

Mr. President, this letter reminds us that terrible ethnic persecution takes place all around the globe. Sadly, it also reminds us that the potential for genocide still exists in the world today. And, although Americans detest such oppression, our Nation has not done all that it could to end this heinous practice.

Mr. President, since 1967 I have daily urged the Senate to ratify the convention for the Prevention and Punishment of Genocide. While it has remained in legislative limbo in our Senate, over 80 other nations have ratified it.

By neglecting to ratify the treaty, the United States fails short of its duty as a leader in the area of international human rights. No human right is more fundamental to all racial, religious, and ethnic groups than the right to exist. While the United States abstains from ratifying the treaty, thousands fear ethnic obliteration. We cannot afford to wait any longer—I urge the Senate to act now.

9.

[October 3, 1983 (Senate), p. 26855]

THE KURDISH SITUATION AND THE GENOCIDE CONVENTION

Mr. PROXMIRE. Mr. President, recent media accounts of Kurdish involvement in the Iranian-Iraqi war brings again to our attention the plight of the Kurdish people, who have for decades been oppressed by the governments which rule them. This situation illustrates the acute need for the Genocide Convention.

Some 10 million Kurds inhabit the mountainous region where Iraq meets Iran and Turkey. Although Kurdistan is divided by these national boundaries, its inhabitants constitute a separate nationality. They speak a distinct Indo-European language, practice unique cultural traditions, and claim ethnic distinction from the peoples which surround them.

Yet the Kurds have been, and continue to be, the target of systematic efforts—most recently, in particular by Iraq—to uproot, disperse, and extinguish their society. Kurdish villages have been destroyed. Kurdish families have been separated. Kurdish patriots and resistance fighters have been imprisoned or executed. Kurdish refugees have been forcibly resettled and detained under subsistence-level living conditions. These acts are clearly designed to literally eliminate the Kurds as a cultural group.

It is not clear that the Kurdish people are victims of genocide according to the Genocide Convention's precise definition. it seems undeniable, however, that many Kurds have been victims of gross violations of human rights, and that these violations are being systematically carried out as a deliberate government policy. These acts certainly border on genocide.

Historical illustrations of the need for a treaty banning genocide are less compelling precisely because they are now history. We may find it too easy to shrug them off as mistakes of the past. I hope my Senate colleagues will remember that acts of a genocidal character are still occurring in the present day. The imperative for a genocide ban remains current. U.S. ratification of the International Genocide Convention would strengthen the message that the international community will no longer tolerate these offenses against humanity. I urge my fellow Senators to lend their support to ratification without delay.

10.

[August 3, 1987 (Extension of Remarks), p. 22147]

KURDISH MILITANTS THREAT TO TURKEY
HON. JIM MOODY
OF WISCONSIN
IN THE HOUSE OF REPRESENTATIVES

Monday, August 3, 1987

Mr. MOODY. Mr. Speaker, I thought my colleagues might find interesting the following article that appeared in the *Christian Science Monitor*. This article deals with the very important and ongoing problems on Turkey's borders with Iran and Iraq. Activity in southeastern Turkey by the Kurdish militants has created, by many accounts, "the most serious threat" faced by that country in the last 50 years. For this reason, I wish to place this piece in today's RECORD . . .

11.

[March 24, 1988 (House), p. 5111]

THE OUTRAGE IN IRAQ

(Mr. LANTOS asked and was given permission to address the House for 1 minute and to revise and extend his remarks.)

Mr. LANTOS. Mr. Speaker, not since the nightmare of Jonestown—when 913 men, women, and children were killed by poison—has the American public been exposed to pictures of deliberate horror like those that are coming from Iraq showing the use of cyanide, mustard gas, and nerve gas by the Iraqi Government against its own people.

Since the media are excluded from access to these events, we do not know whether it is 3,000 or 5,000 children, women, and old men who are dead as a result of this outrageous use of poison gas by Iraqi authorities.

The U.S. Navy is now protecting Iraq and its allies in the Persian Gulf. The administration must use its leverage with the regime in Baghdad to convince them that mass poisoning of its own civilian population is unacceptable in the eyes of civilized nations. The United Nations must send a mission to investigate this barbaric mass murder—and it must do so immediately.

12.

[March 29, 1988 (House), p. 5556]

LEGISLATION CONDEMNING USE OF CHEMICAL WEAPONS BY THE GOVERNMENTS OF IRAN AND IRAQ

(Mr. ATKINS asked and was given permission to address the House for 1 minute and to revise and extend his remarks.)

Mr. ATKINS. Mr. Speaker, I rise to express my concern over the use of chemical weapons by the belligerents in the war between Iran and Iraq. Last week, hundreds of innocent people were killed mercilessly by chemical weapons in the Kurdistan region of Iraq. We have all seen the news reports. Families gathered around the meal table—dead. Parents cradling children to their bosoms as the deadly fumes swept through their towns. It looked as if the fourth horseman of the apocalypse had ridden through the town, and left a swath of death in his wake.

Chemical weapons are horrible. They have been denounced by virtually every nation on the planet. The 1925 Geneva protocol banned their use, and it was hoped that they would never again be used. Yet it is believed that both Iran and Iraq have used these terrible weapons in the gulf war.

Utilizing chemical weaponry as a tool of war is, in itself, barbaric, but apparently the Government of Iraq has also used them against its own civilian population. It appears that this is not the first time that chemical weapons have been used in the Kurdistan region. The killing of innocents can never be justified, and massacres such as the one that occurred last week are beyond the pale.

I will be introducing legislation this week that condemns the use of chemical weapons by the Governments of Iran and Iraq. I urge my colleagues to join me in this effort—to, at least for the innocents, bring sanity back to the war in the gulf. We must not remain silent.

13.

[March 30, 1988 (House), p. 5875]
CONDEMN IRAQI VIOLATIONS OF TURKISH AIRSPACE

(Mr. PORTER asked and was given permission to address the House for 1 minute and to revise and extend his remarks.)

Mr. PORTER. Mr. Speaker, last week Iraq did not stop with its unconscionable chemical attack on its own citizens in the border town of Halabja. They also tool the liberty of violating Turkish airspace to bomb Peshmerga camps only 1 kilometer from the Turkish border.

While the United States should remain neutral in the Persian Gulf war, there is no doubt where we stand with regard to an attack against Turkey. Under the NATO Charter, an attack against one NATO ally is to be regarded as an attack against us all.

The Iraqis should be forwarned that while they gassed their own citizens with apparent impunity, an attack against a loyal ally such as Turkey will result in the gravest consequences.

Let the "heroes" of the Iraqi Air Force, who carried out the attack against the U.S.S. STARK and Halabja, know that they risk antagonizing enemies far greater than the one they face on the Iranian front.

14.

[June 24, 1988 (Senate), pp. 15918-21]

CONDEMNATION OF THE USE OF CHEMICAL WEAPONS BY IRAQ

The PRESIDING OFFICER. Under the previous order, the Senate will now proceed to the consideration of Senate Resolution 408, which the clerk will report. The legislative clerk read as follows:

A resolution (S. RES. 408) to condemn the use of chemical weapons by Iraq.

The Senate proceeded to consider the resolution.

The PRESIDING OFFICER. Under the previous order, there will now be 20 minutes on the resolution to be equally divided and controlled by the Senator from Maine [Mr. MITCHELL] and the minority leader or his designee.

The Senator from Maine is recognized.

Mr. MITCHELL. Mr. President, I am pleased that today my colleagues will have the opportunity to express their support for Senate Resolution 408. I ask unanimous consent that Senators KERRY, PRYOR, SPECTER, and CRANSTON be allowed to join the other 40 cosponsors of this important resolution.

The PRESIDING OFFICER. Without objection, it is so ordered.

Mr. MITCHELL. Mr. President, the resolution condemns the use of chemical weapons by Iraq and urges the President to continue American efforts to achieve an international ban on the production and use of chemical weapons.

It is tragic that there is any need for a resolution of this nature. Yet we cannot ignore the horrifying developments in the Iran-Iraq war. We must place the U.S. Senate firmly on record in condemnation of the use of chemical weapons, and we must express our support for the ongoing efforts to reinstate the moral and legal prohibition against chemical weapons use.

A few months ago, the international community was shocked by the graphic evidence of Iraq's use of chemical weapons against its own citizens. On March 16, Iraq launched a chemical attack on the Iranian-occupied town of Halabja, killing up to 2,000 Kurdish civilians with chemical agents. The resolution praises President Reagan for his prompt condemnation of Iraq's action as a "particularly grave violation" of international law.

The grotesque images of civilians frozen dead in the midst of their daily routine outraged us all. But even before this incident, there had been increasing signs of expanding chemical capabilities in the Middle East.

We knew that in early 1982 Iraq began experimenting with the use of chemical weapons and accidentally poisoned its own troops. United Nations investigators had concluded that Iraq employed chemical weapons against Iran in 1984, in 1986, and again in 1987. Each attack was a flagrant violation of the 1925 Geneva protocol that Iraq had signed. Iran apparently began producing chemical weapons in limited quantities a few years after Iraq's experiments began. Iran has reportedly used chemical weapons, including at Halabja, in retaliation for Iraqi chemical attacks.

Unless both sides forgo the use of chemical weapons, there could be an even more alarming escalation of the nearly 8-year-old gulf war. Iran and Iraq now use conventional missiles in attacks against cities. If they were to arm these missiles with chemical warheads, they could devastate civilian populations in urban centers.

Senate Resolution 408 conveys a strong message to the combatants in the gulf war. It condemns Iraq's pattern of chemical weapons attacks. It expresses concern about reported Iranian use of chemical weapons. It calls upon the President to exert diplomatic efforts to prevent the further development or use of chemical weapons. The Senate should resoundingly support this unequivocal condemnation of chemical weapons use by any country.

The recent Iraqi chemical attack symbolizes the failure of the international community to effectively prevent the transfer of chemical capabilities and the failure to prevent the use of weapons that were outlawed by the 1925 Geneva protocol.

While the United Nations has repeatedly condemned Iraq's use of chemical weapons, that body has never invoked sanctions of any sort against a violator of the Geneva protocol.

The use of chemical weapons is not yet routine, but it threatens to become widespread as chemical production technology crosses borders and as the strictures against chemical use weaken with every reported violation. Clearly, it is time for a strengthening of both international law and national policy to prevent the spread and use of chemical weapons.

Many countries, particularly in the Middle East, are fast acquiring chemical weapons and chemical production capabilities. For example, Syria is upgrading its chemical capabilities and has built a new production facility to ensure its own chemical supplies. Libya reportedly has also acquired chemical weapons.

Chemical weapons are attractive to such states because they pose a serious military threat, but are relatively cheap and easy to make. The manufacturing technology is not highly complex, and much of it can be bought on the open market-in the name of seeking an industrial chemical capability.

Of course an effective delivery system is required to actually use chemical weapons. But as ballistic missile technology proliferates throughout the Third World and particularly the Middle East, so too does the capability to deliver chemical munitions across great distances.

The increasing range and sophistication of delivery vehicles and the expansion of chemical capabilities are a potentially devastating combination.

Therefore, the resolution urges the President to seek allied cooperation to further tighten controls on the export of chemical technology to countries seeking to develop a chemical weapons capability.

The United States has already recognized the need to closely monitor and control the spread of chemical weapons capabilities. The 1984 Chemical Weapons Export Control Act prevents the sale to Iraq and Iran of industrial chemicals that could be used to manufacture chemical weapons. In 1987, the State Department extended the ban to include Syria. But more can be done. For example, it seems obvious that Libya should be added to this list.

Anticipating which countries may seek to acquire chemical weapons is crucial for successfully preventing proliferation. But it is equally important that other industrialized nations participate fully in the application of export controls.

Our allies, many of whom have large domestic chemical industries, have not enthusiastically joined our effort to limit access to chemical weapons capabilities. They should be encouraged to help prevent increasing numbers of nations from becoming chemical weapons producers and distributors.

In addition to restricting access to chemical weapons components, we must focus attention on the need to achieve a comprehensive and verifiable chemical arms control agreement.

World War I, in which chemical weapons killed at least 90,000 and wounded well over a million, convinced the world that chemical weapons should never be used and led to the signing of the 1925 Geneva protocol.

But the protocol bans only the use-not the production or stockpiling-of chemical weapons. Furthermore, the law lacks enforcement mechanisms and the ethical strictures against chemical weapons use have been undermined by the increasingly violent means of modern warfare. It is time to strengthen international law's prohibition against chemical warfare.

The resolution expresses the Senate's support for American efforts to reach an international agreement banning the use, production, development, stockpiling, transfer, and acquisition of chemical weapons.

Since the mid sixties, the United States has been engaged in such negotiations. Today the primary forum is the 40-nation Conference on Disarmament in Geneva.

The Soviets, who have a huge stockpile of chemical weapons and even dedicated chemical warfare forces, have long expressed reservations that posed serious obstacles to agreement.

However, there have been some hopeful signs. During the 1985 Reagan-Gorbachev summit meeting, the two leaders vowed to pursue a worldwide chemical weapons agreement and agreed to discuss ways to stem the proliferation of chemical weapons. In 1987, the Soviet Union announced that it had halted production of chemical weapons. The Soviets have also adopted a more open attitude in the Geneva chemical arms negotiations.

Although this altered Soviet attitude has led to encouraging progress at Geneva, many hurdles must be overcome before an agreement can be reached.

The subject of chemical weapons control is exceedingly complex. Verification in particular poses a very difficult problem.

National technical means—photoreconnaissance satellites—clearly are not sufficient to verify compliance with a ban on chemical weapons. The overlap between legitimate commercial chemical plants and weapons production facilities would enable chemical munitions to be surreptitiously stored in conventional munitions depots.

The United States has correctly insisted that onsite inspection, including provisions for challenge inspections, is a critical prerequisite for meaningful chemical arms control. The Soviets appear more open to the possibility of challenge inspections. Furthermore, the unprecedented onsite verification provisions incorporated in the INF Treaty provide additional reason for hope that this prime obstacle can be overcome.

As the recent Iraqi chemical weapons attack reminds us, banning the production, stockpiling, and use of chemical weapons must remain a high international priority.

I hope that this resolution will help convince all nations that the U.S. Senate condemns in no uncertain terms the use of chemical weapons by any country. It is also my hope that this call for an international chemical weapons ban will help bring this issue the immediate attention it surely deserves.

Mr. HATFIELD. Mr. President, it is with great pleasure that I rise this morning in support of the resolution submitted recently by Senator MIT-CHELL. He deserves great credit for submitting the resolution, as does the Senate Foreign Relations Committee for acting on it. The pictures of Kurdish villagers frozen in their tracks by poisonous, deadly nerve gas jarred us all out of our complacency last March, and this resolution offers us all the opportunity to express our outrage in a genuinely bipartisan manner. My hope is that it will pass unanimously.

Before we cast our votes, however, I would like to share a couple of brief observations with my colleagues.

First, Mr. President, the nerve gas attack in Kurdistan must be considered in the broader context of the 8-year-old war between Iran and Iraq. A headline in the Economist said it all: "If you can think of something even beastlier, do it." Who will ever forget-can ever forget-the stories about Iran's use of children to sweep minefields? The atrocities come from both sides, Mr. President, and so do the victims. More than 1 million people have lost their lives in this crazy war, and even more have been permanently injured. In fact, of the more than 100 wars fought since World War II, this one is already the most deadly. As we cast our votes for this resolution, let us also cast our votes for international efforts to bring an end to this war.

My second observation, Mr. President, is that I am surprised that ghastly attacks like these do not happen more often. Nerve gas is a poor man's neutron bomb-it just kills people, and this crazy world is full of countries and terrorist groups that love the strategic implications of that. This crazy world is awash with nerve gas-all shapes and sizes, all models and makes. As an aside, Mr. President, I might point out that that includes us-the United States of America. Although President Richard Nixon declared a moratorium on nerve gas production in 1969, this Congress—this very Congress—gave the green light to production of an entirely new generation of nerve gas weapons just last year.

I hope this bears on the conscience and on the minds of this Senate.

All this brings me to my final observation, Mr. President. In my opinion, the most important section of the resolution now before us is the one that urges the President to pursue a multilateral agreement banning the use, production, development, transfer and acquisition of nerve gas weapons. Our choice is clear-either we sit around and wait for the inevitable-the next nerve gas attack-or we actively and aggressively pursue an agreement today that seeks to prevent that next attack tomorrow.

Again, Mr. President, as we cast our votes for this resolution-let us also cast our votes for an end to the Iran-Iraq war, and for the complete and final destruction of the world's nerve gas arsenals.

Mr. MURKOWSKI. Mr. President, I rise to support the important resolution offered by my colleague from Maine.

As we reflect on the hideous realities of the Iran-Iraq war, which have touched members of our own U.S. Navy, we must consider that the greatest of those horrors is the use of chemical weapons by both sides.

This legislation is important because it highlights that particular aspect of the Persian Gulf situation. I am afraid, Mr. President, that with the constant television pictures of ships burning in the gulf, with the discussion in this Chamber and in other places of the rightness of our U.S. reflagging policy, and with the vigorous discussions that we have had on the meaning and application of the War Powers Resolution, we and the American people may lose sight of the real horrors of the war which has dragged on between Iran and Iraq.

That war, in terms of casualties and, in terms of the disruption of people's lives is rapidly becoming one of the most horrific events in this already horrific century.

Mr. President, much has been said here in the course of this session of Congress about the reduction of nuclear arms. This resolution provides an important moment, however, for us to focus on a threat which is older and in some ways more terrifying than nuclear weapons, that is chemical weapons.

Mr. President, it is incredible that in the late 20th century, we can witness the barbarity of chemical weapons being used in the Iran-Iraq war. It is also incredible that civilized nations must maintain chemical warfare arsenals at this late date.

I do not have to remind my colleagues of the horrors of chemical warfare. The history of the First World War tells us that, but we must not content ourselves with believing that the flow of gas in the trenches is an event which occurred three quarters of a century ago and is therefore irrelevant to our times.

In these days of terrorist activities, we have all heard of the possibilities of nuclear weapons being employed by terrorists. We have read that it is possible to develop a nuclear bomb in a relatively unsophisticated laboratory with relatively sophisticated materials.

It is much simpler, Mr. President, to develop and field chemical weapons.

As we reflect on the recent major step which the United States has taken in arms control with the ratification of the INF Treaty, it is essential that the administration place the highest emphasis on the achievement of a ban on chemical arms. I particularly call the attention of our colleagues and of the administration to the language in this resolution which calls on the President to put a chemical weapons ban at the top of the list. I also urge the other nations of the world, friends and adversaries, to join in this effort.

The tale of suffering which has been written across the record of this century must end.

We in Congress must support this effort, first of all by assuring that our own Armed Forces have adequate defenses against nuclear weapons and then seeking every opportunity to call for a chemical weapons treaty.

It is also our duty to call barbaric behavior to the attention of the world. The resolution offered by my friend from Maine is timely and I urge our colleagues to support it.

Mr. HATFIELD. Mr. President, I know of no one else anxious to speak at this time on my side.

If the Senator from Maine [Mr. MITCHELL] wishes additional time, I would be happy to yield time under my control.

Mr. MITCHELL. Mr. President, I simply want to thank the distinguished Senator from Oregon, who, with his usual directness, forcefulness, and clarity, has presented the issues clearly before the Senate.

I have no further remarks at this time and am prepared to vote.

Mr. PELL. Mr. President, I would like to commend my colleague from Maine, Senator MITCHELL, for his initiative in sponsoring Senate Resolution 408, a resolution condemning Iraq for its use of chemical weapons.

The 1925 Geneva Convention outlawed the use of chemical weapons in warfare. This convention grew out of the horrors of the First World War where hundreds of thousands of soldiers succumbed to mustard gas and other chemical weapons. Since 1925 the ban on chemical weapons has been honored with only a few relatively minor exceptions. Even Hitler, murderous as he was, did not use poison gas against the allies because he understood the potentially catastrophic consequences for Germany if these relatively accessible weapons were introduced into combat.

The ban on the use of chemical weapons has been largely honored for the last 60 years. That is, until the current Iran-Iraq war. As Iraq's military position deteriorated after 1982, it has made increasing use of poison gas to offset the greater numbers and zeal of the Iranians. Tragically, poison gas has become a standard part of the Iraqi arsenal. Today it is used not only against Iranians but also against Iraq's rebellious Kurdish population. Last March, some 5,000 civilians-children, women, men, old people-were brutally murdered when Iraqi forces deployed chemical weapons on the Kurdish village of Halabja. Even as Iraq's military position improves, as it has over the last 4 months, Iraq continues to deploy chemical weapons.

The breakdown of the norms against the use of chemical weapons could have catastrophic consequences. The raw materials for chemical weapons are readily available, and poison gas is easy to make and easy to use. Chemical weapons are truly the poor man's nuclear bomb. Unless the world community is firm in its condemnation of Iraq's violation of international law, there is every likelihood Iraq's example will be followed by other countries.

Iraqi diplomats defend their country's use of chemical weapons by arguing that the Iran-Iraq war is the source of the problem. End the war, they say, and there will be no further use of chemical weapons. There can be no doubt but that Iran is responsible for the continuation of the war. Iraq has accepted U.S. Resolution 598 to end the war; Iran seems intent on continuing this cruel and pointless conflict. However, Iran's conduct cannot excuse Iraq's use of chemical weapons. The 1925 Geneva Convention governs the conduct of war. The fact of war cannot be used as an excuse for violating this convention.

Once again, I commend Senator MITCHELL for bringing this matter to the attention of the U.S. Senate. In agreeing to Senate Resolution 408 we are sending a message to Baghdad. I hope our message will be heard.

The PRESIDING OFFICER. Without objection, the committee amendments are agreed to en bloc.

The question is on agreeing to the resolution, as amended. On this question, the yeas and nays have been ordered and the clerk will call the roll.

The legislative clerk called the roll.

Mr. CRANSTON. I announce that the Senator from Connecticut [Mr. DODD], the Senator from Hawaii [Mr. MATSUNAGA], and the Senator from Mississippi [Mr. STEN-NIS] are necessarily absent.

I also announce that the Senator from Delaware [Mr. BIDEN] and the Senator from Oklahoma [Mr. BOREN] are absent because of illness.

Mr. SIMPSON. I announce that the Senator from Washington [Mr. EVANS], the Senator from Pennsylvania [Mr. HEINZ], the Senator from Idaho [Mr. SYMMS], and the Senator from California [Mr. WILSON] are necessarily absent.

The PRESIDING OFFICER. Are there any other Senators in the Chamber desiring to vote?

The result was announced-yeas 91, nays 0, as follows:

[Rollcall Vote No. 201 Leg.]
YEAS-91
NAYS-0
NOT VOTING-9

So the resolution (S. RES. 408), as amended, was agreed to.

The preamble was agreed to.

The resolution, as amended, with its preamble, reads as follows:

S. RES. 408

Whereas the international community recognized the dangers of chemical warfare during World War One, in which at least 90,000 were killed and well over 1,000,000 wounded by chemical weapons;

Whereas the 1925 Geneva Protocol outlawed the use of chemical weapons;

Whereas Iraq has been producing and stockpiling chemical weapons;

Whereas United Nations investigators concluded in 1984, 1986, and 1987 that Iraq had employed chemical weapons, and the United Nations Security Council has condemned the use of chemical weapons in the Iran-Iraq war;

Whereas Iraq's chemical weapons attack on March 16, in which hundreds of Kurdish civilians were killed on Iraqi soil, underscores the horror of these weapons and their impact on noncombatants;

Whereas the United States condemned that Iraqi attack as a "particularly grave violation" of international law; and

Whereas it has been reported that Iran may be producing chemical weapons, and Iran has also used chemical weapons in retaliation for Iraqi use of such weapons: Now, therefore, be it

Resolved, That the Senate—

(1) condemns the use of chemical weapons by Iraq and declares that such action violates international law;

(2) calls upon Iraq to halt immediately and permanently the use of all chemical weapons;

(3) commends the President for his prompt condemnation of Iraq's recent chemical weapons attack on civilians;

(4) urges the President to seek allied cooperation to further tighten controls on the export of chemical compounds to countries seeking to develop a chemical weapons capability;

(5) expresses concern about reported Iranian use of chemical weapons and urges the President to make appropriate diplomatic efforts to prevent Iran from developing or using chemical weapons; and

(6) urges the President to pursue American efforts at the Geneva Conference on Disarmament to reach an arms control agreement banning the use, production, development, stockpiling, transfer, and acquisition of chemical weapons.

15.

[September 8, 1988 (Senate), p. 22877]

STATEMENTS ON INTRODUCED BILLS AND JOINT RESOLUTIONS

By Mr. PELL:
S. 2763. A bill entitled the "Prevention of Genocide Act of 1988"; read the first time.

PREVENTION OF GENOCIDE ACT

Mr. PELL. Mr. President, on the Iraqi-Turkish border evidence of a crime of unthinkable proportions is emerging. For the second time in this century a brutal dictatorship is using deadly gas to exterminate a distinct ethnic minority. In this case the victims are the Kurdish minority of Iraq and the perpetrators are the Iraqi Army.

The Kurds are a distinct ethnic group, with an ancient history and rich culture, comprising some 20 million people. Although many have long aspired to an independent Kurdish homeland, the Kurds have the great misfortune to be divided among Iraq, Iran, Turkey, Syria, and the Soviet Union. It is hard to imagine a less agreeable set of masters.

While Iraq's treatment of its Kurdish minority has in the past been somewhat better than that of its neighbors, the condition of the Iraqi Kurds has in recent years taken a turn for the catastrophic. With the onset of the Iran-Iraq War, Kurdish insurgents in both countries saw an opportunity for greater autonomy, if not independence. In Iraq the Kurdish insurgency made great progress, taking effective control of much of the countryside in mountainous northeast Iraq.

However, with the tides of war changing in Iraq's favor early this year, the Iraqi Army launched a major offensive against the Kurds. The offensive was accompanied by the dynamiting of Kurdish villages throughout the region. Poisonous gas was used on the people. In March in the Kurdish town of Halabja, some 5,000 Kurdish civilians were gassed.

With the August 20 cease-fire in the Iran-Iraq War, the Iraqi Army has turned its firepower and its ample stocks of poison gas almost entirely against the Kurds. Refugee accounts provide incontrovertible evidence of massive use of poison gas. Because the region is closed to all foreign observers we can only speculate at the death toll, but it clearly is in the tens of thousands.

The campaign against the Kurdish people is continuing as we speak. There can be no doubt but that the Iraqi regime of Saddam Hussein intends this campaign to be a final solution to the Kurdish problem.

While a people are gassed, the world is largely silent. There are reasons for this: Iraq's great oil wealth, its military strength, a desire not to upset the delicate negotiations seeking an end to the Iran-Iraq War.

Silence, however, is complicity. A half century ago, the world was also silent as Hitler began a campaign that culminated in the near extermination of Europe's Jews. We cannot be silent to genocide again.

I am today introducing legislation that would cut off credits to Iraq, require the United States to vote against loans to Iraq in the international financial institutions, and prohibit the importation of Iraqi oil. These sanctions will continue as long as Iraq uses poisonous gas in violation of the 1925 Geneva protocols and as long as Iraq's campaign of genocide against the Kurdish people continues.

It is said we do not have much influence over Iraq. This may be true, but I believe we must use whatever means at our disposal to get their attention. The Iraqi regime is a vicious dictatorship toughened by years of conflict. Hand wringing alone will not change their course; immediate action is essential.

16.

[September 8, 1988 (House), p. 22929]

OUTRAGEOUS USE OF POISON GAS BY IRAQ

(Mr. PEASE asked and was given permission to address the House for 1 minute and to revise and extend his remarks.)

Mr. PEASE. Mr. Speaker, I rise to express outrage by the use of Iraq of posion gas against its Kurdish minority.

The reports are especially disturbing because they follow on confirmed reports, carefully confirmed reports, that Iraq also used poison gas against Iran.

Poison gas was outlawed by the international community 60 years ago, because poison gas is unacceptable in a civilized world. Because it is unacceptable, civilized people must condemn Iraq in every forum, in the House of Representatives, in the Senate, in the White House, in the United Nations and in every other possible forum.

The message must be clear, unequivocal, unrelenting. Poison gas is unacceptable as a weapon of war.

17.

[September 9, 1988 (House), p. 7331]

THE GASSING OF THE KURDS

(Mr. PORTER asked and was given permission to address the House for 1 minute and to revise and extend his remarks.)

Mr. PORTER. Mr. Speaker, Iraq has stooped to new lows in human rights by using mustard gas to strike down its Kurdish minority. Secretary of State Shultz has appropriately informed the Iraqis that the continued use of these weapons and the other human rights violations will come at the expense of improved United States-Iraqi relations.

This latest Iraqi chemical atrocity is a symptom of a much larger problem. Today, at least 15 nations, including Iran, Libya, Iraq, Syria, and North Korea, have obtained chemical weapons. Apparently, many nations of the world have forgotten the horrors of mustard phosgens and chlorine gas used in World War I. It is imperative that the international community takes steps to stop the proliferation of these weapons.

IKE SKELTON and I introduced H.R. 2880, to establish a new U.S. chemical and biological weapons nonproliferation regime to help direct attention to the importance of controlling the spread of these weapons. I urge Members to cosponsor this legislation.

In the meantime we must ensure that countries like Iraq which use these illegal weapons face the full weight of international condemnation-and, if necessary, isolation.

18.

[September 9, 1988 (Senate), pp. 23065-66]

KURDISH GENOCIDE

Mr. BOND. Mr. President, the news reports we have been hearing out of northern Iraq in recent days are truly appalling. It is clear that the Iraqis are systematically carrying out a campaign to eradicate the Kurdish minority in that country.

Since the signing of the cease-fire agreement between Iran and Iraq on August 20 freed up Iraqi troops, the Iraqi Government has turned its force against its own citizens. Over the past 2 weeks, refugees arriving in Turkey have told of more than a thousand Kurds being machinegunned, and even worse of huge areas coming under chemical attack.

News reporters are not allowed access to the area so details are sketchy. However, estimates of those killed by the Iraqis range into the tens of thousands, with many more wounded. More than 100,000 others have been forced to seek refuge in neighboring Turkey. The government of Turkish Prime Minister Turgut Ozal deserves commendation for its effort to accept those fleeing the Iraqis and to move them away from the dangerous border area.

This is not the first time the regime in Iraq has used gas against its own citizens. Most recently, on March 16, they gassed hundreds of innocent men, women and children in the town of Halabja. The pictures we saw from that horrible event shocked the world.

Mr. President, civilized people in this country and throughout the world cannot simply sit by while crimes of this magnitude are perpetrated against innocent people. I have been concerned over the past few days by the lack of concern expressed by international leaders. Yesterday, I was very pleased that our distinguished chairman of the Foreign Relations Committee introduced a bill which would force the United States to take action against Iraq. It is a good bill, and I hope my colleagues will approve it before we recess. I believe, however, that further action is necessary. I urge the President to issue the strongest possible condemnation of Iraq's action and to call upon our allies to do the same. In addition, I urge the President to seek a United Nations Security Council investigation into the Kurdish massacres and to push for a U.N. vote condemning the Iraqi actions.

Too many times in this century we have witnessed the horror wrought by madmen bent upon exterminating an ethnic or religious group-Idi Amin's massacres in Uganda; Pol Pot's extermination of 3 million of his countrymen; and the worst, Hitler's killing of 6 million Jews. We cannot allow it to happen again.

I ask unanimous consent to have two articles printed in the RECORD following my remarks. One is by Jim Hoagland and is entitled "Make No Mistake: This is Genocide" [*The Washington Post*, Sept. 8, 1988]. The other, by William Safire, is titled "Stop the Iraqi Murder of the Kurds" [*New York Times*, September 9, 1988]. I urge my colleagues to read these articles, and to not just let this issue fade away.

There being no objection, the articles were ordered to be printed in the RECORD ...

Mr. BOND. I yield the floor.

19.

[September 9, 1988 (Senate), pp. 23116-21]

PREVENTION OF GENOCIDE ACT OF 1988

Mr. BYRD. Mr. President, I ask unanimous consent that the Senate proceed to the consideration of S2763, this having been cleared by the distinguished Republican leader.

The PRESIDING OFFICER. The clerk will report. The legislative clerk read as follows:

A bill (S2763) entitled "The Prevention of Genocide Act of 1988."

The PRESIDING OFFICER. Without objection, the Senate will proceed to its immediate consideration.

The Senate proceeded to consider the bill.

AMENDMENT NO. 2946

Mr. PELL. I send to the desk an amendment on behalf of Senators FORD and BRADLEY and ask for its immediate consideration.

The PRESIDING OFFICER. The clerk will report the amendment.

The legislative clerk read as follows:

The Senator from Rhode Island, Mr. PELL, for himself, Mr. FORD, Mr. BRAD-

LEY, Mr. PROXMIRE and Mr. HELMS, proposes an amendment numbered 2946.

Mr. PELL. Mr. President, I ask unanimous consent that reading of the amendment be dispensed with.

The PRESIDING OFFICER. Without objection, it is so ordered.

The amendment is as follows:

After sec. 6 insert the following:

SEC. —. UNITED NATIONS.-The Secretary of State is requested to immediately bring before the Security Council of the United Nations the matter of Iraq's use of poison gas against its own nationals, most of whom are defenseless civilians, and demand that, in accordance with U.N. Security Council Resolution 620, appropriate and effective measures be taken against Iraq for its repeated use of chemical weapons.

Mr. PELL. I ask unanimous consent that Senator PROXMIRE be added as a cosponsor.

The PRESIDING OFFICER. Without objection, it is so ordered.

Mr. PELL. Mr. President, the RECORD should show the principal cosponsors of the resolution are Senator HELMS and myself.

Mr. FORD. Mr. President, the amendment Senator PROXMIRE and I propose this afternoon needs little elaboration. It directs Secretary of State Shultz to immediately bring the matter of Iraq's repeated use of poison gas against defenseless civilians before the Security Council of the United Nations.

Last month that body passed a resolution sponsored by four Western countries-Britain, West Germany, Italy, and Japan-which not only condemned, once again, the use of chemical weapons in the Iraq-Iran war, but also stated for the first time that "appropriate and effective measures will be taken" if such weapons are used again by anyone anywhere in the future. The time to take these measures, Mr. President, is now.

The bill before us imposes sanctions on Iraq that will remain in force as long as that country uses poisonous gas in violation of the 1925 Geneva protocols and as long as it continues to commit genocide against the Kurdish people. It is an excellent measure-I commend its author, Senator PELL, and it is the least we, the leader of the free world, a country founded upon the principle of the protection of individual rights, should do.

But expressing our deep outrage at the horrible crime that is being committed against the Kurdish people is not enough. This is a crime against the international community and that community must sit in judgment on it. The matter must be taken up by the Security Council so that the strongest international sanctions may be imposed upon Iraq. The United States and the world must not fail to speak out and act against the use of chemical weapons and the crime of genocide.

I ask unanimous consent that an article from yesterday's *Washington Post* by Jim Hoagland, entitled "Make No Mistake: This Is Genocide" be printed in the RECORD. I also ask unanimous consent that two appeals to the Security Council from Massoud Barzani, leader of the Kurdistan Democratic Party in Iraq, also be printed.

There being no objection, the information was ordered to be printed in the RECORD . . .

———

MASSOUD BARZANI APPEALS TO THE NATIONS OF THE SECURITY COUNCIL

Following the recent events in Northern Iraq, during which chemical weapons were used by the Iraqi military against the civilian Kurdish population, Mr. Massoud Barzani, leader of the Kurdistan Democratic party, wishes to lodge an appeal to the nations of the Security Council on behalf of the Kurdish people.

We request the Security Council to fulfill its recent resolution to take immediate action against any nation using chemical warfare. We feel it is imperative that the civilized world intervene in this issue which involves a violation of human rights amounting to genocide.

We are decimated in an atrocity such as has rarely been seen in modern times. We realize that the Security Council does not intervene in a country's internal affairs, and our request is in no way politically motivated, but it is a desperate appeal on behalf of the unarmed citizens who will die if the Iraqi government is allowed to continue its current onslaught.

This issue, we feel, has wider implications than those just affecting our beleaguered people. If Iraq is allowed to continue unchallenged, this may well act as a sanction for other nations who cannot resolve their conflicts by civilized means.

In the volatile atmosphere of the Middle East and other areas of the world, nations may take silence by the international community on this matter as permission to do likewise.

We trust, for the sake of our people and in the interest of world peace, our plea does not go unanswered, and we have every confidence that the Security Council will live up to its mandate in this matter.

MASSOUD BARZANI,
LEADER OF THE KURDISTAN
DEMOCRATIC PARTY,
Iraq, 1st September, 1988.

———

IRAQI KURDISTAN FRONT POLITICAL LEADERSHIP,
Kurdistan, Iraq, August 15, 1988.

Memorandum to:
His Excellency, Mr. Javier Perez de Cuellar,
  Secretary General of the United Nations,
His Excellency, Representative of the
  U.S.S.R. at the Security Council,
His Excellency, Representative of the U.S.A.
  at the Security Council,
His Excellency, Representative of the United
  Kingdom at the Security Council,
His Excellency, Representative of the People's
  Republic of China at the Security Council,
His Excellency, Representative of France at
  the Security Council.
Subject: Escalation of the Racial War of
  Genocide against the Kurdish People of
  Iraq.

DEAR SIRS: We send you our greetings and would like to express our appreciation of your good efforts towards ending the Iraq-Iran war, and rescuing the peoples of these two countries from human and material catastrophes which have lasted almost eight years. We hope that a just and lasting peace will be accomplished between Iraq and Iran, and that the desire of the Iraqi people for liberty, democratic and human rights will be respected.

Allow us to remind you, as we have done in the past, of the fact that there is another war going on, which successive Iraqi governments have pursued since 1981, against the Kurdish people in Iraq. In this chauvinistic war which has taken the form of a total war of genocide since April, 1987, the Iraqi government uses different means of destruction, especially Chemical weapons, as the world witnessed in the Kurdish town of Halabja in the middle of last March. We would like to add that while this war goes on, the Iraqi authorities follow a policy of repression and terror against the people of Iraq, whether they are Arabs, Kurds, or from other ethnic minorities. The Iraqi government carries on this unnecessary bloody violence against a people deprived of its basic rights, and demands simple national rights which are legitimate according to many international and human rights conventions. It is noteworthy that while the international media were carrying information from United Nations experts reporting about the use of Chemical weapons by the Iraqi forces in the Gulf War, as well as against civilians in Halabja and other Iraqi Kurdish towns and villages, at the same time, the Iraqi government was using Chemical weapons against civilians in other Kurdish villages; e.g. on 30th and 31st of last July, Iraqi forces bombed the villages of the valley of Balisan, Heeron and Simaqooli, north east of Arbil, by Chemical weapons. It did the same thing on the 2nd of August in the villages of Arai, Sero and Zarwa near the Turkish border. Indeed, the use of Chemical weapons against our people by the Iraqi regime was going on until the time this memorandum was written. It seems that nothing will deter the Iraqi government from using Chemical weapons against the Kurdish people, at present and in the future, unless the world community, especially the Security Council, takes some serious measures in this respect.

We believe that the Iraqi government has committed grave crimes against the people of Kurdistan which can be considered crimes against humanity. They together make a war of genocide carried out by several different means, among them the following:

(A) Use of Chemical weapons extensively since 14 April, 1987 when they were used for the first time in the villages of Sheikhwassan and more than a dozen other villages.

(B) Declaration of the major part of the Kurdish villages and countryside as a "forbidden" area where the armed forces have been given instructions to kill any human being or even any animal on sight.

(C) Destruction of more than three thousand villages, towns and townships, and the deportation of their population by force. A group of these displaced people have been transferred to the deserts in the south and southwest parts of Iraq, where they have been detained in collective camps in very unsanitary and harsh social conditions.

(D) Burning of farms, orchards and forests in these areas.

(E) Tightening of the economic blockade around the "forbidden" areas with the purpose of destroying the people living there.

(F) Continuation of the policy of torture and mass executions where tens, indeed sometimes hundreds of people are killed, including children, for the simplest of reasons, such as political, religious or national affiliation.

During the military campaign on the Kurdish villages in the provinces of Kirkouk, Sulaimania and Arbil last spring, the authorities detained tens of thousands of families. Then they put old people and children in separate camps, while men were taken to an unknown destination. There is grave concern about their fate. Meanwhile, young women were transferred to other places, and we have received unmentionable news about their situation.

Mr. Secretary General,

Messr. Representatives of the permanent members of the Security Council,

Iraqi Kurdistan Front, which includes six parties, appeals to your Excellencies:

(1) To intervene with the Iraqi government to put an immediate end to the use of chemical weapons against the people of Kurdistan.

(2) To take measures to stop this racial war of genocide against our people, and to nullify all acts of deportation, Arabisation, and other forms of changing the national character of Kurdistan. The indigenous people of Kurdistan should be allowed to return to their villages. A democratic, just and peaceful solution should be found for the Kurdish problem.

Allow us to refer to the promise which the League of Nations gave to the Kurdish people to safeguard their national rights when southern Kurdistan was annexed to Iraq.

(3) To intervene with the Iraqi government to respect human rights, personal and civil liberties of Iraqi citizens, irrespective of their nationalities. All political detainees and prisoners should be released.

Please accept our deepest respect and appreciation.

Yours sincerely,
MASOUD BARZANI,
On Behalf of The Political Leadership of the Iraqi Kurdistan Front.

Enclosed:

1. A list of the military operations carried out by the Iraqi forces in which they used chemical weapons between 15/4/87 and the beginning of August 1988.

2. An Iraqi government directive ordering its forces to kill any human being or animal on sight in the "forbidden" area of Kurdistan.

ARAB BAA'TH SOCIALIST PARTY LEADERSHIP OF ZAKHO SECTION COMMITTEE OF ORGANIZING, NATIONAL DEFENSE BATTALIONS, Date 14/6/1987.
TOP SECRET AND PERSONAL

To all the Party Organizations.
Subject: A Decision.

Comradely greetings, With reference to the letter of Committee of Organization National Defense Battalions S/Sh/1175 dated 9/6/1987 which refers to the letters of the Bureau of the Organization of the North (top secret and personal) 28/2650 dated 3/6/1987 which include the following:

1. It is totally forbidden to let any foodstuff or person and/or machine to reach the forbidden villages which are included in the second stage of the collecting villages. Villagers are allowed to come to the national fold if they wish, but their relatives are not allowed to contact them without prior information of the Security Apparatus.

2. Existence is totally taboo in the forbidden villages of the first stage. It starts on 21/6/1987 for the second stage of collecting villages.

3. After harvesting the winter crops which ends before the 15th of July, cultivation is forbidden for the following summer and winter seasons.

4. Animal grazing is also forbidden in these areas.

5. It is the duty of military forces, everyone according to his section, to kill any human being or animal that exists in these areas which are considered totally forbidden.

6. Those who are included in the deportation orders should be informed and they will be responsible for any misbehavior towards fulfilling these orders.

For your information and to do accordingly every one according to his specialty.

With respect,
COMRADE, ALI MOASHNA KAZIM,
Secretary of the committee.

Mr. PELL. Mr. President, today the Senate will take up "The Prevention of Genocide Act of 1988" which I introduced yesterday and which has as its principal cosponsor the distinguished ranking minority member of the Foreign Relations Committee, Senator HELMS.

It is almost unprecedented for the Senate to take up a bill of this magnitude so swiftly. The situation in Iraqi Kurdistan, however, demands immediate action. As we speak, the Iraqi army is waging a campaign that can only be described as genocide against its Kurdish population. Kurdish villages in northeast Iraq are being dynamited, often with the people still there. Even more unspeakable, the Iraqi army has been using lethal gas in massive and effective attacks on defenseless Kurdish civilians.

Iraq's conduct is a crime against humanity. It must be met with the toughest possible response. The sanctions imposed on Iraq in this bill are tough. The United States will vote against loans to Iraq in international financial institutions. For a country that is some $60 billion in debt and which seeks international financing to help recover from a costly war, this can be a tough sanction.

The bill cuts off all credit and all credit guarantees from the United States to Iraq. These amount to some $800 million a year. The bill would prohibit the export of any item to Iraq, the export of which is controlled by any agency of the United States Government. Potentially this could deny Iraq equipment it needs to run its oil industry and to start up infrastructure that has been idled by the war. The bill also prohibits the importation of Iraqi oil.

Some American businesses will pay a price as a result of the enactment of this bill. However, this is a matter of life and death for hundreds of thousands, this is a moral issue of the greatest magnitude. To do the right thing the American people have in the past been willing to pay the price.

After the holocaust that consumed Europe's Jewish population, the world said "never again." Sadly, it is happening again in Iraqi Kurdistan. We must do whatever we can to let the Iraqi dictatorship know that the United States will not stand idly by while they massacre the Kurds. This bill sends that message.

Mr. PROXMIRE. Mr. President, I strongly applaud the Senator from Rhode Island [Mr. PELL] for the initiative he has taken with regard to the plight of the Kurdish people. His leadership and foresight on this issue have been remarkable.

The Kurds have often been the forgotten people-caught within national boundaries of hostile regimes, used by the superpowers for their own ends, with little or no constituency in the West. That is why it took the State Department so long to respond to the tragic events in northern Iraq-that and a fear that to speak out strongly would somehow undermine the peace effort.

That is just the latest in a long line of excuses and justifications for ignoring an entire culture, for looking the other way at repression, for failure to take action.

In the mid-1970's it was the policy of the United States to support the Kurdish resistance movement by supplying military equipment and other supplies to the Barzani front through Iran. Then Henry Kissinger reached an agreement with the Shah of Iran that closed that border, forced a capitulation of the rebellion and crushed the very people we had supported.

Not a very pretty picture for a superpower but just another example of what has happened to the Kurds over the decades. The Russians, by the way, have treated the Kurds no better and in some ways worse.

Now the Iraqi Government is using chemical weapons against the Kurdish people-not only military forces but civilian groups, villages, refugees. This comes on top of massive relocation efforts plus attempts to stamp out the Kurdish culture and even systematic killings of Barzani family members.

Mr. President, this is genocide. This is the intent to destroy in whole or part a national, ethnic population. And it is occurring with the most ruthless of weaponry. With gasses and chemicals that sear the body, disfigure the young and old, and cause lingering, painful death; or if the victim is mercifully fortunate, a quick death by nerve agents.

We are witnessing the beginning of what I fear will become a weapon of choice in developing countries-chemical agents. Within the technological grasp of any nation producing pesticides or fertilizers, chemical agents have been proven to be tactical and strategic assets. They not only turned the tide in the Iran-Iraqi war and set the stage for the current truce but they have been found to be effective against national resistance populations.

How long will it be before that lesson is learned in Ethiopia or Libya or within the PLO or in Zaire, Burundi, Sri Lanka, Peru, or any other country with hostile domestic opposition groups?

Mr. President, if Nicaragua were using chemical agents against its own population or a neighboring state, the outcry by the public, politicians, and our own Government would drown out all other news. The President would be speaking out about such a barbarity as would the Secretary of State and certainly the Defense Department would not remain silent. We would be pounding the doors of the United Nations and the world community.

We should expect no less when genocide is being conducted against a people far away, of faint familiarity, who do not touch our daily lives, but who are no less victim to the inhumanity of chemical warfare.

I urge the passage of this bill and pray that in some small measure it will alleviate the suffering of the Kurdish people.

Mr. HELMS. Mr. President, during the past week, millions of Americans have become aware of the horrible efforts of the Iraqi Government in systematically eliminating its own citizens of Kurdish descent. This is a crime against humanity, and the United States must not sit by and idly watch it proceed.

It is appalling to contemplate how cruel and vicious radical regimes-such as the Saddam Hussein regime in Iraq-can be. Often utilizing chemical weapons, the Iraqi Government has killed literally thousands of Kurds, and has forced tens of thousands more to flee to neighboring countries.

This is by no means the first time the Iraqi regime-which, by the way, gets most of its arms from the Kremlin-has employed chemical weapons against its own civilians. In March of this year, Iraq dropped chemical weapons on a Kurdish city. According to U.S. News and World Report, this attack took the lives of 5,000 innocent civilians. News reports suggest that this attack was meant to punish Kurdish Iraqi citizens.

In the last month, however, the Iraqi regime's attack against its own Kurdish citizens intensified. According to the *New York Times*, the regime took advantage of its August 20 cease-fire with Iran to launch a military offensive against the Kurds.

Mr. President, the United States should not sit idly by and watch the Iraqi regime undertake an offensive against their 3 to 4 million Kurdish citizens. The American people do not want us to sit idly by. In fact, I am proud to say that the church Dot and I attend here in Virginia, the First Baptist Church in Alexandria, is currently giving shelter to three Kurds

who are on a hunger strike to protest the actions of the Iraqi regime.

This legislation, of which I am proud to cosponsor with the distinguished chairman of the Foreign Relations Committee, will help demonstrate to the Iraqi regime just how serious our country views its campaign against the Kurds. In addition, it will help assure that United States tax dollars do not subsidize the Iraqi regime.

Specifically, the legislation would require that the U.S. representative to all international financial institutions-such as the World Bank-be instructed to vote against all loans to Iraq. In addition, all United States assistance, sales of military equipment, credits and credit guarantees to Iraq would be banned, and imports of oil from Iraq-which account for 1.3 percent of our oil imports would be prohibited.

These sanctions would continue until such time as the President certifies that Iraq has ceased its campaign of genocide against the Kurds and has stopped using chemical weapons.

Mr. President, I ask unanimous consent that an article [By Caryle Murphy] from the *Washington Post* of September 7, reporting on the provision of sanctuary to three Kurds by the First Baptist Church in Alexandria be printed in the RECORD, in addition to a most insightful piece by William Safire which ran in the *New York Times* on September 9, 1988.

There being no objection, the articles were ordered to be printed in the RECORD . . .

The PRESIDING OFFICER. Is there further debate on the amendment? If not, the question is on agreeing to the amendment of the Senator from Rhode Island.

The amendment (No. 2946) was agreed to.

Mr. HELMS. Mr. President, I move to reconsider the vote by which the amendment was agreed to.

Mr. PELL. I move to lay that motion on the table.

The motion to lay on the table was agreed to.

The PRESIDING OFFICER. The question is on the engrossment and third reading of the bill.

The bill was ordered to be engrossed for a third reading, was read the third time, and passed, as follows:

S. 2763

Be it enacted by the Senate and House of Representatives of the United States of America in Congress assembled,

SECTION 1. SHORT TITLE.-This Act may be cited as "The Prevention of Genocide Act of 1988."

SEC. 2. FINDINGS.-The Congress finds:

(i) The Kurdish people constitute a distinct ethnic group of some 20 million, with an ancient history and a rich cultural heritage;

(ii) Three to four million Kurds are citizens of Iraq, residing in the northern part of that country;

(iii) The Iraqi army has undertaken a campaign to depopulate the Kurdish regions of Iraq by destroying all Kurdish villages in a large part of northern Iraq and by killing the civilian population;

(iv) Conclusive evidence exists that the Iraqi army has been and is continuing to use chemical weapons against Kurdish insurgents and unarmed Kurdish civilians;

(v) Tens of thousands of Kurdish survivors of the Iraqi army assaults have taken refuge in Turkey;

(vi) Iraq's use of chemical weapons is a gross violation of international law; and

(vii) Iraq's campaign against the Kurdish people appears to constitute an act of genocide, a crime abhorred by civilized people everywhere and banned under international law.

SEC. 3. SANCTIONS AGAINST IRAQ.-

(a) The United States Executive Director or representative at all international financial institutions of which the United States is a member is instructed to vote against all loans to Iraq.

(b) The United States shall provide no assistance, shall make no sales of any kind of military equipment, shall provide no credits, and shall provide no guarantees of any credits to Iraq.

(c) No item subject to export controls by any agency of the United States shall be sold or otherwise transferred to Iraq.

(d) No oil or petroleum products produced in Iraq shall be imported into the United States.

SEC. 4. WAIVER.-The President may waive the sanctions contained in section 3 if he determines and so certifies in writing to the Speaker of the House of Representatives and the Chairman of the Committee on Foreign Relations of the United States Senate that:

(i) Iraq is not committing genocide against the Kurdish population of Iraq; and

(ii) Iraq is not using chemical weapons banned by the 1925 Geneva Conventions and has provided reliable assurances that it will not use such weapons.

SEC. 5. COMMENDATION OF TURKEY. The Congress commends the Government of Turkey for its humanitarian decision to host thousands of Kurdish people fleeing extermination in Iraq. The President is requested to convey to the Government of Turkey this commendation.

SEC. 6. ASSISTANCE TO KURDISH REFUGEES.-It is the sense of the Congress that the United States should provide assistance to Kurdish refugees in need of medical treatment and other humanitarian aid.

SEC. 7. UNITED NATIONS.-The Secretary of State is requested to immediately bring before the Security Council of the United Nations the matter of Iraq's use of poison gas against its own nationals, most of whom are defenseless civilians, and demand that, in accordance with U.N. Security Council Resolution 620, appropriate and effective measures be taken against Iraq for its repeated use of chemical weapons.

SEC. 8. EFFECTIVE DATE.-This act shall take effect on enactment.

Mr. PELL. Mr. President, I move to reconsider the vote by which the bill, as amended, was passed.

Mr. HELMS. I move to lay that motion on the table.

The motion to lay on the table was agreed to.

Mr. PELL. I thank the Chair. I yield the floor.

20.

[September 9, 1988 (Senate), pp. 23139-41]

GAS WARFARE AND THE PROLIFERATION OF WEAPONS OF MASS DESTRUCTION: THE NEED FOR AMERICAN ACTION

Mr. McCAIN. Mr. President, I believe I join all my colleagues in condemning Iraq's use of poison gas. I do not believe that our opposition to Iran's fanatic ambitions in the Iran-Iraq war, and to dominate Islam, lead any of us to believe this Nation should excuse or ignore Iraq's use of poison gas.

THE IRAQI DRIFT TOWARD MURDER AND GENOCIDE

I do not believe that there is a single Member of the Senate who believes that Iraq was justified in using poison gas for military purposes. War is horrible enough without adding another weapon of mass destruction to the appalling total of killing mechanisms available to modern armies. This is particularly true when the weapon is one whose effects may last for decades and lead to a slow and painful death years after the conflict in question is over.

What is even more horrifying, however, is that Iraq has used poison gas in areas where it knew Iranian civilians would suffer, and is now using poison gas in a genocidal campaign against its Kurdish minority.

We already have seen a steady increase in the willingness of both Governments and armed movements to make civilians, including women and children, the target of military action and terrorism. We have only to think of Cambodia, the long agony of Lebanon, or the current atrocities in Burundi, to realize that the murderous heritage of World War II continues in many parts of the world.

The introduction of poison gas, however, adds a new and even more horrifying dimension to this process of total war. It is one thing to see ethnic and tribal conflicts explode into hatred and violence. It is another thing to see weapons of mass destruction used methodically in continuing acts of cold-blooded murder.

Iraq has plainly embarked upon this course. For all its evasions, and its night and fog approach to trying to hide the facts, it is patently clear that thousands of innocent people are being murdered solely because of their ethnic group.

Mr. President, I wonder if they were not Kurds whether we would not be a lot more exercised than we are at this time.

AMERICA'S STRATEGIC INTERESTS IN CONDEMNING THE USE OF POISON GAS AND THE PROLIFERATION OF WEAPONS OF MASS DESTRUCTION

It is true that the Kurds are half a world away, it is true that some Kurds have conducted a state of civil war filled with acts of terrorism and the murder of other civilians, and it is true that the Kurds have become a pawn of history whose only strategic value lies in the ability to use them against the governments of the nations where they reside. This in no way, however, excuses what is happening or can lead us to turn away from the fact that mass murder is mass murder.

Further, we need to take a longer term view of the strategic threat that the use of poison gas and weapons of mass destruction pose to our interests. This is true whether we define that long term interest in terms of our relations with Iraq, our position in the gulf, or the search for stability and development within the Third World.

THE NEED FOR THE RIGHT KIND OF RELATIONS WITH IRAQ

In the most narrow sense, we want to establish friendly relations with Iraq. We have every interest in seeing a strong, independent, and secular buffer state in the northern gulf. We have every interest in encouraging Iraq to become more moderate, to expand its trade ties with the West, and to become a developed nation.

We will do nothing, however, to build a stable and lasting relationship by turning a blind eye to genocide. We must be prepared to confront Iraq every time it departs from a moderate course. We must not tolerate any return to the support of terrorism, and we must do everything in our power to deter it from its present use of poison gas.

THE NEED TO ENCOURAGE STRATEGIC STABILITY IN THE GULF REGION

As for our position in the gulf, we need to recognize that a strong and independent Iran is as important to our strategic interests as a strong and independent Iraq. Our quarrel with Iran is not its choice of governments, but the fact that Government has sought to subvert or conquer other states by force, and has perverted and twisted Islam into the glorification of fanaticism. The moment Iran turns away from subversion and conquest, it is in our interest to encourage the development of a state that is strong enough to preserve its own security and any relations that will lead to the development of a more moderate and less repressive regime.

We need to recognize that the end of the Iran-Iraq war leaves no pro-Western "pillars" in the region. Bahrain, Kuwait, Oman, and Saudi Arabia are friendly states, but they are relatively weak and cannot either formally grant us bases or assume the role of defending an area with over half the world's proven oil reserves. Our "over-the-horizon" reinforcement capabilities must be the last, not the first, resort in ensuring the flow of oil.

The key factor that can bring stability to the region is the kind of balance between Iraq and Iran that will checkmate any ambitions either state has to dominate its neighbor or the gulf. This, however, means that we must be as willing to condemn the use of poison gas by Iraq as we are to condemn Khomeini's butchery of hundreds of thousands of his own youth in a pointless attempt at conquest.

We cannot afford to isolate Iran, or let Iraq threaten any other nation with acts of genocide. The end result would be to give Sadam Hussein the same powers we have denied Khomeini, and risk changing Iran from an independent state that acts as a buffer between East and West and a checkmate to Iraq, to a nation which is forced to turn to the Soviet Union or which becomes too weak to help stabilize the region.

THE NEED TO FIGHT THE PROLIFERATION OF WEAPONS OF MASS DESTRUCTION WHILE WE STILL CAN

We also need to realize that it we ignore limited use of poison gas now, or the broader proliferation of weapons of mass destruction, we will ultimately license massive threats to our friends, our strategic interests, our own forces, and ultimately our own territory.

Iraq's use of poison gas has already accelerated the efforts of other nations to create major stockpiles of such weapons. Iran is actively engaged in creating its own production facilities, as is Syria. Many nations throughout the Third World have reactivated research efforts in this area, and some may well be moving toward the production and stockpiling of such weapons.

There can be no question that the use of poison gas is also accelerating efforts to develop low cost biological weapons, and is interacting with efforts at nuclear proliferation. The moment the international community tolerates Iraq's use of poison gas, it tacitly tolerates the use of small nuclear weapons or biological agents like the mycotoxins. It also encourages every Third World nation to find its own cheapest path to obtaining weapons of mass destruction, regardless of type.

We also have already seen a friendly state like Saudi Arabia turn to the PRC for the kind of IRBM whose only military merit lies in the eventual acquisition of chemical, biological, and/or nuclear warheads. We have seen Israel, Egypt, and Syria all renew their own search for long range missiles, and this is only the tip of the iceberg. For all its ritual denials, the PRC has become actively involved in selling long-range missiles and it has been joined by nations like Brazil.

If we let poison gas be used against the Kurds today, it will almost certainly be used against Israel or Saudi Arabia in the years to come, and eventually against our own forces in some low-level conflict. More broadly, however, we will repeat the mistakes the world made in tolerating Japanese use of poison gas against the Chinese, Italy's use of poison gas against Ethiopia, or Germany's experiments in the use of airpower to destroy civilians at Guernica, and Neville Chamberlain's indifference to the people of Czechoslovakia.

No part of the world has been far enough away for us to safely ignore for more than half a century. If we allow Iraq's example to fester and breed, and to contaminate the world, we will eventually reap the whirlwind. We will find ourselves in a world where every major regional conflict and tension leads to a new kind of proliferation. Ultimately, we will find ourselves thrust into one of these conflicts and ultimately, we will be the target.

Admittedly, we ourselves are still dependent on nuclear and chemical weapons for deterrence, and cannot ignore the need for research in biological warfare. We also, however, are beginning to make real progress in moving toward the reduction or elimination of these weapons and we have a quarter of a century's experience in guiding us to avoid their use. The proliferation of weapons of mass destruction is not a sane form of nationalism in the Third World, and it may ultimately destroy the validity of our own efforts at arms control.

TAKING ACTION TO HALT THE PROLIFERATION OF WEAPONS OF MASS DESTRUCTION

The question is what we can do about the process. It is obvious that mere protests and resolutions will do little, if anything. At the same time, we have learned through our efforts in regard to the Non-Proliferation Treaty that we cannot simply force our will on other nations through threats.

I believe, therefore, that we should adopt a three point program that does not single out Iraq, but which attacks the problem on a global basis and which addresses the proliferation of all the elements of weapons of mass destruction: chemical weapons, nuclear weapons, biological weapons, and advanced delivery systems.

COMPREHENSIVE REPORTING ON THE PROLIFERATION OF WEAPONS OF MASS DESTRUCTION

The first step should be the kind of report on the proliferation of such weapons that goes far beyond the kind of summary report that is common in the U.S. Government. To be specific, the President should be required to issue an annual report on each country in the world that is deliberately designed to embarrass the buyers and sellers of mass destruction in detail.

In the case of the buyers, it should require that the President report on the current activities of each Third World country in trying to develop or acquire chemical weapons, nuclear weapons, biological weapons, and missiles or other delivery systems suited for the use of such weapons. This legislation should require the disclosure of any holding and stockpiles of such weapons, and that the U.S. name the responsible officials in each country. It should cut through the vagueness and hypocrisy in most such reports, and deliberately shame the nations involved in the eyes of world opinion.

Further, the President should be required to notify the Congress in unclassified form of any major development in acquiring weapons of mass destruction by any country in the world within 30 days of the confirmation of such developments.

In the case of the sellers, the President should be required to provide a similar report any country, company, or individual selling weapons or technology which can be, or is, used to develop weapons of mass destruction. Once again, this report should name names. It should name the responsible official or officials in any seller country, the firms involved, and the individuals involved. Further, the President should be required to provide notification to the Congress of such sales within 30 days.

SANCTIONS AGAINST NATIONS ACQUIRING WEAPONS OF MASS DESTRUCTION

The second step should be to take more tangible steps to act on this report. In the case of any Third World nation that is acquiring weapons of mass destruction, we should make it firmly clear that the United States will not extend any form of credit, aid, or technology transfer in any form to a nation that is acquiring such weapons for the first time, or adding to its present stockpile, for a period of 5 years after the most recent Presidential notification of such action, and will halt support to any international institution that will provide such aid.

Further, we should maintain a public international "blacklist" of the officials and individuals in a country that are involved in acquiring weapons of mass destruction, and permanently deny them visas to the United States. This would brand those responsible for life, and end the kind of personal secrecy that is an essential part of today's efforts at proliferation.

SANCTIONS AGAINST NATIONS SELLING WEAPONS OF MASS DESTRUCTION

Finally, we must take equally firm action against the seller. We cannot shut off all trade with other nations for selling such weapons and technology, but we can target several key aspects of our relations. One is to deny technology transfer for all military technology. Another is to deny all forms of aid and credits, including both civil and military.

We also can target the selling firms to force them to divest any holdings in the use and to prevent any goods containing any component they manufacture from being imported to the United States. We can demand that they be blacklisted from any overseas contracts involving U.S. aid or international aid to which we contribute, and we can demand that this blacklisting be so broadly defined that it includes the parent company, any company with any holding of any kind in the selling company, and any company with agreements for technical or financial cooperation on an international level.

We also should expand the international blacklist on entry to the United States to include sellers, and establish much harsher criminal penalties to any Americans that may violate U.S. law in these areas.

THE NEED TO BE FIRM WITH OUR FRIENDS AS WELL AS OUR ENEMIES

These measures may not prevent the proliferation of weapons of mass destruction, but they will make it far more difficult and put far more pressure on other nations to halt the new arms race toward weapons of mass destruction. They will establish a firm basis for seeking support for similar policies from our NATO allies, the PRC, and the Soviet bloc. They will greatly strengthen the many people in the Third World who fully recognize the dangers of such action, and that the Third World does not need to repeat the mistakes of the West and East.

We must, however, recognize that we cannot play favorites. We cannot condemn Iraq or the PRC and ignore the actions of Pakistan, Saudi Arabia, or Israel. We cannot deal in cliches or half truths, or excuse our own firms or the actions of our major Western allies. We must act firmly and decisively, and leave no ambiguity or uncertainty on the part of other nations as to the firmness of our response. We cannot hope to be successful in safeguarding our most vital long-term interests if we are willing to take short-term advantage of failing to be honest about what friendly nations are doing.

THE AGENDA FOR ACTION

We cannot hope to do more than acknowledge the problem as we move toward adjournment and a Presidential election. We lack the time for the kind of hearings and careful drafting of legislation that will be vital in making such legislation successful.

Nevertheless, as we move toward adjournment, I believe that as many Members of this body and the House as possible should condemn Iraq for what are clearly crimes against humanity. Further, regardless of the outcome of the Presidential election, I feel it is clear that we need to act early in the new year to hold hearings on the proliferation of weapons of mass destruction and to take firm and decisive legislative action. I will be discussing how to best take this action with Senator Nunn and Senator Warner of the Senate Armed Services Committee and I sincerely hope that the House will join us in this effort.

Mr. President, I ask to have printed in the Record, Senate Resolution 408, which I submitted.

There being no objection, the resolution was ordered to be printed in the Record, as follows:

S. RES. 408

Whereas the international community recognized the dangers of chemical warfare during World War One, in which at least 90,000 were killed and well over 1,000,000 wounded by chemical weapons;

Whereas the 1925 Geneva Protocol outlawed the use of chemical weapons;

Whereas United Nations investigators concluded in 1984, 1986, and 1987 that Iraq had employed chemical weapons, and the United Nations Security Council has condemned the use of chemical weapons in the Iran-Iraq war;

Whereas Iraq's chemical weapons attack on March 16, in which hundreds of Kurdish civilians were killed on Iraqi soil, underscores the horror of these weapons and their impact on noncombatants;

Whereas the United States condemned that Iraqi attack as a "particularly grave violation" of international law; and

Whereas it has been reported that Iran may be producing chemical weapons, and Iran has also used chemical weapons in retaliation for Iraqi use of such weapons: Now, therefore, be it

Resolved, That the Senate —

(1) condemns the use of chemical weapons by Iraq and declares that such action violates international law;

(2) calls upon Iraq to halt immediately and permanently the use of all chemical weapons;

(3) commends the President for his prompt condemnation of Iraq's recent chemical weapons attack on civilians;

(4) urges the President to seek allied cooperation to further tighten controls on the export of chemical compounds to countries seeking to develop a chemical weapons capability;

(5) expresses concern about reported Iranian use of chemical weapons and urges the President to make appropriate diplomatic efforts to prevent Iran from developing or using chemical weapons; and

(6) urges the President to pursue American efforts at the Geneva Conference on Disarmament to reach an arms control agreement banning the use, production, development, stockpiling, transfer, and acquisition of chemical weapons.

Mr. McCAIN. Mr. President, I suggest the absence of a quorum.

The PRESIDING OFFICER. The clerk will call the roll.

The legislative clerk proceeded to call the roll.

Mr. LEVIN. Mr. President, I ask unanimous consent that the order for the quorum call be rescinded.

The PRESIDING OFFICER. Without objection, it is so ordered.

21.

[September 9, 1988 (Extension of Remarks), p. 23409]

IRAQI USE OF CHEMICAL WEAPONS AGAINST THE KURDS
HON. BENJAMIN A. GILMAN
OF NEW YORK
IN THE HOUSE OF REPRESENTATIVES

Friday, September 9, 1988

Mr. GILMAN. Mr. Speaker, today's newspapers reveal that the Department of State has concluded that Iraq is using chemical weapons against Kurdish civilians and armed insurgents inside Iraq.

If the Iraqis ever felt the Kurds were a threat, in that many Iraqi Kurds had allied themselves with Iran, the time for such a concern has passed; and Iraq and Iran have agreed to a cease-fire. In any event, the use of chemical weapons is prohibited by the 1925 Geneva Convention. With respect to civilians within Iraq who have not joined in any uprising, the use of chemical weapons against Kurdish civilians is all the more offensive.

I applaud the administration for its forthright declaration on this matter, and for its prior, repeated condemnation of Iraq-as well as Iran-using these weapons in the Iran-Iraq war. We cannot allow the use of weapons of mass killing, such as chemical weapons and long range missiles, to become a matter of routine. The implication of their routine use for the peace and stability of the world are too horrible to contemplate. Many countries around the world-and in the unstable Middle East in particular-are in the process of stockpiling such weapons. We cannot allow this trend to continue without interruption.

We should certainly continue to evaluate the evidence of the use of chemical weapons and other kinds of weapons against the Kurds, and we should consider the use of various kinds of pressure against the Iraqi Government in order to affect a change in current practices.

The American people applaud the Turkish Government for giving sanctuary to Kurds fleeing Iraq and hope that it will continue this humanitarian for as long as necessary.

Mr. Speaker, for humanitarian reasons, and for the sake of the peace and stability of the world, the Iraqi Government must reverse its current policies.

22.

[September 12, 1988 (Senate), p. 23423]

IRAQ'S USE OF CHEMICAL WEAPONS

Mr. GORE. Mr. President, according to extensive and apparently well-documented reports, the Government of Iraq may right now be in the midst of trying to impose a final solution on its Kurdish population. Upward of 100,000 Kurds have already fled the Iraqi Army by crossing over the border into Turkey. Something on the order of 50,000 Kurds remain trapped inside a forbidden zone said to have been marked by the Government of Iraq for depopulation. These people are now the object of a military program, which, according to many reports, includes the use of chemical weapons.

If the world does not respond to these developments, we may again be forced to look on as yet another act of mass atrocity is committed by yet another government whose behavior will yet again stain the honor of humanity and of civilization. At such times, there can be no such thing as innocent bystanders. For governments to have knowledge of such events, and not to cry out, is to become complicit with them.

Last week, the United States finally broke the silence, cynicism and indifference which, until then, typified the world's response to repeated charges of inhumane behavior by Iraqi forces, involving the use of chemical weapons. The Secretary of State-convinced by information at his disposal-bluntly laid it on the line for Iraq. Thanks to Senator PELL, the Senate did likewise, by approving legislation aimed at cutting off United States aid to Iraq, and ending United States imports of Iraqi oil.

It is a beginning, but it is not enough. To achieve results, we should focus world opinion on a demand that Iraq desist from the use of chemical weapons; that it allow international inspection to follow up on claims that chemical weapons have been used; and that it conform its behavior toward the Kurdish population within its borders to norms acceptable under the U.N. Charter and international law.

To that end, Mr. President, there are certain actions I urgently recommend:

First, our Government should immediately issue a statement which presents the evidence against Iraq in the fullest possible detail.

Second, we should request an immediate session of the Security Council to address the charge that Iraq is in the process of carrying out a genocidal policy.

Third, we should call upon our allies, some of whom are deeply involved with Iraq as trading partners and/or military suppliers, to demand that Iraq be responsive to these charges.

Fourth, we should directly confront the nations of the neutral-nonaligned movement with their silence in the face of the evidence and demand that they speak out.

Fifth, we should ask the Soviet Union to speak out in the same manner as have we. Parallel United States and Soviet approaches will do more than anything else to signal Iraq's leaders that they must change course.

Sixth, we should communicate with every nation that is a party to the Geneva Protocol on the Prohibition of the Use of Chemical Weapons, to advise that silence in the presence of such a challenge to this agreement will make it a dead letter.

Seventh, we should move speedily to determine the needs of Kurdish refugees in Turkey, and of agencies seeking to aid them, including both the United Nations and the Government of Turkey itself. We should make sure that these needs are met.

To promote these actions, Mr. President, there are certain steps which we in this body can take.

First, the Senate should call upon the Secretary of State to provide public testimony as to the nature of information at his disposal, and as to the administration's ongoing plans.

Second, I suggest that both parties through their leaders consider setting up a clearinghouse process to collect and analyze information on behalf of the Senate as a whole.

Third, we can communicate with the Turkish Government through its ambassador here, to express appreciation for what it has done so far to provide refuge for Kurdish refugees, and to indicate that the Senate is ready to respond to their material needs for our part in this process.

Fourth, we can communicate with the Soviet Government through its ambassador here, urging them to join the United States in public condemnation of Iraqi behavior.

Fifth, we can and should communicate with governments of Iraq's trading partners, suppliers, and supporters; appealing to them to speak out and to use their influence.

Sixth, we can and should make sure that the American people are alerted to what is going on. To this end, we can use not only our own resources, but we ought to ask the two Presidential candidates to speak out.

Mr. President, ruthless as it may be, the Government of Iraq is not irrational. Its leaders are aware of world opinion, and understand that their vital interests can be damaged by a hardening of that opinion against them. Recognizing this, we can influence the outcome of these events. But only if we shake world opinion awake.

I yield the remainder of my time.

23.

[September 13, 1988 (House), p. H7529]

USE OF POISON GAS BY THE IRAQIS

The SPEAKER pro tempore. Under a previous order of the House, the gentleman from Ohio [Mr. PEASE] is recognized for 5 minutes.

Mr. PEASE. Mr. Speaker, I rise to commend Secretary Shultz, the Reagan administration, and the U.S. Senate for action taken recently to call attention to the use of poison gas by Iraq. I, for some months earlier in this year, looked on with distress and disgust week after week as reliable reports came out that Iraq was using poison gas against Iran in that longstanding war.

It seemed to me that much of the civilized world, most especially the United States Government, was standing by and doing far too little to protest and take action against the outrage of Iraq using poison gas, a practice that has been outlawed and condemned for the last 60 years.

The war in Iran and Iraq has ended, at least for the time being, with a cease-fire. So the reports of Iraq using poison gas against Iranian soldiers in the few days and weeks leading up to the cease-fire have little relevance right now. There are no current hostilities between Iran and Iraq.

But just as soon as that use of poison gas against Iran died down, Iraq began a war against some of its own people, those who are Kurds and who occupy one corner of Iraq. It is probably not too much to say that Iraq is trying to wipe out its own Kurdish population.

That is bad enough. Genocide is always to be condemned. But it is even worse when Iraq is using poison gas to do so. There have been increasingly reliable reports in the last couple of weeks that that is indeed going on, and I have a fistful of clippings from newspapers and magazines in the United States reporting on Iraqi use of poison gas.

Mr. Speaker, a civilized world cannot tolerate the use of poison gas against Iranians or

Kurds or anyone else. I was delighted when the Senate last week passed legislation that cuts off $800 million in trade and credits to Iraq to protest that country's use of poison gas. Companion legislation has been introduced in the House by the gentleman from California [Mr. LANTOS] and the gentleman from Illinois [Mr. PORTER]. I want to commend them for that action on their part, and I hope very much that the House Foreign Affairs Committee and the full House will both take up this legislation very soon and that we will pass it and send it to the President.

In the meantime, I commend Secretary Shultz for the statement that he made, a very strong statement last Thursday or Friday. I ask that he and President Reagan follow up that action in the United Nations by seeking to send an investigative team from the United Nations to Iraq to determine for sure that poison gas has been used against the Kurdish guerrillas, and if that is proved, I ask Secretary Shultz and President Reagan to take the strongest possible position within the United Nations to exercise multilateral sanctions of the strongest kind against Iraq.

We simply have to make it clear that poison gas has no place, no place in the civilized world, and that any nation, Iraq or any other which uses it, must expect swift and sure action by the rest of the civilized world.

24.

[September 13, 1988 (Extension of Remarks), pp. 23678-79]

CHEMICAL GENOCIDE OF KURDS
HON. STENY H. HOYER
OF MARYLAND
IN THE HOUSE OF REPRESENTATIVES

Tuesday, September 13, 1988

Mr. HOYER. Mr. Speaker, two articles appeared in the *Washington Post* [Jim Hoagland. "Make No Mistake: This is Genocide," Sept. 8, 1988] and the *New York Times* [William

Safire. "Stop the Iraqi Murder of the Kurds," Sept. 5, 1988] this week that I would like to submit for the RECORD. The thrust of both is clear. Genocide is being committed by the armed forces of Iraqi President Saddam Hussein against the Kurdish populace of northern Iraq.

Mr. Speaker, we cannot remain indifferent to this wholesale slaughter. Indifference in the past has allowed ruthless dictators to murder millions of people, and indifference today will allow countless more to die. The ceasefire in the gulf war has ended a conflict that claimed hundreds of thousands of lives, and we should not allow this ceasefire to be used as an opportunity for renewed bloodletting. The systematic use of chemical weapons in gas attacks against civilian populations centers is an outrage with little precedent, and should be met with a firm response if similar affronts to humanity are to be avoided in the future . . .

25.

[September 13, 1988 (Extension of Remarks), p. 23695]

KURDS BEING GASSED
HON. JIM BATES
OF CALIFORNIA
IN THE HOUSE OF REPRESENTATIVES

Tuesday, September 13, 1988

Mr. BATES. Mr. Speaker, despite the Iraq-Iran cease fire agreement of August 20, 1988, U.S. intelligence sources have confirmed that Iraq has used chemical weapons against its Kurdish minority. This is a barbaric act which will have serious ramifications.

The use of poison gas was outlawed by the 1925 Geneva protocol, as a result of World War I casualties caused by poisonous gas, and has not been used extensively by any form of government since. Yet, it has been confirmed that poison gas has been used by the Iraqi Government as a means of quelling any potential uprising by its Kurdish minority.

The violations against these 3.5 million people seeking to gain autonomy is reminiscent of the horrors the world witnessed during the Jewish Holocaust. We must "never again" allow a nation to attempt the physical elimination of a faction of its people.

For these reasons, I have introduced a resolution in the House of Representatives, House Resolution 5320, which expresses a sense of outrage at the Iraqi Government for its use of poison gas against the Kurds, and calls upon Iraq to immediately and permanently halt the use of all chemical weapons.

The Kurdish people constitute a distinct ethnic group of 20 million people. The 1922 establishment of a Turkish Republic ended the Kurd's hopes of an independent homeland known as Kurdistan and they currently reside in Turkey, Iran, Iraq, Syria, the Soviet Union, and Lebanon. Due to the use of the chemicals, 100,000 Iraqi Kurds have recently fled to Turkey. Mr. Speaker, Iraq's use of chemical weapons against the Kurdish people appears to constitute an act of genocide in gross violation of international law, and I urge my colleagues to support the resolution.

26.

[September 14, 1988 (Senate), pp. 23710-11]

IRAQ'S REPEATED USE OF CHEMICAL WEAPONS

Mr. MITCHELL. Mr. President, I am saddened to once again rise on the Senate floor to condemn Iraq's use of chemical weapons. Iraq has continued to flagrantly violate international law and basic humanitarian principles by using chemical weapons.

It is testimony to the lack of international concern and action that Iraq has dared to repeatedly employ these weapons-weapons that the international community, including Iraq, banned over 50 years.

The 1925 Geneva protocol reflected the world's belief that the effects of chemical agents are so inhumane that they must not be used even in war. Yet Iraq has insisted on using these weapons both in its war against Iran

and more recently in its campaign to eliminate an entire ethnic group of Iraqi citizens.

These actions constitute a callous and cruel assault on the principles of law and respect for human rights that have been painstakingly codified over many years. Iraq's actions cannot be rationalized, cannot be defended, cannot be dismissed. They must not go uncensured.

The international community must protect the principles on which it has been painstakingly trying to build a more gentle and just world. Iraq's actions threatens to gravely harm the progress slowly won during the past century.

On June 24, the Senate unequivocally stated its view of Iraqi violations of international law. In passing Senate Resolution 408, which I offered, this body unanimously condemned Iraq's use of chemical weapons and urged the administration to apply diplomatic pressure to prevent their future use.

The resolution was enacted after the world witnessed the graphic evidence of Iraq's use of mustard and nerve gas against Kurdish civilians in the Iranian-occupied town of Halabja.

Yet, the March attacks, in which thousands were killed, were part of a larger pattern that had long been ignored. The United Nations has concluded in 1984, 1986, and again in 1987 that Iraq had used chemical weapons against Iran.

The international community did nothing.

The aftermath of the attack on Halabja, documented by camera, made it impossible to ignore Iraq's atrocities. The undeniable evidence challenged the community of nations to act.

It is tragic that the Senate's outrage was not more widely shared, tragic that the opportunity to exert effective international pressure was squandered. While responsibility for the slaughter of innocent civilians lies with Iraq and Iraq alone, the international community failed to act forcefully to dissuade Iraq from further chemical attacks.

The world overlooked Iraq's actions and instead focused its hopes on an end to the Iran-Iraq War. In a cruel irony, the gulf ceasefire offered Iraq an opportunity to turn its chemical arsenal against its own citizens. In what appears to be a campaign of genocide against its 3 million Iraqi Kurds, government forces have reportedly killed thousands of Kurdish people and forced some 50,000 to 100,000 to flee the country.

Where is the international outrage? Where is the will to act against such slaughter?

The Senate has again moved quickly to condemn Iraq and propose a United States response to the repeated violations of international law. S2763, introduced by the distinguished chairman of the Senate Foreign Relations Committee, Mr. PELL, would implement tough economic sanctions against Iraq.

It would end all credit and credit guarantees to Iraq, require the United States to vote against loans to Iraq by international financial institutions and prohibit imports of Iraqi oil. The sanctions would be lifted only if Iraq halts the use of chemical weapons and ends its campaign against the Kurds.

The legislation also requests the administration to bring the issue of Iraqi chemical weapon use before the U.N. Security Council and demand that appropriate and effective measures be taken against Iraq.

I confess my disappointment in the administration's failure to take stronger action against Iraq before thousands of civilians were deliberately killed. The United States had learned of Iraq's violations of the Geneva protocol during the years in which the United States-Iraqi ties grew stronger. Our tilt toward Iraq in the gulf war, symbolized by the convoying of ships belonging to Iraq's allies, should have bought us some leverage, some authority with which to dissuade the Iraqis from employing chemical arms.

Thankfully, President Reagan condemned the attack on Halabja as a "particularly grave violation of international law." Secretary Shultz called the more recent poison gas attacks "unjustifiable and abhorrent," and told Iraq that continued attacks would affect United States-Iraqi relations.

It is time to translate these words into deeds.

It is time to marshal international support for the censure of Iraq.

It is time for nations to restore the legal and moral prohibition against the use of chemical weapons.

I support the administration's effort to prompt the Government of Iraq to declare a policy of opposition to the use of chemical weapons.

But such a statement will not suffice. First of all, it would not be believed. Iraq had long denied using chemical weapons against Iranian forces. The Iraqi Government continues to deny using chemical weapons against the Kurds, despite the statements and physical testimony provided by fleeing refugees and despite the evidence that convinced our State Department that such use had in fact occurred.

Moreover, such a policy statement would not constitute a penalty for killing thousands of civilians with weapons long banned by international agreement.

The Senate has correctly called for the United States to bring this issue before the U.N. Security Council and demand that effective measures be taken against Iraq. An issue of grave international concern like this one should be boldly addressed in this forum of nations.

At the very least, the crime must be named and Iraq held responsible.

The ominous silence cannot continue.

We must not turn our heads as a government attempts to eliminate an entire segment of its own citizenry.

We must not passively allow the Geneva protocol to also all force and meaning.

We must not squander this opportunity to push for stronger international prohibitions against chemical weapons.

Clearly, the Geneva protocol is flawed. It lacks enforcement mechanisms. It bans only the use of chemical weapons. There is an urgent need to go further—to ban the production, transfer and stockpiling of these weapons—if we are to effectively prevent their use.

Cheap and easy to manufacture while posing a horrific military threat, chemical arms are the poor man's nuclear bomb. Chemical production technology continues to proliferate, eased across borders by Western commercial chemical exports. As nations rapidly acquire chemical weapons, the risk of their use in the next conflict increases.

The Senate has already expressed its unanimous support for American efforts to achieve an agreement banning the use, production, development, stockpiling, transfer and acquisition of chemical weapons.

The time to push forward in chemical negotiations is now.

Sadly, the Reagan administration has not demonstrated a seriousness about pursuing a chemical weapons ban, even though chemical weapons pose an increasing threat to the people and environment of this planet.

The need for leadership on this issue is clear.

The next administration must make a strong commitment to pursuing a comprehensive chemical weapons ban. No one pretends that it will be easy. But given political will and good faith negotiating, a chemical weapons treaty is well within reach.

The next administration should set itself a clear goal: attain a chemical weapons agreement within the next few years.

The next administration should make American policy consistent with that goal and discontinue the production of binary chemical weapons on our own soil.

If nothing else, Iraq's egregious use of chemical weapons, including its use against its own citizens, should convince the world of the need to successfully conclude the Geneva negotiations to prohibit the production and stockpiling of chemical weapons.

We must learn from our own human failures. We can act to prevent future deaths by poison gas.

I urge the nations of the world to join together to condemn and punish any country that violates the Geneva protocol banning the use of chemical weapons.

I sincerely hope that this President, the next President, and all national leaders will bring urgency and purpose to the ongoing chemical weapons negotiations. The need for immediate action has never been so clearly and tragically demonstrated as in the graphic deaths of innocent civilians poisoned by their own government.

27.

[October 7, 1988 (Senate), p. 29361]

KURDS AND CHEMICAL WEAPONS

Mr. GORE. Mr. President, with permission, I am submitting a copy of an opinion piece I authored for the *Christian Science Monitor* yesterday [Oct. 6, "Clamping Down on Chemical Weapons"], on chemical weapons, for publication in the RECORD.

A wall of silence surrounds the fate of scores of thousands of Kurds trapped in Iraq by the armed forces of that country, and cut off from escape into Turkey. Anything may be happening: from the "mere" possibility that Kurdish culture within this region is being eradicated by scattering the populace, to the possibility of a final solution, involving the use of chemical weapons.

Indeed, there is no question but that chemical weapons have been used: the issue, rather, is to what extent; whether the deaths should be estimated in the hundreds, the thousands, or tens of thousands. Civilization, always thin in Iraq, has worn entirely through. The protestations of that government are fiction; their show of righteous indignation is the snarl of the guilty, exposed in the commission of their crime.

Iraq expects to get away with it. Because that country is victorious over Iran. Because it has oil money. Because there is big business to be done in provisioning its economy, reconstructing war damage, and equipping its armed forces. Because it has used chemical weapons before without penalty: indeed because it used them successfully, to break the morale of Iran's army and civilian population.

Our Government has acted correctly in condemning Iraq. But the question of next steps is blank.

All of us are united in our feeling of revulsion against the use of chemical weapons by Iraq. Hopefully, Congress will agree before much longer on compromise legislation to impose sanctions. Perhaps then the administration will reconsider its opposition to them. I respect the administration's desire to see whether persuasion and diplomacy can work—but it seems to me that this is a situation where delicacy has little scope, and where we have already been patient enough.

Meanwhile, there is the administration's proposal for an international conference. In principle it has merit, but as yet there is no discernable agenda. Some of us have already signed a letter to the President, originating with Senators KASSEBAUM, COHEN, BIDEN, and BRADLEY, which makes certain suggestions. My editorial column makes others. Since the Government of France has agreed to host such a conference it can be made a reality, and the present administration should be encouraged to work out a set of proposals which will reinforce existing prohibitions concerning the use of chemical weapons.

Mr. President, I deeply believe that if this episode is allowed to slide, then governments contemplating the acquisition or the use of chemical weapons will conclude that they may do so with impunity. This situation is an important test of the will and the ability of nations to exert themselves for the sake not only of a moral imperative, but also for the sake of their common security.

I ask unanimous consent that the article be printed in the RECORD.

There being no objection, the article was ordered to be printed in the RECORD . . .

28.

[October 12, 1988 (Senate), pp. 29907-08]

A "FURLOUGH" FOR IRAQ

Mr. PELL. Mr. President, on occasion a regime will commit a crime so heinous that the world community speaks vehemently in protest. Iraq's use of poison gas against its Kurdish population is such a crime.

Translating our sense of moral outrage into action becomes more difficult. On September 9, the Senate voted to impose on Iraq the most sweeping sanctions put forward for any country in decades. Yesterday the Senate voted for the third time for sanctions. This time, however, the package had been watered

down after intense pressure from the House of Representatives and a variety of American business interests. I regret the weakening of the sanctions bill but I do believe yesterday's legislation has teeth and will cause Iraq and other countries to think twice about using chemical weapons.

Now we hear that the State Department opposes even this watered down sanctions bill. Apparently they would take the word of Iraq's foreign minister, Tariq Aziz, who promised Secretary Shultz that Iraq would not use chemical weapons. Unfortunately, this promise of future good conduct was accompanied by an assertion that Iraq had not used chemical weapons against the Kurds-an assertion that is demonstrably false. Can we really be expected to overlook the gassing of thousands of people on the basis of an assurance that is itself predicated on a lie?

As a former Foreign Service officer, I am sympathetic to the State Department's desire to maintain good relations with Iraq. Iraq is a rich and strategically important country and much work has gone into rebuilding the United States-Iraq relationship.

Some conduct, however, is beyond the pale for civilized nations. If we are not prepared to respond to Iraq's use of poison gas, will we ever be prepared to act?

Jim Hoagland has written a splendid column on these issues which appears in today's *Washington Post* [Oct. 12, 1988, "A "Furlough" for Iraq."]. He concludes by saying that President "Reagan should not veto sanctions against Iraq and become a party to the refusal to confront evil." I endorse these sentiments wholeheartedly and would like to call the Senate's attention to the Hoagland article.

Mr. President, I ask unanimous consent that the Hoagland article be printed in the RECORD.

There being no objection, the article was ordered to be printed in the RECORD . . .

Mr. PELL. Mr. President, I suggest the absence of a quorum.

The PRESIDING OFFICER. The clerk will call the roll.

The legislative clerk proceeded to call the roll.

Mr. PRYOR. Mr. President, I ask unanimous consent that the order for the quorum call be rescinded.

The PRESIDING OFFICER. Without objection, it is so ordered.

29.

[October 20, 1988 (House), p. H10670-77]

ANTI-TERRORISM AND NATIONAL SECURITY AMENDMENTS ACT OF 1988

Mr. FASCELL. Mr. Speaker, I move to suspend the rules and pass the bill (H.R. 5550) to combat international terrorism and otherwise further the national security and foreign policy interests of the United States.

The Clerk read as follows:

H.R. 5550

Be it enacted by the Senate and House of Representatives of the United States of America in Congress assembled,

SECTION 1. SHORT TITLE.

This Act may be cited as the "Anti-Terrorism and National Security Amendments Act of 1988".

SEC. 2. TABLE OF CONTENTS.

The table of contents for this Act is as follows:

TITLE II-SANCTIONS AGAINST IRAQ

SEC. 201. SHORT TITLE.

This title may be cited as the "Sanctions Against Iraqi Chemical Weapons Use Act".

SEC. 202. FINDINGS AND PURPOSE.

(a) FINDINGS.-The Congress finds that-

(1) the Kurdish people constitute a distinct ethnic group of some twenty million, with an ancient history and a rich cultural heritage;

(2) three to four million Kurds are citizens of Iraq, residing in the northern part of that country;

(3) the Iraqi Army has undertaken a military campaign against Kurdish regions of Iraq and has destroyed Kurdish villages in northern Iraq;

(4) substantial evidence exists that the Iraqi Army has been using chemical weapons against Kurdish insurgents and unarmed Kurdish civilians;

(5) by these and other actions against the Kurds, Iraq has violated their internationally recognized human rights;

(6) tens of thousands of Kurdish survivors of the Iraqi Army assaults have taken refuge in Turkey;

(7) several United Nations teams have confirmed that Iraq has used chemical weapons in its war with Iran; and

(8) Iraq's use of chemical weapons is a gross violation of international law.

(b) PURPOSE.-It is the purpose of this title to mandate United States sanctions against Iraq because of its use of chemical weapons in violation of international law.

SEC. 203. IMPOSITION OF SANCTIONS AGAINST IRAQ.

(a) INITIAL SANCTIONS.-(1) The United States Government may not sell to Iraq any item on the United States Munitions List.

(2) Licenses may not be issued for the export to Iraq of any item on the United States Munitions List.

(3) The authorities of section 6 of the Export Administration Act of 1979 shall be used to prohibit the export to Iraq of any goods or technology on the control list established pursuant to section 5(c)(1) of that Act.

(4) Licenses may not be issued for the export to Iraq of any chemical that the President determines may be used primarily in the production of chemical weapons or may be otherwise devoted to chemical warfare purposes.

(5) The United States shall oppose any loan or financial or technical assistance to Iraq by international financial institutions in accordance with section 701 of the International Financial Institutions Act.

(6) This subsection takes effect on the date of enactment of this Act.

(b) REQUIREMENT FOR ADDITIONAL SANCTIONS.-Not later than December 31, 1988, the President, after consultation with the Congress, shall impose appropriate additional sanctions against Iraq unless the President certifies in writing to the Speaker of the House of Representatives and the chairman of the Committee on Foreign Relations of the Senate-

(1) that the Government of Iraq is not using chemical weapons in violation of international law, including the 1925 Geneva Protocol (relating to the use of chemical weapons in war) and Common Article 3 of the 1949 Geneva Conventions (relating to the protection of victims of war); and

(2) that the Government of Iraq has provided reliable assurances that it will not use chemical weapons in the future in violation of international law; and

(3) that-

(A) the Government of Iraq is willing to allow on-site inspections by United Nations observers or other internationally-recognized, impartial observers, or

(B) other reliable means exist,

to ensure that the Government of Iraq is not using chemical weapons.

(c) DESCRIPTION AND AUTHORIZATION OF ADDITIONAL SANCTIONS.- (1) To the extent they are not otherwise authorized, the sanctions described in paragraph (2) of this subsection are hereby authorized to be imposed against Iraq pursuant to subsection (b). In imposing sanctions against Iraq pursuant to subsection (b), the President shall exercise authority described in one or more of the subparagraphs of paragraph (2). Sanctions described in paragraph (2) shall be in addition to any other sanctions imposed on Iraq pursuant to subsection (b).

(2) The sanctions referred to in paragraph (1) are the following:

(A) DENIAL OF ACCESS TO THE EXPORT-IMPORT BANK.-Denying credits or credit guarantees through the Export-Import Bank of the United States to Iraq.

(B) RESTRICTIONS ON IMPORTS.-Prohibiting or otherwise restricting the importation into the United States of one or more kinds of articles (which may include petroleum or any petroleum product) that are the growth, product, or manufacture of Iraq.

(C) ADDITIONAL RESTRICTIONS ON EXPORTS.-Prohibiting or otherwise substantially restricting, using the authorities of section 6 of the Export Administration Act of 1979, exports to Iraq of goods and technology (excluding agricultural commodities and products).

(D) DOWNGRADING DIPLOMATIC RELATIONS.-Using the President's constitutional authorities to downgrade or suspend diplomatic relations between the United States and Iraq.

(d) CONTRACT SANCTITY.-(1) For purposes of export controls imposed in accordance with subsection (a)(3) of this section, the date described in section 6(m)(1) of the Export Administration Act of 1979 shall be deemed to be September 18, 1988.

(2) In imposing any additional sanction under subsection (c) of this section, the President may not prohibit or curtail the execution of any contract or agreement entered into before the earlier of the date on which notice of intent to impose the additional sanction is printed in the Federal Register or the date on which the President notifies the Congress of such an intent.

(e) REPORTS TO CONGRESS.-The President shall report to the Congress periodically on the actions taken pursuant to this section.

SEC. 204. CONDITIONS FOR LIFTING
          SANCTIONS.

The President may waive any sanctions imposed pursuant to section 203 (a) or (b), including sanctions described in section 203(c), if the President determines and so certifies in writing to the Speaker of the House of Representatives and the chairman of the Committee on Foreign Relations of the Senate-

(1) that the Government of Iraq is not using chemical weapons in violation of international law, including the 1925 Geneva Protocol (relating to the use of chemical weapons in war) and Common Article 3 of the 1949 Geneva Conventions (relating to the protection of victims of war); and

(2) that the Government of Iraq has provided reliable assurances that it will not use chemical weapons in the future in violation of international law; and

(3) that-

(A) the Government of Iraq is willing to allow on-site inspections by United Nations observers or other internationally-recognized, impartial observers, or

(B) other reliable means exist,

to ensure that the Government of Iraq is not using chemical weapons.

SEC. 205. RESPECT BY THE GOVERN-
          MENT OF IRAQ FOR INTERNA-
          TIONALLY RECOGNIZED HUMAN
          RIGHTS, ESPECIALLY THOSE OF
          THE KURDISH MINORITY.

Not later than December 31, 1988, the President shall submit to the Speaker of the House of Representatives and the chairman of the Committee on Foreign Relations of the Senate an assessment of whether the Government of Iraq is respecting internationally recognized human rights, in particular the rights of the Kurdish minority in Iraq. This assessment shall be accompanied by a report which includes-

(1) all available information regarding the Government of Iraq's respect for internationally recognized human rights;

(2) a detailed description of the Government of Iraq's treatment of the Kurdish minority, including a detailed account of civilian killings and depopulation activities against the Kurds;

(3) a review of whether the Government of Iraq is committing gross violations of internationally recognized human rights;

(4) a description of the steps which the United States has taken to promote respect by the Government of Iraq for internationally recognized human rights; and

(5) a description of the steps which the United States has taken to discourage practices by the Government of Iraq which violate internationally recognized human rights, especially the rights of the Kurdish minority in Iraq.

SEC. 206. ACTIONS BY THE GOVERNMENT OF TURKEY.

The Congress-

(1) urges the Government of Turkey to cooperate with any United Nations or other appropriate investigation of Iraqi use of chemical weapons; and

(2) commends the Government of Turkey for its humanitarian decision to host thousands of Kurdish people fleeing Iraq.

SEC. 207. MULTILATERAL ACTIONS.

(a) UNITED NATIONS.—The Congress calls upon the President—

(1) to bring immediately to the attention of the Secretary General of the United Nations, and to pursue before the Security Council of the United Nations, the matter of Iraq's use of poison gas against its own nationals, most of whom are defenseless civilians; and

(2) to demand that, in accordance with United Nations Security Council Resolution 620, appropriate and effective measures be taken against Iraq for its repeated use of chemical weapons.

(b) OTHER MULTILATERAL EFFORTS.-(1) The Congress calls upon the President to seek multinational cooperation in imposing sanctions and otherwise bringing pressure on Iraq in order to obtain a cessation of Iraq's use of chemical weapons.

(2) The Congress also call upon the President to seek multilateral cooperation in order to obtain Iraqi respect for the internationally recognized human rights of the Kurdish minority in Iraq.

(3) It is the sense of the Congress that the United States should cooperate with and, as appropriate, participate in multilateral efforts to assist Kurdish refugees who are in need of medical treatment and other humanitarian aid.

SEC. 208. CERTAIN UNITED STATES EXPORTS.

It is the policy of the United States to prohibit the export to Iraq of goods and technology that would significantly contribute to the military potential of Iraq. The President should review, under section 6 of the Export Administration Act of 1979, any proposed export to Iraq of goods or technology valued at over $50,000,000.

SEC. 209. TERMINATION.

No provision of this title, and no sanction imposed by or under the authority of this title, has force and effect after June 30, 1991 . . .

30.

[May 31, 1989 (Senate), p. S5867]

SUPPORT FOR WRITERS AND JOURNALISTS

Mr. HATFIELD. Mr. President, among the many freedoms we all too often take for granted is the freedom of writers and journalists to report, comment, and oftentimes even criticize. In a great many countries around the world, writers and journalists are detained without charge, jailed without trial, and some times even put to death for doing no more than writers and journalists in our country do every day.

During the last session of Congress, Representative Bill Green, Representative John Lewis, Senator Bob Graham, and I formed the Congressional Committee to support Writers and Journalists in an effort to focus attention on the persecution of writers and journalists and to protect the closings of newspapers, magazines, and television and radio stations. The Congressional Committee now includes 15 Senators and 74 Representatives.

I recently came across an article in the *International Herald Tribune* which illustrates the urgent need for the Congressional Committee and the spotlight of attention it focuses on individual cases. The article, by Lois Whitman and Thomas Froncek, describes the plight of the editor of a Turkish magazine who now sits in prison facing a variety of charges involving articles her magazine has printed. I ask that the article be printed in the Record following my remarks.

The article follows: . . .

31.

[November 2, 1989 (Extensions of Remarks), pp. E3666-68]

AMNESTY INTERNATIONAL CRITICAL OF TURKEY'S HUMAN RIGHTS VIOLATIONS
HON. WM. S. BROOMFIELD
OF MICHIGAN
IN THE HOUSE OF REPRESENTATIVES

Thursday, November 2, 1989

Mr. BROOMFIELD. Mr. Speaker, I want to call the attention of my colleagues to a recent Amnesty International Report which documents the tragic violations of human rights in Turkey. It is time for Turkish officials to honestly assess their human rights practices and quickly put an end to the ongoing abuses of fundamental human rights in that country. Turkish officials should also realize that their military occupation of northern Cyprus has violated the human rights of thousands of Greek Cypriots on that once united island. It is time for those Turkish forces to go back home.

In particular, the current Amnesty International Report on human rights practices around the world talks about the imprisonment of prisoners of conscience and the use of torture which has resulted in the deaths of some prisoners in Turkish jails. In addition, Iranians who tried to escape from the tyranny of the Ayatollah Khomeini by fleeing to Turkey were denied asylum and forcibly returned to Iran. These human rights practices are truly regrettable.

Over the years, I and other Members have been deeply concerned about the Turkish invasion of Cyprus and the impact which that military action had on the human rights of Greek Cypriots. That 1974 intervention resulted in the deaths of thousands of Greek Cypriots. Many are missing and unaccounted for. Among them is Andrew Kassapis, a young Michigan resident, who was visiting his family on Cyprus at that time. Nearly 200,000 Greek Cypriots were displaced from their homes in the north of that island. They lost their residences, and their land and are now forbidden from visiting their birthplace. They are strangers in their own country. Nearly 30,000 armed Turkish troops still occupy the northern half of Cyprus. On many occasions, I have called for the withdrawal of those troops and a return to normalcy on that island.

All around the world, there is a growing respect for human rights. Events in the Soviet Union and Eastern Europe reveal this trend. It is time for Turkey, a friend and close NATO ally, to participate in this international effort. Let us hope that Turkish authorities will join the family of nations who are ending human rights violations. Now is the time for Turkey to stop violating human rights both at home as well as Cyprus.

I commend the following 1989 Amnesty International Report to my colleagues in the Congress:

AMNESTY INTERNATIONAL REPORT
1989
TURKEY

Thousands of people were imprisoned for political reasons, including hundreds of prisoners of conscience. The use of torture continued to be widespread and systematic, in some cases resulting in death. Civilian and military courts passed at least 18 death sentences. In November 228 death sentences were awaiting ratification by parliament, all legal remedies having been exhausted. Iranian asylum seekers were returned to Iran without their claims for asylum having been assessed by the competent authorities. Recognized refugees awaiting resettlement in third countries were also forcibly returned to Iran, where some were reported to have been executed despite the Turkish Government's stated commitment to the principle of non-refoulement.

In November the government lifted emergency legislation in Istanbul. At the end of the year a state of emergency was in force in eight provinces in southeastern Turkey where the security forces had been engaged in counter-insurgency operations against Kurdish secessionist guerrillas. The guerrillas were reported to have carried out attacks on the civilian population and to have taken prisoners, some of whom they tortured and killed.

In February Turkey signed and ratified the European Convention for the Prevention of Torture and Inhuman or Degrading Treatment or Punishment and in August it ratified the United Nations Convention against Torture and Other Cruel, Inhuman or Degrading Treatment or Punishment.

Some prisoners of conscience were released but many others remained in prison and arrests and trials of prisoners of conscience continued throughout the year. Among several hundred prisoners of conscience were members of political organizations, trade unions and illegal Kurdish groups, journalists and religious activists.

A number of people were prosecuted during the year for membership of illegal political parties which did not espouse violence. They were tried on charges brought under Article 141 of the Turkish Penal Code prohibiting "membership of an organization trying to establish the domination of one social class over the others". Five alleged members of the Turkish Socialist Workers' Party (TSIP) who had been detained since July 1987 were released in March. In April Izmir State Security Court acquitted them, together with two other defendants who had also been released earlier (see Amnesty International Report 1988). Alleged members of the Turkish Communist Party (TKP) were also prosecuted under Article 141. The trial of 13 alleged TKP members who had been detained in August and September 1987 ended in November at Izmir State Security Court. At that time six defendants were still in prison. Ali Ugur received a sentence of six years, eight months' imprisonment and remained in Buca Prison; the other five were each sentenced to four years', two months' imprisonment but were released pending appeal. Another defendant who had been released earlier received the same sentence.

Six defendants were acquitted (see Amnesty International Report 1988).

The trial of Haydar Kutlu, the TKP's Secretary General, and Dr. Nihat Sargin, Secretary General of the Turkish Workers' Party (TIP), both imprisoned since November 1987, started in June in Ankara State Security Court and was still continuing at the end of the year.

Some TIP and TKP members who had been convicted by Istanbul and Ankara Military Courts but had been released pending appeal were reimprisoned after the Military Appeal Court confirmed their sentences. In June three of 46 TIP defendants in Istanbul facing reimprisonment were taken to high-security prisons for political prisoners in order to serve the remaining 22 to 24 months of their sentences. In Ankara, eight out of 75 TKP defendants facing reimprisonment were taken to various prisons to serve between seven and 24 months. Amnesty International adopted all these prisoners as prisoners of conscience.

Aziz Celik, educational director of Kristal-Is, the glass-workers' union, and Huseyin Bas, a former official of Maden-Is, the banned mine-workers' union, were detained in the first week of May in Istanbul and charged with membership of the TKP. When their trial began in September in Istanbul State Security Court they were released from custody although their trial continued.

In November the Minister of the Interior announced that during the first nine months of the year 2,120 people had been detained in southeastern Turkey, where most of the population is of Kurdish origin. Of these, 593 had been charged and formally arrested. Most of the Kurdish activists known to Amnesty International were charged with violent offences but they included prisoners of conscience imprisoned on account of their non-violent political or cultural activities.

Mehmet (Sehmuz) Cibran had been detained in October 1986 on return from exile. In July 1987 Diyarbakir Military Court convicted him of membership of the Kurdistan Workers' Party [PKK] and sentenced him to 14 years' imprisonment under Article 171 of the penal code for membership of a "secret association formed in order to commit crimes". Three separate trials have reportedly since started in which he has faced charges such as making separatist propaganda in his oral and written defence and shouting in court. During one of the hearings in August he was expelled from the courtroom when he tried to defend himself in Kurdish.

Trials of religious activists charged under Article 163 with "attempting to change the secular nature of the state" continued. In May Hasan Damar, who had been in prison since October 1986, was sentenced by Ankara State Security Court to four years, two months' imprisonment under Article 163(4) for anti-secular propaganda. In September the same court sentenced him to another four years, two months' imprisonment under Article 163(2) for membership in the Federal Republic of Germany of an anti-secular organization, Milli Gorus, National View, which is legal there. He remained in Ankara Closed Prison as a prisoner of conscience (see Amnesty International Report 1988).

Writers, publishers and journalists were prosecuted or remained in prison under provisions of the penal code including Article 142, "making communist propaganda"; Article 159, "insulting the State authorities"; and Article 312, "incitement to commit a crime". In June five people were detained in Ankara and charged under Articles 142, 311 and 312 in connection with articles they had written for the political journal Toplumsal Kurtulus, Social Liberation. After 10 days in incommunicado detention one was released. Of the remaining four, Dr. Yalcin Kucuk and Husnu Ondul—a defence lawyer in many political trials—were freed in August and the other two defendants in September. The trial of the five continued at Ankara State Security Court.

Political prisoners were sentenced to imprisonment or death after trials which did not meet internationally recognized minimum standards of fairness. Although martial law was lifted in 1987 trials before military courts have continued. In April the Ministry of Justice disclosed that 5,309 defendants—1,392 of whom were in prison—were being tried by such courts; some had been in pre-trial detention for more than seven years. A total of 61,220 people had been sentenced by military courts between December 1978 and April

1988. Since May 1984 political prisoners have been tried in state security courts established in eight Turkish cities. Both military and state security courts have failed to investigate allegations of torture and in some cases have permitted statements extracted under torture to be used as evidence. Most defendants have not been granted facilities for an adequate defence.

There were many new allegations of torture of political and criminal detainees and prisoners. In June Mustafa Dilmen, President of the Mersin branch of Kristal-Is, the glassworkers' union, was arrested and taken to Ankara. He alleged that he was tortured by being stripped and hosed with ice-cold water, suspended by his hands and given electric shocks. Even children were among the reported victims. In June Ozgur Cem Tas, aged 13, was taken to Diyarbakir Police Headquarters and interrogated for two hours about the whereabouts of his cousins, who were suspected of supporting Kurdish guerrillas. He alleged that he was blindfolded and handcuffed, and then beaten on the soles of the feet. Later he was suspended from hooks and electric shocks were applied to his penis.

In most cases torture was said to have occurred while victims were held incommunicado in police stations but allegations of torture and ill-treatment also came from high-security prisons for political prisoners known as E- and L-type prisons. Some 60 political prisoners in Gaziantep L-type Prison and around 70 in Bursa E-type Prison were reported to have been injured in September following arbitrary beatings by prison guards and members of the security forces.

In some cases people were reported to have died in custody as a result of torture. Mustafa Gulmez was detained in June by Istanbul Political Police while doing his military service, suspected of being a TKP member. After two days he was taken to Edirne, where he was found dead in his cell. The official explanation was suicide by hanging with a bedsheet, an article not usually provided in detention centres. Relatives and lawyers claimed the death had been caused by torture and made an official complaint. Sadik Celebi, who died in November, had been detained on 16 November and taken to Mardin Gendarmerie Station. When, after 19 days, his corpse was handed over to his family, they were told he had died in an armed encounter with guerrillas. His family claimed that the body had been bruised and that a hospital official had told them the corpse had been brought to the hospital one day before the clash with the guerrillas.

At least 18 people were sentenced to death by military and civilian courts. Other death sentences, among over 700 imposed during the previous nine years, were confirmed by appeal courts with the result that, by November, the number of people under sentence of death who had exhausted judicial appeals had reached 228.

Throughout the year Amnesty International continued to call for the release of prisoners of conscience, for fair and prompt trials for all political prisoners, and for an end to torture and the death penalty. In November Amnesty International published a report, Turkey Briefing: Human Rights Denied, detailing its concerns, launched an international campaign for an end to human rights violations in Turkey, and pressed the Turkish Government to take effective measures to protect human rights.

The campaign followed a long period during which Amnesty International had sought to raise its concerns with the Turkish authorities and to obtain effective action by the government to end torture, deaths in detention, the imprisonment of prisoners of conscience and other human rights abuses. In June an Amnesty International mission visited Turkey and met the Minister of Justice, the Minister of the Interior and other government officials. Before the mission Amnesty International submitted a list of 229 names of prisoners who had reportedly died in custody between September 1980 and April 1988. The organization asked to be informed of the cause of death in each case, as it appeared that some of the deaths might have been the result of torture. At the end of the year replies on 56 cases had been received, acknowledging torture in 13 cases.

The Turkish authorities also responded to a number of specific torture allegations raised by Amnesty International. In some cases they stated that investigations were still in progress, in others that there were no grounds for prosecution of police officers allegedly responsible for torture because medical reports had shown that torture had not been inflicted. In most cases no response was received. The number of responses increased after the publication of the Turkey Briefing and the launch of the campaign calling on the Turkish Government to stop human rights abuses.

In June Amnesty International observers attended the trial of Dr. Nihat Sargin and Haydar Kutlu, and in December attended the trial before Ankara Criminal Court of 11 leading members of the Human Rights Association in Turkey who had been charged after their campaign in 1987 for a general amnesty and the abolition of the death penalty—the prosecutor had viewed this campaign as political activity proscribed by the Law on Association. All the defendants were acquitted.

Amnesty International appealed in a number of individual refugee cases and sought clarification from the government of a report published in the Turkish press that at least 40 of a group of 58 Iranians forcibly returned to Iranian border guards by Turkish police in July had been executed in Iran. No response was received. The organization was also concerned by the forcible return (refoulement) of refugees recognized by the United Nations High Commissioner for Refugees (UNHCR), some of whom had apparently been accepted for resettlement in countries other than Turkey. In July and December it issued reports which described shortcomings in procedures for Iranian asylum-seekers and the serious lack of protection from refoulement. In November Amnesty International also made an oral statement about these concerns to the Committee on Migration, Refugees and Demography of the Council of Europe. It called for improvements in the situation of refugees and asylum-seekers in Turkey faced with refoulement and urged the international community to assist in the resettlement of Iranian refugees in countries in which their protection from refoulement would be assured.

In April Amnesty International submitted information about its concerns in Turkey to the United Nations procedure (under Economic and Social Council Resolutions 728F/1503) for confidentially reviewing communications about human rights violations and also referred to torture in Turkey in one of its oral statements to the 44th session of the UN Commission on Human Rights.

32.

[April 20, 1990 (Senate), p. S4726]

THE ANTICS OF A MISGUIDED DESPOT

Mr. PELL. Mr. President, many of my fellow Senators have been disappointed, if not surprised, by the drumbeat of disclosures in recent weeks indicating that Iraq's thoroughly unpleasant leader, Saddam Hussein, seems determined to make that nation a full-fledged outlaw.

We have all read recent press reports regarding Iraqi efforts in the fields of chemical, biological, and nuclear weapons. Saddam Hussein has lent credence to it all by mouthing vile threats to use chemical weapons against Israel. Since Iraq already has used chemical weapons repeatedly against Iran, in clear violation of international law, and has felt free to gas its own citizens, the Kurds, these recent threats have to be taken seriously.

We also must treat seriously apparent efforts to get parts for nuclear devices and other weapons, no matter how bizarre the reports may sound.

Unfortunately, Saddam Hussein's rantings have struck a responsive chord in some quarters of the Arab world. I would urge those in that part of the world to beware the siren song of this fellow, for his is not the way to a fair peace but to conflict and continued suffering.

Frankly, I believe that responsible Arab leaders will see through Saddam Hussein and recognize him for what he is-a murderous despot lacking common sense, who is leading his nation along a very risky course in which the lightest penalty he can expect is ostracism by much of the civilized world.

Mr. President, the world is becoming increasingly aware of and disgusted by Saddam Hussein's activities. In this connection, I would like to bring to the attention the text of a resolution approved earlier this month by the European Parliament. I ask unanimous consent that the text of the resolution be printed in the RECORD following my remarks.

Thank you, Mr. President.

There being no objection, the resolution was ordered to be printed in the RECORD, as follows:

RESOLUTION

The European Parliament,

A. Having regard to the genocide policy ruthlessly and consistently applied by the Iraqi regime against the Kurdish people and recalling the chemical bomb attacks carried out by the Iraqi Air Force on the civilian population of Halabja on 17 March 1988, causing 5,000 deaths,

B. Having regard to the responsibility that lies with the foreign states which have equipped and are still equipping the Iraqi Army with deadly offensive weapons for its genocide policy against the Kurdish people, unclassified,

C. Deeply shocked at the barbarous decree issued by the Iraqi Revolutionary Command Council on 28 February 1990, abolishing all forms of punishment for men who kill female members of their family-mothers, daughters, sisters, aunts, nieces or cousins-who have committed adultery,

D. Recalling execution on 15 March 1990 of Mr. Farzad Bazoff, a British journalist, on the orders of Saddam Hussein and on a false conviction of espionage,

E. Taking a serious view of the Iraqi attempt to import nuclear weapon components, as reported in London on 28 March 1990, which confirms the Iraqi regime's intention of equipping itself with nuclear weapons, despite having signed the International Nuclear Non-Proliferation Treaty,

F. Denouncing the statement on 2 April 1990 in which Saddam Hussein put into words the threat to deploy chemical weapons against the population of the state of Israel,

G. Recalling its many previous resolutions on human rights violations in Iraq,

(1) Condemns Saddam Hussein's regime for its aggressive attitude to foreign countries

and the Iraqi population and in particular for the massacres perpetrated against the Kurdish people;

(2) Insists that it is imperative that member states, through the foreign ministers meeting in European political cooperation, consider ways of preventing Iraq from acquiring nuclear weapons in defiance of its obligations under the Nuclear Non-Proliferation Treaty, and submit proposals to this end at the review of the working of the treaty in August 1990;

(3) Calls on all member states immediately to impose a ban on the export and delivery to Iraq of all material essential for the production of weapons of mass destruction;

(4) Calls on the Secretary-General of the United Nations to make the necessary arrangements for the convening of the U.N. Security Council as soon as possible so that consideration may be given to an appropriate response by the international community to the treaty posed by the Iraqi regime to world security;

(5) Urges in this context the member states to promote cooperation with other states, especially with permanent members of the Security Council, willing to consider joint measures to prevent Iraq from acquiring more weapons of mass destruction;

(6) Calls on the Council and the foreign ministers meeting in European political cooperation to take the appropriate measures vis-a-vis Iraq;

(7) Instructs its President to forward this resolution to the Commission, the Council, the foreign ministers meeting in European political cooperation, the governments of the member states, the Secretary-General of the United Nations and the Iraqi Government.

33.

[June 28, 1990 (Extension of Remarks), p. E2206]

SUFFERING OF KURDISH REFUGEES IN TURKEY
HON. JOHN EDWARD PORTER
OF ILLINOIS

IN THE HOUSE OF REPRESENTATIVES

Thursday, June 28, 1990

Mr. PORTER. Mr. Speaker, Kurdish refugees in Turkey continue to suffer.

It has been almost 2 years since 70,000 Kurds fled Saddam Hussein's chemical attack. Tragically, they have been treated not much better in Turkey.

News reports indicate that Turkish refugees camps are in miserable condition, lack basic amenities and isolate Kurds from employment opportunities. Since Turkish authorities refuse to grant Kurds refugee status, they live in squalor. International efforts to build them permanent housing were canceled by the Turkish government. President Ozal appears to want Kurds to return to Iraq. There they will undoubtedly face further persecution.

Mr. Speaker, Kurdish refugees in Turkey must be granted access to international refugee agencies and proper care in addition, we must insist that Iraq, Iran, and Turkey respect fully the rights of their Kurdish citizens.

34.

[July 12, 1990 (Senate), p. S9661]

IRAQI KURDISH REFUGEES IN TURKEY FACE CONTINUED HARDSHIP

Mr. DECONCINI. Mr. President, I wish to voice my growing dismay at actions taken by the government of Turkey with regard to 30,000 Iraqi Kurdish refugees living in southeast Turkey. These unfortunate people have already suffered enormously at the hands of Iraqi's ruler Saddam Husayn, who gassed them, murdered them, and deported those who survived far from their destroyed homes and villages. Because these outrages received little attention by the media, few outside the Kurdish community realize what is occurring in this relatively inaccessible region. Unfortunately, this abhorrent behavior, an affront to all humanity, continues because the United States and other western nations refuse, or are unable to pressure the despotic Iraqi regime.

After thousands of Kurds were massacred by Iraqi troops, tens of thousands of survivors fled and sought refuge in Turkey. Here, however, they encountered an entirely new set of problems. The government of Turkey refused to recognize them as refugees, referring to them as "temporary visitors." as such, they were made ineligible for certain forms of humanitarian assistance. Three years later, these temporary visitors still reside in camps in southeastern Turkey, and the Turkish government persists in its attempts to make their stay temporary and difficult. Last August, Senator Lautenberg and I visited one of the three camps which was supposedly in the best condition. Thirty to forty people shared three-room apartments, sanitation conditions were appalling, refugees could not work. Furthermore, the government does not allow the formal teaching of Kurdish to refugee children, and the boredom and uncertainty of the future fosters a pervading atmosphere of oppression, frustration, and tension.

Recently, the government of Turkey canceled a long-sought agreement with the United Nations High Commissioner for Refugees [UNHCR] which would have permanently sheltered thousands of the most needy. Governments around the world had pledged money for the settlement project at the behest of the UNHCR and the Turkish government. This Congress recommended the expenditure of $5 million, and our state department played a significant and commendable role in securing the cooperation of other nations in this endeavor. While domestic politics figured prominently in the last minute cancellation of the much-needed settlement, anti-Kurdish bias and continued unwillingness to deal constructively with this group of refugees is reflected in the actions of the Turkish government. In addition to canceling the project without official explanation, the Turkish government has also refused to allow remaining donations to be used to upgrade conditions in existing camps. To make matters worse, since the beginning of this year, the Turkish government has restricted access to the camps by United States diplomats and UNHCR officials.

Turkish officials are now suggesting that the Iraqi Kurds take advantage of Saddam Husayn's offer of amnesty and return to Iraq. The refugees now claim that supplies to the camps are being withheld by Turkish officials in an attempt to coerce them into returning to Iraq. Human rights groups familiar with the situation have also voiced concerns over possible forced repatriations of the refugees. Mr. President, the fear is very real that if these individuals return to Iraq, they will share the fate of their brothers and sisters who have been murdered, or deported far from their homes.

Mr. President, I returned from Turkey last August a strong supporter of our mutually beneficial relationship with that nation and I value our long friendship. Over the centuries Turkey, not unlike the United States, has provided a safe haven for millions of refugees. In fact, 1992 will mark the 500th anniversary of the establishment of a Jewish community in Turkey, which had fled the destruction of the Spanish Inquisition. The government of Turkey faces important domestic political and security considerations in any matters pertaining to Kurds living in southeastern Turkey. However, the government's actions with regard to the Iraqi Kurdish refugees have demonstrated an insensitivity that only exacerbates existing tensions in the region. I urge the government of Turkey to reconsider its policy vis-a-vis this refugee group, and do all that it can to welcome these refugees and allow them to enjoy the freedom and opportunity Turkey offers.

35.

[September 11, 1990 (Extensions of Remarks), p. E2779]

HUSSEIN'S REPRESSIVE REGIME POSES THREAT TO MILLIONS HON. JOHN EDWARD PORTER OF ILLINOIS IN THE HOUSE OF REPRESENTATIVES

Tuesday, September 11, 1990

Mr. PORTER. Mr. Speaker, we are all aware of the threat to world economic stability posed by Iraq's illegal invasion of Kuwait. But Saddam Hussein's repressive regime poses an equally urgent threat to millions of human lives in the Persian Gulf.

Since Saddam Hussein came to power in 1979, the Kurds, Iraq's largest minority, have been brutally repressed for seeking recognition of their distinct ethnicity. Over the past 5 years, hundreds of children, whose parents were reportedly political activists have been arrested and tortured; hundreds of thousands of Kurds have been relocated in efforts to diminish a collective Kurdish presence; and hundreds of villages were destroyed, killing thousands, by a chemical offensive aimed against Kurdish civilians. Any voice of dissent has been violently suppressed.

We must ignore Saddam's words, for the truth means nothing to him, and look instead at his deeds. In light of his dismal human rights record against his own children, it is our duty to ensure the safety of both foreign nationals held hostage in Kuwait, and the citizens of Kuwait and neighboring countries.

The following articles [David Mutch, "Experts Familiar with Nation's Record Express Concern Over Welfare of Foreign Hostages," *The Christian Science Monitor*, Aug. 28, 1990; Glenn Frankel, "Suppressed at Home and Dismissed Abroad," *The Washington Post*, Aug. 27, 1990] outline Saddam Hussein's abysmal record on human rights and how this accord may affect current events: . . .

36.

[September 28, 1990 (Senate), p. S14237-38]

WILL TURKEY LOOK EAST?

Mr. SIMON. Mr. President, recently [July 7, 1990], the *National Journal* carried an article by David C. Morrison titled simply "Will Turkey Look East?" The conclusion of the article is that Turkey is likely to look east.

The United States has failed to treat Turkey like one friend should treat another friend. That is to help when help is needed but, to speak candidly.

And so, we have been obsequious to Turkey in matters that relate to Greek-Turkish relations. We have been reluctant to talk candidly about the Armenian massacre.

That does not make for a good, normal relationship between countries.

I think, inevitably, Turkey will look both to the East and to the West for here commerce and her culture.

I want to maintain a good relationship with Turkey.

But, I do not want to do it by turning my back on Greece and Cyprus, and I do not want to do it by pretending that the events that occurred 75 years ago against Armenian people did not occur.

So let us develop a good, healthy, candid relationship with Turkey in which Turkey can talk to us candidly about her concerns, and we can do the same.

I ask that the article by David Morrison be printed in the RECORD.

The article follows: . . .

37.

[January 12, 1991 (Senate), pp. 323-69]

UNITED STATES POLICY TO REVERSE IRAQ'S OCCUPATION OF KUWAIT

TESTIMONY BY JOSHUA R. GILDER, PRINCIPAL DEPUTY ASSISTANT SECRETARY FOR HUMAN RIGHTS AND HUMANITARIAN AFFAIRS, JUNE 15, 1990

U.S. RELATIONS WITH IRAQ

Human rights, as such, are not recognized in Iraq. As our report details, the ordinary Iraqi citizens knows no personal security against government violence. Disappearances, followed by secret executions, appear to be common. In some cases, a family only learns that one of its loved ones has been executed when the security services return the body and, in line with the Iraqi regime's view of justice, require the family to pay a fine.

The penalty for expressing opinions deemed objectionable by the regime is swift and brutal. We believe that over the past ten years many thousands to tens of thousands-and I will speak to the inexactitude of our figures in a moment-have been arrested by the secret police on suspicion of opposition to the government. While the judicial system seems to function fairly well by regional standards for people accused of crimes with no political implications, there is not even the charade of due process for those charged with security-related offenses. I should add that security-related offenses are broadly defined to include such routine criminal matters as currency violations.

Torture is routine, for security offenses and ordinary crimes alike, and confessions extracted under torture are admissible in court. Treatment is reported to be the worst immediately following arrest and during the period of interrogation and investigation, which can last for months.

Compiling accurate information on human rights in Iraq is made extremely difficult by the highly secretive and repressive nature of the regime. Diplomatic travel is severely restricted, and most Iraqis are, quite understandably, fearful of speaking their minds to foreigners-or to anyone else for that matter.

The Iraqi regime is authoritarian in the extreme. There are some exceptions. The practice of religion is largely free. There has been some attempt to relax the worst aspects of the statist command economy. In general, however, the regime is ruthless in its efforts to maintain absolute control over the population.

Control is exercised in part through the Baath Party apparatus. The party is a secretive one. While it has a large grass roots membership, decisionmaking is concentrated among the few at the top. The lower ranks serve as informers on the political reliability of their neighbors. There are many other intelligence networks through which the government monitors the citizenry, as well as keeps a careful eye on the military and the Baath Party itself. I have already described the punishment for stepping out of line, or being deemed unreli-

able by the government. Periodically, over the last two years, the regime announced that it had uncovered incipient coup plots within the military. Hundreds were arrested. We do not know how many were executed.

The Baath Party is a Pan-Arabist party. As such, it has integrated Arabs of various religions and sects quite well, but has had trouble finding an ideological niche for Iraq's non-Arab citizens, most of whom are Kurds. The disaffection of elements of the Kurdish population did not begin with Baath Party rule, but the current government's policy has resulted in enormous human rights abuses.

With respect to the Kurds, the Iraqi government has followed a policy of carrot and stick. It has sought to gain the support of as many Kurdish tribes as it can, using the carrot of ethnic cultural freedom. There is a Kurdish Autonomous Region with its own institutions, providing patronage for Kurdish tribes that support the regime. Kurdish language and culture are fostered, and education in Kurdish is available through the secondary level.

But the stick of Iraqi policy has been brutal. During the Gulf War, in which Iran took advantage of the dissatisfaction among Kurdish tribes, the Iraqi Government began a campaign of destroying suspect villages, relocating the populations to closely-watched cities and new settlements. After the ceasefire with Iran, Iraq's campaign to dislodge rebels from the areas they controlled was accompanied by the shocking, indiscriminate use of chemical weapons-killing thousands of men, women, and children. After Iraqi troops regained these areas, destruction of villages and towns, and population transfers were speeded up, until finally some 500,000-about one-seventh of the entire Kurdish population of Iraq-were displaced. Although we understand Iraqi authorities are now allowing displaced villagers to commute to their lands to cultivate the fields and orchards, we remain extremely concerned about the overall effects of this massive displacement.

Let me stress that in detailing our concerns over the treatment of Iraqi Kurds we are not taking a position on the roots or aims of Kurdish rebellions, but rather on abuses of internationally recognized human rights. The United States Government supports the territorial integrity of the states in this region, and holds that Kurds should seek to fulfill their aspirations peacefully within this context.

During the last two years the Government of Iraq has announced its intention to institute reforms. Wartime travel restrictions have been relaxed, permitting large numbers of Iraqis to travel abroad for the first time in eight years. Elections for the National Assembly and the Kurdistan Autonomy Council were held in April and September 1989, respectively. Independents were allowed to run, and some Baath Party members were defeated. However, all candidates were carefully screened for support for the Government, and in any event neither body has any real power or legislative function as we would understand the terms.

A new constitution has been drafted and was submitted to the President last January. According to a recent Iraqi press report, the draft has undergone the finishing touches by a panel of six members of the Iraqi leadership, and it will soon be submitted to the National Assembly and to a popular referendum.

It is, however, one thing to adopt a constitution and another thing to respect it. The current Iraqi constitution includes clauses on respect for human rights, a ban on torture, and the independence of the judiciary-none of which has any apparent effect in practice. If Iraq wishes to end international criticism of its human rights record, it must take steps that are real, not cosmetic. It must end the climate of fear imposed by its security apparatus and hold meaningful elections that are more than a mere charade. It must institute a truly independent judiciary and allow for a truly free press that does more than simply parrot the government line.

Most important of all, it must treat its citizens with dignity and give them the chance to live secure in their own homes and persons-free from the omnipresent threat of government repression and violence.

———

U.S. DEPARTMENT OF STATE, COUNTRY REPORTS ON HUMAN RIGHTS PRACTICES FOR 1989

Iraq is in effect a one-party state governed by the Arab Ba'ath Socialist Party (ABSP) through a Revolutionary Command Council (RCC) which has both executive and legislative authority under the provisional Constitution of 1968. Saddam Hussein holds decisive power as President of the Republic, Chairman of the RCC, and Secretary-General of the Regional Command of the ABSP. Two other small parties are essentially support groups for the Government. In 1989 the Government announced its intention to adopt a multiparty system enshrined in a new constitution. Elections for the National Assembly-which has few powers-were held April 1. A draft constitution which would reportedly allow a multiparty system was completed in 1989 and is expected to be put to a referendum in early 1990. It remains to be seen, however, whether this will dilute the monopoly of power held by Saddam Hussein and the ABSP. Iraq's population comprises many disparate groups, most notably Shi'a and Sunni Muslim Arabs, Kurds, Turcomans, and various Christian sects, predominantly Assyrians and Chaldeans.

Iraq's military is large and well trained, and parts of it, notably the Fursan, or Kurdish tribal levies, have responsibility for security within the Kurdish autonomous region. The National Police is responsible for civil order.

The Government exerts a high degree of control over the economy, dominated by the petroleum sector, and owns all major industries. The Government has been carrying out a program of divestiture and privatization in agriculture, tourism, services, and light industry, and is trying to attract investor capital and expertise in the operation of the economy. However, close government regulation of economic activity is expected to continue.

Iraq's human rights record remained abysmal in 1989. Effective opposition to government policy is stifled; the intelligence services engage in extensive surveillance and utilize extralegal means, including torture and summary execution, to deal with antiregime activity. The civil rights of Iraqi citizens continue to be sharply limited, and Iraqis do not have the right to change their government. The freedoms of speech and press and of assembly and association are virtually nonexistent. Other important human rights problems include continuing disappearances and arbitrary detentions, lack of fair trial, widespread interference with privacy, excessive use of force against Kurdish civilians, and an almost total lack of worker rights. In addition to the repressive domestic controls that predate the war with Iran, tight wartime controls, including travel restrictions, remain in effect despite the August 1988 cease-fire with Iran.

An armed Kurdish insurgency continued in 1989, but at a reduced level. Although there were no allegations that the Government used chemical weapons against Kurdish civilians in 1989, as it did in 1988, in its efforts to crush the rebellion, it continued to violate the human rights of elements of the Kurdish population. The Government announced in June that in its campaign to suppress the rebellion it has pursued a program since 1987 of establishing a depopulated security zone along the full length of Iraq's borders with Iran and Turkey. Under this program, the Government has destroyed villages within a 30-kilometer-wide zone and relocated approximately 500,000 Kurdish and Assyrian inhabitants into more easily controlled and protected towns, cities, and newly constructed settlements in traditional Kurdish areas.

RESPECT FOR HUMAN RIGHTS

Section 1. Respect for the Integrity of the Person, Including Freedom from:

a. Political and Other Extrajudicial Killing

For years execution has been an established Iraqi method for dealing with perceived political and military opponents of the government, including, but not limited to, members of the outlawed Da'wa organization (an Iran-supported fundamentalist Shi'a Muslim group that has engaged in acts of international terrorism). In some cases, a family only learns that one of its members has been executed when the security services return the body and require the family to pay a fine.

Amnesty International (AI), in its presentation before the U.N. Subcommission on the Prevention of Discrimination and Protection of Minorities in August, stated that it had received allegations that some 80 army deserters

were executed in December 1988 and charged that the Government executed 11 of its Kurdish opponents in March and April 1989.

In its February report, "Iraq: Children: Innocent Victims of Political Repression," AI stated that it receives allegations of hundreds of executions in Iraq each year. AI cited the case of 29 Kurdish children and youths allegedly executed in January 1987. In addition, AI, in its 1989 Report covering 1988, cited allegations that hundreds of civilians, including women and children, were executed at Tanjaro Military Garrison, Sulaimaniya province. Independent information to confirm the allegations cited in AI reports is not available.

b. Disappearance

In the February report, AI asserted that thousands of people arrested over the years by Iraqi security or intelligence forces reportedly have "disappeared" while in detention, with many feared executed. In its August presentation to the U.N. Subcommission, AI reported the disappearance in mid-April of Mulla Muhammad Dalgayi, described as the imam of Qal'at Diza, who was among delegates from Kurdistan who reportedly met with government officials to appeal against forced settlement of the Kurds at Qal'at Diza. He was reportedly arrested in Baghdad and has since disappeared. An Assyrian organization based in the United States charged in March that the whereabouts of 33 Assyrians, who took advantage of the amnesty issued by the Government and returned to Iraq from Iran and Turkey, were unknown.

c. Torture and Other Cruel, Inhuman, or Degrading Treatment or Punishment

The Constitution prohibits torture and prescribes stiff punishment for it, but it is clear that both physical and psychological torture are used by the authorities, especially the security policy. Given the rigid chain of command within the Government and the security services, torture could not be practiced without the knowledge or authorization of senior officials.

Emigre groups and former prisoners assert that persons detained by the security police for political or security-related matters are frequently tortured and mistreated. Treatment is reported to be worst immediately following arrest and during the period of interrogation and investigation, which can last for months. Torture and brutal treatment are not limited to political cases.

Security-related offenses are broadly defined and include such routine criminal matters as currency violations.

In its 1989 Report, AI stated that the routine torture and ill-treatment of prisoners continued to be widely reported. It said the victims included detainees below the age of 18 who were reportedly beaten, whipped, given electric shocks, and deprived of food. The Government categorically denied any use of torture against children as an official policy or as a practice, and stated its readiness to consider fully any individual allegation with a view to bringing perpetrators to justice. Impartial observers have so far been unable to look into these allegations.

d. Arbitrary Arrest, Detention, or Exile

While the Constitution and legal code provide for the rights of citizens and place checks on police powers in such areas as arrest, detention, imprisonment, and search, these provisions have virtually no weight in political or national security cases, although they are generally respected in ordinary criminal cases. Security police not only make arbitrary arrests but also secretly detain suspects, whose fate sometimes becomes known only after they have been executed. Security charges have included espionage, treason, and conspiracy against Iraq, in collaboration with unnamed foreign enemies.

The relocation of 500,000 Kurdish villagers to other areas of Kurdistan since 1987 may be considered a form of internal exile. The Government declared in June 1989 that it was creating an uninhabited security zone to ensure the safety and security of citizens in the border regions (who were subjected to shelling and military operations during the war with Iran) and to provide better services to the villagers.

Although the Government has ceased expelling Iraqis of supposed Iranian descent, most of the few remaining Iranians have been imprisoned or live under the fear of deportation or incarceration. Spouses of Iraqis of Iranian origin are required to obtain a divorce or

suffer the same consequences. Moreover, other Iraqis, whose grandparents are shown not to be of Iraqi origin, are subject to arbitrary detention and deportation.

With regard to forced or compulsory labor, see Section 6.c.

e. Denial of Fair Public Trial

Iraq's legal system provides for investigation by police and then by an inquiry judge who may refer a case to the courts or dismiss it. Judges try criminal cases; there are no juries. Convictions may be appealed to the Court of Appeal and then to the Court of Cassation, the supreme court. There are no Shari's courts per se in Iraq; however, family courts administer Shari's law modified by Iraqi custom.

Trials of ordinary cases are held in civil, criminal, and religious courts and are open. Defendants are entitled to counsel-at government expense if the defendant is indigent. Charges and evidence are available for review by the lawyer. Appellate courts hear cases not under the jurisdiction of the Revolutionary Courts.

In contrast to ordinary cases, security cases are handled by the Revolutionary Courts, which usually hold closed trials. Security cases include espionage, treason, smuggling, currency exchange violations and drug trafficking. The right of defense in such courts is said to be severely restricted. The "special courts" constituted by the RCC for specific incidents, such as the reported conspiracy against the regime in 1979, are also closed. These special tribunals are apparently exempt from constitutional safeguards of defendants' rights; defendants are held incommunicado, and confessions extracted by torture are admissible. Appeals can be taken only to the chairman of the RCC. However, the utility of this appeal is questionable, since there are reports that executions take place shortly after trial.

Political dissent in Iraq is taken by the authorities to encompass a wide range of activities and, in an environment where public acknowledgement of arrest or imprisonment is rare, it is extremely difficult to estimate the number of political prisoners. In its 1989 Report, AI stated that "thousands" of political prisoners continued to be arbitrarily arrested and detained, especially members of prohibited political parties, Army deserters, and draft resisters. Relatives, including children of suspects, are said to be held as hostages to compel confessions.

f. Arbitrary Interference with Privacy, Family, Home, or Correspondence

The Constitution provides protections for the inviolability of the home, and strong cultural values reinforce these protections. Police must obtain a search warrant before entering the home of a criminal suspect. However, warrants are not required for the arrest of security suspects. Although most arrests occur outside the home, there have been reports of forced entry and arrest by the security police, particularly of suspected members of the outlawed Da'wa organization.

Although the Constitution provides for the confidentiality of mail and telegraphic and telephone correspondence, many Iraqis believe that the monitoring of telephones is a common practice and that all mail is subject to review by censors. The security services and Ba'ath Party maintain pervasive networks of informers. The Government maintains a close watch against Iranian attempts to exploit dissatisfaction among Iraqi Shi'a, who adhere to the branch of Islam prevalent in Iran.

g. Use of Excessive Force and Violations of Humanitarian Law in Internal Conflicts

Elements of Iraq's Kurdish population have engaged in armed struggle with all governments of Iraq periodically since the 1920's. The outbreak of the Iran-Iraq war in 1980 sparked a new antigovernment insurgency by Kurdish elements, many of whom fought with or aided Iran during the war. From 1981 to 1989, the Government's efforts to crush the rebellion militarily resulted in approximately 8,000 deaths, many of them civilians killed indiscriminately by chemical weapons in 1988.

Although the fighting was at a reduced level in 1989, Kurdish military operations continued, as did government measures to contain them. Kurdish rebels continued to announce their hostility towards the central Government. On August 29, 1989, the leader of one group of insurgents stated to the press in Geneva that his group would target foreign interests in Iraq supporting the Iraqi regime. At year's end, the cycle of Kurdish rebellion and government repression remained unresolved.

Section 2. Respect for Civil Liberties, Including:

a. Freedom of Speech and Press

The freedoms of speech and press are not respected. The Constitution prohibits "any act aimed at undermining the national unity of the people, provoking racial, sectarian, and regional bigotry, or violating gains and achievements of the country." The Government views political dissent as a threat to its security and strictly controls speech and all information media. All publications are subject to censorship. The Government and the Ba'ath Party own and operate the press, radio, and television. The media do not criticize the Government, and news reporting is strongly biased. There is no presentation of opposition viewpoints.

Few foreign periodicals reach Iraq and those that do may be censored. Western newspapers are not sold. Foreign visitors' magazines, newspapers, cassettes, cameras, and video cassettes may be confiscated at the airport. To control the dissemination of political leaflets, word processors and computers must be registered. Failure to register is a criminal offense. Iraqis no longer need to register their typewriters or photocopiers, but foreigners in Iraq must do so. Taking photographs of military installations, government buildings, or areas near sensitive locations is forbidden and punishable by imprisonment. Journalists and photographers visiting Iraq at the invitation of the Government are required to present film taken in Iraq for inspection by the authorities.

b. Freedom of Peaceful Assembly and Association

These freedoms are severely limited. Public meetings may only be organized under the auspices of the Government or the Ba'ath Party. Association for nonreligious purposes and demonstrations without government approval have met with severe repression. Professional organizations are subject to control by the Ba'ath Party Central Vocational Bureau.

For a discussion of freedom of association as it applies to labor unions, see Section 6.a.

c. Freedom of Religion

Iraq is an ethnically and religiously diverse society. Since its rise to power in 1968, the Ba'ath Government, while carefully controlling religious groups, has enforced tolerance of religious diversity, seeking to submerge religious differences in the promotion of secular nationalism. A 1981 law gave the Ministry of Endowments and Religious Affairs the authority to promulgate laws and regulations governing places of worship, appointment of clergy, publication of religious literature, and participation in religious councils and meetings. Muslim religious leaders operate under close government supervision, are considered government employees, and receive their salaries through the Government. The Government administers the principal Muslim shrines and mosques and has provided allotments to them and to churches for maintenance and refurbishing. There are no penalties under Iraqi law for changing one's religion, although there is a social stigma for Muslims who convert to another faith.

While the Government has assumed much greater authority in Islamic religious affairs since 1981. It has been less intrusive into the religious affairs of Iraq's Christians, who number more than 500,000 and constitute nearly 4 percent of the population. Their freedom of worship in churches of established denominations is legally protected, but they are not permitted to proselytize or to hold meetings outside church premises. Convents and monasteries exist, and some new churches have been constructed, in some cases with government financial support. The Jewish community has decreased from 150,000 following World War II to under 400. There is no evidence of recent persecution. One synagogue in Baghdad still functions.

d. Freedom of Movement Within the Country, Foreign Travel, Emigration, and Repatriation

Iraqis are generally free to travel within the country and to change their residences of workplaces. However, they are likely to be constrained by social, cultural, and religious traditions which define the areas occupied by the various ethnic and religious groups. Sensi-

tive border and other security areas are off limits. There are police checkpoints on highways and outside major towns, but Iraqis and nondiplomatic foreigners travel freely in nonrestricted areas.

The Government's harsh campaign to suppress Kurdish rebels, involving mass relocations of Kurdish villagers, has nullified the right of hundreds of thousands of Kurds to choose their place of residence. Since the Government began its programs of forced relocation in 1987, an estimated 500,000 people have been uprooted. Since traditional Kurdish culture has been deeply embedded in the rural village, the forced removals and razing of villages has had a destructive impact on the lives of some half a million Kurds.

Most foreigners who remain in the country for more than 30 days and all Iraqis must obtain exit permission. Travel has been severely limited since September 1986, when the Government imposed tight restrictions on currency exchange. These restrictions were eased somewhat in 1989, but the most an Iraqi may exchange is 1,000 dinars ($3,220). Because of the drain on the economy caused by the war and reconstruction, permission to travel abroad is restricted to a few categories of Iraqis, including officials, businessmen, government-approved students, and persons needing medical treatment. In 1989 the Government eased restrictions to permit one parent to visit his or her offspring who is studying or working abroad.

While permission for medical treatment abroad may be granted, permission to transfer hard currency abroad to pay for it may not be. In cases of those desiring medical treatment in the United States, the Government now requires a bend to be posted by an American friend or relative with the Iraqi embassy in Washington before exit permission is granted. The minimum amount of this bond is $10,000. The Government sometimes limits the countries an Iraqi traveler may visit and, should the traveler visit a nonauthorized country, a small fine may be levied upon his return. Iraqis who have residences abroad may depart the country, provided they originally left before the war began. A married woman must have the permission of her husband to travel abroad.

The Government can require a prospective traveler to post a substantial bond to assure his return. The RCC decreed in 1987 that Iraqi students abroad who refuse to return to Iraq must reimburse the Government for all education received in Iraq or abroad at government expense. The decree is applicable retroactively to students who have refused to return since May 16, 1983, the date the Government began requiring employees leaving government jobs before 20 years of service to reimburse the State for the cost of their education. Amounts due can be recovered by confiscation; nonpayment may result in imprisonment. Each student must provide a guarantor before traveling abroad. This guarantor and the student's parents may be held liable if the student fails to return.

There is no specific ban on emigration or special restrictions for members of minority groups; however, emigration is discouraged. For the past several years, almost all of those given permission to emigrate have been Christian Iraqi wives of former Iraqi citizens now living abroad as citizens of another country. Prospective emigrants have had travel permission delayed and have been harassed. Many emigrants leave behind substantial property because of the difficulty of exporting assets. Currency exchange violations are considered national security offenses, and penalties can be severe.

Non-Iraqi spouses of Iraqi citizens who have resided in Iraq for 5 years are required to take Iraqi nationality or leave Iraq. Many people, including several Americans, have thus been obliged to accept Iraqi citizenship and are therefore subject to the present travel restrictions. In March 1984, an order by the RCC reduced the residency period before naturalization to 1 year for the spouses of Iraqi citizens employed in government offices. The Iraqi spouse faces penalties for noncompliance, including loss of job, a fine of approximately $10,000, and repayment of the costs of education. Iraq does not recognize the concept of dual nationality, and many Iraqi "dual nationals," especially the children of an Iraqi father and a mother of non-Iraqi birth, have

been denied permission to leave Iraq to visit the country of their other nationality.

In recent years, the Government has instituted special programs to encourage repatriation of qualified professionals. Aliens of Iraqi origin can apply for a document permitting them to enter and exit from Iraq without a visa.

Other persons of Iraqi origin are permitted to return, including many persons who were admitted to other countries as refugees. A number of such people, especially Assyrian Christians, have returned on temporary visits. They are free to come and go, within the limits of the present travel restrictions, since they are not considered to have violated Iraqi laws. However, those who emigrated only after the beginning of the Iran-Iraq war, including several U.S. permanent resident aliens, have been unable to depart from Iraq after returning. In September and November 1988 and in February and March 1989, the Government announced amnesties for Kurds who fled the country for any reason. Approximately 2,000 have voluntarily returned from refugee camps in Turkey.

Section 3. Respect for Political Rights: The Right of Citizens to Change Their Government

Iraqi citizens do not have the ability peacefully to change their government. President Saddam Hussein and the RCC rule Iraq through the Ba'ath Party. It reportedly has some 1.5 million adherents, representing about 9 percent of the population.

There are two other small legal political parties, both Kurdish. They and the Ba'ath Party constitute the Patriotic and Progressive National Front, essentially a vehicle of support for the Government. Members of the military or security services may engage in political activities only within the Ba'ath Party. Association with the party is not required for appointment to senior government positions or military ranks or election to National Assembly, but is normally necessary to attain political influence. Opposition groups, including various Kurdish groups and splinter parties, are severely repressed. The Communist Party was removed from the National Front and declared illegal in 1979. The Da'wa organization, a violent Shi'ite group, is still proscribed, and its members are subject to incarceration and execution, as are members of other parties believed to be cooperating with Iran. Plans the Government announced in 1988 to permit legal formation of opposition parties were not implemented in 1989.

General elections were held for the 250-seat National Assembly in April. Though in theory possessing a wide range of official duties, the Assembly exercises little real authority. The majority of the more than 900 candidates were independents, although all supported current government policies. The elections by secret ballot were more open than in the past, and some high-ranking Ba'ath party officials were defeated.

The biennial elections for the Legislative Assembly of the Kurdish Autonomous Region were held in September 1989. All 174 candidates, from the three legal parties and independents, had to satisfy the same requirements as National Assembly candidates. The Legislative Assembly does not exercise meaningful authority.

In October 1989, an Experts Commission finished drafting a new Constitution to replace the Provisional Constitution of 1970. Iraqi officials assert that the new Constitution will provide more guarantees of human rights. However, the new Constitution has not yet been made public pending approval by President Saddam Hussein and the RCC . . .

U.S. DEPARTMENT OF STATE, COUNTRY REPORTS ON HUMAN RIGHTS PRACTICES FOR 1988

Iraq is in effect a one-party state governed by the Arab Ba'ath Socialist Party (ABSP) through a Revolutionary Command Council (RCC) which has both executive and legislative authority under the provisional Constitution of 1968. Saddam Hussein holds decisive power as President of the Republic, Chairman of the Council, and Secretary General of the Regional Command of the ABSP. Two other legal parties are essentially support groups for the Government.

Iraq's population comprises many disparate groups, most notably Shi'a and Sunni Muslim Arabs, Kurds, Turcomans, and various Christian sects, predominantly Assyrians and Chaldeans.

Iraq's military is large and well trained, and parts of it have security responsibilities, notably the Fursan, or Kurdish tribal levies, which have responsibility for security within the Kurdish Autonomous Region. The national police is responsible for civil order. In addition, Iraq's intelligence services are widely feared, and have engaged in extensive surveillance and extralegal means to deal with antiregime activity, including torture and summary execution.

The Government exerts a high level of control over the economy, which is dominated by the petroleum sector. The state owns all major industries, including petroleum and banking. In agriculture, tourism, the services industry, and light industry, the Government is engaged in a program of divestiture and privatization. Close government regulation of economic activity will be maintained, but the Government is trying to attract investor capital and expertise in the operation of the economy.

Iraq's abysmal human rights record remained unacceptable in 1988. Political and individual rights continued to be sharply limited, and the news media remained largely under government control and subject to censorship. In addition to repressive domestic controls that predate the war with Iran, tight wartime controls remained in effect after the cease-fire. These included a decree which prescribes the death penalty for anyone who damages the country's military, political, or economic position. Wartime travel restrictions, which prevent most Iraqis from departing the country, also remained in force.

Most significant in 1988 were the grave human rights violations that occurred when the Iraqi armed forces moved to crush a long-standing Kurdish rebellion after the August 20 cease-fire with Iran. The campaign was marked by the use of chemical weapons against guerrillas and civilians alike. It marked an intensification of the program begun in 1987to destroy villages and hamlets in Kurdish areas of northern Iraq, and to relocate approximately half a million Kurdish and Assyrian villagers to more easily controlled towns and cities. In addition, there are unconfirmed reports that tens of thousands of Kurds have been removed from their homes to camps located outside traditional Kurdish areas of northern Iraq.

RESPECT FOR HUMAN RIGHTS

Section 1. Respect for the Integrity of the Person, Including Freedom from:

a. Political Killing

Execution has for years been an established method for dealing with perceived political and military opponents of the Government, particularly members of the outlawed Da'wa Organization (an Iran-supported fundamentalist Shi'a Muslim group that has engaged in acts of international terrorism). The Government has been accused of murdering Iraqi political opponents in the United Kingdom and Sudan; in the case of Sudan, the victim was a leader of the opposition Supreme Assembly of the Islamic Revolution in Iraq, based in Tehran and closely linked to the Da'wa Organization.

The Government's intensified efforts to crush a Kurdish rebellion in northern Iraq resulted in approximately 8,000 deaths, many of them civilians, according to Kurdish sources. The Iraqi armed forces made extensive unlawful use of chemical weapons against both military and civilian targets in Iran and Iraqi Kurdistan. In the course of a March 16 battle between Iraqi forces and Iranian Revolutionary Guards in and near the Kurdish city of Halabja in northern Iraq, an estimated 600 to 3,000 civilians were killed by Iraqi chemical weapons. The United States condemned Iraq's action as a particularly grave violation of the 1925 Geneva Protocol on chemical weapons, to which Iraq is a party, while noting that Iran also appears to have employed chemical weapons in the same battle. Several international teams, including a U.N. team and a team of Belgian doctors, confirmed the use of chemical weapons in this battle. Twice in 1988 the U.N. Security Council condemned use of chemical weapons in the Iran-Iraq War.

With the cessation of hostilities between Iran and Iraq in August, the Iraqi armed forces launched an offensive against Kurdish rebel forces. Combat troops from the Iranian front carried the battle to villages, which they claimed rebels were using for sanctuary.

On several days in August, chemical weapons were used in this campaign. Immediately thereafter, at least 60,000 Kurds fled across the border into Turkey. On September 8, the U.S. Department of State announced that it had conclusive evidence that Iraqi forces used chemical weapons unlawfully against Kurds and condemned its use. Since then, several groups including a U.S. Senate staff delegation, Physicians for Human Rights, and a British laboratory that analyzed soil samples, confirmed Iraq's use of chemical weapons in this campaign. The Iraqis have denied using chemical weapons against Kurds.

In its 1988 Report, covering 1987, Amnesty International (AI) noted that at least 17 Kurdish children aged 14 to 17 were executed in November and December 1987. AI also reported the poisoning of Kurdish opponents in November 1987 by security forces.

b. Disappearance

Iraqi emigrants have reported that some persons, particularly those detained by the security police for subversion, disappear following detention. Kurdish rebels in northern Iraq have occasionally kidnaped foreign workers and businessmen. In its 1988 Report, AI noted that the "disappearance" of large numbers of people continued to be widely reported, and that many of them were feared to have been executed.

c. Torture and Other Cruel, Inhuman, or Degrading Treatment or Punishment

The Constitution prohibits torture and prescribes stiff punishment for it, and the Government rejects charges that it practices torture. Nevertheless, reliable reports make clear that both physical and psychological torture are used by the authorities, especially the security police. Given the rigid chain of command within the Government and security services, torture could not be practiced without the authorization of senior officials.

According to emigre groups and former prisoners, persons detained by the security police for political or security-related matters are frequently tortured and mistreated. Treatment is reported to be worst immediately following arrest and during the period of interrogation and investigation, which can last for months. Torture and brutal treatment are not limited to political cases. Security-related offenses are broadly defined to include such routine criminal matters as currency violations.

The security forces' methods of torture, often employed to extract confessions or information about the suspect and his colleagues, reportedly include beatings with fists and rubber truncheons, electrical shocks to the genitals and other parts of the body, and the extraction of fingernails and toenails, as well as psychological torture. AI has reported that over the years the Government had denied allegations of torture even when the allegations were supported by detailed medical evidence and that the Government had also failed to show that such allegations were ever investigated or that any perpetrators were brought to justice. In its 1988 Report, AI noted that the routine use of torture by the security forces continued to be widely reported. It said that the victims included political prisoners, and cited a report that the bodies of 29 youths-who allegedly had been tortured shortly before being executed without trial in January 1987- were returned to their families bearing marks of torture. They had been among 300 Kurdish children and young people arrested in 1985.

d. Arbitrary Arrest, Detention, or Exile

The Constitution and legal code provide for the rights of citizens and place checks on police powers in such areas as arrest, detention, imprisonment, and search. These provisions are generally respected in ordinary criminal cases, but have little weight in political or national security cases. Security police not only make arbitrary arrests but also secretly detain suspects, whose fate sometimes becomes known only after they have been executed. Security charges have included espionage, treason, and conspiracy against Iraq, often in collaboration with unnamed foreign foes.

As part of its campaign to eliminate the Kurdish rebellion and to clear a security zone along its northern border, the Government continued the policy of relocating, sometimes forcibly, several hundred thousand Kurds. While most were moved to or near Kurdish towns and cities south of the mountains, there are unconfirmed reports that others were exiled to non-Kurdish parts of the country. The campaign involved widespread destruction of Kurdish villages, and some Turcoman and Christian villages near the front lines.

In the past, Iraq has expelled to Iran large numbers of Iranians and Iraqis of supposed Iranian descent. These deportations ceased in the early 1980's; however, most of the few remaining Iranians have been imprisoned or live under the fear of deportation or incarceration. Spouses of Iraqis of Iranian origin are required to obtain a divorce or suffer the same consequences. Moreover, other Iraqis, whose grandparents are shown not to be of Iraqi origin, are subject to arbitrary detention and deportation. Assyrian religious groups in the United States alleged in 1987 that many Iraqi Assyrians were expelled to Turkey under this rule.

With regard to forced or compulsory labor, see Section 6.c.

e. Denial of Fair Public Trial

Iraq's legal system provides for investigation by police and then by an inquiry judge who may refer a case to the criminal court. A judge tries criminal cases; there is no jury. Convictions may be appealed to a court of cassation or, in the case of major crimes, the High Court of Appeals.

Trials of nonsecurity cases are held in civil, criminal, and religious courts and are open. Defendants are entitled to counsel. A lawyer is provided if a defendant cannot afford one. Charges and evidence are available for review. Appellate Courts hear cases not under the jurisdiction of the Revolutionary Courts. The Revolutionary Courts, which usually hold closed trials, deal with espionage, treason, smuggling, and drug trafficking. The right of defense in such courts is reportedly severely restricted.

The "special courts" constituted by the RCC for specific incidents, such as the reported conspiracy against the regime in 1979, are also closed. These special tribunals are apparently exempt from constitutional safeguards of defendants' rights; defendants are held incommunicato, and confessions extracted by torture are used. Appeals can be taken only to the Chairman of the RCC. However, the practical availability of this appeal is open to question, since there are reports that executions take place shortly after trial.

Political dissidence in Iraq is taken by the authorities to encompass a wide range of activities and, in an environment where public acknowledgment of arrest or imprisonment is rare, it is extremely difficult to estimate the number of political prisoners. In its 1988 Report, AI noted that "thousands of political prisoners" continued to be arbitrarily arrested and detained.

f. Arbitrary Interference with Privacy, Family, Home or Correspondence

The Constitution provides protections for the inviolability of the home, and strong cultural values reinforce these protections. Police must obtain a search warrant before entering the home of a criminal suspect. However, warrants are not required for the arrest of security suspects. Although most arrests occur outside the home, there have been reports of forced entry and arrest by the security police, particularly of suspected members of the outlawed Da'wa Organization. As their campaign against Kurdish rebels intensified, government forces conducted large-scale searches of homes in Kurdish towns, and arrested and relocated large numbers of people.

There is no legal protection against the monitoring of telephones, which many Iraqis believe to be a common practice. All mail is believed subject to review by censors. The security services and the Ba'ath Party are generally assumed to maintain pervasive networks of informers.

Section 2. Respect for Civil Liberties, Including:

a. Freedom of Speech and Press

These freedoms are not respected. The Constitution prohibits "any act aimed at undermining the national unity of the people, provoking racial, sectarian, and regional bigotry, or violating gains and achievements of the country," and the Government views political dissent as a security threat and strictly controls speech, all information media, and assembly. The Government owns and operates the press, radio, and television. The media do not criticize the Government, and news report-

ing is strongly biased. Opposition viewpoints are not heard. Few foreign periodicals reach Iraq, and Western newspapers are not sold. Foreign visitors magazines, newspapers, cassettes, cameras, and video cassettes may be confiscated at the airport. To control the dissemination of political leaflets, typewriters and photocopying machines must be registered. Taking photographs of military installations, government buildings, or areas near sensitive locations is forbidden and punishable by imprisonment. Journalists and photographers visiting Iraq at the invitation of the Government are required to present film taken in Iraq for inspection by the authorities.

b. Freedom of Peaceful Assembly and Association

These freedoms are severely limited. Public meetings may only be organized under the auspices of the Government or the Ba'ath Party. Association for nonreligious purposes and demonstrations without government approval have met with severe repression. Professional organizations are subject to control by the Ba'ath Party Central Vocational Bureau.

For a discussion of freedom of association as it applies to labor unions, see Section 6.a.

c. Freedom of Religion

Iraq is an ethnically and religiously diverse society. However, many non-Muslims, principally Jews and Christians, left Iraq under previous regimes. Since its rise to power in 1968, the Ba'athist Government, while carefully controlling religious groups, has enforced tolerance of religious diversity, seeking to submerge religious differences in the promotion of secular nationalism. A 1981 law gave the Ministry of Endowments and Religious Affairs the authority to promulgate laws and regulations governing places of worship, appointment of clergy, religious literature, and participation in religious councils and meetings. Muslim religious leaders operate under close government supervision, are considered government employees, and receive their salaries through the Government. The Government administers the principal Muslim shrines and mosques and has increased allotments to refurbish and maintain them in an apparent attempt to win support from the devout.

While the Government has assumed much greater authority in Islamic religious affairs since 1981, the law has not been invoked against Iraq's Christian sects. Iraq's Christians number more than 500,000 and constitute nearly 4 percent of the population. Their freedom of worship in churches of established denominations is legally protected, but they are not permitted to proselytize or to hold meetings outside church premises. Convents and monasteries exist, and some new churches have been constructed, in some cases with government financial support. The Jewish community is believed to have decreased from 150,000 following World War II to under 400. It was severely persecuted in the past, but there is no evidence of recent persecution. One synagogue in Baghdad still functions.

d. Freedom of Movement Within the Country, Foreign Travel, Emigration, and Repatriation

Iraqis are generally free to travel within the country and to change their residences or workplaces. However they are likely to be constrained by social, cultural, and religious traditions which define the areas occupied by the various ethnic and religious groups. Sensitive border and other security areas are off-limits. Civilian travel in the war zone is restricted. Curfews are in effect where Kurdish insurgents have been active. There are police checkpoints on highways and outside major towns, but most Iraqis and foreigners travel freely in nonrestricted areas.

The Government's harsh campaign to suppress Kurdish rebels, involving mass relocations of Kurdish villagers, has nullified the right of hundreds of thousands of Kurds to choose their place of residence. An estimated 250,000 to 300,000 Kurdish villagers were forcibly relocated in 1988; since the Government began its program of forced relocation in 1987, an estimated 500,000 people have been uprooted. Since traditional Kurdish culture has been deeply embedded in the rural village, the forced removals and razing of villages has had a destructive impact on the lives of some half a million Kurds.

All Iraqis and most foreigners who remain in the country for more than 2 weeks must obtain exit permission. Travel has been even further limited since September 1986 when severe restrictions on currency exchange were imposed. Because of the war's drain on the economy, permission to travel abroad is restricted to a few categories of Iraqis, including officials, government-approved students, and medical treatment abroad may be granted, permission to transfer hard currency abroad to pay for it usually is not. The Government seeks to limit the countries an Iraqi traveler may visit and, should the traveler visit a nonauthorized country, a small fine may be levied upon his return. Iraqis who have residences abroad may depart the country provided they originally had left before the war began. In general, a married woman must have the permission of her husband to travel abroad.

The Government can require a prospective traveler to post a substantial bond to assure return. The RCC decreed in 1987 that Iraqi students abroad who refuse to return to Iraq must reimburse the Government for all education received in Iraq or abroad at government expense. The resolution is applicable retroactively to students who have refused to return since May 16, 1983, the day the Government began requiring those employees who left government jobs before completing the required 20 years of work to reimburse the State for the cost of their education. Amounts due can be recovered by confiscation; nonpayment may result in imprisonment. Each student must provide a guarantor before traveling abroad. This guarantor and the student's parents may be held liable if the student fails to return.

There is no specific ban on emigration or special restrictions for members of minority groups; however, emigration is discouraged. For the past several years, almost all of those given permission to emigrate have been spouses of foreign nationals. Prospective emigrants have had travel permission delayed and have been harassed. Many emigrants leave behind substantial property because of the difficulty of exporting assets. Currency exchange violations are considered national security offenses, and penalties can be severe.

Alien spouses of Iraq, citizens who have resided in Iraq for at least 5 years are required to become naturalized or leave Iraq. Many people, including several Americans, have thus been obliged to accept Iraqi citizenship and are therefore subject to the present travel restrictions. In March 1984, a resolution by the RCC reduced the residency period before naturalization to 1 year for the spouses of Iraqi citizens employed in government offices. The Iraqi spouse faces penalties for noncompliance, including loss of job, a fine of approximately $10,000, and repayment of the costs of education. Iraq does not recognize the concept of dual nationality, and many Iraqi "dual nationals," especially the children of an Iraqi father and a mother of non-Iraqi birth, have been denied permission to leave Iraq to visit the country of their other nationality.

In recent years, the Government has instituted special programs to encourage the repatriation of qualified professionals. Aliens of Iraqi origin can apply for a document permitting them to enter and exit from Iraq without a visa. Former Iraqis can more easily obtain visitors' visas than can other aliens, who generally must have a sponsor.

Other persons of Iraqi origin are permitted to return, including many persons who were admitted to other countries as refugees. A number of such people, especially Assyrian Christians, have returned on temporary visits. They are free to come and go, within the limits of the present travel restrictions, since they are not considered to have violated Iraqi laws. However, those who emigrated only after the beginning of the Iran-Iraq War, including several U.S. permanent resident aliens, have been unable to depart Iraq after returning. AI reports that in November 1987 the Government declared an amnesty "for Iraqis living abroad who had been convicted or suspected of political or criminal offenses. It was not known whether anyone took advantage of it." In September the Government announced an amnesty for Kurds who fled the country during the August campaign. Approximately 1,400 returned from refugee camps in Turkey.

Section 3. Respect for Political Rights: The Right of Citizens to Change Their Government

Citizens do not have the right to change their government in Iraq. The Ba'ath Party, whose limited membership is dominated by the President and the party's Regional Command, rules Iraq. The party reportedly has some 1.5 million adherents, representing about 10 percent of the population; but only some 50,000 "active" or full members, less than 0.33 percent of the population, participate influentially in party activities. There are two other legal political parties, both Kurdish. They and the Ba'ath Party constitute the Patriotic and Progressive National Front, essentially a vehicle of support for the Government. The two minor parties carry on only limited activity. Members of the military or security services may engage in political activities only within the Ba'ath Party. Association with the party is not required for appointment to senior government positions or military ranks or election to the National Assembly, but is normally necessary to attain political influence. Opposition groups, including various Kurdish groups and splinter parties, are severely repressed. The Communist Party was removed from the National Front and declared illegal in 1979. The Da'wa Organization, a violent dissident Shi'ite group, is still proscribed, and its members are subject to incarceration and execution, as are members of other parties believed to be cooperating with Iran. The Government announced in November plans to permit the legal formation of opposition parties. However, this development is unlikely to have a major effect on the nature of the regime.

General elections were last held for the 250-seat National Assembly in 1984. The Government screened all the candidates for consonance with Ba'ath Party ideology. Though in theory possessing a wide range of official duties, the Assembly exercises little real authority. The most recent local elections were held in the Kurdish Autonomous Region in 1986. With the term of the National Assembly having expired, elections are scheduled for March 1, 1989.

Section 4. Governmental Attitude Regarding International and Nongovernmental Investigation of Alleged Violations of Human Rights

Iraq denies charges that it violates human rights. Iraqi officials claim that the information on which AI and other human rights groups base their charges comes from pro-Iranian and Kurdish Iraqi exile groups in London and Paris. In its 1988 Report, AI noted several instances in 1987 in which Iraqi authorities had commented on AI reports or responded to AI inquiries, but in each case these authorities had defended their actions as justifiable. Iraq refused to permit any independent investigation, including one under U.N. auspices, of charges related to the use of chemical weapons in its campaign to suppress Kurdish rebels. Iraq adamantly denied such use.

There is no government office or official charged with investigating human rights and coordinating with other governments and international organizations on human rights. Iraq cooperates with the International Committee of the Red Cross in efforts to resettle Iranian civilian refugees in third countries. The U.N. High Commissioner for Refugees (UNHCR) in previous years sent several representatives to Iraq for brief periods to register refugees and to work for their resettlement. A UNHCR representative has been in Baghdad since April 1988.

Section 5. Discrimination Based on Race, Sex, Religion, Language, or Social Status

The Ba'ath Party has been committed to the equality of the sexes, and a series of laws since it came to power in 1968 has steadily improved the status of women. Such laws have protected women from exploitation in the workplace; granted subsidized maternity leave; permitted women to join the regular army, Popular Army, and police forces; and equalized women's rights on divorce, land ownership, taxation, suffrage, and election to the National Assembly. In the 1970's, the Government imposed legal penalties on families that opposed sending their women to literacy schools, and on men who were seen harassing women. However, women may still travel abroad only with the permission of their husbands. School enrollment of females has been increasing in recent years, reaching 45 percent in elementary schools and 36 percent in secondary schools in 1985-86.

Women represent about 47 percent of agricultural workers and about 25 percent of the total work force. The war accelerated the Government's drive to elevate the status of women, and some Iraqis believe it has permanently broken cultural barriers to the acceptance of women in traditional male roles. Women have become increasingly visible as architects, construction engineers, oil engineers, air traffic controllers, factory and farm managers, and Air Force pilots. Some 40,000 women were reportedly volunteers in the Popular Army in 1982.

The use of minority languages is unrestricted. Kurdish, an official language, is used in schools and media in Kurdish areas. Turcomans publish in their dialect of Turkish. The Shi'a, who make up roughly 55 percent of the population, have historically been economically, politically, and socially disadvantaged throughout the Middle East. The Government has a declared policy to raise their living standards and equalize opportunities for their economic and professional advancement. For four centuries, political power in Iraq has been concentrated in the hands of the Sunni minority. Sunni Arabs, who comprise 20 to 25 percent of Iraq's population, dominate the RCC, the Regional Command of the Ba'ath Party, and the Cabinet. However, many Shi'as hold prominent positions, and the economic status of the Shi'a has improved. Nevertheless, the Government maintains a close watch against Iranian attempts to exploit dissatisfaction among the Iraqi Shi'a, who adhere to the branch of Islam prevalent in Iran.

Although Christians sometime allege discrimination in education and jobs, adherence to their religion has not prevented many from obtaining wealth and professional advancement. The Deputy Prime Minister and Foreign Minister, a Chaldean Christian, has represented Iraq even at meetings of the foreign ministers of the Organization of the Islamic Conference. Other Christians hold important official and private positions. Citizens considered to be of Iranian origin carry special identification, and they are often precluded from desirable employment and their advancement may be impeded. Many "Iranian" families have been in Iraq for generations. Some say their forebears were not from Iran but claimed

Iranian nationality to evade Ottoman military conscription.

Section 6. Worker Rights

a. The Right of Association

Industrial workers do not constitute a significant part of the total work force, whose principal components are agricultural workers, shopkeepers, and government employees. Under the Trade Union Organization Law of June 2, 1987, a new single trade union structure was prescribed for organized labor. Workers in private and mixed enterprises and in cooperatives-but not public employees or workers in state enterprises-have the voluntary right to join a local trade union committee. The trade union committees form trade unions which in turn are part of provincial trade union federations. At the top is an umbrella organization, the Iraqi General Federation of Trade Unions, which is organically linked to the Ba'ath Party and required to promote party principles and policies among union members. The General Federation is affiliated to the International Confederation of Arab Trade Unions and to the Soviet-controlled World Federation of Trade Unions. It is also active in the tripartite Arab Labor Organization which is currently headquartered in Baghdad.

Although workers legally have the right to strike, after providing notice to the Labor Ministry, no strikes have been reported for almost 20 years.

b. The Right to Organize and Bargain Collectively

Even before the abolition of the Labor Federation, the right to bargain collectively was not recognized. Labor legislation and practice is uniform throughout the country. There are no export processing zones in Iraq.

c. Prohibition of Forced or Compulsory Labor

The Popular Army, the militia of the Ba'ath Party, employs press-gang methods to draft recruits. It sets up roadblocks and inducts eligible men on the spot; they are sometimes not allowed to contact their families for weeks afterwards. Popular Army personnel perform duties in rear areas, freeing regular army personnel for front line duty; they also perform many functions, such as reconstruction work, which would normally be done by the civilian labor force. However, on October 30 the Gov-

ernment announced that the Popular Army would cease recruiting drives and begin to release Popular Army inductees who were currently in training camps. There has been no evidence of recruiting into the Popular Army since this announcement, and measures are under way to significantly reduce its size.

d. Minimum Age for Employment of Children

Children are frequently encouraged to work as necessary to support the family, a common social practice in the Middle East. The employment of children is forbidden in all enterprises other than small-scale family enterprises . . .

38.

[January 15, 1991 (Senate), pp. 529-30]

KURDISH REFUGEES

Mr. LEAHY. Mr. President, as the possibility of war in the Persian Gulf grows more real every day I want to call attention to the plight of a group of people whose past suffering at the hands of Saddam Hussein have too readily been ignored by the world community, including the Bush administration.

Today there are approximately 12,000 Kurdish refugees living in squalor in the Kiziltepe camp in Turkey, just 100 miles from the Turkey-Iraq border. They are among an estimated 30,000 Kurdish refugees living in camps inside Turkey along the Iraqi border. They fled Iraq in 1988, after Hussein bombed their villages with chemical weapons.

Although that has often been cited as an example of the barbarity that Saddam Hussein is capable of, it was only one of many outrages he inflicted on the Kurds. Their villages were flattened by tanks and their people tortured and executed in mass.

Mr. President, the Kurds are truly forgotten people, at least forgotten by the world's leaders. There are over 20 million Kurds, yet they are without a country or land of their own. They have learned to expect persecution wherever they go.

The Kurdish refugees on the Iraqi border are in grave danger if war erupts in the Persian

Gulf. They are confined to closely guarded camps from which they cannot leave. If war spreads in their direction they will have no way of protecting themselves.

Three years ago the Bush administration was silent when Saddam Hussein ordered mustard gas to be used against the Kurds. I urge the administration to use its influence with Turkey and the governments of Western Europe, and the U.N. High Commissioner for Refugees, to ensure that these vulnerable people will not suffer again such a terrible fate.

Mr. President, I ask unanimous consent that a recent editorial from the Burlington Free Press on the Kurdish refugees in Turkey be printed in the Record.

There being no objection, the article was ordered to be printed in the Record, as follows: [See *Burlington Free Press*, January 2, 1991, THE FORGOTTEN KURDS].

If you're going to be a victim of Saddam Hussein, it helps to control a flock of oil wells. It helps to be a Kuwaiti, not a Kurd.

When Saddam rolled over the Kuwaitis, world leaders shivered with horror and dispatched half a million troops. President Bush discovered a new Hitler in his erstwhile ally.

Kuwaiti sheiks relocated their limousines and counting houses to Saudi Arabia and await deliverance in comfort.

The Kurds don't control any oil. So, when Saddam gassed them, razed their villages in northern Iraq and turned their land into a desert, nobody paid much attention. Nobody paid ANY attention.

This was not a new experience for the Kurds. About 17 million Kurds—a people of Indo-European roots and Muslim faith—inhabit the dusty plains and hills where the borders of Iraq, Iran, Syria and Turkey come together.

When the Ottoman Empire was dismantled after World War I, the Kurds were promised an independent Kurdistan. Instead, their territory was split among the four neighbors and a nearby area of the Soviet Union—almost all of whom set out to annihilate the Kurds' culture. Turkey, where about half the Kurds live, refuses to acknowledge their ethnicity, calling them "mountain Turks." In Turkey, it's a jailable offense to speak Kurdish in the street.

So there is some irony—lost on the Kurds—in the fact that Iraqi Kurds fleeing Saddam's poison gas sought refuge in Turkey. Saddam apparently decided to decimate the Kurds because they sided with Iran in the Iran-Iraq war.

"On 28 August 1988, they (the Iraqis) started bombing. They dropped chemical weapons on 70 points. I was there," said Akram Mayi, a Kurdish leader who is in the United States to receive a human rights award.

"The color of the gas was between white and yellow," he said, describing mustard gas. "It smelled of garlic. Thousands of men and women and children died. Thousands fled to Turkey."

And there they sit, about 30,000 of them, in three refugee camps, although Turkey calls them "guests" and declines international aid on their behalf. They have lived in tents and crude apartment blocks for two years, several families to a room. The food is plain but acceptable, Mayi said, but schooling is forbidden, and there is no work for the adults.

What the Kurds would really like, Mayi said wistfully, is to be given an autonomous region in northern Iraq if the United States destroys Saddam.

Short of that, the Iraqi Kurds would like to be accepted as refugees in Western Europe and North America.

The United Nations refused to discuss the Kurds or Saddam's campaign of genocide. Until recently, the United States showed no interest in accepting them as refugees—although who could better show "a well-founded fear of persecution"? This month, Mayi said, the United States agreed to accept 300 families.

"Every day the Iraqis killed thousands of Kurds and nobody talked about it," he said with bitterness.

"And now they talk about 'human rights.' Human rights! It appears it is petrol rights, not human rights, that matter."

39.

[February 28, 1991 (Senate), p. 2505]

THE PERSIAN GULF

Mr. PELL. Mr. President, the war in the Persian Gulf now appears to be over. It has been a stunning triumph for American arms and for the forces of our coalition partners. I would like to commend our brave service men and women who served with such professionalism and with such commitment in the gulf. All Americans salute them for their role in the liberation of Kuwait.

We are also very grateful that American and coalition casualties have proved to be extremely light. Never in history has such a major military campaign been waged with so much damage inflicted on the enemy and so few lost by the victorious side. However, my heart goes out to the families and friends of the 79 men and women who died for our country and for freedom in Operation Desert Storm. The world deeply appreciates their sacrifice.

We also sympathize with the terrible suffering from which the people of Kuwait have now been delivered. They have endured unspeakable hardships over the last 7 months. And we should not forget Saddam Hussein's other victims: the Kurds who have been attacked by poison gas and seen their villages destroyed by the thousands.

And I would also like to offer a thought for the people and ordinary soldiers of Iraq. They too are victims of Saddam Hussein. The Iraqi people have been subject to aerial bombardment and have seen services in their cities go back nearly a century, all because of Saddam Hussein's megalomaniacal ambitions. The ordinary Iraqi soldier was a conscript, he was poorly fed and subject to fire from his own side to keep him from surrendering. He too is a victim of Saddam Hussein.

Now, however, our attention must shift to the postwar situation. We will profit little from the success of our arms if we fail now to secure the peace.

First on our list of postwar issues must be the political future of Iraq. In my view Saddam Hussein's days are numbered. He has brought unprecedented misery on his own country, first through an 8-year war with Iran that cost 250,000 dead and put his country deep into debt. Now he has brought ruin on his country's infrastructure, the destruction of his military and produced thousands of Iraqi deaths. This is a record no leader can long endure.

We should do what we can to encourage a democratic alternative to Saddam Hussein. Already there is a coalition of Kurdish, Shi`a Arab and other groups which has outlined a program for a democratic alternative in Iraq, an alternative that also guarantees autonomy for the long suffering Kurdish minority. We should encourage these efforts. And above all we should not accept the replacement of Saddam Hussein with another general from the Sunni Arab 15 percent minority who will run yet one more authoritarian Iraqi regime. The Government of Saudi Arabia is sponsoring its own alternative to Saddam Hussein. While I have the greatest admiration for our Saudi allies, theirs is not a government that knows about democracy. Their alternative for Iraq should not be ours.

Our next priority in the postwar world must be to contain the unrestrained transfer of weapons to countries in the Middle East. It is ironic that all the countries that supplied Iraq with its vast arsenal of modern weapons formed part of the international coalition against Iraq. These arms sales to Iraq may have encouraged Iraq to be more aggressive; it certainly made an aggressive Iraq more dangerous. The countries in the Middle East should be devoting their resources to their own development; it is the diversion of scarce resources to wasteful and dangerous military expenditure that is the cause of so much instability in the region.

Finally, in the postwar period we must redouble our efforts to find peaceful solutions to regional problems: the Iraq-Kuwait dispute, the Arab-Israel conflict, the civil war in Lebanon and, I would add, the legitimate aspirations of the Kurdish people.

Mr. President, this has been a great triumph for America and for the United Nations. Now we face a new challenge. I hope our policymakers can show the same courage and same professionalism that did our service men and women in the Persian Gulf.

40.

[March 7, 1991 (Senate), pp. 2991-93]

KURDS, TURKS, AND CYPRIOTS: A NEW WORLD ORDER FOR WHOM?

Mr. Cranston. Mr. President, for those of us who opposed Saddam Hussein both before his August 2 invasion of Kuwait and after, the plight of Iraq's 3 million Kurds has been of special interest.

Few peoples in modern history have received such systematic mistreatment and neglect. In the mid-1970's Henry Kissinger's State Department and the Shah of Iran cut a deal that effectively turned our backs on our former Kurdish allies, paving the way for their bloody suppression.

In recent years, tens of thousands of Kurds have been imprisoned, tortured and murdered by Saddam and his brutal forces. Half a million have been expelled from their ancestral mountain homelands in Kurdistan.

In this morning's *Washington Post*, former foreign service officer, David A. Korn, wrote a compelling account of the plight of these people. The title of his article was "Don't Ignore Iraq's Kurds—It's Wrong, and It's Shortsighted Policy" [*The Washington Post*, March 7, 1991]. That such an article needed to be written at all is particularly disquieting. Yet, according to Korn:

When Kurdish leader Jalal Talabani visited Washington recently, no official of the State Department or the White House would receive him. The administration would not even talk with Talabani about human rights; the assistant secretary for human rights wouldn't see him. Other Kurdish representatives sit in Washington anxiously waiting to learn whether they can get a hearing even at a junior level in the State Department.

In Korn's view, an opinion I share, the administration's standoffishness has a lot to do with our relationship with Turkey, which has waged its own campaign of repression against its Kurdish population. As Korn states:

The Turkish government would be deeply apprehensive if the United States were to be seen to be doing anything to help Iraq's Kurds gain the kind of autonomy that it denies its own Kurdish citizens.

Mr. President, no one denies Turkey's importance as a member of NATO; or its contribution during the recent Gulf War.

However, I question just how close a relationship we should have given the Turkish government's well-documented record of human rights abuse. And as even greater proof of the folly of this course, I would draw attention to the continued occupation by Turkey of part of Cyprus.

Victory in the Persian Gulf was an important triumph for international law. Yet, just as the United Nations spoke with one voice against Iraqi aggression against Kuwait, so too has the security council issued many resolutions calling on the Turks to withdraw from Cyprus.

The world awaits the time Turkish troops leave the island, and Cyprus' sovereignty, independence, and territorial integrity are respected.

Mr. President, I call on the administration to stay the course in establishing the international rule of law. I urge that it give the Kurds a fair shake, while telling Turkey the world awaits a just solution for Cyprus.

Mr. President, I ask for the *Washington Post* article to be reprinted in the record, as well as a recent speech given by Senate Foreign Relations Committee staffer Peter Galbraith on the plight of the Kurds.

The material follows:

REMARKS BY PETER GALBRAITH

To day the world focuses on Saddam Hussein's latest victim, the people of Kuwait. The Kurds, however, were his first and longest suffering victim. Sadly, much of what the Kurds endured occurred in places inaccessible for political and geographic reasons to the world media. I had a brief window on some of what has happened to the 3 million people of

Iraqi Kurdistan and this is the focus of my remarks today.

In connection with Senate Foreign Relations Committee assessments of the Iran-Iraq war, I twice had occasion to visit Iraqi Kurdistan, in 1984 and 1987. Between those visits I was able to witness the sharp deterioration in the treatment of the Kurdish population by the Iraqi government.

In 1988 the plight of the Iraqi Kurds burst onto the international consciousness, first with the graphic reports of a poison gas attack on the Kurdish city of Halabja and then with the massive outflow of refugees from northern Iraq in September, bringing with them tales of a broad chemical weapons offensive by the Iraqi army.

In connection with legislation that Senator Pell introduced to sanction Iraq for this use of chemical weapons against the Kurds, the Senate Foreign Relations Committee asked me to lead a mission to report on and document the use of chemical weapons.

First, to restate the principal conclusions of our fact-finding mission, we found overwhelming evidence that Iraq did use chemical weapons on Kurdish civilians in northern Iraq in a major offensive that began August 25, 1988. The offensive was intended to break the Kurdish insurgency and accomplished that objective.

These chemical weapons attacks were part of the an Iraqi military policy intented to depopulate large parts of Iraqi Kurdistan. Elements of the policy include: (1) the destruction of villages and towns throughout Kurdistan: (2) the relocation of the Kurdish population into concentrated new settlements were military control can be exercised; (3) the deportation of Kurds to areas outside of Kurdistan; and (4) the use of terror tactics, including lethal poison gas to drive civilians out of the areas to be depopulated.

The policy has been carried out with great brutality and with a cynical disregard for world opinion and international law. Our fact-finding mission documented chemical weapons attacks on 49 villages; we believe the actual total to be much higher. The chemical weapons attacks were followed by military operations in which many survivors who chose to remain in Iraq (or could not reach Turkish sanctuary) were massacred. Drawing on interviews, we estimated that the total cumulative civilian casualties from the chemical weapons attacks and the follow-on military operations were in the thousands. However, our information comes from only that part of Iraq where Kurds had access to refuge in Turkey. If the same kinds of military operations took place deeper in Iraqi Kurdistan as took place in the border areas, the Kurdish death toll could have been in the tens or hundreds of thousands.

We do not know the total casualties. We do not know with any degree of certainty what has happened in Iraqi Kurdistan since 1988. Iraqi soldiers sealed the border with turkey at the beginning of September 1988, a deadly silence has descended on Iraqi Kurdistan.

In the last week of August and the first week of September, 1988, some 65 thousand people came unexpectedly across the Iraq-Turkey border. Although they came from many different villages spread over a very mountainous terrain, they described essentially the same pattern of attacks. Let me say a word about what these attacks were like.

Beginning around dawn on August 25, Iraqi warplanes and helicopters dropped bombs containing chemical weapons on villages in the Dihok, Zakho and Amadiyah regions of Iraq. The aircraft would drop four to eight bombs each. The bombs, often described as green cannisters, created a weak sound as they detonated, and then a cloud spread out from the center of the explosion. The cloud was alternatively described as white or yellowish. The air then filled with the smell of bad garlic, rotten onions, bad apples, or rotten parsley.

Those exposed to the gas dropped dead instantly or very quickly. The bodies, according to some, appeared frozen and, in some cases, turned blue or black. Living or dying was often determined by where one was standing and or on the direction of the wind. On one occasion I heard from a mother whose children had perished 20 yards away while she emerged physically unscathed.

According to the survivors, livestock died and birds fell out of the sky. Later, troops wearing protective clothes entered the villages. In some places, such as the village of Baze, Iraqi forces opened fire with machine guns on the survivors and then bulldozed the bodies into mass graves.

This general description is a synthesis of hundreds of interviews conducted by my team with survivors in all the principal camps and gathering areas. The interviews took place within two weeks of the events described and included all sorts of people: Kurdish insurgents (the Pesh Merga), civilian men, women, and children. We had no trouble finding witnesses; indeed, I would estimate that one-half to three-fourths of the refugee population were eye-witnesses to the events I described.

Under our system of law eye-witness accounts are usually considered the best evidence. However, there was also physical evidence of the attacks. A team of American doctors examined wounded survivors and found symptoms consistent with the use of chemical weapons. A British television crew, led by Gwynne Roberts whose film we will see later, entered Iraq and unearthed bomb fragments containing traces of mustard gas. When on September 8, 1988, Secretary Shultz denounced Iraq's use of chemical weapons he did so, according to the press, on the basis of technical information available to him.

Indeed, while the issue of an appropriate response to Iraq's chemical weapons attack was hotly contested between the Senate which favored tough sanctions and the Reagan administration which favored no action at all, there was never any disagreement about the facts of Iraq's use of chemical weapons.

Let me make two further points about Iraq's use of poison gas against its Kurdish minority. First, these attacks began August 25, 1988—that is to say five days after a ceasefire went into effect in the Iran-Iraq war. Second, the targets of the attacks were not the Kurdish insurgents. The insurgents were located in bases in the mountains in the northern part of Iraq. It is a treeless and barren terrain and presumably the insurgent camps were visible from the air. However, the Iraqi regime chose to attack the villages in the valleys. Thus, the victims were overwhelmingly women, children, and non-combatant men.

Iraq's chemical weapons attacks were gratuitous. The Kurdish insurgency could have been suppressed without the use of chemical weapons and without massacring innocent civilians. Instead Iraq chose to punish a population it saw as disloyal by the most brutal and most inhumane means possible.

Poison gas was only one part of Iraq's Kurdish policy. During my September 1987 trip, on the road from Baghdad to Jalawla to Darbandikhan to Sulamanyeh to Kirkuk, I counted more than forty Kurdish villages that had been destroyed recently. This part of Kurdistan presented an eerie landscape where utility poles, graveyards, and abandoned orchards were the main reminders of recent human habitation.

These villages were not in remote areas. They were on the principal roads of Iraqi Kurdistan. As such, there was no military rationale for the destruction of the villages. Rather, it was another example of a punitive policy aimed at innocent civilians.

Kurdish leaders have documented 3,897 villages that have been destroyed along with thousands of schools and hundreds of ancient churches and mosques. The population has been relocated to the handful of surviving cities, to new townships that are in effect concentration camps under the supervision of the Iraqi military, and in some cases, to new settlements in the southern desert, far from mountainous Kurdistan. It is impossible for me to estimate the death toll of such a policy, but one can reasonably conclude it must be high. The depopulation program was certainly cruel and destructive of an ancient and rich culture.

Finally, I would note that the Kurds have been particularly victims of the kinds of human rights abuses that have afflicted all Iraqis. This includes summary execution, torture, detention without trial, and denial of basic freedoms. A particular Iraqi innovation is the torture and murder of children as a means of punishing or pressuring their parents. Amnesty international has documented cases where parents have been obliged to pay money for the return of the mutilated corpses of their young children.

In the case of the Kurds, Iraq quite literally got away with murder. By and large, the world community has reacted to the destruction of Iraqi Kurdistan, and even to the use of poison gas against innocent civilians, with silence. As many of you know, in 1988, immediately after receiving the reports of the massive chemical weapons attacks on the Kurds, Senators Pell and Helms introduced legislation to impose comprehensive financial and economic sanctions against Iraq. That legislation, "the prevention of genocide act of 1988" passed the Senate one day after its introduction, a speed of action almost unprecedented for this body. Sadly, however, "The Prevention of Genocide Act" did not become law. It was opposed by every special interest that did, or wanted to do, business with Iraq. It was vehemently opposed by the Reagan administration, and failed due to parliamentary maneuvering on the final day of the 100th Congress.

"The Prevention of Genocide Act" was the only attempt any place in the world to respond concretely to Iraq's appalling violation of Kurdish human rights and of international law. Few other countries went even as far as the United States, which through Secretary Shultz at least condemned the poison gas attacks.

When Saddam Hussein invaded Kuwait, he clearly believed the world would not respond in a forceful manner. Perhaps our failure to act when he gassed his own people contributed to that belief.

As Kuwait's independence is restored, I hope we will not forget Saddam Hussein's first and longest suffering victims, the Kurds. It is improbable that Kurdish rights can be accommodated within an Iraq headed by authoritarian regimes. Kurdish cultural survival, and indeed the physical survival of the Kurds, depends on enduring arrangements for Kurdish autonomy. Autonomy was guaranteed to the Kurds by the instruments that ended World War I and by the League of Nations when it terminated the mandate over Iraq. The world community, however, was neither willing nor able to enforce those guarantees. Perhaps in the context of the broader post-war settlement more binding international arrangements can be found to protect the Kurdish minority in Iraq.

More fundamentally, Kurdish rights are best protected in an Iraq that respects the human and political rights of all its citizens. The usually fragmented Iraqi opposition including the major Kurdish parties has come together with the outlines of a democratic political program in a post-Saddam Iraq. I believe this initiative is promising. I certainly believe the United States and its coalition partners should do what we can to encourage a democratic alternative in Iraq. Such an alternative provides the best hope for the Kurds.

I grew up in the aftermath of the Holocaust and as we learned about these terrible events, I remember well the resolution of my generation: never again. By this we meant that such evil events should never again go unnoticed and unopposed.

No one can encounter a tragedy of the magnitude of that which occurred in September of 1988 and remain unmoved. I have many images of the five days I spent along the Iraq-Turkey border: in a high mountain valley a women seated atop a small bundle constituting all her possessions waiting for a very uncertain future; donkeys with gaily woven saddlebags wandering aimlessly after being abandoned by their refugee owners; and old man crying as he told of the deaths of his children and grandchildren. These are images that will remain with me as long as I live. And I hope that we will never again let such suffering go unnoticed and unopposed . . .

41.

[March 20, 1991 (House), p. 1853]

HOMELAND FOR KURDS

(Mr. BILBRAY asked and was given permission to address the House for 1 minute and to revise and extend his remarks.)

Mr. BILBRAY. Mr. Speaker, as we sit here in relative comfort, the people in northern Iraq are suffering from bombardment. The Kurds who, in World War I, were promised a homeland, have been denied that homeland, and are fighting for their independence from a tyrant in Baghdad.

We now waffle whether or not we want to see the Iraqi republic broken into maybe two or three different countries. I say the Kurds, who have suffered so much over the last period of the last few years, need that homeland. They need a homeland where they do not have to worry about being gassed by a tyrant, their children killed, their women killed, and their men killed.

The Kurds have been there long before the Arabs came to Iraq, before the Turks invaded the Anatoly Plateau. As Alexander's armies marched out of Persia, they talked about being fought mile by mile by a tribesman called the Kurd. They have been there for 4,000 years, these people, and they deserve our help.

Mr. Speaker, the President of the United States should give to the Kurds, the people they need, and not only shoot down their fixed wing planes, but the helicopters being used to deliver that massive destruction against the Kurdish tribesmen.

42.

[April 9, 1991 (House), p. 2096]

RESOLUTION TO HALT MASSACRE OF IRAQI KURDISH POPULATION

(Mr. LEVINE of California asked and was given permission to address the House for 1 minute and to revise and extend his remarks.)

Mr. LEVINE of California. Mr. Speaker, today I am introducing a resolution calling on the President to take immediate action to halt the massacre of the Iraqi Kurdish population. We are moving much too slowly to stop this tragedy. Hundreds of thousands of Kurds have fled their homes, thousands have died, and thousands more are at imminent risk of death from starvation, disease, exposure, and further attack by Saddam Hussein's helicopter gunships and ground troops.

The reluctance of the administration to act by firing upon Saddam's helicopters earlier as they ruthlessly attacked the civilian Kurdish population has already cost innumerous lives. If we hesitate any longer, there will be no one left to benefit from the proposed U.N. buffer zones in Iraq.

Mr. Speaker, President Bush rightly could and did claim the moral mantel for America in our important effort to defeat Saddam Hussein. He should not allow that victory to be compromised now by abandoning the Kurdish population, who so desperately needs help from the international community.

Mr. Speaker, I submit for the RECORD the text of my introduction, and urge Members to support immediate protection and assistance for the Iraqi Kurds.

H. CON. RES. 112

Whereas Saddam Hussein has brutally attacked the Kurdish population of northern Iraq with helicopter gunships and armored ground forces in retaliation for their rebellion against his dictatorship;

Whereas the civil conflict in Iraq has displaced hundreds of thousands of Iraqis, primarily members of the Kurdish minority population;

Whereas many of these displaced persons, as well as those Kurds and other rebel groups still in Iraq are at imminent risk of death due to starvation, exposure, injury and disease;

Whereas the medical personnel stationed currently with the multilateral forces in the Persian Gulf area could provide urgently needed medical care on a timely basis;

Whereas Iraq has continued to keep its borders closed to international relief efforts, severely impeding efforts to ameliorate human suffering: Now, therefore be it

Resolved by the House of Representatives (the Senate concurring), That it is the sense of Congress that-

(1) the President should immediately request the deployment of United Nations forces in Iraq to escort international humanitarian relief providers, such as the Red Cross, the Red Crescent, the U.N. Children's Fund and other U.N. relief agencies and private voluntary humanitarian relief organizations to provide services to Kurds and other Iraqis;

(2) the President should call upon coalition medical teams stationed in the Persian

Gulf to provide humanitarian relief and medical assistance to Iraq's Kurdish population in areas where urgently needed;

(3) the President should call upon the United Nations to station peacekeeping forces in Iraq to protect the Kurdish population and other groups who have suffered attacks by Iraqi government forces.

43.

[April 9, 1991 (House), p. 2098]

ENFORCE AGREEMENT CONCERNING IRAQI HELICOPTERS

(Mr. KOSTMAYER asked and was given permission to address the House for 1 minute and to revise and extend his remarks.)

Mr. KOSTMAYER. Mr. Speaker, the agreement signed by General Schwarzkopf and Saddam Hussein's military prohibits the use of helicopter gunships except for administrative purposes by the Iraqis. Yet, these helicopters are being used as we speak to drop napalm and phosphorus bombs on Kurdish civilians as one of the 20th century's great tragedies unfolds before our eyes.

Why does not the President enforce the agreement, Mr. Speaker? His failure to do so after encouraging Kurdish Iraqis to revolt makes a mockery of his high-sounding moralizing during the Gulf war. To call Saddam Hussein Hitler and then to stand aside while he murders the Kurds brings shame on America.

I say to President Bush: "Enforce the agreement. The whole world is waiting and watching."

44.

[April 9, 1991 (Senate), p. 4169]

IRAQI REFUGEES

Mr. LEAHY. Mr. President, I wish to speak of a situation in the Middle East today, and that is the human tragedy of terrible proportions that is occurring in Iraq. Hundreds of thousands of Kurds and Shiites and other refugees are fleeing Saddam Hussein's tyranny. They are seeking sanctuary in Turkey, in Iran, and some in occupied Iraq. There are reports that thousands of men and women and children are being injured and many perishing in the icy mountain passes leading into Turkey or in the squalid and overcrowded refugee camps in Turkey and Iran.

I praise President Bush's decision to send emergency food and other aid to these refugees, including the air drops from our U.S. military aircraft. But we all know that these air drops can sustain only a handful of the masses that are streaming out of Iraq. The United Nations and individual countries like Britain and France are also responding to the genocidal savagery that Hussein is using against his very own people.

But as so often in the case in these all too familiar tragedies-like the countries of Africa and Asia are prone to-unfortunately too little comes too late for thousands of these suffering refugees.

My information is that the Emergency Refugee and Migration Account at the State Department now has less than $40 million. In fact, much of that is already committed to meet urgent needs of thousands of starving refugees in the horn of Africa and Southeast Asia, and sub-Sahara Africa.

Funds that might be available to help the Kurds and the Shiites and others who are fleeing murder, torture, brutality, and starvation in Iraq are just not adequate. We know that. But yet the United States has to provide large-scale immediate and effective help for these suffering people.

I urge President Bush to submit an emergency supplemental request for these refugees now. As chairman of the Foreign Operation Subcommittee with jurisdiction over the Emergency Refugee and Migration Account, I pledge my cooperation to help move an emergency supplemental for the Iraqi refugees to the President's desk without delay.

We know that the Kurds and the Shiites claim the rebellion against Hussein was at the urging of the Bush administration. President Bush said he never gave these oppressed people any reason to believe that the United States would intervene on their behalf. That is not the debate. That issue no longer even matters. Let the historians sort out the arguments later on.

The brutal reality is that those who rebelled are paying a terrible price for their courage. To remain in Iraq under Saddam's control means more killings, more torture, more savagery. They have no choice but to flee. Their only hope is that they might get help from the world community. It is one of those times in history for American good will and generosity to come forth.

Mr. President, as we recall, at the height of the Desert Storm bombing, we were spending perhaps as much as a billion dollars a day to wreak destruction. Let us now spend a fraction of 1 day of that amount to save the lives of the people who had the courage to stand up against their Government, hoping to depose the dictator who remains in control of their country.

Is there any American who, when they watch these pictures, when they watch a mother carrying a badly burned child, when they see families walking through the icy streams, when they see children scratching, trying to find another little twig to burn to keep warm, when they see whole families huddled together in the cold hoping they may all be alive the next day and not frozen to death, is there one single American who would not be willing to help? I doubt it very much.

We helped during the war. The United States spent an enormous amount of money. Let us be willing to spend at least a tiny fraction of that to help the people who are still suffering under the oppression that we fought against in Desert Storm. It is what America is best at. It is something that we can do well. Let us show the rest of the world once again the difference between Saddam Hussein and us. Let us go to their aid. It can be done. It should be done. I hope it will be done soon.

45.

[April 9, 1991 (Senate), pp. 4169-71]

THE KURDISH TRAGEDY

Mr. GORE. Mr. President, I would like at this point to address a problem which a few others have discussed already this afternoon, and that is the tragedy involving the Kurds as they attempt an exodus from the Kurdish areas of Iraq.

It is gratifying that the United States has decided to recognize the fact that events in Iraq are leading toward what is potentially one of the great, politically induced disasters of our time. Our contribution of the resolution of this issue, however, is to this point minuscule in relation to the dimensions of the problem and also in relation to our responsibility for these events. Moreover, we are still concentrating on immediate next steps while continuing to ignore the long-term requirements of a solution.

All figures are suspect, and we must use a great deal of caution when dealing with the estimates of other governments. Nevertheless, a snapshot of how things stand at this moment would look something like this: Perhaps 300,000 Kurds have crossed into Turkey and almost a like number are located in border regions of nearby Iraq. Iran has accepted about 300,000 Kurds also and says it is preparing to admit about 200,000 more. Iran has also received about 40,000 refugees from the southern regions of Iraq. Finally, there are perhaps 15,000 to 20,000 persons currently located in the part of southern Iraq presently controlled by the coalition.

An international relief effort of some dimension is now being organized for the relief of Kurds who have fled to the vicinity of Turkey. Whether that relief effort will arrive in time and in the amounts needed to stave off the threat of immediate disaster is an open question. It is also an extremely heavy responsibility for the world community but in particular for the wealthy nations of the world-I might add especially for nations like Kuwait and Saudi Arabia, on whose salvation the Kurds' resistance was focused in the immediate past.

Meanwhile, so far as I know, there is no similar response under way to aid those who have fled in the direction of Iran. Now that the Government of Iran has asked for this assistance, it ought to be provided with the same sense of urgency as the aid now moving toward the Iraq-Turkish border region. Certainly, if there was ever a moment for the world to respond to an Iranian request, this is it.

Meanwhile, attention is being focused on the proposal from Prime Minister Major of the United Kingdom for enclaves in which refugees could find safety and relief. That is an excellent idea but it has ramifications and limitations which have not yet been explored. I doubt, for example, that it is possible to set up enclaves in very shallow areas along the Turkish and Iranian borders. There is no infrastructure there; no way to mount a relief effort for so many people. The logistics of this problem have their own iron logic. Any such enclave must be deep enough to encompass towns which can then serve as the focal point for massive relief efforts.

I believe therefore that the enclaves concept probably requires us to think in terms of a fairly deep region extending well into the Kurdish regions of Iraq, and therefore right back within reach of Saddam Hussein's forces. If I am correct in this assumption, then the survival of hundreds of thousands of men, women, and children depends precisely upon being able to create zones of safety and relief that cannot exist without the cooperation of the Iraqi Government.

The idea of enclaves does not therefore allow us to delay consideration of precisely the one issue which the administration has not wanted to face; that is, what exactly do we expect of the Government of Iraq in order to allow this crisis to be resolved on terms we can live with as a principled people, and what actions are we prepared to take if they will not?

In my opinion, we have several tools at our disposal. First, the Secretary General has been authorized to involve himself in this issue by Resolution 688.

Second, Resolution 678, which authorized the use of force, also clearly and for reasons that are certainly valid now, spoke of the need not merely to force Iraqi troops out of Kuwait, but to take such steps as would be needed to restore international peace and security in the region. Certainly, a mass flight of peoples such as has now occurred constitutes a threat to security in the region well within the sense of this language.

Third, there is Saddam Hussein's own declaration of amnesty, which opens the door to hard-nosed conditions for outside supervision of any such amnesty within the area of a declared enclave. Since Saddam Hussein has so spectacularly demonstrated that he is far from honest in declarations of this sort, the world community must address itself to enforcing the sincerity of that declaration.

Let me make sure that I am perfectly understood on the latter point about these enclaves. If my assumptions are correct, an enclave big enough to be able to sustain the refugee population we now have must extend to some depth within the Kurdish areas of Iraq. At its farthest reaches nearest the borders of Turkey and Iraq, Saddam Hussein's power is attenuated, weakened, and blunted.

But the farther down into the Kurdish areas of Iraq this enclave reaches the more within Saddam Hussein's grip it is, and consequently the more clearly we have to deal with his behavior.

If we do not push this issue hard at the United Nations, exerting the kind of leadership we did in order to assemble backing for the use of force, it will not be possible to deal with the present crisis effectively. As was also the case then, we must be prepared to exert new and extra forms of pressure on Iraq to secure the kind of compliance we require.

By this, I certainly do not mean that we should stop the withdrawal of our troops, but I do have some other ideas to offer. Specifically, No. 1, we should still demand an end to those helicopter flights. If anything can enable Saddam Hussein to pursue the Kurds into the mountains, it will be helicopter gunships. That has already been demonstrated.

There is still something to be gained by taking this step, late as it is.

And it is worth noting again, Mr. President, that the terms of the case-fire explicitly prohibited the use of helicopter gunships for the purpose to which they are now being put. The spokesman for the State Department, when pressed after the slaughter became evident, said, "Is our policy ambiguous? Yes."

Mr. President, by that time, the administration, exercising its authority in these circumstances to establish policy on behalf of the country, granted in effect a specific easement to allow the helicopter gunships to be used to slaughter the Kurds. They knew it was going on day after day, and from reports as late as yesterday, it is still going on; as late as yesterday.

We have the power to order them to stay on the ground. Everybody is aware of what is at stake. But some are reluctant to take the step because they are afraid of a straw man. The straw man says that if we shoot down the helicopter gunships, then we are on a slippery slope which leads to the introduction of U.S. ground forces, and then on to our entanglement in an internal civil war. Nonsense.

As recently as this Nation's superb achievement during the Persian Gulf war, we demonstrated the capacity to make careful, even subtle, judgments in holding together an international coalition and exerting force with precision, with devastating effect, and avoiding complications that were there, were obvious, and were dealt with.

This straw man should not be allowed to prevent us from saving the lives of these people. It was wrong to allow these gunships to fly. We should stop these flights now.

Second, we should remind Iraq that failure to comply with Resolution 688 can lead to a Security Council recommendation to the General Assembly that Iraqi membership in the United Nations either be suspended or even, in the extreme case, revoked. If anyone thinks that these are relatively mild threats for Saddam Hussein, I believe the connection could be made that these are steps toward the point at which at least some important members of the United Nations may question whether an Iraq that can only be held together by extreme violence can ever be regarded as other than a threat not only to its our people but to its region.

Third, the United States, acting for itself, should consider whether or not to warn Iraq that failure to allow this matter to be settled in a humane way could increase the chance that assistance will reach the Kurdish rebels of a sort that would even the odds should they confront a much less powerful Iraqi Army in the future. And by this, I do not mean, again, the straw man which has been asserted, that we would then become entangled in the internal affairs of Iraq.

Mr. President, the argument that we should not involve ourselves in the internal affairs of Iraq is being made now at a time when, as has been noted by one acute observer:

We control and occupy 20 percent of the territory of Iraq; at a time when we control totally 100 percent of the airspace of Iraq; at a time when we propose, in concert with the other members of the coalition, to control 100 percent of the flow of oil out of Iraq and take such percentage of its oil revenues as we deem appropriate in order to satisfy war reparations; at a time when we, in concert with others, propose to regulate every single import Iraq seeks from the rest of the world community.

So the assertion that we do not wish to interfere in the internal affairs of Iraq when it comes to preventing the slaughter of tens of thousands of people-and potentially, even more-that complaint, that excuse seems a little hollow.

Fourth, the United States, acting for itself, should make clear that we intend to apply the sanctions to their maximum extent short of denying the necessities of life to the people of Iraq; not just until Saddam Hussein is gone, but until such time as a new government is formed which takes account of the human rights and political rights of Iraqi citizens.

As to the question, what kind of government-again, a straw man-the answer is, the design is not up to us, but the world community will know it when it sees it by the absence of the kind of terror now going on, and, until then, Iraq should not expect an easing of the sanctions beyond the level necessary for humanitarian reasons.

Fifth, the United States, having taken the step of ending our present state of involvement with Saddam Hussein's survival, should begin to press for the establishment of an international fact-finding tribunal to record and analyze what can be learned of Iraqi behavior in

Kuwait and during the current uprising. If these crimes are allowed to be hidden, believe me, we will again see processions of world leaders heading to Baghdad one day to shake Saddam Hussein's hand or the equally bloody hand of some Baathist lieutenant who succeeds him in control of the very same apparatus of terror and oppression of which Saddam Hussein is the principal, but not the only, architect.

Mr. President, there are many complex legal and ethical issues involved here. Whole new chapters of international law are about to be written. Let us focus, however, on certain immediate realities. Thousands upon thousands of lives are in our hands. We have the authority and international law to engage the United Nations in this matter. We have the authority and the Security Council resolutions to define conditions that will avert disaster. We have the power to impose these conditions. What we do not yet have is the one ingredient without which all else is inert and useless, and that is American leadership. Hopefully, though delayed, it will eventually be provided.

(The remarks of Mr. GORE pertaining to the introduction of S95 are located in today's RECORD under "Statements on Introduced Bills and Joint Resolutions.")

The PRESIDING OFFICER (Mr. CONRAD). The Senator from New York is recognized.

Mr. MOYNIHAN. I thank the Chair.

(The remarks of Mr. MOYNIHAN pertaining to the introduction of S786 are located in today's RECORD under "Statements on Introduced Bills and Joint Resolutions.")

46.

[April 9, 1991 (Senate), pp. 4171-72]

THE REFUGEE CRISIS IN IRAQ

Mr. LIEBERMAN. Mr. President, on January 12 of this year, I voted to give the President the power to go to war against Saddam Hussein. I did so believing Kuwait must be liberated. But, most important, I cast my vote believing the evil of Saddam Hussein must be destroyed.

I said in my speech in this Chamber on that important day "international morality is at stake." A victory by Saddam would have been a victory of anarchy over order, war over peace, brutality over liberty, immorality over morality.

We achieved our goal of liberating Kuwait. And we achieved our goal of diminishing Saddam's capacity to wage war against any neighbor for years to come. For that, the American people and people and nations around the world are grateful to President Bush and to our heroic troops, all of whom performed magnificently.

But has international morality been restored? Has Saddam been truly defeated? One look at the anguished faces of the refugees struggling to escape Saddam's terrorism-one look at the bruised, bloodied, and burned faces of Kurdish children-tells us that the immorality of Saddam Hussein continues to snuff out innocent lives within Iraq, even if it no longer threatens our own.

Saddam cannot wage war upon his neighbors. He no longer controls the fourth largest army in the world. But he still controls one of the most brutal armies in the world. He can and does attack the innocent, defenseless people of Iraq: the Kurds in the north, the Shiite Moslems in the south, indeed any citizen who dares challenge his rule. It is being reported today that Iraqi forces massacred 2,000 to 3,000 people in the village of Kara Henjir alone this week. Up to 2 million Kurds are refugees and may face starvation if their needs are not met. Every hour more and more Kurds die from exposure, disease, malnutrition, and injuries suffered at the hands of Iraqi troops.

In the face of such terrible news, it must be said: Final victory in the gulf cannot be proclaimed until Saddam is gone from power and his regime no longer engages in the mass murder of innocent Iraqi people.

During the gulf war, we saw televised images of Iraqis decrying the allied bombing. We now know much of that was stage-managed propaganda, designed to weaken our resolve. In the real world of Iraq, millions of its citizens must fervently pray for the final defeat of Saddam Hussein. I understand why we ceased hostilities just a few short weeks ago. But frankly, I believe our troops would have received a hero's welcome throughout much of Iraq had they marched further into that nation. Few advocated continuing the war-I did not-but it is becoming clearer that many people in Iraq actually wanted us to do more. They wanted us to free them from Saddam's evil rule.

But the United Nations did not mandate the liberation of Iraq. Marching all the way to Baghdad was not part of mission of Operation Desert Storm. One Saddam Hussein recognized that fact; once he saw that his troops and even his helicopters could operate freely throughout all but the southern portion of the country that we occupied, he moved swiftly. He has taken full advantage of the cessation of hostilities to consolidate his hold on his country, a hold that was in doubt following the war, thanks to Shiite and Kurdish rebellions-rebellions overtly encouraged by the United States.

We defeated Saddam's army, liberated Kuwait, occupied part of Iraq, and encouraged the Iraqi people to rebel against Saddam Hussein, all because we saw in Saddam the kind of evil that once before in this century created a Holocaust and threatened the security of the civilized world. Do we have the moral right now to stand silently by as Saddam butchers thousands of innocent Iraqi men, women, and children?

I did not speak out and vote for the use of force against Saddam Hussein on January 12 only to remain silent on April 9 while Saddam's murderous rampage rages on.

I believe the United States must pursue final victory over Saddam. We must use all reasonable diplomatic, economic, and military means to achieve his removal from power. Until that end is realized, the peace and stability of the region will not have been fully accomplished.

If we do not act, if we neglect our duty to humanity, we would, as Dwight Eisenhower once said in speaking about a failure to confront evil in the world, "outrage our own conscience. In the eyes of those who suffer injustice we would become partners with their oppressors."

There is more, much more, we can and should do now to confront the evil of Saddam Hussein and avert further loss of innocent lives.

First, we must dramatically expand our airlift operation to feed, clothe, and shelter the enormous refugee populations created by Saddam's aggression, within and outside of Iraq. That humanitarian response to a tragedy of historic proportions is something the world community simply must undertake with all possible speed.

Second, the President should declare that Iraqi helicopters will be shot down if they fly. That is our policy for Iraqi fixed-wing aircraft. That should be our policy for helicopters. Such action would not in itself lead to rebel victories over Saddam. But we could, in that simple step, end one horrific tool of Saddam's suppression of the Iraqi people. We could, in short, save many lives.

Third, we should encourage passage of a new Security Council resolution as proposed by British Prime Minister John Major. That resolution would create U.N.-sponsored "safe havens" within Iraq to provide immediate relief for the beleaguered refugees. But there will be no safe havens unless their safety is assured by a military presence or capability. The security of those buffer zones must be protected by the use of force if they are violated. One thing we have learned about Saddam is that he will respect nothing unless compelled to do so by the threat of force, or the actual use of force.

Fourth, we must consider such a threat or use of force to stop the wholesale slaughter of mass numbers of civilians even outside the safe havens. While we should not become militarily involved in a civil war in Iraq, we have an obligation to prevent the creation of new "killing fields." We have a duty to protect the truly innocent from annihilation at the hands of a modern, mechanized army.

Fifth, at some point the concept of safe havens must be transformed into a policy of safe passage home for the Kurds and other refugees of Saddam's aggression. Some way of assuring that the Iraqi refugees can return home without being strafed or bombed must be worked out by the United Nations. We cannot tolerate the long-term institutionalization of refugee camps. The refugees of Iraq deserve to go home and live in peace.

Sixth, we should make clear to Iraq that all costs associated with the refugee problem will be added to the bill Iraq owes the world community as a result of Saddam's aggression. Saddam and his clique must realize that every action they take against their own people will delay their ability to rejoin the community of nations and rebuild their nation. Frankly, I cannot see letting Iraq reconstitute its normal oil export business as long as Saddam remains in power.

Finally, if Saddam manages to survive in the months ahead, we should realize that getting him out of power may involve providing more than just verbal support for the Kurdish rebels and others who seek to establish a legitimate government in Baghdad. While the logistics of providing military and financial aid to rebels are complex, the concept must be explored.

There are those who say that all this discussion about what to do with Saddam Hussein and the refugees of Iraq is fruitless, because we have no business meddling in the internal affairs of a sovereign nation.

Iraq has sovereignty. But Saddam Hussein does not. We have no obligation to consider him, or treat him, as a legitimate head of state. He is a thug, a terrorist who is claiming to rule a nation, not a legitimate ruler in his own right.

We have every right to come to the aid of Iraqi people who want to be rid of this criminal and who want to restore a legitimate government in Iraq. We have a right and an obligation to use our influence at the United Nations, among our coalition partners, and through our military supremacy to rid Iraq and the world of Saddam Hussein so that the difficult path toward peace and security in the region will not be littered with the corpses of thousands-perhaps millions-of innocent victims of Saddam's evil rule.

The liberation of Kuwait has been achieved. But the work of the community of nations will not be done until the liberation of Iraq from Saddam Hussein is also won.

Frankly, I cannot imagine us allowing Iraq to begin selling its oil again on world markets so long as Saddam Hussein leads that country.

Finally, if Saddam manages to survive in the months ahead, we should realize that getting him out of power, which must remain our goal, may involve providing more than just verbal support for the Kurdish rebels and the Shiite rebels, and others who seek to establish a legitimate government in Baghdad.

I understand that the logistics of providing military and financial aid to rebels are complex, but it is a concept that we must actively explore. There are those who say all this discussion about what to do with Saddam Hussein and the refugees of Iraq is fruitless because we have no business meddling in the internal affairs of a sovereign nation. Iraq has sovereignty but Saddam Hussein does not. We have no obligation to consider him or treat him as a legitimate head of state. He is a terrorist who rules by brutal force. He is not a legitimate ruler in his own right, chosen by his own people. We have every right to come to the aid of the Iraqi people who want, clearly, to be rid of this criminal and who want to restore a legitimate government in Baghdad.

We have a right and an obligation to use our influence within the United Nations, among our coalition partners and through our military supremacy, to rid Iraq and the world of Saddam Hussein so that the difficult path toward peace and security and stability in that region will not be littered with the bodies of thousands, perhaps millions of innocent victims of Saddam's rule.

The liberation of Kuwait has been achieved, but the work of the community of nations will not be done until the liberation of Iraq from Saddam Hussein is also won.

I yield the floor.

The PRESIDING OFFICER. The Senator from Maryland.

47.

[April 9, 1991 (Senate), pp. 4196-97]

THE KILLING SANDS OF IRAQ

Mr. DOLE. Mr. President, a decade ago, the world witnessed the killing fields of Cambodia. Today's headlines portray the grim reality of the killing sands of Iraq. All of us have been appalled by the scenes of tragedy among the Kurdish refugees in the north, and the Shiite refugees in the south. So many of these helpless people-women, children, the elderly-are victims, not of war or rebellion, but of Saddam Hussein's genocidal persecution of his political opponents.

As a humane and caring people, we Americans join all civilized people in crying out for an end to the killing. We join with other nations, and people, in providing assistance to the displaced and endangered hundreds of thousands now crowding Iraq's northern and southern borders.

I commend the President for his decision to provide $11 million in emergency relief for this massive new population of refugees. In particular, the use of airdrops is an appropriate response to this true emergency, and sends exactly the right kind of visible message of our concern.

It is my understanding that the President will also take additional steps to respond to the needs of the refugees.

At the same time, I also believe the President has made the right decision in resisting the urging of some for a unilateral military intervention in this complex and tragic situation.

Indeed, it is ironic that some-who only a dozen weeks ago refused to vote to authorize the use of force against Saddam's naked and brutal aggression against a neighboring country, arguing passionately about the dangers of involving America in a quagmire of Arab politics-some of those same voices are now calling on President Bush to get the United States directly involved.

I hope, and believe, the President will continue to resist those calls. This time, the quagmire is real.

The struggle of the Kurds and the Shiites against Saddam Hussein did not start on the day the United States launched military operations against Iraq. It did not escalate into open warfare because of something someone said, but because the defeat of Iraq's forces in the gulf war gave Saddam's enemies reason to believe he was ripe for the picking.

Were we to intervene with anything less than a massive use of our forces-which I believe no one advocates-the result would not be a quick and easy victory, but a growing American involvement in an unending war of attrition; and the kind of chaos inside Iraq that would invite the intervention of others, such as Iran.

Even more to the point, as one astute observer pointed out in an op-ed in the *New York Times*, the likely result of an American intervention would be that, and I quote, "the suffering of the Kurds and other Iraqis would become even more tragic."

Mr. President, I ask unanimous consent that the full text of that op-ed [*The New York Times*, Apr. 5, 1991, "Stay Out of Iraq's Civil War"], by Prof. Shibley Telhami of Cornell University, be printed in the RECORD.

There being no objection, the text was ordered to be printed in the RECORD . . .

The debate over the U.S. obligations to the Kurds has pointed up a moral quandary: No one should watch bloodshed like that in northern Iraq without considering options to stop it. U.S. military action, which is not the right choice, would pose even more troubling moral problems.

There are alternatives. We can continue to use the U.N. to affect Iraqi behavior, as it did this week in setting punishing cease-fire conditions. The unprecedented resolutions cannot be carried out without world cooperation. The U.S. must also take a lead in guaranteeing that humanitarian aid reaches all suffering Iraqis, including refugees-under U.N. supervision. In the end, we must recognize that there are limits to what the U.S. can do, even as its power stands without equal in the world today.

Mr. DOLE. But, Mr. President, not intervening does not mean not caring.

We do care, and we care deeply. Our caring is manifest in the steps the President has taken and the efforts of so many private groups and citizens to offer aid for the needy.

Nor does it mean we do nothing. There are steps we are taking and should take. As we all know, Secretary Baker is in the region now, exploring with Iraq's neighbors what steps are appropriate and realistic, and meeting with the Kurdish refugees.

The United Nations has already passed one resolution, strongly condemning Saddam's latest outrage. The weight of nearly unanimous international opinion, and the pressure of tough economic sanctions, must continue to be brought to bear on Iraq. And certainly, in my view, if we cannot get some satisfaction from Saddam Hussein I see no rush to lift the sanctions.

We should also give serious consideration to the British proposal to establish refugee sanctuary zones, under U.N. auspices, within Iraq.

Meanwhile, as long as the refugees remain in jeopardy of Saddam's butchery, we should strongly urge Turkey and Iran to provide them temporary safe haven; and we should do all we can to make sure that the international community helps affected nations bear the burden of these large refugee populations.

Mr. President, we won a great victory in the gulf war. But the tragedy that has unfolded in Iraq is a poignant reminder that the challenge of establishing peace, stability, and security for the people of the Middle East, and the Persian Gulf, is still very real.

All Americans joined in our successful effort in the gulf war-the President, the Congress, and above all the people.

Let us find that same unity of purpose, and determination, as we seek to achieve, and to secure, a broader and more lasting peace.

I thank the Chair, and I yield the floor and suggest the absence of a quorum.

The PRESIDING OFFICER. The clerk will call the roll.

The legislative clerk proceeded to call the roll.

Mr. SIMPSON. Mr. President, I ask unanimous consent that the order for the quorum call be rescinded.

The PRESIDING OFFICER. Without objection, it is so ordered.

48.

[April 9, 1991 (Senate), pp. 4237-38]

STATEMENTS ON INTRODUCED BILLS AND JOINT SESSIONS

By Mr. MOYNIHAN (for himself, Mr. D'AMATO, Mr. PELL, Mr. BRADLEY, Mr. GORE, Mr. DECONCINI, Mr. BINGAMAN, Mr. FORD, Mr. LIEBERMAN, Mr. WELLSTONE, Mr. LEVIN, and Mr. SARBANES):

S786. A bill to amend the Foreign Assistance Act of 1961 to authorize the provision of medical supplies and other humanitarian assistance to the Kurdish peoples to alleviate suffering; to the Committee on Foreign Relations.

THE KURDS AND A NEW WORLD ORDER

Mr. MOYNIHAN. Mr. President, I rise to offer legislation which will authorize $50 million of humanitarian assistance to the Kurds of Iraq. It also expresses the sense of the Congress that the United States should seek to have the Security Council adopt effective measures under Chap. VII of the U.N. Charter to stop the illegal attacks on Iraqi civilians.

The recent attacks on Iraqi civilians-and our response to them-raise fundamental questions about whether we intend to pursue a new world order beyond the immediate crisis posed by Iraq's invasion of Kuwait. Under the U.N. Charter (specifically article 2(7)) certain events are considered to be "essentially within the domestic jurisdiction" of a state and, therefore, beyond the competence of the Security Council. That is not the case here. Iraqi troops are driving before them perhaps 2 million Iraqi Kurds. These refugees are spilling over into Turkey and Iran, raising tensions and destabilizing the region. There can be little doubt that these events are-in the words of article 39-a "threat to the peace". In the words of Alan Riding's report to the *New York Times* which appeared this morning, Turkish officials note that-

They expected the number of Kurds fleeing Iraq to swell to one million in the coming weeks and that those are numbers that are simply beyond the scope of any sustained international relief effort. Thirty thousand refugees is a humanitarian problem, but one million, they argued, is a political problem.

Iranian officials reportedly expect as many as 1.5 million Kurdish refugees from Iraq.

Moreover, international law now governs even the conduct of a civil war.

Under the Fourth Geneva Convention Relative to the Protection of Civilians in Time of War of 1949, it is absolutely prohibited to attack persons taking no part in the conflict. This prohibition applies even in the case of "armed conflict not of an international character". Iraq is a party to this Convention as are virtually all the nations of the world. These ruthless attacks on civilians are more than simply immoral-they are illegal.

The Security Council has taken the first step at the initiative of the French. They have in fact concluded that this situation constitutes a "threat to the peace". They have ordered the Iraqi army to cease these attacks. That order is binding on Iraq under article 25 of the charter. If Iraq refuses to comply, then the United States should do what it did so brilliantly in the Persian Gulf crisis: It should use the mechanisms of the charter to collectively confront a threat to the peace. The tools are at hand: international law, article 39, article 41 on sanctions and article 42 on the use of U.N. forces. Article 42, for instance, allows for "demonstrations" of the use of force when sanctions have been determined to be inadequate. The Security Council could order Iraqi helicopters to cease their attacks. If the Iraqis refused to comply, then the council could direct that the allied forces in the region should down some of the Iraqi helicopters as a "demonstration" of possible additional U.N. action to enforce the Security Council's decree.

When Saddam Hussein massacred the Kurds in 1988 using poison gas he violated one of the most solemn international agreements ever entered into, namely, the 1925 Geneva Protocol on the Use of Poison Gas. The United States did nothing to prevent this. On the contrary the State Department opposed economic sanctions on Iraq until the day that country invaded Kuwait. During the subsequent crisis, however, we saw the strong reassertion by the United States of the concepts of international law. The administration used the mechanisms of the charter, imposing a total economic embargo on Iraq. The present crisis presents us with the question of whether this commitment to a new world order will outlive the expulsion of Iraqi troops from Kuwait. I support the President's call for a return to the rule of law and I hope that the United States will continue to act as if it truly believes that chapter VII of the charter can be used to enforce the rule of law.

Mr. President, I am far from confident that the amount of aid authorized in this legislation will prove to be sufficient. Estimates of the cost of caring for as many as 2 million refugees already range to 10 times this amount. But it is a beginning. I congratulate the administration on its decision to begin sending aid and I hope that it will embrace this measure as well.

Mr. President, in his very able, forceful remarks about the situation of the Kurdish refugees and others in Iraq and the bordering areas, the Senator from Tennessee, Mr. GORE, observed there will be new chapters of international law written in the course of our dealing with this issue.

As I am sure he will agree, and the thrust of his remarks implied, it is even so the case that we have an international law that applies today. It is that part of the Fourth Geneva Convention of 1949 which deals with the case of conflict of an internal nature.

The Geneva conventions, as the President knows, were basically treaties drawn up in the aftermath of the Second World War intended to codify as war crimes the behavior of the Nazi Government and others which were the subject of the Nuremberg tribunals, for example, following World War II.

These acts by Iraq are illegal under international law, as it exists today, as it has for the better part of half a century. I remind the President, and he does not need to be reminded of that, as a treaty the United States is bound to pursue this matter. We have signed that treaty and a treaty, under our Constitution, is the supreme law of the land. We have no more choice in this matter than with respect to pursuing enforcement of any law. It is not always possible that you will succeed, but that you should try, it seems to me, is beyond question.

It is a question that deeply involves the issue of what we have in mind when we speak of a New World order, because within years we have seen comparable events and we have chosen not to respond, given the statement in the U.N. Charter, specifically article 2, section 7, that events that are essentially within the domestic jurisdiction of a State are beyond the competence of the Security Council. We have chosen to simply ignore events which otherwise clearly command our response as in the case of the Iraqi troops which are now driving as many as 2 million Iraqi Kurds into internal or foreign exile.

Kurdistan is a large region that has had the unhappy experience, if that is the term, to exist on the general regional borders of the Arab world, the Persian world, and the world of Turkey, the Ottoman Empire of old. They will be found in all three of those countries, as left over from the borders drawn in the aftermath of the Treaty of Sevres, which ended the war between the allies and the Ottoman Empire.

I would make a point, Mr. President, that the United States in 1917 did not declare war on the Ottoman Empire. They did on Germany, and also Austro-Hungary, but not the Ottomans. As a consequence, we were not party to that treaty. We simply find ourselves involved in this latter period.

There can be no doubt, sir, that this present situation was to be foreseen, was foreseeable, and is simply unacceptable, surely, that a human convulsion of this order should pass by with mere pronouncements of concern and distress. It was the United States that took the lead with Britain in drawing up the Geneva Conventions of 1949. The Fourth Geneva Convention is relative to the protection of civilians in time of war. It absolutely prohibits attacks on civilians who are not taking part in a conflict.

And what prohibition extends even in the case, as I have said, to "armed conflict not of an international character." It applies explicitly, if you will, to situations such as the one with which we are dealing now, particularly because it is a situation that rises in the aftermath of an international conflict. In that conflict, the U.N. forces pursued a policy of following step by step the provisions of chapter VII of the charter. And it is now clear that we have an equal obligation to pursue the aftermath-which the regime in Iraq brought about-which would not have existed had there not been the U.N. response to the situation.

Mr. President, I would accordingly introduce for myself, Mr. D'AMATO, Mr. PELL, Mr. BRADLEY, Mr. GORE, Mr. DECONCINI, Mr. BINGAMAN, Mr. FORD, Mr. LIEBERMAN, Mr. WELLSTONE, Mr. LEVIN and Mr. SARBANES, a bill to amend the Foreign Assistance Act of 1961 to authorize the provision of medical supplies and other humanitarian assistance to the Kurdish peoples to alleviate suffering.

We act on humanitarian principles and on legal principles. We do not have an option to stand by. We are obliged under our laws. The Geneva Convention of 1949 is a treaty we have signed. Under the Constitution it is the supreme Law of the Land. And I cannot suppose that we will wish to fail in this matter.

I have already heard this afternoon the Senator from Vermont speak to the point; the Senator from Tennessee speak to the point. I have introduced a bill here which has 11 cosponsors on this first day of our return from the Easter recess, and we may hope that it is addressed in the very early part of next week.

I ask unanimous consent that the text of the bill be printed in the RECORD at this time.

There being no objection, the bill was ordered to be printed in the RECORD, as follows:

S786

Be it enacted by the Senate and House of Representatives of the United States of America in Congress assembled,

SECTION 1. KURDISH HUMANITARIAN RELIEF.-Chapter 9 of part I of the foreign Assistance Act of 1961 (relating to international disaster assistance) is amended by adding at the end thereof the following new section:

"SEC. 495L. KURDISH HUMANITARIAN RELIEF.-(a) The Congress recognizes that prompt United States assistance is desirable to help alleviate the suffering of the Kurdish people and other civilian refugees who have been attacked by Iraqi troops.

"(b)(1) The Administrator of the Agency for International Development shall-

"(A) furnish, in accordance with the authorities of this chapter, humanitarian assistance for the relief of the Kurdish people;

"(B) solicit private sector donations of humanitarian assistance for Kurdish and other refugees fleeing Iraq; and

"(C) cooperate with private relief agencies attempting to provide such humanitarian aid.

"(2) The Commander-in-Chief of the United States Transportation Command is authorized to provide all airlift and sealift necessary to transport such United States public and private donations of medical supplies on a regular basis.

"(c)(1) In addition to funds authorized to be appropriated to carry out this chapter, there are authorized to be appropriated by the President $50,000,000 to carry out subsections (b)(1) and (b)(2).

"(2) Funds appropriated pursuant to paragraph (1) are authorized to remain available until expended.

"(3) The authority contained in the Foreign Assistance Act of 1961 to transfer funds between accounts shall not apply with respect to funds appropriated pursuant to paragraph (1).

"(d) Assistance may be provided under this section notwithstanding any other provision of law.

"(e) The Congress urges the President to begin discussions with the nations surrounding Iraq as may be necessary regarding the importation of such humanitarian assistance.

"(f) Humanitarian assistance may also be provided under this section to civilian refugees in Saudi Arabia, Kuwait and the Allied occupied areas of southern Iraq.

"(g) For purposes of this section, the term 'humanitarian assistance'
includes but is not limited to-

"(1) oil, gas, and fuel;

"(2) water purification supplies, materials for immunization, and other materials needed to prevent the outbreak of contagious diseases and to safeguard public health;

"(3) medical supplies; and

"(4) food and clothing".

SEC. 2. Sense of the Congress Concerning the Iraqi Army's Attacks on Kurdish and other Iraqi Civilians.

It is the sense of the Congress that-

(a) The attacks upon civilians in Iraq constitute a violation of Article 3 of the Fourth Geneva Convention Relative to the Protection of Civilian Persons in Time of War of August 12, 1949;

(b) The attacks upon civilians in Iraq constitute a threat to peace and stability in the region; and

(c) The United States should request the Security Council of the United

Nations to take measures to prevent these attacks pursuant to Chapter VII of the United Nations Charter.

49.

[April 9, 1991 (Senate), pp. 4261-2]

HUMANITARIAN RELIEF FOR THE KURDS IS THE LEAST WE CAN DO

Mr. WELLSTONE. Mr. President, I thank the Senators from New York for their bill authorizing the provision of medical supplies and other humanitarian assistance to the Kurdish people and to Iraqis seeking refuge in the allied occupied zone. Their speedy effort to address a horrific situation is to be commended. I am pleased to join them on this legislation.

In reprisal for a short-lifed Kurdish uprising, Kurdish people are being driven from their homes and slaughtered wholesale by forces loyal to Saddam Hussein. Hundreds of thousands of Kurds-civilians and rebels alike-are desperately trying to escape Saddam Hussein's genocidal rampage. For the refugees massed at the Iraqi border, food is scarce, medicine unavailable, and fear and cold are pervasive.

This bill represents a first modest step, but it is an important step which will set U.S. policy on the right and moral path. The $50 million in humanitarian assistance authorized by this bill is the very least we can do. Unfortunately, $50 million won't go very far in meeting the needs of the refugees.

The United States, and the international community, did not react in the past when Saddam Hussein massacred Iraqi Kurds or violated basic human rights of the whole population. But this time the United States has a special responsibility and a special opportunity.

The United States actively encouraged the Kurds and the Shiites to rebel against Saddam Hussein. The United States bombing campaign-that, in the words of a U.N. report, pounded Iraq back into the preindustrial age-created the conditions for Iraq's collapse into internal war and chaos. During the early phases of the uprising, President Bush made much of the fact that the cease-fire forbade Hussein any military use of the Iraqi Air Force. He promised to shoot down any Iraqi aircraft used to attack the rebels.

But as the Kurdish and Shiite insurrections were brutally suppressed and the civilians populations slaughtered, the United States turned its back. As forces loyal to Hussein made extensive use of helicopter gunships to shell civilian populations, the United States stood by.

The reason offered by President Bush for our lack of response to Hussein's slaughter is that he does not want to intervene in Iraq's internal affairs. But we are already deeply involved. The United States extensively bombed the country, invaded it, killed 100,000 conscripts and thousands of civilians, and called on its people to overthrow its dictator. American forces now occupy 20 percent of Iraq, we control all of its airspace and we are proposing to regulate by fiat all their oil revenues and arms trade. We are deeply involved.

I am encouraged by the European Community and the United Nations' efforts to provide relief for the victims of Iraq's civil chaos. The European Community has pledged $180 million in assistance and the United Nations is going to appoint a senior diplomat as coordinator of a widespread humanitarian effort. Britain and other nations are proposing the establishment of a Kurdish enclave under international protection. I would hope that the United States would assume a leadership role in addressing this tragedy. But short of that, the United States can encourage these efforts with a generous pledge of U.S. aid and military troops for a multilateral peacekeeping force.

One of the reasons I opposed this war was that I feared the administrative had no strategy for achieving long-term political objectives in the Middle East. Indeed, I feared the administration had little conception of the potential political consequences of a war.

The bill proposed by Senator MOYNIHAN and D'AMATO will start to address these consequences. Finally, Mr. President, I want to on record expressing my concern that the funding provided in this bill will not put at risk existing refugee disaster assistance and relief funds.

50.

[April 10, 1991 (House), p. 2114]

THE TRAGIC SITUATION OF THE IRAQI KURDS

(Mr. KENNEDY asked and was given permission to address the House for 1 minute and to revise and extend his remarks.)

Mr. KENNEDY. Mr. Speaker, a crisis exists in which thousands of Iraqi Kurds could die of starvation and disease almost immediately. It is a tragic situation that was clearly avoidable.

The United States bears much of the blame for what has happened to these innocent people. We set the stage for the overthrow of Saddam Hussein, but failed to deliver once these brave men and women rose to the challenge. As a result, some estimate that at least 30,000 civilians may have perished at the hands of Saddam's war machine.

To many Americans, this is an unacceptable conclusion to a war that was fought on behalf of human rights and freedom. By failing to reply to their cries for help, a moral wrong was done. Now we must take responsibility to correct it.

A safe haven must be established to protect these persecuted people—adequate relief must be provided to stop the children and elderly from dying—and Saddam Hussein must be made to understand that this brutality will be challenged wherever it exists—both inside and outside Iraq.

Unless we face this human tragedy now, we risk witnessing a modern holocaust. Unless we act on this moral disgrace at once, people a hundred years from now, will be talking about a new film entitled "Dances With Kurds."

We are now in a position to influence events in the Middle East—let us not waste this opportunity—let us save the real victims of this war.

51.

[April 10, 1991 (House), p. 2115]

INTRODUCTION OF LEGISLATION APPROPRIATING $150 MILLION FOR KURDISH AND SHIITE REFUGEES

(Mr. DICKS asked and was given permission to address the House for 1 minute and to revise and extend his remarks.)

Mr. DICKS. Mr. Speaker, I am introducing legislation today that authorizes and appropriates $150 million in emergency humanitarian funds for Kurdish and Shiite refugees escaping from Iraq.

As all of you surely know, more than a million Kurds and Shiites are fleeing the genocidal persecution of the Iraqi Army. Women, children, and the elderly continue to be the target of Saddam Hussein's ruthless campaign against these populations. Those fortunate enough to escape violent death, now face starvation, freezing temperatures, and disease. Because of the primitive environment, it is impossible to know how many refugees are currently seeking protection in the mountain passes of northern and eastern Iraq, but the need for humanitarian aid is critical. Two

days ago, Secretary of State Baker received a firsthand look of the horrific living conditions the refugees must endure. Clearly, the living conditions and the pleas of its inhabitants were extremely dishearting to the Secretary as they are to all of us here in this chamber. I believe former Prime Minister Margaret Thatcher was correct when she said:

It should not be beyond the wit of man to get planes there with tents, food, and warm blankets. It's not a question of legal niceties. We should do it now.

It is important to note that Britain has already pledged $40 million to help the refugees. This legislation allows the President to demonstrate the sympathy of the American people, as well as our flexibility to act quickly before the refugee conditions decay further. It provides a total of $150 million-immediately-to the President to use as the U.S. contribution to the international relief effort. We cannot hesitate another day, the lives of thousands depend on this Government to take action, and I urge your support for this measure.

52.

[April 10, 1991 (House), p. 2127]

WHERE IS THE UNITED STATES IN THE MIDDLE EAST?

The SPEAKER pro tempore. Under a previous order of the House, the gentleman from Ohio [Mr. McEwen] is recognized for 5 minutes.

Mr. McEWEN. Mr. Speaker, I ask the question: Where is the United States since January and February? Since the Congress went into session a little over an hour ago, over a thousand people have died, Kurdish refugees trying to avoid helicopter gunships under the control of Saddam Hussein.

America stood against that 30 days ago, and yet we have the capacity to stop it and are not doing it. We have on location, in sight, enough water, bottled water for 500,000 troops. We have enough food for 500,000 troops. We have enough medical supplies for

500,000 troops. We have blankets, we have tents, we have transportation. We have the C-130's. We have the maps in the helicopters and in the cockpits and we have the pilots. We have the capacity to take those supplies to them, and I do not know why we are not.

Three weeks ago they were chanting, "God bless George Bush." We encouraged them to stand firm and to assert their independence. We encouraged them to stand against the miserable tyrant, Saddam Hussein, and I do not know where we are.

Pilots and soldiers coming back for their parades at home break down in tears about seeing those poor refugees being gunned down in their sights, and they can do nothing. The euphoria of 3 weeks ago is being wiped out by a policy that I am at a loss to understand. I would encourage the Chairman of the Joint Chiefs of Staff to reassess what we are and what we are standing for, the lack of leadership that the United States is exerting today. The leadership that George Bush exerted from August 2 to March 3 is unprecedented in history. I submit there is not another person on this planet who could have held the coalition of forces, from Syria to Israel, from the Soviet Union to China to stand together against tyranny in the Middle East. George Bush and the United States had a bright and shining moment.

Now, in this lack of action by our country, we see the Prime Minister of Britain stepping forth, we see the President of France stepping forth, five flights yesterday by the French. We see the Foreign Ministers of all of the European nations speaking this morning about starting refugee aid and efforts.

The United States is standing idly by and I do not understand why. I call upon our Nation to take those supplies that are there, those soldiers who wish to deliver them. I am not calling for troops. I do not want to instigate a war. I have no desire to send troops. I have no desire to take American marines and drop them between Sunnis and Shiites and Kurds.

I simply am saying that Saddam Hussein is in his bunker. We should have been allowed the additional 12 hours to finish him, but that is history. He is there, and we control the air. If we allow them to use the air to do that, then we are culpable. It is our airspace, and it will be for a year. We should say to Saddam Hussein, park your helicopters, read my lips, do not fly again, and do not shoot those people. Then what I think we should do is to take those blankets, and those tents, and that food, and those medical supplies and that water and drop them to those dear people who are sitting there with their children dying of starvation, a thousand an hour every day as we speak. Unless someone can give me a reason why we should not, then we should have done it yesterday.

53.

[April 10, 1991 (Extension of Remarks), p. 1176]

**URGENT ASSISTANCE NEEDED FOR IRAQI REFUGEES
HON. BILL GREEN
OF NEW YORK
IN THE HOUSE OF REPRESENTATIVES**

Wednesday, April 10, 1991

Mr. GREEN of New York. Mr. Speaker, I want to express my deep concern at the failure of the United States to restrain Iraq from indiscriminate attacks on noncombatants in both the Shiite and Kurdish regions of Iraq. I support the President's decision to shoot down Iraqi fixed-wing military aircraft, and I believe it would be wise to extend that policy to include helicopters. As the United States troops begin moving out of positions in southern Iraq, many civilians there fear a new wave of slaughter by Saddam Hussein's regime.

We can be proud that through United States strength and resolve we accomplished what we set out to accomplish in the Persian Gulf with respect to Kuwait. But that does not absolve us from the responsibility to speak out and act about our other concerns in the region. The international community that supported Iraq's ouster from Kuwait must now stand united in ensuring that the hundreds of thousands of Iraqi Kurds, Shi'as, and others fleeing Iraq are not turned back to face Saddam Hussein's torture. The Iraqi leader's gruesome legacy of dealing with dissenters reminds us all that the refugees need international protection.

Although it may be too little, too late, the United States, individually and through the United Nations, must act swiftly to do everything it can to assist all refugees with urgently needed humanitarian assistance. Massive assistance is needed to prevent large numbers of refugees from dying, and it must be undertaken with urgency. Estimates are that at least a million people have massed on the borders in just a few days. The Governments of Turkey and Iran will need enormous support from the international community in responding to the overwhelming refugee crisis, and I appeal to President Ozal of Turkey to keep his nation's borders open to the refugees.

54.

[April 11, 1991 (House), p. 2144]

NO TIME TO WASH OUR HANDS OF THE KURDS

(Mr. GLICKMAN asked and was given permission to address the House for 1 minute and to revise and extend his remarks.)

Mr. GLICKMAN. Mr. Speaker, the national news last night was a dark reminder of the terror and tragedy that is the aftermath of Iraq's invasion of Kuwait.

While we negotiate a cease-fire and request hostilities against the Kurds cease, while humanitarian aid arrives on Iraq's borders in a fashion far less efficient than sending thousands of troops to that area, while all this happens, children are dying in their parents' arms.

It was Edmund Burke who said, "The only thing necessary for triumph of evil is for good men to do nothing." I suppose something is being done, but like so many who have read and seen the horrors perpetuated against a people, we would paraphrase Burke and say, "The only thing necessary for the triumph of evil is for men and women to do too little, too late."

The Kurds are apparently not a priority on this administration's agenda. I am not certain what we should do. I am certain something dramatic must be done or we will see the extinction of a religious minority in that part of the Middle East.

The killing of people because of their religion is not new to this world. The slaughter of innocents is not new to history. Evil is not new.

Surely we can act in some way to alter the course of this horror. Surely, Mr. President, you can give the same organization and commitment to saving the Kurds that we gave to saving Kuwait.

55.

[April 11, 1991 (Senate), pp. 4298-301]

SUPPORT FOR CRANSTON-MOYNIHAN WAR CRIMES BILL GROWS

Mr. CRANSTON. Mr. President, the scenes of horror and human suffering emanating from Iraq have served as a fresh reminder-as if any were needed-of why the comparison of Saddam Hussein to Hitler was an apt one.

The plight of the Kurds has shown us the extent to which President Bush's call for a new world order has been ignored by the White House itself.

The hope offered by the administration's apparent promise of international order through strict observance of international law has foundered on the shoals of a geostrategic view of the world divorced from our own best instincts as a people.

The policy, noted David S. Broder in yesterday's *Washington Post*, shows "something of the character of this President, who has demonstrated over and over again that he is ready to 'rise above principle' when it collides with power realities."

Fortunately this policy of calculated callousness has been met with cries of outrage from our colleagues, Democrat and Republican alike. Half a million men and women from our Armed Forces did not risk everything in the Persian Gulf to restore the Kuwaiti monarchy.

Nor was their sacrifice made so that they could now sit idly by as Saddam's military henchmen-whose troops broke ranks and surrendered by the tens of thousands when confronted by a real army-turn their vengeance on innocent old people, women, and children in Basra, Kurdistan, and scores of forgotten towns that are known to us now only because of their suffering.

Mr. President, it is clear that Congress must make itself heard to ensure that that moment of unity and sense of higher national purpose that characterized our battlefield victory over Saddam is not lost to us now.

On Tuesday, my good friend and distinguished colleague, the Senator from Rhode Island [Mr. PELL], took an important step in this direction by convening a hearing in the Foreign Relations Committee he ably heads, to look at the issue of war crimes.

Perhaps the administration was too busy denying its own role in encouraging the Kurdish rebellion, then leaving these valiant partisans twisting slowly in the wind, to have sent a representative to the hearing. Or perhaps someone over at Foggy Bottom remembered President Bush's March 7 address to the joint session of Congress, where he declared that:

It's time to put an end to micromanagement of foreign and security assistance programs, micromanagement that humiliates our friends and allies and hamstrings our diplomacy.

Whatever the case, there were no administration witnesses; they were, apparently, speechless. Instead the committee was treated to the wise and eloquent words of Nobel Laureate Elie Weisel, as well as to the well-informed counsel of two international legal scholars, Robert Woetzel, president of the Foundation for the Establishment of an International Criminal Court, and Anthony D'AMATO, international law professor at Northwestern University.

One of the bills which was discussed was the Cranston-Moynihan War Crimes Prevention Education Act of 1991.

Our bill would cut off all foreign assistance except for humanitarian aid to any government that commits gross violations of international standards governing the conduct of armed conflict. I realize that this bill does not cover all the situations foreseen in the Geneva Conventions, only those involving situations of armed conflict, but this, of course, is what we are concerned with today.

The bill also does something more. It would make American security assistance conditional on the recipient governments teaching the Geneva Conventions and other relevant rules of war to all its military personnel.

According to Dr. D'AMATO, the Cranston-Moynihan bill "supplies an important missing element to the very progressive legislation on the books prohibiting assistance for countries that violate fundamental human rights."

In a similar vein, I would like to point out that the Cranston-Moynihan bill has been endorsed by two prestigious human rights groups, the Human Rights Watch and the Washington Office on Latin America.

In a letter to my office, Kenneth Roth, deputy director of the Human Rights Watch, said that our war crimes bill is viewed by his office "as an important effort to ensure that the United States does not, through the provision of foreign assistance, become a party to systematic violations of international humanitarian law, or the laws of war."

The State Department, he noted, "has implicitly recognized the importance of guiding U.S. foreign policy not only by reference to international human rights law but also by reference to international humanitarian law when, 2 years ago, it began including a section on violations of the laws of war in its annual Country Reports on Human Rights Practices. However, no comparable change has been made in the legislation guiding U.S. foreign assistance."

Mr. President, once again I urge my colleagues to reaffirm our commitment to an international order based on international law by supporting the Cranston-Moynihan bill.

I ask unanimous consent that a statement of mine that was entered into the record of the Foreign Relations Committee hearing Tuesday be now entered into the RECORD. I also ask that the letters of support I have received from the Human Rights Watch and the Washington Office on Latin America, together with a paper on war crimes written by American University legal scholar Robert K. Goldman, be entered into the RECORD as well.

There being no objection, the material was ordered to be printed in the RECORD, as follows:

STATEMENT ON WAR CRIMES, U.S. SENATOR ALAN CRANSTON, SENATE FOREIGN RELATIONS COMMITTEE, APRIL 9, 1991

The brutal suppression of anti-regime insurgents in Iraq and Kuwaiti reprisals against Palestinians and other foreigners in the wake of the allied victory show that the issue of war crimes-and what to do about them-is not going away.

The terrible reports of criminal brutality against Kurdish civilians and Shiite dissidents in Iraq, in particular, show that more concerted efforts by nations are needed if the 1949 Geneva Conventions are going to work.

The current campaign by the Butcher of Baghdad against Kurdish freedom fighters is only the latest in a string of outrages committed by Saddam against both international standards of decency and the rules of the conduct of warfare.

Today's civilian massacres, a specter of evil in and of themselves, are also an indictment of earlier failures to deal forcefully and convincingly with Saddam's brutality.

Both before and after Iraq's invasion of Kuwait last year, Saddam Hussein oversaw the massive violation of all civilized conduct regarding warfare.

The use of weapons of mass destruction against both Iraqi Kurds and against Iranian combatants; the rape of Kuwait and the unprovoked Scud attacks against Israel's civilian population; the abuse of American and other allied POW's-all these acts of barbarism reaffirmed the need for a new resolve in dealing with war crimes.

The general purpose of the Geneva Conventions and other rules concerning the conduct of warfare is to persuade nations that they should, in times of war, avoid certain inhumane acts while ensuring the performance of other fundamental guarantees.

The four Geneva conventions provide for the protection of the sick and wounded on land, the protection of the sick and wounded at sea and of those who become shipwrecked, the treatment of prisoners of war, and the protection of civilians in times of war.

Currently U.S. aid is conditioned on a country's respect for human rights and its nonsponsorship of terrorism.

There is, however, a gaping hole in our foreign assistance legislation. There are no explicit provisions for a cutoff of assistance for those countries which commit war crimes.

Last month I introduced, together with Senator Daniel Patrick Moynihan, a bill-the "War Crimes Prevention Education Act"-that would plug this gap.

My bill would cut off all foreign assistance except for humanitarian aid to any government that commits gross violations of international standards governing the conduct of armed conflict.

The bill would also make American security assistance conditional on the recipient governments teaching the Geneva conventions and other relevant rules of war to all its military personnel.

They should be warned that orders by superiors to violate those rules are illegal and should be disobeyed. Following orders is no defense against war crimes.

As American University legal scholar Robert K. Goldman has noted, just as human rights legislation seeks to avoid this country's identification with governments that grossly violate internationally recognized human rights, the Cranston-Moynihan bill distances the United States from governments whose armed forces grossly violate fundamental guarantees of international humanitarian law.

The Gulf War should have taught us the lesson that the old idea-that "the enemy of my enemy is my friend"-is a false standard upon which to base our foreign policy. it was part of our Cold War strategy, and it didn't work very well then either.

Because Saddam was the enemy of our enemy, Iran, in the 1980s, we helped him help himself to our technology, our financial credits and even our intelligence.

Had the Cranston-Moynihan war crimes bill been law then, we would have stopped aiding in the 1980s a country we went to war against in 1991.

We would have disassociated America's good name and international standing from Iraq at a time when the Kurds and the Iranians were slaughtered by Saddam's weapons of mass destruction.

And it would have served as a signal that not only does the United States expect compliance with the Geneva Conventions governing armed conflict by our own troops, but also by those receiving our security assistance.

Just how seriously we take war crimes, however, is not just a matter of legislation. it also requires leadership.

The brave partisans in the mountains of Kurdistan and in the streets of Basra deserved better than they received from us.

Under the 1949 Geneva Conventions we are responsible, as a party to this conflict, to assure that the victims of the conflict are treated humanely and cared for to the best of our ability.

That is an international legal responsibility, I fear, that the U.S. government has not adequately met, particularly in the case of the Kurds and other ethnic rivals to Saddam.

One is left with the impression that the events of the last weeks is nothing less than a sad repetition of those in Budapest in 1956.

Only a few short weeks ago we and our allies were talking about bringing Saddam up on war crimes charges.

Now the question seems to be shifting to: Can we deal with an Iraqi Government still led by Saddam and his military henchmen?-with the implication being that the answer might be, yes.

The answer in keeping with our best selves and with our own outrage about war crimes should be, no.

———

HUMAN RIGHTS WATCH,
Washington, DC, April 9, 1991.
Hon. ALAN CRANSTON,
U.S. Senate,
Washington, DC . . .

56.

[April 11, 1991 (Senate), pp. 4320-22]

WHAT HAPPENED TO PRINCIPLES?

Mr. DECONCINI. Madam President, the war in the Persian Gulf has been won, yet Hitler remains in power. That is the situation we find ourselves in today in Iraq. To compound the moral dilemma, as A.M. Rosenthal wrote in the *New York Times* last week, "They are killing the Jews again. This time the slaughter, the torture and the forced marches to death are taking place in Iraq and the killers have different names for the Jews. They call them Kurds and Shiites as they spit in their faces and tear the beards of men and throw the women down for rape, before the day's killing."

I did not vote to authorize force after the lengthy and I thought deliberate debate in the Senate. At the time, I believed in the merit of the argument that sanctions had not yet had time to work. Also, it was not clear to this Senator whether the war would guarantee the removal of Saddam and a clean end to the despotic rule he has imposed in that part of the world. Yet, once the President committed U.S. forces to offensive action, I wholeheartedly supported the troops and the President's policy. As a member of the Defense Appropriations Subcommittee, I strongly supported the necessary funding requests for our forces to get the job done. President Bush and the brave, well-trained American servicemen and women earned a brilliant military victory in the Persian Gulf. Kuwait has been liberated. Iraq has apparently pledged to accept the United Nations' imposed cease-fire with its stiff terms. Yet it appears that this victory may be a hollow one. The job is not yet done.

President Bush spoke eloquently before and during the war about the need for a "new world order." He correctly framed the debate in terms of moral principles, not oil. He described our objectives in the region as the liberation of Kuwait and the pursuit of freedom from Iraq's tyrannical violation of international law which that country had imposed on others. These principles, he argued, are the ones under which our Nation was founded and in which the American people believe.

President Bush also called upon the people of Iraq-all of the people-to remove Saddam Hussein, their modern-day Hitler, from power. On February 15, in a speech at the Raytheon Missile Systems Plant, President Bush called upon "the Iraqi military and the Iraqi people to take matters into their own hands to force Saddam Hussein, the dictator, to step aside and to comply with the United Nations resolutions." Yet, when the Iraqi people heeded his call, President Bush acted like Ronald Reagan walking away from a helicopter. He cupped his hand to his ear and mouthed the words, "I can't hear you."

The man who called for ending Iraq's aggression on moral grounds became blind, deaf, and dumb. He became blind to the sight of thousands of women and children stumbling into American hospitals after being attacked by Iraqi forces. He became deaf to the cries from the Kurds for assistance in their attempts to topple Saddam. And he became dumb when the world began to ask why a nation so eager to go to war to end one aggression was so slow to respond to another aggression-from the same regime.

The media has speculated that the President and his intelligence advisors had counseled the Kurds into planning military action against Saddam. This is not beyond the realm of possibility. In the mid-1970's, the CIA provided arms to another group of Kurds in Iraq to fight Saddam. An article in the *Washington Post* details the establishment of clandestine radio broadcasts into Iraq after the invasion of Kuwait compelling the people, including Kurds and Shiites, to rebel.

Regardless of actual contacts between the Bush administration and the Kurdish rebels.

This intrepid brand of Iraq Kurds and others were inspired by the President's words, our President's words. These long-suffering people proved their worth in battle and made significant progress in just a few weeks' time. They took advantage of the chaos among Saddam's Republican Guards and captured key cities, Kirkuk and Irbil. They also asked for our assistance, any kind of assistance. The request fell again on deaf ears.

In reality the rug was pulled from under them by an administration which only weeks earlier had implicitly rallied them to arms to overthrow Saddam Hussein.

I understand the concerns that by supporting the Kurdish rebels we would be dragged into another Vietnam-type situation. There are creative methods and channels however to assist rebels and others opposed to Saddam Hussein without committing U.S. forces. We apparently provided the Kurds with arms in 1975. After the cessation of hostilities last month we could have turned over to the rebels captured Iraqi equipment. We could have provided air cover for the rebels to prevent Iraqi troops from using their helicopters against them.

After all, Iraq violated its vows to use its helicopters solely for transporting government officials and supplies. It used them as gunships against their own people. Even General Schwarzkopf admitted that he was suckered by the Iraqis on this particular issue. We therefore should not feel constrained from responding.

It also has been reported that the Kurdish leadership officially requested the Bush administration to allow its volunteers to fly captured Iraqi Mig's. I am not aware that this request has been acknowledged even as of today.

All that is required is some creative planning on our part. But this planning has not taken place even as of today. In fact, the administration even ignored the initial pleas for help from the refugees facing genocide who fled to the borders of Iran and Turkey, and who are being slaughtered by helicopter gunships manned by Saddam's elite forces.

But it was the French and the British who raised the issue in the United Nations, not our own Government. It is also the British who are now calling for an area of Kurdish autonomy and safe haven in northern Iraq. We may get dragged into finally supporting that. Is not it long overdue?

Where is the leadership that we once had in successfully prosecuting a war, bringing it to a conclusion, and extracting and forcing the

Iraqi military from Kuwait? Where is the U.S. leadership?

We were great in leading the war. Indeed we were. But what about U.S. leadership on peace?

This was a war about principles. We went to the United Nations and we argued our cause on the basis of these salient beliefs. Why then does the administration not raise the principle of human rights at the United Nations when Saddam is committing genocide on his own people? Is this yet another example of the Bush administration making policy as it goes along?

It seems to me it cannot be the logical conclusion. The Iraqi troops were in their elements, shooting and gassing fellow Iraqis who happened to be Kurds or Shiites. These are the same brave troops who crumbled and fled under the lightning attack of the U.S. forces in the international coalition. These feared Republican Guards are quick to use phosphate weapons against helpless women and children. It is easy to win when you shoot your target in the back.

Instead of the ounce of prevention which President Bush could have offered the Kurds in their fight against Saddam Hussein he seems to have settled for a pound of cure. He has suggested a little more than $10 million in refugee assistance for these estimated half-a-million Kurdish and other refugees. But this is just a down payment on the hundreds of millions of relief dollars which will be needed.

Just 2 years ago Senator BYRD and I were successful in having $5 million appropriated for the Kurdish refugees who fled into southern Turkey from Saddam Hussein's last chemical attack. While Congress and the State Department heeded the Turkish Government's call for aid to the refugees, the Turkish Government unfortunately refused to allow this and other international assistance to be distributed to the refugees.

The money President Bush now offers is a Band-Aid approach to a problem which requires major surgery. In what could have been a defining moment in U.S. history, the Bush administration has returned to its old practice of developing foreign policy as it goes along.

A couple of days ago Secretary Baker flew to the Turkey-Iraq border to witness the refugee problem firsthand, and I am glad he did so. I congratulate him on going there and seeing these people as I have seen in the refugee camps in eastern Turkey of Kurdish refugees who have been gassed and run out of their own country. I congratulate him for doing it.

I was there. I saw it, and I know what he saw. And it absolutely shakes you to the marrow of your bones.

I am convinced that this trip of Secretary Baker was a last-minute addition to a schedule because of the pressure the administration has been receiving on this particular issue. If the administration has demonstrated a little foresight and planning perhaps we would not be facing this horrendous refugee problem. But the problem is real. It must be confronted forcefully. Once again it is the case of too little too late because the administration is constructing its foreign policy on an as-it-goes basis and not with any foresight and long-term planning.

I am truly outraged. I encourage the Bush administration in the strongest possible terms to tell Saddam Hussein to end his genocide of his own people within a specified timeframe or face removal by U.S. forces if necessary. This action can be justified. U.N. Resolution 678 authorizes the use of "all necessary means to restore international peace and security in the area."

Saddam Hussein's continued brutal attacks against the Shiites, Kurds, and other opposition forces are preventing peace from coming to this region. His actions force the United States and other coalition members to maintain a military presence in the area. Also opportunistic forces from Iran and Syria are taking advantage of the turmoil within Iraq to improve their own international standards, and in the long term this does not bode well for regional international peace and security, which was our goal in the first place.

Our troops are already in Iraq. The argument is that you cannot meddle with the internal affairs of a country. We are already there. We are inside that country with a sizable military force. It is not like we are on the outside suggesting that we invade, or we go in. We are already there.

They have told reporters that they feel powerless and frustrated-our own troops as they watch the Republican Guard forces fire tank rounds into hospitals and shell hundreds of civilians in refugee camps who huddle in the ditches and alongside the road. This is what our troops who are there in Iraq, not outside, are telling the news media and the American people.

A U.S. Army captain from Toledo was quoted in the *Washington Post* on March 31 saying that an 18-month-old girl was "shot with a pistol in her chest," up close enough so the powder burn could still be seen.

Another soldier expressed his frustration by saying "There isn't a soldier here who does not want to finish it. They hate this." S. Sgt. Jonathan Santy talked about the Iraqi citizens he had met who were fleeing their country and he voiced his concern that "If Saddam Hussein remains in power these people will truly be destroyed. I do not see Saddam letting these people live and continue and come back to the country. Does anybody?" In essence, our troops feel that they are prevented from completing the job they were sent to do, a job that they did very well.

If the President refuses to issue this ultimatum to Saddam Hussein, then he must fully explain to the American people and to the world the administration's policy and future goals for this region. Where is that new world order?

What is the President's vision for this region of the world? Do we have a blueprint for the future, or even a road map to indicate the direction we are going? Can President Bush look the United States soldier currently in the buffer zone in southern Iraq in the eye and justify his lack of action? Can he congratulate these men and women for fighting the good fight in January and February only to allow Saddam Hussein to gas his own people, commit genocide, and ruthlessly remain in power in March and April of the same year?

I also urge President Bush, at the very least, to use his authority to ensure the broader issue of the Kurdish human rights and self-determination is made an integral part of the regional peace talks. The Kurdish people must not be forgotten once again, as they have been in the past.

In fact, President Bush could expand upon the concept of a safe haven in northern Iraq. He could call upon the United Nations to establish an independent semiautonomous Kurdish entity in this region. This area, whose security could be guaranteed by U.N. forces, would provide a homeland for the Kurds and a sanctuary for a people which have known only suffering and animosity through almost all of their history.

It also would ease the crush of refugees currently crossing the border into Turkey and Iran. This would do that if they had a safe haven, one that was going to be backed up by the United Nations and the United States, if necessary. It would be a costly effort but, again, a principle that this country could stand tall, as we did in the end of February when this war came to a conclusion at that time.

I recognize that taking this step would cause considerable concern within the Turkish Government and others in the region. But again, this is a moral issue. It must be raised with our friends as well as our adversaries.

In the end, human rights must be respected. The United States can stand tall, and does stand tall, in the world because it has never relented on talking about human rights, particularly in Eastern Europe and the Soviet Union.

Where are we when it comes to human rights in the Middle East? In our beliefs as Americans, we need a vision and leadership, and we need that leadership and vision to include human rights.

Madam President, if you do not do this, we send the dangerous signal to Saddam Hussein that it is once again business as usual in the Middle East, that human rights only apply in Europe, or in other areas, but not here. We won a war on a principle, and even maybe human rights was discussed during those debates. But now that the war was won, and the Iraqis are out of Kuwait, where is the human rights issue now? Not to be discussed. Not to be impressed by the President of the United States. Not to be a fundamental moral principle, once again, as it relates to dealing with Saddam Hussein.

We tell those who are oppressed in the rest of the world that the United States lacked the backbone to resolve the tough issues which cannot be easily resolved at the end of a gun. We say human rights one day, yes; but the next day, no. Human rights as to the Kuwaitis so that they can have their country back? Absolutely.

This Congress supported the President unanimously in his action, once he took that action. And yet, that "Hitler," Saddam Hussein, is still in power. Where is the human rights principle now, as it should be applied against him? We are losing more than we know by not finishing the job. It is one thing to win the military war; it is something else to lose the peace.

Mr. D'AMATO addressed the Chair.

The PRESIDING OFFICER. The Senator from New York is recognized.

57.

[April 11, 1991 (Senate), p. 4323]

U.S. HUMANITARIAN AID TO IRAQI REFUGEES

Mr. BINGAMAN. Madam President, we have watched over the last week as the plight of the Kurdish refugees from Iraq has gone from bad to worse. Questions of whether we should have continued military action with Desert Storm longer than we did, or whether we should have denied Iraqi forces the use of the air against the Kurdish, will only be answered by history. However, we can, here, today, answer the question of whether the United States bears some responsibility for the Kurdish refugees. We do bear the responsibility of aiding these people, of doing what we can to ensure that they are not starving, and not freezing to death, or dying of disease due to the conditions of the camps along the border.

We bear that responsibility not only because of what we did in the Persian Gulf but because of why we did it. Because it is here, in the faces of these men, women, and children living in terrible conditions along a desolate border, where the new world order really begins. We flexed our muscles and showed the world that aggression will not be tolerated. Now we need to open our hearts and show the world that we will fulfill our responsibilities in peacetime as well as in war. It is past time that the United States lift its full part to aid these refugees and begin providing humanitarian aid with the same enthusiasm with which we provided military aid.

Madam President, by March 27 Iraqi forces had defeated the Shiite rebels in the south and begun attacks against Kurds in the north. By April 1 the Kurdish rebels had been forced into retreat. On April 5 the United Nations adopted Resolution 688 calling upon Iraq to stop its attacks against Kurds and seek a dialog with the rebels, the same day that the first of the refugees began crossing the Turkish border. The trickle of refugees during the first few days of April quickly became a flood; yet little was done to assist them.

As of last Monday, April 8, Turkey and a handful of other countries had provided $67 million in aid to the refugees, which presumably included the $11 million in aid President Bush proposed on April 5. On April 8 Secretary of State Baker saw firsthand the terrible conditions in which the refugees are living; at the same time an assistant to the U.N. High Commissioner for Refugees was describing the U.N. relief efforts to that point to be totally inadequate. The European Community responded by immediately pledging $180 million in aid.

The United States, also, has undertaken a relief effort over the last 2 days. The U.S. Air Force has been active in air dropping supplies provided by the international relief effort, and efforts are under way to identify more supplies that could be gathered and air dropped to the refugees. The United States is responding to the plight of the Kurds, but it is late, and it is simply not enough. A reported 1.5 million Kurdish refugees have entered or are trying to enter Turkey and Iran. As the numbers swell, the U.N. relief effort remains inadequate, and the U.S. response continues to be dwarfed by the magnitude of the suffering.

Madam President, if the United States can mount an international effort to oust Saddam

Hussein from Kuwait, surely we can mount an international effort to provide food and shelter to helpless refugees. We can help these people, and we must help these people, but to do that requires leadership, a leadership that we have not seen from the administration. We must lead by example, as we did in Desert Shield and Desert Storm. An immediate, large-scale effort to provide aid must begin now. We must begin now to bring the international community together to focus on the plight of the refugees, just as we brought the international community together to focus on the plight of the Kuwaitis.

This is where the new world order begins, Madam President. The international community reacting to a threat, as it did to Saddam, is one thing. The international community reacting to fellow humans who are suffering is another. I hope that we will react with as much unity and sense of purpose as we did in Desert Storm. And I urge President Bush to provide the leadership.

58.

[April 11, 1991 (Senate); p. 4324]

SADDAM HUSSEIN'S GENOCIDE

Mr. D'AMATO. Madam President, today we have a beautiful memorial in the Capitol rotunda. It was a memorial to the 6-million people who lost their lives in the Holocaust. There were sentiments expressed of the fact that we will never forget. As part and parcel of that, it seems to me, are interwoven certainly an expression of our outrage and our shared outrage and our shared commitment to see that this kind of genocide, that was forgotten that somehow people looked the other way while it was taking place, never take place again regardless of to whom or to what group.

Madam President, I have to say to you I am shocked, I am appalled, I have a difficult time understanding how it is that this Nation and the world community indeed sits back again and allows genocide to take place, allows Saddam's killing machine to kill people,

women, children, civilians, because they may be Shiites or because they are Kurds, because they are sympathetic to those who seek to break the shackles of oppression.

The world inaction today takes on even more ominous terms because there can be no excuse. People cannot claim that they do not see it or they did not know. It is happening. It is taking place.

So that beautiful memorial and all the memorials and tributes that we give in the name of those whose lives have been snuffed out really become empty rhetoric as long as we fail to deal with Saddam Hussein.

I am not going to get into the particulars of whether or not there should be an enclave to represent sanctuary for innocent women and children.

It seems to this Senator, though, that that would be a rather modest thing. It seems to me that the great power that the allies have in that region certainly could be used to stop the killing machine, and that he and his generals should be told quite clearly: If you are going to use your power against innocent civilians, we will crush that power. That is the voice of righteousness and the action of righteousness, not a lost of biased, sanctified prayers without backing them up with action.

How dare we talk about we are going to hold the memory of whoever has been oppressed in the Holocaust or in any other genocide dear and sacred, and we will never forget, when that is exactly what we are doing. Well, we are doing it in a much more despicable way because we turn our back on that which we see on our own TV screens.

Yes, the world may have claimed 50 years ago: We had no knowledge; we did not know. We never had any idea. Well, do we have any idea now? Do we make ourselves feel better because we are going to send $10 million or $20 million or $30 million or 50 million dollars' worth of humanitarian aid? Do we make ourselves feel better, and say: Who knows; we might have somebody who is even worse then Saddam Hussein.

I have reporters tell me, "Well, Senator; my gosh. Who will take his place?" Is that a reason not to deal with evil; not to crush him;

not to stand up for those who are being oppressed?

Madam President, while we like to say how appalled and shocked we are, and we commit ourselves that never again will we allow this to take place, I suggest that all of us have a great deal of work to do to see to that that becomes a reality rather than empty rhetoric.

I yield the floor.

The PRESIDING OFFICER. The Senator from Vermont is recognized.

Mr. JEFFORDS. I thank the Chair.

(The remarks of Mr. Jeffords pertaining to the introduction of S. 812 are located in today's Record under "Statements on Introduced Bills and Joint Resolutions.")

Mr. JEFFORDS. Madam President, I yield the floor.

I suggest the absence of a quorum.

The PRESIDING OFFICER. The clerk will call the roll.

The assistant legislative clerk proceeded to call the roll.

Mr. MOYNIHAN. Madam President, I ask unanimous consent that the order for the quorum call be rescinded.

The PRESIDING OFFICER. Without objection, it is so ordered.

59.

[April 11, 1991 (Senate), pp. 4325-7]

PROTECTION OF REFUGEES IN IRAQ-SENATE—RESOLUTION 99

Mr. MOYNIHAN. Mr. President, for myself and Mr. D'AMATO and others, I send to the desk a sense-of-the-Senate resolution. There are 15 Senators who joined in an earlier resolution concerning the plight of the Kurds which I submitted on Tuesday: My distinguished colleague and friend from New York;

Senator PELL, the distinguished chairman of the Foreign Relations Committee; and Senators BRADLEY, GORE, DECONCINI, BINGAMAN, FORD, LIEBERMAN, WELLSTONE, LEVIN, SARBANES, INOUYE, JEFFORDS, and KERRY.

Today I rise to introduce another resolution concerning this crisis. This resolution simply states that with respect to the situation that is developing in Iraq with the Iraqi Kurdish refugees in the northern part of the nation, it is the sense of the Senate that we support action of our Government in supporting the recent resolutions of the Security Council. The Security Council has called upon the Iraqi Government to cease its extraordinarily brutal treatment of Kurdish refugees in Iraq at this time.

I would make one point-I ask the distinguished Republican leader if he would hear me on this, and I am sure he would agree with me-that the United States in supporting the Security Council resolution, which I believe was introduced by the French, called for a halt to these attacks. We are all aware that the attacks violate article 3, "Common Article 3" as it is called, of the Fourth Geneva Convention of 1949, and that is the convention relative to the protection of civilians in time of war. Each of the four Geneva Conventions has the same article 3. It is specifically provided that the absolute prohibition upon attacking persons "taking no part in hostilities" applies even in the case of a civil war. And this is a treaty of which Iraq is a part, of which we are a part.

It was our initiative, and it arises out of the Nuremberg Tribunals. As a treaty this is the supreme law of the land, and we must congratulate the President and his administration for taking this position at the Security Council.

Under article 25 of the U.N. Charter, member states are obliged to abide by such Security Council resolutions. The Security Council resolution found that Iraqi attacks internally had posed a threat to international peace and security. This is one of the very few times the Security Council has ever invoked that provision of the charter with respect to an internal matter.

It is an important action and deserves, in my view, to be acknowledged here in the Senate and to be supported.

This language, contained in Security Council Resolution 688, has important legal consequences. It triggers the provisions of chapter VII of the U.N. Charter. That is the section of the charter which deals with "action with respect to threats to the peace, breaches of the peace, and acts of aggression". Article 39 of the charter states that-

The Security Council shall determine the existence of any threat to the peace, breach of the peace, or act of aggression and shall make recommendations, or decide what measures shall be taken in accordance with Articles 41 and 42, to maintain or restore international peace and security.

The Security Council has now determined that such a threat to the peace exists. It has ordered, not requested, not pleaded with, but ordered Iraq to immediately end this repression of the Iraqi civilian population and to cooperate with the Secretary General and humanitarian organizations in providing for the relief of Iraqi refugees. As I have mentioned, Iraq is absolutely bound by article 25 of the charter to obey this order of the Security Council. Yet Iraq has continued its attacks. We have some reports that in the last 2 days the Iraqi Army has not conducted operations against civilians in the extreme north of the country, but we have no assurance whatsoever that attacks on all civilians have stopped, that they will not resume with their former intensity or that Iraq will cooperate with the Secretary General and humanitarian organizations.

Under these circumstances the United States has the right to ask the Security Council to fulfill its mandate under the charter to "decide what measures shall be taken in accordance with Articles 41 and 42 to maintain international peace and security." It most certainly should do so. And swiftly, before there is further loss of life.

There are those who may argue that the Security Council will not act.

This seems a curious argument given the history of the last 9 months. The Security Council, having shaken off the lethargy of the cold war, moved swiftly to enact chapter VII sanctions against Iraq when it invaded Kuwait. At the initiative of the French, it has now ordered Iraq to cease its illegal attacks on its citizens. If Iraq refuses, or if it fails to cooperate with the Secretary General and the U.N. High Commissioner for Refugees, chapter VII contains the tools to enforce the order of the Security Council.

Mr. President, the resolution I am introducing today strongly encourages the administration to press the Security Council to enforce Resolution 688 immediately. The situation is desperate. These attacks are illegal. The charter, created in the midst of the greatest conflagration in human history, provides the tools to deal with a threat to the peace. With the cold war over we have seen a new willingness to use these tools to keep and restore the peace. If we are to have a new world order it must mean that we truly commit ourselves to using those tools. A blueprint for the new world order exists. It is called the United Nations Charter. It can, it should and it must be used to stop the illegal slaughter of the Kurdish people.

Mr. DOLE addressed the Chair.

The PRESIDING OFFICER. The Republican leader.

Mr. DOLE. Mr. President, I am not certain whether there will be a unanimous-consent request propounded to consider the resolution, but I advise my colleagues there are a couple of minor areas we could resolve if we could get consent. Otherwise, I would be constrained to object.

Mr. MOYNIHAN. Mr. President, I sent the aforementioned resolution to the desk and I ask unanimous consent for its immediate consideration. I believe it requires unanimous consent.

Mr. DOLE addressed the Chair.

The PRESIDING OFFICER. The Republican leader.

Mr. DOLE. I have no objection to sending it to the desk. But I do object to its immediate consideration, I again say.

The PRESIDING OFFICER. The clerk will report.

The legislative clerk read as follows:

A resolution (S. RES. 99) concerning the protection of refugees in Iraq.

The PRESIDING OFFICER. Objection is heard.

Mr. DOLE. Mr. President, I object. And I point out as I did before that there are a couple of minor areas we hope to be able to resolve in the language. If we do that, then there would be no objection to the resolution. I am not certain it can be done yet this evening. We are willing to work on it.

The PRESIDING OFFICER. The Chair understands the resolution will be held over under the rules.

Mr. D'AMATO addressed the Chair.

The PRESIDING OFFICER. The Senator from New York.

Mr. D'AMATO. Mr. President, I was very pleased that our staff had the opportunity to work together with the senior Senator from New York [Mr. MOYNIHAN] as it relates to the resolution which was sent to the desk and which will not be taken up for immediate consideration.

I believe that the issue is one that cannot be put on the back burner or put to the side. Indeed, it has been put to the side. It has been put on the back burner for too long by the world community. I think our country has lacked the fervor and direction necessary to deal with the slaughter of innocent men, women, and children.

I have heard these arguments about, well, my gosh, who is going to take over if Saddam is not there? May it not be a situation that would be catastrophic? I think the catastrophe is now, and that we are really literally doing little, if anything, to stop that killing, to stop the annihilation of people simply because they are Kurds or they are Shiites.

One of the areas that we speak to that I do not believe is objectionable in this resolution is maintaining economic sanctions against Iraq.

Here we are, the United Nations, about to pat itself on the back. It is about to say job well done, and, that provided Saddam meets certain requirements called for by the U.N., economic sanctions will be lifted. That means he is going to be able to sell oil. He is going to be able to raise about $300 million a week worth of revenue-$300 million a week. That is what he will raise when he sells oil.

Why should we be supplying this killer, this thug, this international terrorist, with the means by which to keep himself in power? Oh, yes, he is going to have to meet certain requirements. He will have to pay some reparations so a percentage of that money-and obviously since the money goes through pipelines that flow through Turkey and Saudi Arabia we will be able to set up a formula whereby some of these moneys will go to help pay reparations for the rebuilding of Kuwait.

What about the innocent people now? Do we just turn our backs? It defies logic to say that we are going to make believe that it is not happening. It is just like we made believe that Saddam Hussein was not using chemical weapons to kill Iranians. But after all, those were only Iranians. That was the argument. This is the enemy of my enemy.

So we made him a friend-political expedience. I remember when Senator MOYNIHAN, Senator PELL, and myself were here on the floor saying, my gosh, what are we doing? What are we trading? Why are we subsidizing this madman? I was met by a bevy from both sides of objections. "We should not stop trade. Let us give the killer a chance. He has promised he is reformed."

We repulverized most of his army but we left some of it off the hook for whatever reason. But it happened. Who would have thought they would have undertaken to continue the maniacal conduct of Saddam Hussein after they saw the power that we could exercise in the free world. But they did.

I am not going to second guess that. I do not think one person is going to second guess the fact we brought the war to a conclusion. I support the President. As a matter of fact, if he had continued another 24 hours the media of the world would have come down on him and it would have been George Bush, the President, who was unnecessarily killing people. That is what would have happened in the real world we live in. Let us make no mistake about it.

So all of those wonderful, gifted Communists would have condemned him if he had not stopped. He stopped at the right time. No one could have really recognized or foreseen what is taking place. But we see it happening.

Now there is no excuse. Are we going to stop and say well, the sanctions will be lifted because he has agreed to the terms of the U.N. resolution? Are we going to give him $300 million a week? That is what the revenue stream will be for the sale of his oil so he can continue to buy the armaments, to buy the loyalty, and to rebuild himself-not the people.

This is incredible. This is madness. And what are we attempting to do? I will tell you. We compound the madness because just like the idiot who has lost his way and has a headache. He is trying to deal with his headache by pounding his head with a hammer.

We do not want to go in, and it should not be our place to try to establish the format of government. But I think the world body does have an obligation and an opportunity to see to it that we do not support in any way, and yes that we penalize and punish a government that is killing its own, punish it-deny it trade, deny it sanctuary in the world community.

We cannot give the Kurds sanctuary but we are going to give Saddam Hussein and the Iraqis sanctuary. We are going to give him cover. We are going to let him have normal trade and intercourse with the world community. It is incredible.

I would like to see all of those other things we call for in the U.N. cease-fire resolution be carried out. I do not think it will happen if we cannot deal with this situation now. It is not too late. We have hundreds of thousands of people living in caves, mountainsides, roads, in ditches, babies being born, babies dying, innocent women and children dying. We cannot find the moral courage to do what is right. I say "we" because we are part of this acquiescence. We have to wait for the French to come forward and exercise this resolution.

You know, springtime is here with the opening of baseball season. We are all interested in games going on. Everything is being conducted just like all is right in the world. All is not right in the world. This is a tragedy. I think that each and every one of us have a very shared responsibility.

Why are we here if we can treat this with such indifference? Why are we here if we are afraid to raise our voice to this tragedy? Is it because there are no Kurds in the United States? Is it because there is no great political support for Shiites in the United States? Is it because we have such a fear of the Iranians and the Shiites, and the Iranians who are Shiites for the most part might constitute some kind of problem? Is that why we can just stand by to see them slaughtered, to see the innocent being victimized? Is that why we find it easy? Are we practicing again the failed policy that brought us over the past decade to this situation, the politics of practical political expedience? Are we adopting the philosophy that the enemy of my enemy is my friend? That is the policy that got us into this situation. I do not mean to personalize it.

But the same people who advised the State Department and our Secretary of State are the architects who are carefully crafting out and carrying out the what if's, what if Saddam is gone, what about the Lebanonization? The Lebanonization of Iraq could not be worse than what is happening today.

So while I do not want troops and soldiers to spill their blood in Iraq, I think that the United Nations has an obligation and we have an obligation to see to it that we come to the aid of these people.

Certainly by saying to the leaders of Iraq, "We will not allow your oil to be sold on the world economy, we will keep economic sanctions in place," at the very least that may sober them to the point of recognizing that Saddam cannot be continued in power.

I thank my distinguished colleague, the Senator from New York [Mr. MOYNIHAN] for his leadership in this role, and I look forward to continuing to work with him and Senator PELL and others who demonstrated a concern. This is a test of what we are about.

Mr. MOYNIHAN. Mr. President, I would like to acknowledge the implacable integrity of my colleagues from New York and his willingness to say what has to be said when it has to be said on this subject. I thank him for his remarks.

I yield the floor.

Mr. President, I ask unanimous consent that Senate Resolution 99, placed over under the rule earlier, be modified with the changes I now send to the desk, and that Senators PELL and DOLE be added as cosponsors.

The PRESIDING OFFICER. Without objection, it is so ordered.

The resolution (S. RES. 99), as modified, is as follows:

S. RES. 99

Whereas Kurds, Shiites and others throughout Iraq began an armed uprising against the government of Saddam Hussein;

Whereas since the uprising began Iraqi forces have employed indiscriminate force against civilian populations throughout the country, including the use of weapons such as napalm and phosphorous, and have killed thousands, and displaced and put at risk of starvation perhaps one million people;

Whereas the United Nations Security Council on April 5, 1991, adopted Resolution 688 which condemns the repression of Iraqi civilians and states that this repression threatens international peace and security in the region, demands that the Iraqi Government immediately end its repression of civilians, insists that Iraq allow immediate access by international humanitarian organizations to those in need of assistance and demands that Iraq cooperate with the Secretary General to address urgently the critical needs of the refugees;

Whereas the United Nations and the United States, as the leader of the international coalition opposing Iraqi aggression, have a unique responsibility and ability to address the plight of the Iraqi refugees; Now, therefore, be it hereby

Resolved by the Senate, That:

The Senate strongly condemns Iraq's continuing military atrocities, its slaughter of thousands of innocent civilians, and its blatant violations of international standards of human rights and the Fourth Geneva Convention of 1949;

The Senate calls for a United States policy in support of democracy and respect for human rights and international law in Iraq;

The Senate believes that the United States has a moral obligation to provide sustained humanitarian relief for Iraqi refugees and urges the President to continue his efforts to garner international support for those fleeing Iraqi repression;

The Senate notes the assistance Turkey and Iran have provided to Iraqi refugees, encourages them to continue to assist the refugees in every appropriate manner, and pledges United States assistance to international relief efforts for the refugee populations;

The Senate calls upon the President immediately to press the United Nations Security Council to adopt effective measures to assist Iraqi refugees as set forth in Resolution 688 and to enforce, pursuant to Chapter VII of the United Nations Charter, the demand in Resolution 688 that Iraq immediately end its repression of the Iraqi civilian population. Such measures could include: (1) establishing temporary enclaves to provide sanctuary to those fleeing Iraqi troops, (2) developing procedures to verify the full implementation of any Iraqi government offer of amnesty to Iraqi citizens, (3) maintaining economic sanctions against Iraq, and (4) using effective means to protect refugees pursuant to Article 42 of the United Nations Charter.

Mr. PELL addressed the Chair.

The PRESIDING OFFICER (Mr. FORD). The Senator from Rhode Island.

60.

[April 11, 1991 (Senate), pp. 4327-8]

STOP IRAQI GENOCIDE

Mr. PELL. Mr. President, a catastrophe, without precedent since World War II, is now taking place inside Iraq. Up to 3 million Kurdish Iraqis face the triple threat of death through exposure, through starvation, or through military assault by a vengeful Iraqi Army.

Eye witnesses, including a staff member of our Foreign Relations Committee, have reported on Iraqi tactics. They include relentless bombardment of Kurdish cities by artillery and helicopter gunships, the massacre of civilians in areas recaptured by the army, and the use of such unconventional weapons as phosphorous artillery shells and napalm.

Several million Kurds have left the cities of northern Iraq to seek shelter in the high mountain valleys and, now, in Turkey and Iran. Because the Ba'ath regime systematically destroyed every village in Kurdistan, the refugees inside Iraq have no shelter and there is no source of food in this once rich agricultural region. The refugees who reached the mountain areas did so mostly on foot and such food as they had they brought with them. By now this food is gone.

We need to provide relief to the millions of Kurds on the Iraq-Turkey border, inside Turkey, on the Iraq-Iran border, and inside Iran. I appreciate the efforts both Turkey and Iran have made to help the Kurds but both countries must do more. It is not acceptable to leave starving people in a freezing cold environment exposed to military attack. And the United States has an obligation to endeavor that the financial burden of these refugees is borne not by Turkey and Iran but by the whole world community.

Most of all, the world must take effective action to stop the killing now. We should communicate to Saddam Hussein that killing of civilians is not acceptable and that he must stop. To do this, I would prefer the use of United Nations sanctioned force but, if necessary to save lives, the United States could shoot down helicopters and conceivably bomb the artillery that is now chewing up Iraqi civilians. In saying this though, I must emphasize that I would oppose the use of any United States ground troops.

The United States has some responsibility for what is now going on inside Iraq. The slaughter of civilians is one of the unintended consequences of our military intervention. Further, the Iraqi rebellion was encouraged by the administration with statements that unintentionally led Kurds and Shi'a to believe the United States would help them overthrow Saddam Hussein. As it now turns out, President Bush did not mean to help. But at a time when the United States is aiding rebels opposed to the Governments of Angola, Afghanistan, and Cambodia, it is understandable that the Iraqis believed that the American President's statements also meant they would be helped.

Not since World War II have so many people found themselves in such peril so quickly. We must act now to stop the slaughter. More than a million live may depend on what we do in the coming days.

I yield the floor.

The PRESIDING OFFICER. The Senator from New York.

Mr. MOYNIHAN. Mr. President, I ask unanimous consent that Senators GORE, LEAHY, and MITCHELL be added as co-sponsors to the resolution that is now before the body.

The PRESIDING OFFICER. Without objection, it is so ordered.

Mr. MOYNIHAN. May I also take just a moment to express the great appreciation which we have for the efforts Senator GORE has made, and the contributions he has made in drafting this measure. He is necessarily absent from the Senate at this hour but wants very much to be recorded as being part of this debate.

Mr. President, I yield the floor.

61.

[April 11, 1991 (Senate), p. 4377]

SENATE RESOLUTION 99-CONCERNING THE PROTECTION OF REFUGEES IN IRAQ

Mr. MOYNIHAN (for himself, Mr. D'AMATO, Mr. GORE, Mr. PELL, Mr. LEAHY, Mr. SANFORD, Mr. MITCHELL, Mr. DOLE, Mr. PACKWOOD, Mr. CRANSTON, and Mrs. KASSEBAUM) submitted the following resolution; which was considered and agreed to.

S. RES. 99

Whereas Kurds, Shi'ites and others throughout Iraq began an armed uprising against the government of Saddam Hussein;

Whereas since the uprising began Iraqi forces have employed indiscriminate force against civilian populations throughout the country, including the use of weapons such as napalm and phosphorous, and have killed thousands, and displaced and put at risk of starvation perhaps one million people;

Whereas the United Nations Security Council on April 5, 1991 adopted Resolution 688 which condemns the repression of Iraqi civilians and states that this repression threatens international peace and security in the region, demands that the Iraqi government immediately end its repression of civilians, insists that Iraq allow immediate access by international humanitarian organizations to those in need of assistance and demands that Iraq cooperate with the Secretary General to address urgently the critical needs of the refugees;

Whereas the United Nations and the United States, as the leader of the international coalition opposing Iraqi aggression, have a unique responsibility and ability to address the plight of the Iraqi refugees: Now, therefore, be it hereby

Resolved by the Senate, That the Senate strongly condemns Iraq's continuing military atrocities, its slaughter of thousands of innocent civilians, and its blatant violations of international standards of human rights and the Fourth Geneva Convention of 1949;

The Senate calls for a United States policy in support of democracy and respect for human rights and international law in Iraq;

The Senate believes that the United States has a moral obligation to provide sustained humanitarian relief for Iraqi refugees and urges the President to continue his efforts to garner international support for those fleeing Iraqi repression;

The Senate notes the assistance Turkey and Iran have provided to Iraqi refugees, encourages them to continue to assist the refugees in every appropriate manner, and pledges United States assistance to international relief efforts for the refugee populations;

The Senate calls upon the President immediately to press the United Nations Security Council to adopt effective measures to assist Iraqi refugees as set forth in Resolution 688 and to enforce, pursuant to Chapter VII of the United Nations Charter, the demand in Resolution 688 that Iraq immediately end its repression of the Iraqi civilian population. Such measures could include: (1) establishing temporary enclaves to provide sanctuary to those fleeing Iraqi troops, (2) developing procedures to verify the full implementation of any Iraqi government offer of amnesty to Iraqi citizens, (3) maintaining economic sanctions against Iraq, and (4) using effective means to protect refugees pursuant to Article 42 of the United Nations Charter.

62.

[April 11, 1991 (Senate), p. 4383]

MIDDLE EAST RELIEF EFFORTS

Ms. MIKULSKI. Mr. President, I would like to speak in support of a more aggressive relief effort in the Middle East.

I do not want to discuss today the policy of whether or not we actively support the insurrection in Iraq. Or whether we support a separate Kurdistan or the separatist movements in Africa. Those are complicated issues for anther time.

Starvation is not a complicated issue. Neither is death from exposure.

As Americans, we cannot stand by and ignore the pictures of Kurdish refugees or the starving millions in Somalia, Ethiopia, and the Sudan.

Today we have tons of equipment in the region that can help these people. Tents, food, aircraft, generators.

We do not need a consultant to make a "needs assessment." We do not have time for studies.

We know what they need. We know what we have close by. The only question is how to deliver it.

I call on officials in the Agency for International Development and the Department of Defense to use all the creativity, resourcefulness, and common sense at their disposal to find a quick, efficient way to deliver desperately needed goods to these people.

63.

[April 11, 1991 (Extensions of Remarks), pp. 1210-11]

THE ADMINISTRATION'S DANGEROUS DEFERENCE TO RIYADH
HON. MEL LEVINE
OF CALIFORNIA
IN THE HOUSE OF REPRESENTATIVES

Thursday, April 11, 1991

Mr. LEVINE of California. Mr. Speaker, in her commentary in yesterday's *Wall Street Journal* ["Led Astray by the Saudis in Iraq," April 10, 1991], Laurie Mylroie reveals disturbing evidence of Saudi Arabia's influence over American policy in the Middle East.

Ms. Mylroie asserts that the administration agreed to a Saudi plan to stage a military coup against Saddam. When the coup failed to materialize, the Saudis panicked and warned the administration that Islamic fundamentalists might take over the rebellion in the south.

According to Ms. Mylroie, the Saudis are largely responsible for President Bush's unconscionable abandonment of the Kurds and other Iraqi dissidents.

In response to the Saudi's concerns, the administration reversed its course and left the rebels on the northern and southern Iraqi borders to be mercilessly slaughtered by Saddam's army, after having encouraged the Iraqi people to rebel and signaling that the United States would assist in that effort. The betrayal of the Kurds will no doubt go down as one of the most tragic chapters in American history, and one that could have been avoided.

As Ms. Mylroie notes, American deference to the Saudis has historically hindered American interests in this region. The current crisis is no exception. It is time American policy in the Middle East was based on American interests-including the promotion of democratic values-rather than on that of a monarchical and self-serving regime.

I strongly urge my colleagues to review the following insightful and revealing article: .

. .

64.

[April 16, 1991 (House), p. 2191]

KURDISH SITUATION: THERE IS NO NOBILITY IN SILENCE

(Mr. PETERSON of Florida asked and was given permission to address the House for 1 minute and to revise and extend his remarks.)

Mr. PETERSON of Florida. Mr. Speaker, today we bear witness to the suffering of children. We hear stories of cruelty beyond our human comprehension, and we turn away in horror. We must turn back and face the children. We can do no less.

I introduce the Kurdish resolution so that we may encourage the President to take immediate action to save lives, feed starving children, and assume moral, as well as tactical, leadership in the Middle East.

As 2 million Kurdish people are fleeing from Saddam Hussein, and 1,000 are dying with each passing day, there is no more time to deliberate.

We are faced with a test of our values, as a nation, as an institution, as individuals. As long as we stand silent as the Kurdish people cry out for help, we betray our own hearts. As long as we turn away from the sight of their pain, we belie our own history. There is no nobility in silence.

Today, we urge the President to treat the Kurdish situation as his highest national priority and to lead the United Nations in a dual effort to provide protection and massive relief for the Kurdish people. As we condemn crimes against humanity that recall the blackest periods in the history of our civilization, we can do no less.

65.

[April 16, 1991 (House), pp. 2192-3]

AMERICA'S RESPONSE TO HOLOCAUST II

(Mr. RAVENEL asked and was given permission to address the House for 1 minute and to revise and extend his remarks.)

Mr. RAVENEL. Mr. Speaker, what is the matter with us? For the third week now, we see Holocaust II occurring before our eyes in Iraq. Yet America's response to the misery, dying, and desperation of those children, pregnant women, the old, the sick, and indeed all those pinned there like animals in those freezing mountains has been shamefully small.

Why is the rhetoric of our leaders so defensive and apologetic? Are the deaths of these infants and innocents weighing on our consciences? Of course they are. Why is a Gus Pagonis or Schwartzkopf in Turkey not coordinating massive relief that only we can give? Why is Secretary Baker in Ankara and Tehran not urging increased efforts? Why have our plentiful hospitals, soup kitchens, doctors, nurses, and support personnel not been adequately deployed? Have we won a great war to now lose our honor and reputation as a compassionate nation in what tragically has become not a peace, but a genocide?

66.

[April 16, 1991 (House), p. 2193]

COMMENDING THE PRESIDENT FOR HIS INVOLVEMENT IN IRAQ

(Mrs. KENNELLY asked and was given permission to address the House for 1 minute and to revise and extend her remarks.)

Mrs. KENNELLY. Mr. Speaker, yesterday the Vice President of the United States had occasion to go to my State of Connecticut to visit. On the way to the event that he was attending, he stopped at a restaurant by the name of Friendly's to say hello. After he left, a young woman was heard to say over and over again, "I can't believe it. I am going to be on television. I can't believe it. I am going to be on television."

For good or ill, what we have to realize is that our young people see what they see on television as more real than life itself. And that is the reason this morning that I stand here to commend our President for getting involved once again in the situation in Iraq. There is no doubt that what is happening to the Kurds is one of the worst things we have seen in modern times, and at the same time that the young people see our people be so proud of our soldiers as they come home, we show our pride in our excitement, at the same time our young people see these refugees and see what they are suffering. So I think it is only right and proper that we involve our armed forces in

helping these people, and I thank you, Mr. President, for getting us involved once again.

67.

[April 16, 1991 (House), p. 2194]

ACTION MUST BE TAKEN IMMEDIATELY TO PROTECT AND SAVE KURDS

(Mr. HOYER asked and was given permission to address the House for 1 minute.)

Mr. HOYER. Mr. Speaker, I rise with so many other of my colleagues to express my outrage and my compassion and my desire that the administration move quickly and decisively with respect to the problems of the Kurds. After World War II, we decided that collectively as an international community we would not only condemn genocide, which had been condemned before, but that we would join together to act against it.

More recently, Saddam Hussein was compared to Hitler. Day after day that analogy, I think, is more apt than the President made initially. We see the terror that he visits on his own people. We see them fleeing, the creation of refugees.

Mr. Speaker, we waited, frankly, too long. We responded too late. But it is never too late to do the right thing, and we are responding now. I hope the President and this Congress and this country use the same kind of decisive, direct, able creation of coalition in the international community to go in and protect and save innocent people and lives.

Mr. Speaker, we have moved late, but move now we must.

68.

[April 17, 1991 (House), p. 2268]

UNITED STATES MUST NOT STAND BY WHILE INTERNATIONAL OUTLAWS COMMIT GENOCIDE

(Mr. KENNEDY asked and was given permission to address the House for 1 minute and to revise and extend his remarks.)

Mr. KENNEDY. Mr. Speaker, the world continues to witness Saddam Hussein's annihilation of the Kurdish people. What he has failed to achieve by gassing and bombing, he now tries to accomplish by mass starvation and freezing. No less than 1,000 innocent refugees are dying in the mountains each day. Many, maybe most, of these victims are children under 5 years old.

If the new world order means anything, it is that the United States will not stand by while international outlaws commit genocide.

After urging the Iraqi people to rise up, our President has finally stood up for them. He is to be congratulated for his decision yesterday to provide greater relief and safety to Kurds in northern Iraq.

But our efforts to bring peace to Iraq will not end in a month. Nor will they stop at the 36th parallel. Peace will only come once the Kurds and Shiites can return home without the threat of massacre. And peace will only come once these persecuted peoples have a say in how their country is run.

Mr. Speaker, as the moral leader of the free world, the United States should immediately place before the United Nations a resolution demanding that sanctions against Iraq will not be lifted until the Iraqi people have food, safety, and free elections. That is what our soldiers fought for, that is what the people of Iraq deserve, and that is what it takes to bring real peace and stability to this region.

69.

[April 17, 1991 (Senate), p. 4523]

SADDAM HUSSEIN, UNNATURAL DISASTER

Mr. LIEBERMAN. Mr. President, yesterday the President of the United States announced a policy of establishing safe havens within Iraq for the orderly distribution of food, medicine, clothing, and shelter to the Kurdish refugees. Those havens will be protected, at least on a temporary basis, by United States and allied military forces.

This is an important, significant step in the right direction. In my remarks in this Chamber a week ago, I called for a dramatic increase in our assistance to the Kurds, saying, "there will be no safe havens unless their safety is assured by a military presence (and) protected by the use of force if they are violated." I hope that this new international effort will quickly provide relief for a devastated people. The scale of this disaster is immense, and an enormous, unprecedented humanitarian effort must be made.

But the problem goes beyond hunger, disease, shelter. The problem goes to the doorstep of Saddam Hussein. This is no ordinary relief campaign. We are not dealing with the consequences of an earthquake, tornado, hurricane or other natural disaster. We are dealing with an unnatural disaster by the name of Saddam Hussein. And unlike an earthquake or hurricane that comes and goes, Saddam continues to afflict his people to this day. He is the reason Kurds are dying. He must go. And more can and must be done to get rid of him.

Safe havens are only a temporary solution. The Kurds deserve safe passage home. They have homes, beds, farms, food, clothing in their villages in Iraq-at least in villages that have not been destroyed by Saddam's aggression. But they are afraid to go home. They are risking death from natural causes because of their fear of death by Saddam Hussein. The fact that a human being would choose to confront hunger, thirst, homelessness, and disease rather than confront Saddam Hussein is strong testimony to how evil he is, and how important it is for us to get him out of power. We must do more to lift from there afflicted people the terrible choice they face. We must give them hope, where currently there is none.

I wish we had acted sooner. I wish we have shot down the helicopters the minute we saw them fly against the rebels in Iraq. I wish we had called for a stop to the armed assaults against Iraqi civilians, and used air power to stop them if our warnings did not suffice. While such acts might not have kept the rebels from losing their battle against Saddam's forces, we could have prevented the wholesale slaughter of innocent lives, and perhaps we could have prevented the mass exodus of Kurds from their homeland.

Even now, we should make clear to Iraq's ruler and to his terrorized people that there will be no more killing fields. The Kurds cannot go home until they know they have no more to fear from Saddam Hussein.

We need not get involved in a ground war or a civil war to come out on the side of innocent people and against a one-sided slaughter. But we cannot pretend that we have nothing to do with the internal affairs of Iraq. Yesterday's announcement by the President provides proof that we have been involved in Iraq's internal affairs, and we are about to become more involved.

The people of Iraq want our help. Our troops have been greeted as liberators by nearly every Iraqi they see. The regime in charge of Iraq does not deserve our respect or our deference. A terrorist is claiming to run a country, and the international community of civilized nations cannot let him get away with it. We must use all reasonable economic, diplomatic and military means to bring about the downfall of Saddam's regime.

America, with its allies, must pursue a concerted policy of defeating the menace of Saddam Hussein once and for all, and bringing him to justice for his crimes. The people of America and of Iraq want such justice. International morality demands it.

70.

[April 17, 1991 (Senate), pp. 4598-9]

IRAQ

Mr. D'AMATO. Mr. President, I would like to make several observations.

Much has been said recently about the United States action, lack of action, lack of world reaction to what is taking place in Iraq. Let me first say that we should not take exception with the efforts that are being undertaken at this time. Reasonable people may second guess and offer their own conclusions or solu-

tions to a very complex problem. They may say we should have acted sooner, but we are acting and that is what is important, and it is necessary.

I say that I am pleased that the President has undertaken an action that will at least give some temporary refuge to the poor Kurds and to other innocent civilians who have been victimized by this madman, this terrorist, this butcher, Saddam Hussein.

Let me offer this as not a total solution, but at least as a manner by which we can address some of the problems.

Recently we heard that Iraq has petitioned the United Nations to lift the sanctions, to allow it to sell a billion dollars' worth of oil, so that it can buy desperately needed food, medical supplies, and other things for its people. Let me suggest that we do lift the sanctions, but we see to it, because we can control the flow of both oil and revenues, by way of agreement, that those moneys go for the refugees first, for the Kurds, for the Shiites, to pay for this massive effort. And it will be a massive effort, it will be an effort probably bigger than any we have seen in our lifetime in such a short period of time.

So let us use that money and see to it that that money goes to its rightful purpose.

Second, if we are going to say that is the end of this situation because we have nicely washed our hands and we have provided safe haven—and let us hope that we can—that is not going to be an easy job; it is going to be a job that takes time, effort, and money, and I can suggest some of the ways we get some of those moneys and I think it is appropriate that we have to stand up for something.

Let me also suggest that it is hard for me to believe that our European allies in the European Community had the good sense and judgment to finally step up to the plate, not needing us as a prod, to say Saddam Hussein should be tried as a war criminal. I think he should. I think we should tell the Iraqi generals who are still following him that we will not lift the sanctions as it relates to the normal intercourse of business, that they will be treated as the pariahs that they are. Make no mistakes about it, that we will use the world power economically and militarily if necessary to protect innocent civilians. You cannot have it two ways.

So while we commemorated just a week ago and had a great ceremony to the memory of 6 million people who perished because the world stood by indifferently, I do not think that what we are undertaking is sufficient to meet the needs of these people or to really cleanse ourselves of what is an obligation that each and every one of us has, the United States has and the world community.

I hope that we would be in the forefront of this effort.

Mr. President, I yield the floor.

Mr. President, I suggest the absence of a quorum.

The PRESIDING OFFICER. The clerk will call the roll.

The legislative clerk proceeded to call the roll.

Mr. MITCHELL. Mr. President, I ask unanimous consent that the order for the quorum call be rescinded.

The PRESIDING OFFICER. Without objection, it is so ordered.

71.

[April 17, 1991 (Senate), p. 4647]

HOLOCAUST MEMORIAL DAY

Mr. Simon. Mr. President, I would like to spend a few moments talking about Holocaust Memorial Day, which was commemorated April 12, 1991. Holocaust Memorial Day serves as a reminder of the atrocities committed against humanity. And we need to remind ourselves that the scourge of inhumanity still plagues us as we approach the 21st century.

The millions of humans that suffered and died under the Nazi regime must never be forgotten. Their memory must live in our hearts and souls as a reminder of the evils of racism. All of Europe was caught in the horrible conflagration of World War II, and many people suffered because of their religion and nationality—but none more than the Jewish people. European Jewry was singled out for extermi-

nation, and, as we know all too well, Hitler succeeded in murdering 6 million Jews.

The day we have chosen to remember the Holocaust has come at a time when we are witnessing another brutal attack on humanity in the form of Saddam Hussein's vicious assault on the Kurdish people. The scale and scope are clearly different than the Nazi Holocaust, but the horrors are starkly reminiscent. In Cambodia in the mid-1970's, Pol Pot decimated his own people in a wild killing spree that boggles the mind. International condemnation followed the disclosure of this genocide, with vows that the world cannot and will not stand by and allow such crimes to occur, or to go unpunished.

We are now in a situation in Iraq where Saddam seems to be exacting vengeance for those opposed to his rule—Shiites in the south, Kurds in the north, Sunnis who joined the insurrection. Just as it is important to understand what happened 45 years ago, we must recognize what is happening now—and act before it is too late. Saddam's military attacks against the Kurds have resulted in a huge exodus, with tragic results. The United States ought to take the lead worldwide in ensuring that humanitarian aid on an adequate scale reaches the Kurds as quickly as possible. I join with my colleagues here in the senate, and with all Americans, in hope and prayer that the world shall never witness such atrocities again. While great strides have been made, anti-Semitism has not been eradicated from the world scene. Holocaust Remembrance Day is an important occasion to remember the horrors of anti-Semitism, genocide, racism, and aggressive war, because it is our collective memory of the Holocaust that will prevent future holocausts. We can never forget.

72.

[April 17, 1991 (Senate), pp. 4647-9]

TERRY ANDERSON

Mr. MOYNIHAN. Mr. President, I rise to inform my colleagues that today marks the

2,223d day that Terry Anderson has been held captive in Lebanon.

Mr. MOYNIHAN. Mr. President, as the distinguished Republican Leader BOB DOLE records in his estimable "Historical Almanac of the United States Senate," the Senate created its first staff position, the post of Doorkeeper, on April 7, 1789. James Mathers-"an Irish immigrant who earlier had distinguished himself in the Revolutionary War"-was chosen for this post which he held for 22 years until his death.

In the two and more centuries since, the staff of the Senate has grown, and with it the number of exceptionally able and devoted persons who have given some or all of their working careers to the institution. But I would not know of any whose service can be compared to that of Peter Galbraith of the staff of the Committee on Foreign Relations who has, quite literally, risked his life in the performance of his duties.

On Easter weekend, March 30-31, Mr. Galbraith crossed the Tigris River-under bombardment-from Syria into northern Iraq. There he spent two harrowing, incredibly heroic days among the Kurdish inhabitants of that region. This included one hellish night in the city of Dihok, then held by the Kurdish resistance and under continuous bombardment from the forces of Saddam Hussein.

This bombardment included the use of phosphorus shells.

In utter disregard of his own safety, Mr. Galbraith met with Kurdish leaders, spoke with refugees, watched and recorded the unimaginable devastation of that region and those people. The Mathers spirit is still alive in this Chamber.

Somehow, he survived. He crossed back into Syria and returned to the United States where he reported his experiences to the American public on television programs and in a graphic article in the current New Republic. He has of course provided even more information to the Committee on Foreign Relations itself.

In any organization within the executive branch there would surely exist a form of recognition for such service above and beyond the call of duty. A military medal, a departmental citation. We have nothing of that sort

for members of the Senate staff. This is no dereliction on our part. It is simply that in two and more centuries we have not seen the like of young Galbraith:

The indifference to his own welfare and safety; the all-consuming concern for the welfare and safety of an oppressed people caught up in a ghastly travail. At minimum I would wish to record this Senator's admiration for an incredible display of grace under pressure. I ask unanimous consent that His *New Republic* article be printed in the RECORD at this point ["Last Stand," Apr. 29, 1991].

There being no objection, the article was ordered to be printed in the RECORD, as follows: . . .

73.

[April 17, 1991 (House), p. 2342]

INTRODUCTION OF RESOLUTION TO REPLACE IRAQI GOVERNMENT WITH UNITED NATIONS ADMINISTERED GOVERNMENT

The SPEAKER pro tempore (Mr. TAYLOR of Mississippi). Under a previous order of the House, the gentleman from Florida [Mr. BACCHUS] is recognized for 5 minutes.

Mr. BACCHUS. Mr. Speaker, my first vote as a Member of this House was a vote for a new world order.

In January, I voted to authorize the President of the United States to use military force to end the occupation of Kuwait by Saddam Hussein.

I did so because I seek a new world in which our American dream of freedom and democracy can one day become a reality for everyone, everywhere.

I did so because I believed our President when he said that he believed in that same new world.

But today that new world we sought in January looks very much like the same old world. Today, when I listen to our President, I am not sure what he believes.

The new world I envisioned is not one where armies are allowed to slaughter their own people with helicopter gunships and chemical weapons. It is not one where starving, freezing children are allowed to die on remote mountains. It certainly is not one where the United States of America turns away from its responsibility to a brave and helpless people, offering only the hollow excuse that we cannot interfere in the internal affairs of another nation.

There is a word from the old world order to describe what is happening in Iraq. That word is genocide. The mountains of Iraq are the new death camps, the new killing fields. One thousand precious lives are lost every day.

I'm far more interested in saving real lives than I am in the heartless nuances of heedless *real politik*. If the new world order is to mean anything at all, we must use all reasonable diplomatic, economic, and military means to end the mass murder of the Kurds, prevent the mass sacrifice of the Shiites, and remove Saddam Hussein from power. We must send a message once and for all that we value the fundamental human rights of oppressed people more than we value the territorial rights of oppressive governments.

President Bush did a superb job in bringing the world community together to drive Saddam Hussein from Kuwait.

Rarely has the moral and military might of the United States been so effectively and properly applied.

Why has the President not shown the same leadership in bringing the world community together to help the innocent people of Iraq? Can we truly celebrate victory amid reports of mass starvation and mass execution? Can we truly treasure the homecoming of our troops while children are tortured before the eyes of the world? Are the yellow ribbons we have worn so proudly beginning to fray?

I applaud the actions the President took yesterday to protect the Kurdish refugees. I wish that those and other urgently needed actions had come sooner. In recent weeks, I've been deeply disappointed in the President. He called on the people of Iraq to rise up against Saddam Hussein. I heard him. The whole world heard him. America must not abandon them now.

So today I have joined my distinguished colleague from New York, Mr. SOLARZ, in a letter to the President urging him to seek a Security Council resolution calling for the resignation of the brutal government of Saddam Hussein and its replacement by a government administered by the United Nations that would hold free and fair elections. We believe that this resolution must authorize the use of whatever means are necessary to enforce this demand.

In concert with other members of the allied coalition, we must do all we can to stop the slaughter in Iraq. We should destroy Iraqi helicopters, warplanes, and artillery when used against civilians. We should arm and finance what remains of the resistance against Saddam Hussein.

Building on the belated efforts of recent days, we should expand our relief efforts to feed, clothe, and shelter the vast refugee populations fleeing oppression. We should work through the United Nations to create safe havens for refugees inside Iraq. We should move quickly to provide American troops to protect the Kurds in Northern Iraq, and we should not remove our remaining troops from southern Iraq at this time, for that would allow Saddam to slaughter the Shiite refugees we left behind, even as he has slaughtered the Kurds.

I am not advocating solely unilateral action by the United States. I am not advocating that we march on Baghdad and impose a government on the people of Iraq.

I am advocating that we help give the Iraqi people the means to accomplish what President Bush encouraged them to do: Overthrow Saddam Hussein, and establish a new government that will live in peace with its own people and with the rest of the world. I am advocating that we live up to the principles that our brave men and women have been defending in the Persian Gulf.

America must continue to stand for what America is supposed to stand for. Only then will we have a victory truly worth celebrating. Only then will we have real hope for the new world we seek.

74.

[April 18, 1991 (Senate), pp. 4720-4]

RECENT EVENTS IN IRAQ

Mr. GORE. Madam President, if there is no other business my colleagues would like to pursue at this point, I want to address the Senate on the subject of recent events in Iraq and in the areas along the border between Iraq and Turkey, and between Iraq and Iran.

The world community has been moved by the precarious struggle for existence of hundreds of thousands of innocent men, women, and children forced by their fear of Saddam Hussein into the harsh mountains of northern Iraq. As part of that world community, we have watched young babies perish and the elderly succumb to the cold, the hunger, the brutality of a dangerous and difficult exodus.

I wish our Government's responses had displayed more foresight and more alacrity. Our President, who displayed such brilliant initiative in summoning others to make war, needed to be pleaded with before he would confront one of the war's unintended consequences. But, at last, he has.

Americans support President Bush's warning to Iraq to stop military action north of the 36th parallel, which now becomes the de facto southern boundary of the safe zone. Americans also support President Bush's parallel warning to Iraq not to interfere in any way with the efforts to provide relief to those Kurds who are enduring such terrible suffering.

I believe Americans will support efforts to enforce this demand if Saddam Hussein does not comply. The President's decision, announced earlier this week, to fully engage our own military forces in the rescue effort, has its risks, but it seems to me that most Americans will also feel that this was an act well taken in the name of the United States, even if belatedly.

It is essential now, however, to take stock of what else needs to be done, not only in the coming days but also in the longer term. We must plan better or be continuously forced to improvise. The suffering of the Kurds and others should be warning enough to us about the costs of being constantly overtaken by events. The President is having to make up for lost time now, and that, among other things increases the risk factor for our own troops. It is essential that planning for the relief operation overcome the disabilities of a late start. There are indications that the President has caught even the United Nations off guard, and it is not clear whether he has made sure that Saddam Hussein will stay out of the way.

I, myself, would like to go on record in support of the difficult calculation just made by the President, that the risks to our personnel-who are now asked to help distribute the relief supplies and to provide some semblance of security and order while that process takes place-are acceptable during the time period when this operation can be expected to take place and then conclude.

I believe that the military units of Iraq which have so recently been enduring the devastation of the war in the southern part of Iraq understand very clearly what will happen to them if they should ignore the clear warnings provided by President Bush. I believe our country will be just as united in support of this operation as we were in support of some very difficult and risky operations during the Persian Gulf war. But there are steps that we need to take to minimize these risks and to define the outcomes we are now seeking. For example, at a minimum, we need to settle any doubt that the United Nations is in support of this operation and is ready to accept the responsibility for taking it over once we and our allies have made it a going proposition. That is now in some doubt and that doubt must be quickly resolved.

In the near term, a successful relief effort may well require steps beyond those already taken. The continued presence of Republican Guard units north of the 36th parallel is one of the most immediate sources of concern. The presence of such units can undermine efforts to build any sense of confidence among the refugees or to provide for the security of relief personnel.

As long as these units can remain in the region, even if we take no overt action, we may have trouble persuading the Kurds to relocate far enough away from the Turkish border down to areas where food and medical care and some kind of shelter can be provided. Certainly, if our plan is one day soon to have the Kurds leave the encampments we are now building and return to their dwellings in Iraq, it is hard to realize their agreeing to do so if it means passing through the ranks of their worst, most feared enemies. Ultimately, the President may find he has to tell Iraq that such units must withdraw.

According to the President's announcement, we will establish several encampments the size of small cities. I take it as a given that we cannot allow either the Iraqi military or civilian police authorities to operate in these encampments or in their vicinity. Consequently, it seems clear that those providing relief, whether it is the United States and some of our allies, or the United Nations, must also be prepared to provide for public order.

Arguably, the authority for this action comes from Resolution 688 on the refugee crisis. If there is any doubt about that, then steps must be taken to strengthen and clarify the resolution. It would, of course, be absurd for the United Nations to try to save lives while Saddam Hussein is trying to take them all in the same territory.

Meanwhile, attention must also be paid to the refugee crisis near and in Iran. That country is straining its resources to deal with an immense number of desperate people. Conditions appear to be as urgent there as they are in the north. But the international response to date has been ineffective, in large measure, because of Iran's own estrangement from the rest of the world.

Nonetheless, Iran has a problem on its doorstep almost as bad or the one on the Turkish border. Indeed, the number of people is as great or greater. It is only the apparently more efficient efforts by Iran compared to those of Turkey which have kept the suffering from reaching quite the horrendous levels as we see on the Turkish border. Thousands of innocent lives are at stake. We should be clear about that. Iran is asking for help. If ever there is a time for the world community to respond to a request from Iran, now is that time. We and other nations should extend ourselves and move fast.

Also, there appear to be continuing skirmishes involving units of the Iraqi military and Kurds on this part of the Iraqi border. This must also be dealt with, notwithstanding the fact that it is south of the 36th parallel, because the relief operations are going to be underway there, just as they are on the Turkish border. Indeed, they are already underway, albeit without our full participation on the part of Iraq, and spilling over the border into Iran.

What is perhaps most disturbing is what seems to be a lack of clear focus on this problem at the Iranian border which, I repeat, is as great in its human dimension as measured by the number of people involved, as is the problem on the Turkish border. The issue for here and for now is not our dislike of Iranian policy but the saving of lives. Iran does appear to be doing a more effective job, as I said before, but it should specify exactly what it would like to see from the world community in assisting them in their efforts to deal with the suffering now underway.

In the south of Iraq, there is yet another different kind of problem. As we withdraw our military forces from the occupied zone, it seems to me inconceivable that the almost 40,000 individuals who have left that zone and put their lives in our care should be turned over to Iraqi authority against their will. The image of men, women, and children in that part of Iraq, on the Kuwaiti border, hanging on to the trousers' legs of American soldiers as they withdraw, looking over their shoulders at Iraqi machine guns poised to deal with those who have in some cases been demonstrating publicly against the regime of Saddam Hussein, that cannot be allowed to take place. It is not too extreme to say that their blood would be on our hands if we were to acquiesce in such a tragedy.

In addition, many of the people who normally live in that area are expressing fear about what will happen after we leave. It is good that Secretary Cheney has publicly pledged that we are going to take care of the safety of these people, but there seems to be a great deal of confusion as to the details. And that is where the difference between life and death will be found, in those details. What are they?

Having inquired, Madam President, I would like to say I am not satisfied that our Government is clear about what those details are.

In particular, I think our arrangements may be inadequate at the point where our protection is withdrawn and the safety of refugees becomes dependent upon the United Nations. In theory, there is some protection from the presence of U.N. peace-keeping forces after they replace United States forces on the Iraqi side of the demilitarized zone. But their mandate may at present be inadequate. They appear authorized only to monitor Iraqi observance of the demilitarized zone, but not to concern themselves with what happens to people inside that zone.

There is a danger that we may eventually see U.N. forces passively standing by while Saddam Hussein's civilian police round up the innocent for slaughter. Do we doubt that he is capable of doing precisely that? He is right now engaged in an effort to reestablish the extent of his power over the people of Iraq, in all of its parts. He has and will continue to have less ability to threaten his neighbors than he had before the start of the war. But his power inside of Iraq, the base from which he will seek to rebuild power in the region and the world, is now being reestablished.

One of the means by which he reestablishes his power is to slaughter those who disagree with him. Having seen these people, chanting against Saddam Hussein's rule, on television, what will his reaction be?

I do not think it is a difficult question to answer. But we cannot pretend that vague arrangements will suffice. We need to be clear, as we were not clear about what was happening to the Kurds when this tragedy began to unfold, and about what was happening to the Shiites just east of the area we are now discussing.

And again here it seems clear additional steps are now needed. The behavior of Iraqi civilian police toward the people within the demilitarized zone needs to be officially included within the mandate of the U.N. forces. Kuwait's border with Iraq must be porous enough to permit flight and relocation to an emergency zone in the north of Kuwait, should that prove to be necessary.

Now, there is another matter involving the suffering of Iraqi citizens which we should also anticipate and not allow ourselves to be surprised by when it occurs.

Temperatures will continue to climb in the weeks ahead. The public health threat in the heart of Iraqi population centers, including Baghdad and those cities and towns up and down the river valley, could well become critical as warming temperatures bring the threat of cholera and other communicable diseases, which threaten precisely because of the devastation visited upon the water systems, sewer systems, and other parts of the infrastructure of the nation.

What will be our reaction if we witness widespread deaths from a pandemic in the populated regions of Iraq's center? We need to address these questions now. The world community needs to think about and prepare for addressing such questions right now.

Critics say that as we address questions such as that one, or the problems surrounding the establishment of these encampments in the north, or the relief efforts on the Iranian border, or the fate of those refugees along the Kuwait border, that in doing so we are now simply dividing Iraq into segments and in the process destroying the territorial integrity of that country.

The President points out that creating safe zones is not the same thing as promoting the establishment of regions that are fully and permanently independent of Iraq. Arguably, however, the steps he has taken reduce the sovereign authority of the Government of Iraq to act as it pleases within its own borders, and the further steps that I am discussing here would have a similar, and additive, effect. But the cease-fire itself already crosses that line.

The government in Baghdad essentially retains only those sovereign powers not claimed by the U.N. Security Council. And if we have already denied the Government of Iraq the power to use oil to rebuild its military force, how much farther is it to deny the Government of Iraq the power to exploit the circumstances of the postwar environment to spill the blood of its own people in a never-ending sacrifice to the power of the Baathist regime in Baghdad.

Imagine, then, that we do take the necessary steps to prevent the vast calamity which is rising to engulf the Kurds and others. Obviously, any success we have in stabilizing the situation is a mere holding operation. We are not going to accept the idea of hundreds of thousands of people indefinitely huddled together on the perimeter of Iraq; indefinitely at the mercy of events. True, we have stood by and witnessed other mass tragedies:

In Cambodia and in the Sudan, for example. But in this situation we have the ability to decide otherwise.

The whole world realizes what is going on. Our allies-to their credit-are in the front ranks of those pressing for action and are telling us more needs to be done.

We are dealing with a government in Iraq that defied the United Nations even to the point of warfare, and which has now been defeated as a result. We are able to bring tremendous force to bear on the Government of Iraq, because even after our ground forces leave the gulf, we will continue to control the air space of Iraq, and we control its economic future with the continued application of the sanctions.

We have, in other words, the power to influence events in Iraq. But that power can be wasted if it is not directed toward clear objectives.

What is it we would like to see in Iraq? We want the people of Iraq to be able to return to their homes and to live at least in relative safety. Saddam Hussein has made offers of amnesty. But who will believe him? And who should? Previous offers of amnesty have been followed quickly by betrayal and murder.

Even the words of this offer of amnesty clearly spell out wide exceptions large enough to accommodate whatever violence Saddam Hussein wishes to visit upon the people who so unwisely believe in the simple word "amnesty" coming from his lips.

Who will urge the Kurds and the Shiites and others who have fled to return and to place their lives and the lives of their families in the grip of this man simply because he has given his "word"?

Clearly, the minimal requirement here is to secure not only a statement of the terms of an unconditional amnesty, but also to put in place a network of observers who will monitor the situation. That is a thin reed to lean on, of course: mere words juxtaposed to the reality of a regime which will sacrifice anything, commit any crime, and go to any length to preserve its power; a regime which would prefer to rule a valley of the dead rather than allow the living their freedom.

In the end, I believe we will finally have to confront the central questions, questions the administration still apparently hopes to escape; namely, what will happen to the political organization of Iraq, and how can we encourage change?

In any such analysis, it is necessary to grasp something which continues to elude many people. Saddam Hussein may be a singular personality, but alone his removal from power will not end Iraq's Government by terror. We must be clear about this point. He and his lieutenants, including the Army command, are united in crime and culpability for what has happened to Iraq and its people.

The removal of Saddam Hussein alone will not reveal a layer of honest and decent underlings to lead Iraq. It will only reveal the next layer of those who are complicit in his crimes. Anyone who has studied the history of his rule understands that fact. If we look the truth in the eye, we will see it is not only Saddam Hussein who must be removed from power, but his government.

Until Saddam Hussein is gone, until his government is gone, and until the Iraqi state is reestablished on a new footing, there can be no solution on an enduring basis for the hundreds of thousands of refugees, nor durable basis for regional security and stability.

We must recognize that simple, if difficult fact.

This conclusion leads to clear operational consequences for American policy. We must decide that our goals in this region cannot be mortgaged to the survival of a government which has demonstrated time and time again a capacity for mass, unconscionable violence, against its own people and against its neighbors.

On the contrary, our efforts must be focused on isolating that government internationally, and on encouraging its downfall at the hands of authentic forces from within Iraq.

Madam President, the force which we are in a position to exercise right now in Iraq, by virtue of the sanctions, by virtue of our leadership of an international coalition, by virtue of our control of the airspace in Iraq, by virtue of the international community's control of its oil revenue, by virtue of our ability to communicate with elements inside Iraq-all must be organized and orchestrated toward the objective of removing Saddam Hussein from power, and removing his government from power.

That is necessary in order to achieve our goals and the just goals of the world community, and the aspirations of the Iraqi people-even Iraqis who have, in the past, been supporters of Saddam Hussein. He is reestablishing his power by exercising continued terror against them as well.

One of the most important things we can do to isolate the government of Saddam Hussein is to document, through testimony and evidence gathered under international auspices, its criminal nature and deeds. This may or may not lead to indictments and trials in absentia.

The President seemed, the day before yesterday, to hint he would trade the equivalent of immunity in return for Saddam Hussein's prompt departure into permanent exile. But the only way to seal the door to any return to international acceptability for Saddam Hussein and for his regime is to thoroughly document their crimes and lay them on the public record for the world to see.

Then, if we wish to plea bargain with Saddam Hussein, which is how I would characterize the offer of immunity in return for his departure-and I do not do that in a way that is designed to cast prejudice upon that, because I think the President is right to consider that possibility-but, if we wish to even consider such an arrangement, the best way to do it is to first indict him and lay out the record.

Meanwhile, every effort should be made to emphasize that under the present govern-

ment, Iraq will exist as a pariah state. Iraq's suspension from the United Nations, a process which begins with a Security Council resolution, would be a useful expression of that status, with both symbolic and practical consequences, that should increase the discomfort and isolation of Saddam Hussein and his government.

The process of nurturing internal forces capable of bringing down Saddam Hussein and his government should begin with a clear statement that the United States will never relent on sanctions until a new government has been formed; one which will arguably give voice to the peoples of that nation, and respect their basic rights and needs.

Why are we so reluctant to speak out in favor of democracy and the principles we hold most dear in seeking a resolution for this crisis, which is lingering past the time when we all hoped it would end?

Let me emphasize, we must demand not just the downfall of Saddam Hussein, which the President has been doing in words, but the replacement of his system of government as the condition for modifying the sanctions beyond those forms of relief necessary for the health and basic sustenance of the Iraqi people. We must underscore that our fundamental dispute is not with the people of Iraq, but with their government.

Of course, even if that government were to be replaced, Iraq must still bear responsibility toward other nations and people for damages and crimes, but certainly a decent government in Baghdad should invite a reassessment of those obligations.

It is also time for the Government of the United States, at the highest levels, to contact those who are in a position to speak out for the oppressed peoples of Iraq. We do not have to recognize them as a government in exile, or formalize their position. But it is shameful that for years we have refused to even meet these people in the open; that we have refused to even allow them to state their case publicly here in the United States in a forum of our choosing.

Why do we seem automatically to assume that neither they nor the peoples of Iraq are capable of self-discipline and self-government? That assumption betrays our most basic leap of faith which led to the establishment of this country and its revolutionary form of government.

When did we come to think that self-government was beyond the capability of certain peoples? How did we come to accept that we could export sophisticated equipment, including advanced weaponry to Iraq, but that these same people, who could master these advanced devices, are somehow incapable ever of mastering the techniques of democracy?

Why, when representatives of the Kurds explicitly say they are not seeking independence from Iraq, but some form of autonomy for themselves within Iraq, does our Government brush that extraordinary series of statements aside?

It is not just moral outrage that should lead us to reappraise our policy. Iraq is a potentially wealthy and powerful nation. It has a large and talented population, and it has, in addition to its resource base in oil, another resource base in the form of fertile agricultural regions.

As we have seen, if these resources are under the control of a totalitarian state, they can menace the entire region. We cannot risk allowing such hostile power to again take root and grow in Iraq.

But vigilance is not enough. That is essentially a defensive waiting game, and dictators have notoriously long lives and long careers. The resources of the Iraqi State must be directed to peaceful purposes under the guidance of a different regime which exists to meet the needs of its people. Until there is such a regime, there will remain the ultimate risk of Saddam Hussein's reemergence.

Moreover, if we believe that a stable Iraq is in our interest, surely we now can see that dictatorship there is not the cure for internal instability, but the cause. If our objective is to make sure we do not have to face another Iraqi bid for regional hegemony and for world influence based on aggression, the reconsolidation of Saddam Hussein's control over Iraq is precisely the wrong outcome.

If we are concerned about Kurdish irredentism as a threat to Turkey, and Shiite fundamentalism as a threat to the gulf states, then we should understand that oppression nurtures extremism. And yet, it seems to me that our Government completely discounts the possibility that the solution to the stability of Iraq is that its peoples must live at peace with each other within a democratic and just framework.

Instead, we seem to have banked entirely on the survival of the existing system of government, even though we say we would like to see it under a different individual leader.

We should request nothing from Saddam Hussein, but rather state our demands and be prepared to enforce them. We are not asking him to avoid military operations north of the 36th parallel; we are telling him. The clear implication is that if he refuses to comply, we will use force to enforce it.

Similarly, we must make it clear that in the end, we will never be reconciled either to him or to his government; that even after our ground forces are withdrawn, unless he prepares the way for his own departure, we will grease the skids.

In this connection, let me note that American covert assistance to the Afghan resistance was highly effective in changing the balance in that struggle, even though there was never any thought of a direct United States military engagement. We have options that do not at all depend on a sustained U.S. military presence. We should be considering them. The exercise of power begins with a correct understanding of its extent as well as its limits.

I fully agree with the President that the United States should remove its ground forces from the occupied zone as planned and from the region, but the President is confronting us with a false choice when he says that to complete that withdrawal, we must be passive about the internal affairs of Iraq. We are already deeply involved in those internal affairs and must, of necessity, remain so for some time. We must pick our preferred course of action. If we do not succeed in imposing an agenda that reflects American goals of regional and international security, Saddam Hussein will have an opportunity to impose his. He is seeking to do so right now.

The withdrawal of our armies does not require us to leave Saddam Hussein to his own devices. We have to believe that he not only intends to survive on power but to recover what he has lost and then to grasp for another opportunity to dominate. He is gaining strength again right now. Therefore, if we do not want to be forced at some future time to reintroduce our armies, we must recognize that the removal from power of Saddam and his government are vital pieces of unfinished business.

In my opinion, Madam President, and I want to state this clearly, President Bush should not be blamed for Saddam Hussein's survival to this point. There was throughout the war a clear consensus that the United States should not include the conquest of Iraq among its objectives. On the contrary, it was universally accepted that our objective was to push Iraq out of Kuwait, and it was further understood that when this was accomplished, combat should stop. That is also why, after it became apparent that Iraqi forces were being routed, pressure mounted rapidly here and abroad to proclaim a cease-fire.

If it was a mistake to believe that Saddam Hussein would be a prompt political casualty of the war, as the debacle it turned out to be for Iraq, that his rule would end shortly after the defeat of his armies, then that was a mistake widely shared throughout our country.

But only the President could speak on behalf of the United States to suggest that Saddam Hussein ought to be overthrown, and only the President could decide on behalf of the United States to permit the use of Iraqi combat helicopters to suppress rebellion, in clear violation of the understanding of the conditions agreed to at Safwan. The President's appeal was, therefore, arguably a factor in stirring up rebellion.

The President's decision not to ground the Iraqi combat helicopters conferred an important, perhaps decisive, advantage to Saddam Hussein in overcoming rebellion and then in generating the mass, panicked flight with which we are now confronted.

There have been published reports that the United States took other steps to encourage rebellion. I do not know whether that is the case or not. We should know.

Certainly, I am prepared to accept that the President, as an individual, is as shocked and angered at what is happening before our eyes as any American. I believe, however, his initial refusal to act was the result of a conviction he has held and continues to hold about basic American interests in this situation. The President believes the United States must withdraw its ground forces from the region in the shortest possible time, and I agree. And he evidently believes that the collapse of centralized authority in Iraq would put that withdrawal in doubt. He also believes that the territorial integrity of Iraq is important to the future stability of the entire region.

So far, I believe most Americans agree, but, unfortunately, the President also appears to have believed that Saddam Hussein's government was critical to these purposes because Saddam Hussein could commit Iraq to a cease-fire, which was the necessary condition for our withdrawal, and because Saddam Hussein, or preferably in the President's mind his associates, could prevent the collapse of Iraq.

Madam President, why do we seem so frequently to strike an alliance with dictators of the worst stripe?

Mr. SPECTER. Will the Senator yield for a question or does he prefer to finish before yielding?

Mr. GORE. I prefer to finish the statement because I do not have longer to go and then I will yield.

In my previous comments in the past few weeks, I have tried to deal with aspects of the President's thinking that I believe misjudged how we ought to respond in the specific context of Iraq. But others have noticed that the President's approach to developments in Iraq reflects an even larger pattern in his approach to events in other parts of the world. The President speaks of a new world order, but he confronts a tension between a world order based on correct and cooperative relations among governments and the nature of those governments.

The President has tried to escape this dilemma by applying a strict interpretation of the doctrine of noninterference in the internal affairs of other states. Our business, he seems to have been saying, has to do only with the external behavior of the government in Baghdad. What that government does internally may be vile, but it is not our business, and we should keep out. This is not an improvised position on the part of the President but a statement of real principle, clearly of major importance in the President's thinking. It is the way he reacted to the Government of China after Tiananmen Square. He placed so much importance on that principle that he sent close associates to have a very pleasant exchange of views and even raise their glasses in toast to those who were responsible for Tiananmen Square, very soon after the tragedy occurred.

The same principle governed the way he reacted to the Soviet Union in the wake of efforts to destroy the movement for full independence in the Baltics. The same principle guides, I believe, the overly prolonged attachment to Gorbachev in preference to some greater lines of communication to other emerging centers of power within the Soviet Union.

We should speak out for democracy. We should be willing to stand for the principles upon which our Nation is based and for which our Nation stands throughout the world. We should not be too quick or too righteous in that regard to deny that the President's approach does have its values, even in complex international tradeoffs on issues of right and wrong. At the hour of choice in the Security Council, would China and the Soviet Union, for example, have facilitated American policy against Iraq if the United States had earlier disrupted its ties with those governments? The President is within his rights to believe that the world is often too ambiguous a place for crisp moral certainties. And yet, is a cool amoralism to be the foundation of the new world order? Is our objective nothing more than peaceful relations among states, no matter what may be going on within those states?

Even the Charter of the United Nations seems to point in that direction.

I had to reread that document, and it is clear that the United Nation was brought into being to regulate relations among states and not to regulate their internal behavior, except if it becomes a threat to international stability.

At least that would be what you might call a strict constructionist reading of the Charter.

(Mr. LAUTENBERG assumed the chair.)

And yet again we need to recognize that there is wisdom in this restraint. All governments wish to be treated as sovereign equals, despite the gross disparities that exist among them in terms of power. In particular, when they participate in an international organization, they must take care not to be exposed to a "tyranny of the majority." So, although some countries taking shelter behind the doctrine of noninterference are using this to cover their crimes, others may need this doctrine to protect themselves against bloc voting intended to victimize them.

What is happening in Iraq catches us and the world community at a point where our thinking about international order and international justice is thin. We do not know how to handle this kind of issue very well. But I believe we all share a sense that statesmen who deal in tightly sealed compartments with issues of national interest on the one hand, and with issues of international justice on the other, are not building anything durable for future generations. The debate which has erupted over the President's original course of official noninvolvement with the fate of the Kurds is driven by the sense that this was a step away from the path we must follow.

It would be unseemly to treat the ongoing suffering of hundreds of thousands of people as an abstraction. For the moment, we must focus on how to successfully respond in the present instance, to the plight of those whose fate is in our hands. But I want to point out that this crisis is certainly not going to be the last time we have to confront a disastrous misalignment between the principle of nonintervention in the internal affairs of states and our deepest impulses about what is humane, morally imperative behavior.

As we witness the tragedy of the Kurds and others who wished to escape domination in Iraq, and who have instead become a nation of the dispossessed, we must wonder whether there is a golden mean whereby justice and order can be reconciled; not in an imaginary world suddenly repopulated by a new and better kind of humanity, but in our own world populated by the descendents of Adam.

It is not enough, in this situation we now face, to declare that the future of Iraq is entirely the business of its present government. Our leaders once told our troops that the way home was figuratively "through Baghdad," meaning that the Government of Iraq had to be checked. It is time for our statesmen to take that remark as a guide for themselves.

We cannot deal with our problems in this part of the world merely by attempting to contain such evil. It will not let us alone, even if we turn away from it. No one is talking about ensnaring American military forces in an unending civil war. We are talking about using American influence and power to speed, rather than delay, the end of a regime and a system of government which we cannot tolerate either morally or in terms of our fundamental interests.

The stories we read now record the deaths of children, of infants. Every morning, they bury the children first, we are told. These stories confound our sense of justice, our sense of compassion and conscience. They make clear the need for actions the President is now taking, but they also point toward other steps that must eventually be taken, although-it seems to me-they are still being resisted by the administration.

Mr. President, I yield the floor.

Several Senators addressed the Chair.

The PRESIDING OFFICER (Mr. LAUTENBERG). The Senator from Pennsylvania.

Mr. BUMPERS. Will the Senator from Pennsylvania yield for one minute?

Mr. SPECTER. I had already stated to my colleague from Arkansas that I would on the condition that I retain the right to the floor. I had stated earlier that I had some questions for the distinguished Senator from Tennessee, so if the Senator from Tennessee would stay, I would ask unanimous consent that I retain my right to the floor after the Senator from Arkansas concludes.

The PRESIDING OFFICER. The Senator from Arkansas.

75.

[April 18, 1991 (Extensions of Remarks), pp. 1337-38]

TO PUT TEETH INTO THEIR WORDS
HON. MICHAEL G. OXLEY
OF OHIO
IN THE HOUSE OF REPRESENTATIVES

Thursday, April 18, 1991

Mr. OXLEY. Mr. Speaker, I commend to the attention of my colleagues a recent article written by columnist and scholar Ben Wattenberg regarding the hypocrisy demonstrated by certain of the critics of the President's Persian Gulf policies.

The sniping we have heard from some Members of Congress is just that-risk-free armchair quarterbacking from politicians who vigorously opposed U.S. military action when the President needed their support the most.

I urge any colleagues attention to this article.

TO PUT TEETH INTO THEIR WORDS

Some leading Democrats and liberals have said they were shocked, dismayed and distressed that President Bush did not help the Kurds in their moment of military agony. They say we should do something now. Fair enough.

But lest the waves of hypocrisy climb dangerously toward nostril-level, there are some questions that should be asked of Democrats and liberals. Answers may yield a serious and sustainable American policy.

Question: Are Dem/libs in favor of intervening in civil wars?

In Vietnam, they were not. Not intervening in a civil war was offered as the prime reason for opposition. We were told that America should abstain even when the bad-guy side in a civil war was communist, expansionist and backed by our nuclear-tipped adversary, the Soviet Union.

In Nicaragua, ditto. Moreover, this time the conflict was "in our back yard." But the Dem/lib line was that civil wars were out of bounds for America.

Question: Are liberals prepared to use force?

Liberals made the Democratic Party the Dove Party. They opposed use of force under almost any circumstance. Iraq's invasion of Kuwait was cross-border aggression, a sin of the first magnitude, without ambiguities of "internal affairs" that come with civil wars. Liberals said: Thou Shalt Not Use Force. And so, when the president asked for congressional approval to blast Iraq out of Kuwait, two-thirds of the Democrats voted no.

Question: If Mr. Bush had helped the Kurds militarily, would liberals have said, "Kurdistan is another Vietnam?"

If we had grounded Saddam's helicopters, wouldn't he have used artillery and tanks against the Kurds? If we then pounded Saddam's artillery and tanks, wouldn't he have likely used ground troops against the Kurds? What then? Escalation, in order to prevail.

How would liberals have responded? Because many of the same players said that (a) Nicaragua, (b) Angola, (c) Kuwait, and (d) El Salvador "was another Vietnam," it is likely that if involvement in Kurdistan had lasted a while, it too would have been Vietnamized by liberals.

Question: Why don't the critical Democrats put their money where their mouths are? If they did, they would help their party, their country and the world. A "sense of the Congress" resolution, if passed with a majority of Democrats, could help rescue the current tragic situation.

The resolution should formalize the logical results of current liberal rhetoric. It could say that America made a mistake in not helping the Kurds earlier. It could say that the United Nations should do the job. (The letter to the president circulated by Rep. Stephen Solarz, New York Democrat, is a wise first step.) In the event the United Nations does not act with sufficient force (alas, likely), the resolution should seek allied support.

It should say America should now help the Kurds, with low-casualty military action if necessary, in order to halt potential genocide and to achieve Kurdish autonomy within an Iraqi federal democracy. And it should say we will not betray the brave Kurds if the going gets tough.

Such a resolution would resonate everywhere. It need not announce in a rub-noses-in-it manner that liberals have recanted. But its implication would be clear. It would mean that in the post-Cold War world, liberals and Democrats are prepared to selectively support the good guys in civil wars.

Upon what principle could such a resolution be based? That America is the only superpower, that superpowers have unique responsibilities and can act unilaterally.

What might Mr. Bush do with such a resolution?

He would have to seriously rethink his policy regarding the Kurdish situation. He says we shouldn't get bogged down in a civil war. That is reasonable; after all, he knows that if it happened, America could be split apart again in hawk-dove discord, as in Vietnam and Nicaragua. But if liberals were seriously supportive, new possibilities would emerge. In fact, America could move with dispatch toward creating a new world order.

76.

[April 23, 1991 (Extensions of Remarks), p. 1396]

THE EMERGENCY ASSISTANCE FOR IRAQI REFUGEES ACT
HON. JULIAN C. DIXON
OF CALIFORNIA
IN THE HOUSE OF REPRESENTATIVES

Tuesday, April 23, 1991

Mr. DIXON. Mr. Speaker, I rise today to bring to your attention legislation that I introduced last week to provide immediate humanitarian aid to the suffering Kurdish refugees and displaced persons in Iraq-the Emergency Assistance for Iraqi Refugees Act. This measure calls upon the United States and the international community to step up their humanitarian aid efforts to the suffering Kurdish refugees and displaced persons in Iraq, and condemns the ruthless slaughter of the Iraqi people by Saddam Hussein.

Thousands of Iraqi men, women, and children have died-and continue to die everyday-from exposure due to freezing temperatures, hunger, and diseases associated with malnutrition. As human beings, we cannot just stand by and watch it happen.

The Emergency Assistance for Iraqi Refugees Act affirms Congress' support for humanitarian, refugee assistance and emergency relief. It also supports the United Nations Security Council Resolution 688 which condemns the repression on Iraqi civilians and demands that such repression end. This resolution insists that the Iraqi government allow immediate access by international humanitarian organizations to those in need of assistance and cooperate with the Secretary General to address urgently the critical needs of the refugees.

The full text of the bill follows:

H. CON. RES. 131

Whereas Congress condemns the ruthless slaughter and heinous human rights abuses against the Iraqi people, particularly the Kurdish minorities in the north and Shiites in the south, by Iraqi President Saddam Hussein and his troops;

Whereas the United Nations Security Council on April 5, 1991, adopted Resolution 688 which condemns the repression of Iraqi civilians and states that this repression of civilians threatens international peace and security in the region, demands that the Iraqi Government immediately end its repression of civilians, insists that Iraq allow immediate access by international humanitarian organizations to those in need of assistance, and demands that Iraq cooperate with the Secretary General to address urgently the critical needs of the refugees;

Whereas the President of the United States has warned the Iraqi government against any attacks on refugees and refugee assistance operations;

Whereas hundreds of thousands of refugees are fleeing their homes in terror in the aftermath of the civil war in Iraq and are desperately seeking safe haven and sanctuary and an estimated 1.7 million people have been displaced in Iraq or have been forced to seek refuge in neighboring countries;

Whereas hundreds of men, women, and children have died from exposure due to freezing temperatures, hunger, and diseases associated with malnutrition;

Whereas countries neighboring Iraq, such as Turkey and Iran, have established temporary camps within their borders for the refugees that have fled northern and southern Iraq, and thousands more are amassed at the 206-mile frontier border between Iraq and Turkey, and others are in southern Iraq in the area previously occupied by coalition forces and now occupied by the United Nations peacekeeping force, the United Nations Iraq-Kuwaiti Observation Mission (UNIKOM);

Whereas the United States, European and other countries, the United Nations, and private voluntary organizations have witnessed the dire need for medical supplies, shelter, food, blankets, and potable water for the refugees and the necessity for a massive international relief effort;

Whereas the United States and United Nations have sent experts to the Gulf region to assess the crisis and determine the immediate needs of the Kurdish, Assyrian, Chaldean Christians, Shiite and other refugees and displaced persons;

Whereas the United Nations international appeal effort calls for over $500 million for humanitarian refugee assistance to address the needs of the estimated 1.7 million Iraqi displaced persons and refugees in Iran, Turkey, Syria, and Jordan;

Whereas the United States has pledged $10 million for immediate humanitarian assistance and other international donor countries are making similar pledges;

Whereas Congress is supportive of the humanitarian outreach efforts by Turkey and other countries, and supports United States Operation Provide Comfort that is providing desperately needed food and supplies to the refugees and the humanitarian relief efforts by France, Britain, Germany and other countries; but believes there should be a greater coordinated international effort and

Whereas Congress is deeply concerned and committed to providing additional humanitarian aid immediately for these suffering people: Now, therefore, be it

Resolved by the House of Representatives (the Senate concurring), That the Congress

(1) supports humanitarian, refugee and emergency assistance for Iraqi refugees and displaced persons; and

(2) recommends that the United States provide additional assistance for a sustained international humanitarian relief effort.

77.

[April 24, 1991 (Extensions of Remarks), p. 1424]

HUMAN TRAGEDY FACING THE KURDISH AND SHIITE PEOPLE
HON. BARBARA B. KENNELLY
OF CONNECTICUT
IN THE HOUSE OF REPRESENTATIVES

Wednesday, April 24, 1991

Mrs. KENNELLY. Mr. Speaker, I want to express my deepest concern about the human tragedy facing the Kurdish and Shiite people today, as they attempt to flee from the terror of President Saddam Hussein and his loyalists. At the same time I want to commend President Bush for his announcement last week to substantially expand the relief efforts to the Kurds in northern Iraq. This represents a profound and positive shift in the administrations policy toward the Kurds.

With every war comes stories of human tragedy. The brutal mistreatment of the Kurds and the Shiites is fast becoming the greatest tragedy of this war. Those that managed to escape death at the hand of President Hussein's forces, have been dying of starvation, disease, and exposure as a result of that escape.

Nine months ago, we acted quickly and decisively to contain Iraqi aggression. We freed Kuwait. We all take pride in the efforts and accomplishments of our men and women in the Armed Forces in that effort. But once

again, we must act quickly and decisively on behalf of a people facing death.

The Shiite refugees who fled into the United States occupied zone in southern Iraq for protection deserve our attention. In every way, they continue to suffer the same devastation as the Kurds, and have fled with as much pain and suffering to the Iranian and the Kuwaiti borders.

I support the continuation of sanctions against Iraq, except for food and medicine, and welcome long-term United Nations efforts to protect the Kurdish and Shiite people against attacks and reprisals by the Iraqi Government. I also support efforts to further attempt to bring order back to Iraq. As always in war, innocent people continue to suffer long after the major battles, and it is our humanitarian duty to help in ending this suffering.

78.

[April 25, 1991 (Senate), pp. 5321-2]

THE PLIGHT OF THE KURDS

Mr. LIEBERMAN. Mr. President, the news of Iraq's Kurdish population continues to be grim. It is being reported that 500 Kurdish refugees are dying each day along the Iraq-Turkey border.

Such horror is a searing reminder of the brutality of Saddam Hussein, the evil force behind this disaster of Biblical proportions.

As grave as the situation is for the 850,000 Kurds near the Turkish border, the life and death struggle may be worse for the 1.5 million Kurds near Iran. We do not know how many Kurds die along that border each day. We can only imagine that the tragedy must be great.

And the future of Shiite refugees in southern Iraq, protected up until now by United States forces, is in some doubt, as reports surface about Iraqi secret police amassing lists to hand over to Saddam's military forces. Will they, too, die, as the American military shield is withdrawn?

It is likely many refugees now dead would be alive today had the international community, including the United States, acted more quickly in response to their plight, if we had stopped the horrific slaughter of innocent life in the aftermath of the gulf war through a series of air strikes against helicopter gunships and tank columns, for example. The act, while not necessarily tipping the strategic balance of power in favor of dissident forces in Iraq, would have saved many civilian lives, and might have prevented the wholesale, panic-driven flight of Kurds to the Turkish and Iranian borders.

But we cannot remake the past, no matter how recent it is. We can only deal with present reality. The President has begun to act on behalf of the Kurdish refugees, and that is a positive sign. We are establishing camps where their immediate needs can be met. More and more food and other supplies are being airlifted in. The death rate should continue to fall.

But there is more to do. We must continue to explore ways to help those Kurds situated near the Iranian border. The administration is pursuing discussions with Iran, through Swiss intermediaries, about how we can help. Those discussions should be speeded up, so that we can lead an international effort to supply the desperate Kurds, despite our longstanding problems with the Iranian regime. The scope of this disaster is so great that it overwhelms the politics of international relations. We do not abandon our legitimate concerns about Iran's Government by acting to help feed, cloth, shelter, and heal hundreds of thousands of Kurds displaced by the tyranny of Saddam Hussein. Perhaps cooperation in this humanitarian effort can even help close the gap between Washington and Tehran, and help us solve the hostage crisis in Lebanon. Nonetheless, we have a moral responsibility to do more to help the Kurds, and that responsibility should drive our policy in the days and weeks ahead.

We must also plan for the security of the Kurds over the long term. We cannot simply set up tent cities, move the Kurds in, and then leave without in some way safeguarding their lives against a renewed murderous rampage by Iraqi forces. Already there are scenes of so-called Iraqi police hovering nearby the new camps. What will they do if and when we leave? Will a U.N. peacekeeping force be sufficient protection against the might of Saddam's military? The international community, led by the United States, must outline our policy regarding the protection of the Kurds from renewed attacks by Saddam more clearly. The President has acted properly by ordering armed Iraqi forces from the neighborhood of our safe haven, but we need to ensure they will not easily return once we are gone.

We must also recognize that safe havens-even if we make them truly safe-are but temporary solutions. The Kurds deserve safe passage home, where they have beds, clothes, food, work. It should be our goal to help them go home in peace.

I suspect that will not be possible until Saddam Hussein and the Baathist regime are out of power. There is no room for cosmetic or symbolic changes. American policy must be clearly enunciated: President Bush must say loudly and unmistakably that we want Saddam and all his men gone from power in Iraq.

To this end, we should change our overly timid policy toward the Iraqi political exile community. In the past, out of fear of offending Saddam, we avoided contacts with these exiled leaders. It was only this month that the State Department met with them to discuss political issues, as opposed to strictly humanitarian concerns. Such contacts should continue and be broadened. We must encourage the creation of the next generation of Iraqi leadership-leaders who will seek to establish democracy, a free market economy, and respect for human rights within Iraq. We can also back up our support for Iraqi rebels with actual commitments of arms and funding. We gave them so much verbal support in months following Saddam's invasion of Kuwait that they rose up against Saddam, only to find the depth of our support skin deep. If we truly want Saddam's regime overthrown, we must do more than say so; we must take all reasonable actions necessary to bring it about. To do so is not only in America's interest: it is in the interest of the community of nations, and the people of Iraq itself. The news that Saddam has reached an accord with some Kurdish leaders is being welcomed in some quarters. But I remain deeply suspicious of Saddam's intentions, as I am sure many Kurds do, too. I simply do not trust him. We cannot rely on his word as we formulate and apply America's foreign policy regarding Iraq.

Regarding contacts with members of the Iraqi regime, we must make clear that we will have no normalized discussions with them. As long as we continue to control Iraq's airspace, we can continue to tell Iraqi officials what they can and cannot do with their oil and their military. That is a policy of common sense when one accepts that Iraq's rulers are terrorists, not legitimate officials. Truthfully, many of them belong in the dock of international war crime trials, and we should keep that uppermost in mind every time we must have contact with them.

Our embargo of Iraqi exports and imports must continue as long as Saddam's regime remains in power. The sanctions were not a weapon strong enough to force Saddam out of Kuwait, but their continued application can serve as a signal to Iraq that we will not tolerate Saddam's rule. The more we make life easier for Saddam, the stronger he will become. There is a news report that Saddam would like the prohibition on oil exports lifted in time for his 54th birthday. That is one birthday present I don't believe we should be giving Saddam Hussein. I urge the President to use America's veto power to stop any attempt to let Saddam get his birthday wish.

Beyond the use of sanctions as a weapon against Saddam, we must retain our air supremacy and use it to coerce proper Iraqi military behavior toward civilians under their control. As we leave southern Iraq, we must be prepared to respond quickly to any reports of atrocities committed in our absence. If we leave northern Iraq, the threat of air strikes against any armored movements against civilians must remain. An umbrella of American air power must exist over Iraq as protection against the slaughter of innocent lives. It is not an easy task; it comes with some risk. But it is an obligation we must undertake if we are to remain true to the principals which moved us to take arms against Saddam's forces in Kuwait.

Humanitarian aid for Kurdish and Shiite refugees. Military protection of their lives against Iraqi army aggression. Continued control of Iraqi airspace. Continued prohibition against Iraqi imports and exports, with minor exceptions to provide essentials for the health of Iraqi citizens. More diplomatic, economic, and military support for Iraqi rebels. And an unwavering commitment to the removal of Saddam Hussein and his henchman, and to their trial for war crimes.

That is the stay-tough policy America needs. That is the policy I urge the administration to adopt, in the national interest. For our national interest extends beyond the narrow calculus of material gain and political or military advantage. It extends to the restoration of international morality, to the destruction of evil forces that threaten the stability of a civilized world. The total destruction of Saddam's regime in Iraq is the one truly humanitarian act that Americans, Iraqis, and people of conscience throughout the world, want to see accomplished.

79.

[April 25, 1991 (Senate), pp. 5512-3]

IF SADDAM IS HITLER, THEN WE MUST SUPPORT THE KURDS

Mr. CRANSTON. Mr. President, I thank the distinguished chairman of the committee. I rise today to urge in the strongest possible way a vigorous U.S. policy in support of the Kurdish people and other dissidents in Iraq.

I rise also to call attention to an overlooked issue in the Kurdish drama: The widespread human horror of Kurds living in concentration camps in northern Iraq.

These are the Kurds you do not see on CNN.

They live in what the Iraqis euphemistically call "Victory Cities"-as many as 50 such cities.

Best available estimates say there may be as many as 1 million forgotten people starving in these cities that are actually in effect, concentration camps.

Mr. President, one of the main objectives of the war in the Persian Gulf should have been to get rid of Saddam Hussein, who President Bush properly likened to Adolf Hitler.

Well, "Adolf" Hussein is still in power, he is still the unbowed dictator of Iraq, and he still rules with the bloodied iron hand of the heavily armed Republican Guard.

The atrocities Saddam Hussein has committed against the Kurds both before and since the war are as bad or worse than his invasion of Kuwait. We must not give him the opportunity to resume the savagery of genocide.

Mr. President, I call on President Bush to make clear that the United States has a firm commitment to the Kurds and others who rebelled against Saddam Hussein that we and other coalition forces will stay in Iraq until Saddam is out of power, or until we are told by the leaders of autonomous Kurdistan our presence is no longer needed.

The news today is that the Kurds are struggling to achieve some accommodation with Saddam Hussein in order to avoid a continuation of the genocide.

U.S. policy must do nothing to undercut Kurdish aspirations-and I urge President Bush to do everything he can to make Saddam understand that the Kurdish position-self-determination and multiparty pluralism-is our position.

In the meantime, amid the horror and the anguished pleas for help, we should not act as though Kurdish refugees realistically can return to their villages.

The fact is that Saddam Hussein's forces leveled those villages at a time when the Reagan-Bush State Department was cozying up to the Iraqi dictator.

They've wiped the villages out like Hitler wiped out the Czechoslovakian town of Lidice during World War II.

The United States and its allies ought to be expanding the refugee safe-haven zone in northern Iraq.

We should step up the pace of relief efforts to an estimated 800,000 Kurds living in fields and camps near the Turkish border.

And we should not be turning a blind eye, using the most specious arguments, to the plight of another 1.5 million refugees on the border with Iran.

Mr. President, for years the democratic, partisan forces fighting the Saddam dictatorship have looked to the United States for help and for support. Even in the worst moments of terror, in the streets of Basra and in the mountains of Kurdistan, brave men and women secretly thrilled to the same ideas of democracy and respect for the rights of man that motivated Jefferson and Lincoln.

Unfortunately, the United States failure to respond to the desperate cries of Iraqi freedom fighters this year, in 1991, is not the first time Iraqi democrats have felt betrayed by American actions.

In the mid-1970's Henry Kissinger's State Department and the Shah of Iran cut a deal that effectively turned our backs on our former Kurdish allies, paving the way for their bloody suppression. Kissinger later callously dismissed complaints about the human cost of this cynical betrayal by saying: "Covert action isn't missionary work."

In recent years, tens of thousands of Kurds have been imprisoned, tortured, and murdered by Saddam and his brutal forces. Deference to Turkey, and to Saddam himself, made our response to these outrages shamelessly muted.

Today, representatives of Physicians for Human Rights suggest that every day as many as 1,000 refugees on the Iraq-Turkey border alone are dying.

Iran claims it is spending $10 million a day on refugee relief.

Yet, to date, no direct U.S. aid has been given to the people there.

President Bush mustered world opinion ably and well against the Iraqi invasion of Kuwait. Yet, his administration seems positively wimpish about calling on the international community to show the same concern about Saddam's victims in Iraq.

Mr. President, this is not a new world order; this is a brave new world, where in order to save Iraqi national sovereignty have ended up as silent accomplices in the destruction of Iraqis; where big brother Saddam continues to receive our deference, and where human freedom is merely a slogan mouthed by policymakers, not a policy itself.

It is shameful, and it must stop.

80.

[April 29, 1991 (House), p. 2568]

PLACES OF REFUGE FOR THE KURDS

(Mr. GEKAS asked and was given permission to address the House for 1 minute and to revise and extend his remarks.)

Mr. GEKAS. Mr. Speaker, I have written a letter to the President of the United States in which I have expressed my fullest support for his actions and that of our allies in establishing the places of refuge for the Kurds and for other displaced persons, in providing security for them and assuring clothing and shelter and all the amenities of life itself. And further I have indicated to the President that I would support him 100 percent if he should decide in the near or further future that the use of force will again be necessary to assure that these Kurds and other displaced persons will remain secure, that he has my support in that regard.

If Saddam's people dare to even fire one shot at the coalition or American forces, we ought to be in a position to hunt him down and to remove him from power forever.

81.

[April 30, 1991 (House), p. 2576]

RELIEF FOR THE KURDISH REFUGEES

(Mr. MAZZOLI asked and was given permission to address the House for 1 minute and to revise and extend his remarks.)

Mr. MAZZOLI. Mr. Speaker, later today the House will take up the bill, H. R. 2122, which is an emergency bill to provide assistance to the Kurdish refugees who are in the camps in Iraq and in Turkey and in Iran. This bill provides for some $400 million in assistance to these refugees through the United Nations and through other multinational disaster relief agencies.

We hope, of course, after seeing the plight of these people that has been so clearly demonstrated on TV, that once their plight has been eased and once their situation is stabilized that most, if not all, will be repatriated, which is to say returned to their hometowns to take up the lives that they had before the war began. But for many of these people, return home will not be possible for a number of reasons.

Accordingly, at my request as chairman of the Subcommittee on International Law, Immigration, and Refugees, I have asked the General Accounting Office to send a team to the camps to assess the needs not just for assistance that the refugees need now but to gather information concerning whether or not the United States has a responsibility to resettle some or all of these people. The obvious likelihood is not all can or should be resettled but perhaps some would have to have a place to go other than their hometowns.

I will report to the House and to the country as this investigation proceeds.

82.

[April 30, 1991 (House), pp. 2584-90]

EMERGENCY SUPPLEMENTAL PERSIAN GULF REFUGEE ASSISTANCE ACT OF 1991

Mr. BERMAN. Mr. Speaker, I move to suspend the rules and pass the bill (H.R. 2122) to authorize emergency humanitarian assistance for fiscal year 1991 for Iraqi refugees and other persons in and around Iraq who are displaced as a result of the Persian Gulf conflict.

The Clerk read as follows:

H.R. 2122

Be it enacted by the Senate and House of Representatives of the United States of America in Congress assembled,

SECTION 1. SHORT TITLE.

This Act may be cited as the "Emergency Supplemental Persian Gulf Refugee Assistance Act of 1991".

SECTION 2. EMERGENCY ASSISTANCE FOR REFUGEES.

(a) Authorization of Appropriations.—There are authorized to be appropriated as supplemental appropriations for fiscal year 1991 for emergency humanitarian assistance for Iraqi refugees and other persons in and around Iraq who are displaced as a result of the Persian Gulf conflict, and to reimburse appropriations accounts from which such assistance was provided before the date of the enactment of this Act—

(1) up to $150,000,000 for "International Disaster Assistance" under chapter 9 of part I of the Foreign Assistance Act of 1961; and

(2) up to $200,000,000 for "Migration and Refugee Assistance" for the Department of State.

(b) Emergency Migration and Refugee Assistance.—For purposes of section 2(c)(2) of the Migration and Refugee Assistance Act of 1962, the limitation on appropriations for the "United States Emergency Refugee and Migration Assistance Fund" for fiscal year 1991 shall be deemed to be $75,000,000.

(c) Contributions to International Peacekeeping Activities.—There are authorized to be appropriated as supplemental appropriations for fiscal year 1991 for peacekeeping activities in the Persian Gulf region and to reimburse accounts for which such activities have been funded before the date of enactment of this Act up to $50,000,000 for "Contributions to International Peacekeeping Activities" for the Department of State.

(d) Other Authorities.—

(1) International disaster assistance.—Amounts obligated for fiscal year 1991 under the authority of section 492(b) of the Foreign Assistance Act of 1961 to provide international disaster assistance in connection with the Persian Gulf crisis shall not be counted against the ceiling limitation of such section.

(2) Special authority.—The value of any defense articles, defense services, and military education and training authorized to be drawn down by the President on April 19, 1991, under the authority of section 506(a)(2)(B) of the Foreign Assistance Act of 1961 shall not be counted against the ceiling limitation of such section.

(3) Agricultural trade development and assistance act of 1954 (public law 480).—Notwithstanding subsections (b) and (c) of section 412 fo the Agricultural Trade Development and assistance Act of 1954 or any other provision of law, funds made available for any title of such Act by the Rural Development, Agriculture, and related Agencies Appropriations Act, 1991, may be used for purposes of title II of the Agricultural Trade Development and Assistance Act of 1954.

(d) Waiver of Country Specific Restrictions.—Assistance may be provided under this section notwithstanding any provision of law which restricts assistance to particular countries.

(e) Availability of Funds.—Amounts authorized to be appropriated under this section are authorized to remain available until expended.

(f) Sources of Funds.—Notwithstanding any other provision of law, amounts authorized to be appropriated under this section are authorized to be appropriated from the Defense Cooperation Account of the United States Treasury, the Persian Gulf Regional Defense Fund of the United States Treasury, or the General Rule of the Treasury.

(g) Designation as Emergency for Budgetary Purposes.—Funds authorized to be appropriated under this section may be designated emergency requirements pursuant to section 251(b)(2)(D)(i) of the Balanced Budget and Emergency Deficit Control Act of 1985.

The SPEAKER pro tempore. Pursuant to the rule, the gentleman from California [Mr. Berman] will be recognized for 20 minutes and the gentleman from Michigan [Mr. Broomfield] will be recognized for 20 minutes.

The Chair recognizes the gentleman from California [Mr. Berman].

Mr. BERMAN. Mr. Speaker, I yield myself such time as I may consume.

Mr. Speaker, from April 18 to 22, I traveled with a congressional delegation, ably led by the gentleman from New York [Mr. McHugh] to assess the predicament and needs of Iraqi refugees and displaced persons in Turkey and in northern Iraq.

What we were able to see was only a small part of the appalling tragedy which, by all accounts, has befallen the people of Iraq.

What we quickly came to understand was both what an outstanding job the international community, led by the United States, has done to respond to the needs of the people in this area, and how great a need remains yet to be addressed.

The magnitude of the suffering and humanitarian needs which we witnessed at first hand was such that it is hard to believe that it represents only one part of a much larger humanitarian emergency.

In addition to visiting, and witnessing the plight of, these refugees and displaced persons, we also reviewed the operations and sites of the United States relief effort in the area, spoke with our military personnel involved in these operations, and met with officials including the President and other officials of Turkey, the United States Ambassador to Turkey, United States military commanders, and U.N. officials, including Prince Sadruddin Aga Khan, coordinator of the relief effort.

What we saw and discussed on the border of Iraq and Turkey is, as I said, only one part of the total tragedy. Both further within Iraq, on Iraq's southern borders, and in Iran and Saudi Arabia, are found large populations of persons displaced from their homes, suffering from hunger and medical needs, and usually in fear of their safety. Indeed, in Iran the scale of the problem is even greater than that on the Turkish border of Iraq.

H. R. 2122 would authorize the resources necessary for the United States to adequately fulfill its responsibility in this situation.

This bill would authorize appropriations of $200 million for migration and refugee assistance to the Department of State; $150 million for international disaster assistance under the Foreign Assistance Act; and $50 million for contributions to international peacekeeping activities.

This bill would also—

Allow use of the funds appropriated under it for reimbursement of accounts from which such assistance has already been provided;

Authorize the temporary lifting of the cap on the emergency migration and refugee assistance account from $50 million to $75 million; and

Allow provision of assistance only for these purposes to countries to which assistance is ordinarily prohibited. This would allow assistance for the purposes of humanitarian relief to Iran, which is host to the majority of Iraqi refugees.

This mix of authorities will allow the United States, through international organizations, private voluntary agencies, and otherwise, to address the variety of needs which exists. Only part of the suffering Iraqi population is outside its country of nationality, and therefore entitled to assistance provided by refugee agencies. The resources authorized for migration and refugee assistance will allow that population's needs to be met.

A population with equally compelling needs is that of persons still within Iraq. The resources authorized for international disaster assistance will partially address their needs.

It was also quite clear during our recent trip that one of the most compelling needs of refugees and displaced persons is for basic security. It is also clear that, for better or worse, the United States will not indefinitely assume a role in keeping the peace, with or without allies, unless there is a transition to a United Nations or other multilateral presence. It is for this reason that our bill includes the resources for U.S. contributions, through the Department of State, to international peacekeeping activities.

We are aware that this is an extraordinary initiative, and that it represents an extraordinary amount of resources for a single region. We believe that it is justified, in part by the special role that the United States has assumed in the region, and in part by the extraordinary human needs that must be addressed. It is quite clear from what we saw, and from what we know from public sources of what we were unable to see at firsthand, that the need is indeed compelling.

The committee is aware of other needs elsewhere in the world, and it is certainly not our intention to either allow those needs to be ignored as a matter of policy, or to deprive them of resources. The people of Liberia, Sudan, and Somalia appear to be suffering equally grave humanitarian tragedies, and United States policy will undoubtedly continue to seek resources to meet their needs.

It is to ensure that the present initiative does not detract from our ability to respond elsewhere that H. R. 2122 includes certain elements not directly related to needs of Iraqis.

Section 2(a) of our bill would allow use of the funds authorized to be appropriated under it to reimburse migration and refugee and international disaster assistance money that has already been used for gulf-related needs. This would ensure that the capacity of these accounts to address needs elsewhere would be restored.

Section 2(b) of our bill would temporarily lift the ceiling on funds which may be held in the emergency migration and refugee fund [ERMA] at any one time from $50 million to $75 million. Our bill would also leave ERMA free to respond to other needs by providing sufficient authorizations to meet Iraqi needs through the migration and refugee assistance and international disaster assistance accounts. Although ERMA is a permanently authorized fund, and we do not authorize appropriations for it, we trust that the Appropriations Committee will approve a level up to the new ceiling for that account.

The administration's request for supplemental appropriations, dated April 25, is for a total amount of $150 million. Our bill's authorized level of $400 million is designed to provide room for that and any further appropriations which may be requested for these purposes for fiscal year 1991. In the event that the level we authorize is not necessary, I am sure that we will all be delighted, not only at the fiscal implications of that, but also at the improvement in the humanitarian situation which that would suggest.

Finally, I would like to express appreciation to those colleagues with whom I was privileged to travel to the region, our delegation leader, Mr. McHugh, Mrs. Roukema, Mr. Hall of Ohio, and Mr. Smith of New Jersey.

Their observations and insights contributed immeasurably to my understanding of the situation.

I am happy to note that the administration supports this legislation.

Mr. BERMAN. Mr. Speaker, I yield such time as he may consume to the chairman of the Committee on Foreign Affairs, the gentleman from Florida [Mr. Fascell], who set the hearing and movement on this legislation as soon as we came back from our trip.

Mr. FASCELL. Mr. Speaker, I thank the subcommittee chairman for yielding me some time.

Mr. Speaker, I want to take a moment to simply express my appreciation to the delegation that went to view firsthand this very difficult situation.

Mr. Speaker, I rise in strong support of H. R. 2122, a bill authorizing emergency humanitarian assistance for fiscal year 1991 for Iraqi refugees and other persons in and around Iraq who are displaced as a result of the Persian Gulf conflict.

Mr. Speaker, this legislation, represents an effort by the Committee on Foreign Affairs to provide a quick response to assist refugees in the Persian Gulf, and to provide the administration with the flexibility to continue to respond throughout the remainder of this fiscal year as this crisis continues to unfold.

This bill was drafted after an in-depth hearing where testimony was heard from the executive branch, non-government relief organizations active in the region, and Members of Congress who traveled to the region to witness the human devastation. The assessment of the Speaker's delegation, including that of the distinguished sponsor of this bill, the gentleman from California, is that generous relief is needed on an urgent basis.

Nongovernment organizations have estimated that this crisis will cost the international community upward of $1 billion before the dying will stop. Given such assessments. I believe that this bill is a realistic measure to authorize U.S. funding for the remainder of the fiscal year.

H. R. 2122 provides up to $400 million in urgent authorities for: migration and refugee assistance, disaster assistance, and international peacekeeping authorities. It also temporarily raises the ceiling on the emergency refugee and migration account so that this account may be reimbursed for the drawdowns already made on behalf of the Persian Gulf refugees. A replenishment of this account would enable the Department of State to continue to respond to the situation in the Persian Gulf as well as fund other dire refugee situations in other parts of the world. The authorities in this bill will enable the United States to respond with direct aid, or by contributing to the numerous appeals from international organizations, already in excess of $700 million.

The administration has made it clear that is expects to turn the duties of administering refugee camps and protecting refugee populations over to the United Nations. To assist in that process, this bill includes $50 million in new authority for international peacekeeping activities. Finally, this bill provides that the defense cooperation account and the Persian Gulf regional defense fund may be sources of funding for these humanitarian assistance measures.

I urge my colleagues to support this legislation.

□ 1320

Mr. BROOMFIELD. Mr. Speaker, I yield myself such time as I may consume.

(Mr. BROOMFIELD asked and was given permission to revise and extend his remarks.)

Mr. BROOMFIELD. Mr. Speaker, each day, the bitter legacy of Saddam Hussein's atrocities against his fellow man is evidenced by the suffering of thousands of Iraqi refugees who are mired in squalid refugee camps. This legislation seeks to alleviate that suffering.

This bill has the support of the administration. It has three important features. First, it authorizes the appropriation of $400 million in additional funds for international disaster assistance, migration and refugee assistance, and peacekeeping activities in the Persian Gulf region.

These funds may be appropriated, at the discretion of the executive branch, from three different sources: The defense cooperation account, which was established as the reposi-

tory of foreign contributions to the Persian Gulf war effort; the Persian Gulf regional defense fund, for which $15 billion was appropriated in early April; and the general fund of the Treasury. Any appropriations from the sources may be designated as emergency expenditures and are therefore budget-neutral.

Second, the bill raises the statutory ceilings on the amounts of international disaster assistance, emergency migration and refugee assistance, and military supplies and services that can be made available in fiscal year 1991.

Third, the bill provides authority to increase the amount of funds available to provide food aid to the refugees.

Mr. Speaker, this legislation could not be more timely. I call on Members to support its swift passage.

Mr. Speaker, I yield 2 minutes to the distinguished gentleman from New York [Mr. Gilman].

(Mr. GILMAN asked and was given permission to revise and extend his remarks.)

Mr. GILMAN. Mr. Speaker, I rise to express my strong support for H.R. 2122, a bill authorizing emergency humanitarian assistance for fiscal year 1991 for Iraqi refugees and other persons in and around Iraq who are displaced as a result of the Persian Gulf conflict.

I commend the gentleman from California [Mr. Berman], the distinguished chairman of our Foreign Affairs Committee the gentleman from Florida [Mr. Fascell], the distinguished ranking Republican member the gentleman from Michigan [Mr. Broomfield], and the chairman of our Subcommittee on Europe and the Middle East, the gentleman from Indiana [Mr. Hamilton] for their outstanding, expeditious work on this critically needed and important measure.

Mr. Speaker, this measure comes at a time when, over 1 million Kurdish refugees are seeking safe haven from the barbarity of Saddam Hussein's forces in Iraq. Many of the encampments created by our allied forces are lacking in even the most rudimentary sanitary provisions: no latrines, no camp registration, and no proper medical personnel or supplies to care for the wounded.

This measure will provide up to $150 million for international disaster assistance and up to $200 million for migration and refugee assistance. In addition, a number of other provisions have been made for additional funding from a variety of other sources.

It is also necessary for us to remember than there are 12,000 Assyrian Christians, as well as other minorities such as Chaldeans and Turkomans, who also continue to suffer from Saddam Hussein's brutal and vicious tactics. It is my sincere hope that this measure will be a step toward ameliorating the living conditions of all of these refugees.

According, Mr. Speaker, I urge the causes to full support this measure.

Mr. BERMAN. Mr. Speaker, I yield 3 minutes to the gentleman from Kentucky [Mr. Mazzoli], the chairman of the Subcommittee on Immigration, Refugees, and International Law.

(Mr. MAZZOLI asked and was given permission to revise and extend his remarks.)

Mr. MAZZOLI. Mr. Speaker, I thank the gentleman from California for yielding me this time. Let me salute the gentleman, as others have, on his outstanding work, both as a member of the Committee on the Judiciary, and also as a leading member of the House Committee on Foreign Affairs, for his work today.

Mr. Speaker, I also commend the gentleman from Michigan [Mr. Broomfield], and the gentleman from California [Mr. Lagomarsino], and others.

Mr. Speaker, this bill before us is a very important piece of legislation. I salute the committees for having moved it very quickly.

As the gentleman from California [Mr. Berman] has said, this bill provides over $400 million in immediate assistance to the refugees who are living in these terrible conditions in Iraq and other parts of the Middle East. It provides assistance through the United Nations. It provides assistance through other multinational disaster relief agencies. It helps provide money for the peacekeeping effort, and it certainly does a very commendable job of trying to assist in place, trying to relieve the current plight of these people.

Mr. Speaker, as the gentleman from California [Mr. Berman] and I both know, the issue goes beyond immediate assistance to the refugees. We hope, and it does appear to be somewhat possible, that most of these people can be repatriated, go back to their home villages, where they would be protected from any retribution, and where they could resume the threads of their life that have been exploded by this gulf war.

But there may be some who cannot be repatriated. As a result, we are sending over pursuant to my request a team from the General Accounting Office to take a look at the refugee matter, not just from the perspective of immediate assistance, but also from the long-term perspective of what people in that group cannot be repatriated because of some special problems they might have and what people in that group we may have a special relationship to by reason of their actions on behalf of the United States.

As a result of that team effort, the GAO will report back to us, and we in turn will report to Members here in the House on just what responsibilities the United States might have under the 1980 Refugee Act.

We know, unfortunately, that the 1980 act has not been extended or reauthorized for several years. It has been continued via the appropriations process. I am hopeful that this year we might be able to reauthorize the Refugee Act.

Mr. Speaker, in any event, this bill before us is important, because it addresses the plight of the refugees today. It helps relieve their misery and put them into more habitable settings. But in the long run, there will be other responsibilities we will have to address. I am looking forward to working with the gentleman from California [Mr. Berman], and others, in fulfilling those other additional responsibilities.

Mr. Speaker, I support the bill, and I hope that it has immediate and unanimous support.

Mr. BROOMFIELD. Mr. Speaker, I yield 3 minutes to the distinguished gentleman from California [Mr. Lagomarsino].

(Mr. LAGOMARSINO asked and was given permission to revise and extend his remarks.)

Mr. LAGOMARSINO. Mr. Speaker, I rise in support of this bill which I have also cosponsored authorizing emergency humanitarian assistance for Iraqi refugees and other persons in and around Iraq who are displaced as a result of the Persian Gulf conflict. Clearly, from the testimony the Foreign Affairs Committee has heard, especially from the congressional delegation, and from the very moving pictures on television and in the newspapers, it is clear beyond a doubt that these innocent refugees—Saddam Hussein's latest victims—need help and need it right now.

I am encouraged that the Bush administration has already answered the calls for help from Iraqi Kurds, Shiites and others by providing both humanitarian assistance and creating special safe-haven enclaves where these refugees are protected from Saddam Hussein's terror squads. And, as I personally witnessed during my recent trip to Kuwait, Saddam Hussein's brutality is real and deadly. Today's legislation allows for additional assistance to be provided, including funds for much needed peacekeeping activities.

While I support this measure and urge its immediate adoption, I do hope that it can be followed up with another bill including needed policy language. I recognize that to pass this critical authorization bill as expeditiously as possible and with as little controversy as possible, policy language we discussed in the committee had to be deleted. For example, I had an amendment that would have required Iraqi war reparations be used to help pay for this assistance to Kurdish and other refugees. As citizens of Iraq, they should benefit from their Government's expenditures, particularly since, to date, they have only suffered at the hands of Saddam Hussein's regime. Iraq's resources should be used to help its citizens, not harm them. As I said, I hope we can positively address this and other important policy issues in the very near future.

Nevertheless, I strongly support this bill today and commend my colleagues, Dante Fascell, Howard Berman, Matt McHugh, Bill Broomfield, Olympia Snowe, Ben Gilman, Marge Roukema, and Chris Smith for taking the lead and bringing this measure to the floor.

□1330

Mr. BERMAN. Mr. Speaker, I yield 3 minutes to the gentleman from New York [Mr. McHugh] who, in addition to being a member of the Subcommittee on Foreign Operations that will soon be considering appropriations under this legislation, also led the delegation to visit these refugee camps.

Mr. McHUGH. Mr. Speaker, I want to thank the gentleman from California not only for yielding time to me but for his leadership on this legislation. He and I, as well as Representatives Marge Roukema, Tony Hall, and Chris Smith, had the opportunity of the request of the Speaker within the last 10 days to visit the Iraqi-Turkish border areas and see the human tragedy that has been unfolding there.

We have all observed on television these compelling pictures of families, from very young babies to grandparents, suffering under horrendous conditions. To visit these locations personally one can fully appreciate the individual suffering, and also the remote and rugged locations in which these people are struggling to survive. It is truly a moving experience, and it is important for us to respond to this human crisis as quickly and as fulsomely as we can. In this conclusion, I want to commend the Committee on Foreign Affairs for moving so promptly on a bipartisan basis, and I urge my colleagues to support this legislation.

The delegation which I had the privilege to lead at the Speaker's request reached a number of conclusions, one of which was that President Bush made the right decision in authorizing American military forces to undertake this humanitarian effort. Not only are there an enormous number of refugees who seem to have been dropped on these rugged mountains, which are comparable to the Alps, but they gathered in a matter of days, overwhelming the capacity of neighboring governments and humanitarian relief agencies to respond. Only the U.S. military, with the help of some of our coalition partners, could have delivered the urgent humanitarian relief which is necessary, and even then doctors who have gone into these areas project that people are still dying on an average of between 400 and 1,000 a day.

It is critically important not only to provide this relief, but to get these people off the mountains into the temporary camps in low-lying areas. We have been assuming the primary responsibility for doing that. It costs money. About a week ago when our delegation returned from that region, our Government had already spent about $133 million in this effort. We need to restore that money. There are other problems in the world to which we and the international community must attend.

Therefore, this legislation is important as an initial, critical response to restore what we have been already incurred by way of expense in this humanitarian effort.

Our delegation also concluded that this humanitarian effort should be undertaken as soon as possible by the international community, primarily by the United Nations and other international relief organizations. Our military is not a humanitarian relief organization, but if we expect these traditional relief agencies to take over this effort, it is important that they get the kind of financial support that is necessary, not just from the United States but from other countries. This bill will make that kind of contribution possible.

For all of these reasons, Mr. Speaker, I want to commend the committee for its fine work. My hope is that the Appropriations Committee on which I served will respond quickly as well, as I think we will. I urge my colleagues to support this legislation.

Mr. BROOMFIELD. Mr. Speaker, I yield 3 minutes to the distinguished gentlewoman from New Jersey [Mrs. Roukema] who was a part of the congressional delegation who went along with the gentleman from New York [Mr. McHugh] to northern Iraq to visit the Kurdish refugees.

Mrs. ROUKEMA. Mr. Speaker, I thank my colleague for yielding me this time.

Mr. Speaker, this morning as I picked up my *New York Times*, I noticed on the front page a picture of a small Kurdish girl. The child was riding on what appeared to be a United States military vehicle as it carried her to the newly established "safe havens" in the Iraqi city of Zakho. The joy in her face and those riding with her was heartwarming. It was also in stark contrast to the horrors of the mountain refugee camps that we visited last weekend as members of House leadership delegation, led by Representative Matt McHugh.

The name Operation Provide Comfort is a misnomer. The United States is not there to provide comfort but rather to establish a life support system for the hundreds of thousands of Kurdish refugees who fled the brutal oppression of Saddam Hussein. This is just the latest episode in a long history of nationalistic and ethnic hatred of the Kurdish people. As we viewed it last week, conditions were deteriorating rapidly and, if left unattended, would have accelerated and grown exponentially with massive starvation, disease, and death. Absent the swift actions of President Bush in providing assistance, the situation had the potential for a genocidal catastrophe.

Phase 1 of our relief effort is the immediate delivery of emergency supplies in an effort to stave off disease and death. Phase 2 is the relocation of the refugees to these safe haven camps established by the U.S. military. As these efforts get underway, I want to address two areas lacking attention as I witnessed during my visit.

Although foodstuffs in general are lacking, particularly distressing is the fact that there is no distribution of prepared infant formula. Mothers are no longer lactating and the babies cannot digest the jarred baby food that has been provided to the camps. In the Kurdish culture it is not uncommon to find a mother who breast feeds her children up to 2 years old. Therefore, we must provide prepared infant formula. Toward that end, I have personally spoken with Dr. Ronald Roskens, the Administrator of the Agency for International Development, to stress the importance of this.

Dr. Roskins also assured me that basic staples will be on the way. Namely, wheat, rice, and other high protein foods available under the Public Law 480, Food for Peace Program.

It also pains me to report that medical care is grossly inadequate. We must provide the resources to bring in medical experts immediately. While medical supplies are in seriously short supply, some vaccines and antibiotics have made it to the mountain regions.

However, these camps need the medical personnel to deliver care.

Finally, Mr. Speaker, I cannot emphasize enough that the U.S. military should not be in the long-term business of operating refugee camps. Make no mistake, our service people are to be commended for their swift and professional efforts. However, it is the United Nations that is the appropriate organization to run these camps and provide protection for the Kurdish people. The United States should be out of Iraq as soon as possible.

Mr. Speaker, I support this emergency relief package under consideration today and I urge my colleagues to vote in favor of it.

□1340

Mr. BERMAN. Mr. Speaker, I yield 2 1/2 minutes to the gentleman from Ohio [Mr. Hall].

(Mr. HALL of Ohio asked and was given permission to revise and extend his remarks.)

Mr. HALL of Ohio. Mr. Speaker, I rise in support of H.R. 2122. I commend the gentleman from California [Mr. Berman], for introducing this important piece of legislation to authorize emergency assistance for the Iraqi refugees. I also want to thank the Foreign Affairs Committee for reporting this supplemental authorization which will be an important step in helping to alleviate the suffering I and four of my colleagues witnessed on our recent trip to the refugee camps at the Turkish border.

This legislation authorizing supplemental funds for the Iraqi refugees will be a valuable contribution to the excellent relief efforts currently being undertaken by the United States military. As we saw during our trip, it is vital to continue the relief operations now underway to move the refugees from the mountaintops, to more accessible areas where they can receive the necessary food and medical assistance.

This supplemental is particularly important, not only because of the Kurdish refugee crisis, but because of all the other pressing refugee problems around the world which are all competing for our scarce resources. Right now in the Sudan, around 10 million people are now at risk of starvation. People are already dying there, and large numbers of deaths can be expected soon. Therefore, it is critical that we provide these additional funds for the Iraqi refugees and not deplete the emergency resources for Africa.

I would also like to underline the importance of the waiver of country specific restrictions in the bill. This is vital regarding assistance to Iran, which is now facing a larger influx of Iraqi refugees than Turkey. There are reports of over 1 million refugees inside Iran, with another 500,000 to 800,000 along the border.

I urge my colleagues to support this resolution and support the Iraqi refugees.

Mr. BROOMFIELD. Mr. Speaker, I yield 5 minutes to the distinguished gentleman from New Jersey [Mr. Smith], who also accompanied the gentleman from New York [Mr. McHugh] on the recent trip to northern Iraq.

Mr. SMITH of New Jersey. Mr. Speaker, I rise in strong support of the Emergency Supplemental Persian Gulf Refugee Assistance Act of 1991 which will authorize $400 million in aid to the refugees including the Kurdish population displaced by Saddam Hussein and his government. The administration, as well, is in strong support of this measure.

At the Speaker's behest, I had the privilege of joining my colleagues, the gentleman from New York [Mr. McHugh], the gentleman from Ohio [Mr. Hall], the gentleman from California [Mr. Berman], and the gentlewoman from New Jersey [Mrs. Roukema], on a 5-day factfinding mission to assess the Iraqi refugee crisis and efforts under way to help the Kurdish people. Upon our return, in testimony before the Committee on Foreign Affairs and in meetings with Deputy Secretary of State Lawrence Eagleburger, we urged the Congress and the administration to proceed quickly on the request for additional humanitarian aid and to do so without diminishing the important work in our commitment to work with such refugee assistance in Africa and other parts of the world, and move quickly they have, as evidenced by this bill.

Mr. Speaker, the explosion of displaced persons inside Iraq and the hundreds of thousands of refugees fleeing into Turkey and Iran is unprecedented in modern history. Within a span of 2 or 3 days in early April, hundreds of thousands of Iraqis fled their homes in a desperate attempt to escape the brutality of Saddam Hussein. I will point out that none of the experts in the international relief community anticipated the magnitude nor the rapidity of the exodus. All were caught off guard.

Mr. Speaker, it became very clear to me during the visit that two events were instrumental in beginning to alleviate the suffering of Iraqi refugees. The first was Secretary of State Baker's trip to the area of April 7 and 8 which galvanized the administration and the world into according to higher priority to the refugee situation, and the second was President Bush's decision to fly United States military forces to Turkey to take charge of the relief operations. These operations, as we saw firsthand, have proven to be absolutely essential in preventing a tragedy of even greater catastrophic proportions.

Mr. Speaker, thousands would have died but for the U.S. military's rapid response to the crisis. Mr. Speaker, the allied provision of security for the refugees in the north of Iraq and the withdrawal of Iraqi troops has clearly eased fears, and the refugees are beginning to return to their homes. Without the confidence of our security, however, and the need of that security, the refugees will understandably not be willing to endanger their families and venture back to their villages and their homes.

Mr. Speaker, the crisis in the refugee camps that we visited in Cukurca cannot be overstated. At the refugee camp there and elsewhere, disease has been rampant, a circumstance that is especially chilling in light of the fact that over 50 percent of the refugee population is comprised of children under the age of 12.

Officials of the U.N. High Commissioner for Refugees reported in their handouts to us in Geneva that there are 7 to 10 deaths each day for every 10,000 refugees. Thankfully the number has been mitigated.

Many victims, I would point out, are children, and babies are especially vulnerable.

Mr. Speaker, the troops that are engaged in the intensive and heroic mission to stabilize the refugee population ought to be congratulated by this body for their outstanding efforts.

The initial results are no less spectacular than those achieved in Operation Desert Storm.

Mr. Speaker, as the immediate efforts to stop the dying and suffering continue, the United States must be committed and is committed to its priority of relocating the refugees from their often inaccessible mountain campsites to the lower terrain where they can be adequately cared for and shielded from the elements. Providing the needed protection to encourage families to continue their return is undoubtedly one of the greatest challenges of all. The refugees look to the United States and they look to our allied partners to be their guarantors against renewed savagery by Saddam Hussein.

Mr. Speaker, the provision of refugee assistance contained in this bill is absolutely necessary, and I hope we get a unanimous vote in favor of it.

Finally, I would like to thank the gentleman from California [Mr. Berman] for his responsiveness in helping to bring this legislation to the floor. It was a real honor and a privilege to travel with the other four members of this delegation led by the gentleman from New York [Mr. McHugh] and the gentleman from Ohio [Mr. Hall] and the gentlewoman from New Jersey [Mrs. Roukema] and, of course, the gentleman from California [Mr. Berman]. I think we worked in an extraordinarily bipartisan way.

We were there to assess the situation to try to glean as quickly as we could during the visit what was truly going on and how we might be a part of the effort to make it better.

Also, I want to commend our excellent staff who were on board who provided us with a tremendous amount of assistance including our own staffer, David Laufman, who was a very valuable addition to the delegation.

I would also like to thank the gentleman from Illinois [Mr. Michel] and the gentleman from Michigan [Mr. Broomfield] for recommending the gentlewoman from New Jersey [Mrs. Roukema] and I make this trip as a part of the Speaker's delegation.

Mr. Speaker, I urge passage.

Mr. BROOMFIELD. Mr. Speaker, I have not further requests for time, and I yield back the balance of my time.

Mr. BERMAN. Mr. Speaker, I yield 3 1/2 minutes to the gentleman from New York [Mr. Scheuer].

(Mr. SCHEUER asked and was given permission to revise and extend his remarks.)

Mr. SCHEUER. Mr. Speaker, I strongly support the emergency aid to Iraqi refugees. I wish to strongly commend the gentleman from Florida [Mr. Fascell], chairman of the full committee, the gentleman from California [Mr. Berman], and the gentlewoman from New Jersey [Mrs. Roukema] on the minority side for their splendid and enthusiastic support.

Mr. Speaker, words and deeds have consequences. When our President exhorts the Iraqis to rise up and throw out their depraved leader and when our country, in a correct decision, unleashes a hail of bombs on that beleaguered country, those words and deeds have consequences. They are reasonably predictable consequences. For us at the end of the 100-hour war to want to turn our backs and walk away from the scene and get the troops home before we have adequately evaluated the postwar challenge in that area does not show America in its best light.

There was a vacuum there, and thank the Lord the Committee on Foreign Affairs, the gentleman from California [Mr. Berman], and the gentleman from Florida [Mr. Fascell] and the distinguished minority supporters met that vacuum and came in with a fine program for emergency aid to Iraq.

But there is yet much more to be done. Mr. Speaker, I have talked to the gentleman from California [Mr. Berman], and I know how deeply he feels about the essential need for an arms-denial program for the Middle East, to create some of the conditions for peace there and prevent vast imports into the area of weapons of mass destruction to be used all too frequently by despots, by authoritarians, and states that do not have the remotest semblance of democracy.

□1350

The second challenge that I hope and I am confident that the Committee on Foreign Affairs will take up is the challenge of putting together a regional development program to bring science and technology and aid to the countries of the Middle East that do not have the wherewithal to develop their resources now.

I hope that our Nation will encourage the countries of the Persian Gulf, especially Saudi Arabia and Kuwait, to reach into their pockets, and give of their resources to help achieve a greater degree of well-being and improved standard of living, improved joint cooperation in the area. That could be the precursor to peace between the Arabs and the Israelis.

Right now, we seek to alleviate immense human suffering.

Our reaction to the plight of the Iraqi refugees, the Kurds and the Shi'as has been sadly deficient.

We must reclaim the moral high ground, answer our obligations, and provide protection and aid to these brave peoples, and we must answer our critics who say this war was fought only for oil. The Kurds and the Shi'as answer to President Bush's exhortations for the overthrow of Saddam Hussein, brought down the wrath of Saddam Hussein's murderous army on top of them. To escape massacre, the Kurds fled on a death march through the frozen, muddied mountain passes.

We must not, cannot, and will not turn our backs on the desperate state of these refugees. Passage of this aid package is but a drop in the bucket, but a much-needed drop.

Mr. BERMAN. Mr. Speaker, I yield myself such time as I may consume to add that the gentleman from New York has raised some very important broader geopolitical questions surrounding this issue, and there are important questions. The use of our military for humanitarian purposes, the philosophical underpinnings of our refugee policy, and the extent to which that has worked in the past, the very important question of whether or not our goals here can be met with Saddam still in power, but we cannot let any of those broader questions stop the United States or cause the United States to get caught up in a failure to act about what we know to be the desperate need that exists now.

This bill provides the framework for this Congress helping the administration to meet that need. I think it is very important that we do so.

Mr. Penny. Mr. Speaker, I rise in strong support of this legislation authorizing emergency aid for Iraqi refugees.

The refugee situations on both the northern and southern borders of Iraq are unprecedented. The number of Kurds fleeing into such dangerous terrain and unfavorable weather conditions illustrates the political reasons for refugee situations and the fear these people have of Saddam Hussein.

We responded to the invasion of Kuwait and now we must respond to the human injustice the Kurds are trying to escape. Our efforts, although too late for some Kurdish refugees, many of them children, must continue at all urgency to help the thousands of other Kurdish refugees still caught in the refugee crisis. As world leaders we have the responsibility to protect the human rights of these people. The need for shelter, food, medical supplies, water, adequate clothing, and manpower with the necessary skills to help the refugees cannot be underestimated.

As we all are aware, refugee camps are being established in the northern areas of Iraq. We must not abandon these people once the camps are established. They have many obstacles before them as they seek to resettle permanently. Safety and security must be ensured for these people for we have seen the destruction the Iraqi leaders can bestow on innocent people. We hope the United Nations and the international community will accept their responsibilities to help the refugees with basic life support, resettlement assistance, and security.

As a member of the House Select Committee on Hunger, I caution us not to let our actions here today on behalf of the Iraqi refugees minimize the need to act on other critical refugee situations throughout the world, especially in the horn of Africa. Chairman TONY HALL has worked tirelessly on behalf of the world's refugees and recently traveled to the Iraq-Turkey border to observe the refugee situation firsthand. Representative Dorgan has

also taken a keen interest in the refugee situation in east Africa. I applaud their efforts.

Again, I commend the Foreign Affairs Committee for bringing this situation to our attention and expediting the passage of this critical legislation.

Mr. Weiss. Mr. Speaker, I rise in strong support of this legislation to provide desperately needed emergency assistance to the refugees fleeing Saddam Hussein's brutality in Iraq.

Approximately 850,000 Kurdish refugees are now stranded on the Iraq/Turkey border, and more than 1.5 million Kurds have fled to areas along the border with Iran.

In addition to these Kurdish refugees, there are also 100,000 Iraqi Shiites who have fled Southern Iraq—mostly into Iran and the allied-controlled zones where they are being fed and sheltered by United States forces.

Mr. Speaker, we have all seen the news reports about the desperate conditions under which these refugees are now living. Their situation is dire—they face malnutrition, disease, and completely inadequate living conditions. Some reports indicate that thousands may be dying each day. This human tragedy demands a response from the international community and from the United States.

This legislation—of which I am proud to be an original cosponsor—authorizes over $400 million in emergency assistance to Iraqi refugees in and around Iraq. Most of this assistance is in the form of aid to United Nations relief agencies or for other international disaster relief activities. The bill also permits the transfer of additional food assistance from the Food for Peace Program to the refugee zones in and around Iraq.

Mr. Speaker, this is not the first time these people have suffered as a result of Saddam Hussein's tyranny. Over the last decade, they have felt political repression, egregious human rights abuses, and even chemical attacks by the Iraqi government. These beleaguered refugees have suffered enough.

I strongly support this legislation and urge my colleagues to join with me and the other cosponsors in approving this desperately needed relief.

Mr. DE LA GARZA. Mr. Speaker, I rise in support of H.R. 2122, a bill to provide emergency assistance to the Kurdish people.

This legislation was jointly referred to the Committee on Agriculture because it contains a provision which provides more flexibility to transfer funds from other titles of the Food for Peace Act—Public Law 480—to Title II of that act for emergency feeding programs during fiscal year 1991.

In order to accommodate expeditious action by the House on this legislation, the Committee on Agriculture did not schedule a public hearing or markup on this legislation. However, we have discussed in full the need for this legislation with representatives of the Agency for International Development and are fully supportive of the legislation.

Mr. Speaker, this provision makes a necessary change in the existing limits on the transfer of funds within the Food for Peace Program.

Section 412(c) of the Agriculture Trade Development and Assistance Act of 1954 provides that up to 15 percent of the funds available in any fiscal year for carrying out any title of the act may be used to carry out any other title of the act. Section 412(b) of the act also requires that of the total amount of funds made available for titles I and III, not less than 40 percent of such funds shall be allocated to title I and not less than 40 percent shall be allocated to title III.

Finally, I would also note that the Rural Development, Agriculture, and Related Agencies Appropriations Act for fiscal year 1991—Public Law 101-506—prohibits the use of more than 10 percent of the funds made available to carry out any title of the act to carry out any other title of the act.

The increased flexibility provided by H. R. 2122 will not affect already planned title I and title III programs. Transfer of the unallocated funds from these programs, however, together with the availability of wheat from the Food Security Wheat Reserve, will help tremendously in addressing the increasing food needs of those facing emergency political, economic, and natural disaster situations.

The authorizing committees of jurisdiction are pleased to address these concerns through this legislation.

I commend Congressman BERMAN and our colleagues at the Committee on Foreign Affairs for their initiative to help the Kurdish people.

Mr. Speaker, H. R. 2122 deserves the support of each member of the House.

Mr. REED. Mr. Speaker, I rise today in support of emergency aid for those Iraqis now facing starvation and disease after fleeing the brutal campaign of repression carried out by Saddam Hussein.

In the wake of our military victory, we are beginning to comprehend the long-term costs associated with Operation Desert Storm.

Over the last few weeks, people throughout the United States and the world have seen the images of pain and suffering occurring along Iraq's borders with Turkey and Iran. They have been moved deeply by the sight of men and women burying their children. Families striving to survive on the limited supplies they could carry on their backs as they fled. And the omnipresent anguish on the faces of young and old alike.

True to our nation's spirit of compassion for the oppressed, U.S.' military personnel along with our coalition partners are establishing safety zones and refugee camps. At the same time, the distribution of direly needed food and medical assistance has begun.

While we must provide immediate aid for those in need, we must also begin the task of creating a stable environment which will allow for the pullout of our troops. We must also ensure that the burden of our aid and diplomatic efforts are shared equally by our coalition partners.

Mr. BILBRAY. Mr. Speaker, I rise today to not only acknowledge and commend the Congress' support for the Iraqi refugees but to also remind my fellow members of the questions that still remain about the political future of this dangerous situation.

There is no question in any of our minds that what the Kurdish and Shiite refugees need at this very minute is the food, shelter and security that our forces and our efforts are providing. This aid will cement our support to stop the slaughter by the Iraqi troops of these refugees. These brave citizens of the new world order answered the call to arms to overthrow the dictatorship of Saddam Hussein. As the Iraqi troops reorganized, these patriots of their cause, their wives and their children were murdered for standing up for freedom in Iraq.

In the mountains of the Turkish and Iranian border, we are now faced with the prospect of over 3 million refugees, forced out of their towns and villages in order that they could protect their families and their future from complete eradication by Saddam Hussein. The aid we are providing will stop the 500 to 1,000 men, women, and children who were dying every day. Yet, much will be left to do.

Our efforts have mainly concentrated on the Turkish and Iraqi border areas. There are over a million and a half people on the Iranian border who are just barely beginning to receive aid. We need to encourage the relief efforts to concentrate in this previously forgotten area. However, of dire importance is a lasting political solution in the area. The Kurdish and Shiite refugees in the region will not feel secure, and have no reason to feel secure until the threat of Saddam Hussein has been removed or extinguished. The international community needs to provide these people with a set of guarantees that will assure them of their continued safety and stability. As we encourage settlement of the political situation in the Palestinian/Israeli question let us also take up the instability of Iraq.

Again, I commend the efforts of Chairman FASCELL and the Foreign Affairs Committee to aid the Iraqi refugees. It is important that this Congress take the lead and initiative to help those who are in such dire need. I urge my fellow members to support this vital measure.

Mr. LEVINE of California. Mr. Speaker, I rise in strong support of the emergency supplement Iraqi Refugee Assistance Act of 1991, and commend Chairman FASCELL and Subcommittee Chairman HOWARD BERMAN for the appropriate speed with which this bill has been moved to the floor.

The horror of the human suffering on the Iraqi-Turkish border demands immediate and effective action. It is tragic that the President did not take earlier action in an attempt to prevent this catastrophe. The assistance we approve today will not help the thousands who were killed by Saddam Hussein's helicopter gunships, or who died of starvation and exposure in a desperate attempt to flee the genocidal policies of the Iraqi dictator.

But the thousands upon thousands of innocent civilians displaced as a result of the civil war in Iraq who survived the trek to the border regions continue to face the threat of death every day. Aid for these individuals is more urgent and necessary than ever.

I am pleased the President, at congressional urging, has involved our Armed Forces in the effort to protect the Kurds and other refugees and assist emergency relief supplies in getting through to where they are so desperately needed. But clearly, the catastrophic situation faced by these long-suffering people urgently demands the additional assistance provided for in this legislation.

Unquestionably, difficult policy choices remain about how to safeguard the Iraqi Kurdish population over the long term. I share the concerns of many of my colleagues that United States forces not be caught in a permanent holding pattern to protect Iraqi minorities, who will never be safe so long as Saddam Hussein remains in power. I welcome the moves from the United Nations indicating it will soon take greater responsibility for administering the refugee facilities.

But regardless of whatever thorny policy questions may arise, the human tragedy that presently exists requires humanitarian action.

I once again commend the authors of this legislation, and urge its unanimous acceptance by my colleagues.

Mr. BERMAN. Mr. Speaker, I have no further requests for time, and I yield back the balance of my time.

The SPEAKER pro tempore (Mr. McNulty). The question is on the motion offered by the gentleman from California [Mr. Berman] that the House suspend the rules and pass the bill, H. R. 2122.

The question was taken; and (two-thirds having voted in favor thereof) the rules were suspended and the bill was passed.

A motion to reconsider was laid on the table.

83.

[April 30, 1991 (Extensions of Remarks), p. 1502]

LET'S SAVE AMERICA'S KURDS
HON. PETER H. KOSTMAYER
OF PENNSYLVANIA
IN THE HOUSE OF REPRESENTATIVES

Tuesday, April 30, 1991

Mr. KOSTMAYER. Mr. Speaker, Mr. Leslie Gelb wrote in Sunday's *New York Times* ["Look Homeward"] of the plight of millions of Americans who go unhoused, uneducated, unfed, and unnoticed. If the United States can protect the Kurds of Iraq, and we must; if we can make sure they are fed and housed, cannot we do the same for millions of our own countrymen, many of them children?...

84.

[April 30, 1991 (Extensions of Remarks), p. 1504]

SO LITTLE TIME TO SAVE SO MANY LIVES
HON. BYRON L. DORGAN
OF NORTH DAKOTA
IN THE HOUSE OF REPRESENTATIVES

Tuesday, April 30, 1991

Mr. DORGAN of North Dakota. Mr. Speaker, last week, the Hunger Committee held a hearing to review the plight of the world's refugees and to see whether we are investing enough to respond to the situation. We learned that we have not.

The General Accounting Office testified that the number of refugees worldwide has more than doubled from 7 million to 15 or 16 million. That amount has now jumped to over 18 million with the refugee crisis in Iraq, Turkey, and Iran. During the same period, according to GAO, our overseas refugee relief has hovered at around $200 million and actually declined in real dollars.

This is not to say that the United States is lagging behind others. We contributed about $10 billion at home and abroad for all kinds of refugee relief in the 1980's. The United States was also the largest donor to all but one of four major international refugee relief organizations.

However, I believe that the growing refugee problem requires that we do even more to help. I, also, think that we can do so without adding to the budget deficit. Reallocating foreign aid from security assistance to refugee and food aid accounts can help to save lives and reduce human misery without straining our budget. The end of the cold war means that we can prudently make such a reallocation.

May I also emphasize that this is not a debate about statistics-whether money or refugees. It is a plea to save human lives-one at a time.

Right now, the international media have focused their cameras on the refugee crisis in Iraq. That's as it should be. I would like to include in the RECORD an article that describes the Kurdish refugee emergency by Lionel Rosenblatt, executive director of Refugees International ["The Race Against Time to Save Kurdish Refugees," *The Christian Science Monitor*, Apr. 19, 1991].

Mr. Rosenblatt testified at our hearing last week this is a case "of the failure of early warning and rapid international response to refugee crises." The House next week will authorize additional emergency relief but we must also explore how to establish an international emergency relief corps, which can help to prevent the deaths and suffering now taking their grim toll in the Kurdish encampments.

Mr. Rosenblatt also urged that we not forget the "looming famine in the Horn of

Africa that threatens to kill millions" and that "we must insure that the international community does not divert funds from that impending disaster. We should not rob the East Africans to pay for the refugees from Saddam." I could not agree more: . . .

85.

[May 6, 1991 (Senate), pp. 5335-6]

KURDISH REFUGEES

Mr. LEVIN. Mr. President, every American who has seen the pictures of the Kurdish refugees clinging to the sides of mountains has been moved and enraged. Squalid conditions, diarrhea, malnourishment, and disease have brought the Kurds the death and devastation they sought to escape when they fled Saddam Hussein's army.

But, Mr. President, some Americans are expressing emotions of a different sort. Let me quote, from this morning's *Washington Post*, the words of Army Reserve Lt. Patricia Lessor. She spoke of her worries from a United States-built tent camp near Zakhu, Iraq, as she processed Kurdish refugees.

Said Lieutenant Lessor:

I feel good about what I'm doing here, but I also feel like I'm leading lambs to the slaughter. We're taking care of them and everything's fine for now, but what happens when we go?

That is the question of the hour for the Kurds and for our military. It is a question Saddam Hussein would like the world to leave unanswered. But it is a question that can no longer be avoided.

I have just returned from visiting the border areas of Turkey and Iraq, with Senators EXON and ROBB where we witnessed firsthand the tragedy of the Kurdish people.

We stood in a makeshift graveyard below one camp and watched a family dig an infant daughter's grave. We visited a Dutch hospital tent where dying babies lay motionless next to their mothers. Despite his failure in war, these are the signs of success for Saddam Hussein in this effort to destroy the Kurdish people once and for all.

Amid the appalling tragedy there are heroic efforts to ease the suffering of the Kurds. We witnessed the awesome logistical might of the U.S. military and its lifesaving results. When finally ordered to the task of saving Kurdish lives, the U.S. military brought rations, water, blankets, and tents with impressive efficiency.

Huge tent cities are being built quickly. Tens of thousands of people will be saved from a slow death caused by malnutrition and disease, by harsh elements of cold and snow and, later heat and drought.

The death rate is now dropping, but the potential for devastating epidemics remains.

To escape the vengeance of Saddam Hussein, over a million Kurds left their cities and villages for the harsh uncertainties of the high country. Right now, to save lives, the primary goal of our military lifesavers and the international community is to convince the Kurds to leave the mountains.

And the Kurds are now coming off the mountains to these tent-cities for one reason: They trust the United States to protect them from Saddam Hussein's retribution. That was the message given to us over and over again by the refugees.

But a great uncertainty remains: will the Kurds use the tent cities as temporary homes as they hope? Can they ever find permanent safety in their own hometowns?

In Friday's *New York Times*, a young man newly returned to his village under the protection of U.S. troops was asked, "Do you feel safe now?" Given the permanent state of war that Saddam Hussein has maintained with the Kurds, his answer was predictable: "If you want the truth, no. We are scared they will do something to us."

Our Government has not yet said how long the Kurds will be protected by U.S. and allied forces. The tent cities' internal administration is being turned over to the United Nations. But the U.N. unit is a civilian operation rather than a protective military unit.

Clearly, it is vital to maintain military security in the refugee camps and the zones surrounding them. They are two ways to guarantee this security: keep allied and U.S. forces in place, or work to authorize an unprecedented U.N. military presence.

The United Nations has not sent protective forces to a nation without a request from that country. But the circumstances in Iraq demand some new approaches in the United Nations. It is necessary to begin shaping new principles of law.

These new principles should allow protection of refugees on the sovereign soil of a country, even without its agreement: First, by a U.N. protective force that is an adjunct to the civilian refugee administration; and second, where that refugee problem has been created as the result of a U.N. resolution authorizing the use of force against that country.

If there is to be a new world order, it should begin in this place and at this time, along the Iraq-Turkey border with or without the agreement of Saddam Hussein.

After too long a delay, the United States and the allied forces responded in an appropriate manner intervening to alleviate the massive suffering of the Kurdish people.

The PRESIDENT pro tempore. The time of the Senator has expired.

Mr. LEVIN. I ask unanimous consent that I be allowed to proceed for 2 additional minutes.

The PRESIDENT pro tempore. There being no objection, the Senator is recognized for 2 additional minutes.

Mr. LEVIN. I thank the Chair.

Decency, compassion, and a sense of moral responsibility demanded that we do so. It is now time for the United Nations to establish a precedent and take an important step toward achieving an orderly and peaceful world. The civilized world, through the United Nations, should guarantee the safety and security of the Kurds from Saddam Hussein.

It is important for U.S. forces to withdraw as early and as quickly as possible. Our troops want to come home and I do not blame them. For this to happen, however, the United Nations will have to fill the military role now being played by the United States and allied forces in protection of the refugee enclaves.

President Harry Truman presided over this Nation in the difficult early years between the end of World War II and the beginning of the United Nations. In 1946 he said, "We are convinced that the preservation of peace between nations requires the United Nations Organization composed of all the peace-loving nations of the world who are willing jointly to use force, if necessary, to ensure peace."

Mr. President, the necessity of international force remains, and so must the willingness to deploy these U.N. protective forces if we are in fact going to carry out that responsibility which we have now undertaken along the Turkish and Iraqi border.

I thank the Chair. I yield the floor.

I note the absence of a quorum.

The PRESIDENT pro tempore. The absence of a quorum has been observed.

The clerk will call the roll.

The legislative clerk proceeded to call the roll.

Mr. METZENBAUM. Mr. President, I ask unanimous consent that the order for the quorum call be rescinded.

The PRESIDENT pro tempore. Without objection, it is so ordered.

86.

[May 9, 1991 (House), p. 2909-17]

DIRE EMERGENCY SUPPLEMENTAL APPROPRIATIONS FROM CONTRIBUTIONS OF FOREIGN GOVERNMENTS AND/OR INTEREST FOR HUMANITARIAN ASSISTANCE TO REFUGEES AND DISPLACED PERSONS IN AND AROUND IRAQ AS A RESULT OF THE RECENT INVASION OF KUWAIT AND FOR PEACEKEEPING ACTIVITIES AND OTHER URGENT NEEDS ACT OF 1991

Mr. WHITTEN. Mr. Speaker, pursuant to the order of the House of Wednesday, May 8, 1991, I call up the bill (H. R. 2251) making dire emergency supplemental appropriations from contributions of foreign governments and/or interest for humanitarian assistance to refugees and displaced persons in and around Iraq as a result of the recent invasion of Kuwait and for peacekeeping activities, and for other urgent needs for the fiscal year ending September 30, 1991, and for other purposes, and ask for its immediate consideration.

The Clerk read the title of the bill.

The text of H. R. 2251 is as follows:

H. R. 2251

Be it enacted by the Senate and House of Representatives of the United States of America in Congress assembled, That the following sums are appropriated, out of any money in the Treasury not otherwise appropriated, to provide dire emergency supplemental appropriations for the fiscal year ending September 30, 1991, and for other purposes, namely: . . .

CHAPTER II

The bill includes $235,500,000 for emergency international disaster assistance, emergency refugee assistance, and emergency peacekeeping activities of which $85,000,000 is from a rescission of unearmarked funds in the Economic Support Fund which were not going to be obligated for the purposes for which appropriated. The balance of $150,500,000 is from foreign contributions, and/or interest on those contributions, made by foreign governments to support the effort to free Kuwait.

FUNDS APPROPRIATED TO THE PRESIDENT
BILATERAL ECONOMIC ASSISTANCE
Refugee crisis

Since 1985 the number of refugees worldwide has grown from 10 million to 16 million. That already difficult situation has now been compounded by the tragic plight of as many as two million Kurdish and other Iraqi civilians fleeing from the Iraqi military to border areas and into neighboring countries.

The current refugee crisis in and on the border of Iraq is a rapidly developing and changing situation. United States actions to date can be credited for saving the lives of many of these refugees. It appears that some of the Iraqi refugees are now beginning to return to Iraq, either to temporary camps being constructed under the supervision of the United States or to their own homes. However, many uncertainties remain and this process will continue to require resources both from the United States and other international donors.

Once the United States has stabilized the Iraqi refugee situation, it should become the responsibility of traditional international relief agencies to assume humanitarian relief efforts. It is uncertain at this time the exact amount of refugee and disaster assistance, that will be needed to address the current problem. International relief agencies have already appealed for more than $700 million to meet the initial few months of the Iraqi refugee crisis. The United States has made a large bilateral contribution to this refugee effort, but it may be necessary to provide additional multilateral assistance to assure continuing relief on a timely basis to the refugee population. Efforts should be made to accelerate donations by other countries to meet the international appeals.

The Administration has requested $125,000,000 to address the Iraqi refugee crisis. The bill includes $210,000,000. In order to meet the Iraqi refugee situation and to be able to address other disaster situations, the bill includes, as described below, additional funding for both the Disaster Assistance and the Emergency Refugee and Migration Assistance accounts.

INTERNATIONAL DISASTER ASSISTANCE

The bill includes $67,000,000 in additional assistance for International Disaster Assistance. The Congress originally appropriated $40,000,000 in the fiscal year 1991 bill for International Disaster Assistance. However, by mid-April all of the funding under the Disaster Assistance account had been committed.

The Administration requested an additional $27,000,000 to provide assistance related to the Iraqi refugee situation. The bill would immediately provide additional assistance for relief associated with the needs of displaced Iraqis. However, there is a question whether the $27,000,000 is sufficient to meet these needs and to address other disasters in Africa. Bangladesh, Costa Rica, and the Soviet Union. Therefore, the bill includes sufficient funding to meet the Administration's request, plus funds necessary to restore the disaster assistance account to the $40,000,000 level originally appropriated.

The Agency for International Development is to use funds appropriated in this Supplemental for disaster assistance prior to using borrowing authority for disaster assistance purposes.

DEPARTMENT OF STATE
MIGRATION AND REFUGEE ASSISTANCE

The bill includes supplemental funding of $75,000,000 for the Migration and Refugee Assistance account, as requested by the Administration.

UNITED STATES EMERGENCY REFUGEE AND MIGRATION ASSISTANCE FUND

The bill includes $68,000,000 for the Emergency Refugee and Migration Assistance Fund. This is an increase of $45,000,000 over and above the $23,000,000 requested for the Emergency account. The amount included in the bill for the Emergency account will permit funding to be increased to the ceiling included in the recently passed authorization bill for the Emergency Refugee and Migration Assistance account. The bill has provided the additional assistance in the Emergency Fund in order to give the President the flexibility to meet additional costs associated with the Iraqi refugee situation and other refugee emergencies around the world.

INTERNATIONAL ORGANIZATION AND CONFERENCES

Contributions to international peacekeeping activities.

The bill includes a supplemental appropriations of $25,500,000 as requested for the Contributions to International Peacekeeping Activities appropriation in the Department of State to pay the United States assessed contribution of the United Nations Iraq/Kuwait Observer Mission (UNIKOM). The assessment, as requested and recommended by the Committee, is to be derived by transfer from interest earned on balances in the Defense Cooperation Account, Department of the Treasury.

Contributions of foreign governments to such account will not be used to pay this assessment.

The United Nations Iraq/Kuwait Observer Mission (UNIKOM) was established by United Nations Security Council Resolution 687 to monitor, observe, and report on violations of the demilitarized zone between Iraq and Kuwait and on potential threats to the peace. UNIKOM consists of unarmed observers from thirty-four countries including the United States, armed infantry to provide for their security and engineering and logistics units. Substantially all members of UNIKOM are in place and the first observation post was manned as of May 1, 1991.

The United Nations preliminary cost estimates for UNIKOM total $61,000,000 for the first six months of operation. Assessments are levied on member states according to the special peace and security scale of assessments. The United States share, at approximately 31 percent, is $18,700,000 under this scale. The remaining funds totaling $6,800,000 are provided toward the United States share of follow-on assessments for UNIKOM which is expected to continue into FY 1992.

SOURCE OF FUNDS

The bill includes the following recommendations of the Administration to make a portion of the funds requested for refugees, disaster assistance, and peacekeeping available from the balance, including interest, in the Defense Cooperation Account. Additionally, a rescission has been included to offset any funds not provided by the use of the interest on the Defense Cooperation Account.

GENERAL PROVISIONS—CHAPTER II

The bill includes a number of general provisions that allow the following: (1) designates funds as costs associated with Operation Desert Storm; (2) allows disaster and refugee assistance provided in the Supplemental to be used to reimburse accounts that have been previously drawn down; (3) waives the limitation on disaster borrowing for funds borrowed for Persian Gulf area assistance; (4) excludes

Persian Gulf area drawdowns for Department of Defense equipment and supplies from being counted against the $75,000,000 annual limitation on drawdowns; (5) waives restrictions on providing assistance to countries; and (6) waives requirement for authorizations.

CHAPTER III

The bill includes language directing the Office of Management and Budget to provided a report on the costs of damage resulting from natural disasters in the United States. Sufficient funding to respond to the needs of the Nation due to the impacts of tornadoes, floods, freezes, and other natural disasters is not available. Additionally emergency appropriations will be necessary. In order to develop these emergency appropriations, pending receipt of a budget request, additional information it to be provided by OMB within ten days after enactment of this law.

Similarly, several major natural disasters have occurred around the world, outside the United States. It is also felt that insufficient funds exist to make the proper response to these events. Additional information, to be provided by OMB, pending receipt of a budget request, it also required to develop the appropriate response.

The oil well fires in Kuwait continue to burn impacting the environment and possibly the health of the people of the Persian Gulf region. Also, production from the fields appears to be severely impacted. The bill calls for a report on this solution within ten days of enactment. While it realized that a comprehensive study cannot be accomplished in this time frame an assessment and plan of study can be developed and submitted so that additional congressional action can be developed.

CHAPTER IV—FUNDING WITHIN BUDGET ALLOCATIONS

All funds appropriated in the bill are either incremental costs of Operation Desert Storm, dire emergencies, or are offset and therefore would not result in any sequestration.

Mr. Speaker, I reserve the balance of my time.

Mr. MCDADE. Mr. Speaker, I yield myself such time as I may consume.

(Mr. MCDADE asked and was given permission to revise and extend his remarks.)

Mr. MCDADE. Mr. Speaker, I rise in support of this supplemental appropriations bill. It provides urgently needed funding of our relief efforts by the Departments of State and Defense for the Kurds and other refugees in Iraq. It also replenishes the State and Agency for International Development programs that are likely to be needed in other troubled areas like Sudan and Bangladesh.

Mr. Speaker, the distinguished chairman of the committee has explained the provisions of this bill, so I will just make a few points in that regard.

In total, the bill provides $572 million, all of it paid for either out of the special funds put together to pay for Operation Desert Storm out of rescissions of other 1991 appropriations.

The administration requested an open-ended appropriation for the costs of the Defense Department's relief operation, known as Operation Provide Comfort. We recommend a specific amount, $320.5 million, to cover those costs through the end of May, by which time we hope the operation will be wrapping up, and the United Nations taking over.

The administration requested $150.5 million for State and AID refugee and peacekeeping programs, to be paid for out of the interest that has accumulated in the Defense cooperation account. We approved that $150.5 million, and allow it to be paid for either out of the account itself or out of the interest.

It is my expectation that the administration has the flexibility it needs to assure the allies that we are using only the interest for these humanitarian relief programs, so as not to discourage further contributions to the cooperation account.

The Foreign Operations Subcommittee recommended an additional $85 million for humanitarian relief, and put the funds in programs that can be used both for the needs of refugees in Iraq and for other emergencies around the world, like the tragic cyclone in Bangladesh and the desperate food shortages in Sudan and other parts of Africa.

That addition would be paid for by rescinding moneys in the 1991 foreign operations appropriation bill that cannot be used for their intended purpose.

Mr. Speaker, this supplemental is meant to respond to a dire situation. Once Saddam Hussein's forces had been expelled from Kuwait, he turned upon his own people.

More than 2 million Kurds fled their homes out of fear of death and retribution at the hands of that tyrant. Having once trained poison gas on the Kurds, Saddam Hussein now trained the remnants of his army on them, using their weapons, and the weapons of fear, starvation, and destruction to put an entire people in jeopardy.

The United States took the lead in extending our protective umbrella under difficult circumstances in a remote part of the world.

The United States did not wait for congressional action to put resources into helping the refugees, as, indeed, it could not. Estimates put the U.S. contribution to date at $207 million.

There are 29 nations participating in this effort.

Of the 17,000 coalition forces on the ground supporting this humanitarian effort, 10,000 are American.

Of the 7,900 forces on the ground in northern Iraq, over 3,000 are American.

Of the 2,795 missions flown, 1,597 have been by the Americans.

Of the 13,000 tons of supplies delivered, over half are from the Americans.

Even as the United States mobilizes to build secure refugee camps in Iraq, hundreds of thousands of refugees remain stranded in Turkey, Iraq and Iran.

And so, while we provide funding to pay the bills for what has already been done, we also must provide the funding to keep this effort going.

That is what this supplemental does, Mr. Speaker, and I am pleased that the committee has responded in a timely way and in a responsible way to the administration's request to support these efforts.

Obviously, it is not 100 percent to the administration's liking, but I think it gets the job done, and I believe the administration will ultimately agree.

I will support this bill, and urge my colleagues to do likewise.

Mr. Speaker, I reserve the balance of my time.

AMENDMENT OFFERED BY MR. WHITTEN

Mr. WHITTEN. Mr. Speaker, I offer an amendment.

The Clerk read as follows:

Amendment offered by Mr. WHITTEN: On page 5 of the bill, strike out lines 1 through 14.

The SPEAKER pro tempore. The question is on the amendment offered by the gentleman from Mississippi.

The amendment was agreed to.

Mr. WHITTEN. Mr. Speaker, I yield 6 minutes to the gentleman from New York [Mr. MCHUGH], a member of the Committee on Appropriations.

(Mr. MCHUGH asked and was given permission to revise and extend his remarks.)

Mr. MCHUGH. Mr. Speaker, I rise in strong support of the bill and urge its adoption by the House. The crisis which this supplemental appropriation addresses is both compelling in human terms and time sensitive, and I want to commend the House leadership and the committee for moving this bill to the floor so swiftly.

All of us are fully aware of the plight of the Kurds and other Iraqi refugees. The media has given us a stark view of families, from very young children to their grandparents, suffering under horrendous conditions in rugged border regions far from their homes. At the request of the Speaker, I recently led a small bipartisan delegation to the Iraqi-Turkish border areas to assess the crisis. I can tell you that the media coverage does not begin to capture the full dimensions of the human suffering involved.

At the end of March, as many as 2 million Kurdish and other Iraqi civilians fled their homes, often with nothing more than the clothes on their backs. They did so in mortal fear of Iraqi military forces. In the border areas our delegation visited, we saw tens of thousands of people perched on the tops of mountains that were virtually inaccessible. Most of them were malnourished, ill-clothed, and exposed to the elements without adequate shelter. Potable water and medical care were in painfully short supply. Sanitary conditions were atrocious and, despite the valiant efforts of our military to provide emergency relief, many people were dying. The best estimates were that between 400 to 1,000 people were being lost each day in the Turkish border areas alone.

To help alleviate this crisis, the administration devised a three-phase plan, with which our delegation fully concurred. The first phase was to deliver humanitarian relief to the refugees in their remote mountain locations to help stabilize the situation. The second phase, now underway, is to convince the refugees to come down from the mountains to temporary camps in lower lying areas as in northern Iraq where they can be better cared for. The final phase will be to persuade the people to return to their homes.

Essential to the success of phase 1 has been the use of our military forces. Clearly, the President made the right decision in authorizing American forces to undertake this job with the help of other coalition military personnel. They have been doing an extraordinary job under daunting conditions, and there can be no doubt that many more refugees would have died without their intervention. Traditional relief agencies, as well as neighboring governments, were simply incapable of coping with the massive numbers that gathered in a matter of days in areas that were virtually inaccessible to any but our military.

It is also clear that our military forces will also be critical in implementing phase two and possibly phase three. This is because the refugees will not leave their mountain retreats and ultimately return home without some credible guarantee of security. At the moment, our forces represent the only credible assurance they have. They do not trust the Iraqi Government, and the coalition forces are all that stand between the refugees and Saddam Hussein's military. This poses a real dilemma for us, because while we are willing to provide both relief and security in the short term, it is not in America's interests to be in northern Iraq indefinitely or to be seen as an occupying force.

Our delegation concluded that responsibility for the relief effort should be assumed as soon as possible by the United Nations and other traditional relief agencies. This is a role they are fully capable of performing once the refugees are off the mountains, hopefully within the next few weeks. They have said that they will undertake this responsibility so long as they receive adequate financial support.

With respect to security, we also believe that the international community should assume responsibility if necessary. Ideally, a political agreement can be reached between the Iraqi Government and the Kurds which will provide the Kurds with adequate political and security assurances, perhaps with international endorsement. However, if that cannot be achieved in the short term and the Kurds still require military protection, a serious effort should be made to get U.N. or regional peacekeeping forces to replace the U.S. and coalition forces. This may not be easy to achieve, but the alternatives of abandoning the Kurds or staying in Iraq indefinitely are unacceptable.

In the meantime, Mr. Speaker, we and others are incurring financial obligations which must be met. As of Monday, the United States had already spent about $207 million. The chairman of our subcommittee [Mr. OBEY] has given us the specific breakdown of those costs. In addition, the United Nations and certain other international relief agencies have issued an appeal for contributions of about $722 million. If we expect them to assume the burden of providing humanitarian relief, we and other governments will have to help.

On April 26, the President submitted to Congress his supplemental budget request for $150.5 million to meet the costs of this operation. Frankly, our subcommittee concluded that this would not be adequate, and therefore we added to that request an additional $85 million, bringing the total in this supplemental bill to $235.5 million. None of these funds would break the spending ceilings imposed by the budget, because the amount requested by the President would be derived from the interest earned on the Defense Cooperation Account associated with Desert Shield and Desert Storm. The $85 million we have added represents money originally appropriated for Pakistan which cannot be spent.

Finally, Mr. Speaker, it is important to note that there are other disasters in the world which we and others must respond. There is continuing famine in Africa, a recent earthquake in Costa Rica, and the truly cataclysmic disaster that struck Bangladesh in recent days. We believe that this supplemental appropriations bill will give the President adequate flexibility in the short term to respond, particularly since he has authority to draw an additional $50 million from development accounts. However, if additional funds are required to meet these or other unanticipated emergencies, the President has discretion to come back to Congress with further requests, and I would encourage him to do so.

Mr. Speaker, I urge my colleagues to support this bill.

Mr. MCDADE. Mr. Speaker, I have no further requests for time, and I yield back the balance of my time.

Mr. WHITTEN. Mr. Speaker, I yield 1 minute to the gentleman from Wisconsin [Mr. OBEY].

Mr. OBEY. Mr. Speaker, I simply want to say that, as has been already explained, chapter 2 of the bill provides for $210 million in refugee assistance and disaster assistance, as recommended by our Subcommittee on Foreign Operations, Export Financing and Related Programs. The committee added $85 million to the administration's request, all of which is offset by a rescission.

I would hope, and I would fully expect that the administration would use the ample authority which this bill provides for them to deal with all the refugee problems around the world, not just the Kurdish refugee situation, but the North African situation, as well as most certainly the Bangladesh emergency which has just arisen.

I think this bill gives ample opportunity to deal with all of them, along with other authority that they have in existing law.

Mr. WHITTEN. Mr. Speaker, I yield 2 minutes to the gentleman from Ohio [Mr. HALL].

(Mr. HALL of Ohio asked and was given permission to revise and extend his remarks.)

Mr. HALL of Ohio. Mr. Speaker, I rise in support of this most important bill, and I want to thank the staff for their splendid work, especially the chairman, the gentleman from Mississippi [Mr. WHITTEN], and the gentleman from Wisconsin [Mr. OBEY] for doing an excellent job on this bill.

Mr. Speaker, refugees and displaced people around the world are the most miserable, neglected people in our world. As chairman of the Select Committee on Hunger, I have visited many refugee camps and have seen the suffering of displaced people around the world, along with the gentleman from New York [Mr. MCHUGH] and three other Members of the Congress, who witnessed firsthand a few weeks ago the Kurds in both Iraq and Turkey, and the situation that they are in, the dying of exposure, malnutrition, and the tremendous problems they are dealing with.

This is not a problem that is just central to Turkey and Iraq. All over the world, we are talking about 18 million people that are refugees, and another 15 million that are displaced. In the Sudan, around 10 million people are at risk of starvation. People are already dying there, and large numbers of deaths can be expected soon. Millions more are at a risk of death in Ethiopia and Somalia, Sudan's neighbor in the Horn of Africa. Millions of Bangladeshis urgently need assistance to help survive the devastating cyclone that struck only last week.

Therefore, it is critically important that this bill provide additional funds for Iraqi refugees while also adding emergency resources to Africa, Asia, and other refugee humanitarian emergencies.

I want to thank the chairmen, Mr. WHITTEN and Mr. OBEY for really stepping up to this most important challenge of helping so many people in the world that are in need. I urge my colleagues to also support this in a really strong way.

Mr. WHITTEN. Mr. Speaker, I yield 2 minutes to the gentleman from Illinois [Mr. DURBIN] a member of the committee.

Mr. DURBIN. Mr. Speaker, H. R. 2251 is a good bill. It does some important things. It provides assistance for our troops overseas. It provides assistance to the families of those troops who have suffered hardships because of their service.

As my colleague from Ohio [Mr. HALL] has said so eloquently, and my colleague from New York [Mr. MCHUGH], it provides refugee assistance to people who are suffering, people we see on the television screen every night. The United States is a caring nation. We reach out. We help people. By doing so, we send a message as to what kind of people we are.

However, I would like to raise a point which I think should be made in this debate. This is the sixth piece of legislation this year which has been classified "emergency" legislation. This legislation and all the preceding emergency bills have related to foreign aid and military assistance. They are all deserved causes. However, I want to ask this question: Why is it, when it comes to questions of military spending and foreign aid, the administration and this Congress continue to consider it an emergency? An emergency which sets it apart from the otherwise strict budget process around here? In fact, what we are doing, time and again, is making exceptions to the rules.

So far, some $45 billion has been tied up in emergency bills. Here today, we will debate a motion to instruct from the President's party which says that when it comes to emergencies in the United States of America, when it comes to emergencies in schools and emergencies in health care, we are not going to step aside from the budget process. We are going to make it more difficult to find ways to solve problems here in the United States. I am for solving problems, but we should have equity. We should have some caring not only for the people overseas, we should have some caring for the people at home.

I think if we do that and show some balance in our approach, we will literally serve America and send a message as to what we stand for.

Mr. WHITTEN. Mr. Speaker, I yield 1 minute to the gentleman from Nevada [Mr. BILBRAY].

Mr. BILBRAY. Mr. Speaker, I rise today in full support of the appropriation for the Iraqi refugees. It is clear to every Member of this Chamber that the immediate need is to protect the Kurds and the Shiites from the weather, famine, and disease.

However, this crisis will not, will absolutely not be resolved until there can be a suitable international guarantee that the Kurdish and Shiite people will not be persecuted. We can feed them today but we also have to ensure that they will continue to live in peace. The history of the Saddam Hussein regime proves that periods of relative lull have been followed by massive repression by his troops upon these people. Let us not be tricked by this madman once again. Let us now finally settle the question of freedom and democracy for all of the people of Iraq and free them from the brutal domination of Saddam Hussein.

I ask my colleagues to supply this much needed aid to the women, children, and families of Iraq's Kurdish and Shiite peoples. But I also remind you that this will not be over until we can guarantee that it will not happen again.

Mr. WHITTEN. Mr. Speaker, I yield 5 minutes to the gentleman from California [Mr. FAZIO], a member of the committee.

Mr. FAZIO. Mr. Speaker, while I applaud the President's request for aid for their victims of this very real human tragedy in Kurdistan, I would like to know where the President's empathy is for those affected by disasters here at home?

Yes, this will aid critical assistance to the starving Kurdish children stranded in the mountains of Northern Iraq, but the President has failed to extend a hand of hope and assistance to thousands of men and women and children who are going hungry each day, within our own borders, and within my own State of California.

Specifically, the President has done little to respond to the human suffering resulting from the winter freeze in California which destroyed most of the State's citrus crop. Eighty percent of the crop in three counties alone-Tulare, Kern, and Fresno-was destroyed. Whole communities that depend on the agricultural industry have been devastated. Several unemployment rates in those areas have exceeded 50 percent. Families are being evicted from their homes, an estimated 70,000 agricultural workers and their families are in danger of going hungry each day because there is no work in the fields.

Farm workers have even been sending their children back to Mexico to stay with relatives because they fear that their children will starve if they stay here in the United States.

This is not a neat and graphic television story of human suffering that seems to be the type of problem that gets our attention, gets the President's response. However, the human suffering which grows worse each day is no less real and no less a tragedy just because it is not the lead story on the evening news each night or the cover story of national news magazines.

The President has it within his power to provide the necessary aid to these communities. In H. R. 2251 we are directing the President to inform the Congress, within 10 days of enactment of this measure, of what should be included in a dire emergency supplemental appropriations bill to respond to all domestic disasters, including disasters resulting from freezes and floods and other natural disasters.

Most importantly, for those impacted by last winter's freeze, the President should use this opportunity to request a dire emergency supplemental appropriation for the Crop Disaster Assistance Program, authorized in last year's farm bill. Funding that program will help some 4,500 citrus growers get back on their feet and allow them, in turn, to reemploy tens of thousands of farm workers in the San Joaquin Valley.

This assistance will put food on the tables and into the mouths of those who now feel the pain of hunger and deprivation as efficiently as any other Federal relief program. It will have the long-term benefit of helping to ensure future employment for those workers in the years to come.

The recordbreaking freeze that hit California last December was the third worst natural disaster in our State's history, surpassed only by the Loma Prieta earthquake of 1989 and the San Francisco fire and earthquake of 1906.

But the President and his administration have turned a deaf ear to the desperate cries of thousands of hungry and homeless farm workers in California. It is time for the President to refocus his attention to the serious problems we face here at home.

I urge approval of the bill and I urge the President to send Congress a domestic emergency relief bill as soon as possible.

I would also like to thank the chairman of the committee, the gentleman from Mississippi [Mr. WHITTEN] who without a great deal of promoting because of his awareness of the situation, not just in California but across the South and in the upper Midwest, has included this language once again, similar to language included in the earlier supplemental to try to get the attention of the administration to focus on our domestic problems.

The chairman has always been attentive to the needs of constituents of Members from across the country. I applaud his efforts and I certainly hope within the next few days we will get a response from OMB and from the agencies directly affected who have within their power the ability to help resolve these issues.

The SPEAKER pro tempore. The time of the gentleman from California has expired.

Mr. WHITTEN. Mr. Speaker, I yield 1 additional minute to the gentleman.

Mr. LEWIS of California. Mr. Speaker, will the gentleman yield?

Mr. FAZIO. I am happy to yield to the gentleman from California.

Mr. LEWIS of California. Mr. Speaker, in the interests of time, I say to my colleague, the gentleman from California, I was going to raise similar questions that the gentleman is addressing himself to about concern for emergency circumstances. I presume the gentleman includes within those concerns the emergency that focuses around freeze impacts on agricultural products in our State as well as other parts of the country.

Mr. FAZIO. Absolutely. I mentioned the freeze specifically. There has to be no doubt that freezes should be considered as all other natural disasters. Certainly there are many counties in our State that have been impacted.

Mr. LEWIS of California. I should have known my colleague would have included the parts of the State that are impacted. I am sorry that I was not in the room, but I should have known my colleague would focus on that important item.

Mr. FAZIO. I appreciate the gentleman's assistance. The gentleman may not want to associate his remarks with all of mine, but at least the gentleman may want to help focus on at least the problem area.

Mr. LEWIS of California. With the gentleman, I seldom have much reserve, but I do have reserve.

Mr. WHITTEN. Mr. Speaker, I yield 3 minutes to the gentleman from Ohio [Mr. TRAFICANT].

(Mr. TRAFICANT asked and was given permission to revise and extend his remarks.)

Mr. TRAFICANT. Mr. Speaker, I do not think anybody in the Congress would oppose trying to help the Kurds, and actually they deserve help.

I oppose the policy. We are the United States, not the United Nations. We are the United States, not the International Welfare Department. They deserve help, but let me just say something to the Congress.

Members do not see this because we live in pretty much, nice white ivory towers. But there are people in America who eat dog food to make sure their little bit of money lasts them for the month. There are some people who actually live and sleep on steel grates. They do not have any other choice. There are more poor children in America than any other industrialized nation.

Where is the domestic aid package for America? Over 50 percent of the people in parts of my district are on some form of assistance, barely making it.

By God, you have got the Nation's Capital on fire. Cities and States are asking for a little revenue sharing.

I am not going to complicate your bill. This is a great chairman, and I do not want anybody hurting my district.

But, I oppose the policy of emergency supplementals every week or two weeks for people overseas. We are broke. Our banks are teetering, our savings and loans have folded.

Why don't we come up with a little domestic aid? If we could find it in our reservoir of moneys somewhere, why not find it for the home team?

I do not oppose the measure. It has money in it for the military. We have 10,000 troops over there, and to tell you the truth, I think that is enough. We already saved their behinds. I think it is time for everybody else to pay their fair share.

I want to commend the committee on one thing. At least they are pushing these other contributors to pay their fair share, but I do, and will continue to oppose the policy.

Mr. WHITTEN. Mr. Speaker, I yield 2 minutes to the gentleman from Wisconsin [Mr. OBEY], a member of the committee.

Mr. OBEY. Mr. Speaker, the gentleman who just spoke is perfectly correct in indicating that this country ought not to play Winston Churchill abroad and Scrooge at home.

I absolutely totally agree with that, but I would simply point out for the benefit of anyone who wants to know the facts, there is not one new additional dollar of foreign assistance in this bill. Every dollar which is provided for humanitarian assistance to the somewhere from 400 to 1,000 people a day who are presently dying on the borders of Iran, every dollar here is provided by making reductions in other foreign assistance programs, and as the chairman of the committee has indicated there is an ability in the bill to use the International Fund which has been accumulated because of contributions from other countries to pay the remainder of the costs associated with the bill; so there is not one new additional dollar of American tax money going for aid in this bill. We are simply moving other foreign assistance around to cover these costs. I think it is in the national interest and in the humanitarian interest of this country to do so.

Ms. SLAUGHTER of New York. Mr. Speaker, today we are passing funding desperately needed to save the lives of Iraqi refugees. This assistance is targeted for Kurdish refugees fleeing their own country upon fear of death, only to meet death in the inhospitable mountains bordering Iraq. The funds for humanitarian relief operations in this supplemental appropriation can mean the difference between life and death for these refugees.

But H. R. 2251 also contains important provisions for funding domestic issues of urgency. Chapter III requires the Office of Management and Budget [OMB] to report back to Congress 10 days after this bill is enacted on the status of unfunded dire emergencies because of natural disasters here in the United States.

This report will show that the Federal Emergency Management Agency [FEMA] is so short of funds that it has stopped paying out approved funding for qualified public assistance needs. FEMA has publically reported that it has a shortfall of about $600 million because of the unexpectedly high number of disasters. There are normally 23 major disasters per year, but in the first 7 months of this fiscal year there were 24, with an estimated cost of $270 million.

In my congressional district there is an urgent need for FEMA funds which are now being held up indefinitely. FEMA estimates that it will need about $35 million to respond to the devastating ice storm that crippled Rochester, NY, area on March 3, 1991. The ice storm was a natural as well as an economic disaster. In a single night we witnessed the wholesale destruction of our historic landscape. Tens of thousands of healthy, bountiful trees-which required generations to grow were killed within a few short hours. In the city of Rochester alone, it is estimated that at least 30,000 trees have been lost. No neighborhood street in the city escaped the devastation of this ice storm.

My district is struggling to clean up, restore public safety, and begin to restore the tens of thousands of trees that were damaged or destroyed by the storm. FEMA has reimbursed localities $130,000. It has approved another $6 million and anticipates approving an additional $28 million. Now, FEMA has announced that it cannot provide this funding.

Mr. Speaker, the towns, cities, and counties of my district are desperate. They are making heroic efforts to comply with FEMA deadlines, and have submitted their applications for reimbursement in good faith. FEMA promises to approve these needs, but that promise is meaningless if FEMA has no funding available.

I urge OMB to report back on the status of funds for responding to domestic disasters and to declare this need a dire emergency. Then Congress will have the opportunity to ensure that communities responding to disasters in New York and elsewhere across the country receive the Federal disaster assistance they deserve.

Mr. DORGAN of North Dakota. Mr. Speaker, I will gladly support the supplemental appropriation for Iraqi refugees. The bill responds to the tragedy unfolding in the mountains of Iraq and Turkey where some 320,000 Kurdish refugees have moved to escape the oppression of Saddam Hussein and the Iraqi army. Many of these distressed people are at risk of death from severe malnutrition and related diseases. Particularly vulnerable are the infants and elderly, who have been dying at alarming rates in these camps.

The bill will provide some $236 million in humanitarian aid for Kurdish refugees and for international peacekeeping operations. This is $85 million above the President's request and every penny is needed. However, the bill is funded in a fiscally responsible way because $150 million comes from foreign contributions or interest on them and the $85 million balance is transferred from unobligated economic support funds.

The bill also permits the Defense Department to draw upon $321 million from the Persian Gulf defense cooperation fund to cover the cost of the U.S. military forces being used in the relief effort. Interest on the gulf fund will also support activities of military service organizations that provide hardship grants to financially strapped families of U.S. service personnel.

This is the right kind of aid for the right purpose. Let's vote it out unanimously and speed relief to the hundreds of thousands suffering Kurds. It will also relieve some of the pressure on some on overall refugee and disaster relief accounts, so that is also helpful.

Permit me, however, to make several observations.

First, we would not be debating aid to the Kurds had not the international media spotlighted their tragic plight and mobilized world opinion to support emergency relief.

Second, that same spotlight has not shone brightly on the even greater number of Kurdish refugees at risk in the Iranian-Iraqi border areas. Nor has it highlighted the enormous tragedy unfolding in Africa, where some 35 million people-or dozens times more people-are at risk of famine.

Third, we move with dispatch to aid the Kurds because the media has propelled us into action, because of our military interest in a solution, and because we have demanded and obtained help from the international community. That is not happening with respect to the cyclone victims of Bangladesh, the famine victims of Africa or some 15 million other refugees.

The United States has committed a meager $6 million to aid the 10 million homeless Bangladeshis, many of whom face peril from epidemics or starvation. The main champions of relief in Bangladesh are private relief organizations such as CARE, and Save the Children. But they can't possibly cope with a tragedy of this magnitude without the active and generous support of our Government, the United Nations, and other world donors.

Likewise, the United States Committee on Refugees has predicted that even if disaster relief is effective, some 300,000 Sudanese will still die. Certainly, we must find the will and the means to prevent such tragic losses of human life.

But we will not do so as long as our foreign policy and foreign aid programs are mired in political constraints and dominated by security aid and defense concerns. We must liberate our foreign policy so that our aid can focus on the real needs of people, and at no additional cost. We ought to be transferring some security aid funds to expand food aid and development programs.

Not only will that aid hungry people and afford a better way to promote the national interest. It will help American family farmers who can't get a decent price for their crops-as the administration negotiates away price supports-and who can't find markets for their abundant production-as artificial trade barriers continue to impede exports.

Let's start turning this around with the right kind of foreign aid. Let's start moving our agricultural abundance around the world to hungry people.

Mr. VISCLOSKY. Mr. Speaker, I rise today to express my reluctant opposition to H. R. 2251, the supplemental appropriations for Iraqi refugees.

I am very sympathetic to the plight of the Kurds and all those who have been displaced due to the recent Persian Gulf war. I am not opposed to helping them. However, in this era of a spiraling national deficit and shrinking Federal resources, I cannot in good conscience support this $572 million foreign aid bill.

While I do not advocate that we adopt a purely isolationist policy, we must ensure that the needs of all Americans are met first. In 1990, there were 25,000 cases of mostly preventable measles reported. Seventy percent of those students eligible to participate in Head Start cannot because we cannot afford to expand this vital and proven program; 37 million Americans are without proper health insurance. Can we afford to give $573 million away while too many Americans are hungry, homeless, and helpless?

I do not make this vote easily, but this legislation will just dig a deeper hole for our children and grandchildren. We have a responsibility to the next generation of Americans to address our problems now. If our Nation hopes to remain a world leader and power, we cannot ignore our domestic problems, pay the way for other countries and pass the bill onto our children.

Mr. MURTHA. The defense chapter of the refugee assistance supplemental provides for the transfer of $320,500,000 from the Persian Gulf regional defense fund to the military personnel and operation and maintenance accounts of the Defense Department in order to finance the defense costs of Operation Provide Comfort. These funds will cover the military personnel costs, supplies, transportation and other support costs associated with the relief effort for refugees and displaced persons in and around Iraq.

Also $16 million is appropriated from the interest earned on balances in the defense cooperation account, a gift fund, to the military relief societies. These funds will provide additional aid to members of our Armed Forces which have incurred added hardships based on the deployment relating to Operation Desert Shield/Desert Storm. These societies provide interest free loans or grants to military personnel and their dependents to help finance food, rent or utility expenses, emergency transportation expenses, vehicle repairs, funeral expenses, medical and dental expenses, and other emergency assistance.

Mr. PENNY. Mr. Speaker, I rise in strong support of this Iraqi refugee supplemental appropriation.

The refugee situations on both the northern and southern borders of Iraq are unprecedented. The number of Kurds fleeing into such dangerous terrain and unfavorable weather conditions illustrates the political reasons for refugee situations and the fear these people have of Saddam Hussein.

We responded to the invasion of Kuwait and now we must respond to the human injustice the Kurds are trying to escape. Our efforts, although too late for some Kurdish refugees, many of them children, must continue at all urgency to help the thousands of other Kurdish refugees still caught in this crisis. As world leaders we have the responsibility to protect the human rights of these people. The need for shelter, food, medical supplies, water, and adequate clothing cannot be underestimated.

As we all are aware, refugee camps are being established in the northern areas of Iraq. We must not abandon these people once the camps are established. They have many obstacles before them as they seek to resettle permanently. Safety and security must be ensured for these people.

As a member of the House Select Committee on Hunger, I caution us not to let our actions here today on behalf of the Iraqi refugees minimize the need to act on other critical refugee situations throughout the world, especially in the Horn of Africa. Chairman TONY HALL has worked tirelessly on behalf of the world's refugees and recently traveled to the Iraq-Turkey border to observe the refugee situation first hand. Representative DORGAN has also taken a keen interest in the refugee situation in East Africa. I applaud their efforts.

Again, I commend the Appropriations Committee for expediting the passage of this critical legislation.

Mr. WHITTEN. Mr. Speaker, I have no further requests for time, and I yield back the balance of my time.

The SPEAKER pro tempore (Mr. MCNULTY). Pursuant to the order of the House of Wednesday, May 8, 1991, the previous question is ordered.

The question is on the engrossment and third reading of the bill.

The bill was ordered to be engrossed and read a third time, and was read the third time.

MOTION TO RECOMMIT OFFERED BY MR. MILLER OF OHIO

Mr. MILLER of Ohio. Mr. Speaker, I offer a motion to recommit.

The SPEAKER pro tempore. Is the gentleman opposed to the bill?

Mr. MILLER of Ohio. In its present form, yes, Mr. Speaker.

The SPEAKER pro tempore. The Clerk will report the motion to recommit.

The Clerk read as follows:

Mr. MILLER of Ohio moves to recommit the bill, H. R. 2251, to the Committee on Appropriations.

The SPEAKER pro tempore. Without objection, the previous question is ordered on the motion to recommit.

There was no objection.

The SPEAKER pro tempore. The question is on the motion to recommit.

The motion to recommit was rejected.

The SPEAKER pro tempore. The question is on the passage of the bill.

The question was taken; and the Speaker pro tempore announced that the "ayes" appeared to have it.

Mr. WALKER. Mr. Speaker, I object to the vote on the ground that a quorum is not present and make the point of order that a quorum is not present.

The SPEAKER pro tempore. Evidently a quorum is not present.

The Sergeant at Arms will notify absent Members.

The vote was taken by electronic device, and there were-yeas 384, nays 25, not voting 21, as follows:

[Roll No. 84]
YEAS-384
NOT VOTING-21

Messrs. RAY, GEREN of Texas, and ROHRABACHER changed their vote from "yea" to "nay." Mr. KOLTER changed his vote from "nay" to "yea."

So the bill was passed. The result of the vote was announced as above recorded. A motion to reconsider was laid on the table.

87.

[May 9, 1991 (Senate), p. 5598]

EMERGENCY SUPPLEMENTAL PERSIAN GULF REFUGEE ASSISTANCE ACT OF 1991

Mr. BUMPERS. The Senate has just adopted a Kurdish relief authorization bill, which I strongly support. It is one of the gravest tragedies in history, and we, as a country, with the values that we all share, have a moral obligation to address it, which we are prepared to do here, apparently.

I also support sending $1-1/2- billion in credits to the Soviet Union because if Gorbachev does make it you would be able to cut 10 times that much off the defense bill in the immediate future.

But I rise, Mr. President, to say that while I strongly support both of those items I want to point out that the people in my State and the people of Louisiana and Mississippi are suffering greatly from a very big flood and many of these people have lost virtually everything they had for the third year in a row.

Last year we put $600 million in the Ag appropriation bill for disaster loans and as of a few weeks ago, the Department of Agriculture has loaned a whopping $38 of that $600 million.

I do not think many of these people are even going to qualify for loans. They are go-

ing to have to have additional help, and the reason Senator COCHRAN and I did not put a hold on this Kurdish relief bill is that we do not want to mix it up, we do not want to hold that hostage, but there is a supplemental appropriation coming through here in about 5 weeks, and I tell you, Mr. President, and I tell my colleagues that there has to be some relief, there has to be relief provided for these farmers in the delta areas of those three States that I have just mentioned.

I yield the floor.

88.

[May 9, 1991 (Senate), p. 5606]

REFUGEE RELIEF AUTHORIZATION BILL

Mr. KENNEDY. Mr. President, I give my strong support to H. R. 2122, the dire emergency supplemental authorization bill. This bill authorizes $4 million in emergency assistance to the 1.5 million Kurdish refugees who are suffering under desperate conditions in Iran, Turkey, and Iraq.

Rarely, if ever, has the world witnessed a refugee crisis of this magnitude. Rarely has there been such a tragic exodus of men, women, and children from their homes and their homeland.

I urge all my colleagues to join me in supporting this supplemental appropriation and ensuring that immediate humanitarian assistance is provided to the long-suffering Kurdish people.

Mr. RIEGLE. Mr. President, I suggest the absence of a quorum.

The PRESIDING OFFICER. The clerk will call the roll.

The legislative clerk proceeded to call the roll.

Mr. BUMPERS. Mr. President, I ask unanimous consent that the order for the quorum call be rescinded.

The PRESIDING OFFICER [Mr. LEAHY]. Without objection, it is so ordered.

89.

[May 9, 1991 (Senate), p. 5608]

PASSAGE OF THE KURDISH RELIEF BILL

Mr. PELL. Mr. President, this legislation provides authorization for essential assistance to the Kurdish people made homeless by the brutal policies of the Saddam Hussein regime. More than 2 million people have sought refuge along Iraq's borders with Turkey and Iran. We have all been deeply moved by the television images of dehydrated babies lying listless on the ground, staring hollow eyed into an uncertain future.

After a too long delay, the international community is now taking care of the material needs of the 800,000 refugees along the Turkey border. There is an urgent need for assistance to the larger number of refugees along the Iranian border and this, in turn, will require greater cooperation from the Iranian Government.

This legislation addresses the humanitarian needs of the Kurdish people. The larger problem, however, is a political and military one.

As long as Saddam Hussein is in power, the Kurds will be at risk of slaughter by the Iraqi Army. The United States and its coalition allies now occupy a significant part of northern Iraq. This safe haven, which I hope will soon be expanded to include the city of Dihok, can accommodate up to 1 million of the Kurdish refugees. To accommodate all refugees a further expansion to the east and south is required.

This is not a situation from which we can easily extricate ourselves. If we pull out while Saddam is still in power, the Kurds will leave with us or face death. I would hope, therefore, that a very high diplomatic priority be given to creating an international force, preferably under the auspices of the United Nations, to protect the Kurdish population of Iraq from the Iraqi police and army.

If the current negotiations between the Baghdad regime and the Kurds produce agreement on Kurdish autonomy, then there is a way for the United States to get out of Iraq. But we can only do so if there are credible international guarantees for the autonomy arrangement including a mandate for the use of force if Iraq violates the terms of any Iraq-Kurd deal.

Ultimately, we cannot forget that Saddam Hussein is the root of our problem in this region. Unfortunately, we may have lost our best opportunity to get rid of him, and he is now much stronger than he was 2 months ago.

Saddam Hussein and his regime have committed grievous violations of international law of which the slaughter of the Kurds and the occupation of Kuwait are but two examples. So far, Iraq has not even honored the conditions contained in U.N. Resolution 687 for the cease-fire. Among other things, all Kuwaiti prisoners have not been returned home or accounted for. The list of Iraq's weapons of mass destruction sent to the United Nations is incomplete.

A regime with this sort of record cannot be reintegrated into the international community. It is a pariah regime and should be treated as such. The world community must not treat Saddam Hussein and his Ba'ath Party clique as the legitimate rulers of Iraq, but rather, should in every way emphasize its illegitimacy.

The PRESIDING OFFICER. The Senator from South Dakota.

Mr. PRESSLER. Mr. President, I ask unanimous consent to speak as in morning business.

The PRESIDING OFFICER. The Chair informs the Senator we are in morning business at this time.

90.

[May 9, 1991 (Senate), pp. 5693-8]

DIRE EMERGENCY SUPPLEMENTAL APPROPRIATIONS

Mr. BYRD. Mr. President, this request has been cleared with the leaders on both sides.

I ask unanimous consent that the Senate proceed to the immediate consideration of H. R. 2251.

The PRESIDING OFFICER. The bill will be stated by title.

The assistant legislative clerk read as follows:

A bill (H. R. 2251) making dire emergency supplemental appropriations from contributions of foreign governments and/or interest for humanitarian assistance to refugees and displaced persons in and around Iraq as a result of the recent invasion of Kuwait and for peacekeeping activities, and for other urgent needs for the fiscal year ending September 30, 1991, and for other purposes.

The PRESIDING OFFICER. Is there objection to the immediate consideration of the bill?

There being no objection, the Senate proceeded to consider the bill.

Mr. BYRD. Mr. President, I have certain amendments which I will offer on behalf of other Senators and myself. These have been cleared on both sides.

I ask unanimous consent that no other amendments be in order.

The PRESIDING OFFICER. Without objection, it is so ordered.

Mr. BYRD. Mr. President, I ask unanimous consent that the time on the bill and the amendments thereto be limited to not to exceed 20 minutes to be equally divided between Mr. HATFIELD and myself.

The PRESIDING OFFICER. Without objection, it is so ordered.

(Mr. ROCKEFELLER assumed the chair.)

Mr. BYRD. Mr. President, H. R. 2251 provides appropriations totaling $487,000,000 in budget authority and $367,269,000 in outlays. Of this amount, $150,500,000 in budget authority is provided from the Defense Cooperation Account for emergency international disaster assistance, emergency refugee assistance, and emergency peacekeeping activities in the Persian Gulf region. Senators will recall that the Defense Cooperation Account con-

tains the contributions of our allies in the Desert Shield/Desert Storm effort.

Appropriations totaling $320,500,000 are to be derived from the Persian Gulf regional defense fund to cover the DOD costs of the refugee relief effort.

The bill also contains $85,000,000 for reimbursement of international disaster and refugee assistance accounts drawn down in support of Kurdish aid.

All of the funds provided in the bill are within the limitations for DOD and for international affairs for fiscal year 1991 and will not break the caps nor cause a sequester.

The bill also contains a provision requiring OMB to submit a report on domestic disaster assistance needs within 10 days after enactment. Mr. President, Senator HATFIELD and I have been working with the administration on determining the amount of emergency funding that will be needed to cover these disasters. On May 1, 1991, I wrote a letter to OMB Director Darman concerning the funding shortfall for programs such as the disaster relief fund of the Federal Emergency Management Agency [FEMA]. Mr. Darman responded on May 7, 1991. In his response, Mr. Darman indicated that "it is highly likely that we will recommend a FEMA supplemental of some amount. It is also likely that we will recommend a further Desert Shield/Storm supplemental."

In light of the need for OMB to complete its assessment of domestic disaster assistance needs, and in order to work out acceptable funding levels so that these domestic needs will be treated as "emergencies" under the Budget Enforcement Act, I urge my colleagues to withhold such amendments on this bill. To do otherwise would likely cause a sequester on all domestic discretionary programs and this would cut into our domestic discretionary outlays in fiscal year 1992 and beyond.

Mr. President, this dire emergency supplemental appropriations bill supports the policy of the United States, to provide emergency relief, support and relocation of the Kurdish refugees in northern Iraq. This unusual, but absolutely necessary and commendable action, swiftly put into place by the Department of Defense, has been joined in by many other nations-a wide combination of nations, including our coalition partners in Desert Storm, but also other nations, international private relief organizations and the United Nations.

The care, feeding, sheltering, medical relief, and counseling of some half a million Kurds in the high mountains on the Iraq-Turkish border have been accomplished through a professional, humane, and even heroic effort by United States military forces. Senators and staff who have traveled to the region within the last few days have reported to me that our efforts have stabilized the situation, saving hundreds and perhaps thousands of Kurds, particularly children from what otherwise would have been certain death. I am particularly proud of the role that U.S. Special Forces men and women have played, living in the makeshift camps on those high mountains, organizing the distribution of food, developing a sense of confidence in those people that their future is not hopeless. I am also told that our forces there have high morale and are very proud of the role that they are playing. In addition, we are, together with our allied partners, establishing a security zone in northern Iraq that will provide some safety for the return of those people, having been driven by desperate fear from the marauding destruction of Iraqi Armed Forces.

Mr. President, it is unclear where American policy will go from here. In the rush to stabilize the situation, long-term questions naturally have been delayed and are only now coming into focus. How long will America provide the lion's share of the guarantee of Kurdish survival? What will be the cost of our efforts beyond May 31? How effective will the turnover of security responsibility from the U.S.-led coalition to the United Nations be?

Mr. President, the United States has done absolutely the right thing to provide for and, in effect, guarantee the survival of those Kurdish refugees. That is the message of our presence and our operations in establishing an adequate security zone in northern Iraq, and in our effort to convince the Kurdish people to come down from their mountain sanctuary and resume normal life in their towns and farms in northern Iraq. Our policy does not mean that

we are going to dictate the politics or economics of that region, or that we are taking sides in traditional rivalries, or supporting claims of any kind by the various parties in the region. It does not mean that we are going to support, indefinitely, an American occupying force in that region. That is a matter which demands a long-term solution under the United Nations umbrella, and may or may not include the presence of peacekeeping forces, or other forces under that umbrella to ensure that Saddam Hussein does not try to resume his armed attacks against the Kurds. We should not stay on any longer than it takes for the international community and the U.N. High Commission for Refugees to get their acts together. The transition should occur rapidly, consistent with the need to guarantee the survival of the Kurds, but not so as to entangle the United States in the prospects of redrawing lines of national sovereignty in that region.

Mr. President, I also commend the actions of the Government of Turkey and the people of Turkey in this effort. Despite isolated press reports of incidents involving Turkish troops, the overall efforts by Turkey have been consistent with her effort from the opening hours of this war, which has been to rise to the occasion, to do her duty, and to make a central and continuing contribution to resolving problems. I am told that Turkish villages on the Iraqi border have provided all kinds of relief to the refugees. The Turkish Government has allowed Turkish bases and territory to literally be taken over by more than 10,000 United States forces, allied forces of many nations, and international organizations to organize this tremendous, unprecedented relief operation. It would not have been possible to succeed as we have without that support. I say, this, Mr. President, knowing that there have been historical tensions and problems between Turkey and the Kurds-this is all the more reason to commend the Government of President Turgut Ozal, for providing the support that it has given.

Mr. President, we came to the relief of the Kurds because it was the right thing to do. I believe that we incurred substantial responsibility, other than on moral grounds, to engage in this operation. First, this mass human migration was an outcome of the war, an outcome of the devastation that Saddam Hussein invited, and got, from the United States and our partners. The Kurds, then are in some sense, victims of that war, and in helping them, we are responsibly acting to attend to one unfortunate outcome of our actions. Second, we encouraged the Kurds, perhaps indirectly, to revolt against the Iraqi regime, and they may have presumed that we would come to their aid, and relied on the words of President Bush to assume that we would support their revolt.

Now, Mr. President, the legislation that is before us provides that the American taxpayer pay 100 percent of the costs of the Department of Defense in this relief effort, some $320.5 million, as calculated through the end of May. We are going to be there well beyond the end of May, certainly into the summer, in all likelihood, before we can extract ourselves and leave the security task to the United Nations. So there will be further costs, perhaps amounting to several hundred additional millions of dollars. The administration, in making the request in the way it has, is saying that the money our allies have so far contributed to the American war effort should not be going to the Kurdish relief, so the taxpayer is paying for it. I suppose the rationale for this is that it is not a direct cost of the war, and the allies are contributing some forces and supplies bilaterally to the relief operation. While this may be true, the facts are that American taxpayers are footing almost the whole tab. And even the State Department costs, amounting to some additional $150 million, are coming from the interest on the allied contribution account and, in a deft exercise in fine distinctions, the administration argues that the interest is U.S. money and not allied money, so the fiction is preserved that allied contributions are not being used for the American operation.

Mr. President, our allies, particularly the Persian Gulf states, are still in arrears to us for some $17.8 billion that they pledged to help defer the war costs. That is from a total pledge of some $54 billion. We fully expect that our allies will help pay the war costs and keep their promise. I understand that the State Department has asked that they help pay our

share of the relief effort as well. I do not have any idea whether our allies have agreed to pay any of our relief costs, but collecting from them has been a rather disappointing experience to date. In addition, I understand that the money pledged by the Persian Gulf states to Turkey to help defer her war costs are not materializing, and I hope that the Secretary of State, Mr. Baker, will continue to press and remind those states of their obligations not only to us but also to the Turks, who were so instrumental in protecting allied interests from the outset of the Iraqi attack last August 2, 1990.

Mr. President, the United States cannot remain indefinitely in northern Iraq and we have to set up an international guarantee of Kurdish survival that is not borne by the American taxpayer forever. We need to devise ways to relieve the burden on our taxpayers. We are acting rightly and superbly in Turkey and Iraq, but the American taxpayer has a right to know where it all stops. Our allies have a continuing obligation to shoulder their share of the liabilities.

Mr. President, I think it would be very appropriate for the record to state at this time how the allied financial contributions are coming along. Saudi Arabia made a total pledge of $16.839 billion. The total received to date in cash and in kind, $7.595 billion, or 45 percent of the commitment, leaving an amount owed by Saudi Arabia of $9.244 billion.

Kuwait made a total pledge of $16.006 billion, and has paid $9.271 billion, or 58 percent of her pledge, leaving an amount owing of $6.735 billion.

Germany made a total pledge of $6,572,000,000. She has paid to date $6,554,000,000, or 99.7 percent of her commitment, leaving $18 million. Japan pledged $10,740,000,000, has paid $9,448,000,000, or 88 percent, leaving owed $1,292,000,000. The total pledges to date are $54,557,000,000. The total received to date is $36,798,000,000, or 67 percent of the total, leaving $17,759,000,000.

Mr. President, I ask unanimous consent that a letter dated May 1, 1991, to Richard Darman from myself and his response dated May 7, 1991, be printed in the RECORD.

There being no objection, the letters were ordered to be printed in the RECORD, as follows:

U.S. SENATE,
COMMITTEE ON APPROPRIATIONS,
Washington, DC, May 1, 1991. . .

91.

[May 14, 1991 (House), p. 3031]

PROVIDE RELIEF AND PROTECTION TO IRAQI KURDS AND OTHER REFUGEES FLEEING SADDAM HUSSEIN'S REPRESSION

The SPEAKER pro tempore (Mr. LANCAS-TER). Under a previous order of the House, the gentleman from Hawaii [Mr. ABERCROMBIE] is recognized for 5 minutes.

Mr. ABERCROMBIE. Mr. Speaker, I come before the body today fully in support and resolved with respect to the use of United States military forces to provide relief and protection to the Iraqi Kurds and other refugees fleeing the repression of Saddam Hussein. Especially gratifying was the decision to move American forces into position to protect the routes and temporary sites used by the refugees.

I believe that Americans of all political persuasions share this view, and commend the action of the President and the administration to forestall death and suffering on a scale so huge as to be scarcely comprehensible. I think the action of the Congress in providing funding for this shows that we are a caring people and that our hearts are gladdened by the sight of American troops delivering food, ministering to the sick, erecting shelter, and deploying troops to shield an entire people in mortal distress.

The scale of calamity is so vast and the peril so immediate that the U.S. Armed Forces are the only agency capable of rising to the challenge. We believe that even more needs to be done, taking advantage of this moment when our presence in the Middle East has never been stronger.

Mr. Speaker, therefore, in addition to the steps I have outlined, I urge, One, that we continue and expand the scope of humanitarian aid to the Iraqi Kurdish refugees, both inside and outside of Iraq, and enlist the aid of the United Nations in that effort;

Two, direct the U.S. Armed Forces to expand and vigorously enforce the prohibition against Iraqi military operations north of the 36th parallel, and through all of Iraqi Kurdistan. These include the Provinces of Kirkuk, Sulaymaniyah, Arbil, Dahuk, the portion of Ba'qubah Province northeast of the Hamrein Mountains, and those parts of Mosul Province north and east of the Tigris River.

Those who have been watching television in recent days will know this means we have to expand from this small refugee area in the northern part of Iraq to all of that territory which constitutes Iraqi Kurdistan.

Three, we need to use American resources and enlist United Nations aid to facilitate the return of all Iraqi Kurds who fled their homes after the March 1991 uprising, as well as those who previously were forced to relocate in southern Iraq by the regime of Saddam Hussein.

Four, lead a United Nations effort to establish a new government in Iran, which will respect international human rights norms for all Iraqi citizens, including Kurds, Assyrians, Turkomans, Chaldeans, and other minorities.

Five, we must take steps to include the plight of Iraqi Kurds on the agenda of a comprehensive Middle East peace conference.

Mr. Speaker, these steps would single out a commitment to a Middle East policy that accepts the moral obligations that flow from our involvement in that region. Concern for justice, human rights, democratic values, and compassion are not factors to be relegated to peripheral consideration. They must lie at the heart of any settlement. To ignore these considerations would doom the area to a state of continued turmoil. Only by recognizing those unquenchable aspirations can peace and stability be restored.

Mr. Speaker, it might fairly be asked why should we pay attention to people whose name we possibly had not even heard before this war? The reason is that this war is not over and will not be over. The United States, by aiding and assisting in the ejection of the Iraqis from Kuwait, has opened the floodgates of freedom loving people throughout the region to try to attain a measure of justice that we say that we can provide for the emirs and all of those in Kuwait who now find themselves being asked to leave Egypt, for example, from luxury hotels there, and come back to their homeland.

The Kurds are asking the same thing. We will not find ourselves able to be out of this war, to be out of this territory, without the Iraqis reasserting themselves in the territories in a manner which has been the hallmark of the regime in Baghdad ever since it came to power in Saddam Hussein. Saddam Hussein is in power today. Saddam Hussein will be in power when we leave, if we do not take the steps that I have outlined.

Mr. Speaker, we cannot extricate ourselves simply by saying the war is over. It is not over.

My point, Mr. Speaker, is that we will find ourselves in a situation in which thousands upon thousands of Kurds will find themselves in the path of the murderous regime of Saddam Hussein, and we will wonder why did we fight this war? Why did we not have as our object ridding the area of Saddam Hussein. If that was not our object, then what was it? If we did not urge the people of Iraq to rise up in opposition to Saddam Hussein, maybe we would have something to say today about our leavetaking. But we cannot say it, because we did urge them to do it.

Mr. Speaker, that is the reason they had this uprising, and that is the reason we see the refugees on the Turkish border and on the Iranian border.

Mr. Speaker, we must take steps to see to it that the United States carries out its moral obligations with respect to the Kurds, and that we finish the war. The only way it could be finished is by seeing to it that Saddam Hussein is removed from power and the people in revolt against him aided and assisted.

92.

[May 22, 1991 (Senate), pp. 6421-22]

SENATE RESOLUTION 132- COMMENDING HUMANITARIAN RE- LIEF EFFORTS FOR IRAQI REFUGEES

Mr. KENNEDY (for himself, Mr. SIMP- SON, Mr. DECONCINI, and Mr. PELL) submitted the following resolution; which was referred to the Committee on Foreign Relations:

S. RES. 132

Whereas beginning on March 28, 1991, nearly two million Kurdish and Shia men, women, and children in Iraq fled to their nation's borders in the aftermath of the failed uprising against Saddam Hussein;

Whereas the past policies of Saddam Hussein against the Iraqi people and attacks on the population since the defeat of Iraqi forces instilled terror in the population and led to the largest and swiftest flight of refugees in modern history;

Whereas an estimated 700,000 Kurdish refugees sought safety from Iraqi forces in the mountains along the Turkish-Iraqi border; 1.3 million Kurdish refugees sought safety along the Iranian-Iraqi border; 100,000 Shiites sought refuge along the Iranian-Iraqi border; and 25,000 Shiites who sought refuge along the Kuwaiti-Iraqi border have been relocated to Saudi Arabia;

Whereas an unknown number of Iraqis have been displaced internally inside Iraq;

Whereas an estimated 1,000 Kurdish refugees died each day in the early days of the refugee crisis along the Turkish-Iraqi border from exposure, malnutrition, and disease;

Whereas on April 5, 1991, President Bush ordered United States forces to begin providing assistance to the refugees along the Turkish-Iraqi border;

Whereas on April 16, 1991, in response to the overwhelming humanitarian needs of the Kurdish refugees along the Turkish-Iraqi border, President Bush, following consultations with Prime Minister Major of the United Kingdom, President Mitterand of France, President Ozal of Turkey, Chancellor Kohl of

Germany, and the United Nations Secretary General Perez de Cuellar, announced a greatly expanded relief effort, named "Operation Provide Comfort", to provide adequate food, medicine, clothing, and shelter to the Kurds living in the mountains along the Turkish-Iraqi border;

Whereas consistent with United Nations Security Council Resolution 688 and in conjunction with European nations, the United Nations and international relief organizations, the United States forces established encampments in northern Iraq to provide relief supplies to the refugees;

Whereas "Operation Provide Comfort" saved the lives of more than 20,000 Kurdish refugees in northern Iraq and Turkey by reducing the death rate to less than 10 per day; and

Whereas the performance of the allied forces involved in this effort have accomplished an extraordinary humanitarian relief effort in a brief period of time: Now, therefore, be it

Resolved, That (a) The Senate—

(1) commends the United States and allied troops who are participating in

Operation Provide Comfort in northern Iraq and Turkey and those who ably assisted thousands of refugees in Kuwait and southern Iraq, and who have demonstrated exceptional dedication, professionalism, and compassion in accomplishing this humanitarian task;

(2) supports the continuation of the benefits enacted by Congress for "Operation Desert Storm" to the participants of "Operation Provide Comfort" for the duration of that operation;

(b) It is the sense of the Senate that—

(1) the United States and the international community should continue to assist and protect the refugees and to support the goal of enabling all the refugees, including those along the Turkish-Iraqi border, the Iranian-Iraqi border, and in Saudi Arabia, to return home with adequate assurances of peace and security;

(2) increased efforts should be made to assist the remaining 900,000 refugees in Iran and the Iranian Government should cease impending international relief efforts; and

(3) the United States should respond immediately to the United Nation's appeal for increased assistance to the refugees.

SEC. 2. The Secretary of the Senate shall transmit a copy of this resolution to the President.

Mr. KENNEDY. Mr. President, a month ago, the world watched in shock and horror as nearly 2 million Iraqi men, women, and children fled their homes and villages in terror to escape Saddam Hussein's murderous retribution and violence.

Their panic flight into the harsh winter conditions where they faced death, starvation and diseases is a telling indictment of the brutality of Saddam Hussein and his henchmen. Never in recent history has a refugee tragedy of this magnitude exploded upon the world in so short period.

Who among us can ever forget the pictures night after night on television and in the Nation's newspapers of tens of thousands of Kurds on the mountain tops along the Turkish-Iraqi border? For too long, the United States delayed in coming to the assistance of these refugees. Our desire to bring our troops home quickly from the war clouded our duty to these innocent people.

But the plight of starving Kurds touched the conscience of the Nation and the world. On April 16, President Bush ordered the United States to act, and sent troops into northern Iraq and Turkey to assist the Kurds.

This relief effort, called "Operation Provide Comfort," was an international humanitarian mission unlike any seen before. Over 20,000 U.S. and allied troops worked together to bring food, clothing, shelter and medicine to the Kurds suffering from exposure, disease and starvation in the mountains on the border between Turkey and Iraq.

In a matter of days, the tide of misery and death was turned. At the beginning, as many as 1,000 Kurds-mostly children and the elderly-were dying each day in the mountains. Within days after the commencement of Operation Provide Comfort, the death rate plummeted to less than 50 a day. Today, it is less than 10 a day. Never before in history has such an enormous human disaster been alleviated so quickly or so effectively.

A delegation from the Senate Subcommittee on Immigration and Refugee Affairs has recently returned from the region. It estimates that our efforts saved some 20,000 lives. The only regret is that we did not act sooner and save an even larger number of lives.

Our troops also provided critical assistance to the nearly 40,000 refugees who fled Saddam Hussein in southern Iraq. These refugees, mostly Shia, feared reprisals from Iraqi forces after the Shia in the region rose up unsuccessfully against Saddam Hussein. Our troops, in conjunction with our allies and private voluntary agencies provided basic assistance and medical care to these individuals.

In one of the most efficient and rapid relocation of refugees ever, one half of these refugees in southern Iraq-25,000-were airlifted to a refugee camp in Rafhah, Saudi Arabia. The United States has since turned over responsibility of the remaining refugees in the Demilitarized Military Zone along the Iraqi Kuwait border to the United Nations, but we must not forget the extraordinary success of this operation.

The resolution I am introducing today with Senator SIMPSON commends the United States and allied troops who participated in these extraordinary relief operations. Their exceptional dedication, professionalism and compassion has made them heroes to not only the Kurds but also the world. Many of these troops had served in Operation Desert Storm, and some were on their way home when they were diverted to assist in the refugee crisis.

I urge my colleagues to join me in applauding these men and women who demonstrated once again the outstanding capabilities of our military forces. Trained for combat and war, they showed how well our military can adapt to changing circumstances and changing missions.

They deserve our full support and I am pleased that the administration has decided to extend the benefits enacted by Congress for the participants of Operation Desert Storm to those involved in Operation Provide Comfort. I urge the administration to ensure that these benefits continue for the duration of this important relief effort.

United States Armed Forces are now also coming to the aid of the victims of the tragic cyclone in Bangladesh. The success of these recent operations may well pave the way for institutionalizing a new role for the U.S. military in responding to international disasters. I hope the administration will begin to look at ways to facilitate similar relief efforts in the future.

There is new hope that adequate security measures will be put in place to enable the remaining 200,000 refugees in northern Iraq and Turkey to return home. The United States must not withdraw from the region until this critical goal can be achieved.

U.S. troops have arrived in the city of Dohuk, and the United Nations may soon be able to assume positions around the area and enable U.S. troops to withdraw. The Kurdish leadership continues to negotiate an autonomy agreement with the Iraqi Government, which will enhance their security throughout northern Iraq. Once these steps occur, virtually all of the refugees along Iraq's northern border will be able to return home.

There remain deep concerns about the presence of the Iraqi secret police in the region. Even in towns controlled by allied forces, such as Zakho, secret police regularly infiltrate the area to harass and intimidate the population. So long as Saddam Hussein remains in power, the people of Iraq are at risk and the international community must remain engaged in efforts to provide for their peace and security.

The United Nations plan to station hundreds of blue helmets throughout Iraq in order to enhance the security of the Iraqi people and to deter any repressive actions by the Iraqi Government, military or secret police. While the U.N. personnel will not perform the functions of security police, they will provide a tripwire system that can alert the international community to abuses by Saddam and his forces. Such a system will reassure the returning refugees and the Iraqi people that the international community intends to stay engaged in the struggle for human rights and democracy.

Stability in Iraq will not be possible until security and democracy is established throughout the country. The administration should lend its full weight to the ongoing negotiations between the Kurdish leadership and the Iraqi Government until a satisfactory agreement is in place. It must also press the Iraqi Government to provide adequate protection to populations outside the zone of current negotiations in order to permit the return of the refugee population from Iran and Saudi Arabia and to ensure long-term stability in Iraq.

U.S. Government policy toward democracy in Iraq remains unclear.

Administration policy continues to advocate an overthrow of Saddam Hussein by his own Ba'ath party officials, not democratic elections to permit the people of Iraq to chose their own leaders. The Ba'ath make up only 20 percent of Iraq's population and thus 80 percent of the Iraqi people would continue to be denied a choice in their leadership. Our goal, even after Saddam Hussein leaves power, must be democracy in Iraq and respect for human rights.

The United States and the international community must also remain mindful of the 900,000 Kurdish refugees and the 100,000 Shia refugees who remain along the Iranian-Iraqi border. There are also another 25,000 refugees now in Saudi Arabia. We must not neglect these individuals. Instead we must work to establish conditions within Iraq to enable their return, too. The crisis cannot be considered ended, when over 1 million Iraqi refugees remain.

As the refugee crisis continues in Iran, there are reports that deaths in the refugee camps continue to number between 140 to 450 a day. While international relief efforts have succeeded in dramatically reducing the large death toll along the Turkish-Iraqi border, no similar success has occurred in Iran.

The Iranian Government bears a heavy responsibility for impeding relief efforts to the Iraqi refugees in its care. Despite its pleas for international assistance, the Iranian Government has blocked humanitarian organizations from access to the camps, slowed assistance by insisting on lengthy bureaucratic processes, intimidated relief workers and politicized our own shipment of blankets.

It denied a visa request from a delegation of the Subcommittee on Immigration and Refugee Affairs to visit the refugee camps, put several Americare relief workers under house arrest for 5 days, interrogated one American member of the private U.S. Committee for Refugees overnight, and harassed the American volunteers in the region to the point where they were forced to abandon their critical work. Ironically, Kurdish and Shia refugees continue to perish because of these obstacles to relief.

Nevertheless, the U.S.-led relief operation to assist the Iraqi refugees is one of the most extraordinary achievements in recent times. Let us take this step today to commend the dedicated men and women serving on our Armed Forces who made it possible. They deserve our whole-hearted praise and support, and I urge my colleagues to join me in this tribute to them.

93.

[May 23, 1991 (Senate), pp. 6761-63]

COMMENDING HUMANITARIAN RELIEF EFFORTS FOR IRAQI REFUGEES

The resolution (S. RES. 132) commending the humanitarian relief efforts for Iraqi refugees, was considered and agreed to.

The preamble was agreed to.

The resolution, and the preamble, are as follows:

S. RES. 132

Whereas beginning on March 28, 1991, nearly two million Kurdish and Shia men, women, and children in Iraq fled to their nation's borders in the aftermath of the failed uprising against Saddam Hussein;

Whereas the past policies of Saddam Hussein against the Iraqi people and attacks on the population since the defeat of Iraqi forces instilled terror in the population and led to the largest and swiftest flight of refugees in modern history;

Whereas an estimated 700,000 Kurdish refugees sought safety from Iraqi forces in the mountains along the Turkish-Iraqi border; 1.3 million Kurdish refugees sought safety along the Iranian-Iraqi border; 100,000 Shiites sought refuge along the Iranian-Iraqi border and 25,000 Shiites-who sought refuge along the Kuwaiti-Iraq border have been relocated to Saudi Arabia;

Whereas an unknown number of Iraqis have been displaced internally inside Iraq;

Whereas an estimated 1,000 Kurdish refugees died each day in the early days of the refugee crisis along the Turkish-Iraqi border from exposure, malnutrition, and disease;

Whereas on April 5, 1991, President Bush ordered United States forces to begin providing assistance to the refugees along the Turkish-Iraqi border;

Whereas on April 16, 1991, in response to the overwhelming humanitarian needs of the Kurdish refugees along the Turkish-Iraqi border, President Bush, following consultations with Prime Minister Major of the United Kingdom, President Mitterand of France, President Ozal of Turkey, Chancellor Kohl of Germany, and the United Nations Secretary General Perez de Cuellar, announced a greatly expanded relief effort, named "Operation Provide Comfort", to provide adequate food, medicine, clothing, and shelter to the Kurds living in the mountains along the Turkish-Iraqi border;

Whereas, consistent with United Nations Security Council Resolution 688 and in conjunction with European nations, the United Nations and international relief organizations, the United States forces established encampments in northern Iraq to provide relief supplies to the refugees;

Whereas "Operation Provide Comfort" saved the lives of more than 20,000 Kurdish refugees in northern Iraq and Turkey by reducing the death rate to less than 10 per day; and

Whereas the performance of the allied forces involved in this effort have accomplished an extraordinary humanitarian relief effort in a brief period of time: Now, therefore be it

Resolved, That (a) The Senate-

(1) commends the United States and allied troops who are participating in Operation Provide Comfort in northern Iraq and Turkey and those who ably assisted thousands of refugees in Kuwait and southern Iraq, and who have demonstrated exceptional dedication, professionalism, and compassion in accomplishing this humanitarian task;

(2) supports the continuation of the benefits enacted by Congress for "Operation Desert Storm" to the participants of "Operation Provide Comfort" for the duration of that operation;

(b) It is the sense of the Senate that-

(1) the United States and the international community should continue to assist and protect and refugees and to support the goal of enabling all the refugees, including those along the Turkish-Iraqi border, the Iranian-Iraqi border, and in Saudi Arabia, to return home with adequate assurances of peace and security;

(2) increased efforts should be made to assist the remaining 900,000 refugees in Iran and the Iranian Government should cease impeding international relief efforts; and

(3) the United States should respond immediately to the United Nation's appeal for increased assistance to the refugees.

SEC. 2. The Secretary of the Senate shall transmit a copy of this resolution to the President.

Mr. SIMPSON. Mr. President, I rise to join my colleague in support of this resolution commending the performance of our military and the other allied forces in providing emergency relief to the Kurdish and Shia refugees who fled the depredations of Saddam Hussein's army.

Operation Provide Comfort has saved the lives of tens of thousands of refugees, and that is something that every participating country can be proud of.

I also want to pay tribute to President Bush for his decisive and resolute action in ordering our forces to provide the lifesaving assistance to the Kurds in the mountains along the Turkish-Iraqi border.

I know that President Bush told our military to determine what could be done to help-not what could be done "if we had the money," but what could be done. Well, what was done was effective, lifesaving and another example of the superb skills, training and ability possessed by our men and women in uniform.

What our troops did was historic. Never before have our military forces taken on a humanitarian assistance task of this scale and under such harsh conditions as existed in the mountains along the Iraqi-Turkish border.

Our forces carried out their duties in Operation Provide Comfort with the same dedication, professionalism and effectiveness that we saw in Operation Desert Storm.

Our troops fought two extraordinary campaigns, and won them both. We are all so proud.

I urge my colleagues to support this resolution which recognizes this fine humanitarian accomplishment of our Armed Forces.

Mr. KENNEDY. Mr. President, yesterday, Senators SIMPSON, DECONCINI and I introduced a resolution to commend the extraordinary humanitarian relief mission of our troops in aiding the Iraqi refugees. The Senate Foreign Relations Committee reported the resolution unanimously earlier today, and I urge my colleagues to join in paying tribute to this historic relief operation.

I am grateful to the chairman of the Senate Foreign Relations Committee for considering this resolution in such an expedited manner. The strong support it received today in the committee underscores the overwhelming appreciation in this body and across the Nation for the lifesaving mission our forces carried out to save Kurds and other refugees fleeing Saddam Hussein's murderous retribution and violence.

Only a month ago, the world watched a massive tragedy unfold, as hundreds of thousands of Iraqi Kurds and Shia fled their homes and villages. Never before in modern times has such a massive and sudden exodus of innocent men, women, and children occurred. Their flight is a chilling testament to the brutal and ruthless regime of Saddam Hussein.

None of us will ever forget the heartwrenching pictures night after night on the evening news of starving Kurds rushing to grab the initial deliveries of relief supplies, or the faces of the dying children, and grief stricken parents. Rather than face Saddam Hussein, the Kurds preferred to face death and disease in the harsh mountains along the Turkish-Iraqi border.

At first, the administration hesitated to come to the assistance of these innocent victims of the war. But the plight of the Kurds touched the conscience of the Nation and the world. On April 16, President Bush ordered the United States to act, and sent troops into northern Iraq in an unprecedented military mission of mercy. Within days, the number of Kurds dying in the mountains dropped from 1,000 a day to less than 50. Today, the rate is less than 10.

This extraordinary effort, Operation Provide Comfort, saved an estimated 20,000 lives, as United States and allied troops provided food, clothing, shelter, and medicine to the Kurds. The only regret is that we did not act sooner and save an even larger number of lives.

In addition, beginning in the early days after the war, the United States, together with the allied forces and international relief agencies, assisted the 40,000 mostly Shia refugees in southern Iraq. In one aspect of that most impressive operation, the United States military airlifted 25,000 Iraqi refugees to a camp in Saudi Arabia. We have now turned over the responsibility of the remaining refugees to the United Nations within a demilitarized military zone along the Iraqi-Kuwait border. The committed men and women involved in this impressive effort deserve recognition for their extraordinary performance and the tremendous success of their operation.

The resolution before us commends these men and women for their skill, courage and dedication. It also urges that the benefits enacted by Congress for Operation Desert Storm be extended to the participants of Operation Provide Comfort for the duration of the relief mission.

Trained for war, our troops demonstrated the outstanding capability and flexibility of our military to adapt to changing circumstances and changing missions. Never before has the military conducted such a massive humanitarian relief effort. And never before

Simple

have relief efforts been so extraordinarily successful and saved so many lives so quickly.

The resolution also urges the United States and the international community to continue to assist and protect the refugees and to support the goal of enabling all the refugees to return home with adequate assurances of peace and security. The arrival of allied troops in the critical city of Dahuk and the eventual transfer of authority to the United Nations officials provide a needed sense of security for the returning Kurds. That action, coupled with the ongoing autonomy negotiations between the Kurdish leadership and the Iraqi Government, will enable the vast majority of the Kurds along the Turkish-Iraqi border to return home.

But long-term problems persist and the United States has a responsibility to remain engaged in the process of establishing peace and stability throughout Iraq. Secret police remain active throughout the country, even in the allied controlled areas, and threaten and harass the Iraqi people. One million Kurdish and Shia refugees remain along the Iran-Iraq border and another 25,000 Shia remain in the refugee camp in Saudi Arabia. No one knows how many more Iraqis are displaced within Iraq. We must continue to work for conditions that will enable them to return home, too.

Finally, our policy toward Iraq cannot be based solely on the overthrow of Saddam Hussein. Peace and stability will never come to Iraq until all the people of that troubled country have a role in choosing their own leaders. Our current policy of supporting an internal coup within the Ba‘ath party structure disenfranchises 80 percent of the population. The Shia, who make up 55 percent of Iraq's people, and the Kurds, who make up another 25 percent, must also participate in governing the nation. The United States must put itself clearly on the side of democracy and human rights in Iraq.

I thank the majority leader for allowing this important resolution to be considered by the Senate, and I urge my colleagues to join in giving the support of the Senate to this historic relief effort and to our forces who made it all possible.

94.

[June 12, 1991 (Senate), pp. 7702-3]

INTERNATIONAL EFFORTS TO PROTECT THE KURDISH PEOPLE

Mr. KERREY. Mr. President, in the past 72 hours we have immersed the military participants of Operation Desert Storm with an unprecedented homecoming. In Washington, DC, it was one of the largest demonstrations; in New York City they broke all previous records.

The success being celebrated is the military victory over the Iraqi army. American and allied forces drove the Iraqi occupiers out of Kuwait just as they promised to do. It was a very impressive operation and we now welcome home those who impressed us so much.

The language of our speakers describe this as a victory for liberty and freedom. However, as stunning as the military victory was, the fight for freedom has just begun, Reports of ongoing human rights abuses in Kuwait indicate that we need to sustain our concern for the freedom of the Kuwaiti people. Further, as grateful as I am for the safe homecoming of our men and women, the most impressive movement home has been the return of Kurdish refugees to northern Iraq. Mr. President, I hope and pray we do not forget them.

In this morning's *Washington Post* there is an editorial by Mr. Sadruddin Aga Khan, the executive delegate of the Secretary General for the United Nations interagency humanitarian program for Iraq, Kuwait, and the Iraq-Turkey and Iraq-Iran border areas. I ask that Mr. Khan's text appear at the conclusion of my statement.

Mr. Khan explains the purpose and history of the United Nations "guards contingent" formula being used in Iraq to protect the freedom of the Kurdish people. These 500 U.N. guards are in Mr. Khan's words "to be assigned wherever a U.N. humanitarian presence is needed it is a small step for peace, a tentative but instructive idea of how innovation, even within the United Nations somewhat rigid structures, can unblock the impasse."

These 500 guards operate according to a May 23 U.N. agreement with Iraq and the framework agreement signed in Baghdad on April 18. It is a humanitarian operation which can only be successful if the United States stands watchfully and forcefully behind it. Unfortunately, thus far the voluntary fundraising effort has fallen short of needs. The United States must lead the world to make certain this shortage evaporates. It would be a tragic and bitter end if the freedom of these refugees was sacrificed to complacency.

Mr. Khan's vision for a new kind of response is worthy of our support. His words are more than worthy; they inspire. He says:

The debate over a right of humanitarian intervention has been given a good airing recently. Compassion and self-interest find temporary common cause in international action to alleviate suffering that knows no frontiers. In a vacuum of authority, responsibility must be assumed, and services disrupted by disasters must be restored. Yet imposed concern remains largely unwelcome. Once again, innovation and flexibility are crucial. Life-saving and face-saving may have to go hand in hand.

Mr. President, not only do we have the opportunity through this effort to finish the job we began, we also have the opportunity to learn how to use force to prevent wars from beginning. In the postcontainment world we must provide the means to make these kinds of operations as big a success as Desert Storm ...

95.

[June 25, 1991 (Senate), pp. 8557-8]

DON'T DESERT THE KURDS

Mr. PELL. Mr. President, for more than 2 months, United States and coalition forces have been saving lives in northern Iraq. These service men and women have fed the hungry, ministered to the sick, and sheltered the homeless. Most important, our troops have protected the Kurdish, Assyrian, and Chaldean peoples from wholesale slaughter by Saddam Hussein's defeated but still murderous army.

Now, however, the allied mission in northern Iraq appears to be drawing to a close.

And without adequate arrangements to protect the peoples of the region, we are likely to see a reprise of the tragedies that got us into northern Iraq in the first place.

For the last 2 months, Kurdish leaders have been negotiating in Baghdad with Saddam Hussein. These negotiations seem to be producing an agreement for substantial Kurdish autonomy. According to press reports, the Kurds are to have democratic elections in the autonomous region within 3 months, will obtain a portion of the revenues from Kirkuk oil fields, and will be allowed to operate their own press, radio, and television stations. Within 6 months to a year, democratic elections are to be held in all of Iraq.

It is a deal, in short, that seems too good to be true, and it almost certainly is. In earlier periods of weakness, such as in the early 1970's and during the Iran-Iraq War, Saddam Hussein entered into comparable negotiations with the Kurdish leaders. However, as his regime regained strength, agreements were discarded and the killing resumed.

There is no reason to believe anything different of the current situation. For the moment, Saddam Hussein is likely to adhere to at least part of his deal, although it defies belief that he would have truly democratic elections in Iraq.

Not only does Saddam want to get the foreign forces out of Iraq, he also wants the international community to turn its attention away from Iraq. This he knows will not happen as long as the international community is seized with the Kurdish issue. Therefore, he has adopted a very transparent strategy: conclude a deal with the Kurds, get the international forces out of Iraq, let international opinion move from the Kurds to other issues, and then settle scores with the Kurdish rebels and the people that backed them.

There is no reason why we should play into Saddam's strategy. We must recognize that no deal with a man who our President has said is worse than Adolf Hitler can be trusted not to resume persecution of the Kurdish people. Protection of the Kurdish people must be the guiding principle of our policy in northern Iraq.

The Kurds are at risk because of the action the international community took against Iraq. By decimating Saddam's army, we created a situation that made the Kurdish rebellion inevitable. More than this, however, we actively encouraged the Kurdish rebellion in the public statements of President Bush calling for the Iraqi people to overthrow Saddam Hussein, in the promise of military support-"You fly, you die"-and in the broadcasts of a clandestine United States-supported radio station. We cannot and must not walk away from our responsibility to people who are at risk because of our actions. The rebellions following the ground war are direct consequences of the war, and we cannot escape our responsibility.

The Kurdish people rebelled en masse against Saddam Hussein. In 1988, a much smaller rebellion provoked extensive chemical weapons attacks against more then 60 villages. This time, whole cities were part of the rebellion and whole cities are at risk for retribution. The Kurds will be at risk as long as Saddam Hussein and his regime are in power. This fact presents the United States with some very unpleasant choices: Either we find a way to keep an international presence in Iraq indefinitely or we abandon the Kurds to a cruel fate. Because the second alternative is, in my view, inhumane and immoral, we have little choice but to stay in northern Iraq.

Ideally, we should be working with the other members of the Security Council to establish an international force with a mandate to protect the Kurdish population. This force must go far beyond the 500 lightly armed UN police who are there at the sufferance of the Iraqi regime and whose mandate is limited to the protection of the international relief workers. It will take time to create the appropriate kind of international force.

In the meantime, we should not be so eager to get out of northern Iraq. Our troops are quite literally lifesavers. As much as we want them home, I do not believe they would want to leave knowing all they accomplished will be quickly undone. The parades we will hold this July 4 will honor the great achievements of our men and women in Operation Desert Shield and Desert Storm. Let us not besmirch

this triumph by a premature withdrawal from northern Iraq.

96.

[August 2, 1991 (House), p. 6320]

REMEMBER THE KURDS

(Mr. BILBRAY asked and was given permission to address the House for 1 minute and to revise and extend his remarks.)

Mr. BILBRAY. Mr. Speaker, tomorrow, August 3, the Kurdish National Congress of North America will convene in Washington, DC, in order to discuss and map out future strategy to resolve the continuing Kurdish crisis in northern Iraq. I am greatly honored to have been invited to address this gathering.

Although we do not continue to see nightly pictures of dying refugees, tent cities, and food drops, there are still a number of issues that need to be settled. Although we now have a rapid action force in Turkey, we can still not guarantee the safety of these people. The Iraqi Government's past actions have shown an incredible disdain for the existence of the Kurds.

Of utmost importance is the fact that people are still dying. Our economic embargo upon Iraq is necessary and justified. However, we must devise ways in which to deliver the assistance and subsistence that every human deserves.

And finally Saddam Hussein is still in power. No one, especially Kurds, will be safe until this dictator is removed. I hope my colleagues will join me in commending the continuing actions of the Kurdish front and I hope that we will not forget their struggle.

97.

[October 7, 1991 (Extensions of Remarks), pp. 3290-91]

THE HUMAN RIGHTS SITUATION IN TURKEY
HON. LEE H. HAMILTON
OF INDIANA

IN THE HOUSE OF REPRESENTA-TIVES

Monday, October 7, 1991

Mr. HAMILTON. Mr. Speaker, I wish to draw to the attention of my colleagues a recent exchange of letters with the Department of State regarding the human rights situation in Turkey. In recent months, reports of widespread use of torture and other human rights violations in Turkey have increased, raising serious questions about the commitment of the Government of Turkey to addressing these problems.

I believe it is important that the United States take an objective and critical view of human rights development in Turkey. The State Department response to my letter of July 17, 1991, speaks of some positive advances on human rights issues in Turkey, but fails to mention other developments which undermine the impact of some of these steps.

Turkey is an important friend and NATO ally. It is in our interest and in the interest of the future of United States-Turkish relationship to ensure that serious human rights violations cease to occur in Turkey.

The correspondence follows:

U.S. DEPARTMENT OF STATE,
Washington, DC, August 5, 1991.
Hon. LEE H. HAMILTON,
Chairman, Subcommittee on Europe and the Middle East, Washington, DC.

DEA MR. HAMILTON: Thank you for your letter of July 17, 1991, to the Secretary expressing concern over the human rights situation in Turkey.

There have been some positive advances on human rights issues in Turkey this past year, but some problems remain. On the positive side the Turks took the following actions: Parliament repealed the ban on use of the Kurdish language; amnested 20,000 prisoners; and repealed the "thought-crime" laws (although a recent constitutional court decision leaves the practical effect of this last move somewhat questionable). Parliament also established a human rights commission which has taken an active role in investigating allegations of human rights abuses.

On the negative side, the continuation of incommunicado detention and the recent incidents in the southeast are cause for concern. The latest southeastern violence was sparked by the murder of Vedat Aydin, President of the Diyarbakir branch of the People's Labor Party [HEP] and a member of the local Human Rights Association. He was picked up from his home by four individuals who identified themselves as members of the police force, something they would be most unlikely to do if they really were members of a security force and intended to kill him. We do not know whether they produced any identification. Mr. Aydin's body was found 3 days later. Masquerading as members of the security forces has been a frequent ploy for Turkish terrorists, including the individuals who murdered an American citizen in Istanbul several months ago. The opposition parties and the Human Rights Association have yet to reach any consensus regarding the motive for the killing or the possible identity of the killers. Two official investigations are underway, one by parliament and the other by the Ministry of the Interior.

Mr. Aydin's funeral in Diyarbakir on July 11 sparked a violent demonstration which included gunfire. The police claim the first shot came from the crowd which, newspaper accounts make clear, was already pelting them with stones. The demonstration took place in narrow streets bordering on the city's medieval walls. Some people were shot; others were trampled, pushed off the walls, or otherwise injured. At least three people were killed and thirty eight injured, some seriously. The police detained over three hundred people. this incident, too, is under investigation.

Mr. Aydin's murder and the violence at his funeral came in the aftermath of a bombing at the Diyarbakir Human Rights Association; a car bomb which wounded another human rights activist (and his son) in the region; and a second car bomb incident in Diyarbakir in which no one was hurt.

While it is unclear whether these latest events involved human rights violations, there is no doubt we have conveyed our concerns on this subject repeatedly to the highest levels of the Turkish government, most recently during the visit of President Bush. I can assure you that Ambassador Abramowitz made human rights one of his top priorities, as will Ambassador-designate Barkley. You should also be aware that our Embassy in Ankara has initiated a program of human rights seminars, the first of which was held in May. It was attended by human rights activists, government officials, and parliamentarians. We hope to hold two more seminars in the next year.We believe the new Turkish government will continue to take steps to improve its human rights record. This was a subject of discussion between President Bush and Turkish leaders during the recent state visit; the discussion followed a mention of human rights in President Bush's arrival statement. We have an open and continuing dialogue with the Turks and believe the open and continuing dialogue with the Turks and believe the government is determined to improve its generally excellent democracy-free elections, courts and parties-with police reforms.

Sincerely,
JANET H. MULLINS,
Assistant Secretary, Legislative Affairs.

98.

[November 25, 1991 (Extensions of Remarks), p. 4058]

NEW TURKISH GOVERNMENT OFFERS ENCOURAGING PACKAGE OF HUMAN RIGHTS REFORMS HON. STENY H. HOYER OF MARYLAND IN THE HOUSE OF REPRESENTATIVES

Monday, November 25, 1991

Mr. HOYER. Mr. Speaker, the new government in Turkey, led by Suleymin Demirel, recently unveiled a package of wide ranging reforms which addresses many concerns voiced by human rights observers including the Commission on Security and Cooperation in Europe. The sweeping proposals would make amendments to the 1982 Constitution and abrogate or change existing laws. The measures, if adopted by the Turkish Parliament and fully implemented, would secure for Turkey a place alongside the most advanced democracies in the world.

The "democratization package" as it is called, would do the following: Lift the state monopoly on television and radio broadcasts, expand academic independence, reform voting laws, provide added police training, redraft existing laws concerning torture, remove all forms of censorship, reduce maximum periods of pretrial detention, enforce a detainee's right to counsel at all stages of detention, limit martial law and emergency rule powers, expand permissible activities for trade unions, students and associations, televise parliamentary debate and ensure judicial autonomy. Other specific reforms addressed in the package include one which directly relates to commitments undertaken by the Government of Turkey within the Conference on Security and Cooperation in Europe [CSCE]: and I quote, "The legal and de factor restrictions and obstructions on free expression of ethnic origin, use of language and promotion of culture by all citizens, will be eradicated within the concept of national unity and in conformity with the Paris Charter to which Turkey is a party".

Mr. Speaker, Prime Minister Demirel stated publicly today that "torture is a crime against humanity and it is our duty to prevent this." The Helsinki Commission applauds this public condemnation by the newly elected Prime Minister as an important and critical signal to those who engage in torture that such practices will no longer be tolerated.

Mr. Speaker, this promising, if yet enacted, set of proposals by the new coalition government indicates a determination on the part of Mr. Demirel and his partners to address the major sources of problems which have seriously clouded Turkey's past human rights performance. Given the economic difficulties facing Turkey and the violent conflict in the southeastern regions inhabited by Kurds, this proposal is even more remarkable and courageous. It is likely, as was previously the case when even less sweeping reforms were introduced, conservative elements in government will offer objections to the package. In the past, similar types of legislation were often delayed for years, haphazardly implemented or allowed to fall from the agenda. I sincerely hope that the new government will work hard to adopt these proposals, knowing that they have the full support of the United States. The stated intentions of the new government to make the Kurdish issue a priority is a most positive indicator.

Mr. Speaker, I would also like to note what I consider to be a significant incentive for Turkey to pursue these reforms and see that they reach fruition. Turkey's historic ties with Central Asia provide it with a unique opportunity. As the Muslim republics of the former Soviet Union strive to further develop their own political and economic systems, Turkey could serve as a model of democratic development and economic achievement. I sincerely hope that such ties will be developed, as they will certainly benefit not only Turkey and the Central Asia nations, but regional and global stability.

99.

[November 26, 1991 (Extensions of Remarks), p. 4123]

THE HUMAN RIGHTS SITUATION IN TURKEY
HON. LEE H. HAMILTON
OF INDIANA
IN THE HOUSE OF REPRESENTATIVES

Tuesday, November 26, 1991

Mr. HAMILTON. Mr. Speaker, I wish to draw to the attention of my colleagues the latest in a series of letters exchanged with the Department of State regarding the human rights situation in Turkey. The last exchange appeared in the CONGRESSIONAL RECORD on Monday, October 7, 1991. In their current response, the State Department addresses a number of individual concerns raised by human rights groups regarding the earlier State Department letter on this issue.

Once again, I wish to reiterate that Turkey is an important friend and NATO ally of the United States. It is in our interest and in the interest of the future of the United States-Turkish relationship to ensure that serious human rights violations cease to occur in Turkey.

The correspondence follows:

CONGRESS OF THE UNITED STATES,
HOUSE OF REPRESENTATIVES,
Washington, DC, October 24, 1991.
Hon. JAMES A. BAKER III,
Secretary of State, Department of State, Washington DC.

DEAR MR. SECRETARY: I write to follow-up on our exchange of letters this summer on the human rights situation in Turkey. I recently received correspondence from the human rights organization Helsinki Watch regarding continued serious violations of human rights in Turkey. The Helsinki Watch letter paints a very different picture of this problem from that portrayed in the Department's August 5, 1991 response to me.

Helsinki Watch asserts that:

Premeditated torture of political detainees is a routine practice in Turkey today;

Twelve political prisoners have died in detention under suspicious circumstances since January 1-twice the number of deaths in detention in 1990;

In recent months 19 people have died in house-to-house police raids and 10 demonstrators have died as a result of indiscriminate use of live ammunition by Turkish security forces;

Restrictions on freedom of expression persist and the recent enactment of a broad Antiterror law represents a step backward in this area; and,

Human rights violations against the Kurdish minority continue. Despite the publicized repeal of the ban on Kurdish, it continues to be a crime to use the Kurdish language in official settings, including family visits to prison detainees.

I have enclosed a copy of the Helsinki Watch letter for your information.

I would appreciate it if you would have your staff review the points made in this letter and get back to me.

I appreciate your prompt consideration of this matter and I look forward to hearing from you.

With best regards,
Sincerely yours,
LEE H. HAMILTON,
Subcommittee on Europe and the Middle East.

———

UNITED STATES DEPARTMENT OF STATE,
Washington, DC, November 22, 1991.
Hon. LEE H. HAMILTON,
Chairman, Subcommittee on Europe and the Middle East, House of Representatives.

DEAR MR. CHAIRMAN: This is in reply to your letter of October 24 to Secretary Baker concerning allegations of human rights abuses in Turkey as reported to you by Helsinki Watch.

Torture of detainees in Turkey does occur-most typically during periods of incommunicado detention before a suspect is brought before a court. The government recognizes that torture occurs but asserts it is neither widespread nor systematic. The Justice Ministry maintains that the Turkish government is pursuing an all-out fight against torture and does not tolerate anyone who mistreats suspects and inmates. While the government has introduced some reforms that could contribute to a reduction of abuse, these reforms have not been effectively implemented. There were no known political killings attributable to the government or opposition political parties in 1991. However, figures compiled by the Human Rights Foundation show that as of October 31, eighteen persons have died while in police custody. At least some of these deaths may have been due to police torture.

Turkey has taken important steps recently to combat human rights abuses. Turkey has signed several international conventions against torture and the Turkish Constitution outlaws torture. In December 1990 the Turkish Grand National Assembly established a multi-party "Human Rights Commission,"

empowered to investigate any allegations of human rights abuses that are submitted to it. The Commission began operating early in 1991. In September 1991 the Justice and Interior Ministries announced that each would establish a Human Rights section within their respective ministries. The Parliament sponsored an October 4-5 symposium on "International Protection of Human Rights and the Turkish Grand National Assembly." The Police Academy announced in October that human rights is being taught as the first course in its fall semester.

The assertion by Helsinki Watch that 19 people have died in house-to-house police raids, and that 10 demonstrators have died as a result of indiscriminate use of live ammunition by Turkish security forces must be considered in the light of the dismaying frequency of political murders perpetrated by terrorists in Turkey. These have included in this past year, five retired generals, an Ankara physician, an archaeology professor, a British businessman, two American civilian contract employees, an American Air Force staff sergeant, and 20 Istanbul policemen. The radical left terrorist group Dev-Sol claimed to have committed many of the killings. The Kurdish Workers' Party (PKK) a Marxist terrorist separatist organization active in Turkey's southeast claimed to have murdered the archaeologist and also killed dozens of policemen, soldiers, teachers, and villagers in 1991. The PKK has fired rockets at night into the centers of Turkish towns, ostensibly aiming at security establishments or the homes of Turkish officials; in fact, the rockets frequently miss and cause death, injury or damage in surrounding neighborhoods. The PKK has also continued its attacks against the Turkish education system, killing or threatening to kill ethnic Turkish teachers in many districts. As a result, schools did not reopen in most rural areas of southeast Turkey at the beginning of the 1991-92 school year. The tense political situation leads to accusations of overreaction by security forces in crowd situations. The facts in such cases are disputed by different sources and are almost impossible to establish.

With some significant exceptions, the freedoms of speech and press are widely and vigorously practiced in Turkey. The privately owned press does not hesitate to criticize the government and reflects a broad range of opinion. Parliament passed a new "anti-terror" law in April 1991. While this law quashed previously-stipulated capital sentences, amnestied thousands of prisoners, commuted sentences, decriminalized the use of the Kurdish language and nullified articles 141, 142, and 163 of the Penal Code; it also introduced a broad and ambiguous definition of "terrorist" activities that could invite abuses of power by security authorities. The opposition Social Democratic Populist Party [SHP] submitted portions of the new law to the Constitutional Courts, asking that they be struck down as unconstitutional. As yet, the Court has rendered no opinion, but a decision is expected before the end of the year.

Concerning alleged human rights violations against the Kurdish minority, our embassy reports that it has never heard allegations that families are being denied the right to use Kurdish in conversations during visits to detainees. Millions of Turkish Kurds who have moved to industrialized cities in the western part of the country are by and large fully integrated into the political, economic, and social life of the nation. Most Parliamentary representatives from southeastern Turkey are ethnic Kurds, but representatives of Kurdish ethnic origin have been elected from districts far removed from the southeast. A number of cabinet ministers, as well as other government officials, claim an ethnic Kurdish background.

The Turkish Constitution proclaims Turkey to be a secular state, regards all Turkish citizens as equal, and prohibits discrimination on ethnic, religious, or racial grounds. It is legal to speak Kurdish, sing or record Kurdish songs and publish books, newspapers or other material in the Kurdish language. Materials dealing with Kurdish history, culture, and ethnic identity, however, continue to be subject to confiscation and prosecution under the "indivisibility of the State" provisions of the antiterror law. The question of Kurdish cultural identity within Turkey is more and more openly debated, however, both in government and among the general public.

In summary, it is fair to say that much progress has been made with respect to human rights in Turkey. However, much remains to be done. The activities of terrorist groups and the Kurdish separatist movement in southeastern Turkey certainly complicate efforts at reform. The United States government continues to press the Turkish government to improve its human rights record, and the situation is closely monitored by Ambassador Barkley and his staff in Turkey.

Sincerely,
JANET G. MULLINS,
Assistant Secretary, Legislative Affairs.

100.

[February 7, 1992 (Senate), pp. 1495-6]

SADDAM HUSSEIN IS AT IT AGAIN

Mr. LIEBERMAN. Mr. President, Saddam Hussein is at it again. We learned yesterday that the dictator of Iraq is thumbing his nose at the United Nations resolutions that are designed to curb his appetite for war.

Saddam is now unwilling to allow the United Nations to fully monitor his military forces. Specifically, Iraq has refused to submit a detailed report on its defense industries. Saddam does not want the world to know whether he still has the capacity to make nuclear, chemical, and biological weapons. But because he does not want us to know we know.

We know he will turn again to acquiring weapons of mass destruction the minute our gaze is averted. Clearly, he is testing us. He is testing the resolve of the international coalition, less than a year after our victory in Operation Desert Storm. He is probing for weakness.

We must let him find only strength and preparedness. And strength lies in the unity of nations. And preparedness lies in our willingness to use force against Saddam again. As we have learned so well, it is only the believable threat, or actual application of force that gets Saddam's attention.

This turn of events-not surprising to those who understand the true nature of Saddam Hussein-underscores what I believe were crucial errors in American policy in the aftermath of Operation Desert Storm. I fully supported our actions following Saddam's invasion of Kuwait in 1990. I supported Operation Desert Shield, and I supported the massive buildup of forces in November 1990. I voted for the resolution authorizing the President to use force against Saddam.

But at the conclusion of the conflict, we missed several crucial opportunities to rid the world of Saddam's despotic rule. We could have destroyed more of his army in the final hours of Operation Desert Storm. And we could have used allied air power to protect the Kurds and the Shiites from the slaughter they endured at the hands of Saddam's army in the weeks and months following our victory in the gulf.

I understand that there were legitimate concerns at the time about igniting armed rebellions among Kurds in Turkey and creating a Shiite regime in southern Iraq that could have become an Iranian satellite. But all these considerations should have been outweighed by the opportunity to get Saddam Hussein out of power.

Saddam's aggression against the Kurds and the Shiites continues. Fighting has broken out again in southern Iraq, and the north has been largely blockaded by Saddam, who seems not to care if the Kurds freeze or starve to death. We should respond to his actions by providing weapons and other material support to Kurdish and Shiite guerrillas and Sunni dissidents, both inside and outside the army. There are also 20,000 Iraqi soldiers in Saudi Arabia, including hundreds of officers, who have up until now refused to return to their country. They might be urged to work with us and other opponents of Saddam within Iraq and form the basis of an opposition army. And, should Saddam's aggression against his own people escalate to widespread proportions, we should be prepared to introduce air power in their defense. We should not become involved in a full-scale land war again within Iraq, but we continue to dominate the skies,

and can still wreak havoc on Saddam's forces from above. We must clearly state our willingness to do so if the need arises.

And the economic sanctions must continue. While Iraqi propaganda continues to blame those sanctions for malnutrition and disease among Iraqi children, we know where the blame lies for any such tragedy-it lies with Saddam himself, who has it within his power to provide immediate relief to all who suffer. Yet we also learn today that Saddam is not even interested in allowing Iraqi oil to be sold to provide food and medicine to his own people. He believes our guidelines for the money from such a sale are too stringent. Clearly that is because we would spend that money on Iraqi children, and not on Iraqi armaments, as he would like to do.

The economic noose must tighten; we must pressure Jordan to staunch the flow of goods from that nation into Iraq. We should consider having U.N. inspectors play a role in monitoring the borders to ensure that the tools of war are not entering Iraq.

A tight embargo must also be maintained because it can help us limit Saddam's ability to acquire weapons of mass destruction. David Kay, the American nuclear specialist who led the United Nations inspection team in Iraq after the war, has stated that the Iraqi nuclear program involved 20,000 people and that nearly all of them are still in Iraq. We cannot yet conclude that all of Iraq's nuclear equipment has been discovered and destroyed. We have not yet shut down Iraq's capacity to build nuclear bombs.

In the wake of Saddam's new violations of the United Nations resolutions, I hope the Security Council will take strong steps to counter Iraq's intransigence. Saddam needs a fresh reminder that we have the power to back up those resolutions with force.

Iraq is a test for the post-cold-war world. It is a test for the United Nations, and for the United States. We can only pass this test when we achieve the downfall of Saddam Hussein. Until that happens, true peace and stability will not prevail in the gulf and the Middle East. Until that happens, the gulf war will have been a great victory, but not a final one.

101.

[March 4, 1992 (Senate), pp. 2810-12]

THE ANNIVERSARY OF THE GULF WAR CEASE-FIRE AND THE NEED TO SET A NEW DEADLINE FOR SADDAM HUSSEIN

Mr. LIEBERMAN. Mr. President, it was 1 year ago last Friday that American and allied forces ceased their fire on the army of Saddam Hussein, and the end of Operation Desert Storm was proclaimed. It was-and remains-a tremendous moment in our Nation's history, a genuine and worthy cause for pride.

Of course, there are revisionists who denigrate the war and the heroic accomplishments of those who waged it. And the deep troubles of our economy may obscure, for the moment, the war's true meaning. But had Desert Storm not been unleashed against the forces of Saddam Hussein in the gulf, there is no doubt in my mind that our recession would be much worse, and the world would be dealing with a dictator in Iraq who had at his grasp the capacity to wage nuclear war. Because Desert Storm did occur, we are a safer world, thanks to the courage of those who fought in it, especially those who fought and died.

Yet our euphoria is tempered on the occasion of this anniversary because we know that the work of Desert Storm will not actually be completed until we achieve total victory over Saddam Hussein himself. In considering the sacrifice of those who died, we are reminded of Lincoln's words at Gettysburg: "It is for us, the living, rather to be dedicated there to the unfinished work which they who fought here have thus far so nobly advanced."

The unfinished work is represented by the person of Saddam himself. His power has been tremendously cut by our bombs and rockets and tanks and gunfire, and by the embargo that continues to deprive him of many goods and much money. But if we abandon our determination to achieve total victory over Saddam, if we neglect the unfinished work of the gulf war, we will allow him to reinvigorate his capacity to wage war-a capacity which he will, no doubt, exercise at the appropriate time to fulfill his dreams of conquest.

To those who doubt that Saddam should be dealt with now, consider this:

Iraqi officials this week said the lives of U.N. inspectors may be in danger from angry Iraqis. We all know that any attacks against U.N. inspectors would only result from direct orders from Saddam Hussein himself. We must view the words of the Iraqi officials in that light-not as a friendly warning, but an ominous threat from the dictator's lips.

United National inspectors report that up to 20,000 people were involved in Saddam's nuclear weapons programs-20,000 people who are still in Iraq. At the right time-namely, the minute our grip on Iraq is loosened, Saddam will issue a back-to-work order, and they will surely resume the deadly task in which they had been so successfully engaged. Already, he has reportedly reinstated his son-in-law-Gen. Hussein Kamel al-Majid-as head of Iraq's arms and oil industries. He is the same man responsible for Iraq's secret campaign to develop a long-range nuclear and chemical weapons capability. Make no mistake: If we leave Iraq alone, it will create a nuclear bomb. And if Saddam has the bomb he will use it.

U.N. human rights official Max Van der Stoel recently charged the Iraqi regime with having the worst human rights violations since World War II. New evidence give credence to accusations that Saddam was engaged in the wholesale slaughter of Kurdish civilians in the 1980's. And fears are widespread and well-founded that Saddam will not hesitate to resume the slaughter-against Kurds and Shiites and others-once we look the other way. Today, in fact, Iraq's brutal defense minister, Ali Hassan al-Majeed, who masterminded attacks on the Kurds in the 1980's, is stepping up an attack on dissent within Iraq, and has told the army to be alert against what he called foreign lackeys.

Saddam has refused to allow outside agencies to relieve the suffering of the truly innocent Iraqi people-especially the children, who have paid a terrible price for Saddam's intransigence. Iraqi's propaganda machine churns out stories about the plight of Iraqis, ignoring the fact that Saddam is believed to control billions of dollars hidden around the world-funds that he uses to keep his clique well fed and in power.

Saddam has balked at complying with the U.N. resolutions that call for the destruction of his weapons of mass destruction. Iraqi officials have said they do not want to cooperate unless the United Nations relaxes its embargo, and they claim they are not obligated to destroy their ballistic missile factories. The Security Council is now awaiting the arrival of an Iraqi delegation led by Tariq Aziz on March 11 to determine whether Iraq will comply with these crucial resolutions. But it is fair to say that, thus far, Saddam has displayed the same kind of arrogant disregard for the rule of law that led Iraq to invade Kuwait 18 months ago.

Saddam has thumbed his nose at U.N. resolutions calling for the return of all prisoners of war and confiscated military equipment. More than 1,000 Kuwaiti men and women are missing-and believed to be in the hands of Iraqi captors. Needless to say, last week's 1 year anniversary brought little joy to the families of those missing Kuwaitis. Indeed, Kuwait's ambassador sent us a message last week, in which he said celebration of Kuwait's liberation was suspended out of concern for that nation's POW's. And Saddam still holds the keys to more than 200 British tanks his troops removed from Kuwait, and 150 advanced Hawk missile systems, which could be deployed against American planes.

In short, we have no sign-no sign whatsoever-that Saddam has changed, has repented, has learned any lessons in the year since the gulf war hostilities came to an end. Just look at the recent newsletter from the Iraqi defense ministry, which loudly proclaims Saddam's military genius in leading what they still call the Mother of Battles. Saddam himself had recently said of the Shiite opponents of his regime, "I want the doors to be opened and machineguns to emerge from them to chop off their treasonous heads." We cannot reward the obstinacy of his evil with any lessening of effort to remove him. As Franklin Roosevelt said to Hitler, "No man can tame a tiger into a kitten by stroking it. There can be no ap-

peasement with ruthlessness. There can be no reasoning with an incendiary bomb"

There can, in fact, be no final end to what Saddam has wrought since August 2, 1990, until Saddam himself is gone from power.

Last year, as the cease-fire took hold, and as Kurdish and Shiite revolts began, we missed opportunities to further weaken-and possibly eliminate-Saddam Hussein. We missed opportunities-but we have not lost them altogether. That is why I believe we should take action through the United Nations as follows:

First, no easing of sanctions while Saddam rules. The Security Council should firmly reject Iraq's proposal to negotiate a phase-out of sanctions in exchange for a promise to destroy weapons of mass destruction. No deals with this devil. Keep the sanctions on.

Second, to give the sanctions more bite, U.N. inspections of traffic between Jordan and Iraq should be established. It is believed that the gates of trade between these nations have been opened wide. A crackdown will hurt Saddam where it counts. Saddam's own embargo of the Kurds within Iraq is tighter than the U.N. embargo of his regime. I urge the President to make the embargo a top priority in his upcoming talks with Jordan's King Hussein.

The sanctions can also be supplemented by seizure of up to $5 billion in frozen Iraqi assets, a move now being considered by the Security Council. We should also accelerate our search for additional, hidden assets around the globe.

Third, because we know that Saddam is capable of brutal human rights abuses against innocent Iraqi people-U.N. human rights inspectors should be stationed throughout Iraq, especially in Kurdish and Shiite territories to monitor the behavior of Saddam's regime. Their right to travel where they need to should be backed up by the military.

Fourth, American support of Iraqi opponents to Saddam-Kurdish, Shiite and Sunni-should be expanded at both the official and covert levels. We can look to the thousands of Iraqi soldiers who refuse to return to Iraq for signs of a nascent anti-Saddam force. There are also elections coming up in the Kurdish region that we should encourage and protect.

We must make clear our willingness to support all serious dissident groups in their efforts to undermine Saddam's dictatorial regime.

Fifth, consideration should be given to granting recognition to a provisional government, comprised of Kurds, Shiites and Sunnis, and protecting that government's existence in areas of Iraq outside of Saddam's control. It is unclear at this date whether the various opposition groups can find common ground, but we should give them every opportunity to do so, and demonstrate that we are prepared to flood such a new regime with diplomatic, moral and material support. Saddam's outlaw regime deserves no measure of respect or recognition from the civilized world.

Sixth, we must do all we can to covertly assist any significant effort to topple Saddam Hussein from within. That might include equipping Kurds with weapons with which to protect themselves against Saddam's forces. The more we can strengthen the Saddam-free zones of Iraq, the easier we can weaken Saddam himself. And we should lend whatever high-tech support we can-satellite phones, fax machines, night vision equipment-to allow Iraqi dissidents within territory Saddam controls to survive and flourish.

Seventh, because Saddam Hussein understands nothing less than the use of force, we should give him a new deadline. He routinely forces the United Nations to give him deadlines for compliance with specific requests, such as last Friday's deadline in connection with the destruction of Scud factories-a deadline Saddam ignored. I believe the time may be right to put all our specific demands into one overall ultimatum: a date certain by which he must provide immediate, broad, and complete compliance with every U.N. resolution, or face the prospect of air attacks again. Saddam knows our mastery of Iraqi airspace is complete, and he knows many of his forces are exposed, and far away from civilian sectors.

Eighth, in setting such a date, it must be clear that we have the power and the willingness to act if Saddam does not back down. We can begin by sending more air power to the region, to back up our words with the capacity for action.

Ninth, we can then improve our inspection and destruction of Saddam's chemical, biological, nuclear, and ballistic missile capabilities. In view of the resistance they have experienced whenever they get close to new and dangerous sites, U.N. inspectors should have heavily armed escorts when necessary.

Tenth, American surveillance flights over Iraq should be supplemented by flights of combat aircraft as a vivid reminder to Saddam that we are fully capable of keeping him in check-and a reminder to Saddam's opponents within Iraq that we mean business.

Eleventh, we should make clear to Saddam, in no uncertain terms, that if any major offensive occurs against Kurdish or Shiite populations, we will strike, hitting his helicopters and his tanks from above, which he knows we can do so well. Any military offensive Saddam launches against his people should also be met with full-scale electronic warfare, inhibiting his ability to control his forces.

Twelfth, efforts to try Saddam Hussein and his henchmen for war crimes should be revived. The European Community called for such action after the gulf war, and this body went on record in support of war-crimes trials. The evidence of Saddam's crimes against humanity is enormous, and any failure to pursue him as the international criminal he is only dilutes the force of international morality, which was at the heart of the gulf war itself. Some might argue that war-crime trials are merely symbolic without Saddam in the dock, but symbols are important in matters such as this. We must not let the world forget what a monster we are dealing with.

The path I have outlined is not neat; it is not easy. It is not a path without risks. But, I would argue, it is far riskier to do nothing. As FDR said more than 50 years ago, "normal practices of diplomacy are of no possible use in dealing with international outlaws."

Mr. President, while we observe this first anniversary of the gulf war with quiet pride and honest recognition of the unfinished work before us, Saddam Hussein observes it with martial music and perverted celebration of his victory. Let us here dedicate ourselves as Lincoln said, to the "unfinished work so nobly advanced" by those who fought the gulf war, so that on the occasion of the second anniversary of Desert Storm, next year, we might join with the liberated peoples of Iraq in a shared celebration of freedom, as we embark on a common course toward peace in the Persian Gulf and throughout the world.

102.

[March 12, 1992 (Senate), p. 3581]

THE UNINTENDED VICTIMS OF THE GULF WAR

Mr. RIEGLE. Mr. President, last month marked the first anniversary of President George Bush's declaration of victory in the Persian Gulf war. Certainly we can be proud of the brave American men and women who served their country in the gulf. However, 1 year after the President declared Kuwait liberated, not only is Saddam Hussein still in power, but we have also lost sight of the war's unintended victims. In the wake of the war, there remain hundreds of thousands of displaced peoples from many ethnic groups including Palestinians, Kurds, Shiites, and Christian Chaldeans, and Assyrians.

This humanitarian problem has been deemed the "fastest growing refugee situation in modern history." (U.N. Chronicle, September 1991.) Since the end of the gulf war, it is estimated that over 5 million persons have been displaced. The mass exodus of the Kurds from Iraq, which received much media attention, and the expelling of non-nationals from Kuwait are only part of the current gulf refugee crisis.

Despite the Kuwaiti Government's assurances that there have been no general expulsions, hundreds of thousands of Egyptians, Yemenis, Palestinians, and other nationals are being evicted from Kuwait without any opportunity for deportation hearings and without any legal recourse to resist their expulsion. In fact, the al-Sabahs, the restored Kuwaiti royal family, seem to have forgotten that in their absence, many of those being deported stayed behind and resisted the cruel Iraqi regime while they fled the country.

Moreover, despite first-hand knowledge of Saddam Hussein's atrocities, the Kuwaiti Government has mandated the return of nonnational workers carrying foreign passports to their country of origin. In many cases, those expelled are people who were born in Kuwait or had lived there for several decades. Moreover, they are being sent to countries without the capacity to absorb them, such as Jordan, or nations with poor human rights records, such as Iraq. Having fought for the liberation of Kuwait, many Americans are deeply disturbed by the Kuwaiti Emir's lack of respect for ethnic minorities living in his country.

Palestinian refugees, in particular, face a unique economic and political crisis. Prior to the gulf war over 400,000 Palestinians lived and worked in Kuwait. The majority of those were part of a highly educated work force that had lived in the emirate for decades. Until the gulf crisis, the Palestinians were considered valuable members of the Kuwaiti community.

Following Saddam's invasion of Kuwait, more than 230,000 Palestinians either fled or have subsequently been forced out of the country. Those who escaped during the invasion have been denied visas to allow them to return. Those who remained in Kuwait are now being forced to leave. For the Palestinian people, this mass expulsion has created a new trauma. Not only are they a people in diaspora around the Middle East, but Palestinians from Kuwait have been forced to leave their jobs and the homes in which they have lived for decades.

During the war, President Bush called upon Iraqi minorities, such as the Kurds and Shiites, to rise up and overthrow Saddam Hussein and his Ba'thist government. The uprisings failed to dislodge the Iraqi Government and Saddam Hussein's response was swift and brutal. With his remaining tanks and infantry, Saddam crushed the popular rebellions with a ruthless application of military force.

Nevertheless, after calling on the Kurds and Shiites to overthrow Saddam, George Bush failed to support them in their moment of need-resulting in the waves of refugees flowing into Iran and Turkey. Not only have these people faced inhospitable mountain and desert terrain, but they remain entrenched in refugee camps, and have little food, medical, or fuel supplies. The Bush administration, moreover, has been unwilling to enforce Iraqi compliance with U.N. Security Council resolutions designed to alleviate the Kurds' deplorable conditions.

Other ethnic minorities also continue to suffer greatly in the wake of the Persian Gulf war. There are over 12,000 Christian Assyrians and Chaldeans, as well as other minorities, who fled Iraq during and after the war and remain refugees. Fearing negative consequences if they return to Iraq, they remain stranded in foreign lands.

Despite the Bush administration's proclamation of victory, for these forgotten victims, the gulf crisis persists. Those who continue to suffer in the aftermath of the gulf war must receive the full attention of the United States and must no longer be ignored by the current administration. On this 1-year anniversary of the end of the Persian Gulf war, while we should not forgo commemorations of America's victory, let us recall the war's unintended victims.

103.

[March 17, 1992 (Senate), p. 3763]

SADDAM HUSSEIN, THE KURDS, AND GENOCIDE

Mr. DOLE. Mr. President, this week marks the fourth anniversary of one of the most heinous acts of the 20th century. On March 17-18, 1988, the military forces of Saddam Hussein exterminated thousands of innocent women, children, and old men in a mountain village in Iraq called Halabja. This massacre was accomplished with chemical weapons, the same kinds of chemical weapons that the United Nations is seeking to find and destroy in Iraq today.

Since that awful moment in 1988, Saddam Hussein and his Republican Guard military units have struck repeatedly at the Kurdish people in northern Iraq with chemical weapons, with mass executions, with almost every form of torture imaginable.

These atrocities were shown to much of the world on television but somehow these matters are quickly forgotten. Just this month the television program "60 Minutes" covered the latest atrocities which Saddam Hussein's military has visited upon the Kurdish people. It seems the Iraqi troops had video cameras to record the slaughter so that they could be rewarded for their successes. The video footage has been captured along with thousands of pages of documentation. The graphic detail was horrifying-revolting. An estimated 60 million Americans watched "60 Minutes" and yet there is hardly a mention in Washington of what can only be called genocide in progress.

Even now the focus of the United States and the Western powers is on the technologies and the factories that produce weapons of mass destruction rather than the people who have been and may soon again become the victims of Saddam Hussein's weapons.

In the past week, news accounts have covered the arrogant and defiant stance of Saddam Hussein's Deputy Prime Minister as he tells the United Nations what Saddam will and will not allow with respect to the United Nations' search for weapons.

There is pressure building in both Great Britain and the United States for some kind of military action. However, the hostile reaction to Saddam seems more motivated by an embarrassment that Saddam is thumbing his nose at the West than by a genuine outrage at the murderous, ongoing genocide against the Kurdish people in northern Iraq.

Where is the outrage? Have we not learned from Hitler's Holocaust, from the killing fields of Cambodia? Continued indifference to the determined and systematic genocide of the Kurdish people should not be permitted.

104.

[March 17, 1992 (Senate), p. 3789]

FOUR YEARS AGO: SADDAM GASSES THE KURDS

Mr. DECONCINI. Mr. President, long before Saddam Hussein's atrocities gained widespread notoriety, his brutal regime had waged a campaign to annihilate Kurds living in northern Iraq. Villages were razed, thousands were killed, and tens of thousands forced to flee their homes. Today marks the fourth anniversary of an episode in that brutal and ongoing campaign which horrified the world and foreshadowed Saddam's barbarous tactics of terror which we now know all too well. Four years ago the Iraqi dictator used chemical weapons on the residents of Kurdish villages, killing thousands of men, women, and children.

Mr. President, the vivid pictures of this massacre still haunt all who have seen the victims lying in the streets and homes of their villages. Whole families lay together frozen in death, and despite irrefutable evidence, the Iraqi regime to this day refuses to acknowledge its heinous actions. Even now Saddam's regime continues its attempts to destroy the Kurds with a strangling economic blockage and constant military pressure.

Saddam Hussein's willingness to use chemical weapons to slaughter his own citizens leaves little doubt about the depths of cruelty he will descend to in order to maintain his evil rule. The Kurds in northern Iraq have scheduled elections next month and the United States should support this effort to bring a measure of democracy to a country where freedoms have been abused for so long.

Four years ago much of the world remained silent, and indeed continued to support Saddam, in the aftermath of the gas massacres. Mr. President, we now realize that the Kurds are our natural allies against Saddam Hussein and they deserve our political and moral support, as well as continued humanitarian assistance. This grim anniversary should serve as a marker of this Nation's resolve to keep alive the hope of Kurds in Iraq struggling for freedom and democracy. Never again should they, or anyone else, have to suffer from the brutal hand of Saddam Hussein.

105.

[March 18, 1992 (Senate), pp. 3857-8]

FOURTH ANNIVERSARY OF THE GASSING OF THE KURDS

Mr. GORE. Mr. President, Monday, March 16, was the fourth anniversary of the gassing of the Kurdish city of Halabja, at the order of Saddam Hussein. More than 5,000 men, women, and children died in that attack. Today, Saddam Hussein-having survived even his military defeat at our hands-remains in power. He continues a genocidal war against any group that would stand against him: against the Shiites holding out desperately in the southern marshes of Iraq, and especially, against the entire population of the Kurdish region in the north.

There are no words to adequately or fully explain the nightmare of Saddam Hussein's continuing reign of terror, the suffering of innocent men, women, and children who have been methodically tortured-literally and figuratively-by a government that has them frightened, paralyzed, and smothered by despair.

For a description of these events, I especially commend to you and to all Members of this body, a staff report issued in November 1991, to the Senate Committee on Foreign Relations, entitled "Kurdistan in the Time of Saddam Hussein." When this report was issued, 600,000 Kurds had fled to the Turkish border with Iraq and were facing mass death from exposure, epidemic disease, and hunger. After a belated start, but to its credit, the Bush administration ultimately acted. Operation Provide Comfort prevented a major calamity from becoming a catastrophe.

Thanks to that effort, the Kurdish people escaped the worst, but they continue to face a deadly threat.

For months, Saddam Hussein has imposed a land blockade on the Kurdish regions, literally starving to submission or death his own people-simply because he is afraid that if their voices are not silenced, they will overpower his. Food, fuel, and medicine are in critically short supply. The United Nations, which has taken over responsibility for humanitarian relief, is not-according to my information-responding at a level commensurate to the need.

Meanwhile, Iraqi military forces are reportedly beginning to press in upon the Kurdish regions. It is clear that Saddam Hussein is going to use every means at his disposal to destroy the Kurds. The question is: Can he get away with it?

Our country cannot turn its back on this cruel, inhuman, unthinkable repression. We alone can make a difference to millions of human beings-to men, women, and children, to parents and grandparents and the new generations they are struggling to protect and nurture.

We could bring food, fuel, and medicine to the Kurdish people-even as we and others must now undertake to help Turkey deal with the effects of the recent earthquake. We have the ability to make Saddam Hussein pay for any military infraction of the cease-fire. And, in my opinion, we have the ability ultimately to dispose of him and his entire wretched system of government.

But President Bush has created an obstacle to action by creating an obstacle in our thinking; namely, the sense that Saddam Hussein is somehow essential to the stability of his region and that we must take care to deal with him only within carefully weighted limits. We must get over it and beyond it. Saddam Hussein and those who serve him are war criminals. The people in the region will not begin to know safety until Saddam and his cohorts have met the fate of all tyrants, as one day they assuredly will.

Long ago, we should have started to prepare for that day of reckoning. Instead, based on the misguided notion that we needed Saddam Hussein's regime, the administration literally gave him the means to save himself, and to beat down those who rose up against him. It took a long time-too long-for the administration to accept that this man is a permanent menace, and to begin to cast about for ways to bring him down.

Better late than never, maybe, but more than the administration's timing is off-the policy is still lagging and haphazard. Once the administration finally came to appreciate the need to depose Saddam Hussein, you would think that it would grasp any and all tools for that purpose. One of those tools, it seems to me, is to convene a formal war crimes tribunal to document crimes against humanity, committed by Saddam Hussein and his associates. But no tribunal was convened. Why?

This should have been done immediately after the liberation of Kuwait. That it was not done is extremely curious. But perhaps more curious still is the administration's slowness to act on another major opportunity to document without question the criminal nature of the Baathist regime. The possibility exists to remove from the Kurdish region all the necessary and terrifying documentation to keep a tribunal fully occupied investigating and prosecuting crimes against the Kurds alone.

These are the records kept by the Iraqi police themselves, of torture and death visited upon thousands of men, women, and even little children. In some cases there are videotapes of these atrocities-videotapes too brutal even for American television. Recently, there has been some press and television coverage of these matters, but it is only the tip of the iceberg.

Starting in late November, I have appealed privately on more than one occasion for the administration to act to secure these documents and tapes. I have even provided the administration with the promised support of one of our greatest universities to help speedily organize and release this information. But the administration delays, and with each day, the risk increases that some portion of this information will be lost.

I understand that there are impediments of one sort or another. But even making allowances for that-generous allowance-it baffles me and disappoints me deeply that so much time has been lost, and still the administration plods along on a spiral bureaucratic track. Where is the passion for justice that one should find here?

Does our Government find it acceptable that this record should be lost, and that these voices of the dead be silenced forever? We have it without our capacity to document these atrocities and to make this information available. Does this administration really endorse a policy of inaction that threatens to erase a brutal record that must be remembered and prosecuted rather than being whispered away and forgotten? Does it wish to risk becoming Saddam Hussein's accomplice by helping him escape exposure and condemnation? Surely, not. That cannot be the explanation, and it is not. Surely, the administration will act eventually to make sure that the one imperishable memory of Saddam Hussein will be the precisely documented and cataloged record of his crimes against humanity.

Tomorrow, Mr. President, the Senator Foreign Relations Committee will be holding a hearing on the subject of mass murder in Iraq. In doing this, they perform a sacred duty to the dead whose blood, as the Bible says, cries out from the earth on which it was spilled. But there are the living to remember as well as the dead. Hopefully, during this week of remembrance, our Government will reaffirm its support for the living: by stating bluntly that we will not stand idle while the Kurds perish by degrees, as Saddam Hussein tightens the noose. Instead, let us provision the Kurds, let us warn Saddam Hussein against violating their sanctuary, and let us take every necessary step to expose to world opinion what has been done to them by the powers that be in Iraq.

In the aftermath of the gulf war, President Bush decided not to react in the face of the uprising he had encouraged and, as a result, thousands of lives were unnecessarily lost. A brilliant war strategy was dimmed by the disarray of lackluster post-war confusion. We have an urgent opportunity before us. We cannot allow mistakes of policy or a loss of courage. We cannot ignore the voice of conscience for the sake of expediency.

Mr. President, I yield the floor.

The PRESIDING OFFICER. The Senator from Massachusetts is recognized.

106.

[March 26, 1992 (House), p. 1983]

INTRODUCTION OF THE SPRING MOUNTAIN LEGISLATION

. . .

PROTECTION OF THE KURDS

Mr. BILBRAY. Mr. Speaker, I also introduced today a resolution which has interna-

tional significance. I, as the prime sponsor, but cosponsored by the gentleman from Florida [Mr. FASCELL], chairman of the Committee on Foreign Affairs, the gentleman from New York [Mr. GILMAN], the ranking minority member of the Subcommittee on Europe and the Middle East of the Committee on Foreign Affairs, the gentleman from Indiana [Mr. HAMILTON], chairman of the Subcommittee on Europe and the Middle East, the gentleman from New York [Mr. SOLARZ], who is also the chairman of the Subcommittee on Asian and Pacific Affairs of the Committee on Foreign Affairs, have introduced a resolution calling for the United Nations to extend the date that they will have observers and peacekeeping forces in Kurdistan in northern Iraq.

We also call upon the Turkish Government to extend the time that bases can be used in Turkey for overflight over the Kurdish protected area.

We third call upon the United States to extend the time that our forces will be available to help protect the Kurds because, if this deadline is not extended, Saddam Hussein and the Iraqi Army is poised to go into Kurdistan, crush the Kurds, and inflict hundreds of thousands of casualties. And we will again have a terrible, terrible refugee problem and thousands of dead.

I urge my colleagues in the House of Representatives to look at this resolution, which will be heard either next week or the following week in the Subcommittee on Europe and the Middle East of the House Committee on Foreign Affairs and to join with us that want to see this area preserved and the Kurds protected as one of the oldest races on the face of the Earth, dating back to the ancient Samaritans. The Kurds are the largest ethnic group in the world that has no homeland.

We ask our colleagues to help us and help the Kurds and to help them be protected by the United Nations and the United States in overflying the areas.

107.

[March 30, 1992 (Extensions of Remarks), p. 875]

A HUMAN RIGHTS TRAGEDY: TURKEY'S TREATMENT OF THE KURDS
HON. WM. S. BROOMFIELD
OF MICHIGAN
IN THE HOUSE OF REPRESENTATIVES

Monday, March 30, 1992

Mr. BROOMFIELD. Mr. Speaker, the world was shocked to learn of Saddam Hussein's brutal treatment of the Kurdish minority in northern Iraq. Now, the world is seeing the true facts about an even more shocking development, the brutal suppression of the Kurds by Turkey, a close NATO ally of the United States.

During the past few weeks, Turkish security forces have used massive force to put down separatist Kurdish guerrillas. In the most recent fighting, Turkish units used German-supplied weapons in their skirmishes with the Kurds. Berlin strongly condemned the Ankara Government's use of the German origin equipment against the civilian Kurdish community and called upon the European Community to protest against Turkish violations of the human rights of the Kurdish minority there.

Germany provided the military equipment to Turkey on condition that it be used only for NATO defensive purposes and has halted arms shipments to Turkey pending an investigation of the incident. A junior party in Germany, the Free Democrats, has called on the EC to reject Turkey's application for membership in that organization.

The Kurdish Workers' Party has sought to have an independent state in what is now Turkey since 1984 and over 3,400 people have been killed in fighting between Turkish security forces and Kurdish separatists.

Although the Turkish Government has security problems that it must deal with, Ankara's security forces appear to operate like a bull in a China shop and many Turkish troops and police units have been involved with illegal killings, torture and related human rights abuses. Although the new Turkish Prime Minister, Suleyman Demirel, promised to redress the wrongs done to the Kurdish minority, he apparently decided to increase military operations against them rather than negotiate a peaceful resolution of that long standing conflict.

I am particularly disturbed that Turkey has again chosen to use equipment supplied for NATO purposes to put down its own citizens. This reminds me of Ankara's unfortunate decision to use United States-supplied weapons for the tragic invasion of Cyprus in 1974, an occupation that still continues today.

108.

[March 31, 1992 (Senate), pp. 4435-6]

ESCALATION IN IRAQ

Mr. PELL. Mr. President, I am deeply concerned by reports in today's press that Iraq is carrying out renewed attacks against the Kurds. The reports indicate that Iraq is bombarding the Kurdish inhabited areas surrounding Irbil, causing as many as 40,000 Kurdish people to flee their homes. The reports also assert that Iraq is flying helicopters over Kurdish-controlled areas, including the U.N.-mandated safe haven, and moving Republican Guard units into the region. U.N. officials have indicated the latest Iraqi actions are violations of the U.N. cease-fire resolutions.

This marks an alarming escalation of Saddam Hussein's continuing campaign against the Kurds. During the past year, the traditionally Kurdish area of northern Iraq has been subjected to a harsh economic embargo and to periodic harassment by Iraqi forces. The Kurds have mandated nonetheless to establish de facto control over most of the territory, and have gone as far as to organize elections to establish a unified Kurdish leadership, scheduled to be held later this month.

Undoubtedly, the latest Iraqi attacks are designed to force a cancellation of the Kurdish elections. Even more troubling, however, is the fact that these attacks adhere to a demonstrated pattern of Iraqi persecution against the Kurds. Earlier this month, I chaired a Senate

Foreign Relations Committee hearing on mass killings in Iraq under the Saddam Hussein regime. The committee heard graphic testimony describing indiscriminate killings of Iraqi Kurdish civilians, based on official Iraqi documents and on tests conducted by forensic specialists. The available evidence suggests that the total number of Iraqi Kurdish deaths and disappearances may be as high as 200,000 to 300,000, or roughly 5 percent of the Iraqi Kurdish population. In my view, the information demonstrates that Iraqi actions against the Kurds are tantamount to an official policy of genocide.

The United States has an abiding responsibility to help protect the Kurds. During the gulf war, the President urged the Iraqi people to "take matters into their own hands" and overthrow Saddam Hussein, leading directly to the Kurdish uprising last year. The international community, too, assumed responsibility when it urged the scores of thousands of Kurdish refugees to return home under the protection of allied air cover. Now that U.N. Security Council resolutions-and, evidently, the borders of the safe haven-are being violated, the international community must ensure that its words are not meaningless. We must reaffirm our commitment to protect the Kurds under Operation Provide Comfort and see that the Kurds are not left open to the brutality of the Iraqi Army. It is not only in our interest, but our moral responsibility to do so.

109.

[April 7, 1992 (Senate), p. 4971]

TURKEY'S POLICIES REGARDING ITS KURDISH CITIZENS

Mr. DECONCINI. Mr. President, I rise today to voice concern over the situation in southeast Turkey which has seemingly degenerated in recent weeks to a state of civil war. The recently elected Prime Minister of Turkey, Suleyman Demirel stated that a resolution of the Kurdish situation would be a top priority of his government. During a much publicized trip to the Kurdish area of Turkey last year he reached out to Turkey's Kurdish citizens, offering them greater cultural autonomy and promising increased economic development. Mr. Demirel's government has removed obstacles to printing Kurdish publications and has lifted other restrictions on the use of the Kurdish language hoping that increased cultural autonomy would diminish support for Kurdish PKK terrorists attempting to form their own state.

Unfortunately, Mr. Demirel's efforts to address the Kurdish situation have not resulted in a reduction of tensions. Instead, massive discontent has erupted in southeast Turkey, and the level of violence between security forces and terrorists has taken an increasing and unacceptable toll of innocent lives. While the tactics of the PKK terrorists are abhorrent, the group appears to be gaining support among a population weary of constant harassment by security forces. Recently, 14 Kurdish deputies withdrew from the ruling coalition in the Turkish Parliament to protect the Government's policy toward Kurdish citizens. The new Government of Turkey and its program of wide ranging democratic reforms now appear jeopardized by the chaos and destruction in the southeast.

Turkish military incursions into northern Iraq, ostensibly to attack PKK bases, have, in fact, also killed civilians who do not support the PKK. Actions taken by security forces against terrorists have been heavy-handed and have served to further incite the Kurdish population and destabilize the entire region. Turkey's NATO ally, Germany, has recently halted shipments of arms to Turkey because of Turkey's use of German equipment for offensive purposes against the Kurds. Germany has announced its intentions of raising the Kurdish issue during the Conference on Security and Cooperation meeting taking place in Helsinki.

Mr. President, it is in the best interests of all parties that extreme caution be exercised by the Turkish Government as it continues to counter the efforts of the PKK. While Turkey, and indeed, all nations have a right to protect the security of their citizens and the sovereignty of their borders, Turkey is also obligated to protect the human rights of the its citizens. Unfortunately, as the PKK has stepped up its violent attacks, the human rights of civilians in the southeast are becoming increasingly threatened by the increasingly violent actions of security forces.

This is particularly regrettable because, under President Demirel's leadership, the Government of Turkey has taken several important steps toward improving the civil and human rights of its citizens. This process must continue and the implementation of reform measures should be vigorously enforced at all levels of Government. The actions of the PKK terrorists are deplorable, yet the Turkish Government should move even more swiftly and earnestly to protect the legitimate human and civil rights of its citizens and ensure that its security forces act according to international and democratically established procedures. Violence only begets violence and support for the PKK may grow unless President Demirel takes decisive action to protect the rights of all of Turkey's citizens.

110.

[April 9, 1992 (Senate), pp. 5317-20]

STATEMENT OF SENATOR J. BENNETT JOHNSTON, CHAIRMAN, COMMITTEE ON ENERGY AND NATURAL RESOURCES DEPARTMENT OF ENERGY NATIONAL LABORATORY PARTNERSHIP ACT OF 1992

. . .

SENATE CONCURRENT RESOLUTION 108—RELATIVE TO THE KURDS IN NORTHERN IRAQ

Mr. MACK submitted the following concurrent resolution; which was referred to the Committee on Foreign Relations:

S. CON. RES. 108

Whereas the Government of Iraq brutally suppressed a Kurdish uprising in February and March 1991, forcing hundreds of thousands of Kurds to flee across the border into Turkey;

Whereas this sudden, massive refugee flow into Turkey resulted in shortfalls of shelter, food, medicine, and potable water that placed thousands of Kurdish lives at risk;

Whereas the best solution to this humanitarian crisis was to encourage the Kurds to return to their homes in northern Iraq by creating a security zone in northern Iraq in which the United States guaranteed that they would not be attacked by Iraqi aircraft or other forces;

Whereas in response to the extraordinary humanitarian need of the Kurds, the United States took the lead in organizing Operation Provide Comfort, in which the United States and other forces undertook a major relief effort for the Kurds both within Turkey and in the designated security zone in northern Iraq;

Whereas in June 1991 the United Nations High Commissioner for Refugees took over the prime responsibility for all relief operations in northern Iraq;

Whereas the United Nations High Commissioner for Refugees still maintains a large presence in northern Iraq, including over a thousand civilians involved in relief activities as well as hundreds of United Nations guards;

Whereas the United Nations High Commissioner for Refugees is currently negotiating with the United Nations Children's Fund and other United Nations organizations to take over the functions being performed in northern Iraq by the United Nations High Commissioner for Refugees;

Whereas the memorandum of understanding between Iraq and the United Nations which authorizes the United Nations presence expires in June 1992;

Whereas the severe shortages of food within the security zone as a result of the Iraqi blockade of northern Iraq make a continued international relief effort essential in order to prevent famine among the Kurdish population;

Whereas the courageous decision of the Government of Turkey to permit the stationing of United States military forces in southern Turkey, despite the possibility of Iraqi retaliation against Turkey, was essential to the success of Operation Provide Comfort;

Whereas Operation Provide Comfort is still necessary in order to deter Iraqi attacks against the Kurdish population in the security zone in northern Iraq;

Whereas the agreement between the United States and Turkey that permits the stationing of United States military forces in southern Turkey expires in June 1992; and

Whereas if this agreement is not extended and if Operation Provide Comfort is terminated, it is extremely likely that Iraqi forces will attack the security zone, resulting in substantial loss of lives and possibly generating another massive wave of Kurdish refugees into Turkey: Now, therefore, be it

RESOLVED BY THE SENATE (THE HOUSE OF REPRESENTATIVES CONCURRING), That it is the sense of the Congress that—

(1) the United States should seek Turkish permission to extend beyond June 1992 the agreement that permits the stationing of United States military forces in southern Turkey for purposes of Operation Provide Comfort;

(2) the Government of Turkey, whose continued commitment to Operation Provide Comfort is essential if the operation is to be continued, should respond positively to a United States request to extend that agreement;

(3) the United Nations presence in northern Iraq should be extended; and

(4) the United States and the international community should attach priority to persuading the Government of Iraq to lift the economic boycott of northern Iraq.

Mr. MACK. Mr. President, I am gravely concerned about the potential of attacks against the Kurdish peoples of northern Iraq should the United Nations withdraw its forces in June 1992, upon the expiration of the current agreement with the government of Turkey.

I encourage the administration to maintain the United States' commitment to protecting the Kurds through Operation Provide Comfort as long as necessary. There is ample evidence that Saddam Hussein is prepared to move swiftly against these innocent people should our commitment waiver, including recent reports that Iraqi air defense batteries have begun tracking allied flights within the security zone, and their fighters have begun flying training missions for the first time since Saddam's surrender at the end of Operation Desert Storm.

I recognize that no congressional action is required to extend the commitment of American forces to Operation Provide Comfort. I simply wish to convey, in the strongest possible terms, my recommendation we take all steps required to do so.

To that end, I rise to introduce this resolution, and encourage my colleagues on both sides of the aisle to take a stand on behalf of the Kurdish people of Iraq and support this vital effort.

111.

[May 6, 1992 (Extensions of Remarks), pp. 1265-66]

HUMAN RIGHTS SITUATION IN TURKEY
HON. LEE H. HAMILTON
OF INDIANA
IN THE HOUSE OF REPRESENTATIVES

Wednesday, May 6, 1992

Mr. HAMILTON. Mr. Speaker, I wish once again to draw the attention of my colleagues to the latest in a series of letters with United States and Turkish officials regarding the human rights situation in Turkey. Two earlier exchanges with the Department of State appeared in the CONGRESSIONAL RECORD on Tuesday, November 26, 1991, and Monday, October 7, 1991. The current exchange is with Turkish Ambassador to the United States, Nuzhet Kandemir.

While several months have passed since this exchange with the Turkish Ambassador, I believe the Ambassador's comments will still be of interest to Members. Concerns over human rights practices in Turkey have not diminished since December. There have been a number of violent incidents between Turkish authorities and the local population in southeastern Turkey in recent months. The United States continues to maintain an enhanced military presence in this region as part of Operation Provide Comfort. For this and other reasons, I believe we have a special responsibility to work with Turkey to improve its human rights record in this and other areas.

The correspondence follows:

TURKISH EMBASSY,
Washington, DC, October 15, 1991.
Hon. LEE HAMILTON,
Chairman, Subcommittee on Europe and Middle East, Washington, DC.

DEAR MR. CHAIRMAN: Having become aware of your interest in human rights practices in Turkey through your remarks in the Congressional Record of October 7, 1991, detailing your correspondence with the Department of State on that subject, I am taking the liberty of providing you further information on democracy and human rights in my country.

In Turkey, we have a relatively young democracy. But our experience dates back to 1946, when we had the first multi-party free elections. The road travelled in the last decades has not been without difficulties, not even without interruptions. However, the Turkish people was not deterred from its determination to live in a domestic society.

Turkey's democratic evolution is unique; in fact, Turkey is the only preponderantly Muslim country where democracy has flourished. Turkey has compressed into mere decades a democratization process that, in the west, spanned at least two countries and gestated centuries before that.

The establishment of the Turkish Republic 68 years ago, and the initiation of Ataturk's revolutionary reforms, set in motion a strong wave of political modernization, which continues unabated in Turkey today. Ataturk, the founder of modern Turkey, established the foundations of a modern state and society. The Turkish governmental system rests firmly on the twin pillars of justice and the supremacy of law, both of which guarantee the free and peaceful exercise of human rights and ensure human dignity.

We know from experience that free and fair elections are not sufficient to sustain democracy and ensure the protection of human rights. We are aware that democracy is a continuous process, that laws need to be revised and updated, that the implementation of legislation and administrative actions require constant vigilance.

In recent years, Turkey has become party to various international control mechanisms in the field of human rights. In 1987, we recognized the individual right of application to the European Commission on Human Rights. In 1988, Turkey became party to the European Convention Against Torture. The following year she became party to the UN Convention Against Torture. The same year Turkey ratified the European Social Charter. Last year we recognized the compulsory jurisdiction of the European Court of Human Rights. Less than a year ago Turkey signed the 9th Additional Protocol to the European Convention on Human Rights which provides for the right of individual petition to the European Court of Justice. And we signed the European Social Code.

These actions, which involve greater international controls, reflect the determination and the openness of the policy of the Turkish Government in fighting human rights violations and abuses.

Parallel to international control mechanisms, new national legislation was enacted to provide additional safeguards for the protection of human rights. The Penal Code reform of this year lifted restrictions on the freedom of expression, conscience, and assembly. In another legislative act, the Turkish Parliament abrogated the law banning publications in languages other than Turkish. Thus publication and other forms of cultural expression in Kurdish as well as in other regional and local languages and dialects are now free.

The death penalty has been de facto abolished. In fact, there has been no implementation of the death penalty since 1984.

The Turkish legal system guarantees that defendants have access to their lawyers at all times. Detention periods may extend from one to 15 days only in specific instances of collective crimes against state security involving 10 or more individuals. This is done to prevent the destruction of evidence. Nevertheless, police are not authorized to prolong custody beyond 24 hours without the written authorization of the prosecutor of competent magistrate.

A draft bill to reduce the period of detention for collective crimes from 15 days to 4 days has been presented to the parliament. The new parliament, which will be formed following this month's general elections, will take up this issue and enact new legislation. As most cases of alleged torture and other abuses of human rights take place during the period of detention, a significant shortening of the detention period, coupled with continuous access to defense attorneys will, we hope, be a major contribution to combatting human rights violations.

A human rights commission was established in the Turkish Parliament last March. It monitors human rights practices in Turkey and the world, investigates allegations and complaints, and introduces amendments to existing legislation. The commission receives petitions from individuals and organizations. It carries out visits to prisons and police stations to supervise the conditions of detainees and imprisoned persons. The commission shall also examine existing legislation and draft bills with a view to determining their conformity to human rights standards.

Recently, through a law enacted by Parliament, more than 20,000 prisoners were released.

Additionally, human rights classes have been introduced in the curricula of police colleges and academies.

The new Minister of Justice, in his first public statement on the 3rd of September, announced his plan to organize regional human rights seminars for judges and prosecutors to update them on Turkey's human rights commitments.

Mr. Chairman, these changes and reforms will, we hope, lead to further improvements in the area of human rights. We still have persisting problems and difficulties in this area. Despite governmental policy, sporadic violations of human rights occur in Turkey. I can assure you that we are determined to reduce such occurrences and we believe that we will succeed. Because Turkey is a democratic society based on rule of law with an independent judiciary. The Turkish public is increasingly sensitive to human rights violations. The Turkish

press is an important means of revealing and reporting abuses. The transparency of Turkish society, both to Turks and non-Turks, provides the best guarantee for the protection of human rights. Such transparency can, however, occasionally lead to exaggeration of the abuses that take place.

We take no offense from criticism of Turkey's human rights record, provided that such criticism is fair and objective; that is, that it take into account the progress achieved as well as those problems that remain.

Finally, Mr. Chairman, I would like to mention one factor that is a direct challenge to basic human rights-that is the persistence of terrorism in southeastern Turkey.

The activities of foreign-based terrorism are directed against the territorial integrity of our country and to the most basic rights of the individual-the right to life. But we are determined to combat terrorism with rule of law and democracy.

Mr. Chairman, we are determined to continue to improve the human rights situation in Turkey. It is gratifying that a consensus on this issue has emerged among the eight political parties competing in this month's general elections.

Turkey, in full cooperation with its partners in democracy, is firmly committed to raising the standards of human rights in the country.

With my best personal regards,
Sincerely,
NUZHET KANDEMIR,
Ambassador.

———

CONGRESS   OF   THE   UNITED STATES,
Washington, DC, October 28, 1991.
His Excellency NUZHET KANDEMIR,
Embassy of the Republic of Turkey, Washington, DC.

DEAR MR. AMBASSADOR: Thank you for your letter of October 15, 1991 regarding my October 7, 1991 insert in the Congressional Record on the human rights situation in Turkey. I appreciate hearing from you and receiving your further comments regarding democracy and human rights in Turkey.

Your letter makes many good points and I am pleased to learn about the steps you mention. As you point out, Turkey stands virtually alone in the Muslim world as a country where free elections, free press and rule of law have taken root.

Turkey has made important progress in improving its democratic institutions and practices in the last forty years, but many people consider your democracy to continue to be young and in some respects fragile.

I appreciate the fact that Turkey lives in a tough neighborhood and that you face special challenges from internal terrorist groups and Kurdish separatist groups operating in the southeastern part of the country. Nevertheless, I remain concerned by the information I receive regarding continued and persistent violations of human rights in Turkey. Specifically, let me raise a few issues of most concern:

Despite the fact that Turkey is now party to the European and U.N. Conventions Against Torture, I am informed that some 95 percent of all political detainees are believed to be subject to torture in Turkey today;

One of the most common methods of torture is reportedly electric shock treatment-which requires special equipment and is clearly a premeditated, not an accidental, part of an interrogation process;

There has been a significant increase in deaths in detention in 1991, with 12 political prisoners dying in detention under suspicious circumstances since January 1, 1991;

There has also been an increase in deaths of individuals as a result of excessive police force. Nineteen people have died in house-to-house police raids and 10 demonstrators have died as a result of indiscriminate use of live ammunition by Turkish security forces since June, 1991;

Restrictions on freedom of expression persist and the recent enactment of a broad anti-terror law represents a step backward in this area; and

Human rights violations against the Kurdish minority continue. Despite the publicized repeal of the ban on the Kurdish language, it continues to be a crime to use the Kurdish language in official settings, including in family visits to prison detainees and in prisoner-lawyer consultations.

I applaud the Turkish Government's encouraging public statements regarding the need to end torture in Turkey and improve human rights practices, but I must also admit that, to my knowledge, there have been no legal or other action taken against individuals alleged to have tortured detainees. I have no information to indicate that police or prison personnel have been sentenced, dismissed or punished as a result of any of the abuses mentioned above. This is difficult for many Members to understand, and it stands in contrast to the sort of record and commitment you outline in your letter.

I appreciated hearing from you, and I would welcome any additional comments you have in response to the concerns I have outlined.

With best regards.
Sincerely yours,
LEE H. HAMILTON,
Chairman, Subcommittee on Europe and the Middle East.

TURKISH EMBASSY,
Washington, DC, December 3, 1991.
Hon. LEE HAMILTON,
Chairman, Subcommittee on Europe and the Middle East, Washington, DC.

DEAR MR. CHAIRMAN: In my letter dated October 15, 1991, I tried to give you some information on democracy and human rights reforms in Turkey. Your response of October 28, 1991 was indeed gratifying, in that a distinguished member of Congress has acknowledged that human rights reforms have taken root in my country.

As I have stated in my previous letter, Turkish Governments are dedicated to the promotion of human rights standards in Turkey. We are fully aware of our shortcomings. Despite governmental policy, sporadic human rights violations occur. We are determined to reduce such occurrences and firmly believe that we will succeed.

In this context, I would like to draw your attention, Mr. Chairman, to the package of wide ranging reforms recently unveiled by the new Government, formed following the October general elections in Turkey, which addresses many of the concerns voiced by human rights observers.

The "democratization package," as it is called, would do the following:

All legal documents, including the Constitution, will be further reformed to ensure that their provisions irrevocably meet the principles embodied in the Paris Charter and other international documents, thereby broadening the existing democratic political atmosphere for all levels of state and society.

Freedom of the press and people's right to have access to true and reliable information will be reinforced.

Without waiting for the constitution to be redrafted, all of its provisional articles that impede the lawful nature of the state will be abolished.

The voting age will be reduced to eighteen and the eligible age to be elected to Parliament will be reduced to twenty-five years.

Educational staff of universities will be permitted to enroll in political parties and to take part in their governing bodies.

All restrictions preventing leaders of trade unions and other professional organizations from being elected to Parliament in that capacity will be removed.

All restrictions that prevent students from becoming members of political parties will be abolished.

Labor and trade union rights will be expanded.

All members of Turkey's work force, including civil servants, will be permitted to set up unions.

The independence of the judiciary and the guarantee that members of the judiciary will be free from all considerations in discharging their duties will be truly safeguarded. The principle of "natural judge" will be established throughout the judicial system. The High Council of Judges and Prosecutors will be rearranged according to the principle of the independence of the judiciary.

All restrictions on political parties to establish women, youth and professional branches will be removed.

Police forces will be further educated on individual rights and liberties and their authority will be reorganized.

Amendments to the Penal Code and related laws will be made to guarantee individuals who are under arrest the right to refuse to testify in the absence of their lawyers. Persons under arrest or in detention will have the right to confer with their lawyers at any stage of the proceedings. As a result, torture allegations will be eliminated and testimonies made in the preparatory stage of an investigation will be credible and valid.

Pre-trial detention periods will be reduced.

Martial law and emergency rule powers will be limited and put in compliance with the rule of law.

The Anti-terrorism Act will be radically modified in order to bring its provisions in line with the basic principles of fundamental freedom and human rights.

The legal and practical obstacles and restrictions that citizens face in the free expression, preservation and development of their ethnic, cultural and linguistic identities will be eliminated within the concept of national unity and in accordance with the spirit of the Paris Charter, to which Turkey is also a signatory.

Mr. Chairman, Prime Minister Demirel stated publicly on November 25, 1991, and it is clearly underlined in the Government Programme, that "torture is a crime against humanity and it is a Government's duty to prevent torture."

The coalition Government's encouraging democratization package attests to Turkey's determination to eradicate the sources of problems in the human rights field. With 48 percent of the vote, the coalition has the strongest public mandate of any Government formed in the last 11 years. Therefore, we hope that these reforms will lead to further improvements in human rights.

Please do not hesitate to contact me, Mr. Chairman, if you have any further questions in this respect.

Yours sincerely,

NUZHET KANDEMIR,
Ambassador.

112.

[May 7, 1992 (Senate), p. 6302]

ELECTIONS IN KURDISTAN

Mr. KERRY. Mr. President, May is a month of spring, of hope, and of rebirth. So too in Northern Iraq, the month of May holds promise for the birth of democracy. On May 17, the Kurdish people of northern Iraq will hold an election for a regional legislative assembly. This election will mark the first ever genuinely democratic election in the history of Iraq.

Sadly, this election represents only a small step forward, for the Kurdish people of northern Iraq still face a serious threat from Iraq's brutal dictator, Saddam Hussein. Saddam's military forces continue to impose a total economic blockade of the Kurdish areas of Iraq and have continued to engage in military attacks against Kurdish villages.

It may well be only the presence of United States, British, and French airpower and the establishment of a protection zone that has prevented Saddam Hussein from implementing a policy of virtual genocide against the Kurdish people in northern Iraq.

Despite this terrible situation, the Kurds in Iraq have not given up. They are seeking to hold the first ever democratic elections and establish a Kurdish legislative assembly. The government of Iraq has withdrawn all civil administration from northern Iraq, and the Kurds are seeking to establish a legitimate, elected government to handle civil administration, and other governmental responsibilities.

Mr. President, the election in Kurdistan, Iraq, is an important event and deserves the recognition and support of the United States and the international community. The Kurdish people in Iraq have seen their rights violated and their legitimate aspirations denied for far too long. They deserve our admiration for their courage, their willingness to embark upon the democratic path against great odds, and their determination to stand up against Saddam Hussein.

113.

[May 13, 1992 (Senate), p. 6590]

DEMOCRATIC ELECTIONS IN IRAQI KURDISTAN

Mr. SPECTER. Mr. President, I want to bring to the attention of the Senate an event which will be taking place later this month in Iraq. On May 17 there will be a first ever democratic election in Iraq. Despite the fact that Saddam Hussein remains in power in Baghdad, the Kurdish people of northern Iraq are going to hold an election for Kurdish Legislative Assembly.

With so many other international events unfolding, it would be easy to miss an event which will take place so far away, but this election deserves the attention and support of the United States.

Mr. President, an estimated 200,000 Kurds-men, women, and children-have been murdered by Saddam Hussein and his ruthless military. Even after the military defeat of Iraq in Desert Storm, Iraqi troops have continued to attack Kurdish villages and it is only the threat of British, French, and United States military retaliation that protects the Kurdish people.

Despite this horrendous situation and a virtual economic blockade of Kurdish areas, the Kurds have established a liberated zone and would hold democratic elections.

Mr. President, this election, if it is held, will hopefully mark a true turning point for the Kurdish people. Hopefully, a democratic election can be the start of a brighter future for a people that have endured a denial of their most basic human rights for more than 70 years.

It is my hope that the United States Government will give encouragement to a process which will give to the Kurdish people in Iraq the right of self-determination-a fundamental human right. The government of Saddam Hussein has clearly forfeited any right to control or govern the Kurdish people and even now it pursues an economic blockade of northern Iraq which is intended to starve the Kurdish people out of existence.

Mr. President, I realize that a proper United States policy toward Iraq is a complicated matter. I realize that there are regional concerns, border disputes, and the genuine threat of Islamic fundamentalism. However, the United States has always stood for the right of self-determination and against the violation of human rights. In Iraq, the issues seem clear. The Kurdish people of northern Iraq deserve the continued protection from the genocidal attacks of Saddam Hussein and they deserve encouragement for seeking to hold the first ever democratic election in the territory now know as Iraq.

114.

[May 14, 1992 (Extensions of Remarks), pp. 1391-92]

IN RECOGNITION OF KURDISH HUMAN RIGHTS AND THE UPCOMING ELECTIONS
HON. JAMES H. BILBRAY
OF NEVADA
IN THE HOUSE OF REPRESENTATIVES

Thursday, May 14, 1992

Mr. BILBRAY. Mr. Speaker, I rise before you today to appraise the Members of this House about the dire situation that continues to rage in the Kurdish occupied areas of the northern Iraq.

There continues to be nearly a million refugees stranded in the peaks of the treacherous Iraqi/Turkish border with the very real fear that death is what they face if they return to their homes. It is only the continued presence of the United Nations and overflights by our American planes, that has kept the Iraqi Army at bay and allowed these people a slight measure of security and safety.

However, a deadline is looming. Next month the United Nations mandate in that area will expire and what will follow will surely be a genocide of the Kurdish people. Saddam Hussein has had no qualms about expressing his disdain for the Kurdish people through gassing the town of Habladja and the continued slaughter of innocent women and children.

Yet, we now have the opportunity to bring to the Bush administrations notice an historic event. This Sunday, May 17, the Kurdish people will take an historic step toward expressing their desire to be part of the democratic community by holding parliamentary and presidential elections. In this way, they hope to provide the world with concise proof that what we have is a freedom loving people who want the same guarantees of freedom and security that the rest of the democratic world shares.

At this time, a delegation of congressional staff members, foreign affairs specialists and human rights activists have departed for Turkey in order to travel into the Kurdish areas and observe these elections. Led by the former two-time Governor of Nevada and current editor of the Las Vegas Sun Mike O'Callahan, this delegation will report back to myself and other Members of Congress about the continued plight of these people and the need to afford them continued security.

Currently I have introduced legislation before the Congress, with the cosponsorship of Chairman DANTE FASCELL, LEE HAMILTON, and STEPHEN SOLARZ, that will express the sense of Congress that the United Nations presence should be extended and that this conflict should be resolved once and for all in order to afford these people the security that they deserve. I urge my colleagues to support House Concurrent Resolution 299 and call for its immediate enactment.

I would also like to submit for the RECORD today's article from the *New York Times* [Leslie Weaver, "Iraqi Kurds Prepare for First Free Elections," May 13, 1992] which covers the upcoming election so that my fellow members will be aware of the historic events occurring in the region. I urge them not only to read this article but to make the choice to support an end to the violence perpetrated against these people . . .

115.

[May 14, 1992 (Extensions of Remarks), p. 1400]

DEMOCRATIC ELECTIONS IN KURDI-STAN
HON. MEL LEVINE
OF CALIFORNIA
IN THE HOUSE OF REPRESENTA-TIVES

Thursday, May 14, 1992

Mr. LEVINE of California. Mr. Speaker, this Sunday, May 17, the Kurdish minority of northern Iraq will be holding elections to choose a national legislative assembly. This is an important event for the population of Kurdistan and the entire international community.

The Kurds of Iraq have suffered immensely as a result of the Bush administration's failed Iraq policy. It is estimated that 200,000 Kurds have been murdered by Saddam Hussein's military forces. Hundreds of thousands more have been uprooted and live in the inhospitable terrain of northern Iraq where food and shelter are scarce. And amidst this despair, Saddam's regime continues to attack Kurdish villages throughout Iraq.

Despite these hardships, the Kurdish people have not given up hope for a better life. Carrying out democratic elections that will create democratic institutions is a manifestation of these desires. Additionally, free and fair democratic elections in Kurdistan would also set an important example for democracy in the Iraq and the Persian Gulf region.

Mr. Speaker, the Kurdish people are suffering great hardships at the hands of Saddam Hussein and an international community that has shown little inclination to help. On May 17, the Kurds will take measures to help themselves. The U.S. Government and the international community should pay close attention to the elections in Kurdistan and encourage its neighbors to pursue a similar democratic course.

116.

[May 19, 1992 (Extensions of Remarks), p. 1438]

LEGISLATIVE ELECTIONS IN KURDI-STAN
HON. MEL LEVINE
OF CALIFORNIA
IN THE HOUSE OF REPRESENTA-TIVES

Tuesday, May, 19, 1992

Mr. LEVINE of California. Mr. Speaker, today, in northern Iraq, the Kurdish people are voting to establish a national legislature for the first time. Despite the hardship of their plight, the Kurds of Iraq are displaying their commitment to an enlightened form of government that is the exception, not the rule, in the Middle East. For this, the Kurdish people deserve our deepest admiration, respect, and most of all, support.

The administration, however, views the Kurds in a different light. To the Bush-Baker team, the Kurds of Iraq are one of the most visible examples of its failed and misguided policy toward Saddam Hussein. Instead of seizing the opportunity to encourage democratic practices in a region that has been particularly resistant to human rights concerns and political freedoms, the Bush administration has tried to down play the elections in Kurdistan.

A.M. Rosenthal describes the administration's activity in an article that appeared in Friday's *New York Times*. This administration should be ashamed of itself. By trying to sweep the failures of its previous Iraq policy under the rug, it is exacerbating the misery and displacement of the Kurds.

THE ABSENT AMERICANS

The chance was lying there for weeks-the opportunity for the United States to make a gesture in support of a people it had betrayed.

It was a chance important politically, and important morally, and cost-free. No announcement has been made yet, but the United States has taken its decision. It has refused.

The opportunity was for the U.S. to do what other countries are doing-send observers to witness as the Kurdish people carry out an astonishing political gamble.

On May 17 about one million Kurds are expected to vote, choosing a legislative assembly. Never before has there been an election like it-by a persecuted people, in the midst of a war for their survival, in the face of the enemy, within range of his guns.

The Kurds are a Muslim, non-Arab people scattered through Iraq, Turkey, Iran, Syria, and some of the southern republics of the former Soviet Union. Now and then one western or mid-eastern nation or another decides the Kurds might be useful as pawns in one war or another.

During the gulf war President Bush mused aloud about wishing the Iraqi people would rid him of Saddam Hussein. The Kurds, trusting America, rose against the man who had murdered all the years of his reign.

So, after Saddam was defeated, the U.S. allowed him to keep and use the helicopters, artillery and divisions he needed to try to destroy the Kurds altogether. He failed that time, but the sight of Kurds dying in the mountain passes shocked the world, for a while.

The Kurds now hold part of the Iraqi areas where they seek self-government-autonomy, not statehood.

According to U.S. sources, Saddam has been told that still another fullscale attack against the Kurds will bring U.S. reprisals. He does not seem terrified. The same sources also say that he has doubled the size of his forces ranged against the Kurds.

The Kurds, we are often reminded by some of the American specialists who built up Saddam Hussein, are a quarrelsome, fractious lot. Perhaps, but maintaining unity and delicacy under centuries of massacre can be a bit difficult.

Anyway, the Kurds will hold an election in the midst of ongoing war day-to-day danger and deprivation. The Kurds say that Saddam's blockade means that they get only about 25 percent of the food and supplies available to other Iraqis.

The Kurds thought the U.S. might like to witness such an election. They asked the U.S. to send observers, as it has for elections in Nicaragua, Bangladesh, Albania, Namibia, Chile, among other places.

The State Department said no. Why, Saddam Hussein might say American were involved in the election. And one fellow on the Iraqi desk actually trotted out the "Arab streets" again and how they might rise if the U.S. dared send observers.

Then the Department began warning off Congressional aids and other Americans who planned to go privately.

They were told that it would be dangerous. Saddam Hussein may try same election-day nastiness. But as on Californian said after Los Angeles, that did not freeze his blood.

The Americans were also warned they could be prosecuted under an executive order barring commerce with Iraq. That neatly lumps Saddam and his victims together as the enemy, which must tickle him.

Representative Lee Hamilton of Indiana tried to get the State Department to allow private Americans to go. Back came a letter from Assistant Secretary of State Janet G. Mullins saying that if the Kurds wanted observers, let them go ask any of the "growing number of democracies around the world." She wrote it, unembarrassed. I have the letter and will cherish it.

One Administration official said observers had been vetoed because Turkey, which has problems with Turkish Kurds, would be upset. Apparently he did not have the late news:

A few Americans who were warned off are going anyway-among them Mike O'Callaghan, the former Governor of Nevada, an amputee of the Korean War; but the U.S. Government will be studiously absent.

For the Kurds, official witness would have meant that the Bush Administration was not only acknowledging their willingness to gamble on democracy but giving them some respect and dignity. Those things seem to have value to those fractious Kurds.

117.

[May 21, 1992 (House), p. 3682]

PROTECTING KURDISH PEOPLE DURING ELECTIONS

(Mr. BILBRAY asked and was given permission to address the House for 1 minute and to revise and extend his remarks.)

Mr. BILBRAY. Mr. Speaker, this week for the first time in the history of the Kurdish people, free elections were held in Kurdistan. It was done to establish the fact that they can have a central government in Kurdistan, not asking for independence from Iraq, but for an autonomous region where the Kurds can be protected against the onslaught of the brutal dictator from Baghdad, Saddam Hussein.

Today in the Foreign Affairs Committee they are marking up a bill and in this bill they are marking up this resolution which calls for the United States to continue overflights above the 36th parallel in Iraq to protect the Kurds, asking for the Turks to continue to allow our planes to fly out to protect the Kurds and for the United States to continue the peacekeeping operations in Kurdistan.

The Kurdish people have been inflicted with tremendous brutality from this regime. Saddam Hussein is massing troops along the 36th parallel just waiting for the United Nations to get out and Americans to stop overflights.

Mr. Speaker, I urge all my colleagues when this bill comes to the House floor next week or the week after to support the Kurdish resolution which urges us to help continue to protect the Kurds from this brutal dictator of Baghdad, and hopefully the Kurdish people who have a 4,000-year history will continue to prosper under U.N. protection.

118.

[June 2, 1992 (House), pp. 3933-8]

EXPRESSING SENSE OF CONGRESS REGARDING KURDS IN IRAQ

Mr. HAMILTON. Mr. Speaker, I move to suspend the rules and agree to the concurrent resolution (H. CON. RES. 299) expressing the sense of the Congress regarding the Kurds in northern Iraq, as amended. The Clerk read as follows:

H. CON. RES. 299

Whereas the Government of Iraq brutally suppressed a Kurdish uprising in February and March 1991, forcing hundreds of thousands of Kurds to flee across the border into Turkey;

Whereas this sudden, massive refugee flow into Turkey resulted in shortfalls of shelter, food, medicine, and potable water that placed thousands of Kurdish lives at risk;

Whereas the best solution to this humanitarian crisis was to encourage the Kurds to return to their homes in northern Iraq by creating a security zone in northern Iraq in which the United States guaranteed that they would not be attacked by Iraqi aircraft or other forces;

Whereas in response to the extraordinary humanitarian need of the Kurds, the United States took the lead in organizing Operation Provide Comfort, in which the United States and other forces undertook a major relief effort for the Kurds both within Turkey and in the designated security zone in northern Iraq;

Whereas in June 1991 the United Nations High Commissioner for Refugees took over the prime responsibility for all relief operations in northern Iraq;

Whereas the United Nations High Commissioner for Refugees still maintains a large presence in northern Iraq, including over a thousand civilians involved in relief activities as well as hundreds of United Nations guards;

Whereas the United Nations High Commissioner for Refugees is currently negotiating with the United Nations Children's Fund and other United Nations organizations to take over the functions being performed in northern Iraq by the United Nations High Commissioner for Refugees;

Whereas the memorandum of understanding between Iraq and the United Nations which authorizes the United Nations presence expires in June 1992;

Whereas the severe shortages of food within the security zone as a result of the Iraqi blockade of northern Iraq make a continued international relief effort essential in order to prevent famine among the Kurdish population;

Whereas the courageous decision of the Government of Turkey to permit the stationing of United States military forces in southern Turkey, despite the possibility of Iraqi retaliation against Turkey, was essential to the success of Operation Provide Comfort;

Whereas Operation Provide Comfort is still necessary in order to deter Iraqi attacks against the Kurdish population in the security zone in northern Iraq;

Whereas the agreement between the United States and Turkey that permits the stationing of United States military forces in southern Turkey expires in June 1992; and

Whereas if this agreement is not extended and if Operation Provide Comfort is terminated, it is extremely likely that Iraqi forces will attack the security zone, resulting in substantial loss of lives and possibly generating another massive wave of Kurdish refugees into Turkey: Now, therefore, be it

Resolved by the House of Representatives (the Senate concurring), That is the sense of the Congress that-

(1) the United States should seek Turkish permission to extend beyond June 1992 the agreement that permits the stationing of United States military forces in southern Turkey for purposes of Operation Provide Comfort;

(2) the Government of Turkey, whose continued commitment to Operation Provide Comfort is essential if the operation is to be continued, should respond positively to a United States request to extend that agreement;

(3) the United Nations presence in northern Iraq should be extended;

(4) the United States and the international community should attach high priority to persuading the Government of Iraq to lift the economic boycott of northern Iraq; and

(5) in working to ameliorate the conditions of the Iraqi Kurds, the United States should continue to support the sovereignty and territorial integrity of all states, and the inter-

nationally recognized human rights of all peoples, in the region.

The SPEAKER pro tempore. Pursuant to the rule, the gentleman from Indiana [Mr. HAMILTON] will be recognized for 20 minutes, and the gentleman from Michigan [Mr. BROOMFIELD] will be recognized for 20 minutes.

The Chair recognizes the gentleman from Indiana [Mr. HAMILTON].

(Mr. HAMILTON asked and was given permission to revise and extend his remarks.)

Mr. HAMILTON. Mr. Speaker, I yield myself such time as I may consume.

Mr. Speaker, I rise in support of House Concurrent Resolution 299, as amended, which deals with issues concerning the Kurdish community in northern Iraq. This resolution was considered by the Foreign Affairs Committee on May 20 and passed by voice vote.

Mr. Speaker, this resolution addresses four issues. First, it urges the continuation beyond June 1992 of the stationing of United States forces in southern Turkey for purposes of Operation Provide Comfort. Second, it calls for extension of the United Nations presence in northern Iraq. Third, it underscores the need for continued humanitarian help for the Iraqi Kurds. And, finally, it urges the administration to take efforts to gain the immediate lifting of the economic embargo by Baghdad of northern Iraq.

On May 19, 1992, the Iraqi Kurds successfully held local elections in northern Iraq. This is a trend toward greater democracy that we would like to see repeated in the rest of Iraq, and elsewhere throughout the Middle East. These elections would not have been possible without the presence of Operation Provide Comfort in southeastern Turkey. I think this is a particularly appropriate time to recognize the need to continue Operation Provide Comfort and to work for peaceful and democratic change elsewhere in Iraq.

I commend our colleagues, Mr. BILBRAY and Mr. SOLARZ, for their leadership on this issue and I urge adoption of House Concurrent Resolution 299, as amended.

I recognize Mr. GILMAN for his work on behalf of this resolution.

Mr. Speaker, I reserve the balance of my time.

Mr. BROOMFIELD. Mr. Speaker, I yield myself such time as I may consume. I support this timely resolution, which urges continuation of Operation Provide Comfort and the security zone in northern Iraq, along with the United Nations presence there. I commend the sponsor, Congressman BILBRAY, as well as Mr. SOLARZ and Chairman FASCELL of the Foreign Affairs Committee, and Congressmen HAMILTON and GILMAN of the Europe and Middle East Subcommittee.

Saddam Hussein's regime has a terrible record of brutality toward the Kurds in Iraq. Every day, new evidence is uncovered that reveals systematic efforts to murder, torture, and maim innocent Kurds who are supposedly citizens of Iraq.

In addition to maintaining the current security zone, our Government is now also assisting the Kurds by removing detailed Iraqi security records which carefully document the extent of Saddam Hussein's atrocities. Soon, the world will know the truth about these horrible human rights abuses.

We cannot forget Iraq's brutal suppression of the Kurdish uprising in early 1991. I believe that Saddam Hussein is ready, willing, and able to launch another military operation against the Kurds if international protection were withdrawn. We must do everything possible to ensure that Operation Provide Comfort continues and that the security zone remains intact.

The Kurdish people have recently shown their commitment to the democratic process and their wish for greater autonomy by conducting free and fair elections. Massive numbers of Kurds voted and elected a Kurdish National Assembly and a leader of the Kurdish movement. Despite threats from Baghdad, the Kurds in Iraq bravely set out on the road to a democratic future.

As long as the current regime in Iraq retains power, the Kurdish people there remain threatened by further repression. I urge my colleagues to join me in supporting this resolution.

□ 1300

Mr. Speaker, I yield such time as he may consume to the gentleman from New York [Mr. GILMAN].

(Mr. GILMAN asked and was given permission to revise and extend his remarks.)

Mr. GILMAN. Mr. Speaker, I rise to express support for House Concurrent Resolution 299, a resolution expressing the sense of Congress regarding the Kurds in northern Iraq. I join in commending the gentleman from Nevada [Mr. BILBRAY], the gentleman from New York [Mr. SOLARZ] as well as the gentleman from Indiana [Mr. HAMILTON], the distinguished chairman of our Foreign Affairs Subcommittee on Europe and the Middle East, and our committee's distinguished minority member, the gentleman from Michigan [Mr. BROOMFIELD] for their outstanding work on this measure.

The plight of the Kurds has received some attention; but, in my view, not enough attention.

Mr. Speaker, it is obvious that Operation Provide Comfort remains necessary in order to deter Iraqi attacks against the Kurds in northern Iraq.

I believe the United States should seek Turkish permission to extend beyond June 1992, the agreement that permits the stationing of United States military personnel in southern Turkey for purposes of Operation Provide Comfort.

Mr. Speaker, the United Nations and the entire international community should use the forces of moral suasion to pressure the despicable government of Saddam Hussein to lift its economic boycott of northern Iraq.

Accordingly, as a proud cosponsor of this resolution, I urge its unanimous adoption.

Mr. HAMILTON. Mr. Speaker, I yield 5 minutes to the gentleman from New York [Mr. SOLARZ], one of the chief sponsors of this resolution.

Mr. SOLARZ. Mr. Speaker, I want to pay tribute to the distinguished chairman of the Subcommittee on Europe and the Middle East for bringing this resolution before us, and also to my very good friend, the gentleman from Nevada [Mr. BILBRAY], who has been the driving force behind the formulation of this resolution. I am also pleased to thank our friends on the other side of the aisle; that great statement, the gentleman from Michigan [Mr. BROOMFIELD], that extraordinary Member of the House, the gentleman from New York [Mr. GILMAN], and some of my other friends whom I see over there; the gentlewoman from Kansas [Mrs. MEYERS], the gentleman from Nebraska [Mr. BEREUTER], and the gentleman from Illinois [Mr. PORTER], who are supporting it as well.

Mr. Speaker I attach considerable importance to the adoption of this resolution. It underscores, in my judgment, two very significant and enduring realities in that part of the world. The first is that there are literally hundreds of thousands of Kurds now living in northern Iraq whose security and perhaps even whose lives would be in jeopardy if Operation Provide Comfort were to come to an end in June.

I was in northern Iraq several months ago, where I had an opportunity to witness for myself the enormous devastation which Saddam and his forces had inflicted upon the Kurdish people in the late 1980's. Thousands of villages which had existed for centuries were literally leveled. Chemical weapons were used not just in Halabja, the village where several thousands were killed and about which we all know, but in literally dozens of other villages as well. And there can be little doubt that if Operation Provide Comfort comes to an end, and the deterrent presence of the United Nations is removed from northern Iraq, not to mention the potential deterrent presence of coalition air forces in Turkey, Saddam will move once again against these people. And if he does, then once again tens of thousands, and perhaps even hundreds of thousands, will be rendered homeless, and many of them may even lose their lives.

So the objective of this resolution, which calls for the extension of Operation Provide Comfort, is an objective of enormous humanitarian significance. But the resolution underscores one other significant and perhaps enduring reality, and that is the extent to which any satisfactory resolution of the problem in the Persian Gulf will clearly require the continued cooperation of Turkey.

Had it not been for Turkey, it would not have been possible to impose effective sanctions against Iraq after the Iraqi invasion of Kuwait, inasmuch as it was Turkey's willingness to cut the oil pipeline from Iraq which made sanctions viable. And Turkey, of course, cooperated fully with us during the course of the war and made it possible for us to stage air raids against Iraq during the course of Desert Storm. In a similar sense, had it not been for the willingness of Turkey to make its territory available, Operation Provide Comfort simply would not have been possible.

That is why I believe this resolution, which calls upon not only our government to urge Turkey to agree to an extension of Provide Comfort, but which also urges our Turkish friends to provide their consent for a continuation of Provide Comfort is so important. I am hopeful that Turkey will continue to be as cooperative in the future as they have been in the past, and I believe that if we are able to continue working together we will be able to continue making it possible for the Kurdish people, who have perhaps suffered more than almost any other peoples in the history of that tortured and troubled part of the world, to at least have some security in the year ahead.

Mr. Speaker, for all of these reasons, I urge the adoption of the resolution.

Mr. BROOMFIELD. Mr. Speaker, I yield 3 minutes to the distinguished gentleman from Nebraska [Mr. BEREUTER].

Mr. BEREUTER. Mr. Speaker, as ranking member of the Human Rights Subcommittee, I rise in strong support of this resolution.

Mr. Speaker, the ongoing turmoil in northern Iraq, and the extremely precarious situation of the Iraqi Kurds, is a situation that troubles us all. Saddam Hussein has demonstrated his intent upon punishing the Kurds for their disloyalty to his ruthless regime. All that stands in his way is the international relief effort known as Operation Provide Comfort.

But, as my colleagues have mentioned, the mandate of Operation Provide Comfort is about to expire. The U.N. peacekeepers who have stood as a barrier against Saddam Hussein may have to be withdrawn very soon. If the international community abandons the Kurds at this point in time, this Member believes we can accurately predict what will happen to them. The Kurds can expect a reign of terror that exceeds their worst nightmare.

House Concurrent Resolution 299 seeks to prevent that devastation. It expresses the sense of Congress that the United States should seek to extend Operation Provide Comfort, and work with the Turkish Government to ensure that international relief efforts in northern Iraq are not terminated. It makes the important statement that the United States simply cannot forget about the vicious nature of the Iraqi regime, and the vulnerability of the Kurdish people.

This Member would note that House Concurrent Resolution 299 was amended at full committee to recognize the territorial integrity of the states in the region. Again, Mr. Speaker, this is consistent with United States policy, and addresses the legitimate concerns that the Turkish Government has regarding a Kurdish separatist movement. This change of language strengthens the resolution, and increases the likelihood that the Turkish Government will respond favorably.

Mr. Speaker, this important resolution would not have been possible had it not been for the diligent efforts of its author, the gentleman from Nevada [Mr. BILBRAY]. The chairman of the Subcommittee on Europe and the Middle East [Mr. HAMILTON], and the chairman of the Subcommittee on Human Rights and International Organizations [Mr. YATRON] deserve acknowledgment for moving this House Concurrent Resolution 299 in an expeditious manner. This Member would also point to the important contributions of the gentleman from New York [Mr. GILMAN] and the gentleman from Michigan [Mr. BROOMFIELD] in preparing the legislation before this body today. House Concurrent Resolution 299 is indeed a bipartisan effort.

Mr. Speaker, this Member urges the adoption of House Concurrent Resolution 299.

Mr. HAMILTON. Mr. Speaker, I yield 3 minutes to the gentleman from Nevada [Mr. BILBRAY], who is one of the chief sponsors of this resolution.

□ 1310

Mr. BILBRAY. Mr. Speaker, I want to thank Chairman HAMILTON and Chairman SOLARZ along with the assistance of Chairman FASCELL and Congressman GILMAN for helping those of us who have cared for the Kurdish cause for so long to finally send a message to the administration that the American Government intends to keep their promise to the Kurds.

For well over a year, a million Kurds, mostly women and children, have known only cold and hunger as they were forced to flee to the Turkey-Iraq border in order to avoid the genocide that the Saddam Hussein had in mind. Well over a year ago, we encouraged these ancient and proud people to assist us in the overthrow of Saddam Hussein and when all did not go well, our administration left them to the wolves of the Iraqi army. Only through U.N. intervention and Operation Provide Comfort have we been able to maintain the troops of Saddam's army at bay and prevented the slaughter.

But time is once again running out. Soon deadlines will expire and these people will once again be left to their own resources, with no one to turn to but themselves, and facing the much better equipped Iraqi army.

House Concurrent Resolution 299 takes the position that this administration has avoided for many months, to defend those we asked to assist us in our hour of need and to ask the pertinent international organization, the United Nations, to continue their peacekeeping role in the area. This is not a call for money. This is not a call for sending our troops over there. It is a call for the U.S. leadership to once again lead the international community to continue the protection that is already in place and has been to critical to the continued safety of the Kurds.

I would like to take the opportunity to congratulate the Kurds, who only 2 weeks ago took the opportunity to express their democratic dreams, and held their free election, without fraud and without violence. I would like to submit for the RECORD, a series of articles that former two term Governor of Nevada Mike O'Callahan wrote after monitoring those elections. Not only do his writings offer us a true insight into the violence and misery in the world around us, but also the hope. It is clear from his writing and other reports that I have received, that it is the United States that these people admire and look to.

Let us keep our promises and ask our administration to finally take a position in support of the Kurds. These proud people have already proven their thirst for democracy, and their desire for a lasting peace in the region. Let us finally ask the administration to keep their promises to these people.

Let us make sure that what happened to the Armenians does not happen to the Kurds. They need a democratic, free-elected area, an autonomous area within Iraq. We must show our support.

Mr. Speaker, I would like to thank all those who have expressed their support for the Kurdish people.

Mr. Speaker, I include an article by Mike O'Callahan, as follows:

. . .

Mr. BROOMFIELD. Mr. Speaker, I yield 3 minutes to the gentleman from Illinois [Mr. PORTER].

(Mr. PORTER asked and was given permission to revise and extend his remarks.)

Mr. PORTER. Mr. Speaker, I thank the distinguished gentleman from Michigan for yielding me this time.

Mr. Speaker, I rise in support of this concurrent resolution.

Mr. Speaker, the congressional human rights caucus that I am privileged to cochair throughout its almost entire 10-year history has directed great interest and concern for the Kurds. That has occurred both prior to and since Desert Storm.

Several years ago, we brought Mrs. Francoise Mitterrand to Washington, the First Lady of France, to tell of her great concerns about the Kurdish people and their mistreatment in all of the countries in which they find their population spread. That discrimination and suffering has been great in each of these countries, but it has been most profound in Iraq where Saddam Hussein turned his toxic chemical weapons upon his own people, the Kurdish people, killing thousands of them and where that suffering and discrimination has been intensive throughout this entire period.

So I want to commend my colleagues in the Congress, the gentleman from Nevada [Mr. BILBRAY], the gentleman from New York [Mr. GILMAN], the gentleman from New York [Mr. SOLARZ], the gentleman from Indiana [Mr. HAMILTON], the gentleman from Michigan [Mr. BROOMFIELD], the gentleman from Nebraska [Mr. BEREUTER], and the gentleman from Pennsylvania [Mr. YATRON], all of whom have shown great concern for the suffering of the Kurdish people, and for bringing this resolution to the floor of the House.

Elections have now been held in northern Iraq. We commend the people for their courage and for taking this important step, but our support for the Kurdish people must continue to provide the protection for them that is absolutely essential, and this resolution points us in the right direction, Mr. Speaker, and I would urge its adoption by the House of Representatives.

Mr. Speaker, history has been very unkind to the Kurds. For centuries they have been in ethnic limbo, split between as many as four different nations and always prevented from fully expressing their political will. In times of political or military uncertainty, the Kurds frequently have been brutally repressed by leaders who fear that they will rise up and demand representation or independence.

The latest chapter in the sad tale of the Kurds has been the gulf war. Following Saddam Hussein's crushing defeat at the hands of the U.S. military, he sent his forces north to crush a fledgling Kurdish uprising. With the help of the United States and the United Nations, Saddam's aggression against the Kurds was checked and relief supplies were made available to them through Operation Provide Comfort. In addition, a security zone was established in Iraq north of the 36th parallel to provide a haven for the Kurds. This zone is patrolled by U.N. observers. In addition, the Turkish Government has agreed to allow United States forces to use bases in southern Turkey to provide assistance to the Kurds. Unfortunately, the agreements allowing the United States to operate in southern Turkey and the United Nations to operate in northern Iraq both expire in June 1992.

House Concurrent Resolution 299 urges the United States to seek an extension of the agreement with Turkey which will allow United States forces to continue to assist the Kurds. This legislation also urges the United Nations to continue to operate in northern Iraq.

Mr. Speaker, the Kurds must not be forgotten. If the United States and United Nations turn their backs on the Kurds, Saddam will have a free hand to commit the types of human rights abuses that we all know he is capable. I urge members to support House Concurrent Resolution 299 and to support the human rights of the Kurdish people.

Mr. FASCELL. Mr. Speaker I rise in support of House Concurrent Resolution 299 regarding the Kurds in northern Iraq. I am pleased to be an original cosponsor of this measure and commend the author, the distinguished gentleman from Nevada [Mr. BILBRAY] for his commitment to alleviating the plight of the Kurds in Iraq. I also commend the distinguished chairmen of the Human Rights and International Organizations Subcommittee, Mr. YATRON, and the Subcommittee on Europe and the Middle East, Mr. HAMILTON, for their willingness to take prompt action on this timely measure so that it could be considered by the full House today.

Mr. Speaker, the agreement that allows the United States to station military forces in southern Turkey in order to provide protection to the Kurds in northern Iraq expires this month. Furthermore, the agreement between the United Nations and the Government of Iraq, which established humanitarian centers and safe areas in northern Iraq for Kurds and others, also expires at the end of this month. It is imperative that both these agreements be extended immediately. The lives of thousands of Kurds, who have suffered massively under the brutal regime of the Iraqi dictator Saddam Hussein, depend on the protection afforded them by the United Nations presence in the north of Iraq and by the coalition forces stationed in Turkey. We cannot allow Saddam Hussein to once again unleash his tyranny on these beleaguered people.

House Concurrent Resolution 299 addresses this urgent need. It calls upon the Turkish Government to permit the continued stationing of United States and other coalition forces on its territory. The measure calls for the extension of the United Nations presence in northern Iraq and calls upon the Iraqi Government to lift the economic boycott of northern Iraq. I believe firmly that the U.S. Government should work vigorously toward these ends.

Mr. Speaker, that Iraqi Kurds took a giant step toward the realization of their democratic aspirations last month when they conducted, under difficult conditions, what are acknowledged to be free and fair elections. We, in the United States, who have rightly made democratic reform and respect for human rights a cornerstone of our foreign policy, cannot now abandon those who, at great personal risk, seek to exercise those rights. The Kurds deserve our support and protection. I urge unanimous consent of House Concurrent Resolution 299.

Mr. YATRON. Mr. Speaker, House Concurrent Resolution 299 expresses the sense of the Congress that the international community should extend the mandate of Operation Provide Comfort in northern Iraq and southern Turkey.

Provide Comfort, a U.N.-sponsored operation, has supplied security, food, and shelter for hundreds of thousands of Kurdish refugees now living in northern Iraq and Turkey. These refugees were forced to flee their homes in February and March of 1991 when Iraqi forces brutally suppressed a Kurdish uprising.

Operation Provide Comfort's mandate has been relatively successful in protecting the Kurds against Iraqi attacks.

Turkey has permitted United States forces to be stationed on its soil to provide air cover for the Kurds and the U.N. High Commissioner for Refugees has been administering the camps.

However, Ankara's agreement with the United States military and the United Nations accord with Iraq to administer the refugee camps are both set to expire in June.

The Government of Turkey is currently considering whether it should extend the agreement with the United States beyond June.

The United Nations High Commissioner for Refugees will soon be transferring its responsibilities for administering the camps to UNICEF which must reach a new agreement with Baghdad on the continued presence of the United Nations in the security zone.

This resolution calls on all parties to extend the mandate and also calls on Iraq to end its economic boycott of northern Iraq which is responsible for the massive suffering of thousands of civilian Kurds.

Mr. Speaker, while it is critically important to support Operation Provide Comfort, it is clear that as long as Saddam is in power the Kurds will never be safe from Iraqi aggression.

The resolution complements U.S. policy objectives with respect to this issue. The administration has informed us in writing that they have no objection to this resolution.

Mr. Speaker, I would like to commend Chairman FASCELL, Congressman BROOMFIELD, Chairman HAMILTON, Congressman BEREUTER, Congressman BILBRAY, and Congressman GILMAN for supporting this resolution.

I urge my colleagues to adopt this resolution.

Mr. BROOMFIELD. Mr. Speaker, I have no further requests for time, and I yield back the balance of my time.

Mr. HAMILTON. Mr. Speaker, I have no further requests for time, and I yield back the balance of my time. The SPEAKER pro tempore (Mr. MONT-GOMERY). The question is on the motion offered by the gentleman from Indiana [Mr. HAMILTON] that the House suspend the rules and agree to the concurrent resolution, House Concurrent Resolution 299, as amended.

The question was taken; and (two-thirds having voted in favor thereof) the rules were suspended and the concurrent resolution, as amended, was agreed to.

A motion to reconsider was laid on the table.

119.

[June 3, 1992 (Senate), pp. 7474-5]

EXTEND THE MANDATE TO PROTECT THE KURDS

Mr. PELL. Mr. President, the next several weeks will be a crucial period in the history of the Kurdish people. In the wake of the recent watershed elections for an Iraqi Kurdish parliament, the Kurds face a difficult road ahead as they attempt to consolidate their democratic achievement. The task, however, is being compounded by the fact that the mandate for Operation Provide Comfort-the allied air protection for the Kurds north of the 36th parallel in Iraq-is set to expire at the end of the month.

Operation Provide Comfort is the salvation of the Kurds. Without international protection, the Kurds would once again find themselves at the mercy of the Saddam Hussein regime. From experience, we know all too well what that means. It means oppression and torture by Saddam Hussein's security forces. It means Kurdish women will be hauled into secret police headquarters to be raped. It means the resumption of chemical weapons attacks. It means Kurds-old or young, dissident or nonpolitical-will again disappear without a trace.

As ugly and distasteful as all this sounds, I do not exaggerate. We know this to be true because, as incredible as it seems, the Iraqis documented their persecution of the Kurds on videotape, in print, and on cassette tapes. Just last month, the Senate Foreign Relations Committee participated in an effort to transport the documentation of Iraqi atrocities, which consists literally of tons of records and other evidence, to the States for safekeeping. Just a cursory study of some of the documents, now in the custody of the Foreign Relations Committee, has revealed untold horrors wrought by the Iraqi security network against the Kurds under what is now known as the "al-Anfal" campaign. A more detailed study over time ought to provide the basis for obtaining judgments against Saddam Hussein and his cronies for crimes against humanity and genocide.

We must continue the air cover for the Kurds not only to prevent them from being subjected to further savagery, but also to help them reap the benefits of their experiment with democracy. Last month, Iraq's 5 million Kurds took to the polls in exemplary fashion to elect a unified leadership. While the elections produced a split result between the two main political parties, they were an extraordinary exercise in democracy in the face of adversity and will help establish the Iraqi Kurd claim for self-government.

In April, I, along with six of my colleagues in the Senate, wrote to President Bush to urge continued protection for both the Iraqi Kurds and Shi'a. I ask unanimous consent that our letter to the President and the reply from National Security Adviser Scowcroft be included in the RECORD upon conclusion of my remarks. I also ask unanimous consent to include a recent editorial from the *Washington Post* that addresses this same subject ["The Kurds' New Democracy," June 1, 1992].

Mr. President, the expiration of the mandate of Operation Provide Comfort looms over the Kurdish people as a proverbial sword of Damoclese. The anti-Iraq coalition has within its hands the means to ensure that Saddam Hussein's fury is not once again unleashed on the Kurds. The United States, as the preeminent player in the coalition, must take the lead in seeing that the mandate is extended.

There being no objection, the material was ordered to be printed in the RECORD, as follows:

U.S. SENATE,
COMMITTEE ON FOREIGN RELATIONS,
Washington, DC, April 14, 1992.
The PRESIDENT,
The White House,
Washington, DC.

DEAR MR. PRESIDENT: We are writing to express our deep concern over the current situation in Iraq, particularly regarding the safety of the Kurds in northern Iraq and the Shi'a muslims in southern Iraq.

Recently, the Senate Foreign Relations Committee held a hearing to receive testimony on mass killings in Iraq under the Saddam Hussein regime. The Committee heard graphic and convincing reports of indiscriminate killings of Iraqi Kurdish civilians, particularly during the past several years. The testimony, based on official Iraqi documents and on tests conducted by forensic specialists, confirms the Committee's own research in this area. The available evidence suggests that the total number of Iraqi Kurdish deaths and disappearances may be as high as 200,000 to 300,000, or roughly 5 percent of the Iraqi Kurdish population. This information indicates that Iraqi actions against the Kurds are tantamount to an official policy of genocide.

The Kurds have effectively established a liberated zone in most of the traditionally Kurdish areas of northern Iraq. However, it is only the threat of allied military retaliation that protects this liberated zone from renewed Iraqi attack. And, from what we know, a renewed attack threatens the Kurdish people with extermination.

We therefore strongly support an extension of allied air cover under Operation Provide Comfort, currently set to expire at the end of June. We also hope the United States will urge the government of Turkey-whose support is a critical element of Operation Provide Comfort's success-to support an extension of the mandate.

In addition, we hope that the United States will make an effort to address the situation of the Shi'a population in Iraq. While the plight of the Kurds is becoming increasingly prominent, relatively little attention has been paid to the fate of the 13,000,000 Shi'a muslims who have struggled under Saddam Hussein's rule. Last year, following the uprising in the south, many of the Shi'a combatants, their civilian supporters, and Iraqi army deserters were forced into the southeastern marshlands at the confluence of the Tigris and Euphrates rivers. There they have been subject to harsh retribution from Iraqi forces, leading to numerous deaths and causing serious refugee problems. Accordingly, we would urge the United States to examine possibilities for expanding the United Nations' presence in southern Iraq and extending appropriate international protection to the Shi'a.

We appreciate your attention to these matters.

Sincerely,
Claiborne Pell, Harris Wofford, James M. Jeffords, Joseph R. Biden, Jr., Albert Gore, Jr., Paul Simon, Daniel Patrick Moynihan.

———

THE WHITE HOUSE,
Washington, May 26, 1992.
Hon. CLAIBORNE PELL,
Chairman, Committee on Foreign Relations, U.S. Senate, Washington, DC.

DEAR MR. CHAIRMAN: The President and I fully share your concerns about the current situation in Iraq which you enumerated in your letter of April 14, 1992. As we have said publicly on many occasions, United States policy toward Iraq seeks to maintain international sanctions until there is a change in leadership in Baghdad and a new government prepared to live at peace both with Iraq's neighbors and with the Iraqi people. We fully support United Nations Security Council Resolution 688 which calls on Iraq to cease repression of all Iraqi citizens.

As you noted, the coalition's Provide Comfort air cover has been critical to preventing an Iraqi attack on the areas of northern Iraq under Kurdish control. We are proud of the role coalition forces have played in curtailing the suffering of the population of northern Iraq. Let me assure you that we and our allies in Operation Provide Comfort have already begun consultations on extending the mandate for the presence with the Turkish leadership.

Our concern about the suffering of the Iraqi people naturally extends to the Shia population of the south as well. We have been engaged in a dialogue with the United Nations about expanding the U.N. presence in that area for some time and will continue to do so.

Sincerely,
BRENT SCOWCROFT

. . .

120.

[June 12, 1992 (Senate), p. 8133]

RELIEF FOR KURDS IN NORTHERN IRAQ

Mr. REID. Mr. President, yesterday, the Senate agreed to House Concurrent Resolution 299—a concurrent resolution originally submitted in the House by Representative JAMES BILBRAY. The resolution asks Turkey to continue beyond June 1992 the agreement that permits the stationing of United States forces in southern Turkey; it states that the United Nations presence in Northern Iraq should be extended; it states that the United States and the United Nations should attach a high priority to persuading Iraq to lift its boycott of northern Iraq; and it states that the United States should support the sovereignty of all the states in the area.

The United States encouraged the uprising of the Kurds, and then forgot about them-left them to Saddam Hussein's butchery. Millions of Kurds-mostly women and children-have been forced to flee their homes because of threats from the Iraqi Army. They have experienced much suffering, much hunger. Saddam Hussein has used gas attacks against the Kurds, and he has massacred entire villages.

If the United States and United Nations move out of the region, we can expect wholesale slaughter of the Kurds.

Through the United Nations and Operation Provide Comfort, we have been able to keep the wolves from the door. But time is running out. Soon, deadlines will expire, and the United States needs to act. This is not a call for money, nor a call for military intervention. This is a call for leadership.

Recently, the Kurds expressed their desire for democracy by holding free elections free of violence or fraud. The United States must keep its promises to these freedom-loving people. That is why the adoption of House Concurrent Resolution 299 yesterday was so important. Representative BILBRAY is to be praised for his efforts to remind the administration of its promises and to send a message of support to an embattled culture. It is the least we can do.

Mr. LEVIN addressed the Chair.

The ACTING PRESIDENT pro tempore. The Senator from Michigan is recognized.

121.

[July 8, 1992 (Extensions of Remarks), p. 2110]

OPERATION PROVIDE COMFORT EXTENDED BY TURKEY
HON. MATTHEW F. MCHUGH
OF NEW YORK
IN THE HOUSE OF REPRESENTATIVES

Wednesday, July 8, 1992

Mr. MCHUGH. Mr. Speaker, I would like to take this opportunity to publicly commend the Government of Turkey for its recent decision to extend Operation Provide Comfort for another 6 months.

As you know, Operation Provide Comfort is the international program of protection and assistance for the Kurds of northern Iraq. On June 26, by a vote of 228 to 136, the Turkish Parliament approved this latest extension as our own Government had been urging.

At your direction, Mr. Speaker, I led a bipartisan congressional delegation to the region last year to assess the plight of the Kurds following the conclusion of Operation Desert Storm. The situation the Kurds faced at the time of our visit was desperate and it was quite apparent that no effort to assist them could succeed without the cooperation and support of the Turkish Government.

That support was promptly forthcoming and Operation Provide Comfort has been successful in providing protection and assistance to the Kurds. By approving this latest 6-month extension, the Turkish Parliament has once again displayed the humanitarian concern of the Turkish people for the Kurds of northern Iraq.

122.

[July 9, 1992 (House), p. 6151]

CONGRATULATING TURKEY ON EXTENSION OF OPERATION PROVIDE COMFORT

(Mr. BILBRAY asked and was given permission to address the House for 1 minute and to revise and extend his remarks.)

Mr. BILBRAY. Mr. Speaker, this morning, I would like to take the opportunity to congratulate the people of Turkey and in particular their parliament under the leadership of Prime Minister Suleyman Demirel for their courageous vote to extend Operation Provide Comfort. By a vote of 228 to 136, coalition forces will be allowed to continue their overflights and provide safety and security for the hundreds of thousands of Kurdish refugees that remain in northern Iraq.

This vote continues to show Turkey's desire to be a partner with the United States and to join forces with us to bring democracy and stability to the region. Their acknowledgement of the Kurdish situation and their efforts to alleviate and resolve the problem have clearly placed them as a leader of a democratic and peaceful Middle East.

Again, my thanks and those of all the Members of this Congress who have joined me in supporting the Kurdish people go to the people of Turkey. I look forward to the continued partnership between our two countries and to Turkey's assistance as we strive to find a peaceful and democratic solution for the future of the Kurds.

123.

[July 9, 1992 (Extensions of Remarks), p. 2150]

OPERATION PROVIDE COMFORT
HON. BENJAMIN A. GILMAN
OF NEW YORK
IN THE HOUSE OF REPRESENTATIVES

Thursday, July 9, 1992

Mr. GILMAN. Mr. Speaker, following the gulf war, the world was faced with a refugee crisis when Iraqi Kurds, fearing their fate at the hands of a defeated dictator, fled to the borders of Iran and Turkey. As a response, the allies established a security zone in northern Iraq and encouraged Kurds to return to their homes. The United States, with international cooperation, organized a relief effort which became known as Operation Provide Comfort. In order to facilitate this operation, the Turkish Government agreed to station United States military forces in southern Turkey. This decision was heroic, given the possibility of Iraqi retaliation. The agreement was first extended through June 1992 with the Understanding that, because Turkey is a parliamentary democracy, additional extensions would have to be approved by Parliament.

Mr. Speaker, many of us in the Congress are pleased that our Turkish friends in Parliament voted decisively this month to extend the agreement authorizing support for Operation Provide Comfort. This vote, the most recent example of Turkey's cooperation with the West, will encourage stability in the region and give new hope to tens of thousands of people.

This reaffirmation of support for Operation Provide Comfort underscores Turkey's importance in the region. Turkey, whose cooperation was essential to the success of the international coalition during the gulf crisis, will play a crucial role in building a peaceful future. Turkey is a good role model, not just for the newly independent republics of the former Soviet Union, but for the Arab world as well. Committed to the idea of peace through greater economic cooperation and trade, Turkey recently hosted leaders of 11 nations, including those of six former Soviet republics, to sign a Black Sea economic cooperation declaration. Included in the group were Armenia and Azerbaijan, two countries at odds over Nagorno-Karabaugh.

Mr. Speaker, Turkey's decision to extend the Operation Provide Comfort agreement will give Iraqi Kurds new hope. Turkey's decisive stand is a reminder that the West can count on Turkey and that it will play an increasingly important role in regional and world affairs.

124.

[September 10, 1992 (Extensions of Remarks), p. 2582]

THE NO-FLY ZONE: TAKING THE NEXT STEPS
HON. LES ASPIN
OF WISCONSIN
IN THE HOUSE OF REPRESENTATIVES

Thursday, September 10, 1992

Mr. ASPIN. Mr. Speaker, the creation of the no-fly zone to ground Iraqi aircraft in southern Iraq was a necessary step, both to help protect the persecuted Shia minority there and to reply to Saddam Hussein's aggressive challenges to the United Nations authority. But it has by no means tied his hands. How the United States and its coalition partners answer Saddam's countermoves will greatly influence our prospects for success.

Saddam may, of course, hunker down for a while. He may believe that President Bush is gunning for a fight and decide to deny him one.

If nothing happens for a few months, the no-fly policy is a winner. This is clearly what the administration is hoping will happen. We, however, should not rely on Saddam Hussein's political acumen. Furthermore, let's not kid ourselves, even if Saddam goes away for a while, eventually he'll come back. It is just a question of when and how he will challenge, not if.

That's why we should remember that we don't do very well when we are surprised. We must start thinking now about how we might respond to Saddam's countermoves.

We've already made one mistake that may hamper our responses to Saddam in the future. That was our failure to build political support at the United Nations and in the region for the no-fly zone. Whatever else we have to do will now be that much more difficult.

And, Mr. Speaker, we should realize that Saddam is not without options, both military and nonmilitary, to which we may have to respond.

SADDAM'S MILITARY OPTIONS

Militarily, Saddam can do little to directly challenge the no-fly zone. The superiority of the coalition air forces is overwhelming. He can, however, pursue other military strategies in the north and south that can cause us difficulty.

First, the Iraqis could ratchet up the ground attacks against the Shi'as in the marsh area of southern Iraq to see how far the coalition is willing to go in their defense. A no-fly zone will alleviate some of the suffering in the south, but it will not necessarily prevent artillery and tank attacks in the area.

Fortunately, more ground attacks against the Shi'as may turn out to be ineffective. The large number of lakes and streams in the southern marshes make the terrain very inhospitable to heavy armor.

Saddam could also opt for increased attacks against the Kurds in northern Iraq. Such a move could be tougher for us and for the targets-the Kurds.

For one thing, about a third of the Kurdish enclave lies below the 36th parallel, and therefore beyond the official protection of coalition air cover. An air-ground attack against this portion would not violate our prohibition of military activity north of the 36th parallel and would severely test the extent of our commitment to the Kurds.

For another, such an attack would also test our relationship with the Turks, who remain skittish about any actions that could lead to the breakup of Iraq. The Turkish Government is not yet on board with the no-fly zone, raising a question about whether we can use coalition planes located at the air base in Incerlik.

U.S. RESPONSES

I believe the United States and its coalition partners should be ready to use air power to blunt an Iraqi attack in either the north or the south. This would be a significant escalation, but I am not sure we can afford to do otherwise.

First, the establishment of the no-fly zone reinforces the notion that the coalition members have a commitment to protect the Iraqi people from Saddam. Renewed ground action would be devastating, especially for the Kurds below the 36th parallel, and could prompt another mass exodus. Once we have taken the step of setting up the zone, we cannot stand by and watch Saddam renew the genocide in another part of the country.

Moreover, it is very likely that air power would effectively blunt such an attack. During Operation Desert Storm, sustained air attacks destroyed the Iraqi Army's ability to fight effectively. There is no indication now that the Iraqis would have the will to fight when attacked by coalition aircraft.

Finally, our failure to protect persecuted minorities in Iraq would strengthen Saddam when we are trying to weaken him.

SADDAM'S NONMILITARY OPTIONS

In addition to his military options, Saddam also has nonmilitary cards to play.

For example, Saddam Hussein is already using an aggressive propaganda campaign to undermine support for the zone. Saddam's efforts to portray the coalition's no-fly zone as a direct attempt to partition Iraq plays on the fears of both his Sunni political base within Iraq, and the concerns of many other states in the region with their own sectarian divisions to worry about.

Saddam's claim that George Bush has demanded the zone for his own domestic political purposes also resonates throughout the international community. The Iraqi press has described the no-fly zone as "one of the dirtiest games" ever. No country wants to be seen as the lackey for United States election year politics.

Saddam is also in the grimly paradoxical position of being able to strengthen his position by increasing the hardship on segments of his own population, especially in the northern and southern protected zones. To do this, he could tighten the internal embargoes; further restrict humanitarian access to the people; and continue road construction projects in the south to make the area more accessible to Iraqi ground forces.

In addition, Saddam may respond to the no-fly zone by increasing his noncompliance in other areas. We have already seen some evidence of this.

The Iraqis have already banned all non-U.N. relief organizations from the country and even the U.N. relief workers cannot enter most of southern Iraq.

Further, in response to the no-fly zone, Iraq has threatened to expel all remaining U.N. guards, now there to protect United Nations and private relief workers. The number of guards in Iraq has already dwindled to just over 100 from an earlier total of 500, largely because the Iraqis have refused to issue visas and travel papers.

Saddam's noncompliance, however, probably will not stop there. I expect him to continue to reject the recommendations of the U.N. boundary commission working on a border between Iraq and Kuwait and to obstruct the inspection and destruction of Iraq's weapons of mass destruction.

U.S. RESPONSES

The United States and the rest of the coalition must be equally vigilant in responding to these kinds of nonmilitary moves. We have taken the first step toward countering Saddam's propaganda in Iraq and the region by stressing our commitment to Iraq's territorial integrity. We will have to do more.

First, to dull the effects of Saddam's repressive tactics, the United States should consider providing some direct humanitarian relief to the Iraqi people within the northern and the southern zones.

In the north, the United States could encourage the United Nations to partially lift the economic embargo in the Kurdish enclave, perhaps permitting limited exports to finance the care and feeding of the people in the zone. In the south, the coalition partners should mute the effects of Iraqi actions by air-dropping supplies, food, and medicine in southern Iraq.

Also, we should continue high-level meetings and close cooperation with the Iraqi opposition, particularly the Iraqi National Con-

gress. Such support will help to demonstrate to the Iraqi people that there is a credible alternative to Saddam Hussein.

In addition, we should press harder to borrow against frozen Iraqi oil revenues to finance U.N. operations in Iraq. This would alleviate some of the financial pressure on U.N. operations in Iraq and begin the reparations process. These assets would be repaid once Iraq decides to start pumping oil.

Finally, we have to be prepared to deal more forcefully and quickly with any repeat of the delaying tactics Saddam used on U.N. inspectors looking for evidence of programs for weapons of mass destruction at the Agricultural Ministry. Saddam Hussein must understand that we, our allies, and the United Nations will not tolerate his continued cheat-and-retreat tactics on the U.N. inspections.

These steps will mute the effects of any Iraqi response to the no-fly zone and show Saddam that we mean business. But it is going to take both political will and political muscle on the part of the United States and our coalition partners to make it work.

REBUILDING THE COALITION

Imposing the no-fly zone in southern Iraq was a good move. I fear, however, that building support for whatever we have to do next will now be much more difficult. By not pushing for another Security Council resolution authorizing the action, the Bush administration chose the path of least resistance. That bit of expediency may cause us problems in the future.

The coalition forces have invoked the no-fly zone under U.N. Resolution 688, which condemns Iraq's repression of its citizens and demands its cessation.

The administration, at least initially, believed that it needed another resolution authorizing all necessary means to enforce Resolution 688. In fact, on July 29, U.S. Ambassador to the United Nations, Edward Perkins, testified before Congress that the United States intended to approach the Security Council for such a resolution within the next week.

Initial soundings at the Security Council, however, convinced administration officials that such a resolution would be a tough fight. Therefore, the day after Ambassador Perkins' testimony, an unnamed administration official told reporters that Ambassador Perkins had been mistaken.

The administration then decided to try a different tact and set up the no-fly zone without an additional resolution.

The administration convinced the British, the French, and the Russians that Resolution 688, coupled with all of the other resolutions against Iraq, already provided sufficient authority to set up the no-fly zone.

They argued further that ongoing operations in northern Iraq, including a ban on Iraqi aircraft and helicopters above the 36th parallel, provided a precedent for enforcing Resolution 688 without obtaining an additional Security Council resolution.

The French, the British, and the Russians may have accepted this argument, but many experts, both within and outside the United States, do not. They insist that the no-fly zone is beyond the legal scope of Resolution 688 and, therefore, lacks U.N. authorization.

First, the Security Council passed Resolution 688 under Chapter 6 of the U.N. Charter, which deals with pacific settlement of disputes. Resolutions passed under Chapter 6 are generally nonbinding recommendations, intended to be persuasive rather than coercive. For this reason, Resolution 688 does not carry the weight of Resolution 687 and the other U.N. resolutions against Iraq, which were invoked under Chapter 7 of the U.N. Charter and are mandatory and binding upon all members of the United Nations.

Furthermore, since Resolution 687 outlines the terms under which the war ended, Iraq's noncompliance could effectively nullify the ceasefire and makes a resumption of hostilities legally possible. The demands of Resolution 688 are not a part of this ceasefire agreement.

Do these legal technicalities matter? Perhaps not, in and of themselves. But our failure to win support for another U.N. resolution suggests that we may be in a weak position when further action against Iraq becomes necessary.

Since August, 1990, a clear mandate from the Security Council has undergirded the collective response to Saddam Hussein's outrageous behavior. Taking the path of least resistance may have gotten the no-fly zone up and running more quickly, but it may come back to haunt us in future confrontations with Saddam Hussein.

As we saw in the lead up to the gulf war, solid U.N. authority provides important political cover to our regional allies. Our lack of convincing United Nations authorization may, in part, explain the lack of regional support for Operation Southern Watch.

Presently, only Kuwait has stated publicly its support for Operation Southern Watch. Syria has flatly rejected the zone, and the Egyptians are sitting on the sidelines. By imposing a total news blackout, the Saudis seem to be trying to pretend they aren't even participating.

This does not bode well for the future. Eventually Saddam will respond and we must be ready. By failing to do the heavy political lifting to get more countries on board, we may have made the next job-whenever and wherever that might be-much more difficult.

125.

[September 22, 1992 (Extensions of Remarks), pp. 2747-48]

HUMAN RIGHTS IN TURKEY
HON. LEE H. HAMILTON
OF INDIANA
IN THE HOUSE OF REPRESENTATIVES

Tuesday, September 22, 1992

Mr. HAMILTON. Mr. Speaker, I wish to draw to the attention of my colleagues the latest in a series of letters exchanged with the Department of State regarding the human rights situation in Turkey. The last exchange appeared in the CONGRESSIONAL RECORD on Tuesday, November 26, 1991. The current exchange deals with the question of the existence of political prisoners in Turkey.

The Department's August 3, 1992 response is striking for the number of places where the Department states that information is lacking about the nature of human rights in Turkey. It underscored the need to improve our information and knowledge about this situation.

Once again, I wish to reiterate that Turkey is an important friend and ally of the United States. We have a broad agenda with the Government of Turkey. It is in our interest and in the interest of the future of the United States-Turkey relationship to ensure that serious human rights violations cease to occur in Turkey.

U.S. DEPARTMENT OF STATE,
Washington, DC, August 3, 1992.
Hon. LEE H. HAMILTON,
Chairman, Subcommittee on Europe and the Middle East, Committee on Foreign Affairs.

DEAR MR. CHAIRMAN: I am pleased to respond to the questions you raised in your letter of July 10 to Assistant Secretary Niles regarding the issue of political prisoners and other human rights abuses in Turkey.

On the overall human rights situation in Turkey, there is no better source of information and analysis than the Department's Report on Turkey in its Country Reports on Human Rights Practices for 1991. It provides as complete a review of human rights abuses in Turkey as available information permits.

Despite the care and attention to detail that characterizes that report, it does not establish the number of political prisoners in Turkey at that time or whether, in fact, there are such. In this connection, I can confirm Mr. Niles's statement June 23 that we have no information that there are people in prison in Turkey for specifically "political" offenses, such as, for example, belonging to a political organization. There are persons imprisoned in Turkey for activities which the government considers illegal, and which could be regarded as politically motivated: for example, members of the Kurdish Workers Party (PKK) convicted of carrying out terrorist acts. I do not, however, consider those detained for terrorist activity to be political prisoners. Rather, the PKK is a terrorist organization, recognized

as such by most governments in the world, including the United States. As a consequence of intensified terrorist action in the southeast by the PKK, the parliament recently extended the state of emergency in that area for another four months.

We have no information on new cases of persons sentenced for what we would consider political activities since April 1991, when new anti-terrorist legislation abolished features of the criminal code which defined advocacy of beliefs, such as communism and Islamic fundamentalism, as "crimes." As are you, we are aware that the security courts still have the authority, in theory, to indict and convict persons who advocate separatism, threaten the unity of the state, or conduct "armed propaganda." The Turkish claim that such persons would not be political prisoners does not conform with international standards.

In this regard, we believe that Turkish state security prosecutors take an impermissibly broad view of what constitutes "separation"-as, for example, in their thus far unsuccessful efforts to prosecute Kurdish members of parliament for speaking Kurdish at the rostrum and for wearing Kurdish colors at their swearing-in ceremonies. As a consequence, the security courts may in the past have convicted and sentenced people for what outside observers would consider to be the legitimate expression of opinion. However, there are no estimates of the numbers of such convictions any more definite than those offered by the reports you cite, and these cannot be confirmed. Such estimates are made more difficult by pardons and amnesties (exact number unknown) that have been issued since the passage of the anti-terrorist law.

As regards the other specific questions you raised in your letter:

We do not accept a definition of "terrorist" drawn as broadly as in the Turkish anti-terror law. Our Human Rights Report characterized the Turkish definition as "broad and ambiguous" and susceptible to abuse. As noted in that report, the law's provisions are still pending judicial review.

In whatever manner "political prisoner" may be defined, we consider anyone detained for freedom-of-expression "offenses"-whether through ambiguity of the law, or abuse of the law by authorities-to be an appropriate subject of our concern.

Our working definition of "political prisoner" is broadly inclusive. To summarize, it includes persons who are incarcerated without charges, or on charges for offenses commonly held to be matters of belief, or for membership in a religious, social, racial, or national group. This definition extends our concern to persons prosecuted even under an ostensibly internationally acceptable law when the charges are trumped-up, or the trial unfair. Our definition also includes those convicted of politically-motivated acts in cases where the punishment is unduly harsh because of the person's race, religion, nationality, or social group. It does not include those who, regardless of their motivation, have gone beyond advocacy and dissent to commit acts of violence.

We are aware of the problem of torture in Turkey. Turkish Government figures show that more than 1400 cases of torture we investigated in 1991. The Turkish Human Rights Association reported 18 deaths of persons in police custody that same year. We continue to receive reports of torture, but the process of compiling full statistics for 1992 is not yet complete. We shall again report fully on this abuse, but we believe the record has improved since our last report in terms of the number of cases.

Thus the Department takes a very comprehensive view of what constitutes human rights abuses, as our annual reports amply demonstrate. We feel that abuse of human rights, as you suggest, does not depend solely on definitions of offenses, nor on numbers of convictions. Indeed, the whole range of issues involving human rights is a matter of serious concern in our bilateral relations with Turkey. We follow closely, for example, reports of unjustified detention, torture, and unsolved deaths of Kurdish activists. Since Mr. Niles met with the Subcommittee on June 23, Ambassador Barkley again discussed our human rights concerns with the Turkish Minister for Human Rights on July 14 and urged Turkey's compliance with international human rights standards to which it has subscribed.

At the same time, we are encouraged by improvements that have occurred in Turkey since the restoration of democratic government. Although Turkey has faced during that period a growing threat from Dev Sol, PKK, and other terrorist groups, we believe that the long-term trend is good. Turkey has taken many significant steps, and we believe that the present government is committed to implementing democratic standards of human rights. As Mr. Niles stated in his testimony on June 23, the Government of Turkey is actively seeking ways in which those human rights abuses can be put in the past. For example, the government has presented to the parliament for its consideration judicial reform legislation which would limit pre-trial detention and guarantee attorney access at all stages of detention. I believe the Turkish authorities recognize that some of their procedures are simply unacceptable, not just because of international pressure but because of what kind of a country they want Turkey to be. We intend to continue to discuss abuses with Turkey in order to support that trend.

I hope this letter has been responsive to your concerns.

Sincerely,
JANET G. MULLINS,
ASSISTANT SECRETARY
Legislative Affairs

126.

[October 2, 1992 (Extensions of Remarks), p. 2906]

ETHNIC CLEANSING BY TURKEY IS SYSTEMATICALLY IGNORED
HON. NICHOLAS MAVROULES
OF MASSACHUSETTS
IN THE HOUSE OF REPRESENTATIVES

Thursday, October 1, 1992

Mr. Mavroules. Mr. Speaker, much of the world has been focused on ethnic cleansing efforts being undertaken in parts of the former Republic of Yugoslavia. In reaction to the many reports of these atrocities, Serbia and Montenegro have been targeted by a U.N.-initiated international blockade, a U.N.-sponsored peacekeeping task force and strong international condemnation. As a strong supporter of this type of international pressure, i am pleased that the United States and the European Community have received such wide international support for their efforts to end ethnic cleansing in the Balkans.

It seems tragically ironic, however, that ethnic cleansing by a country nearby Yugoslavia has been systematically ignored by the Bush administration and many of our allies. The atrocities I refer to are being committed by the Government of Turkey against its Armenian, Greek, Cypriot and Kurdish minorities.

In 1915, Turkey took ethnic cleansing to the extreme, and the result was the Armenian genocide. This action alone, combined with the refusal by Turkey to admit culpability, makes me shudder to think that we gave this supposed "ally" $1 billion in foreign aid last year.

But it does not end there. For generations the Greek population living under Turkish rule has suffered the abuse of government-directed ethnic cleansing policies. In 1992 the Turks burned Smyrna and slaughtered its residents. Pogroms have been organized against Greeks in Istanbul and Izmir. Even today, Greeks residing within Turkey continue to exist as an oppressed minority.

Cypriots are another prominent example of an ethnic group that has suffered ethnic cleansing at the hands of Turkey. On a day-to-day basis for the past 18 years, the Turkish government has actively removed Cypriots from their homes, detained Cypriots on political grounds, and concealed the whereabouts of missing Cypriots and Americans. The Turkish government has also worked to undermine U.N.-sponsored talks aimed at finding a peaceful resolution to the dilemma. I have included for the record a copy of a *New York Times* editorial concerning ethnic cleansing in Cyprus. This editorial explains the situation that has arisen since the 1974 invasion of the sovereign nation of Cyprus by Turkish armed forces.

It is also painfully ironic that the United States has actively opposed ethnic cleansing by Iraq of its Kurdish minority. The United States provides air protection for Kurds residing in northern Iraq while ignoring military action being undertaken by Turkey against this same Kurdish minority, both in Turkey and across the border in northern Iraq. Amnesty International has repeatedly condemned Turkey for its use of torture, among other inhumane actions, against its Kurdish minority. This double standard cannot continue. The United States is spending millions of tax dollars to protect a group of people who are under daily attack by our "ally" Turkey. We, as a people, cannot afford to allow this outrage to persist.

The cold war is over. Communism and the U.S.S.R. are dead. Turkey demonstrated reluctance to assist the United States and United Nations during the Persian Gulf crisis and war. The political reality of the "new world order" is simply that Turkey is not the strategic ally that the Bush administration claims.

Even worse, Turkey has violated the United Nations charter, the NATO treaty, the human rights sections of the Foreign Assistance Act of 1961, the European Convention on Human Rights, the fourth Geneva Convention, the United Nations Universal Declaration of Human Rights, and the Treaty of Guarantee under the London-Zurich Agreement of 1959-60. Their human rights abuses have been documented by Amnesty International, the Freedom House annual survey, the Human Rights Watch Report, the Humanitarian Law Project Report, the Helsinki Watch, and numerous international news organizations. This list of grievances reads like the rap sheet of an international criminal, not a close ally of the land of the free.

President Bush cannot continue to ignore these continued human rights violations. Ethnic cleansing in the Balkans, as horrible as it is, pales in comparison to almost a century of similar efforts by the regimes of Turkey and the Ottoman empire.

Mr. Speaker, I call on each and every one of my colleagues to stand up for human rights around the globe and to stop allowing this deadly double standard to continue. We, as a body, cannot and will not allow Turkey's despicable record of abuse, torture, genocide, and ethnic cleansing to go without response.

127.

[October 3, 1992 (Extensions of Remarks), pp. 2959-60]

SITUATION IN SOUTHEASTERN TURKEY
HON. LEE H. HAMILTON
OF INDIANA
IN THE HOUSE OF REPRESENTATIVES

Saturday, October 3, 1992

Mr. HAMILTON. Mr. Speaker, I wish to draw to the attention of my colleagues a written response from the Honorable Thomas M.T. Niles, Assistant Secretary of State for European and Canadian Affairs, regarding the security situation in southeastern Turkey and human rights abuses in Turkey. Since the mid-1980's, Turkey has been combatting the activities of the PKK, a terrorist organization committed to the creation of a separate Kurdish state in southeastern Turkey. Turkish security forces have used increasingly violent methods to try to deal with the PKK threat. Innocent civilians are being killed by both sides in this conflict.

Secretary Niles remarks were submitted to the Subcommittee on Europe and Middle East in response to questioning during a subcommittee hearing on September 29, 1992, on recent developments in Europe.

Secretary Niles' response differs notably from his earlier testimony before the subcommittee on these issues and from earlier letters from the Department of State on the human rights situation in Turkey. The response goes further than any other statement of administration policy to date in acknowledging that a serious problem exists in southeastern Turkey, not only in terms of terrorist violence, but in terms of the heavyhanded official Turkish policy for dealing with the situation in the southeast. The response also notes, for the first time, that the trend today regarding the practice of torture in Turkey is not one of improvement and may in fact be one of increased violations.

Once again, I wish to reiterate that Turkey is an important friend and ally of the United States. We have a broad agenda with the Government of Turkey. It is in our interest and in the interest of the future of the United States-Turkey relationship to ensure that serious human rights violations cease to occur in Turkey.

REMARKS BY HON. THOMAS M.T. NILES

The level of terror and political violence in Turkey is notably elevated from last year. In the southeast, the focus of the PKK insurgency, this violence has clearly increased: more than 4000 military, insurgents, and civilians have died since the insurgency began in 1984, almost half of them in 1992 alone. More than 300 civilian deaths have been reported this year-85 of them in July 1992.

Underlying this violence lies the emotionally charged issue of Kurdish-Turkish relations. The Kurdish Workers Party (PKK), which has tried to claim the mantel of Kurdish leadership in Turkey, frequently uses terror to pursue its separatist goals-extortion and murder, kidnapping and assassination, targeting innocent civilians as well as security forces. PKK attacks on teachers have closed more than 1200 schools in southeastern Turkey. It has assassinated more than 50 local officials, most recently on September 21, when it murdered two Diyarbakir officials. On September 27, the PKK gunned down a prosecutor and a judge in Diyarbakir. In August, the PKK attacked a social club in Adana, killing a pregnant woman and wounding several others. The violence has driven many Kurds to seek refuge in western Turkey, but even such refugees are victimized-a 29 year old man was murdered in Izmir on September 3, reportedly after fleeing PKK recruitment efforts.

The government of Turkey is attempting to deal with this threat to its security, while maintaining a functioning, democratically-elected parliamentary system and a free press which criticizes the government and debates alternative futures in an unfettered fashion. Within their Parliament, representatives from the Kurdish areas of southeastern Turkey have formed a political group which outspokenly advocates cultural and economic rights for Turks of Kurdish origin.

As you know, the 1991 Human Rights Report discusses inadequacies in Turkey's human rights performance, especially torture and excessive use of force by security personnel. I have previously expressed our satisfaction that laws on thought crimes have been abolished, and are no longer a basis for arrests. In addition, political prisoners have been released. On the issue of torture, it had previously been our impression that, reflecting the policy of the new government, the trend was in a favorable direction. Recent reports, however, indicate that allegations of torture have not diminished, and torture may have actually increased.

Parliament has failed to move forward with a package of judicial reforms which would address many of our concerns over human rights protection. The reform program, by limiting pre-trial detention and providing those accused access to legal counsel, could significantly improve this situation. President Ozal vetoed the bill because he believed it would hamper investigations and operations against terrorists and their sympathizers. We have been assured that the government intends to pass this law in the next two weeks.

Clearly, part of the problem of southeastern Turkey is economic. For decades that part of the country has been neglected with the result that it has been economically deprived and is far less developed than the western part of the country. The GOT has promised to address these inequities with institutional reforms and development programs for the region. Unfortunately, the upsurge in violence over the past year has reached the point where these reforms have been set aside.

The Turks are also addressing the PKK problem directly, by using their security forces to root out PKK strongholds. There is no question that the Turkish government is uncompromising on the issue of separatism, as is

every other country in the region. We strongly support Turkey's territorial integrity, and that of Iraq. The Government of Turkey has consistently said that its Kurdish population is free to express itself politically within the established parliamentary system. We support the many efforts of Turkish Kurds to work through the Parliament and other legitimate institutions; it is vital that those institutions be sufficiently flexible to allow the full expression of concerns of all Turkish citizens.

We must not forget that there are Kurds willing to oppose the PKK and its methods. The Kurdish leaders of northern Iraq have met with Turkish officials about the problem of PKK bases in Iraq, and have said they will no longer tolerate PKK activities from Kurdish-controlled areas. We are in touch with these leaders, who are committed to a united Iraq. Within the context of maintaining Iraq's territorial unity, we, the Turks, and other allies continue to work to maintain freedom from repression for all the people of northern Iraq. Turkish cooperation remains a vital ingredient for the astonishing humanitarian success of Operation Provide Comfort. We will continue to work with both Turks and Iraqi citizens in the difficult days that lie ahead in order to build a stable peace, within establish borders for all the citizens of that troubled region. In an area where we have important interests-in the Middle East, the Balkans, the Caucasus and Central Asia-Turkey is emerging as a regional power. We seek to cooperate with Turkey in these areas.

It is also clear that third-world countries are supporting PKK activities. We are working with Turkey in its efforts to end the support this group gets from other states.

At the same time, and in the spirit of our long friendship with Turkey, we remain uncompromising in our defense of the human rights of all Turkish citizens. We are particularly concerned by the frequency of reports of extrajudicial killings and torture. We will expand our dialogue with the Turkish government on the subject of human rights. Believing that the rule of law and the fight against terrorism must be pursued simultaneously, we have urged the Turks to pass and implement urgently needed reforms which would protect the human rights of all Turkish citizens. Turkey's battle against the PKK is one in which we are not directly involved, but in which we clearly have a stake. We will cooperate with the Turks in reminding third-world countries that it is unacceptable that they harbor terrorist camps from which attacks are mounted on a friend.

In summary, the deep-rooted economic, political and security problems of southeastern Turkey must be addressed in reinforcing fashion. We support Turkey's democratic parliamentary system. We applaud its willingness to allow these problems to be discussed openly in a free press. As always, we deeply regret the loss of life, often innocent, as a result of the cycle of terror and violence.

128.

[October 8, 1992 (Senate), pp. 17763-66]

THE FOREIGN RELATIONS COMMITTEE'S RECORD IN THE 102D CONGRESS AND ITS AGENDA FOR THE 103D

Mr. PELL. Mr. President, last week the Senate gave its advice and consent to the START Treaty and approved a House-Senate conference report on aid to the countries of the former Soviet Union. These actions are the most significant achievements of the Foreign Relations Committee during the 102d Congress. Today, I would like to review that record and to discuss how the committee and the Senate as a whole can build on the record of the past 2 years in the 103d Congress.

Mr. President, this Congress has coincided with extraordinary events in the world. At the beginning of the Congress, we had great hopes for a new world order. In some ways, the results far exceeded our expectations, and in other ways, the new world order has proved bitterly disappointing. The Persian Gulf war which entailed the very first and probably most difficult decision of this Congress gave us both high hopes and keen disappointments. That war liberated Kuwait with very low coalition casualties. But it also ended

with Saddam Hussein still in power bent on the destruction of his Kurdish and Shi'a populations and still determined to acquire nuclear and other weapons of mass destruction.

At the beginning of this Congress, the Foreign Relations Committee prepared for the Senate vote on going to war to liberate Kuwait. It was a tough vote for every Member in this Chamber, and I was deeply impressed by the seriousness with which all Senators made and explained their votes. I believe our committee played an important role in framing the issues for that historic debate.

After the end of the war, the committee reflected on the policy errors that preceded Saddam Hussein's invasion of Kuwait. Through the hearing process and staff investigations, the committee documented the ill-founded assumptions and mistaken policies that led to a war that might well not have occurred.

The committee was also deeply concerned with the catastrophe that threatened to overtake the Kurdish people. On the day that Desert Storm ended, the Foreign Relations Committee played host to a delegation of Kurdish leaders and learned of their plans to try to oust Saddam. We tried, without success, to persuade the administration to meet with the Kurds and, had they done so, the United States might have been better prepared to help the rebellion that followed a few days later. The committee sent its staff to collect firsthand information on the rebellion and, as a result, had some of the earliest information on the flight of the Iraqi Kurds to the mountains.

Also in the aftermath of Desert Storm, the committee sought to strengthen international law by legislation directing the administration to pursue war crimes actions against Iraq. This year the committee arranged for 14 tons of Iraqi secret police documents captured by the Kurds to be turned over and brought to the United States. This extraordinary archive of genocide is now in the custody of the committee and being held at the National Archives.

In 1991, the committee moved expeditiously to dispose of its regular legislative responsibilities. Under the leadership of Senators KERRY and BROWN, we enacted authorizations for the State Department, USIA, the Arms Control and Disarmament Agency, and the Board for International Broadcasting. This legislation contains many important innovations, and I am proud of our role in the creation of the Voice of American Kurdish service and in strengthening educational exchange programs. More recently, just last week in fact, the committee, acting on the advice of a prestigious advisory commission, approved legislation to create a Radio Free Asia to broadcast to China, Tibet, Vietnam, and Burma. The 102d Congress was not able to act on this legislation, but it will be a priority objective to enact it in 1993 . . .

129.

[October 9, 1992 (Extensions of Remarks), pp. 3095-96]

LEGISLATION TO WITHDRAW MOST-FAVORED-NATION STATUS FROM TURKEY
HON. ROBERT T. MATSUI
OF CALIFORNIA
IN THE HOUSE OF REPRESENTATIVES

Friday, October 9, 1992

Mr. MATSUI. Mr. Speaker, I rise today to introduce legislation to address the ethnic cleansing and human rights abuses in Turkey and Cyprus.

The United States and the world community have noted with alarm and have imposed sanctions regarding the ethnic cleansing in the former Republic of Yugoslavia. It is time that we and the rest of the world also focus attention on ethnic cleansing by Turkey in Turkey against its Kurdish and Greek minorities and in Cyprus against the Greek Cypriots.

The United States has never actively condoned Turkey's actions, but the simple fact is that money is fungible, and thus all of our military and economic aid to Turkey indirectly supports Turkey's ethnic cleansing actions against its Kurdish citizens who constitute a 20-percent minority and against the Greek Cypriots.

Unfortunately, Turkey has been involved in a reportedly consistent pattern of gross violations of internationally recognized human rights, and is in obvious violation of sections 116 and 502B of the Foreign Assistance Act of 1961, as amended. According to a *New York Times* editorial in April of this year,

> [T]urkish Kurds have been subject to systematic human rights violations including torture. The international community is morally bound to demand that Ankara cease [its] ugly repression of Kurdish civilians before it becomes genocide. (April 1, 1992.)

In Cyprus, the Turks still reportedly maintain 35,000 occupation troops and have brought 80,000 illegal colonists to Cyprus in violation of international law. While the U.N. has been sponsoring Cyprus talks, these talks were adjourned in mid-August until October 26, 1992, and are stalled. Turkey and Rauf Denktash, the Turkish Cypriot leader, have been the main obstacles to progress in those talks. According to a *New York Times* editorial on September 5, 1992, entitled "Ethnic Cleansing, Cypriot Style," "Rauf Denktash shredded all proposals for powersharing and justice for refugees." Talks may be resuming this month, but the simple fact is that Cyprus remains divided because no one is really pressing Turkey to withdraw its illegal occupational forces and illegal colonists.

At present, Representative GREEN and 64 colleagues have legislation pending which puts several conditions on United States foreign aid to Turkey. I believe that more stringent sanctions may also now be necessary so I am introducing legislation to withhold most-favored nation [MFN] treatment for Turkey. MFN status would be suspended so long as Turkey continues its ethnic cleansing by its massive violations of human rights of its Kurdish and other minorities, and so long as that nation continues to occupy Cyprus illegally and does not cooperate in the U.N.-sponsored talks.

I encourage my colleagues to join Representatives DOWNEY, PELOSI and me in sponsoring this important legislation. It is time to let the Turkish Government know that the aid spigot has closed and that trade sanctions will be used pending positive Turkish action to stop its ethnic cleansing actions and all human rights abuses.

130.

[January 05, 1993 (Extensions of Remarks), p. 69]

TURKEY'S SHAMEFUL RECORD ON HUMAN RIGHTS
HON. JOHN EDWARD PORTER
OF ILLINOIS
IN THE HOUSE OF REPRESENTATIVES

Tuesday, January 5, 1993

Mr. PORTER. Mr. Speaker, despite Turkey's best efforts to align itself with the Western world, including its application for membership in the European Community, and its stated desire to receive huge amounts of U.S. military and economic assistance it continues to maintain an unconscionable human rights record.

In fiscal year 1993, partly because of Turkey's horrendous treatment of its own people, its treatment of the Kurds, and its intransigent stance on reunification of the tiny island nation of Cyprus, Congress eliminated all military grant aid to Turkey.

The article reprinted below, which originally appeared in the January 5, 1993 *Washington Post*, ["The Cries that Haunt Turkey," by Jack Healey and Maryam Elahi] clearly outlines the types of abuse being perpetrated in Turkey and Prime Minister Demirel's refusal to address this essential issue in a meaningful way.

I join the authors of this article in calling on Turkey to adhere to internationally recognized standards of human rights and on President-elect Clinton to make clear to Prime Minister Demirel that he will oppose providing any assistance to Turkey until it dramatically improves its human rights record.

I commend this important article to Member's attention and urge all Members to op-

pose aid to Turkey until it substantially improves its shameful human rights record . . .

131.

[May 25, 1993 (Senate), pp. 6393-4]

KURDS

Mr. REID. Madam President, one of the things I remember well during my time here in the Senate is the debate that took place on this floor regarding President Bush's authority to allow American troops to go and thwart the efforts of Saddam Hussein. It was truly a proud moment of this body and our country.

We halted the aggression of a modern-day Stalin or Adolf Hitler. The problem is we cannot rest on our laurels with regard to Saddam Hussein.

I read in the *New York Times* yesterday-and I have heard numerous accounts-that Saddam Hussein is planning to attack the Kurds again in northern Iraq. Such an assault can begin as early as next week. We cannot let this happen.

A year ago, the Kurds held a democratic election. One of the people there to count the votes to make sure the vote was conducted fairly and properly was a former Governor of Nevada, Michael O'Callaghan.

I looked at the photographs he took while he was there. I have listened to him recount the stories of his days in the Kurdish areas of Iraq, where people on election day lined up for blocks and blocks, in spite of the threats from Saddam Hussein. They were willing to take a chance and vote, and they did; they now have a democratically elected government.

The United Nations, though, is planning to remove its minuscule peacekeeping force from northern Iraq, and they are planning to do it very soon. What kind of a message does this send to the madman, Saddam Hussein?

I believe, Madam President, that President Clinton and Secretary Christopher should instruct our Ambassador to the United Nations to encourage an increase in the forces, not tell them to leave. We must let Saddam Hussein know we are serious. We must let him know that he cannot get away with murder, as he has most of his adult life.

The United States has already made, as I have indicated, a large investment in this area. We have sacrificed American lives, equipment, and significant amounts of money.

If Saddam Hussein is allowed to invade, or encouraged to invade by our inaction, the entire region will be destabilized.

The *New York Times*, for example, reports:

"The Iraqi forces have moved long-range artillery, trucks, and tanks up to the front in the last few days," said Jabar Farman, Defense Minister for the Kurdish Government.

Kurds along the front line, which are subject to daily shelling and gunfire, wait nervously.

In nearby Awena, witnesses said Iraqi troops, in a March raid, mutilated and shot 17 people to death.

This, Madam President, is serious.

"The United Nations and America told us to come back, that it was safe," said Nadir Ali, a 22-year-old vegetable vendor. "But now it looks like we are being left alone, us against Saddam. There is nothing we can do in front of an Iraqi attack but run."

Madam President, the Turks and Iranians do not want, cannot support, and should not have to support 3.2 million Kurds who will leave in the face of violence from Saddam Hussein.

The Kurds are now low on supplies. The World Food Program and the United Nations have said their supplies are running low. Relief agencies are shutting down.

They are also dealing with a deteriorating infrastructure. Some of the pictures I talked about earlier are certainly graphic, illustrating how this old part of the world is falling apart in the light of the fact that they have had no ability to have a stable government due to the fact that Saddam Hussein continually harasses them. Roads, sewers, bridges, and power lines are all in trouble. There are shortages of basic materials for life.

According to reports, a teacher in northern Iraq makes $10 a month, yet a bag of rice costs $20. They are simply starving to death in front of us.

It is no wonder Saddam Hussein is moving his troops closer. Saddam Hussein is an expert at preying on the weak. He has done it, as I have indicated, his whole life. He did it when he was head of the secret police, where he killed and had killed thousands and thousands of people.

During Saddam Hussein's reign of terror in this region, hundreds and hundreds of villages were wiped out. We all can recount in our mind's eye the gas attacks, where little babies in their mothers' arms were found dead because this man of brutality, this sinister man, allowed gas attacks on these villages.

Are we going to stand by and let women and children flee into the bitter cold mountains? Are we going to allow this to happen again? We cannot allow this to happen. We must increase the U.N. presence, and we must send a message to Saddam Hussein that he cannot do this.

Last year, this body and the other body appropriated $70 million to aid the Kurds. Unfortunately, the Defense Department has refused to implement the plan we directed them to implement. This is a plan that included medical clinics, mobile grain silos, and automatic building machines which would allow these metal buildings to be put up very, very quickly.

We have focused attention, as we should, on 400 terrorists the Israelis expelled. We can see the pictures of them out in the desert air-400 terrorists. Should we not focus a little bit of attention on 3.2 million people who are trying to maintain a way of life they have maintained for over a thousand years? Are we going to turn our head?

I call upon Secretary Aspin to review this situation and take appropriate action.

In addition, we need to consider a winterization program and a long-term basic human needs program. This is the kind of message we should send to Saddam Hussein-that we support the Kurds and that we support democracy.

Unless we want to see the destruction, gas attacks, torture, and execution of people striving for democracy and a chance to live in peace, we had better do something about it. Humanity cannot let the modern-day Stalin flourish. Humanity must not let the modern-day Hilter exercise his sadistic brutality.

132.

[May 28, 1993 (Senate), pp. 6816-18]

WITH OUR HELP, THE KURDS CAN HELP THEMSELVES

Mr. PELL. Mr. President, in northern Iraq, where the Kurdish people have been freed for more than 2 years from the yoke of Saddam Hussein's oppressive rule, the Kurds have made remarkable advances in their quest to lead a normal life. It appears, however, that their success has not gone unnoticed in Baghdad, and reports indicate that the Kurds may once again face the prospect of an Iraqi invasion.

In April 1991, the world community was galvanized into action by the tremendous suffering of the Kurds who fled Iraq in the wake of a failed uprising against Saddam's Ba'athist regime. Motivated in part by our collective guilt for leaving the Kurds exposed for so long to Saddam's genocidal designs, the anti-Iraq coalition finally made a commitment to protect the Kurds. With the onset of Operation Provide Comfort, the allied effort to patrol the no-fly zone over northern Iraq, the Kurds found the necessary degree of protection to begin their drive toward self-sufficiency.

The Kurds' effort, which was chronicled recently in a *Wall Street Journal* piece by Geraldine Brooks ["Out of Harm's Way: For Kurds, at Least, "Safe Area" Designation Provides Protection," May 19, 1993], is both compelling and instructive. One theme of the article, which I shall submit for the RECORD upon the conclusion of my remarks, is that the Kurdish example might prove useful in the policy debate on Bosnia. Now that the United States and its allies are looking toward a strategy involving the use of safe havens in Bosnia, they could draw upon the experience of the safe haven effort in northern Iraq. I urge my colleagues to read the piece with some care.

At the same time, I do not wish to give the impression that the Kurdish issue is solved. As this week's news reports have shown, the Kurds are still at considerable risk of retribution from the Iraqi army. Iraqi troops are deployed in a threatening pattern, and harassment of Kurds and foreigners alike has increased. The Kurds have grown nervous and many international humanitarian organizations have pulled out of northern Iraq altogether. This is particularly troubling, given the fact that the Kurds are struggling under the weight of two embargos: The U.N. blockade of all of Iraq, and an additional Iraqi blockade on the Kurdish-held areas.

If an attack comes, it is likely to target the city of Sulaimaniya and its environs, which, although controlled and governed by the Kurds, is south of the 36th parallel, which marks the southern-most limit of the no-fly zone. Sulaimaniya has a population of 800,000; any attack would likely spark an exodus of refugees reminiscent of the Kurdish flights of 1987 and 1991.

An Iraqi attack, and the subsequent refugee flight, would be catastrophic. With the situation in Bosnia already diverting so much of our attention from the domestic agenda, the United States does not need another international crisis. We must act swiftly to prevent this from occurring.

First, the United States and its allies in Operation Provide Comfort must continue to affirm that they will not tolerate an attack on any Kurdish-held area, including the territory below the 36th parallel. This week the United States took a significant step in this regard, when Secretary of State William Christopher said the United States would enforce the U.N. resolutions "with great resoluteness."

I applaud the Secretary, as well as other State Department officials who underscored his warning and indicated that the United States would respond to attacks on Kurdish territory even south of the 36th parallel. If the buildup to the Persian Gulf war demonstrated one thing, it is that Saddam Hussein is capable of making the wrong decision when faced with the least bit of uncertainty. Our allies must be encouraged to follow Secretary Christopher's lead, so that Saddam Hussein understands the scope of allied resolve and avoids making yet another colossal misjudgment.

Second, the United States must press the international community to reiterate its commitment to protect and assist the Kurds. U.N. Security Council Resolution 688, adopted April 5, 1991, codified international support for the protection of Iraq's minorities. The Security Council should be convened to demonstrate a continued sense of purpose, perhaps through the adoption of an updated resolution that explicitly provides for the protection of Kurdish-held areas south of the no-fly zone. The Security Council should also consider a partial lifting of the U.N. blockade for the Kurdish-held areas in northern Iraq, provided there is a verifiable commitment from the Kurdish leaders not to trade with Baghdad.

Third, the world must endorse the Kurdish drive to reach self-sufficiency. The Kurds are more than willing to wean themselves off of international aid and protection, but they need a little help before they are able to do so. The Kurdish-held areas, for instance, are endowed with significant oil reserves. With the provision of a refinery capability, international donors can help the Kurds begin to pay their own way. In addition, the Kurds have made tremendous strides in developing a unified army and police force. With the provisions of some additional financial assistance, the Kurds can begin to take on responsibility for their own self-defense.

None of these steps would require substantial new commitments from the United States or its allies; in fact, quite the contrary. These steps are designed to help the Kurds stand on their own two feet, where they will be prepared to assume a prominent place in a federated, post-Saddam Iraq. By implementing these cost-effective steps now, we can avoid having to deal with the consequences of another Iraqi attack and refugee crisis later.

I ask unanimous consent that the *Wall Street Journal* article, "Out of Harm's Way," be included in the RECORD at this point.

There being no objection, the article was ordered to be printed in the RECORD, as follows: . . .

133.

[June 30, 1993 (Senate), p. H4280]

ASSISTING THE KURDS

(Mr. BILBRAY asked and was given permission to address the House for 1 minute and to revise and extend his remarks.)

Mr. BILBRAY. Mr. Speaker, as we speak Kurds and Kurdistan are suffering. We pledged to help the Kurds. We brought aid into them, humanitarian aid, but the boycott that Saddam Hussein has established against the Kurds is stifling them and strangling them.

We approved $15 million in aid for the Kurds, but bureaucracy has tied that money up. Saddam Hussein has abolished the 25 dinardo that was the only currency of large amounts that the Kurds had. They cannot even buy the products from their farmers to feed the people, and unless the United States does something rapidly, Kurdistan will turn into a starving field, and we will see that same humanitarian airlift be needed to be done for lots more than the $15 million.

I ask the administration, the Department of State to do something to help the Kurds. Lift the boycott against northern Iraq and the Kurdistanish areas and help the Kurds to establish themselves as an independent body, autonomous body in that area. If not, the Kurds will starve this winter again.

134.

[July 30, 1993 (Senate), p. S9972]

IRAQI BOMBING PUTS KURDS AT RISK

Mr. PELL. Mr. President, Iraq is once again in the forefront of the news. Yesterday, United States warplanes fired missiles on Iraqi antiaircraft positions, possibly after being illuminated by Iraqi radar. Earlier, an Iraqi plan to assassinate President Bush while he was in Kuwait was confirmed by United States intelligence, and the United States retaliated with missile attacks on Iraqi intelligence headquarters.

Yet Saddam Hussein again seems to be pounding his chest in Baghdad; unfortunately, the Iraqi Kurds could well be his next victims.

In March 1991, in the aftermath of the Persian Gulf war, the Kurds rose up against Saddam Hussein to reclaim a centuries-old homeland which had been rendered unlivable by his regime. In April, a renewed Iraqi onslaught sent the Kurds fleeing for cover to the mountainous Turkish border region. Thousands of Kurds, and especially those most vulnerable, the children, perished from hunger and exposure.

As it had in years past, the suffering of the Kurds attracted the attention of the world. This time, under U.S. leadership, the allied coalition Operation Provide Comfort supplied the Kurds with the protection and provisions needed to begin to rebuild and recover. It has provided for the protection of human rights and the growth of democracy in Iraqi Kurdistan, including the first truly democratic elections in the Middle East, aside from those in Israel.

But these are desperate days for the Kurds. Despite the allied air cover, there are now more than 100,000 Iraqi troops massed south of the allied-protected safe haven. Since July 1991, when the last of the allied ground troops pulled out, AID workers have been the only expatriate ground presence. Attacks directed against them have prompted one group, Doctors Without Borders, to withdraw its physicians to protest the Iraqi Government's determination to get rid of all independent witnesses.

The face-off with Saddam continues today, north of the 36th parallel. It is possible that Saddam Hussein will attack the Kurds in response to the recent flareups. It is evident that his forces are willing and able to do so.

President Clinton's authorization of the Tomahawk missile attack on Baghdad sent the right message to Saddam. The next message should say to Saddam, in terms he understands, that our commitment to the democratic aspirations of the Kurds is real, not merely a sympathetic reaction to television images, and not postwar bravado.

When the Security Council meets in September, the United States should seek, as a matter of priority, a United Nation resolution that would reaffirm protection of Iraq's Kurdish and other minorities.

The United States with its coalition partners should seek an indefinite extension of the present air cover, and provide financial assistance to enable the Kurds to defend themselves and AID workers.

We need also look for ways to assist the economic development of Iraqi Kurdistan which, like Saddam's Iraq, remains subject to the United Nations embargo. A selective lifting of the economic sanctions for Iraqi Kurdistan would increase its access to world markets, open a way round Saddam's worsening internal blockade, and provide some insurance against Saddam's sabotage of the Kurdish economy.

Mr. President, the Senate Foreign Relations Committee recently approved the Foreign Relations Authorization Act, fiscal years 1994 and 1995. That act contains an amendment I authored concerning United States policy toward the Iraqi Kurds; in my view it outlines the type of long-term, cost-term, cost-effective approach that we should adopt towards Kurdistan. I ask unanimous consent that the amendment be printed in the RECORD at this point.

There being no objection, the amendment was ordered to be printed in the RECORD, as follows:

Sec. 709. UNITED STATES POLICY CONCERNING IRAQI KURDISTAN.

(a) FINDINGS.-The Congress finds that-

(1) The international community, pursuant to United Nations Security Council Resolution 688, and with the continuation of Operation Provide Comfort, support the protection of Iraq's Kurdish and other ethnic and religious minorities;

(2) Notwithstanding the international community's resolve, certain areas of Iraqi Kurdistan remain at risk of an Iraqi invasion;

(3) Despite the threat of an Iraqi invasion, the Kurds, along with other minority ethnic and religious groups, have initiated a drive toward self-sufficiency, including-

(A) holding free and fair democratic elections to establish a parliament, which supports Iraq's territorial integrity and the transition to a unified, democratic Iraq,

(B) planning for an administering public services,

(C) reconstructing and rehabilitating the basic infrastructure of Iraqi Kurdistan, and

(D) establishing unified police and security forces;

(4) Despite the provision of substantial international humanitarian assistance, and despite the fact that the United Nations blockade on Iraq contains exceptions for humanitarian-related items, the inhabitants of Iraqi Kurdistan still face difficulties because of an internal Iraqi government blockade;

(5) the Kurds and other ethnic and religious minorities, with appropriate additional support, would have the ability to meet their goal of self-sufficiency and move beyond the need for international assistance.

POLICY.-It is the sense of the Congress that the President should-

(1) take steps to encourage the United Nations Security Council-

(A) to reaffirm support for the protection of all Iraqi Kurdish and other minorities pursuant to Security Council Resolution 688, and

(B) to consider lifting selectively the United Nations embargo on the areas under the administration of the democratically-elected leadership of Iraqi Kurdistan, subject to the verifiable conditions that-

(i) the inhabitants of such areas do not conduct trade with the Iraqi regime, and

(ii) the partial lifting of the embargo will not materially assist the Iraqi regime,

(2) Continue to advocate the transition to a unified, democratic Iraq,

(3) take steps to design a multilateral assistance program for the people of Iraqi Kurdistan that supports their drive for self-sufficiency through the provision of-

(A) financial and technical aid through the democratically-elected Kurdish administration to enable the exploitation of natural resources such as oil, and

(B) financial assistance to support the legitimate self-defense and security needs of the people of Iraqi Kurdistan, and

(4) take steps to intensify discussions with the Government of Turkey, whose support and cooperation in the protection of the people of Iraqi Kurdistan is critical, to ensure that the stability of both Turkey and the entire region are enhanced by the measures taken under this section.

135.

[February 10, 1994 (Extensions of Remarks), pp. 171-72]

UNITED STATES POLICY TOWARD TURKEY
HON. LEE H. HAMILTON
OF INDIANA
IN THE HOUSE OF REPRESENTATIVES

Thursday, February 10, 1994

Mr. HAMILTON. Mr. Speaker, I wish to draw to the attention of my colleagues a recent exchange of letters with the Department of State regarding United States policy toward Turkey and Turkish efforts to combat the insurgency of the Kurdistan Workers' Party [PKK] in the southeastern part of the country. This exchange was prompted by a VOA editorial late last year on United States policy toward the situation in southeast Turkey.

In a number of respects, the situation in Turkey appears to be worsening in recent months. The economic situation has deteriorated. The government's military offensive in the southeast against the PKK is not making much progress despite recent Turkish cross-border bombing in Iraq and Iran against PKK strongholds.

As a key friend and NATO ally of the United States, the situation in Turkey is of intense United States interest. It is in our interest and in the interest of the United States-Turkish relationship to ensure that Turkey successfully resolve the problems in the southeast. Military force alone will not solve this problem. A political and social solution is critical to the long-term resolution of the situation of the Kurds in southeast Turkey.

The Secretary of State,
Washington, January 15, 1994.
Hon. LEE. H. HAMILTON,
Chairman, Committee on Foreign Affairs, House of Representatives.

Dear Mr. Chairman: Thank you for your December 7 letter expressing concern about U.S. policy toward Turkey and Turkish efforts to combat the insurgency of the Kurdistan

Workers' Party (PKK) in the southeastern part of the country. I apologize for the delay in our reply.

You are correct that the situation in the southeast is deteriorating, primarily because the PKK has accelerated its terrorist campaign over the past six months. Increasing PKK attacks have involved acts of murder and extortion against innocent civilians. The PKK has kidnapped foreign tourists, including a young American who was held for seven weeks late last year. PKK terrorism also has an international dimension. Last fall's spate of terrorist attacks in several European capitals led Germany to ban the organization.

We also share your concerns about human rights violations committed by Turkish forces in the southeast. There are reports of significant human rights violations, including extrajudicial killings and torture, committed by the Turkish military in its counterterrorism campaign.

Our Post-Cold War policy toward Turkey is evolving away from an emphasis on security toward a broader bilateral partnership to more fully develop our economic ties. Our concern for Ankara's security nevertheless remains an integral part of U.S. policy, given Turkey's strategic importance. Within that context, the U.S. supports Turkey in its fight against terrorism. At the same time, we continue to urge Turkey's leaders to seek political and social solutions to the problem of their Kurdish citizens in the southeast, and to prevent violations of human rights in its military campaigns. The President addressed these issues during Prime Minister Ciller's visit to Washington in October. Assistant Secretary Oxman reiterated our message to Mrs. Ciller as well as Turkish military leaders during the visit last month to Ankara.

The November 13 Voice of America editorial to which you refer in your letter was prepared by USIA and was approved by the Department's Office of Southern European Affairs. The editorial's condemnation of terrorism by the PKK and the non-Kurdish Dev Sol organization accurately reflects U.S. policy as does its reference to Prime Minister Ciller's recognition that "lasting solutions to the problems of southeastern Turkey will be found in economic and political initiatives, not simply through security measures." It is important to note that this editorial's focus on terrorism was prompted in part by the PKK's terrorist campaign in Western Europe in early November.

I agree with your views on the need for balance in both our policy and public statements. The November 13 editorial could have addressed our concerns about human rights. Overall, we believe that VOA's reporting is balanced. For example, a VOA editorial of June 18, 1993 (copy attached) addressed the need for political solutions in more detail.

Regarding your concern about future U.S. military assistance to Turkey, the principal goal of our transfers of excess defense articles is to strengthen the defense of a NATO ally. We assess each request for the transfer of defense material in light of our broader security interests in the region, and we monitor the use of EDA equipment through reports from our military and diplomatic representatives in Turkey, as well as from the press and non-governmental organizations. We will continue to consult with Congress before undertaking sensitive transfers.

I appreciate having your views about Turkey's need to adopt a more flexible approach to the problems in the southeast and to correct human rights abuses. Please be assured that we will continue to urge the Turks publicly and privately to balance the need to fight terrorism with the equally important goals of seeking a political solution and protecting human rights.

With best regards,
Sincerely,
Peter Tarnoff,
Acting Secretary.

————

Date—June 18, 1993,
Type—Editorial,
Number—0-05443,
Title—U.S.-Turkey Partnership,
CONTENT—THIS IS THE SECOND OF TWO EDITORIALS BEING RELEASED FOR BROADCAST JUNE 18, 1993.

Anncr: Next, an editorial reflecting the views of the U.S. Government.

Voice: Secretary of State Warren Christopher recently visited Turkey, a long-time friend and ally of the United States. With more than fifty million people. Turkey is a strategically located military and economic power. And with a democratic, secular government, this predominantly Muslim country is also a bridge between Europe and the Middle East.

In his meetings with President Suyleman Demirel and other Turkish officials, Secretary of State Christopher discussed the strengthening of political, military and economic ties between the U.S. and Turkey. He announced that the U.S. will transfer fifty-nine million dollars' worth of surplus military equipment to Turkey. It was also announced that Turkey will purchase two hundred seventy-seven million dollars' worth of helicopters and aircraft parts and supplies from the U.S.

In addition to discussing diplomatic ties, Secretary of State Christopher stressed the need for continued improvement in Turkish human rights practices, particularly in regard to Turkey's large Kurdish minority. The U.S. has often pointed out to the Turkish government that the rights of the Kurds , like those of all citizens, must be fully respected. The U.S. has been encouraged by recent steps by the Turkish government toward more respect for the human and cultural rights of the Kurds.

Unfortunately, the situation of Turkey's Kurds has been harmed by the violent actions of the Kurdish Workers Party, or PKK, a Marxist-Leninist group established in the mid-1970s. The PKK has received aid from Iran, Syria and Iraq, and has carried out terrorist attacks in Turkey, as well as throughout Western Europe. Last month, the PKK ambushed and killed a group of Turkish soldiers in Bingol province in eastern Turkey. This savage action ended a two-month-old PKK cease-fire and appeared to be intended as a provocation to stop the process of political accommodation that the Turkish government had been considering. Despite the renewed PKK terrorism, the Turkish government has decided to move forward with an offer of limited amnesty for some PKK members. The U.S. welcomes this move. The long-term solution to the problems

in southeastern Turkey must be found through political, not military, means.

As Secretary of State Christopher noted, Turkey is "a strong regional power, which can be a positive force in the peaceful settlement of regional disputes." Turkey played a major role in the international effort to reverse Iraq's invasion of Kuwait. In addition, Turkey supports the international community's efforts to bring humanitarian relief to the people of northern Iraq, who are blockaded by the Baghdad government. More recently, Turkey has worked with the U.S. and Russia to try to end the conflict between Armenia and Azerbaijan. For these and other reasons, as Secretary of State Christopher said, the U.S. looks forward to an "expanded partnership" with Turkey.

Anncr: That was an editorial reflecting the views of the U.S. Government.

————

Date: November 13, 1993
Type: Editorial
Title: Terrorism Against Turkey and the West
Content: This is the Only Editorial Being Released for Broadcast November 13, 1993

Anncr: Next, an editorial reflecting the views of the U.S. Government.

Voice: Of the democratic nations threatened by international terrorism few have been hit harder than Turkey. Terrorists recently attacked Turkish citizens and interests across Western Europe. The attacks killed one person and wounded twenty-three in cities in Germany, Switzerland, Britain and Denmark. In June, a similar campaign of murder and bombing was launched against Turkish citizens in six European nations.

One of the groups that has waged a war of terrorism against Turkey in recent years is the Kurdistan Workers Party, or PKK, which poses a growing threat to U.S. interests in Turkey. This terrorist group is composed primarily of Turkish Kurds seeking to establish a Marxist state in southeastern Turkey. Established in the mid-1970s, the PKK has carried out numerous attacks inside Turkey and has escalated its attacks on Turkish interests in Western Europe and against rival Kurdish groups. The PKK has received aid and safe-haven from Syria, Iran, and Iraq, and has used training camps in Lebanon's Syrian-controlled Bekaa Valley.

Competing with the PKK in terrorist murder and destruction is Devrimci Sol, or Dev Sol. Formed in 1978 as a splinter faction of the Turkish People's Liberation Front, Dev Sol espouses a Marxist ideology, is intensely xenophobic and is virulently anti-American and anti-NATO. Financed chiefly by robbery and extortion, Dev Sol terrorists have attacked Turkish officials, foreign businessmen and NATO military officers and bombed dozens of Western diplomatic, commercial, and cultural facilities. The group claimed responsibility for killing two American contractors and attempted to kill a U.S. air force officer in 1991. Dev Sol was responsible for two rocket attacks against the U.S. consulate in Istanbul in 1992.

Like the PKK, Dev Sol has failed in its effort to intimidate the government of Turkey through a campaign of arson, kidnapping, and murder. To its credit, Turkey has refused to negotiate with terrorists or concede to the demands. Prime Minister Tansu Ciller recently reaffirmed her government's determination to eradicate the "terrorist plague" that has afflicted the people of Turkey. At the same time, Prime Minister Ciller has made it clear that lasting solutions to the problems of southeastern Turkey will be found in economic and political initiatives, not simply through security measurers.

The U.S. condemns the most recent acts of terrorism directed against Turkey. The U.S. has an ongoing anti- terrorist training assistance program with Turkey, one of the largest such programs offered by the U.S. Respect for Turkey's territorial integrity and its right to self-defense against terrorist violence is long-standing U.S. policy. The U.S. calls on all nations to join Turkey in its fight against a common enemy—international terrorism.

Anncr: That was an editorial reflecting the views of the U.S. Government.

———

House of Representatives,
Washington, DC, December 7, 1993.
Hon. WARREN M. CHRISTOPHER,

Secretary of State, Department of State, Washington, DC.

DEAR CHRIS: I write regarding the situation in the predominantly Kurdish -area in southeast Turkey and U.S. policy toward Turkey on this issue.

By many accounts, the political and economic situation in southeast Turkey today is deteriorating. It is my impression that the Turkish government's response to this situation has been to focus primarily on a military solution to the problem. Efforts to eliminate the PKK organization through use of force over the last decade—and, more aggressively since December 1992—appear to have produced few positive results. The PKK maintains significant grassroots support within southeast Turkey and, by some accounts, this support is growing due, in part, to the methods employed by the Turkish gendarme and military against the civilian population.

I have serious concerns about U.S. policy toward Turkey on this issue. Specifically, I draw your attention to two issues: (1) a statement of U.S. policy presented in a Voice of America editorial on PKK terrorism broadcast on November 13, 1993; and (2) the provision of U.S. military equipment to Turkey for use in the military campaign in the southeast.

First, the VOA editorial addresses only one aspect of the Kurdish problem in Turkey—that of PKK terrorism. By presenting the issue in this way, it leaves the impression that the United States government views the problem in southeast Turkey as predominately, if not exclusively, one of terrorism. By endorsing eradication of the 'terrorist plague' and crediting Turkey's unwillingness to "concede to terrorist demands", the United States is seen as endorsing the tactics of the Turkish military to address the problems of southeast Turkey.

I would like to raise a number of questions about this VOA editorial and its implications for U.S. policy:

Who approved the text of the VOA editorial?

Does the language of the editorial represent U.S. policy on this issue?

Why was there no attempt in the editorial to balance Turkish concerns regarding terrorism with often-stated U.S. concerns regarding human rights in this area?

Why does the editorial fail to address more directly the central importance of opening political and economic opportunities and options for the Kurdish population in Turkey?

How has the message of this editorial been interpreted in Ankara?

Second, the United States continues to provide military hardware to Turkey for use in its military campaign in the southeast. I understand that there is consideration being given to providing additional U.S. military assistance for this purpose. I believe we should approach with great caution the question of further involving the United States in the conflict in southeast Turkey under present circumstances.

I understand the desire to be helpful to Turkey, a NATO ally and friend, on this difficult issue. I condemn the terrorist tactics employed by the PKK and I have no doubt that the PKK represents a serious security problem for the Government of Turkey. Nevertheless, I believe we must be careful, both in our statements and in our actions, not to be drawn into a Turkish Government military campaign that may not fully be consistent with broader U.S. interests in the region.

I appreciate your consideration of this matter. I look forward to a future dialogue with you on this matter.

> With best regards,
> Sincerely yours,
> Lee H. Hamilton,
> Chairman.

136.

[March 2, 1994 (Senate), pp. 2231-32]

TURKISH DEMOCRACY IMPERILED

Mr. DECONCINI. Mr. President, I rise today to voice concern over Turkey's political future. Because Turkey is an important friend and ally in an unstable region, this Congress and administration should be deeply troubled by increasing violence in southeast Turkey. This predominantly Kurdish region has become a virtual war-zone where basic human rights have been suspended and fear and death

mount. Since 1991, more than 5,000 have died in an increasingly brutal battle between Kurdish guerrillas, Moslem fundamentalists and Turkish security forces. The vicious cycle threatens to expand, tearing at the fabric of Turkish democracy and straining delicate regional relations. And while I have no doubt that Turkey's democratic institutions are currently stronger than ever, rumors of a coup have already surfaced in the Turkish press, stirring unpleasant memories of three such previous setbacks to democracy since 1960.

Since modern Turkey's establishment in 1923, Kurds, who presently comprise about 11 million of Turkey's 57 million population, have faced varying pressure to deny their cultural distinctiveness. While Moslem, they maintain distinct language and cultural forms. Through expressions of their Kurdish identity, civil disobedience, or at the extreme, open rebellion, Kurds have sought to promote and preserve their culture and rights. Since 1987, eight provinces where Kurds reside have withered under a state of emergency which authorizes a regional governor and the military to curb political, media and cultural activity.

In 1984, the Kurdish Workers Party [PKK] initiated a violent campaign in support of Kurdish autonomy. Funded in part by groups in Europe, the PKK operates from Syria, Iraq, Iran, and hideouts in Turkey and is considered a terrorist organization by the United States and most other governments. Recently, the group has targeted Turkey's tourist industry. Civilians in areas where the PKK operates often face a terrible choice between aiding the guerrillas and risking violent reprisal by Turkish security forces—or not helping and facing equally harsh PKK retribution. On the one hand, locals suspected of collaborating with Turkish authorities are executed by the PKK. On the other, security forces arbitrarily round up villagers and subject them to beatings, mass arrests, and intimidation. A particularly disturbing tactic, which has caused substantial hardship and displacement, has been the forced evacuation of hundreds of villages and the destruction of entire towns in response to alleged terrorist incidents.

While Turkey, and indeed all states, is entitled to protect their citizens from terrorism and to preserve the integrity of its borders, Turkey has also obligated itself to uphold basic human rights principles. Unfortunately, as the PKK steps up its attacks, civilians are also increasingly threatened by reactions of security forces, and indeed, legitimate rights of Turkey's Kurdish citizens are being denied under the mantle of combating terrorism. The violence is polarizing Turks and Kurds, creating an unprecedented level of fear and mistrust. Kurds, resentful of security abuses, become more supportive of Kurdish nationalism and the PKK. Turks, angered by the costs and brutality of terrorism, are increasingly intolerant of the legitimate rights of Kurdish citizens.

The Turkish Government's military efforts to address the Kurdish situation have only escalated tensions. Massive discontent has resulted in an increasing and unacceptable toll of innocent lives. The one-dimensional military approach stifles even moderate Kurdish political voices, enabling the PKK to gather support among a population weary of constant harassment and with no power or representation to put forward legitimate cultural and political aspirations.

The violent prelude to upcoming local elections has highlighted threats to the democratic process and underlined the inability of Kurds to gain political representation or exercise other basic rights. In the past 2 years, shadowy death squads have killed 70 members of the pro-Kurdish Democratic Party [DEP], which holds 18 of 450 seats in the Turkish Parliament, including a Member of Parliament. Twenty party offices have been bombed. Over 300 DEP election candidates have been arrested and changes in electoral laws—reportedly made on security grounds—have made it extremely difficult for voters in Kurdish regions to cast their ballots. On February 23, DEP members decided to boycott the March 27 elections. International human rights organizations and the European Parliament have announced intentions to send election observes to Turkey.

Mr. President, just yesterday the Turkish Parliament lifted the immunity of four DEP parliamentarians in order to prosecute them for the contents of speeches or writings. Two were detained outside parliament on charges which could bring the death penalty. Prosecutors want to charge a total of eight Kurdish parliamentarians. Such policies are contrary to basic principles of free speech and an affront to the rights of Kurds throughout Turkey. While Turkey remains a NATO ally and major recipient of U.S. military and economic assistance, this Congress and administration should not be deterred from voicing serious concerns over the deteriorating human rights situation and the Turkish Government's inability or unwillingness to constructively address abuses.

Mr. President, while there are no easy solutions to the complex Kurdish issue, fortunately some voices of moderation are heard among civilian policy makers who call for redressing Kurdish grievances and meeting Turkey's commitments to a society based on rule of law. Such voices have called for continued economic investment in the southeast; rescinding the state of emergency; abolishing the restrictive antiterror law and village guard system; reaffirming Kurdish cultural rights; and removing restrictions on Kurdish broadcasting, publishing and other forms of free speech. Major causes of frustration and discontent, which have swelled the ranks of the PKK, could be significantly alleviated by permitting Kurdish political and cultural expression, restoring civil and economic institutions and withdrawing soldiers from city streets and village. Such actions, in my view, could help establish the foundation of a more peaceful, prosperous, and stable Turkish democracy for all its citizens.

Last October, as Turkey's Prime Minister Ciller visited Washington, I joined the cochairman of the Helsinki Commission, Steny Hoyer, and a number of congressional colleagues on a letter suggesting that the Government of Turkey pursue political, as opposed to military, solutions to the Kurdish situation. Six months later, I am disappointed not to have received a reply to our views. Cochairman Hoyer discussed and passed the letter to a senior Turkish official who indicated a response would be forwarded. I would like to insert a text of that letter into the Record following my remarks, and reiterate my hope that a response will soon be forthcoming.

Meanwhile, as the violence escalates, I again urge the Turkish Government to use more carrot and less stick to address underlying roots of Kurdish discontent. The heavy-handed security presence has disrupted normal life and crippled economic viability in the southeast. The military approach drains Turkish coffers, strains relations with neighboring countries, and draws criticism from human rights observers worldwide. Members of the 53 State Conference on Security and Cooperation in Europe have been asked to consider sending official human rights monitor missions to Turkey, and given the present level of hostilities in the southeast, I believe such CSCE missions are warranted.

Mr. President, we in the United States often look with pride upon our heritage as a "melting pot" of ethnicity and culture. We should appreciate that Turkey has been a "melting pot" far longer. Tolerance and understanding, ingredients crucial to keeping such societies from boiling over, are in great need today in Turkey. Violence will certainly beget more violence and further imperil Turkish democracy. Support for the PKK will grow until the Government pursues political solutions and acts to protect the rights of all Turkey's citizens.

There being no objection, the letter was ordered to be printed in the RECORD, as follows:

October 14, 1993.

DEAR MADAME PRIME MINISTER: We respectfully offer our congratulations on your appointment as Prime Minister. We hope your term will be marked by peace and prosperity, and look forward to working with your government to strengthen the bonds of friendship which exist between our two governments and peoples.

As a NATO ally, trusted friend of the United States and signatory to the Helsinki Final Act, Turkey occupies a unique position between East and West. We appreciate that while developing its resources and society. Turkey has also proved committed to strengthening its democratic institutions and protecting and promoting human rights.

We understand that Turkey faces a difficult security situation, and has a legitimate need to counter the terrorist actions of the Kurdish Workers Party [PKK]. At the same time, we are deeply troubled by the apparent escalation of restrictive measures and government-sanctioned violence against Kurdish civilians in southeast Turkey.

The recent decision by the Turkish Constitutional Court to outlaw the People's Labor Party [HEP] and official attempts to suppress Kurdish publications and broadcasting indicate that free expression remains restricted for those who peacefully support the promotion and protection of Kurdish rights.

The unsolved assassinations of Kurdish leaders, human rights activists and journalists have created a climate of fear and mistrust of the government among Turkey's Kurds. The assassination of Mehmet Sincar, a member of Parliament, is a prominent reminder of the danger facing those who promote legitimate cultural and political rights for Kurds.

Under the mantle of combatting terrorism, Turkish government security forces are reported to have forcibly evacuated thousands of Kurdish civilians from their homes and destroyed hundreds of Kurdish villages. We believe this use of military extremism encourages other kinds of extremism and hinders development of moderate Kurdish political views and organizations.

The U.S. government clearly condemns acts of terrorism employed by any people, organization or government, and is against any action which threatens Turkey's stability and sovereignty. However, we also believe it is imperative that Turkey uphold the rights and freedoms of all its citizens, including those of Kurdish origin. In view of the spiraling levels of violence in southeast Turkey, it appears that a political solution, rather than continued reliance on military force, offers the best chance of reestablishing security and peace throughout Turkey and the region.

As friends and supporters of Turkey, we sincerely hope that you will be successful in addressing this critical issue.

Sincerely,

137.

[March 22, 1994 (Extensions of Remarks), pp. 507-08]

THE FUTURE OF DEMOCRACY IN TURKEY
HON. DAN BURTON
OF INDIANA
IN THE HOUSE OF REPRESENTATIVES

Tuesday, March 22, 1994

Mr. BURTON of Indiana. Mr. Speaker, there has been much discussion about the future of democracy in Turkey. In a March 14, 1994, Washington Times editorial, Turkey's Ambassador to the United States points out that Turkey's fight against the terrorist PKK should not be viewed as a threat to democracy. The Marxist-Leninist, PKK has murdered thousands of civilians, many of whom are Kurds who were unwilling to support their terrorist agenda, in an effort to carve a Kurdish state out of the sovereign territory of Turkey.

I also believe that it is important not to confuse Kurds who have been oppressed under the rule of Saddam Hussein in Iraq and those who reside in Turkey. As Ambassador Nuzhet Kandemir explains in his editorial, "Turkish citizens of Kurdish origin live throughout Turkey and participate without discrimination in all walks of life." "Kurds have served as presidents and prime ministers of the Republic of Turkey" and currently, "they serve in large numbers in Parliament," he adds. While it is natural to be sympathetic to the plight of Kurds in Iraq, I must emphasize that the terrorist activities of the PKK do not have the support of the great majority of Turkish citizens of Kurdish origin.

For those Members of Congress who want a realistic picture of PKK terrorism in Turkey, and who want to know about some of the positive steps which Turkey has taken to benefit its citizens of Kurdish origin, I highly recommend Ambassador Kandemir's editorial [See *The Washington Times*, March 14, 1994,

TURKEY HAS A RIGHT TO PROTECT ITS DEMOCRACY, by Nuzhet Kandemir].

Recent press commentary, such as Sen. Dennis DeConcini's (Op-Ed, March 8) has expressed anxiety about the future of democracy in Turkey. Democracy has been a rare, precious and often fragile institution throughout human history, so attentive concern for its preservation is always in order. But it is not correct to view. Turkey's fight against terrorist criminals as a sign of democracy in danger. On the contrary, true danger would be signified if a democratic government were unwilling or unable to protect its country's territorial integrity or its citizen's human rights from the depredations of a terrorist organization.

A much-misconstrued event has prompted some of the current concerns: The vote of the General Assembly of the Turkish Parliament on March 2 and 3 to lift the immunity of eight Turkish parliamentarians. The vote, taken pursuant to the legal process prescribed in the republic's constitution, occurred in connection with judicial investigations of charges that the eight individuals have engaged in activities against the country's constitutional democratic system and its territorial integrity. The issue is not the political views the parliamentarians have been expressing. None of the individuals have been arrested and none has been stripped of membership in the Parliament. The action regarding their immunity is consistent in principle with the immunity provisions of the U.S. Constitution (Article 1, sections 3 and 6).

The Turkish constitution provides that all citizens have the same political rights and civil liberties which they may exercise equally, without impediment, regardless of ethnic or religious background. Allegations that the immunities of the eight parliamentarians were lifted because of their pro-Kurdish politics are completely unfounded. Turkish citizens of Kurdish origin live throughout Turkey and participate without discrimination in all walks of life; this is a crucial fact that is widely and wildly misunderstood. Kurds have served as presidents and prime minister of the Republic of Turkey. They serve in large numbers in Parliament, belonging to a wide range of political parties. They enjoy full political representation, and all Turkish citizens, including the great majority of citizens of Kurdish origin, do not support Kurdish extremism.

Such extremism manifests itself most virulently in the violence perpetrated by the PKK, an antidemocratic, indeed Marxist-Leninist, terrorist organization. The violence aims at carving a Kurdish state out of the sovereign territory of Turkey, thereby undermining the peace and stability of the entire region. Since its inception in 1984, the PKK has based its operations on intimidation and extortion. After the Gulf War, the PKK increased its atrocities and intensified its attacks on the human rights of Turkish citizens of Kurdish and non- Kurdish origin. It has killed thousands of civilians, many of whom are Kurds whom the PKK claims to serve and represent. The PKK took full advantage of the post-war power vacuum in the areas of Iraq bordering Southeast Turkey, which became a breeding ground for terror. The U.N. Human Rights Commission, in its March 2 resolution, recognized that terrorist organizations perpetrate grievous human rights violations. It condemned such violations and asked its members to cooperate to fight terrorism, as required in a large number of international agreements and resolutions, including those of the Conference on Security and Cooperation in Europe (CSCE) and NATO.

The Turkish government has accelerated its reform programs for the southeast region. These programs—economic, social and political—have been severely hampered by PKK terror. But the government, operating within the rule of law, is determined to eradicate terror and to continue its reform programs for the region. Economic and social programs claim nearly 17.5 percent of Turkey's total investment capital for enormous development projects in the Southeast, such as the Southeastern Anatolia Project (GAP). GAP alone consumes the equivalent of $1.7 million daily (at 1992 exchange rates). Turkey invests in the southeast 13 times more than it collects in taxes from the region. In 1993, investment there was 1.6 times greater than investment in the Western regions.

Despite the challenges, democracy in Turkey remains strong. The Turkish democratic system is the foundation for existing open, secular, pluralistic society and an expanding free market economy. Since the republic's establishment, the Turkish people and their successive governments have dedicated themselves to furthering these values.

Supporting a strong democratic Turkey in a generally volatile region has long been recognized as an important interest of the United States. For over half a century, Turkey has been a staunch ally of the United States and NATO. In the evolving new world order after the collapse of Soviet communism, U.S.-Turkish bilateral relations are a major force for good in a vast region stretching from Central Asia through the Middle East to the Balkans. Turkey's heightened strategic importance at the epicenter of important geopolitical changes increases its potential to expand and deepen its "enhanced partnership" with the United States. Military and economic assistance to Turkey should be evaluated with respect to NATO requirements as an investment in bolstering Turkish democracy.

Turkey's local elections on March 27 will be conducted according to law, as appropriate for an open, free and democratic society, notwithstanding any attempts by terrorist organizations to poison the country's political climate. We are vigilant and have the wisdom not to play into the hands of those who would undermine Turkish democracy or damage Turkey's deep-rooted relations with its democratic friends and allies in the United States.

138.

[April 12, 1994 (House), pp. 2198-99]

THE CONTINUING TRAGEDY IN IRAQ

Mr. BILBRAY. Mr. Speaker, will the gentleman [Bonior] yield?

Mr. BONIOR. I yield to my friend, the gentleman from Nevada.

Mr. BILBRAY. Mr. Speaker, I agree with what the gentleman stated and the fact is that the suffering of the Iraqi people is the direct result of the callousness of their dictator. We also have the problem in Kurdistan, Iraqi Kurdistan, where the embargo that we placed against Iraq is being enforced by the United

Nations against the Iraqi Kurds, the people that are being protected by us north of the 36th parallel, and I think it is a shame that we do not lift the embargo to those people in that area that have certainly suffered the most along with the Shiites in the south from the oppression of this brutal regime.

Mr. Speaker, even over the last decade, he has gassed with nerve gas and mustard gas huge portions of that population. The Kurds can be self-sustaining, they certainly are not asking for independence from Iraq, but they are certainly asking for the help that we give them, that we lift the embargo to allow them to sustain themselves during this time of crisis.

Mr. Speaker, I commend the gentleman for bringing this to the President's attention and hopefully in the next bipartisan meeting, the gentleman will bring up the plight of the Kurds also who need desperately our help there in Iraq.

Mr. BONIOR. Mr. Speaker, I thank my colleague for his contribution, and let me assure him that I will in fact discuss the issue in its totality. We will make the case for that, that for those who are suffering because of lack of medicine and other basic essentials, we find ways through the efforts of humanitarian and religious organizations to get them the aid so they can sustain themselves and so they can in fact have the wherewithal when and if the time arises, to take their political place in opposition to Saddam Hussein in a strong way.

Mr. BILBRAY. Mr. Speaker, I thank the gentleman from Michigan.

Mr. BONIOR. Mr. Speaker, I thank the gentleman from Nevada, and I yield back the balance of my time.

139.

[May 17, 1994 (Senate), pp. 5849-50]

TURKISH DEMOCRACY? FREE MEHDI ZANA

Mr. DECONCINI. Mr. President, I am compelled to recount to this body an incident which reflects a growing and most disturbing trend by the Government of Turkey to restrict free speech on the Kurdish issue. As I speak today, I sadly recall similar statements I have made on behalf of political prisoners who spoke out and then suffered at the hands of authoritarian Communist rulers behind the iron curtain.

Last Friday, Mehdi Zana, a man whom I have met and for whom I hold deep respect, was jailed for 4 years for a speech he delivered at the European Parliament in October 1992. Mr. President, Zana is a man of honor and peaceful intentions who has struggled for more than 30 years for the cause of human rights in Turkey. He has already spent 15 years in jail and has been tortured because he refused to remain silent about the injustices visited upon his Kurdish brothers and sisters. Leyla Zana, his wife, is one of six Turkish parliamentarians who face the death penalty for statements they made in support of Kurdish rights.

Mr. President, I am frightened not only for the fate of the Zana family, but for the future of Turkish democracy itself. The situation in southeast Turkey has deteriorated to the point where violence has become the most common form of discourse between Turks and Kurds. It is a tragic irony that thousands of Turkish Kurds are presently being forced to seek refuge in northern Iraq—taking the reverse route of Iraqi Kurdish refugees who fled Saddam Hussein's war machine. Turkish security forces seem to be creating a buffer zone along the Iraqi border to prevent infiltration by the PKK and hundreds of villages have been destroyed and their inhabitants forced to flee—a pattern which has been compared to ethnic cleansing conducted by the Serbs in Bosnia.

Mr. President, as I have in the past, I once again condemn PKK terrorism. Terrorist violence is never, I repeat, never, a legitimate means of securing political objectives in a democratic state. I am acutely aware of the severity of the PKK threat, but firmly believe all of Turkey's Kurdish citizens cannot be labelled PKK supporters. The fight against terrorism must not be waged at the expense of the legitimate rights of all Turkish citizens.

Turkey's Kurds, whether in Istanbul or Diyarbakir, must be allowed to express their cultural identity and to participate in the political process.

Aside from my overriding human rights concerns, however, my major motivation for speaking out is that, given my belief that Turkey is a most valuable ally, I cannot remain silent as Turkey's Government pursues policies which have no hope of ending the violence. I am convinced that these policies further threaten democracy and regional stability. The $7 billion the Turkish Government spends each year to fight the PKK could be better used to address Turkey's serious economic woes. As a friend and supporter of Turkey, I have to express my frustration with the Government for not seeking a political solution to a crisis which cannot be solved by military means or crude attempts to restrict free speech.

Mr. President, yesterday, STENY HOYER and I, as Chairmen of the Helsinki Commission, sent a cable to Prime Minister Ciller urging the immediate release of Mehdi Zana. I wish to submit to the RECORD a copy of the appeal he delivered before the European Parliament which resulted in his 4-year jail sentence. Successive Turkish Governments have committed themselves to upholding numerous international human rights conventions which include free speech protections. The increasingly frequent practice of arresting those who speak out peacefully for Kurdish rights is an affront to democracy and violates Turkey's stated international commitments. What follows is the text of the speech which serves as the basis for Mehdi Zana's being in jail now as I speak. So again, Mr. President, I call for his immediate release, and urge my colleagues to follow suit.

The text follows:

October 26, 1992.
AN APPEAL FROM MEHDI ZANA TO
    THE EUROPEAN PARLIAMENT, TO
    ALL HUMAN RIGHTS ADVOCATES,
    AND TO THE PRESS

Ladies and Gentlemen, let me first heartily thank you for your presence here today at this press conference.

My name is Mehdi Zana. I am 52 years old. For 30 years I have fought for the recognition of the rights of the Kurdish people in Turkey. In spite of the fact that I was never involved in any act of violence, I had to spend 15 years of my life in Turkish prisons because of my opinions and pacifist struggle for my people. I am one of the few miraculous survivors of the sinister Diyarbakir prison where so many of companions died under torture. My eye-witness account of the unspeakably brutal and sadistic torture proceedings is included in the publication "Journal of Barbarity" currently being translated from Turkish to French. I owe my survival to the mobilization of public opinion, to NGOs and to the Western mayor colleagues in my favor.

I say colleagues, because I was mayor of Diyarbakir, the politico-cultural capital of Turkish Kurdistan. The population of this city which amounted to 400,000 inhabitants in 1977 had elected me mayor by direct universal suffrage. At that time, I practiced the trade of tailor and I was an independent activist. The military coup d'etat of September 1980 dissolved my municipal council. I was arrested and incarcerated only to be released in May 1991. Since then, I have again been arrested twice. At this time, I, like all other Kurds condemned of the "crime of separatism", am deprived of my political rights for the rest of my life. Such is democracy—Turkish style! Finally I must emphasize that while continuing to struggle pacifically for the recognition of the rights of 15 million Kurds of Turkey, I am not a member of any party or movement.

Thus, it is as an independent Kurdish activist, that I address myself to you and through you to public opinion to the conscience of the civilized world, so that a cry of alarm may be sent forth.

The Kurds of Turkey are experiencing at this time one of the most dramatic moments in their history. Our cities and villages have been systematically destroyed, our forests burned. Using military and economic means, Turkey has forced the Kurdish people to evacuate their ancestral lands. Girls and women of the villages are insulted and raped by Turkish soldiers. Homes are looted, Kurdish journalists and intellectuals are assassinated one after another in broad daylight. People arrested on the pretext of interrogation are tortured to death by barbaric methods. Prisons are filled with children and youth under 18. Legal and illegal state organizations known as counter-guerilla units or as special units have the authorisation to act freely as they please. They have the power of life and death over those questioned. The last measure taken by the National Security Council protects members of the security forces against prosecution for actions committed in the exercising of their functions and prohibits the press from reporting these incidents.

Our maternal language, Kurdish, still remains prohibited. Offenders are arrested and mistreated at police stations. One example among so many others, illustrates this prohibition de facto: barely 15 days ago in Diyarbakir, the security forces intervened in the wedding ceremony of a Kurdish lawyer, Fikret Akias, broke the Kurdish musical instruments and arrested several people including 7 lawyers.

State television by way of propaganda programs incites the Turkish people to rise up against the Kurdish population established in Anatolia. The ideas which suggest a ban on doing business with the Kurds, on furnishing them with work have appeared on these openly distributed tracts. The latest violent events against the Kurds in the city of Fethiye in the West of the country give evidence of the severity of the situation. Chased by the violence perpetrated in their region, the Kurdish population no longer knows where to shelter themselves, where to live in security. In fear they wait to die at any moment. The risk of a Kurdish-Turkish racial war is growing larger every day.

Whole hours would not suffice were I to begin to enumerate for you the cases of assassination, of torture and destruction which I have witnessed, the tragedy which my people are experiencing even as I stand before you. In the press kit, you will find numerous facts, figures and eye-witness accounts on this subject.

Is it still possible to imagine that at the dawn of the twenty-first century, a people can still be deprived of the use of its own mother tongue, of the expression of its identity?

The democratic promises, the speeches on the respect of human rights which thoroughly dominated the October 1991 legislative elections, over the course of moving electoral meetings, promises for the respect of the rights and demands of the Kurdish people made by the governmental coalition of the DYP and the SHP which emerged from the elections, which had worried over the massive support of Kurdish voices for the candidates of the HEP party, gave birth to real hope. The current Prime Minister Demirel, barely 5 days after his nomination, publicly affirmed during a televised speech which surprised everyone, that henceforth Turkey would recognize the Kurdish reality in the East and West of the country, that it would establish an egalitarian policy permitting a common life between the Kurdish and Turkish people.

Mr. Demirel also displayed his faith in a henceforth unrestricted democracy and his willingness to put an end to all anti-democratic laws, to develop a new Constitution which would take contemporary reality and values into consideration.

Since then, not only has not a single anti-democratic law inherited from the military junta and aiming to wipe out the rights of the Kurdish people been abolished, but on the contrary, the promulgation of new repressive laws almost inspire a nostalgia for the military regime.

At this time in Turkey not a single investigation nor trial is underway concerning so many journalists and intellectuals, against the forces which destroyed and set fire to cities such as Sirnak, Cizre, Kulp, Vario and so many others which you will find listed in the press kit.

Meetings on democracy and on human rights have been prohibited in the Kurdish provinces. Censorship rages in full force to prevent the circulation of independent news on the barbarity of the war running rampant in Kurdistan. Not a single journalist is authorized to go to the scene of army operations. Even the parliamentarians of the region are denied the right to approach the regions concerned.

A new administrative measure has just transferred the prerogatives of the Regional Prefect to the military. Kurdistan is now governed by an undeclared State of siege administration and completely left to the good well of the army.

About three weeks ago, the IFHR delegation which visited Turkish Kurdistan was not authorised to go to the cities of Sirnak and Cizre. They will be able to testify to the situation themselves.

I sincerely believe that the Turkish regime never opted for democracy. This notion remains only in the speeches destined to mislead the civilised world. If we make a careful assessment of the current government over the past year, we will not find any arrangements made to further the respect of human rights.

I send forth publicly an appeal to all those who are enamoured of liberty and democracy to act to stop the Turkish government's policy which aims at the pure and simple extinction of the Kurdish people, to act in order to finally permit this people to live in dignity and in peace.

I invite journalists, parliamentarians, NGOs to investigate on the spot, to pierce the wall of silence which surrounds the destruction of my country and my people.

140.

[May 23, 1994 (Extensions of Remarks), p. 1022]

**TURKEY'S LATEST DEMOCRATIZA-
TION PACKAGE
HON. STENY H. HOYER
OF MARYLAND
IN THE HOUSE OF REPRESENTA-
TIVES**

Monday, May 23, 1994

Mr. HOYER. Mr. Speaker, on May 18 Turkey's coalition government unveiled a package of reforms intended to liberalize political activity. The program includes revisions of the constitution, and 62 amendments to existing laws or new pieces of legislation. A major thrust of the package aims to remove obstacles that bar political activity by labor unions, associations, students and academics, which were imposed under military rule. The reforms also include creation of an Undersecretary's Office for Human Rights. The package is intended to improve Turkey's human rights image abroad and help prepare for closer links with the European Union when a customs union enters into force in 1995.

Mr. Speaker, this latest initiative represents a significant attempt to strengthen Turkish democracy. It comes at a time when Turkey faces major economic difficulties and an increasingly violent confrontation with Kurdish militants. I would point out however, that previous democratization packages have either failed to be adopted by the Turkish parliament, or have not been implemented. Given the seriousness of the problems facing the government, I hope that this package is swiftly approved and fully implemented.

Mr. Speaker, while I do not wish to detract from this positive initiative on the part of Turkey's ruling coalition, I am obligated to point out that democratization is seriously undermined when individuals are arrested for nothing more than exercising freedom of speech. Six Turkish parliamentarians, Hatip Dicle, Orhan Dogan, Sirri Sakik, Leyla Zana, Ahmet Turk, and Mahmut Alinak are facing the death penalty for non-violent pro- Kurdish expressions. Last week, Mehdi Zana, an independent Kurdish rights activist was also jailed for speech crimes. Mr. Speaker, a key benchmark of democracy is a tolerance of all non-violent expression and a free exchange of ideas—however unpopular they might be. Despite the intentions of those who crafted Turkey's elaborate new reform proposals, Turkey's commitment to democracy will continue to be questioned as long as political prisoners remain incarcerated for simply expressing their beliefs, however unpopular.

141.

[June 23, 1994 (Senate), pp. 7588-89]

ADDITIONAL STATEMENTS

**TURKISH DEMOCRACY: ONE MORE
STEP TOWARD THE ABYSS**

Mr. DECONCINI. Mr. President, I am compelled once again to voice my grave concerns over the state of affairs in Turkey. Were I not convinced that Turkey is one our Nation's most important allies, I would not express such frustration when the government contravenes its own constitution and international human rights commitments. Last Thursday, June 16, when Turkey's highest court banned the pro- Kurdish Democracy Party [DEP], and kicked 13 DEP members out of Parliament because of statements they made, my concern and frustration reached new heights.

The 13 duly elected members of Turkey's legislature have been removed from Parliament because of a party communique issued last year appealing for a peaceful solution to the Kurdish problem. Five deputies, who have been jailed since early March without being indicted, face the death penalty for speaking out for the rights of Turkey's Kurdish citizens. Six others have fled Turkey and, I am informed, will seek political asylum in Belgium. Two others face imminent arrest in Turkey. Mr. President, I have met with some of these individuals and others now in Turkish jails for simply expressing their views, and I am appalled. Mr. President, what kind of democracy finds its own legislators either in prison or fleeing arrest to seek political asylum?

A perhaps unintended consequence of the court decision relates to constitutional requirements that by-elections be held when 24 vacancies occur in the 450-seat Parliament. If the four Kurdish deputies who resigned from DEP before legal action was taken should leave Parliament, it would appear that elections would have to be held within 3 months. Mr. President, I want to make it clear from the outset, that should such elections take place, and it seems likely, our Government and the many non-governmental election monitors, should be prepared to send observers to ensure that international standards are met. Furthermore, in light of recent developments, the Helsinki Commission, of which I am chairman, will, in upcoming meetings of the Conference on Security and Cooperation in Europe [CSCE], press for official CSCE missions to be sent to Turkey to monitor the deteriorating rights situation.

Mr. President, what is most alarming about the deteriorating rights situation in Turkey is this increasingly frequent trend to criminalize free speech. Words and ideas, regardless of their content, are tolerated in democratic systems. As signatory to the Conference on Security and Cooperation in Europe [CSCE], the United Nations Universal Declaration on Human Rights and the International Covenant on Political and Civil Liberties, Turkey has obligated itself to protect all forms of nonviolent expression. The decision to remove 13 duly elected parliamentarians because of speeches they made or documents they sign is an affront to all democratic legislatures.

Mr. President, obviously no country, including our own, is immune from situations where human rights are jeopardized. Turkey's Kurdish issue has a long and complex history, which has unfortunately become increasingly clouded by violence. In the midst of a severe economic crisis, Turkey's government and military are spending over $7 billion a year to fight the PKK—yet the PKK continues to operate and draw followers. Regrettably the heavy-handed tactics of security forces, who have destroyed over 1,000 Kurdish villages in the past 18 months, alienate local Kurds and fuel sympathy and support for the radicals. Additionally, by criminalizing even moderate expressions of Kurdish discontent, the government stifles legitimate discourse within a democratic framework and denies its citizenry an outlet through which to legally articulate their frustration. And while no one denies Turkey's sovereign right to protect its citizenry from terrorism, this must not be pursued at the expense of other fundamental human rights.

Mr. President, in the interests of peace and regional stability, I appeal to Turkey's civilian and military leaders to reconsider increasingly intolerant and unproductive policies toward Turkey's Kurdish citizenry. There can be no hope of peace if voices on all sides are silenced and forced into more radical positions. Such policies raise serious questions about the ability of Turkish democracy to meet the pressing needs of a modern multiethnic society. Furthermore, Mr. President, despite a confluence of foreign policy interests with our Government on numerous issues, Turkey's deteriorating human rights situation makes it increasingly difficult to support a leading role for Turkey in regional political undertakings.

In conclusion, Mr. President, I would urge Turkey's government to pursue political solutions to the Kurdish situation. So as not to be criticized for simply pointing out the problem without offering my own thoughts on a solution, I will share some thoughts on defusing the mounting crisis. I believe a key element of any political approach must be official willingness to distinguish between PKK terrorism and nonviolent expression promoting rights for Turkey's Kurdish citizens. Similarly, the PKK must abandon the use of violence for political objectives and renounce aspirations for outright independence. A bilateral cease-fire could be a first step toward establishing a political dialog, not with the PKK, but with moderate Kurdish elements. In such a climate, I would urge the Turkish Government to take the following steps:

First, allow all nonviolent political parties to participate in political life.

Second, abolish restrictions on free expression including those within the Antiterror law.

Third, repeal the state of emergency.

Fourth, dismantle the village guard system.

Fifth, remove all restrictions on Kurdish linguistic and cultural expression.

Sixth, lift constraints on dissemination of Kurdish language television and radio broadcasts, print, music, and other mediums.

Seventh, develop a government-sponsored Institute of Kurdish Studies and allow schools to offer instruction in Kurdish , and

Eighth, convene an official, high-profile, conference examining all aspects of Turkish-Kurdish relations.

Mr. President, I believe such actions would bolster Turkey's civilian democracy, stem violence, marginalize the PKK by providing moderate alternatives, lift an oppressive climate which has stifled political and economic life throughout Turkey, and begin to reverse the destructive polarization of Turks and Kurds. I sincerely hope Turkey's government will seek to protect free speech and pursue nonmilitary approaches to the Kurdish dilemma to avoid plunging the nation into further turmoil.

142.

[July 28, 1994 (House), p. 6385]

U.S. FOREIGN POLICY—BASED ON MORALITY OR GEOGRAPHY?

(Ms. FURSE asked and was given permission to address the House for 1 minute and to revise and extend her remarks.)

Ms. FURSE. Mr. Speaker, today Leyla Zana is in prison, and she faces the death penalty. She along with six elected Kurdish leaders are charged with treason. They all face the death penalty.

What is their crime, Mr. Speaker? It is exactly what I am doing today. They spoke out on the issue of human rights.

Mr. Speaker, these Kurdish parliamentarians are not in Iraq whose treatment of the Kurdish people we have called rightly crimes against humanity. No, these parliamentarians are in Turkey, a country that the United States supports with massive aid and military assistance.

Mr. Speaker, every time Members of Congress protest the conditions of repression and torture and human rights we are told that we must remember that Turkey is strategically important to us. Does our morality depend on geography rather than on conviction?

It is time that Congress demands the release of the six Kurdish parliamentarians.

143.

[August 4, 1994 (Senate), p. 10601]

DEMOCRACY ON TRIAL IN TURKEY

Mr. DECONCINI. Mr. President, this day marks a sad milestone on Turkey's path toward democracy. Today, before a court in

Ankara, six Kurdish parliamentarians face capital punishment for expressing political views deemed treasonous by Turkey's civilian and military leadership. Altogether, 13 duly-elected deputies of the Democracy Party [DEP] have been thrown out of parliament, including six who fled the country so they could not be silenced.

Mr. President, I am flabbergasted that such a spectacle is taking place in Turkey, a staunch friend, a NATO ally, and CSCE participating state whose officials regularly express commitments to democracy and international human rights standards. This trial will take place before the world press and hundreds of lawyers, foreign parliamentarians, human rights activists and others on hand to demonstrate their concern and support. In addition to starkly illustrating how free speech and political activity is restricted in Turkey, the trial will bring attention to other underlying obstructions to democracy.

Mr. President, I was initially dismayed at the widespread popular support for the Government's dogmatic campaign against the DEP members. But what is becoming increasingly clear is that public opinion is being openly manipulated by major media outlets controlled by government or other political sources.

With respect to Kurdish rights issues and the war in southeast Turkey, informed debate has fallen victim to inflammatory prefabrications or severely restricted information. I believe, as long as major media sources remain controlled by political and military interests, and journalists and others remain silenced, informed public debate will be impossible.

Mr. President, free expression and an unrestricted press are prerequisites of democratic societies. The Turkish press must be enabled to report responsibly on Kurdish issues and other human rights concerns.

The DEP trial will also likely underscore the deficiencies of the Government's unrealistic military approach to the Kurdish question—a cornerstone of which is the criminalization of Kurdish -based political parties. When political parties are banned, the pattern in Turkey is that like-minded groups form on their heels or members move to more extreme parties. It would seem that allowing Kurds to form legal political parties would be a plausible way of diminishing support for the PKK and other extremist groups.

The CSCE Copenhagen Document clearly outlines commitments taken by 53 participating states regarding unrestricted political party activity. The campaign against the Democracy Party and its predecessors raises serious questions about the Government of Turkey's commitment to these principles.

Mr. President, while the start of this political trial marks a dark day for Turkish democracy, one can hope that the attention drawn by this event will bring added pressure on the Government to pursue nonmilitary resolutions of the Kurdish crisis and to address other pressing rights issues.

I would remind my colleagues, that two of the deputies face the death penalty for statements made at a Helsinki Commission briefing right here on Capitol Hill in the Rayburn Building.

I find it truly unfathomable that a professed democratic government could press capital charges against elected parliamentarians simply for their speeches or writings which advocate neither violence, secession nor solutions outside of a democratic framework. On this inauspicious occasion, I urge my colleagues to join me in expressing to the Government of Turkey our disappointment at their irrational campaign to squelch free speech.

This is one of the greatest atrocities that is occurring. Several of these parliamentarians came before the Helsinki Commission of the U.S. Congress. They did not advocate a violent overthrow of the government. They did not advocate any treasonous activities toward the government, and yet now their party has been banned, and they are under indictment, and some of them have fled the country because they spoke out to a committee of the U.S. Congress.

Once again, I thank sincerely my friend from Vermont.

The PRESIDING OFFICER. Under the previous order, the Senator from Vermont is recognized.

Mr. LEAHY. Mr. President, I want to commend the Senator from Arizona for his comments. He has been a voice at times in a lonely place on the subject, from the early days of the Helsinki Commission on through.

He is certainly as aware of the situation as any Member of the Senate, not only because of his personal interest and the travels he has made there, and personal observations, but as chairman of the Senate Select Committee on Intelligence. I think the Senate should listen to him.

I have refrained reluctantly from supporting unilateral action of the United States to lift the arms embargo. I must say that I no longer feel comfortable doing that. We have waited for the others to join with us in lifting the embargo. These people should be allowed the means to defend themselves.

Should we have to vote again on the question of whether we lift the arms embargo, I suspect I will be changing my vote.

144.

[August 4, 1994 (Senate), p. 10644]

ADDITIONAL STATEMENTS

DEMOCRACY ON TRIAL IN TURKEY

Mr. DECONCINI. Mr. President, this day marks a sad milestone on Turkey's path toward democracy. Today, before a court in Ankara, six Kurdish parliamentarians face capital punishment for expressing political views deemed treasonous by Turkey's civilian and military leadership. Altogether, 13 duly elected Deputies of the Democracy Party [DEP] have been thrown out of Parliament, including 6 who fled the country so they could not be silenced.

Mr. President, I am flabbergasted that such a spectacle is taking place in Turkey, a staunch friend, a NATO ally, and CSCE participating State whose officials regularly express commitments to democracy and international human rights standards. This trial will take place before the world press and hundreds of lawyers, foreign parliamentarians, human rights activists and others on hand to

demonstrate their concern and support. In addition to starkly illustrating how free speech and political activity is restricted in Turkey, the trial will bring attention to other underlying obstructions to democracy.

Mr. President, I was initially dismayed at the widespread popular support for the Government's dogmatic campaign against the DEP members. But what is becoming increasingly clear is that public opinion is being openly manipulated by major media outlets controlled by government or other political sources. With respect to Kurdish rights issues and the war in southeast Turkey, informed debate has fallen victim to inflammatory prefabrications or severely restricted information. I believe, as long as major media sources remain controlled by political and military interests, and journalists and others remain silenced, informed public debate will be impossible. Mr. President, free expression and an unrestricted press are prerequisites of democratic societies. The Turkish press must be enabled to report responsibly on Kurdish issues and other human rights concerns.

The DEP trial will also likely underscore the deficiencies of the Government's unrealistic military approach to the Kurdish question—a cornerstone of which is the criminalization of Kurdish -based political parties. When political parties are banned, the pattern in Turkey is that like-minded groups form on their heels or members move to more extreme parties. It would seem that allowing Kurds to form legal political parties would be a plausible way of diminishing support for the PKK and other extremist groups. The CSCE Copenhagen Document clearly outlines commitments taken by 53 participating States regarding unrestricted political party activity. The campaign against the Democracy Party and its predecessors raises serious questions about the Government of Turkey's commitment to these principles.

Mr. President, while the start of this political trial marks a dark day for Turkish democracy, one can hope that the attention drawn by this event will bring added pressure on the Government to pursue nonmilitary resolutions of the Kurdish crisis and to address other pressing rights issues. I would remind my colleagues, that two of the deputies face the death penalty for statements made at a Helsinki Commission briefing in the Rayburn Building. I find it truly unfathomable that a professed democratic Government could press capital charges against elected parliamentarians simply for their speeches or writings which advocate neither violence, secession nor solutions outside of a democratic framework. On this inauspicious occasion, I urge my colleagues to join me in expressing to the Government of Turkey our disappointment at their irrational campaign to squelch free speech.

145.

[August 11, 1994 (Senate), p. 11361]

ADDITIONAL STATEMENTS

PKK ATTACKS ON CIVILIANS MUST STOP

Mr. DECONCINI. Mr. President, I wish to express my anger and frustration over recent killings of innocent civilians by members of the Kurdish Workers Party [PKK]. Yesterday, 12 innocent civilians, including women and children, were machine gunned by PKK guerrillas while riding a bus. This, and similar attacks, only propel forward the senseless cycle of violence responsible now for over 12,500 lives and widespread destruction and dislocation throughout southeast Turkey. I fail to see how the killing of innocent men, women and children serves the interests of anyone who professes to want human rights and democracy.

Mr. President, violence certainly begets violence and murder can never become an acceptable means of achieving political objectives. Mao Tse Tung believed that political power emanated from the barrel of a gun, but Mr. President, in the 21st century, political power will be built on words and the free flow of information. The force of ideas is ultimately more powerful than the force of arms. So, just as I have called upon the Government of Turkey to peacefully and democratically redress the grievances of its Kurdish citizens, so too

must the PKK abandon its armed struggle. I cannot understand how PKK leaders expect their calls for political solutions to the Kurdish problem to be taken seriously as long as the PKK slaughters civilians. To the contrary, their terrorist tactics only besmirch the legitimate efforts of Kurdish leaders who are genuinely seeking a peaceful political solution.

Mr. President, the human rights situation in Turkey is not getting any better. A virtual state of civil war exists in southeast Turkey. Kurdish villages burn and tens of thousands are made refugees. Human rights and pro-Kurdish activists are regularly murdered or disappear. A relentless campaign against free speech is silencing parliamentarians, journalists and other and stifling informed public debate. Mr. President, amidst the haze of war and propaganda emanating from all sides, the truth is becoming increasingly difficult to discern.

Mr. President, for the sake of human rights and the future of democracy in Turkey, I urge Turkish and Kurdish combatants to consider an immediate ceasefire. Their military debate must end and a political debate be allowed to begin. Only after the violence and terror has ceased can the process of bringing peace and prosperity to all of Turkey's citizens commence.

146.

[October 6, 1994 (Senate), p. 14381]

TURKEY'S RELEVANCE IN WORLD ORDER

Mr. COCHRAN. Mr. President, I would like to call my colleague's attention to a recent column by Turkish Ambassador Nuzhet Kandemir which appeared in the *Washington Times*.

The relationship between the United States and Turkey is one of the most important bilateral relationships in the world. Turkey was a valuable ally and NATO partner when the free world was united in resisting Soviet expansionism, and Turkey's importance has not diminished in the changing and uncertain world we face today. On the contrary, friendship between our two countries may be more important today than it was in the bipolar world we leave behind.

Turkey is located where Europe, Asia, the former Soviet Republics in the Caucasus and the Middle East converge. To the extent that the United States has vital interests at stake in each of these regions, a friendly and stable Turkey is essential to the protection of those interests.

Ambassador Kandemir provides valuable insights into Turkey's perspective in this transitional era. As with any friend, we might not always agree with Turkey, but its views are always relevant to our foreign policy deliberations. I commend his column to the attention of the Senate and ask unanimous consent that Ambassador Kandemir's column be inserted in the Record.

There being no objection, the article was ordered to printed in the RECORD, as follows:

Turkey's Relevance in World Order

Five years after the end of the Cold War and three years after the end of Operation Desert Storm, the international community continues to struggle with the myriad problems confronting it; identifying new priorities, resolving regional conflicts, dealing with humanitarian disasters, stabilizing the international economic system, allocating foreign assistance, and halting the proliferation of weapons of mass destruction and the spread of terrorism and violent Islamic fundamentalism. This is particularly true of two areas of critical interest to Turkey and the United States— Southern Europe and the Middle East.

Turkey is more relevant to the important interests of the United States and Turkey's other friends in the international community than it was during the less complex, but no less threatening, Cold War. Turkey straddles both Southern Europe and the Middle East and is a position to exert a positive influence on events in each. This is the reality with which Turkey's friends and critics should assess the prospects for regional peace and stability, or conversely, the danger of a destabilized Turkey.

Turkey wants to make it clear that in an era in which a shrinking U.S. foreign aid and an emphasis on domestic matters calls for more self-reliance by America's friends, Turkey remains prepared to shoulder its share of the burden. Further, my government can assure the U.S. that there are no fundamental differences in our respective foreign policies on the key issues of peacekeeping, human rights, economic stabilization, and humanitarian assistance.

I would like to clarify certain issues that have led to misinformation that could tarnish the relations between the United States and Turkey.

First, on the controversial issue of human rights, the Turkish government introduced an additional package of democratic reforms in 1994 that will further ensure there are no possible abuses of the rights of Turkish citizens of Kurdish origin.

Second, on the issue of terrorism, my government is engaged in a conflict with the Kurdistan Workers Party (PKK), an organization often misportrayed as a band of romantic nationalists, representing all Kurds. This is the same PKK singled out in the U.S. State Department's most recent report on terrorism. Turkey is engaged in a conflict with the PKK, not "the Kurds," and makes no apologies for attempting to safeguard democracy for all elements of Turkish society.

Just as recent acts of terrorism in London, Panama and Buenos Aires demonstrate the intent of some to derail peace in the Middle East, it was the PKK that blew up all initiatives by my government to resolve the conflict. Within the democratic process, Turkey has always maintained a constructive dialogue with those segments of society who reject violence and dismemberment of the Turkish state.

Finally, my government's stance has been clear from the outset on the recently concluded debate on U.S. foreign aid. Recently, we announced that Turkey would not accept the 10 percent portion of assistance linked to the administration's report on Cyprus and human rights. Still, my government, though puzzled and dismayed, wants to get past the misinformation and emotion of the debate and focus on Turkey's future. Looking ahead, it is important for U.S. decision-makers and taxpayers to recognize that foreign assistance advances the causes of regional peace, economic stability and growth. Turkey provides peacekeeping forces in Europe and Africa and grants humanitarian assistance in Europe, Africa and the Middle East. Assistance to Turkey and the country's economic stability has a direct impact on developments in Southern Europe and the Middle East.

In this regard, my government implemented a series of domestic economic reforms that led to a new accord with the International Monetary Fund, created jobs for all Turkish citizens, and enabled Turkey to re-establish itself as an emerging market. These reforms will allow Turkey to serve as an engine of economic growth in the region in cooperation with several nations, including Israel.

However, I trust that decisionmakers will recognize that a measure of the economic instability afflicting Turkey today is a result of its unwavering support for sanctions against Iraq since 1991. This support terminated trade with one of Turkey's largest trading partners—an action comparable to the United States ending trade with Canada. During this time, foreign aid was reduced dramatically, resulting in a shortfall that had an obvious impact on Turkey, but did not undercut our commitment as a reliable partner.

In the spirit of future cooperation, there could soon be an opportunity in the United Nations to rescue a significant economic asset for the international community, the Turkey- Iraq pipeline, which was shut down as part of the sanctions. Turkey hopes that a U.N. resolution will soon be approved to flush the pipeline; it would prevent further damage to that asset and provide revenue that would fund humanitarian assistance to all Iraqis, but would not violate any U.N. sanctions regime. The passage of a new resolution would also illustrate the ability of Turkey and the international community to negotiate a solution to delicate diplomatic and economic problems.

Turkey is struggling with the difficult tasks of defining its diplomatic, security and economic roles in the new world order, as well as combating terrorism and the expansion of violent Islamic fundamentalism. Turkey welcomes its friendship with the United States. Turkey also would welcome a balanced examination of the facts as the United States copes with instability in Europe and the former Soviet Union, monitors future events in Turkey and considers the unpalatable alternatives to a stable, friendly Turkey.

147.

[October 6, 1994 (Extensions of Remarks), p. 2089]

AMNESTY INTERNATIONAL BARRED FROM TURKEY
HON. STENY H. HOYER
OF MARYLAND
IN THE HOUSE OF REPRESENTATIVES

Wednesday, October 5, 1994

Mr. HOYER. Mr. Speaker, in what is becoming an all too frequent occurrence, I again rise to protest actions by the Turkish Government which raise serious questions about professed human rights commitments. Amnesty International's leading researcher on Turkey, Jonathen Sugden, has been declared persona non grata and is now barred from entering Turkey to look further into the deteriorating human rights situation of Turkey's Kurdish population.

Mr. Speaker, I do not need to detail for this body the excellent work Amnesty International does around the world. As cochairman of the Commission on Security and Cooperation in Europe, I know the value of Amnesty's human rights research and reporting. Its grassroots membership around the world often serve as the eyes, ears, and conscience of governmental and nongovernmental efforts to promote human rights protections, indeed to save lives.

Over the years, the Government of Turkey has understandably resented Amnesty's attention to widespread torture, political prisoners, and the brutality used to suppress Kurds . Yet through Turkey's leadership denounced Amnesty's findings as being politically motivated and often refused to meet with Amnesty officials, they nevertheless allowed Amnesty researchers access to the country. If leaders of Turkey now believe that by barring human rights investigators they will escape embarrassing scrutiny, they have again seriously miscalculated. Such action will only draw increased interest and attention to the very practices the Government seeks to keep out of view. This issue will surely be raised at the upcoming CSCE Budapest Review Meeting Conference and will likely contribute to calls by a number of states to invoke the Moscow Human Rights Mechanism to mandate a CSCE monitoring mission to Turkey.

Mr. Speaker, the Turkish Government continues to view its human rights problems as a result of terrorism employed by the Kurdish Workers Party [PKK]. For years Turkish Governments have vowed to crush the PKK militarily. And while this objective is understandable, in the process of combating the PKK, the Government has waged war upon its own citizens—razing Kurdish villages, destroying livestock and crops, and forcing over 1 million Kurds to become refugees in their own country. In effect, their actions have generated more recruits for the PKK than the PKK could have ever enlisted itself.

Mr. Speaker, I am coming to believe that despite our mutual strategic and economic interests we should express serious reservations about continuing to provide the weapons Turkey uses on its own citizens. The action taken by this Congress to condition 10 percent of Turkey's foreign assistance on human rights performance indicates growing concern, yet affects only a small amount of favorable loans. Turkey also receives billions of dollars of excess defense equipment and other assistance, and perhaps it is time that we consider conditioning this.

148.

[October 8, 1994 (Extensions of Remarks), pp. 2220-21]

LEYLA ZANA
HON. ELIZABETH FURSE
OF OREGON
IN THE HOUSE OF REPRESENTATIVES

Friday, October 7, 1994

Ms. FURSE. Mr. Speaker, I have spoken out in the past on the House floor about the egregious situation Leyla Zana finds herself in.

Leyla is the first and only Kurdish woman parliamentarian deputy in Turkey's history. She has been held in solitary confinement by Turkish authorities since March 2, nearly 7 months now. Her crime? Public speech, for which the Turkish government wants her sentenced to death.

Leyla was first arrested and severely tortured by the Turkish police in 1988 for engaging in peaceful demonstrations on behalf of prisoners against the barbarity of torture, and for respect for human dignity and the Universal Declaration of Human Rights.

I want to read from Leyla's September 15 letter to me and I ask permission to submit it in its entirety to the RECORD.

I came to realize that war and violence, inflicted by a society based on macho values—worship of power and destruction of the weak, had brought the Kurdish and Turkish peoples to the point of civil war and to the brink of social and moral disaster. I therefore resolve to take an active part in political life in order to send a different message.

In October 1991, I was elected deputy to the Turkish Parliament with 82% of the vote.

During my swearing-in ceremony, a phrase I spoke in Kurdish, on friendship and coexistence between Kurds and Turks within the context of equality and of respect for the identity of the other [caused me to be] described as a "separatist," and "ally of terrorists," a "traitor." My photo was used in the target practice of the Turkish police.

I am determined to continue, by peaceful means, the struggle for peace between Kurds and Turks, for democracy, and for respect for human rights. These, I believes, are the universal values which must unite us, beyond differences of language or religion.

Mr. Speaker, I appreciate the leadership Congressman Porter is taking on behalf of Leyla Zana, as well as the other five duly elected parliamentarians representing Kurdish populations who are also being detained. As elected officials, we all must speak out against this abuse of humanity.

Ankara, 15 September 1994
Ms. Elizabeth Furse,
House of Representatives, Washington, DC.

DEAR COLLEAGUE, I read in the Turkish press that you are considering taking action to demonstrate your solidarity with me. I am very touched, and would like to express my warmest thanks.

I am the first and only Kurdish woman parliamentary deputy in Turkey's history. My political experience began outside the gates of the Turkish prison where my husband, mayor of Diyarbakir (the main Kurdish city), was imprisoned for 10 years and 8 months. Prisoners' wives organized peaceful demonstrations against the barbarity of torture, and for respect for human dignity and the Universal Declaration of Human Rights. For the activity I was harassed and persecuted by the Turkish police, who finally arrested me in July 1988. I was severely tortured for 59 days, and still bear the scars, both psychological and physical.

I came to realize that war and violence, inflicted by a society based on macho values—worship of power and destruction of the weak, had brought the Kurdish and Turkish peoples to the point of civil war and to the brink of social and moral disaster. I therefore resolved to take an active part in political life in order to send a different message, one of respect for human beings, their dignity and their inalienable rights, and of the need for dialogue about the deep problems in our society. In October 1991 I was elected deputy from Diyarbakir to the Turkish Parliament, with 82% of the votes.

My first clash with the Turkish political establishment, dominated by generals and men who deny the very existence of the Kurdish people, took place during my swearing-in ceremony in Parliament. A phrase I spoke in Kurdish , on friendship and coexistence between Kurds and Turks within the context of equality and of respect for the identity of the other, elicited a violent attack from the media. I was described as a "separatist", an "ally of terrorists", a "traitor", etc. My photo was used in the target practice of the Turkish police. After that, I barely escaped two attempts on my life. (In fact, eighty-four national and regional leaders of our Democracy Party have already been assassinated).

On 2 March 1994, on my return from a European trip during which I had been received by President Mitterrand of France and Jacques Delors, President of the European Community Commission, I was arrested along with five other deputies. Since then we have been held in preventive detention. We are criticized for our statements in Turkey and abroad, including those before the Helsinki Commission. The Turkish Government want us sentenced to death for our opinions. For 7 months I have been in solitary confinement. My only contacts with the outside world are my lawyers and a few authorized visitors.

In spite of these difficulties and the poor state of my health, I am determined to continue, by peaceful means, the struggle for peace between Kurds and Turks, for democracy, and for respect for human rights. These, I believe, are the universal values which must unite us, beyond differences of language or religion.

Any support from the Untied States is of great importance to us. I count in particular on the solidarity of my feminist sisters, those admirable American women to whom the struggle for democracy, peace and equality is so greatly indebted. Come and be with us as observers of the trial. Write via the Kurdish Institute of Paris, which will see that the message gets to me.

Thanking you again, and awaiting your reply, I remain.

Sincerely yours,
LAYLA ZANA.

149.

[November 30, 1994 (Senate), p. 15254]

TURKEY

Mr. DECONCINI. Mr. President, in October, I visited Turkey as chairman of the Helsinki Commission and the Senate Intelligence Committee. I wanted to follow up on issues examined during my last visit in 1989, including human rights, the Kurdish situation, conflicts in the Balkans and the Middle East peace process. Following the visit, I joined President Clinton at the signing of the Jordanian-Israeli peace agreement—an historic milestone in the quest for regional peace, and a priority of both the United States and Turkey.

I met with parliamentary leaders, a foreign ministry official and representatives of human rights organizations. I was disappointed, however, that I was not allowed to meet with jailed Kurdish parliamentarians and other political prisoners, a departure from the openness with which I was received during my 1989 visit.

I expressed concern for the heavy toll on commerce caused by the enforcement of U.N. sanctions against Iraq and believe our Government should seek further compensation for Turkey's losses from Gulf States who have benefited most from continued allied pressure on Saddam Hussein. I also expressed my belief that Turkey can play a critical role in promoting a CSCE-like regional framework for the Middle East, especially if it finds a non-military solution to the Kurdish issue. Turkey's Government has already taken a leading role in supporting a CSCME as a means of fostering a lasting and comprehensive regional peace.

Mr. President, terrorism threatens Turkey's stability and remains a major factor in the cycle of violence plaguing all its citizens. The apparent unwillingness and inability of Turkey's leadership to seek new approaches to the Kurdish situation, however, were evident and disturbing, as was evidence of continued widespread use of torture and restrictions on free expression. Despite these problems, I left Turkey with an appreciation of mutual interests and shared democratic values and believe both our governments should work towards strengthening bilateral relations.

I discussed ongoing efforts by security forces to evacuate and destroy Kurdish villages while fighting the PKK. While I was encouraged by official claims that investigations have been launched, at this point, no such public examination has occurred. I also discussed restrictions on free expression and was told that pending legislation could result in the release of many currently detained for speech crimes. I expressed hope that concrete measures decriminalizing all forms of non-violent expression would take place to bring Turkey into compliance with stated CSCE commitments. I reiterated that the rights of ordinary citizens and duly elected legislators to freely express themselves could not be curtailed in a democratic society.

I also discussed continued widespread use of torture. During my 1989 visit, officials indicated that concrete measures would be taken to reduce torture and educate police officers about proper and acceptable interrogation methods. Today, however, heightened tensions and violence seem to have lessened the political will and urgency of eradicating torture. Human rights advocates say torture is routinely used in political cases and forced confessions are widely used to obtain convictions. I urged officials to redouble torture prevention

and monitoring efforts, especially during pre-trial detention periods when detainees have no access to lawyers and most torture is alleged to occur. A recent incident further underscores my concerns. On November 3, a Turkish court ordered the confiscation of "File of Torture" a booklet published by the Human Rights Foundation which documents deaths in detention since 1980 and other torture cases. Prosecutors are determining whether to charge Yavuz Onen, who met with the delegation, and Fevzi Argun for disseminating separatist propaganda, a crime carrying a 2-to-5 year prison sentence.

The very measures Turkey is employing to safeguard the State from threats of separatism are polarizing Turkish society even further. Rising nationalism and the tendency to view reforms as concessions to terrorism intimidate any who speak of compromise. The tactics of the PKK do nothing to engender support yet it is the PKK that finds itself the beneficiary of increased sympathy by a people who view themselves with no choices. Voices of moderation are squelched by threats of repression and even assassination.

The delegation left Turkey very concerned as to whether Turkey can accommodate the interests and aspirations of its Kurdish citizens within the present political framework. For years Turkey has repressed, often brutally, a separate Kurdish cultural identity in favor of a secular Turkish identity. Whereas Turkey is not the same as it was only 5 years ago, the steady progression from denying the mere existence of Kurds to granting certain restricted liberties, has been accompanied by a growing gulf of mistrust between Kurds and Turks. The armed insurgency and the counter measures by the military are approaching the dimensions of a civil war. The Kurdish issue is a critical one for Turkey and all its citizens with very serious long-term repercussions for not only Turkey but the Middle East. Old unresolved questions are reemerging in Turkey and how it deals with those questions today will largely determine the state of democracy in Turkey tomorrow.

I believe the Turkish Government must consider non-military approaches to meet the concerns of Kurdish citizens who do not support the use of violence and who are presently victimized by both sides. Moderate political voices, whether Turkish or Kurdish, must be legitimized and heard—and they must condemn terrorism. Policies and attitudes which fail to differentiate between terrorism and protected forms of expression threaten the foundations of Turkey's democracy. A ceasefire should be the first step towards peacefully resolving the Kurdish issue. Should the PKK declare a unilateral ceasefire, as it did in March 1993, the Government of Turkey should reciprocate. Only when the guns have been silenced, can the difficult task of reconciling Turks and Kurds victimized by war begin. Until the Kurdish question is peacefully resolved, Turkey's efforts in many other areas will be jeopardized—as will continued close cooperation and relations with Western allies.

150.

[December 20, 1994 (Senate), pp. 15479-80]

TURKEY'S CONFIDENT LEADER

Mr. SIMON. Mr. President, recently, Lally Weymouth had a piece in the *Washington Post* about Turkey's remarkable prime minister ["Turkey's Confident Leader," Nov. 23, 1994)]. It is a great tribute to her.

The political storms are not easy to weather in Turkey, but one of the things that our friends in Turkey must understand is that an improved relationship with the United States, and much of Western Europe, is in the interest of all of us. But it is not likely to happen until Turkey faces up to the Cyprus question and the Armenia question.

I recognize that is easy for a politician of the United States to say, and not easy for a political leader in Turkey to say because of the decades of emotion on these issues. [*S15480]

But if the people in the Middle East can get together, even though it is not all smooth, and if the people in Northern Ireland can get together, then it seems to me, the Turks, the Greeks, and the Armenians ought to be able to work out a better relationship than the one

they now have, and that is in the interest of all parties.

I ask the Lally Weymouth column be printed in the Congressional Record.

The column follows: . . .

151.

[January 20, 1995 (Extensions of Remarks), p. 145]

TURKEY'S ASSAULT ON HUMAN RIGHTS CONTINUES
HON. CHRISTOPHER H. SMITH
OF NEW JERSEY
IN THE HOUSE OF REPRESENTATIVES

Friday, January 20, 1995

Mr. SMITH of New Jersey. Mr. Speaker, over the years the Helsinki Commission has closely monitored human rights developments to Turkey. I have supported Commission efforts and have joined my colleagues in speaking out about suppression of free speech, torture, and fundamental human rights questions concerning Turkey's Kurdish citizens. As the new Chairman of the Commission, I will continue to speak out on these and other such developments.

I rise today to protest the arrest of seven leaders of the Human Rights Association of Turkey's Diyarbakir branch. Prosecutors want to jail these individuals for no less than 10 years on charges that a publication they produced which documented human rights cases constitutes "separatist propaganda." One of those detained, Neymetullah Gunduz, an attorney and association leader, had met with members of a Helsinki Commission delegation last October. Just weeks ago, several other human rights leaders were acquitted of similar charges. Mr. Speaker, international scrutiny has and should continue to focus on these draconian speech restrictions and other human rights problems which continue to tarnish Turkey's democratic credentials.

For years now, Human Rights Association members throughout Turkey, but especially in the southeast, have been harassed, gunned down, and have had their offices forcibly closed. The Diyarbakir branch was the last allowed by authorities to function in the region, and now, it too has been silenced. Mr. Speaker, the deteriorating human rights situation facing residents of southeast Turkey can only be described in terms of fear and violence. The freedoms and liberties of all citizens have been stripped in an effort to fight terrorism, and residents are victimized by both terrorist and security forces.

Mr. Speaker, Turkish leaders have expressed dismay at efforts to slow Turkey's integration into the European Union, and yet that Government has continued to pursue policies contrary to accepted international human rights norms. Their protests about congressional conditioning of U.S. aid on human rights performance ring equally hollow given the flagrant disregard for Turkey's stated human rights commitments, including those undertaken with the Organization for Security and Cooperation in Europe.

Mr. Speaker, I call upon the Government of Turkey to immediately drop its case against the seven activists and to release all those political prisoners who presently languish in Turkish prisons simply for expressing their opinions.

152.

[January 20, 1995 (Extensions), pp. 146-47]

TURKEY: HERE WE GO AGAIN
HON. STENY H. HOYER
OF MARYLAND
IN THE HOUSE OF REPRESENTATIVES

Friday, January 20, 1995

Mr. HOYER. Mr. Speaker, last October, the Chairman of the Helsinki Commission, Dennis DeConcini, lead a delegation to Turkey to examine human rights issues in that country. While in Diyarbakir, the largest city in the predominantly Kurdish southeast, dele-gation members visited the offices of the local Human Rights Association [HRA] branch. The delegation had met with HRA leaders in Ankara and the Helsinki Commission has often worked with the HRA and has found its publications extremely useful and reliable.

While meeting with the Commission delegation, HRA leaders explained how the organization's members operated at great risk to their personal safety. HRA members around the country, but especially in the southeast, face constant danger and persecution. Dozens of activists had been threatened, kidnaped, murdered and disappeared with the collusion of security forces. The Diyarbakir HRA branch was the only office in 10 state of emergency provinces allowed to remain open. HRA leaders believed authorities wanted to use the open office to demonstrate their tolerance of human rights organizations. Now, even that Potemkin village has been pulled down by authorities bent on eradicating all criticism of Kurdish polices.

Mr. Speaker, last Tuesday, seven leaders of the HRA chapter in Diyarbakir were arrested and charged with disseminating separatist propaganda. Prosecutors are seeking jail sentences of more than 10 years for these activists because of their publication which detailed human rights cases in 1992. One of those now in prison awaiting trail is Neymetullah Gunduz, an attorney who met with members of Chairman DeConcini's delegation and who visited the Helsinki Commission in 1993 while on a USIA grant. Mr. Gunduz is highly regarded and is considered a dedicated human rights lawyer and reliable source of information concerning rights abuses by both the Government and the PKK.

Mr. Speaker, just recently the Government abandoned a similar case brought against a group of well known Turkish activists. The move was widely hailed as a positive development in an otherwise bleak human rights picture. What this new case seems to indicate is that the recent acquittal stands merely as an aberration as opposed to a genuine effort to dismantle restrictions on free expression. I have said it before, and I reemphasize it now, Turkey cannot be considered a truly democratic nation as long as individuals like Neymettulah Gunduz, Mehdi Zana, Halit Gerger, former parliamentarians and other are jailed for exercising their rights to free expression.

Mr. Speaker, a recent commentary in a large Turkish daily purports that the Government has spent five times more money fighting terrorism than on the giant GAP water project supposed to be the cornerstone of development in southeast Turkey. Tens of billions of dollars have been used to institute policies which have left the region more devastated than ever and its population more resentful than ever. Meanwhile, Turkey continues to fact mounting economic and political crises tied directly to failed Kurdish policies. Unless Turkish leaders bit the bullet and seek political approaches to the Kurdish situation, there can be no hope for peace, prosperity or democracy in Turkey. As a friend and ally of Turkey, such a dismal prognosis can bring no happiness to anyone in this country either.

153.

[February 9, 1995 (Extensions of Remarks), p. 313]

TURKEY ESCALATES WAR ON FREE EXPRESSION
HON. CHRISTOPHER H. SMITH
OF NEW JERSEY
IN THE HOUSE OF REPRESENTATIVES

Thursday, February 9, 1995

Mr. SMITH of New Jersey. Mr. Speaker, last October, a Helsinki Commission delegation met with Turkish officials and others in Ankara. With one exception, each and every official, including the Speaker of Parliament, produced a copy of the pro-Kurdish newspaper *Ozgur Ulke* and waved it in the air as proof that, despite what critics alleged, free expression was alive and well in Turkey.

Last week, Mr. Speaker, Turkish officials decided that the costs of allowing the paper to air its pro-Kurdish sentiments outweighed its value as a token of free expression. On February 3, a Turkish court forced the paper to shut

down. This blatant assault on free speech comes within a week of the decision to prosecute Turkey's most widely known author, Yasar Kemal, for publicly stating his thoughts on the government's handling of the Kurdish situation. He now faces charges of separatist propaganda, and now, even those who favor the government's uncompromising hardline towards the Kurds are beginning to question whether the government hasn't gone too far.

Mr. Speaker, *Ozgur Ulke's* closure culminates an orchestrated campaign which began as soon as the newspaper appeared to fill the void left when a likeminded predecessor was forcibly closed. Censorship of the paper included violent attacks that left 20 reporters and distributors killed by unidentified death squads. At least four others have been kidnapped. The tortured, bullet-ridden body of one reporter was found weeks after he had disappeared. At least 35 journalists and workers of the newspaper have been imprisoned and 238 issues seized. The campaign against the newspaper went into high gear on November 30, 1994, when Prime Minister Ciller issued a secret decree, which was leaked and published, calling for the complete elimination of the newspaper. On December 3, 1994, its printing facility and headquarters in Istanbul and its Ankara bureau were bombed. One person was killed and 18 others were injured in the explosions.

On January 6, 1995, policemen started to wait outside the printing plant to confiscate the paper as soon as it was printed. Copies were taken directly to a prosecutor who worked around the clock to determine which articles were undesirable. Often some three to four pages of the paper, mostly articles about security force abuses, were censored and reprinted as blank sections. Since December, five reporters, who were detained and later released, spoke of being tortured by police attempting to force confessions against the newspaper's editorial board.

Mr. Speaker, last week, the State Department issued its annual human rights report, and only China had as many pages devoted to it as Turkey. While the report indicated that human rights conditions in Turkey had worsened significantly over the past year, the publication of *Ozgur Ulke* was cited as a positive example of press freedom. Responding to the report, an official spokesperson dismissed its report as biased and based on one-sided information. The spokesperson, repeating assertions made whenever Turkey is criticized for human rights violations, insisted that significant improvements had taken place and other important reforms were being undertaken. Given the countless times we have heard such assertions, it is a wonder that Turkey is not a model of freedom and democracy.

Mr. Speaker, now that Turkish officials do not have copies of *Ozgur Ulke* to wave at visiting delegations, they will likely search for other props to convince skeptics of their good intentions. I would suggest, Mr. Speaker, that instead of tolerating certain types of expression in order to placate foreign observers, Turkish officials should take real steps to bring policies in line with stated human rights commitments. Free expression and other rights cannot be viewed simply as products of public relations campaigns. If Turkish officials are unwilling to work seriously towards implementing such rights to bring their laws into conformity with international standards, then they cannot expect their pronouncements on human rights to be viewed sympathetically. In this context, Turkish denunciations of the State Department human rights report are as puzzling as they are absurd.

154.

[March 20, 1995 (Senate), pp. 4199-201]

STATEMENTS ON INTRODUCED BILLS AND JOINT RESOLUTIONS

By Mr. D'AMATO (for himself and Mr. Pressler):

S. 578. A bill to limit assistance for Turkey under the Foreign Assistance Act of 1961 and the Arms Export Control Act until that country complies with certain human rights standards; to the Committee on Foreign Relations.

TURKISH HUMAN RIGHTS COMPLIANCE ACT

Mr. D'AMATO. Mr. President, I rise today to introduce legislation which will help restore credibility to our foreign assistance program by ensuring that one of the largest recipients of United States aid, the Republic of Turkey, adheres to internationally accepted standards for human rights and humanitarian practices.

The time has come, after years of fruitless quiet diplomacy, for the Congress to take the lead in addressing a broad range of issues dealing with Turkey, including its worsening human rights record, its continued blockade of humanitarian supplies to Armenia, its refusal to work toward a lasting and equitable settlement in Cyprus, its denial of basic rights to its Kurdish minority, and its continued persecution of Christian communities in Turkey. The hundreds of millions of dollars that the United States sends to Turkey each year provides us with the necessary leverage to bring about positive change in each of these five areas.

In each of these areas, Turkey has consistently violated international treaties and agreements to which it is a signatory. Among these are the U.N. Universal Declaration of Human Rights, the final act of the Conference on Security and Cooperation in Europe, and the European Convention on Human Rights.

The Congress, in the fiscal year 1995 foreign aid bill, withheld 10 percent of the principal amount of direct loans for Turkey based on its human rights record and the situation in Cyprus. The Turkish Government has spoken clearly on this issue—they will reject any United States aid tied to its human rights record. While the de-linking of United States assistance and human rights may be in the interests of the Turkish Government, it is surely not in the interest of the United States or the international community. It is clear, given the Turkish Government's response, that we must move beyond symbolism and fundamentally reassess our relationship with Turkey.

On the question of human rights, we need only to look at the State Department's recently released 1995 country reports on human rights, to see that years and even decades of behind the scenes efforts by the State Department have not produced any improvement in the human rights situation in Turkey. This report concludes, in fact, that "the human rights situation in Turkey worsened significantly in 1994."

Mr. President, the full spectrum of human rights monitoring organizations have condemned Turkey for its systematic and widespread abuse of human rights, including the use of torture. Amnesty International, Human Rights Watch, the U.N. Committee Against Torture, the European Parliament, the International Human Rights Law Group, the Lawyers Committee for Human Rights, Physicians Without Frontiers, Freedom House, the humanitarian law project, the Turkish Human Rights Association, and other organizations have documented the deteriorating human rights situation in Turkey.

My legislation would link the level of United States assistance to Turkey's willingness to allow free and unfettered monitoring of the human rights environment within its territory by domestic and international human rights monitoring organizations. Among the groups which have been denied full access in the past are the Turkish Human Rights Association, the Conference on Security and Cooperation in Europe, Amnesty International, and Human Rights Watch.

I would like to address Kurdish rights, or lack thereof. Nowhere is the case for cutting aid to Turkey more compelling than on the question of the Kurds. To this day, Turkey continues to deny the very existence of its 15 million Kurdish citizens. The Turkish military has systematically emptied over 2,000 Kurdish villages and uprooted over a million Kurdish citizens from their homes. The Turkish Government's systematic and deliberate eradication of the Kurdish identity within its borders is, in many ways, a high-technology version of the massacres and deportations of the Armenian genocide earlier this century.

If Turkey is to continue benefiting from the generosity of the American taxpayer, it must take demonstrable steps toward the full recognition of the civil, cultural, and human rights of its Kurdish civilians and demonstrate

that it will resolve the Kurdish question peacefully.

Important too is the question of Cyprus which remains unresolved more than 20 years after Turkey's illegal 1974 invasion of the island nation. Despite countless U.N. resolutions and international agreements, Turkey continues its illegal military occupation and has obstructed efforts toward a peaceful settlement. The division of the island and the massive uprooting of Greek Cypriots caused by the 1974 invasion remain a constant reminder of the failure of the international community to enforce a lasting and equitable resolution to the conflict.

The Turkish Government must take demonstrable steps toward the total withdrawal of its military forces from Cyprus. In addition, Turkey must demonstrate its support for a settlement recognizing the sovereignty and territorial integrity of Cyprus with a constitutional democracy based on majority rule, the rule of law and the protection of minority rights.

Mr. President, I must state that the failure of quiet diplomacy on the part of the State Department is nowhere more apparent than in its failure to lift the Turkish blockade of humanitarian aid to Armenia. In violation of international law and in defiance of the United Nations, Turkey continues to blockade its border with Armenia. For close to 2 years, the Turkish Government has refused to allow desperately needed United States and other international assistance reach the people of Armenia. Unable to cross Turkish territory or transit its airspace, relief supplies have been rerouted through Georgia, where due to widespread instability, large portions of the aid has been either lost or stolen.

The United States simply can not tolerate the obstruction of its humanitarian relief efforts by another recipient of its foreign aid. Until the blockade is lifted, the provisions in this bill cutting the level of United States assistance to Turkey would be in force.

The Turkish Government continues to place prohibitive restrictions on the Christian communities within Turkey. Among the communities which have suffered from official persecution are the Armenians, Greeks, Syrian Orthodox, and the Assyrians. The religious leaderships of these communities, in particular, have been subject to official restrictions which significantly limit their ability to serve their people. In addition, the Turkish Government has failed to adequately protect them from acts of violence and vandalism.

The United States must ensure that Turkey lifts any official restrictions on Christian churches and schools and offers sufficient protection against acts of violence and harassment against the clergy and vandalism against church and school property.

The Turkish Government must understand that the United States will not continue to subsidize its illegal and irresponsible conduct. By withholding $500,000 a day in our assistance until they have taken steps toward resolving each of the five issues I have just addressed, we will send the Turkish leadership a clear signal that our foreign assistance programs will not extend aid to those nations which regularly violate human rights and international law.

Mr. President, I ask unanimous consent that the text of the bill and an article [John Darnton, "Rights Violations in Turkey Said to Rise," *The New York Times*, March 6, 1995] be printed in the Record.

There being no objections, the material was ordered to be printed in the Record, as follows:

S. 578

Be it enacted by the Senate and House of Representatives of the United States of America in Congress assembled,

SECTION 1. SHORT TITLE.

This Act may be cited as the "Turkish Human Rights Compliance Act".

SEC. 2. FINDINGS.

The Congress makes the following findings:

(1) The Department of State, in its 1995 report entitled "Country Reports on Human Rights", documented a systematic and widespread pattern of human rights abuses by the Government of Turkey. According to the portion of the report relating to Turkey, "the human rights situation in Turkey worsened significantly in 1994".

(2) Amnesty International, Human Rights Watch, the United Nations Committee Against Torture, the European Parliament, the International Human Rights Law Group, the Lawyers Committee for Human Rights, Physicians Without Frontiers, Freedom House, the Humanitarian Law Project, the Turkish Human Rights Association, and other human rights monitoring organizations have documented extensive and continuing human rights abuses by the Government of Turkey, including the widespread use of torture.

(3) The actions of the Government of Turkey are in violation of several international human rights agreements to which Turkey is a party, including the United Nations Universal Declaration of Human Rights, the Final Act of the Conference on Security and Cooperation in Europe, and the European Convention on Human Rights.

(4) The Government of Turkey continues to deny the existence of its 15,000,000 Kurdish citizens and has used military force to deny them an identity, destroying more than 2,000 Kurdish villages and uprooting more than 2,000,000 Kurds.

(5) Turkey continues its illegal military occupation of Cyprus and has obstructed efforts to reach a just and lasting resolution to the division of Cyprus and the massive uprooting of Greek Cypriots caused by the 1974 invasion by Turkey of Cyprus.

(6) The Government of Turkey continues to blockade Armenia, obstructing the delivery of American and international humanitarian relief supplies.

(7) Turkey continues to place prohibitive restrictions on the religious leadership of Christian communities within Turkey and has failed to protect these communities adequately from acts of violence and vandalism.

(8) The Congress, in the fiscal year 1995 budget for foreign assistance, withheld 10 percent of the principal amount of direct loans to Turkey because of that country's human rights record and the situation in Cyprus. The Government of Turkey has stated that it would reject any United States assistance tied to its human rights record, which, according to in-

dependent human rights monitoring organizations, has continued to deteriorate.

SEC. 3. RESTRICTIONS ON ASSISTANCE FOR TURKEY.

(a) Restrictions.—Of the funds made available for fiscal year 1996 for assistance for Turkey under the Foreign Assistance Act of 1961 and the Arms Export Control Act, the President shall withhold, first from grant assistance, if any, and then from loan assistance, $500,000 for each day that Turkey does not meet the conditions of section 4

(b) Waiver—The President may waive the application of subsection (a) if the President determines that it is in the national security interest of the United States to do so.

SEC. 4. CONDITIONS.

The conditions of this section are met when the President certifies to Congress that the Government of Turkey—

(1) allows free and unfettered monitoring of the human rights situation within its territory by domestic and international human rights monitoring organizations, including but not limited to, the Turkish Human Rights Association, the Conference on Security and Co-operation in Europe, Amnesty International, and Human Rights Watch;

(2) recognizes the civil, cultural, and human rights of its Kurdish citizens, ceases its military operations against Kurdish civilians, and takes demonstrable steps toward a peaceful resolution of the Kurdish issue;

(3) takes demonstrable steps toward the total withdrawal of its military forces from Cyprus and demonstrates its support for a settlement recognizing the sovereignty, independence, and territorial integrity of Cyprus, with a constitutional democracy based on majority rule, the rule of law, and the protection of minority rights;

(4) completely removes its blockade of United States and international assistance to Armenia; and

(5) removes official restrictions on Christian churches and schools and offers sufficient protection against acts of violence and harassment directed at members of the clergy, and offers sufficient protection against acts of vandalism directed at church and school property . . .

155.

[March 23, 1995 (Senate), pp. 4516-7]

SENATE RESOLUTION 91—RELATIVE TO TURKEY

Mr. PELL (for himself, Mr. Kerry, Mr. Feingold, and Ms. Snowe) submitted the following resolution; which was referred to the Committee on Foreign Relations:

S. Res. 91

Whereas as a signatory to the Charter of the United Nations, the Government of Turkey is obligated to maintain international peace and security, to develop friendly relations among states based on respect for the principle of equal rights and self-determination of peoples, and to achieve international cooperation through the promotion and encouragement of respect for human rights and fundamental freedoms for all;

Whereas the Government of Turkey, as a party to the International Covenant on Civil and Political Rights and the International Covenant on Economic, Social, and Cultural Rights, has made additional and firm commitments to observe and uphold the rights of all peoples;

Whereas as a member of the North Atlantic Treaty Organization, the Government of Turkey undertook to refrain in international relations from the threat or use of force in any manner inconsistent with the purposes of the United Nations;

Whereas as a member of the Organization of for Security and Cooperation in Europe, Turkey is obliged to respect the territorial integrity of other states, and to support the human rights, fundamental freedoms and the self-determination of peoples;

Whereas on March 21, 1995, more than 35,000 Turkish military troops, with tanks, armored personnel carriers, and air support, began an invasion of Northern Iraq;

Whereas the Government of Turkey declares that the invasion is in response to acts of terrorism by the Kurdistan Workers Party, also known as the PKK, and constitutes the hot pursuit of terrorists;

Whereas reports indicate that the Turkish army has penetrated 25 miles into Iraq along a 150 mile front, and that hundreds of ethnic Kurds have been killed thus far;

Whereas independent international observers claim that some of those killed are innocent civilians, and accuse Turkey of torturing prisoners, and of forcibly evacuating and destroying villages;

Whereas U.S. government officials have suggested that Turkey's invasion could last more than 3 weeks in duration;

Whereas in scope, scale and duration, Turkey's invasion of Iraqi Kurdistan appears to be an illegal act of aggression and inconsistent with Turkey's obligations under the U.N. Charter;

Whereas Turkey's actions jeopardize U.S. and international efforts under Operation Provide Comfort in Northern Iraq, and threaten the provision of vital humanitarian assistance by nongovernmental organizations to the Kurds;

Whereas the U.S. Department of State reports that the general human rights situation in Turkey "worsened significantly" in 1994, and that in many human rights case, the specific "targets of abuse were ethnic Kurds or their supporters;"

Whereas according to the U.S. Government, specific violations of human rights by the Government of Turkey in its campaign against the PKK include the illegal use of torture, excessive force, and political and extra-judicial killings of non-combatants;

Now, therefore be it resolved, That the Senate—

(1) Condemns Turkey's invasion of Northern Iraq as an illegal act of aggression and a violation of international law, inconsistent with Turkey's obligations under the Charter of the United Nations, the North Atlantic Treaty, and other international agreements;

(2) Calls upon the President of the United States to express strong U.S. opposition to Turkey's invasion of Northern Iraq;

(3) Urges the United States at the United Nations Security Council to condemn Turkey's illegal act of aggression and bring about an immediate and unconditional withdrawal;

(4) Denounces Turkey's consistent pattern of human rights violations against ethnic Kurds;

(5) Condemns all acts of terror, including those by PKK forces against Turkish civilian, military and other targets;

(6) Supports the maintenance of Operation Provide Comfort and the continuation of other non-governmental humanitarian assistance for the Kurds of Northern Iraq.

Mr. PELL. Mr. President, five years ago, when Iraqi forces crossed the border and invaded Kuwait, the international community—with the United States at the forefront—condemned the aggression and vowed that it would not stand. This week, more than 35,000 Turkish forces invaded Iraqi Kurdistan under the assertion of being engaged in hot pursuit of Kurdish terrorists. The truth is that Turkey's action is no less a violation of international law than Iraq's invasion of Kuwait.

The official United States position is that Turkey faces a legitimate threat from the Kurdish Workers Party—also known as the PKK—a Kurdish separatist group based in Turkey that advocates the establishment of an independent Kurdish state.

The PKK is a terrorist organization, and Turkey has a right to defend its citizens against the unlawful use of terror. Where I draw the line, however, is Turkey's use of terrorism as a pretense for its full-scale invasion of Iraqi Kurdistan and as justification for its consistent pattern of human rights violations against innocent Kurdish civilians in southeast Turkey.

There is no way that the Turkish forces can distinguish between the Turkish Kurds and Iraqi Kurds that presently reside in Northern Iraq. Nor can they reasonably determine which Turkish Kurd is an armed terrorist, and which is an innocent civilian refuges. The result is that innocent Kurds—be they Iraqi or Kurdish—are being harassed, terrorized, and killed by Turkish forces.

I think that there is a fundamental truth that Turkey attempts to obscure in its approach to the Kurdish issue. The fact is that Kurdish experiment with self-rule in Northern Iraq threatens and undermines Turkey's identity. By conducting this invasion, Turkey has exposed that it cares little about Iraq's territorial integrity, and only wants to keep the Kurdish people in check.

The United States apparently has given the green light to Prime Minister Ciller's military adventure. Moreover, it is nearly certain that the Turkish military is using equipment and supplies of United States origin in its brutal war against the Kurds.

Turkey's militaristic policy towards the Kurds goes beyond the pale of civilized behavior. It is time for the United States to take a principled stand, express its opposition to Turkey's invasion of Iraqi Kurdistan, and cut off supplies of United States military equipment to Turkey. If, as reports today suggest, this operation is to extend for the next 3 to 5 weeks, then it is an outright falsehood to say that Turkey is engaged in hot pursuit. We should condemn this invasion for what it truly is—a clear act of aggression and a threat to international peace.

In this regard, I am submitting today with Senators Kerry, Feingold, and Snowe a resolution that does just that. In addition to condemning the invasion, the resolution calls upon the President to oppose Turkey's action, and urges the United States to lead an effort at the United Nations Security Council calling for an immediate and unconditional withdrawal. The resolution denounces both Turkey's consistent pattern of human rights violations against the Kurds and the violence perpetrated by terrorists, including the PKK. Finally, the resolution calls for the continuation of Operation Provide Comfort, which is crucial to the protection of civilians in Iraqi Kurdistan.

Mr. President, I would urge my colleague to join me in sponsoring this resolution.

156.

[March 28, 1995 (Senate), p. 4741]

TURKEY'S INVASION OF IRAQ

Mr. KERRY. Mr. President, I commend the Senator from Rhode Island for his principled stand on this issue and am pleased to join him as an original cosponsor of Senate Resolution No. 91, which condemns Turkey's invasion of Iraq.

On March 20, an estimated 35,000 Turkish troops poured across Iraq's northern border in a massive assault on the Kurdish guerrilla group known as the Kurdistan Workers' Party, or PKK. Although Turkish Prime Minister Tansu Ciller defended the invasion as a legitimate act of self-defense, the nature and extent of Turkey's invasion of northern Iraq belie this assertion. Accordingly, this resolution calls on President Clinton to express strong opposition to Turkey's invasion and to request that the United Nations Security Council condemn the invasion and seek an immediate and unconditional withdrawal of Turkey's forces back to Turkey.

Turkey's invasion contradicts its obligations under the United Nations Charter and the Organization for Security and Cooperation in Europe which oblige Turkey to respect the territorial integrity of other states, and to support the human rights, fundamental freedoms, and the self-determination of all peoples.

I and many of my colleagues sympathize with Turkey's struggle to defeat the Marxist PKK which has been engaged in a struggle for over a decade to establish an independent Kurdish state and has adopted terrorism as the principle means toward that end. However, the nature and brutality of the tactics Prime Minister Ciller and the military have adopted to combat the PKK are unacceptable, counterproductive, and unlikely to succeed.

The invasion, besides violating the fundamentals of international law, is likely to exacerbate the conflict rather than calm it. Moreover, Turkey's action seriously detracts from its standing in the international community. For a nation seeking to convince the world—and the European Union in particular—that it is committed to democracy, the rule of law, and respect for human rights, the invasion of Iraq and the ongoing military campaign to eliminate the PKK undermine Turkey's commitment to these principles and raises legitimate questions about the nature and extent of our relationship with Turkey.

Turkey, I fear, has fallen victim to the temptation to combat terrorism with reciprocal and punitive acts of violence more destructive than PKK acts of terrorism. The Turkish military has systematically emptied Kurdish villages and uprooted many Kurdish citizens from their homes. Human rights organizations have documented extensive human rights abuses, including torture and political assassination. The military's actions often wreak havoc and destruction on innocent Kurds and provide an incentive for Kurds to support the PKK.

I fear that relations between our two nations will deteriorate unless Turkey takes demonstrable steps to improve its human rights record, abandon the military campaign, and seek alternative solutions to the Kurdish problem. Turkey's recognition, that its Kurdish civilians have civil, cultural, political, and human rights is an essential first step. Failure to recognize these rights would be folly, for it is simply inconceivable for Turkey, if it is to remain committed to the fundamentals of democracy, the rule of law, and respect for human rights, to seek a military solution where one-fifth of the Turkish population—15 million—is Kurdish.

Turkey has long been a loyal and trusted allay and a valuable member of NATO. Like all nations, Turkey is struggling with the difficult task of defining its diplomatic, security, and economic roles in the post-cold-war era. This task is compounded by the need to combat PKK terrorism and the expansion of violent Islamic fundamentalism. However, these challenges, difficult though they may be, in no way legitimize Turkey's invasion of northern Iraq, and the United States must make it clear to Turkey that such behavior is damaging to our relationship and inconsistent with the announced goals of democracy, human rights, and the rule of law.

157.

[March 28, 1995 (Extensions of Remarks), pp. 705-06]

DELEGATION DETAILS HUMAN RIGHTS CONDITIONS IN TURKEY HON. CHRISTOPHER H. SMITH OF NEW JERSEY IN THE HOUSE OF REPRESENTATIVES

Tuesday, March 28, 1995

Mr. SMITH of New Jersey. Mr. Speaker, earlier this month members of a Parliamentary Human Rights Foundation delegation returned from a fact-finding mission to Turkey. The human rights situation in that country has significantly deteriorated in recent years despite assurances otherwise by Turkey's leaders.

At present, internal tensions have reached new heights, threatening to tear apart the multiethnic fabric of Turkish society while destabilizing the entire region. Turkey's campaign against the Kurdish Worker's Party [PKK] has been used to justify the recent invasion of Northern Iraq as well as sweeping restrictions on pro-Kurdish expression and peaceful political activity. And, while the PKK continues to operate and gather support, Turkey's democratic credentials are increasingly questioned.

Mr. Speaker, at this time I ask that the report of the Parliamentary Human Rights Foundation delegation, which outlines many of the human rights problems in Turkey and offers constructive recommendations on how Turkey's Government might better address such problems be printed in the Record.

REPORT ON HUMAN RIGHTS CONDITIONS IN TURKEY, MARCH 2, 1995

I. SUMMARY

The Parliamentary Human Rights Foundation (formerly the Congressional Human Rights Foundation) organized a human rights fact-finding mission to Turkey (2/25-3/1/95). The delegation was led by the Honorable J. Kenneth Blackwell, a Member of the Board of Directors and former U.S. Ambassador to the United Nations Human Rights Commission

(UNHRC). The delegation also included David L. Phillips, President of the Foundation. The purpose of the trip was to investigate reported human rights violations committed by the Government of Turkey, particularly the abuses against its citizens of Kurdish origin. The delegation also investigated violations by the PKK, a separatist organization committed to armed struggle. Based on the delegation's findings, a report has been submitted to officials in Geneva, Members of the U.S. Congress, the European Parliament, and National Assemblies in Europe.

II. PROGRAM

The delegation visited Istanbul, Diyarbakir, and Ankara. In order to consider a broad range of views, the delegation spoke with Turkish officials from the Office of the Prime Minister, the Ministry of Justice, the Ministry of Foreign Affairs, the Turkish Grand National Assembly, the Governor and Deputy Governor of the Emergency Region, and Turkish Army personnel. The delegation also met with representatives of the Turkish Human Rights Association, the Turkish Human Rights Foundation, the Diyarbakir Bar Association, HADEP officials, a DEP Parliamentarian, lawyers representing the DEP MPs, former MPs of Kurdish origin, and Kurdish citizens.

Our official request for meetings with Layla Zana and Ahmet Turk, imprisoned parliamentarians and members of the Foundations Interparliamentary Human Rights Network (IPN), was declined. Despite assurances from the Governor of the Emergency Region, our travel to Kurdish villages outside of Diyarbakir was blocked at military checkpoints. The office of the Diayarbakir Human Rights Association was closed and four members were arrested within 24 hours of the delegation's meeting with representatives of the Association.

III. SUMMARY OF OBSERVATIONS

Turkish authorities are systematically violating the rights of Turkish citizens, including those of Kurdish origin. The Anti-Terror Act and the State of Emergency provide legal sanction for gross human rights violations, particularly in Southeast Turkey.

Turkish authorities state that their objection is to the non-combatants terrorism. However, many civilian non-combatants suffer human rights violations as a result of the struggle between Turkish authorities and the PKK. The PKK is an extremist, militant organization responsible for acts of terrorism in which Turkish military and police personnel are targeted, as are Kurdish civilians. It should be noted, however, that the PKK has recently called for a "civilian solution" to the Kurdish question and has recognized Turkey's borders.

The Government of Turkey believes all persons who seek political and cultural expression for the Kurds are "separatists" and PKK sympathizers. Suspected by Turkish authorities as bases for PKK operations, more than one thousand Kurdish villages have been destroyed. Human rights monitors report instances of arbitrary detention, torture, extrajudicial killing, and restrictions on freedom of expression. In addition, democratically elected parliamentarians of Kurdish origin have been jailed and convicted for disseminating "separatist" propaganda and supporting an "armed band" while, in reality, they were merely representing the interests of their constituents. There are serious shortfalls in Turkey's administration of justice.

IV. SUMMARY OF FINDINGS

The Interior Ministry indicates that 1,046 villages in the emergency region have been evacuated; human rights monitors say several thousand villages have been destroyed; homes and their claimed inhabitants have been burned; use of chemical agents and poison gas are reported. The Government acknowledges that 940 combatants have been killed; however, other reports claim that thousands have died. The population of Diyarbakir has doubled to more than 1.2 million as internally displaced persons have sought refuge in the city.

The DEP parliamentarians were convicted in proceedings many observers labelled a "show-trial." The Government of Turkey indicates that 8,682 persons have been sentenced under its Anti-Terror Act, which permits arbitrary arrest. Many of those known to be arrested, as well as persons who have disappeared, were just attempting to peacefully exercise freedoms of speech, association, or other internationally recognized human rights. The Turkish Human Rights Association reports instances of extrajudicial killings and torture of persons held in incommunicado for political crimes. There are 250 cases/appeals presently before the European Court of Human Rights and the European Commission on Human Rights.

The Constitutional Court of Turkey has no right of review for "decrees with the force of law" issued under the state of emergency. The Anti-Terror Act, adopted in 1991, restricts many civil liberties, including attorney access to, as well as the rights of, persons in detention. The Anti-Terror Act and state of emergency provisions also restrict freedom of expression. Government agencies harass and imprison human rights minors, journalists, lawyers, and professors. The Act's broad and ambiguous definition of terrorism, particularly Article 8, has led to widespread abuses of innocent civilians.

In addition, the Constitutional Court has banned the DEP party, a vehicle for the expression of Kurdish cultural identity and full citizenship rights. In the past two years, 26 DEP and HADEP members have been killed. In the run-up to recent elections, the DEP headquarters was bombed. The press law permits banning of publications with a court order and states that "responsible editors" bear responsibility for the content of their publications; 19 journalists have been tried under the Anti-Terror Act. On December 3, 1994, a journal reputed to be pro-PKK, the "*Izgur Ulke*" was bombed. There are no independent Kurdish language newspapers, television, or radio. Regarding cultural expression, the Constitution does not recognize Kurds as a national, racial, or ethnic minority. Two hundred Kurds were arrested during Newroz New Year celebrations in Diyarbakir.

It is important to note that the PKK, itself, is responsible for gross human rights violations by targeting village officials, guards, informants, teachers, and young men who refuse to take up arms against the authorities. By the admission of its own representatives, the PKK has recently killed 179 village guards, 66 collaborators, and police officials. The well-being of almost every Kurd is adversely affected by the conflict.

As a result of the conflict, Turkey's citizens of Kurdish origin have become bereft of many democratic rights and are denied effective political and cultural expression. The resulting radicalization of the Kurds is contributing to a worsening security situation throughout the country. An increasing number of Kurds are turning to the pro-Muslim Welfare Party.

V. RECOMMENDATIONS

The international community should promote improvement in human rights conditions in Turkey by encouraging a dialogue between Turkish authorities and legitimate representatives of Kurdish interests. To this end, amnesty should be provided to convicted DEP parliaments so that they can participate in a dialogue concerning the reduction of tensions and the normalization of relations between Turkish authorities and Turkey's citizens of Kurdish origin.

Within the competence of the UNHRC, the Working Group on Arbitrary Detention, and the Special Rapporteurs on Torture and Freedom of Expression should investigate human rights conditions in Turkey. The Government of Turkey has "invited" the Special Rapporteur on Summary Executions to visit Turkey. A suitable itinerary and near term date should be finalized.

Efforts should be made by the U.S. and the E.U. to establish mutual reinforcing restrictions on the sale of military equipment which might be used against civilian populations. The US and EU should also coordinate the extension and/or relaxation of tariff and trade privileges based on Turkey's overall human rights performance.

Technical assistance programs in the rule of law should be undertaken among Members of the Turkish Grand National Assembly, European Parliament, and U.S. Congress in order to strengthen democratic institutions and assist in constitutional and legislative reform. The Anti-Terror Act should be amended so that the rights of Turkish citizens are safeguarded, as is the right of the state to protect its territorial integrity. Electronic computer networks should be established between the TGNA and parliamentary bodies in other countries.

These recommendations are provided so that the international community can become fully seized by the worsening human rights conditions in Turkey. The authors of this report hope for reconciliation through dialogue so that peace, prosperity, and democracy may flourish for all citizens of the Turkish Republic.

158.

[March 30, 1995 (Extensions of Remarks), p. 745]

TURKEY MUST CEASE ITS RELENTLESS ATTACKS AGAINST THE KURDISH PEOPLE
HON. BOBBY L. RUSH
OF ILLINOIS
IN THE HOUSE OF REPRESENTATIVES

Thursday, March 30, 1995

Mr. RUSH. Mr. Speaker, I rise today to express my extreme dismay and strong concerns about the recent actions of the Turkish Government.

The government in Turkey has once again decided that it is easier to address dissention around its borders with military force than to sit down to talk with those whose only wish is to seek freedom from overwhelming oppression.

You will hear from the Turkish Government that this recent excursion into Kurdish-held areas in Iraq is only aimed at stopping Kurdish rebel groups from making raids into Turkey. We must not be fooled by what they say.

It is accepted policy in that country to deny official acknowledgement of a group that comprises close to 20 percent of its total population. Because they have no special protection under Turkish law, Kurdish civilians have been victim to a policy of discriminate harassment, persecution, even killing and wounding at the hands of the Turkish establishment.

The Turkish Government has been condemned time and time again by the United Nations, Helsinki Watch, and Amnesty International for denying Kurds the basic civil liberties. These include the right to freedom of self-determination and the right to freely express the richness of their cultural heritage.

Mr. Speaker, this current situation is no different. Thousands of Turkish-born Kurds are now living in northern Iraq, after fleeing Turkey last year because of harassment from Turkish officials. Their lives have been shattered because of the incessant attacks on their heritage, culture, and indeed, their very existence.

These civilians have been caught in the crossfire for too long. These civilians only seek the freedom to choose their own destinies. At the very least, this Government's response should be to say in no uncertain terms that they be allowed to pursue this very basic right.

However, Mr. Speaker, we may be also partly to blame for the ongoing crisis in the mountains of Iraq.

Not only does the Turkish Government receive vast amounts of United States financial aid, we and our allies also supply their government with large amounts of military hardware. These weapons are in turn being used to wipe out whole villages, to kill innocent women and children. We should follow the lead of the German Government and look to end our weapons trade with Turkey.

I believe, Mr. Speaker, all United States aid to Turkey should be reviewed in light of their history with other ethnic groups in Cyprus and Armenia. And just as important, that government's current activities in the mountains of Iraq should further make us question our priorities in that region.

Mr. Speaker, Turkey does have the right to protect its borders and to protect its citizens from terrorism. However, this very right cannot be used to justify continued harassment and persecution of innocent civilian populations.

We have supported the right of Iraqi-born Kurds to pursue independence from the regime in Baghdad. Our troops are in the mountains of northern Iraq at this moment, protecting Kurds from the Iraqi military. However, Mr. Speaker, we should look to protect the rights of all Kurds, regardless of where they were born.

The United States has warned the Turkish Government that we are watching. I will say also that the whole world should watch this situation very closely. This will not only hold that government accountable but will also force this country to reevaluate its foreign priorities and practices.

159.

[April 5, 1995 (Senate), pp. 5189-93]

TURKEY MUST WITHDRAW

Mr. PELL. Mr. President, on March 23, together with Senators Kerry, Feingold, and Snowe, I submitted Senate Resolution 91 condemning the Turkish invasion of Northern Iraq. Since then, Senators Biden, D'AMATO, Sarbanes, and Simon have become cosponsors. With such strong bipartisan support, I hoped to move this resolution to Senate passage. Until today, I had intended to offer it as an amendment to the pending legislation. Given the fluidity of the floor situation—particularly the difficulties involving the Jordan debt amendment, and the need to send that matter to the President as soon as possible—I think it best not to offer a foreign policy amendment to this bill.

I remain deeply concerned, however, about Turkey's continued military operations in northern Iraq, and I wish to address that subject now. In the past several days, I have had occasion to pursue this issue at the highest levels of both the United States and Turkish Governments. I have had an exchange of letters with both the President and the Secretary of State, and just this morning, I and other members of the Foreign Relations Committee met with the Turkish Foreign Minister.

Specifically, I am disturbed by Turkey's continued military presence in Iraqi Kurdistan, and by the Government's unwillingness to set a date certain for withdrawal. Turkey should withdraw now.

While I appreciate Turkey's legitimate desire to combat the terrorist threat posed by the PKK, I believe the military action in Northern Iraq goes beyond mere self-defense, and furthermore offers virtually no prospect of eradicating PKK terror. The vast majority of terrorist attacks in Turkey are carried out not from Northern Iraq, but from inside Turkey itself. Turkey's repressive treatment of its own Kurds has forced thousands of civilian Kurds to flee to Northern Iraq. This has made it easier, in fact, for a small number of PKK terrorists to use civilian settlements in Northern Iraq as cover.

The Turkish incursion puts at risk thousands of Kurdish civilians living in Northern Iraq. To my mind, the Turkish incursion is a violation of international law, that must be brought to an end.

Furthermore, reports indicate that Turkey has made difficult access to areas of the conflict to representatives of international relief organizations, such as the International Red Cross. At a minimum, Turkey should take immediate steps to ensure the protection of innocent civilians and refugees. It also appears that Turkey has restricted journalists' access to critical areas of the conflict.

I must say that I took small comfort in the thought that Turkey is arranging tours for journalists and that it must place limits on access to the ICRC to ensure that the PKK does not receive assistance. I believe that the ICRC has vast experience in these matters, and certainly is as capable as the Turkish Government in determining how best to assist civilians caught in the fighting.

I will say that in my consultations with the U.S. Government on these matters, I have been pleased to see an acknowledgment of—and a concerted effort to—address my concerns. The President has assured me that United States officials in Washington and Ankara are pressing Turkey daily to protect innocent civilians and to withdraw at the earliest possible date.

The Secretary of State acknowledges that Turkey has been denying access to journalists and nongovernmental organizations, and informs me that the United States is working at the highest levels to rectify this situation. I am pleased to learn that United States embassy officials are visiting Iraqi Kurdistan this very week, and that Secretary Talbott and Secretary Holbrooke will travel to Ankara where they will pursue our concerns. I await their reports anxiously.

I welcome the apparent shift in the administration's approach to the troubling aspects of the invasion. The administration seems much more willing to question Turkey's motives and behavior, and to confront Turkey on these troubling issues. Although I still intend to pursue adoption of my resolution at the earliest practical time, I do believe U.S. policy is moving in the right direction. I yield the floor . . .

160.

[May 24, 1995 (House), pp. 5502-52]

AMERICAN OVERSEAS INTERESTS ACT OF 1995

. . .

II. U.S. Weapons at War

A comparison of the Pentagon's own data on deliveries of weapons through the U.S. Foreign Military Sales (FMS) and Commercial Sales (CS) programs over the past decade with a list of 50 significant wars that were under way during 1993- 94 indicates that U.S. weapons exports have played a major role in fueling the ethnic and territorial conflicts that have become one of the most difficult security challenges of the post-Cold War era [18]:

In the past ten years, parties to 45 current conflicts have taken delivery of over $42 billion worth of U.S. weaponry;

Of the significant ethnic and territorial conflicts going on during 1993-94, 90% (45 out of 50) of them involved one or more parties that had received some U.S. weaponry or

military technology in the period leading up to the conflict;

In more than half of current conflicts (26 out of 50), the United States has been a significant arms supplier, accounting for at least 5% of the weapons delivered to one party to the dispute over a five year period;

In more than one-third of all current conflicts (18 out of 50), the United States has been a major supplier to one party to the dispute, accounting for over 25% of all weapons imported by that participant in the most recent five year period;

Despite the popular perception that it is U.S. policy to cease deliveries of weapons once a conflict is under way, as of the end of 1993 (the latest year for which full statistics are available) the United States was shipping military goods and services to more than half (26 out of 50) of the areas where there were wars being fought.

The data outlined above demonstrate that contrary to the assertions of key policymakers, academic analysts, and industry lobbyists, the United States is sustaining the warfighting capabilities of a substantial number of the parties to the world's current conflicts. In a number of volatile areas the United States has been the primary supplier to governments that are involved in either internal or regional conflicts. In cases where the United States has supplied a majority of a client government's imported weaponry over an extended period of time, it is likely that some U.S. systems will be utilized in future conflicts involving these nations (see Table I, below)

Among the most serious conflicts in which the United States has been the primary weapons supplier are Turkey, Morocco, Somalia, Liberia, Kenya, Zaire, Pakistan, Indonesia, the Philippines, Haiti, Guatemala, Colombia and Mexico. Official U.S. weapons deliveries to Haiti, Guatemala, Liberia, and Zaire were cut off as of the early 1990s, but U.S. deliveries to conflict zones in Turkey, Morocco, Somalia and Kenya have actually increased over the past few years. In the case of Somalia, the increase is explained by the fact that a new government has been installed as a result of a UN peacekeeping mission in that nation. But continuing U.S. deliveries to Morocco, Turkey, and Kenya have no such rationale: in these cases, U.S. arms are shoring up regimes that have been intransigent in their pursuit of military solutions to sensitive ethnic and territorial disputes. Last but not least, in both Haiti and Guatemala, legislative attempts to terminate U.S. military assistance were subverted by the implementation of covert aid programs that were actually larger than the overt programs that were eliminated by Congress (see sections II and III for further discussion) . . .

While data on the total volume of U.S. weapons supplies to areas of conflict is readily available, specific information on how U.S. weaponry is being put to use in today's wars is harder to come by. This is in part because neither the media nor the armed forces have made it their business to identify the specific types of weaponry utilized in a given conflict or to document the origins of these armaments. Even if gathering such data was a priority, the reality of warfare, particularly multi-sided civil conflicts involving light weaponry, would make it difficult to obtain comprehensive information. Nonetheless, accounts in the mainstream and specialty press have uncovered a number of recent examples of how U.S.-supplied weaponry is being put to use on the battlefield, and a number of arms control and human rights researchers have recently begun a concerted effort to gather more information on the patterns of deliveries of light weaponry to ethnic conflicts. The following examples are illustrative of the ways in which U.S. weapons are being utilized in current conflicts: a more comprehensive accounting would require more open reporting of the nature of U.S. weapons transfers to these areas.

TURKEY: Turkey received over $6.3 billion worth of military equipment and services from the United States between F.Y. 1984 and F.Y. 1993.[19] The United States supplied 76% of all weapons imported by the Turkish government between 1987 and 1991, a figure which increased to 80% for the period from 1991 to 1993. The majority of U.S. weapons supplies to Turkey have been paid for by U.S. taxpayers as part of an extensive military aid program that has provided over $5 billion in assistance from F.Y. 1986 through

F.Y. 1995.[20] Turkey has also received large deliveries of U.S. weaponry for free or at minimal cost as part of the NATO "cascading" program, which involves redistributing surplus weapons rendered redundant by the Conventional Forces in Europe Treaty (CFE).[21] Last but not least, a number of U.S. weapons systems are produced in Turkey under coproduction and licensing agreements with U.S. firms, including Lockheed's F-16 fighter plane and the FMC Corporation's M-113 armored personnel carrier.[22]

There have been reports in the international and Turkish press indicating that U.S.-supplied weaponry has been used extensively by the Turkish government in its war on the Kurdistan Worker's Party (PKK) in southeastern Turkey. A wide range of U.S. systems, including F-16, F-4, F5, and F-104 fighter aircraft, Cobra and Black Hawk helicopters, cluster bombs, and M-60 tanks and M-113 armored personnel carriers have been used in the conflict, which has claimed over 15,000 lives since 1984.[23]. The Clinton Administration and other supporters of the Turkish government have argued that the PKK is a terrorist organization, not a legitimate political movement. However, regardless of their views on the PKK, most independent observers agree that the politico-military strategy of the Turkish government—strafing and depopulating entire villages in the southeast—entails unnecessary suffering and repeated violations of the human rights of civilian noncombatants. Human Rights Watch has reported that as of October 1994, the Turkish government has depopulated as many as 1,400 villages and hamlets and displaced several hundred thousand people in its prosecution of the war against the PKK.[24] Major encounters involving U.S.-supplied weaponry have included May 1993 bombing raids in the Karliova valley that utilized F-4 fighter plans and Cobra helicopters to kill 44 Kurdish fighters and a January 1994 incursion into Iraq to bombard PKK camps with cluster bombs, 500- and 2000- pound bombs dropped from F-16 and F-4 aircraft.

The Turkish government's March 1995 invasion of Northern Iraq marks the latest chapter in its quest for a military solution to the Kurdish question. A Turkish government spokesperson proudly described the cross-border raid by 35,00 troops as "the biggest military operation in the history of the Turkish Republic."[25] Ironically, the Turkish attack targeted the same sector of Iraq in which the United States had been enforcing a "no fly zone" as part of the United Nations-backed Operation Provide Comfort, an effort designed to protect Iraqi Kurds in the area from Saddam Hussein's regime. Because the United States is far and away Turkey's largest supplier of weapons and military aid, Turkish Prime Minister Tansu Ciller cleared the operation with President Clinton by telephone before sending her military forces into Iraq. White House spokesperson Mike McCurry reported that the President accepted Ciller's explanation that the raids were strictly aimed at PKK "terrorist bases" in Northern Iraq, and that Clinton expressed "understanding for Turkey's need to deal decisively" with the rebel group.[26]

In a move that may prompt debate for some time to come, President Clinton and the Pentagon also ordered U.S. military personnel in Northern Iraq to "stand down" from enforcing the no fly zone against Turkey aircraft for the duration of Turkey's intervention. when a reporter asked Pentagon spokesperson Dennis Boxx whether the Pentagon was "uncomfortable" over the fact that a U.S. ally was "beating up on . . . the same people we've been trying to protect from Iraq for a number of years," Boxx argued that Turkey was taking great care to focus its attacks on PKK terrorist strongholds. When he was asked where U.S. enforcement of the no fly zone would be rendered inoperative for the duration of the Turkish intervention in Northern Iraq, Boxx implied that it would, noting that "it's simply better not to put these people at risk [U.S. military personnel involved in Operation Provide Comfort] until this has been resolved." The chilling implication of Boxx's remark is that the Pentagon actually feared that if U.S. forces had tried to enforce the no fly zone against the Turkish military, Turkish forces would have engaged in an air war against U.S. troops, using U.S.-supplied aircraft. It was almost as if the Pentagon spokesman was acknowledging that Turkey had intimidated the

U.S. into allowing its Iraqi incursion to go forward unhindered.[27]

As has been the case in its major anti-Kurdish operations of the recent past, Turkey's offensive in Northern Iraq has relied heavily on U.S.-supplied equipment. Reports in the European press have indicated that Turkey's air war against the PKK (and against a number of Kurdish settlements and refugee camps) in Northern Iraq has been conducted almost entirely with U.S.-designed fighter planes such as the McDonnel Douglas F-4, the Lockheed F-104, and the Lockheed Martin F-16. Other U.S.-supplied aircraft such as the Textron-Bell Cobra helicopter gunship and the United Technologies/Sikorsky Black Hawk troop transport have also been used in support of Turkey's move into Iraq.[28]

U.S. support of the Turkish intervention is based on the assumption that it is a carefully crafted defensive operation aimed at wiping out PKK bases in Iraq, with little or no negative impact on Kurdish civilians. But press reports from the area have raised serious doubts regarding Turkey's claim that it has been mounting a "surgical strike" against terrorists. Turkey's ongoing war against the PKK, both in Northern Iraq and Southeastern Turkey, is looking increasingly like it may become that nation's Vietnam: a draining, divisive, and ultimately unsuccessful effort to defeat a nationalist movement by military means. An April 2nd news analysis piece by John Pomfret of the *Washington Post*—appropriately entitled "Turkey's Hunt for the Kurds: the Making of a Quagmire?"—captured the dilemma faced by Turkish troops in Northern Iraq as they attempted to sort out Kurdish PKK militants from Kurdish civilians (both Turkish and Iraqi) in the area:

". . . by embracing a military answer to what it considers a terrorist question, Turkey risks bogging its army down in a vicious cycle of incursion and withdrawal, followed by guerilla counterattacks and more incursions again. Such a cycle, Western officials have said, would only empty government coffers overtaxed by an ailing economy and a similar counterinsurgency operation within Turkey."[29]

A western relief worker underscored the futility of Turkey's military strategy when he told Pomfret "you can't wipe out a terrorist operation that operates on two continents by attacking the mountains. It's like killing a fly with a sledgehammer." Turkish soldiers reported a conundrum similar to that faced U.S. forces in Vietnam—an inability to distinguish friend from foe. One soldier told the Post "we have a big problem because we don't know who is a villager and who the PKK is . . . we can't do a thing."[30]

Unfortunately, contrary to the soldier's report, Turkish troops did plenty of things in Northern Iraq, including a number of documented cases of killings and displacement of Kurdish civilians. There is no way of knowing at this point whether these were isolated incidents or part of a larger pattern of abuse, because at a number of key stages in the conflict Turkish military commanders limited access to the combat zones on the part of both journalists and relief workers.[31] At the end of March, during the second week of the Turkish invasion, residents of the Iraqi village of Beshile reported that their village had been bombed and burned to the ground by Turkish forces. Fevzi Rashid, a 43 year old farmer who witnessed the Turkish attack, described it to a reporter from Reuters news service as follows:

"First the planes bombed our village. Then soldiers came some days later and burned our houses. Yesterday they came again and fired at the village with rockets and mortars."[32]

Turkey's claim to be targeting only PKK terrorists has been further undercut by assertions by the Iraqi National Congress, the Iraqi Kurdish organization that controls most of the territory impacted by the Turkish invasion, that on the very first day of the invasion "Turkish soldiers . . . arrested hundreds of refugees as suspected followers of the Kurdish Workers' Party."[33]

Although the Clinton Administration firmly held to its position that the Turkish invasion would be limited in duration and narrow in focus, one expected withdrawal date—Turkish Prime Minister Tansu Ciller's April 19th visit to Washington—came and went with no final timetable for withdrawal in sight. A partial pullback of Turkish troops in late

April of 1995 still left at least 10,000 Turkish troops inside Iraq, and there is some dispute even now as to whether all Turkish troops have cleared out of the area (see discussion below). In contrast to the policy of Germany, which has cut off all weapons shipments to Turkey in response to the Iraqi incursion, the Clinton Administration's position on the Kurdish question appears to be "Turkey right or wrong."[34] The U.S. arms industry has officially weighed in on the side of the Turkish government's tactics as well, in the form of a comment by Joel Johnson, chief lobbyist for the Aerospace Industries Association, to the effect that Turkey's military plan was no different from what other global and regional powers have done in similar circumstances:

"It must be acknowledged that the Turks have not invented Rolling Thunder. We used B-52s to solve a guerrilla problem [in Vietnam]. The Russians used very large weapons platforms [in Afghanistan]. And the Israelis get irritated on a reasonably consistent basis and use F-16s in Southern Lebanon. One wishes that it didn't happen. Sitting in the comfort of one's office, one might tell all four countries they're wrong. It's a lot easier to say that here than when you're there and it's your military guys who are getting chewed up."[35]

Setting aside for a moment the obvious moral issues raised by massive bombing raids as a tool of modern warfare, it must be pointed out that Johnson's statement glosses over a key strategic point: in two of the three examples he cites, Vietnam and Afghanistan, the "Rolling Thunder" tactic was employed by great powers that were ultimately defeated militarily and politically by smaller, better motivated nationalist forces. Even staunch allies of the current Turkish regime might find reason to advise Prime Minister Ciller to abandon her country's current military strategy vis-a-vis Kurdish separatist forces.

In response to a growing international outcry against the Turkish government's tactics in its war against the PKK, the Clinton Administration has repeatedly urged Turkey to stop its indiscriminate approach of bombing and depopulating entire villages. congress has gone beyond rhetoric by withholding 10% of Turkey's U.S. military aid for F.Y. 1995 pending a report on abuses against civilians by the

Turkish military. In December 1994, Human Rights Watch published a report entitled "U.S. Cluster Bombs for Turkey?" which called for a reversal of a plan to provide advanced U.S.-built CBU-87 cluster bombs to Turkey on the grounds that the weapons might be used against civilians. As a result of the pressure generated by the report, the cluster bomb sale has been shelved for the moment.[36]

Despite these efforts to restrict the flow of U.S. arms to Turkey's war against the PKK, the United States remains Turkey's number one weapons supplier, and Turkey's inhumane warfighting tactics continue. As of the first week of May, 1995, Turkish officials claimed to have removed all of their troops from Northern Iraq, but Prime Minister Ciller has stated in no uncertain terms that she retains the right to invade the area again if Turkey detects further PKK activities there.[37] So far, moves to curb Turkey's use of imported weaponry have had no discernible impact on Ciller's approach to the Kurdish problem: she told members of her governing coalition in early April that "we have one thing to say to those who threaten us about using their arms when they should be standing by us—we will use our right to defend ourselves under any circumstances. You can keep your weapons."[38] Maybe it's time for President Clinton to take Prime Minister Ciller up on her offer . . .

FOOTNOTES

19. See Appendix A, Table I.

20. Human Rights Watch Arms Project, U.S. Cluster Bombs for Turkey?, (New York: Human Rights Watch, December 1994), p. 9.

21. Ibid., p. 11; see also British American Security Information Council, Fueling Balkan Fires: The West's Arming of Greece and Turkey, Project on the Arms Trade Report 93.3, (Washington, DC: BASIC, 1993), and British American Security Information Council, "US-German Arms Exports and Greece at a Record High,22M̶a̶y̶2̶0̶, 1994; for a review of Turkey's military industrialization drive and the role of U.S. and other foreign firms in helping to sustain it through coproduction and licensing deals, see Gulay Gunluk-Senesen, "An Overview of the Arms Industry Modernization Program in Turkey," in SIPRI Yearbook 1993: World Armaments and Disarma-

ment (New York: Oxford University Press, 1993), pp. 521-532.

23. For the best review of the evidence on the Turkish armed forces use of U.S.-supplied systems against the PKK, see U.S. Cluster Bombs for Turkey?, op. cit., pp. 4-6.

24. Human Rights Watch/Helsinki, Turkey: Forced Displacement of Ethnic Kurds from Southeastern Turkey (Washington, DC: Human Rights Watch, October 1994), p. 4.

25. "Turkey Unleashes a Massive Raid on Kurdish Bases in Turkey," International Herald Tribune, March 21, 1995.

26. Ibid.

27. Department of Defense News Briefing by Dennis Boxx, March 21, 1995, official DoD transcript.

28. "Turkey Unleashes," op. cit., note 25; "Turkish Army Readies Final Assault on Kurd Pockets," International Herald Tribune, March 25-26, 1995; and John Barham, "Turkish Army Invades Iraq to Strike at Turkish Bases," Financial Times (London), March 21, 1995.

29. John Pomfret, "Turkey's Hunt for the Kurds: The Making of a Quagmire?", Washington Post, April 2, 1995.

30. Ibid.

31. "UN Evacuates Kurds from Path of Turkey's Offensive," International Herald Tribune, March 27, 1995; "Turkey Plays Down Criticism of Assault," International Herald Tribune, March 29, 1995; and Pomfret, "Turkey's Hunt," op. cit.

32. Suna Erdem, "Iraqi Kurds Say Turkey Torched Their Town," Washington Post, March 30, 1995.

33. "Turkey Unleashes," op. cit.

34. "Germany Withholds Materiel Over Drive on Kurds," International Herald Tribune, March 30, 1995.

35. David Morrison, "Turkish War Concern for America," National Journal, April 15, 1995.

36. U.S. Cluster Bombs for Turkey, op. cit., pp .9-10; and Thomas W. Lippman, "Rights Group Seeks to Block Proposed Cluster-Bomb Sale to Turkey," Washington Post, December 28, 1995.

37. "Turkish Aid Says Troops Have Left Iraq," New York Times, May 5, 1995. The article actually cites conflicting reports from two different Turkish officials—Turkish Defense Minister Mehmet Golhan is quoted as saying "We have no one there . . . We have withdrawn them all and we only have security measures on the border." However, the article goes on to indicate that "Deputy Prime Minister Hikmet Cetin said . . . that a few troops still remain in Northern Iraq, but he did not give details."

38. John Pomfret, "Turkish Premier Assails Kurdish Attack's Critics," *Washington Post*, April 5, 1995 . . .

Sincerely,
Cynthia McKinney,
Member of Congress.

161.

[July 27, 1995 (Extensions of Remarks), p. 1521]

TURKEY'S PARLIAMENT TAKES IMPORTANT STEP FORWARD
HON. CHRISTOPHER H. SMITH
OF NEW JERSEY
IN THE HOUSE OF REPRESENTATIVES

Wednesday, July 26, 1995

Mr. Smith of New Jersey. Mr. Speaker, I rise today to commend Turkey's Parliament and Prime Minister Ciller for taking an important step towards strengthening democracy. On Sunday, July 23, Turkey's Parliament approved 16 constitutional amendments which are part of a democratization plan introduced last year. The Parliament also agreed to resume work in September on amending article 8 of the Anti-Terror Law, which is widely used to criminalize anti-government and pro-Kurdish expressions. These reforms are considered prerequisites to Turkey's acceptance into a European Union customs agreement this fall. Mr. Speaker, I am very encouraged by the fact that the amendments were adopted by a vote of 360-32 after weeks of tumultuous debate.

These amendments are significant for the cause of democracy in Turkey. Their passage marks the first time the civilian government in Turkey has altered the 1982 constitution promulgated by the military. Prime Minister Ciller and the junior coalition partner, Republican Peoples Party deserve much praise for standing by the legislation despite strong opposition from Islamic and nationalist parties.

More specifically, Mr. Speaker, the amendments will broaden political participation by lowering the voting age from 20 to 18; adding 100 seats to the 450 seat Parliament; enabling MPs to switch parties; and allowing trade unions, student associations and other groups to engage in political activities. Language in the constitution praising the 1980 military takeover was also removed.

As I have said in the past, Mr. Speaker, it is in our Nation's best interest to maintain close relations with a stable, democratic Turkey. These amendments, and other efforts in the future, will place our bilateral relations on a much more firm footing. While there is more that needs to be done to address free speech issues and the situation of Turkey's Kurdish population, adoption of these amendments by such a wide margin indicates a commitment and willingness in the Parliament to move forward along this path.

Mr. Speaker, as someone who has spoken out in the past against actions taken by the Government of Turkey, I believe it is important to give the Turkish Government credit where credit is due. Reaction in the Turkish press to the amendments was resoundingly positive and public opinion is also likely to view the reforms in a positive light. Given this set of circumstances, I strongly encourage the Turkish MPs to immediately seize upon the momentum of this impressive showing and press on for further reforms.

Last week, Mr. Speaker, it looked as though partisan politics in Turkey would block the passage of any democratic reforms. Successful adoption of the amendments, though, has breathed new life into the reform debate underway in Turkey. Mr. Speaker, I believe that all who are concerned about human rights and regional stability should express support for the continued efforts of Turkey's Parliament and Government to continue this important process.

162.

[July 27, 1995 (Extensions of Remarks), p. 1529]

KURDS IN TURKEY: THE TRUE STORY
HON. DAN BURTON

OF INDIANA
IN THE HOUSE OF REPRESENTA-
TIVES

Thursday, July 27, 1995

Mr. BURTON of Indiana. Mr. Speaker, the relationship between Turkey, its Kurdish population, and the PKK—the Kurdistan Workers Party—is greatly misunderstood. Contrary to what Turkey's critics in the United States Congress would like the rest of the world to believe, Turkey's Kurdish population is not oppressed by the Government. In fact, the Turkish Constitution provides that all citizens, including Kurds, have the same political rights and civil liberties which they may exercise equally, without impediment, regardless of ethnic or religious background.

Turkish citizens of Kurdish origin live freely throughout Turkey, and participate in all walks of life without discrimination. Kurds are doctors, lawyers, teachers, and artists. This is an important fact that is widely misunderstood. Twenty-five percent of the Turkish Parliament is composed of Kurdish Turks, even though only 18 percent of the general population is Kurdish. Turkey's Deputy Prime Minister is Kurdish. Even Turkey's former President Turgut Ozal was Kurdish.

In addition, Turkey works to protect the livelihood of Kurds in northern Iraq. When Saddam Hussein attacked his own Kurdish citizens with poisonous gas years before the gulf war, Turkey opened its doors and clothed, fed, and sheltered them until it was safe for them to return to their homes. After the gulf war, Turkey again accepted half a million Kurds fleeing from Saddam Hussein's tyranny. Today, Turkey hosts Operation Provide Comfort, the international effort which operates from Turkish bases to protect Iraqi Kurds.

These facts, however, are overshadowed by Turkey's fight against the PKK—Kurdistan Workers Party—a Marxist-Leninist terrorist group that is supported by Iran, Iraq, and Syria. Western societies fail to understand that the Kurds now fighting against Turkey are not the same Kurds suffering under the brutality of Saddam Hussein. Although the Kurdish people of Turkey have little sympathy for the PKK, the PKK has the audacity to claim that it represents the Kurdish people.

Another little-known fact about PKK terrorists is that they are not all Kurds. The PKK ranks include mercenaries and the unemployed from a host of other countries. The only support it receives from within Turkey, it extorts from innocent Kurdish businesses. The PKK is only able to continue its war against Turkey by maintaining bases outside of Turkey, such as one in Syria's Bekaa Valley, and training with other extremist organizations. Not only is the PKK unrepresentative of the true aspirations of the Kurdish people, but its goal of "freeing the Kurdish people" is ironic when one considers what the PKK is ultimately seeking to accomplish: To set up an independent Kurdistan State based on Marxist-Leninist ideology. Such a Marxist-Leninist State would endanger the lives of many Turks and Kurdish Turks living in the region and threaten peace and stability throughout the entire Middle East.

Since its inception in 1984, the PKK has based its operations on intimidation. To force its ideology upon the masses, the PKK uses an extensive policy of oppression, and forces villagers, both Turks and Kurdish Turks, who are loyal to the State, to vacate their villages and move elsewhere. It has killed thousands of civilians, many of whom are the same Kurds that the PKK claims to represent, while sabotaging economic development projects that would assist in the strengthening of democracy in Turkey. It has also extorted money from the Kurds. Those who resist are murdered in groups. Their houses are burnt, and their harvests and livestock are destroyed. It is absurd to say that the PKK is an organization waging an armed struggle for the freedom of the Kurdish people.

What we are dealing with is a group that could seriously undermine the future of democracy in Turkey. It has defied the laws that are designed to promote economic opportunity and preserve law and order, in a democratic society that respects the rights and freedoms of all people in the region. Supporting a strong democratic Turkey in a generally volatile region has long been regarded as important to the United States. Therefore, it is in the interest of the United States to support Turkey's policies to combat PKK terrorism. It is not correct, however, to target Turkey's fight against terrorists like the PKK as a sign of democracy in danger. On the contrary, true danger would be signified if a democratic government were unwilling to protect its country's territorial integrity or its citizens' human rights from the inhuman measures of a terrorist organization.

By conditioning and threatening to cut off aid to Turkey, the United States is undermining a democratic government that is only seeking to protect its citizens and its territorial integrity. It is especially counterproductive to condemn Turkey's policies at this critical juncture when the Turkish Parliament is considering a series of constitutional reforms to bring Turkey's laws in line with those of the European Union, and just recently approved a 6-month extension of Operation Comfort to provide relief to Iraqi Kurds in northern Iraq. In order to promote Turkish democracy, the United States should support Prime Minister Ciller in her efforts to fight PKK terrorism and improve democracy. The Turkish people deserve the support of their democratic allies in the face of PKK intimidation.

163.

[September 7, 1995 (Extensions of Remarks), pp. 1721-22]

HUMAN RIGHTS ABUSE AND UNITED STATES-ORIGIN MILITARY EQUIPMENT IN TURKEY
HON. LEE H. HAMILTON
OF INDIANA
IN THE HOUSE OF REPRESENTATIVES

Wednesday, September 6, 1995

Mr. HAMILTON. Mr. Speaker, on June 1, 1995, the State Department released a report on allegations of human rights abuses by the Turkish military. This report stated that United States-origin military equipment has been used in operations in Turkey during which human rights abuses have occurred. This report is the most definitive administration statement linking United States military assistance to human rights violations in Turkey.

I wrote a letter to Secretary Christopher on June 29 asking several questions about that report, and on August 15 I received a reply. I ask that my letter, and the Department's response, be printed in the CONGRESSIONAL RECORD.

HOUSE OF REPRESENTATIVES,
COMMITTEE ON INTERNATIONAL RELATIONS,
Washington, DC, June 29, 1995.
Hon. WARREN CHRISTOPHER,
Secretary of State, Department of State, Washington, DC.

DEAR MR. SECRETARY: I write regarding the State Department's Report onAllegations of Human Rights Abuses by the Turkish Military, released on June 1, 1995. I commend you for the precision and detail of that report, which provides important information to the Congress.

What impresses me about that report is your open acknowledgment of the role of U.S.-origin military equipment in human rights abuse in southeastern Turkey. As your report states: "U.S.-origin equipment, which accounts for most major items of the Turkish military inventory, has been used in operations against the PKK during which human rights abuses have occurred."

I would like to ask you several questions about the June 1 report.

1. I do not recall prior Administration statements or testimony coming to the conclusion that U.S. military equipment provided to Turkey was used in operations during which human rights abuses occurred.

Can you point me to prior statements by this Administration, or previous Administrations, that make a link between U.S.-origin equipment provided to the Turkish military and human rights abuses?

2. For how long has the Turkish military used U.S.-supplied equipment in operations against the PKK?

For how long do you believe human rights abuses in connection with Turkish military operations against the PKK have been occurring?

3. Are Turkey's human rights abuses with U.S.-origin military equipment, as detailed in your June 1 report, consistent with Section 4 of the "Purposes for Which Military Sales by the United States Are Authorized," under Section 4 of the Arms Export Control Act (AECA)?

Do you intend to report under Section 3(c)(2) of the AECA concerning a violation of that Act, through the use of U.S.-origin defense equipment for a purpose not authorized under Section 4 of the AECA?

At what point do human rights abuses with U.S.-origin defense equipment constitute a "consistent pattern of gross violations" and thus, under Section 502B of the Foreign Assistance Act, prohibit AECA sales of defense articles or services?

4. What are the implications for U.S. policy of your determination that Turkey has used U.S.-origin military equipment in operations in which human rights abuses have occurred?

What steps are you taking to address human rights abuses mentioned in your June 1 report?

5. Is it U.S. policy to promote a political solution in southeastern Turkey?

Does Turkey support a political solution?

What is the next step in trying to promote a political solution?

I appreciate the strategic importance of Turkey, and I agree with you that Turkey is a long-standing and valuable U.S. ally. I also appreciate the serious security dilemmas facing that country. Yet I believe that your June 1 report compels the United States to revisit relations with Turkey, to insure that U.S.-origin weapons are not used to commit future human rights abuses, and to insure that every effort is made to work for a political solution in southeastern Turkey.

I look forward to your answers to the questions above.

With best regards,
Sincerely,
LEE H. HAMILTON,
Ranking Democratic Member.

———

U.S. DEPARTMENT OF STATE,
Washington, DC, August 15, 1995.
Hon. LEE HAMILTON,
House of Representatives.

DEAR MR. HAMILTON: On behalf of Secretary Christopher, I am responding to your June 29 letter, which raised a number of questions regarding human rights abuses and the Turkish military's use of U.S.-supplied equipment.

I want to thank you for your comments regarding the State Department's Report on Allegations of Human Rights Abuses by the Turkish Military. The Embassy in Ankara and concerned offices at the Departments of State and Defense made every effort to convey the situation as accurately as possible.

Turning to your questions, we are not aware of statements by this or previous administrations which specifically linked U.S.-origin equipment provided to the Turkish military and human rights abuses. That said, the Administration has frequently expressed concern about human rights abuses in Turkey's conflict with the PKK. We have also noted, in response to Congressional inquiries, the high probability that the GOT has used U.S.-supplied equipment in the southeast. Ambassador Grossman addressed this issue during his confirmation hearings in response to a question from Senator Pell. I have enclosed Ambassador Grossman's response.

The United States has had a military supply relationship with Turkey for over 40 years. It is reasonable to assume, therefore, that Ankara has used U.S.-origin equipment against the PKK since the conflict started nearly 11 years ago. The Turkish military became extensively involved in operations against the PKK in 1992, when the conflict worsened dramatically. Until that time, the military's involvement, as opposed to that of the Jandarma (national guard), was minimal.

With respect to your questions regarding the Arms Export Control Act ("AECA"), section 4 of that Act provides in relevant part that the U.S. Government may provide U.S.-origin defense articles to friendly countries for a number of purposes, including for internal security. Although human rights violations have occurred in the course of operations, those operations appear in fact to have been undertaken for a purpose authorized under the AECA and therefore a report is not required under section 3(c)(2). In any case, the information in our report on alleged human rights abuses is more extensive than what would be provided in a report under section 3(c)(2) of the AECA.

Turkey's human rights record raises serious concerns, but we do not believe that it has engaged in a consistent pattern of gross violations of internationally recognized human rights within the meaning of Section 502B of the Foreign Assistance Act. We must not forget that Turkey is a functioning, albeit troubled, democracy. Although freedom of expression is restricted, Turkey's press is able to criticize the government, and frequently does so.

On July 23, Turkey's Grand National Assembly approved, by the overwhelming majority of 360 to 32, 16 constitutional amendments which will enhance Turkish democracy and broaden political participation. These amendments, among other things, eliminate restrictions on participation in politics by associations, unions, groups and cooperatives; grant civil servants the right to form unions and engage in collective talks; lower the voting age from 20 to 18, and increase the number of parliamentarians from 450 to 550. Both Prime Minister Ciller and Deputy Prime Minister Cetin are committed to going beyond this important step to achieve further reforms, such as modification of Article 8 of the Anti-Terror Law, which has constrained freedom of expression. Additionally, as noted in our report, the Turkish General Staff (TGS) has instituted a program to train soldiers in human rights requirements.

For the past three years, human rights has been a major part of our dialogue with the Turkish government. Every high-level official, both from the State Department and DoD, who has visited Ankara has raised the issue of human rights and its importance to U.S.-Turkish relations. We have started to engage the TGS on this subject as well, and have encouraged visitors from other western countries to support these efforts.

The Turkish government interprets references to the need for a "political solution" in the southeast as encouragement to negotiate with the PKK, which we have not asked Ankara to do. We support Turkey's territorial integrity and legitimate right to fight terrorism. We have emphasized repeatedly that there is no solely military solution to this conflict. We have argued that, in addition to carefully calibrated military operations, resolution will require the expansion of democracy and human rights, including increased civil and cultural rights for Turkey's Kurdish citizens.

While engaged in a difficult struggle with a brutal terrorist organization, the Government of Turkey is making a determined effort to improve its human rights performance. We believe that to promote a settlement in the southeast, our best course is to continue energetically to promote democratization, while supporting Turkey's legitimate struggle against terrorism. In both of these efforts, Turkey needs, and continues to deserve, our help and support.

Please do not hesitate to contact us if we may be of further assistance.

Sincerely,
WENDY R. SHERMAN,
Assistant Secretary, Legislative Affairs.
Enclosure: As stated.

QUESTION FOR THE RECORD SUBMITTED TO MARC GROSSMAN BYSENATOR CLAIBORNE PELL

Question. 2. Is U.S.-origin equipment being used in the Turkish military campaign against Kurdish civilians?

Answer. A large portion of Turkey's inventory of defense items is U.S.-supplied or produced under co-production arrangements. I therefore assume that U.S.-origin equipment is being used in the Turkish military's campaign against the PKK.

I understand that internal security, along with self-defense, is recognized as an acceptable use of U.S.-supplied defense articles. The agreements under which we provide Turkey and other foreign countries with defense articles permit such uses.

There are reports that in the counterinsurgency a large number of civilians have been killed. These reports are troubling, and the Administration has brought them to the attention of the Turkish authorities, and will be looking into them further. Assistant Secretary Shattuck visited Turkey in July and will be going again in October, partly for this purpose.

164.

[September 21, 1995 (Senate), pp. 14060-61]

MCCONNELL (FOR PELL) AMENDMENT NO. 2746, TO ENSURE THAT THE CURRENT PROPORTION OF ECONOMIC ASSISTANCE CONTINUES TO BE CHANNELED THROUGH PRIVATE AND VOLUNTARY ORGANIZATIONS AND COOPERATIVES

AMENDMENT NO 2747

At the appropriate place in the bill, insert the following:

Of the funds appropriated for Turkey under the heading "Economic Assistance", not less than $5 million shall be made available only through non-government organizations to be used only for projects in the ten southeastern provinces currently under a state of emergency, and shall be used only for projects designed to promote economic development, cultural and ethnic tolerance, and human rights activities, and to support the development and activities of non-governmental organizations.

Mr. PELL. Mr. President, I am offering an amendment that directs that a small amount of our overall assistance to Turkey be used by nongovernmental organizations for specific activities in the poorest part of Turkey-the southeast. Specifically, the amendment designates that not less than $5 million of our aid to Turkey be used for projects designed to promote economic development, cultural and ethnic tolerance, and human rights activities, and to support the development and activities of nongovernmental organizations in the southeast. The southeast, of course, is a traditionally Kurdish area where Kurds are caught

in a vise between PKK terrorism and the Turkish military.

Earlier this week, I released a report on Turkey prepared by members of the minority staff of the Foreign Relations Committee. The report, which was based upon a trip that the staff conducted in August, found, among other things, that the Kurdistan Workers' Party [PKK] poses a grave threat not only to Turkey, but to regional stability as well. According to the report, the PKK bears direct responsibility for much of the tensions in southeast Turkey and for prompting the recent Turkish invasions of Iraq. The report also found, however, that the Government of Turkey bears much of the responsibility for the continued suffering in the southeast. The report acknowledges the great political challenges Prime Minister Ciller faces as she tries to address the Kurdish problem-a fact borne out by developments of the last several days by the fall of her government. The bottom line, however, is that the government has been unable-or unwilling-to distinguish the genuine threat posed by the PKK from the legitimate rights and aspirations of the Kurdish people. As a result, Turkey refuses to engage in a political dialog with nonviolent Kurdish representatives, and is executing a heavy-handed, indiscriminate military campaign to eradicate what it views as a monolithic threat to the unity of the country.

By equating all Kurdish aspirations with the terrorist designs of the PKK, Turkey effectively has eliminated outlets for nonviolent Kurdish political or cultural expression. As a consequence, Turkey unintentionally may be contributing to the PKK's appeal. I believe it is important to encourage Turkey to offer Kurds and other groups outlets for nonviolent expression.

One response to the well-chronicled Turkish rights violations has been to cut assistance. In fact, as many of my colleagues may be aware, the House voted to limit economic support funds for Turkey to $21 million. I propose that we take a different approach by addressing some of the very real economic needs Turkey is facing in the southeast-and to do so through non-governmental organizations.

The Foreign Relations Committee staff visited Diyarbakir, one of the main cities in the southeast, which in many ways symbolizes the ethnic difficulties that persist within Turkey. That city has become a haven for rural Kurds forced to evacuate neighboring towns and villages destroyed by the Turkish military. By some estimates, the city's population has grown from roughly 300,000 to more an 1,500,000 during the past 5 years. Although Turkish officials, local residents, and some independent observers suggest that tensions have subsided during the past 2 years, it is evident that any existing calm is tenuous and the result of Turkey's overwhelming-and at times oppressive-security presence, which has exacted a high cost in terms of human rights violations. I believe that my amendment would have a positive impact by improving economic conditions in a very unstable area.

This amendment also sends an important message to Turkey-as it faces the challenge of forming a new government-about the need to address other underlying problems such as the lack of ethnic and cultural acceptance and human rights abuses in the southeast. Turkish officials speak of the need to increase stability in the southeast. True stability can only come with increased tolerance. This amendment is intended to bolster that effort . . .

165.

[November 17, 1995 (Extensions of Remarks), pp. 2213-14]

**JUSTICE FOR ALIZA MARCUS
HON. JOHN EDWARD PORTER
OF ILLINOIS
IN THE HOUSE OF REPRESENTATIVES**

Friday, November 17, 1995

Mr. PORTER. Mr. Speaker, I am pleased and relived that on November 9, Turkey's State Security Court voted unanimously to acquit American citizen Aliza Marcus. Justice

has been served with this complete vindication.

Ms. Marcus never should have been arrested in the first place. She committed no crime. Ms. Marcus only was guilty of reporting the truth about the ongoing Turkish military campaign of forced evacuation and destruction of Kurdish villages. She was merely doing her job—and doing it well.

Ms. Marcus' acquittal is an encouraging indication that Turkey may be willing to reform its ways. However, this is one small step down a long road. Turkey's prosecution of speech, writing, and other peaceful expressions violates numerous international human rights commitments undertaken by Turkey. Change will truly be evident not when the Aliza Marcuses are acquitted, but when they are not arrested in the first place.

166.

[November 27, 1995 (Senate), pp. 17534-5]

ADDITIONAL STATEMENTS

IRANIAN HUMAN RIGHTS ABUSES

Mr. D'AMATO. Mr. President, I rise today to deplore Iran's abominable human rights practices, and to remind my colleagues that Iran's continued abuse of the fundamental rights of its own citizens is one of the reasons why I have offered legislation intended to increase economic pressure on this outlaw regime in Tehran.

Human rights organizations all over the world have been deploring the Islamic Republic of Iran's human rights abuses against women, religious and ethnic minorities for years.

This is a country that sentences women to death for adultery, and then carries out the death penalty by bundling them into a postal sac and throwing them from the roof of a 10-story building.

This is a country that still carries out public stonings, and even has a strict legal code to govern the size stones citizens are to use to stone their fellow citizens. Stones too large are not to be used, because death will be inflicted too quickly. Stones too small are to be avoided, because death doesn't come at all. The stones have to be just the right size to allow the victim to suffer for a very long time, and to ensure that they will die of their wounds.

This is a country that continues to use paramilitary security forces to harass and intimidate people in the street, and that closes newspapers because of a political cartoon comparing the Supreme Leader to a comic strip figure.

This is a country where to be a candidate in an election you must first be deemed to be a supporter of the sitting Government. And this is a country, Mr. President, that continues to be cited, year after year, by the Special Representative of the U.N. Subcommission on Human Rights for its systematic use of torture, arbitrary arrests, and summary executions.

These practices were described in an article appearing in a Paris-based newsletter nearly 5 years ago, which I ask to have printed in the Record at the conclusion of my remarks, along with more recent material supplied to my office by the Foundation for Democracy in Iran, a human rights advocacy group.

Mr. President, I would like to call your attention to a few of the lesser known human rights abuses of the clerical regime in Tehran: its repression of religious and ethnic minorities.

As cited by the 1995 report of Middle East Watch, and the February 1994 report of U.N. Special Representative on Human Rights for Iran, the Iranian security forces conduct arbitrary arrests of Kurdish, Balouch, Turkomen, and other ethnic minorities, and to subject these minorities to cruel and degrading punishments in Iranian jails, including torture and summary execution.

Similarly, as the State Department's February 1995 Report on Human Rights points out, the clerical regime discriminates against citizens of other religious persuasions than the dominant Shiite Moslem faith. Baha'is, Jews, and Sunni Muslims have been arrested over the past year for no other reason than their faith, and some of these individuals have been executed.

In fact, the Islamic Republic has engaged in a deliberate policy to suppress the rights of its Sunni minority, and in particular members of the Balouchi tribes in eastern Iran. On February 1, 1994, riots broke out in Zahedan, Mashed, and Khaf after 500 municipal workers demolished a Sunni mosque in the Zahedan district. On January 10, 1993, Iranian Revolutionary Guards troops attacked Balouchi residents in the village of Robat, when the homes of an estimated 50 families were set on fire in an attempt to secure a single individual, Haji Pirdad. The U.N. Special Representative for Human Rights reported on February 2, 1994 that 20 Balouchis were executed in December 1992 and February 1993 in Zahedan prison, while Amnesty International reported that 42 Balouchis including minors were executed between November 1991 and March 1992.

I believe, Mr. President, that this behavior by the Islamic Republic just goes to show that we are dealing with an outlaw regime that cares little about its own people. If it cares so little about its own people, how will it act toward others?

Iran is isolated and universally viewed as a pariah state. Its actions are abhorrent to the civilized world. As long as this warped, terroristic regime continues to punish the Iranian people with its misrule, this condition will continue. The tyrants in Tehran must understand their aggression and abuse of the good people of Iran will not last, and one day they will be brought to task for their actions.

While the tyrants continue to rule in Tehran, sanctions are a clear way to keep up the pressure on Iran and to deny them the ability to carry out their aggression on the outside world as well as against their own people. We do not take these issues lightly. It is a pity that the regime cannot act like a civilized country and not be so abusive. If only Iran would not conduct these brutal actions, we would not have to place sanctions on it.

The article follows: [see *Mednews*, no. 4, 4, December 3, 1990, HUMAN RIGHTS ABUSES IN IRAN].

———

October 20, 1995.
Subject: Execution and arrest of Kurds in Iran.

FOUNDATION FOR DEMOCRACY IN IRAN

The Foundation for Democracy in Iran is concerned over recent reports from Iranian Kurdistan regarding the execution of 10 Kurds and the arrest of at least 26 others.

According to the opposition Democratic Party of Iranian Kurdistan (DPIK). 10 Kurdish political prisoners accused by the regime of being DPIK supporters were executed or died under torture in late September.

Six of the prisoners, Kurdish villagers from north-western Iran, were executed by firing squad after a year of detention in Orumiyeh prison, the group said. Three others died under torture. The tenth, a Kurdish villager identified as Rashid Abubakri, was hanged on Sept. 21, also in Orumiyeh prison. All were detained and executed on the grounds they were supporters of a banned political opposition group.

In early October, the Iranian press reported that 345 persons had been arrested in Orumiyeh district at the same time as the alleged DPIK sympathizers were executed. On October 7, 1995, the DPIK released the names of 26 Kurdish civilians it claims have been arrested over the past two months in the Orumiyeh and Salmas regions in northwestern Iran, on charges of cooperating with a banned political opposition group. Those arrested were identified as follows:

1. Asgar Darbazi, son of Omar, native of the village of Barazi.
2. Aziz Hayavani, son of Shino, native of the village of Barazi.
3. Pros Azizi, son of Hussein, native of the village of Barazi.
4. Dino Ibrahimi, son of Saleh, native of the village of Barazi.
5. Salahaddin Faghapur, son of Saleh, native of the village of Barazi.
6. Ghamar Mirazai, son of Timur, native of the village of Dostan.
7. Saleh Amini, son of Khaled, native of the village of Gozek.
8. Yunes Amini, his son, born in the same village.

9. Naji Mohammadi, son of Mohammad, native of the village of Gozek.
10. Omar Mohammadi, son of Timur, native of the village of Gozek.
11. Doctor Shirvan, son of Mostafa, native of the village of Haraklan.
12. Sadigh Alizadeh, son of Abubakr, native of the village of Haraklan.
13. Afshar Laal, son of Abdul Rahman, native of the village of Kalarash-Sofla.
14. Shafigh Hakkari, son of Reza, native of the village of Kalarash-Sofla.
15. Bakra Hakkari, son of Sultan, native of the village of Kalarash-Sofla.
16. Taghsim Mirzai, son of Mirza, native of the village of Tarikan.
17. Nuraddeen Taheri, son of Jahanghir, native of the village of Tarikan.
18. Farhad Zareh, son of Sayda, native of the village of Sharvani.
19. Tajaddeen Faghazadeh, son of Sadigh, native of the village of Sharvani.
20. Nasser Zarch, son of Mullah Sultan, native of the village of Sharvani.
21. Majid Husseini, son of Mullah Sayed, native of the village of Sharvani.
22. Nosrat Hassanzadeh, son of Khaled, native of the village of Sharvani.
23. Faysal Zareh, son of Tamo, native of the village of Sharvani.
24. Sadigh Majidi, son of Mamo, native of the village of Hamamlar.
25. Zaher Ahmadi, native of the village of Koran.
26. Ahmad Sultani, son of Smeh, native of the village of Islamabad.

The Foundation condemns the execution of individuals for their political beliefs, and calls on the UN Rapporteur for Human Rights to investigate these reports. The Foundation further condemns the recent round-ups of Kurdish civilians by the Iranian authorities as a clear attempt to intimidate citizens from the legitimate non-violent expression of their political beliefs . . .

167.

[December 12, 1995 (Extensions of Remarks), pp. 2340-41]

OPPOSE THE SALE OF ADVANCED MISSILES TO TURKEY
HON. CHRISTOPHER H. SMITH
OF NEW JERSEY
IN THE HOUSE OF REPRESENTATIVES

Tuesday, December 12, 1995

Mr. SMITH of New Jersey. Mr. Speaker, on December 1, DOD's Defense Security Assistance Agency notified the House International Affairs Committee of the sale of 120 Army Tactical Missile Systems [ATACMS] to Turkey. Essentially a massive, guided cluster bomb, each missile is accurate at a range of up to 100 miles and delivers 950 small bombs. Many of the munitions fail to detonate, remain on the ground, and become a mortal threat to noncombatants. I rise today to voice grave concerns about this sale and question the rationale and timing of this deal. I also want to point out possible consequences of this sale and underscore the danger of unconditional military support for an unstable regime which routinely commits massive human rights abuses against its own citizenry.

Mr. Speaker, my main concern about this sale is that Turkey's regime could use these missiles against civilians as it pursues its ruthless campaign against Kurdish guerrillas. Tragically, Kurdish terrorists have killed hundreds of innocent civilians. Yet in response, Turkey's military has killed thousands, tortured and maimed countless others, destroyed almost 3,000 Kurdish villages and forced 3 million people from their homes. On November 20, 1995, Human Rights Watch detailed in a 171-page report the Turkish military's widespread use of United States-supplied equipment in campaigns which inflict death and destruction against civilians. The atrocities detailed in this report are appalling. The report cites more than two dozen eyewitness accounts and substantiates a June 1995 State Department report which also concluded that U.S. equipment was used to violate the human rights of civilians.

Mr. Speaker, advocates of the missile sale argue that Turkey would not use ATACMS against civilians because of the system's high cost and because such use can be easily detected. Both rationales are preposterous. Over recent years, Turkey has spent an estimated $7 billion per annum fighting its internal war. The supposed deterrence due to United States detection capabilities also rings hollow given that this administration, despite overwhelming evidence that Turkey uses United States-supplied weapons against civilians, refuses to condition Turkey's use of United States equipment. I am particularly disturbed that the State Department's Office on Democracy, Labor and Human Rights has lent its support to this sale when it had opposed the sale of ordinary cluster bombs to Turkey earlier this year. The sale of such weapons appears to indicate that the United States Government is willing to ignore Turkey's ruthless suppression of its Kurdish population because of Turkey's value as a strategic and economic partner. It is worth pointing out, Mr. Speaker, that the prime beneficiary of this $132 million contract will be the LORAL Corp., which manufactures ATACMS in Camden, AR.

Mr. Speaker, Turkey is undeniably located in a troubled and unstable region of the world. But Mr. Speaker, extending assistance to a fellow member of NATO does not mean we must shut our eyes to their violations of basic human rights. This administration has prioritized the halt of missile proliferation, and I would further question the introduction of advanced missile technology into this unstable region on these grounds.

On October 17 of this year, Mr. Speaker, a *New York Times* editorial entitled "America Arms Turkey's Repression" concluded that "[A]ny further [military] aid should carry human rights conditions that would promote a political solution to a war that has undermined Turkish democracy, boosted the power of the military, drained the economy and divided Turkey from its European allies. Placing such conditions on assistance would also reduce America's complicity in Turkey's repressive internal war." Administration representatives, many of my colleagues, and political leaders around the world are urging the Government of Turkey to pursue nonmilitary solutions to the Kurdish crisis because Turkey's purely military approach has failed to do anything but prolong the bloody, divisive and costly conflict. Mr. Speaker, I would also ask how the transfer of an advanced, destructive weapons system serves long-term United States interests in promoting nonmilitary solutions to Turkey's internal conflict?

Mr. Speaker, on December 24, national elections will be held in Turkey which will have far reaching implications for United States-Turkish relations and the course of democracy in Turkey. Most observers believe the Islamic-based Welfare Party is poised to win more votes than any other party and will play an important role in, if not lead, Turkey's post-election government. This anti-Western party has declared its intentions to reevaluate the foundations of Turkey's strategic and economic relationship with the United States. This raises the question of whether United States policy makers have thought about the consequences should Turkish voters bring the fundamentalists to power? If the Turkish military is to remain subordinated to civilian authorities, then should we not think twice about providing sophisticated weaponry to a regime whose leaders have stated their opposition to United States interests in the region?

Mr. Speaker, I want to reiterate my opposition to this sale on the grounds that it is amoral and undermines U.S. security interests. Turkey's leaders have not sought to assuage concerns that such weapons would be used internally, by publicly committing to nonuse of this United States-supplied weapon on its own territory, against its own citizens. Mr. Speaker, I believe the sale of ATACMS to Turkey is a mistake we will come to regret. It is shameful that these implements of civilian death and destruction will be labeled "Made in the USA."

168.

[December 20, 1995 (Senate), pp. 18996-97]

MISSILE SALES TO TURKEY

Mr. PRESSLER. Madam President, on Monday, December 18, my good friend from New York, Senator D'AMATO and I, sent a letter to Secretary of State Warren Christopher, urging the Clinton Administration to reconsider its decision to sell 120 Army tactical missile systems [ATACMs] to the government of Turkey.

I was troubled to learn last night that the Clinton Administration intends to proceed with the sale. This transfer is ill-advised, to say the least. I strongly urge the Administration to reconsider its decision or at the very least, place clear, indisputable restrictions on deployment and use of these weapons.

This transfer does not make sense. Generally, it is disturbing because the Turkish government has used U.S. and NATO military equipment repeatedly in the past to advance policy and military objectives that are clearly not in our best interests.

As all of us are well aware, the Turkish government in 1974 used NATO military equipment when it invaded the island of Cyprus. More than two decades later, Cyprus remains divided, with one side subjected to an occupation force of 35,000 Turkish troops. I have held a great interest in resolving the Cyprus dispute. This is a matter of strong, bipartisan interest. The Clinton Administration has stated that it intends to make a serious effort to reunite Cyprus. Frankly, I cannot see how the proposed missile sale helps our nation achieve this goal. I believe the opposite is true, and that is very unfortunate.

I also am concerned about American made military equipment being used to prolong the conflict between Armenia and Azerbaijan. It has been documented that Turkey has transferred U.S. and NATO military hardware to the Azeris, who have made use of this equipment against civilian populations in the besieged Nagorno-Karabagh region. It is my understanding that it is contrary to U.S. policy for a buyer of U.S.-made military equipment to transfer such equipment to a third party. What assurances do we have from Turkey that it intends to abide by this policy?

Finally, I am concerned that this missile sale could serve to prolong continued violence between the Turkish Army and the Kurds. For more than a decade the Turkish government has waged a brutal war against the Kurdish people. Human rights watch [HRW] estimated that the conflict has resulted in the death of 19,000 Kurds, including 2,000 civilians, and the destruction of 2,000 villages. More than 2 million Kurds have been forced from their homes.

HRW also reported that in 29 incidents from 1992 and 1995, the Turkish Army used U.S.-supplied fighter-bombers and helicopters to attack civilian villages and other targets. Further, U.S. and NATO-supplied small arms and armored personnel carriers have been used in a counter-insurgency campaign against thousands of Kurdish villages.

Clearly, these instances stretching over a period of more than two decades are contrary to our nation's interests as well as our own moral sensibility. In the face of this evidence, the President now wishes to supply the Turkish Army with 120 ATACMs. What exactly are ATACMs? Basically, the U.S. Army handbook describes the ATACM as a conventional surface-to-surface ballistic missile launched from a M270 launcher. Each missile has a warhead that carries a combined payload of 950 small cluster bomblets, which can spray shrapnel over a large area.

The practical use of an ATACM does not leave much to the imagination. This kind of missile can be used to disable numerous human and material targets at once and very quickly. Kurdish villages and organized teams of Kurdish dissidents easily could be targets for ballistic missile attack. This would be a terrible tragedy.

The Administration has argued that these missiles are a necessary deterrent against two potential aggressors along Turkey's borders—Iran and Iraq. I believe these missiles are far from necessary. Consider the following: Turkey is an ally of the United States. It is a member of NATO. The Turkish military's Incrylik air base is a launching point for our enforcement of the no-fly zone over Northern Iraq. And Turkey will participate in the enforcement of the Dayton peace accord in Bosnia. I would think that the strategic importance of Turkey to the United States and Europe is enough to deter any foolish military action by either Iran or Iraq. If our nation can mobilize the world to expel Iraq from the tiny nation of

Kuwait, imagine our response if Iraq or Iran even made a hostile gesture toward Turkey. Clearly, the Administration's "deterrent" argument to justify the missile sale is hollow at best.

Indeed, I can find no credible political, economic or strategic cause that is furthered by the sale of the ATACMs to Turkey.

Madam President, just last month, Congress took a strong stand against Turkish aggression in the region by voting to cap US economic support funds for Turkey. This is an important step. My friend from New York, Senator D'AMATO, and I are sponsors of legislation that would take even tougher action. It is my hope that we in Congress can all agree that there must be an added price for US economic and military assistance to our allies, particularly our NATO allies, and that price is morally responsible use of U.S. assistance. I do not see how the Administration's missile sale fits even that basic standard.

We have seen a number of different initiatives designed to bring peace to troubled regions, such as Bosnia-Herzegovina, Northern Ireland, Cyprus, and the Middle East. However, the Administration needs to demonstrate our nation's strong interest in bringing the violence in Kurdistan and Nagorno-Karabagh to an end. The sale of 120 ATACMs moves our nation in the wrong direction and could further fuel the war and destruction in both regions.

Though the Administration has announced it intends to pursue the sale, I make one last plea to urge it to reconsider its decision. If the Administration intends to complete the sale, I would urge at the very least that it impose a few basic conditions. In short, if these missiles are for national self-defense, the sale should be conditioned solely for that purpose. More to the point, the missiles should not be placed so as to pose a threat to the people of Greece and Cyprus. Further, the Turkish government should promise that none of the missiles be transferred to Azerbaijan. And finally, the missiles should not be used to prolong the violence in Kurdistan. The Clinton Administration at the very least should insist on these conditions at the very least. The Clinton Administration also should make clear that failure to abide by these conditions could undermine future economic and military assistance.

Again I believe this sale to be bad policy. It is a mistake. However, if the Administration intends to pursue this sale, it should at the very least make clear that this nation insists on this equipment being strictly limited to self-defense. If we are going to be forced swallow this very bitter bill, the Administration should try to make it less bitter.

I ask unanimous consent that the text of the letter to Secretary Christopher be printed in the RECORD.

There being no objection, the letter was ordered to be printed in the RECORD, as follows:

U.S. Senate,
Washington, DC, December 18, 1995.
Hon. Warren M. Christopher,
Secretary of State,
Washington, DC.

DEAR MR. SECRETARY: We are writing to express our strong opposition to the Clinton Administration's proposed sale of 120 army tactical surface-to-surface missiles (ATACMS) to Turkey.

As you well know, for more than a decade the Turkish government has waged a brutal war against the Kurdish people. According to recent data from Human Rights Watch (HRW), the conflict has resulted in 19,000 military and civilian dead, 2,000 villages destroyed and more than 2 million being forced from their homes.

What concerns us deeply is the use of American-made military equipment to commit these atrocities and to prolong the war against the Kurdish people. Specifically, it has been reported that in 29 incidents from 1992 and 1995, the Turkish Army has used U.S.-supplied fighter-bombers and helicopters to attack and fire against civilian villages and targets. Further, U.S. and NATO-supplied small arms and armored personnel carriers have been used in a counter-insurgency campaign against thousands of Kurdish villages.

The Kurds are not the only ones to have been subjected to attack with U.S. or NATO equipment from Turkey. Indeed, the record of the last twenty years is disturbing. Most notably, the Turkish military used NATO military hardware when it invaded and occupied the now-divided island of Cyprus. Further, Turkey has transferred US and NATO weapons to Azerbaijan, where they have been used against civilian Armenians residing in Nagorno-Karabagh.

In the face of this history, the President now wishes to supply the Turkish Army with 120 ATACMS, each of which is capable of carrying a warhead payload of 950 small cluster bombs. With these weapons, the Turkish Army has the capability to launch a horrendous ballistic missile attack on the Kurdish people. The results would be equally disturbing if any of these missiles ended up in the hands of the Azeris, or were deployed within range of either Cyprus or Greece.

Mr. Secretary, the Clinton Administration has taken a great interest in achieving peace in troubled regions, such as Bosnia-Herzegovina, Northern Ireland, Cyprus, and the Middle East. However, the Administration needs to demonstrate our nation's strong interest in bringing the violence in Kurdistan and Nagorno-Karabagh to an end. By arming Turkey with 120 ATACMS, we would send the opposite message and further fuel destruction in both regions.

The time has come for the United States to take a stand for peace throughout the entire Middle East. For that reason, we urge the Clinton Administration to reconsider its proposed sale of tactical surface-to-surface missiles to Turkey.

Thank you for your attention to this important issue.

Sincerely,
Larry Pressler.
Alfonse M. D'AMATO.

169.

[December 22, 1995 (House), pp. 15619-20]

SALE OF ATACMS MISSILES TO TURKEY

The SPEAKER pro tempore. Under a previous order of the House, the gentleman from New Jersey [Mr. Pallone] is recognized for 5 minutes.

Mr. PALLONE. Mr. Speaker, as soon as today, or at least by the middle of next week, our Department of Defense will sign a letter of offer and acceptance [LOA] with the Government of Turkey, to complete the sale of 120 Army Tactical Missile Systems [ATACMS]. The ATACMS—pronounced attacks 'ems—is a ground-launched surface-to-surface, conventional, semiguided ballistic missile which carries an antipersonnel/antimateriel cluster warhead capable of spraying shrapnel over a 150-square-meter area. Turkey already has the multiple launch rocket system from which to launch these very nasty, destructive weapons. What this weapon does is essentially deliver 950 small bombs, some of which do not immediately detonate and remain on the ground, posing a threat to noncombatants—including children.

Mr. Speaker, this is the wrong weapon sale to the wrong country at the wrong time.

Earlier this month, I circulated a letter with the gentleman from Florida [Mr. Bilirakis] which was signed by 35 Members from both sides of the aisle, calling on President Clinton to reconsider this sale, based on our very serious concerns over how these weapons would be used. The Turkish Government's domestic and international behavior—including the ongoing campaign against the Kurdish people, the occupation of Northern Cyprus, and the blockade of Armenia—makes us deeply concerned that providing such destructive power to that Government has the potential to cause terrible, and preventable, human suffering.

Today I am joining with my colleagues, Mr. Torricelli and Mr. Bilirakis in introducing House Concurrent Resolution 124 expressing the sense of Congress that the President should suspend the proposed sale of the Army Tactical Missile System to the Government of the Republic of Turkey until the Government takes significant and concrete steps to end the military occupation of Cyprus, lift its blockade of Armenia, cease its ongoing campaign

against the Kurdish people, and demonstrate progress on the protection of human and civil rights within Turkey.

Mr. Speaker, the timing of this sale is peculiar to say the least. The Foreign Operations appropriations bill includes a cut in economic assistance to Turkey. This provision, which has strong bipartisan support, was enacted in response to the concerns cited above. We believe that the message we are trying to send with this provision would be undermined by approving a new sale of military hardware at this time. In Ankara, the conclusion would inevitably be that, beyond limited symbolic measures, Americans do not take seriously the shocking breaches of international law and decency committed in the name of the Turkish Government.

The proposed transaction represents the first sale of these weapons to any foreign nation. The Turkish military track record is not consistent with what we would expect of any recipient of United States arms, much less a NATO member. The Human Rights Arms Project has cited numerous examples of the indiscriminate use of weapons by Turkish forces in Kurdish civilian areas. We are also concerned about the evidence strongly linking Turkey to unauthorized transfers of United States and NATO weapons to the Republic of Azerbaijan.

While it is our contention that the weapons sale should be halted entirely, in our letter to the President we recommended that, are the very least, strong conditions governing the use and transfer of these weapons be attached to any sale, and that these conditions be strongly enforced.

Mr. Speaker, this sale has been strongly opposed by Greek-American, Armenian-American, and Kurdish-American organizations, as well as Human Rights Watch, the Council for a Liveable World, and the Federation of American Scientists. And for good reason.

Turkey claims it needs the ATACMS as a deep strike weapon against the threat of tanks in Syria, Iraq, and Iran. Yet, in Greece, Turkey's neighbor to the west, there is deep concern about the threat posed by these offensive weapons. In the regional arms race, Turkey already has a substantial edge, with F-16 fighter jets, attack helicopters, and antiarmore missiles. In addition Turkey has imported more than 1,000 tanks from the United States alone in the past 5 years.

The Government of Turkey is conducting a war against the Kurds within Turkey and has made incursions into Kurdish areas of Iraq, resulting in thousands of civilian casualties and millions of refugees. This cruel war is one part of an overall effort to essentially negate the Kurdish people as a distinct entity within Turkey. Many people are concerned that these missiles could be used as part of this military campaign, resulting in terrible civilian casualties.

Also, Turkey continues its occupation of one-third of the territory of Cyprus, having declared a "Northern Republic of Cyprus," an entity that has no international recognition, and resisting good-faith efforts of the United States, Greece, and other nations and international bodies to end the conflict. The occupation of Cyprus is well into its 21st year. There is no sign that it will end if we continue to send the message to Ankara that there are no significant consequences to this illegal occupation, and that our protests are largely symbolic and rhetorical.

Another illegal and immoral Turkish Government policy is the blockade of its border with the Republic of Armenia. This blockade has blocked the delivery of American humanitarian aid to Armenia and complicated its delivery. In the foreign ops bill, we have language, with strong bipartisan support, known as the Humanitarian Aid Corridor Act, which restricts aid to those countries that block the delivery of aid to other nations. Although the language does not mention Turkey by name, clearly that is the country that would be targeted.

Why are we taking these seemingly significant legislative steps—Humanitarian Aid Corridor Act, cutting aid to Turkey—and then turning around and giving them this terrible weapon system?

Mr. Speaker, we also have to worry about whether Turkey will see fit to transfer this technology—our technology—to other nations. Strong evidence has linked Turkey to the unauthorized transfer of Untied States and North Atlantic Treaty Organization weapons to the Republic of Azerbaijan. Azerbaijan and Armenia are engaged in a tense conflict over the region of Nagorno-Karabagh. A tenuous cease-fire is holding, and the administration has recognized the importance of resolving this crisis by appointing a special negotiator with the rank of Ambassador. Why, again, do we turn around and take steps that will potentially undermine our efforts to negotiate a just and lasting resolution to this conflict?

International human rights organizations continue to cite Turkey for egregious violations of the basic human rights and freedoms of its own citizens. Earlier this year, an American journalist was jailed in Turkey because of her reporting on the campaign against the Kurds. She was released, thank God. Unfortunately, there has not been such a happy ending for those few brave Turkish journalists and human rights activists who try to tell their countrymen and the world the truth about what's going on. These brave souls languish in prison, largely forgotten by all but a few friends and supporters.

Mr. Speaker, I am very discouraged and disappointed by the reaction of Western governments—not only our own—to Turkey's continued flouting of international law and standards of decency. Just last week, the European Union admitted Turkey into its Customs Union, a likely first step toward full membership in the EU—despite the strong objections from many legislators and activists on the other side of the Atlantic.

Why are we doing this? Sadly, we are witnessing the triumph of Realpolitik, in other words, putting economic or strategic interests ahead of our own values. The argument is that we need Turkey because of its strategic location and as a bulwark against Islamic fundamentalism. Well, in the first place, I believe that these goals could be achieved by more positive means than weapons sales. But I also wonder whether we're making a terrible strategic mistake over the long term, investing billions, sending our most advanced weapons and otherwise hurting America's good name by associating with a regime that isn't very stable and may collapse anyway.

While it may be too late to stop this ill-advised weapons sale, I urge all my colleagues to work with me and other Members of this House to stop coddling the regime in Ankara, to stand with Turkey's neighbors, and to stop basing our foreign policy on the bad bet represented by the Government of Turkey.

It may be too late to stop this ill-advised weapons sale to Turkey. I urge all of my colleagues to work with me and other Members of this House to stop coddling the regime in Ankara, to stand with Turkey's neighbors, and to stop basing our foreign policy on the bad debt represented by the Government of Turkey.

170.

[January 25, 1996 (Extensions of Remarks), pp. 95-6]

SUPPORT PEACE, DEMOCRACY, AND JUSTICE FOR ALL OF TURKEY'S CITIZENS
HON. CHRISTOPHER H. SMITH
OF NEW JERSEY
IN THE HOUSE OF REPRESENTATIVES

Thursday, January 25, 1996

Mr. SMITH of New Jersey. Mr. Speaker, I rise today to offer a resolution advocating a peaceful end to the conflict between the Turkish Government and Kurdish militants. The ongoing war undermines the very foundations of both the Turkish State and our bilateral relations and its persistence challenges the desires of the United States and Turkish Governments to establish a secure, long-term relationship. For the sake of the people of Turkey, the end of the conflict will strengthen Turkish democracy, help eliminate the scourge of terrorism, resuscitate a shaky economy and promote regional stability.

Mr. Speaker, Turkey is home to half of the world's 25 million Kurds and has experienced 28 Kurdish uprisings in the past century. Since 1984, more than 20,000 people have died in clashes among security forces, the Kurdistan Workers Party [PKK] and shadowy Moslem fundamentalist groups. In the past 3 years, security forces forcibly evacuated or destroyed more than 2,650 villages in southeast Turkey and displaced more than 3 million people. Villagers have been rounded up by security officials and subjected to beatings, mass arrests and intimidation. Death squads, believed connected to security forces and fundamentalists, have been responsible for hundreds of extrajudicial killings and disappearances. PKK fighters have also snuffed out the lives of innocent civilians. Each month there are reports of individuals killed in detention and torture remains widespread in cases involving political charges. Eight southwestern Turkish provinces are under a constant state of emergency authorizing local authorities to curb political and media activity.

Mr. Speaker, successive Turkish Governments have viewed the PKK solely as a terrorist phenomenon undermining its sovereignty and dividing the country along ethnic lines. The Government has dismissed as propaganda recent PKK statements renouncing violence and separatism and calling for peaceful and lasting political solutions. Turkey's Government has given the military free reign in responding to the PKK, and its heavy-handed approach has also stifled legitimate Kurdish political voices.

Mr. Speaker, in southeastern Turkey, citizens are often forced to choose between supporting the guerrillas and risking violent reprisal by Turkish security—or not helping and facing equally harsh PKK retribution. Locals believed to be sympathetic to Turkish authorities have been executed by the PKK. Eleven years of violence has polarized Turks and Kurds and threatens to rend Turkish society along ethnic lines. Kurds, resentful of military abuses, become more supportive of the PKK. Turks, angered by the costs and brutality of terrorism, become increasingly intolerant of the rights of Kurdish citizens.

Mr. Speaker, no one disputes Turkey's key role in preserving U.S. strategic, political and economic interests in a critical region. However, the inability of successive Turkish

Governments to resolve the Kurdish crisis remains an obstacle to improved ties and enables persistent human rights problems to stunt Turkey's democratic development. The time has come for Turkey's true friends and supporters to call on all sides in the conflict to abandon violence and settle their differences peacefully, democratically and within the framework of the territorial unity of the Republic of Turkey. Following recent elections, Turkey's Government finds itself in a state of protracted paralysis. Observers believe that any new government is unlikely to offer substantially new approaches to the Kurdish issue because of prevailing nationalist sentiments and the possibility of new elections in the near future. Additionally, Turkey's military supports the war in southeast Turkey, although its approach has failed to do anything but foster local support for the PKK.

Mr. Speaker, I have learned from our experiences dealing with the PLO and Israel, the ANC and South Africa, and the IRA and Britain, that the longer it takes to begin reconciliation, the harder it becomes to look beyond the bloodshed and suffering. Mr. Speaker, violence will not resolve this conflict. The time for dialog is long overdue.

Mr. Speaker, the U.S. Government has often been instrumental in promoting peace in troubled areas. So too should we demonstrate our commitment to encouraging the resolution of this destructive and bloody conflict. The resolution which I am introducing, along with Mr. Steny Hoyer, ranking minority member of the Helsinki Commission, is an important first step in this direction. I would ask our colleagues to join us in cosponsoring this resolution. I ask that the language of the resolution be printed in the RECORD at this time.

H. CON. RES. [136]

Whereas armed conflict has existed in southeastern Turkey since 1984, and the entire region has been placed under a state of emergency since 1987;

Whereas the human toll of this conflict has been great, with the loss of more than 20,000 lives, the displacement of more than 3,000,000 civilians, and the destruction of more than 2,650 Kurdish villages;

Whereas free expression in Turkey is restricted by laws which criminalize nonviolent expression, resulting in the incarceration of journalists, writers, academics, human rights activists, and others as political prisoners;

Whereas in the past 2 years, 13 Kurdish members of Turkey's parliament have been removed from office, jailed, or exiled for expressing political opinions or having alleged contacts with the illegal Kurdistan Workers Party (PKK);

Whereas Kurdish citizens of Turkey have been denied certain basic political and civil rights such as the right to full and free participation in political life, the right to be educated in their mother language, and the right to freely write and publish materials in the Kurdish language;

Whereas the conflict between Kurdish guerrillas and Turkish armed forces has spilled over Turkey's borders and threatens the stability of the region;

Whereas the escalating conflict poses grave threats to economic stability and the existing political order and prevents realization of full-fledged democracy;

Whereas international and local humanitarian organizations, including the International Committee of the Red Cross, have been denied access to southeastern Turkey;

Whereas terrorism poses a grave threat to human rights and violates international law;

Whereas Turkey's leaders have made commitments to building a democratic society and have made significant progress in realizing this goal;

Whereas the Government of Turkey has acceded to upholding international human rights agreements, including the United Nations Universal Declaration of Human Rights, the Geneva Conventions, and the Helsinki Final Act;

Whereas Turkey, a member of the North Atlantic Treaty Organization and the Organization for Security and Cooperation in Europe, is an important strategic and economic partner of the United States;

Whereas long-term strategic and economic interests of the United States are jeopardized by the continuing conflict in Turkey;

Whereas after 11 years, Kurdistan Workers Party (PKK) guerrilla leaders have offered to lay down their weapons;

Whereas a military solution to the Kurdish question in Turkey is not possible, and only a nonviolent political solution can bring peace, stability, full democracy, and prosperity to Turkey; and

Whereas such a solution must be sought and implemented within the framework of the territorial unity of the Republic of Turkey: Now, therefore, be it

Resolved by the House of Representatives (the Senate concurring), That it is the sense of the Congress that—

(1) the Government of Turkey should immediately release all political prisoners and lift restrictions on free expression and thereby enable all Turkish citizens, including those of Kurdish origin, to enjoy the political and cultural rights of peoples in all democratic countries;

(2) the President should take every opportunity to encourage the Government of Turkey to initiate steps to end the armed confrontation in that country;

(3) the Kurdistan Workers Party (PKK) should declare a cease-fire and restate support for resolution of the conflict through democratic means and within the framework of the territorial unity of the Republic of Turkey;

(4) the Government of Turkey should declare a cease-fire and reaffirm a foundation upon which its Republic is based: "Peace at home. Peace in the world";

(5) upon cessation of hostilities, the International Committee of the Red Cross and other appropriate humanitarian and monitoring organizations should be given access to southeastern Turkey;

(6) the Government of Turkey should take steps to further reduce the potential for future confrontation, including—

(A) allowing all political parties committed to nonviolence to participate in Turkish political life;

(B) repealing the state of emergency in southeastern Turkey;

(C) dismantling the paramilitary "village guard" system;

(D) lifting all constraints on the dissemination in the Kurdish language of television and radio broadcasts, print, music, and other media;

(E) allowing schools to offer instructions in the Kurdish language; and

(F) establishing consultative mechanisms to defuse sources of conflict and propose strategies to resolve current crisis in southeastern Turkey; and

(7) the President should support providing technical assistance to carry out paragraphs (1) through (6).

171.

[February 1, 1996 (Extensions of Remarks), p. 132]

SUPPORT PEACE AND DEMOCRACY IN TURKEY: SUPPORT HOUSE CONCURRENT RESOLUTION 136 HON. STENY H. HOYER OF MARYLAND IN THE HOUSE OF REPRESENTATIVES

Wednesday, January 31, 1996

Mr. HOYER. Mr. Speaker, on January 25, 1995, I joined the chairman of the Helsinki Commission, Chris Smith, in introducing H. Con. Res. 136, legislation which advocates a peaceful end to the conflict between the Government of Turkey and Kurdish militants. I urge my colleagues to join us as cosponsors of this important resolution aimed at ending a vicious cycle of violence and terror which has claimed so many lives over the past decade and has eroded the impressive strides made by a government committed to achieving full-fledged democracy.

Mr. Speaker, for more than a decade Turkey's citizens, especially those residing in the southeast, have suffered the horrors of terrorism and the excesses of a government committed to eradicating terrorism at any cost. More than 20,000 people have died in clashes among security forces, the Kurdistan Workers

Party [PKK] and shadowy Muslim fundamentalist groups. Turkish troops in southeast Turkey have forcibly evacuated or destroyed more that 2,650 Kurdish villages, burned crops, killed livestock, and displaced more than three million people. Citizens are detained, tortured, extrajudicially executed or disappear without a trace. The PKK has also killed innocent civilians, mined local roads, and set off bombs in populated areas—contributing to the cycle of violence and the climate of fear that pervades southeast Turkey.

Mr. Speaker, earlier this month, European newspapers printed color pictures of Turkish soldiers posing with the heads of decapitated Kurdish guerrillas. These gruesome and despicable photos all too graphically underline the hatred and brutality fueling this conflict. But even more, the pictures reinforce the urgent need for reconciliation. Violence and terrorism will not resolve this conflict. Only dialog can help overcome bitterness inspired by 12 years of war. House Concurrent Resolution 136 promotes an end to violence and a beginning for efforts promoting reconciliation and understanding.

Mr. Speaker, Chairman Smith and I are sending letters to officials of the Organization for Security and Cooperation in Europe [OSCE] urging them to initiate and support steps to resolve the escalating conflict in Turkey. We believe the OSCE should establish a million of long-duration to monitor human rights abuses and help defuse sources of conflict and have asked that the OSCE chairman-in-office send a personal representative to develop recommendations concerning the mandate and scope of future OSCE activities in Turkey. We have also asked the president of the OSCE Parliamentary Assembly to designate a parliamentary delegation to Turkey to assist in this task. The OSCE has played a critical role in conflict prevention, mediation, and human rights monitoring in the former Yugoslavia, the Caucasus, the Baltic States, and elsewhere. An OSCE presence in Turkey would be especially helpful as local nongovernmental organizations, international humanitarian groups, including the International Committee of the Red Cross, and even journalists are not allowed by authorities to operate freely in this region.

Mr. Speaker, Turkey and Israel are the only functional democratic states in the Middle East. Turkey is a NATO ally and OSCE member. The government's inability to peacefully and democratically resolve the Kurdish conflict jeopardizes Turkey's democratic foundations, drains a stumbling economy, threatens regional stability, and makes closer relations with Europe and the United States problematic. Our Government has been instrumental in helping resolve conflicts in the Middle East, the Balkans and elsewhere. Mr. Speaker, if we truly value our strategic, economic and political partnership with Turkey, and I believe we do, we must act now to help end this brutal conflict. It is precisely because of that partnership that we seek to assist Turkey in ending this conflict.

Mr. Speaker, I urge my colleagues to review House Concurrent Resolution 136. I believe it represents a balanced and thoughtful first step that our Government can and should take to promote peaceful resolution of a difficult and divisive conflict. I call on all my colleagues who value human rights and our partnership with Turkey to cosponsor this resolution. We must try to help stop the violence.

172.

[March 14, 1996 (Senate), pp. 2095-97]

REMEMBERING HALABJA

Mr. PELL. Mr. President, this weekend will mark the anniversary of one of humanity's darkest moments. Eight years ago, on March 16, 1988, Iraqi President Saddam Hussein's forces, besieged by Iranian forces on the Faw Peninsula and losing ground to Kurdish insurgents in northern Iraq, commenced an attack on the Kurdish city of Halabja. There, Iraqi forces used poison gas resulting in the death of as many as 5 to 6 thousand Kurds, most of whom were innocent noncombatants.

In the 8 years since the poison gas attack, Halabja has become the single most important symbol of the plight of the Kurdish people— the very embodiment of Iraq's brutality towards the Kurds. The unforgettable images of the victims—a man frozen in death with his infant son; a little girl wearing a scarf, her face swollen in the first stages of decomposition—remain seared in the Kurdish psyche. Much as the Bosnians will never forget the ethnic cleansing of Srebrenica, the Kurds will never forget the attack on Halabja.

Incredibly, as we now know, Halabja was not the only instance when Iraq employed chemical weapons against the Kurds, nor was it the end of Iraqi repression against the Kurds. Although clearly the most dramatic, Halabja was but one of a series of Iraqi atrocities against the Kurds. Beginning in the mid to late 1980's—and culminating in the infamous Anfal campaign of 1988—Iraqi forces systematically rounded up Kurdish villagers and forced them into relocation camps, took tens of thousands of Kurds into custody where they were never heard from again, and destroyed hundreds of Kurdish villages and towns. By some estimates as many as 150,000 Kurds are missing from this period and presumed dead. Collectively, these actions amount to an Iraqi campaign of genocide against the Kurds.

I, along with the distinguished chairman of the Foreign Relations Committee, Senator Helms, have tried very hard to call attention to the persecution of the Kurds, including by introducing the first-ever sanctions bill against Iraq in 1988 for its use of poison gas against the Kurds.

Since then, a wealth of evidence has been uncovered documenting Iraq's brutality against the Kurds, much of which was written in Iraq's own hand. The Foreign Relations Committee—particularly through the vigorous efforts of former staff member, now United States Ambassador to Croatia Peter Galbraith—led an effort to retrieve more than 18 tons of Iraqi Secret Police documents captured by the Kurds in 1991, which charts out Iraq's criminal behavior in excruciating detail. Human Rights Watch, the independent human rights organization, has done a superb job of analyzing those documents to mount an overwhelming case that Iraq has engaged in genocide against the Kurds.

This is a story that must be told. As some of my colleagues may know, the issue of genocide has a particularly strong resonance for me. Just after World War II, my father, Herbert Claiborne Pell, played a significant role in seeing that genocide would be considered a war crime. Although he met stiff resistance, my father ultimately succeeded and I learned much from his tenacity and commitment to principle. The world must oppose genocide wherever and whenever it occurs; Halabja cannot be forgotten, and Iraq must be held accountable for its atrocities against the Kurds. We simply cannot afford to let this opportunity pass by.

I wish I could say that there is a happy ending to the tragic story of the Kurds in Iraq, that there was a lesson learned by the Iraqi leadership. Sadly, I cannot. Although the Iraqi Kurds now control a significant portion of Kurdistan—a consequence of the Persian Gulf war—Saddam's ill treatment of the Kurds continues. Iraqi agents continually carry out terrorist acts against Kurdish targets, and Iraq maintains an airtight blockade of the Kurdish-controlled provinces. Since there also is a U.N. embargo on all of Iraq, the Kurds are forced to live under the unbearable economic weight of a dual embargo. In addition, Kurds in other portions of the region—particularly in Iran and Turkey—have been subjected to serious abuses of human rights and outright repression, demonstrating that the Kurdish plight knows no boundaries. The situation has become so dire that for the past 18 months, the Iraqi Kurds —once united in their quest for autonomy and their hatred for Saddam Hussein, have resorted to fighting amongst themselves.

The situation does not seem right or fair to me. Nor does there seem to have been a proper response by the international community to the horrifying legacy of Halabja. I think there should be a much greater effort to look at ways to help the Iraqi Kurds dispel the painful memories of the past, to graduate from the status of dependency on the international donor community, and to confront our common enemy—Saddam Hussein. Only then can Iraqi Kurdistan emerge as the cornerstone of a free and democratic Iraq.

At a minimum, the international community—and the United States in particular—

must reaffirm its commitment to protect the Kurds. Under Operation Provide Comfort, an international coalition including United States, British, and French forces, continues to provide air cover and protection to the Iraqi Kurds, and to facilitate the supply of humanitarian relief. The recent political changes in Turkey, however, have cast new doubt on the long-term viability of Provide Comfort, and overall economic conditions in Kurdistan continue to deteriorate. The current situation does not serve United States or international interests, nor does it help to rectify the sad history of repression against the Kurds. Our work in Iraq—both against Saddam and in support of the Kurds—is not yet done.

Mr. HELMS. Mr. President, I join with my distinguished friend, Senator Pell, the able ranking member of the Foreign Relations Committee, in recalling the massacre of thousands of Kurdish civilians 8 years ago at the town of Halabja.

On March 16, 1988, Iraqi jets, without warning, dropped chemical weapons on Halabja, a Kurdish village in northern Iraq. The attack, horrific even by Iraq's barbaric standards, killed thousands of unarmed men, women, and children.

The massacre at Halabja drew attention to Saddam Hussein's campaign of genocide directed against the Kurds of northern Iraq. However, that attention was not enough to prevent the systematic killing of hundreds of thousands of Kurdish civilians by the Government of Iraq.

Mr. President, I must commend Senator Pell for being one of the few willing to speak out about the plight of the Kurds. I worked with him in 1988 to sanction Iraq for its reprehensible behavior. Had more people around the world, and especially here in the United States, heeded Senator Pell's pleas to protect the Kurds, perhaps more could have been saved.

The final act of this tragedy, however, has not yet played out. Saddam Hussein has not abandoned his crusade against the Kurdish citizens of Iraq. If he cannot eliminate them, he will do all he can to deprive them of their basic human rights.

Mr. President, thanks to Senator Pell, the plight of the Kurds has the attention of the world. They must never be forgotten.

Mrs. FEINSTEIN. Mr. President, 8 years ago this week, in the closing weeks of the Iran-Iraq war, Saddam Hussein sent Iraqi forces to crush a rebellion among the Kurds of northern Iraq. In the assault, centered on the city of Halabja, Saddam's forces rained poison gas down upon the city, and over 5,000 Kurds, many of them civilians, lost their lives in horrifying fashion.

As research since the end of the Iran-Iraq war has shown, Halabja was only the most brutal chapter in Saddam's genocidal campaign against the Kurds of northern Iraq. From the mid-1980's through the end of the war, Iraq forced hundreds of thousands of Kurdish citizens into detention camps, kidnapped tens of thousands of others, most of whom are presumed dead, and attacked Kurdish towns and villages, often with deadly poison gas. Some 150,000 Kurds lost their lives in this infamous Anfal campaign—which can only be described as a campaign of genocide by Saddam Hussein against the Kurds of Iraq.

Sadly, this is not the only incident of Saddam's brutality against his own people. The threshold crossed by Iraq during the Anfal campaign laid the groundwork for Saddam's most recent genocidal killing spree, this time against the Marsh Arabs of southern Iraq. In the years following the gulf war, as Iraqi Shiite rebels took refuge in the remote communities of the Marsh Arabs, Saddam turned his army on this community. In the last 3 years, thousands of Marsh Arabs have disappeared, never to be heard from again, and entire villages have been burned to the ground. This time, the genocide was accompanied by an environmental outrage, as Iraqi engineers drained thousands of acres of marshlands in order to reach remote villages, wiping out a fragile ecosystem and obliterating the centuries-old way of life of the Marsh Arabs.

The Kurds, too, continue to suffer at Saddam's hand. They narrowly escaped a new round of massacres at the end of the gulf war in 1991, thanks to the intervention of the United States and our allies. Today, although the Kurds of Iraq govern the northern provinces autonomously under the protection of

Operation Provide Comfort—a cooperative effort by the United States, Britain, and France—they remain subject to an internal blockade by Saddam's forces, as well as the U.N. embargo against all of Iraq, and periodic Iraqi attacks against Kurdish towns and individuals.

No Member of this body has done more to publicize and address the plight of the Kurds than the distinguished ranking member of the Foreign Relations Committee, Senator Pell. Thanks in large part to his efforts, and those of the distinguished Chairman of the Foreign Relations Committee, Senator Helms, over 18 tons of Iraqi Government and secret police documents detailing Iraq's genocidal campaign against the Kurds—after being captured by Kurdish rebels in 1991—were brought to the United States for research and analysis. The result has been a well-documented history of Iraqi atrocities against the Kurds, including the horrific use of poison gas.

On this tragic anniversary, I want to commend Senator Pell and Senator Helms for their leadership on this issue. I hope that the United States will continue to take a leadership role in working to ensure a better life for the Kurds of Iraq, both until and after Saddam Hussein is driven from power.

173.

[March 26, 1996 (House), pp. 2853-55]

ANNIVERSARY OF MASSACRE OF KURDS BY IRAQI GOVERNMENT

Mr. GILMAN. Mr. Speaker, I move to suspend the rules and agree to the resolution (H. Res. 379) expressing the sense of the House of Representatives concerning the eighth anniversary of the massacre of over 5,000 Kurds as a result of a gas bomb attack by the Iraqi Government.

The Clerk read as follows:

H. RES. 379

Whereas over four million Kurds live in Iraq, composing 20 percent of the population;

Whereas the Iraqi Government has continually taken violent actions against Kurds living in Iraq;

Whereas, on March 17, 1988, the Iraqi Government, by its own admission, used chemical weapons against Iraqi Kurd civilians in the Kurdish frontier village of Halabja, resulting in the death of over 5,000 innocent persons;

Whereas this terrible, inhumane act by the repressive Iraqi Government provoked international outrage;

Whereas the Iraqi Government continued its use of chemical weapons against a defenseless Kurdish population throughout 1988;

Whereas over 182,000 Iraqi Kurds were killed by the Iraqi Government during the Anfal campaigns in 1988;

Whereas it was not until the international response to Iraq's invasion of Kuwait in 1990 that the international community instituted measures to destroy Iraq's arsenal of weapons of mass destruction;

Whereas the Iraqi Government has laid over 20 million mines throughout the Kurdish countryside which continue to hamper efforts of rehabilitation of the displaced population;

Whereas United Nations Security Council Resolution 688 of April 1, 1991, demanded that Iraq cease repression of its citizens and called for an international relief program for the Iraqi civilian population and, in particular the Kurdish population;

Whereas, since the spring of 1991, the United States, Britain, and France have enforced by daily overflights a no-fly zone over Iraq north of the 36th parallel;

Whereas, in addition to the allied air umbrella, the United Nations carries out relief and security operations in Iraq, with emphasis on the Kurdish region;

Whereas, since 1991, the United States has provided approximately $1.2 billion to support humanitarian and protective activities, known as Operation Provide Comfort, on behalf of the Iraqi Kurds; and

Whereas there will never truly be peace for the Iraqi Kurds without justice being carried out against their Iraqi perpetrators: Now, therefore, be it

Resolved, That it is the sense of the House of Representatives that the United States Administration should—

(1) mark the eighth anniversary of the death of over 5,000 Iraqi Kurds in the 1988 chemical attack by the Iraqi Government on Halabja by commemorating all those innocent men, women, and children who lost their lives;

(2) reaffirm the United States' commitment to protect and help the Kurdish people in Iraq, thus ensuring that the tragedy of Halabja will never be repeated;

(3) support efforts to promote a democratic alternative to the present regime in Iraq which will assure the Kurdish people the right to self-government through a federal system; and

(4) renew efforts to establish an international war crime tribunal to prosecute Iraqi leaders involved in crimes against humanity and war crimes.

The SPEAKER pro tempore (Mr. UPTON). Pursuant to the rule, the gentleman from New York [Mr. Gilman] and the gentleman from Virginia [Mr. MORAN] will each be recognized for 20 minutes.

The Chair recognizes the gentleman from New York [Mr. GILMAN].

(Mr. GILMAN asked and was given permission to revise and extend his remarks.)

Mr. GILMAN. Mr. Speaker, I yield myself such time as I may consume.

Mr. Speaker, I rise in strong support of House Resolution 379, legislation introduced by our distinguished colleague the gentleman from Illinois [Mr. PORTER], which expresses the sense of Congress regarding the eighth anniversary on March 17, 1996, of the massacre of 5,000 Iraqi Kurds as a result of a gas bomb attack by the Iraqi Government.

The United States is well aware of the brutal actions of Saddam Hussein's regime against Iraqi minorities, particularly Iraqi Kurds, who are now protected in northern Iraq by Operation Provide Comfort. United States support for Operation Provide Comfort is substantial, through our participation in monitoring the no-fly zone over Iraq north of the 36th parallel, and through our approximately $1.2 billion in humanitarian and protective activi-

ties there to assist the Kurds in the north, in which we are also able to deter Saddam's aggression.

House Resolution 379 recalls the events of March 17, 1988, and calls upon the administration to: Commemorate the memories of those innocents who lost their lives in that tragic attack; reaffirm the United States commitment to protect and assist the Kurdish minority in Iraq, to ensure that the Halabja massacre does not happen again; support efforts to promote a democratic alternative to the present regime in Iraq which will assure the Kurds the right to self-government through a federal system; and renew efforts to establish an international war crimes tribunal to prosecute Iraqi leaders involved in crimes against humanity.

Mr. Speaker, the gentleman from Illinois [Mr. PORTER] is to be commended for his sponsorship of this resolution, and for his consistent leadership in fighting for human rights. Accordingly, I support the gentleman's resolution, and urge my colleagues to support it as well.

Mr. Speaker, I reserve the balance of my time.

Mr. MORAN. Mr. Speaker, I yield myself such time as I may consume.

The minority applauds this resolution introduced by the gentleman from Illinois [Mr. PORTER] and appreciates the gentleman from New York [Mr. GILMAN], the chairman, bringing it to the floor. It is appropriate that we express our sense of outrage over the massacre of 5,000 Kurds by gas bomb attack. It is a timely reminder that we have to continue our vigilance and pressure against Iraq with and on behalf of the international community.

This resolution reaffirms our commitment to protect and to help the Kurdish people in Iraq. It supports efforts to promote a democratic alternative to the present regime in Iraq which will assure the Kurdish people the right to self-government through a federal system, and it calls on the administration to renew efforts to establish an international war crimes tribunal to prosecute Iraqi leaders involved in crimes against humanity and war crimes and their principal leader, in particular, Saddam Hussein.

So this is a good resolution, and we would urge its adoption.

Mr. Speaker, I reserve the balance of my time.

Mr. GILMAN. Mr. Speaker, I yield such time as he may consume to the distinguished gentleman from Illinois [Mr. PORTER], distinguished co-chairman of our human rights caucus, who has been a leader in our battle for human rights and has brought this Kurdish problem to our attention for a number of years.

Mr. PORTER. Mr. Speaker, I thank the distinguished chairman for yielding time to me. I particularly thank him for his tremendous leadership in fighting for the rights of minorities all across the world.

He has been steadfast in his support for the Kurdish people, the largest ethnic group in the world not to have a country of their own, 25 million people divided between Turkey, Iraq, Iran and Syria. The gentleman from New York has been absolutely outstanding in his leadership, to draw our attention to their plight in several of these countries and to fight for their basic human rights.

Mr. Speaker, 8 years ago on March 17, 1988, Saddam Hussein's regime attacked the Kurdish town of Halabja using poison gas and nerve gas. Over 5,000 civilians, including women and children, perished in this attack. Following the attack, the Iraqi Government demonstrated just how terrible and inhumane it is by continuing its reign of terror against the Kurds.

Throughout 1988, over 182,000 Iraqi Kurds were killed by the Iraqi Government in vicious gas attacks. It was not until Iraq's invasion of Kuwait in 1990 that the international community stepped forward and took measures to destroy Iraq's arsenal of weapons of mass destruction.

Today the United States and the international community support efforts to protect the Iraqi Kurds. the United States has been instrumental in ensuring that humanitarian assistance reaches Kurds in Iraq and that they are protected from Iraqi Government attacks.

The plight of the Iraqi Kurds, however, remains precarious at best. Saddam Hussein continues to terrorize the Kurdish region through acts of sabotage and economic embargo. Additionally, over 20 million land mines laid by the Iraqi Government throughout the Kurdish countryside continually hamper relief efforts. Today there are posed on the edge of the Kurdish area 100,000 Iraqi troops threatening those areas.

Mr. Speaker, the Iraqi Government refuses to guarantee its citizens basic human rights and the right to live under the rule of law. The United Nations imposed sanctions as a result of Iraq's 1990 invasion of Kuwait. Saddam Hussein continuously refuses to comply with the U.N. Security Council resolutions.

As a result, the economy continues to deteriorate, but it is not Saddam Hussein who suffers the terrible cost of a debilitating economy, Mr. Speaker. Instead, those who bear the burden of a dictator's cruel and senseless policy are the innocent citizens who are refused the right to change their government and whose freedoms of expression and association are denied. Basic human rights only exist in the Kurdish-controlled areas in the north because of the protection of international forces.

Iraq must continue to be ostracized from the community of nations, Mr. Speaker, until its conduct begins to approach a respect for basic rights of each human being to live, to worship and to speak according to the dictates of his or her own conscience.

We must never ever forget those Iraqi Kurds who lost their lives as the result of the terrible, despicable acts of a repressive dictator. Mr. Speaker, the responsibility falls to us to ensure that their memory forever remains alive.

Mr. Speaker, past events make crystal clear that Saddam Hussein would attack the Kurds tomorrow if the United States did not protect them. Since 1991, Operation Provide Comfort has provided humanitarian assistance and protective activities on behalf of the Iraqi Kurds.

Without the support both morally and economically of the United States, I believe without the slightest doubt that many more innocent Kurdish men, women, and children would have lost their lives. The United States must continue to stand with those like the Iraqi Kurds who refuse to surrender their basic human rights to the present repressive and monstrous ways of dictators like Saddam Hussein.

Mr. Speaker, with the passage of this resolution today, Congress will go on record as commemorating the March 17, 1988 attack on the Iraqi Kurds and reaffirming strong United States support for the Kurdish people of Iraq. I strongly urge the adoption of this resolution.

Mr. Speaker, let me also comment upon a related matter. Recently our ally, Turkey, has chosen a new prime minister, Mesut Yilmaz. He has recently called for a new dialog with Greece that would intend to resolve many ongoing disputes and to bring Turkey and Greece into the kind of relation, or allies with one another, that would reflect well upon both countries and would lead to a lessening of tensions in the geographic region.

As part of that announcement, Prime Minister Yilmaz also said that he would like to open a border gate with Armenia, if he saw clear signs of progress toward a peace settlement between Armenia and Azerbaijan in their 5-year war over Nagorno-Karabakh.

He also said, Mr. Speaker, that regarding the repression of the Kurds in southern Turkey by the Turkish Government, that he would put upon the table a plan that would include granting the Kurds in Turkey cultural liberties such as the Kurdish language education that moderate Kurdish groups have long sought.

Mr. Speaker, he said also that the state of emergency would gradually be lifted in the southeast region and that measures would be taken to stimulate its economy which has suffered during the long conflict.

Mr. Speaker, he said that, and I quote, "after having witnessed such terrible events in the past, after losing 15,000 people. I believe we have come to a common understanding that this problem can be solved only by peaceful means and not by military means."

Mr. Speaker, this is extremely good news. This is what the United States and those of us in Congress concerned with the plight of the Kurds in Turkey have long sought. If the Turkish Government can follow through and the Turkish people can support their new

prime minister in this endeavor, I believe that the lives of thousands and thousands of innocent people, part of the Kurdish minority as well as the lives of Turkish citizens will be spared.

I commend the new prime minister, Mr. Yilmaz, on taking this initiative. I know that it takes great political courage in Turkey to do so. We will promise that we will work together with the Turkish Government to achieve the settlement of differences with Greece, the opening of a positive relationship with Armenia and on the resolution of the terrible conflict in southeast Turkey that has claimed so many lives, made so many people homeless and refugees in their own country and had plagued the entire country for such a long, long time.

□ 1500

Mr. SMITH of New Jersey. Mr. Speaker, I yield myself such time as I may consume.

I want to commend the gentleman from Illinois [Mr. Porter] first and foremost for this fine resolution and for his leadership on these issues. He has been tenacious over the years in raising the issue of the such maligned and troubled Kurds who have suffered so much, and I want to thank him for remembering, through this resolution, that horrible day when some 5,000 people were killed by poison gas.

I will never forget the picture of that mother clutching her young child, with the child's mouth gaping open. As a result of the gas, the impact of the gas, there was a look of absolute fright on both mother and baby; just one of the Kurds killed by Saddam Hussein, one of the many.

I also want to remind everyone that the regime of Saddam Hussein continues to kill, torture and illegally imprison members of the Kurdish minority in Iraq, as well as anyone else who displeases the regime. Relief workers who have gone in to help the Kurdish refugees have also been the victims of extrajudicial executions as well as disappearances.

Mr. Speaker, back in the early 1990's I was part of the Speaker's mission that went to the refugee camps on the border of Turkey and Iraq and met with many of the Kurds who were fleeing the repression. It was right in the aftermath of the Persian Gulf War, and the

Republican Guard were in hot pursuit of this Kurdish minority. It was very compelling and encouraging for me to see how our military carried on Operation Provide Comfort." They came in, they organized, and they were able to provide the logistical support for medicines and food to be dispersed, and thousands of Kurds were spared because of the humanitarian efforts of the United States military as part of "Operation Provide Comfort". After several months, the situation was stabilized, and the baton was passed to the nongovernmental organizations that then carried on the good work of providing this important relief.

Mr. Speaker, as my good friend and colleague, the gentleman from Illinois [Mr. Porter], pointed out, the Kurds do suffer much in Turkey as well. We have had hearings, on the subject including one just this morning. The gentleman from Virginia [Mr. Moran] was there, the gentleman from New York [Mr. Gilman], the gentleman from Illinois [Mr. Hyde] and other members of our committee and subcommittee, and we focused on one of these areas, the proposed sale of Cobras to Turkey. As the chair of the Subcommittee on International Operations & Human Rights I believe that it would be outrageous to send Cobras to Turkey after the military might of the Turkish regime has been used in an ethnic cleansing effort against the Kurds, again another sad chapter in the kind of cruelty that these people have had to endure.

What is pointed out in this resolution, the massacre of the 5,000, is but one rather large and very terrible event in a series of tragedies that have been visited upon the suffering Kurdish minorities. So this is an important resolution, and I urge its passage.

Mr. GILMAN. Mr. Speaker, I have no further requests for time, and I yield back the balance of the time.

Mr. MORAN. Mr. Speaker, I yield myself such time as I may consume.

Mr. Speaker, let me just say I am encouraged by what the gentleman from Illinois [Mr. Porter] shared with us in terms of the new leadership in Turkey. That is major progress, to consider opening up the supply lines, economic and humanitarian supply lines, to Armenia if we can make progress in terms of the conflict with Azerbaijan. Certainly, starting to hear the relationship with Greece is a step in the right direction. Some of us would like to see a recognition of the Armenian genocide, which has been a problem in terms of improved relations with Turkey. But perhaps with new leadership we will continue to move forward.

This resolution, however, is entirely in order, and we strongly support it.

Mr. Speaker, I yield back the balance of my time.

The SPEAKER pro tempore (Mr. Upton). The question is on the motion offered by the gentleman from New York [Mr. Gilman] that the House suspend the rules and agree to the resolution, House Resolution 379.

The question was taken.

Mr. PORTER. Mr. Speaker, on that demand the yeas and nays.

The yeas and nays were ordered.

The SPEAKER pro tempore. Pursuant to clause 5, rule I, and the Chair's prior announcement, further proceedings on this motion will be postponed.

174.

[March 28, 1996 (Extensions of Remarks), pp. 469-70]

UNITED STATES—ORIGIN MILITARY EQUIPMENT IN TURKEY
HON. LEE H. HAMILTON
OF INDIANA
IN THE HOUSE OF REPRESENTATIVES

Wednesday, March 27, 1996

Mr. HAMILTON. Mr. Speaker, on September 8, 1995, I wrote to Secretary of State Christopher, asking several questions about the use and possible misuse of United States-origin military equipment by Turkey. This letter was a followup to an exchange of letters on the same issue earlier in the year, which I inserted in the Record at that time.

I have now received a response from the State Department to my September letter, which sets out the administration's position on the human rights situation in Turkey and its relationship to the issue of U.S.-supplied military equipment in the country.

Since I believe that other Members will find the administration's views informative and useful in formulating their own approach to this important issue, I would like to insert both my letter and the administration's response in the RECORD.

DEPARTMENT OF STATE,
Washington, February 29, 1996.
HON. LEE HAMILTON,
U.S. House of Representatives.

DEAR MR. HAMILTON: This is a follow-up reply to your letter of September 8, 1995, to Secretary Christopher about human rights in Turkey. As stated in our November 1, 1995 interim response, you raised a number of serious questions in your letter. Thank you for your understanding in allowing us time to prepare this reply.

In your letter, you state that human rights abuses in Turkey are a matter of real concern to the U.S. Congress. We appreciate your interest and that of your colleagues in these issues. Congressional hearings, reports, and statements are a valuable way for the U.S. government to indicate concern about human rights in Turkey.

As we consider how best to pursue our objectives in Turkey, it is important to understand just what Turkey is up against. The Kurdistan Workers' Party (PKK) has stated that its primary goal is to create a separate Kurdish state in part of what is now Turkey. In the course of its operations, the PKK has frequently targeted Turkish—civilians. It has not hesitated to attack Western—including American—interests.

The Turkish government has the right to defend itself militarily from this terrorist threat. The Turkish military has said it seeks to distinguish between PKK members and ordinary Kurdish citizens in its operations. We remain concerned, nevertheless, about the manner in which some operations in the southeast have been conducted. As we have docu-

mented in our annual human rights reports and in the special report we submitted to Congress last June on the situation in the southeast, these operations have resulted in civilian deaths, village evacuations and burnings.

You ask what the U.S. is doing about information that U.S. supplied defense articles may have been used by Turkey's military against civilians during the course of operations against the PKK. We discussed those issues at length in our June "Report on Allegations of Human Rights Abuses by the Turkish Military and the Situation in Cyprus."

These reports trouble us deeply. We have frequently cautioned the Turkish government to exercise care that its legitimate military operations avoid targeting civilians and noncombatants. We have made it clear that, in accordance with both the Foreign Assistance and Arms Export Control Acts, human rights considerations will continue to be very carefully weighed in considering whether or not to approve transfers and sales of military equipment.

With regard to death squad activities in the southeast, as we stated in our report last June, we have found reports of government involvement in these incidents to be credible. Others have also been involved. In this regard, a number of Turkish "Hizbullah" terrorists are now on trial for alleged involvement in "mystery killings." According to Turkey's prestigious Human Rights Foundation, these sorts of killings were down sharply in 1995.

We have told the Turks repeatedly that we do not believe a solely military solution will end the problems in the southeast. We urge them to explore political and social solutions which are more likely to succeed over time. These should include fully equal rights—among them cultural and linguistic rights—for all of Turkey's citizens including the Kurds. We have been encouraged by incremental actions toward granting the Kurds such rights. For example, Turkey's High Court of Appeals ruled in October that Kurdish former members of Parliament had not committed crimes when they took their oaths in the Kurdish language, wore Kurdish colors, and stated that Turkish was a foreign language for them. The Appeals Court's decision on these matters, which are very sensitive and emotional in Turkey, may send an important signal to the lower courts and may help expand Kurdish rights.

We believe it is important for those individuals who have been displaced to be compensated for their losses and to be able to return to their homes without fear. If the security situation prevents their return, it is important for the villagers to be compensated and resettled elsewhere. Like you, we are disturbed by Turkey's failure to date to adequately provide for the displaced. We will encourage the new Turkish government to do so.

In the long run, an improved dialog between the government and Kurdish representatives is needed to bring a lasting solution to the southeast. It is important that those who purport to speak for the Kurds do so sincerely and constructively. In this context, you asked whether former DEP members of the Turkish Parliament who were stripped of their immunities and fled to Europe could speak for the Kurds. Unfortunately, some of them associated the "Kurdistan Parliament in Exile" (KPIE), which is financed and controlled by the PKK. We cannot, therefore, advocate negotiations with the so-called KPIE.

There are legitimate interlocutors with whom the government could discuss Kurdish concerns. Although the Pro-Kurdish People's Democracy Party (HADEP) fell substantially short of obtaining the ten percent of the national vote required to take seats in the Turkish Grand National Assembly, the party campaigned well and carried a large number of votes in the southeast. In addition, other parties, politicians, academicians, businesspeople, and journalists also raised Kurdish concerns during the recent election campaign.

These developments are positive, and there are other signs that our active engagement with the Turks on human rights issues are meeting with success. The constitutional amendments enacted this past summer broadened political participation in several ways, including by enfranchising voters over eighteen and those residing outside of Turkey. There is also a move to devolve more authority from the central government to the local authorities. And, on October 27, the Turkish government—with encouragement from the U.S. and Europe—amended Article 8 of the Anti-Terror Law, which had been used to constrain freedom of expression substantially. As a result of this revision, over 130 people were released from prison and many pending cases are being dropped.

U.S. officials will continue to monitor closely human rights developments in Turkey. Our observations on Turkish human rights are the result of a constant, energetic effort by our Embassy and others in our government to stay informed. Our officials meet regularly with elected officials in the Turkish Administration and Parliament. We also speak frequently with critics of the government—including Turkish and international NGOs, bar and medical associations, lawyers, and other human rights activists. U.S. officials travel to the Southeast periodically where they see government officials and the affected parties.

We will also continue to encourage change by supporting those who are committed to human rights and democratic reforms, including Turkish NGOs. This is a long-term effort that will require continued engagement. The important point to keep in the forefront is that the real impetus behind democratic change in Turkey must come from Turkish citizens themselves. Our objective must be to give them all the constructive help we can.

I hope this information is useful. If I can be of further assistance, please do not hesitate to contact me.

Sincerely,
WENDY R. SHERMAN,
Assistant Secretary,
Legislative Affairs.

———

COMMITTEE ON INTERNATIONAL RELATIONS, HOUSE OF REPRESENTATIVES,
Washington, September 8, 1995.
HON. WARREN CHRISTOPHER,
Secretary of State, Department of State,
Washington, DC.
DEAR MR. SECRETARY: Thank you for your reply of August 15th to my letter of

June 29th concerning the use and possible misuse of U.S.-origin military equipment by Turkey. I wanted to follow-up that correspondence with two general lines of questioning.

First, I continue to have deep concerns about the use of U.S.-supplied military equipment in Southeast Turkey and about the reports of the misuse of that equipment, the wholesale destruction of villages, and the indiscriminate firing on civilian populations. Such abuses can erode support for Turkey in the Congress.

In your response to my letter, you indicated that internal security, along with self-defense is recognized as an acceptable use of U.S.-supplied defense articles but that the United States is troubled about reports that a large number of civilians have been killed in Turkish government counter-insurgency operations against the PKK. Questions remain:

What precisely are you doing about these reports?

Is it the U.S. policy, for example, to tell the Turks when we see reports of the destruction of villages or the killing of civilians, that we do not like it and cannot tolerate such abuses in the use of U.S.-supplied equipment?

What is the U.S. strategy to insure that such practices end?

Second, I have further questions regarding a related aspect of U.S. policy toward Turkey—resolution of the Kurdish issue in southeast Turkey.

There is considerable sympathy in Congress for the plight of the Kurdish population in Turkey, although none for terrorist acts by the Kurdish Worker's Party (PKK). I do not know of any Member support for Kurdish separatism or the break up of Turkey, but there is strong support for full equality of rights, including cultural and linguistic rights, for all Turkish citizens, including the Kurds. Members are troubled by the Turkish government's dominant reliance on force to put down the insurrection in the southeast, and would like to see the United States take a more active role in promoting negotiations among a broad base of Turkish citizens to end the violence.

I am concerned that if the present situation persists, the United States will have difficulty sustaining its Turkey policy. An amendment this summer to the Foreign Operations Appropriations bill in the House which limits aid to Turkey because of human rights concerns illustrates some of the problems that arise if these issues are not adequately addressed.

I understand that it is U.S. policy to support Turkey's territorial integrity and its legitimate right to combat terrorism, including terrorist acts by the PKK. I also understand that the U.S. supports democratic reform in Turkey as an integral part of the effort to improve human rights conditions and to undercut support for PKK violence. In this context, I would like to pose the following questions:

What is the United States doing to push efforts in Turkey to amend Article 8 of the antiterrorism law?

What are the implications for U.S. policy and for the situation in the Southeast if efforts to amend Article 8 fail or are abandoned?

What is the United States doing to promote efforts to provide Kurds with equal rights in Turkey? Is it United States policy to support the legitimate political, cultural and linguistic rights of Turkish citizens of the Southeast of Kurdish origin? How do you react to recent comments by senior Turkish officials that the extension of such rights are not a priority of the Turkish government?

In our human rights dialogue, is the U.S. pressing the Turkish government and General Staff to abandon tactics that target the Kurdish civilian population, such as forced evacuation and burning of Kurdish villages?

What is United States policy doing to address allegations that the Turkish government is either sponsoring or tolerating the activities of death squads reported to have killed hundreds of Kurdish activists in the southeast?

What is United States policy on meeting and dealing with the elected representatives of Turkish citizens in the Southeast regardless of whether they are able to sit in the National Assembly at this time? Does the United States support negotiations between several exiled Turkish Kurdish parliamentarians and the Turkish government? With whom do you think the Turkish Government should negotiate?

What kind of political engagement between the Turkish government and Kurdish nationalists does the United States seek to promote in order to encourage Turkey to move away from reliance on a solely military solution?

I look forward to your reply.

With best wishes,
Sincerely,
LEE H. HAMILTON,
Ranking Democratic Member.

175.

[September 5, 1996 (House), pp. 10091-92]

SECURITY OF KURDISH MINORITY

The SPEAKER pro tempore. Under a previous order of the House, the gentleman from Illinois [Mr. Porter] is recognized for 5 minutes.

Mr. PORTER. Mr. Speaker, the Kurdish people are an ancient people. There are 30 million of them. They live in Turkey, in Iraq, in Iran, in Syria, and they are an oppressed people within each of those societies.

None of those countries wants the Kurdish people to be united. They see it as in their interest to keep them divided and fighting. Whenever possible they supply arms to various sides and take advantage of them through propaganda and other means to manipulate them.

Today the media may be focused on what has been done with cruise missiles, but innocent Kurdish people are being killed and the situation in northern Iraq is extremely grave, Mr. Speaker. That situation was precipitated, I believe, by our State Department's failure to take seriously the need to bring the Kurdish sides, the Kurdish factions, together and to stop their exploitation by all sides and to respect their rights as human beings.

Mr. Speaker, when I sat down with representatives of the State Department in July, they had no information that Iran might attempt to cross the border in northern Iraq to attack the KDPI bases there, and when Iran in fact did so, less than a week later, no protest was heard from our Government, no action was taken. Yet at that time when Iran crossed the border, it was inevitable, Mr. Speaker, that the Iraqis would see that incursion into their territory as violating their sovereignty and would move north.

They have done so obviously in great force, but the fact that they had not done so during the previous 5 years, since the beginning of Operation Provide Comfort, is clear evidence that the reason that they did so at that time was the incursion of Iran into northern Iraq.

We did nothing about it, to head it off. We did nothing to take the division of the Kurds seriously between the PUK and the KDP, and I believe that was the beginning of the problems that we are now experiencing in that area.

Today the Iraqi Republican Guards, many of them dressed in Kurdish garb, are in Kuysangaq, they are in Sulaimaniya, they are going door-to-door looting Kurdish homes, and innocent people are being killed and dying and we are doing nothing about it.

On the northern border, the Turkish border, Turkey has taken advantage of the situation to declare a 3- to 6-mile wide zone, not in Turkey but in Iraq, that they are presently clearing, with 35,000 Turkish troops and armored personnel carriers in that region, moving out people who are living in villages, killing those that resist and creating a no-man's-land along their border.

Mr. Speaker, this situation is a grave and serious one for which the United States has great responsibility, and it is not enough just to send cruise missiles to the southern part of Iraq and say that we are stopping aggression. The aggression is continuing to this moment. It is continuing almost on all sides. And the people that are caught in the middle are innocent people who have been taken advantage of for centuries by the places where they are found within societies where in each case they are in the minority and are being severely oppressed. It is time that the President of the United States and that this country stand up for the rights of these people who need our help as perhaps never before.

176.

[September 5, 1996 (House), pp. 10093-99]

WHEN WILL WE STOP THE IMPERIAL PRESIDENCY?

The SPEAKER pro tempore. Under the Speaker's announced policy of May 12, 1995, the gentleman from California [Mr. Dornan] is recognized for 60 minutes as the designee of the majority leader.

Mr. DORNAN. Mr. Speaker, we adjourned regular legislative business, or ended regular legislative business, so early that it is in the middle of the day. It is only 10 minutes to 1 out in California and still the morning in Hawaii, so I am going to take advantage of this opportunity and try to keep my good friend from Texas, Mr. Gonzalez, interested by covering three different topics. The first thing I would like to cover is Iraq.

I want to associate myself with the remarks of Mr. Porter of Illinois. There is great suffering going on in northern Iraq. I thought that the Kurdish people would maybe reach a period of tranquility here. They are one of these sad ethnic groups that spread over three, actually four, nations, with the geographic lines changing over the past several centuries multiple times. The only Nation that I can think of that has been cut up into four different nations like this is the once great nation of Armenia, now down to less than a fourth of its original size; the first nation as a nation to embrace Christianity in the 300's, the fourth century, and now we learn about these Kurdish people dividing among themselves, starting to kill one another. We had an opportunity here diplomatically to move in after Operation Provide Comfort was sent to that area of northern Iraq by President George Bush. Secretary of State Jim Baker visited. I recall telling President Bush when he called me for the only hospital visit I remember having in my life, and I was in the hospital for 3 or 4 days for some surgery, and President Bush called me on my birthday, April 3, 1991, and he said:

"Bob, we need you, get out of there."

And I said, "Can we talk business?"

And he said, "What?" He said, "In the hospital you want to talk business?"

I said, "Mr. President, draw a line in the hills. The way you drew a line in the sand, draw a line in the mountains."

And he said, "Bob, there are forces in Washington that would like to see Iraq spin into at least three different nations."

And I said, "Well, if you'll look at the television, which I have been looking at a lot in the last 2 days, you will see that they are beating your brains out. Kurdish women are coming into our camps along the Turkish-Iraqi northern border with children on their shoulders that have already frozen to death."

Fortunately with each day it was getting a fourth of a degree warmer, and he said, "Well, we're looking at it."

The media then began to just savagely attack President Bush. This is within days of the 4-day land war in Iraq ending on the 27th of December. Here it was less than 5 weeks later and they are beating his brains out. Within a few days he did draw that line in the hills of northern Iraq and organized Operation Provide Comfort.

Well it is hard to believe that 6 years ago this coming March, 5\1/2\ years ago now, and the Kurds are still suffering. Iraqi troops in the north, as Mr. Porter said, are beating in doors, shooting people. They opened up with savage artillery fire a few days ago into Irbil, the so-called capital of the Kurdish people in the northern area.

Why Mr. Clinton neglected this area of the world for almost his entire first term is beyond me. We do have strategic interests in the area because a dictator like Saddam Hussein can just destroy oil prices around the world. He was driving faster than anybody believed toward nuclear, biological and chemical warfare capability. It remains a fact that we were never able to discover a single Iraqi scud missile.

This last week I have been in Great Britain visiting some of the best intelligence sites outside of the United States proper in the world. There is a new news center at the RAF base at Moesworth, which was our second GLCM base in Great Britain. Fortunately with the dissolution of the evil empire out of the Kremlin, we were able to shut down those GLCM bases in Sicily and the two in Great Britain and stop the one in Germany before it had even gone operational, and we had all of these new facilities built for the GLCM, the GLCM missiles in Great Britain, and we put in there something that is called the JAC, the Joint Analysis Center. I went in there last Thursday, watched in the clearest way possible, beyond anything I have ever seen of intelligence capability so far, watched the buildup of the Iraqi troops. Unless the President has taken the course of Jimmy Carter and disregarded his daily intel briefings, which Carter did in a few instances, then he could claim ignorance. But I have to believe his National Security Council was keeping him briefed on this buildup of power, and I managed to evaluate for the third time the F-16—excuse me the F-15 E, the strike eagle fighter at Lakenheath, which is not only the world's greatest operational fighter but the best we have in all of Europe, Asia, and Africa, and flew a simulated bombing mission up to Scotland, fought our way through British tornadoes electronically defending the area.

That is just absolutely astounding how you can accomplish a real mission all electronically, bomb a target, shoot down aircraft or get shot down yourself. We did the shooting now this time, fought our way back from aggressor F-15 E's, and as amazing as this system is, the strike eagle, constantly updating the software packages in it from the time that I first flew it in March 1990, just a few months before Saddam Hussein came across the Kuwaiti border, the southern border of Iraq, on August 2. In spite of its capabilities, not a single F-15 E was able to find in the field a scud missile during the whole course of the air war and the 4 days of the ground war in 1991.

And at Farmborough, the air exposition there, the Russian Su-37 did not debut during Monday's open in the Farmborough exposition, but that night, as I was walking and looking at some of the Russian equipment on the flight line, the Su-17 taxis out. It is a beautiful looking aircraft. It still astounds me how a nation so poverty stricken, so incapable of making a class radio, a television, a refrigerator, an automobile; this is Russia I am speaking of; how they can make a fighter this beautiful and capable is beyond me.

The Su-37 taxis out, it is dusk, its landing lights and all of its lighting equipment is on. It makes a match performance takeoff, racks it over the orange cones that they set up to have as the line beyond which you cannot fly near the crowd. I realized then that they were probably putting on a performance for the authorities, the British authorities, at Farmborough to show their max demonstration, a flight which are not allowed to do in our military because it is so beyond the envelope, as pilots say, so on the danger edge.

If you lose one engine in that two-engine aircraft, it is a definite crash, and this Su-37 that is now available for export to countries like India, through an arrangement with China, where after the first few they would start building an aircraft totally capable of equaling the performance of our F-15 E strike eagle. The pilot goes through some opening maneuvers, then comes across the field in powered slow flight, pulls up or powers up, rather, into perfectly vertical flight and expecting to see him do what is called the cobra, which he pushes the tail up beyond the vertical and then slowly powers back and recovers. Instead he goes through the cobra manuever, flops on its back and does what I can only call a snap loop.

I mean only a biplane, a little tiny highly stressed sports biplane can do what this massive, maybe 20-ton aircraft could do, and that is pull through and turn on its axis, on the horizontal axis wings in the tightest loop—it is not even a loop, a snap loop—and recover and power out of it and accelerate.

The point is the Russians are in the field before we are, even though we have done this at our test center at Edwards Air Force Base with vectored thrust, where you take the engine nozzles at the rear of the aircraft and vary them so that you get this vectored thrust change, thereby augmenting in an amazing way the control services, your air runs, your elevator and the rudder on the vertical stabilizer.

The Russians making this airplane available for export means that on this floor in the 105th Congress next year we must again protect against the shortsighted FR-22 Lockheed-

Boeing-General Dynamics Lightning 2, is what I think they will finally nickname the F-22.

It is amazing how people in this country, with all of the history that has taken place just in this century, from the Wright Brothers flying at Kittyhawk on December 17, 1903, to this December 17, in 93 years from a little aircraft that could only be powered 120 feet. That is almost the wingspan of one of our new unmanned aerial vehicles, the Global Hawk, which I spent the better part of a morning examining in its hangar. The first one is due to fly soon down at Teledyne Ryan in San Diego. I stole some time away from the convention. This Global Hawk can loiter for almost 2 days without a man, bringing this dazzling type of data downlinked to our intelligence facilities so we can observe the brutal antics of a dictator like Saddam Hussein.

So here we are in a fast-moving world, all in this the bloodiest century in history. We see a dictator bragging that he has outlasted George Bush, Brian Mulroney, Margaret Thatcher, Francois Mitterrand, Prime Minister Ohara in Japan. He has outlasted them all, in some cases double turnovers like Mulroney to KimCampbell to now the new, let us call it labor liberal government in Ottawa. He is so cocky. He is there on television yesterdaysaying that we will not face him man to man, as though we had not cleaned his clock in Desert Storm. Heis talking about we are hitting him with technology.

Then, of course, in Tehran, on Tehran radio and television they are talking about us, the Great Satan, child pornography, 1.5 million abortions a year, runaway divorce, runaway pornography. And now we are killing humble Iraqi soldiers, who they killed millions of in their war back in the 1980's; that we are doing it with technology that comes in out of the night that no one can see. It is just astounding how the Clinton administration has rallied the Arab world against us.

Jordan, who is getting some of our advanced military equipment, will not support us in this. Great Britain always stands beside us, but in all the French papers today are saying that this is nothing more than a cynical election final quarter stunt by Clinton.

Mr. Speaker, it is with some trepidation that I criticize the moves that Mr. Clinton has made, but I am going to just ask 10 questions today that I want the 1 million-plus audience that follows C-Span, particularly on a day when we are through with legislative business so quickly, I want to ask these questions. If somebody wants to take them down, Mr. Speaker, be my guest. I would recommend you call them in to the successful talk shows around this country and ask these questions, as some of the more important ones come toward the end. Some of them people have already thought about.

Here is the first of the 10: Why was Congress not notified? Constitutionally he should get our permission for aggressive activities like this. This is not defending the United States. This is not what Thomas Jefferson talked about when people yelled at him to use our young embryonic Navy to punish the Barbary pirates along the Tripoli coast of North Africa.

Jefferson said very clearly, I can only use our small military and our Navy, and there was not much Armyat all, in a defensive way if the United States, the colonies, the 13 colonies, are attacked. Only then. By then it was 14 colonies, the 15th about to become a State. Only with these young 15 American States can I use our military, small military power defensively. Offensively, like sailing across the Atlantic to the Mediterranean and punishing the Barbary pirates, for that I need congressional authority.

And he got it 10 times, through John Adams, his predecessor, through Jefferson, through his successor, Madison, up through John Quincy Adams. Ten times this Congress, in that Chamber just a few yards away, authorized, the Chamber that we were in from 1807 through 1857, and the small rooms on the Senate side before that, through the British burning it August 24, 1814, 10 times this Congress said, you will, by order, as the President, go after the Barbary pirates.

Now all of a sudden where is that congressional authority? We have a scholar at the Library of Congress, professor Lewis Fisher, who has written a brilliant book. and I hope next year we have a 2-year, 3-year debate, multiple special orders like this with dialog back and forth on why we have allowed an imperial Presidency to grow through Republicans and Democrats. Now we have a President burning up 50 million dollars' worth of cruise missiles, sea-launched Tomahawks and air-launched Alcum, 50 million dollars' worth with no loss of life on our side.

But I had a very long commentary with Regis Philbin and Kathie Lee, holding up these New York headlines this morning saying "Victory for Clinton, War is Over," and Regis flippantly, I am sure he thought better of it later, said "I like wars where nobody dies." There is no such thing as nobody dying. Peasants, personnel in Iraq who man these surface to air sites we destroyed, they are dead. It is their misfortune that they live in a country with an evil dictator.

Mr. Speaker, our official reporters of debate are excellent in titling these 5-minute or 1-minute or 60-minute special order speeches. If we choose, they will use our title. I would say that the title of this first section of my special order would be "When do we stop the imperial Presidency?"

That is question No. 1. Why was Congress not brought into the decision process; subquestion: why were we not even notified, those of us on the intelligence committees: Senator Strom Thurmond, chairman of Armed Services, the gentleman from South Carolina, Floyd Spence, both ex-Army and Navy officers, chairman of National Security, why was not Mr. Spence notified? Why were not the two chairmen, Medal of Honor winner Bob Kerrey, Senator from Nebraska, the gentleman from Texas, Larry Combest, chairman on our side; why were we not notified of this operation?

No. 2. Why has there been no attack against the actual Iraqi army in the North that violated the United Nations amendments and has done the killing? The forces in the North are untouched. We attacked targets in the South. Is that because they are softer targets? Maybe, because we have more air power out of the South? Is it because Turkey will not support us in this?

We have now a fundamentalist government in Turkey. The brilliant lady President in

Turkey was defeated, so I guess it is that Turkey will not let us use Incirlik, the equivalent of Operation Proven Force. I was there the day the land war started in Incirlik on February 24.

Because of a courageous Air Force officer who will not be named, I was able to go on a combat mission with a KC-135 out of Dias Tek, right over the Iraqi-Turkey border, refueling our F-111's, our 15's, our 16's. They were going down the very flight we refueled went down to Sulaimniya and blew up a nuclear missile facility just on the outskirts of Baghdad.

Incirlik was important. More Iraqi fighters were shot down by our fighter pilots who came down from Spangdahlen and Bitburg and Shusterburg than were shot down by the fantastic 33rd fighter wing out of Eglin Air Force Base, FL. In the North they were the ones that captured or shot down the Iraqi fighters fleeing to Iran, where they were confiscated anyway, in that peculiar relationship between this Persian nation and this Arabic nation, Iran and Iraq, but no punishment for the Iraqi army that has done the killing, and is killing today. Or it will be morning soon over there, and it will be another day of killing, and Clinton is claiming victory here in the United States.

He did it in the most unseemly way: in the Oval Office, with Vice President Gore at his side, not a briefing at the Pentagon, not bringing Shalikashvili, our four-star Chairman of the Joint Chiefs into his office, but sitting there, for all the world like two aging schoolboys, discussing this technological short combat with 44 cruise missiles and one F-16 Falcon punishing a surface-to-air site for painting them with their radar.

If the Clinton administration did know of the troop movements before-hand and failed to act, was the administration then encouraging through its nonaction, encouraging this Iraqi attack to counter a growing influence in the region by Iran?

No. 3. Was there some geopolitical reasoning behind this? I rather doubt it, but it is a fair question.

No. 4. If the U.S. actions were a response to the Iraqi attack on one of the two major

Kurdish factions, why was the no-fly zone not extended in the North? Why was the no-fly zone extended in the South? The Kurdish cities of Sulaimaniya and Kirkuk, they are both outside of the no-fly zone in the North. Now are they going to be the likely targets for next week if Saddam Hussein decides that is his course of action? Which leads me to other questions later on.

No. 5. Iraq, as I said from my own intelligence fact-finding in the field in Great Britain just these last few days. If Iraq has been moving troops to that region for at least half a month, 3 weeks, did the Clinton administration warn Iraq that the U.S. was going to respond militarily if any attack occurred against the Kurds?

We could see the artillery pieces lining up. There was almost a feeling in Europe that, well, maybe they were not going to do it, it was just a show of force. You could see the way the troops were deployed they were going to attack Irbil. So where was the warning here? Where is the discourse between nations to say to Saddam Hussein, if you do that, here is the result? Or is there a suspicion that it was politically advantageous to let Saddam Hussein move, and then you have a quick little action, and a certain person running for the highest elected office in the world suddenly looks decisive? It is more than cynicism to analyze that in a fair way.

No. 6. Why did the administration not respond when Iran recently attacked one of the two Kurdish factions, the one backed by Baghdad, which led to Iraq's decision to retaliate against the Iranian-backed Kurdish faction? Why did we not respond then when the initial fighting started a while ago? It was not ever in the press. They were busy at the Democratic convention.

No. 7. Why is our military response only minimal and nonthreatening to the Iraqi forces in the North?

No. 8. Will the United States escalate its response if Iraq attacks the aforementioned Sulaimaniya or Kirkuk? Or what if its forces just remain in the region? They are still occupying Irbil. There are some reports they are pulling out, but not all of their forces.

They are still occupying what is considered the capital of the Kurdish part of Iraq.

Irbil is where the two helicopters that were shot down April of 1994 in that horrible friendly fire mess where two F-15 pilots destroyed their careers, they are through flying, got either out of the Air Force or leaving it. One is gone and one is about to leave. We shot down two U.N.-controlled H-60 Blackhawks with 13 people on each one, and the majority of those people were Americans: a tragedy. Where were they heading? Toward Irbil, which is above the no-fly zone. So now Saddam Hussein has total control, if he chooses over Sulaimaniya and Kirkuk.

No. 9. What attempts are made to gather allied and other Middle Eastern support for further action? This is where former President George Bush shined. He brought together not a dozen nations, not 15, not two dozen, 28 nations in the allied coalition. He even brought the declining Gorbachev on board. It was an amazing feat of diplomacy for George Bush and Jim Baker, the Secretary of State, to build this coalition. Who is with us? As I mentioned, not the French, not Turkey. Just our standby mother country, Great Britain . . .

177.

[September 5, 1996 (Senate), pp. 9934-38]

UNITED STATES RESPONSE TO IRAQI AGGRESSION

Mr. DASCHLE addressed the Chair.

The PRESIDING OFFICER. The minority leader.

Mr. DASCHLE. According to the unanimous consent agreement, the final issue to be disposed of at approximately 9:30 deals with the resolution relating to Iraq. I would like to address that resolution at this time.

I send it to the desk.

The PRESIDING OFFICER. The clerk will report.

The bill clerk read as follows:

A resolution (S. Res. 288) regarding the United States response to Iraqi aggression.

The Senate proceeded to consider the resolution.

Mr. DASCHLE. Mr. President, on Tuesday, I spoke briefly about my views on President Clinton's decision to retaliate against Iraq for its unprovoked, unjustified, and brutal attack on the civilian population of Irbil, a city in northern Iraq.

At that time, I also indicated I planned to introduce a resolution condemning Saddam Hussein's behavior and expressing the Senate's support for the President's actions.

I must say I never dreamed it would take this long and be this difficult to arrive at a simple resolution in support of the actions taken earlier this week.

For several days now, we have been attempting to resolve issues relating to language and have been thwarted and frustrated in that effort for a lot of reasons, in large measure because many of my colleagues on the other side wish not to laud the President or find any way with which to praise the President's actions. In fact, for the last several hours the issue has been, do we even use the word "President" in the resolution? There was an adamant feeling on the part of many on the other side that we could not use the word "President," and so you will not find that word used as a result of the requirements by many of my colleagues on the Republican side.

In fact, the only reference to the President is a reference to the Commander in Chief, and I must say that that is suitable to many of us, but I do believe that it is a very unfortunate set of circumstances that could have caused some partisanship, in fact a great deal of partisanship, to enter into these deliberations.

Let me at the same time applaud the majority leader for his willingness to continue to work with me to resolve those outstanding questions and to come to some compromise on the language that has now been presented to the Senate. His work and his cooperation as well as that of some of our colleagues on the other side have brought us to this point tonight.

Let me also thank the distinguished Senator from Georgia, the ranking member of the Armed Services Committee, Senator Nunn, and the distinguished Senator from Michigan, Senator Carl Levin. Let me also thank Senator Pell and many others—Senator Biden, who had a lot to do with the wording of this legisla-

tion; in addition, Senator McCain, Senator Warner, and others who were very helpful in bringing us to this point.

Let me make it very clear that in spite of what I consider to be the pettiness involved with whether you use the word "President" or not, this resolution very clearly and strongly and wholeheartedly supports the measures taken by this President in the last 72 hours.

Last Saturday, in spite of clear warnings from the United States and the international community, Iraqi forces commenced their vicious attack on the defenseless civilian Kurdish population in and around Irbil. Casualties reportedly numbered in the thousands. Reports of door-to-door searches resulting in executions were rampant and, unfortunately, all too credible.

In addition to this obvious toll on human life, Saddam's invasion also threatens the interests of the United States and its allies in this crucial region of the world. The prospect for factional strife has been greatly increased while regional stability has been called into question, thereby enhancing the risk of a larger scale conflict in the region.

Saddam's aggression is in direct contravention of the United Nations Resolution 688 which was enacted in 1991 at the end of the Persian Gulf war. At that time the Security Council empowered the United States, Britain, and France to protect the Kurdish population from human rights abuses by the Iraqi regime through the establishment of a no-fly zone over large portions of northern and southern Iraq.

Saddam's attack on Irbil blatantly violates international norms and is by itself sufficient justification for the President's decisions to strike four critical Iraqi targets with 44 cruise missiles and to expand the no-fly zone northward to the very suburbs of Baghdad.

Unfortunately, the aggression in Irbil is but the latest in a string of ruthless and provocative actions undertaken by Saddam before, during, and after the Persian Gulf war.

Mr. President, I will not outline the entire catalog of violent and reprehensible acts undertaken by Saddam and his henchmen since he ascended to power in Iraq. Needless to say, the list is as chilling as it is long. President Clinton succinctly noted in his statement on Tuesday, "Saddam Hussein's objectives may change but his methods are always the same—violence and aggression against the Kurds, against ethnic minorities, against Iraq's neighbors."

It is for these reasons that I support and our colleagues support the President's decision to take action. I am very confident the American people feel exactly as we do tonight.

The President's actions served a twofold purpose. First, they showed Saddam that he will pay a price for his latest act of aggression. In mounting the largest attack on Iraqi territory in the 5 years since the end of the Persian Gulf war, president Clinton has appropriately reminded Saddam that violations of international norms will not go unpunished.

Secondly, by destroying air defense assets in central Iraq and extending the no-fly zone northward toward Baghdad, the United States has greatly reduced the threat Saddam poses to his opponents within Iraq and his opponents in adjoining nations.

By restraining Saddam's bloody hand, the President's decisive action has limited the ability of an oppressive regime to disrupt the volatile center of a Middle East region that is vital to American foreign policy interests. The response was measured, appropriate, and absolutely necessary.

I also want to indicate at this time my strong support for the men and women in uniform who are asked repeatedly to go in harm's way to protect our national interests. Early damage reports from the latest attack on Iraq indicate another mission accomplished without a hitch and without a casualty.

It is noteworthy that despite the end of the cold war, the military forces of the United States continue to play a crucial role around the world in advancing and protecting our national interests. This dedicated group of men and women have been called upon repeatedly since the collapse of the Soviet Union and the onset of the post-cold-war era. They have never failed the American people or our friends abroad.

The resolution before us is an extremely crucial matter for all of us because our enemies and friends must see that we speak with one voice when it comes to our policy for containing and defeating Saddam Hussein. As we have learned only too painfully in the past, domestic discord on important national security issues only plays into the hands of those who seek to undermine our resolve. It is critically important to demonstrate national unity when our military forces are in harm's way.

Even in this most intense political season, politics for all Americans still ends at the water's edge.

President Clinton was faced with a broad array of choices when deciding how to respond to Saddam's aggression, everything from doing nothing to inserting United States ground troops and forcefully evicting Iraqi troops from Irbil. Obviously, each end of this spectrum constitutes an unacceptable and inappropriate response. Only something between the two extremes makes any sense, precisely the course chosen by President Clinton.

This resolution puts the Senate forcefully behind the President's measured decision. The President opted both to weaken Iraqi air defenses and simultaneously expand the area in which the Iraqi Air Force will not be permitted to operate. These actions clearly demonstrate the United States is prepared to impose real costs on Saddam Hussein for his aggression. As noted by Gen. Colin Powell, the President did exactly the right thing.

Of our friends and allies abroad, we ask they stand with the United States as we seek to faithfully implement the U.N. resolutions adopted at the end of the Persian Gulf war. Saddam's actions demonstrate he still represents a direct threat to his people, his neighbors, and the security of the entire vitally important region. If the world were to look the other way now and allow Saddam to go unpunished, we would encourage more blatant and damaging incursions in the future. There must be no doubt in Saddam's mind that the international community is united in its opposition to such unacceptable behavior.

Finally, to Saddam Hussein, let us state for the record the position of this administration and this Congress, as plainly and as simply as we can. Although we may belong to different political parties and have opposing views on some issues, we stand united and indivisible on this. Iraqi aggression must not go unpunished, now or in the future. We will insist on Iraq's compliance with international norms of behavior, regardless of the circumstance.

To this end I have worked with the distinguished majority leader to draft a resolution condemning Saddam's behavior and indicating our strong support for the U.S. response to this latest incident. With the adoption of this resolution by the Senate, there should be no doubt in anyone's mind, least of all Saddam Hussein's, that the American people are united in their opposition to this conduct. Passage of this resolution is one way to demonstrate to our friends and enemies alike, our resolve on this crucial issue.

I ask for its support tonight. I hope we could indicate our support unanimously.

I yield the floor.

Mr. LOTT. Mr. President, just briefly, this Senate Resolution 288 recognizes that the United States and its allies have vital interests in ensuring regional stability in the Persian Gulf. It recognizes that:

On August 31, 1996, Saddam Hussein, despite warnings from the United States, began an unprovoked, unjustified, and brutal attack on civilian population in and around Irbil in northern Iraq.

It recognizes:

the United States responded to Hussein's aggression on September 3, 1996 by destroying some of the Iraqi air defense installations and announcing the expansion of the southern no-fly zone.

Those are the whereas clauses in the resolution. And the resolved says:

The Senate commends the military actions taken by and the performance of the United States Armed Force under the direction of the Commander-in-Chief, for carrying out this military mission in a highly professional, efficient and effective manner.

There are those who would have liked for it to have said a lot more. There are those who were not comfortable saying anything at this time, who have some questions about the policy and what the future holds. But I do think it is appropriate that we have a bipartisan resolution on this subject matter, that we commend our men and women for the job they have done. They have done a wonderful job in the air and on the sea in this instance, as in all other instances. And whenever American forces are introduced, we do come together and partisanship stops at the shoreline, and that is the case here.

We have been working since Tuesday to craft a resolution that condemns what happened there in Iraq, under Saddam Hussein's actions, again, and to commend these troops.

There is no doubt in any Senator's mind that we have 100 percent support by the American people and by us in support of our men and women who have participated in this military action.

The United States has led the multinational coalition which defeated Hussein's aggression in 1991. When President Clinton came into office, he inherited a policy toward Iraq that included a weakened Saddam Hussein, a united international coalition, a solid international sanctions regime and a united Iraqi opposition.

There is concern now about the move toward lessening sanctions, although I had an opportunity to personally ask the President about the sanctions, and he assured me that the sanctions were not being lifted and that the Iraqi oil sales were not going to go forward under these conditions.

We are also concerned about our international coalition, what is going to be their role in the new no-fly zone in the southern part of Iraq.

So there is work to be done in this area, but I am sure both the Congress will be paying attention to that, as will the administration.

There is unanimous condemnation by the American people and by the Senate of the brutal attacks on the Kurdish areas in northern Iraq. That is as it should be. While it is a complicated situation, with interests by Turkey and interests by Iran and by different factions within the Kurds, it still is a situation that we cannot ignore. Any leader of a country, however that person obtained that position, that will exercise that kind of brutality in his own country or threaten military action against its neighbors or, in fact, invade a neighbor must be consistently watched and very serious and strong actions taken against them.

I want to also say I am concerned—and I discussed this with the Democratic leader—about the lack of prior consultation with the Congress about this action. The War Powers Act is very clear about the need for notification, consultation and also a report on what happened. It did not happen in this instance, and I don't believe it happened on either side of the aisle. That is unacceptable. Perhaps there were reasons for it, but I have expressed my concern to the administration, to the NSC, and I believe that we will have more consultation and notification in the future. We must not have the commitment of military power without even a word of consultation with the Congress. We have to continue to insist on that.

Our resolution is a modest step tonight. Many of our Members would like it to have been much more. I think it is fair. It has been worked out in a bipartisan way. I think it is time we stepped up to this issue, we have this resolution and we move on. So I appreciate the cooperation we did have.

Mr. President, I yield the floor.

Ms. MIKULSKI. Mr. President, I rise to support the resolution on Iraq. This resolution states the Senate stands with our troops, and our President, as they respond to Saddam Hussein's brutality.

The President was right to act to contain Saddam Hussein's aggression. Saddam Hussein's actions threaten American interests and peace in the Middle East—as well as the safety of his own people. He must be taught that his reckless acts have consequences. He must pay the price for his brutal and immoral actions.

The U.S. response is swift, specific and limited. The President responded swiftly and strategically after Iraq seized the city of Irbil in the Kurdish safe haven. Our objectives are clear and limited: to force Saddam Hussein to pay a price for his brutality and to make it safer for our pilots to patrol the no-fly zones in Iraq by destroying Iraqi air defense systems. To achieve these objectives, only specific military sites are targeted.

We have already paid a great price to contain Saddam Hussein in Operation Desert Storm. If we ignore Saddam Hussein's latest aggression, he will only be emboldened to take further reckless actions that threaten our national interests—and the lives of his own people.

Mr. President, my thoughts and gratitude are with our brave troops. They are once again called upon to stand sentry for those who would otherwise stand alone. The men and women of our Armed Forces have performed their mission with great skill and courage. I pray for their safe and swift return.

Mr. KERRY. Mr. President, last weekend Saddam Hussein sought to test the international community's tolerance and resolve yet again. Some 30,000 Iraqi soldiers, led by the elite Republican Guards, attacked and captured the Kurdish-controlled city of Irbil in northern Iraq. Saddam undertook this action despite warnings from the United States and other members of the international community and in defiance of our collective commitment, born out of the Persian Gulf war, to protect the Kurds.

None of us knows why Saddam decided to test us now. But if the history of the last six years has taught us anything, it is that Saddam Hussein does not understand diplomacy, he only understands power, and when he brandishes power in a manner that threatens our interests or violates internationally accepted standards of behavior, we must be prepared to respond—and with force, if necessary.

President Clinton's response to Saddam's latest challenge was the right one—decisive, measured, and carefully calculated to take the strategic advantage away from Saddam. By expanding the southern no-fly zone to the 33d parallel, we have denied him the ability to use two key military air bases and to control Iraqi airspace from the Kuwaiti border to the southern outskirts of Baghdad. This significantly reduces his capacity to launch offensive operations against Iraq's neighbors and the Persian Gulf oil fields. By attacking his air defense and command and control systems we have increased our capacity to patrol the no-fly zone and reduced the potential treat to our pilots and those of our British and French allies.

Saddam Hussein has tried to explain away this latest aggressive move by contending that his forces entered Irbil at the request of the Kurdistan Democratic Party [KDP], one of the two warring factions in northern Iraq. It is hard to understand why any Kurdish faction would willingly ally with Saddam, given the many years in which his forces have repressed, tortured and abused the human rights of the Kurdish people. However, if the KDP did request Iraqi intervention, that request does not justify the use of force against Kurdish civilians in Irbil. The international community has made it clear since April 1991, when the United Nations Security Council passed Resolution 688, that it would not tolerate the repression of the Kurds and other Iraqi civilians. That is why the United Nations established the no-fly zone in northern Iraq. The Iraqi attack on Irbil, and the continued threat posed by Iraqi forces positioned to attack again in support of the KDP, contravenes the letter and the spirit of this resolution.

For months the United States has led a diplomatic effort to try to mediate the conflict between two warring Kurdish factions, the Kurdistan Democratic Party led by Massoud Barzani and the Patriotic Union of Kurdistan [PUK] led by Jalal Talabani. There is no doubt that the PUK's flirtation with Iran earlier this year and the raw power politics played by these groups opened the door for Saddam Hussein. Hundreds of innocent Kurdish civilians have died, and others could die as long as Saddam has de facto control over Irbil and Iraqi forces remain poised to attack other PUK-controlled areas.

The United States has a moral interest in preventing the abuse of the Kurdish people, but our strategic interests go beyond this. We have strategic interests in denying Saddam the capability to take action against Kuwait and other states in the region or to threaten the world's oil supply. We also have a strategic interest in supporting the Iraqi opposition as a way to counter Iran's growing influence and limiting its ability to control a post-Saddam Iraq. That is why we did not—and should not—side with either of the Kurdish factions.

The U.S. military response was deliberately designed to accomplish two objectives: first, to make Saddam Hussein pay a steep price for his aggressive moves against Kurdish civilians in Irbil, and second, to weaken his capacity to undertake offensive action in the region. Time and again in the last six years, Saddam has tried to test the international community's commitment to peace and stability in the region. Each and every time he has met a forceful response.

Iraq's August 1990 attack on Kuwait resulted in defeat for Iraqi forces at the hands of a U.S.-led coalition. Suppression of the Kurdish revolt in northern Iraq at the end of the Persian Gulf war led to the establishment of the northern no-fly zone by the international community. Iraqi threats against United States and allied planes enforcing the no-fly zone in January 1993 led to missile strikes against Iraq's southern air defense systems. Six months later President Clinton ordered United States forces to strike at an Iraqi intelligence facility when he learned of an Iraqi plot to assassinate former President Bush. In October 1994, the United States and its allies sent forces to the region as Iraqi troops began to move south toward Kuwait. We did the same thing the following fall when Iraqi troops appeared to

The United States, under President Bush and then President Clinton, led these earlier efforts to contain Saddam. Whereas some of our allies in the region are constrained from acting on this occasion, we are not. Our interests, and the long-term interests of peace and stability in the region, dictate that we respond to this latest test of wills with Saddam.

The Iraqi attack on Irbil has had serious ramifications for the people of Iraq. It has resulted in the deaths of innocent civilians. It has set back the possibility of resolving differences and reaching a viable political settlement between the Kurdish factions. It has forced the United Nations Secretary General to suspend implementation of U.N. Security Council Resolution 986, which provides for the sale of some Iraqi oil to generate funds to buy food and medicine for the Iraqi people. Irbil is one of the key distribution centers for this humanitarian assistance. Needless to say that plan cannot go forward in the shadow of Iraqi forces.

President Clinton made it clear that we intend to judge Saddam Hussein by his actions, not his words. Saddam has said that Iraq will not respect the expanded no fly zone and yesterday, Iraqi radar locked on a United States plane enforcing the zone. What this means is unclear. Clearly the rational response on Saddam's part would be to refrain from any action that will escalate this crisis. I know that all of us hope that rationality will prevail.

Mr. WARNER. Mr. President, I join the majority leader today in expressing the Senate's support for the accomplishments by the men and women of the Armed Forces who planned and executed the recent air strikes against Saddam Hussein and the Iraqi military. At times of international crisis, it is essential that our troops in the field—those who are assuming high personal risks—know that they have the support of Congress and the American people. Having myself served in, and later with our military, as Secretary of Navy, I know the vital need for this support for our troops and their families.

Since Saddam Hussein's forces invaded Kuwait in August 1990, I have been a consistent supporter of U.S. military, using force if justified, to stop Iraqi aggression throughout that region. It is clearly in the national security interests, and the economic interests, of the United States—and indeed the international community—to ensure that the Government and military of Iraq do not threaten the stability of a region which contains an estimated 70 percent of the world's known oil reserves. That is why the United States, under the leadership of President Bush, was able to put together the most significant military coalition since World war II to force Iraqi invaders out of Kuwait, restore Kuwait sovereignty, impose severe restrictions and prohibitions on Saddam Hussein's military capability and aggressive behavior, and restore a measure of stability to this ever troubled region.

I was privileged to work with Senator Dole in drafting the legislation and managing the floor debate resulting in Senate approval of the resolution which authorized President Bush to employ U.S. Armed Forces—using force—in the Gulf War. It is hard to image today—when a consensus generally exists in this country for taking military action against Iraqi aggression—that in 1991, with 500,000 U.S. troops in the Gulf ready to use force that the Senate supported the authority for the President to use force by a mere 5 votes. Thankfully, after Desert Storm was launched, the Congress, the nation quickly rallied behind our troops. The missions, as set out in U.N. resolutions, were successfully accomplished.

Today, the crisis in Iraq is not simply about a tragic civil war between factions of the Kurds. It is about maintaining the regional security balance that our troops fought—and died—for in 1991. Almost 6 years after the gulf war, the international community is still fighting to secure Saddam's compliance with the agreements demanded from him and his government at the end of the war. Yet today, Saddam continues to defy U.N. weapons inspectors; refuses to account for Kuwaitis missing since the war; refuses to return Kuwaiti property seized during the Iraqi occupation; and continues to repress Iraqi citizens. Such actions must not be tolerated.

The United States has already made a substantial investment, in the Sacrifices, casualties of our troops and their families, to contain Saddam's aggression. During Desert Storm, almost 150 U.S. military personnel were killed, and over 460 were wounded. In addition, the American taxpayer invested heavily in the U.S. major military effort, and has continued to pay—an average of at least a half billion dollars a year since 1991—to contain Saddam Hussein.

That investment must be preserved, so a U.S. response to Saddam's latest transgression had to be made. The timeliness, the magnitude, and the process by which the Presidential decisions were made must be fully reviewed. But for now, a "well done" to the U.S. military.

I commend the majority leader, Senators Thurmond and McCain for their leadership on this resolution.

Mr. CRAIG. Mr. President, Saddam Hussein's movement into northern Iraq was yet another direct threat to U.S. national interest: to maintain security and stability in the Middle East. American cruise missiles have struck various Iraqi military installations with the purpose of deterring Iraq from further violence against the Kurds and to take out air-defense systems that posed a danger to our air patrols.

I support the President as our Commander in Chief and his decision to attack Saddam Hussein's military installations to provide greater protection for our personnel enforcing the current and expanded no-fly zone. I stand 100 percent behind the brave men and women in our Armed Forces. Therefore, I support the resolution we are voting on this evening which condemns Saddam Hussein's actions and expresses support for our troops and the President's efforts to curb further actions by Iraq. It is my understanding that after intelligence reports disclosed the Iraqi military buildup, clear warnings were sent that he should not use any military force—warnings that were not heeded.

Mr. President, Saddam Hussein's actions and our response didn't come out of the blue. They are an extension of ongoing efforts to enforce the restraints placed on Iraq at the end of the Gulf war. Therefore, while the use of force should always be a last resort tool of foreign policy, the reckless and aggressive pattern of actions Hussein has carried out, required the only warning he would respond to: force.

While we can understand these recent events, the future of this situation remains a concern for us all. U.S. interests in the region have not changed. In addition, the various conflicts among neighboring nations and the division within the Kurdish people, further complicates our ability to stabilize the situation. It is critical and in our national interest that the administration work with our allies, especially those in the region, to bring this incident to a peaceful conclusion.

Finally, while the cold war has come to an end, it is clear that we continue to live in an unstable world where our national security interests will be tested. We must continue to fully fund our Armed Forces so they remain strong. When we ask American men and women to put their lives on the line for our country, they better have the best equipment and training possible.

Mr. President, there is no doubt that we have strong national security interests in this very volatile and unstable region of the world. Any further hostility by Saddam Hussein's forces against our personnel, or in violation of Operation Provide Comfort or the other restraints established by the international community must be met with a swift and decisive response from the United States.

Mr. BIDEN. Mr. President, 2 days ago the President ordered a forceful response to Iraq's aggression against its own Kurdish minority.

The question before us is whether the Senate supports the action taken by our President.

Some have expressed concerns that go beyond the scope of that question. They have raised points that could be the matter of legitimate debate—but that debate should be reserved for another day. We are not debating the history of American diplomacy with respect to Iraq.

We are not debating the future of American security policy in the Persian Gulf. We are simply being asked to state whether or not we support the actions initiated by the Commander in Chief; Whether we support the troops fulfilling his orders; and, whether we condemn Saddam Hussein's aggressive actions.

These are weighty matters in and of themselves. We should not cloud the debate by injecting extraneous issues.

I intend to support the resolution before us because I believe that the forceful response ordered by the President was both necessary and appropriate. Saddam Hussein has demonstrated repeatedly that he only understands the language of force.

He was warned explicitly by the United States when evidence mounted of a threatening Iraqi military mobilization. He chose to ignore those warnings and enter an area that has been the site of past Iraqi transgressions. His actions violated universal human rights norms as well as U.N. Security Council Resolution 688, which demanded that he cease his oppression of the Kurds.

Had this aggression gone unanswered, it would have strengthened his position internally and emboldened him to strike elsewhere. Thankfully, it did not go unanswered.

President Clinton's decisive action sent a strong signal that the United States will not condone Iraqi military adventurism. It sent the message that there is a price to pay for aggression. It served to protect vital interests in the Persian Gulf by reassuring key allies of America's commitment to regional stability. And by extending the Southern no-fly-zone, the President has constrained Saddam Hussein's ability to make greater mischief.

Upholding these interests transcends the concerns that I and many of my colleagues have over becoming enmeshed in the internecine warfare between Kurdish factions. The saga of the Kurds is a long tale of struggle, betrayal, and oppression. It is one that is further complicated by a regional dynamic involving Iran, Iraq, Syria, and Turkey. The Kurdish question does not lend itself to an easy solution.

However, we should not allow the complexities of Kurdistan to cause us to lose sight of our broader objectives. The President's action is not about involving the United States in Kurdish intrigue. It is about containing a dangerous tyrant who is a continuing threat to international peace and security. It is about preserving stability in a region vital to American national security. In short, it is about protecting American interests.

I urge my colleagues to join me in standing with the President as he confronts a ruthless dictator.

178.

[September 5, 1996 (Senate), pp. 9955-56]

UNITED STATES RESPONSE TO IRAQI AGGRESSION

The Senate continued with the consideration of the resolution.

The PRESIDING OFFICER. The question before the Senate now is Senate Resolution 288, offered by the majority leader and minority leader regarding the United States response to Iraqi aggression. There are 2 minutes equally divided.

The minority leader is recognized.

Mr. DASCHLE. Mr. President, there are a number of Senators on both sides of the aisle who deserve our gratitude for the effort put forth in the last couple of days to bring us to this point. I will not name them now. I will name them later.

Let me simply read the resolving clause:

The Senate commends the military actions taken by and the performance of the United States Armed Forces, under the direction of the Commander in Chief, for carrying out this military mission in a highly professional, efficient and effective manner.

The PRESIDING OFFICER. The Senator from Arizona.

Mr. McCAIN. Mr. President, I thank the majority leader and the Democratic leader for framing a very difficult compromise which has, given the proximity to a Presidential election, a great deal of emotion associated with it.

I believe this resolution achieves the goal that we seek of expressing our appreciation and our gratitude for the outstanding men and women who serve in the military. It is obvious that those men and women serve under the Commander in Chief, and that is appropriate to be mentioned in this resolution.

Mr. President, I don't know how this whole situation is going to evolve, nor do we know exactly what has taken place. But I do know, as always, we can thank and be grateful and in our prayers be grateful that we have the finest men and women that this world has ever seen serving in our military who, again, responded to the call of the Commander in Chief in such an outstanding fashion.

Mr. President, I am pleased to join my colleagues in supporting this resolution. When the President, in his unique capacity as Commander in Chief, orders our Armed Forces into action, Congress has an obligation to both affirm our support for the men and women of the United States military who have been ordered to undertake the mission, and our respect for the President as the constitutional officer responsible for the conduct of our military and foreign policies. This is the purpose of the resolution before us, and it is wholly appropriate that the Senate adopt it without dissent.

Such an affirmation does not, however, signal Congress' intention to relinquish our responsibility to make critical judgments about the President's decision, the goals which his decision are intended to achieve, and the efficacy of his administration's policies to secure United States security interests in the Persian Gulf region. Political custom and the importance of assuring our servicemen and women of Congress' support, as well as the necessity of presenting a united front to America's adversaries oblige Members of Congress to refrain from criticizing the administration while military operations are underway. But, we are not expected to permanently defer our constitutional responsibility to either concur with or oppose the President's policy.

I have never shied away from criticizing administration policies in the Persian Gulf or elsewhere when I found them wanting. Neither have I refrained from offering my support to this administration when I believed such support was warranted. I am on record criticizing administration policies for Iraq and the region prior to the initiation of the recent military operation there. I stand by that criticism, but will refrain from elaborating it further until I am confident that the immediate military exigency has passed.

I will reserve judgment on the efficacy of these strikes, and the advisability of the President's subsequent policies in the region until the administration has provided Congress with sufficient information upon which to base an informed judgment.

Toward that end, Mr. President, let me suggest that the administration in briefings and testimony before Congress be prepared to answer certain obvious and basic questions about its purposes and policies in the region beyond simply providing bomb damage assessments and analyses of Iraqi responses to our missile strikes.

Speaking for myself, and, I suspect, many of my colleagues, the necessity of taking some military action against Iraq is apparent. Whether the action ordered by the President was the appropriate response to the threat posed by Saddam Hussein cannot be determined until we have a much fuller understanding of the administration's overall strategy for reducing instability and countering threats to our security interests in the region.

The administration should explain what precise purposes our cruise missile strikes were intended to serve. Were they intended to compel Iraq's complete withdrawal from the Kurdish city of Irbil in the north of Iraq and to cease all aggression against Kurds? Were they intended to persuade Saddam against contemplating renewed aggression against his neighbors to the south? Were they intended to foment opposition to Saddam within the Iraqi military? Was the limited dimension of this operation dictated by the opposition of our allies in the region or does it represent some other consideration which the administration has yet to disclose?

Should Saddam test American resolve further by continuing hostilities in the north, launching new operations against the Shiite minority in the south, flaunting the new no-fly restrictions, firing missiles at U.S. and allied warplanes, or again threatening the territorial integrity of U.S. allies in the region, is the administration prepared to take significantly greater military actions? Will they rebuild the coalition of Desert Storm allies that will almost certainly be necessary if we are obliged to increase our military response? Without the use of bases in Turkey and Saudi Arabia, our military options are obviously very severely limited.

Most important, Mr. President, what are the geopolitical circumstances which the administration wishes to obtain in the Persian Gulf region, and what is its overall, coherent strategy for achieving them which integrates our bilateral policies for all the countries of the region? Until these basic questions are answered, neither I nor any Member of Congress, nor the public we serve can judge not only the efficacy of these strikes, but the administration's ability to protect our most vital security interests in the region, interests for which this country has already paid a very high price to defend.

Mr. President, let me reiterate that none of these unanswered questions cause me nor should they cause any Member of Congress to withhold his or her support for our military personnel tasked with executing the President's decision. Nor should we begrudge the President our respect for his authority or our prayers for the success of his policy. This is the time to give voice to that support as I am confident we will do when we shortly vote on this resolution. The time for critical analysis also begins now. Our conclusions must await another day. That day, however, will not be too distant.

I urge my colleagues to support the resolution.

I ask for the yeas and nays.

The PRESIDING OFFICER. Is there a sufficient second?

There is a sufficient second.

The yeas and nays were ordered.

The PRESIDING OFFICER. The question is on agreeing to the resolution. The yeas and nays have been ordered. The clerk will call the roll.

The assistant legislative clerk called the roll.

Mr. NICKLES. I announce that the Senator from Oregon [Mr. Hatfield] and the Senator from Alaska [Mr. Murkowski] are necessarily absent.

I further announce that, if present and voting, the Senator from Oregon [Mr. Hatfield] would vote "nay."

Mr. FORD. I announce that the Senator from Hawaii [Mr. Inouye] is necessarily absent.

The PRESIDING OFFICER. Are there any other Senators in the Chamber desiring to vote?

The result was announced—yeas 96, nays 1, as follows: . . .

The resolution (S. Res. 288) was agreed to.

The preamble was agreed to.

The resolution with its preamble, reads as follows:

S. RES. 288

Whereas the United States and its allies have vital interests in ensuring regional stability in the Persian Gulf;

Whereas on August 31, 1996, Saddam Hussein, despite warnings from the United States, began an unprovoked, unjustified, and brutal attack on the civilian population in and around Irbil in northern Iraq, aligning himself with one Kurdish faction to assault another, thereby causing the deaths of hundreds of innocent civilians; and

Whereas the United States responded to Saddam Hussein's aggression on September 3, 1996 by destroying some of the Iraqi air defense installations and announcing the expansion of the southern no-fly zone over Iraq. Now, therefore, be it

Resolved by the United States Senate, That: The Senate commends the military actions taken by and the performance of the United States Armed Forces, under the direction of the Commander-in-Chief, for carrying out this military mission in a highly professional, efficient and effective manner.

Mr. BOND. I move to reconsider the vote.

Mr. ABRAHAM. I move to lay that motion on the table.

The motion to lay on the table was agreed to.

179.

[September 6, 1996 (Senate), p. 10016]

EXPLANATION OF VOTE—SENATE RESOLUTION 288

Mr. GORTON. Mr. President, last evening my vote was the only negative vote on the resolution relating to the President's military intervention earlier this week in Iraq. As there was little if any time last night to explain the reason for that vote, I intend to do it at this time.

It is the conventional wisdom, led perhaps by the President of the United States, that George Bush severely erred in not completing the war in the gulf against Iraq by the total defeat of its armed forces and the replacement of the Saddam Hussein government. Because I did not make such a criticism at the time, I do not join in that criticism now and regard it as essentially irrelevant to the activities of this week.

President Clinton, when he took that office, inherited the situation as it existed then, when that was no longer a real possibility. Since taking office, however, President Clinton's policies have caused the deterioration, if not the entire unraveling, of the coalition that was put together against Iraq at the time of the war in the gulf. Most particularly, his administration's indifference to the peculiar burdens imposed upon our ally, Turkey, and the particular problems and challenges that it faces, have caused us to be in a position in which we have been unable to use our bases in that country for any kind of response to Iraq. In fact, the coalition has unraveled to such an extent that we were not permitted to use the bases of any of our allies other than the United Kingdom in that response.

Earlier this summer we totally and completely ignored an incursion by Iranian forces, aimed to support its Kurdish partisans, into Iraq, across an international border. Earlier this summer we completely ignored Iraq's defiance of a U.N. search for prohibited weapons, both chemical and nuclear in nature.

Nevertheless, we did respond in a military fashion to a contest between Iraqi-backed Kurds and Iranian-backed Kurds earlier this week, and we responded, Mr. President, in a totally inappropriate fashion.

It seems to this Senator that at the time of the recent Iraqi incursion in support of its own faction in Kurdistan, we had essentially two choices: We could have made the choice that we have no dog in that fight, that there was no favorite in a contest between a group backed by Iran and a group backed by Iraq. On the other hand, we could have responded militarily by showing that aggression does not pay. Under those circumstances, however, the only appropriate military response would be one which would exact a price substantially greater than the hoped-for goals of the aggression itself on the part of Iraq.

We did neither. We responded to this fight among Kurdish partisans in a way that could not possibly help the victims of that Iraqi aggression. In fact, we clearly stated that we were not attempting to reverse what Saddam Hussein was doing in the northern part of his own country.

The net result is this: The net result is that Iraq has regained control over much of Iraqi Kurdistan. It has slaughtered its rebels, many of whom were under our implicit protection and have been abandoned by us. It has shown the United States to be a paper tiger. And what cost has it paid, Mr. President? A handful of radar sites.

We have been abandoned by all of our allies in the Middle East, none of whom was willing to publicly support our military response. We have been repudiated by France with respect to our new no-flight zone. Our President has now terminated the military adventure and has proclaimed victory.

Mr. President, a few more victories like this and we will be announcing a no-flight zone over Riyadh.

The best analogy I can think of is this one: It is as if the Mayor of the District of Columbia was warned of an incipient drug war in some part of this city and expressed severe warnings against any violence in connection with that drug war. Faced with great violence and a number of murders, the Mayor then imposed $100 fines on each one of the murderers and announced that the drug war was over and that the streets of Washington, DC, were safe. That, in effect, has been what our response was.

Mr. President, the United States has been defeated and humiliated. We have added to the instability of the Middle East and have whetted Saddam Hussein's appetite for further adventures.

No consultation, no advance notification was given to any Member of Congress in connection with this adventure. Under the circumstances, Mr. President, I do not believe that any resolution of support, even one so cautious, so reluctant, so absent in praise as the one passing last night was warranted.

I believe that within a short period of time, a majority of my colleagues will wish that they had voted the way in which I voted last night. It was an inappropriate resolution, an inappropriate response to an inappropriate action on the part of the President of the United States.

180.

[September 10, 1996 (Extensions), pp. 1549-50]

TURKEY: NEW GOVERNMENT, SAME OLD REPRESSION
HON. CHRISTOPHER H. SMITH
OF NEW JERSEY
IN THE HOUSE OF REPRESENTATIVES

Tuesday, September 10, 1996

Mr. SMITH of New Jersey. Mr. Speaker, in the last few weeks, the new Government of Turkey has demonstrated a familiar disregard for international human rights commitments and earlier promises made to secure entry into a European Union customs agreement. On August 26, 41 members of the Peoples Democracy Party [HADEP], including its leadership, were charged for alleged ties with the outlawed Kurdistan Workers Party [PKK]. The same day, two editors of the Turkish Daily News were charged with "damaging the prestige of the armed forces" by publishing an opinion poll. And, on September 3, Akin Birdal, president of the Human Rights Association of Turkey, was detained for participating on a delegation negotiating the release of Turkish soldiers captured by the PKK.

Mr. Speaker, the HADEP case follows an all too familiar pattern. The Turkish Government is stepping up efforts to delegitimize and dismantle HADEP, Turkey's only Kurdish-based political party. Supported by more than 1.2 million votes in last December's elections, HADEP was increasingly viewed as a possible interlocutor in the bloody conflict between government forces and Kurdish militants. Yet, like its director predecessor, the Democracy Party [DEP], whose 13 parliamentarians were imprisoned or exiled for speech crimes, HADEP has now become the government's target. In June, following a party convention at which a Turkish flag was torn down, 28 HADEP leaders were detained and have been held ever since, without being charged—despite their disavowal of any connection to the flag incident. Following the convention three HADEP members were murdered and party offices in Izmir were bombed. Two men accused of tearing down the flag have been charged with treason and could face the death penalty.

Mr. Speaker, nationalist hysteria over the flag incident also had negative consequences for a former DEP Member of Parliament, Sirri Sakik, who has been charged for saying, "People who desire that a certain respect be paid to their own flags should also be respectful of others' flags". Prosecutors deemed this statement to be advocating separatism and charged Sakik under article 8 of the Anti-Terror law. Mr. Speaker, you may recall that article 8 was amended with great fanfare last fall to mollify European concerns about Turkey's human rights record in advance of the vote on Turkey's customs union entry. Dozens of people have since been jailed under the new and improved article 8, and hundreds of others under similarly restrictive statutes.

Mr. Speaker, the Turkish Daily News case demonstrates how mainstream journalists also face continued repression. Ilnur Cevik, who participated in a Helsinki Commission briefing on Turkish elections, and Hayri Birler face up to 6 years in prison for publishing results of a poll on preferences for government alternatives following last year's elections. The polls were published in February and some speculate that the belated decision to prosecute was based on growing displeasure in military circles with Cevik's perceived support of Refah, the Muslim-based party.

Mr. Speaker, another troubling case involves Human Rights Association [HRA] President Akin Birdal, who participated in a 1995 Helsinki Commission briefing. A valuable source of information on human rights abuses in Turkey, the Association and its president, Akin Birdal, have received numerous awards in the United States and Europe. Since its inception, HRA activists have faced severe repression. Fifteen branches have been closed in southeast Turkey, activists and leaders have been murdered by government-supported death squads, and hundreds of HRA members have been arrested and imprisoned.

The absurd justification for the latest detention, however, made the authorities look even more capricious than usual.

Akin Birdal participated in a delegation seeking the release of Turkish soldiers captured by the PKK. The delegation, led by a Member of Parliament from the ruling Refah Party and including other well-known human rights activists, was discussed in the press and government circles for weeks. Although unsuccessful, the delegation's mission fueled speculation that the government might be reconsidering its purely military approach to the Kurdish insurgency. Such speculation caused sufficient consternation in ruling circles to order detention of delegation members. Although the government released the delegation members on September 6, it remains unclear whether they will be charged under Penal Code Article 169 for aiding an illegal organization, for which they could face up to 5 years in prison.

These recent incidents, Mr. Speaker, punctuate the routine repression occurring daily in Turkey. None accused in these incidents committed acts of violence, but are being silenced rather for speaking against government-sponsored violence and policies that have prolonged a bloody internal war. And, if the pattern of past convictions of former parliamentarians and others repeats itself, the only evidence that will emerge to suggest support for terrorism will be clumsy fabrications and testimony coerced under torture.

Our important ally Turkey, Mr. Speaker, is facing a serious multidimensional crisis. If we are to help Turkey address this crisis, we must be firm in our support for a political solution to the conflict which has claimed more than 21,000 lives and created more than three million internal refugees. Recent events in northern Iraq have underscored regional instability complicated in no small part by Kurdish unrest in Turkey. Clearly, Turkey's leaders will pay little more than lip service to human rights commitments when it become necessary to secure cooperation with Western governments. They will continue such policies as long as Western governments remain willing to overlook abuses in order to advance security or economic objectives. Turkey's allies should undertake every effort to support the victims of this peculiar form of democracy. Mr. Speaker, I urge my colleagues to speak out against recurring restrictions imposed on free speech in Turkey and call upon the Turkish Government, once again, to release all those imprisoned for nonviolent expression, including the HADEP members and former DEP parliamentarians.

181.

[September 11, 1996 (Senate), p. 10279]

UNITED STATES MILITARY ACTION AGAINST IRAQ

Mr. McCAIN. Mr. President, this morning we learned that Iraq fired a surface-to-air missile at American F-16's patrolling the no-fly zone over what has now become an imaginary Kurdish safe haven in northern Iraq. This latest challenge to the safety of American pilots and to the credibility of American security guarantees in the Persian Gulf region comes on the heels of Saddam Hussein's rejection of United States warnings not to repair his air defense systems damaged by our cruise missile strikes in southern Iraq.

The necessity of further United States military action against Iraq is now obvious. And by his actions, Saddam Hussein has made the strongest argument for a disproportionate U.S. response of considerably greater military significance than our military action last week.

Furthermore, Saddam's aggressive challenges to the United States, and his success in reasserting his control in northern Iraq as his troops and the troops of his new Kurdish allies, the KDP, completed their conquest of the region on Monday, reveal the critical importance of curbing the Clinton administration's tendencies to rhetorical inconsistency in defining its objectives, disingenuous explanations of its policy choices, and exaggerated claims of success.

Our strikes last week were in response to Iraq's conquest, in alliance with the KDP, of the Kurdish city of Irbil. But by striking targets in the south, the administration chose not a disproportionate response to Iraqi aggression, but a minimal response that was disconnected from the offense it was ostensibly intended to punish. As one administration official put it: "We know that we did the right thing in terms of stopping Saddam Hussein in whatever thoughts he might about moving south and in letting him know that when he abuses his people or threatens the region, that we will be there . . . We really whacked him."

Evident in that statement [is] the three harmful administration tendencies cited above. Our stated purpose to stop Saddam's abuse of his people was quickly overridden by, in the words of another administration official, the judgment that "we should not be involved in the civil war in the north." And while administration officials at first suggested that our strikes in southern Iraq would affect Iraq's action in the north, they now emphasize that the strikes were intended only to serve our strategic interest in restricting Saddam's ability to threaten his neighbors from the south.

It is clear now that the erosion of coalition unity, evident in Turkey and Saudi Arabia's refusal to allow United States warplanes to undertake offensive operations from bases in those countries, had a far more important influence on our choice of targets and the level of force used than administration officials have admitted.

Most importantly, the President's claims that our strikes were successful in achieving their objectives are belied by the events of this week. By what measurement can we assert that Saddam has been persuaded to treat his people humanely; that he has been compelled to abide by U.N. resolutions and the terms of the cease-fire agreement; that the containment of Iraq has been further advanced; and that the United States and our allies are strategically better off since we fired 44 cruise missiles at Iraqi air defense systems in the south?

Since those strikes, Saddam's Kurdish allies have achieved a complete victory in the north, and Saddam has regained control of an area from which he has been excluded for several years. Kurdish refugees are again flooding across the border. Saddam, in utter contempt for U.S. warnings, has begun repairing the

radar sites we struck last week. He, at least temporarily, split the Desert Storm coalition. And in violation of the cease-fire agreement and U.N. Security Council resolutions, he has fired missiles at U.S. planes patrolling an internationally established no-fly zone. As successes go, this one leaves much to be desired.

Clearly, Iraq's attempted downing of American planes requires a military response from us. I have little doubt that the President will order a response. Given that Iraq's action represents a challenge not just to the United States, but to the international coalition responsible for enforcing the no-fly zone, I would expect that we will have greater cooperation from our allies than we experienced last week. Thus our ability to take the disproportionate, truly punishing action which is clearly called for under the circumstances should not be limited by the consequences of our failure to maintain coalition unity.

Decisions about the dimensions of our response are, of course, the President's to make. I pray that he will choose wisely.

The PRESIDING OFFICER. The Senator from Nebraska is recognized for 5 minutes.

182.

[September 13, 1996 (Senate), pp. 10538-39]

THE RESOLUTION OF SUPPORT FOR MILITARY OPERATIONS IN IRAQ

Mr. GORTON. Mr. President, a week ago, I was the only Member of this body to vote against a mild resolution of support for our military operations in Iraq last week. I did so, Mr. President, because it seemed to me that our response fell between two more appropriate responses and, as a consequence, was totally ineffective and inappropriate.

Mr. President, I felt last week—and I continue to feel the same way today—that we could have determined that in a civil conflict between two groups of fighting Kurds, one backed by Iraq and the other by Iran, that we had no interest, simply that we had no dog in that fight.

On the other hand, by reason of the protection that we have provided for Kurds, however uncivil in their conduct to one another, we could also have responded militarily. Almost without exception, however, Mr. President, thoughtful academics, military scholars, and national security experts have felt that the United States should not use its Armed Forces in combat in response to a challenge from another nation without doing so disproportionately.

What does that mean, Mr. President? It means that we should make absolutely certain when we use our Armed Forces that the cost exacted of an aggressor, of an enemy, is considerably greater, measurably greater, than the gains sought by that aggressor. If we don't use it with that philosophy, we almost certainly will be disappointed in the results of the use of our armed services and, of course, with respect to our national prestige.

I was convinced, Mr. President, that what we did last week was 5 cents worth of damage in response to a dollar's worth of gain on the part of Saddam Hussein and his Iraqi forces.

We launched 44 cruise missiles against Iraq last week in response to military adventures on the part of Iraq in a northern protected zone in Kurdistan. The act, as I have said, came in the midst of a civil war between two Kurdish factions, one backed by Iran and one by Iraq. We responded not only inadequately, but we responded in the south part of Iraq, while the fighting and the brutality was occurring in the north. The result, according to the administration, was a U.S. victory. As one administration official described it, "We really whacked him." Now, a little more than a week later, the reality is considerably different.

Saddam Hussein has regained control over the northern part of his country. After many years of oppression of its people, whom he has bitterly oppressed, thousands of whom he has killed, he is continuing to fire at U.S. warplanes in the south. The administration is in the midst of a review of its policy. Under most circumstances, Mr. President, when you are victorious, when you really whack them, it is the other guy who changes what he is doing—not us.

But this is precisely the flaw in the administration's policy; rather than respond to Iraq's military adventure in a manner that ensures that any such adventure costs far more than it is worth, we offered Band Aid solutions. The result has been less than glowing. Almost certainly at this point a reaction which will cost Iraq more than it has gained will require a greater investment and a greater risk than the investment and the risk which we engaged in a week ago.

Let us reflect for just a moment on what last week's military response achieved. Is Saddam Hussein treating his people better? Has he been compelled to abide by a U.N. cease-fire? Has Iraq been contained? Is the United States better off now than it was before the military action? Do we have solid support from the allies and the anti-Iraq coalition? The answer to each one of these questions is clearly no.

The coalition, masterfully constructed during the gulf war by President Bush, is frayed, if not defunct. Saddam Hussein is brazenly flaunting both U.S. and U.N. warnings and is scurrying to rebuild the very sites we destroyed last week and told him not to rebuild. In the last 2 or 3 days he has fired missiles at the aircraft patrolling the no-fly zone.

My friend, the Senator from Arizona, Senator McCain, said night before last that "decisions about the dimensions of our response are, of course, the President's to make."

Yet, the confusion continues. The day before yesterday the Secretary of Defense said that our response would be "disproportionate." Yesterday the Department of Defense says that the response will be "measured." Perhaps today we will have action that is "disproportionately measured."

In any event, Mr. President, it seems to me that it is vitally important, first, that the President consult with our allies in the Mideast in the coalition—something that he did not do earlier—second, that he follow the War Powers Act and consult with the Congress. Whether he believes the War Powers Act to be constitutional or not, he would be extremely wise to consult with the representatives of the people of the United States before such an action rather than simply to ask for ratification after that action.

We are worse off than we were a week ago, Mr. President. We face very serious dilemmas. We are almost without bases from which to mount any military attack. The President is simply going to have to pay much more attention to the issue than he has in the past and build a much broader coalition if we are not to lose everything that we gained at such high cost during the gulf war.

183.

[September 13, 1996 (Senate), p. 10552]

THE SITUATION IN IRAQ

Mr. CRAIG. Mr. President, I have been glued to the television today in order to keep myself updated on the situation in Iraq. Needless to say, I am more than a little frustrated that no attempts have been made by the President to consult the Congress on this swiftly evolving situation. I do not say this lightly, Mr. President, but CNN reporting is not what I would consider fulfillment of the President's reporting obligation in the War Powers Act.

The War Powers Act states that the "President in every possible instance shall consult with Congress before" introducing troops into imminent hostilities and shall also consult with Congress regularly after the introduction of combat troops. Mr. President, that also applies when situations develop into hostilities. This obligation was easily overlooked for the incident on August 31. The Congress was adjourned on recess, making it difficult, if not impossible to brief Members prior to taking action. The Congress stood with the President in an effort to fully support our troops and his decision as Commander in Chief. However, the current situation is quite different. The Congress is here, and we are waiting. Let me be clear, Mr. President, support for our troops is steadfast. But the President cannot assume the continued support of Congress if he fails to keep us informed.

Mr. President, the President acted to counter Saddam Hussein's aggression against

the Kurds, and quickly declared victory. The President's policy to-date is not a victory. In less than a week's time, the premature declaration has soured into a situation that has our pilots being shot at in the Northern No-Fly Zone, Hussein gaining a strong foothold in the former Kurdish safe-haven, and a movement of American personnel and equipment into the Persian Gulf. If a strong and clear policy is not defined soon, the President's policy in the gulf will most assuredly become an abject failure. It's time to come to the Congress and the American people with a defined mission, goals and exit strategy. It is time for the President to fulfill his obligations under the War Powers Act.

In my speech on the situation in Iraq, just a week ago today, I expressed concerns about the President's failure to maintain the alliance with our gulf war partners. Without the coalition, we risk losing the necessary strategic advantage we how hold, and our defensive presence in the gulf will necessarily deteriorate. Saddam Hussein is testing our resolve in the Persian Gulf by his efforts to play divide and conquer with the United States and our coalition partners from the gulf war. Without a clearly defined missioned and policy, we will continue to be pulled into a situation that will isolate us in the region and leave few, if any, positive options to resolve the situation.

Saddam Hussein is not an individual to be toyed with. He understands little other than aggression, and we should be wary that for him, embarrassing the United States at any cost may be considered a victory. This is very important, Mr. President, because that cost could include American lives.

Mr. President, the reporting on CNN provides good and timely information, but it does not provide insight, direction, or a clear message about the policy you intend to pursue. Therefore, it is my hope and my purpose to encourage the President to fulfill his obligation to the Congress under the War Powers Act for the American people and for our troops.

184.

[September 17, 1996 (Senate), pp. 10624-25]

USE OF FORCE AGAINST IRAQ

Mr. SPECTER. Mr. President, I have come to the floor immediately after attending a meeting with President Clinton, the Secretary of State, the Secretary of Defense, the Chairman of the Joint Chiefs of Staff, and Members of both Houses from both parties on the subject of Iraq. I would like to comment about an issue which I raised specifically with the President, and that is my urging him to submit to the Congress of the United States the issue as to whether there should be force used against Iraq in the gulf.

In time of crisis there is no question, under our Constitution, that the President as Commander in Chief has the authority to take emergency action. Similarly, it is plain that the Congress of the United States has the sole authority to declare a war, and that involves the use of force, as in the gulf operation in 1991, which was really a war, where the President came to the Congress of the United States in January 1991, and on this floor this body debated that issue and, by a relatively narrow vote of 52 to 47, authorized the use of force. It is my strong view that the issue of the use of force in Iraq today ought to be decided by the Congress of the United States and not unilaterally by the President where there is no pending emergency and when there is time for due deliberation in accordance with our constitutional procedures.

I note when the first missile attacks were launched 2 weeks ago today, on September 3, the President did not consult in advance with the Congress, which I believe was necessary under the War Powers Act. That is water over the dam. At the meeting this morning there were comments from Members of Congress about the need for more consultation. I believe the session this morning was the first time that there had been a group of Members of the House and Senate assembled to be briefed by the administration, by the President, and by the Secretary of State and Secretary of Defense.

We know from the bitter experience of the Vietnam war that the United States cannot engage in military action of a protracted nature without public support, and the first place to seek the public support is in the Congress of the United States in our representative capacity. It is more than something which is desirable; it is something which is mandated by the constitutional provision that grants exclusive authority to the Congress of the United States to declare war. We have seen a transition as to what constitutes a war—in Korea, where there was no declaration of war by the Congress, in Vietnam, where there was no declaration of war by the Congress. And we have seen the adoption of the War Powers Act as an effort to strike a balance between congressional authority to declare war and the President's authority as Commander in Chief; and, as provided under the War Powers Act, where there are imminent hostilities, the President is required to consult in advance with the Congress and to make prompt reports to the Congress, although the President does have the authority to act in case of emergency.

My legal judgment is that the President does have authority as Commander in Chief to act in an emergency, even in the absence of the War Powers Act. But when there is time for action by the Congress of the United States, then that action ought to be taken by the Congress on the use of force, which is tantamount to war, which we saw in the gulf in 1991 where the Congress did act. And we may see—we all hope we do not see it—but we may see that in Iraq at the present time.

The Congress is soon to go out of session in advance of the November elections. While we are here, this issue ought to be considered by the Congress of the United States as to whether we are going to have the use of force.

In the meeting this morning, attended by many Members of the House and Senate, both Democrats and Republicans, there was considerable question raised on both sides of the aisle as to what our policy is at the present time, whether we have a coherent policy as to what we are going to do there, not only how we get in but how we get out, and what our policy ought to be.

Those policy issues are really matters which ought to be debated by the Congress of the United States and acted upon by the Congress of the United States.

We know there is a considerable problem that we face today on getting support from our allies, and that is an indispensable prerequisite, it seems to me, for action by the United States military forces. We have seen the deployment of air power all the way from Guam for missile strikes, and yet we wonder why we are not using air power from Saudi Arabia or from Turkey, and the question is raised as to whether the Saudis or the people in command of Turkey are willing to allow us to use their bases for these air strikes.

When it comes to the issue of containment, representations were made by key administration officials that there is a full and total support by the Saudis for our efforts to contain Saddam Hussein, but that when it comes to the issue of air strikes, the same cannot be said; there is less than a full measure of support from the Saudis. So that when we deal with the issue of how much force the United States of America ought to use in the gulf against Saddam Hussein, those are the issues which ought to be considered by Congress, and we ought to have a statement of particularity as to just how much support we are going to get from our allies.

We know the French, illustratively, will refuse to supply in the expanded zone to the 33d parallel. There have been reports from Kuwait that the Kuwait Government is not prepared, not really willing to have us expand our military forces there. There is some dispute about that, with representations being made by the administration that the media reports have been overblown and that there is really cooperation from Kuwait and from Bahrain and from others. But on the face of what is at least the public record, there is a serious question as to whether we do have real support among our allies. That is something which has to be considered in some detail.

In our meeting this morning, reservations were expressed by Members on both sides of the aisle, and there was a question as to what we ought to be doing with Saudi Arabia in

terms of long-range policy and long-range planning. When we moved into the gulf war in 1991, it was an emergency situation, but the plan was supposed to enable the Saudis to have time to defend themselves and to take action in their own defense, and that has not happened. Every time Saddam Hussein moves, there is significant expenditure of U.S. resources and U.S. money.

In the middle of the discussion, we had the point raised about whether the defense budget is adequate and a very blunt reference to the Chief of Staff, Mr. Panetta, as to agreeing to the figures which have come from the appropriators, and that also was obviously a matter of fundamental importance by the Congress because we are the appropriators and we have had the administration take the position that the administration does not like what the Congress is doing by way of appropriations. But the administration is coming in with a very expensive operation, and it may be justified, it may be warranted, it may be necessary, but that is a matter for the Congress to decide as to what our policy should be and how much money we are prepared to spend.

In the meeting today, the question was raised rather bluntly about the credibility of the administration in expanding the no-fly zone to the south when the actions come against the Kurds in the north, and there seems to be a consensus that the action taken thus far by the administration has not weakened Saddam Hussein but has strengthened Saddam Hussein and that he did, in fact, receive cover when certain Kurdish leaders invited him in; and there is a distinction to be made about what the United States will do for a vital U.S. interest contrasted with what we might do for humanitarian purposes, and that while U.S. military personnel may be placed in harm's way where we have an issue of a vital national interest, there may be a difference of opinion if we are dealing with a humanitarian consideration.

Mr. President, all of this boils down to the judgment, my judgment, that the American people today are not informed about what the administration is seeking to do in the gulf and what the administration is seeking to do against Saddam Hussein, and the Congress has not been consulted in advance of the initial missile strikes and has been, in my view, inadequately informed as we have proceeded. When you deal with the use of force, which is tantamount to war, that is a matter to be decided by the Congress of the United States, leaving to the President his constitutional authority as Commander in Chief to act in cases of emergency. But at this time we do not have an emergency. We have time for deliberation in the Congress, for debate in this Chamber and the floor of the House of Representatives to decide what our policy should be, what we are prepared to spend, and how we ought to proceed. That is why in the meeting I asked the President to submit to the Congress his request for an authorization for the use of force so that matter could be decided by the Congress in accordance with constitutional provisions.

Mr. President, I noted that I made that request to the President, and I commented about a letter which I had sent to the President yesterday on that subject. I ask unanimous consent that the text of that letter be printed in the Record.

There being no objection, the letter was ordered to be printed in the RECORD, as follows:

U.S. SENATE,
SELECT COMMITTEE ON INTELLIGENCE,
Washington, DC, September 16, 1996.
HON. WILLIAM JEFFERSON CLINTON,
President of the United States, The White House,
Washington, DC.

Dear Mr. President: I am writing to you to express my growing concerns over the escalation of U.S. military activity in and around the Persian Gulf and to urge you to promptly seek a resolution from Congress authorizing the use of force in the Gulf. There is no emergency which would require escalation of the use of force by you in your role as Commander-in-Chief. The constitutional role of Congress as the sole authority to declare war should be respected, as it was in 1991, with the Congress

determining national policy on our objectives, the conditions of allied burden sharing, an exit strategy and an overall policy which is lacking at the present time. A further statement of my reasons follows.

First, let me repeat my publicly stated support for the policy of containment of Saddam Hussein's regime and for the practice of United States military involvement in the enforcement of the United Nations' ordered no-fly zone in southern Iraq. No less than in 1991, when I voted to support the use of force in the Gulf War, the United States has vital interests in this region which must be protected.

Second, I strongly support the bravery and professionalism of our military men and women who are carrying out your orders at substantial risk to their lives.

All this having been said, I believe your current course of gradual escalation against Iraq, starting with the missile attacks on September 4, (for which you sought no prior authorization from Congress) constitutes the involvement of our armed forces in the sorts of hostile and potentially hostile situations so as to trigger the limit of your authority as commander-in-chief established by the War Powers Act.

Moreover, this present course of escalation—especially the reported possible dispatch of 3-5,000 ground troops to Kuwait—could well lead to a renewal of full scale war between the United States and Iraq. For example, if, heaven forbid, our Army units were to sustain losses from any form of Iraqi attack, this country would be duty-bound to respond with massive force.

I know you understand, particularly in view of this country's bitter experiences with undeclared wars in Korea and Vietnam, the paramount importance of the constitutional principle that only Congress can declare war. It is an unavoidable concomitant of this principle that the President cannot have unilateral authority to set up a trip-wire which, if breached, would surely commit this nation to war. Your present posture toward Iraq, however, may be creating just such a trip-wire.

Beyond the always vital matter of honoring basic constitutional principle, I urge you to promptly seek Congressional authority for the use of force against Iraq because, just as in 1991, this democratic exercise is by far the best way to clarify both the legitimate means and the legitimate ends which underlie our national policy towards Saddam Hussein.

A congressional debate now will focus you and the Congress, and ultimately the American people, on what our policy should be at this time in the Persian Gulf. It will define national understanding and hopefully shape a national consensus on the key questions which must be answered as the potential for deeper conflict grows—questions such as the proper burden sharing we must demand from our allies in the region and around the world and, most importantly, about an exit strategy to ensure a way back home, in reasonable time and at reasonable cost, for the troops we so rapidly send today into harm's way.

Thank you for your consideration.
Sincerely,
Arlen Specter.

185.

[September 24, 1996 (Extensions of Remarks), p. 1676]

EUROPEAN RIGHTS COURT RULES AGAINST TURKEY IN VILLAGE BURNING
HON. CHRISTOPHER H. SMITH
OF NEW JERSEY
IN THE HOUSE OF REPRESENTATIVES

Tuesday, September 24, 1996

Mr. SMITH of New Jersey. Mr. Speaker, on September 16, the European Court of Human Rights for the first time rules that the Government of Turkey must compensate Kurdish villagers whose houses had been destroyed by security forces. The Court found that the burning of homes violated European Human Rights Conventions. The Court also found that the Turkish Government had inter-fered with the applicants' right to appeal to the European Commission on Human Rights.

Mr. Speaker, presently, more than 150 cases involving more than 400 individuals have been submitted to the European Commission. These cases relate to the destruction of Kurdish villages, extra-judicial executions, disappearances, rape, and torture. Already, 56 such cases have been deemed admissible by the European Commission, and a handful have proceeded to the European Court.

Mr. Speaker, the sheer volume of cases brought against Turkey and declared admissible, as well as the circumstances surrounding each, leave little doubt that the Government of Turkey is not only conducting a violent campaign against its own citizens, but also trying to cover up its abuses with intimidation and propaganda. Earlier this year, Human Rights Watch/Helsinki released a report which documented efforts by Turkish authorities to prevent individuals from pursuing cases at the European Commission and Court. The report referenced numerous incidents in which applicants, as well as their family members and lawyers, had faced harassment, torture and murder in attempts to prevent them from pursuing their cases.

Mr. Speaker, Turkish officials often recognize the European Court's jurisdiction and the right of Turkish citizens to appeal to the Court as proof of a commitment to human rights. Yet following this first ruling against Turkey, officials have called the ruling wrong and criticized the Court as being politically biased. Following a familiar pattern in which public proclamations bear little resemblance to actuality, other international human rights commitments are similarly dismissed when implementation would bring attention to serious abuses. Last July, at the Organization for Security and Cooperation in Europe [OSCE] Parliamentary Assembly meeting in Stockholm, members of the Turkish delegation agreed to invite an assembly delegation to Turkey. One week later, Turkey's Ambassador to the OSCE in Vienna stated that his government would not cooperate in issuing such an invitation. Not only has Turkey reneged on the OSCE invitation, efforts by the International Committee of the Red Cross [ICRC] to discuss questions of access to conflict areas have also been rebuffed.

Mr. Speaker, the ruling by the European Court will surely be the first of many. The longer Turkish rulers refuse to acknowledge the true reality of the Kurdish situation the more all citizens will pay in precious blood and resources. Turkish economic and political development has been stunted by the crisis in southeast Turkey and its human dimension; 21,000 lives have been lost, 3,000 villages have been destroyed and approximately 3 million people forced from their homes in Kurdish regions by Turkish troops. And, despite what officials and their mouthpieces in the media claim, restrictions on free speech and the media persist. The U.S. Government should use every opportunity to press for real reform. If we want to fully develop a deep and lasting relationship with NATO ally Turkey, our policymakers must not continue to downplay human rights problems to advance economic and strategic interests.

186.

[May 1, 1997 (House), pp. 2152-53]

SELF-DETERMINATION FOR THE KURDS

The SPEAKER pro tempore. Under the Speaker's announced policy of January 7, 1997, the gentleman from California [Mr. Filner] is recognized for 60 minutes as the designee of the minority leader.

Mr. FILNER. Mr. Speaker, I want to focus my colleagues' attention this evening on the plight of the Kurds, an ancient people living in the Middle East in a land that should be a nation called Kurdistan, a proud people numbering some 30 million, perhaps the largest people in the world today lacking in the exercise of their right to self-determination.

The Kurds have resided in their present homelands for thousands of years. Kurdish Guti kings ruled Persia and Mesopotamia over 4,000 years ago. Before that, the Neolithic revolution probably first took place in Kurdi-

stan, around 7000 B.C., 3,500 years before similar developments in Europe.

Some of the earliest towns and villages, as well as other human settlements, have been discovered in Kurdistan. Yet, one of the largest nations in the Middle East is prevented from exercising sovereignty over any part of its own land. It is an international colony, governed over by the states of Turkey, Iraq, Iran, and Syria.

The Kurdish people suffer from ghastly atrocities committed by all four regimes. Over one half of Kurdistan and nearly two-thirds of the Kurdish population are under Turkish control, an occupation legitimized in the 1923 Treaty of Lausanne, which reneged on a promise to Kurds and Armenians in the earlier 1920 Treaty of Sevres. That promise envisioned the creation of a Kurdish state on Kurdish territory in the aftermath of World War I. The Lausanne Treaty legitimized the Turkish massacres against the Armenians which had already taken place and set the stage for a stepped-up campaign of genocide against the Kurds in subsequent years.

Turkish states have been responsible for a long string of ethnic cleansings ever since. Historian James Tashjian has estimated that over 2\1/2\ million people perished in a 100-year period between 1822 and 1922.

□ 1800

Among them were Greeks, Nestorians, Maronites, Syrians, Bulgarians, Yezidis, Jacobites, and Armenians. He acknowledged that these figures did not include over 500,000 Kurds murdered, deported, or displaced in the same period.

Between 1925 and 1938, an additional 1 million Kurds were reported slaughtered. Almost the entire Armenian population under Turkish control had previously been exterminated, over 1\1/2\ million people.

Today, Turkish Special Komandos actually collect rewards for the severed heads of Kurdish guerrillas and others, casually referring to their victims as Armenians, leaving no doubt as to what is in store for the Kurds and their national aspirations.

"Special action teams," as they are called, color their faces green and white. The paint, as well as 80 percent of Turkey's military hardware and equipment, is furnished by the United States, much of it at the taxpayer's expense.

Today, seven Kurdish members of parliament are in prison in Turkey. Most prominent among them is Leyla Zana, the recipient of the Sakharov Freedom Award. Andrei Sakharov came to the defense of the Kurds in 1989, when he declared, and I quote, "The tragic struggle of the Kurdish people, which has continued for so long, originates in the principle of the right of peoples to self-determination, and for this reason, it is a just struggle."

Human Rights Watch, Helsinki Watch, Amnesty International and a variety of other human rights groups have devoted much attention to Turkish depredations against the Kurds in recent years. They note that over 20,000 people have been killed since 1984, over 3,000 villages destroyed with rampant torture, murder, displacement and imprisonment directed at the Kurdish population.

The repression by the Saddam Hussein regime in Iraq has been more widely publicized. Over 200,000 Kurds were killed in the wake of the Iran-Iraq war, and over 4,000 Kurdish villages have been destroyed over the past three decades by Iraqi forces. Three tons of documents and other materials related to the post-Iran-Iraq war "Anfal" campaign are stored away by the U.S. Government. I call upon the State Department to release them for general inspection by interested parties. I believe they would confirm the crimes against humanity carried out by the Iraqi regime in Kurdistan.

It is imperative that we affirm a human rights linkage with any foreign aid given by the United States and to oppose the furnishing of lethal equipment to those who would use it for repressive purposes. Never again should United States-made chemical weapons be used against the Kurds or against anybody else, as they were at the ancient Kurdish city of Halabia, where over 5,000 Kurdish civilians, mostly women and children, were gassed to death in March 1988.

It is time, Mr. Speaker, to reverse our longstanding policy and recognize the existence of Kurdistan and the rights of its citizens to exercise the prerogatives and liberties which every people without exception should and must enjoy.

We should use our influence to help resolve the Kurds' internal conflict and support their unity in the effort to achieve their inalienable right to self-determination. We must stop looking at whole nations in terms of the profitability of oil companies and as assets to be deployed in big power maneuvering. We must ban the export of chemical weapons. Both Iraq and Turkey have used lethal weapons against the Kurds which were furnished by the United States. Cluster bombs are continuing to be sold to Turkey and continuing to be used in bombing runs against Kurdish villages and areas.

Iran also continues to oppress the Kurds in its territory. The Shah's father, a Fascist sympathizer who was removed from his throne by the Allies in 1941, oversaw what was called the "sedentarization" policies which resulted in the disappearance of many Kurdish and other tribes. Khomeini's regime went after the Kurds almost immediately upon assuming power over Iran in 1979. Leaders of the major Kurdish party resisting Iranian domination have been repeatedly assassinated by agents of the government, often in European settings.

The Kurdish plight at the hands of Iran has received surprisingly little notice in America, givenour oft-stated concerns over the human rights violations of that regime.

We must stop viewing freedom for the Kurds as being some kind of threat to stability and instead welcome such freedom.

As was stated by Michael van Walt van Praag, an adviser to the Dalai Lama of Tibet, and again I quote, "The potential for explosive disintegration lurks in all states where the people are prohibited from exercising their right to self-determination. We must move away from our misguided view of stability premised on immediate short-term economic and political considerations to a long-term perspective which will ensure the peaceful coexistence of all peoples. Universal recognition is the cornerstone and, indeed, the sine qua non of a truly peaceful and stable world."

According to Justice William O. Douglas, who visited the Kurds nearly 50 years ago, "The Kurds have a saying: The world is a rose; smell it and pass it to your friends."

The source of such resources as water, oil, gas and agricultural wealth, Kurdistan has much to share with neighboring peoples in the world, once the pall of oppression has been lifted and they can manage their own affairs and control their own resources and their own destiny.

President John F. Kennedy was right when he said that "There can be no doubt that if all nations refrain from interfering in the self-determination of others, the peace would be much more assured."

And Dwight D. Eisenhower underscored the point when he declared that "Any nation's right to a form of government and an economic system of its own choosing is inalienable. Any nation's attempt to dictate to other nations their form of government is indefensible."

We must apply these principles to our dealings with the Kurds and their aspirations. United States military aid to Turkey should be halted pending a review of Turkish policies toward Kurdistan. Kurdish initiatives for peaceful resolution of conflicts related to the occupation of Kurdistan should be supported.

Above all, we must recognize the Kurds as a people with the right to self-determination, a right held sacred by liberty-loving Americans, a right that should be enjoyed by all people in the world.

Mr. Speaker, I hope to speak about this at a later time.

Mr. PALLONE. Mr. Speaker, I rise to join in this effort to focus more attention on the plight of the Kurdish people. I want to thank my colleague from California, Mr. Filner, for taking this time to discuss the ongoing human tragedy in the mountains of Kurdistan.

About half of the worldwide Kurdish community lives within the borders of the Republic of Turkey, where their treatment is an absolute affront to the basic fundamentals of human rights. At least one-quarter of the population of Turkey is Kurdish. Yet, in Turkey, the Kurds are subjected to a policy of forced assimilation, which is essentially written into the Turkish constitution. To date, 3,124 Kurdish villages have been destroyed, and more than 3 million of their residents have been forced to become refugees, either in Kurdistan or abroad.

While the situation for the Kurdish people in such nations as Iraq, Iran, and Syria is also deplorable, I wish to draw particular attention to the situation in Turkey for some basic reasons. Turkey is, after all, a military ally of the United States, a member of NATO. As such, Turkey has received billions of dollars in military and economic assistance—courtesy of the American taxpayers. In addition, Turkey aspires to participate in other major Western organizations and institutions, such as the European Union.

Mr. Speaker, I believe that most Americans would be frankly appalled to know that a country that has received so much in the way of American largesse is guilty of so many breaches of international law and simple human decency. I have joined with many of my colleagues in denouncing Turkey's illegal blockade of Armenia, its failure to acknowledge responsibility for the Armenian Genocide of 1915-1923, its ongoing illegal occupation of Cyprus, and its threatening military maneuvers in the Aegean Sea. The brutal treatment of the more than 15 million Kurds living within Turkish borders offers a major argument for cutting back on military and economic aid to Turkey, or to at least attach very stringent conditions to the provision of this aid. If Turkey wants the benefits of inclusion in Western institutions that are supposed to be founded on the defense of democracy and human rights, then that country should start living up to the agreements it has signed.

Mr. Speaker, I want to say a few words on behalf of one of the most prominent victims of Turkey's cruel irrational anti-Kurd policies. Mrs. Leyla Zana was elected to a seat in the Turkish Parliament in 1991, representing her hometown of Diyarbakir. She was elected with 84 percent of the total vote. She became the first Kurd to break the ban on the Kurdish language in the Turkish Parliament, for which she was later tried and convicted. She had uttered the following words: "I am taking this [constitutional] oath for the brotherhood of the Turkish and Kurdish peoples."

On May 17, 1993, she and her colleague Ahmet Turk addressed the Helsinki Commission of the United States Congress. This testimony was used against her in the court of law. On March 2, 1994, her constitutional immunity as a member of Parliament was revoked, and she was arrested, taken into custody, tried, in a one-sided mockery of justice, convicted and sentenced to 15 years in prison. Leyla Zana, who is 35 years old and the mother of two children, is in the third year of her 15-year sentence at a prison in Ankara, the Turkish capital.

Leyla Zana's pursuit of democratic change by non-violent means was honored by the European Parliament, which unanimously awarded her the 1995 Sakharov Peace Prize. She has twice been nominated for the Nobel Peace Prize. I know that some of my colleagues are circulating a letter to the President on her behalf, and I hope a majority of the Members of this House will join with the European Parliament in defending the human and civil rights of this brave woman—and, I might remind my colleagues—a fellow Parliamentarian, a fellow-elected official. We owe her our moral support, and to urge our ambassador in Ankara to raise Mrs. Zana's case with the Turkish authorities at the highest levels.

Mr. Speaker, I would like to share with the Members of this Body, and anyone watching us, some of the basic goals of Mrs. Zana and of the repressed Kurdish people of Turkey: The Kurdish identity must be recognized; The use of the Kurdish language in conversation and in writing should be legalized; All cultural rights should be conceded; Kurdish political parties must be given full Constitutional rights; and A general amnesty for all political prisoners must be granted.

Mr. Speaker, we often hear—from our own administration, from other apologists for Turkey—about what a great democracy the Republic of Turkey is. Yet this is how a duly elected representative of that so-called democracy is being treated, for the crime of speaking

her language and defending the rights of her people.

Mr. Speaker, this cannot go on. For many years we have witnessed a clear pro-Turkish tilt on the part of the State Department. We often hear about the strategic importance of Turkey, its pivotal location. I don't discount these arguments completely. But we have to balance these factors against some other very important considerations. Turkey continues to spend billions of dollars on obtaining sophisticated weapons systems, not only from the United States, but from France, Russia, and elsewhere. Much of this military hardware is then used to repress and terrorize the Kurdish people, citizens of Turkey who should be extended the protection of their country's armed forces, and not be victimized by those armed forces. Meanwhile, Turkey does not have a strong industrial base and is lacking in infrastructure in many key areas. Why is Turkey, our ally, throwing away so much of its limited resources on sophisticated weapons to use against its Kurdish residents, when it could be investing in better schools, health care and other services that could help put Turkey on a par with the Western nations it seeks to be associated with?

Mr. Speaker, last week I led a special order in this House commemorating the Armenian Genocide of 1915-1923, committed by the Ottoman Turkish Empire. Just yesterday, I joined with members of the Armenian-American community for an observance of the anniversary of the unleashing of the Genocide. In recalling this well-documented part of history, the existence of which Turkey continues to officially deny, we often point out that the importance of remembering the past is to prevent similar tragedies from occurring in the future.

Mr. Speaker, we are currently witnessing a similar tragedy in Kurdistan. True, the Kurdish people have not been slaughtered on the scale that the Armenians were in the early part of this century. To some extent, the greater scrutiny that exists today—through satellite imaging and instantaneous communication—may be playing some role in restraining the Turkish Government. But there is a certain similarity to the pattern: A concerted effort by a Turkish government to wipe out the presence of a non Turkish people which has lived in the region for centuries.

Mr. Speaker, I would like to close my remarks with a statement from Lord Eric Avebury, the chairman of the Parliamentary Human Rights Group of the British House of Lords, who recently visited Turkish and Iraqi Kurdistan. He cited a quote, dating from AD 84, from the Roman historian Tacitus describing the Roman conquest of Britain: "Ubi solituneinem faciunt, pacem appelant." "They made it a desolation and called it peace." Mr. Speaker, let us resolve not to let the entire land and nation of Kurdistan be made into a desolation.

187.

[October 30, 1997 (Extensions of Remarks), pp. 2134-35]

THE DISMAL STATE OF HUMAN RIGHTS IN TURKEY
HON. CHRISTOPHER H. SMITH
OF NEW JERSEY
IN THE HOUSE OF REPRESENTATIVES

Wednesday, October 29, 1997

Mr. SMITH of New Jersey. Mr. Speaker, yesterday several of my colleagues on the Helsinki Commission—Representatives Hoyer, Markey, Cardin, and Salmon—joined me in introducing a sense of the Congress resolution with respect to the human rights situation in the Republic of Turkey and that country's desire to host the next Summit Meeting of the Heads of State or Government of the Organization for Security and Cooperation in Europe [OSCE]. Turkey—an OSCE country since 1975—first proposed to host the next summit meeting nearly a year ago. Shortly after this proposal surfaced, I wrote to then-Secretary of State Christopher on November 22, 1996, together with the Helsinki Commission's co-chairman, Senator D'AMATO, to raise concerns over human rights violations in Turkey and to urge rejection of the Turkish proposal

unless the human rights situation improved. We wrote to Secretary Albright on July 15, 1997 expressing concern over the lack of human rights progress in Turkey. Unfortunately, Turkey has squandered the opportunity to demonstrate its determination to improve implementation of Ankara's freely undertaken OSCE commitments over the past 11 months.

Without reciting the lengthy list of Turkey's human rights violations, including the use of torture, it is fair to say that Turkey's record of implementation of OSCE human dimension commitments remains poor. The Committee to Protect Journalists has documented the fact that at least 47 Turkish journalists—the largest number of any country in the world—remain imprisoned. Four former parliamentarians from the now banned Kurdish-based Democracy Party [DEP], including Leyla Zana, remain imprisoned. Turkey has pursued an aggressive campaign of harassment of non-governmental organizations over the past year. The Department of State has found that serious human rights problems persist in Turkey and that human rights abuses have not been limited to the southeast, where Turkey has engaged in an armed conflict with the terrorist Kurdistan Workers Party [PKK] for over a decade.

Last week, Mr. Speaker, the Congress honored His All Holiness Bartholomew, the leader of Orthodox believers worldwide. The Ecumenical Patriarchate, located in Istanbul the city proposed by Turkey as the venue for the next OSCE summit, has experienced many difficulties. The Ecumenical Patriarchate, has repeatedly requested permission to reopen the Orthodox seminary on the island of Halki closed by the Turkish authorities since the 1970's despite Turkey's OSCE commitment to "allow the training of religious personnel in appropriate institutions." The Turkish Embassy here in Washington viewed the visit, according to its press release, "as an excellent opportunity to forge closer ties of understanding, friendship and cooperation among peoples of different faiths and ethnicities." Unfortunately, this spirit has not characterized the Turkish Government's relations with the Patriarchate and Orthodox believers in Turkey.

Mr. Speaker, the United States should encourage the development of genuine democracy in Turkey, based on protection of human rights and fundamental freedoms. Those who would turn a blind eye toward Turkey's ongoing and serious human rights violations hinder the process of democratization in that important country. Poised at the crossroads of Europe, the Caucasus, Central Asia and the Middle East, Turkey is well positioned to play a leading role in shaping developments in Europe and beyond. But to be an effective and positive role model abroad—as some have suggested Turkey might be for the countries of Central Asia—Turkey must get its house in order. Uncorrected, Turkey's human rights problems will only fester and serve a stumbling block along the path of that country's further integration into Europe.

It is also important to keep in mind, Mr. Speaker, that Turkey is not new to the OSCE process. The Turks are not the new kids on the block. Turkey's current President, Suleyman Demirel, was an original signer of the 1975 Helsinki Final Act. The time has come for Turkey to focus on putting into practice the human rights commitments Ankara has freely accepted over the past 22 years.

The privilege and prestige of hosting an OSCE summit should be reserved for participating States that have demonstrated steadfast support for Helsinki principles and standards—particularly respect for human rights—in word and in deed. Such linkage is not new in the OSCE. When, in the mid-1980's Moscow expressed an interest in hosting a human rights conference of Helsinki signatory states, the United States and several other OSCE countries insisted on specific human rights improvements before they would agree to the Kremlin's proposal. This approach contributed to a tremendous improvement in Russia's human rights record. Should we expect any less from our allies in Ankara?

For starters, the United States should insist that Turkey release the imprisoned DEP parliamentarians, including Leyla Zana, as well as journalists and others detained for the nonviolent expression of their views; end the persecution of medical professionals and NGO's who provide treatment to victims of torture and expose human rights abuses; abol-

ish Article 8 of the Anti-Terror Law, Article 312 of the Penal Code, and other statutes which violate the principle of freedom of expression and ensure full respect for the civil, political, and cultural rights of citizens of Turkey, including ethnic Kurds ; and begin to aggressively prosecute those responsible for torture, including members of the security forces.

A key ingredient to resolving these and other longstanding human rights concerns is political will. Developments in Turkey over the past few days underscore the sad state of human rights in Turkey. Last week we learned of the imprisonment, reportedly for up to 23 years, of Esber Yagmurdereli, for a speech he made in 1991. The same day, a three-judge panel backed down after police officers accused of torturing 14 young people back in 1995 refused to appear in court. Frankly, such developments have become almost commonplace in Turkey, dulling the appreciation of some for the human tragedy of those involved in such cases.

A decision on the venue of the next OSCE summit will require the consensus of all OSCE participating States, including the United States.

The resolution we introduced, Mr. Speaker, does not call for an outright rejection of Ankara's bid to host an OSCE summit, but urges the United States to refuse to give consensus to such a proposal until such time as the Government of Turkey has demonstrably improved implementation of its freely undertaken OSCE commitments, including their properly addressing those human rights concerns I have touched on today. Our resolution calls for the President to report to the Congress by April 15, 1998 on any improvement in the actual human rights record in Turkey. We should be particularly insistent on improvements in that country's implementation of provisions of the Helsinki Final Act and other OSCE documents.

Simply put, Mr. Speaker, Turkey's desire to host an OSCE summit must be matched by concrete steps to improve its dismal human rights record. Promises of improved human rights alone should not suffice.

Mr. Speaker, I ask that correspondence between the Helsinki Commission and the State Department be included in the Record.

Commission on Security and Cooperation in
Europe,
Washington, DC, July 15, 1997.
Hon. Madeleine Korbel Albright,
Secretary of State,
Washington, DC.

Dear Madam Secretary: We write to reiterate and further explain our steadfast opposition to Turkey as the venue for an Organization for Security and Cooperation in Europe (OSCE) summit meeting and ask the Department, which we understand shares our view, to maintain the United States' refusal to give consensus to the Turkish proposal that the next summit should be held in Istanbul. We also observe that a rigid schedule of biennial summit meetings of the OSCE Heads of State or Government appears to be unwarranted at this stage of the OSCE's development and suggest that serious consideration be given to terminating the mandate which currently requires such meetings to be held whether circumstances warrant them or not.

Last November, the Republic of Turkey—an original OSCE participating State—first proposed Istanbul as the site for the next OSCE summit. At that time, we wrote to Secretary Christopher urging that the United States reject this proposal. A decision was postponed until the Copenhagen Ministerial, scheduled for this December, and the Lisbon Document simply noted Turkey's invitation.

The United States should withhold consensus on any proposal to hold an OSCE summit in Turkey until and unless Ankara has released the imprisoned Democracy Party (DEP) parliamentarians, journalists and others detained for the non-violent expression of their views; ended the persecution of medical professionals and NGOs who provide treatment to victims of torture and expose human rights abuses; and begun to aggressively prosecute those responsible for torture, including members of the security forces.

In addition, the United States should urge the Government of Turkey to undertake addi-

tional steps aimed at improving its human rights record, including abolishing Article 8 of the Anti-Terror Law, Article 312 of the Penal Code, and other statues which violate the principle of freedom of expression and ensuring full respect for the civil, political, and cultural rights of members of national minorities, including ethnic Kurds .

Regrettably, there has been no improvement in Turkey's implementation of OSCE human rights commitments in the eight months since our original letter to the Department. Despite a number of changes in Turkish law, the fact of the matter is that even these modest proposals have not translated into improved human rights in Turkey. Ankara's flagrant violations of OSCE standards and norms continues and the problems raised by the United States Delegation to the OSCE Review Meeting last November persist.

Expert witnesses at a recent Commission briefing underscored the continued, well-documented, and widespread use of torture by Turkish security forces and the failure of the Government of Turkey to take determined action to correct such gross violations of OSCE provisions and international humanitarian law. Even the much heralded reduction of periods for the detention of those accused of certain crimes has failed to deter the use of torture. The fact is that this change on paper is commonly circumvented by the authorities. As one U.S. official in Turkey observed in discussion with Commission staff, a person will be held in incommunicado detention for days, then the prisoner's name will be postdated for purposes of official police logs giving the appearance that the person has been held within the period provided for under the revised law. Turkish authorities also continue to persecute those who attempt to assist the victims of torture, as in the case of Dr. Tufan Kose.

Despite revisions in the anti-Terror Law, its provision continue to be broadly used against writers, journalists, publishers, politicians, musicians, and students. Increasingly, prosecutors have applied Article 312 of the Criminal Code, which forbids "incitement to racial or ethnic enmity." Government agents continue to harass human rights monitors. According to a recent report issued by the Committee to Protect Journalists, 78 journalists were in jail in Turkey at the beginning of 1997—more than in any other country in the world.

Many human rights abuses have been targeted at Kurds who publicly or politically assert their Kurdish identity. The Kurdish Cultural and Research Foundation offices in Istanbul were closed by police in June to prevent the teaching of Kurdish language classes. In addition, four former parliamentarians from the now banned Kurdish-based Democracy Party (DEP): Leyla Zana, Hatip Dicle, Orhan Dogan, and Selim Sadak, who have completed three years of their 15-year sentences, remain imprisoned at Ankara's Ulucanlar Prison. Among the actions cited in Leyla Zana's indictment was her appearance before the Helsinki Commission. The Lawyers Committee for Human Rights has expressed concern over the case of human rights lawyer Hasan Dogan, a member of the People's Democracy Party (HADEP), who, like many members of the party, has been subject to detention and prosecution.

The Government of Turkey has similarly pursued an aggressive campaign of harassment of non-governmental organizations, including the Human Rights Foundation of Turkey and the Human Rights Association. An Association forum on capital punishment was banned in early May as was a peace conference sponsored by international and Turkish NGOs. Human Rights Association branch offices in Diyarbakir, Malatya, Izmir, Konya, and Urga has been raided and closed.

As the Department's own report on human rights practices in Turkey recently concluded, Ankara "was unable to sustain improvements made in 1995 and, as a result, its record was uneven in 1996 and deteriorated in some respects." While Turkish civilian authorities remain publicly committed to the establishment of a rule of law state and respect for human rights, torture, excessive use of force, and other serious human rights abuses by the security forces continue. It is most unfortunate that Turkey's leaders, including President Demirel—who originally signed the 1975 Helsinki Final Act on behalf of Tur-

key—have not been able to effectively address long-standing human rights concerns.

Madam Secretary, the privilege and prestige of hosting such an OSCE event should be reserved for participating States that have demonstrated their support for Helsinki principles and standards—particularly respect for human rights—in both word and in deed. Turkey should not be allowed to serve as host of such a meeting given that country's dismal human rights record.

While some may argue that allowing Turkey to host an OSCE summit meeting might provide political impetus for positive change, we are not convinced, particularly in light of the failure of the Turkish Government to improve the human rights situation in the eight months since it proposed to host the next OSCE summit. We note that several high-level conferences have been held in Turkey without any appreciable impact on that country's human rights policies or practices.

Promises of improved human rights alone should not suffice. Turkey's desire to host an OSCE summit must be matched by concrete steps to improve its dismal human rights record.

We appreciate your consideration of our views on this important matter and look forward to receiving your reply.

Sincerely,
Christopher H. Smith,
Co-Chairman.
Alfonse D'AMATO, *Chairman.*
U.S. Department of State,
Washington, DC, 20520 August 13, 1997.
Hon. Christopher H. Smith,
Co-Chairman, Commission on Security and Cooperation in Europe, House of Representatives.

Dear Mr. Chairman: I am responding on behalf of the Secretary of State to your July 15 letter regarding your concerns about the possible selection of Turkey as the venue for the next summit meeting of the Organization for Security and Cooperation in Europe (OSCE).

The Department of State shares your concerns about Turkey's human rights record. All states participating in the OSCE are expected to adhere to the principles of the Helsinki Final Act and other OSCE commitments, including respect for human rights and fundamental freedoms. The U.S. Government has consistently called attention to human rights problems in Turkey and has urged improvements. It does not in any way condone Turkey's, or any other OSCE state's, failure to implement OSCE commitments.

The OSCE, however, is also a means of addressing and correcting human rights shortcomings. As you note in your letter, the issue of Turkey's human rights violations was raised at the November OSCE Review Meeting, and will likely continue to be raised at such meetings until Turkey demonstrates that it has taken concrete measures to improve its record. Holding the summit in Turkey could provide an opportunity to influence Turkey to improve its human rights record.

As you note, the Turkish government has made some effort to address problem areas, through the relaxation of restrictions on freedom of expression and the recent promulgation of legal reforms which, if fully implemented, would begin to address the torture problem. These measures are only a first step in addressing the problems that exist, but we believe they reflect the commitment of the Turkish government to address its human rights problems. We have been particularly encouraged by the positive attitude the new government, which came to power July 12, has demonstrated in dealing with human rights issues.

As you know, the fifty-four nations of the OSCE will discuss the question of a summit venue. As in all OSCE decisions, any decision will have to be arrived at through consensus, which will likely take some time to achieve. In the meantime, the Department of State welcomes our views, and will seriously consider your concerns about the OSCE summit site. I welcome your continuing input on this issue, and thank you for your thoughtful letter.

We appreciate your letter and hope this information is helpful. Please do not hesitate to contact us again if we can be of further assistance.

Sincerely,
Barbara Larkin,
Assistant Secretary, Legislative Affairs.

188.

[October 31, 1997 (Senate), pp. 11550-3]

SENATE CONCURRENT RESOLUTION 59—RELATIVE TO THE ORGANIZATION FOR SECURITY AND COOPERATION IN EUROPE

Mr. D'AMATO submitted the following concurrent resolution; which was referred to the Committee on Foreign Relations:

S. Con. Res. 59

Whereas the Republic of Turkey, because of its position at the crossroads of Europe, the Caucasus, Central Asia, and the Middle East, is well positioned to play a leading role in shaping developments in Europe and beyond;

Whereas the Republic of Turkey has been a longstanding member of numerous international organizations, including the Council of Europe (1949), the North Atlantic Treaty Organization (1952), and the Organization for Security and Cooperation in Europe (1975);

Whereas Turkey's President, Suleyman Demirel, was an original signer of the 1975 Helsinki Final Act of the Conference on Security and Cooperation in Europe;

Whereas the Republic of Turkey proposed in late 1996 that Istanbul serve as the venue for the next OSCE summit, a prestigious gathering of the heads of state or government of countries in Europe, Central Asia, and North America, including the United States;

Whereas a decision on the venue of the next OSCE summit will require the consensus of all OSCE participating states, including the United States;

Whereas the OSCE participating states, including Turkey, have declared their steadfast commitment to democracy based on human rights and fundamental freedoms, the protection and promotion of which is the first responsibility of government;

Whereas the development of genuine democracy in Turkey is undermined by ongoing violations of international humanitarian law as well as other human rights obligations and commitments, including provisions of the Helsinki Final Act and other OSCE documents, by which Turkey is bound;

Whereas the Department of State has found that serious human rights problems persist in Turkey and that human rights abuses have not been limited to the southeast, where Turkey has engaged in an armed conflict with the terrorist Kurdistan Workers Party (PKK) for over a decade;

Whereas flagrant violations of OSCE standards and norms continue and the problems raised by the United States Delegation at the November 1996 OSCE Review Meeting in Vienna persist;

Whereas expert witnesses at a 1997 briefing of the Commission on Security and Cooperation in Europe (in this concurrent resolution referred to as the "Helsinki Commission") underscored the continued, well-documented, and widespread use of torture by Turkish security forces and the failure of the Government of Turkey to take determined action to correct such gross violations of OSCE provisions and international humanitarian law;

Whereas the Government of Turkey continues to use broadly the Anti-Terror Law and Article 312 of the Criminal Code against writers, journalists, publishers, politicians, musicians, and students;

Whereas the Committee To Protect Journalists has concluded that more journalists are currently jailed in Turkey than in any other country in the world;

Whereas the Government of Turkey has pursued an aggressive campaign of harassment of nongovernmental organizations, including the Human Rights Foundation of Turkey; branch offices of the Human Rights Association in Diyarakir, Malatya, Izmir, Konya, and Urfa have been raided and closed; and Turkish authorities continue to persecute the members of nongovernmental organizations who attempt to assist the victims of torture;

Whereas four former parliamentarians from the now banned Kurdish -based Democracy Party (DEP) Leyla Zana, Hatip Dicle, Orhan Dogan, and Selim Sadak remain imprisoned at Ankara's Ulucanlar Prison and among the actions cited in Zana's indictment was her 1993 appearance before the Helsinki Commission in Washington, D.C.;

Whereas the Lawyers Committee for Human Rights has expressed concern over the case of human rights lawyer Hasan Dogan, a member of the People's Democracy Party (HADEP), who like many members of the party, has been subject to detention and prosecution;

Whereas many human rights abuses have been committed against Kurds who assert their Kurdish identity, and Kurdish institutions, such as the Kurdish Cultural and Research Foundation, have been targeted for closure;

Whereas the Ecumenical Patriarchate has repeatedly requested permission to reopen the Orthodox seminary on the island of Halki closed by the Turkish authorities since the 1970s despite Turkey's OSCE commitment to "allow the training of religious personnel in appropriate institutions";

Whereas members of other minority religions or beliefs, including Armenian and Syrian Orthodox believers, as well as Roman Catholics, Armenian, Chaldean, Greek and Syrian Catholics, and Protestants have faced various forms of discrimination and harassment;

Whereas the closing of the border with Armenia by Turkey in 1993 remains an obstacle to the development of mutual understanding and confidence, and friendly and good-neighborly relations between those OSCE participating states;

Whereas the Republic of Turkey has repeatedly rebuffed offers by the Chair-in-Office of the OSCE to dispatch a personal representative to Turkey for purposes of assessing developments in that country;

Whereas, despite the fact that a number of Turkish civilian authorities remain publicly committed to the establishment of rule of law and to respect for human rights, torture, excessive use of force, and other serious human rights abuses by the security forces continue; and

Whereas the Government of Turkey has failed to meaningfully address these and other human rights concerns since it first proposed to host the next OSCE summit and thereby has squandered this opportunity to demonstrate its determination to improve implementation of Turkey's OSCE commitments: Now, therefore, be it

Resolved by the Senate (the House of Representatives concurring), That it is the sense of Congress that—

(1) the privilege and prestige of hosting a summit of the heads of state or government of the Organization for Security and Cooperation in Europe (OSCE) should be reserved for participating states that have demonstrated in word and in deed steadfast support for Helsinki principles and standards, particularly respect for human rights;

(2) the United States should refuse to give consensus to any proposal that Turkey serve as the venue for a summit meeting of the heads of state or government of OSCE countries until the Government of Turkey has demonstrably improved implementation of its freely undertaken OSCE commitments, including action to address those human rights concerns enumerated in the preamble of this resolution;

(3) the United States should encourage the development of genuine democracy in the Republic of Turkey based on protection of human rights and fundamental freedoms; and

(4) the President of the United States should report to Congress not later than April 15, 1998, on any improvement in the actual human rights record in Turkey, including improvements in that country's implementation of provisions of the Helsinki Final Act and other OSCE documents.

Sec. 2. The Secretary of the Senate shall transmit a copy of this concurrent resolution to the President of the United States.

Mr. D'AMATO. Mr. President, I rise to submit a concurrent resolution on the human rights situation in Turkey. This resolution is prompted by that country's desire to host the next summit meeting of the heads of state or government of the Organization for Security and Cooperation in Europe [OSCE]. This summit meeting is scheduled to take place in 1998. The issue is which country will host this most important OSCE gathering.

Last November, the Republic of Turkey—an original OSCE participating state—first proposed Istanbul as the site for the next OSCE summit. At that time, I wrote to then-Secretary of State Christopher, together with Commission Co-Chairman Christopher Smith,

urging that the United States reject this proposal based on Turkey's dismal human rights record. I also wrote to Secretary Albright in July to reiterate my concerns regarding the state of human rights in Turkey and Ankara's failure to improve its implementation of OSCE commitments.

Ankara has squandered the past year, failing to meaningfully address a series of long-standing human rights concerns. Regrettably, there has been no meaningful improvement in Turkey's implementation of its OSCE human rights commitments in the 11 months since our original letter to the State Department. Despite a number of changes in Turkish law, the fact of the matter is that even these modest proposals have not translated into improved human rights in Turkey.

Mr. President, my resolution does not call for outright rejection of the Turkish proposal. Rather, the resolution calls for the United States to refuse consensus to such a plan until the Government of Turkey had demonstrably improved implementation of its freely undertaken OSCE commitments, including action to address those human rights concerns I will describe in more detail later in my remarks. Under OSCE rules, decisions require that all participating states, including the United States, give their consensus before a proposal can be adopted. The resolution we introduce today calls upon the President to report to the Congress by April 15, 1998, on any improvement to Turkey's actual human rights performance.

Expert witnesses at a Commission briefing earlier this year underscored the continued, well-documented, and widespread use of torture by Turkish security forces and the failure of the Government of Turkey to take determined action to correct such gross violations of OSCE provisions and international humanitarian law. Even the much heralded reduction of periods for the detention of those accused of certain crimes has failed to deter the use of torture. The fact is that this change on paper is commonly circumvented by the authorities. As one United States official in Turkey observed in discussion with Commission staff, a person will be held in incommunicado for days, then the prisoner's name will be postdated for purposes of official police logs giving the appearance that the person had been held within the period provided for under the revised law. Turkish authorities also continue to persecute those who attempt to assist the victims of torture, as in the case of Dr. Tufan Kose.

Despite revisions in the Anti-Terror Law, its provisions continue to be broadly used against writers, journalists, publishers, politicians, musicians, and students. Increasingly, prosecutors have applied article 312 of the Criminal Code, which forbids "incitement to racial or ethnic enmity." Government agents continue to harass human rights monitors. According to the Committee to Protect Journalists, at least 47 Turkish journalists are in jail in Turkey today—more than in any other country in the world.

Many human rights abuses have been committed against Kurds who assert their Kurdish identity. The Kurdish Cultural and Research Foundation offices in Istanbul were closed by police in June to prevent the teaching of Kurdish language classes. In addition, four former parliamentarians from the now banned Kurdish -based Democracy Party [DEP]: Leyla Zana, Hatip Dicle, Orhan Dogan, and Selim Sadak, who have completed three years of their 15-year sentences, remain imprisoned at Ankara's Ulucanlar Prison. Among the actions cited in Leyla Zana's indictment was her 1993 appearance before the U.S. Commission on Security and Cooperation in Europe here in Washington, DC. The Lawyers Committee for Human Rights has expressed concern over the case of human rights lawyer Hasan Dogan, a member of the People's Democracy Party [HADEP], who, like many members of the party, has been subject to detention and prosecution.

The Government of Turkey has similarly pursued an aggressive campaign of harassment of nongovernmental organizations, including the Human Rights Foundation of Turkey and the Human Rights Association. An Association forum on capital punishment was banned in early May as was a peace conference sponsored by international and Turkish NGO's. Human Rights Association branch offices in Diyarbakir, Malatya, Izmir, Konya, and Urfa have been raided and closed.

Mr. President, last week the Congress honored His All Holiness Bartholomew, the leader of Orthodox believers worldwide. The Ecumenical Patriarchate, located in Istanbul—the city proposed by Turkey as the venue for the next OSCE summit—has experienced many difficulties. The Patriarchate has repeatedly requested permission to reopen the Orthodox seminary on the island of Halki closed by the Turkish authorities since the 1970's despite Turkey's OSCE commitment to "allow the training of religious personnel in appropriate institutions."

As the State Department's own Country Report on Human Rights Practices for 1996 concluded, Turkey "was unable to sustain improvements made in 1995 and, as a result, its record was uneven in 1996 and deteriorated in some respects." While Turkish civilian authorities remain publicly committed to the establishment of rule of law state and respect for human rights, torture, excessive use of force, and other serious human rights abuses by the security forces continue. As our resolution points out, the United States should encourage the development of genuine democracy in the Republic of Turkey based on protection of human rights and fundamental freedoms.

Mr. President, it is most unfortunate that Turkey's leaders, including President Demirel—who originally signed the 1975 Helsinki Final Act on behalf of Turkey—have not been able to effectively address these and other longstanding human rights concerns.

The privilege and prestige of hosting such an OSCE event should be reserved for participating states that have demonstrated their support for Helsinki principles and standards—particularly respect for human rights—in both word and in deed. Turkey should not be allowed to serve as host of such a meeting until and unless that country's dismal human rights record has improved.

While some may argue that allowing Turkey to host an OSCE summit meeting might provided political impetus for positive change, we are not convinced, particularly in light of the failure of the Turkish Government to meaningfully improve the human rights situation in the months since it offered to host the next OSCE summit. We note that several high-level conferences have been held in Turkey without any appreciable impact on that country's human rights policies or practices.

Mr. President, promises of improved human rights alone should not suffice. Turkey's desire to host an OSCE summit must be matched by concrete steps to improve its dismal human rights record.

I ask unanimous consent that the two letters I mentioned earlier, to Secretary Christopher and Secretary Albright, and a copy of the State Department's August 13, 1997, reply signed by Assistant Secretary of State for Legislative Affairs, Barbara Larkin, be inserted in the Record.

In closing, I urge my colleagues to join in supporting this concurrent resolution and to work for its passage before the end of this first session of the 105th Congress.

There being no objection, the material was ordered to be printed in the Record, as follows:

COMMISSION ON SECURITY AND COOPERATION IN EUROPE,
Washington, DC, July 15, 1997.
Hon. Madeleine Korbel Albright,
Secretary of State, Department of State,
Washington, DC.

Dear Madam Secretary: We write to reiterate and further explain our steadfast opposition to Turkey as the venue for an Organization for Security and Cooperation in Europe (OSCE) summit meeting and ask the Department, which we understand shares our view, to maintain the United States' refusal to give consensus to the Turkish proposal that the next summit should be held in Istanbul. We also observe that a rigid schedule of biennial summit meetings of the OSCE Heads of State or Government appears to be unwarranted at this stage of the OSCE's development and suggest that serious consideration be given to terminating the mandate which currently requires such meetings to be held whether circumstances warrant them or not.

Last November, the Republic of Turkey—an original OSCE participating State—first proposed Istanbul as the site for the next OSCE summit. At that time, we wrote to Secretary Christopher urging that the United States reject this proposal. A decision was postponed until the Copenhagen Ministerial, scheduled for this December, and the Lisbon Document simply noted Turkey's invitation.

The United States should withhold consensus on any proposal to hold an OSCE summit in Turkey until and unless Ankara has released the imprisoned Democracy Party (DEP) parliamentarians, journalists and others detained for the non-violent expression of their views; ended the persecution of medical professionals and NGOs who provide treatment to victims of torture and expose human rights abuses; and begun to aggressively prosecute those responsible for torture, including members of the security forces.

In addition, the United States should urge the Government of Turkey to undertake additional steps aimed at improving its human rights record, including abolishing Article 8 of the Anti-Terror Law, Article 312 of the Penal Code, and other statutes which violate the principle of freedom of expression and ensuring full respect for the civil, political, and cultural rights of members of national minorities, including ethnic Kurds .

Regrettably, there has been no improvement in Turkey's implementation of OSCE human rights commitments in the eight months since our original letter to the Department. Despite a number of changes in Turkish law, the fact of the matter is that even these modest proposals have not translated into improved human rights in Turkey. Ankara's flagrant violations of OSCE standards and norms continues and the problems raised by the United States Delegation to the OSCE Review Meeting last November persist.

Madam Secretary, the privilege and prestige of hosting such an OSCE event should be reserved for participating States that have demonstrated their support for Helsinki principles and standards—particularly respect for human rights—in both word and in deed. Turkey should not be allowed to serve as host of such a meeting given that country's dismal human rights record.

While some may argue that allowing Turkey to host an OSCE summit meeting might provide political impetus for positive change, we are not convinced, particularly in light of the failure of the Turkish Government to improve the human rights situation in the eight months since it proposed to host the next OSCE summit. We note that several high-level conferences have been held in Turkey without any appreciable impact on that country's human rights policies or practices.

Promises of improved human rights alone should not suffice. Turkey's desire to host an OSCE summit must be matched by concrete steps to improve its dismal human rights record.

We appreciate your consideration of our views on this important matter and look forward to receiving your reply.

Sincerely,
Christopher H. Smith,
Member of Congress, Co-Chairman.
Alfonse D'AMATO,
U.S. Senate, Chairman.

————

COMMISSION ON SECURITY AND COOPERATION IN EUROPE,
Washington, DC, November 22, 1996.
HON. WARREN CHRISTOPHER,
Secretary of State, Department of State, Washington, DC.

Dear Mr. Secretary: We have recently learned that the Republic of Turkey may offer Istanbul as the venue for the next summit meeting of the Heads of State or Government of the Organization of Security and Cooperation in Europe (OSCE). We write to urge that the United States reject this proposal. A decision on this important matter is extremely urgent as the OSCE Review Meeting concludes today and drafting for the Summit document will begin next week.

The privilege of hosting such a prestigious OSCE event should be reserved for participating States that have demonstrated steadfast support for Helsinki principles and standards—particularly respect for human rights—

in word and in deed. The U.S. should deny consensus on Turkey's proposal to serve as host of an OSCE summit meeting because of that country's dismal human rights record.

The United States Delegation to the OSCE Review Meeting has raised a number of specific examples that illustrate Turkey's flagrant violation of OSCE human rights commitments and international humanitarian law, including the well-documented use of torture. The European Committee for the Prevention of Torture has found that incidence of torture and ill-treatment in Turkey to be "widespread." The UN Committee on Torture has referred to "systemic" use of torture in Turkey. Earlier this week, Amnesty International released a report documenting the torture of children held in detention in Turkey.

Despite Turkey's revisions to the Anti-Terror Law, it provisions continue to be broadly used against writers, journalists, publishers, politicians, musicians, and students. Increasingly, prosecutors have applied Article 312 of the Criminal Code, which forbids "incitement to racial or ethnic enmity" to suppress expression of dissenting views. Government agents continue to harass human rights monitors. Many human rights abuses have been committed against Kurds who publicly or politically assert their Kurdish identity.

As the Department's own report on human rights practices in Turkey concluded, while Turkish civilian authorities remain publicly committed to the establishment of a state of law and respect to human rights, torture, excessive use of force, and other serious human rights abuses by the security forces continue.

Regrettably, lone overdue reforms of Turkey's human rights policies and practices announced in mid-October by the Turkish Deputy Prime Minister and Foreign Minister, Mrs. Ciller, have not materialized and the prospects for genuine change in the near term appear remote.

Another key factor in our urgent call for rejection of Turkey's proposal to host an OSCE summit is Turkey's continuing illegal and forcible occupation of Cypriot territory in blatant violation of OSCE principles. A substantial force of 30,000 Turkish troops remains in Cyprus today in a clear breach of

Cypriot sovereignty. In recent months, we have witnessed the worst violence against innocent civilians along the cease-fire line since the 1974 invasion, resulting in at least 5 deaths. In addition, Turkish and Turkish Cypriot authorities have failed to fully account for at least 1,614 Greek Cypriots and five Americans missing since 1974.

While some may argue that allowing Turkey to hose an OSCE summit might provide political impetus for positive change, we are not convinced, particularly in light of the fact that several high-level conferences have been held in Turkey without any appreciable impact on that country's human rights policies or practices. Allowing Turkey to host an OSCE summit based upon an inference of increased leverage to improve Turkish human rights performance, when they are in current, active violation of solemn international commitments would be wrong.

Turkey's desire to host an OSCE summit must be matched by concrete steps to improve its dismal human rights, to end its illegal occupation of Cypriot territory, and to contribute to a reduction of tensions in the eastern Mediterranean. Absent demonstrable progress in these areas, the United States should withhold consensus on any proposal to hold an OSCE summit in Turkey.

Sincerely,
Alfonse D'AMATO,
U.S. Senator, Co-Chairman.
Christopher H. Smith,
Member of Congress, Chairman

U.S. DEPARTMENT OF STATE,
Washington, DC, August 13, 1997.
Hon. CHRISTOPHER H. SMITH,
Co-Chairman, Commission on Security and Cooperation in Europe, House of Representatives.

Dear Mr. Chairman: I am responding on behalf of the Secretary of State to your July 15 letter regarding your concerns about the possible selection of Turkey as the venue for the next summit meeting of the Organization for Security and Cooperation in Europe (OSCE).

The Department of State shares your concerns about Turkey's human rights record. All states participating in the OSCE are expected to adhere to the principles of the Helsinki Final Act and other OSCE commitments, including respect for human rights and fundamental freedoms. The U.S. Government has consistently called attention to human rights problems in Turkey and has urged improvements. It does not in any way condone Turkey's, or any other OSCE state's, failure to implement OSCE commitments.

The OSCE, however, is also a means of addressing and correcting human rights shortcomings. As you note in your letter, the issue of Turkey's human rights violations was raised at the November OSCE Review Meeting, and will likely continue to be raised at such meetings until Turkey demonstrates that it has taken concrete measures to improve its record. Holding the summit in Turkey could provide an opportunity to influence Turkey to improve its human rights record.

As you note, the Turkish government has made some effort to address problem areas, through the relaxation of restrictions on freedom of expression and the recent promulgation of legal reforms which, if fully implemented, would begin to address the torture problem. These measures are only a first step in addressing the problems that exist, but we believe they reflect the commitment of the Turkish government to address its human rights problems. We have been particularly encouraged by the positive attitude the new government, which came to power July 12, has demonstrated in dealing with human rights issues.

As you know, the fifty-four nations of the OSCE will discuss the question of a summit venue. As in all OSCE decisions, any decision will have to be arrived at through consensus, which will likely take some time to achieve. In the meantime, the Department of State welcomes your views, and will seriously consider your concerns about the OSCE summit site. I welcome your continuing input on this issue, and thank you for your thoughtful letter.

We appreciate your letter and hope this information is helpful. Please do not hesitate to contact us again if we can be of further assistance.

Sincerely,
Barbara Larkin,
Assistant Secretary, Legislative Affairs.

189.

[November 7, 1997 (House), pp. 10328-34]

FAST TRACK AUTHORITY

The SPEAKER pro tempore. Under the Speaker's announced policy of January 7, 1997, the gentleman from New Jersey [Mr. Pallone] is recognized for 60 minutes as the designee of the minority leader.

Mr. PALLONE. Mr. Speaker, I want to spend some time tonight initially talking about the fast track legislation which we are likely to be voting on either tomorrow or Sunday. I am very much opposed to the fast track legislation for a number of reasons, and I wanted to use part of the hour tonight to outline some of those reasons and begin with a local situation in Monmouth County, which is one of the two counties that I represent in the State of New Jersey, because I think it illustrates the types of problems that I have with fast track by reference to NAFTA. Many of those who are opposed to fast track and who will be voting against fast track legislation, if it comes up over this weekend, are doing so because of the experience with NAFTA.

I want to comment on why Congress really should resist the pressure being put on us to grant the fast track authority, to expand NAFTA and essentially put even more Americans out of work . . .

TURKISH STUDIES CHAIR AT UCLA

Mr. Speaker, I wanted to just talk briefly about a few other issues. First of all, I should say that my colleague from California [Mr. Sherman], touched on two issues that I wanted to mention briefly also this evening. He mentioned that the University of California at Los Angeles, UCLA, is establishing a Turkish Studies Chair, funded I may add, by the Government of Turkey. I wanted to join the gentleman in expressing my serious concern about this unfortunate use of a major prestigious university as a vehicle of indoctrination by another country.

In my home State of New Jersey, we had a similar situation where Princeton University set up a study program that was financed by the Government of Turkey. As a result, the information that was coming out of the study program essentially denied the Armenian genocide. There has been a history with the Ottoman Empire and the Republic of Turkey to basically deny that the Armenian genocide ever occurred.

My concern, and I know that of Mr. Sherman as well, is that by establishing these chairs or these Turkish study programs in different parts of the country, in my case at Princeton, in his case at UCLA, the Turkish Government is using these study programs to basically deny history and deny the facts of the Armenian genocide. In fact, it is really a brazen opportunity, if you will, a brazen attempt by a foreign government, to manipulate an American university for the denial of the historically verified genocide of the Armenian Nation.

The Turkish Government is not setting up scholarships. These are propaganda and propaganda alone. It would be like a German Government that had not acknowledged the Holocaust funding a Nazi studies program at an American university. Of course, the difference is that Germany at least accepts responsibility and apologizes for the Holocaust of the Jewish people. The Turkish Government, still defying the historical record, denies that the Armenian genocide ever happened.

I just wanted to join this evening with the Armenian community in the United States in appealing to the officials at UCLA, in the same way that I did at Princeton University about a year ago, and ask the board of regents to stop the effort of filling the heads of young Americans with revisionist propaganda in the name of so-called scholarship.

This is something that we have seen happen more and more where the Turkish Government has been financing these study programs or chairs at various American universities in order to basically deny the Armenian genocide.

PLIGHT OF THE KURDISH PEOPLE

I know Mr. Sherman also mentioned earlier this evening, and another of my colleague from California, Bob Filner, has basically spearheaded this effort, there has been a group of Kurdish Americans who have been fasting on the steps of the Capitol, on the main steps of the Capitol now for a number of days, probably more than a few weeks, in order to highlight, if you will, the ongoing tragedy in the mountains of Kurdistan , where, again, the Turkish Government, which is, of course denying the Armenian genocide and continues to, is also basically trying to essentially obliterate, not only individually by killing Kurds in Turkey, but also by denying Kurds the ability to speak their language, to learn about their culture, to go to school in Kurdish , and this fast, conducted by supporters of the Turkish people on the Capitol steps, includes the human right activist Cameron Porter, who is the spouse of one of our colleagues, the distinguished gentleman from Illinois [Mr. John Porter].

I just want to say these fasters deserve tremendous credit for the dedication, courage and perseverance. It has been getting cold lately here in Washington, but that has not deterred them.

Last Friday I joined with a group of my colleagues, members from both sides of the aisle, to visit with the fasters and supporters. I know Congressman Sherman and Congressman Filner were out there with me. Every day as we pass by these people sacrificing for the causes of peace and human rights, the sight of these protestors on the Capitol steps is a reminder to all people of conscious of the plight of the Kurds and the governments that hold them down, most notably the Government of the Republic of Turkey.

In particular, Mr. Speaker, as we come into the Capitol to cast votes on legislation, sent here to do a job by the constituents who elected us, I hope we will remember one of our fellow elected legislators who does not have the opportunity to represent her constituents, Mrs. Leyla Zana, one of the most prominent victims of Turkey's cruel, irrational anti-Kurd cruel policies.

Leyla Zana was elected to a seat in the Turkish Parliament in 1991 representing her hometown. She was elected with 80 percent of the total vote, and she became the first Kurd to break the ban on the Kurdish language in the Turkish Parliament, for which she was later tried and convicted. She had uttered the following words: "I am taking this Constitutional oath for the brotherhood of the Turkish and Kurdish peoples."

On May 17, 1993, she and one of her colleagues addressed the Helsinki Commission of the U.S. Congress. The testimony was used against her in a court of law. On March 2, 1994, her constitutional immunity as a member of Parliament was revoked and she was arrested, taken into custody, tried in a one-sided mockery of justice, convicted, and sentenced to 15 years in prison.

Leyla Zana, who is 35 years old and the mother of two children, is well into the third year of her 15 year sentence at a prison in Ankara, the Turkish capital.

Leyla Zana's pursuit of Democratic change by nonviolent means was honored by the European Parliament, which unanimously awarded her the 1995 Sakharov Peace Prize. She has received major consideration for the Nobel Peace Prize. More than 150 Members of this House, my colleagues, have written to President Clinton on her behalf, and I hope a majority of the Members of this House will join with the European Parliament in defending the human and civil rights of this brave woman, and I might remind my colleagues, a fellow Parliamentarian, a fellow elected official. We owe her our moral support and to urge our ambassador in Ankara to raise Mrs. Zana's case with the Turkish authorities at the highest levels.

Mr. Speaker, I just want to share with the Members of this body and anyone watching this some of the basic goals of Ms. Lasagna, of the fasters outside this building, and of the repressed Kurdish people of Turkey. The Kurdish identity must be recognized. The use of the Kurdish language in conversation and in writing should be legalized. All cultural rights should be conceded. Kurdish political parties must be given full constitutional rights and a general amnesty for all political prisoners must be granted.

Mr. Speaker, we often hear from our own administration and other apologists for Turkey about what a great democracy the Republic of Turkey is. Yet this is how a duly elected representative of that so-called democracy is being treated for the crime of speaking her language and defending the rights of her people.

Mr. Speaker, this cannot go on. For many years we have witnessed a clear pro-Turkish tilt on the part of the State Department. We often hear about strategic importance of Turkey and its pivotal location, and I do not discount those arguments completely. But we have to balance those factors against some other very important considerations.

Turkey continues to spend billions of dollars in obtaining sophisticated weapons systems, not only from the United States, but from France, Russia and elsewhere. Much of this military hardware is then used to repress and terrorize the Kurdish people, citizens of Turkey who should be extended the protection of their country's armed forces and not be victimized by those armed forces.

Meanwhile, Turkey does not have a strong industrial base, and is lacking in infrastructure in many key areas. So why is Turkey, our ally, throwing so much of its limited resources on sophisticated weapons to use against its Kurdish residents, when it could be investing in better schools, health care and other services that could help put Turkey on a par with the western nations it seeks to be associated with?

About half of the worldwide Kurdish community lives within the borders of the Republic of Turkey, where their treatment is an absolute affront to basic fundamentals of human rights.

At least one-quarter of the population of Turkey is Kurdish . Yet in Turkey, the Kurds are subjected to a policy of forced assimilation which is essentially written into the Turkish Constitution. To date, 3,134 Kurdish villages have been destroyed and more than 3 million of their residents have been forced to become refugees, either in Kurdistan or abroad.

Mr. Speaker, I would venture to say that in many ways what we are seeing happen in Kurdistan today is in some ways the prelude to the same type of genocide that occurred by the Turks against the Armenian people 80-some years ago.

While the situation for the Kurdish people in such nations as Iraq, Iran and Syria is also deplorable, I wish to draw particular attention to the situation in Turkey for some basic reasons. Turkey is, after all, a military ally of the United States, a member of NATO. As such, it has received billions of dollars in military and economic assistance, courtesy of the American taxpayers. In addition, Turkey aspires to participate in other major western organizations and institutions, such as the European Union.

Mr. Speaker, I believe most Americans would be frankly appalled to know a country that has received so much in the way of American largesse is guilty of so many breaches of international law and simple human decency. I have joined with many of my colleagues in denouncing Turkey's illegal blockade of Armenia, its failure to acknowledge responsibility for the Armenian genocide of 1915 through 1923, its ongoing illegal occupation of Cyprus and its threatening military maneuvers in the Aegean Sea.

The brutal treatment of the more than 15 million Kurds living within

Turkish borders offers a major argument for cutting back on military and economic aid to Turkey, or to at least attach very stringent conditions to provisions of this aid.

If Turkey wants the benefits of inclusion in Western institutions that are supposed to be founded on the defense of democracy and human rights, then that country should start living up to the agreements it has signed.

Again, the situation in Kurdistan is just another example of the type of treatment that Turkey has done historically with the Armenian people and other peoples, and it must stop . . .

190.

[November 8, 1997 (Extensions of Remarks), pp. 2251-52]

TURKEY LOOKS OUTSIDE ITS BORDERS TO SOLVE ITS KURDISH QUESTION, WHEN THE PROBLEM

CLEARLY RESTS WITHIN
HON. STENY H. HOYER
OF MARYLAND
IN THE HOUSE OF REPRESENTA-
TIVES

Friday, November 7, 1997

Mr. HOYER. Mr. Speaker, over the past several years, Turkey, a NATO ally and United States friend, has made repeated incursions into Iraq. The invasions, which violate international law, are undertaken ostensibly against Kurdish guerillas waging a violent insurgency in Turkey. In reality, these military campaigns result in countless civilian casualties, widespread population displacement, severe economic hardship, and if anything, encourage local support for the guerrillas. While the Turkish military declares the guerrillas eradicated after each incursion, repeated cross-border attacks expose this as a fiction.

The latest invasion raises new cause for concern. For more than three weeks, Turkish forces have actively supported the Kurdistan Democratic Party (KDP), which has been engaged in years of bloody fighting with its rival, the Patriotic Union of Kurdistan (PUK). Widespread reports indicate Turkey is using napalm and cluster bombs, despite international covenants banning their use. The PUK receives significant United States funding, so in effect, our ally Turkey is attacking a party which receives funds from the United States Government. I question why our Government refuses to acknowledge this inconsistency. And even more importantly, I question our Government's silence when a United States-supplied ally violates a United States-imposed 'no-fly zone' to kill Kurdish civilians and destroy their villages in the so-called safe haven.

Mr. Speaker, Turkey along with the United States and Great Britain, had been participating in the "Ankara Process" in an effort to bring the two feuding Kurdish factions to the negotiating table. Turkey's military support for the KDP ends any hope that it can serve as a neutral regional peace-broker. Furthermore, Turkish plans to establish a "buffer zone" in Iraqi Kurdistan , with at least 8,000 troops, will destabilize the entire region and invite intervention by Iraq, Iran and Syria. Mr. Speaker, I would like to submit for the record an editorial by Jim Hoagland from last Sunday's *Washington Post* that further questions the logic of U.S. policy in this area ["Before Turkey Joins Europe," Nov. 2, 1997].

It is tragic and ironic that Turkey seeks answers to its " Kurdish question" outside its borders, when in reality it should be working these issues out at home. Turkey's 15 million Kurds have faced oppression since modern Turkey was forged in 1923. Since then, there have been 28 major Kurdish uprisings. The most recent, underway since 1984, has claimed almost 30,000 lives. According to Turkish Government sources 3,185 Kurdish villages have been evacuated and up to three million people have been internally displaced from southeast Turkey. Despite the severity of the conflict, Turkey refuses access by the International Red Cross to the stricken region. The conflict costs billions of dollars each year and destroys hopes of economic development that is greatly needed in the region.

Mr. Speaker, the Turkish regime must put flesh on its skeletal democracy, or the Kurdish problem and other pressing issues will fester and continue to prevent Turkey from moving closer to Europe. Turkey's civilian and military leaders have repeatedly stated their intentions to address human rights problems, yet the problems persist and reform efforts seem little more than public relations exercises. Meanwhile, our Government continues business as usual, sending billions of dollars worth of security assistance to Ankara while refusing to acknowledge increasing signs of political instability. Such unequivocal support is unwise because it reinforces the military and other non-democratic forces in Turkey, and sends a message that the United States Government will support the Turkish Government no matter how deficient it remains in human rights areas.

Mr. Speaker, as I stand before this distinguished body, a group of Kurds and Americans, including Kathryn Cameron Porter, are fasting in front of this building to protest human rights violations in Turkey. They too believe our Government has remained silent in the face of growing threats to democracy in Turkey. A major impetus for their protest is the continued imprisonment of four Kurdish parliamentarians, including Leyla Zana, whose indictment included charges related to her appearance at a Helsinki commission briefing. All Kurdish -based political parties in Turkey are suppressed, even though Kurdish political opinions must be considered if political institutions are to be truly representative. Nonviolent Kurdish parties must be allowed to participate in political life. Individuals should not be jailed for expressing opinions deemed harmful by the Government. Open debate and dialogue is imperative.

Mr. Speaker, another democratic measure is freedom of the media. On October 21, the Committee to Protect Journalists (CPJ) issued a report entitled "The Anatolian Archipelago" which details the fate of 78 journalists jailed for speech crimes in Turkey. CPJ, which does meticulous research and seeks Turkish Government input before publishing, has concluded in each of the last 3 years that more journalists are jailed in Turkey than in any other country.

Human rights defenders and Kurdish peace activists are also subject to harassment, imprisonment or worse. This past week, Yavuz Onen and Akin Birdal, two internationally recognized rights leaders, and Ahmet Turk, a Kurd, were charged for reading in public a report detailing the ongoing scandal linking officials to death squads and face up to 3 years in prison. On October 20, well-known peace activist, Esber Yagmurdereli, was jailed for 22 years. On October 21, the president and 7 other Human Rights Association (HRA) executives were sentenced to between 1 and 2 years in prison for speeches made during human rights week in 1996. In recent years, 20 HRA branches have been closed, including all that serve Kurdish communities in Southeast Turkey.

Free expression is only one area where Turkey is deficient in meeting its stated human rights commitments. Local NGOS, Amnesty International, Human Rights Watch, and our own State Department conclude that torture remains widespread and few accused of torture are brought to justice. Last week, a panel of judges presiding over an internationally publicized trial, refused to make police accused of torturing 14 young people, some as young as 13, appear in court. Also pending is the legal appeal of the human rights foundation doctor who refused to turn over to the government information on victims of torture.

Mr. Speaker, I have joined more than 160 of our colleagues in signing a letter calling for the release of imprisoned parliamentarians in Turkey. At the very least, as Members of an elected legislature, we should demand that our colleagues in Turkey be freed, for it is unthinkable that legislators in a democratic society would be jailed for speaking out on behalf of democratic society would be jailed for speaking out on behalf of their constituents. I urge my colleagues to sign the "Dear Colleague" letter and to visit those fasting on the steps of this building.

I have also joined my colleagues on the Helsinki Commission in introducing a resolution expressing the sense of the Congress that Turkey should not be chosen as the host of the next summit meeting of the Organization for Security and Cooperation in Europe. As long as Turkey continues to violate international law and its own commitments to OSCE principles, Turkey should not be considered an appropriate venue for a human rights summit. Such a privilege, Mr. Speaker, should be reserved for participating States that have demonstrated, in word and in deed, steadfast support for Helsinki principles and standards, particularly respect for basic human rights . . .

191.

[November 10, 1997 (Extensions of Remarks), p. 2305]

**FREE LEYLA ZANA, KUDISH PARLIAMENTARIAN JAILED IN TURKEY
HON. JOHN EDWARD PORTER
OF ILLINOIS
IN THE HOUSE OF REPRESENTATIVES**

Sunday, November 9, 1997

Mr. PORTER. Mr. Speaker, I come to the floor today to express my profound outrage at the treatment of an elected official in Turkey. Leyla Zana—a Kurdish parliamentarian, duly elected by the people of her district—has been arrested and jailed in turkey for the crime of expressing her political opinions and beliefs. To be precise, Ms. Zana had the temerity to express her views at a meeting of the Commission on Security and Cooperation, here in Washington. Her prosecution is a crime against democracy and a crime against freedom. For nearly 3 weeks, a group of Kurds and Americans have been fasting in front of the Capitol in silent protest of Leyla Zana's incarceration. One of these individuals was forced to end his vigil yesterday because his health was threatened.

Last week, over 150 of my colleagues and I sent a letter to President Clinton asking him to demand Leyla Zana's freedom. I regret to say, however, that I do not have high hopes that our Government will take her case seriously. Our administration—like those before it—has maintained a policy of ignoring outrageous Turkish human rights abuses, and papering over the fault lines in Turkish democracy.

For the past week, many of my colleagues and I have taken to the floor to express our genuine outrage at the human rights abuses in China. The litany of human rights abuses that we heard about is, unfortunately, what we have come to expect from countries like China. What we should not expect or tolerate is for a country like Turkey— ostensibly a western, European, democratic country—to have the same type of human rights problems. Yet Leyla Zana's case demonstrates that freedom of expression, freedom of thought and political dissidence are nearly as dangerous in Turkey as they are in China today. Turkey is our close ally, a partner in NATO and the European theater. How can we criticize China, but expect so little from Turkey? This hypocrisy must end.

It is even more shameful that Turkey's harassment of the Kurdish people does not end at its own borders. In the past 3 weeks, Turkey has openly waged an indiscriminate attack on Kurdish villages in Northern Iraq. Turkey has said that they are merely pursuing the PKK into Northern Iraq, but the facts bear out a different story. The use of napalm and cluster bombs against civilians in Northern Iraq is irrefutable evidence that turkey does not care who it hurts in its mindless military effort to eradicate the Kurds . I am ashamed to say that our Government—the same government that marshaled the entire international community when these same Kurds were attacked by Saddam Hussein—has done nothing to criticize this lawless behavior on the part of our ally Turkey. Instead we have allowed Turkey to willfully disrupt our own efforts to negotiate a peaceful settlement between the Kurdish groups in Northern Iraq.

The United States has a moral responsibility to speak out against such behavior whether it comes from China or Turkey. I hope that my colleagues will join me in expressing their outrage at Turkey's outrageous actions at home and beyond its borders, and our own administration's "see no evil" policies.

192.

[November 10, 1997 (Extensions of Remarks), pp. 2310-11]

FREE LEYLA ZANA
HON. BOB FILNER
OF CALIFORNIA
IN THE HOUSE OF REPRESENTATIVES

Sunday, November 9, 1997

Mr. FILNER. Mr. Speaker, as I speak here tonight, members of the Kurdish community are conducting a vigil for peace and a hunger strike to spotlight the continuing oppression of the Kurdish people. I rise tonight for one simple reason: to express my solidarity with the hunger strikers and my support for the Kurdish people's struggle for freedom, justice—and self-determination. The symbol of that struggle is a fellow democratically elected representative, the imprisoned Kurdish leader, Leyla Zana.

In Turkey today, Mr. Speaker, innocent Kurdish civilians are being massacred, entire Kurdish villages are being destroyed, and millions of Kurds are forced from their homes, forced to the cities where unemployment and inflation are extremely high. The entire region of southeastern Turkey has been ravaged—it has become an economic and humanitarian disaster area. This is simply unacceptable. This is a cause for alarm for a country that uses American arms to commit such crimes. United States-made weapons should never again be used against the Kurds or against anybody else, as they were at the ancient Kurdish city of Halabia, where over 5,000 Kurdish civilians, mostly women and children, were gassed to death. Never again.

Leyla Zana has committed her life's work to pursuing a peaceful and just resolution to the enduring Kurdish question. I hope my colleagues will learn her story—an incredible story of self-education, political growth, heroism and courage.

The Turkish Government feared Leyla Zana was progressing too far in her endeavors for peace and now she shares a prison cell with a convicted murderer. But they cannot imprison her picture, her words, her courage, and her inspiring story.

An initiative has been undertaken in the U.S. House of Representatives in pursuit of Leyla Zana's freedom. I, and 143 of my colleagues in Congress have signed a letter to President Clinton urging him to seek Leyla Zana's immediate and unconditional release from prison. More Members of Congress are standing with Leyla Zana and the Kurdish people now than ever before. Without a doubt, the U.S. Congress is becoming more aware of, and more sympathetic to, the plight of the Kurdish people.

Kurds in Iran, Iraq, Syria, as well as Turkey live as second class citizens, denied the basic human rights of life, liberty, and the pursuit of happiness. Because of the inspiring work of Leyla Zana and thousands of others, the oppression of the Kurdish minority will someday come to an end. To achieve this result, it is far better to use peaceful measures and end the longstanding violence. Thus, we

must embrace Leyla Zana for risking her life for the Kurdish people, not through violence, but through peaceful and democratic activism.

So, Mr. Speaker, I salute those who are fasting today in support of the freedom of Leyla Zana. And I say to the Government of Turkey: in the name of humanity, free Leyla Zana.

193.

[November 13, 1997 (House), pp. 10870-73]

EXPRESSING SENSE OF HOUSE CONCERNING NEED FOR INTERNATIONAL CRIMINAL TRIBUNAL TO TRY MEMBERS OF IRAQI REGIME

Mr. GILMAN. Madam Speaker, I move to suspend the rules and agree to the concurrent resolution (H. Con. Res. 137) expressing the sense of the House of Representatives concerning the urgent need for an international criminal tribunal to try members of the Iraqi regime for crimes against humanity.

The Clerk read as follows:

H. Con. Res. 137

Whereas the regime of Saddam Hussein has perpetrated a litany of human rights abuses against the citizens of Iraq and other peoples of the region, including summary and arbitrary executions, torture, cruel and inhumane treatment, arbitrary arrest and imprisonment, disappearances and the repression of freedom of speech, thought, expression, assembly and association;

Whereas Saddam Hussein and his associates have systematically attempted to destroy the Kurdish population in Iraq through the use of chemical weapons against civilian Kurds , the Anfal campaigns of 1987-1988 that resulted in the disappearance of more than 182,000 persons and the destruction of more than 4,000 villages, the placement of more than ten million landmines in Iraqi Kurdistan , and the continued ethnic cleansing of the city of Kirkuk;

Whereas the Iraqi Government, under Saddam Hussein's leadership, has repressed the Sunni tribes in western Iraq, destroyed Assyro-Chaldean churches and villages, deported and executed Turkomen, massacred Shi'ites, and destroyed the ancient Marsh Arab civilization through a massive act of ecocide;

Whereas the status of more than six hundred Kuwaitis who were taken prisoner during the Gulf War remain unknown and the whereabouts of these persons are unaccounted for by the Iraqi Government, Kuwait continues to be plagued by unexploded landmines six years after the end of the Gulf War, and the destruction of Kuwait by departing Iraqi troops has yet to be redressed by the Iraqi Government;

Whereas the Republic of Iraq is a signatory to the Universal Declaration on Human Rights, the International Covenant on Civil and Political Rights, the Convention on the Prevention and Punishment of the Crime of Genocide and other human rights instruments, and the Geneva Convention on the Treatment of Prisoners of War of August 12, 1949, and is obligated to comply with these international agreements;

Whereas Saddam Hussein and his regime have created an environment of terror and fear within Iraq and throughout the region through a concerted policy of violations of international customary and conventional law; and

Whereas the Congress is deeply disturbed by the continuing gross violations of human rights by the Iraqi Government under the direction and control of Saddam Hussein: Now, therefore, be it

Resolved by the House of Representatives (the Senate concurring), That it is the sense of the House of Representatives that—

(1) the Congress—

(A) deplores the Iraqi Government's pattern of gross violation of human rights which has resulted in a pervasive system of repression, sustained by the widespread use of terror and intimidation;

(B) condemns the Iraqi Government's repeated use of force and weapons of mass destruction against its own citizens, as well as neighboring states;

(C) denounces the refusal of the Iraqi Government to comply with international human rights instruments to which it is a party and cooperate with international monitoring

bodies and compliance mechanisms, including accounting of missing Kuwaiti prisoners; and

(2) the President and the Secretary of State should—

(A) endorse the formation of an international criminal tribunal for the purpose of prosecuting Saddam Hussein and all other Iraqi officials who are responsible for crimes against humanity, including unlawful use of force, crimes against the peace, crimes committed in contravention of the Geneva Convention on POW's and the crime of genocide; and

(B) work actively and urgently within the international community for the adoption of a United Nations Security Council resolution establishing an International Criminal Court for Iraq.

The SPEAKER pro tempore. Pursuant to the rule, the gentleman from New York [Mr. Gilman] and the gentleman from Florida [Mr. Hastings] each will control 20 minutes.

The Chair recognizes the gentleman from New York [Mr. Gilman].

Mr. GILMAN. Madam Speaker, I yield myself such time as I may consume.

(Mr. GILMAN asked and was given permission to revise and extend his remarks.)

GENERAL LEAVE

Mr. GILMAN. Madam Speaker, I ask unanimous consent that all Members may have 5 legislative days within which to revise and extend their remarks on this measure.

The SPEAKER pro tempore. Is there objection to the request of the gentleman from New York?

There was no objection.

□1400

Madam Speaker, the resolution before us today, House Concurrent Resolution 137, which I introduced, along with our colleague the gentleman from Illinois [Mr. Porter], cochairman of the Human Rights Caucus, expresses a sense of the House concerning urgent need for an international war crimes tribunal to try Saddam Hussein and members of his Iraqi regime for crimes against humanity.

I want to thank the gentleman from Illinois [Mr. Porter] for his leadership on this important issue. The critical need for this measure is highlighted by the events taking place just as we speak. House Concurrent Resolution 137 notes that dictator Saddam Hussein has perpetrated a litany of human rights abuses against the citizens of Iraq, including arbitrary executions, torture, cruel and inhumane treatment, arbitrary arrest and imprisonment, and disappearances.

Saddam Hussein has attempted to destroy the Kurdish population in Iraq through the use of chemical weapons. He has repressed Sunni tribes in western Iraq, destroyed Assyro-Chaldean churches and villages, executed Turkomen, and massacred Shiites. Saddam Hussein has also continued to commit ecocide against the ancient Marsh Arab civilization.

Saddam Hussein's brutality is not limited only to his fellow Iraqis. We recall the dark days of the Gulf War, which witnessed Saddam's holding Kuwait and its innocent citizens hostage for so many months. The whereabouts of more than 600 Kuwaitis who were taken prisoner during the Gulf War still remains unknown and unaccounted for by the Iraqi Government.

House Concurrent Resolution 137, therefore, expresses a sense of Congress deploring the Iraqi Government's pattern of gross violations of human rights and denounces Saddam's refusal to comply with international human rights documents to which Iraqi is signatory. This bill also endorses the creation of an international criminal tribunal to prosecute Saddam Hussein and his henchmen and urges the President and Secretary of State to work actively toward the adoption of a United Nations Security Council resolution establishing an international criminal court for Iraq.

Accordingly, Mr. Speaker, I urge our colleagues' strong support for the adoption of House Concurrent Resolution 137.

Mr. Speaker, I reserve the balance of my time.

Mr. HASTINGS of Florida. Mr. Speaker, I yield myself such time as I may consume.

Mr. Speaker, I commend the Chair and the gentleman from Illinois [Mr. Porter] for their efforts on this timely resolution. And I know that I speak for my colleagues, particu-larly the ranking member, the gentleman from Indiana [Mr. Hamilton], in indicating our feelings with reference to this particular resolution.

We do not oppose this resolution. I join the chairman at this time in condemning Iraq's gross violation of human rights. Those who commit such crimes should be brought before an international criminal court, as this resolution correctly states. I do question, however, and several of us do, whether this resolution is likely to have much impact.

The resolution calls for an international court to bring Saddam Hussein to justice. But this resolution does not tell us how we get from here to there. The chief concern that I wish to express is that this resolution will raise expectations, especially in Kuwait, that such an international court will be created. But we do not, by our actions today, create a court or make it significantly more likely that such a court will be created.

I do, however, strongly support the resolution. It urges the United States to work for a U.N. resolution creating an international criminal court for Iraq. I would hope that we would continue in a vigorous manner to urge the United Nations to do that.

Mr. Speaker, I yield 3 minutes to the distinguished gentlewoman from Oregon [Ms. Furse].

Ms. FURSE. Mr. Speaker, I thank the gentleman from Florida [Mr. Hastings] for yielding me the time.

I rise in support of this bill. What I would like to say, though, is that every great human rights struggle has involved personal responsibility and sacrifice. Today, Mr. Speaker, a brave group of hunger strikers are highlighting the human rights issues posed by the Turkish Government against the Kurdish population, also the Kurdish population, you notice a connection with this bill, the Kurdish population and Kurdish elected officials.

I would like to quote to my colleagues from a letter which was sent to President Clinton and signed by 153 Representatives which highlights the terrible situation of a Kurdish politician who was elected by her people and who is in prison for violating Kurdish law. All she did was speak out, as any Parliamentarian does. As I today speak out for human rights, she was speaking out.

In our letter to Mr. Clinton we say, one of the charges against Mrs. Zana was her 1993 appearance, here in Washington, at the invitation of the U.S. Congress. We say, we find it outrageous that although she had been invited to participate, her activities led to her imprisonment. We actively today, Mr. Speaker, seek and call on the administration to look for the release of Leyla Zana and to look at the terrible situation of the Kurdish people in Turkey.

I got a letter just the other day from our Representative to the United Nations, former Congressman Bill Richardson; and he said, Leyla Zana's case is one of four convictions which are being appealed to the European Human Rights Commission. Four of those convictions.

Mr. Speaker, I say today that we must focus the light of the American conscience on those people who are standing today in solidarity with the Turkish citizens, whether they be in Iraq or Turkey. And especially I want to draw attention to those brave citizens who have decided to take their lives at stake, their own health, by standing with Mrs. Zana and other Kurdish officials who have been imprisoned in Turkey.

I thank the chairman for allowing me to speak on this issue. This is an issue, just as the bill is an issue, of human rights violations to the Kurdish population. It is up to us, as Members of Congress and members of the greatest democracy in the world, to speak out when we see human rights violations, whether it be our friends or our enemies who are creating these violations.

I thank the gentleman from Florida [Mr. Hastings] for letting me use this time, and I thank him for his great work for human rights, as also the chairman the gentleman from New York [Mr. Gilman], who have stood for human rights in this country, in this body. And together, I think that we will all join to try and get the release of these Turkish elected officials who are Kurdish and who are speaking for their own citizens.

So, today, I join in solidarity with those hunger strikers. And I have heard them say,

"Oh, well, these are terrorists." I remember when Nelson Mandela in South Africa was termed a "terrorist." A terrorist is also a freedom fighter. These people are seeking freedom for their people.

Mr. GILMAN. Mr. Speaker, I yield 7 minutes to the gentleman from Illinois [Mr. Porter], the distinguished cochairman of the Human Rights Caucus.

Mr. PORTER. Mr. Speaker, let me thank the able and distinguished chairman the gentleman from New York [Mr. Gilman] for yielding me this time, but more importantly, for bringing this very significant legislation to the floor today.

In light of what is going on in Iraq at this moment, this could not be a more timely resolution. Once again, Saddam Hussein is showing his true colors as a ruthless dictator who will attempt to do anything to manipulate his way out of sanctions and weapons monitoring through whatever means he can.

Mr. Speaker, I grew up in an era characterized, unfortunately, by ruthless dictators— Hitler, Mussolini and Stalin—individuals who committed crimes of unspeakable horror against their own people, against their minorities. And the regime in Iraq is identical to the types that were run in Nazi Germany, in Fascist Italy, and in Communist Soviet Union under Stalin.

We must stop Saddam Hussein now. We must isolate him and make certain that the world understands the nature of his ruthless regime. We must make certain that Saddam Hussein and every one of his henchmen are indicted as war criminals and individuals who commit crimes against humanity.

I am pleased to be an original cosponsor of this legislation to bring him to justice for the crimes he has committed against the Iraqi people and against the citizens of other countries whom he has harmed, including our own people. The Kurdish people, the Marsh Arabs, the Assyrian minority, the members of the Iraqi National Congress, the Kuwaiti prisoners of war, these are just a few of the victims of Saddam and his ruthless regime.

Mr. Speaker, he has used chemical weapons against his own people. In 1988, 8,000

Kurds were killed in Halabja by one poison gas attack using the chemical agent sarin that he had produced. Now we are in Iraq trying to determine where he keeps those supplies and of an even worse nerve agent, VX, that just like sarin can kill people in the way he killed Iraqi Kurds in Halabja—mercilessly and indiscriminately.

He has waged ecological war against his own people, the Marsh Arabs. He has tortured, murdered, and kidnapped to maintain power. Saddam Hussein has clearly committed, in my judgment, crimes against humanity, crimes against the peace, and gross breaches of humanitarian law. If there is any individual in the world who deserves to be brought to justice today, it is Saddam Hussein.

I would commend this resolution to my colleagues and urge all of them to join me in sending a strong message to Saddam Hussein and the international community that the United States has not forgotten his crimes, that we hold him accountable for these abuses, and we demand justice for his victims.

Mr. Speaker, on the steps of the Capitol right now there are people, Kurds, who are starving themselves. They are I believe 25 days into a hunger strike to free Leyla Zana, a Turkish Parliamentarian who was elected in 1991, came to the United States in 1993 to testify about human rights abuses against the Kurdish minority in her country, testified before a standing committee of Congress and before the Congressional Human Rights Caucus, went home, was then stripped of her office by her government, placed in jail, tried for what is equivalent to treason, and given a 15-year sentence for merely speaking her mind and testifying before the United States Congress.

Turkey and Iraq together at this moment, Mr. Speaker, are attacking the Kurds in northern Iraq. Turkey has come across the line with tens of thousands of their elite troops, using napalm and cluster bombs against the Kurdish minority that has fled their country. Iraq is joining in on the other side. Both are persecuting the Kurds at this moment. Each of the countries in which the Kurds exist as a minority, in Turkey, in Iraq, in Iran, in Syria, each one of them oppresses that minority. Each one of them turns Kurd against Kurd in an effort to

oppress them, and each one of them calls the Kurdish people, who would seek only basic human rights, terrorists, when they are only protecting themselves from oppression.

Mr. Speaker, the oppression must end. The Kurds are not terrorists. There may be some who believe they have no other way out, but the Kurdish people are not terrorists. They are people simply seeking their rights, their rights against the Turkish Government, their rights against the Iranian Government, their rights against the Syrian Government, and their rights also against the Iraqi regime of Saddam Hussein.

It is the governments who oppress them that are the terrorists. It is the governments who deny them their basic human rights, deny them respect and standing in their communities, kill them and their children on a daily basis, attempt to drive them out of their societies—those are the true terrorists, Mr. Speaker.

The chief among them is Saddam Hussein, whose regime responds to nothing, not to public pressure, not to resolutions from the Security Council. It is time that we isolate this regime. It is time that we declare Saddam Hussein to be what he is, a person who commits crimes against humanity that all of us abhor. It is time that we indict him and try him and remove him from power, and that we return Iraq to a State that can live in the world community at peace with its neighbors and stop this murderous, ruthless dictatorial regime from further oppressing its people and threatening its neighbors.

Mr. HASTINGS of Florida. Mr. Speaker, I am pleased to yield 3 minutes to the distinguished gentleman from California [Mr. Lantos], a continuing champion for human rights around the world.

□ 1415

Mr. LANTOS. Mr. Speaker, I thank the gentleman for yielding me this time. I want to commend the cochairman on the Republican side of the Congressional Human Rights Caucus, the gentleman from Illinois [Mr. Porter], for his powerful and eloquent statement, and I want to commend the chairman of the Committee on International Relations, who has been indefatigable in his fight for human rights, in bringing H. Con. Res. 137 before us.

I fully concur with all previous statements made concerning Saddam Hussein and his despicable regime. It is remarkable, Mr. Speaker, that even at this late date there are apologies for Saddam Hussein and his brutal and cruel regime in the West. There are countries that can hardly wait to renew on a large scale their lucrative business deals with Iraq, despite the fact that the Saddam Hussein regime has been attempting to conceal, hide, obfuscate its continuing development of weapons of mass destruction.

Later this afternoon, this body will have an opportunity of dealing with a resolution that expresses the view of the House that if peaceful and diplomatic measures do not succeed, military action, preferably on a multinational scale, be undertaken to eliminate Hussein's chemical, biological, nuclear and missile capability. But while that is a military issue, this is a human rights issue. A regime which has poison gassed its own people, a regime which perpetrates the worst human rights violations of the 20th century against its own people, does indeed need to be hauled before an international tribunal and tried for crimes against humanity. If there was central casting's appropriate person to be hauled before the international community for crimes against humanity, it is Saddam Hussein. His brutality, his ruthlessness, his bloodthirstiness, knows no bounds.

I call on all of my colleagues across the aisle to vote to approve this important measure.

Mr. GILMAN. Mr. Speaker, I yield 3 minutes to the gentleman from California [Mr. Rohrabacher], a member of our committee.

Mr. ROHRABACHER. Mr. Speaker, I rise in strong support of the Porter amendment to indict Saddam Hussein for crimes against humanity and war crimes as well. I voted for the gulf war, and I did so reluctantly but I knew that our national well-being and our national security were at stake. I then cheered the troops when they came home victorious, what seemed to be one of the greatest and most glorious victories in our country's history.

Yet the job was not finished. If President Bush has anything to regret, it should be the fact that he sent our troops by the hundreds of thousands to the Persian Gulf and we did not finish the job when our people were there.

It is clear that the enemy of the United States was not the people of Iraq. The Porter amendment today focuses on the real enemy of not only the United States but people who believe in democratic rights and human rights, Saddam Hussein and his clique of thugs that control Iraq. During the gulf war we killed hundreds of thousands, perhaps hundreds of thousands of young men, and perhaps some women and children as well, who were not enemies of the United States. Many of those people had just been drafted into the army by a tyrant named Saddam Hussein.

This amendment goes straight to the heart of the issue. Saddam Hussein is our enemy. We should indict this man. He should be brought to trial like any other war criminal, whether it was Adolf Hitler or some of the Serbian gangsters who have committed genocide more recently in Bosnia.

Again, this underscores and what has happened underscores that there is a relationship between peace and freedom and prosperity. If we go for short-term peace and we try to bring our troops home too soon or we cut deals with tyrants, it will bring us neither peace nor freedom. We cannot compromise the value of freedom because in the end it will bring us to a situation where our security is under attack.

Let us not forget, as well, that over 600 Kuwaiti POW's have yet to be accounted for. There are thousands upon thousands of Kuwaiti families who are missing a member of their family who have never been accounted for, who were killed or taken away by the Iraqis when they invaded that country and occupied it for that year. That is the equivalent of millions of Americans who would have a family member lost and unaccounted for. There must be an accounting of the Kuwaiti prisoners of war. There must be an accounting of Saddam Hussein for all of his crimes.

Let us remember that when the Soviet Union began to evolve into what is now a democratic Russia or continues to struggle to try to be a democratic Russia, the chances for peace went up. A demand for freedom in Iraq and an elimination of this tyrant, Saddam Hussein, will increase the chances for peace in that entire region and secure the United States of America as well. I strongly support the amendment of the gentleman from Illinois [Mr. Porter] to bring Saddam Hussein to task.

Mr. GILMAN. Mr. Speaker, I thank the gentleman from California [Mr. Rohrabacher] for his eloquent words.

Mr. Speaker, I yield 2 minutes to the gentleman from Virginia [Mr. Wolf].

(Mr. WOLF asked and was given permission to revise and extend his remarks.) Mr. WOLF. Mr. Speaker, I rise in very strong support of H. Con. Res. 137, which condemns the government of Iraq for its continued reign of terror against the Kurds , and that is what it has basically been for the last several years, a reign of terror that unfortunately the West has not focused on. But with this resolution and with the effort that the Kurds are now making, I think more and more people are focusing on it.

What this would do is encourage the establishment of a war crimes tribunal to try Saddam Hussein and the other Iraqi officials for their crimes against humanity. I want to commend the gentleman from Illinois [Mr. Porter], the gentleman from New York [Mr. Gilman], and the other Members for sponsoring this resolution. Hopefully this resolution will send a message not only through the United States, but to the Kurdish population around the world and particularly in that area, that the United States Congress, the people's House, cares very, very deeply.

Iraq is a bad actor government. Saddam Hussein is a brutal dictator who cares about nothing more than hanging onto his power. He has persecuted the people of Iraq. He is engaging in a dangerous showdown with the West. He is not afraid to murder members of his own family who threaten to tell the truth about his brutality or threaten his reign.

He is seeking to wipe out the Kurds of northern Iraq who are trapped because of their geography. The Kurds of northern Iraq have nowhere to go to escape their plight. They have been and are being murdered, imprisoned, tortured and repressed. Hopefully with this resolution, sponsored by the gentleman

from Illinois [Mr. Porter] and supported by the gentleman from New York [Mr. Gilman] and so many other Members, it will send a message to Saddam Hussein that the West cares, and send a message to the Kurds that are going through this problem that we deeply care and that we stand with them.

Mr. GILMAN. I thank the gentleman from Virginia [Mr. Wolf] for his kind remarks in support of the resolution.

Mr. Speaker, I yield 4 minutes to the gentleman from Texas [Mr. Paul].

Mr. PAUL. I thank the gentleman for yielding me this time.

Mr. Speaker, I agree certainly with the sharp criticism against the government and the leaders of Iraq. I do disagree with what we are trying to do here, not because it is not well motivated, but I do not see that we have the authority to all of a sudden impose our system of justice across the entire world. I do not think it is effective. I think it drums up anti-American hostility more than it achieves justice.

But there is a bit of inconsistency here. Earlier it was mentioned that it is not only the Iraqis that abuse the Kurds , the Turks do it as well. Why are the Turks not included in this? Why do we not call them out and put them on the carpet and demand justice from the Turks? But they happen to be our allies.

At the same time, we ignore other major problems. What did we do with China? The leaders of China came here, they got the red carpet treatment and a promise of more money. But how do they treat their people at Tiananmen Square and currently throughout their whole country? They abuse civil liberties there.

But are we going to do the same thing? Do Members think we can do that? We pick and choose and pretend that we are going to perform this great system of justice on the world. Indonesia today, they are getting bailed out by the American taxpayer to the tune of tens of billions of dollars. They mistreat in a serious manner the people in East Timor. But here we decide all of a sudden that we are going to, through the United Nations, expose the American taxpayer, expose young American soldiers, because how are we going to enforce these things? Where do we get this authority to be the policeman of the world?

I do not believe we have this authority. I believe it is detrimental overall to our national security. I believe it is a threat to the American people and indirectly, in many ways, to the taxpayer. I object. I object generally to so many of these amendments, so well-intended. I do not disagree with the challenges, the charges made against Iraq and the leadership. I strongly criticize the approach to trying to solve this very serious problem.

Mr. ROHRABACHER. Mr. Speaker, will the gentleman yield?

Mr. PAUL. I yield to the gentleman from California.

Mr. ROHRABACHER. First, would the gentleman suggest that there is not a relationship between freedom and peace?

Mr. PAUL. Mr. Speaker, I am not sure what the gentleman is getting at. I know the most important thing for freedom and peace is for me to obey the Constitution. Where is it the authority of the Constitution for us to police the world?

Mr. ROHRABACHER. The gentleman is suggesting, then, that this body should not have condemned Adolf Hitler until he actually attacked the United States, is that what he would suggest? Is that his foreign policy?

Mr. PAUL. I think that is not the debate on the floor right now. I think when our national security is threatened, the American people have a right to vote through their Congressmen for a declaration of war.

This is the kind of thing that leads to Vietnam War-type wars and U.N. sanctions. This is the kind of thing that leads to Koreas, Vietnams and useless wars. This is why we did not win the war in the Persian Gulf and why we are still faced with this problem.

Mr. ROHRABACHER. Short of a declaration of war, the gentleman does not think the United States Government should do anything about tyranny?

Mr. PAUL. I believe in the responsibility of this U.S. Congress to assume that they are the ones that declare war in a proper manner.

Mr. Speaker, in closing, I have no criticism about those who are challenging the leadership in Iraq. I condemn them. I challenge, though, the technique that we are using, the process that we are using. I do not believe we have the authority. Long-term, it is not effective.

It is totally inconsistent when we are dealing with China. These token resolutions that we dealt with on China will have nothing to do with solving the problem. At the same time, we give them more money, we give the Turks more money, we give China more money, we give Indonesia more money, and they are all in the process of abusing civil liberties. I just think that we have conveniently picked a whipping horse and we are pretending that we are doing some good.

Mr. HASTINGS of Florida. Mr. Speaker, I yield 2 minutes to the gentleman from Illinois [Mr. Porter].

Mr. PORTER. Mr. Speaker, I just wanted to say to the gentleman who just finished speaking that I certainly respect the consistency of his ideas, but I disagree. If he had expressed those ideas as a member of the parliament in Turkey or if he expressed them in Iraq or in Indonesia, he might well find himself in the same situation as Leyla Zana and the Kurdish parliamentarians found themselves and, that is, behind bars. It seems to me that if we do not recognize that we are our brothers' and sisters' keeper, that our freedoms and theirs are in some way connected, we will invite the kind of terrorism that Saddam Hussein practices on his people and others practice on their people throughout this world.

Let me agree with him, however, in part. Let us stop giving money to the Turks as long as they repress their people. Let us stop giving money to the Indonesian Government that takes away the religious freedoms of the people of East Timor. Let us stop supporting dictators that deny the basic human rights of their people.

I believe that we attempt very strongly to be consistent. We passed nine bills dealing with China. Those bills do have a potential, particularly the one on Radio Free Asia that will broadcast to China and Tibet and North

Korea and Burma. I think we have a potential for positively impacting their society.

Let us never give up our ideals and our beliefs in human freedom, the very foundation of this society, because we might see a little inconsistency or cannot find the exact words we want to give us authority. The authority is moral authority, and it has a great power in this world if only we will exercise it.

Mr. HASTINGS of Florida. Mr. Speaker, I yield back the balance of my time.

Mr. GILMAN. Mr. Speaker, I yield back the balance of my time.

The SPEAKER pro tempore (Mr. Snowbarger). The question is on the motion offered by the gentleman from New York [Mr. Gilman] that the House suspend the rules and agree to the concurrent resolution, House Concurrent Resolution 137.

The question was taken. Mr. PORTER. Mr. Speaker, on that I demand the yeas and nays.

The yeas and nays were ordered.

The SPEAKER pro tempore. Pursuant to clause 5 of rule I and the Chair's prior announcement, further proceedings on this motion will be postponed.

194.

[February 4, 1998 (Extensions of Remarks), p. E95]

CONCERN ABOUT "THE TURKISH UNDERWORLD"
HON. ELIOT L. ENGEL
OF NEW YORK
IN THE HOUSE OF REPRESENTATIVES

Wednesday, February 4, 1998

Mr. ENGEL. Mr. Speaker, I rise to call attention to a growing problem in Turkey. Although it is a member of NATO and a democracy, Turkey is currently experiencing a growth of government-connected crime. Indeed, a recent official report has found that former Prime Minister Tansu Ciller's administration conspired with a broad range of criminal organizations to eliminate political

enemies of the Turkish government domestically and abroad. I commend the following editorial, "The Turkish Underworld," published in the *New York Times* on January 30, 1998, to my colleagues for a fuller explanation of this serious dilemma.

I ask unanimous consent that the text of the article be printed at this point in the Congressional Record . . .

195.

[March 12, 1998 (Senate), pp. 1867-69]

INDICTMENT AND PROSECUTION OF SADDAM HUSSEIN

Mr. President, I have been asked by our distinguished majority leader to request that we now proceed to Calendar No. 322, relative to the war crimes, under the provisions of the consent agreement entered into on March 9, 1998.

The PRESIDING OFFICER. The clerk will state the concurrent resolution by title.

The legislative clerk read as follows:

A concurrent resolution (S. Con. Res. 78) relating to the indictment and prosecution of Saddam Hussein for war crimes and other crimes against humanity.

The Senate proceeded to consider the concurrent resolution.

Mr. SPECTER. Mr. President, the majority leader has asked me to express his intention to have a vote on this resolution occur tomorrow at around 9:30 a.m. and the majority leader notes that he will inform all Members as to when that vote is set by unanimous consent.

The majority leader has also asked me to announce—if I may have the attention of the majority leader on this part—the majority leader has asked me to announce that there will be no further rollcall votes this afternoon. I hesitate to do that on my own, but, with Senator Lott here—and he says, now, the vote will be fixed with precision at 9:30 in the morning.

The PRESIDING OFFICER. The Senator from Pennsylvania.

Mr. SPECTER. Mr. President, this resolution has been offered by Senator Dorgan and myself. The most expeditious way to move to the import of the resolution is to read the "resolved" clause. It is as follows:

That the President should:

(1) call for the creation of a commission under the auspices of the United Nations to establish an international record of the criminal culpability of Saddam Hussein, and other Iraqi officials;

(2) call for the United Nations to form an international criminal tribunal for the purpose of indicting, prosecuting, and imprisoning Saddam Hussein and other Iraqi officials who are responsible for crimes against humanity, genocide, and other violations of international law; and

(3) upon the creation of such an international criminal tribunal, take steps necessary, including the reprogramming of funds, to ensure United States support for efforts to bring Saddam Hussein and other Iraqi officials to justice.

This move to try Saddam Hussein as a war criminal is the most recent in a series of moves to establish the international rule of law with an international criminal court. The antecedent for this activity lay in the international military tribunal at Nuremberg, which was convened to try individuals for crimes against international law committed during World War II. The Nuremberg tribunal provisions stated that:

Crimes against international law are committed by men, not abstract entities, and only by punishing individuals who commit such crimes can the provisions of international law be enforced.

That statement is as valid today as it was in 1946. For more than a decade, many of us in the Congress of the United States have sought to create an international criminal court to deal with crimes against humanity and other international crimes. Senator Dodd and I have authored a series of resolutions in the U.S. Senate. In the House of Representatives, under the leadership of Congressman Jim Leach, a number of resolutions have been offered. The international criminal court is moving forward,

with a realistic likelihood of the establishment of such an international criminal court in the not too far distant future. And, in the interim, the War Crimes Tribunal has been established by the United Nations to try crimes against humanity from the former Yugoslavia, the offenses committed in Bosnia and related territories, and for crimes against humanity committed in Rwanda.

The War Crimes Tribunal is in existence. I have had the opportunity to visit it on three occasions to see the operation of the Tribunal. It would be merely an extension of the War Crimes Tribunal to include the import of the current resolution so that Saddam Hussein could be tried as a war criminal.

The specifics are that in 1988 the Iraqi Government, under the direction of Saddam Hussein, carried out a systematic campaign to destroy the Kurdish population in Iraq. Kurdish leaders estimated the death toll of this campaign at between 50,000 and 182,000.

On March 16, 1988, Iraqi aircraft bombed the city of Halabja, then in the hands of Iranian-supported Kurdish rebels. That bombing was with chemical weapons, and more than 5,000 women and children died in that attack.

Iraqi chemical weapons were used in 1982 to 1984 in the Iran-Iraq war. The Iraqis developed their proficiency in chemical weapons gradually during the war with Iran. The Iraqis initially used chemical weapons against the Iranians in 1982, and the next recorded deployment was in July 1983, when the Iraqis used mustard gas against an Iranian force. Large quantities of mustard gas were used in November 1983 and February 1984. They may also have used a nerve agent in the February 1984 attack.

With respect to the Iraq-Kuwait crisis, from January 18, 1991, to February 25, 1991, Iraq fired 39 Scud conventional warhead missiles at Israel in 18 separate attacks, killing 2 persons directly, killing 12 people indirectly, and injuring more than 200 persons.

On December 18, 1990, Amnesty International issued a report that stated Iraq tortured or executed hundreds of Kuwaitis suspected of conducting guerrilla warfare against Iraqi forces. Thousands of Kuwaitis were arrested for resisting Iraqi orders. Amnesty International also reported that some 312 premature babies died after the Iraqi troops stole their incubators.

Iraq committed deliberate and calculated crimes of environmental terrorism in the region by its willful ignition of more than 700 Kuwaiti oil wells in February 1991.

In the spring of 1993, the Government of Kuwait informed the U.S. administration that it had discovered evidence that Iraq sponsored an attempt to assassinate former President Bush and destabilize Kuwait during his April 14, 15, and 16 visit to Kuwait. The Federal Bureau of Investigation and other U.S. intelligence agencies were sent to Kuwait to conduct their own investigation and reported back to the President on June 24, 1993, that their findings confirmed the view that Iraq was behind the plot.

Iraq denied that it attempted to assassinate the President. But the proof, being overwhelming, led the United States, on June 26, 1993, to launch 23 Tomahawk missiles at Iraqi intelligence headquarters.

On June 28, 1993, President Clinton sent the Congress a letter describing the missile attack on Iraq being "consistent with the War Powers Resolution."

This is a very brief summary of the war crimes committed by Saddam Hussein and others. We have found on the international scene the conduct of Saddam Hussein to be reprehensible in many other respects. Saddam Hussein has flagrantly violated the U.N. resolutions, carrying the world to the brink of conflict and then backing down at the last minute. It would be a very salutary matter to have Saddam Hussein indicted and tried as a war criminal. It is obvious that taking Saddam Hussein into custody is a very complex matter and perhaps impossible without an enormous military force. By 20/20 hindsight, Saddam Hussein should have been taken into custody in the 1991 Persian Gulf war, but that is 20/20 hindsight.

There have been a number of calls to have Saddam Hussein toppled. It is not beyond the realm of possibility that insurgent forces within Iraq could lead a revolution. The United States could lend the Voice of America to those efforts. The United States could, con-

sistent with international practices, support those who would move against Saddam Hussein, and in the context where action is contemplated against Saddam Hussein, a resolution for the trial of Saddam Hussein as a war criminal, the indictment itself, the trial, even if in absentia, could give the United States a high moral ground and warrant our action in toppling Saddam Hussein.

I am joined at this time by my distinguished colleague, Senator Dorgan, who is a cosponsor of the resolution. I yield the floor to Senator Dorgan.

The PRESIDING OFFICER (Mr. Bennett). The Senator from North Dakota.

Mr. DORGAN. Mr. President, first, I compliment Senator Specter from Pennsylvania, since he is the original author of this resolution on an international criminal tribunal for Iraq. I very much appreciate his leadership, and I know the Senate appreciates that leadership as well.

This is the right subject. It is something the Senate needs to be discussing. I hope very much that tomorrow, when we vote on this resolution, the Senate will overwhelmingly approve it.

Recently, in the country of Iraq, a state-controlled newspaper proposed that Saddam Hussein be given the Nobel Peace Prize. I doubt whether many Americans would believe that Saddam Hussein would qualify for the Nobel Peace Prize. The only ceremony I believe Saddam Hussein ought to attend in the near future is a war crimes trial. And I expect, in the future, if there were a war crimes trial to be held—and I hope this legislation will be the catalyst to make that happen—I expect in the future no one will again suggest a Nobel Peace Prize for a convicted war criminal.

Why do we say there should be an international tribunal to try Saddam Hussein and other leaders of Iraq for war crimes?

First of all, there is precedent for it, as Senator Specter indicated. In Nuremberg, at the end of World War II, over 200 Nazi leaders were tried between 1945 and 1949. Thirty-seven of them were sentenced to death, 23 to life in prison, and 101 to shorter prison terms.

There is an international tribunal for Rwanda at work right now. Three trials are underway. Thirty-one suspects have been indicted, and nearly all of them are in custody.

The international tribunal for the former Yugoslavia has indicted 79 suspects, of whom 24 are now in custody.

I believe that an international tribunal to try Saddam Hussein and other Iraqi leaders for war crimes should follow on these models. A tribunal for Iraq should be constituted by the United Nations, and war crimes trials should begin.

Iraq's crimes against peace include two wars of aggression: the Iran-Iraq war in which Iraq invaded Iran, and the Persian Gulf war, in which Iraq invaded its southern neighbor, Kuwait.

War crimes committed by Iraqi forces against civilians in Kuwait include extrajudicial and political killings, acts of torture, rapes of civilian women, pillage and looting—all crimes under the Fourth Geneva Convention, which requires wartime protections for civilians.

Iraqi troops committed crimes against third country nationals. They prevented Western and Arab refugees from leaving Iraq and Kuwait. They carried out arbitrary arrests and detentions. Iraq even resorted to hostage taking and use of hostages as human shields.

The Iraqi government committed crimes against prisoners of war. It used physical and mental torture to coerce POWs to reveal information. It used prisoners of war as human shields, and it displayed injured prisoners of war on Iraqi TV.

Iraq committed crimes against diplomats and embassies: it abducted people with diplomatic immunity, and it seized and blockaded embassies in Kuwait.

So Mr. President, the list of war crimes during the Persian Gulf War is a lengthy one. However, Iraq's criminal record goes back further than that.

Human Rights Watch has written extensively about the Anfal campaign against the Kurds living in northern Iraq. This campaign was a policy of systematic and deliberate murder. Human Rights Watch concluded that the Iraqi government killed at least 50,000 and perhaps as many as 100,000 Kurds.

The Anfal campaign involved the destruction of thousands of Kurdish villages and the murder, disappearance, and extermination by chemical weapons or the forcible resettlement of hundreds of thousands of Kurds. This was ethnic cleansing before the term was invented.

Even worse, the Anfal campaign included chemical weapons. A U.S. Government white paper says there were "numerous Iraqi chemical attacks against civilian villages in 1987 and 1988." The white paper lists 10 instances of Iraqi chemical attacks and says that Iraq "delivered...Mustard 5 agent and the nerve gases Sarin and Tabun in aerial bombs, spray dispensers, 120-mm rockets and several types of artillery."

Iraq possesses a chemical weapons program and a biological weapons program. Its chemical stockpile contained 40,000 chemical weapons munitions; 480,000 liters of chemical weapons agents; and 8 delivery systems.

Iraq's biological weapons arsenal included 8,500 liters of anthrax; 19,000 liters of botulinum toxin; and 2,200 liters of alfatoxin. This program was in violation of the Biological Weapons Convention, to which Iraq is a party.

And the list of Iraqi crimes and treaty violations goes on at some length. I ask unanimous consent to have the list printed in the Record at the conclusion of my remarks.

The PRESIDING OFFICER. Without objection, it is so ordered.

(See Exhibit 1.)

Mr. DORGAN. Mr. President, let us look at the behavior and the actions of Saddam Hussein and the regime in Iraq through the horror of what happened to a young boy, now dead, named Dejwar, 5 years of age. In reading Dejwar's story, I am relying on the wonderful reporting work done by Middle East Watch and the Physicians for Human Rights. Human Rights Watch has published this work in a book called, "The Anfal Campaign in Iraqi Kurdistan."

This book tells a terrible story about happened to Dejwar.

On August 25, 1988, at dawn, this 5-year-old boy, with his father, a farmer, was awake inside their house in Birjinni. Hassan, the boy's father, lived there with his father and mother, his four brothers, his wife and four children, of whom Dejwar was one.

Hassan, Dejwar's father, was preparing to go to the orchards that morning. Then the bombs began to drop. The father said that the explosions that morning were not as strong as other bombs that had been dropped on their village by the Government of Iraq.

The surviving villagers described the smoke that morning rising from the bombs as "white, black and then yellow" smoke. Those columns of smoke from the bombs rose 50 to 60 meters in the air.

The smell of gas was "pleasant, at first" that morning. "It smelled of apples," they said, smelled of "something sweet." Several men said it smelled like "pesticides in the fields." Shortly after that, they said "it became bitter. It affected our eyes, and our mouths, and our skin. All of a sudden," they said, "it was hard to breathe. Your breath wouldn't come. You couldn't breathe" at all.

The people of that village—and this is one study of one village, one attack on one morning by the Iraqi Government—did not know what to do when those bombs fell. They began to understand these were not usual bombs, these were chemical bombs.

As the smoke from the chemical bombs settled into the lower land, they said "it drifted down the valley toward the fields and the orchards." The father said, "I took my family, three of my children and my wife, and we ran to higher ground. We went the other direction from the smoke." There was complete panic; people ran in all directions. Families were separated, children lost from their parents. Everyone "was trying to save themselves, each one himself, even the mothers of children, because they couldn't breathe."

But Hassan's father and other family members at first stayed in the house because "they didn't know what the smoke could do." When they realized they were under gas attack, many of them ran down from the village to an orchard in a ravine. The smoke followed them into the ravine.

Hassan and his wife realized that one of their four children was also separated from them, and that was the 5-year-old boy I mentioned, Dejwar. He was missing. He had gone with his grandfather to the orchard in the ravine and stayed there.

When some of the smoke lifted, after about a half an hour, Hassan and other survivors thought it was safe to come to the village. He found his mother and sister "lying on the ground, overcome by the gas." Symptoms: Hands, legs paralyzed, trembling, shaking. They tried to swallow water and couldn't. Their throats were burning. They were vomiting. Hassan later said, "My mother whispered, 'I think there's a hole in my head.'" Within several hours after exposure to the smoke, both mother and sister went blind, according to family members.

Hassan went down from the village and found his father and his son Dejwar lying dead outside the orchard. There were no marks on them. "It was like they were sleeping," he said, "except their faces were blue." Then he found his two brothers dead in a small cave where they had taken refuge.

Mr. President, these are just a few paragraphs in a book describing the experience of one village under attack with chemical weapons by the country of Iraq.

Name another leader on the face of this Earth who has decided, not once but on numerous occasions, to use weapons of mass destruction against his own people and his neighbors. Name one other country. Only Iraq, only Saddam Hussein.

The Senator from Pennsylvania and I and others say it is time, long past the time, when there should be constituted an international tribunal to try these people, who have committed such atrocities, for war crimes. That tribunal will give a much longer presentation of evidence than the Senator from Pennsylvania or I will give today. Maybe then, maybe all of the world will see the systematic presentation of evidence, and hear of the unspeakable horrors that have been visited upon innocent men, women and children. Not just tens of thousands, but hundreds of thousands of people, who have disappeared and been killed and murdered. Some of them were killed by poison gas.

Maybe then the rest of the people in the world will understand this is not just a foreign leader, this is not just the leader of Iraq, this is a convicted war criminal.

A war crimes trial should have happened after the Gulf War. Whether Saddam Hussein is tried in absentia or not is irrelevant to me. The fact that he is tried is very important. We must, as a world, come together and judge actions of this type.

The unspeakable horrors that have been visited upon so many innocent people by this government must not go unnoticed and must not remain unprosecuted. We can, we should, and we will convene an international tribunal. We have done that in the past, and there are two such tribunals ongoing right now.

With the leadership of the Senator from Pennsylvania, we can and will and should convene that international tribunal for Iraq and do the right thing.

This resolution may be controversial for some, who say that the foggy world of diplomacy does not accommodate this kind of decisive and important action. I think the foggy world of diplomacy demands this kind of action.

When diplomatic initiatives occur in the Persian Gulf in the future, it ought not occur between respectable diplomats on one side and Saddam Hussein as a national leader on the other side. It ought to be Saddam Hussein, a convicted war criminal, on the other side, a war criminal convicted by evidence all the world will have seen. That is the purpose of this resolution.

Mr. President, I yield the floor . . .

GENOCIDE AND CRIMES AGAINST HUMANITY

The violations of international law in Kuwait were

systematic and widespread. But the international tribunal should not confine itself simply to the Persian Gulf War—to do so would be to ignore the larger pattern of Saddam Hussein's crimes, of which the invasion of Kuwait was only a part. Criminals, after all, have records—and the criminal record of Saddam Hussein is a long one. It goes back to before the Persian Gulf War, and it continued after the war.

The most enormous crime that Iraqi leaders have committed was the genocidal Anfal campaign against Kurds in rural areas of northern Iraq. Relying on over 300 interviews, field work in Iraqi Kurdistan, and forensic material, and using a captured cache of official Iraqi documents, Human Rights Watch has concluded that the Anfal campaign against Iraqi Kurds involved the "systematic, deliberate murder of at least 50,000, and possibly as many as 100,000, Kurds." The campaign involved the destruction of thousands of Kurdish villages, and the murder, disappearance, extermination by chemical weapons, or forcible resettlement of hundreds of thousands of Kurds.

A Human Rights Watch report describes how this campaign of genocide worked, village by village. "A village was often first shelled or bombed, sometimes with chemical weapons, evidently of the type used in the Iran-Iraq war. The inhabitants, attempting to flee, were trapped by troops enveloping the village." Iraqi security forces would cull out the men and the boys, who disappeared. Eyewitness reports suggest that they were taken south by truck, killed, and buried in mass graves.

These acts against its own Kurdish population make the Iraqi government guilty of genocide, as that crime is defined by the Genocide Convention, to which Iraq became a party in 1959. The Convention prohibits the mass murder of people based on their ethnicity. It is clear from Iraq's own documents that on a mass scale, the Government of Iraq attempted to eliminate Kurds simply because they were Kurds. This is the definition of genocide.

In its campaign against its own Kurdish population, the Iraqi government used chemical weapons left over from its wartime stockpile. A U.S. government white paper on Iraqi weapons of mass destruction says that there were "numerous Iraqi chemical attacks against civilian villages in the 1987 and 1988 time frames... in areas close to both the Iranian and Turkish borders." That same white paper also lists 10 instances of Iraqi chemical attacks against Iranian troops or Kurdish civilians. To quote the report:

"Iraq had an advanced chemical warfare capability that it used extensively against Iran and against its own Kurdish population during the 1980s. Iraqi forces delivered chemical agents (including Mustard 5 agent and the nerve agents Sarin and Tabun 6) in aerial bombs, aerial spray dispensers, 120-mm rockets, and several types of artillery both for tactical military purposes and to terrorize rebellious segments of the population." . . .

196.

[May 14, 1998 (Extensions of Remarks), p. E 867]

CONDEMNING THE ATTACK ON AKIN BIRDAL: TURKEY'S LEADING RIGHTS ADVOCATE
HON. STENY H. HOYER
OF MARYLAND
IN THE HOUSE OF REPRESENTATIVES

Thursday, May 14, 1998

Mr. HOYER. Mr. Speaker, yesterday morning Akin Birdal, the President of the Human Rights Association of Turkey (IHD), was gunned down in his Ankara office. A right-wing squad has claimed responsibility for the attack which left Turkey's most vocal human rights critic comatose.

Since 1986, under Akin Birdal's leadership, the IHD has established itself as the largest independent human rights monitoring NGO in Turkey. Akim Birdal has appeared before the Helsinki Commission and met with its staff in Washington and Ankara. He is in high regard by legislators and diplomats around the world. In recent years he has received awards from the Lawyers Committee for Human Rights, the International Human Rights Law Group and NGOs in Europe. Last year, he was elected Vice-President of the prestigious International Federation of Human Rights Leagues (FIHD).

This vile assault takes place against a backdrop of repression and intimidation against rights workers throughout Turkey. The Government of Turkey has criminalized non-violent human rights advocacy. Security forces and right-wing death squads have collaborated in the murders of human rights activities, Journalists, Kurdish dissidents and others. More than a dozen IHD offices have been closed by authorities and IHD leaders, including Mr. Birdal face continuous legal and other harassment.

Mr. Speaker, despite great personal danger, Akin Birdal and his colleagues dared to continue speaking against human rights violations by the State. The IHD has been especially critical of the "dirty war" waged against Turkey's Kurdish rebels. In recent weeks, the climate of intimidation escalated. Mr. Birdal reported numerous death threats against himself and his family. Unsubstantiated allegations by security officials leaked to the media stated that Birdal took orders from the PKK, an outlawed Kurdish guerrilla group. Mr. Birdal vigorously denied such allegations and denounced the "primitive conspiracy" orchestrated by Turkey's military rulers against their "enemies list."

Mr. Speaker, the shooting of Akin Birdal is a great tragedy for all who cherish human rights. His steadfast support for peace and non- violence is an inspiration to many in Turkey and abroad. IHD was working with NGOs around the world to commemorate the 50th anniversary of the Universal Declaration of Human Rights. On this auspicious occasion, it is sad to note deteriorating human rights conditions in Turkey and a steady slide towards outright military rule. Instead of supporting the work of independent human rights NGOs, which make significant contributions to development of civil society and the rule of law, the Government of Turkey instead represses them, labels their members "terrorists," and makes them open targets.

Mr. Speaker, the United States Government supports Turkey militarily, economically and politically. Turkey is a NATO ally and member of the Organization for Security and Cooperation in Europe. I therefore welcome the settlement by the State Department spokesperson condemning the attack and urging that the perpetrators be brought to justice.

However, our government must do more to demonstrate our commitment to democracy in Turkey. If we truly value a stable and long-term relationship, we must not continue to ignore the fact that the military's predominance in politics precludes true democracy. The inability of military or civilian administrations to peacefully address the Kurdish problem or the rise of Islamic political activism remains a recipe for disaster. The resulting political instability fuels the climate in which human rights activists are attacked, free speech is curtailed and other fundamental freedoms eroded.

Mr. Speaker, as I speak today, my thoughts and prayers are with Akin Birdal, his family, his colleagues at IHD and all those in Turkey committed to the ideals of human rights and democracy. It is a sad day for all, and we can only hope that this incident will make people think and act seriously about the state of human rights in Turkey.

197.

[August 4, 1998 (House), 7004]

U.S. CONTINUES TO IGNORE PLIGHT OF KURDISH PEOPLE

The SPEAKER pro tempore. Under the Speaker's announced policy of January 21, 1997, the gentlewoman from Oregon (Ms. Furse) is recognized during morning hour debates for 2 minutes.

Ms. FURSE. Madam Speaker, I rise today on behalf of 40 million people who have an identity, but do not have a country. The Kurdish people. Their land continues to be a setting for war and destruction that has lasted for decades.

The Kurds are a persecuted minority. It is a crime in Turkey to talk about Kurds or Kurdish issues. One cannot fly a Kurdish flag or even address another by his Kurdish name.

Madam Speaker, I am outraged wherever violations of human rights occur, but I am particularly enraged and distressed that our country continues to ignore the Kurdish people and their plight. For years, the U.S. has neglected reports and testimony from the Kurdish people about the human rights viola-

tions. Madam Speaker, our government must engage in and develop a Kurdish policy. We cannot continue to stand by as millions of their people suffer.

Now, Turkey is an important partner of the United States. It is a NATO member, gets huge amounts of money from us, but its abuses of the Kurdish people are unacceptable.

I would like to draw my colleagues' attention to Leyla Zana, who is an elected member of the Turkish Parliament. She is the first Kurdish woman to ever be elected. She is also a nominee for the Nobel Peace Prize. But Leyla Zana was arrested and severely tortured by the Turkish police in 1988. What was her crime? She engaged in peaceful demonstrations on behalf of prisoners who were also being tortured, and for respect for human dignity and the universal declaration of human rights, Leyla Zana, a parliamentarian, is currently serving a 15-year sentence with 4 other Kurdish members of the Turkish Parliament.

Leyla Zana writes, and I quote, that she is determined "to continue by peaceful means the struggle for peace between Kurds and Turkey, for democracy and for respect for human rights." She goes on to say, "These are the universal values which must unite us."

As elected officials here in the United States, we must speak out against abuses and develop a Kurdish U.S. policy.

198.

[October 7, 1998 (Senate), p. S11811]

ESTABLISHING A PROGRAM TO SUPPORT A TRANSITION TO DEMOCRACY IN IRAQ

I ask unanimous consent that the Senate now proceed to the consideration of H.R. 4655, which is at the desk.

The PRESIDING OFFICER. The clerk will report.

The assistant legislative clerk read as follows:

A bill (H.R. 4655) to establish a program to support a transition to democracy in Iraq.

The PRESIDING OFFICER. Is there objection to the immediate consideration of the bill?

There being no objection, the Senate proceeded to consider the bill.

Mr. LOTT. Mr. President, I am pleased the Senate is about to act on H.R. 4655, the Iraq Liberation Act of 1998. I introduced companion legislation, S. 2525, last week with 7 co-sponsors. Last Friday, the House International Relations Committee marked up the legislation and made only minor, technical changes. On October 5, the House passed H.R. 4655 by an overwhelmingly bipartisan vote of 360 to 38. That vote, and our vote in several moments, is a strong demonstration of Congressional support for a new policy toward Iraq—a policy that overtly seeks the replacement of Saddam Hussein's regime through military and political support for the Iraq opposition.

The United States has many means at its disposal to support the liberation of Iraq. At the height of the Cold War, we support freedom fighters in Asia, Africa and Latin America willing to fight and die for a democratic future. We can and should do the same now in Iraq.

The Clinton Administration regularly calls for bipartisanship in foreign policy. I support them when I can. Today, we see a clear example of a policy that has the broadest possible bipartisan support. I know the Administration understands the depth of our feeling on this issue. I think they are beginning to understand the strategic argument in favor of moving beyond containment to a policy of "rollback." Containment is not sustainable. Pressure to lift sanctions on Iraq is increasing—despite Iraq's seven years of refusal to comply with the terms of the Gulf War ceasefire. Our interests in the Middle East cannot be protected with Saddam Hussein in power. Our legislation provides a roadmap to achieve our objective.

This year, Congress has already provided $5 million to support the Iraqi political opposition. We provided $5 million to establish Radio Free Iraq. We will provide additional resources for political support in the FY 1999 Foreign Operations Appropriations Act, including $3 million for the Iraqi National Congress.

Enactment of this bill will go farther. It requires the President to designate at least one Iraqi opposition group to receive U.S. military assistance. It defines eligibility criteria such a group or groups must meet. Many of us have ideas on how the designation process should work. I have repeatedly stated that the Iraqi National Congress has been effective in the past and can be effective in the future. They represent the broadest possible base of the opposition. There are other groups that are currently active inside Iraq: the Patriotic Union of Kurdistan, the Kurdish Democratic Party and the Supreme Council for the Islamic Revolution in Iraq. The State Department seems to believe there are more than 70 opposition groups, many of which do not meet the criteria in H.R. 4655. Many barely even exist or have no political base. They should not be considered for support. We should also be very careful about considering designation of groups which do not share our values or which are simply creations of external forces or exile politics, such as the Iraqi Communist Party or the Iraqi National Accord.

I appreciate the work we have been able to do with the Administration on this legislation. But we should be very clear about the designation process. We intend to exercise our oversight responsibility and authority as provided in section 4(d) and section 5(d). I do not think the Members of Congress, notified pursuant to law, will agree to any designation that we believe does not meet the criteria in section 5 of the Iraq Liberation Act of 1998.

This is an important step. Observers should not misunderstand the Senate's action. Even though this legislation will pass without controversy on an unanimous voice vote, it is a major step forward in the final conclusion of the Persian Gulf war. In 1991, we and our allies shed blood to liberate Kuwait. Today, we are empowering Iraqis to liberate their own country.

Mr. HELMS. Mr. President, I am an original co-sponsor of H.R. 4655, the Iraq Liberation Act, for one simple reason: Saddam Hussein is a threat to the United States and a threat to our friends in the Middle East.

This lunatic is bent on building an arsenal of weapons of mass destruction with a demonstrable willingness to use them. For nearly eight years the United States has stood by and allowed the U.N. weapons inspections process to proceed in defanging Saddam. That process is now in the final stages of collapse, warning that the U.S. cannot stand idly by hoping against hope that everything will work itself out.

We have been told by Scott Ritter and others that Saddam can reconstitute his weapons of mass destruction within months. The *Washington Post* reported only last week that Iraq still has three nuclear "implosion devices"—in other words, nuclear bombs minus the necessary plutonium or uranium to set them off. The time has come to recognize that Saddam Hussein the man is inextricable from Iraq's drive for weapons of mass destruction. For as long as he and his regime are in power, Iraq will remain a mortal threat.

This bill will begin the long-overdue process of ousting Saddam. It will not send in U.S. troops or commit American forces in any way. Rather, it harkens back to the successes of the Reagan doctrine, enlisting the very people who are suffering most under Saddam's yoke to fight the battle against him.

The bill requires the President to designate an Iraqi opposition group or groups to receive military drawdown assistance. The President need not look far; the Iraqi National Congress once flourished as an umbrella organization for Kurds, Shi'ites and Sunni Muslims. It should flourish again, but it needs our help.

Mr. President, the people of Iraq, through representative organizations such as the INC, the Patriotic Union of Kurdistan, the Kurdish Democratic Party and the Shi'ite SCIRI, have begged for our help. The day may yet come when we are dragged back to Baghdad; I believe that day can be put off, perhaps even averted, by helping the people of Iraq help themselves.

Opponents of this initiative—I shouldn't call them friends of Saddam—have said that the Iraqi opposition exists in name only, that they are too parochial to come together. They are not entirely wrong— which is why Senator Lott and Chairman Gilman (the lead House sponsor) have carefully crafted the designation requirement in H.R. 4655 to insist that only broad-based, pro-democracy groups be selected by the President to receive drawdown assistance. I would go further, and suggest to the President that he designate just one group, the Iraqi National Congress, in which the Kurds, the Shi'ites and the Sunnis of Iraq hold membership. The opposition must be unified, but it may just take the leadership of the United States to bring them together.

Finally, this bill gives the Congress oversight over the designation and drawdown authorities. As Chairman of the Foreign Relations Committee, I intend to exercise vigorously that authority. The White House and the State Department have indicated that they support this bill. We have a unique opportunity, and I intend to do everything in my power to ensure that opportunity is not frittered away. The price of failure is far too high.

Mr. KERREY. Mr. President, I rise to urge the passage of H.R. 4655, the Iraq Liberation Act. Thanks to strong leadership in both Houses of Congress and thanks to the commitment of the Administration toward the goals we all share for Iraq and the region, this legislation is moving quickly. This is the point to state what this legislation is not, and what it is, from my understanding, and why I support it so strongly.

First, this bill is not, in my view, and instrument to direct U.S. funds and supplies to any particular Iraqi revolutionary movement. There are Iraqi movements now in existence which could qualify for designation in accordance with this bill. Other Iraqis not now associated with each other could also band together and qualify for designation. It is for Iraqis, not Americans to organize themselves to put Saddam Hussein out of power, just as it will be for Iraqis to choose their leaders in a democratic Iraq. This bill will help the Administration encourage and support Iraqis to make their revolution.

Second, this bill is not a device to involve the U.S. military in operations in or near Iraq. The Iraqi revolution is for Iraqis, not Americans, to make. The bill provides the Administration a potent new tool to help Iraqis toward this goal, and at the same time advance America's interest in a peaceful and secure Middle East.

This bill, when passed and signed into law, is a clear commitment to a U.S. policy replacing the Saddam Hussein regime and replacing it with a transition to democracy. This bill is a statement that America refuses to coexist with a regime which has used chemical weapons on its own citizens and on neighboring countries, which has invaded its neighbors twice without provocation, which has still not accounted for its atrocities committed in Kuwait, which has fired ballistic missiles into the cities of three of its neighbors, which is attempting to develop nuclear and biological weapons, and which has brutalized and terrorized its own citizens for thirty years. I don't see how any democratic country could accept the existence of such a regime, but this bill says America will not. I will be an even prouder American when the refusal, and commitment to materially help the Iraqi resistance, are U.S. policy.

Mr. McCAIN. Mr. President, I ask unanimous consent the bill be considered read a third time and passed, the motion to reconsider be laid upon the table, and any statements relating to the bill appear at this point in the Record.

The PRESIDING OFFICER. Without objection, it is so ordered.

The bill (H.R. 4655) was considered read the third time, and passed.

199.

[October 9, 1998 (Extensions of Remarks), p. E 2007]

ANKARA'S DECISION TO SENTENCE LEYLA ZANA A BLATANT VIOLATION OF FREEDOM OF EXPRESSION
HON. ELIZABETH FURSE
OF OREGON
IN THE HOUSE OF REPRESENTATIVES

Thursday, October 8, 1998

Ms. FURSE. Mr. Speaker, I rise today to express my indignation over the decision of the Turkish government to sentence Leyla Zana, the Kurdish parliamentarian who is currently serving a 15-year sentence, to 2 additional years in prison as a blatant violation of the freedom of expression and an insult to her supporters worldwide.

This time, the Turkish authorities charge that Leyla Zana broke the law in a letter she wrote to the People Democracy Party (HADEP) to urge them to be forthcoming, diligent, decisive and to push for individual and collective freedoms. The fact that Leyla Zana has been charged with inciting racial hatred reveals that Turkey is a racist state and continues to deny the Kurds a voice in the state.

As my colleagues know, Leyla Zana is the first Kurdish woman every elected to the Turkish parliament. She won her office with more than 84 percent of the vote in her district and brought the Turkish Grand National Assembly a keen interest for human rights and a conviction that the Turkish war against the Kurds must come to an end. Last year, 153 Members of this body joined together and signed a letter to President Bill Clinton urging him to raise Leyla Zana's case with the Turkish authorities and seek her immediate and unconditional release from prison.

Leyla Zana was kept in custody from March 5, 1994, until December 7, 1994 without a conviction. On December 8, 1994, the Ankara State Security Court sentenced her and five other Kurdish parliamentarians to various years in prison. Leyla Zana was accused of making a treasonous speech in Washington, DC., other speeches elsewhere, and wearing a scarf that bore the Kurdish colors of green, red, and yellow. This year marks her fifth year behind the bars.

Today, in Turkish Kurdistan, 40,000 people have lost their lives. More than 3,000 Kurdish villages have been destroyed. Over 3 million residents have become destitute refugees. Despite several unilateral cease-fires by the Kurdish side, the Turkish army continues to pursue policies of hatred, torture and murder, and genocide of the Kurdish people.

Mr. Speaker, as I finish my sixth year in office as a Member of the United States Congress, I find it outrageous that the government of Turkey, after so much outcry, after so much petitioning and after so much publicity would dare to punish her again incensing her friends and supporters all over the world. There is only one word that comes to my mind and it is, fear, Mr. Speaker. The government of Turkey is afraid of Leyla Zana and it thinks it can lock her away forever. That was the story of those who locked Nelson Mandela. The longest nights, Mr. Speaker, give way to bright dawns. Mr. Mandela is a public servant now. And the world is grateful.

People like Leyla Zana who utter the words of reconciliation and accommodation need to be embraced, validated, and freed. I urge the government of Turkey to set aside its conviction of Leyla Zana and free her immediately, and I urge my colleagues and government to condemn her conviction and make her release a priority.

200.

[October 15, 1998 (House), p. H 10987]

THE KURDISH CEASE-FIRE: AN OPPORTUNITY THAT SHOULD NOT BE SQUANDERED

The SPEAKER pro tempore. Under a previous order of the House, the gentleman from California (Mr. Filner) is recognized for 5 minutes.

Mr. FILNER. Mr. Speaker, I rise today to express my support for what many in this country do not know has occurred, but is exceedingly important. That is the unilateral cease-fire that was declared on August 28, 1998, by the Kurdish rebel leader, Abdullah Ocalan.

Taking part in a live broadcast on Med-TV from his base in the Middle East, Mr. Ocalan noted that, effective September 1, 1998, he has ordered his guerillas to cease their operations and silence their guns until further notice. This is a momentous opportunity, Mr. Speaker, for the advocates of peace, the defenders of human rights, and the champions of

trade with the oil-rich countries that surround this explosive region called Kurdistan.

For several years now, Mr. Speaker, I have risen on this floor to draw the attention of my colleagues to the enduring struggle of the Kurds for peace, democracy, and human rights. I have strongly supported their inalienable right to self-determination. Who among us has not heard of the brutality exercised against the Kurds by Saddam Hussein?

The theocracy in Iran has targeted the top leadership of the Kurdish resistance, and murdered many of its ablest leaders. Turkey, a country that we supported as a bulwark against the Soviet expansion during the Cold War, has left its own trail of desolation in the land of the Kurds.

We cannot afford to call a country a friend, ally, and partner, Mr. Speaker, if it refuses to practice the most basic dictates of democracy, such as the freedom of expression and assembly. Kurds, who constitute one-third of the population of Turkey and number some 20 million, are denied their basic human rights, such as the expression of their identity, the use of their own language, the practice and perpetuation of their culture, as a distinct and indigenous people that has its roots in the dawn of history.

The Turkish constitution, the solemn document binding the peoples of Turkey together, makes no reference to the existence of the Kurds. Its Article 3 expressly forbids the use of the Kurdish language in print and in official settings. The Kurds, thus, can write books in English, French, or German, but not in their native Kurdish. Those who do end up with a prison sentence that can run into a century. The noted Turkish sociologist, Ismail Besikci, who has merely written about the Kurds, has accumulated prison sentences of more than 100 years.

Many of us are well aware, Mr. Speaker, of the historical abuse of the Armenians. In 1915, the Armenians were systematically exterminated in the Ottoman Empire. A similar strategy is now being carried out against the Kurds.

Mr. Speaker, the time has come for a bold departure from the old policy of entrusting a blank check to Turkey to do whatever it wishes with its Kurdish minority. The government in Ankara has abdicated its responsibility, and entrusted the entire Kurdish region to the rule of uncompromising Turkish generals for the last 18 years. They have killed more than 40,000 people, and have driven 3 million from their homes. More than 3,000 Kurdish villages have been destroyed. Duly-elected Kurdish parliamentarians are now rotting in jails. The voices of compromise and reconciliation have been silenced. We are witnessing an historical tragedy.

Now the offer of the cease-fire by the Kurdish rebel leader has the potential to bring peace to this troubled region, and open the way for the coexistence of the Kurds with the Turks. Mr. Ocalan has stated that he is ready to disband his forces if Turkey takes steps to constitutionally recognize its 20 million Kurdish population.

Some courageous leaders in Turkey now recognize the crisis must be solved. On September 11, 1998, Husamettin Cindoruk, leader of the Democratic Turkey Party, a member of the ruling coalition in the Turkish government, actually admitted that negotiations must begin. As he said, Turkey will get nowhere by masking this problem and delaying a solution.

He suggested that the talks that produced the good Friday agreement between Ireland and Britain can be the model for his own country. Members of the largest Turkish party, the Virtue Party, Recai Kutan and Hasim Hasimi, have also expressed similar sentiments. These deputies ought to be commended for their courage. Their words carry the real promise of peace.

Mr. Speaker, I cannot help but bring to the attention of this body the plight of a group of Turkish and Kurdish women who have gathered in front of Galatasaray High School to protest the disappearance of their loved ones over the last 3 years. Known as the Saturday Mothers, they were visited this past January by our colleagues, the gentleman from Illinois (Mr. John Porter) and the gentleman from Maryland (Mr. Steny Hoyer), and the President of the Human Rights Alliance, Kathryn Porter.

Under the U.N. Declaration of Protection of All Persons from Enforced Disappearance,

the authorities are obliged to carry out prompt, thorough, and impartial investigations into every report of disappearance. According to Amnesty International, no investigations satisfying these criteria have been carried out. This sad state of affairs was compounded on August 29 when police detained 150 people.

With the declaration of this Kurdish cease-fire, we now have an opportunity. We helped to make possible the Good Friday Agreement, the Dayton talks, and the Israeli-Palestinian accords. We must do no less for the Kurds.

201.

[October 21, 1998 (Extensions of Remarks), p. E2289]

CLINTON ADMINISTRATION'S DOUBLE STANDARD OF FOREIGN POLICY
HON. MICHAEL PAPPAS
OF NEW JERSEY
IN THE HOUSE OF REPRESENTATIVES

Tuesday, October 20, 1998

Mr. PAPPAS. Mr. Speaker, I rise today to voice my concern on the Clinton Administration's double standard of foreign policy application toward Turkey. I fail to understand why the same policy that is now being implemented against the Bosnian Serbs, who are denying basic human rights and imposing death sentences upon hundreds of ethnic Albanian women and children in Kosovo, is not being implemented upon Turkey.

For 14 years, the Turkish military has been conducting an inhumane campaign of ethnic cleansing and oppression on its own Kurdish people in no different a way than the Serbs are. The Turks' war of horror against the Kurds has killed over 30,000 Kurds and has left over two million refugees without homes and lives.

The situations in Kosova and against the Turkish Kurds are unacceptable and must be dealt with swiftly, so that more innocent people will not die. If the United States military is ready to intervene in Kosova, then someone could ask are we ready to do the same against Turkey? A double standard foreign policy is not good policy, especially when innocent lives are at stake. I ask that the Administration end this doublespeak, and act now in Turkey.

Mr. Speaker, I also ask that the following letter from the A.H.I. be inserted in the Record following my statement.

American Hellenic Institute, Inc.,

October 15, 1998.
Hon. William J. Clinton,
President of the United States, Washington, DC.
Re: Double Standard on the Application of the Rule of Law to Turkey

Dear Mr. President. The present crisis in Kosovo impels me to write to you once again on the double standard that underlies the Administration's foreign policy approach to Turkey. At a time when our nation has invoked the threat of military intervention over the application of UN Security Council Resolution 1199 on Serbia, we utterly fail to apply the same standard of the rule of law to Turkey.

The American Hellenic Institute is appalled by and wholly condemns the violence in Kosovo. We welcome the Administration's efforts to address the Kosovo crisis as being in the best traditions of our nation's moral and humanitarian values. These values, however, as also under attack in Turkey where the Turkish military is conducting a ruthless campaign of ethnic cleansing and repression against its own Kurdish citizens. Just as we acted in Kosovo, so our country needs to undertake similar efforts in Turkey in defense of U.S. interest and values.

Turkey's fourteen year war of terror against its 20% Kurdish minority in Turkish Kurdistan is no secret. The Turkish armed forces have killed over 30,000 Kurds and destroyed 3,000 villages resulting in over two million refugees. Ethnic cleansing has taken place on a vastly wider scale than in Kosovo. And yet our government does nothing.

On Bosnia and Kosovo, high officials of our government have repeatedly spoken out in protest. We have mobilized our armed forces.

Over turkey the same officials are conspicuously silent.

If, as demonstrated over the past weeks, we are ready to intervene militarily on behalf of the Kosovo Alabanians, we should be ready to apply the same principles on behalf of the Kurds in Turkey. If we do not and instead continue U.S. support for Turkey, then we are turning ourselves into an accessory to Turkey's massive human rights violations in Turkey. This is a stain on U.S. honor.

Mr. President, our country cannot live by double standards. In 1991 the U.S. went to war with Iraq to eject it from Kuwait. What is the difference in principle between the Iraqi invasion and occupation of Kuwait in 1990 and Turkey's invasion and occupation of 37.3% of Cyprus in 1974? There is none. Indeed, the military controlled government of Turkey is in violation of more laws than Saddam Hussein in his invasion of Kuwait.

The Administration's vigorous actions and resolve in Kosovo stand in harsh contrast to its willingness to support Turkey's repression (some would say genocide) against its own Kurdish citizens and to its unwillingness to enforce a series of UN Security Council and General Assembly resolutions condemning Turkey's illegal invasion and occupation of Cyprus dating back to 1974. Why is our country so selective in enforcing certain resolutions and disregarding others?

The answer, I regretfully have to conclude, is that the Administration is mesmerized by Turkey. Consider the following recent examples:

When in October 1998 Turkey threatened military action against Syria and mobilized its armed forces on the Syrian border, the Administration did not condemn Turkey's action as a violation of the UN Charter article 2 (4) and a threat to regional stability. Instead it referred once again to the PKK as a "terrorist" organization and called upon Syria to "cease its support of the PKK." In effect, this denies the Kurds the right to autonomy which we are championing for the Kosovo Albanians.

When in August 1998, President Demirel issued a statement claiming unspecified Greek sovereign territories in the Aegean, the Administration made no statement condemning this irresponsible irredentism of Turkey against an American NATO ally.

When in December 1997 the European Union unanimously found itself unable to accept Turkey's application for membership on the deeply seated grounds of Turkey's fundamental lack of normal democratic governance and adverse human rights record, the Administration took Turkey's side.

When in early 1997 the Republic of Cyprus announced its intention to acquire a modest increase in its self-defense capability, the Administration created the S-300 controversy by taking the lead in criticizing Cyprus. It subsequently allowed to go uncontested Turkey's absurd interpretation that this challenged the balance of power in the Eastern Mediterranean.

The sad fact is that the Administration has thrown its lot in with the Turkish military controlled government. We supply them with the arms needed to oppress their own citizens, we take their side against the European Union; we fail to condemn their repeated challenges to international law in the Aegean and over Cyprus; we stand by when Turkey time and time again demonstrates it is the primary source of regional instability.

The explanation AHI is regularly offered for this bizarre policy that so obviously contradicts both American interests and values is that Turkey is a secular Islamic state and that any alternative U.S. approach might risk delivering Turkey into the hands of Islamic fundamentalists.

Mr. President, this analysis is fundamentally erroneous. The true fault line in Turkey is not between secularism and fundamentalism but between military rule and democracy. The Administration's current policy supports the military and ignores democracy. In Iran we found at great cost that this approach did not work. We should not make the same mistake in Turkey.

The Turkish constitution affords the military political powers far exceeding anything than would be acceptable in the U.S. or other normal democracies. Instead of siding with the military and its political and diplomatic puppets, the Administration should support, as does AHI, the brave Turkish citizens within

Turkey struggling for human rights and the rule of law.

A guiding principle in foreign affairs for the U.S. should be the words of President Dwight D. Eisenhower in the 1956 Middle East crisis, when he condemned and reversed the invasion of Egypt by Britain, France, and Israel. In a memorable address to the nation on October 31, 1956 Eisenhower said:

"There can be no peace without law. And there can be no law if we invoke one code of international conduct for those who oppose us and another for our friends."

The need for a change in our policy toward Turkey is critical in the interests of the U.S.

Respectfully,
Eugene T. Rossides.

202.

[March 24, 1999 (Extensions), p. E 540]

REMEMBERING THE MASSACRE AT HALABJA
HON. STENY H. HOYER
OF MARYLAND
IN THE HOUSE OF REPRESENTATIVES

Wednesday, March 24, 1999

Mr. HOYER. Mr. Speaker, I rise today to remember a horrifying event in our world's recent history. Eleven years ago, Saddam Hussein bombed the Kurdish town of Halabja with chemical weapons. Clouds of poison gas including mustard gas and sarin were rained down on Saddam's own people, merely because they were Kurds.

This heinous act resulted in the death of over 5,000 innocent civilians and injury to approximately 10,000 others. However, Halabja was neither the first nor the last of the chemical warfare attacks Saddam Hussein unleashed against the Iraqi Kurds. Throughout 1988, Saddam's brutal regime continued to use chemical weapons against its own people. In only 6 months, over 200 Kurdish villages were attacked and 25,000 people were killed by chemical weapons during the vicious Anfal Campaign. This campaign ultimately led to the destruction of 4,500 Kurdish villages and the death of 500,000 Kurdish people. More than 200,000 Kurds remain missing and 500,000 have been internally displaced.

Although the people of Halabja undoubtedly suffered beyond words when this horrifying event occurred 11 years ago, their children and their children's children will feel the effects of this one action of Saddam Hussein for generations to come. For, 11 years hence, the Halabja attack has not really ended. Many people in the region continue to suffer from respiratory problems, eye conditions, neurological disorders, skin problems, and cancers. All of these effects are attributable to long-term damage to DNA caused by the chemicals used by Saddam in the attack.

The Iraqi regime has never expressed remorse for Halabja, nor have Saddam Hussein and his thugs ever been called to account for these crimes they have committed against their own citizens. We do know that whether in attacks on Iraqis or neighboring states, inhumanity is precisely the common element of Saddam Hussein's policies. We must never forget the innocent people who died and those who continue to suffer from Saddam's ruthlessness.

203.

[Thursday, March 25, 1999 (House), pp. H 1792-93]

NEEDED: JUSTICE AND A POLITICAL SOLUTION FOR THE KURDISH PEOPLE

The SPEAKER pro tempore. Under a previous order of the House, the gentleman from New Jersey (Mr. Pallone) is recognized for 5 minutes.

Mr. PALLONE. Madam Speaker, before we adjourn for our spring district work period, I wanted to draw attention to the plight of the Kurdish people.

There was a lot of attention to this otherwise usually ignored issue last month with the apprehension of Abdullah Ocalan, the leader of the Kurdistan Workers Party, the PKK.

Mr. Ocalan has been fighting for autonomy for the Kurdish people who are the victims of oppression by Turkey, as well as Iraq, Iran and Syria. The Turkish regime refuses to even acknowledge the Kurds' existence, referring to them as Mountain Turks, prohibiting all expression of Kurdish culture and language in an effort to forcibly assimilate them, and jailing, torturing or killing Kurdish leaders.

The Iraqi regime has used poison gas on its Kurds and has destroyed 4,000 Kurdish villages. The Iranian regime has lined them up against firing squads, while the Syrian regime barely tolerates them with no rights.

Madam Speaker, while the treatment of the Kurds in Iraq, Iran and Syria is deplorable, the Turkish mistreatment of the Kurdish people is particularly shocking for a very basic reason. Turkey is considered an ally of the United States, a member of NATO, and the recipient over many years of millions in economic and especially military assistance courtesy of the American taxpayer. This embarrassing record of American support for the Turkish regime reached a new low last month when our intelligence and diplomatic services actually helped a Turkish commando team to capture Mr. Ocalan in Kenya. This action violates the spirit of the torture convention to which the United States is a signatory.

Mr. Ocalan, had he been here in the United States I cannot imagine that he would have been turned over to Turkey, just as Italy refused to do so when he was in Italy. This shameful collaboration with Turkey has resulted in Mr. Ocalan being held in solitary confinement on an island prison in Turkey with no access to his international team of lawyers.

Plans call for him to be tried in a secret military-type court with no jury and no foreign observers.

Given the unlawfulness of this abduction and the illegitimacy of the state security court's tribunal, there is ample reason to assume that Mr. Ocalan will not receive a fair trial.

Madam Speaker, I want to note that the injustice of the Ocalan abduction and trial and the much larger issue of the oppression of the Kurdish people has not gone unnoticed around the world. Here in Washington over the past weekend, a rally was held across the street from the Turkish Embassy. The Congressional Human Rights Caucus and the Human Rights Alliance recently commemorated the 11th anniversary of Saddam Hussein's massacre of over 5,000 Kurds in the village of Halabja.

The suffering of the Kurdish people has not gone completely unnoticed but we need to do more for the Kurdish people. The government of Turkey's undeclared war on the Kurds has claimed close to 40,000 lives and caused more than 3 million people to become refugees.

Mr. Ocalan's appearance in Rome with a pledge that he was ready to renounce violence presented an opportunity for peace but neither Turkey nor the United States took him up on his offer.

Madam Speaker, let me say it is not too late. We should use our leverage over Turkey to demand that an international tribunal prosecute Mr. Ocalan since Turkey is at war with the Kurds and cannot be expected to conduct a fair trial. I hope that the European Union to which Turkey is seeking admission will also put pressure on Turkey. We must demand a fair trial for Mr. Ocalan but this should only be a first step in our efforts to press Turkey to enter into negotiations to achieve a political solution to this ongoing struggle. This is fundamentally in Turkey's interest, too, in the long run, since they cannot continue to keep down 35 million people living in their midst.

On January 21, we celebrated, or the Kurds celebrated their new year, which is called Newroz, symbolizing a day of resistance and deliverance from tyranny for the Kurds. In that spirit, I hope that we will soon witness a turning point from the terrible tragedies that the Kurdish people have experienced and instead see the rebirth of a strong and free Kurdistan.

Madam Speaker, this week U.S. forces have gone into the battle in the former Yugoslavia in an effort to prevent the genocide of the Kosovar people. I strongly support that effort which shows America at its best and I hope that the same resolve and sense of outrage that caused us to act to protect the Kosovars will finally motivate America and the free world to put an end to the genocide of the Kurdish people.

Let me point out that the Kurdish new year, Madam Speaker, was actually last Sunday, March 21, Newroz, and that was the day when the Kurds celebrate their new year.

204.

[May 11, 1999 (House), pp. H 2930-31]

TURKISH-KURDISH CONFLICT MUST BE RESOLVED

The SPEAKER pro tempore. Under the Speaker's announced policy of January 19, 1999, the gentleman from New Jersey (Mr. Pallone) is recognized during morning hour debates for 5 minutes.

Mr. PALLONE. Mr. Speaker, as our military campaign in the Balkans continues, with the noble goal of stopping the ethnic cleansing that the dictator Milosevic has perpetrated against the Kosovar Albanian people, another similar atrocity continues to be perpetrated in the mountains of eastern Turkey against the Kurdish people.

There is a crucial difference between the situations in Kosovo and in Kurdistan. In the case of Kosovo, the forces of NATO are being used to stop the murderous rampage unleashed by Milosevic. But the Turkish regime that is responsible for the war against the Kurds is actually a member of NATO.

Unfortunately, because Turkey is viewed as a strategic ally of the U.S. and the West, the plight of the Kurds in Turkey has not been given adequate attention by the United States. In fact, Mr. Speaker, we may actually be contributing to the oppression of the Kurds.

The issue of Turkey's war on the Kurds and American support for Turkey was brought into sharp focus earlier this year with the apprehension of Abdullah Ocalan, the leader of the Kurdish independence movement. Mr. Ocalan has been fighting for autonomy for the

Kurdish people, who are the victims of oppression by Turkey as well as Iraq, Iran and Syria.

Mr. Speaker, the Turkish regime refuses to even acknowledge the Kurds' existence, referring to them as "mountain Turks", prohibiting all expression of Kurdish culture and language in an effort to forcibly assimilate them, while jailing, torturing, and killing Kurdish leaders.

It is true that the Kurdish communities in Iraq, Iran and Syria also suffer terribly, and we should keep in mind the fate of the Kurds in those countries—indeed, the U.S.-led Operation Provide Comfort in Northern Iraq is an action we can all be proud of. But, frankly, we tend to expect egregious human rights violations to occur under the Iraqi, Iranian and Syrian regimes. Turkey, on the other hand, is a member of NATO, touted as a democracy, a participant in Operation Allied Force. Turkey has received over the years millions of dollars in economic and, especially, military assistance courtesy of the American taxpayer. We have a right to expect better, and Turkey, as a member of NATO and a candidate for the European Union has an obligation to do better.

Furthermore, the mistreatment of the Kurdish population of Turkey is not the only example of Turkey's blatant violation of American values, ideals or interests. The continued occupation of Northern Cyprus and the blockade against Armenia are two other glaring examples where Turkey pursues the kind of policies that we should not accept from any nation, but particularly one of our allies.

Mr. Speaker, I was appalled when it was reported that American intelligence and diplomatic services actually helped a Turkish commando team to capture Mr. Ocalan in Kenya in February of this year. This shameful collaboration with Turkey has resulted in Mr. Ocalan being held in solitary confinement on an island prison in Turkey. He will be tried in a secret military-type court with no jury and no foreign observers.

The prosecutors are seeking the death penalty. There is little hope that Mr. Ocalan will receive a fair trial. In fact, the debate in the Turkish press is not about whether he will get a fair trial but rather when he will be executed.

According to a recent report by Amnesty International, Mr. Ocalan's defense lawyers are routinely beaten and harassed by Turkish police. The police have even tried to incite public riots against the defense team. The lawyers and their families have received telephone threats.

I should point out that this is in violation of the United Nations Basic Principles on the Role of Lawyers, which states that lawyers shall not be identified with their clients or their clients' causes as a result of discharging their functions.

In the United States and in other countries where the rule of law is respected, we believe that everyone, even the most unpopular defendants, has a right to a fair trial. There is no place for a lynch mob mentality.

After 3 months in solitary confinement, denied proper access to his lawyers and being constantly guarded by armed soldiers wearing ski masks, Mr. Ocalan may be suffering a psychological breakdown. All of his meetings with his lawyers are monitored. It is quite possible that he has been subjected to torture.

But if Turkey does go ahead and hang Mr. Ocalan, the result would be to create a martyr for the Kurdish people and to unleash an all-out civil war that would be disastrous for all the people of the region, both Turks and Kurds. Such an outcome is not in anyone's interests, not that of Turkey, not the Kurdish people, not the neighboring countries, certainly not the United States.

Mr. Speaker, in order to encourage the U.S. Government to play a constructive role in heading off a crisis in Turkey, my colleague, the gentleman from California (Mr. Filner), and I will be circulating a letter this week asking our colleagues to sign a letter to President Clinton urging his intervention, to implore that the Turkish authorities show some basic fairness in trying Mr. Ocalan and to spare his life.

The government of Turkey's undeclared war on the Kurds has claimed close to 40,000 lives and caused more than 3 million people to become refugees. Before his arrest, Mr. Ocalan had announced that he was ready to renounce violence and negotiate, but Turkey did not even consider the request. Even worse, Mr. Speaker, the United States did not encourage such negotiations to begin.

Mr. Speaker, it is my belief that it would be more appropriate to have an International Tribunal prosecute Mr. Ocalan since Turkey is at war with the Kurds and cannot be expected to conduct a fair trial. Seeking a fair trial for Mr. Ocalan should be the first step in our efforts to press Turkey to enter into negotiations to achieve a political solution to this tragic struggle.

What is truly tragic about the conflict between the Turkish regime and the Kurdish people is that the Turkish and Kurdish people have not always lived in conflict. There is hope that reconciliation could occur but only if the Turkish authorities recognize the rights and distinct identity of the Kurds and finally halt their goal of controlling and conquering the Kurds.

205.

[May 20, 1999 (House), p. H 3442]

ON THE OCCASION OF THE INAUGURATION OF THE NATIONAL CONGRESS OF KURDISTAN

The SPEAKER pro tempore. Under a previous order of the House, the gentleman from California (Mr. Filner) is recognized for 5 minutes.

Mr. FILNER. Madam Speaker, I rise today to speak about democracy, a form of government which was invented in the 5th century B.C. by the Greeks in Athens, great city of Athens. The British honor democracy through their parliament, the Japanese have their Diet, the Duma serves the Russians, and of course here in the United States democracy is exercised right here on the floor of Congress. Democracy still remains the best hope for troubled humanity throughout the world.

With the end of the Cold War, Madam Speaker, we have seen a great expansion of the boundaries of democracy. The world is a better place today because many former Soviet republics now enjoy self determination and are given their rightful seats in the Hall of Nations. But auspicious as has been the forward march of liberty, the world remains far from being free. Nations remain in captivity. The color of one's skin still bars some from feeling our common humanity. But the hope that we can rise to the challenge of total equality is enduring. People of goodwill are risking their lives against great odds. They know the rewards are worth the risks.

Madam Speaker, on May 24, 1999, just a few days from now, a nation whose voice has been silenced for too long will convene its first congress, unfortunately not in its own land but in Brussels, Belgium, and 150 delegates from around the world representing the Kurdish people of Turkey, Syria, Iraq, Iran and the former Soviet republics will assemble for the purpose of raising their voice for their brothers and sisters who are denied a voice in Kurdistan. I salute the birth of this congress that represents a people as old as the dawn of history.

Madam Speaker, the Kurds are natives of the Middle East who inhabit a mountainous region as large as the State of Texas. They speak Kurdish, which is distinct from Turkish and Arabic but is closely linked with Persian. Having survived in mountain strongholds and ancient empires, they are now persecuted, denied their identity and forced to become Turks or Arabs or Persian by the states that were born in the early 20th century. Thirty million strong, they are viewed as beasts of burden or as cannon fodder, but never as Kurds who should enjoy human rights that we take for granted in this country.

It is a crime to be a Kurd in Turkey, Madam Speaker. Saddam Hussein has used chemical and biological weapons against them in Iraq. The theocracy in Tehran often machine guns the Kurdish dissidents in the city squares. The poignancy of the Kurdish situation hits closer to home when we realize that our own government is sometimes involved in their misery. Turkey boosts of American F-16 fighter planes, Sikorsky attack helicopters and M-60 battle tanks. Saddam Hussein, according to some declassified U.N. documents, had the support of 24 European companies to produce his deadly chemical fumes and biological fumes. Tehran's opposition to the Kurds has gone beyond Iran with the assassination of Kurdish leaders in Vienna and Berlin.

We all revere the words of Thomas Jefferson when he wrote in the Declaration of Independence: "When in the course of human events, it becomes necessary for one people to dissolve the political bonds which have connected them with another, and to assume among the Powers of the earth the separate and equal station to which the Laws of Nature and of Nature's God entitle them, a decent respect to the opinions of mankind requires that they should declare the causes which impel them to the separation."

Madam Speaker, given the lot of the Kurds, it is more than understandable that they set up their own Congress and take charge of their own destiny. They have the people, the resources and the political understanding to succeed in their dream of statehood.

Madam Speaker, I need also at this time to address the situation of Abdullah Ocalan, the Kurdish leader who, according to a recent *New York Times* article, was handed over to the Turks with the help of our intelligence services. As you may recall, he had ventured to Europe from his home base in the Middle East to seek a political solution to the enduring Kurdish struggle for basic human rights. I spoke on this floor welcoming his declaration of cease-fire and hoped, it now seems against hope, to see the debate on the Kurdish question change from war to peace and from confrontation to dialogue.

Mr. Ocalan, denied a refuge in Rome, was promised the safe passage through Greece to the Hague where he intended to sue the Government of Turkey at the International Court of Justice for its crimes against the Kurds. But the laws of granting asylum to political figures, as old as the time of prophets, were suspended in this case. Abdullah Ocalan, the most popular Kurdish figure of the day, was arrested. Through a deal that smacks of political venality at its worst, he was handed over to the Turks and now awaits his most likely execution as the sole inmate in the Imrali Island prison in the Sea of Marmara.

Madam Speaker, it is unbecoming of this great power to aid and abet dictatorships which are merely disguised as democracies. Those who imprison duly elected representatives such as Layla Zana in Turkey for testifying before a standing committee of this Congress cannot and should not enjoy our support. Leaders such as Abdullah Ocalan, despite his violent past, still hold the promise of peace and reconciliation for the Kurds with their neighbors. The euphoria that we all felt for the freedom of captive nations in the former Soviet Union now must extend to our allies and their subjects as well.

So we welcome the convening of the National Congress of Kurdistan. They are dreaming what to many may seem an impossible dream, the dream of a united Kurdish people in the Nation of Kurdistan.

206.

[May 27, 1999 (Senate), p. S 6438]

PLIGHT OF THE KURDISH PEOPLE

Mr DODD. Mr. President, I rise today out of concern for the plight of the Kurdish people living in Northern Iraq and Eastern Turkey. They have been victims of some of the most egregious human rights abuses in recent years including brutal military attack, random murder, and forced exile from their homes. While American efforts in Northern Iraq have greatly improved the plight of the Kurds, there is certainly much room for improvement both there and in Turkey.

In 1988, the world was stunned by the horrific pictures of the bodies of innocent Kurds disfigured by the effects of a poison gas attack by Saddam Hussein. We may never know exactly how many people died in that particular attack due to Saddam Hussein's efforts to cover up his culpability. The number of victims, however, is most likely in the thousands.

This was certainly not Iraq's first deplorable attack on the Kurds and, sadly, it was not destined to be the last. Yet, this attack continues to represent a stark milestone in the long list of deplorable deeds Saddam Hussein has perpetrated against his own people.

In recent years, however, the United States has come to the aid of the Kurds of Northern Iraq. At the conclusion of the Gulf War, the United States and our allies established "no-fly" zones over Northern and Southern Iraq. These zones, plus the damage the Iraqi military sustained during Operation Desert Storm, have mercifully curtailed Saddam Hussein's ability to attack the Kurds in Northern Iraq. Mr. President, the men and women of the United States Air Force who risk Iraqi anti-aircraft fire over Iraq each day in order to enforce these no-fly zones deserve our support and commendation. Not only do their efforts protect nations throughout the region and around the world from Saddam Hussein's aggression, but their daily flights serve as sentries against human rights abuses.

Mr. President, the United States has taken other, more direct actions to help the Kurds of Northern Iraq. Following the Gulf War, the United States Agency for International Development worked to provide important humanitarian assistance to Iraqi Kurds. When Iraqi incursions into the region once again threatened the lives of thousands of innocent civilians, the United States worked to evacuate more than 6,500 people to the safety of Guam. Many were later granted asylum in the United States.

Our relationship with the Kurdish people of Northern Iraq is not a one-way street. More than 2,000 of the Kurds who the United States evacuated in 1996 were either employees of American relief agencies or family members of those employees. Others have provided invaluable intelligence information to the United States.

As I mentioned earlier, many Kurds also live in Eastern Turkey. A minority of Turkish Kurds have taken up arms against the democratically elected Turkish government in a bid for independence. Unfortunately, both sides in this internal conflict are guilty of human rights abuses against innocent Kurdish civilians.

The Kurdistan Workers Party, or PKK, has devolved into a terrorist organization targeting not only Turkish military and police forces but innocent Kurdish civilians as well. While reliable estimates of the number of victims are extremely hard to come by, it is clear that thousands, probably tens of thousands, have died at the hands of the PKK.

As is often the case, neither side in the dispute holds a monopoly on human rights abuses. The PKK's actions unquestionably demand a response from the Turkish government. Rather than a measured and targeted response, however, Turkey has declared a state of emergency in a large portion of Eastern Turkey, directly affecting more than 4 million of its citizens.

Under the state of emergency, Turkey has severely rationed food, leading to great hardship amongst innocent civilians. In addition, Turkey has forced hundreds of thousands of people out of their homes, leaving more than 2,600 towns and villages mere ghost towns.

These actions are all aimed at suppressing the PKK's terrorism. Yet, the government has actively targeted not only known terrorists but those believed to agree with the PKK's goal of independence—although perhaps not their methods—as well. Even those who support neither the PKK's goals nor their means suffer at the hands of the Turkish military and police forces. Thus, Turkey's Kurdish population is under attack from both sides without any place to hide.

Turkey is both a democracy and an important ally of the United States. In Kosovo and Bosnia, Turkey has stood firmly with other NATO members against human rights abuses. In recent weeks, Turkey has opened its borders to tens of thousands of innocent Kosovars desperate to escape Slobodan Milosevic's murderous rampage. Turkey, along with our other NATO allies, deserves a great deal of credit for its principled stand in the Balkans. In fact, Turkey has allowed the United States to enforce the no-fly zone over Northern Iraq from our air force base on Turkish soil.

Yet, it would be inappropriate for us to overlook Turkey's human rights abuses against its own people simply because of its commendable actions elsewhere. Mr. President, the intentional murder of innocent noncombatants is an anathema to the United States regardless of where it occurs or who the perpetrator is. Thus, the PKK's efforts to intimidate others by random murder, certainly not indicative of all Kurds, deserves our condemnation as does Turkey's abuse of its own innocent citizens in the pursuit of terrorists.

Mr. President, we must never let our nation's commitment to the protection of human rights lapse. As we sit here today, the human rights of an entire race of people in Turkey and Iraq are under assault. I urge my colleagues to join me in condemning these abuses.

207.

[June 8, 1999 (House), p. H 3768]

TURKEY MUST ACCEPT KURDISH PEACE OFFER

The SPEAKER pro tempore. Under the Speaker's announced policy of January 19, 1999, the gentleman from New Jersey (Mr. Pallone) is recognized duringmorning hour debates for 5 minutes.

Mr. PALLONE. Mr. Speaker, there are some who call it the trial of the century." Abdullah Ocalan, the imprisoned Kurdish rebel leader, is on trial before a Turkish military tribunal. The trial could hardly be called fair. Mr. Ocalan, who faces the death penalty if convicted, has been denied access to his lawyers. His legal team has faced a pattern of harassment and threats.

The Turkish government and media have stirred up nationalistic passions against Mr. Ocalan. If the Turkish government forges ahead with legally railroading Mr. Ocalan and the threat to hang him is carried out, the result would be disastrous for all the people of the region. Yet interestingly enough, the trial of Mr. Ocalan has created a potentially positive and long overdue opening towards reconciliation between the Turkish and Kurdish peoples.

Standing in the dock at his show trial, Mr. Ocalan made a brave plea for a negotiated, Democratic solution to the Kurdish question. Mr. Ocalan's organization, the Kurdish workers's party known as the PKK, has announced its support for Mr. Ocalan's peace offer. With the media attention that the trial is attracting,

putting the Kurdish issue in the spotlight to an almost unprecedented degree, Turkey could vastly improve its international standing by simply agreeing to begin negotiations with the Kurdish leaders but, sadly, Mr. Speaker, so far the Turkish government has rejected the path to peace insisting that it will not negotiate with Mr. Ocalan or any leaders of the Kurdish movement.

Yesterday's *Washington Post* had an editorial entitled, "Turkey's Kurdish Opening," which begins with these words: "Turkey may have a once in a generation opening to treat its national cancer, the problem of its aggrieved Turkish minority."

The editorial in the Post, a paper that has previously shown sympathy to the Turkish point of view on a number of issues, notes that the Turkish policy of relentless military and political attack on the Kurdish movement dooms Turkey to a conflict that sets it at odds with the human Democratic values of the western nations whose company it most values.

That is the bind, Mr. Speaker, that Turkey has put itself into. Turkey is a member of NATO and has sought membership in the European Union, so far unsuccessfully. At the same time, Turkey continues not only to wage a dirty war against a minority community within its borders but to repress and essentially deny the existence of a distinct Kurdish identity, language or culture.

In the meantime, Turkey's economic development, levels of education, infrastructure, development and standard of living, lag far behind European standards while scarce resources are squandered on its ongoing war against the Kurds. It is a cycle that must be broken.

As The *Washington Post* editorial concludes, "Friends of Turkey must hope it can muster the courage to broaden its perspective and to conduct an honest exploration of the Ocalan initiative."

Mr. Speaker, two recent articles in the *New York Times* suggest unfortunately that the Turkish political and military establishment is a long way from making this major leap. Last Friday, it was reported that Turkey's best known human rights advocate, Akin Birdal, entered prison to serve a 9 ½ month sentence for giving speeches judged subversive.

What was his subversive activity? Mr. Birdal, chairman of the Human Rights Association, has repeatedly urged the Turkish state to reach a peaceful settlement with Kurdish rebels. Now, as the article reports, such statements constitute support for terrorism under Turkish law. This same law has recently been used to convict two journalists, a university professor and an aide to Mr. Birdal. While some brave Turks, including the country's top judge, have called for repeal of the law, the hardline regime refuses to give in.

Mr. Speaker, in an effort to encourage the U.S. Government to play a constructive role in heading off the crisis in Turkey, my colleague, the gentleman from California (Mr. Filner) and I, are circulating a letter this week asking our colleagues to sign a letter to President Clinton urging his intervention to implore that the Turkish authorities show some basic fairness in trying Mr. Ocalan and to spare his life. Seeking a fair trial for Mr. Ocalan should be the first step in our efforts to press Turkey to enter into negotiations to achieve a political solution to this tragic struggle.

Mr. Ocalan and his Kurdish organization have offered an olive branch to the Turkish government. It would be both the decent and the smart thing to do for Turkey to accept this good faith offer and to embark on the path of peace.

In fact, Mr. Speaker, Mr. Ocalan made several previous cease-fire offers prior to his arrest—all of which were summarily rejected by the Turkish government and military officials.

An article in Sunday's *New York Times* further describes the hardening of official attitudes in Turkey. According to the article, the Turkish Interior Ministry has issued a directive listing terms that must be used when discussing Mr. Ocalan, his movement or Kurds in general. The rules are binding on all reporters for state-run news agencies. It represents another example of the ongoing pattern of inciting nationalistic fear and distrust of the PKK, while trying to blind the Turkish people to the Kurds, their history, their culture and the validity of their struggle.

Mr. Speaker, the Turkish regime refuses to even acknowledge the Kurds' existence, referring to them as "mountain Turks," prohibiting all expression of Kurdish culture and language in an effort to forcibly assimilate them, while jailing, torturing and killing Kurdish leaders. The Government of Turkey's undeclared war on the Kurds has claimed close to 40,000 lives and caused more than 3 million people to become refugees.

208.

[March 9, 2000 (Senate), p. S 1436]

COMMEMORATING THE TWELFTH ANNIVERSARY OF THE HALABJA MASSACRE

Mr. President, I ask unanimous consent that the Senate now proceed to the immediate consideration of S. Con. Res. 95, submitted earlier by Senator Lott for himself and others.

The PRESIDING OFFICER. The clerk will report the resolution by title.

The legislative clerk read as follows:

A concurrent resolution (S. Con. Res. 95) commemorating the twelfth anniversary of the Halabja massacre.

There being no objection, the Senate proceeded to consider the concurrent resolution.

Mr. GRAMS. I ask unanimous consent that the concurrent resolution be agreed to, the preamble be agreed to, the motion to reconsider be laid upon the table, and any statements relating to the resolution be printed in the Record.

The PRESIDING OFFICER. Without objection, it is so ordered.

The concurrent resolution (S. Con. Res. 95) was agreed to.

The preamble was agreed to.

The concurrent resolution, with its preamble, reads as follows:

S. Con. Res. 95

Whereas on March 16, 1988, Saddam Hussein attacked the Iraqi Kurdish city of Halabja with chemical weapons, including nerve gas, VX, and mustard gas;

Whereas more than 5,000 men, women, and children were murdered in Halabja by

Saddam Hussein's chemical warfare, in gross violation of international law;

Whereas the attack on Halabja was part of a systemic, genocidal attack on the Kurds of Iraq known as the "Anfal Campaign";

Whereas the Anfal Campaign resulted in the death of more than 180,000 Iraqi Kurdish men, women, and children;

Whereas, despite the passage of 12 years, there has been no successful attempt by the United States, the United Nations, or other bodies of the international community to bring the perpetrators of the Halabja massacre to justice;

Whereas the Senate and the House of Representatives have repeatedly noted the atrocities committed by the Saddam Hussein regime;

Whereas the Senate and the House of Representatives have on 16 separate occasions called upon successive Administrations to work toward the creation of an International Tribunal to prosecute the war crimes of the Saddam Hussein regime;

Whereas in successive fiscal years monies have been authorized to create a record of the human rights violations of the Saddam Hussein regime and to pursue the creation of an international tribunal and the indictment of Saddam Hussein and members of his regime;

Whereas the Saddam Hussein regime continues the brutal repression of the people of Iraq, including the denial of basic human, political, and civil rights to Sunni, Shiite, and Kurdish Iraqis, as well as other minority groups;

Whereas the Secretary General of the United Nations has documented annually the failure of the Saddam Hussein regime to deliver basic necessities to the Iraqi people despite ample supplies of food in Baghdad warehouses;

Whereas the Saddam Hussein regime has at its disposal more than $12,000,000,000 per annum (at current oil prices) to expend on all categories of human needs;

Whereas, notwithstanding a complete lack of restriction on the purchase of food by the Government of Iraq, infant mortality rates in areas controlled by Saddam Hussein remain above pre-war levels, in stark contrast to rates in United Nations-controlled Kurdish areas, which are below pre-war levels; and

Whereas it is unconscionable that after the passage of 12 years the brutal Saddam Hussein dictatorship has gone unpunished for the murder of hundreds of thousands of innocent Iraqis, the use of banned chemical weapons on the people of Iraqi Kurdistan, and innumerable other human rights violations: Now, therefore, be it

Resolved by the Senate (the House of Representatives concurring), That Congress—

(1) commemorates the suffering of the people of Halabja and all the victims of the Anfal Campaign;

(2) condemns the Saddam Hussein regime for its continued brutality towards the Iraqi people;

(3) strongly urges the President to act forcefully within the United Nations and the United Nations Security Council to constitute an international tribunal for Iraq;

(4) calls upon the President to move rapidly to efficiently use funds appropriated by Congress to create a record of the crimes of the Saddam Hussein regime;

(5) recognizes that Saddam Hussein's record of brutality and belligerency threaten both the people of Iraq and the entire Persian Gulf region; and

(6) reiterates that it should be the policy of the United States to support efforts to remove the regime headed by Saddam Hussein from power in Iraq and to promote the emergence of a democratic government to replace that regime, as set forth in Public Law 105-338.

209.

[April 6, 2000 (House), p. H1943]

KURDISH RIGHTS

The SPEAKER pro tempore (Mr. Shimkus). Under a previous order of the House, the gentleman from New Jersey (Mr. Pallone) is recognized for 5 minutes.

Mr. PALLONE. Mr. Speaker, I rise to join my esteemed colleague in introducing a resolution calling for democratic, linguistic and cultural rights for all Kurds living in Turkey today.

The lands of Kurdistan are considered by many to be the birthplace of the history of human culture. Some of the earliest settlements as well as the earliest indications of the Neolithic Revolution have been found among the hills and valleys of this beautiful landscape. Yet even as one ponders the cultural advancements made on Kurdish soil thousands of years ago, one cannot help but wonder what lies in store for the Kurds' future.

For Kurds living in the Middle East, recent history has brought far less reason to celebrate. Kurds in Iraq, Iran, Syria, and Turkey have been persecuted by the regimes in power, with the most brutal assault being the poison gas attacks made by Saddam Hussein in 1988 which decimated an entire section of a city and its 5,000 inhabitants.

Although Saddam Hussein's heinous attacks caused unimaginable death and biological destruction, his regime, ironically, has not launched an all-scale offensive on the culture of the Kurds. It is unfortunate that the most comprehensive assault on the Kurdish language and culture has stemmed from our own ally and fellow-NATO member, Turkey.

Mr. Speaker, in 1997 I addressed this body on the cultural oppression of Kurds by the Turkish government and on the existence of democratically-elected Kurdish Parliamentarians unjustly jailed in Turkey. It is with a heavy heart that I stand before you today and recall recent events and happenings in Turkey, all of which suggest that nothing has changed. The Kurdish language and culture is still on Turkey's most wanted list and Kurdish Parliamentarians elected to give voice of their constituents, are still being silenced.

When I addressed this body three years ago, Turkish Kurdistan was under a declared State of Emergency, patrolled by the Gendarmerie. Torture and abuse of the Kurds, the searching of Kurdish homes without a warrant, and the persecution of assemblies and demonstrations were the norm. This situation, in flagrant breech of democracy, continues today. The 1999 U.S. Department of State Human Rights Report for Turkey states that members of the Gendarmerie continue to commit serious human rights abuses including the torture of Kurds, well-aware that the likelihood of their personal conviction is extremely slim.

Such lax prosecution is not the case, however, for Kurds. Six years ago four former members of Parliament, stripped of their official duties, were imprisoned for the crime of representing the will of Kurdish citizens. As I stand here today, Mrs. Leyla Zana, Mr. Hatip Dicle, Mr. Orhan Dogan, and Mr. Selim Sadak are still in jail. Labeled "Prisoners of Conscience" by Amnesty International, these four are guilty only of attempting to invigorate a true spirit of democracy in Turkey.

Three years ago 153 Members of Congress expressed their disapproval of the anti-democratic treatment of elected Kurdish representatives in the Turkish Parliament. I humbly stand before you to question whether it was enough. Today these four individuals are still in jail. Even more disturbing, the harassment of democratically-elected officials seems to be expanding from the national level to encompass local levels as well.

In February of this year, in a move that shocked many of us in this room, the Turkish Gendarmerie arrested three Kurdish mayors from cities in Turkish Kurdistan. One, the mayor of Diyarbakir, had just met with the Swedish Foreign Minister the day before his arrest in order to discuss hopes for a lasting and solid peace between Turks and Kurds. Although the mayors have since been released, their trials are pending, and if convicted, they too will face prison sentences. The arrests raise questions, not only about the legitimacy of Turkish democracy, but about the sincerity of Turkey's commitment to forging peace.

When I addressed the body three years ago, the Kurdish language could not be broadcasted or taught, even as a foreign language, in schools. I am saddened to say that this negation of a people's language continues today. But, here I must add that the criminalization of speech and expression is not necessarily limited to Kurdish citizens communicating in their native tongue. High numbers of journalists, human rights workers, doctors, and lawyers who expose injustices committed by the military, police, or state are also subject to prison sentences and illegal torture making the anti-sedition legislation perhaps the most "equal opportunity" of all laws in Turkey.

Mr. Speaker, the Kurdish Question, touches upon the very nature of democracy in Turkey and carries serious implications for the whole of Turkish society. Illustrations of how excessive laws mitigating Kurdish culture can spill into the mainstream, ultimately curtailing the freedoms of all citizens, are easy to find. Just last week authorities in Istanbul detained nearly 200 Kurds for illegally celebrating the Kurdish New Year, Newroz. Following their detention, authorities launched investigations of 6 Turkish newspapers that had reported on Newroz activities, for their crimes of spelling the holiday with a Kurdish "w" rather than the "v" found in the Turkish appellation. (the v is not the only letter charged with criminality—p and k have been banned from text books)

This persecution of a language and a culture, committed with such diligence that even individual letters come under fire, would be lamentable in any region of the world. But, that it occurs in the very Cradle of Civilization which bore witness to the first creative sparks of human culture and innovation instills the situation with a sense of tragedy so compelling that I believe it presents a direct challenge to those of us assembled here today.

Mr. Speaker, this resolution, supported by my esteemed colleagues Bob Filner, John E. Porter, Frank Wolf, and Anna Eshoo, was written with the hope that the future of the Kurds need not be wrought with even greater persecution and suffering. It was written with the knowledge that democracy, rather than being a simple destination, needs to continually be nurtured. And it was written with the promise that peace and justice may be cultivated. I ask my friends and esteemed colleagues to join in support of this resolution so that language, culture and democracy will be permitted to flourish on the very ground that holds our common humanity's cultural roots.

210.

[April 6, 2000 (House), pp. H1953-54]

A FUTURE OF HOPE FOR TURKEY: ONE OF PEACE AND JUSTICE FOR THE KURDS

The SPEAKER pro tempore (Mr. Thune). Under the Speaker's announced policy of January 6, 1999, the gentleman from California (Mr. Filner) is recognized for 60 minutes as the designee of the minority leader.

Mr. FILNER. Mr. Speaker, yesterday I introduced a resolution, House Resolution 461, to ask for the freedom of Leyla Zana, Hatip Dicle, Orhan Dogan and Selim Sadak as well as the lifting of the ban on the Kurdish language and culture in Turkey. Now, these names may be unfamiliar to some, but the names I just read are those of Kurdish parliamentarians, Kurdish Congress members who have been in prison, yes, Mr. Speaker, in prison as Congresspeople for the last 6 years. The language and culture that they represent are the Kurds, an indigenous people of the Middle East who live in an ancient land called Kurdistan. These representatives are in prison solely because they are Kurds, and the Kurds are not free because their land is ruled by Turkey, Syria, Iran, and Iraq.

Now, this body has previously heard of the name Leyla Zana who, according to The New York Times, is the most famous Kurdish dissident in the world. This country has heard of the Kurds because Saddam Hussein gassed them with his chemical and biological weapons in 1988 and threatened to do so again in 1991. But neither this country nor this body has really paid any attention to the plight of the Kurds living as they still do on their ancient lands and still persecuted now even as I speak by the governments in Ankara, Damascus, Tehran, and Baghdad.

Mr. Speaker, I am going to restrict my commentary today to Turkey, because it is a country we honor as an ally, we support as a friend and we favor as a partner. Turkey boasts of having a sophisticated U.S. arsenal in its inventory: M-16 machine guns, M-60 battle tanks, Cobra attack helicopters, and F-16 fighter planes. American Special Forces in fact train Turkish commandoes in Turkey. Turkish leaders are fond of referring to their people as an "army nation" and talks are now under way to supply Turkey with an additional 145 attack helicopters worth $4 billion.

Now, is Turkey really worthy of these investments? Have our fighter planes, our attack helicopters, our battle tanks, and our machine guns protected the liberty of its citizens? Why are we training Turkish commandoes who are known to behead their victims and haul their dead bodies behind armored vehicles? In Turkey today, Mr. Speaker, I note with trepidation that liberty is under assault. Cultural genocide is the law of the land. A way of life known as Kurdish is disappearing at an alarming rate.

Mr. Speaker, we are not always as a country indifferent to the plight of the Kurds. Our 28th President, Woodrow Wilson, supported the right of subject peoples to self-determination. In an address to the Senate on January 22, 1917 he said:

No nation should seek to extend its policy over any other nation or people but that every people should be left free to determine its own polity, its own way of development, unhindered, unthreatened, unafraid, the little along with the great and powerful.

Three months after this statement, the United States entered the war on the side of the Allies. The war cry "making the world safe for democracy" resonated with subject peoples all over the world and families from North Africa to Central Europe and people who named their sons after our President. But the prophetic words of President Wilson were disregarded, especially in the Ottoman provinces. The Armenians were massacred and the Kurds were subdued after the emergence of the Turkish republic. What followed has been chronicled as nothing other than a slow-motion genocide.

In Turkey, a people known to historians as the Kurds and a land known to geographers as Kurdistan simply disappeared from the official discourse overnight just 1 year after the inception of the young Turkish republic. The Kurds, said the Turkish officials, were not really Kurds but mountain Turks and their land was not really Kurdistan but eastern Tur-

key. This act of social engineering and historical revisionism has been propagated as the law of the land ever since. Thousands of Kurds have died in rebellion after rebellion. Millions have been uprooted. Some wish to raise a Rest in Peace sign over the entire Kurdish nation.

Perhaps of all the stories that have come out of the Kurdish land administered by the Turks, that of Layla Zana captures the essence of what it means to be a Kurd in Turkey. She was born in 1961 in a small Kurdish village near Farqin. Her earliest recollections of the Turks were either as tax collectors or as soldiers. In elementary school the lone Turkish teacher that she had told her she should learn Turkish because it was the language of the civilization. She was able to go to school for only 3 years. Then she worked on a farm, helped out in the house and occasionally heard of the name Mehdi Zana, who was her future husband, as the rising star of Kurdish politics.

In fact in 1976, she married Mehdi Zana and moved to the largest Kurdish city in the world known as Amed, or Diyarbakir, in northern Kurdistan. In 1977, Mehdi Zana was elected to the post of mayor of the city. Turkish officials were appalled. Here was an ardent Turkish nationalist who managed to earn the trust of his fellow Kurds. The city Amed was put under siege. Its funds were frozen. Mayor Zana appealed to his European colleagues for help. French mayors responded by giving 30 buses and trucks filled with office supplies and for a short while the bus fares in the city were simply abolished. Leyla Zana's education in politics began in those tumultuous years.

On September 12, 1980, a general in the Turkish army named Kenan Evren declared himself the supreme leader of the country. He deposed the elected government and dissolved the parliament. His soldiers then began arresting dissidents, especially the Kurds. The rising star of Kurdish politics, Mehdi Zana, was high on their list. Twelve days later, he was arrested without any charges being posted. And for the next 8 years, he would be tortured in the infamous Diyarbakir military prison. He would witness the death of 57 of his friends. But through it all he did not break, he endured as did his wife and small children.

Mehdi Zana was kept in prison for 3 additional years in various Turkish prisons in Turkey proper. He has chronicled his ordeals in a book entitled Prison No. 5, now available in bookstores in this country as well as on amazon.com. I had the fortune of meeting this nonviolent champion of Kurdish rights a couple of years ago and was humbled by the generosity of his feelings toward his tormentors. Like President Nelson Mandela in South Africa, Mehdi Zana does not seek revenge. He wants peace for himself and his family and his people.

In words that still haunt me, he urged me to speak out against the slow motion genocide against the Kurds. "The Armenians," he noted, "were massacred. The Kurds are being put to permanent sleep."

Mr. Speaker, Leyla Zana's schooling consisted of adversity, torture, humiliation, and State-sanctioned persecution that has never slackened to this day. She had given birth to a son when Mehdi was the Mayor of Amed and would later give birth to a daughter after her husband's arrest. She would learn Turkish the hard way, from the police who harassed her for being the wife of a popular mayor, and the courts who ruled that he was a trader and deserved to die.

In 1998, she herself was thrown into jail and endured abuse, humiliation, and torture for organizing the wives of Kurdish political prisoners to demand visitation rights. Although behind bars, the authorities, fearing a chain reaction, gave in to these mothers' demands, and Layla Zana has related this brush with the police as a turning point in her awakening as a political activist. She began reading voraciously, wrote for various publications, passed a proficiency exam for a high school diploma; in fact, the first Kurdish woman to do so in her city.

These were the years when the wall in Berlin came down, the Soviet Union let go of its subject nations, the Cold War that had dominated international politics was supplanted with a rapprochement between the East and the West. The winds of change that brought democracy to former communist nations, people now hoped with visit the lands administered by "our dictators" in such places as South Africa, Indonesia and Turkey.

We all know that South Africa has made its transition to democracy. And just last year, the official world welcomed one of its smallest nations to the fold, the people of East Timor. But the Kurds, the Kurds, thus far, have been kept off of this forward march toward liberty. The adversaries of the Kurds and their misguided friends have managed to define them as the misfits of the world. But this cause of liberty is a just one, and the veil of oppression over the Kurds must come down.

There was a time when the prospects of peace and reconciliation between the Kurds and the Turks almost became a reality. In October 1991, the country held a general election. Twenty-two Kurds were elected to the Turkish parliament. The names I mentioned when I first began tonight, Leyla Zana, Hatip Dicle, Orhan Dogan and Selim Sadak were part of that group. Hopes were raised that these newly and duly elected representatives would be the mediators with the Turks and peace and justice might once again come to the land of the Kurds.

But these hopes were dashed when Mehmet Sincar, a newly-elect Kurdish member of the parliament, was murdered in broad daylight on September 3, 1993. One year later, 6 Kurdish parliamentarians were arrested for their advocacy of a peaceful resolution of the Kurdish question. Six others, who were feeling the sword of Damocles hanging on their shoulders, fled abroad to seek political asylum in Europe, and the remaining nine Kurdish deputies in the parliament either resigned from their posts or changed parties to save their lives.

An all-out war was then declared with devastating results. Turkish troops using American weapons wanted to silence the Kurdish resistance once and for all. The Kurdish cease-fire offers were spurned. The Kurdish villagers were forced to either take up arms against their family members, the Kurdish rebels, or face the consequences of the destruction of their villages. Over 3,400 villages have been destroyed; 37,000 people, mostly Kurds, have been killed; 3 million Kurds have become refugees.

Mr. Speaker, 3 years ago our distinguished colleague from Illinois (Mr. Porter) sent out a "Dear Colleague" letter which was signed by 153 Members of the 105th Congress to President Clinton urging him to intervene on behalf of Leyla Zana. A year later, in fact, the gentleman from Illinois (Mr. Porter) visited her in Turkish prison and urged the Turkish authorities to do the same. Unfortunately, nothing came of these efforts. Her imprisonment continues and the intransigence of the Turks is still at an all-time high.

The Porter letter, which was dated October 30, 1997 addresses some of the concerns of the resolution I have introduced in this Congress, and I would like to read that "Dear Colleague" for the Record.

It states: "Dear Mr. President: We want to draw your attention to the tragic situation of Leyla Zana, the first Kurdish woman ever elected to the Turkish parliament. Mrs. Zana, who is the mother of two children, was chosen to represent the Kurdish city of Diyarbakir by an overwhelming margin in October 1991. She was arrested by Turkish authorities in March of 1994 in the Parliament Building and subsequently prosecuted for what Turkish authorities have labeled "separatist speech" that is stemming from her exercise of her right to free speech in the defense of the rights of the Kurdish people. She was sentenced to 15 years in prison in December 1994 and remains in Ankara today.

One of the charges against Mrs. Zana was her 1993 appearance here in Washington before the Helsinki Commission of the United States Congress. We find it outrageous that although she was invited to participate at the request of Members of Congress, her participation was one of the activities that led to her imprisonment.

Mrs. Zana's pursuit of democratic change through nonviolence was honored by the European Parliament which unanimously awarded her the 1995 Sakharov Peace Prize. In addition, Amnesty International and Human Rights Watch have raised concern about her case.

"Mr. President," the letter goes on, "Turkey is an important partner of the United States, a NATO member, and a major recipient of our foreign aid, but its abuse of its Kurdish citizens and their legitimately-elected representatives is unacceptable. Mrs. Zana's majority Kurdish constituency gave her the mandate to represent them, but the government of Turkey has made an unconscionable effort to stop her. Her voice should not be silenced. This is just one of the many cases in which the Turkish Government has used the power of the State to abuse people, based on their political beliefs.

We ask you and your administration, Mr. President, to raise Mrs. Zana's case with the Turkish authorities at the highest level and seek her immediate and unconditional release so that we may, once again, welcome her to our shores."

Mr. Speaker, that was the letter that 153 of us wrote recently. Since then, Amnesty International has adopted Leyla Zana and her duly-elected members of parliament as prisoners of conscious. In 1995 and 1998, the Noble Peace Committee that assigns its prestigious Peace Prize to people who embody our most deepest aspirations for a more tolerant world acknowledged that Leyla Zana was one of their finalists. The City of Rome has awarded her honorary citizenship. European organizations have bestowed on her numerous awards of their own.

In 1867, Mr. Speaker, a great American, Frederick Douglas, in his "Appeal to Congress for Impartial Suffrage," summarized the situation of his family which is akin to what this resolution is demanding from the Turkish Government. Reflecting on Mr. Douglas's historical remarks, I was reminded of my encounter with Mehdi Zana and how he too echoed the same sentiments as our own great emancipator. Mr. Douglas wrote that, "We have marvelously survived all of the exterminating forces of slavery, and have emerged at the end of 250 years of bondage, not morose, misanthropic, and revengeful, but cheerful, hopeful and forgiving. We now stand before Congress and the country, not complaining of the past, but simply asking for a better future." Simply asking for a better future.

Mr. Speaker, my resolution, supported at this time by my esteemed colleagues, the gentleman from Illinois (Mr. Porter), the gentleman from New Jersey (Mr. Smith), the gentleman from Virginia (Mr. Wolf), the gentlewoman from California (Ms. Eshoo), the gentleman from Michigan (Mr. Bonior), and the gentleman from New Jersey (Mr. Pallone), calls for a better future for the Kurds. In that future, public service is not rewarded with punishment, but honored with gratitude. In that future, languages are not banned, but cultivated as a gift of God to a people and of a people to its offspring. And only in that future, Mr. Speaker, lies the promise of peace and justice for the Kurds and a brighter future with the Turks.

Mr. Speaker, I ask my friends to support us as we help the peoples of Turkey to leap into the future for the good of themselves, as well as our battered humanity.

Mr. Speaker, asking for a better future is what we are doing here tonight.

211.

[April 10, 2000 (Extensions), p. E 521]

RELEASING FOUR KURDISH MEMBERS OF PARLIAMENT OF THE REPUBLIC OF TURKEY
HON. JOHN EDWARD PORTER
OF ILLINOIS
IN THE HOUSE OF REPRESENTATIVES

Monday, April 10, 2000

Mr. PORTER. Mr. Speaker, I am supporting a resolution introduced today calling for the immediate release from prison of four Kurdish members of the Parliament of the Republic of Turkey. I want to thank the gentleman from California (Mr. Filner) for sponsoring this resolution of which I am a proud co-sponsor.

Currently, four Turkish parliamentarians of the now banned Kurdish based Democracy Party DEP, Leyla Zana, Hatip Dicle, Orhan Dogan, and Selim Sadak, are serving prison sentences simply because they are Kurds. Leyla Zana, the first Kurdish woman ever elected to the Turkish Parliament, was chosen to represent the city of Diyarbakir by an over-

whelming majority in October in 1991. In 1993, she travel to the United States to speak to officials about human rights abuses against the Kurdish minority in Turkey and to testify before the Congressional Human Rights Caucus. She was arrested on March 2, 1994 in the Parliament building and subsequently prosecuted for a so-called "separatist speech." Ever since then Ms. Zana, along with Hatip Dicle, Orhan Dogan, and Selim Sadak have been jailed for the simple act of specaking out for their people—the Kurds—the very people by whom they were elected.

Turkey is a country which claims to be a democracy and is continuously taking steps to be accepted as a western partner, as seen with its current European Union candidacy. However, its recent actions do not show any concrete effort to abide by international human rights standards. In the last week, it has been reported that the Turkish military has been massing troops and tanks along the Iraqi border in an apparent pending offense against the Kurds. Equally as disturbing is the re-arrest of Turkey's most prominent human rights figure, Akin Birdal, for a speech he made in 1996 calling for a peaceful resolution to the conflict between the Turkish state and the Kurdish Workers' Party PKK.

If Turkey wants to be treated as an equal partner with the west, it is time for it to treat all of its citizens with equal rights and a general respect for human rights. The time has come for Turkey to allow the Kurdish people the right to speak their language and practice their culture. Releasing these parliamentarians would show Turkey and the world that Turkey is ready to respect the human rights of all its citizens and that it is on the right path to be accepted by the international community.

We must not continue to ignore or apologize for Turkey's outrageous behavior. Six years is far too long for these parliamentarians to be in jail, for speaking out for rights which are guaranteed under the United Nations Declaration of Human Rights. We must speak out strongly against these attacks and unfair acts and demand that Turkey end this lawless assault.

212.

[Wednesday, October 11, 2000 (House), pp. H 9804-05]

OPPOSING THE SALE OF ATTACK HELICOPTERS TO TURKEY

Under a previous order of the House, the gentleman from Florida (Mr. Bilirakis) is recognized for 5 minutes.

Mr. BILIRAKIS. Mr. Speaker, I rise today to voice my fierce opposition to the sale of 145 Bell-Textron attack helicopters to Turkey, as planned by the administration.

First and foremost, there is simply no need to proceed with this sale. Turkey is already the most militarized state in that region, and it has the second largest army in NATO after the United States. Despite these facts, Turkey plans to spend $150 billion over the next 25 to 30 years on military weapons; and it plans to implement the first $31 billion phase in the next 10 years. This money could be better used to build schools, hospitals, or housing for the victims of last year's destructive earthquake. Mr. Speaker, the list is endless.

Previous experience leaves no room for any optimism regarding legitimate use of such weaponry by Turkey. Quite the contrary, the record shows that the Turkish military has consistently failed to distinguish between civilian and military targets. For the last 16 years, the Turkish military has been using American weaponry, most notably attack helicopters, to kill more than 30,000 civilians, destroy over 2,000 ethnic Kurdish villages and displace more than 2 ½ million ethnic Kurds.

The Turkish military has misused its equipment even though its government has signed numerous international agreements guaranteeing freedom of religion and human rights. Recently, Turkey used an American COBRA attack helicopter in its campaign against the Kurds in southeast Turkey, in direct violation of the Arms Export Control Act and the Foreign Military Sales Agreement which Turkey signed with the United States.

Despite its repeated pledges and promises to make improvements, Turkey's record of human rights violations remains dismal. In a December 1997 meeting with U.S. officials, Turkish diplomats pledged to meet certain benchmarks for improving human rights in Turkey. In subsequent meetings, U.S. officials pledged to oppose the sale of U.S. attack helicopters or other military equipment to Turkey unless the Turkish government met these standards.

And to what degree did Turkey honor its promises? According to the State Department's 1999 Country Report on Human Rights, Turkey has failed to meet any of the benchmarks set forth by the administration. How can we allow this sale to proceed when Turkey has repeatedly failed to live up to its promises? Our Nation risks a loss of credibility in permitting this sale while repeatedly proclaiming our commitment to respect and promote human rights and our opposition to Turkey's violations.

Other countries have refused to sell Turkey weapons because of its human rights records. According to a report by Reuters on September 8, 2000, Germany's ruling Social Democrats said their government would veto a $7.1 billion order to supply Turkey with 1,000 tanks because of Turkey's human rights violations. If Germany is willing to forego a lucrative arms deal based on these concerns, why should we feel any differently? Is our Nation any less committed to protecting human rights? Are our principles more "flexible" when a significant dollar amount is involved? I would hope not.

Mr. Speaker, some values transcend geopolitical barriers, and respect for human rights is one of them. People around the world look to the United States for leadership and guidance precisely because of our strict adherence to such principles. The proposed arms sale to Turkey, viewed in the light of its past record on human rights, is contrary to the values we espouse, harmful to our imagine abroad, and threatens the security of a strategically important region.

For these reasons, Mr. Speaker, I urge Members to join me in opposing this arms deal and in calling for its immediate cancellation.

Mr. McGOVERN. Mr. Speaker, I have long been concerned about the level of U.S. military aid and arms sales to Turkey. On average, the U.S. provides Turkey with more than $1 billion each year in direct military assistance and training and commercial arms exports. There are more particular reasons, however, for why I am opposed to the recently announced agreement for Turkey to purchase 145 attack helicopters worth $4.5 billion from U.S. arms manufacturers. Nothing could be more destructive to the efforts by the U.S. and the international community to bring peace and stability to the eastern Mediterranean region that this major arms purchase by Turkey.

Human rights organizations inside and outside of Turkey have documented that Turkey has used American Cobra attack helicopters in its campaign against the Kurdish people in southeast Turkey. The Turkish military consistently fail to distinguish between civilian and military targets. For the past 16 years, the Turkish military has used American weaponry and especially attack helicopters to kill over 30,000 civilian non-combatants, destroy over 2,000 ethnic Kurdish villages, and displace over 2.5 million ethnic Kurds. In its "Report 2000," Amnesty International states that the practice of torture has actually increased in the past year.

At a time when the world hopes for a break-through in negotiations on Cyprus, the U.S. approves a massive military sale to Turkey. At a time when the world is attempting to lessen the attacks and repressive actions taken against the Kurdish minority by the Turkish government, the U.S. approves a massive military sale to Turkey.

Why is the Administration allowing this commercial sale to go forward? Turkey is already the most militarized state in the Mediterranean. It possesses vast military superiority over all its neighbors. There is no need to increase its military arsenal.

Rather than spending $4.5 billion on the purchase of attack helicopters, the Government of Turkey might better target those funds toward rebuilding the communities ravaged by earthquakes, building more schools and health clinics, and addressing other basic economic needs of its people.

I urge the Administration to revoke this export license and move away from the long-standing policy of militarizing Turkey—a pol-

icy supported by Republican and Democratic Administrations alike. What might have once made sense during the Cold War is now counter- productive to efforts to demilitarize the region.

The pursuit of regional peace and stability and respect for basic human rights are not helped by arms sales.

213.

[December 7, 2000 (House), pp. H 12040-41]

TURKISH GOVERNMENT MUST RECOGNIZE BASIC HUMAN RIGHTS OF KURDISH PEOPLE

The SPEAKER pro tempore (Mr. Hulshof). Under a previous order of the House, the gentleman from New Jersey (Mr. Pallone) is recognized for 5 minutes.

Mr. PALLONE. Mr. Speaker, today I want to speak about the need for the Turkish government to recognize the basic human rights of the Kurdish people, and I rise this afternoon to condemn recent, though ongoing, violations of these rights in Turkey.

I have always said the Kurds must be respected as a people, the world must finally listen to and respect their aspirations, and that they should enjoy the same right of choosing their representatives as other people do all over the world. The Turkish government has not accepted the validity of the Kurdish struggle or even of the Kurdish people. They have jailed leaders, but the message of these leaders continues to ring loud and clear.

Mr. Speaker, in the past few weeks, the Turkish government has extended a 13-year-old state of emergency in four mainly Kurdish provinces for an additional 4 months, and who knows what will happen at the end of those 4 months in terms of another extension. Further, the extension of emergency rule occurred despite the European commission's formal expression that the lifting of emergency rule is an objective for Turkey to achieve.

On December 4, *The Washington Post* reported that the director of a Kurdish linguistics institute in Istanbul is facing a trial on charges that the institute is an illegal business. The charges come despite the fact that Turkish security courts have hired interpreters from this very institute for the past 8 years. This incident illustrates the type of human rights violations infringements that continue to occur but that must be halted immediately against the Kurdish people.

I call upon my colleagues to join me, Mr. Speaker, in urging the Turkish government to immediately grant basic rights to Kurdish citizens in Turkey and more formally and fully recognize the Kurdish people. This should include lifting the extension of emergency rule, lifting all bans on Kurdish-language television, cinema, and all forms of fine arts and culture.

Bans on language and culture are particularly disturbing because the lands of Kurdistan are considered by many to be the birthplace of the history of human culture. It saddens me that there is still a need to be on the floor protesting violations of these most basic yet essential human rights.

Mr. Speaker, back in 1997, I addressed the American Kurdish Information Network on the cultural oppression of Kurds by the Turkish government and on the Turks' squelching of Kurdish language and culture. At that time, 153 Members of Congress expressed their disapproval of the antidemocratic treatment of elected Kurdish representatives in the Turkish parliament.

In April of this year, a number of my colleagues joined me in introducing a House Resolution calling for the immediate and unconditional release from prison of certain Kurdish Members of the Turkish parliament and for prompt recognition of full Kurdish cultural and language rights within Turkey.

Now, Mr. Speaker, I am continuing the fight on behalf of the Kurdish people, because their voices are still repressed, although the conflict between the government and separatist Kurdish guerrillas in the southeast has subsided significantly since the arrest last year of the Kurdish Workers Party leader, Abdullah Ocalan. Fears by hard-line Turkish nationalists that any recognition of Kurdish identity will fragment Turkey and strengthen separatism seem unwarranted based on the decline in tensions.

Mr. Speaker, Turkey must negotiate with the Turkish leaders. Turkey must lift its blockade of Armenia also. Turkey must end its military occupation of northern Cyprus. Such a change in behavior would benefit everyone in the region, including the Turkish people.

I hope my colleagues will join me in delivering these important messages to the Turkish government at every possible opportunity.

[In a separate press release, dated December 7, 2000 [not published in *Congressional Record*], Pallone asks Turkey to lift an extended state-of-emergency in four Kurdish provinces and grant Kurdish citizens basic rights. Below is the text of the press release:

Congressman Blasts Recent Human Rights
Violations in Turkey During Statement on
House Floor

Washington, D.C. ---U.S. Rep. Frank Pallone, Jr. (D-NJ) today asked the Turkish government to recognize the basic human rights of the Kurdish people and to condemn recent violations of these rights in Turkey during a speech on the floor of the U.S. House of Representatives.

The Congressman also wrote Turkish Ambassador Baki Ilkin today urging the Turkish government lift the extended state-of-emergency in four mainly Kurdish provinces. Pallone also requested that the government should "instead immediately grant basic rights to Kurdish citizens in Turkey and more formally and fully recognize the Kurdish people."

Pallone's letter to Ambassador Ilkin and his remarks on the House floor follow.

December 7, 2000

The Honorable Baki Ilkin
Embassy of Turkey
2525 Massachusetts Avenue, NW
Washington, DC 20008

Dear Ambassador Ilkin:

I am writing to urge your government to lift the extended state-of-emergency in four mainly Kurdish provinces in Turkey. The provinces include Diyarbakir, Hakkari, Sirnak and Tunceli. The extension of emergency rule occurred despite the European Commission's formal expression that the lifting of emergency rule is an objective for Turkey to achieve.

Your government should instead immediately grant basic rights to Kurdish citizens in Turkey and more formally and fully recognize the Kurdish people. This should include lifting bans on and/or facilitating access to Kurdish-language television, cinema, and all forms of fine arts and culture.

On December 4, the *Washington Post* reported that the director of a Kurdish linguistics institute in Istanbul is facing trial on charges that the institute is an illegal business. The charges come despite the fact that Turkish security courts have hired interpreters from this very institute for the past eight years. This incident illustrates the type of human rights violations and infringements that have been occurring, but that must be halted immediately against the Kurdish people.

The changes I am urging are particularly timely and appropriate, because the conflict between the government and separatist Kurdish guerrillas in the southeast has subsided significantly since the arrest last year of Kurdish Workers Party (PKK) leader Abdullah Ocalan. Fears by hard-line Turkish nationalists that any recognition of Kurdish identity will fragment Turkey and strengthen separatism seem unwarranted, based on the decline in tensions.

Thank you for the opportunity to present my views.

Sincerely,

Frank Pallone, Jr.
Member of Congress

FOREIGN RELATIONS OF THE UNITED STATES

214.

[1936, Volume III, pp. 387–89]

The Chargé in Iran (Merriam) to the Secretary of State

TEHRAN, May 1, 1936.
[Received May 27.]

781. Sir: I have the honor to report that according to Reverend Henry Mueller of the Lutheran Orient Mission at Mehabad (formerly Saujbulak), Azerbaijan, which is now in the process of liquidation at the desire of the Iranian Government, it was decided at the World Missionary Conference held at Edinburgh in 1910, that evangelistic missionary work among the Kurds should be undertaken by the Lutheran Church. Accordingly, the Lutheran Orient Mission is "accredited" to the Kurds as a people, and its field of effort is therefore in the areas in Iraq, Iran, and Turkey, which are inhabited by Kurds. The location of the Mission in one of these countries rather than in either of the other two is, therefore, governed by reasons of expediency and not of principle, and as the Mission is now being sent away from Kurdish territory in Iran, there is good reason to believe that an attempt may be made to relocate it in Kurdish Iraq. Of course, the attitude of Turkey toward Christian missionaries during the past quarter-century places Kurdish Turkey fairly out of the picture.

Mr. Mueller has himself mentioned such a possibility to me, adding that of course the ultimate decision will be up to the home Board. It is his understanding that missionary work in Iraq is regulated by treaty and he appears to think that as the policy of the Iraqi Government towards the Kurds is both lenient and enlightened, at least by contrast with the severe Kurdish policies of the Iranian and Turkish Governments, the presence of the Lutheran Mission would be welcomed by tile Government of Iraq. I have suggested to Mr. Mueller that he call at the American Legation at Baghdad on his way home in order that he may be able to inform himself not only of the cold text of a treaty, but also of the political atmosphere in which missionaries carry on their work in Iraq and of any special factors which might effect working in the Kurdish areas of that country.

It may as well be said here that the Iranian authorities are aware of the possibility that the Lutherans may become established across the frontier and are disturbed at the prospect. Their information was probably obtained by reading correspondence of the Lutheran Mission. Iran is acutely conscious of the fact that Kurdish nationalism, while perhaps not a matter of great immediate concern, may raise its head in any one of the three countries in which the Kurds dwell, and it has done and is doing everything possible to prevent this from happening in Iranian territory. The task is rendered difficult by the indeterminate nature of the frontier for although the boundary was laid down in the Treaty of Erzerum of 1847,[26] and is understood to have been demarcated in 1914 by Perso–Turkish Commissioners, assisted by British and Russian Commissioners having arbitral powers, Mr. Mueller, who has traveled through the country, says that it is not possible to say where the authority of one country ends and that of another commences.

I do not think that the Iranian Government suspects the Lutheran Mission of political involvement in a Kurdish nationalistic movement. I do think that it is entirely unsympathetic to the evangelistic and other work of the Mission, on the ground that whereas the Iranian Government seeks to disestablish contact between the Kurds of Iran and those of Iraq and Turkey, to make them forget that they are Kurds and to realize that they are primarily Iranians—in a word, to wear down and finally to obliterate the differences between the Kurds and the Iranians—on the other hand, the worn of the Mission serves to emphasize and deepen the differences which already exist. If the Mission does not actually foment Kurdish nationalism, at least it tends to prepare the soil for its growth. Mr. Mueller fully appreciates this point of view and, indeed, does not blame the Iranian Government in the least for desiring to see the Mission depart. He appears to realize that there is a fundamental conflict between the purposes of the Mission and those of the Government, and that the latter has the secular power to eliminate those who oppose its aims, which it is quite within its rights to utilize.

Mr. Mueller, it may be added, has the greatest admiration for the Kurds, whom he describes as a proud, simple, vigorous, clean-living mountain people. According, to him, the policy adopted by the Iranian and Turkish Governments towards the Kurds within their borders have been severely oppressive. They have been continuously harried and thousands, even some women, have been shot. On the contrary, the Iraqi Government, while maintaining a firm hand, has encouraged the Kurds as a people, and desires to see them advance and develop as such. For this reason, many Iranian Kurds have emigrated to the Iraqi side.

Respectfully yours,

GORDON P. MERRIAM

---

[26] Signed May 19/31,1847, *British and Foreign State Papers*, vol. XLV, p. 874.

215.

[1942, Volume IV, pp. 318–19]

891.00/1862: Telegram

Concern of the United States Regarding Kurdish Disorders in Soviet–Occupied Province of Azerbaijan

The Minister in Iran (Dreyfus) to the Secretary of State

TEHRAN May 1, 1942—4 p. m.
[Received 8:32 p. m.]

134. Kuniholm[66] reports deterioration of situation at Rezaieh where Kurds are attacking 800 gendarmes outside city and demand (1) a treaty (2) right to circulate armed in city and (3) abolition of gendarmes' posts. He is of opinion that Iranian troops must be allowed to proceed to that region if conditions are to improve. He fears if Russians suffer reverses in Caucasia whole of Azerbaijan will, in absence of strong military forces, fall prey to attack and pillage by Kurds. Situation he says might improve were Soviets to let Kurds know they disapprove of their action.

Seriousness of situation in Rezaieh is confirmed by other sources and it is said several towns are surrounded by Kurds. Prime Minister[67] gave me copy of note he is addressing to Soviet Ambassador in which he attributes alarming conditions at Rezaieh to Soviet refusal to permit troops to proceed there. He stated Iranian Government has right to expect to receive such permission in view of its treaty with Russia. Shah called me yesterday and talked at length along some *[same]* lines. He suggested bitterly than *[that]* Iran is treated in this shabby manner because she is small and weak and that Russians and British would not dare to treat Turkey in similar manner. Iran he said is in treaty relations with Russia as an oversize *[a sovereign]* state and there is no reason why Iranian troops should be denied right to maintain law and order. He expressed hope that help from United States in this regard would be forthcoming. I feel that representations to the Soviet Government along these lines would be helpful.

I discussed matter with Soviet Ambassador who; expressed belief that Iranian gendarmes are sufficient in number to maintain order at Rezaieh if they really tried. I do not agree with this opinion.

Press apparently in fear of Soviet or under their domination plays down conditions in north and refers frequently to Iran's good relations with northern neighbor.

In British zone in central Kurdistan there have been large scale clash[es] between Iranian troops and Kurds under leadership of

Hamarashid with many casualties. It is reported that morale of Iranian troops there is low and that Kurds have firm grip on some sections.

Strong military action seems to be necessary if Kurdish disturbances are to be put down. However, a long range solution must be found along lines suggested by British (see end of my despatch 212, February 19[68]). Iranian Government recognize necessity of this and a committee has already been set up to examine into tribal grievances and seek broad solution.

DREYFUS

---

[66] Bertel E. Kuniholm, Consul at Tabriz
[67] Ali Soheily
[68] Not printed.

216.

[1942, Volume IV, p. 320]

891.00/1866: Telegram

The Minister in Iran (Dreyfus) to the Secretary of State

TEHRAN, May 3, 1942—4 p. m.
[Received May 3—9:53 a. m.]

139. Kuniholm reports as follows: May 2, 2:00 pm. Soviet Consul General, commanding officer Red troops, Iranian officials, and Kurds have met at Askerabad village near Rezaieh. Kurds have resented [presented] series of demands which must be discussed further at Tehran as well as by Russians. Soviet Consul General has appealed to Kurds to disband and go home. Kurdish depredations continue.

DREYFUS

217.

[1942, Volume IV, pp. 320–21]

891.00/1867: Telegram

The Ambassador in Turkey (Steinhardt) to the Secretary of State

ANKARA, May 4, 1942—4 p. m.
[Received 9 p. m.]

362. Iranian Ambassador called on me this morning, and informed me as follows: Iranian Government is seriously concerned with disturbances taking place among Kurds in Azerbaijan, principally in neighborhood of Urmia and Lake Urmia. Although large Soviet forces believed to number 20,000 troops including mechanized units are occupying Azerbaijan they have taken no steps to suppress or discourage activities of about 3,000 Kurds but are believed to be encouraging their rebellious conduct. Repeated requests by Iranian Government for permission to send its own forces into this area for purpose of dealing with Kurds have been refused by the Soviets. Iranian Government continues desirous of suppressing these disorders and would be glad to send necessary forces [to] accomplish this purpose if Soviet authorities will grant necessary permission. Iranian Government is suspicious of motives of Soviet force of occupation in not taking necessary measures.

Ambassador expressed opinion that motive of Soviet Government in refusing permission to Iranian authorities to enter area where disturbances have been taking place or in alternative taking action themselves is to bring pressure to bear on Turk Government in connection with future demands by engendering fear that disorders will spread to Kurds on Turkish side of frontier.

I have learned from his son–in–law that Iranian Ambassador in Kuibyshev called on Stalin in Moscow about 2 weeks ago to discuss foregoing subject.

Repeated to Tehran and Kubyshev.

STEINHARDT

218.

[1942, Volume IV, pp. 321–22]

891.00/1862: Telegram

The Secretary of State to the Ambassador in the Soviet Union (Standley)

WASHINGTON, May 6, 1942—11 p. m.
203. The Legation at Tehran reports that activities of rebellious Kurdish tribes in

Rezaieh section of Azerbaijan are creating a serious situation, which Iranian Government is unable to handle because of Soviet refusal to permit return of Iranian troops to that region. Iranian Government has protested to Soviet and requested their collaboration in accordance with letter and spirit of the Anglo–Russian Iranian treaty of alliance. The Shah has expressed the hope that the United States would support the Iranian position.

If you perceive no objection, please endeavor to find an occasion to discuss the concern of your Government at the disorder which appears to have prevailed recently in North Kurdistan. In the course of your conversation you may advance the following as some of the reasons for your Government's anxiety:

1. As the Soviet Government is undoubtedly aware, the Axis propaganda agencies have been making great capital out of the Kurdish uprisings, which they charge are fomented and encouraged by the Russians as part of a plan to annex the portions of Iran now occupied by Soviet forces. This propaganda, which is directed especially at Turkey and Iraq, as well as Iran, might well have very unfortunate repercussions on the position of the United Nations in that vital area.

2. American lives and property are endangered. The wife of an American correspondent has already been killed by Kurds not far from Tabriz.

3 On one occasion the Axis radio stated that forces of Rashid Ali Gailani, rebel Iraqi leader, had joined the Kurds in Iran. While this may not be true, it is felt that the Kurdish revolt nevertheless offers a potential opportunity which could be exploited by the enemy and might even create difficulties in connection with the maintenance of the supply line to Russian via Iran.

In the light of the above, this Government hopes that the Soviet Government will take such steps as may be necessary to enable the authorities responsible for the maintenance of law and order to put an end to the existing disorders.

The Iranian Government is not being informed of this communication and you should not indicate to the Soviet Government that the intervention of the United States was requested by Iran.

For your information, local Soviet and Iranian officials in Azerbaijan met with Kurdish leaders a few days ago, and it is understood that demands of the Kurds have been referred to Tehran and the appropriate Russian authorities. Please keep Department promptly informed of developments.

HULL

219.

[1942, Volume IV, p. 323]

801.00/1871: Telegram

The Minister in Iran (Dreyfus) to the Secretary of State

TEHRAN, May 12, 1942—noon.
[Received 9:55 p.m.]

151. Following from Kuniholm: May 11, noon. Governor General, War Minister, Iranian and Soviet army officers returned last night from Rezaieh. Kurds have now ceased pillaging. Twenty–one mixed police posts each staffed by about 20 Soviet soldiers and officers and 3 or 4 Iranian gendarmes to be established at once between Rezaieh and Khoi to protect settled localities. Soviets have agreed tentatively to dispatch of one Iranian regiment from Tehran to Rezaieh. No disposition here to grant concessions to Kurds who have no just complaints. Some of pillaged property has found its way to Iraq.

DREYFUS

220.

[1942, Volume IV, p. 324]

740.0011 European War 1939/24546: Telegram

The Minister in Iran (Dreyfus) to the Secretary of State

TEHRAN, September 28,1942—4 p. m.
[Received 11:17 p. m.]

302. Soviet military authorities have asked Iran Government to send a brigade of troops to Tabriz to which Iranians replied they

have not a brigade available. To Iranian suggestion that a brigade be recruited from former Azerbaijan troops Soviets replied that "this would take too much time." I understand, however, that such recruiting is now taking place. Soviet request is interpreted by British here as indication Soviet forces in Azerbaijan are being or are about to be reduced.

Kuniholm reports considerable Russian troop movements in Azerbaijan in last 2 weeks. He states that while most of this is normal reshuffling of units there are in fact indications that troops are being reduced to point where they constitute no more than token force. Kuniholm also reports Soviets adopting sterner attitude regarding Kurds. This is substantiated in Tehran where it is reported Soviets have told Iranians they would not object to disarming Kurds "providing it can be done peacefully".

DREYFUS

221.

[1945, Volume V, pp. 901–08]

761.00/10–2345

The Ambassador in the Soviet Union (Harriman) to the Secretary of State [78]

No. 2215

MOSCOW, October 23, 1945.
[Received November 6.]

SIR: I have the honor to review below current trends of Soviet policy with respect to the Near and Middle East.

General

Soviet aims in this area are primarily strategic: security and aggrandizement. These aims are not defined in hard and fast terms. They are accommodated to time and circumstances. The endless, fluid pursuit of power is a habit of Russian statesmanship, ingrained not only in the traditions of the Russian State but also in the ideology of the Communist Party, which views all other advanced nations as Russia's ultimate enemies and all backward nations as pawns in the struggle for power.

Particularly is this true in the kaleidoscopic Near and Middle East where a realistic policy must take into account not only national factors but also such extra–national forces as the Orthodox Church, the Armenian and Jewish communities, the Kurds and the Arab League.

Turkey

Turkey represents the principal westerly gap in the Soviet system of defense in depth along its borders. Until Turkey is under Soviet domination and the Black Sea a Soviet lake, the USSR will feel itself strategically vulnerable from the southwest. Furthermore, Turkey lies athwart any Soviet ambitions for expansion into the Mediterranean.

More for reasons of security than of expansion it may be assumed that the Soviet program for Turkey is a matter of 'relative urgency. Yet thus far, aside from an irritable press campaign against a Turkish editor, which has now subsided and Mr. Molotov's heavy–handed overtures regarding cession of territory and bases, [79] the U.S.S.R. has remained remarkably inactive with regard to Turkey. The only recent manifestations of interest are the domestic intimations of Communist Party political agitators that certain issues with Turkey are to be joined and that this may lead to war.

But although the U.S.S.R. will probably use its full stock of political stratagems, it is scarcely likely to resort to outright military attack because of the far–reaching international repercussions that such action would have.

Through negotiation, the Soviet Union will presumably seek a favored position with regard to the Straits. But because the Straits are internationally the most explosive of Turkish issues and because the relative strategic importance of the Straits is greatly diminished in an age of airpower, the Soviet Union's ambitions regarding tile Straits may well, in final analysis, play a secondary role. The U.S.S.R. may approach a fundamental revision of the status of the Straits from the Turkish flanks rather than frontally.

The absence of any significant leftist opposition in Turkey means that the Soviet Union must rely principally on other discontented elements real and artificially created. They are

414 KURDISH QUESTION IN U.S. FOREIGN POLICY

the Kurds and the Armenians. Both overlap national borders and so possess a wide utility. Although practically no Armenians remain in eastern Turkey, an Armenian irredenta movement based on Soviet Armenia has already made its implausible presence known. If vigorously developed, it may help to detach the eastern provinces from Turkey by various peaceful pressures or to provoke fatal Turkish exasperation.

While the principal impetus for Armenian separation must originate from outside Turkey, the Kurds are sufficiently strong within Turkey to constitute, if given direction and arms, a considerable disruptive force. This Embassy has seen nothing to indicate that the Kurds of Turkey are being organized and armed by the Soviet Union. But when the time comes, their natural potential utility is not likely to be overlooked by the U.S.S.R.

The Kurds

The utility of the Kurds as an extra–national force extends into Iraq and Iran. This means that if the Soviet Union wishes to exploit the Kurdish potential, there might be developed a regional separatism splitting off contiguous corners of three nations.

The Armenians

With the Armenian SSR constituting an Armenian homeland, the Soviet Union possesses a politically magnetic force tending to draw Armenian communities in the Levant and the western world in the direction of support of Soviet policy. Despite the anti–Soviet sentiments of some Armenian groups outside of the U.S.S.R., it may be assumed that a full–fledged crusade for Armenian SSR recovery of historical Armenian territory would draw popular Armenian support abroad.

Syria and the Lebanon

Soviet strategic objectives in Asia Minor logically extend from Turkey and Iraq to Syria and the Lebanon. Oil pipelines, access to the Mediterranean and propinquity to the Suez Canal are obvious long–range objectives in the Levant States.

The principal obstacle to the realization of these aims is French influence and continued British interest in this area Soviet policy in the Levant States is therefore directed at the

undermining of what remains of the French position in those states, both through local elements friendly to the U.S.S.R. and through French Communists. At the same time the U.S.S.R. is engaged in cautious exploration for and encouragement of indigenous groups amenable to Soviet guidance.

In opposing French influence in Syria and the Lebanon, Moscow is inhibited by the danger that it may inadvertently give aid to elements friendly to the British. For this reason, it must tread a particularly wary path. The U.S.S.R. appears, nevertheless, already to have assumed something of the role of protector of the rights of the Aleppo Armenians and the Orthodox Church, notwithstanding the stubborn attitude of the Patriarch of Antioch. Furthermore, Syrian grievances against Turkey over Alexandretta would seem to tempt Soviet exploitation.

The Orthodox Church

With communities in Turkey, Syria, the Lebanon, Palestine and Egypt, the Orthodox Church is an important extra–national force in the Near East. [81] At present, it offers an opportunity for apparently innocent cultural penetration and propaganda, which opportunity the U.S.S.R. is assiduously cultivating. Having traditionally entertained a keen appreciation of temporal as well as spiritual powers, the Orthodox Church in the Levant does not view the courtship of the Soviet State with excessive distaste. Eventually the Church in the Near East may, despite factional jealousies, serve as a ponderable political force operating in response to Soviet direction.

The Jews and Zionism

In seeking to enlist Jewish support of Soviet policy in the Near and Middle East, Moscow is confronted with complicated and far-reaching issues. For the Jewish problem is not only an international Phenomenon; it is also an important domestic issue in the U.S.S.R. A false Soviet step with regard to the Jews in the Near and Middle East would cause repercussions inside the U.S.S.R., as well as among world Jewry from Wall Street to the Dead Sea. Therefore Moscow is treading softly among Levantine Jews.

In seeking to assess Soviet tactics toward the Jews, it may first confidently be said that the U.S.S.R. does not encourage nationalist sentiments among the Jews as it does among the Armenians. As evidence of this, one need only point to the melancholy position of the Jewish Autonomous Province. [82] Bounded by the Amur on one side, by Siberian desolation on the other, and far from Jewish population and historical centers, the Jewish Province can hardly serve either as a focus of world Jewry's longing for a homeland or as a base for "Jewish national" expansion.

Secondly, it seems clear that the U.S.S.R. does not look with approval on Zionism. The reasons for this attitude are Moscow does not wish to offend the Arabs, and the Zionist movement is not now amenable to Soviet direction. Soviet opposition to Zionism is, however, cautiously expressed. That is to say, it is revealed openly in certain Arab communities, and inferentially in the Soviet press. But it is not manifested so broadly as to provoke the united antagonism of Zionist sympathizers. The U.S.S.R. may be expected to continue this generally noncommittal course until such time as developing events bring Soviet policy into sharp open conflict with Zionism, or—what is far less likely—Moscow is able to capture the Zionist movement.

Having rejected nationalism as a basis for rallying Jewish support in the Levant, Moscow appears to be concentrating on class and ideological appeal. The Soviet program for Jews in the Near and Middle East seeks to enlist the support of laborers and intelligentsia.

Palestine

Soviet policy in Palestine is directed at the elimination of British influence and, however discouraging the task may now appear, the building up of pro–Soviet Arab and Jewish elements to a point where they can eventually be reconciled with each other and united in making a bid for power in that area. The Russians cannot now afford to take sides outright either with the Arabs or the Jews. Their aim is therefore to split both.

Accordingly, they oppose Jewish "reactionaries" in Palestine without opposing the Jews as a body. As has been noted, leftist Jewish intelligentsia labor groups serve Soviet purposes in this enterprise. With the Arabs the U.S.S.R. has been more careful, but the beginnings of a similar distinction are visible

there. Landless Arabs and Arab members of the Orthodox Church are elements which the Soviet Union may turn to its use.

Meanwhile the Soviet Union is not averse to allowing the Arab world to draw from official Soviet reticence on the problem of Palestine the deduction that the U.S.S.R. alone, of all the great powers, has no interest in Jewish immigration into Palestine and is therefore the friend of the Arabs.

The Arab League

The Soviet Government made no reply to the official notification which was given to it of the establishment of the Arab League. [83] The Soviet press has subsequently criticized it somewhat obliquely on the general grounds that it was supported by the British. In so far as the League may outgrow British tutelage and support, it might look for favor in Moscow; and the possibility of such a development may have been one of the reasons for Soviet caution in openly opposing it. But the recent expression of the League's opposition to a Soviet trusteeship in Tripolitania will not go unforgotten, and such merit as the Soviet Union may be able to acquire in Arab eyes by its relative reticence on the Palestine question will probably be exploited toward the disruption rather than the support of the present League leadership.

Egypt

Soviet interest in Egypt is presumably focussed in long range terms on the Suez Canal. That interest is less economic than strategic; less in shipping and other economic benefits which would flow from influence or control over the Canal than in the strategic advantage of being able to compromise or sever the vital British Empire communications line through Suez. Soviet attempts to acquire influence or control over the Canal must, because of extreme British sensitivity regarding Suez, proceed cautiously and slowly—probably through negotiations for financial participation in the Suez Company and through bids to outflank the Canal, as have already been made in the proposals for Soviet trusteeship over Eritrea and Tripolitania.

In the domestic Egyptian scene the Soviet Government is feeling its way. It is trying to build up Soviet prestige through cultural propaganda and a display of interest in Mohammedanism and at the same time is endeavoring to find internal elements sufficiently reliable to be used as effective vehicles of Soviet influence in Egyptian domestic politics. This last has apparently not been easy. The anti–British elements in Egypt are for the most part even more hostile to the U.S.S.R. than to Great Britain. The Soviet Union has a long way to go before it can hope to play an influential role in Egypt.

Iraq

Oil and access to the Persian Gulf and to the Arabian peninsula constitute motivations for Soviet expansion into Iraq.

The Russians are probably fairly well convinced by this time that they cannot do business with the Arab elements which are now in control in Iraq. They have only recently succeeded in establishing diplomatic relations with the Iraqi Government, and they are still hesitant about attacking it openly for fear of involving themselves in trouble with the Arab world in general. They are therefore treating the Iraqi Government with great caution.

This does not hinder them, however, from exploiting the deficiencies of the Iraqi minority policy with respect to the Kurds, who, it is important to note, are strongest in the vicinity of the northern oil fields. It must be expected that Kurdish grievances will be nurtured by Moscow and will some day be exploited by the Russians as a means of pressure on the Iraqi central government. For the moment Soviet policy is to aggravate to the utmost the conflict between the Kurds and the Arabs. At the same time a vigorous effort is being made to obtain influence in Baghdad among the Arab intelligentsia. It must be expected that if this effort is successful, a day will come when dissident pro–Soviet Arab elements will also begin to make trouble for the government and to bid, as in Iran, for political power.

Iran

Security, oil and access to the Persian Gulf are to the Soviet Union three incentives for encroachment on Iran. Domination of northwestern Iran is a minimum requirement for the security of the Caucasus area. Acquisition of control over northern Iranian oil is a

goal for the near future. A bid for control over southern oil must wait because such a move at this time would provoke violent British reaction. Eventually, however, the U.S.S.R. may be expected to attempt to obtain control over southern Iranian Oil, not so much because of Soviet need for that oil, but more because the denial of it to the Anglo–Americans would be a strategic coup. Access to the Persian Gulf, the third incentive for Soviet encroachment on Iran, would open a corridor to Arabia and India and a direct trade route between the Ural industrial area and southeast Asian raw material sources.

In Iran the Soviet Union depends on four instruments for attaining its end. One is the Red Army in occupation. It obstructs the functioning of the Iranian Government and protects, if by no other way than through its presence, the native agents and agencies of the U.S.S.R. A second is the Tudeh Party. The U.S.S.R. seeks to utilize it for the discrediting, and eventually the overthrow, of the existing government and its replacement by a regime amenable to the Soviet Union. Thirdly, the Azerbaijan Party is the instrument by which the U.S.S.R. is attempting, as a preliminary move, to separate northwestern Iran from the rest of the country [84] and so insure early Soviet predominance in that particular region. Finally, under Soviet direction, the Kurds are likewise a fissionist force in northwestern Iran. There have been hints that the Kurdish "independence" movement is already fairly well developed—and that certain Iraqi Kurds have made contact with it.

Afghanistan

Security and a gateway to India constitute primary motives for the Soviet Union's seeking dominant influence in Afghanistan. Security is a primary concern because of the close proximity of Afghanistan's present border to the richest portion of Soviet Central Asia. And Afghanistan is the nearest gateway into India, in which the U.S.S.R. has always had a latent but strong interest.

Soviet policy toward Afghanistan is at present one of comparative quiescence. Although evidently now working quietly, as a preparatory measure, toward the penetration of certain border areas of Afghanistan, the U.S.S.R. is not yet ready to act in a big way.

When the time comes, it will probably seek with characteristic flexibility to exploit the open issue of the Oxus boundary and to utilize fully tribal ties across the Afghan–Soviet border and tribal and dynastic conflicts within Afghanistan. Meanwhile it will of course oppose with determination any association of Afghanistan with other Moslem states in which the U.S.S.R. does not itself play the leading and controlling role.

Summary of Soviet Political Tactics in Near and Middle East

One of the outstanding characteristics of Soviet foreign policy is its flexible multiformity. Nowhere, perhaps, is this quality more clearly demonstrated than in the Near and Middle East. It may therefore be useful, in conclusion, to summarize the various lines of Soviet policy in that area.

Nationalism and irredentist sentiments are encouraged among the Armenians. Tribal revolt and autonomy is incited among the Kurds. The export brand of Stalinist ideology is sold to the Jews. The doctrine of Church unity under the patronage of the Soviet State is propagated in Orthodox communities.

In dealing with states, still other techniques are employed as instruments of policy. Tactics of cultural and religious ingratiation are used in Egypt. In contrast, against Turkey the U.S.S.R. has employed diplomatic negotiation, a war of nerves (including a whispering campaign regarding impending military action) and propaganda by foreign agencies (such as the demand of Armenians in the United States for the "return" of eastern Turkish provinces to the Armenian SSR). Finally, toward Iran the U.S.S.R. has resorted to active and passive military intervention and internal political intrigue.

Respectfully yours,

W. A. HARRIMAN

---

[78] This despatch was drafted by George F. Kennan, Counselor of Embassy, and John P. Davies, Jr., Second Secretary of Embassy at Moscow.

[79] For documentation on the Straits question, see vol. VIII, first section under Turkey.

[81] For indication of the rise of Soviet political influence in the Near East through the church, see telegram 1800, May 30, from Moscow, p. 1127 and telegram 2455, July 7, from Moscow, p. 1129.

[82] The Jewish Autonomous Oblast in the Khabarovsk Kray on the Amur River in a corner jutting into Manchuria was established in 1934 with its administrative center at Birobidzhan after an original settlement of about 19,000 Jews in 1927. Conditions were so uncongenial that the project was not a success.

[83] For documentation on formation of the Arab League, see vol. VIII, section entitled "Attitude of the United States toward the question or Arab Unity."

[84] For documentation on the attitude of the United States toward fostering by the Soviet Union of dissident movements in northern Iran, see vol. VIII, first section under Iran.

222.

[1946, Volume VII, p. 340]

761.91/3–546: Telegram

The Vice Consul at Tabriz (Rossow) to the Secretary of State

SECRET
US URGENT   NIACT

TABRIZ, March 5, 1946—1 p. m.
[Received March 6—6:25 a. m.]

40. Exceptionally heavy Soviet troop movements have been going on since yesterday as follows: On night March 3—450 Soviet trucks heavily laden with supplies, mainly ammunition, departed Tabriz toward Tehran. Last night 20 tanks with 100 trucks departed in same direction and had reached Bostanabad early this morning.

Two regiments of cavalry with two attached batteries of artillery, equipped for full field operations, departed Tabriz this morning toward Marand. It is not definitely known whether they will go on to Zhulfa or turn off toward Khoi, Rezaieh and Maku. However very heavy forage shipments made during past week by Soviets from Tabriz particularly to Rezaieh would seem to indicate latter direction of march. It is further reported from Mahabad that Kurds are preparing to assert claim to Turkish Kurdistan and plan to commence military operations to that end soon.

Another strong force of Soviet cavalry was observed 2 days ago marching southward through Girgan with Iraq frontier as reported destination. In apparent conjunction with this movement 9 Soviet tanks left last night in direction of Maragheh.

There remain in Tabriz at least 2 regiments of cavalry and some artillery but no known armored elements. During past 3 nights several large truck convoys loaded with troops have been observed arriving from direction of Soviet frontier.

Sent Department 40, Tehran 55; Moscow 32; London 20; Ankara 7; Baghdad 5.

ROSSOW

223.

[1946, Volume VII, pp. 362–64]

861–24591/3–1746: Telegram

The Chargé in the Soviet Union (Kennan) to the Secretary of State

SECRET. US URGENT

MOSCOW, March 17, 1946—9 p. m.
[Received March 17—5:37 p. m.]

843. Moment is opportune, I feel, for an attempt to recapitulate implications of present Soviet activities in Iran as seen from Moscow.

First of all I consider it almost a foregone conclusion that Soviets must make some effort in immediate future to bring into power in Iran a regime prepared to accede to major immediate Sov demands particularly continued maintenance of Sov armed forces in Iran and granting of oil concessions. This effort will of course be made through subservient Iranian elements without direct responsibility on Sov side. Sov forces in Iran will serve this scheme by sheer force of intimidation and if necessary by preventing any forceful interference with its execution.

Some such development seems probable because:

(*a*) Sov Govt has no intention of withdrawing its troops from Iran. On the contrary, reinforcements, even though not on large scale, have been sent in.

(*b*) Sooner or later the Sov Govt must give some explanation to the world for continued presence there of their forces in violation of treaty engagements.

(*c*) Delay in giving answer to our inquiry indicates Sov Govt is reluctant to base its action solely on security requirements of USSR and is waiting for some sort of development which will make possible a better answer.

(*d*) Answer which would best commend itself to Sov mind would be that Iranian Govt had requested troops to remain.

(*e*) Coming UNO session and string which SC still has to Iranian question make some early solution imperative.

I find it hard to conceive that Sov Govt could be planning overt Sov aggression against Turkey at this juncture. There has been no special political buildup for this here nor as far as I can see any attempt to create a pretext for such action. This is not to say that smashing of Turk power, achievement of Sov bases on Straits [23] and establishment of "friendly" regime in Ankara may not be objectives of Sov policy to be pursued in due course and time. It is also not to say that Sov armed Kurds might not now begin to make trouble along Turkish border leading to disturbances which might later be cited as grounds for Sov interference. But there is not sufficient evidence here for concluding that present Sov military preparations in northern Iranian sector envisage an immediate Sov attack on Turkey.

With respect to Iraq, situation is not so clear. Here there is some evidence which points toward a Sov inspired and Sov armed Kurdish action to seize Mosul district with Sov forces in background prepared to back up insurgents in favorable circumstances and perhaps to come in after them, ostensibly at Kurd request. It must be emphasized that there has been big propaganda buildup here for difficulties with British and to extent such an attempt on Mosul district might cause difficulties with British, it may be considered a possibility from standpoint of psychological preparation here. But we here do not have impression that Sov Govt plans to push this to point of open break with London. Unless there has been some tremendous and fundamental decision taken here to forego all advantages of further cooperation with western world and to enter on path of complete defiance and armed isolation, a turn of events for which we have as yet no evidence, then I feel Russians will try in whatever action they may undertake in

Middle East to keep just this side of the line which would mean a complete diplomatic break with British. They are doubtless prepared to face very serious diplomatic and political difficulties but to attain their objectives they will try to gauge their action, if our hypothesis is correct, in such a way as to stop just short of the decisive point. Naturally this involves a considerable risk that they may not estimate accurately the line of delimitation or that their action may automatically carry them farther than they originally planned to go. But I believe that these are risks which they have probably taken into calculation and which they have deemed to be warranted in view of immediate and ultimate objectives involved.

Thus it appears to me that whatever action may be undertaken in pursuance of present Sov preparations in that area, Russians must try to hold it down to point where it can be given a local character, i.e., where it should not place either Sov or British Govts in a position from which national prestige would not permit withdrawal. Any other line of procedure would, I must reiterate, imply a profound change of Sov policy on a world wide scale of which we here have no evidence. It is not like the Kremlin to blunder casually into situations, implications of WHICH it has not thought through

Sent Dept 843; repeated Tehran 67 and London 146.

KENNAN

---

[23] For documentation on this subject, see pp. 801 ff.

224.

[1946, Volume VII, p. 340]

861.24591/3–1846: Telegram

The Ambassador in Iran (Murray) to the Secretary of State

SECRET

TEHRAN, March 18, 1946—5 p. m.
[Received 11:50 p. m.]

362. Capt. Gagarine[24] and Rossow have requested permission to attempt trip from Tabriz to Rezaieh presumably to check on

disposition Soviet forces and activities of Kurds. I have instructed them not to attempt this or travel anywhere in Kurdistan. [25]

Unless Dept considers it vitally important to have first–hand information on reported Soviet troop concentrations in Irano–Turkish frontier region I do not propose to send any American officer into that area at present. Territory is inhabited by armed Kurds who are apparently under little or no control and I think there would be grave danger of a serious incident which might even be engineered by Russians to divert attention from main issues involved in present crisis. It seems to me we should try to avoid anything which would confuse matters when Iran's case is brought before Security Council.

I should appreciate Dept's comment.

To Dept as 362, repeated to Moscow 110 and Ankara.

MURRAY

---

[24] Alexis M. Gagarine Assistant Military Attaché in Iran. In telegram 362, March 18, 4 p. m. the Ambassador in Tehran reported that "Gagarine arrived Tabriz March 17 having traveled by road from Tehran. Reports having seen personally soviet column of 25 tanks moving direction of Tehran. Says Soviet garrison Qazvin increased and Soviet infantry unit at Zenjan. Observed armed Red troops in same trucks with armed Azerbaijan "Democrats'." (861.24591/3–1846)

[25] In telegram 223, March 19, 7 p. m. to Tehran the Department agreed fully with Murray's view, that "travel of official personnel in Kurdistan is presently unwise." (861.24591/3–1846)

225.

[1946, Volume VII, pp. 442–43]

123 Dooher, Gerald F. P.: Telegram

The Acting Secretary of State to the Vice Consul at Tabriz (Dooher)

CONFIDENTIAL

WASHINGTON, April 29, 1946—7 p. m.
14. Reurtel 137, Apr 27.[11] We feel that it would be undesirable for you or Rossow to make a visit in present circumstances to Mahabad as guests of Qazi Mohammad's[12] since Qazi still is a leader of an independent move-

ment against Central Iranian Govt.[13] Furthermore such visit might be interpreted throughout all Middle East especially in Iraq and Turkey as manifestation of American sympathy for Kurdish aspirations for establishment of independent Kurdish state.

Sent to Tabriz, repeated to Tehran.

ACHESON

---

[11] Not printed.

[12] Chief Kurdish leader in Iran.

[13] In telegram 648, May 6, the Chargé in Tehran recommended that ban on travel of Tehran Embassy and Tabriz Consulate personnel to Kurdistan be lifted on assumption that all Soviet troops would be withdrawn by May 7. The Department, in telegram398, May 7, agreed that ban on travel in Kurdistan be removed as of that date. (124.91/5–646)

226.

[1946, Volume VII, p. 545]

891.00/11–846: Telegram

The Ambassador in Iran (Allen) to the Secretary of State

SECRET

TEHRAN, November 8, 1946—5 p. m.
[Received November 8—1:20 p. m.]

1450. I took Dooher to see Qavam today to give PriMin firsthand information concerning present situation in Azerbaijan. Dooher emphasized that Kurdish leaders particularly Ammar Khan and chiefs of Western Kurds but also including Qazi Mohammad, are strongly opposed to Communism, having been disillusioned by Soviet failures to furnish them promised assistance, and are ready to join Central Govt in attack on Azerbaijan provided they are assured that Tehran Govt will coordinate its military activity with them and will promise that afterwards it will not follow again the repressive tribal policy of Reza Shah.[18] Qavam showed great interest in Dooher's remarks and asked numerous questions about Tabriz govt and loaders. Qavam said he was determined to occupy Zenjan within 10 days, by force if necessary.

I assured Qavam that US had not wavered in its policy of supporting integrity of Iran, in spite of suggestions which had come to me that severance of Azerbaijan from Iran might be preferable to allowing Communist poison permeate Iran. I pointed out, however, that US would hardly be able to continue indefinitely to support Iranian integrity unless Tehran Govt gave evidence of being at least as interested in this subject as we are. Consequently, I welcomed his statement that he would use re sources at his command to extend his authority to Zenjan. I quid I thought Zenjan was not enough but that it would at least be a start. Qavam said he intended to progress "little by little".

An American missionary who returned to Tehran yesterday from Tabriz says that Tabriz forces are digging trenches in front of Zenjan and give every appearance of intending to put up strong resistance.

ALLEN

---

[18] Reza Shah Pahlavi, Shahanshah of Iran until his abdication in 1941.

227.

[1946, Volume VII, pp. 824–25]

761.67/6–1746: Telegram

The Ambassador in the Soviet Union (Smith) to the Secretary of State

CONFIDENTIAL

MOSCOW, June 17, 1946—6 p. m.
[Received June 17—3:44 p. m.]

1907. Embassy's 1899, June 17;[46] pouched to London. Political offensives by USSR against Turkey having made little or no progress on Armenian and Georgian issues, a new offensive appears to be opening on another front—Turkish Kurds. Initial salvo was fired by *Trud*.

If, as seems indicated, USSR follows up *Trud* article with propaganda campaign for autonomous Kurdistan, Kremlin can scarcely expect to make much more progress towards inducing creation of autonomous Kurdistan shall it has in bringing about "return" of Turkish Armenia and Georgia to their Soviet motherlands.

Firstly, according to our understanding, Turkish Kurds have been removed from frontier to interior. USSR will therefore find it difficult, if not impossible, to make contact with and arm Turkish Kurds. Secondly, even were USSR able to do this, Soviet experience with Iranian Kurds would seem to indicate that these individualistic feuding nomads are not wholly dependable instruments of Soviet policy. Kremlin doubtless realizes that, if it is out to establish genuine Kurdistan incitement of Turkish Kurds should practically follow rounded development of Kurdistan movement in Iran and Iraq.

If foregoing is so, then Turkish Kurdistan campaign will not be designed to achieve its pretended aims. Its objectives will be:

(1). Renewing war of nerves against Turkey on new front; and

(2). Raising smoke screen over issues at CFM which may embarrass USSR.

With regard to second point, timing of *Trud* article to coincide with opening of CFM repeats now familiar pattern. It will be remembered that USSR launched propaganda offensives regarding Armenian, Georgian, Greek, Egyptian, Indonesian and other "grievances" to coincide with previous FM and UN meetings. These propaganda offensives, like present one, were at least in part aimed at defending Soviet position by tactics of confusion, irrelevancy and obscurantism.

Department please repeat to Paris as Moscow's 189 and to Ankara as No. 34.

Passed to London as 286.

SMITH

---

[46] Not printed.

228.

[1947, Volume V, pp. 910–11]

761.91/5–1547: Telegram

The Ambassador in Iran (Allen) to the Secretary of State

SECRET

TEHRAN, May 15, 1947—9 a. m.

379. Renewal of intensive Soviet activity in Azerbaijan is reported by several sources including Kurdish contacts and Iran Majlis candidate who has just returned from three month tour of Province. Sources state that there recently has been renewed activity among former Democrat elements, lending weight to one report that reorganization of Democrat Party as underground force may be underway. This latter report gives detailed plan for such reorganization, stating that former Fidayis,[1] certain Muhajirs,[2] who fled Iran with Pishevari last December and who since have returned to Iran, and number of recently arrived Soviet Caucasians have been grouping in regions west of Astara near Soviet border, particularly in Khalkhal, Maku and Khoi districts. These elements are said to be well armed. Majlis candidate referred to above states that through former Democrat friends he visited three recently established headquarters of ex–Democrats; also adds that he was interviewed by Soviet Consul General Krasnik of Tabriz who offered him "all possible support" if he would assist in "democratization" of Azerbaijan.

Certain sub–tribes of Jagali Kurds (Muku region) are reported harboring considerable numbers of Muhajirs and Soviet agents, in return receiving quantities of rifles and ammunition from Soviets. Northward movement of Barzanis[3] reported in Embtel 217, March 24[4] is said to have been instigated by Soviets for purpose of joining reorganized Democrat Partisan movement.

Tehran press in past two weeks has been agitating against reported influx of Muhajirs from Soviet Union and population of Tabriz last week staged demonstration protesting same situation. Iran Army denies any large scale infiltration across border but admits some small groups may have passed over Araxes River into Iran. On the other band American Gendarmerie Mission officers just back from Tabriz report border control virtually non–existent except at such points as Julfa and Astara and state that large scale movement of Soviet Caucasians into Iran is not at all impossible. Same officers report Azerbaijan peasants being conditioned for possible return of Democrats by failure of Iran Government to take any measures to alleviate their desperate poverty and by Government's support of landlord class in province.

While Embassy does not place full credence in these reports it is believed that Soviets have not given up hope of regaining control of Azerbaijan, and that if peaceful political penetration of province is prevented by Majlis rejection of Soviet oil concession, Soviet may resume much more active interference in Azerbaijan and may possibly try to create guerrilla warfare situations similar to that in Greece.

Repeated London 57, Baghdad 57. Department pass Moscow 46 and Ankara 12.

ALLEN

---

[1] Civil armed volunteers of the Soviet-supported Jafar Pishevari régime in Azerbaijani prior to its overthrow by armed forces of the Iranian Government in December 1946.

[2] Immigrants into Iranian Azerbaijan from the Caucasus regions of the Soviet Union.

[3] Kurdish tribal elements, native to northern Iraq, led by Mullah Mustafa Barzani.

[4] Not printed.

229.

[1947, Volume V, pp. 960–62]

761.91/9–2647: Telegram

The Acting Secretary of State to the Embassy in Iran

SECRET

WASHINGTON, September 26, 1947—5 p. m.

584. Urtels recently indicate salutary result of American stand on Iran–Soviet relations re oil. Dept feels that strong Soviet reaction, possibly even before formal Majlis action, is possible in one or more of following forms:

a) Start of Greek–type guerrilla warfare on Iran–Soviet border, probably involving Barzanis, muhajirs, and other Sov–Caucasian elements.

b) Inspired disturbances in Azerbaijan cities, Abadan, Isfahan and Tehran, to give credence to Soviet charges that reign of terror exists, and to divert Iranian military forces from border areas.

c) Intensification of anti–Iranian propaganda by Soviets.

In anticipation such Soviet actions, Dept now actively considering its United Nations strategy for such contingency.

We feel, however, Iran Govt itself must take certain immediate measures (final para Deptel 434 July 29) if it is to reduce possibility initial success Soviet reactions indicated above. These measures might prove more efficacious than any ex post facto UN action. We are herein suggesting certain steps which might be taken by Iran Govt, leaving it to your discretion communicate suggestions to Shah, Qavam, Hekmat,[1] and other patriotic Iranian leaders in position take appropriate action.

We see as most serious obstacle in way of Iranian national unity, which is prerequisite any successful resistance to Soviet expansion in that country, personal fend between Shah and Qavam (Embtel 859 Sep. 6[2]) We feel both are basically patriotic Iranians but they have permitted their mutual distrust retard progress their country and operate against successful unification various elements Iranian nation. We feel Shah has consistently placed too much confidence in obstructionist advice of military leaders. It is apparent much of this advice not motivated by patriotic sentiments but by desire on part of Razmara and others for domination of Iran by military. Consequently, constant need to cope with Shah–Army group intrigues has done much to hinder Qavam in efforts unite Iranian people. Qavam on his part has at time given Shah serious reason suspect motives by vacillation between sometimes strong front against Soviet pressure and other times apparent willingness to intrigue with Soviets. He has also been dilatory in bringing to fruition plans For reform though neither can it be said Shah has shown any effective interest this phase Iranian national life.

It is our belief that personal feud between Shah and his PriMin intolerable and dangerous for preservation Iranian national interests. Shah and PriMin working together can, we believe, unite all elements Iranian nation including peasants, labor and tribes. Your influence with both Shah and PriMin might at this time be used to bring about this desirable internal situation so closely related to Iran's freedom from Soviet domination, without risk of criticism from political leaders, responsible press, or general public in either Iran or U.S.

To the extent to which Shah and PriMin each demonstrates sincere and effective desire to act in Iranian national interest, we feel you should use your influence to keep them working harmoniously together. If Shah displays cooperative attitude and despite this Qavam so conducts himself that distrust cannot be dispelled, and if Shah should therefore consider new PriMin desirable, it is hoped that change of govt could be brought about in manner not to create wide rift in Iranian body–politic.

It would be highly desirable if new spirit of teamwork between Shah and PriMin could be demonstrated at once by termination petty political attacks on latter by Shah's Majlis deputies, and by immediate implementation by Qavam and Majlis of practical program of reforms similar to those proposed by PM during period of autonomous Azerbaijan Govt, such as provincial councils and real land reforms.

In such disposition as might be made of Iranian Army in conjunction with the *gendarmerie* to combat infiltration hostile elements or to meet local disturbances, it is hoped military forces will behave such manner they will receive whole–hearted cooperation local populations. This may call for change of Army command particularly in regions where tribal groups, presently peaceful but hitherto unpredictable, might welcome opportunity prove themselves loyal supporters Iranian Govt.

We repeat our approval Emb efforts encourage tribes use peaceful and parliamentary means to attain what they consider just ends (Deptel 476 Aug 14[3]). We are particularly anxious every encouragement be given Kurds who will very possibly be first target Soviet penetration following rejection oil concession, and who, if alienated from Iran Govt by Army policy of recrimination, might well become Soviet weapon against not only Iran but Turkey and Iraq as well. It seems to us if Kurds were given some recognition by central govt comparable that accorded Bakhtiaris and Qashqais by Qavam, there would be smaller risk of Kurdish disloyalty in eventualities mentioned.

Dept has observed Majlis President Hekmat's seemingly statesmanlike behavior recent weeks and hopes his influence in Majlis can

be used accelerate action on reforms Qavam might initiate.

In conclusion we feel our position in UN would be much stronger and morally' more tenable if: a) Shah–Qavam feud is terminated, b) loyalty of Iran's minorities to their Govt is assured, and c) certain long–overdue economic and social reforms are initiated immediately by Iran Govt.

Rptd London as 4168[4] and Moscow as 1781.

LOVETT

---

[1] Reza Hekmat, President of the Iranian Majlis.

[2] Not printed.

[3] Not printed, but see footnote 6 p. 960.

[4] In telegram 4247, October 2, the Department authorized the Embassy in London to convey the substance of telegram 4168 to the British Foreign Office (761.91/9—3047).

230.

[1950, Volume V, pp. 206–12]

780.00/9–2150

Record of Informal United States— United Kingdom Discussions, London, Thursday Afternoon, September 21, 1950[1]

SECRET

Participants: Foreign Of Office

Mr. M. R. Wright, Assistant Under–Secretary of State

Mr. G. W. Furlonge, Head, Eastern Department

Mr. T. E. Evans, Head, Middle East Secretariat

Mr. L. A. C. Fry, South–East Asia Department

Mr. L. Barnett, Eastern Department

Department of State

Hon. George C. McGhee (Items 12 and 19)

Mr. Samuel K. C. Kopper (All Items)

Mr. W. Sands (All Items)

American Embassy, London

Mr. Joseph Palmer 2nd (Items 12 and 19)

. . .

Kurds

We said that while we were not alarmed, there seemed to be signs of increasing unrest among the Kurds in all the countries in which they are located and that the situation was perhaps potentially dangerous. We felt therefore that it should be watched and that it might be desirable for the US and UK to exchange information in order to keep fully abreast of the situation.

The UK representatives indicated that they were not particularly disturbed by the Kurdish problem. They pointed out that the Kurds were always unstable and divided, and that, while the UK was aware that there was some unrest at the present time, it did not take the matter too seriously. The British representatives said, however, that they were always glad to exchange views and information with us and they agreed that the situation should be watched.

We informed the British that we were in the process of setting up additional consulates throughout the Near East and hoped that through these we could establish closer contacts with the Kurds and other tribesmen. It was agreed by both delegations that all approaches to the Kurds should be through the established governments of the countries concerned and that care should be taken not to build up the Kurds too much as such action would lead to unrest. It was further agreed that the exchange of views and information between ourselves should be through normal channels, and that there is no need at this time to have special conversations on this subject.

231.

[1950, Volume V, pp. 221–30]

780.00/10–2050

Paper Drafted by the Officer in Charge of Egypt and Anglo–Egyptian Sudan Affairs (Stabler) [1]

TOP SECRET

WASHINGTON, October 24, 1950.

This paper covers the attitudes and reactions which may be expected from the Arab States and Israel in the face of the following eventualities and suggests possible lines of action which might be adopted:

1. Soviet invasion and occupation of the Near East.

2 Limited Soviet attacks on certain key points in the Near East.

3. Soviet supported minority uprisings.

4. Soviet–inspired aggression in other parts of the world, similar to Korea.

5. USSR–US hostilities not immediately involving the Near East.

Background
Strategic

The Near Eastern area comprising the Arab States, the independent Arab Sheikhdoms and Israel forms a vast land bridge between the East and the West and is the center of communications] both in terms of land, sea and air, between Europe and Asia. This area borders on Turkey and Iran, which in turn have common frontiers with Russia. On the other side the Near East stands as a shield protecting the African Continent. While it would be possible for Russia to invade Africa through Europe, the operation would presumably be more difficult than an invasion through the Near Eastern countries.

It is assumed that the principal Soviet effort will be in Europe. However, it is also assumed that a secondary effort of importance will be made against Turkey, Iran and the Near East in order to deny to the Western Powers the strategic facilities available in the Near East, such as bases, Suez Canal and oil.

During World War II Egypt, Palestine, Jordan and Saudi Arabia, and later Iraq, Syria and Lebanon were of extreme importance to the Allied Powers, not only in denying that area to the Axis Powers but also as a base for European operations. When Rommel moved across Libya and almost half way across Egypt, the Allied Powers would have been in serious difficulties if they had not had room to maneuver in Sinai Peninsula, Palestine and Jordan. The loss of the Near Eastern area to Russia would adversely affect the plans of the Western Allies for the conduct of the war.

Political

With respect to political considerations it must be recognized that at the present time the prestige and position of the US in the Near Eastern area is at a low ebb. Such friendship and esteem as the US held at the end of World

War II were quickly dissipated through our Palestine policy which in Arab eyes represented the antithesis of everything. which they believed the US represented. Our support of the UK in its relations with Iraq and Egypt and our support of the French in North Africa have done nothing to increase American prestige. The bitterness engendered by these policies is deeply rooted and the attitude of the Arab States towards the US, in fact the Western world, have increasingly reflected their belief that the US support of Israel and the UK in the Near East will govern US policies, even when these are to the detriment of what the Arabs believe to be their legitimate interests. While Communism and Mohammedianism are mutually incompatible and while there is among the Arab States a degree of fear and hatred of Communism, it is necessary to realize that the attitude of the Arab States toward Communism is not based on an under standing of the ideological conflict involved, but on considerations which are more or less those of expediency. Arab public opinion is formed by the Arab leaders and these leaders would be the ones who would have the most to lose in the event that their countries should fall under Communist domination. Certain Arab statesmen have made statements to the effect that an alliance with Russia is possibly a lesser evil than indirect control by Zionist dominated US policies These statements must be viewed in the light of current Arab bitterness towards the US. However, constant repetition of such statements may result in a form of psychological persuasion that some kind of a deal with Russia is preferable, especially if the belief spreads that there can be no fundamental change in what is considered our inimical policies toward the Arab world. Despite the fact that Arab orientation to the West, in terms of a shift toward Russia has not fundamentally altered, cool area reaction to the Korean situation stands as a warning signal.

It is also important to bear in mind, as of political importance, that the Arabs have a traditional admiration for strength and that consequently they will constantly compare East vs. West strength for the purpose of determining the course of action most advantageous to them.

In the case of Israel the situation is somewhat different. After many years of struggle the Zionist movement succeeded in founding a state in the Near East. Present evidence points to a fairly stable political scene, though unlimited immigration and limited resources present danger signals for the future. Largely because of the existence of large Jewish groups in both Eastern and Western blocs and its economic and military dependence on the sources within both blocs Israel at first followed an official policy of neutrality between the East and West in the cold war. Subsequent to the invasion of Korea this policy has been modified to the extent that Israel can react against aggression and cooperate with the UN in its attempts to block aggression. Israeli relations with the US are close and are based upon the strong political, economic and financial support which was given by the US in the creation and development of that State. It is becoming increasingly evident that Israel's sentiments are in the final analysis with the West

While the Communist party in Israel is of insignificant proportions, its affiliation with Left–Wing groups of some strength actively sympathizing with Russia provides the Eastern bloc with the support of 18% of the population. However, notwithstanding certain Communist inspired disorders the present Government appears to hold the confidence of the country and appears capable of controlling the situation.

Military

The Armed Forces of the Near East, although totalling over 200,000 men, are generally weak and are not in a position to do more than police duty for internal security and offer token resistance to invasion by modern army. Some of them could serve as effective auxiliaries to Western armed forces in the defense of their territories, in particular the forces of the small but well trained and equipped army of Israel, the Jordan Arab Legion and the reorganized Egyptian army. However, the armed forces of the Arab States and Israel could not operate under local combined command, nor could the Israeli Army operate in the Arab States.

At the present time the US maintains an air base at Dhahran, Saudi Arabia, which is equipped to handle long–range bombers. US naval units are present in the Mediterranean and the Persian Gulf.

The UK maintains in Egypt's Canal Zone the following forces: 20,700 UK troops, 8,700 Colonial troops, 5 fighter squadrons, 1 photo–reconnaissance squadron, and 5 transport squadrons. Airfields are capable of handling long–range bombers. The UK also maintains small forces at Akaba, Jordan as well as insignificant units of the RAF in Amman and Mafrak, Jordan. In Iraq air bases at Habbianiyah and Shaibah are maintained with smell forces. Other British bases exist in the Mediterranean area and British naval units are also present.

Discussion

1. Soviet invasion and occupation of the Near East.

(*a*) Attitudes and Reactions—Assuming that Western Forces would not be able to move in force and hold positions in the Near East for any length of time, it is believed that the Arab States and Israel would be unable or unwilling to resist and would be obliged to submit to the USSR. Most of the Government leaders and some members of the upper classes would attempt to flee their countries and form governments in exile. Some may take to the desert and throughout the area, and especially on its fringes some more or less temporary islands of resistance may be established. The people could be expected to adopt a passive attitude toward occupation. With ruthless measures the occupation authorities are likely to wipe out the power of present vested interests of' sectarian and clan loyalties which might threaten to remain or become elements of resistance. In as much as these are regarded by many people in the area as selfish interests and divisive forces, such measures could be described as progress by the new regime which could ultimately secure wide cooperation, especially if it initiates land reform, other basic improvements, and makes an effort to appease religious antipathies. Even if the levelling off of the present economic inequality meant Russian exploitation and generally poorer standards of living, the appeal it would hold for the masses might constitute an obstacle to Western liberation of the area after a prolonged Soviet occupation. This would be particularly true if the West had to offer little more shall the return of the present regimes.

This might apply to Israel too if the Russians destroyed active pro–Western and recalcitrant elements.

(*b*) Courses of action—There are a considerable number of individuals and organized groups in the Arab States and Israel, including military personnel who would remain adamantly opposed to Communism and sympathetic to the Western cause. We should inquire what plans the British have made for the formation of groups for desert–raiding, sabotage and general harassment purposes. Covert canvassing of key personnel, terrain, and other studies should be made while we have free access to the area. It is believed that in the event of war such groups could be contacted even under Soviet occupation and formed in all countries.

Consideration could be given at a later stage to the organization of an area uprising, depending upon the success of the smaller groups and on the general reaction of local populations to continued Soviet occupation.

Consideration should also be given to the formation of governments in exile but great care should be taken to support only those groups which might still have the confidence of the people.

Even if most of the Near East were invaded special efforts should be made to retain strongholds on the fringes especially in areas which occupation forces could not effectively control such as the vast Arabian peninsula.

2. Limited Soviet attacks on certain key points in the Near East

(*a*) Attitudes and Reactions—In the event the USSR should attack limited objectives, (e.g. air and/or sea operations against the Dhahran Airbase, Aden, Suez Canal, the oilfields, etc.) the final attitude of the Arab States and Israel would depend on the success which Allied Forces had in repelling these attacks. In the early stages the assistance of local armed forces could be expected. To the extent Allied action was not successful, considerable instability throughout the area could be expected and there would be agitation for pro–Russian alignment Left–Wing groups, Communists, and some Kurds could be expected to increase their activities and call on the people to abandon the Allies

Pro–Western leaders would be discredited. To stave off Russian aggression the governments would try to assert their neutrality or, if the Soviet attacks looked like a prelude of invasion, to make deals with the USSR.

Soviet aggression in the Near East or in its immediate vicinity which would look like a prelude to a full–scale invasion and which would not be countered by effective military action by the West would demoralize the local governments and people and would convince them that the West is unable or unwilling to protect the area. Regardless of their feelings toward East and West, Israel and the Arab States 'would feel helpless and seek means of survival. In any state which could not count on effective Western protection, some leaders would be found to work either for a neutral position or to make a deal with the USSR. In the eventuality of Soviet occupation, internal resistance forces are likely to be insignificant in hampering Soviet operations fronting on the Mediterranean and the Persian Gulf. The ruthless organization by the Soviet of the resources of the area is likely to make Allied reoccupation an extremely costly undertaking.

(b) Course of action—Immediate military action by the British would be required. In addition to strategic considerations this would prevent a complete demoralization of pro–Western elements who otherwise would conclude that the West is unwilling or unable to defend the area. The U.S. should of course support UN action taken against Soviet aggression.

3. Soviet supported minority uprisings.

(a) Attitudes and Reactions—Although the USSR has fostered grievances among most minorities, the Kurds represent the only compact group which are in a position to stage an uprising. But the solidarity of the Kurdish tribes is not great and many of their influential leaders are in and allied to the central governments and their armies. Furthermore, there is little evidence that either the weak Kurdish nationalist movement 'or tribal leaders capable of rising against the government have a definite pro–Soviet orientation.

However, Mulla Mustafa, leader of the 1945 Kurdish revolt in Iraq is harbored by the USSR in the Caucasus and is reportedly being groomed to stage a comeback.

The Iraqi and Syrian armed forces are in a position to deal with a local Kurdish uprising even if this were sponsored and supported by

Russia with only limited quantities of small arms. In such a case the role of the Iraqi air force, especially if supported by units loaned by the RAF, would be decisive. Israel could be expected to view such uprisings with alarm but would probably adopt a "watch and wait" policy unless its security was directly affected. Certain of the extremist groups might take advantage of the situation to further their own ends vis–à–vis the Arab States.

However, the Armed Forces of Iraq and Syria would be incapable of dealing with a major attack by Russian irregulars operating under the guise of a popular Kurdish uprising. In such a case only effective Western military intervention could stop the Soviet incursion which otherwise under one guise or the other might extend to other areas of the Near East. I

(b) Course of action—Immediate and effective Western military assistance to Iraq and Syria would be required in the form of UK forces and US military equipment.

4. Soviet–inspired aggression in other parts of the world similar to Korea.

(a) Attitudes and Reactions—It is believed that in the event of remote incidents Formosa or possibly French Indo–China—the Arab States and Israel would adopt attitudes similar to those that were adopted in connection with the Korea situation. In the event of closer incidents—Iran, Turkey—the reaction would be immediate and would be accompanied by demands for UN–US action and for immediate arms assistance. In the case of an invasion of Iran the governments of Iraq and Syria could easily fall and might be replaced with governments desirous of making the best peace possible with the Soviet force.

(b) Courses of action—It is essential that the United States continue to build up the UN to deal with aggression and emphasize the stake which all the states of the world have in prompt and effective action to suppress aggression. Prompt UN armed assistance should be given to the area against which the aggression took place.

5. USSR–US hostilities not immediately involving the Near East.

(a) Attitudes and Reactions—If such conflict was sufficiently far removed from the Near East area in order that the Arab States and Israel could adopt a "watch and wait" attitude, it is doubtful that full public support to the West would be given, although Government leaders would probably express their identification with the West.

(b) Courses of action—Increased programs for economic and arms assistance would be required. At the same time the information and psychological warfare program should be accelerated.

Conclusions

1. *Soviet invasion and occupation of the Near East.*—Israeli and Arab Armed Forces would be incapable of defending their countries even with the aid of Western Forces presently in the area. The Governments and some members of the upper classes would flee and attempt to form governments in exile. The people would seek survival by a passive attitude, but with the probability that passivity would change to cooperation, especially if the Soviet occupation involved land reform and other basic improvements. Some opposition under occupation might, however, be expected to occur.

2. *Limited Soviet attacks on certain key points in the Near East.*—If Allied action were immediately effective in countering these limited attacks the support of Israel and the Arab States could be expected. If Allied action was not immediately effective considerable instability could be expected throughout the Near East and agitation for pro–Soviet alignment would increase. Some Governments might fall and there might be a tendency to establish opportunistic governments who would make a deal with the USSR or at least be neutral.

3. *Soviet supported minority uprisings.*—The Armed Forces of Iraq and Syria, where minority uprisings are most likely, are in a position to deal with a Soviet inspired but local uprising by the Kurds who, in any event, are neither organized nor generally pro–Soviet. However, the Armed Forces of Iraq and Syria would be incapable of dealing with a major attack by Kurds, Assyrians and Armenians from the Soviet Union and other Russian irregulars operating under the guise of a popular Kurdish uprising of the Near Eastern minorities and traveling via Iran. If, as in Korea, UN action and effective Western military assistance is brought to bear in such a case, the Arab States would solidly support

the West. However, if Western assistance were not forthcoming or were not effective it is believed that Iraq and Syria would have no choice but to accept the resulting state of affairs. Furthermore, with the establishment of such a stronghold in the Near East it is likely that the USSR would make every effort to gain control of the rest of the area. Israel could be expected to view such uprisings with alarm but would probably adopt a "watch and wait" policy unless its security was directly affected.

4. *Soviet–inspired aggression in other parts of the world, similar to Korea.*—It is believed that the Arab States and Israel would in the case of remote events such as in Formosa or French Indo–China adopt the same attitude as they have with respect to Korea, though with increasing concern over the spreading theater of war and their probable involvement therein. In the case of closer events such as in Iran or Turkey the reaction would be immediate and would be accompanied by demands for Western military action and for immediate military assistance. If the Soviet advance were not effectively checked and if reparations for area defense were not immediately forthcoming the leaders would lose faith in the willingness or ability of the West to oppose Soviet invasion and would seek ways to ingratiate themselves with the USSR.

5. *USSR–US hostilities not immediately involving the Near East.*—The Arab States and Israel would probably await developments and not declare themselves for either side in the event of USSR–US hostilities not immediately involving the Near East. While privately Government leaders might be disposed toward the West, they would take no formal action until allied strategy for the area and the role of the Near East were determined.

Proposals

Courses of action discussed in the above section relate to situations involving hostilities and are, therefore, essentially military in character. It is recognized that at the present time US military commitments in other areas of the world as well as the political situation in the Near East preclude any major effort at this juncture to establish or increase Western military potential in the Near Eastern area. Consequently the principal effort must necessarily be of a diplomatic character, designed to achieve and stabilize pro–Western orientation, and to obtain certain limited objectives of a military character.

The principal concern in the Near Eastern States is whether the US and the Western Allies intend to defend that area against Soviet aggression. These States are conscious that Western strategy is focused on Europe and the Far East, and it appears to them that little attention, from the military point of view, has been paid to the Near East area. Doubts are, therefore, inspired that these States are to be left to their own fate, and since such doubts could generate a serious attitude of despair and defeatism, major efforts must be made to counteract them.

The following suggestions are not all inclusive but are indications of what can and should be done to maintain friendship and support of the area as well as to obtain military requirements:

1. At the present time authorization exists only for the extension of cash reimbursable military aid to the Near Eastern area. Since it is conceivable that it might be necessary and desirable at some point to give military aid on a grant basis, consideration should be given to seeking authorization for grant aid. At the same time consideration should be given to providing cash reimbursable aid to the Arab States and Israel.

2. The US should provide material assistance on a grant basis to contribute to the development of area stability along economic, social and political lines, contingent upon the willingness of these countries to apply the maximum of self–help.

3. The US and the UK should collaborate closely in all matters relating to the Near East, particularly the development of area armies. Agreement should be reached on appropriate strengths and on the division of responsibility between the US and the UK for providing necessary assistance. Consideration should be given to sending US military missions and to increasing the rate of training of Near Eastern officers in US service schools.

4. The US and the UK should develop plans for establishing bases in such areas of the Near East as might remain available even though portions of the Near East were under occupation.

5. We should enquire of the British what their plans are for covert canvassing of key personnel, terrain and other studies while we have free access to the area in order that at the appropriate time groups for desert raiding, sabotage and general harassment could be formed. It is believed that in the event of war such groups could be contacted even under Soviet occupation and formed in all countries.

6. The USIE program of psychological warfare should be accelerated so as to stimulate greater understanding in the Near East of the oppressive intention of international communism and to counteract Soviet propaganda.

7. With respect to the UN we should keep in close touch with the Near Eastern States on our plans to strengthen UN against aggression. We must make these States feel that we genuinely want their views and that they have a stake in the success of the UN in combating aggression.

232.

[1950, Volume V, pp. 651–57]
611.87/11–950

Policy Statement Prepared in the Department of State

SECRET

WASHINGTON, November 9, 1950.

IRAQ

A. OBJECTIVES

Iraq is important to the United States and the western democracies because of its strategic location, its vast petroleum reserves, its control of the potentially fertile Tigris–Euphrates valley, and its control of Basra, the largest seaport on the Persian Gulf. The United States also has an important, if indirect, interest in the special treaty position and the strategic military facilities which the UK currently maintains in Iraq.

Our objectives are to bolster Iraq against Soviet penetration from within or without, to assist Iraq in economic and social development generally, to encourage progressive government, to protect western petroleum and other commercial interests in the area and to give effective support to the legitimate desires of the Iraqi people for national expression and development without prejudice to Iraqi defense or the British strategic position.

A further important objective is to encourage harmonious relations, and cooperation in economic and social development among Iraq and other countries of the Near East.

B. POLICIES

The worsening international situation and oil–rich Iraq's proximity to the Soviet Union and to Iran, have greatly increased Iraqi apprehensions of a Soviet thrust in one form or another. Among the conceivable contingencies are: (1) a direct military onslaught by the Soviet Union through northern Iran; (2) subversion of Iraq by the Communist Party; or (3) a Soviet subterfuge by which irregulars in the guise of Kurdish, Assyrian or Armenian exiles would attempt to "liberate" their dissident kinsmen in Iran, Iraq, Syria, and possibly Turkey and form a Kurdish national state.

Unless the Soviet Union is prepared now to risk a major war, contingency (1) seems for the present unlikely, though plans should be made to meet such a contingency should it arise. Contingency (2) is also remote despite discontent with the semi–feudalistic social system prevalent among peasants and low-income groups in Iraq. If, however, the Soviets wish to start a Near Eastern conflagration of serious proportions without assuming direct responsibility themselves, contingency (3) would be a natural choice. The Kurdish tribes of Iraq, Iran, Syria and Turkey are not well organized and local security forces could probably cope with any uprising of purely internal origin and direction. The situation would be changed completely, however, if merely a small well–equipped force of Soviet "Kurds" infiltrated across the inadequately guarded frontiers into Iran, Iraq and Syria as the nucleus and striking force of a general Kurdish uprising. To meet such a contingency Iraq would definitely need better armament and some military technical assistance and would possibly require support from outside military forces.

Since the UK enjoys special strategic facilities in Iraq, we are discussing the foregoing problems on a continuing basis with the UK, emphasizing that we would expect the UK to assume the primary role in providing Iraq with such military assistance as it required if we should become convinced the Iraqi security situation was sufficiently serious and that the UK alone could not provide all the support necessary, we should consider extension of limited timely assistance to Iraq, in whatever manner might there be feasible.

Both the UK and US should also assist Iraq in minimizing the causes of disaffection in the Kurdish areas by encouraging better provincial administration and by providing technical assistance to help solve economic and social problems in the Kurdish areas.

A further urgent need is better UK and US political and military intelligence coverage of sensitive areas, and a greater exchange of information between the UK and US. We should open a small consulate in Northern Iraq to serve primarily as a political listening post. The US and UK should also coordinate their propaganda services in the area, and information activities—especially Kurdish language broadcasts should be increased.

Although solution of Iraq's military problems is an urgent, immediate aim we should emphasize to the Iraqis that the long–range battle against Communism depends upon enlightened economic and social development and progressive government. The trend toward more progressive government was advanced in Iraq, albeit on a very small scale, when the Government began tribal settlement projects, such as at Dujaila and Hawijah, on state lands, and enacted a law to encourage cooperatives. Progress in economic development has also been made in the past year. A $12.8 million IBRD loan for the Wadi Tharthar flood control project was granted and the IBRD is sending a mission in October to consider further projects; a 50% increase in Iraq's oil royalties was granted by the Iraq Petroleum Company; the Iraqi Government enacted a law providing for the creation of an autonomous central development board and assigning oil royalties in totality for development purposes.

We have also succeeded in bringing a number of Iraqi leader specialists to this country under the Smith–Mundt Act. We have notified Iraq that we are ready to implement the Point Four program and that the Iraqi Government has already submitted a considerable number of requests for various technical experts including a request for an American engineer to serve as a full member of the Iraqi Central Development Board which we have accepted in principle. Substantial progress is being made in negotiating a Fulbright Agreement providing for exchange of persons between Iraq and the US.

If these successful beginnings can be expanded, Iraq's future looks bright. Of particular importance, however, is to increase the number of progressive leaders in the Iraqi Government and gradually to elimination reactionary elements. The western democracies should avail themselves of every opportunity discreetly to encourage the development of more liberal government and improvements in the social system such as progressive taxation and better land distribution. The feudal land tenure system constitutes one of the greatest single obstacles to economic progress in Iraq.

We should encourage the activities of American cultural institutions in Iraq such as Baghdad College and give encouragement and cooperation to the several progressive American-trained leaders serving in technical and administrative positions in Iraqi Government.

We should urge Iraq to expand its world trade on a non-discriminating multilateral basis by adherence to GATT and by improving its tariff, exchange and trade practices consistently with the principles set forth in the ITO Charter. We should especially encourage Iraq to conclude a modern Treaty of Friendship, Commerce and Navigation with the US to replace the outmoded 1938 Treaty.

The US Government should avoid the appearance of being an instrumentality of the oil companies. However, in view of the world significance of oil and the role it plays internally in Iraq, the US discreetly should continue to encourage increased development of Iraq oil resources from each of the three concessions at Kirkuk, Mosul and Basra or the relinquishment of territories the companies do not intend to develop; should continue to encourage the Iraq Petroleum Company to improve its public relations and labor practices and conditions; should increasingly identify the development of Iraq oil resources with the people of the country by encouraging the training, education end employment in company positions at all levels of the maximum number of Iraqis; should encourage the US

partners in the Iraq Petroleum Company to place Americans in other than technical positions; and should maximize oil intelligence in the area by maintaining closest liaison with company and government oil officials and with other Iraqis involved in oil operations. It is also an important objective to restore normal operation of the Haifa pipeline which has been shut off as part of the Arab economic boycott of Israel. However, it is unlikely that representations on the Haifa question would be successful until a more favorable political atmosphere develops.

We should take an early opportunity to resume negotiations for an air transport agreement with Iraq based on the standard Bermuda pattern with full fifth freedom rights. We should be sympathetic, however, to the problems of Iraqi Airways in connection with competition along the routes it serves.

C. RELATIONS WITH OTHER STATES

We support the British treaty position in Iraq and believe the British should have primary responsibility in working out with Iraqi authorities arrangements for that country's defense. At the same time we are aware of Iraqi resentment of vestiges of British imperialism in their country, and we should encourage the UK to continue to seek a suitable means to place its relations with Iraq more nearly on a basis of cooperation between equal partners, continue its policy of interpreting liberally the provisions of the Anglo-Iraqi Treaty regarding technical assistance and, whenever practicable, to modify its treaty position in the direction of the unratified Portsmouth Treaty.

We should also counsel the Iraqis to be moderate in their attitude toward the UK and emphasize the importance to Iraq's security of maintaining effective working arrangements with the UK in matters of defense.

We recognize a strong desire among the Arab peoples for greater unity and we believe that this aspiration should be encouraged so long as it does not develop chauvinistic or aggressive characteristics. For the present, however, a political approach to Arab unity, such as the Syro-Iraqi Union plan which Iraq has espoused, appears to have little chance of success in view of the widely divergent attitudes toward and interests in this subject prevailing among current Arab leaders and political groups. On the other hand, we see fruitful possibilities in an economic, social and cultural approach to Arab unity which would leave the political aspects to develop by evolution. We should, wherever practicable, point out the advantages of the economic and social approach to the Iraqis. We should not, however, give the impression that we would oppose peaceful political unions which might emerge from the spontaneous will of the Arab peoples.

If necessary, we should recall in this connection the attitude of the US, UK and France set forth in the Tripartite Declaration of May 25, 1950: "The three Governments take this opportunity of declaring their deep interest in and their desire to promote the establishment and maintenance of peace and stability in the area and their unalterable opposition to the use of force or threat of force between any of the states in that area. The three governments, should they find that any of these states was preparing to violate frontiers or armistice lines, would, consistently with their obligations as members of the United Nations, immediately take action, both within and outside the United Nations, to prevent such violation." This policy applies as well to Iraq's relations with Israel.

While Iraqi attitudes have an influence among Arab League members, Iraq's involvement in the Palestine dispute is for the most part only indirect. Iraq does, however, maintain an interest in two of the three important aspects of the Palestine problem: the refugee question and Jerusalem. Iraq, like the other Arab States, maintains an economic boycott of Israel which has a special application in the problem of the Haifa pipeline and refinery. Having no boundary contiguous to Israel, Iraq is not involved in territorial questions.

With respect to refugees, Iraq holds the position that the General Assembly Resolution of December 11,1948, should be carried out. This Resolution provided that refugees who wish to return to Israel should be permitted to do so and that those not returning should be compensated for their property. Iraq has not thus far agreed to resettle refugees in Iraq, pointing out that Iraq has a sizeable number of its own tribes to settle and that Palestinians

have a difficult time adjusting themselves to the Iraqi climate, terrain and means of livelihood. It thus seems improbable that Iraq can be counted upon at present to assist greatly in the current problems of the refugees. However, in view of the fact that Iraq has a basic population shortage, the time may well come when Iraq will welcome additional manpower, especially if given assistance such as contemplated in the UN Relief and Works Administration report in assimilating it. We should lose no opportunity to give all possible encouragement to such a trend.

With regard to the status of Jerusalem, Iraq, a member of the Trusteeship Council, has taken the lead in pressing for the implementation of the General Assembly Resolution of December 9, 1949, providing for full internationalization of the city. This has been opposed by Israel and by Iraq's sister Hashemite state, Jordan, who jointly occupy the city. We should continue to make clear to the Iraqis that although we originally opposed the General Assembly Resolution of December 9, 1949, on the basis that it was unworkable, we have loyally cooperated with the Trusteeship Council in trying to implement the resolution and in drawing up a satisfactory statute for Jerusalem. We believe, however, that any plan to be successfully implemented must have the substantial support of Jordan and Israel and at the same time the support of a necessary majority of the international community and in the present General Assembly we will support any proposal for this resolution of the Jerusalem problem which satisfies these criteria.

We deplore Iraq's economic boycott of Israel and its recalcitrant attitude on the Haifa question, but any representations we might make would probably meet a negative response and undermine Iraqi good will toward the United States. Accordingly, action on this question should await greater likelihood of a more favorable response.

It is of utmost importance to our relations with Iraq that we maintain a policy of strict impartiality between the Arab States and Israel and that our public officials refrain from giving the impression that United States policy favors either party.

So long as Iraq's present leadership remains in power and provided the western democracies retain the initiative in helping Iraq solve its security and economic problems, there is little chance of the Soviet Union's attaining major diplomatic successes. The western democracies, therefore, should concentrate on assisting Iraqi leadership to solve its internal problems and to combat Soviet subversive activities among dissident groups.

D. POLICY EVALUATION

The Arab grievances against the US because of its Palestine policy, which has overshadowed all other aspects of our relations with Iraq for the past several years, fortunately appear to be sinking into the background, though they are by no means forgotten. This improvement in our relations can in large part be attributed to the progress made in the past year in the field of economic and social development, and to the fact that the Iraqis have been won over to the logic of concentrating on their own internal problems rather than dissipating their resources and energy in futile altercations over Palestine.

However, it is imperative that we recognize that a larger and far graver issue is developing, which may determine the success or failure of our policy in Iraq. Iraq will expect as a quid pro quo for aligning itself and cooperating with the western democracies concrete evidence that the western democracies will effectively assure its security in the present international crisis. So far Iraq has not been given such evidence and although understanding the reasons why the major effort of the western democracies has been directed to improving security in Europe and latterly in the Far East it is naturally most apprehensive over the inadequacy of the defenses of the Near East.

Whatever our ultimate security needs in the area, the western democracies will at all stages need Iraqi good will. The latter will be difficult to retain if the western democracies allow themselves to appear unmindful of Iraqi security problems now.

Despite the undoubted strain on our resources and the undesirability of spreading ourselves too thin, the UK primarily, the US and other like–minded western democracies should urgently explore every practicable means of improving the defenses of Iraq and of the Near Eastern area as a whole.

[1] Department of State Policy [Information] statements were concise documents summarizing the current United States policy toward the relations of principal powers with and the issues and trends in a particular country or region. The statements were intended to provide information and guidance for officers in missions abroad. They were generally prepared by ad hoc working groups in the responsible geographic offices or the Department of State and were referred to appropriate diplomatic missions abroad, under cover of formal instructions from the Secretary of State for comment and criticism. The Policy statements were periodically revised.

233.

[1958–1960, Volume XII, p. 344–46]

138. Telegram From the Embassy in Iraq to the Department of State

BAGHDAD, October 14, 1958—7 a.m

1312. Three months have now passed since coup which brought Brigadier Qassim to power. It might at this stage prove helpful to depict and assess some aspects of present scene and to attempt some forecast, hazardous though it be, of what coming months probably hold in store.

1. Troops are still camped in Embassy compound and stand guard at other foreign missions, though perhaps in lesser force. Diplomatic and private visitors are still challenged at Embassy gates, as are American officials. I myself was denied entrance a few days ago, until identified, although in official car with flag displayed. Administration of Embassy, though perhaps a shade easier than during July, August and September, is still hampered by petty and unreasonable restrictions. GOI has still not yet permitted us free access USIS offices.

2. Press and radio keep up steady attacks on US, its posture in past and its current official policies. Our actions are sweepingly damned as "imperialistic" and usually linked with "British imperialism". Terminology of these attacks is increasingly "Made–in–Moscow". Public added to this fire of hatred almost nightly by the trials of officials, military and civilian, of former governments, these trials being widely publicized by radio,

television and press. It is for us in the Embassy a sickening sight to see our former firm friends and active supporters of the free world pilloried by a petty military "judge" who also conceives of himself as a prosecutor.

3. We have confirmation from a number of sources that grumblings among shopkeepers and particularly among workmen is steadily growing. Promises made so loudly and widely in early days following coup of a fuller and freer life are in no way materializing. That is immediate basis of growing discontent.

4. What of the government? In last analysis no government in western conception of that term exists in Iraq today, three months after coup. Individual cabinet ministers manage now and then to issue regulations. In few instances cabinet as a whole has approved "Laws" but up to now they are on paper only. Content of these laws, many of which are ill–conceived and hastily drafted, has in several cases required repeated clarification (e.g., laws on rent control, labor and cropsharing). There is widespread paralysis of even routine in first weeks following coup of top layer of trained men comparable, in a measure, to our civil service. Their replacements have been found, are of low caliber indeed. In spite of daily cabinet meetings, there is as yet no coordinated government program in any field, and how could there be? Although cabinet includes handful of men with previous experience this level, this government is woefully lacking in men experienced in the challenging task of governing. This lack is particularly noticeable in the economic development field. The individuals holding cabinet positions have right up to today still nothing more to guide them than the oft–repeated general policy statement of the Prime Minister that Iraq is to be independent; Iraq wants to raise the living standards of the people; Iraq wants to be friends with all nations, east and west, that want to be friends with her; and above all Iraq wants to cooperate closely with other Arab states.

5. Economy of country is stagnant chiefly because development program which was main pump primer in past has been allowed to grind to halt. Government's fumbling efforts to manage economy have caused a lack of confidence among the business community which no number of highly publicized but in

substantial trade agreements with Soviet Union and Soviet bloc countries can dispel.

6. Inevitably, even though coup was carried out most effectively by a very small group of conspirators, differences as to the courses to be followed developed early among them. Tensions, primarily among the military but also among certain civilian members of regime, soon came to surface. Momentarily Qassim is on top. Arif, second in July 14 plot, has been deprived of military and political power positions and left October 12 to become Iraqi Ambassador in Bonn. The known Baathist members of the cabinet were removed or demoted at same time as Arif fell from grace. Thus most important elements working toward union with UAR, or at the least toward very close collaboration with Nasser have been removed from center of government. The group that seems to influence Qassim most at present is made up of members of the National Democratic Party led by Kamal Chaderchi and Mohammed Hadid. This group, unfortunately, is naive to the extreme concerning danger which communism holds for Iraq. Qassim, we believe, is anti–Communist, and may be making a sincere effort to hold Communists in check. We do not think, on basis of reports we have received from diplomatic colleagues and reports emanating from Iraqi sources, that Communists played a major role in having Arif and Baathist Ministers removed from power. Communists do not today have that much influence with the regime. By weakening of Baathist influence, however, Communists undoubtedly gain much more room for maneuver. Communists also have potential for attack on another point through returned Kurdish leader Mulla Mustafa Barzani. He has spent last eleven years in exile in Soviet Union. His appeal to a majority of Iraqi Kurds is strong and his ability to disrupt stability almost endless. Thus we believe that today greatest potential threat to stability and even existence of Qassim's regime lies in hands of Communists.

7. As of today, three months after coup, Qassim's regime is by no means firmly entrenched. There exist strong pressures on it from without and within regime; there is no solid unanimity and tensions are rampant. We are in for weeks, perhaps even months, of

uncertainty. Certainly weeks just ahead are critical. Future stability is dependent on Qassim's ability to withstand the various pressures being brought to bear on him and to lead country back to normal existence.

8. Up to now Qassim's regime, whether deliberately or not, has in the main been carrying out a predominately wrecking operation. We think some of those around him are finally beginning to realize that it is much simpler to effect a coup and tear down government than it is to govern.

9. From my personal experience and observation covering these past four years in Iraq, I would say that with the murder of Nuri, illiberal as he may at times have been in dealing with domestic issues, Iraq sacrificed her best leader toward an eventual life of dignity and decency and her strongest bulwark against recurrent chaos, if not savagery. A number of well placed and knowledgeable Iraqis have been quoted to me within the past few days as having said, in effect, that within ten years at most a monument would be erected in Baghdad to Nuri.

I hope, in fact I believe, they are right.

GALLMAN

Source: Department of State, Central Files, 787.00/10–1458. Confidential. Transmitted in two sections and repeated to Amman, Ankara, Beirut, Cairo, Damascus, Jidda, Karachi, London, Tehran, and Tel Aviv.

234.

[1958–1960, Volume XII, pp. 460–63]

191. Memorandum for the Record

WASHINGTON, June 1, 1959—11 a.m.
SUBJECT
Meeting of Special Committee on Iraq
PARTICIPANTS
Assistant Secretary of State William M. Rountree, Chairman
Mr. Parker T. Hart, Deputy Assistant Secretary of State
Mr. Stuart Rockwell, Director, Office of Near Eastern Affairs, Department of State
Mr. Harrison Symmes, Special Assistant to Mr. Rountree

Acting Assistant Secretary of Defense F. Haydn Williams
Dr. Lynford A. Lardner, ISA, Department of Defense
Colonel Butler—JCS (USAF)
[less than 1 line of source text not declassified], CIA
Mr. William J. Handley, Area Director, NEA, USIA
Mr. Philip J. Halla, NSC Staff

In opening the meeting, Mr. Rountree said he thought it would be advisable for the group to meet regularly on Mondays at 11 o'clock until further notice. He remarked that we had probably all seen the cabled report of Ambassador Jernegan's conversation with Kassem following his return from consultations in Washington.[1] Mr. Rountree observed that the Ambassador seemed neither encouraged nor discouraged as a result of his latest discussion with the Iraqi leader. The Assistant Secretary felt that there was slight evidence of improvement, particularly regarding the Communists. There were, however, no signs that Kassem was building up any anti–Communist forces. One encouraging fact was Kassem's decision not to arm the Popular Resistance Forces. At least one could say that the situation has not deteriorated further.

Mr. Rountree continued that the Iraqi decision to cancel our military assistance agreement and the supplemental sales agreement is the latest development. This was done by diplomatic note, which was in itself an innovation, although the note was only delivered[2] shortly before the press announcement was made. The Department is not sure what the "economic assistance agreement" of July 23, 1957 is which the Iraqis have also canceled. Mr. Rockwell said it possibly concerned the police agreement made by the Richards Mission. (Embassy Baghdad's cable 3439 of May 29[3]—copy attached—thought the reference might be to the telecommunications agreement signed in connection with the Baghdad Pact.)

Mr. Rountree's Deputy, Mr. Parker T. Hart, reported on his recent trip to the area. Mr. Hart said he went primarily to discuss the Iraqi situation with the Turks at their request. He had a lengthy conference at the Hilton Hotel in Istanbul with Foreign Minister Zorlou and several other Turkish of officials including the former Turkish Minister to Syria, whom he had known in Damascus.[4] Mr. Hart regards this man, who is now Zorlou's Middle East advisor, as a very sound individual. The discussion showed that Zorlou may have revised his views of Arab nationalism somewhat. He now seemed to agree that the choice was between independence and Communism in Iraq. At the same time, Zorlou hoped that we would not help resurrect Nasser's influence in Iraq. During the conversation, Zorlou appeared moderate and willing to listen. Among other items, the Turkish Foreign Minister agreed to our suggestion that the Turks extend military aid to the Afghanistan Military Academy. The Turks indicated that they were worried about Iran as well as Iraq, regarding the Shah's country as a weak reed.

Zorlou's attitude toward the Kurds was that they were beset by ancient rivalries and always scrapping among themselves. The Turks do not favor Kurdish activity at present and have so informed Kassem. However, Zorlou considers the Kurds a factor to be held in reserve for possible use if the Iraq situation deteriorates.

In Iran, Mr. Hart mentioned meeting with General Paklavan, deputy head of SAVAK, the Iranian intelligence mechanism, whom he found to be very knowledgeable on Iraq.[5] Mr. Hart found the general attitude toward Iraq more relaxed in Tehran than in Beirut and Ankara. The General appeared to have numerous sources in Iraq which Mr. Hart presumed were among the Shiite Muslim community. Paklavan thought a strong force was building up in the Iraqi army, which would be prepared to take anti–Communist action if necessary. He indicated that the Iranians were also attempting to hold back the Kurds and keep them in reserve.

In response to my question as to whether there were still differences of view between Zorlou and Prime Minister Menderes concerning Iraq, Mr. Rountree said he had talked with Zorlou when he was here last week for Secretary Dulles' funeral. He confirmed Mr. Hart's impressions, stressed Zorlou's dislike of Nasser and his feeling that we should not build up the UAR leader, as well as an impression that the Iraqi situation might start to deteriorate quickly. Zorlou wanted to start joint planning

for possible contingencies in Iraq. Mr. Rountree still thinks this would be highly dangerous and said he "finessed" this Turkish request. The Assistant Secretary feels that we should continue to exchange information, but go no further with the Turks at this time.

Mr. Rountree then asked Mr. Rockwell for comments. The Director of Near Eastern Affairs said that he thought things looked a little better than the last time the group had met.[6]

[less than 1 line of source text not declassified] when asked for comments, said things perhaps are improving, although recent events in themselves had not proven the case. He said Kassem has not given the real tip off of his intentions, which might come if current rumors that he is about to remove one or both of the two pro–Communist Taher brothers turn out to be true or if he cracks down on Col. Mahdawi of the military tribunal.

Mr. Handley asked for State's view of Ambassador Jernegan's suggestion that we send a representative to the celebration of the July 14th revolution.[7] Mr. Rountree replied that if invited we would attend. If the USSR is invited and we are not, it would be highly significant. (Mr. Handley told me later that Ambassador Jernegan had suggested that someone like Dr. Elson of the National Presbyterian Church might represent the U.S. Although he had not yet taken up the matter with Mr. George Allen, Handley expressed some doubt of the desirability of this type of appointment and, in fact, wondered whether we should send a special representative at all. I said that perhaps a sensible military representative might make more impression on the present regime in Iraq, although, of course, Dr. Elson is known for his interest in Near Eastern matters.)

Mr. Haydn Williams said he had no substantive comment. He found Mr. Rountree's report interesting and useful. He liked the idea of regular weekly meetings, which would provide useful information for briefing the Council principals, for discussion of whether there will be a report, and, if so, its contents. Mr. Williams favored group discussion of what the reports will contain. He thought it would be useful to include a check off list for the Council on actions taken. The meetings could also permit the input of new ideas from other agencies.

Mr. Rountree agreed in general, noting that the Group would meet regularly and that his office would undertake to supply on an informal basis advance copies of briefing material prepared for the Secretary of State.

I asked whether the Committee would report this week. Mr. Rountree indicated a report would be made along the lines of the previous report. [8]

Mr. Handley said USIA was looking into the Iraqi request that bookmobiles be provided through UNESCO and asked Mr. Rountree's view of the policy implications. Mr. Rountree favored the idea, although he was not happy about the fact that the U.S. would receive no publicity from such an activity. When asked for details Mr. Handley replied that USIA was working with ICA since the equipment would be costly and with the UNESCO relations staff in the State Department. USIA could supply books.

Mr. Lardner of Defense mentioned the problem of certain effects caused by Iraq's abrogation of the military assistance agreements. This raised a question as to what we should try to do about the equipment we had already given them. The discussion brought out the fact that we had given Iraq five F–86 aircraft (which Col. Butler said are not flyable because certain parts have been returned to the U.S.) and thirteen 8" Howitzers [*less than 1 line of source text not declassified*] which are part of the equipment for an armored regiment. These guns are operational, if maintenance has been kept up. Mr. Rountree and Mr. Rockwell agreed that this represented a problem that we would have to take up with the Iraqi. Mr. Rockwell noted that there is a one-year cancellation notice provision in the agreement, but he was not sure there was much the U.S. could do in view of Iraq's unilateral action.

PHILIP J. HALLA

Source: Eisenhower Library, White House Office Files, Project Clean Up, The Middle East. Top Secret. Drafted by Halla.

[1] See footnote 1, Document 185.

[2] The Iraqi Government delivered the note to the U.S. Embassy the morning of May 29.

[3] Not printed. (Department of State, Central Files, 687.00/5–2952

[4] Hart reported his conversation in telegram 3229 from Ankara, May 16. (*Ibid.*, 787.00/5–1659)

[5] Hart reported his conversation in telegram 2303 from Tehran, May 21. (*Ibid.*, 787.00/5–2159)

[6] At the 408th Meeting of the National Security Council on May 28, as part of his briefing on "Significant World Developments Affecting U.S. Security," Allen Dulles briefed the Council along similar lines noting that Qassim seemed anti-Communist and cautiously favorable to the West. Dulles stated that it was still too early to detect any clear trend. (Memorandum of discussion by Gleason, May 28; Eisenhower Library, Whitman File, NSC Records)

[7] As suggested in telegram 3394 from Baghdad, May 26. (Department of State, Central Files, 887.424/5–2659)

[8] See footnote 1, Document 192.

235.

[1958–1960, Volume XII, p. 474]

198. Editorial Note

At the 414th Meeting of the National Security Council, July 23, Director of Central Intelligence Allen Dulles briefed the Council on disorders in Iraq as part of his "Significant World Developments Affecting U.S. Security" briefing as follows:

"Iraq, which Mr. Dulles described as a troubled land was, he said, having still more trouble. Apparently the Kirkuk outbreak had been put down more rapidly than our own or the Egyptian press had indicated. Still, however, no one knows much about why the outbreak began or how it began. On the other hand, further outbreaks could occur at any time. Qasim has condemned all the elements involved in these outbreaks and has especially singled out the Communists. Qasim has been invited to go to Moscow for a state visit and it is reported that he has accepted the invitation without, however, specifying any date." Later on in the briefing was the following exchange:

"Reverting to the Kirkuk disturbances, the President inquired of Mr. Dulles about the ethnic difference between the Turkomans and the Kurds. Mr. Dulles replied that they are different tribes and had a different language and he believed that they are ethnically quite different. He said that he had virtually completed a lengthy study of the Kurds and would be able to report to the President more fully on his question later." (Eisenhower Library, Whitman File, NSC Records)

236.

[1958–1960, Volume XII, pp. 566–69]

240. Memorandum of Conference With President Eisenhower

WASHINGTON, June 30, 1958—2:45–4:25 p.m.

OTHERS PRESENT
His Majesty, The Shah of Iran
Captain Aurand

The President commenced the conversation by asking if the Iranian Army did not consist of ten divisions. The Shah replied: "Yes, ten divisions, plus some brigades."

The Shah then proceeded to outline his concept of the Middle East situation and Iran's strategic importance to the West in the light of USSR moves. He stressed the following points:

(1) Four years ago Iran put aside a 150–year old policy of neutrality and threw its lot with the West.

(2) He emphasized the importance of the strategic location of Iran as a gateway through which any invasion of the Middle East or moves towards southern Asia must come. "If you control Iran, you control the Middle East."

(3) He stressed the unlikelihood of all–out war in view of the mutual deterrence imposed by the H–bomb.

(4) He stated that, two years ago, Russia had no plans for the Middle East, but, since Suez, they definitely have a plan to penetrate and control it. Their objectives are the West's lines of communications to the Far East, Middle East oil, and after Lebanon, Iraq, or Jordan.

(5) Through broadcasts from Radio Cairo, the Communists are now stirring up the Kurds to fight for a free Kurdistan. Such an arrangement would involve territory now held by Iran, Turkey, Iraq, and the USSR. He pointed out that immediately after seizing Azerbaijan, the Russians had divided it into Turkish and Kurdish Provinces. They had established a Kurdish Government, complete with all trappings, including a national anthem. Radio Cairo is now playing this same anthem in their propaganda campaign.

(6) The hesitation of the free world to become involved in limited wars benefits the USSR who can engage and disengage at will without any inhibitions as to what their own people think. The three countries in this area that stand solid with the free world are Turkey, Iran and Pakistan. If these countries are strengthened to cope with any new development in the region, U.S. problems are reduced regardless of the slowness of UN action and U.S. reservations about intervention. If the armies of these three countries are strengthened, the USSR will change their plans to take over the Middle East.

(7) In response to a query by the President about the inclusion of Iraq, the Shah indicated that although they would be delighted to have Iraq participate, he wondered if Iraq can be trusted as a firm ally since Nasser is more popular with the Iraqi people than the Iraqi government.

(8) The Shah stated that in Baghdad Pact meetings all parties were agreed on the concept that the center of defense of the area was Iran, and that all agreed on the forces required.

(9) He expressed worry as to whether, if World War III were started, the U.S. could destroy Russia before Russia was well into Iran. He asked whether the U.S. would bomb Iran to get at Russian forces in this case.

The President replied that destruction of Russia will defeat any such invasion, and that if any major Russian forces ever invaded Iran that it would be considered a major attack on the free world. The President also pointed out that maintenance of too much force for limited war could be self–defeating economically. The President further stated that it was essential that nations such as Turkey, Iran, and Pakistan had to have a clear concept of what to do, to be ready to make sacrifices, and to have a national will to resist in a combined fashion. He said that it was important that they should have an Allied Commander who would command forces in the interest of the coalition and not of any individual nation.

The Shah then set forth in some detail his estimate that in the next ten years he expected great economic progress and prosperity for Iran. He pointed out that he was having some success with selling to his own people what he called "Positive Nationalism" which envisioned the elimination of colonialism and imperialism, but emphasized cooperation as friends for the mutual benefit of the free world and his own country. He pointed out that Nasser had achieved nothing of the material benefit of his people by his ultra–nationalistic policy. He pointed out the very favorable oil agreements that his country had concluded with the Italians and with the Standard Oil Company of Indiana.

The President stated that he agreed with this policy of positive nationalism and stated that the problem was to explain to the people of the various countries the benefits that they could achieve with cooperation with the West and, if successful, that this would be as good as tanks, planes, etc. He further stated that we had not succeeded very well in the Middle East in getting this message to the people. The Shah said that he felt that in Iran they had been able to convince the little man, at least to the degree that his government was able to adopt their Western–oriented policy with the support of the people.

The President asked him about radio stations. The Shah indicated that they were starting on them, that they were trying to educate the people with them, and that they had ordered two more 100 KW stations that would cover all of Arabia and the Moslem area of Russia. He further stated that they broadcast in Turkish and Kurdish as well as Persian. The President stated that he would like to see a station covering the same area as Radio Cairo point out the crimes of aggression that were being committed in the Middle East, and particularly reach the people of Saudi Arabia so as to induce King Saud to show a little more concern for his people. He stated, and the Shah concurred, that King Saud had a great propaganda advantage in the Moslem world as the keeper of the holy places.

The President told the Shah that he hoped that he would really brief the Defense people on the same subjects that they had been talking about and that he would show them on the map his concepts.

The Shah stated that he felt of all of the nations in the area, Iran was the one country that had the economic resources to keep a large army. The Turks, although good soldiers, are having economic troubles, but the Iranians are their brothers, and Iran can serve her own interests and those of the free world by supporting an army of appreciable size.

The President and the Shah discussed affairs in Pakistan. The Shah stated his admiration for the Pakistani people and added that they had proposed to him a federation of his country and theirs with perhaps including Afghanistan. The Shah felt that this would be to their mutual advantage and that perhaps in the process, East Pakistan could be traded to India for Kashmir. The boundaries of this federation were pointed out to the President on the globe.

The President emphasized the importance of mechanical and technical education if any nation were to be able to maintain complex equipment required by modern military forces. The Shah listed in some detail all of the various efforts that they were making in this direction. He stated that he would like very much to see an American university in Tehran such as now exists in Cairo and Beirut. The Shah further stated that he felt the trained U.S. teams in his country were impressed with Iranian mechanics.

The Shah stated that he was concerned about the beefing up of Syrian–Egyptian forces with Russian military equipment. He said that it was far above what they could use and felt that this was possibly a prepositioned arsenal for Syrian "Kurdish volunteers". He stated that Iran and the other western–oriented countries needed arms to be able to immediately cope with such a threat. The President stated that another problem was to have the political agreements ready so that immediate action could be taken and, further, that this had to be backed with the morale and will to resist. The President said that one of the problems all nations in the West share was to balance their growing economies and their armed strength. Armed strength produces nothing except an assurance of the continued existence of the country.

The President then explained, at some length, some of his problems in getting the mutual aid program through.

The Shah asked to come back to the point of military command in the Baghdad Pact area. He suggested an American be the Commander, and that they would welcome an American Commander for the area and be willing to accept him. The President pointed out that such a Commander must have full authority. The President mentioned General Van Fleet. The Shah agreed that he would be a good man. The Shah then took his leave.

G.

Source: Eisenhower Library, Whitman File, International File, Iran. Top Secret. Prepared by Aurand. The meeting was held at the White House. The concluding time of the meeting is from Eisenhower's Appointment Book. (*Ibid.*, President's Daily Appointments)

237.

[1958–1960, Volume XII, pp. 600–04]

256. Memorandum of Discussion at the 386th Meeting of the National Security Council

WASHINGTON, November 13, 1958.

1. Significant World Developments Affecting U.S. Security

. . . In Iran the chief of the Shah's intelligence service had provided the Shah with a report warning him against Soviet–inspired subversive plots. Mr. Dulles thought we needed to watch with particular care developments along the frontier areas, especially those where there were significant Kurdish elements. These latter offer the best possibility to the Soviets for stirring up trouble. In general Soviet–Iranian relations had currently reached their lowest ebb in three years. In conclusion Mr. Dulles mentioned briefly several small steps taken by the Shah to implement the internal reform program. While these were steps in the right direction, they were thus far insufficient in Mr. Dulles's view to syphon off discontent . . .

2. U.S. Policy Toward Iran (NSC 5703/1; NSC Action No. 1998;[1] SNIE 34–58;[2] NSC 5821;[3] Memo for All Holders of NSC 5821, dated November 5, 1958[4])

Mr. Gordon Gray briefed the Council at greater length than usual, stressing particularly those areas in which the newly proposed policy on Iran (NSC 5821) differed from our present policy on Iran (NSC 5703/1).[5]

At the conclusion of Mr. Gray's briefing, he called on Secretary Herter to comment on the new proposed policy. Secretary Herter said that he found the new paper very interesting, the more so because Iran was the one nation in the world with a long border with the Soviet Union with which we have no defensive alliance. We were not even full partners in the Baghdad Pact. Iran obviously held a highly strategic position, and in our dealings with Iran we have been dealing with an individual (the Shah) of very uncertain quality. Evidently, the Shah had been slow in breaking his ties with the old landed aristocracy but he is now making significant moves in a new and desirable direction. These new moves had been the result of friendly urging by the U.S. rather than as the result of putting the heat on the Shah. The latter was so exceedingly temperamental that the State Department feared that if we really attempted to put the heat on him, he might very well tell us to go to hell and proceed to play ball with the other side. The situation was far from a happy one and, moreover, was now complicated by the recent Kurdish agitation.

As to the problem of the size of Iran's military establishment, the State Department felt that this called for a professional military judgment and was a subject on which the State Department was not too intelligent except insofar as the military strength of Iran were to be so increased that it would constitute a heavy strain both on the economy of Iran and our own U.S. resources for the assistance of Iran. The Shah evidently counts on the hope that increase in Iranian oil revenues will be sufficient shortly to put an end to all need in Iran for outside assistance.

The President commented that he was aware of this hope and that the Shah himself had said to the President that Iran could dispense with outside assistance in ten years' time.

Mr. Gray pointed out that as regards inducements and pressures on the Shah to carry out the necessary reforms in Iran, the Planning Board in the present paper was suggesting that we try inducements first and resort to pressures on the Shah only when the State Department deemed this course of action to be appropriate. In short, the Planning Board did not regard the language in the present paper as constituting a restricting directive to the State Department.

Secretary Herter said he was quite willing to accept the language in the paper dealing with this subject, and Mr. Gray then asked General Taylor, as Acting Chairman of the Joint Chiefs of Staff, to comment on the mission of the Iranian armed forces and the fact that while the old policy paper (NSC 5703/1) had mentioned "outside air and logistic support" to Iran in fighting defensive delaying actions, the present policy (NSC 5821) called merely for "outside support" for this purpose.

General Taylor replied that the language referred to by Mr. Gray in Paragraph 36—a related to Baghdad Pact military planning. It seemed to be the view of the Baghdad Pact planners that some 19 divisions—not only Iranian but some supplied by other Baghdad Pact Powers—were required to discharge the military mission of fighting delaying actions against Soviet forces. Accordingly, it seemed to General Taylor that the change of language from "outside air and logistic support" to "outside support" was a reasonable change and simply reflected the views of the Baghdad Pact planners that Iranian ground forces would be assisted by ground troops from Turkey and Pakistan. With regard to the possibility that the term "outside support" might imply a U.S. commitment to provide ground troops as well as air and logistic support in the event of Soviet–armed aggression against Iran, General Taylor invited the Council's attention to Paragraph 43 which contained guidance for U.S. action in the event that U.S.S.R. military forces invaded Iran. After reading this paragraph to the Council, General Taylor said the language clearly left open to decision by the President at the time what kind of assistance would be offered, and specifically whether U.S. ground forces were to be included or not.

Mr. Gray replied that the Planning Board merely wanted to be sure of the significance of this change of phraseology and went on to say that he had one other comment to make. It was the consensus of the Planning Board that the so–called Firbal Project, a dummy corporation of Iranian notables acting as an intermediary between French contractors and the Iranian Ministry of War, was not of sufficient

importance to justify discussion in the Council. Nevertheless, Mr. Gray said he did feel some concern lest by condoning the Firbal Project, the U.S. was not perhaps in effect condoning the very graft and corruption which it was our policy to try to induce the Shah to eliminate. He therefore hoped that the State Department would take a good look at the Firbal Project so that we could be sure of not being embarrassed later by these arrangements.

Secretary Herter replied that Mr. Allen Dulles was the leading authority on Iranian law, having been the author of that country's present code of law. Nevertheless, one of the most encouraging features of late was the Shah's crackdown on corrupt practices within his own family.

The President brought the discussion back to the matter of the deployment of the Iranian Army, and pointed out that when the Shah had visited him last summer, he had talked about the necessity of deploying two good Iranian military units in the Kurdish areas of Iraq [Iran] and he had also talked of the desirability of installing a radio to broadcast in Kurdish to Kurds living in Iran. The Shah had pointed out that the Kurds were constantly bombarded by Soviet propaganda broadcasts and he wanted some kind of counteraction. The President asked if anything had been done by us to respond to the Shah's request for assistance.

The Director of USIA, Mr. George Allen, said that his agency was currently working with the Government of Iran about setting up a 50–kilowatt broadcasting facility. Of course, continued Mr. Allen, it was equally important what the radio broadcasts of this station would say to the Kurdish population of Iran. The Iranian authorities have not yet decided on what line the new radio would take. Accordingly, USIA was trying to help formulate a broadcasting line to which the Kurds would respond favorably. This was not easy because the Kurds have always disliked the Iranians and probably could never be induced to like them.

Apropos of the various paragraphs of the paper which Mr. Gray had read in the course of his briefing, the President expressed approval of the language. He expressed his earnest agreement with Secretary Herter that as long as we propose to play ball with the Shah, we certainly could not hammer at him in order to get him to undertake the reforms. If we did not propose to treat him skillfully, we had better abandon him altogether and get another man. Mr. Allen Dulles pointed out that there was no "other man" in sight at the present moment.

Secretary Anderson suggested that another significant means of influencing the Shah in the right direction was through his many contacts with American businessmen. Unlike most heads of state, the Shah enjoyed very much talking to American businessmen. They were thus in the position of urging reform measures upon him without appearing to be instruments of the U.S. Government carrying out of official U.S. policy.

The National Security Council:[6]

a. Discussed the draft statement of policy on the subject contained in NSC 5821, prepared by the NSC Planning Board pursuant to NSC Action No. 1998–b.

b. Adopted the statement of policy in NSC 5821.

Note: The statement of policy in NSC 5821, as adopted, subsequently approved by the President; circulated as NSC 5821/1[7] for implementation by all appropriate Executive departments and agencies of the U.S. Government; and referred to the Operations Coordinating Board as the coordinating agency designated by the President.

[Here follow agenda items 3 and 4.]

S. EVERETT GLEASON

Source: Eisenhower Library, Whitman File, NSC Records. Top Secret; Eyes Only. Drafted by Gleason on November 13.

[1] see Document 254.

[2] Document 249.

[3] see footnote 5 below.

[4] This memorandum transmitted the financial appendix of NSC 5821 to the NSC. (Department of State, S/S–NSC Files: Lot 63 D 351, NSC 5821 Memoranda)

[5] As Rountree informed Dulles in a memorandum of November 11, NSC 5821 "emphasizes our concern over a possible deterioration of internal stability if the Shah does not move energetically toward certain political, economic, social and administrative reforms. It stresses the need for our representatives in Tehran to assist the Shah in his efforts, wherever appropriate and feasible. The paper reflects the President's decision of July

19,1958, to accelerate deliveries of equipment to, and training of, the Iranian armed forces, and to bring authorized units up to full strength At the same time it emphasizes the need to convince the Shah and others that the attempted creation of forces beyond the country's ability to absorb and support could only be detrimental to Iran's own security interests." (*Ibid.*)

[6] Paragraphs a and b and the Note that follows constitute NSC Action No. 2006, approved by the President on November 15. (*Ibid.*, S/S–NSC (Miscellaneous) Files: Lot 66 D 95, Records of Action by the National Security Council)

[7] Document 257.

238.

[1961–1963, Volume XVIII, pp. 116-17]
49. Telegram From the Embassy in Iraq to the Department of State

BAGHDAD, September 20,1962—noon.
150. Kurdistan Democratic Party officer, known to be responsible for Baghdad, following instruction from Mulla Mustafa called on Embassy of officer privately September 18. Kurd made strong plea for US support of revolution movement. Said it needs money now and possibly arms later. Claimed most Communists have been eliminated from KDP and remainder will be removed soon.

In return for support, Mulla Mustafa would promise (1) purge movement of any persons we consider suspect, (2) cooperate with conservative Arab Iraqi elements and bring Iraq back into Baghdad Pact if we wish, (3) give us immediately full information on internal political or military developments in Kurdistan or Arab Iraq. KDP official claimed Kurdish intelligence extensive and accurate. Said this offer would be binding on Kurds in Syria and Iran as well as Iraq.

Kurd said that KDP maintains "close and friendly" contact Iranians both in Baghdad and Tehran. Iranians have agreed not interfere with border crossings or to stop aid given revolt by Iranian Kurds. Mulla Mustafa pleased but also wants material support from Iran. KDP official said Mulla Mustafa believes proposal bring Kurdistan into Iran as "autonomous republic" is attractive to Shah.

The Kurds also maintain regular contact with the UAR, which is "friendly but unhelpful", and USSR Embassy Baghdad. He said

Kurds were not willing "burn all bridges to Russia" unless they have assurances USG will support their movement. He said that he personally is given ID 1,000 per month by Soviet Embassy for certain Communist sympathizers in KDP but money goes into KDP coffers. Mulla Mustafa does not consider this small sum as assistance to movement.

Kurds have asked Kuwait for assistance but Kuwait refused. British Embassy Baghdad confirms this. Said British have advised Kuwait give no money to rebels.

Israel has offered assistance to Kurds in Europe but this refused—not because Kurds are anti-Israel but because they fear Israel might purposely reveal information and "movement" would be harmed throughout Arab countries.

KDP official said that Mulla Mustafa knows that after downfall Qasim, which he believes imminent, USSR will be anxious help them with money and arms. Kurd said Mulla Mustafa prefers cooperate with West rather than with USSR, "which he does not trust." However, "all Kurds are nationalists" and must win autonomy now or be prepared for racial extinction. Before Kurds will permit this they would take help from USSR or from "devil himself".

KDP official was clearly told that USG policy toward Kurdish rebellion has not changed.[1] He replied that if it does he should be contacted and message can be transmitted immediately to Mulla Mustafa.

MELBOURNE

Source: Department of State, Central Files, 787.00/9-2062 Secret; Limit Distribution No Foreign Eyes. Repeated to Ankara, Damascus, London, Paris, and Tehran.

[1] A September 11 memorandum from Strong to Talbot describes the public U.S. position on Iraq's Kurdish problem as follows: "The United States considers the Kurdish problem in Iraq an internal matter which should be resolved internally. Our Government does not support Kurdish activities against the Government of Iraq in any way and hopes an early peaceful solution will be possible. It is our understanding that some of the Kurdish demands include requests for the reinstitution of certain constitutional guarantees. While the United States' position is clear on the desirability of democratic constitutional life, any comment on these demands in Iraq would be an intrusion into that country's internal affairs. We believe the future well-being of Kurds in Iraq, as well as those in Iran and Turkey is inseparably tied to the well-being of the countries in which they reside. We know Turkey and Iran share this view, and believe the Iraq Government feels the same way." (*Ibid.*, 787.00/9-1162)

239.

[1961–1963, Volume XVIII, pp. 381–82]

173. Memorandum From Robert W. Komer of the National Security Council Staff to the President's Special Assistant for National Security Affairs (Bundy)

WASHINGTON, March 1, 1963.

McGB—

Some of our spies are beginning to get quite worried about risk that Kurdish problem may flare up again to bedevil new Iraqi regime. It's hard to tell whether talks in Baghdad are going well or badly, but there are many—Turks, Iranians, Nasser, and above all Soviets—who might see a stake in egging Kurds on. We're warning Iranians especially to keep hands off, but if Shah should decide that new Iraq regime is too cozy with Nasser, he may not take our advice. I've urged CIA to raise contingency planning issue in Special Group next time and hope you will support their pitch. Preventive diplomacy is what we need most.

CIA is worried, DIA less so, over growing possibility of Nasser ground strike into Saudi Arabia. State thinks this unlikely on balance (Nasser unwilling to risk break with us), but I see Nasser as testing us. Have urged Pentagon in any case to consider preventive or subsequent military counters. Have also ginned up a proposed third JFK warning to Nasser which should be over shortly. I'm hopeful Nasser won't escalate this far but we ought to be ready for a painful decision.

BOB K

240.

[1961–1963, Volume XVIII, pp. 382–89]

174. Circular Airgram From the Department of State to Certain Posts

CA–9411

WASHINGTON, March 2, 1963—1:05 p.m.

SUBJECT

Interim Policy Guidelines for Dealing With Iraq and With the Implications for the Middle East of the Recent Iraqi Coup

Following for guidance all addressees:

SUMMARY

The recent Iraqi coup, described by coup spokesmen as a continuation of the Iraqi revolution of July 14,1958, is a development of potentially fundamental importance for Iraq, the Middle East generally, and the United States. The United States can "live with" the new Iraqi regime, as presently seen.

Internally the GOI must deal with four principal problems, i.e., the Kurdish Revolt, the Iraq Petroleum Company (IPC), Constitutional Development and Economic Development. Failure to find a political solution to the Kurdish problem would benefit only the Soviets and the Iraqi communists. The US regards it as strictly an internal Iraqi matter. We should continue to consult with the UK on IPC matters and quietly encourage US shareholders of IPC to respond with flexibility to GOI initiatives on unsettled issues. We should express pleasure at expressed GOI initiatives on unsettled issues. We should express pleasure at expressed GOI intent to create a Constitutional situation. The GOI has enough resources, if properly managed, to promote economic development. The US should demonstrate willingness to assist Iraq in feasible ways without materially increasing the aid level. US businessmen should be encouraged to seek opportunities in Iraq, and the GOI should be encouraged to abolish Qasim's restrictive measures against foreign business.

Externally, the GOI will have a strong position in the Eastern Arab world if it consolidates power and remains cohesive. Its goals and ideology will attract particularly the Syrians, Jordanians and Yemenis, and to a lesser extent the Kuwaitis, Saudis, and Lebanese. Wishing to concentrate externally on pan–Arabism, the GOI will seek friendly relations with Turkey and Iran to secure its rear. Competition between Iraq and the UAR is likely to occur. Israel will be apprehensive of Iraq's enhanced influence.

The US should encourage friendly Iraqi relations with Turkey and Iran. The latter should be discouraged from intervening in Iraqi affairs. We should avoid use of the term "Fertile Crescent" and continue to maintain mutually beneficial bilateral relations with other Arab countries, remaining strictly impartial as between Cairo and Baghdad. The US (and UK) should encourage an Iraqi–Kuwaiti modus vivendi while continuing to support Kuwaiti independence. If Kuwait freely chooses to federate with Iraq, we should not oppose provided Kuwait retains full power of decision on oil matters. The US should continue strongly to support Jordan. Syria will be attracted to Iraq. The US should not oppose Syrian federation with Iraq, or the UAR; provided force is not used and a majority of Syrians freely approve. We should continue to respond sympathetically to Syrian requests for American assistance. We should use Saudi apprehensions about the GOI to encourage disengagement from Yemen and rapid advances in reform and modernization. We should reassure Lebanon and others, that we support their independence without reservations. We should not encourage Iraqi activities in Yemen because of the former's hostility to the UK in Aden, and to the Saudi throne. Understanding Israel's concern about implications of the Iraqi revolution, we should nevertheless continue to maintain even–handed impartiality between Israel and the Arab countries. At the same time, we should make known to the GOI and other Arab Governments our interest in Israel's security and well–being, its right to exist as a state, and the desirability of eventual permanent peace between the Arabs and Israel.

A. *The Internal Situation*

Assuming that it will prove able to consolidate power, the new Iraqi Government (GOI), a Ba'thi–nationalist coalition, can be expected to emphasize pan–Arabism within the context of Iraqi national interests, and will be neutralist, reformist, and socialist (Scandinavian type). Its aims will appeal to the aspirations of the bulk of the Iraqi people. Following "pacification" of the country, including a Kurdish settlement, it is likely to seek to create a democratic and constitutional base and to devise a sounder approach to economic development.

From the standpoint of internal Iraqi affairs, we expect that the United States will be able to "live with" the GOI. Whatever the Communists may hereafter be called publicly, the GOI will wish to limit their influence. The GOI is expected to move to a non–aligned position which will in effect reduce the Bloc position in Iraq. We are hopeful that the GOI will negotiate reasonably with IPC. However, there are some longer range implications involving Iraq's external policies which are less happy; these are dealt with in Section B.

Guidance follows on the four principal internal issues with which the GOI must deal:

1. Kurdish Revolt. Failure to find a political solution soon would benefit only the Soviets and the Iraqi communists.

US Position: The United States should continue to regard the problem as strictly an internal Iraqi matter in which there is no role for the United States either directly or indirectly. In discussion with Iraqis and others, United States officials should limit themselves to expressions of hope that the GOI and the Kurds will be able to come promptly to a mutually satisfactory agreement and the United States is pursuing a strictly hands–off policy. Our influence should be used with Iran and Turkey to assure a similar hands–off policy on their part.

2. Oil. IPC found it impossible to deal rationally with Qasim. While the new GOI will not be a "pushover", indications are that it does wish to reach agreement with IPC on outstanding issues. A qualified and "reasonable" Minister now heads up the Oil Ministry, and he has taken the initiative to reopen talks with the IPC on one of the issues. We expect this to lead into talks on other issues in which it will become clearer how the GOI may wish to implement Law 80 and what role the Iraqi National Oil Company will play.

US Position: Traditionally, the IPC has been under British management and we see no reason to seek a change. Likewise, negotiations have always been conducted by the Company without UK or US governmental intervention. This should continue, although in the event of serious difficulty, consideration should be given to quiet discussions by UK and/or US of officials with the GOI. The United States should keep in touch with the UK on developments and seek a common understanding at all times. The United States should also keep in touch with the United States shareholders in IPC (Jersey and Socony), and should encourage them to maintain a degree of flexibility in dealing with the GOI.

3. Constitutional Development. Qasim often promised the creation of a Constitution, a referendum thereon, and parliamentary elections, but nothing happened. The new GOI has stated publicly that it proposes to create a constitutional situation as soon as possible after order is restored (including a settlement with the Kurds). Given the Ba'thist stress on national unity, the new GOI hopefully will carry out its program.

US Position: As in the case of the Kurdish problem, creation of an internal political system is strictly a matter for Iraqi decision. In discussions with Iraqis, and others, United States officials should limit themselves to expressions (a) of pleasure at the publicly stated intentions of the GOI and (b) of hope that conditions will soon permit implementation. We should not seek to advise the GOI on the system to be adopted, nor do we need to tell the GOI how to handle its domestic Communism.

4. Economic Development. Properly managed, considerable resources, both public and private, are available to Iraq for internal development. Apart from effective planning, the greatest need is restoration of confidence on the part of businessmen. Ba'thist doctrine calls for a "mixed" economy with private investment permitted in fields other than basic resources. Thus there is wide scope for private enterprise. During Qasim's regime, Iraq linked itself more and more closely to the Soviet Bloc in terms of development and trade.

While it remains to be seen just how far Iraq will turn toward the West in these fields, precedents have been set in the UAR and Syria for continuing to rely on the Soviets for arms but turning away from the Soviets in economic matters.

US Position: Without increasing the level of aid appreciably, the United States should demonstrate willingness to be of assistance to Iraq in any feasible way. In particular US businessmen should be encouraged to seek opportunities in Iraq, and the GOI should be kept appropriately informed of the need to remove or at least to liberalize the restrictive measures imposed by the Qasim regime against foreign business. (See Deptel 251 of February 15, 1963.)[1]

B. Iraqi External Policy

Assuming its consolidation of power, the new GOI will have a strong position in the Eastern Arab world. The goals and ideology which provide a strong popular base in Iraq will attract particularly the Syrians, Jordanians, and Yemenis, as well as to a lesser extent the Kuwaitis, Saudis, and Lebanese. Prior to the 1958 revolution, Iraq's ability to play a key role in the Arab world was hindered by its unpopular connection with the West, and after 1958 was circumscribed by the Government's alignment with the Soviet Bloc. Iraq is the second most populous and potentially powerful state in the Eastern Arab world after the UAR, and has a viable economy.

The new GOI, following Ba'thist policy, will strive for Arab unity on a federal basis, with foreign, military and Palestine affairs developed commonly; domestic policies are to be determined by each member. Differing from Nasser in his desire that one man and one state should dominate an Arab union and that the union should be made up of states modelled internally upon and compatible with the UAR, the GOI nevertheless regards Egypt as crucial to the Arab cause because of its geographic position, population and resources, and the GOI therefore will do everything possible, short of subordinating itself to the UAR, to avoid an open split. Rather, it will seek to modify Egyptian views to reflect its Own.

Guidance follows on the external issues Iraq is likely to create for the United States.

1. Iraqi–UAR Competition. In seeking to consolidate the Eastern Arabs (Syria, Jordan, Kuwait, Saudi Arabia and Yemen), the GOI will create certain problems for the United States. (We think it will take a good many years for the consolidation to occur, but we consider that the trend is running in the Ba'thist direction.) Competition is likely to develop between Iraq and the UAR as the two principal power poles. This will face the United States with the need to walk the tightrope between the UAR and Iraq. Each will tend to interpret US assistance to its rival as an unfriendly act. In addition, the Ba'thist doctrine is highly nationalistic, and it will eventually seek to establish Arab control over Arab resources. Further, Ba'thist doctrine, in common with widespread Arab sentiment, is hostile to the continued existence of Israel, at least as a security threat to the Arabs and as a physical barrier between the two segments of the Arab world. Israel would react to placement of Iraqi forces on its frontier.

US Position: The United States posture should be one of strict impartiality as between Iraq and the UAR, and the United States should continue to conduct its relations with each Arab state on a bilateral basis in light of United States interests. We should avoid in any way furthering the "Fertile Crescent" theory, *nor should the term be used in conversations or documentation.* Since any United States interest in or pressure for regional development in the Eastern Arab world could only favor Iraq, we should avoid pursuing it. The GOI should be informed at an appropriate time of our criteria for Arab unity. Likewise, the GOI should be apprised of our concern for stability in Jordan, Kuwait, Saudi Arabia and Aden, as well as our interest in a rapid tempo of modernization and reform.

2. Turkey and Iran. Wishing to concentrate externally on pan–Arabism, the GOI seems likely to desire friendly relations with Turkey and Iran in order to have a secure rear while devoting itself to the main task.

US Position: The United States should do what it can with all three governments to ensure friendly relations. We should encourage both Turkey and Iran not to interfere in Iraqi affairs. If problems arise over the Shatt al–Arab between Iraq and Iran we should quietly seek to abate them.

3. Kuwait. We consider it likely that Iraq will not renounce its claim to Kuwait, but will seek a modus vivendi which would attract Kuwaiti resources for Iraqi investment, while tacitly recognizing Kuwaiti sovereignty. Such a settlement would be in United States interests. Kuwait and Iraq may later decide to federate.

US Position: If necessary, and in consultation with the United Kingdom, we should discreetly urge the parties to reach a mutually satisfactory resolution of the problem which will safeguard Kuwait's independence. We should avoid any suggestion of United States bias in favor of either side on the terms of any settlement that would be worked out. Should Kuwait freely opt to federate with Iraq, we should not oppose provided Kuwait retains full power of decision over oil matters.

4. Jordan. Although a Ba'thist-dominated Iraqi Government will exert an attraction on Jordanians, we do not believe the Ba'th Party can build from its fragmented groups in Jordan an organization capable of overthrowing King Hussein at an early date. The bulk of the Palestinians have tended to look towards Cairo and Nasser for leadership, rather than to Baghdad. The Officer Corps of the Jordan Arab Army is made up of relatively less-well-educated tribal or semi-tribal elements which are relatively immune to various ideologies, including the Socialist and pan-Arab ideologies of both Cairo and Baghdad.

US Position. We should continue strongly to support an independent Jordan with American economic, military and technical assistance. We should encourage the reformist trends of the present Jordanian Government which is working for economic development and social reform. If Jordan can be persuaded to continue in the present direction, Ba'thist capabilities for developing a strong political organization will be reduced. Our vital interests are involved in the Jordanian status quo and the situation must be watched with care. Israel would be gravely concerned at the prospect of Jordanian unity with either Iraq or the UAR because this would make possible the stationing of a larger, more modern army on her frontier with Jordan.

5. Saudi Arabia. We believe Iraq will exert some attraction in Saudi Arabia, and will wish eventually to create a political mechanism capable of eventually overthrowing the monarchy, but we doubt that an effective Ba'thist-nationalist organization can be built in a short time. While for Saudi Arabia Iraq can be a counterpoise to UAR pressures, we do not believe Iraq would agree to play Saudi Arabia's game against the UAR in Yemen.

US Position: It would not be in our interest to attempt to create any special relationship between Riyadh and Baghdad. Since the Saudi Royal Family can only feel threatened from Iraq, we should use this fact to persuade Faysal to disengage from the Yemen and to move full speed on reform and modernization.

6. UAR. The Ba'th Party, which dominates the present Iraqi Government, has little strength in Egypt and its capabilities to subvert the UAR Government are considered nil.

US Position: We should maintain strict impartiality as between Iraq and the UAR and should continue our aid programs to the UAR provided the UAR does not seriously modify its present policies in an unfavorable way.

7. Syria. The new Iraqi regime will exert a powerful attraction for Syria, which is likely in the short-run to increase Syrian instability. We have little stake in Syria except to prevent Communist influence from dominating and to retain enough influence to be able to discourage Syrian activism against Israel.

US Position: In the probably approaching tug-of-war between Iraq and the UAR for the loyalties of Syria, the United States must studiously avoid any appearance of favoring one side or the other. We should continue to respond with sympathetic interest to Syrian requests for American assistance. We cannot oppose Syrian unity with the UAR or with Iraq, if that unity is approved freely by the majority of the Syrian people and is brought about without the use of force. The disadvantage to the United States of a Syrian union which might be considered potentially a threat to Israel would be partially counterbalanced, in the short-run at least, by probable increased stability in Syria resulting from unity. If Syro-Iraqi federation occurs and if there is a move to place Iraqi forces on Israel's frontier with Syria, we should seek actively to discourage it.

8. Lebanon. Lebanon will probably welcome the Iraqi revolution because it will tend to correct the disequilibrium which has existed in the Arab world. Anxiety will result, however, from fear, at least in the short run, that her always delicate relations with Syria may be adversely affected.

US Position: We should be prepared to reassure the Lebanese and others that we support an independent Lebanon which we would not be prepared to see subverted from any Arab source.

9. *Israel.* Israel must regard the Iraqi revolution with concern. While Baghdad might develop as a counterpoise to Cairo, the result, in any case, may be greater Arab unity, which Israel fears.

US Position: While continuing the cordial United States relationship with Israel, we should maintain our stance of even–handed impartiality between Israel and the Arab countries. We should resist any Israeli attempts to formalize or institutionalize a special American–Israeli relationship in the security field which would undermine American–Arab relations. On the other hand, we should make known to the Iraqi Government as we do to the other Arab states our interest in the security and well–being of Israel, its right to exist as a state, and the desirability eventually of finding a road to a permanent peace between the Arabs and Israel. We should encourage Iraq, as well as the other Arabs, to concentrate on development and reform rather than diverting energies and resources to the Arab–Israel conflict.

10. *Yemen.* The United States has no stake in Yemen per se. Our interest is in averting dominant Soviet or Communist influence in Yemen and use of Yemen as a base by elements hostile to the United Kingdom base in Aden and to the Saudi throne. Iraq is likely to offer the Yemenis an alternative to heavy reliance on either the UAR or the Sino–Soviet Bloc. It seems doubtful that Iraq can do so until UAR forces are withdrawn.

US Position: Since Iraq is likely to be hostile both to the UK in Aden and to the Saudi throne, the United States should do nothing to encourage or assist Iraq to bolster its position in Yemen which is currently based on a small Ba'thist nucleus and ties with Yemenis trained in Iraq. The United States should, at an appropriate time, make known to Iraq its view toward activities in and from Yemen directed at Aden and Saudi Arabia.

RUSK

Source: Department of State, Central files, POL 1 IRAQ–US. Secret. Drafted by Strong and Killgore on February 25; cleared in draft by Knox, Bowling, Nichols (E), Gaud (AID), Morehouse (INR), Connett (S/S), Kearns–Preston (Department of Commerce), and McGhee; and approved by Talbot. Sent to Addis Ababa, Algiers, Amman, Ankara, Athens, Baghdad, Beirut, Belgrade, bone, Cairo, Damascus, Jidda, Kabul, Karachi, Khartoum, London, Mogadiscio, Moscow, New Delhi, Nicosia, Paris, Rabat, Rome, Taipei, Taiz, Tehran, Tel Aviv, Tokyo, Tripoli Tunis, Warsaw, Accra, and Kuwait.

[1] Not printed. (Ibid., POL IRAQ–US)

241.

[1961–1963, Volume XVIII, p. 397]

178. Memorandum From Robert W. Komer of the National Security Council Staff to the President's Special Assistant for National Security Affairs (Bundy)

WASHINGTON, March 6,1963.

McGB—

FYI, Iraqi coup has probably triggered off a period of heightened fluidity in inter–Arab politics which is going to require some fast footwork on our part in next several months.

Possibilities are another Kurdish uprising,[1] a second pro–Nasser Iraqi coup, a pro–Nasser or pro–Iraqi coup in Syria, trouble in Saudi Arabia, etc. One reason why Nasser is so anxious to settle Yemen affair is that with all its costs plus a third to a half of his combat effectives tied down there he's less able to move elsewhere.

Best policy for us is to sit tight and be prepared to deal with whoever comes out on top. Fortunately our policy now allows us this option, and one reason why we shouldn't overtly choose Saudi side against Nasser is simply that it would tend to tie our hands. It's one thing to defend Saudis against aggression. It's another to declare we choose the kings over the bulk of the Arab world; that would be the real way to lose our oil.

BOB K.

Source: Kennedy Library, National Security Files, Meetings and Memoranda Series, Staff Memoranda, Robert W. Komer, Vol. 1. Secret.
[1] On March 7, Deputy Director for Intelligence of the Central Intelligence Agency Ray S. Cline sent McGeorge Bundy a paper prepared on March 5 by the Office of National Estimates, entitled "The Kurdish Problem: New Dangers." In his covering memorandum Cline noted that "the chances appear to be growing that the Kurdish problem will become more acute in the months ahead. Emergence of an anti–Communist regime in Baghdad has removed the main inhibition on Soviet support of Kurdish dissidence and this problem may have important implications beyond the borders of Iraq." (Kennedy Library, National Security files, Countries Series, Iraq, 6/63–8/63).

242.

[1961–1963, Volume XVIII, pp. 445–46]

204. Memorandum From Harold H. Saunders of the National Security Council Staff to the President's Special Assistant for National Security Affairs (Bundy)

WASHINGTON, April 2, 1963.

Answer to the President's query today[1] about what we're doing for the new Iraqi regime is that we're being as helpful as possible without getting into an unwarranted big new aid program. State feels we've gone about as far as we can until the Iraqis can be more specific about their needs.

The new Iraqi regime has made only a vague pitch for economic aid to help justify its crackdown on the Communists. However, it has been tied up with Arab unity negotiations and hasn't yet re–evaluated the Soviet aid program to isolate projects it might turn over to the West. So the next move is the Iraqis'.

We want to keep our aid on the technical assistance and credit sales level rather than getting into development loans. The Iraqis have adequate capital from oil revenue if they use it wisely. AID has already raised its modest allotment for participant training ($600,000 to $800,000). Also, we've told Iraqis we're ready to help them arrange for IBRD, UN, or private US technical aid; to provide Ex–Im credit; to encourage private US investors and perhaps negotiate an invest-

ment guaranty program when Iraqis are ready; and to encourage Western trade.

We've already agreed to sell them the 12 helicopters they asked for, and it's up to them to decide what kind they want (cost range is $4–15 million depending on model). State will probably also approve selling 40 light tanks they've requested to replace some we gave them before 1958. A new policy paper awaiting clearance through the Talbot–Harriman echelons draws the line at selling heavy equipment that could be moved through Syria to the Israeli front. However, we see no serious problem in selling light tanks, small arms and ammo, commo equipment, or even transport aircraft if requested. AID and DOD are also considering civic action possibilities, but this depends on Iraqi willingness to let us work closely with their military.

The Kurds may object to our military sales. (We've already turned down their request for help—see Baghdad 611.)[2] However, we think it's more important to be responsive to the new regime. Besides, we want Kurds to negotiate a settlement with the new government. If that fails, our interests will be better served if the government can control the Kurds than if the Kurdish rebellion is successful enough to invite Soviet or Iranian meddling.

HAL

Source: Kennedy Library, National Security Files, Countries Series, Iraq. Secret.
[1] According to Legere's notes of the daily White House staff meeting on April 2, when Bundy asked Saunders, in Komer's absence, what actions the United States could take to indicate its support of the Iraqi regime, Saunders replied that "Chief MAAG Iraq had recently requested some tanks for Iraq forces, but that the use contemplated for these tanks was probably to help quell Kurdish unrest, and this is something which we do not necessarily want to do. Here the subject dropped." (National Defense University, Taylor Papers, Daily White House Memos)
[2] See footnote 1, Document 208.

243.

[1961–1963, Volume XVIII, pp. 451–52]

208. Telegram From the Department of State to the Embassy in Iraq

WASHINGTON, April 5,1963—9:07 a.m.

331. Embtel 611.[1] Department increasingly concerned by dangerous potentialities of failure GOI–Kurdish negotiations and resumption hostilities. United States policy remains unchanged; we consider problem strictly one between GOI and Kurds. However, consequences break down current negotiations such that effort to persuade both sides of advantages equitable settlement through mutual compromise warranted. You may, therefore, pass word to Talabani that Mulla Mustafa's message transmitted USG, which fully endorses positions taken by Embassy officer. You may also indicate that Embassy authorized to inform each side informally of its hope for equitable solution to problem and its belief that there are many advantages to Kurds in reasonable compromise with GOI in current negotiations. We wish to avoid discussion of details of compromise.

In its contacts with Kurds, Embassy may draw on following points as appropriate:

1. Resumed conflict could vitiate gains achieved so far.

2. There are many advantages to Kurds in forming integral part Iraqi state.

3. USG understanding of and sympathy for legitimate Kurdish aspirations within Iraqi state will in no circumstances be allowed adversely to affect cordial USG relations with new Iraqi regime.

4. Kurdish willingness to accept less than total Kurdish aspirations, which in US view are unrealistic, would create greater degree of confidence necessary to calm and reasonable negotiation of remaining differences.

Concurrently, Embassy should inform GOI of USG representations to Kurds and urge GOI be forthcoming in meeting Kurdish aspirations to reasonable degree. Presentation should stress that USG policy has not changed and continues regard Kurdish dispute as internal GOI matter in which we have not and will not interfere directly or indirectly. We taking present initiative because of our strong interest in seeing GOI consolidate its internal position. While we would not wish deal with question in detail we believe equitable compromise solution to Kurdish problem can and must be found. In our view, mutual suspicions existing between GOI and Kurds constitute greater danger to successful negotiations than substantive differences between two sides. Reassuring GOI gestures could therefore be very important. (FYI. We have in mind release of prisoners and end of economic blockade. End FYI.) We urge GOI negotiate with patience and determination to achieve non–violent settlement.

For London. Inform UK of foregoing and express USG hope that UK Ambassador Baghdad will be similarly instructed.

RUSK

Source: Department of State, Central Files, POL 26 IRAQ. Confidential. Drafted by Killgore and Davies on April 4, cleared by Strong and Judd, and approved by Talbot. Repeated to London, Ankara, and Tehran.

[1] In telegram 611, April 1, the Embassy in Baghdad conveyed the content of a message from Kurdish leader Mulla Mustafa delivered by Jalal Talabani, the head of the Kurdish delegation in Baghdad for negotiations with the Iraqi Government. In the message, Mustafa offered friendship to the United States, requested assistance for the Kurdish revolt, and asked to meet with a U.S. representative. In response, an Embassy officer said that the United States considered the Iraqi revolt an internal matter and would not help the Kurds, and that a U.S. official could not meet with Mustafa. (Ibid.)

244.

[1961–1963, Volume XVIII, pp. 542–43]

251. Memorandum for the Record

WASHINGTON, May 16,1963.

Minutes of the Special Group (CI) Meeting, 2 p.m., Thursday, May 16,1963

PRESENT

Governor Harriman, The Attorney General, Mr. Gilpatric, General Taylor, Mr. Forrestal, Mr. Coffin vice Mr. Bell, Mr. Wilson vice Mr. Murrow, Mr. Karamessines vice Mr. McCone

Mr. Martin and Mr. Belcher were present for Item I

Mr. Bowling was present for Item 3

Mr. Maechling was present for the meeting.

. . .

3. Implications of a Renewal of Kurdish Hostilities[1]

Mr. Karamessines in commenting on the Special Estimate prepared for this item[2] mentioned that there are indications that the Iraqi Kurds and the Iraqi Government are preparing for possible hostilities. We have no firm evidence that Soviet material assistance is being provided to the Kurds.

General Taylor recommended that we should contact the British and French on this matter. The Chairman added that this is a very serious question and he does not believe that the Iraqi Government would be able to successfully cope with a possible Kurdish rebellion. He pointed out that the Soviet interest in these developments was a disturbing sign.

In response to a question by Mr. Forrestal, Mr. Karamessines stated that the Shah is giving some aid and comfort to the Kurds but that material assistance is not significant. The Iraqi Kurds have used border areas of Iran for temporary safe haven. The Shah is providing assistance to the Kurds in Iran.

The Group agreed that this matter should be kept under close scrutiny by CIA and subsequent reports should be submitted to the Group if the situation deteriorates. Mr. Bowling commented that he was concerned over the possibility of an overland link–up with the Soviets which would greatly facilitate the movement of supplies to the Kurds.

The Chairman mentioned that Embassy Tehran had responded to the State cable urging intensified efforts by the Country Team to assist the land reform program and methods by which we can influence Iran to modify its conservative fiscal policy. He suggested that after this response has been studied by the responsible Washington agencies it should be brought to the attention of the group.

[Here follows a short paragraph on the schedule for the next meeting.]

JAMES W. DINGEMAN
Executive Secretary
Special Group (CI)

Source: Department of State, Special Group, Counterinsurgency Files: Lot 68 D 451. Secret. Drafted by Dingeman. Circulated to the Special Group on May 20 under cover of a memorandum from Carol C. Moor, in anticipation of the Group's May 23 meeting.

[1] In early May, the Department of State had instructed the Embassy in Baghdad to renew its démarche to the Iraqi Government to continue negotiations with the Kurds and avoid a resumption of the fighting. (Telegram 583 to London, May 4; ibid., Central Files, POL 26 IRAQ) Additional documentation is ibid., and ibid., POL 27 IRAQ.

[2] SNIE 30–3–63, "Some Implications of a Renewal of Kurdish Hostilities." (Ibid., S/P Files: Lot 70 D 199, Iraq) See the Supplement, the compilation on Iraq.

245.

[1961–1963, Volume XVIII, pp. 665–66]

307. Memorandum From the Department of State Acting Executive Secretary (McKesson) to the President's Special Assistant for National Security Affairs (Bundy)

WASHINGTON, August 6, 1963.

SUBJECT
Letter from Mulla Mustafa Barzani to President Kennedy

Embassy Tehran's Airgram #67 of July 30, 1963[1] (copies of which were sent to the White House) transmitted a copy of a letter addressed to the President from Mulla Mustafa Barzani, leader of Iraqi Kurdish fighting forces, requesting the President's support for Kurdish autonomy within the Republic of Iraq.

In our view, a Presidential reply to Barzani might well damage United States relations with Iraq. We therefore propose having our Consul in Tabriz respond orally to Barzani's intermediary along the lines of our standard guidance with respect to the Iraqi Kurds, i.e., that the United States sympathizes with legitimate Kurdish aspirations within the sovereign state of Iraq, but that our sympathy will not be permitted to prejudice the cordial relations now existing between the United States and Iraq. We propose to go one step further than our Ambassador in Tehran has suggested, by having our Consul state, should he be asked if Barzani's letter was forwarded, that the message was forwarded to the Department and that the Consul is responding as indicated above, on behalf of the United States Government. We believe that if our Consul is asked whether the letter has been forwarded, an affirmative reply will not damage United

States–Iraqi relations. At the same time, such a reply will demonstrate, if only symbolically, United States concern for and interest in the Kurds.

We propose sending to Tehran the attached telegram should the White House approve.[2]

J.W. DAVIS[3]

Source: Department of State, Central Files, POL 13–3 IRAQ. Secret. Drafted by Killgore and concurred in by Talbot. A typed note on the source text indicates that Komer approved the recommendation in this memorandum on August 7.

[1] Not printed. (Ibid.)

[2] The telegram was sent as telegram 91 to Tehran, August 7. (Ibid.) On September 12, Read sent Bundy another letter from Barzani to President Kennedy, dated July 18 and delivered to the Embassy in Tehran on August 27, which was similar to Barzani's July 12 letter. Noting previous action taken on the July 12 letter, the Department of State recommended no action be taken on the July 18 letter. A typed notation on the Department of State's copy of the memorandum quotes a response from Komer as follows: "We told him to acknowledge receipt and say letter passed to Washington and return noncommittal reply."

[3] Davis signed for McKesson above McKesson's typed signature.

246.

[1961–1963, Volume XVIII, pp. 673–75]

311. Memorandum From the Joint Chiefs of Staff to Secretary of Defense McNamara

JCSM–623–63

WASHINGTON, August 15,1963.

SUBJECT

US Assistance for Iraq (U)

1. Reference is made to a memorandum by the Acting Assistant Secretary of Defense (ISA), I–25321/63, dated 2 August 1963, subject as above. [1]

2. The views of the Joint Chiefs of Staff on US Arms Policy for Iraq, as contained in JCSM–197–63, dated 9 March 1963,[1] were predicated on the belief that subsequent developments would confirm the anticommunist nature of the government which came to power in Iraq on 8 February 1963. Subsequent

events have verified that the policy of the Iraqi Government is to decrease its dependence on Soviet support and to control local communist elements. Moreover, the USSR, by supporting an attempt to bring the Kurdish question before the United Nations, has openly demonstrated its support for Kurdish rebel elements, to the further detriment of Soviet–Iraqi relations. There are also a few indications that the Soviets may be deliberately lagging in deliveries of military assistance to Iraq.

3. Another development which could prove favorable to US interests is the ascendancy of the Baath party in Iraq and Syria, and the conflict of Baath and Nasserist ambitions in the Arab world. Identification of Syria with the anticommunist policies of Iraq would be helpful in reducing Soviet influence in the Middle East, and continued disunity between Nasser and Iraq/Syria could ease pressures on the monarchies of the Arab peninsula, as well as on Israel and the regional members of CENTO.

4. Although the Iraqi Government has announced its intention to pursue a neutralist course between the Communist Bloc and the West, the foregoing developments indicate that there is a good possibility for eventual displacement of communist influence and, more remotely, for open alignment of Iraq and Syria with the West. It is recognized that care must be exercised to avoid arousing Arab suspicions of US intentions, upsetting the balance of military power in the Middle East, or otherwise acting to the detriment of US interests in pursuing unrealistic short–term goals in Iraq and Syria. Nevertheless, US arms policy in Iraq should be pursued with the ultimate objective of having Iraq, and hopefully Syria, look to the West as the primary source for necessary armaments.

5. The most immediate military arms requirements facing the Iraqi armed forces stem from government efforts to suppress the Kurdish revolt, and from Iraq's need to be in a position to assist the Syrian Government, if required.

a. As a long–term goal, the United States should continue efforts to promote assimilation of the Kurds within national boundaries, and granting of a measure of local self–government in predominately Kurdish regions. However, prolongation of the conflict in Iraq engenders instability, and provides an opportunity for communist exploitation of the Kurdish problem in Iraq and in neighboring countries. A firm Iraqi military position, coupled with a willingness to accommodate to legitimate Kurdish grievances, appears to be the most promising avenue for an early end to hostilities and advancement of internal stability in Iraq. To this end, the United States should give favorable consideration to reasonable Iraqi requests for equipment and seek to use resultant influence to urge moderation on the Iraqi Government.

b. As was pointed out in paragraph 3, above, an Iraqi capability to provide assistance to the government of Syria in quelling possible major uprisings could also be advantageous for the United States.

6. Although normal Iraqi income should permit absorption of defense costs without undue impact on the economy, a requirement for large cash payments on equipment deliverable in the near future from all Western sources could have an unsettling effect, particularly when compounded by costs of operations against the Kurds. The stability of the Iraqi Government in the short term could be aided, therefore, by acceding to reasonable Iraqi requests for credit.

7. Except for the need for ameliorating present restrictions on extension of credit, the Joint Chiefs of Staff consider that the currently approved US Arms Policy for Iraq is sufficiently flexible to permit a positive application in pursuance of US objectives in the Middle East. With the foregoing in mind, the Joint Chiefs of Staff recommend that:

a. The United States respond favorably to Iraqi requests which fall within the approved US Arms Policy for Iraq, and which are available from US sources.

b. Deliveries of approved items be made as rapidly as possible consistent with availabilities and priority being accorded MAP recipients.

c. Equipment be furnished on a sales basis, but credit terms be arranged as may be appropriate to avoid an adverse impact on the Iraqi economy in the short term.

d. Consultations be undertaken with other potential suppliers of arms among Free World nations to encourage adoption of policies similar to those of the United States.

For the Joint Chiefs of Staff:
JOHN M. REYNOLDS
Major General, USAF
Vice Director, Joint Staff

Source: Washington National Records Center, RG 330, OSD Files: FRC 69 A 3131, Iraq, 1963. Secret.

[1] Not printed. (Ibid.)

247.

[1964–1968, Volume XXI, pp. 4–7]

3. Background Paper Prepared in the Department of State[1]

CWM–B/10
WASHINGTON, April 6, 1964.

TWELFTH CENTO MINISTERIAL
COUNCIL SESSION[2]
Washington, April 28–29, 1964

Background Paper
The Situation in the Middle East

General Developments

After a year of readjustment and realignment among the Arab States a "Summit" meeting in Cairo in January 1964 called by President Nasser created a stronger sense of unity among the Arabs than had earlier and more formal attempts to attach and join states in legal but unhappy union. In Iraq a Ba'th dominated government came in February and went in November of the same year. The Ba'th Party (pan Arab socialists) has held on in Syria only by packing the Syrian army with its adherents. Yemen is still a sensitive problem, with the strength of UAR troops in the country apparently about the same as a year ago. However, the Arab Summit sparked a series of contacts between the Governments of the UAR and Saudi Arabia, and there now seems to be a disposition on the part of the states concerned to settle the dispute over Yemen. Yemen itself will have to endure a drawn out period of organization, consolidation and adjustment. Meanwhile, Israel's forthcoming off-take of Jordan River waters from Lake Tiberias looms as possibly the most acute source of tension in the area.

United States Policy in the Near East

Political instability has been endemic in the Near East for the past several decades. Despite this, there has been considerable economic and social development which gives promise of providing a basis for greater political stability. The United States attempts to conduct its relations with states of the area on a strictly bilateral basis and to avoid being drawn into disputes either in an inter-Arab or an Arab state-Israeli context, except where vital United States interests are affected. The United States is equally interested in the integrity and well-being of all states of the area. It has no "chosen instrument" in its dealings with Near Eastern states; its aid programs, if examined on a per capita basis, have been remarkably evenhanded. The United States economic assistance and other programs are motivated by the belief that Free World interests will be served by economic, social, and political development of the peoples of the area. The United States believes that problems arising among the Arab states should be solved by those states without outside interference.

Arab Unity and the CENTO Countries

Just as the urge to unity is inherent in the Arab Islamic culture, so is the tradition and habit of strong individuality. Inevitably, the two drives clash. The ambitious plans of April 1963 for uniting the UAR, Syria, and Iraq were discarded as unworkable before September. Nevertheless, the January 1964 Arab Summit meeting brought Arab leaders back together long enough for them to remember their common heritage and to take new steps toward increased military, economic, and cultural consultation. Unity, in the strict sense of a single state made up of federated components, is unlikely in the foreseeable future. However the sense of unity, essentially a psychological phenomenon, was never stronger and cannot be ignored. Nevertheless, the United States believes that Arab unity does not pose a threat against CENTO states. It believes that the Arab states in considering the form of association they believe best for their interests should not be subjected to outside influences or pressures. The United States does not take a position for or against unity but would not favor any association brought about against the will of the majority of the peoples involved, brought about by force, or clearly directed against other states. The United States does not believe that, given geographic, organizational, and logistical considerations, a joint military command or other form of association of Arab military forces would appreciably affect the capabilities of these forces.

Saudi Arabia and Jordan

The United States has made clear its interests in the integrity of the kingdoms of Jordan and Saudi Arabia and has encouraged and contributed to the economic and social development of both countries. Jordan has made most satisfactory progress in the economic and social fields over the past several years and the United States believes that prospects for continued development and stability in this country are good. Jordan has recognized the USSR and the two countries are exchanging Embassies. The United States does not believe that this step will have any significant effect on its relations with Jordan nor that the present Government of Jordan intends to shift its international posture basically. In Saudi Arabia, Crown Prince Faysal has initiated a program of modernization, reform, and economic development which should in time serve to meet the aspiration of the Saudi people. The United States considers these programs to be the real first line of defense of these countries against subversive influence. A recent confrontation between Crown Prince Faysal, the effective ruler, and King Saud has resulted in Faysal's convincing the ailing and feeble King to relinquish all active leadership of government to Faysal.

Kuwait

In the past year Kuwait has consolidated its independence and has become a significant source of funds for Arab world economic developments. This use of its financial strength gives tiny Kuwait an opportunity to buy "integrity insurance." The comparatively vast resources of Kuwait as compared with its own needs also offer an Arab alternative to external sources of funding to support economic development. The extent to which Kuwait will be prepared to fund military equipment purchases by Arab states is not yet clear, but this eventuality cannot be overlooked.

Yemen

Despite agreement on July 4, 1963 between the UAR and Saudi Arabia to disengage from involvement in Yemen, UAR troops remain in large numbers (around 30,000), and Saudi Arabia, while stopping material aid to the royalists, is still giving moral encouragement and probably financial assistance. Nevertheless, the disengagement agreement has confined the conflict to within the borders of Yemen, has served to preserve and even strengthen the Saud regime, and has protected Free World interests in the Arabian Peninsula. Precipitate withdrawal of all Egyptian troops at this time would result in chaos in the country, and some form of outside security force will no doubt be required to keep peace in Yemen for years to come. Meanwhile the UAR-Saudi resumption of diplomatic relations on March 3, 1964 and a mutual announcement that neither had designs in Yemen are positive steps in the direction of some kind of a modus vivendi over Yemen. Yemen's economy is not in dire straits at the moment, but a certain amount of outside foreign assistance will be needed for any real economic development. Before this can be effective, however, Yemen needs a governmental mechanism which can make use of outside help.

The Kurdish Situation (Noforn)

After two and a half years of fighting, during which time the Kurds at their peak were able to engage regular units of the Iraq Army and defeat them and at their weakest were able to hold only the more inaccessible high country, the Government of Iraq and Iraqi Kurdish representatives agreed on February 10, 1964 to a cease fire. Unfortunately, a misunderstanding of the terms of that agreement seems already to have arisen, the government taking the position that it has complied with conditions agreed upon and the Kurds asserting bad faith on the government's part for not carrying out its bargain (the Kurds claim more concessions were made than the government is now ready to honor). Nevertheless, the government has been withdrawing Army units and equipment from the north,

giving every indication it is not planning to make war any longer. There are reports of dissidence within Kurdish circles in Iraq, of a lack of cohesion between the tribal fighters and the Kurdish party's educated and more sophisticated cadre. The party militants are said to be threatening to resume the violence if the "autonomy" they fought for is not granted in sufficiently clear detail by the government. A final settlement is not yet clear nor is it in sight.

Meanwhile, there are reports of arrests in Iranian Kurdish areas of persons believed to entertain similar Kurdish aspirations in Iran. These developments will bear close watching. The Kurdish nationalist fever is not new to Iran. The United States would regard Kurdish unrest in Iran, as it has in Iraq, as an internal problem.

---

[1] Source: Johnson Library, National Security File, Komer Files, 12th CENTO Ministerial Council Session, April 28-29, 1964. Confidential. Drafted by Lee F. Dinsmore of the Office of Near Eastern Affairs; cleared by Davies, Jernegan, Deputy Director of the Office of Near Eastern and South Asian Regional Affairs John P. Walsh, and NEA/NR Officer in Charge of CENTO Affairs Matthew D. Smith, Jr.

[2] The Twelfth Session of the Ministerial Council of the Central Treaty Organization (CENTO) was held in Washington April 28-29. The session was attended by Foreign Minister Abbas Aram of Iran, Foreign Minister Zulfikar Ali Bhutto of Pakistan, Foreign Minister Feridum Camal Erkin of Turkey, Foreign Secretary R.A. Butler of the United Kingdom, and Secretary of State Rusk. For text of the communiqué, see *American Foreign Policy: Current Documents*, 1964, pp. 683-685. For documentation relating to the session, see Johnson Library, National Security File, Komer Files, 12th CENTO Ministerial Council Session, April 28-29, 1964, and Department of State, NEA/RA Files: Lot 75 D 312, CENTO Ministerial Files, 1962-1968, 12th CENTO Ministerial Council Session, Washington, D.C., April 28-29, 1964.

248.

[1964–1968, Volume XXI, pp. 333–34]

162. Airgram From the Embassy in Iraq to the Department of State[1]

A-786
BAGHDAD, March 24, 1964.

SUBJECT
Visit of Assistant Secretary Talbot to Baghdad.

Mr. Talbot's truncated and brief visit (9:15 a.m. March 21 to 2:30 p.m. March 22)[2] was politically successful despite its brevity, despite the fact that the bulk of it fell on a Moslem "Sunday," despite the necessity for making arrangements on short notice, despite the twelve-hour delay in reaching here from Ankara, and despite the fact that his arrival coincided with an airport ceremony marking the departure of President Aref and Foreign Minister Abd al-Hamid for Pakistan and India.

Apart from briefings and discussions within the Embassy, and mixed business-culture visits to Babylon and Iraqi museums, Mr. Talbot was able to meet several ministers and other leading military and civilian personalities at social gatherings (including the moderate Kurdish leader, Baba Ali), talk privately with the British Ambassador and Foreign Office Under Secretary Ali Haidar Suleiman, and meet with the Prime Minister and Acting Foreign Minister separately.

The atmosphere, which on Friday could have been interpreted as correct but cool, warmed up considerably on Saturday in the various calls and at the Ambassador's luncheon. At this final event, which just preceded air departure, the several Iraqi ministers present spent a good deal of time arguing US policy on Israel. While more constructive conversation would have been useful, Mr. Talbot was very effective in his responses.

The main event, from which several conclusions can be drawn, was the fifty-minute talk with the Prime Minister, who was pleasant and restrained in his handling of controversial subjects.

Several memoranda of conversations are enclosed.[3] No effort has been made to cover all talks.

Conclusions:
1. Ranking officials from Washington are welcome and will be treated with courtesy (in contrast to past years).

2. The GOI is a moderate regime and does not wish to let the Palestine issue destroy mutually advantageous relations with the US, but we shall hear a good deal from the GOI about our policy in this area.

3. The GOI is expecting continuing and increasing economic and technical benefits from the US, and the field for cultural and educational cooperation is a wide one.

4. The GOI genuinely wants to handle the Kurdish problem[4] in a fashion which will reasonably satisfy the bulk of the Kurds and isolate the extremists. The GOI is likely to want Title II surplus food.

5. The current political situation is the most hopeful in years, and there is good prospect for its continuation. The Prime Minister and President are cooperating.

ROBERT C. STRONG

---

[1] Source: National Archives and Records Administration, RG 59, Central Files 1964-66, ORG 7 NEA. Confidential. Drafted by Strong. Repeated to Amman, Beirut, Cairo, Damascus, Jidda, Kuwait, Taiz, Tel Aviv, Tehran, London, Paris, Moscow, Ankara, Basra, Aleppo, Dhahran, and Jerusalem. Sent by air pouch.
[2] Assistant Secretary Talbot visited a number of Near East countries on this trip.
[3] Attached but not printed.
[4] A cease-fire between the Iraqi Government and the Kurdish insurgents was announced in early February.

249.

[1964–1968, Volume XXI, p. 337]

165. Telegram From the Department of State to the Embassy in Iraq[1]

WASHINGTON, June 5, 1964, 6:01 p.m.

569. Cairo's 2924.[2] Neither Shawqat Aqrawi nor Luqman al-Barzani could advance Kurdish interests in Washington. On the contrary, delicate Kurdish-GOI situation might be irritated unnecessarily by conversations here with avowed Kurdish nationalists. Embassy Baghdad capable of serving as channel for conveying to USG subjects of concern to Iraqi Kurds and of making clear US positions. Department believes Kurdish representatives,

while not unwelcome visit US, would experience only frustration to find reaction USG circles parallel to Embassy Baghdad's replies and counsel.

In response numbered questions reftel: (1) United States surplus commodities are made available only after agreement with the government concerned on means to assure that the donated food will reach the intended recipients. (2) There is no truth to story reported by Kurds to Embassy Cairo officer that US has promised assistance to Kurds through third country in event fighting renewed in Iraq.

Department interested in learning more about identity "new channel" mentioned reftel.

RUSK

---

[1] Source: National Archives and Records Administration, RG 59, Central Files 1964–66, POL 23-9 IRAQ. Secret. Drafted by Dinsmore; cleared by Officer-in-Charge of United Arab Republic Affairs and Syrian Arab Republic Affairs Curtis F. Jones, Davies, William D. Wolle (NEA/NE), Hallpress (AID/MR/ARD), and AID Director of the Office of Near Eastern Affairs James C. Flint; and approved by Jernegan. Also sent to Cairo and repeated to Beirut.

[2] Telegram 2924 from Cairo, June 2, reported that Kurdish representative Aqrawi and Luzman Barzani, son of Kurdish leader Mulla Mustafa Barzani, met with an Embassy officer in Cairo and told him that Mustafa Barzani wanted them to go to the United States to present the Kurdish case to officers in the Department. They also asked how they could be sure that U.S. rehabilitation aid given through the Iraqi Government would reach the Kurds and if it were true that the United States had promised assistance through a third country if the Kurds were driven to renewed fighting. (Ibid.)

250.

[1964–1968, Volume XXI, pp. 340–41]

167. Telegram From the Embassy in Iraq to the Department of State[1]

BAGHDAD, October 26, 1964, 0845Z.

362. On October 23 Masud Muhammad, Minister of State for Northern Affairs, informed me he planned leave same day for north carrying tentative procedural agreement resulting from several meetings between himself, Interior Minister, Army division heads, Army Intelligence Chief and Northern Mutasarrifs. GOI now prepared make first move involving following steps: (1) release of all Kurdish prisoners including those convicted of military crimes; (2) return of government employees of Kurdish origin to former positions, especially in north; (3) removal of Salahaddin cavalry from north; (4) removal of Arab tribes from Kurdish areas and return of Kurds forced from their villages; (5) compensation to those who suffered during recent troubles.

Following these GOI actions, Kurds to (1) withdraw Pesh Merga from major roads and stop harassment; (2) return weapons captured from Iraqi Army (Masud said token amount would satisfy GOI's honor); and (3) permit establishment local administration, made up mainly of Kurds but under GOI supervision. Once these moves completed, GOI and Kurds to sit down and tackle political settlement. Masud expects to return from north in week with Kurdish acceptance since agreement offers sound opportunity test good faith of GOI. Masud emphasized Mulla Mustafa regards USG as key to settlement of Kurdish problem and USG can get what it wants. He had told Iraqi colleagues he lunching with me to discuss tentative agreement.

Comment: Although first steps by GOI do not incorporate acceptance Kurdish political demands, they do include what Kurds have always requested as proof GOI's good faith. Kurds, therefore, should find it easy accept offer provided that only nominal return of weapons will, indeed, be acceptable to GOI. If GOI and Kurds carry out their parts of bargain, political talks likely follow.

Masud identified himself as prime mover in creation new situation but agreed Egypt is big factor as result of delay in unity until internal Iraqi problems met. He gives us large share of credit. In any event, that GOI willing make first move is significant, indicating tacit recognition of strong Kurdish position and effectiveness of Egyptian pressure. Given Embassy's assessment that neither GOI or Mulla Mustafa wish resume hostilities, present GOI offer may mark turning point. In essence I told Minister, who several times during conversation indicated Mulla Mustafa would heed

US advice, that (1) US hopes for peaceful negotiated settlement within framework Iraq without foreign interference, (2) Kurds should cooperate, having nothing to lose, and (3) Kurds must be prepared be patient in long drawn-out negotiations over internal political settlement and must be prepared compromise their extreme demands. Also stated Kurdish cause best served by avoiding appearance of acting as agents; they should avoid entangling themselves in interests of others.

At end of conversation Masud asked in all seriousness whether in event of trouble he could seek political asylum in American Embassy. I told him case would have to be judged on its merits at the time but US did not encourage such action. While he may have been trying create impression he laboring under great pressure, it is possible he believes there is chance Kurdish extremists in Baghdad may start a racial conflict which would be bloody and would endanger his life.

Addendum. At end of my conversation with FonMin October 24 I said that to counteract any rumors he might hear about my luncheon with Masud. I wanted to tell him that I had told Masud (a) USG continues to advocate a peaceful, negotiated settlement of the Kurdish problem; (b) that use of force could not settle it; © that it was evident GOI wished avoid further military action; (d) that Kurds would be well advised concur in procedural agreement reached by Masud with GOI; (e) that it would be possible to observe whether GOI acting in good faith; (f) that if GOI acts in good faith then Kurds obligated do so; (g) that when time for political negotiations came Kurds should recognize these are complicated and must be prepared be patient; (h) and that USG intends continue avoid getting into specifics of problem. Minister commented he understood our position and he appreciated learning what I had said. He gave no sign of objecting to our role and his manner was as friendly and relaxed when I left as it had been throughout.

Comment: Transfer of Iraqi 3rd division to H-3 further strengthens Kurdish position and increases pressure on GOI reach settlement. Was this one of UAR purposes in request by UAC that Iraq move 3rd division?[2]

STRONG

---

[1] Source: National Archives and Records Administration, RG 59, Central Files 1964-66, POL 23-9 IRAQ. Confidential. Repeated to Ankara, Tehran, Aleppo, Basra, Beirut, Cairo, Damascus, London, and Tabriz.

[2] Circular telegram 765, October 28, stated that the developments reported in telegram 362 were encouraging and that the Department concurred in the line taken by the Ambassador. It commented that Masud's call on the Ambassador pointed up a situation where the United States, without seeking the role, had in effect become a psychological support in Kurdish minds. (Ibid.)

251.

[1964–1968, Volume XXI, pp. 343–45]

169. Memorandum of Conversation[1]

Sec Del/MC/28

NEW YORK, December 10, 1964, 4:30 p.m.

SECRETARY'S DELEGATION TO THE
NINETEENTH SESSION OF
THE UNITED NATIONS GENERAL
ASSEMBLY
New York, November 1964

SUBJECT

The Kurdish Problem

PARTICIPANTS
U.S.
The Secretary
NEA—Mr. Walsh

Iraq
Foreign Minister Naji Talib
Under Secretary for Foreign Affairs Kadhim Khalaf

The Minister said that he had one problem which he wished to bring to the attention of the Secretary, namely, the Kurdish situation.

The Minister said that the Kurdish problem fundamentally dominated the Iraqi scene. The Iraqi Government is preoccupied with this issue and has little time or energy to turn to other pressing economic and social issues. He was not sure that they were any closer to a solution now than they were before the fighting started several years ago.

The Minister went on to say that he could not understand certain elements of the Kurdish problem. Manifestly there are unidentified forces supporting the Kurds. The Kurds are poor people and their land has been damaged by war. Where are they getting money from to buy staple foods, arms, and equipment? Who are these mysterious forces? What do they want?

The Minister stated that his Government might be able to deal with Mullah Mostafa Barzani but the Communists and the Democratic Party were much more difficult. In his opinion, the Kurds were controlled by the Communists. If a Kurdish state were established, it would be a Communist enclave which would split the Arab world, pierce the protective CENTO belt, and shatter the stability of Turkey and Iran. He had seen Kurdish maps indicating a Kurdish state stretching from Iskendrun in Turkey to Basra in Iraq.

He said that the Turks had sealed their Kurdish frontier. On the other hand, some support was drifting into Kurdish hands across the long Iranian frontier. This did not appear to be the result of deliberate Iranian Government intent but rather reflects the inability of a weak government to patrol its frontiers.

He asserted that he did not wish to suggest that the U.S. was supporting the Kurds but he did wish to emphasize that his Government is sore-perplexed by the machinations of some mysterious force which is supporting the Kurds.

In reply, the Secretary categorically assured the Minister that the United States was not directly or indirectly supporting the Kurdish movement. The U.S. supported the independence, integrity, and prosperity of Iraq. It had no other interest in Iraq affairs. Furthermore, he shared the Minister's concern about the dangers of Communist penetration of the Near East by means of a Kurdish independence movement.

The Minister said that he was very pleased to have had this exchange of views and to receive this reassurance in respect to what he had known was American policy. He said that the U.S. could help Iraq by determining who is the financing and supplying source

for the Kurds and what the motivation of this source is.

---

[1] Source: National Archives and Records Administration, RG 59, Central Files 1964–66, POL 23–9 IRAQ. Confidential. Drafted by Walsh on December 11. Approved in the Office of the Secretary of State on December 17. The memorandum is Part I of III.

252.

[1964–1968, Volume XXI, p. 345]

170. Telegram From the Department of State to the Embassy in Iraq[1]

WASHINGTON, December 14, 1964, 7:44 p.m.

343. Ref. NIT-6583/Noforn.[2] Department is persuaded that Kurdish participation in any scheme to overthrow Iraq government would not guarantee establishment regime more sympathetic to Kurdish aspirations. Nasser could hardly be expected continue his current role in favor peaceful solution and agreement between GOI and Kurds, particularly in event plot involved Iran. Furthermore even with new government Kurds would still be faced with problem obtaining agreed settlement.

Kurds would have exposed themselves as willing collaborators with Iranian intrigue against government Iraq thus earning deepened Arab suspicion and resentment of Kurdish ambitions. Until now many Arabs have some sympathy for Kurds. No successor Iraqi government could be expected either deal magnanimously or leniently with Kurds or excuse Iranians. Iranian connection with plot bound be uncovered sooner or later, and in view reports recent close GOI monitoring of communist and Baathi attempts overthrow GOI (various CAS reports) there is good reason believe GOI already privy to Iranian subversive activity.

Embassy's view solicited re whether it could or should find way, without revealing knowledge, let appropriate Kurds know how we would view any plans participate in coup d'etat. Attempt seems to us bound backfire and to worsen Kurdish position vis-a-vis GOI.

BALL

[1] Source: National Archives and Records Administration, RG 59, Central Files 1964-66, POL 23-9 IRAQ. Secret; Noforn. Drafted by Dinsmore on December 11; cleared in draft by Deputy Director of the Office of Greek, Turkish, and Iranian Affairs John M. Howison and by Davies; and approved by Talbot. Repeated to Tehran.

[2] Not found.

253.

[1964–1968, Volume XXI, pp. 346–47]

171. Telegram From the Embassy in Iraq to the Department of State[1]

BAGHDAD, December 16, 1964, 3 p.m.

486. Ref: Deptel 343.[2] Kurds have told us Iranians urging them resume fighting (Embtel 458)[3] but they understand Iranian motives. We have already told Kurds they should avoid appearing act as agents of others or entangling themselves in interests of others (Embtel 362),[4] and would be unwise listen to those who want resumption hostilities (Akins' memcon with Aqrawi, Dec. 8).[5] Masud Mohammad and Aqrawi understood what we meant. Should note that in my October 24 talk with ForMin (addendum to Embtel 362) this was the one point made to Masud Mohammad which I did not reveal to Subhi Abd al-Hamid.

Emb officer plans see representative Ibrahim Ahmad faction December 17 and representatives Mulla Mustafa and new political bureau December 19. Without mentioning any specific plot he will refer to their earlier statements that Iranians trying stir up Kurds; he will tell them we think Kurds have wisely resisted Persian blandishments and we hope they will continue remain calm and try work out solution with GOI—many of whose members favorably disposed toward Kurds; we think Kurds cause will be severely damaged in Iraq if Kurds appear to act as agents for interests of others.

Must bear in mind that Kurds need supply line through Iran and can only be attracted by Iranian offers of material assistance, which they also need. These factors will decline in importance only if GOI shows good faith and proves willing enter into genuine negotiations.

If GOI so acts, Kurds likely eschew participation in Iranian-managed plot although some city-based Kurdish nationalists might act independently. Aqrawi believes (and says Mulla Mustafa shares his belief) that Nasser wants peaceful settlement and that almost any conceivable successor regime—particularly military dictatorship—would be less conciliatory than present one. But if GOI does not soon indicate willingness open negotiations Mulla will conclude, as most Kurds have already, that GOI has been acting in bad faith since last February. He will not then need foreign encouragement to resume revolt. While impossible estimate when this conjuncture will arrive, Kurds will not stand still forever.

If war starts would be too much to expect Kurds could be dissuaded accepting Iranian supplies and money including variety of strings Iranians might choose attach. Annoying Nasser or alienating Arabs—many of whom have lack sympathy for Kurds would be least of Kurdish worries. Once war recommences, current limitations on Kurdish objectives might well disappear, in which case would become international with serious implications.[6]

STRONG

[1] Source: National Archives and Records Administration, RG 59, Central Files 1964-66, POL 23-9 IRAQ. Secret. Repeated to Tehran and Ankara.

[2] Document 170.

[3] Dated December 8. (National Archives and Records Administration, RG 59, Central Files 1964-66, POL 2-2 IRAQ)

[4] Document 167.

[5] Not found.

[6] Telegram 350 to Baghdad, December 16, agreed that the Embassy should continue to urge restraint on all Kurdish factions and warned it to avoid appearing to give credence to Kurdish claims that Iran was urging them to resume fighting. (Ibid.)

254.

[1964–1968, Volume XXI, pp. 347–48]

172. Telegram From the Embassy in Iran to the Department of State[1]

TEHRAN, April 12, 1965, 1500Z.

1128. Man who identified himself as Shamsuddin Mofti and his colleague as Masoud Barzani appeared at Emb today with letter of introduction from Mollah Mustafa Barzani and oral message from him. It was essentially a strong plea for direct US assistance. He said Iraqi Kurds need financial and military assistance, especially heavy weapons, and would be willing receive American officials in their area and wanted be regarded as "another state of the union." He also said Barzani considers oil resources should be handled by an American firm in direct arrangement with the Iraqi Kurds.

We of course gave him no encouragement whatsoever. Mofti stated Barzani asked that his message be sent to Washington and that USG henceforth use Tehran as point of contact with Barzani. Baghdad, he said, had become too difficult for Barzani to use because of recent Iraqi Army movements. He also said Barzani would like to have direct channel of communication with US rather than through Iranians whom he did not trust to report his views accurately.

EmbOff pointed out steadfast US policy toward Iraqi-Kurdish dispute along lines CA-9411 of March 2, 1963.[2] Said message would be transmitted to Washington, but said could give no commitment regarding a response nor place any response might be given. Nevertheless, Mofti said he would wait in Tehran. Mofti and Barzani said Iranian authorities are unaware of their presence here.[3]

HERZ

---

[1] Source: National Archives and Records Administration, RG 59, Central Files 1964-66, POL 23-9 IRAQ. Confidential. Repeated to Baghdad, Ankara, and Cairo.

[2] CA-9411 stated that the United States should continue to regard the Kurdish revolt as strictly an internal Iraqi matter in which there was no role for the United States either directly or indirectly. (1961-1963, vol. XVIII, Document 174)

[3] Telegram 938 to Tehran, April 14, instructed the Embassy to continue courteously to refuse to enter into a dialogue with "self-styled Barzani representatives," emphasizing that the U.S. policy of non-involvement in the Iraq-Kurdish dispute was unchanged. It added that through appropriate channels, SAVAK should be informed promptly of the visit and of the reply given. (National Archives and Records Administration, RG 59, Central Files 1964-66, POL 23-9 IRAQ)

255.

[1964–1968, Volume XXI, pp. 348–50]

173. Telegram From the Embassy in Iraq to the Department of State[1]

BAGHDAD, April 30, 1965, 1115Z.
937. Embtels 804,[2] 929.[3] Kurds and Iran.
FonMin Talib had at me again last night at Japanese reception. Obviously he has not wanted to stay "set straight" very long. In presence of Education Minister Zaki he repeated old theme that Iranian policy is in fact CENTO policy, said it was vital to GOI to know what was discussed in CENTO meetings[4] or in private talks. For first time accused Iran of giving material assistance to Kurds, and declared Shah's policy on Kurds would lead to situation which would be dangerous to Iran itself and to CENTO. He pointed out that Iran had had no issues with Iraq when both were members of Baghdad Pact and seemed to imply that an Iranian objective was to create a situation in Iraq through the Kurdish problem which would lead to government willing take Iraq into CENTO. He objected strenuously to Shah's basing of his policy toward Iraq on his allergy to Nasser.

I repeated that Kurdish problem not discussed in CENTO and I unaware of any private conversations. Reminded him Pakistan member of CENTO, yet Pakistan had been doing utmost through good offices role to try bring Iran and Iraq into some degree of harmony. Pakistanis could tell GOI whether Kurds discussed in CENTO and whether Shah amenable to US advice on this matter.

At my request, Talib identified Iranian material assistance to Kurds as comprising several loads of unidentified equipment transported onto Iraqi soil in jeeps without license plates. (Zaki chimed in that Shah was also sending aid to Yemeni royalists, but this was not pursued.)

I then gently chided Talib for backsliding after my previous talks with him. Said would report conversation, including information about material assistance; was gratified at obvious respect Talib showed for power and influence of USG but wished assure him there were great many things US could not control or even influence. Talib said GOI felt USG could get Shah change policy if wished. As we parted, to cheer him up I told Talib our latest report was that armored personnel carriers would be delivered in May, June and July, but since this report conflicted with other information, I was seeking authoritative statement. He was pleased.

Comment: Talib himself probably is pursuing CENTO scent as tactic, but some of his colleagues surely believe it. They all believe US can make Shah change policy on Kurds.

Turkish Ambassador in call April 5 (reported by memcon Dept and Ankara)[5] expressed idea that out of Iraqi Army failure defeat Kurds could come govt willing take Iraq into area pact with Turkey and Iran. In our opinion this is nonsense. If Shah thinks pro-Iranian government can be brought about by helping Kurds, believe he is as wrong as he proved to be in past on imminence of UAR-Iraqi union.

Action request. I still hope to see Talib in his office before long to discuss some other matters. Have about run out of arguments on Kurds-Iran-Iraq triangle except possibly pointing out Arab interference in Khuzistan cannot be ignored by Shah. Would appreciate any thoughts Department may think useful with Talib. Also would be helpful have instructions responsive to his insistent references to Secretary's private talk in Tehran. Seems useless any longer try pretend Iran not helping Kurds.[6]

STRONG

---

[1] Source: National Archives and Records Administration, RG 59, Central Files 1964-66, POL 23-9 IRAQ. Confidential. Repeated to London, Tehran, Kuwait, Jidda, Dhahran, Taiz, Cairo, Ankara, and Karachi.

[2] Dated March 25. (Ibid., POL 15-1 TUN)

[3] Dated April 29. (Ibid., POL 23-9 IRAQ)

[4] The Thirteenth Session of the Ministerial Council of the Central Treaty Organization (CENTO) was held in Tehran, April 7-8; see Document 7.

[5] Not found.

[6] Telegram 655 to Baghdad, May 4, stated that the Department believed the Ambassador had given the Iraqis all the arguments available to convince the Iraqi Government that the U.S. Government was not involved in Kurdish dissidence. It was unlikely that further arguments could erase the Foreign Minister's suspicions, but U.S. officials should continue to reiterate the U.S. policy line.

Strong could also tell Talib that Secretary Rusk had not brought any new element into his discussion of Iranian security with the Shah. (Ibid.)

256.

[1964–1968, Volume XXI, pp. 350–51]

174. Telegram From the Department of State to the Embassy in Iraq[1]

WASHINGTON, May 6, 1965, 4:51 p.m.

661. Your 956.[2] Assume Deptel 655[3] received too late for use May 5 conversation with Fon Min.

Additionally, you may tell GOI (1) Iranians are and have been kept fully aware of US view that Iranian and US interests dictate making every effort improve Iran-Iraq relations and avoid disruptive steps. However, as we have often said to Iraqis, we do not control Iranian foreign policy, just as we do not control foreign policies Turkey, Pakistan, Greece, India, others. We cannot recall any instance where country in free world agreed relinquish control over any element its national policy as result its relations with another nation.

(2) Department recommends Embassy go ahead with procedure suggested reftel concerning recall Vanli from US by Kurds in Iraq. FYI: Meanwhile we checking regulations and implications involved possible deportation including possible bearing registration as foreign agent on deportation proceedings. End FYI.

Jernegan in meeting with Ambassador al-Hani on other matter (reported separately) May 5 conveyed points in 1 and 2 above except for first sentence under 1. He reiterated that our reply to Kurdish petitions is always the same, we regard their problem an internal affair of Iraq. Jernegan said he thought Fon Min over-concerned about Vanli who has been singularly unsuccessful in US. (Ambassador al-Hani volunteered he had reported in same vein to Foreign Office.)

RUSK

---

[1] Source: National Archives and Records Administration, RG 59, Central Files 1964-66, POL 23-9 IRAQ. Confidential. Drafted by Dinsmore and Howison on May 5, cleared by Davies, and ap-

proved by Jernegan. Repeated to Ankara, London, Tehran, and Tel Aviv.

[2] In telegram 956, May 5, Strong reported another meeting with Talib during which the Foreign Minister again raised the question of U.S. policy on the Kurds. Talib also expressed doubt that Kurdish representative Vanli, who was attempting to establish a permanent headquarters in the United States for Kurdish rebels, could be operating there against the will of the U.S. Government. He requested that the United States preclude Vanli from engaging in political activity and expel him from the United States, and persuade Iran to cease encouraging and aiding Iraqi Kurds. Strong commented that it appeared that the Iraqi Government was reaching the point of desperation. He suggested that Vanli's visa be canceled and deportation proceedings started and that he be authorized to pass to Mulla Mustafa Barzani a U.S request that Vanli be instructed to leave the United States. (Ibid.)

[3] See footnote 6, Document 173.

257.

[1964–1968, Volume XXI, pp. 351–52]

175. Telegram From the Department of State to the Embassy in Iran[1]

WASHINGTON, August 11, 1965, 7:15 p.m.

138. Baghdad's 74 to Department.[2]

Iraqi request for support efforts halt flow of arms from Iran to dissident Iraqi Kurds cannot reasonably be refused. Our consistent policy has been Kurdish insurrection matter concerning only Iraq and flow of arms and men across border to bring pressure to bear against Iraqi government incompatible our goal area stability. Kurdish victory in Iraq in pragmatic terms could have only most ominous import for stability if not integrity Iran and Turkey. Indications Iraq now has fairly accurate information nature and extent Iranian assistance insurrectionists makes it probable continuance support will lead to rapid deterioration relations.

At level GOIran you deem appropriate you should note Iraqi demarche and express US concern over pressures by Iraqis arising out of Iranian assistance to Kurds. US desires maintain good relations with Iraq and Department views it also to Iran's advantage that

US limited potential for influence in Iraq not be weakened.[3]

For Baghdad. Embassy may inform Foreign Office Embassy Tehran instructed raise matter with GOI. *For London.* You may apprise Foreign Office of foregoing.

RUSK

---

[1] Source: National Archives and Records Administration, RG 59, Central Files 1964–66, POL 23–9 IRAQ. Confidential. Drafted by Davies and Dinsmore; cleared in draft by Bracken and by Judd; and approved by Deputy Assistant Secretary of State for Near Eastern and South Asian Affairs William J. Handley. Repeated to Ankara, Baghdad, Karachi, and London.

[2] In telegram 74 from Baghdad, August 11, Chargé d'affaires J. Wesley Adams reported that Iraqi Under Secretary for Foreign Affairs Kadhim Khalaf had called him to the Foreign Office to request "in the strongest terms" that the United States intervene with the Iranians to obtain cessation of the flow of arms from Iran to the Kurds. Adams noted that he made the usual disclaimer regarding the U.S. ability to influence Iran but agreed to forward the request. (Ibid.)

[3] In telegram 153 from Tehran, August 13, Charge d'affaires Martin F. Herz reported that on August 12 he had conveyed the Iraqi demand to the Foreign Office with comments as instructed in telegram 138. The next day he was summoned by Iranian Foreign Minister Abbas Aram to his residence to discuss Iran-Iraq relations. Aram had insisted that Iran was not aiding the Kurds, and complained that Iraq seemed to be following a studied policy of annoying Iran. Herz commented that Aram seemed distressed that the United States had become involved in the matter. (Ibid.)

258.

[1964–1968, Volume XXI, pp. 352–55]

176. Telegram From the Department of State to the Embassy in Iraq[1]

WASHINGTON, October 26, 1965, 2:01 p.m.

193. Embtel 255.[2] Following summary of conversations FYI and Noforn. It is uncleared and subject to amendment upon review.

1-a. During October 8 conversation with Secretary,[3] Prime Minister raised Kurdish question. While recognizing matter basically internal problem, noted there were also external aspects to it. Said GOI willing look at Kurdish peoples as nation, however he predicted there would never be Kurdish state including all Kurds. PM suggested progress might be made on problem if US and UK would advise Shah unwisdom his policy.

b. Secretary reiterated US supports territorial integrity Iraq and asked PM try understand limited influence US has in such matters. He cited India-Pakistan as example.

c. In response Secretary's question whether he might consider making discreet probes to learn whether there is mutual desire friendship between Tehran and Cairo, PM claimed Shah has exaggerated fear President Nasser. Nasser would like cooperate with Iran. Iran's provocations cause him react. PM contrasted Shah's professed fear Nasser's ambitions with Shah's ambitions among Arab territories in Persian Gulf. Secretary suggested Iranian Foreign Minister Aram might be engaged in dialogue but PM responded it unrealistic think anyone but Shah could change official attitude toward Egypt and Arab world. He thought only advice from friendly powerful governments could persuade Shah.

d. As first civilian PM Iraq in many years, he felt atmosphere of stability. Secretary said US has elementary interest in welfare and territorial integrity Iraq adding we have no national ambitions in Iraq and that we ready explore ways assist Iraq on road to development.

e. PM raised particular program in which he personally interested, namely building University Baghdad into great institution. Secretary said Department would be glad review possibility US assistance on some aspect of University scheme.

f. PM agreed worthwhile examine possibilities investment guarantee agreement.

2-a. In talk with Vice President October 15,[4] Bazzaz conveyed President Arif's highest regards to President and wished speedy recovery from operation. Stated Iraq after series revolutions is developing and in evolutionary stage as member Free World. Present government is non-aligned. Past governments had interpreted non-alignment badly. Present GOI socialistic but not Marxist or Communist. Recognizes role private enterprise.

b. Bazzaz stated Nasser only Arab world leader who effectively combatting commu-

nism and Marxism. Key to good relations with Arabs is good relations with Nasser.

c. PM alleged Iran encouraging disturbances northern Iraq for purely destructive reasons. Shah's problem is his attitude towards Nasser. US should use good offices convince Iran stop aiding Kurds.

d. Finally PM urged US persuade British adopt better attitude toward South Arabia.

e. VP stated PM was speaking to sympathetic mind. Social reform in US occurs within structure mixed economy. VP emphasized distinction between communism and socialism. Real secret of freedom is right express and exchange opinions.

f. VP noted he had visited UAR and had talked with Nasser as well as having brought message from President Kennedy.[5] We have differences but it is US policy try find ways agree. Recently in response strong feeling on part American people Congress reacted against Nasser. President, Vice President and Secretary had to work hard to reverse Congressional decision in order keep flow food continuing to Egypt. We appreciate frank words such as PM's, however Nasser also needs frank talk.

g. VP did not comment on Kurdish situation, saying he was uninformed details. Finally Vice President referred question British and South Arabia to Assistant Secretary Hare.

3-a. In call on Under Secretary Mann October 15,[6] PM contrasted his own modern liberal interpretation of socialism with rigid views his predecessors. He eschews slogans and doctrinaire theories. Under Secretary said he could agree with PM comments, adding economic doctrines devised hundred years or more ago not applicable today without modification.

b. In response Under Secretary's question re US-Iraqi economic relations, PM said Iraq's policy is true non-alignment, that GOI would examine every case on own merits and according Iraq interests but there would be good opportunities for US cooperation and assistance.

c. Under Secretary raised claims US firms pending in Iraq. Bazzaz' response provided Deptel 168 (to Baghdad).[7]

d. PM reiterated idea re US assistance in building new university. It would cost $30-35 million. Iraq able repay in 7-8 years. Mann said he would look into matter.

e. Bazzaz raised Kurdish problem in economic sense as drain on Iraq's finances. He mentioned building loan program and said existing Iraqi institution needs capital. GOI might request $7-8 million loan from US. Mann said he would also look into this.

RUSK

---

[1] Source: National Archives and Records Administration, RG 59, Central Files 1964-66, POL 7 IRAQ, Confidential. Drafted by Dinsmore; cleared by Staff Assistant Howard V. Funk of M, in substance by John E. Rielly in the Vice President's Office, and Deputy Director of the Office of Near Eastern Affairs Harrison M. Symmes; and approved by Davies. Repeated to Cairo and Tehran.

[2] Dated October 25. (Ibid.)

[3] The Secretary's conversation with Prime Minister Abd al-Rahman Bazzaz took place at the United Nations. Memoranda of conversation recording their meeting are ibid., Conference Files: Lot 66 D 347, CF 2547. Bazzaz became Prime Minister of Iraq on September 21, 1965.

[4] The Prime Minister's October 15 conversation with Vice President Humphrey is recorded in a memorandum of conversation ibid., Central Files 1964-66, POL 7 IRAQ.

[5] For information on Humphrey's meeting with Nasser on October 22, 1961, see 1961-1963, vol. XVII, Document 131.

[6] The Prime Minister's October 15 conversation with Under Secretary of State for Economic Affairs Thomas C. Mann is recorded in a memorandum of conversation. (National Archives and Records Administration, RG 59, Central Files 1964-66, POL 7 IRAQ)

[7] Dated October 18. (Ibid., E 7 IRAQ)

259.

[1964–1968, Volume XXI, pp. 355–56]

177. Airgram From the Embassy in Iraq to the Department of State[1]

A-424

BAGHDAD, October 30, 1965.

Analysis of the Kurdish Problem

Enclosed is an analysis in outline form of the Iraqi Kurdish problem prepared by Ambassador Strong.[2] The analysis sets forth the many and varied competing interests and mo-

tivations involved and should be helpful to all concerned with United States policy on this problem.

The central conclusion from the standpoint of the United States is that a high degree of autonomy or independence for the Iraqi Kurds would be disruptive of area stability and inimical to our interests in the long run. Neither is the continuation of the fighting in United States interests, although the consequences do not, at least for the time being, warrant a major initiative by the United States. That the communists and Soviets will gain control of a large-scale insurrection seems unlikely, as is Kurdish ability to establish an autonomous or separatist regime.

The analysis brings out that while the United States, Soviet and UAR postures advocating a peaceful, negotiated settlement are superficially parallel, the positions are differently motivated and, especially in the United States and Soviet cases, based on different assumptions as to probable results.

Similarly, the Iranians and Israelis—and perhaps the British—appear for varying motivations to favor continuation of the conflict for its debilitating effect on Iraq.

Continued Iranian/Israeli intervention is a threat to the United States position in Iraq but, unfortunately, neither country is likely to be heedful of United States interests in the matter.

For the immediate future, neither the Kurds or the GOI appear able to force a military solution. Similarly even a negotiated solution is not likely to be permanent. The Kurdish problem is long-term.

The current United States policy stance seems the most suitable—that the problem is an internal Iraqi one for which a negotiated political solution is desirable.

For the Ambassador:
ENOCH S. DUNCAN
Counselor for Political Affairs

---

[1] Source: National Archives and Records Administration, RG 59, Central Files 1964-66, POL 13-3 IRAQ. Confidential. Drafted by Strong and Duncan on October 29, and approved by Duncan. Repeated to Adana, Aleppo, Ankara, Basra, Beirut, Cairo, Damascus, London, Tabriz, and Tehran.

[2] Attached but not printed.

260.

[1964–1968, Volume XXI, pp. 357–58]

179. Telegram From the Embassy in Iran to the Department of State[1]

TEHRAN, January 20, 1966, 1440Z.

1044. Iran-Iraq Relations.

1. Shah Relaxed. When I suggested 20th that he must be confident Iran-Iraq situation under control or he would not be making his planned trip to Europe, Shah answered affirmative. He said he felt Iran's main aim been accomplished, i.e. to let Iraqis know that any military action across Iran border would meet with vigorous response and that Iran meant it when it said it would "silence" sources of any such activity.

2. Long Range Aims. Shah said at no time has Iran objective been acquisition any Iraqi territory, two countries have everything to gain by neighborly relations. He mentioned they both oil producers. They have common water resources which should be utilized equitably. Shia community in Iraq inevitably has close affinity for Iranian Shias, etc.

3. Kurdish Problem. Shah indicated he has no intention antagonizing his Kurds by actions against Iraq's Kurds. He described Kurds as "purest Aryan" segment of Persian race. Shah's point was that problem of Kurds in Iraq is an internal Iraqi problem, not solvable by "butchering" Kurds and not exportable to Iran.

4. Shatt in Perspective. While this might be moment, Shah said, to exploit tension with Iraq to force solution of Shatt issue, clearly this not Iran's intention. This question has history of many decades, he said, and Iran can afford to wait few more years. In fact, in few years with development Iran's Persian Gulf ports, Iran will be virtually independent of Shatt. At that time, when few ships come to Iranian ports, Iraqis will have increasing difficulty with financial burden of keeping Shatt navigable. Shah predicted at that time, Iraqis will come to Iran in hope of sharing this burden, and dividing Shatt between them. Shah noted, however, that without some discussion Shatt differences issue likely be source of unending trouble between two countries.

5. Recent Progress. Referring to my lengthy chat (Embtel 1034)[2] with Hassan Dujaili, new Iraqi Ambassador to Iran, I told Shah that although I had not seen this friend for eighteen years I quickly had recalled what a sincere and constructive fellow he is. I told Shah Dujaili made sense to me when he said no Iraqi Govt. could discuss question like Shatt under duress. Dujaili seemed completely earnest in wanting reduce tensions and develop neighborly ties.

6. Give Bazzaz a Chance. Noting that evidence seems to be coming in almost every day that while Iraq Govt. still has long way to go to attain competence and constructive purpose of pre-1958 days, I gave as my impression that Bazzaz, now that he is in chair of responsibility, is acquitting himself relatively well and that Iranians ought to give him fair chance. Shah appeared to agree and noted that since Labor government took over in England it has behaved much more responsibly than what one would have expected from its declarations when it was out of power. Shah seemed also to have better realization than previously that Bazzaz and IRWP are not necessarily subservient to Cairo. He characterized Aref as pro-Nasser and "crazy." He referred this time merely to Iraq's Egyptian "friends." He also agreed that even Nasser must realize that Iraq could prove more indigestible than Syria.

7. Three-point Program. Shah said Iran had tried to move half way by accepting Bazzaz's three-point proposal but he said three points must be reciprocal. Be third point, he said Iran did not wish Iraqis to be left with impression that payment of compensation which joint investigating commission might determine would resolve all outstanding Iraq-Iran differences. Door must be left open for discussion other problems such as Shatt and also distribution of water resources, 65 per cent of which rise in Persian highlands.

8. Comment. My impression is that Shah is leaving here with instructions to his govt. that Iran not take any initiatives to cause resurgence in Iraq-Iran tensions. Re long-range issues, he considers both question of Iran aid to Kurds and Shatt-al-Arab question unresolved, but resolution not imperative now. Purpose of my remarks was to encourage Shah to leave his Ministers in no uncertainty

as to his wish that situation remain calm during his absence.

MEYER

[1] Source: National Archives and Records Administration, RG 59, Central Files 1964-66, POL IRAN-IRAQ. Secret. Repeated to Ankara, Baghdad, Jidda, and London.
[2] Dated January 19. (Ibid.)

261.

[1964–1968, Volume XXI, pp. 359–60]

180. Telegram From the Embassy in Iraq to the Department of State[1]

BAGHDAD, May 17, 1966, 1240Z.

688. Subject: Call on President Aref.[2] Ref: Embtel 677,[3] Deptel 538.[4]

1. Had 35 minute talk with President Aref noon May 17. After my delivery of President Johnson's personal best wishes to Aref and for well being of Iraq, Aref expressed sincere appreciation and asked that his personal best regards and best wishes be transmitted to President Johnson. He then recalled our frequent friendly contacts before he became President and said he wished our relationship to continue on same basis.

2. Briefly described main feature of my mission as further development of US-Iraqi relations and US cooperation in promoting stability and political, economic and social development of Iraq to extent desired by Iraq and within means available. Aref expressed understanding and appreciation and turned conversation to Iranian aid to Kurds.

3. I explained in detail USG position on Kurdish problem, outlined Iranian concerns, recounted our efforts to encourage Iran and Iraq to find way to settle differences peacefully and said I thought only Iran and Iraq could settle their mutual problems. Aref said Iran had nothing to fear from Iraq or from UAR-Iraqi relations, but if Shah, who alone responsible for Iranian hostility to Iraq, for whatever reason persists in helping Kurds, then Iraq will be obliged make as much trouble for Iran as possible (airgram being submitted with more detailed account).[5]

5. Comment: Aref was friendly, relaxed and mild throughout. He showed good sense of humor several times. In no way did he place blame on US for Iranian actions and he acknowledged USG not helping Kurds. When I referred to great principles for which US fighting in Vietnam he expressed understanding and agreement. Interpreter was used throughout except for several brief exchanges of personal nature at beginning and end of talk. His English is adequate for ordinary conversation.

6. Consider talk to have confirmed earlier belief that Aref well disposed toward US, although we cannot expect him to take cordial public posture and there inevitably will be events which will embarrass our relations somewhat.

STRONG

[1] Source: National Archives and Records Administration, RG 59, Central Files 1964-66, POL 15-1 IRAQ. Confidential.
[2] President Abdul Salam Aref was killed in a plane crash on April 13 and succeeded on April 16 by his brother, Major General Abdul Rahman Aref.
[3] Dated May 16. (National Archives and Records Administration, RG 59, Central Files 1964-66, POL 15-1 IRAQ)
[4] Telegram 538 to Baghdad, May 14, instructed Strong to reiterate the President's congratulations on Aref's assumption of office and noted that the initial call should be primarily a courtesy call, although the Ambassador could discuss specific subjects at issue between the two governments if he felt it appropriate. (Ibid.)
[5] Airgram A-959 from Baghdad, May 18. (Ibid., POL 2 IRAQ) Aref expressed gratitude for frank discussion which he said he would hold in confidence. Said he wished our talks to be as friend to friend rather than President to Ambassador. I said I looked forward to quiet, friendly talks from time to time.

262.

[1964–1968, Volume XXI, pp. 362–63]

182. Telegram From the Embassy in Iraq to the Department of State[1]

BAGHDAD, July 2, 1966, 1300Z.

12. State 396.[2]

1. Rather than delivering congratulatory message from USG on thwarting of coup, propose use suitable occasions to express orally to Iraqi leaders USG (a) regret that Iraq has had to suffer another outbreak of violence, (b) hope that GOI efforts maintain stability and proceed with development will be successful, (c) congratulations on GOI political program for Kurds and on gaining Kurdish acceptance, and (d) hope that settlement will be implemented promptly, consistently and in good faith by both GOI and Kurds. Believe foregoing will be appreciated and avoid possibility of embarrassment.[3]

2. Timing of coup attempt could possibly in part have related to Bazzaz June 29 announcement of Kurdish settlement. Coup leaders perhaps hoped other elements such as military officers originating Mosul, many of whom anti-Kurd, would join movement to overthrow regime which "betrayed Iraq by capitulating to Kurds." Participation of Moslawi commander of fourth division Attarbashi perhaps secured this basis (but GOI apparently already aware his unreliability since Brigadier Adnan Abd al-Jalil several days ago said to have been named to replace him). On other hand coup leaders' first radio announcement accepted Kurdish settlement. Fact settlement being reached and general outline of terms widely known more than week before coup attempt. These points lead to belief that other factors more important in selection of time. For example, Bazzaz due leave for Turkey July 1. Also, afternoon June 30 was eve of two-day holiday, government establishments close 1:30 p.m. and by 3:10 p.m. when ruckus started siesta is general rule, and large numbers of officers and troops normally given weekend and holiday leave.

3. From speed and smoothness of reaction by loyal forces seems evident GOI aware of coup plans and preferred catch leaders redhanded rather than try to round them up ahead of time and have them on GOI hands without proven case. This quite in keeping with way Iraqis look at things, particularly when they confident of winning.

STRONG

---

[1] Source: National Archives and Records Administration, RG 59, Central Files 1964-66, POL 23-9 IRAQ. Secret. Repeated to Cairo.

[2] Telegram 396 to Baghdad, July 1, noted that the Department was considering whether it might be useful for the Embassy to convey U.S. congratulations quietly to President Aref or Prime Minister Bazzaz on successful thwarting of the recent coup attempt. It also asked for the Embassy's analysis of the degree to which that attempt had been triggered by announcement of the Kurdish settlement. (Ibid.)

[3] Telegram 1207 to Baghdad, July 3, stated that the Department concurred in the Ambassador's proposed course of action. (Ibid.)

263.

[1964–1968, Volume XXI, pp. 363–64]

183. Telegram From the Embassy in Iraq to the Department of State[1]

BAGHDAD, August 19, 1966, 1015Z.

241. Subject: Talk with New Prime Minister.[2]

1. I saw Talib for 50 minutes August 18. Much of time spent on Kurdish question and Iran at his initiative. I told him USG prepared work with present GOI as with previous Iraqi Governments in pursuit of fundamental goal of stable prosperous Iraq; explained in detail our concern over lack of progress on claims of contractors; and explained basic facts of Vietnam situation, its meaning to free world, and firmness of US purpose; expressed deep disappointment at Bazzaz's alignment of Iraq with Soviet position. Talib made a note to look into handling of claims. He avoided further discussion of Vietnam by saying cabinet absorbed in domestic affairs and had no time, as had Bazzaz in Moscow, to concern itself with world issues such as Vietnam and German question.

2. Talib declared GOI would implement Kurdish program fully, but he dwelt extensively on difficulties and gave no hint how GOI to proceed. Most serious problem he identified is three-way split among Kurds, with Barzani insisting GOI deal only with him; GOI cannot ignore Kurds who sided with GOI or those of old KDP. Talib said Barzani wants to be "King of Kurdistan," but apart from that nobody knows what he really wants.

3. Talib asked my views, whether Kurds serious, what GOI should do. I said GOI had real opportunity settle problem. Kurds not

likely start conflict unless GOI failed act. I urged GOI take very generous attitude over extended period of time in order create confidence in good faith of GOI. As Kurds see GOI serious, support for armed rebellion likely decline. Talib listened, but he again stressed difficulties and need for Kurdish cooperation.

4. Talib expressed conviction Iran still supplying arms to Kurds. He did not ask that USG take action with Iran nor did he imply USG helped Kurds. I said I thought arms supply from Iran cut off sometime after June 29; possibly other types supplies moving in but if so this would stop if GOI would drop economic blockade of north as it promised. Talib took very hard line, asked what Iran wants of Iraq and compared Iranian attitude with that of Turkey. He said GOI wants good relations with Iran; Bazzaz and Taher Yahya had not wanted bad relations but Iran had created them. Now Iran tries to impose impossible conditions; no GOI can even discuss Shatt al-Arab. I explained Iranian concerns and then noted that in past few weeks opportunity has arisen for Iraq to move toward better relations with Iran. I urged Talib to try to capitalize on it. Talib responded neither aye nor nay but listened carefully.

5. I pointed out that Iran gave limited help to Kurds for limited objective, whereas USSR keeps stirring up Kurdish aspirations and so-called clandestine broadcasts hostile to GOI continue from Eastern Europe. These things ultimately more dangerous to Iraq; Soviets have longstanding ambitions in direction Persian Gulf; their agitation of Kurdish question targeted at this objective. Talib admitted this but went on that USSR is friend of Iraq which needs Soviet help.

6. *Comment:*

A. Talib revealed nothing of general lines of policies to be pursued. He said ministerial policy statement will be issued in few days. It is still too early for evaluation of current GOI. Next few weeks should provide clues as to character and direction.

B. As Shi'a, Talib may deem it necessary be extra hardboiled with Iran. He has been antagonised by Iranian Ambassador Pirasteh who has told Talib that as a Shi'a he (Talib) is practically an Iranian and should cooperate closely with Iran. I still hope Iran will pa-

tiently keep door open to genuine efforts toward improvement in relations.

C. Talib was physically tired. He was business-like but friendly in attitude. He failed raise question of PL-480 wheat or relief program for north.

STRONG

---

[1] Source: National Archives and Records Administration, RG 59, Central Files 1964-66, POL 15-1 IRAQ. Confidential. Repeated to Tehran, Algiers, Amman, Ankara, Basra, Beirut, Cairo, Damascus, Dhaharan, Jerusalem, Jidda, Khartoum, Kuwait, London, Moscow, Rabat, Tel Aviv, Tripoli, Tunis, and CINCSTRIKE/CINCMEAFSA.

[2] Bazzaz resigned as Prime Minister on August 6 and was succeeded by Naji Talib.

264.

[1964–1968, Volume XXI, p. 365]

184. Telegram From the Department of State to the Embassy in Iraq[1]

WASHINGTON, October 8, 1966, 3:56 p.m.

2624. FYI. Following summary of Secretary's meeting with Pachachi October 5[2] is drawn from uncleared memcon and is FYI, Noforn and subject to review.

1. Kurdish Problem. Pachachi stated Iraq had been able solve this. Iraq had hoped US could do something about Iranian assistance to Kurds. Pachachi will meet with Aram in New York. Stated, "It would be gesture of great help if US could aid in reconstruction in Northern Iraq."

2. Economic Affairs. Pachachi stated GOI hopes ratify Investment Guarantee Agreement. Hopes USG will work with HMG and US companies involved in IPC to press them to seek agreement with GOI.

3. Arab-Israel Problem. Pachachi complained US arms sales to Israel made US appear pro-Israeli. Stated his Govt rather unhappy about further US reductions in its contributions to UNRWA. Re refugees themselves, noted no genuine attempt had ever been made to ascertain refugees' own views. Attempt by Joseph Johnson good effort, but weakened by linking consultation with implementation. End FYI.

RUSK

[1] Source: National Archives and Records Administration, RG 59, Central Files 1964-66, POL 23-9 IRAQ. Secret. Drafted by Kinsolving, cleared by Atherton, and approved by Handley. Repeated to Beirut and Tehran.

[2] The Secretary's meeting with Foreign Minister Pachachi took place at the United Nations. The memorandum of conversation recording their discussion of the Arab-Israeli problem is in 1964-1968, vol. XVIII, Document 323. Other memoranda of conversations are at the National Archives and Records Administration, RG 59, Conference Files: Lot 67 D 305, CF 83.

265.

[1964–1968, Volume XXI, p. 372]

189. Memorandum From the Executive Secretary of the Department of State (Read) to the President's Special Assistant (Rostow)[1]

WASHINGTON, February 16, 1967.

SUBJECT

Letter from Kurdish Insurgent Leader Barzani to the President[2]

Enclosed is a letter from the leader of the Kurdish insurrection in Iraq, General Barzani, to the President. The letter was brought to the United States by one of General Barzani's chief supporters, Dr. Osman. It was delivered to the Department of State at the desk level, where Kurds and Kurdish emissaries are received.

The letter requests the United States to . employ its influence to urge a final and just settlement of the Kurdish question in Iraq, and also requests material help for the destitute Kurds. In fact, our Ambassador in Iraq, Robert Strong, has discreetly but repeatedly urged the Iraqi Government to take more steps to satisfy legitimate Kurdish requests within the framework of Iraqi sovereignty. Since 1964 we have been carrying on a program of supplying surplus US food to Kurdish refugees in Iraq.

Since June 1966 a de facto truce has existed between the Kurdish insurgents and the Iraqi Government pending an over-all settlement. Toward the end of 1966 Barzani sent a

memorandum to the President of Iraq, a copy of which he also enclosed in his letter to the President, complaining that the Iraqi regime has not been acting in good faith in implementing the truce arrangements.

In view of the fact that Barzani has technically still not submitted to the Iraqi Government, we recommend that no written reply be sent to Barzani's letter to the President. Instead, we recommend that a Department of State officer at the desk level orally acknowledge receipt of the letter on behalf of the President and reassure the Kurds of United States Government's concern on a humanitarian basis as evidenced by the continuing flow of surplus foods to the destitute Kurds in Iraq. Such a reply would be consistent with our previous handling of messages from Barzani.[3]

BR

---

[1] Source: National Archives and Records Administration, RG 59, Central Files 1967-69, POL 23-9 IRAQ. Secret. Drafted by Kinsolving on February 14 and cleared by Davies and Country Director for Lebanon, Jordan, Syrian Arab Republic, and Iraq Robert B. Houghton.

[2] Attached but not printed.

[3] A notation typed on the memorandum dated May 9 states that the White House determined that no action or reply was necessary.

266.

[1964–1968, Volume XXI, pp. 384–86]
197. Intelligence Note From the Director of the Bureau of Intelligence and Research (Hughes) to Secretary of State Rusk[1]

No. 709
WASHINGTON, September 1, 1967.

SUBJECT

New Kurdish Insurgency Threatens

In addition to its many other problems, the Near East may have to face a new round of fighting between the Kurdish guerrillas and the Iraqi army during the next three or four months. Mulla Mustafa's followers are growing restive. Minor clashes are occurring more frequently between the rival Kurdish factions, and between Mustafa's bands and isolated small army units. The Kurds probably would not move in force before late September, when the harvest is in, but action could be triggered earlier by government miscalculation or by outside pressures.

Kurds Feel That They Must Be Militant. Several factors, both local and regional, tempt the Kurds to reopen hostilities at a time of their own choosing.

Locally: *The government is defaulting on peace promises.* The financial strain of the oil cutoff, first in November-December and then during the war with Israel, paralyzed the Iraqi government's plans for extensive reconstruction in the Kurdish area, which were part of the peace agreement with the Kurds.

The Kurds distrust Tahir Yahya, the new Prime Minister who took office July 10. The Kurds feel that he played them false in earlier dealings. Yahya further angered Barzani by appointing as Kurdish minister in the present Cabinet one Abd al-Fattah al-Shali, an opportunist who is soft on the rival Kurdish faction of Jalal Talabani.

The Arab defeat encourages Kurdish militants. Younger Kurdish militants must want to seize the opportunity to pounce on the defeated Arab armies, and Mustafa may be concerned to hold their loyalty.

The government is weak. The Iraqi Cabinet and regime are very shaky. Mulla Mustafa believes that only by demonstrating his readiness and ability to fight can the Kurds make their weight felt politically now or with a successor government. Also, he must maintain his standing against Talabani.

Kurds May Receive Israeli and Iranian Support. Unsupported, the Kurds would probably not attempt full-scale hostilities, even of the guerrilla type. Mustafa's outside supporters, however, seem now in the mood to sustain some limited Kurdish action. At least, they apparently wish to keep alive Mustafa's capability and will to fight.

An Israeli second front? Just before the war started an Israeli agent reportedly visited Mulla Mustafa to arrange, if possible, some Kurdish action to tie down the Iraqi army. He did not succeed. However, convoys of materiel to the Kurds resumed around the end of April. For some months before that time, assistance had been limited to relief supplies. Israel may now be urging on the Kurds in order to keep up pressure on the Arabs. In view of Syrian intransigence they might now want to extend the agitation to Syrian Kurds who had begun to take a minor part in the revolt just before the truce.

Iran suspicious. The Iranian government, once a strong supporter of the Kurdish insurgency, was pursuing a slow and delicate rapprochement with Iraq before the June war. This policy has been shaken by Iraq's extreme pronouncements during the war, and by the appointment of Tahir Yahya, whom Iranians regard as pro-Nasser. Moreover, SAVAK reportedly believes that Nasserite subversive activities have increased since the war. The Iranian government is said to believe that neither Mulla Mustafa nor the Iraqi government has the confidence for a major showdown at this time, but it does not rule out strong harassing action on the part of the Kurds. Iran shares Mulla Mustafa's view that the Iraqi regime is in serious trouble and it may well be tempted to renew its aid to the Kurds in an effort to help topple the present government and get a successor regime more sympathetic towards Iran.

A New Kurdish Rising Potentially Dangerous. Kurdish guerrilla activities against the Iraqi government have occurred periodically for a long time. Just now, however, renewed fighting in the Kurdish area could be a further unsettling factor in an already brittle situation, particularly if unrest were to spill over into Syria. Should any Israeli or Iranian involvement become known, Arab radical propaganda would no doubt claim that this is a new "plot" against the Arabs instigated by the US.

---

[1] Source: National Archives and Records Administration, RG 59, Central Files 1967-69, POL 23-9 IRAQ. Secret; No Foreign Dissem. Prepared in the Bureau of Intelligence and Research.

267.

[1964–1968, Volume XXI, p. 387]

199. Memorandum From John W. Foster of the National Security Council Staff to the President's Special Assistant (Rostow)[1]

WASHINGTON, July 17, 1968.

SUBJECT

The Iraqi Coup

Until things sort themselves out, and until we get better information—we have no representation in Baghdad—it's impossible to tell what the effect of last night's coup[2] will be. We can't even be sure that the coup leaders' claim of military support is true. A counter-coup tomorrow is conceivable.

The intelligence community's initial reading is that the new group—apparently Baathists—will be more difficult than their predecessors, but at this point no one knows how radical they will be. So far, their communiques have taken a fairly moderate line by Iraqi standards, promising economic reforms, honest government, a "wise" solution of the Kurdish problem,[3] and Arab unity against the Zionist and Imperialist threats. On the other hand, if these people are Baathists, their tendencies will be towards moving Iraq even closer to Fatah, the Syrians and the Soviets. From our point of view, the most important question is whether they will continue Iraq's support for King Hussein. Iraq has about 25,000 troops in Jordan and could easily make life difficult for the King.

This is just to give you the best reading we have before you leave.

JOHN

---

[1] Source: Johnson Library, National Security File, Country File, Iraq, Cables & Memos, Vol. I, 12/63-7/68. Secret.

[2] An almost bloodless army coup overthrew the regime of President Aref at dawn on July 17. The new Revolution Command Council assumed absolute powers at 7 a.m. and unanimously elected former Vice President and retired Major General Ahmed Hasan al-Bakr, as President. Baghdad radio subsequently announced that former President Aref had been retired on pension and deported to "join his family" in England. (Intelligence Note 561, July 17; National Archives and Records Administration, RG 59, Central Files 1967-69, POL 23-9 IRAQ)

[3] The Aref government had made little progress on implementation of the June 1966 cease-fire agreement. Barzani had refused to disband his army until the Iraqi Government made good on its promises for limited Kurdish autonomy in the North, Kurdish proportional representation in the still unreconstituted Iraqi Parliament, and disbanding of the government's anti-Barzani Kurdish irregulars. In the meantime, Barzani's forces maintained de facto control of the North and had recently secured renewed military and financial aid commitments from Iran and Israel. (Intelligence Note 488, June 20; ibid.)

268.

[1964–1968, Volume XXI, p. 388]

200. Memorandum From John W. Foster of the National Security Council Staff to the President's Special Assistant (Rostow)[1]

WASHINGTON, July 22, 1968.

SUBJECT

A Clearer Picture of the Iraqi Coup

While you were gone, the situation in Iraq became much clearer. The new government could still be a little harder for us to deal with than the old—if we ever have a chance to deal with it—but if we had to have a Baathist government there, this is probably the best we could expect.

The Baathists are from the right-wing of the party—the opponents of those in control in Syria—and non-Baathists are playing a major role in the new government. The Syrians had nothing to do with the coup; in fact, one of the most interesting questions raised by the coup is whether the Iraqi example will encourage the moderate Syrian Baathists now in exile to take a crack at the Syrian regime.

The inability of the Aref government to deal with Iraq's domestic problems was the reason—or excuse—for the coup, and the new government is talking mainly about economic reforms, eliminating corruption and solving the Kurdish problem. They have made the usual statements about Zionism, Imperialism and Arab unity, but so far there have been no indications that Iraq's foreign policy will become more radical. It's too early to know whether there will be progress on a Kurdish settlement or more trouble—a key determinant of how free Iraqi troops will be to menace Israel.

Until we see these people in action, we won't know for sure what problems we might face, but there seems to be less cause for concern over anything radically different now than there was last Wednesday.

JOHN

---

[1] Source: Johnson Library, National Security File, Country File, Iraq, Cables & Memos, Vol. I, 12/63-7/68. Secret.

269.

[1964–1968, Volume XXII, pp. 3–8]

2. Letter From the Shah of Iran to President Johnson[1]

TEHRAN, January 7, 1964.

Dear Mr. President,

I have been recalling with pleasure impressions of your memorable but short visit to Teheran, in the company of Mrs. Johnson and your daughter. It was indeed gratifying to have had the occasion to meet you again personally. For the citizens of our capital it was a rare and cherished opportunity to have a glimpse of a kind-hearted and affable personality of your stature, to show their genuine admiration for you and to extend to you, as you no doubt witnessed, their spontaneous and cordial welcome. Such personal contacts and human relationships make for more sincere cooperation, still better understanding and closer ties of friendship between our two countries.

Let me express the earnest hope that the United States, under your wise and capable leadership will further succeed in her continued efforts to usher in a new era of peace and prosperity for mankind.

I am quite confident, Mr. President, that your wisdom and high statesmanship, as well as your long and intimate association with American politics and extensive knowledge and experience of world affairs, will prove invaluable assets in the successful discharge of the heavy responsibilities of your high office both in the United States and abroad.

Since your visit, Mr. President, much has happened in Iran. A comprehensive programme of far-reaching social, political and economic reforms, of which you were then given a brief account, has now been fully implemented. These reforms have transformed completely the entire structure of our society, and placed its foundations firmly upon the enlightened and progressive principles of our time. In their application, varying political slogans which essentially cater for the interests of only a certain class of society played no part. The guiding principle of our national policy is the realization of that which is advantageous to the interests of a free and independent society.

That the Iranian people wholeheartedly supported the cause of our revolutionary reforms was amply manifested at the referendum of January 1963, and during our recent general elections. I am certain that you are already familiar with these events.

Our position today, from the point of view of internal stability, national prestige, and our people's confident hope for a better life has reached a point where, if no external dangers should threaten us, gives us reason to look to the future with well-founded optimism and confidence.

Turning to conditions outside Iran, we are thankful that the firm and far-sighted policy of the United States has led the world to the threshold of a period of relaxation of international tension, and that the Soviet Union seems, for the present at least, to have discarded the use of force as an instrument of her foreign policy. In these circumstances, I believe, Mr. President, co-existence with Russia, in the face of the Chinese peril to universal peace, commends itself as the wisest course to adopt; bearing in mind that until such time that complete and general disarmament with full and precise control becomes a reality, the fundamental question of our time, namely the preservation of peace, remains unsolved. Meanwhile, it is a matter of course that we should be well-disposed to undertake any step or action that would contribute to the realization of this goal, provided, of course, that in so doing we do not compromise our principles.

Your illustrious predecessor, in a letter written to me just before his tragic demise, had asked my opinion, in view of our past experiences with the Soviet Union, on the question of the bruited non-aggression treaty between NATO and the Warsaw Pact countries.

You are well aware, Mr. President, that in 1959 we were on the point of signing with the Soviet Union a non-aggression treaty for a period of some 30 or even 50 years. Their rather ridiculous initial conditions, however, delayed the negotiations for a few days. In the meantime, we received messages from the Presidents of the United States, Turkey and Pakistan warning us of the dangers of such a step. We were even reminded of the fate of the

Baltic States. The reason they advanced was that if any action of this nature were to be taken, it would have to be on behalf of all the countries of the free world; in other words, that such an action would have to be collective, if the free world's united front were to remain intact.

This reasoning I found convincing, and I believe that it holds true even today. There can be no objection, in principle, to the conclusion of a non-aggression treaty between NATO and the Warsaw Pact countries; it may even be fruitful; but what, may in that case be asked, will be the impact of such a treaty on the regional member nations of the Central Treaty Organization? Where will American and British obligations to CENTO stand? Will Russia, then, be allowed to have a free hand to do as she pleases elsewhere? In such a situation—should it arise—it is not unlikely that the countries thus exposed will have to see how best they can arrive at a bilateral agreement with the Soviet Union and that, certainly at a price.

It is, therefore, highly advisable that the non-aggression pact between NATO and Warsaw Pact countries—if there is to be one—should cover all member countries of CENTO, in particular those bordering on the Soviet Union and not to leave them outside the agreement. We have also heard of a proposal that all countries of the world should sign a treaty of non-aggression with each other.

There are certain countries in the world, the preservation of whose independence and territorial integrity, because of their characteristic geographic position, does not only constitute a service to those countries alone, but a service also to the stability and peace of an entire area. Iran is an instance of such a country.

Mr. Brezhnev paid a visit to Iran about a couple of months ago. In his talks with me he did his best to be friendly and to leave formality aside. So much so, that on the last day of his stay he went as far as confiding to me that, relations between Iran and the Soviet Union having improved considerably, he would permit himself to express Russia's dislike of Iran's participation in military agreements with the West. My immediate reply, of course, was that one did not have to go too far to seek

the reasons for the existence of such regional defensive agreements. They would automatically lose their force and validity as soon as the numerous military pacts between countries of the world ceased to exist and the dangers of war and aggression no longer posed a threat to the territorial integrity of smaller nations; and that such an ideal situation could only be brought about when general and complete disarmament with proper controls became a reality.

Permit me to say a few words now about developments in some of the countries around Iran. A matter to which I wish, Mr. President, to call your attention is the danger which threatens this area of the world. I refer to the stockpiles of weapons of aggression in the possession of Egypt and the ever increasing delivery of offensive equipment to that country by the Soviet Union, designed to serve, overtly or under cover, as instruments of Egyptian intervention. Yemen, the Morocco-Algeria conflict and the arming of Somalia for expansion are instances in point. Egypt, in fact, has already prepared an "intervention force" of considerable size, equipped with long-range bombers, missiles, heavy troop transport planes, submarines, ships, and torpedo boats armed with missiles, so that if a "change" should happen to occur in any Arab country and President Nasser be asked to "intervene" he would willingly do so and let the world be faced with a fait accompli. I should perhaps add that even Iran does not seem to be too distant for his designs or immune from his subversive activities.

It is in consideration of these compelling reasons that the security of the Persian Gulf poses for us a source of constant concern, not only in the interest of our own country, but in the interest of the West as well. Indeed, the stakes involved are so great that any lack of vigilance on our parts may have disastrous consequences. To this situation, we have endeavoured to draw the attention of the United States Government.

Last year, the Pentagon prepared a Five Year Plan for Iran which was accepted with some reservations and for want of a more satisfactory alternative.[2] This Plan has already proved inadequate for the requirements of the changing situation in this area. The Iranian Army is capable of serious combat neither in the mountainous regions—for lack of adequate material requirements and logistical support—nor in the plains—for being devoid of the required mobility, and armour for such warfare. Our armoured equipment, the M47 tanks, are of type not in current production whose replacement and spare parts can be found with great difficulty. Now, if such is the condition of our equipment in peace time, it is difficult to imagine how they can be of any serious value at times of emergency. We have no military stockpiles of any kind and no reserves, even of machine guns, automatic rifles and ammunition to meet routine demands. Should unforeseen circumstances require us to put our army in a state of mobilization, we shall hardly be able to place ourselves in a state of readiness for the emergency. All our supplies and equipment have been distributed to provide for the army's current requirements.

The responsibilities of the Iranian Air Force, moreover, have never been equal to even the minimum of the Army requirements. Our airfields are limited in number, and where they do exist we are there faced with deficiencies in radar facilities and anti-aircraft protection.

Furthermore, ships and vessels presently in service with our navy, in number as well as in military value, are hardly adequate to carry out their vital responsibilities.

If our armed forces are to function effectively and to perform their allotted duties, and if Iran, a staunch and steadfast ally of the United States, is to play her full part in the changing political climate of the Middle East, then obviously, Mr. President, these shortages have to be met. Otherwise, we must consider as wasted the funds that are presently allocated for maintaining our armed forces.

In my correspondence with you, Mr. President, I wish to be perfectly candid in dealing with matters of mutual interest. If the United States is not in a position to meet our clear and urgent military needs in addition to the Five Year Plan, in order to be able to fulfil our duties, I thought that we might advisedly arrange for the purchase of our additional needs, under favourable conditions, from the United States of America or from elsewhere.

Of course, the question of CENTO strategy, American engagements and a great many related topics will form the subject of discussions by our representatives at the CENTO Ministerial Council. We hope that this forthcoming meeting, due to be held in Washington, will provide a suitable opportunity for clarifying all these points. In the meantime, it would be useful if you should see fit to appoint someone to discuss with me urgent matters of interest to our two countries and to report the result to you.

In the field of economic activity, it is a source of satisfaction that our own potentials are so great that if we can devote all our planned resources to the implementation of our Five Year Plan, we can envisage an annual growth of 8 per cent, with every hope of raising considerably the material welfare of our people. We have received a number of proposals for economic assistance from Western and even Eastern European countries as well as from the Soviet Union. Doubtless, we would be more than gratified to have offers of loan from the A.I.D. with their very generous terms, and also from the Export Import Bank and its subsidiary organizations. We would welcome, further, private American investors who would wish to participate in the development of our economy.

To turn once again to the Middle East, the situation in Iraq seems uncertain. With the fall of Kassem's unwholesome regime, we welcomed with relief what we hoped would be closer ties with Iraq, thinking that since the Baathists at once began to purge their country of Communists, we had been rid of a troublesome neighbour. Our optimism was shortlived however, for we soon discovered in Southern Iran centres of Arab espionage, with their covetous eyes on a certain integral part of our country, namely Khuzistan, the main centre of our oil industry.

With the overthrow of the Baathist Government in Iraq, this danger seems to have abated. Uncertainty however, still persists. For our information indicates that Marshal Aref himself had been fully aware of the above activities and had given them his full support.

I regret to say that already Marshal Aref has shown a tendency to turn towards Egypt. If I lay emphasis on this question and express my concern, it is because we are well aware of the developments in this area and the course they are likely to take.

Here, I must state that our attitude towards Iraq has always been a friendly one, and we have always hoped that Iraq will have a strong and stable Government, capable of preserving its independence and of safeguarding its national interests.

The Kurdish question is still unsettled. Agents of international communism are making every endeavour to exploit the situation to their own advantage, and Cairo is anxious to play its dubious role in any development in this situation.

If negotiations between the Government at Baghdad and the Kurds should fail to reach an understanding, we have reason to expect that the fighting will flare up again in the spring.

We have reports to the effect that President Nasser did try, and is still making efforts to "mediate" between the Kurds and the Central Government of Iraq. This, on the surface, sounds quite harmless, even perhaps commendable. However, the contents of one of his messages to the Kurds fully reveals his ill intentions towards Iran. He has said in effect, according to our information, that it was a pity the Kurds were fighting the Arabs. He would have given them full support if their force were directed against Iran.

Thus with the situation prevailing in Iraq and with the UAR adventures in Yemen and elsewhere likely to erupt in other parts of the Middle East as well, my obligations to my country and my people make it incumbent upon me to take all precautions for the safety of the country and of our national interests. We cannot tolerate Egypt's subversive influence at our doorstep; nor fail to regard it seriously. I think, as referred to above, upon the stability of Iran depends the security of the entire Middle East. While we in Iran are seeking to ensure the security and stability of our own country, and that of the Persian Gulf, we are contributing also to the preservation of peace in this entire area—an area in which the United States has vital interests.

Happily, on these as on other matters, we have always maintained close and cordial contact, and our views have never been far apart.

Again, my best wishes for your happiness and success in the service of the United States of America as well as in the cause of the free world.

With high esteem,
Sincerely,
M.R. PAHLAVI

---

[1] Source: Johnson Library, National Security File, Special Head of State Correspondence File, Iran—Presidential Correspondence. No classification marking. The copy of the Shah's letter in the Department of State is attached to a covering memorandum indicating that the original was delivered by the Iranian Embassy to the Department on January 17. (Department of State, Central Files, POL 15-1 US/Johnson)

[2] For text of the U.S. Five-Year Military Program for Iran, accepted by Iran on September 19, 1962, see 1961-1963, vol. XVIII, pp. 105-109.

270.

[1964–1968, Volume XXII, pp. 13–18]

6. Memorandum From the Acting Assistant Secretary of State for Near Eastern and South Asian Affairs (Jernegan) to the Special Group (Counter Insurgency)

Washington, March 2, 1964

SUBJECT
Progress Report, Internal Defense Plan—Iran

. . .

4. Major Areas of Continuing Concern.
c. Iran's Kurdish problem may well be affected by the recently reported cease-fire between the Iraqi Government and the Iraqi Kurds. At present writing it is too early to judge whether the cease-fire will stick and, if so, whether it will exacerbate or ameliorate Iran's internal security problem . . .

271.

[1964–1968, Volume XXII, pp. 41–52]

23. National Intelligence Estimate

NIE 34-64

Washington, May 20, 1964.

IRAN

Conclusions

. . .

I. Iran's Problems . . .

The Opposition . . .

14. Tribal dissidence remains a potential rather than a present threat to the regime. The Iranian Kurds have yet to overcome their traditional tribal rivalries and lack any widely accepted local leader. Moreover, they have no very serious grievance, and the government is taking some steps to extend to the Kurdish areas the benefits of economic development and to integrate them in greater degree into national life. The Iranian Kurds are unlikely to create serious problems for the government unless Iraqi Kurds win a large measure of autonomy or unless the USSR makes a determined attempt to incite a separatist movement. Neither of these developments now seems likely. While tribal disorders may occur in other parts of Iran, such conflicts are easy to contain and isolate, and it would be extremely difficult for the diverse tribal groupings to coordinate action against the regime. Though there is almost certainly some Egyptian or Iraqi intrigue among the Khuzistan Arabs, they are unarmed, sunk in poverty and apathy, and therefore constitute no threat at present . . .

272.

[1964–1968, Volume XXII, pp. 321–24]

178. Letter From the Ambassador to Iran (Meyer) to the Assistant Secretary of State for Near Eastern and South Asian Affairs (Hare)[1]

TEHRAN, October 22, 1966.

Dear Ray:

Set out in the paragraphs below is the Embassy's assessment of the internal security situation in Iran prepared in accordance with instructions from IRG/NEA (Department Airgram A-11 of July 21).[2] You will note that since last October when we submitted our last formal report on the counter-insurgency situation here (A-281 of October 20, 1965),/2/ no major changes have taken place in the situation as we viewed it at that time. However, the

moves toward settlement of the Kurdish revolt in Iraq this year and some evidence that the growing number of Soviet technicians is outrunning the capacity of the security services for effective surveillance, point to possible longer-term problems. There has also been a negative development in the reorganization of the Army's Counter-Intelligence Corps (CIC), hitherto regarded as the most effective counter-intelligence force in the government, which will bear continuous close scrutiny.

As noted in the Embassy's recently-prepared semi-annual assessment of the political situation in Iran (Embassy's A-104 of August 23, 1966),[3] the period since our last assessment has been characterized once more by the relative placidity of the internal scene. It has been years since the political atmosphere has been as sluggish, as self-satisfied, or as resigned to the status quo. This is related only partly to the effectiveness of political controls. It is in large measure attributable to economic prosperity and to the Shah's success in giving the impression that a reorientation has taken place in Iran's international position. There is more popular confidence in the regime and less carping criticism. A rising new middle class is on the march economically and, in the short run at least, appears to be developing an interest in political stability. This situation could change, of course, if the Shah should be assassinated, or if a serious slowdown in present economic momentum should take place.

The favorable economic situation and the reduced level of popular dissatisfaction have had the effect of dampening political activities of all kinds. The Communists are in disarray, their fortunes probably at the lowest ebb in years. They certainly can take little heart in the increasingly obvious efforts of the Soviets and the Communist orbit of Eastern Europe to deal directly with the Shah himself on a government-to-government level. The religious opposition remains unreconciled to Iran's increasing modernity and, while there have been rumors of an unholy alliance between the right-wing religious oppositionists and left-wing elements, so far nothing actually has materialized. With the surrender of the Qashqai bandit Bahman Khan earlier this year the last vestige of rebellion among the southern tribes disappeared from the scene, at least for the time being.

However, there is some evidence of increasing activity on the part of the Iranian Kurds. The apparent negotiated settlement of the Kurdish revolt in Iraq reached late last June was generally well-received by the Kurds in Iran. The end of hostilities, however, also set in motion a latent nationalist fervor among this minority group due primarily to the expectation that the Iraqi Kurds would gain certain advantages and privileges from their acceptance of the cease-fire. This tendency probably is best reflected in what has been described by Embassy sources as a general increase in political activity, particularly among Kurdish groups in the Mahabad area. The Iranian Government appears to be watching this unsettled situation warily and has developed a renewed interest in the National Resistance Movement (NRM). So far, however, we have no evidence of any major shift in GOI policy vis-a-vis the Kurds.

Although some Iraqi leaders continue to believe to the contrary, the GOI appears to have discontinued purely military assistance to the Iraqi Kurds, and has closed the Iraqi-Iranian border in the Kurdish area. So far, although there are the usual cases of smuggling and banditry, Iranian Kurdistan appears peaceful. We do not believe that political activity on the part of Kurds in Iran which might affect drastically Iranian Kurdistan will develop in the near future. Iran's central security organizations appear quite capable of handling any situation likely to develop.

While Iranian security forces appear capable of handling any political activity likely to develop in Kurdistan, they are having their difficulties elsewhere. At the present time, the greatest security problem is of a long-term character. The Iranian security forces clearly are unable to keep the steadily rising number of Soviet technicians in Iran under effective surveillance. The number of Soviet personnel in Iran in connection with the steel mill, pipeline, and other projects is approaching 600 and likely to surge beyond that figure. The Iranians, however, have taken a number of administrative steps to aid in controlling more effectively the movements of Soviet officials more or less permanently stationed in this country. The Embassy also hears that a number of dossiers concerning suspicious activities on the part of the Soviets are piled up on the desk of the Shah. We believe that Iranian security forces are keeping especially careful tabs on possible contacts between Soviet technicians and Iranian Communists.

Speaking once more of the Communists, Savak is showing interest in long-term threat posed by the Chinese Communists. The latter have not been able to form any organization within Iran, but have been successful in their propaganda activities among Iranian students in Europe. An increasing number of these students have begun to show Communist Chinese sympathies and some of them apparently have even visited China. The Chinese have flooded Europe with publications which are having an effect on Iranian students some of whom can be expected to return to Iran and to attempt to conduct subversive activities. Savak believes that students returning from abroad will have to be checked very carefully lest the Chinese Communists get a foothold in Iran. Although Savak believes that the pro-Soviet group now dominates the Tudeh party, it feels that the Chinese Communists, considering that they have been laboring under the double disadvantage of being newer in the field than the Soviets and of having no official representation in Iran, have done very well to date. For this reason, Savak will continue to observe closely the activities of Chinese Communist elements.

The decentralization of the Counter Intelligence Corps (CIC) of the Iranian Armed Forces has reduced its effectiveness markedly. CIC units in the field have been transferred from the administrative and operational control of CIC Headquarters in Tehran to the units to which previously they had been attached only. Thus, all reporting on security matters now must pass through channels via the unit commander who, if he sees fit to do so, may suppress the reports rather than forward them to the Supreme Commander's Staff (SCS). Given the well-known Iranian penchant for not reporting matters which superiors do not wish to hear, security reports are more often suppressed than forwarded to headquarters. In addition, decentralization takes away the capability of CIC units in the field to respond quickly to an urgent request from CIC Headquarters for operational support on an espionage or subversion case. Under the new arrangement such requests must be dispatched through command channels to the lower CIC unit. In the past CIC Headquarters sent a message directly to the unit concerned. A study is now underway, however, to determine how to retain such support from the field without taking away the prerogative of the major commander concerned. The decentralization has had a deleterious impact on the morale of the CIC as has also the fact that it is still smarting from the incompetence of its previous commander. Although a new commander, a professional intelligence officer, has been recently appointed, it is problematical whether he will be able to restore the CIC to the level of its previous effectiveness when it was regarded as the top security organization in Iran.

We continue to find valid the judgment made at the time of our last report (March 19, 1966 letter to Governor Harriman)[4] that there are no disturbing elements in the present situation requiring counter-insurgency measures. On the program side we continue to be interested in support for the National Police and in communications for the Imperial Iranian Gendarmerie (IIG). In this latter connection we have obtained from the IIG an idea of the program it desires and have forwarded to DOD via Genmish channels our comments and suggestions. The IIG has obtained from the GOI a pledge of support which we believe approaches 50% of the total cost. The total cost of this communications project is $10.2 million. With the GOI apparently prepared to put up $5 million and with $2.2 million already in the program for IIG communications, this means that $3 million needs to be financed over a five to six year period. We would be grateful for any help you feel you might provide in getting this project on the rails. We think it is of the utmost importance in any counter-insurgency situation likely to develop in Iran that we have an effective command and control system for operations in the countryside.

With all best regards,
Sincerely,
ARMIN

---

[1] Source: Department of State, NEA/IRN Files: Lot 70 D 330, Iran 1966. Secret; Official-Informal. A handwritten note on the source text indicates that it was received on October 27.

[2] Not printed. (Ibid., Central Files, POL 23-1 IRAN)

[3] Not printed. (Ibid., POL 2-3 IRAN)

[4] Not found.

273.

[1988, p. 442]

248. U.S. Position on Kurdish National Aspirations

Daily Press Briefing by the Department of State Spokesman (Redman), June 15, 1988 (Extracts)[15]

Q. Last week there was a meeting between a Kurdish leader, Talabani, [16] with a State Department official. In light of that, do we count the State Department or the U.S. Government as mediating the differences between the Kurds and the Iraqi Government, or what was the reasoning behind it?

A. The meeting with Mr. Talabani was at his request. He asked to meet with State Department officials during a visit to the United States and he was received on June 9th by the Director of the Office of Northern Gulf Affairs in the Near East and South Asia Bureau. He also saw some officials dealing with refugees and human rights issues.

On the question of the Kurds, as you put it, U.S. policy is that Kurds should satisfy their aspirations peacefully within the framework of the existing states in the area. The United States does not interfere in the internal affairs of those countries.

Q. Do you see their receiving Talabani as interfering in Iraq's internal affairs?

A. No.

---

[15] Source: Office of Press Relations, Dept. of State. The briefing began at 12:02 PM.

[16] Jalal Talabani, leader of the Patriotic Union of Kurdistan.

274.

[1988, p. 458]

260. U.S. Condemnation of Iraqi of Chemical Weapons

Statement Read by the Department of State Spokesman (Redman), September 8, 1988[32]

As a result of our evaluation of the situation, the U.S. Government is convinced Iraq has used chemical weapons in its military campaign against Kurdish guerrillas. We don't know the extent to which chemical weapons have been used, but any use in this context is abhorrent and unjustifiable.

We condemn this use of chemical weapons as we have consistently condemned Iraq's use of chemical weapons in the conflict with Iran. We expressed our strong concern to the Iraqi Government which is well aware of our position that use of chemical weapons is totally unjustifiable and unacceptable.

The Secretary will be raising this issue with the Iraqi Minister of State. Mr. Saddoun Hammadi, during his meeting with Mr. Hammadi this afternoon.

---

[32] Source: *Department of State Bulletin*, December 1988, p. 44. The statement was read during the Department of State Daily Press Briefing which began at 12:30 p.m.

275.

[1988, pp. 459–60]

262. Congressional Sanctions Against Iraq

Prepared Statement by the Deputy Assistant Secretary of State for Near Eastern and South Asian Affairs (Burleigh), September 22, 1988[34]

We support the objective of this bill,[35] and are determined to prevent Iraq from using chemical weapons again against the Kurds or anyone else. We appreciate the efforts this Committee has made to work with us in designing legislation which meets our common objectives, and we recognize the impact of this legislation would be less severe than that of the Senate.

If we thought new and extensive controls on exports to Iraq would achieve these objectives. we would have no hesitation in supporting their imposition. Prevention of chemical weapons use by anyone, anywhere, is of transcendent importance to this administration. Our relationship with Iraq is important, but the issue of chemical weapons use overrides other bilateral considerations.

We cannot support this legislation because we do not believe sanctions now would bring us closer to the objective we share with this committee of ending chemical weapons use by Iraq once and for all. As the committee is aware, on September 17, the Foreign Minister of Iraq formally, "reaffirmed that Iraq respects and abides by all the provisions of international law and international agreements accepted by the international community, including the Geneva protocol of 1925 . . . and other agreements within the framework of international humanitarian law."[36] We believe this is an important statement and a positive step. We are discussing its significance with the Government of Iraq. Specifically, we are seeking to confirm that Iraq interprets it as applying to the use of chemical weapons internally. Such use is morally repugnant and prohibited by international law, including the 1949 Geneva Convention relative to the protection of civilian persons in time of war.[37]

If the results of our discussions with the Government of Iraq are unsatisfactory, or if there is evidence of further use by Iraq of chemical weapons, we would reconsider this position. But we believe that the passage of this legislation now would undercut our efforts with Iraq and damage U.S. exporters

without furthering the goal of ending use by Iraq of chemical weapons.

---

[34] Source: Legislation to Impose Sanctions Against Iraqi Chemical Use: Markup Before the Committee on Foreign Affairs, House of Representatives, One Hundredth Congress, Second Session (Washington, 1988), p. 21.

[35] H.R. 5337 was approved by the House of Representatives on September 27; no action was taken by the Senate before Congress adjourned. For text, see ibid., pp. 3–9

36 Ellipsis in the source text.

37 Dated at Geneva, August 12, 1949, entered into force October 21, 1950, for the United States, February 2, 1956; 6 UST 3516.

276.

[1989, pp. 182–85]

75. Country Reports on Human Rights, 1989

Prepared Statement by the Assistant Secretary of State for Human Rights and Humanitarian Affairs (Schifter), February 8, 1989 (Extracts)[2]

Although much happened in the Soviet Union during 1988 that even as recently as 3 years ago, we would not have expected to happen so quickly, we have to keep in mind that the Soviet Union has still far to go before it could be deemed to be in full compliance with the provisions of the Helsinki Final Act.[3] It is still a one–party dictatorship. The secret police still play a powerful role in repressing dissent. The rule of law is a stated goal, not a reality. The media remain state–dominated and controlled. And religion remains under state control.

We must also note that the ultimate success of those seeking reform in the Soviet Union is by no means assured. What is clear is that for the first time in many decades the Soviet leadership is no longer monolithic. There are clear differences between those who want the country to move further in the direction of political and economic freedom and those who believe that the new policies have gone much further than they should and that retrenchment is essential.

Among positive developments in 1988 in other parts of the world, we are pleased to see progress toward democracy in Pakistan, the Republic of Korea, and Taiwan. Also, the plebiscite held in Chile on the continuation of General Pinochet in the Presidency was conducted fairly and honestly. It resulted, as we know, in the rejection of the incumbent by the voters. We hope to see Chile's peaceful transition to democracy in the year ahead.

Unfortunately, there is also a negative side to this ledger and the question arises just where to begin in this brief survey. A review of developments in 1988 leads to the conclusion that interethnic disputes resulted in the greatest number of casualties and often involved the most egregious human rights violations.

It is in this context that attention should be drawn to the fate of many Kurds in Iraq. There is no doubt that significant groups of Iraqi Kurds have for years been in revolt against the Iraqi Government. But the nature of the Iraqi Government's response as the war with Iran was drawing to an end was truly shocking. In two attacks on towns populated by Kurds, many noncombatant civilians were killed. Estimates of the dead range up to 8,000. Truly frightened by these chemical warfare attacks, more than 50,000 Iraqi Kurds fled to Turkey within a matter of days late last August. More than 50,000 others have fled to Iran during the last 2 years.

Furthermore, in 1988, Iraq continued its program of forcible relocation of Kurds from their traditional rural regions to urban areas and, reportedly, also to detention camps. The agricultural economic base of this population was totally destroyed. More than 500 villages were completely leveled. The total number of people thus relocated is estimated at more than half a million.

Interethnic strife between the ruling minority of Tutsis and the majority population of Hutus also led to thousands of deaths in Burundi in 1988. Responding to killings of Tutsis initiated by the Hutus Burundi's Tutsi army killed and injured many thousands of completely innocent civilians. Here, too, about 50,000 people, all Hutus fled the country to nearby Rwanda where their ethnic group is in the majority. By year end, however, most of them had returned to Burundi. This is due in

large part to the laudable efforts undertaken by President Buyoya of Burundi, who is obviously trying his best to lay a foundation for true conciliation between the two ethnic groups.

Another African country in which ethnic differences have resulted in many deaths is Sudan. There the struggle has been between the Sudanese Government, largely oriented toward the Arab and Moslem north of the country and the Sudanese People's Liberation Army, the SPLA, made up largely of people from the Black, Christian, and Animist south. In the military efforts in which both sides have been engaged, they have often cut off food shipments to areas controlled by the other side, with the result that many civilians have starved to death. Estimates for 1988 exceed 150,000 such deaths.

In Somalia, government forces responding to an ethnic-based insurgent used artillery extensively in urban areas where insurgents had barricaded themselves, and bombed and strafed zones populated by civilians. There are no reliable estimates of the number who died, but about 400,000 Somalis fled the fighting, and many remain in refugee camps in Ethiopia, where conditions are harsh.

The strife resulting from the system of apartheid in South Africa continued in 1988, with a disturbing increase in attacks on civilian targets within the country. Attacks were suspected of emanating from various quarters, including South African security forces and rightwing sympathizers as well as the African National Congress. The government took steps to curtail peaceful opposition to apartheid: banning the activities of 32 anti-apartheid organizations, and placing everstricter limits on the press. Although the South African Government's agreement to the Angola/Namibia Peace Accord contributed to increased regional stability in 1988, domestically the government continued to avoid serious discussions with credible black leaders about a solution to South Africa's problems.

Interethnic strife also tragically continues to plague Sri Lanka, where the government has for the last 5 years been caught in the middle, as Tamil and Sinhalese extremists have committed serious acts of violence. As in so many other settings, once a government must use its security forces to suppress large-scale violence, these forces, too, no longer play by the rules.

Since 1987 an Indian Peacekeeping Force has been present in Sri Lanka, which has sustained casualties, and which, in turn, hag also been accused of human rights abuses. During 1988 more than 1,500 persons, including civilians, were killed in fighting involving Tamils in north and east Sri Lanka. Approximately 800 persons, many of them government officials, died in political killings perpetrated by Sinhalese extremists. Also, there continue to be reports of so–called disappearances following arrest by security forces. There is no reason for concern that many of the "disappeared" are, in fact, killed.

I shall now turn to two other situations which, as an analysis of the facts will demonstrate, do not belong in the category of the most serious human rights problems to which I have just referred. They have received attention, instead, because of the good relationship between the countries in question and the United States. The first situation is that in the Israeli–occupied territories.

As far as substance is concerned, this case differs from all others in that we are here not dealing with the actions of a government toward its own citizens, but with the action of a military government, applying both civilian and military law, in occupied territories. The underlying problem is not, as in other settings, the relationship between a government and its citizens, but the question of arriving at a peace settlement. Against that background, we have described in our Occupied Territories Report the areas of our concern. They focus on the measures taken by the Israeli Defense Forces to repress the wave of civil unrest which has swept the territories since December 1987. We recognize that the harsh measures taken by the military were provoked by such acts as the throwing of stones and Molotov cocktails, the burning of tires, and the erection of barricades. We believe, however, that the response thereto has been excessive rather than measured, causing many casualties and, during 1988, 366 cases of Palestinian deaths. We have also been concerned about such practices as punishment by deportation and the blowing up of the homes of persons accused of violent acts. Finally, we have noted that disciplinary

measures taken against Israeli soldiers for violating rule' of conduct are far too mild.

The second case in this grouping is that of El Salvador. In passing judgment on human rights violations in that country, it is important to distinguish between facts and disinformation.

Here the backdrop to the human rights problem is furnished by the Communist insurgency, which has continued for an entire decade. In the course of the years, the FMLN, which once was a major threat to the survival of the Salvadoran Government, has lost ground. However, the FMLN has resorted to assassinations of elected officials and urban terrorism to cause instability. There is no doubt that they have lost any appeal they might once have had for the bulk of the population. Their political allies are participating in the Presidential election, but are currently receiving the support of no more than 10 percent of the populace.

During 1988, the number of killings for political reasons averaged roughly 20 per month. Though every single death is a tragedy for the family affected, note should be taken that this figure does not reflect an increase over recent years. The corresponding monthly average was 22 in 1986 and 23 in 1987. It is down substantially from the monthly average of 444, 219, and 140 per month for the years 1981 to 1983. In addition, 34 civilian deaths occurred during combat between the two sides in 1988, and 42 persons died as a result of guerrilla mines. The political killings to which I have here referred are attributable to rogue operations of personnel of the security forces, on one hand, and carefully calculated measures authorized by the FMLN leadership, on the other hand. (The latter has recently focused on the murder of elected mayors.) I need to underline that we are convinced that the elected civilian Government of El Salvador is *not* responsible for extrajudicial killings. Nor do we believe that there is any evidence of culpability by the leadership of the military forces. The problem lies at lower levels in the military and the failure of the top leadership to clamp down hard on those guilty of human rights violations, particularly its failure to prosecute officers

This brings me to the related topic of the operation of the Salvadoran judiciary. I regret to say that criminal cases with political implications have simply been avoided in the Salvadoran justice system, whether the defendant is associated with the political right or with the political left. I should add that El Salvador is not the only country in this category. Strong independent court systems are even more ran throughout the world than are democratically-elected governments.

---

[2] Source: Review of the State Department's *Country Reports on Human Rights*, 1988: Hearings Before the Subcommittee on Human Rights and International Organizations of the Committee on Foreign Affairs, House of Representatives, One Hundred First Congress, First Session (Washington, 1990), pp. 20–24, 26–30. Chairman of the subcommittee, Gus Yatron, presided over the session. Schifter's testimony referred to Country Reports on Human Rights Practices for 1988: Report Submitted to the Committee on U.S Senate, and the Committee on Foreign Affairs, U.S. House of Representatives by the Department of State, One Hundred First Congress, First Session (Washington, 1989).

[3] For text of the Final Act of the Conference on Security Cooperation in Europe, signed at Helsinki, August 1, 1975, see *Department of State Bulletin*, September 1, 1975, pp. 329–350.

277.

[1990, p. 436]

261. "Iraq's Human Rights Remained Abysmal in 1989"

Report by the Department of State, Submitted to the Congress, January 31, 1990 (Extract)[1]

Iraq's human rights record remained abysmal in 1989. Effective opposition to government policy is stifled; the intelligence services engage in extensive surveillance and utilize extralegal means, including torture and summary execution, to deal with antiregime activity. The civil rights of Iraqi citizens continue to be sharply limited, and Iraqis do not have the right to change their government. The freedoms of speech and press and of assembly and association are virtually nonexistent. Other important human rights problems include continuing disappearances and arbitrary detentions, lack of fair trial, widespread

interference with privacy, excessive use of force against Kurdish civilians, and an almost total lack of worker rights. In addition to the repressive domestic controls that predate the war with Iran, tight wartime controls, including travel restrictions, remain in effect despite the August 1988 cease–fire with Iran.

An armed Kurdish insurgency continued in 1989, but at a reduced level. Although there were no allegations that the Government used chemical weapons against Kurdish civilians in 1989, as it did in 1988, in its efforts to crush the rebellion, it continued to violate the human rights of elements of the Kurdish population. The Government announced in June that in its campaign to suppress the rebellion it has pursued a program since 1987 of establishing a depopulated security zone along the full length of Iraq's borders with Iran and Turkey. Under this program, the Government has destroyed villages within a 30–kilometer–wide zone and relocated approximately 500,000 Kurdish and Assyrian inhabitants into more easily controlled and protected towns, cities, and newly constructed settlements in traditional Kurdish areas.

---

[1] Source: *Country Reports on Human Rights Practices for 1989: Report Submitted to the Committee on Foreign Affairs, House of Representatives, and the Committee on U.S. Senate, by the Department of State, February 1990* (Washington, 1990), pp. 1441–1412.

278.

[1990, p. 443]

266. Iraq and Patterns of Global Terrorism

Report by the Department of State, Submitted to the Congress, April 30, 1990 (Extract)[13]

Iraq was removed from the U.S. list of state sponsors of terrorism in 1982. Since the expulsion of the ANO in 1983, Iraq has continued working to improve its international image. Iraq did not sponsor any known acts of international terrorism in 1989. Iraq has continued, however, to provide safe haven to some Palestinian groups, including the Iraqi–created Arab Liberation Front and Abu Abbas' Palestine Liberation Front, responsible for the 1985 *Achille Lauro* hijacking and killing of an American passenger. In addition, press reports indicate that Abu Ibrahim, the former leader of the now defunct 15 May terrorist organization, has returned to Iraq. Abu Ibrahim is known for the skill with which he built highly sophisticated and lethal suitcase bombs. Iraq continues to support anti–Iranian dissident groups including Mujaheddin–e–Khalq (MEK).

There have been questions in the Turkish media about possible Iraqi support for the terrorist Kurdish Worker's Party (PKK). The Iraqi Government maintains it works effectively with the Turkish Government at the local level on the border as well as on a government–to–government basis to significantly reduce PKK violence. A major failure was the December 1989 PKK massacre of Turkish villagers near the Iraqi border.

Several terrorist attacks including bombings, apparently targeting foreigners, have taken place in Baghdad beginning in July. The perpetrators are unknown although one attack, a bombing at the New British Club which injured 20 people, was claimed by the United Organization of the Halabjah Martyrs, a suspected radical Kurdish group. An afternoon bombing in mid–December on a main business street killed and wounded many passers-by.

The Iraqi authorities are working with the FAA to improve security at Baghdad's airport.

----

[13] Sources: U.S. Department of State, *Patterns of Global Terrorism: 1989* (Washington, 1990), pp. 10–11. The report was submitted in compliance with Section 140 of the Foreign Relations Authorization Act, Fiscal Years 1988/89 (P.L. 100–204), which requires the Department of State to provide Congress a full and complete annual report on terrorism for those countries and groups meeting the criteria of Section (a) (1) and (2) of the Act.

279.

[1990, pp. 444–46]

268. Human Rights, as Such, Are Not Recognized in Iraq

Prepared Statement by the Principal Deputy Assistant Secretary of State for Human Rights

and Humanitarian Affairs (Gilder), June 15, 1990[16]

Human rights, as such, are not recognized in Iraq. As our report[17] details, the ordinary Iraqi citizen knows no personal security against government violence. Disappearances, followed by secret executions, appear to be common. In some cases, a family only learns that one of its loved ones has been executed when the security services return the body and, in line with the Iraqi regime's view of justice require the family to pay a fine.

The penalty for expressing opinions deemed objectionable by the regime is swift and brutal. We believe that over the past 10 years many thousands to tens of thousands— and I will speak to the inexactitude of our figures in a moment—have been arrested by the secret police on suspicion of opposition to the government. While the judicial system seems to function fairly well by regional standards for people accused of crimes with no political implications, there is not even the charade of due process for those charged with security-related offenses. I should add that security related offenses are broadly defined to include such routine criminal matters as currency violations.

Torture is routine, for security offenses and ordinary crimes alike, and confessions extracted under torture are admissible in court. Treatment is reported to be the worst immediately following arrest and during the period of interrogation and investigation, which can last for months.

Compiling accurate information on human rights in Iraq is made extremely difficult by the highly secretive and repressive nature of the regime. Diplomatic travel is severely restricted, and most Iraqis are, quite understandably, fearful of speaking their minds to foreigners—or to anyone else for that matter.

The Iraqi regime is authoritarian in the extreme. There are some exceptions. The practice of religion is largely free. There has been some attempt to relax the worst aspects of the statist command economy. In general, however, the regime is ruthless in its efforts to maintain absolute control over the population.

Control is exercised in part through the Ba'ath Party apparatus. The party is a secretive one. While it has a large grassroots membership, decision–making is concentrated among the few at the top. The lower ranks serve as informers on the political reliability of their neighbors. There are many other intelligence networks through which the government monitors the citizenry, as well as keeps a careful eye on the military and the Ba'ath Party itself. I have already described the punishment for stepping out of line, or being deemed unreliable by the government Periodically, over the last 2 years, the regime announced that it had uncovered incipient coup plots within the military. Hundreds were arrested. We do not know how many were executed.

The Ba'ath Party is a Pan–Arabist party. As such, it has integrated Arabs of various religions and sects quite well, but has had trouble finding an ideological niche for Iraq's non–Arab citizens, most of whom are Kurds. The disaffection of elements of the Kurdish population did not begin with the Ba'ath Party rule, but the current government's policy has resulted in enormous human rights abuses.

With respect to the Kurds, the Iraqi Government has followed a policy of carrot and stick. It has sought to gain the support of as many Kurdish tribes as it can, using the carrot of ethnic cultural freedom. There is a Kurdish Autonomous Region with its own institutions, providing patronage for Kurdish tribes that support the regime. Kurdish language and culture e fostered, and education in Kurdish is available through the secondary level.

But the stick of Iraqi policy has been brutal During the Gulf war, in which Iran ok advantage of the dissatisfaction among. Kurdish tribes, the Iraqi Government began a campaign of destroying suspect villages, relocating the populations to closely–watched cities and new settlements. After the cease–fire with Iran, Iraq's campaign to dislodge rebels from the areas they controlled was accompanied by the shocking, indiscriminate use of chemical weapons—killing thousands of men, woman, and children. After Iraqi troops regained these areas, destruction of villages and towns, and population transfers were speeded up, until finally some 500,000—about one–seventh of the entire Kurdish population of Iraq—were displaced. Although we understand Iraqi authorities are now allowing displaced villagers to commute to their lands to cultivate the fields and orchards, we remain extremely concerned about the overall effects of this massive displacement.

Let me stress that in detailing our concerns over the treatment of the Iraqi Kurds we are not taking a position on the roots or aims of Kurdish rebellions, but rather on abuses of internationally recognized human rights. The U.S. Government supports the territorial integrity of the states in this region, and holds that Kurds should seek to fulfill their aspirations peacefully within this context.

During the last 2 years the Government of Iraq has announced its intention to institute reforms. Wartime travel restrictions have been relaxed, permitting large numbers of Iraqis to travel abroad for the first time in 8 years. Elections for the National Assembly and the Kurdistan Autonomy Council were held in April and September 1989, respectively. Independents were allowed to run, and some Ba'ath Party members were defeated. However, all candidates were carefully screened for support for the Government, and in any event neither body has any real power or legislative function as we would understand the terms.

A new constitution has been drafted and was submitted to the President last January. According to a recent Iraqi press report, the drain has undergone the finishing touches by a panel of six members of the Iraqi leadership, and it will soon be submitted to the National Assembly and to a popular referendum.

It is, however, one thing to adopt a con constitution another thing to respect it. The current Iraqi constitution includes clauses on respect for human rights, a ban on torture, and the independence of the judiciary—none of which has any apparent effect in practice. If Iraq wishes to end international criticism of its human rights record, it must take steps that are real, not cosmetic. It must end the climate of fear imposed by its security apparatus and hold meaningful elections that are more than a mere charade. It must institute a truly independent judiciary and allow for a truly free press that does more than simply parrot the government line.

Most important of all, it must treat its citizens with dignity and give them a chance to live secure in their own homes and persons—free from the omnipresent I threat of government repression and violence.

---

[16] Source: *United States Policy Toward Iraq: Human Rights, Weapons Proliferation, and International Law*, pp. 21–22.

[17] Reference is to *Country Reports on Human Rights Practices for 1989*. See Document 261.

280.

[1991, pp. 157–61]

71. Reauthorization of the Refugee Act of 1980

Statement by the Ambassador at Large and U.S. Coordinator for Refugee Affairs (Lafontant–Mankarious), July 11, 1991[4]

Mr. Chairman, on behalf of the administration, I am pleased to have this opportunity to appear before the subcommittee in order to discuss with you reauthorization of the Refugee Act of 1980 and recent developments in the domestic resettlement program which I believe are important. With me this morning are ambassador Princeton Lyman, Director of the State Department's Bureau for Refugee Programs, and also testifying is Chris Gersten, Director of the Office of Refugee Resettlement within the Department of Health and Human Services.

I would like to touch upon several topics concerning our domestic and international refugee programs. Specifically, I would like to:

–discuss the reauthorization of the Refugee Act of 1980 in its current form: and

–report to you on the role and activities of the U.S. Coordinator with regard to relations between interagency, intergovernmental, and private voluntary groups, as well as my activities abroad.

Let me say from the outset, that this administration has viewed the Refugee Act of 1980 as a flexible instrument of policy which has served our national interest well. At the time of enactment, the 1980 Refugee Act attracted considerable attention at home and abroad. Adopted after years of study and in light of the country's post–Vietnam experience in coping with a sustained requirement for large scale refugee resettlement programs, many observers viewed the new law as a watershed in U.S. immigration practice.

The Act declared that the policy of the United States was to encourage all nations to provide assistance and resettlement opportunities to refugees to the fullest extent possible. The objectives of the Act were to provide a permanent and systematic procedure for the admission to this country of refugees of special humanitarian concern, and to provide comprehensive and uniform provisions for the effective resettlement and absorption of those refugees who are admitted.

Throughout the last decade, the 1980 law has worked well in enabling the United States resettlement program to respond to dramatic changes in the world refugee situation. The Act's flexibility has allowed for new ideas and necessary improvements in our domestic refugee program to be implemented through regulatory and administrative means. What the Act has shown in practical terms is that resettlement happens at the community level and that it is impossible to legislate one pattern across the board which would adequately address the variety of needs at the State and local level.

The Act's flexibility has also resulted in ongoing discussions at all levels of government and among many interested private groups about the need for improvements to our domestic resettlement policy as the need arises. As the administration has gained experience in refugee activities at home and abroad, it has become our practice to introduce changes in operating practices from time to time in order to implement the Act's humanitarian and legal principles. I would like to note that these changes have been made after consultations with members of this subcommittee, the full committee, other Senators as well as with Members of the House. I would also like to point out, that in accordance with Title 111, Section 301 (c)(l) of the Act, my office has consulted regularly with States, localities, private nonprofit voluntary agencies, and mutual assistance associations responsible for administering our domestic refugee programs.

In summary, Mr. Chairman, it is the administration's view that the flexible nature of the Refugee Act of 1980 has worked well over the past decade. With regulatory and administrative changes being taken as appropriate, the administration does not recommend changing the 1980 Act. The administration instead recommends to the subcommittee that it reauthorize the Refugee Act of 1980 in its current form.

I wish to use this opportunity to brief the subcommittee on some of the activities and initiatives taken during my tenure as U.S. Coordinator for Refugee Affairs.

Title III, Section 301(b) of the 1980 Refugee Act, describes the policy role and responsibilities of the U.S. Coordinator for Refugee Affairs. In sum, the Act calls on the Coordinator to coordinate all U.S. domestic and international refugee admission and resettlement programs in a manner that assures that policy objectives are met. The Act further calls on the Coordinator to develop an effective and responsive liaison between the Federal Government and voluntary organizations, Governors and mayors, and others involved in refugee relief and resettlement work. My tenure has been guided by these responsibilities delineated in the Act.

In carrying out the duties of the coordinator, I have identified six interested parties which are of primary concern to my office and with whom I interact regularly. These functional groups include:

—various Federal agencies;
—State and local government agencies;
—the Congress;
—voluntary and nonprofit organizations;
—the general public; and
—foreign governments and international organizations.

At the federal level, I chair an interagency Policy Coordinating Committee on refugee issues. This committee meets to discuss and make decisions on a wide variety of refugee policy issues including preparations for the administration's proposal to the Congress for refugee admissions to the U.S. Committee meetings are attended by representatives from the Departments of State, Defense, Justice, Health and Human Services, the Immigration and Naturalization Service, the Office of Management and Budget, the National Security Council and other agencies.

I have also made it my practice to meet weekly with representatives from bureaus and offices within the Departments of State, Justice, Health and Human Services, the Office of Management and Budget, and the National Security Council in order to more effectively coordinate major policy initiatives that require interagency attention. These weekly meetings allow us to avoid problems in policy implementation throughout the federal bureaucracy that may arise.

In addition to federal coordination, my office has held periodic meetings for State and local leaders where the most recent federal policy changes and problems are discussed at length. These meetings bring together the federal agencies with state and local representatives demonstrating the intergovernmental scope of our refugee admissions and resettlement program. I have found these periodic gatherings a useful channel that sensitizes all levels of government to the special needs of our country's most recent arrivals, from the time of their arrival on our shores to the time of self sufficiency.

I am happy to report that I have consulted regularly with members of this sub committee as well as with other committees in the Senate and the House on major policy issues. Our most frequent contact occurs during the period of our annual consultations on refugee admissions to the United States. We have maintained good relations during my tenure and I have always found the Hill supportive of the administration's commitment to doing its fair share to help those in need of safe haven.

With regard to our domestic resettlement groups, I have made it my practice to be accessible to representatives of many resettlement groups, leaders of national and local voluntary agencies, refugee leaders and others concerned with our policies and programs. There have been numerous meetings with individuals and groups of various sizes which have helped me grasp the interests of several very different sectors of our domestic program. These meetings in Washington and throughout the country have also enabled me to convey to the various groups administration policy and initiatives.

As an expression of the U.S. Government's commitment to the world refugee situation, the Congress designated October 30, 1990, as Refugee Day and requested the President to issue a proclamation in observance of this day. The President did so in a

White House ceremony making official the first Refugee Day. I was particularly interested in initiating the Refugee Day because it provided an opportunity to not only bring together all the levels of government and all private and nonprofit groups, but to reach out to the general public. We have recently published the proceedings of this day–long program and my office is currently working on preparations for the second Refugee Day.

The coordination within the Federal Government coupled with our outreach to intergovernmental and private sector groups has been a particularly worthwhile and vital process in ensuring that our commitment to assist refugees remains strong at all levels of government. I take great satisfaction in the spirit of cooperation that now exists between the governmental and non–governmental sectors in providing relief to refugees.

This administration is committed to strengthening and implementing an effective U.S. refugee admissions and resettlement policy consistent with our domestic and international concerns. Receiving input from all concerned groups has been a high priority in fulfilling my mandate.

Internationally, I have concerned myself with having our allies and other foreign governments commit greater resources to help the world's refugee population. I have traveled to many of the world's refugee camps to see first–hand the plight of the needy. In my travels, I have met with leaders of foreign governments and international organizations reporting on my findings and the U.S. Government's views on refugee problems. In so doing, I believe good relations with foreign governments on refugee issues have been established and maintained. These regular contacts coupled with our commitment to international organizations such as the U.N. High Commissioner for Refugees, the United Nations Relief and Works Agency (UNRWA), the International Committee of the Red Cross among others, have enabled us to continue to lead internationally in dealing with world refugee situation.

During May of this year I had the opportunity to travel abroad to observe the refugee situation in several key areas of policy interest to the United States. My travels took me to

Moscow, Israel, Egypt, and to the Iraqi–Turkish border.

A longstanding issue in our bilateral relations with the Soviet Union has been the Soviet Government's restriction on its citizens' ability to emigrate. To illustrate our longrun commitment to this issue, I recall during my tenure as U.S. Representative to the United Nations in 1972,1 advocated to the Soviets, on behalf of the United States that they open the door to those citizens who sought to leave the Soviet Union. In my recent trip to Moscow, now almost 20 years since my U.N. tour, I met with Soviet officials again pressing the emigration issue. The Soviets indicated to me and other U.S. interlocutors that they would need our help and advice on establishing the institutions and mechanisms to deal with the problems of Soviet migration and internal refugees. I was cautiously optimistic when I learned upon my return from Moscow this May that the Supreme Soviet indeed passed a new emigration law which now brings Soviet emigration policies more into line with internationally accepted standards.

During my visit to Israel, I had an opportunity to observe Israeli resettlement programs for newly arrived Jews from Ethiopia, the Soviet Union and elsewhere. I also met with UNRWA to discuss the plight of Palestinian refugees.

While in Egypt, an important area of focus in my discussions was the large number of African refugees and displaced persons within Egypt. I stressed to of officials there the importance the United States places on providing durable solutions for the future of these refugees.

One of the other major focus points of my trip abroad was to see first–hand the plight of nearly half a million Iraqi civilians, mostly Kurds, who fled to the Iraqi–Turkish border. I was very much impressed with the outstanding humanitarian approach of the soldiers, airmen, and seamen of Operation Provide Comfort and the rapport they were able to achieve with the refugees. Thanks to U.S. leadership of international relief efforts and the cooperation of the Government of Turkey, countless lives were saved and hundreds of thousands of Kurds were returned to their homes. Upon my return from the Middle East, I followed up within the administration and with representatives from various international organizations on many of the issues and problems that were observed on the ground.

Another priority during my tenure has been our Private Sector Initiative (PSI). The PSI is a refugee resettlement program funded entirely with private funds. It was founded on the belief that, in a time of significant constraints on all public budgets and expenditures, a privately funded program would enable some refugees to enter and be resettled in the United States who might not otherwise be admitted because of limitations on the funded programs. In the last several years we have established several memoranda of understanding with various groups in accordance with the Presidential determination authorizing this program. By September 30 of this year, we hope to have admitted several thousand refugees under this program, which includes Cubans and Ethiopians.

Mr. Chairman, as I noted in my confirmation hearings in June 1989, I am pleased that the Of Office of the Coordinator is separate from the agencies it coordinates. My office is a small, action–oriented entity which undertakes to minimize bureaucracy in determining where problems lie and in eliminating them. It remains my belief that the coordinator is in the best position to represent the interests of refugees—to encourage generosity on behalf of all who are moved by their plight and to advance on behalf of refugees the most efficient use of resources in a period of increasing constraints. I have always felt that bureaucratic obstacles should not add to the discomfort and trauma that most refugees endure.

The Office of the Coordinator is uniquely capable, by virtue of its independence from the departments and agencies it coordinates to accomplish the responsibilities delineated in the Refugee Act of 1980. As importantly, the Act permits the coordinator to serve in the role which prompted me to take this position and which continues to motivate me, to serve as the voice of the voiceless—to appeal to the conscience of individuals at the highest levels of government and throughout the community of those concerned for the benefit of refugees.

---

⁴ Source: Department of State Files. Ambassador Lafontant–Mankarious testified before the Subcommittee on Immigration and Refugee Affairs of the Senate Committee on the Judiciary.

281.

[1991, pp. 512–13]

280. Repression of Iraqi Civilians

Resolution 688 (1991), Adopted by the U.N. Security Council, April 5, 1991[61]

The Security Council,

Mindful of its duties and its responsibilities under the Charter of the United Nations for the maintenance of international peace an. security,

Recalling Article 2, paragraph 7, of the Charter of the United Nations,

Gravely concerned by the repression of the Iraqi civilian population in many parts of Iraq, including most recently in Kurdish populated areas which led to a massive flow of refugees towards and across international frontiers and to cross border incursions which threaten international peace and security in the region,

Deeply disturbed by the magnitude of the human suffering involved,

Taking note of the letters sent by the representatives of Turkey and France to the United Nations dated 2 April 1991 and 4 April 1991, respectively (S/22435 and S/22442),

Taking note also of the letters sent by the Permanent Representative of the Islamic Republic of Iran to the United Nations dated 3 and 4 April 1991, respectively (S/22436 and S/22447),

Reaffirming the commitment of all Member States to the sovereignty, territorial integrity and political independence of Iraq and of all States in the area,

Bearing in mind the Secretary–General's report of 20 March 1991 (S/22366),

1. Condemns the repression of the Iraqi civilian population in many parts of Iraq, including most recently in Kurdish populated areas, the consequences of which threaten international peace and security in the region;

2. Demands that Iraq, as a contribution to removing the threat to international peace and security in the region, immediately end this repression and expresses the hope in the same context that an open dialogue will take place to ensure that the human and political rights of all Iraqi citizens are respected;

3. Insists that Iraq allow immediate access by international humanitarian organizations to all those in need of assistance in all parts of Iraq and to make available all necessary facilities for their operations;

4. Requests the Secretary–General to pursue his humanitarian efforts in Iraq and to report forthwith, if appropriate on the basis of a further mission to the region, on the plight of the Iraqi civilian population, and in particular the Kurdish population, suffering from the repression in all its forms inflicted by the Iraqi authorities;

5. Requests further the Secretary General to use all the resources at his disposal, including those of the relevant United Nations agencies, to address urgently the critical needs of the refugees and displaced Iraqi population;

6. Appeals to all Member States and to all humanitarian organizations to contribute to these humanitarian relief efforts;

7. Demands that Iraq cooperate with the Secretary–General to these ends;

8. Decides to remain seized of the matter.

---

[61] Source: U.N. Security Council Resolution 688 (1991). The resolution was adopted by a vote of 10 to 3 (Cuba, Yemen, and Zimbabwe), with 2 abstentions (China and India).

U.S. DEPARTMENT OF STATE DISPATCH

282.

Bush, George. "US Humanitarian Assistance to Iraqi Refugees." *US Department of State Dispatch* 2 (April 8 1991): 233.

The human tragedy unfolding in and around Iraq demands immediate action on a massive scale. At stake are not only the lives of hundreds of thousands of innocent men, women, and children, but the peace and security of the Gulf.

Since the beginning of the Gulf war on August 2, the United States has contributed more than $35 million for refugees and displaced persons in the region. Many other countries have also contributed. It is clear, however, that the current tragedy requires a far greater effort. As a result, I have directed that a major new effort be undertaken to assist Iraqi refugees.

Beginning this Sunday [April 7], US Air Force transport planes will fly over northern Iraq and drop supplies of food, blankets, clothing, tents, and other relief-related items for refugees and other Iraqi civilians suffering as a result of the situation there.

I want to emphasize that this effort is prompted only by humanitarian concerns. We expect the government of Iraq to permit this effort to be carried out without any interference.

I want to add that what we are planning to do is intended as a step-up in immediate aid, such as is also being provided by the British, the French, and other coalition partners. We will be consulting with the UN on how it can best provide for the many refugees in and around Iraq on a long-term basis, as necessary. We will continue in this and in other efforts designed to alleviate the plight of the many innocent Iraqis whose lives have been endangered by the brutal and inhumane actions of the Iraqi government.

I also want to add that this urgent air-drop is but one of several steps the United States is taking to deal with this terrible situation. I will shortly be signing an order that will authorize up to $10 million from the emergency refugee and migration assistance fund. These funds will help meet the needs of the burgeoning refugee population in the region. Our military forces in southern Iraq will continue to assist refugees and displaced persons. We are also providing considerable economic and food assistance to the government of Turkey to help it sustain the many refugees who have taken refuge there. We are prepared, as well, to deploy a US military medical unit to the border area in southern Turkey to meet emergency needs.

The United States is also concerned about the welfare of those Iraqi refugees now fleeing to Iran. We will be communicating through our established channel—to the government of Iran our willingness to encourage and contribute to international organizations carrying out relief efforts aiding these individuals.

In an effort to help innocent people and especially the children of Iraq, we will be donating $869,000 to UNICEF for child immunizations in Iraq. We will also be providing a further $131,000 and 1,000 tons of food to the International Committee of the Red Cross (ICRC). In all cases, funds and goods provided to international organizations will be distributed by the organizations themselves to civilians in Iraq.

Finally, I have asked Secretary Baker to travel to Turkey, en route to the Middle East, to meet with President Ozal and visit the border area to assess the refugee situation and report back to me.

283.

Anonymous. "UN Security Council Resolution 688 on Repression of Iraqi Civilians." *US Department of State Dispatch* 2, no. 14 (April 8, 1991): 233-234.

Resolution 688 (April 5, 1991)
The Security Council,
Mindful of its duties and its responsibilities under the Charter of the United Nations for the maintenance of international peace and security,

Recalling Article 2, paragraph 7, of the Charter of the United Nations,

Gravely concerned by the repression of the Iraqi civilian population in many parts of Iraq, including most recently in Kurdish populated areas which led to a massive flow of refugees towards and across international frontiers and to cross border incursions, which threaten international peace and security in the region,

Deeply disturbed by the magnitude of the human suffering involved,

Taking note of the letters sent by the representatives of Turkey and France to the United Nations dated 2 April 1991 and 4 April 1991, respectively (S/22435 and S/22442),

Taking note also of the letters sent by the Permanent Representative of the Islamic Republic of Iran to the United Nations dated 3 and 4 April 1991, respectively (S/22436 and S/22447),

Reaffirming the commitment of all Member States to the sovereignty, territorial integrity and political independence of Iraq and of all States in the area,

Bearing in mind the Secretary-General's report of 20 March 1991 (S/22366),

1. Condemns the repression of the Iraqi civilian population in many parts of Iraq, including most recently in Kurdish populated areas, the consequences of which threaten international peace and security in the region;

2. Demands that Iraq, as a contribution to removing the threat to international peace and security in the region, immediately end this repression and expresses the hope in the same context that an open dialogue will take place to ensure that the human and political rights of all Iraqi citizens are respected;

3. Insists that Iraq allow immediate access by international humanitarian organizations to all those in need of assistance in all parts of Iraq and to make available all necessary facilities for their operations;

4. Requests the Secretary-General to pursue his humanitarian efforts in Iraq and to report forthwith, if appropriate on the basis of a further mission to the region, on the plight of the Iraqi civilian population, and in particular the Kurdish population, suffering from the repression in all its forms inflicted by the Iraqi authorities;

5. Requests further the Secretary-General to use all the resources at his disposal, including those of the relevant United Nations agencies, to address urgently the critical needs of the refugees and displaced Iraqi population;

6. Appeals to all Member States and to all humanitarian organizations to contribute to these humanitarian relief efforts;

7. Demands that Iraq cooperate with the Secretary-General to these ends;

8. Decides to remain seized of the matter.
VOTE: 10 for, 3 against (Cuba, Yemen, Zimbabwe), 2 abstentions (China, India).

284.

Baker, James A. and Ahmet Alptemocin. "Iraqi Refugees: The Need for International Assistance." *US Department of State Dispatch* 2 (April 15 1991): 271.

April 7, 1991
Remarks by Secretary Baker upon arrival at Esenboga International Airport, Ankara, Turkey.

First, let me say that I'm pleased to be back in Ankara. This is my fifth visit since Iraq invaded Kuwait. I think it highlights the significance of the relationship between the United States of America and Turkey.

But once again, the world and the Iraqi people are being subjected to the utter brutality of Saddam Hussein's regime. Once again, the world finds it necessary to respond to Saddam's savage and indecent use of force. Only this time, the victim is not a neighboring country. This time, Iraq's forces are killing, threatening, and committing crimes against the Iraqi people. [UN] Security Council Resolution 688 condemns the repression of the Kurds and other Iraqi citizens, it demands that Iraq end the repression, and it insists that Iraq allow immediate access by international organizations to all of those in need of assistance throughout the country.

We are not prepared to go down the slippery slope of being sucked into a civil war. We cannot police what goes on inside Iraq, and we cannot be the arbiters of who shall govern Iraq. As the President has made repeatedly clear, including, I think, at our press conference yesterday, our objective was the liberation of Kuwait. It never extended to the re-making of Iraq. We repeatedly said that could only be done by the Iraqi people.

However, we cannot be indifferent to atrocities and human suffering in Iraq, and we haven't been. Working with the international community, we will make certain that humanitarian assistance in both northern and southern Iraq gets to those who most need it. And we will not tolerate any interference with this humanitarian relief effort . . .

Q. What will be the US reaction in case there's military intervention - a Turkish military intervention - into Iraq? What will be the US reaction?

Secretary Baker. Well, that's a decision, of course, for the Turkish government to take. I've just given you the position of the US government with respect to this. We are commencing, as you know, a major airlift of humanitarian supplies to the people who are being repressed. And we will not brook any interference with that humanitarian effort.

April 8, 1991
Remarks by Secretary Baker and Turkish Foreign Minister Ahmet Alptemocin, Diyarbakir, Turkey.

Foreign Minister Alptemocin. We've just come back from the border area where we observed with Secretary Baker the tragedy inflicted by Iraq on its own people. What we are seeing is inhuman and totally unacceptable. It is a challenge that defies the international community to stand together and act effectively. [inaudible] That is what Turkey and the United States are doing.

We have decided to issue a joint statement with Secretary Baker. It reflects our impressions of the situation which continues to worsen. It reflects our position and our resolve to do everything in our power to contribute first, to the alleviation and, then, to the solution of this massive human tragedy. It also confirms our appeal to the world to join in efforts to ensure the safe return of the Iraqi people amassed on our borders to their hometowns without fearing further repression by Saddam Hussein. The civilized world is duty bound not to permit the Iraqi regime to get away with what it is doing to its own civilian people and the threat that it constitutes for peace, security, and stability in the region. Thank you.

Secretary Baker. As the Minister has just indicated, we have a written statement that will be distributed. But before that's done, let me simply say that today we have witnessed the suffering and despair of the Iraqi people. We have seen examples of cruelty and human anguish that really do defy description. Women and children up there are battling hunger, thirst, and the elements to escape repression in Iraq. And as you heard up there - those of you who were in the briefing - may have heard, many of those innocents [are] losing this battle. People are suffering, and, tragically, some of them are dying. Only the generosity and the humanity of the American and Turkish people, as well as the international community, stands between these souls and complete despair and complete tragedy.

President Bush, of course, has asked that I come here and see this human drama and report back first hand on the situation. I will be doing that as soon as I can reach him by telephone.

Our relief efforts, including air drops of supplies, have begun, but they alone are not going to be enough. We cannot do this alone. We cannot do this alone with the Turkish government. Together, we simply cannot cope with this mounting human tragedy.

So the international community, as the Minister has indicated, has to respond. And it must respond quickly and effectively. Basic supplies are going to have to arrive soon to sustain these people. And the organization and distribution that are required are going to have to be provided both in Turkey as well as in northern Iraq. Most importantly, as the Minister indicated, hope of returning home has got to be given to these people. And that means freedom from threat by the Iraqi government and safety from further repression.

April 8, 1991
Joint statement by Secretary Baker and Turkish Foreign Minister Ahmet Alptemocin, Diyarbakir, Turkey

We have just returned from a tour of area where we witnessed the great tragedy suffered by the Iraqi people, most of whom are women and children who have been forcibly uprooted from their homes and villages. The dimension of this tragedy require the urgent and generous compassion and contribution of the international community. It is with the aim of bringing this situation to the attention of the world that we decided to issue the present statement.

Once again, the brutality and folly of the Iraqi regime has created yet another gruesome tragedy: hundreds of thousands of refugees and many deaths among Iraqi citizens who sought only their democratic rights. The Saddam regime has not contented itself with more repression but has acted with excessive force, driving its own citizens out of their own land.

And, once again, the world is reacting swiftly and with determination to counter Saddam's indecent use of force. On Friday [April 5, 1991], the [UN] Security Council, acting at Turkish and French request, condemned Iraq in Resolution 688 and called for a large program of international relief. The international community has once again closed ranks in insisting that Iraq end its repression and allow immediate and unimpeded access by international organizations to all in need of aid throughout the country.

Turkey and the United States will cooperate closely to give effect to this resolution. We do not propose armed intervention in a civil war, but we will not tolerate any interference of our humanitarian relief efforts.

From the initial stages of the arrival in areas on both sides of the Turkish-Iraqi border of the cold and hungry men, women, and children, Turkey has offered generous humanitarian aid in the form of food, shelter, and medical care within the limits of her capabilities. These capabilities obviously cannot match the vast dimensions and requirements of the situation. To raise the large sums that are needed, the United States is working closely with the EC [European Community] and others and with the UN Secretary General. So far - in the last few days - $67 million has been pledged to support relief efforts in Turkey and elsewhere.

In addition, working with Turkey, the United States is now moving quickly to provide tents, food, medicine, and other supplies by a dramatic air-drop to groups inside Iraq. Turkey will also cooperate with a relief effort by international organizations to supply food along and across its borders into Iraq - where the greatest and most vulnerable population of displaced persons is located.

Turkey and the United States agree that the goal of relief efforts should be to enable these people to return to their homes. The plight of these refugees creates - as the Security Council Resolution says - a threat to international peace and security and has thus become another important issue in the full implementation of the cease-fire resolution.

285.

Bush, George. "US Expands Kurdish Relief Efforts." *US Department of State Dispatch* 2, no. 16 (April 22, 1991): 273.

Eleven days ago, on April 5th, I announced that the United States would initiate what soon became the largest US relief effort mounted in modern military history. Such an undertaking was made necessary by the terrible human tragedy unfolding in and around Iraq as a result of Saddam Hussein's brutal treatment of Iraqi citizens.

Within 48 hours, our operation was providing scores of tons of food, water, coats, tents, blankets, and medicines to the Iraqi Kurds in northern Iraq and southern Turkey. The scale of this effort is truly unprecedented. Yet the fact remains that the scale of the problem is even greater. Hundreds of thousands of Iraqi Kurds are in difficult-to-reach mountain areas in southern Turkey and along the Turkish-Iraq border.

The government of Turkey, along with US, British, and French military units, and numerous international organizations, have launched a massive relief operation. But despite these efforts, hunger, malnutrition, disease, and exposure are taking their grim toll. No one can see the pictures or hear the accounts of this human suffering—men, women, and most painfully of all, innocent children—and not be deeply moved.

It is for this reason that this afternoon, following consultations with Prime Minister Major [UK], President Mitterrand [France], President Ozal of Turkey, Chancellor Kohl [Germany] this morning, UN Secretary General Perez de Cuellar, I'm announcing an expanded—a greatly expanded—and more ambitious relief effort. The approach is quite simple: if we cannot get adequate food, medicine, clothing, and shelter to the Kurds living in the mountains along the Turkish-Iraq border, we must encourage the Kurds to move to areas in northern Iraq where the geography facilitates rather than frustrates such a large-scale relief effort.

Consistent with UN Secretary Council Resolution 668 and working closely with the UN and other international relief organizations and our European partners, I have directed the US military to begin immediately to establish several encampments in northern Iraq where relief supplies for these refugees will be made available in large quantities and distributed in an orderly way.

I can well appreciate that many Kurds have good reason to fear for their safety if they return to Iraq. And let me reassure them that adequate security will be provided at these temporary sites by US, British, and French air and ground forces, again consistent with UN Security Council Resolution 688. We are hopeful that others in the coalition will join this effort.

I want to underscore that all that we are doing is motivated by humanitarian concerns. We continue to expect the government of Iraq not to interfere in any way with this latest relief effort. The prohibition against Iraqi fixed- or rotary-wing aircraft flying north of the 36th parallel thus remains in effect.

And I want to stress that this new effort, despite its scale and scope, is not intended as a permanent solution to the plight of the Iraqi Kurds. To the contrary, it is an interim measure designed to meet an immediate, penetrating humanitarian need. Our long-term objective remains the same—for Iraqi Kurds and, indeed, for all Iraqi refugees, wherever they are, to return home and to live in peace, free from repression, free to live their lives.

I also want to point out that we're acutely concerned about the problem of the Iraqi refugees now along the Iran-Iraq border and in Iran. I commend the members of the European Community for their efforts to alleviate hardship in this area. We, ourselves, have offered to contribute to international efforts designed to meet this humanitarian challenge.

As I stated earlier, the relief effort being announced here today constitutes an undertaking different in scale and approach. What is not different is basic policy. All along, I have said that the United States is not going to intervene militarily in Iraq's internal affairs and risk being drawn into a Vietnam-style quagmire. This remains the case. Nor will we become an occupying power with US troops patrolling the streets of Baghdad.

We intend to turn over the administration of and security for these sites as soon as possible to the UN, just as we are fulfilling our commitment to withdraw our troops and hand over responsibility to UN forces along Iraq's southern border, the border with Kuwait.

But we must do everything in our power to save innocent life. This is the American tradition, and we will continue to live up to that tradition.

286.

Lyman, Princeton N. "Crisis of Refugees and Displaced Persons of Iraq." *US Department of State Dispatch* 2, no. 16 (April 22, 1991): 274-278.

[A statement by Bureau of Refugee Programs Director Princeton N. Lyman.]

I appreciate this opportunity to address the crisis of the refugees and displaced people of Iraq. As you know, I have just returned from a trip to the region and to Geneva regarding this important and urgent issue.

Everyone here has likely seen the TV footage of the people affected and the horrors of it. From cities and villages; from all across the north and parts of the south of Iraq; Kurds, Assyrians, Chaldeans, Shias, and Sunnis; 1 ½ million people have had to flee their homes. Many, too many by even one, have died in mountain passes shorn of support or before even making it there.

Background to the Crisis

I would note that movements of refugees and displaced persons during the Persian Gulf crisis can be divided into three stages:

- From August 2, the date of the invasion, through mid-January 1991;
- The armed conflict, January 17 February 28; and
- Post-war.

From August to mid-October, more than 1 million people of numerous nationalities fled Iraq and Kuwait into the neighboring states of Jordan, Syria, Turkey, Iran, and Saudi Arabia. Except for the Kuwaitis, who fled to Saudi Arabia and other Gulf states, these people were overwhelmingly third-country nationals. With the aid of the international community or their own governments, it was possible to repatriate these expatriate workers in Iraq and Kuwait out of the region and to their home countries.

The international community organized rapidly to provide humanitarian relief to this sudden and large flow of people. There were no confirmed reports of death due to starvation or disease. Food and water supplies as well as sanitation and health care in the camps were adequate. Finally, the international effort to repatriate the displaced persons, directed by the International Organization for Migration, went very, very well. By mid-October, the flow of displaced persons from Iraq and Kuwait slowed to a trickle, and the burden on the neighboring states and the international community subsided. The international community provided nearly $300 million for the operation.

From October to January, as the potential for hostilities increased, the international community began to plan for a second large migration of refugees and displaced persons. Under the coordination of the United Nations Disaster Relief Organization (UNDRO), the

UN developed a Regional Action Plan to move adequate supplies into the area, upgrade and expand camp sites, and provide a management system in Jordan, Syria, Turkey, and Iran. The International Committee of the Red Cross (ICRC), which had played an important role in the previous assistance activities, also drafted an operational plan. Both UNDRO and ICRC issued funding appeals—for $175 million and $112 million, respectively—predicated on 400,000 refugees. Donors pledged about $136 million to both appeals. The United States provided $7.6 million in cash and food aid.

Migration from Iraq and Kuwait following January 16 was extremely low, which is why the appeals were not fully funded. By the end of March, only about 65,000 people had fled to the neighboring states, most of them (about 45,000) to Iran. Iraq's closure of its border with Turkey, coalition air activity against Scud and other military sites in western Iraq, and the concentration of ground combat to the south all served to limit the migration.

Although some relief infrastructure was, thus, already in place in Turkey and Iran, and more was planned, no one foresaw the magnitude of the civil conflict which caused the latest massive migration of Kurds and other Iraqi civilians.

In addressing the current crisis, I would like to focus on three particular facets of this situation that bear upon how we respond: the magnitude of the problem, the rapidity of the build-up, and the difficulties in reaching these people.

Magnitude. Today, there are more than 1.4 million people who have crossed into Iran and the Turkey border region, and many more displaced from their homes who are fleeing to the border areas. About 1 million of the above have fled to Iran and 500,000-700,000 are just across the border. There are some 400,000 people on the Turkey-Iraq border and perhaps 300,000 more approaching it. The UN places the number of displaced who may need urgent assistance at 1.5 million, but that is only what has been clearly identified so far. Witnesses report empty cities in northern Iraq, suggesting perhaps half or more of northern Iraq's population of 3-5 million may be in flight.

In the south, there are some 27,000 people getting assistance from US forces. Although the numbers here are smaller, there are special problems of protection that I will discuss below.

Rapidity of the build-up. It is not just the numbers but the rapidity of the build-up with which this crisis has unfolded that has made it so enormous. A month after the hostilities ended, February 28, there were no more than 50,000 refugees in surrounding countries. Just 2 weeks before April 8, the day Secretary Baker looked out on 40,000 refugees at Cukurca, Turkey, a UN team had surveyed the same spot and found no one there. Since Secretary Baker's visit, 1 week ago, the number at Cukurca may have doubled. The numbers are mounting so fast that estimates change daily if not by the hour. Perhaps 20,000 persons enter the Turkey-Iraq border area every day. In Iran, the number of refugees went from 300,000 to 700,000 in 5 days and to 900,000 3 days later. Preparations by the UN, as far back as January to receive even as many as 400,000 refugees in the entire region, were swamped by this explosion of human need. A UN appeal issued on April 5 had to be revised dramatically upward April 9, and already it is out of date.

Difficulties. It is not uncommon for refugees to flee into areas bereft of support, areas without good land, water, roads. Refugees cannot choose. In many cases, they are fleeing for their lives. But in this instance, the problems posed are especially difficult. The border areas of Turkey and Iraq are mountainous; the weather is cold; snow and rain are still failing. Few of the areas of concentration are reachable by roads. People are not in camps but stretched out along a line 165 miles long. This is, in short, a logistics nightmare. In Iran, the conditions are only somewhat better, but the numbers are even greater.

Mounting a sufficient relief effort in these conditions takes tremendous resources and—unfortunately—time. There can be short-cuts, such as air drops, and others I will mention below. But to establish a sustained and steady pipeline of the most basic human services for the number of people in this region—food, shelter, water, minimum health care—

demands a logistics effort of enormous scope. This is what the world is rushing to provide.

A major turning point in addressing this crisis was the passage of UN Security Council Resolution 688 on April 5. This resolution condemns Saddam's oppression of the civilian population as a threat to international peace and security in the region. It insists that Iraq allow immediate access by international humanitarian organizations to "all those in need of assistance in all parts of Iraq." It requests the Secretary General to pursue humanitarian efforts in Iraq, to use all relevant UN agencies to address the critical needs of the refugees and displaced, and to report on the plight of all those, especially the Kurds, suffering from the repression. The resolution appeals to all member states and humanitarian organizations to contribute to the relief efforts. Finally, UNSC [Resolution] 688 demands that Iraq cooperate with the Secretary General to these ends.

This resolution gives exceptional scope as well as urgency to the UN humanitarian effort both within Iraq's borders and for the refugees. The Secretary General has appointed Prince Sadruddin Aga Khan as his Executive Delegate [for Humanitarian Assistance for Iraqi Refugees] to oversee the humanitarian programs for Iraq, Kuwait, and border areas. Prince Sadruddin has designated UNHCR [Office of the UN High Commissioner for Refugees] as the lead agency. The Secretary General also has designated Ambassador [Eric] Suy to assess the plight of the repressed and displaced. Donor nations are already providing assistance at increasingly significant levels, in direct response to UNSC [Resolution] 688, requests of the United Nations for assistance, our own approaches to donor governments. It is in this context that I would like to turn to the efforts underway in each theater.

Turkey-Iraq border. I will start with Turkey from which I have just returned following Secretary Baker's visit. As I mentioned, there are more than 400,000 people now in this region and more arriving every day. They are stretched along a border 165 miles long, in perhaps 10-15 concentrations. They are on both sides of the border: in some cases, the border is irrelevant as concentrations spread over both sides.

The government of Turkey has not distinguished between those on either side of the border in this region. Assistance and protection are being provided to all. The Turkish Red Crescent Society, a highly proficient organization, is devoting much of its personnel and resources to this effort and is serving as a principal channel for assistance from many parts of the world. The regional governor is diverting resources from the Turkish population in his area of responsibility to the needs of refugees. Road-building crews are working through the dark of night to open up relief routes. Turkish villagers and citizens from all over the country are donating food, clothing, and other items for the refugees.

But, there is no way the government and people of Turkey could manage this crisis alone. A massive international effort is underway. Because of the urgency and magnitude of the crisis, a two-pronged strategy is being employed.

• A massive effort by the US military is underway at this very moment to save the lives of up to 700,000 people in this region for the next 30 days. This operation involves more than 40 C-130s, close to 60 helicopters, 75-100 small tactical vehicles, a civil affairs battalion, two medical holding companies, a Seabees construction battalion, and massive amounts of food, tents, blankets, and medical supplies. Air drops began over 1 week ago. But the present effort will deliver supplies much more efficiently, directly to sites, first by helicopter and as soon as possible by ground transport.

Other donors are joining in this effort. Australia, Austria, Denmark, Germany, Italy, Japan, New Zealand, Spain, and the EC [European Community] are all participating with planes and helicopters as well as supplies. An international task force coordinates this effort, just as it did during Desert Storm. This past weekend, supplies from this operation began arriving at Uludere, one of the worst sites in the region. Visited last Wednesday by our Ambassador, Mort Abramowitz, together with Governor Kozakcioglu, Uludere contains 80,000 people mired in rain and mud with virtually no shelter or sources of support.

Private agencies such as Medecins Sans Frontieres, Save the Children, the International Rescue Committee, CARE, and others are flying in supplies and personnel as well.

• The second prong is an international effort under UN leadership. The US military and allied operation is a massive but short-term effort. It is designed to save people's lives until the international relief effort, led by the UN, is fully operational. The military effort will greatly facilitate the UN program, by building storage facilities, opening up roads, and stabilizing the condition of the refugees. The UN must take over with a fully organized pipeline of support, reaching down to the refugees, with logistics, health and sanitation personnel, and with the funds to fully support and sustain the program.

The UN effort, supported by donors from all over the world, is already under way. As part of earlier preparations under the UN Regional Plan of Action, the UN had food for 20,000 persons and other supplies for 100,000 when the crisis began. Those, of course, are all now depleted. Millions of dollars of additional supplies are coming in; the international staff is expanding; an information system with donors [is] being established; coordination mechanisms [are] being put in place. A USAID [US Agency for International Development] Disaster Assistance Reconnaissance Team is on the ground in Turkey assisting the US military and providing a technical bridge from the US-led to the UN-led program. Finally, our embassy in Ankara has deployed teams to the field, to provide essential liaison between USAID and DOD [US Department of Defense] officials and Turkish authorities.

Iran. Iran was in some ways better prepared to meet the crisis than Turkey. Its Red Crescent organization had large-scale relief experience from the 8-year Iran-Iraq war and from devastating earthquakes. As many as 10,000 Iranians have had disaster relief training. The build-up also began earlier there, and the UN and the ICRC had begun expanding supplies and personnel as the numbers grew. As noted earlier, the terrain has not been as formidable as that on the Turkish side.

Iran has now called for massive international help. It has announced readiness to receive international relief flights. The ICRC, by the end of this week, will be caring for 200,000 people in this theater, the UNHCR 100,000. More, of course, must be done urgently. Our contributions to date have been through international agencies, primarily the UN and the ICRC. We have asked Iran to define their needs.

Southern Iraq. The area occupied by US forces poses a special problem. Some 27,000 persons have been receiving food, medical care, and other help in this area, and more have received supplies to take to other areas.

The UNHCR has accepted the responsibility for taking over assistance and protection of people in this area once US forces withdraw. The ICRC also will have a presence here. The UN also will have an observer force patrolling a 15-kilometer wide demilitarized zone along the border. We are concerned that Iraq not violate the rights of the people in this area when US forces withdraw. UNSC [Resolution] 688 demands that Iraq cooperate with the UN in carrying out relief and assistance programs. The UN presence will hopefully act as more than a witness to Iraqi behavior but as deterrence to any persecution.

The Scope of the Effort

I noted at the beginning of my testimony that there have been three stages of refugee or displaced persons movement since Iraq's invasion of Kuwait August 2 of last year. The first involved 1 million foreign workers who were repatriated to their home countries. The international community mobilized nearly $300 million for this effort. The second stage, during the hostilities January-February of this year, addressed the needs of 65,000 persons and stockpiled materiel for many more. This stage cost $136 million. Thus, even before the third, current crisis occurred, over $400 million had been spent on refugees and displaced persons in this region.

Now facing this overwhelming new wave of humanity, we are only beginning to grasp its requirements. New UN and Red Cross/Red Crescent appeals have been issued for $700 million, and these cover in most cases no more than 3 months. The costs will surely rise dramatically by year's end.

So far, in a space of 2 weeks, over $270 million has been pledged for this latest period, and more pledges are coming in constantly. The US contribution to the above is over $53 million and growing. Over $28 million of this total has been contributed in food aid, OFDA

[Office of US Foreign Disaster Assistance] assistance, and drawdowns from the Emergency Refugee and Migration Assistance fund. US military assistance to the effort for the refugees from northern and southern Iraq, including operational costs of the massive relief effort, is estimated to be in excess of $25 million and, further, is expected to increase substantially over the next 30 days.

Perhaps one of the most acute shortages is relief management and logistics expertise. The international community was providing protection and assistance to 15 million refugees worldwide when this crisis erupted. The UN, NGOs [non-governmental organizations], and other repositories of such skills were already heavily engaged. Now we need many more such people.

Problems. Even as this major effort gets underway, three special problems will complicate further our task. In the current circumstances, the Turkish government has readily acknowledged the need for international assistance and has asked the UN to organize the relief effort that will succeed current US activities. Problems remain on both the Turkish and UN sides, however, especially in deploying international relief workers into the region and to refugee concentration points. But we are hopeful they will soon be overcome.

Obstacles to repatriation. Everyone agrees that the desired outcome of this situation is for these people to be able to return home voluntarily. Maintaining them on the border for any long period of time conjures up visions of another Gaza Strip. Yet, what is required for people who fled a killer regime to be able to return home safely? One step is to establish a UN and ICRC presence not only to where people have moved but also in the areas from which people fled, under the authority of UNSC [Resolution] 688. Coupled with humanitarian assistance from these organizations, it is hoped that this will enable people to return home safely. We are at the very beginning of this process, and it is too early to know exactly how it will unfold. It goes beyond the concept of an "enclave." It aims at providing an international humanitarian presence and relief wherever needed in the country, so that people can stay as close to, and eventually return, home. We have added to our earlier warning to Iraq that it is not to take any actions which interfere with relief activities in any part of the country.

This crisis has attracted world attention and rightfully world sympathy. Unfortunately, it comes at the same time as other less publicized crises also demanding our attention. Civil unrest in Somalia has uprooted 350,000 people into Ethiopia whose condition is perilous. The number of Liberian refugees has grown beyond the expectations and budget of UNHCR. A drought in Sudan threatens famine of massive proportions. These crises also demand our attention and our resources. Both in money and personnel, international humanitarian responses and capability—and, indeed, attention—will be stretched thin. Yet, as much as possible, we must endeavor to respond to this emergency in Iraq without doing it at the cost of others.

287.

Lyman, Princeton N. "Update on Iraqi refugees and displaced persons." *US Department of State Dispatch* 2, no. 21 (May 27, 1991): 379-382.

[A statement by Bureau for Refugee Programs Director.]

I appreciate this opportunity to provide an update on the crisis of the Iraqi refugees and displaced people. This crisis has been a human tragedy of tremendous proportions, magnified by the rapidity with which it happened. Some 2 million people fled Saddam Hussein's brutal crackdown of unsuccessful rebellions, seeking safety in or on the border of neighboring countries. We and the international community have been committed to providing sustenance, care, and protection to these people. After an initial period in which people suffered and died, we and our coalition partners have provided sufficient life-sustaining humanitarian assistance to have drastically reduced the initial tragic death rate of children, the elderly, and other innocent victims of this terrible situation. Further, we have assisted in fostering conditions to allow many refugees and displaced persons to return to their homes.

In my last appearance before the subcommittee on April 15, I discussed the background to the crisis. Let me now turn to an update of the situation.

Current Situation

Over the past month, there has been considerable improvement in the plight of the refugees and displaced persons in all the areas which have been affected: Turkey, northern Iraq, Iran, and southern Iraq. Relief systems have been put into place, people moved into more accessible and suitable areas, more assistance is being provided more efficiently, and death rates have gone down markedly. The United States and other allied forces have established a safety zone in northern Iraq, and voluntary repatriation, which began about April 30, has turned into a flood. The United Nations has started to move into place and has issued a revised and consolidated appeal.

We are now working to assure a transition to the medium-term protection and assistance effort under UN auspices and to further the long-term goal of facilitating the ability of all of the refugees and displaced persons to return to their homes in safe and secure conditions.

I will now outline the status of the situation in each of the areas where refugees and displaced have concentrated and the steps we are taking to try to assure an effective turnover to the United Nations.

The Turkey BorderRegion and Northern Iraq

As you know, the tremendously fast buildup of this crisis started following the last weekend of March and coincided with harsh weather and logistical conditions. This region of southeastern Turkey, one of the poorest and most inaccessible in the country, was woefully ill-equipped to support such a massive population influx. Local villagers, generous in their assistance, were coming under an insupportable strain, and government of Turkey resources, even with UN assistance, were overwhelmed by the sheer numbers needing help on the 165-mile-long border.

When an effective international response to the situation on the Turkish border could not be mobillized fast enough, and President Ozal of Turkey requested emergency assistance, the President directed the US military to begin an emergency airdrop relief mission on Sunday, April 7, for the refugees along the mountainous border between Turkey and Iraq. The international community worked to get a relief system in place to provide bulk food, shelter, and medical care.

However, moving food and other emergency aid to the refugees in the mountains along the border could only be a stopgap measure. The only way to save lives and provide adequate shelter, food, and medical care to the refugees was to get them down off the mountains.

Therefore, on April 16, President Bush announced that US troops would enter northern Iraq to create a safe area in the flat lands around Zakhu. This decision followed discussions with our allies, particularly with [British] Prime Minister Major, [French] President Mitterrand, and President Ozal. Taking such a step was fully consistent with UN Security Council Resolution 688, which had been passed on April 5.

In addition, a memorandum of understanding was negotiated between the Secretary General's Executive Delegate [for Humanitarian Assistance for Iraqi Refugees] Prince Sadruddin Aga Khan and the government of Iraq on April 18. This memorandum calls for the United Nations to provide humanitarian assistance throughout the country and requires the Iraqi government both to facilitate relief assistance and to allow the United Nations to work wherever it believes necessary. As part of the memorandum, the United Nations is to establish a series of UN humanitarian centers, staffed with international personnel under the auspices of the United Nations. These centers are to serve as relay stations for refugees who eventually choose to return to their homes under UN protection.

Operation Provide Comfort for the refugees and displaced persons in Turkey and massed at the border has been the largest US relief effort mounted in modern military history. The US military was soon joined by forces provided by United Kingdom, Germany, France, Canada, and the Netherlands, to assist the Turkish government and the Turkish Red Crescent Society in providing food and emergency care for the refugees. UN agencies and private voluntary organizations have also been providing assistance from the beginning of the crisis.

Since early April, the situation along the Turkish border has improved considerably. Up to 20 camp sites were established in Sirnak and Hakkari Provinces. The most vulnerable segments of the refugee population were moved down from the camps with the most serious conditions to better sites inside Turkey at Silopi and Semdinli. By May 3, death rates had dropped, there was a several-day surplus of food in most of the camps, bulk food had increasingly replaced meals-ready-to-eat (MREs), and a measles vaccination program (coordinated by UNICEF) had begun. The UN High Commissioner for Refugees (UNHCR) reported that the death rate at Yekmal had dropped from 30 per day to 3, while the death rate from the worst camps at Isikveren had declined from approximately 50 per day in early April to 16 per day by early May.

As noted earlier, the informal voluntary repatriation from the Turkish border area, which started at the end of April, has turned into a flood. As of May 16, the Department of Defense estimated that 170,300 refugees remained on the border, down from an original total of almost half a million. An average of more than 10,000 refugees a day have been returning to northern Iraq from Turkey. Several camps along the border have been closed, including Isikveren—which held at least 80,000 people on April 21, 40,000 on April 30, and 5,000 on May 13. The camp at Uzumlu held 70,000 refugees on April 30 and had a population of 15,000 on May 15. The only large camp remaining is Cukurca, and it is expected that this site will be closed within a month.

The Turkish government has, throughout the crisis, been a major source of help to the refugees—it spent $93.4 million in April alone for the care of the refugees and is one of the largest donors—despite the burdens, both economic and political, placed on the country. The government has spent about $1.6 million per day for refugee care and has absorbed costs for moving food supplies to remote border locations.

As I have mentioned before, the military contribution has been oustanding, and the cooperation among coalition forces and with the Turkish authorities and military has been excellent. As of May 17, there were 20,700 cellent. As of May 17, there were 20,700 coalition troops from 11 nations—troops from Italy, Spain, Australia, and Belgium have joined those mentioned before—doing humanitarian work in Turkey and northern Iraq; more than half—11,700—are from the United States.

Meanwhile, in the Zakhu area of northern Iraq, US, British, and French military forces worked to secure the area and build temporary encampments, one of which has become a humanitarian center under UN control. Troops from the Netherlands, Spain, and Italy are also working in the area. US military officials also persuaded the Kurdish Pesh Merga resistance to remove roadblocks stopping refugees from returning to Iraq. Many of the returnees appear to have gone to their homes in and around Zakhu town. The population of the three camps at Zakhu was about 52,000 on May 16; Zakhu I and II are now full. Construction of Zakhu III was begun on May 13. The coalition forces are planning to build up to five more camps in the Zakhu area.

US and coalition military forces have secured territory within a 30-kilometer radius from Zakhu east through Amadiyah to Suriya and as far south as the northern outskirts of Dahok. According to the US Agency for International Development (USAID) Disaster Assistance Response Team, preliminary indications are that all but about 30,000-50,000 of the refugees on the Turkish border are from the areas of Zakhu, Dahok, and areas further east.

One reason for the rapid buildup of the population at the encampments at Zakhu is that many of the returnees from the Dahok region continue to express unwillingness to go home under present security circumstances. Dahok-area resident account for up to half or more of those in the Turkish border region, creating a potentially large camp population in the secure zone of northern Iraq if the security situation in Dahok is not resolved.

Truck convoys of relief supplies flying UN flags arrived in Zakhu on April 30 from both Silopi, Turkey, and Baghadad. The UN's Special Envoy in Turkey, Stefan Di Mistura, and 15 staff members accompanied one of the convoys and established a small operations site close to the Zakhu temporary settlement. A week ago today, the UN flag was raised at the first Zakhu camp in a ceremony. Prince Sadruddin Aga Khan, who last week returned from a visit to the region, has told us that UN takeover of the coalition effort would accelerate in the next few weeks.

Iran Border Region

At the same time as the explosion of refugees moving toward Turkey occurred at the beginning of April, there were even more rushing to Iran for sanctuary. The international community has taken major steps to alleviate the plight of these people. At the beginning of the crisis, the government of Iran and the Iranian Red Crescent Society, with help from the International Committee of the Red Cross (ICRC) and the League of Red Cross and Red Crescent Societies (LICROSS), mobilized quickly to meet initial demands. As the number of refugees grew rapidly, the Iranian government publicly appealed for international assistance on April 12.

There are now still about 1 million Iraqi refugees in this region, concentrated in the provinces of west Azerbaijan, Kurdistan, Bakhtaran, Ilam, and Khuzistan. Up to this point, the lead operational international agency in Iran has been the ICRC. However, the ICRC is now shifting its emphasis to inside Iraq as the UNHCR has expanded its capability in the area.

The Iranian Red Crescent Society, with assistance from the ICRC and LICROSS, is providing shelter, food, and medical care to 500,000 refugees located in 56 camps. Others are housed in military facilities, homes, and villages, but about one-third are still lacking shelter. The Iranian Red Crescent Society has sent 6,000 staff members to work in the camps.

The ICRC has had more than a hundred expatriate personnel working in Iran and has provided medical supplies, blankets, tents, and food and has had a primary role in setting up camps.

The UNHCR, in addition to staff in Tehran, has established a presence in west Azerbaijan, Bakhtaran, and Kurdistan, the three provinces with the highest number of refugees. The World Food Program is providing over 48,000 tons of food, sufficient to feed 1 million people for 3 months. A private French medical group is also assisting 10,000 refugees.

While the United States has taken the lead in mobilizing and providing assistance along the Turkish border, the European Community, United Kingdom, Germany, Belgium, and other European donors are providing significant amounts of aid to Iran and proportionately more assistance than to the refugees in Turkey. About 70% of the EC's assistance, for example, is going to the Iran theater.

Despite a lack of relations with Iran, the United States also responded to the Iranian government appeal and offered direct assistance. After modalities were worked out with Iran, a US military flight, loaded with blankets donated by the private sector, arrived in Tehran on April 27. In addition, through the Bureau for Refugee Programs, we have provided multilateral assistance comprising $12 million to the UNHCR and $7 million to the ICRC for the relief activities throughout the region, including Iran.

Informal voluntary repatriation appears to have started from Iran as well as from Turkey. According to the United Nations, the returnee flow appears to be a response to assumptions about security arrangements as well as to agricultural and economic factors. Poor conditions in camps in Iran may also be a motivating factor.

It is still unclear how large the flow of returnees from Iran is. The ICRC believes that there may be up to 5,000-10,000 persons a day returning to Iraq from Iran, mostly along the Piranshah-Irbil route, while the UNHCR estimates that 5,000 refugees are leaving per province per day (for a total of up to 20,000 per day).

The returnees appear to be able to pass Iraqi government checkpoints from Pesh Merga-controlled territory with little difficulty. Most of these returnees seem to be going to areas south of the coaliation secure zone. However, these are preliminary indications.

Southern Iraq

The area occupied by US forces in southern Iraq posed a special problem. With the collapse of the rebellion in southern Iraq in March, about 100,000 people fled the area to Iran and the US-occupied zone. About 30,000

persons received protection, food, medical care, and other assistance from US troops.

As Us forces withdrew from this area, UN observers forces (UNIKOM) were deployed in the demilitarized zone along the Iraqi-Kuwaiti border. The United States worked closely with the ICRC and UNHCR to arrange for their taking over assistance to those who had fled to the occupied zone. However, because of concerns that UNIKOM would not be able to provide adequate protection after the departure of US troops and [because] the area reverted to Iraqi control for those in the occupied zone who had been involved in anti-regime activities, the government of Saudi Arabia—which had been administering a camp just over its border in the occupied zone of Iraq—agreed to provide first asylum protection to persons from that camp, from the Safwan area, and to some displaced civilians in a camp just inside Kuwait by moving them to a new camp inside Saudi Arabia near Rafha.

The movement of displaced civilians in Safwan to the Rafha camp in Saudi Arabia was completed by the US military on May 9; 6,270 people were moved in this operation. About 11,000 displaced civilians in Al Sadah, the Saudi-administered camp in southern Iraq, have also been transported to Rafha.

In addition, the International Organization for Migration (IOM) completed the move of close to 2,000 Iraqi Shias of Iranian descent from the Safwan camp to Iran on April 29.

Although it is now difficult for us to obtain reliable and detailed information on conditions in southern Iraq, we are concerned that health and sanitation conditions could deteriorate in this area. Some of this is clearly the result of the Iraqi government's brutal suppression of opponents and its lack of attention to restoring services in this area. We are hopeful that the UN will be able to convince the Iraqi government to turn attention to this egion.

This is where we are now, about 7 weeks since the crisis began: mostly stabilized situations in the neighboring countries, a relief system in place—extending from the countries of first asylum into the refugees' home areas in northern Iraq—and a flow of voluntary repatriation.

Transition to UN Management

We have also had progress toward moving to the next phase: the turnover of the protection and relief activities to the United Nations. The UN has moved a long way in the last 7 weeks, by purchasing and supplying millions of dollars of relief goods into Turkey and Iran, concluding the memorandum of understanding, setting up a presence in Zakhu and Dahok, issuing appeals, and moving staff into place in the affected region. More has to be done, however, before the United Nations can—in effect—replace the extraordinary bilateral efforts of the US and allied military.

In addition, the United Nations, along with the ICRC, is working to establish humanitarian centers wherever necessary inside Iraq and at the border regions in order to provide humanitarian relief to the refugees and displaced persons. Such a presence is necessary wherever the refugees and displaced happen to be: in northern Iraq, and in the Rafha camp of Saudi Arabia. The ICRC has already established such presence in the border areas, including Irbil, Dahok, and Kani Masi, and plans to expand its presence to Kirkuk and Sulaymaniyah. As noted, the United Nations has begun to establish its presence in northern Iraq, starting with Zakhu and Dahok. The UNHCR plans to have a presence in nine sites in northern Iraq and to send out mobile teams from these sites.

One problem has been funding. Despite an outpouring of generosity from the international community of more than $700 million since the beginning of April—and I would note that this is in addition to the $435 million provided for the two earlier movements of displaced people from Iraq and Kuwait—much of this has been in bilateral assistance or in pledges. It is necessary to turn the pledges into tangible donations so that the United Nations can have the cash to expand its operations. On May 15, the United Nations issued a revised and coordinated appeal, which delineates responsibilities by theater of operations and agency and makes it easier for donors to contribute to programs in each major theater of the UN's humanitarian responsibility. The appeal calls for $415 million for a 4-month period ending August 31, 1991. This 4-month timeframe takes into account that the signifi-

cant movement of returnees will continue to occur through the summer of 1991. About 73% of the programs of the appeal are directed toward refugees or returnees.

To further facilitate the UN takeover of the relief operation, we have suggested that a metting take place in Geneva, UNHCR headquarters, or in the region of all those agencies involved in the humanitarian operation and in the transition planning—representatives from Prince Sadruddin's office, the UNHCR, the European Command, USAID's Office of Foreign Disaster Assitance (OFDA), the State Department, the Department of Defense, and Embassy Ankara—to agree on all aspects of the operational turnover of the relief operation.

Protection

The longer-term goal, as I indicated at the outset of my testimony, is to enable the refugees and displaced to return to their homes. The issue of protection thus is of great importance.

Initially, the presence of US and allied forces, reinforced by the withdrawal of Iraqi military units, for the allied area of operations offers protection for those returning. The next step is for the United Nations and ICRC to establish a presence throughout northern Iraq which can not only provide assistance, but also ensure that Iraq, in accordance with UN Security Council Resolution 688, does not interfere with international humanitarian activities. They would bear witness to any violation of that resolution and to any violation of the resolution and to any persecution of the people in the region. The resolution makes clear that any violation, as well as the general treatment by Iraq of its population, will have a bearing on the lifting of economic sanctions against Iraq.

There is also discussion underway of a lightly armed UN guard force to help protect international humanitarian relief activities. Prince Sadruddin and other UN officials have been discussing this idea with the Iraqi government. We are prepared to examine this proposal once negotiations have proceeded further. Further, the outcome of negotiations between Kurdish rebels and the Iraqi government will be an additional factor affecting the security situation.

US Contribution

Acting on the President's directive of April 5, US military forces have orchestrated the international relief effort in Turkey and northern Iraq. In addition, the United States has been in the forefront of contributors to alleviating this crisis. To date, the United States has committed $207.6 million toward the plight of the refugees. Of this amount, approximately $140 million in goods and service has come from Department of Defense sources, and I would point out that this figure does not include the pay of the nearly 12,000 servicemen and women who are carrying out this program. Their performance has been outstanding as has every level of the US military in carrying out a truly unprecedented humanitarian relief operation. I cannot say enough about the speed, commitment, and effectiveness with which our military is responding. Thousands are alive today because of their rapid response.

OFDA has provided strong support to the military effort and to the establishment of a reliable relief effort inside Iraq. OFDA has obligated $12.9 million toward these objectives. OFDA also assembled a 17-person Disaster Assistance Response Team to provide expertise to assist in very aspect of the relief effort. USAID has also committed nearly 50,000 metric tons of food, delivered or on its way to the region, and valued at $31.6 million, of Food for Peace assistance.

From the President's Emergency Refugee and Migration Assistance account, we have provided $23 million. These funds have gone to the UNHCR and ICRC for the most part, and $2 million were allocated for emergency procurement in Turkey for water, baby food, and other urgently needed items.

The Administration appreciates the prompt action on both houses of Congress in responding to the President's request for supplemental appropriations. The recently passed supplemented appropriations bill provides $125 million for State Department and USAID emergency programs for the Gulf region, $25.5 million for peace-keeping activities, and $85 million in additional funding for the emergency refugee and disaster assistance accounts. We plan to program the funds appropriated for the migration and refugee assistance account to assist in making the next phase of the relief effort—the international phase run by the United Nations—successful in providing assistance to the refugees and returnees and, depending on the security arrangements, in assisting the reintergration of the returnees into their communities.

The $85 million for replenishment of funds expended is also very important. This will enable us to address, I am sorry to say, humanitarian crises of equal or greater magnitude in many parts of Africa and, more recently, Bangladesh.

The bill also includes the authority to transfer such sums as may be necessary from the Persian Gulf Regional Defense Fund to the Department of Defense for the incremental costs of humanitarian assistance in this effort.

Conclusion

In conclusion, let me say that the world should not ever forget the cruelty and destruction caused by the regime of Saddam Hussein that lie at the heart of this crisis. As the United States now commits personnel and resources to respond to the horrible tragedy in Bangladesh, and as we mourn for its many victims, we must not forget that the cause of human suffering in Iraq is wholly different. This tragedy is not from a freak of nature but from the deliberate actions of a ruler against his own people. It need not have happened at all.

288.

Djerejian, Edward. "Meeting with Iraqi Kurdistan Front." *US Department of State Dispatch* 2, no. 40 (October 7, 1991): 751.

This afternoon, NEA [Bureau of Near East and Asian Affairs] Assistant Secretary [Edward] Djerejian met with a delegation of the Iraqi Kurdistan Front, including Jalal Talabani, one of the two principal Kurdish leaders. The group, which also had meetings last week at the State Department and the Pentagon, included representatives of Iraq's Assyrian and Turcoman communities.

Our meetings with the Iraqi Kurdistan Front delegation took place within the context of broadening US Government contacts with a wide range of groups opposed to Saddam Hussein and the present Iraqi regime. We do not back any particular opposition faction, nor is it our aim to shape a government to succeed Saddam Hussein. That is a matter for the Iraqi people. Similarly, the United States supports peaceful political reform within Iraq, not Iraq's breakup.

In talks with the Iraqi Kurdistan Front delegation, US officials stressed our strong support for greater human rights and political participation for all the people of Iraq. We support a pluralistic, democratic Iraq in which no ethnic or religious group is denied full rights of citizenship, full participation in the institutions of government, and the right to honor its distinctive religious and cultural heritage.

Our government is committed ,to humanitarian assistance for the Iraqi people under the aegis of UN Security Council Resolution 688 and the mechanism created by UN Security Council Resolutions 706 and 712. We will insist that Iraq meet its UN-mandated obligations, including the requirement that international relief agencies receive unimpeded access to civilians in need of help in all parts of the country.

We also discussed the residual coalition military force in southeastern Turkey, which will act to preserve peace and stability in northern Iraq and deter Iraqi repression.

We welcome the improvement in relations between the Iraqi Kurdish leadership and the Government of Turkey. We appreciate the clear Iraqi Kurdistan Front statements supporting Turkish sovereignty and denouncing the terrorist tactics of the Kurdish Workers Party (PKK), a terrorist group based in Turkey. Contact with the Iraqi opposition improves mutual understanding and strengthens our long-term relationship with the Iraqi people. We look forward to a continuing dialogue with the Iraqi Kurdistan Front, as well as other Iraqi opposition groups.

289.

Wolcott, Jackie. "Humanitarian Situation in Iraq." *US Department of State Dispatch* 2 (November 18, 1991): 851-853.

I appreciate this opportunity to update you and the other members of the committee on the humanitarian situation in Iraq. There have been several recent developments that I think will be of interest.

Humanitarian Issues

On August 15, the [UN] Security Council adopted Resolution 706 in response to repeated Iraqi requests to be allowed to resume sales of oil for the purchase of urgently needed food and other humanitarian items and to fund other Iraqi obligations. While approving the sale [of] $1.6 billion of oil in order to meet the needs of Iraqi civilians before winter, this resolution imposes certain requirements to ensure that the proceeds are used as intended.

As part of the humanitarian aid component, the resolution requires the Secretary General to establish a system of monitoring and control that would prevent any revenues from this one-time sale of oil from reaching the coffers of the Government of Iraq and ensure that humanitarian supplies are distributed throughout Iraq to the population groups who are most in need. It should be noted that since March 22, when the [UN] Sanctions Committee lifted the embargo on food, the Sanctions Committee has been notified of some 4.2 million metric tons of food to be sent to Iraq. It should also be recognized that the United States has provided over $500 million in humanitarian assistance in Iraq, including our contributions to Operation Provide Comfort which assisted the Kurds in the north.

On September 28, the Security Council adopted Resolution 712, which approved the Secretary General's proposals for implementing Resolution 706. Over 2 months after passage of Resolution 706, and more than a month and a half after passage of [Resolution] 712, Iraq has still neither accepted nor rejected the terms of these resolutions, although various Iraqi officials have made some critical comments concerning their provisions. In addition, a request to visit Iraq by Prince Sadruddin Aga Khan, the Secretary General's Executive Delegate for Humanitarian Assistance in the Gulf area, has been delayed by the Iraqi Government at least until November 18.

A number of international teams have visited Iraq to assess humanitarian requirements. There is general agreement that certain groups in the Iraqi civilian population do, indeed, face serious food shortages and lack adequate medical care. These groups include, in particular, the Shi'a in southern Iraq, Kurds in the north, and poor Sunnis living in central Iraq, especially women and children. There is evidence of chronic malnutrition in Iraq for an extended time, predating the invasion of Kuwait.

While Saddam Hussein cynically calculated that the misery he has inflicted on his own people might serve to sway the international community on the lifting of sanctions, Resolutions 706 and 712 have disappointed and, apparently, annoyed Saddam. However, if Iraq wants to obtain food and other humanitarian items, these resolutions provide the mechanism for that to be done, and it is now up to the Government of Iraq to permit these resolutions to be implemented.

We continue to receive reports from knowledgeable sources that the Iraqi Government is blocking the distribution of needed food and medicine to vulnerable populations inside Iraq by private voluntary organizations. Until now, despite Iraq's non-acceptance of Security Council Resolutions 706 and 712, many PVOs [private voluntary organizations] were able to use health clinics, churches, and mosques as food distribution sites. This now has ended. New pressure on PVO food distribution adds to the evidence that Saddam is pressing for a propaganda showdown over the Iraqi "starvation" issue. Further, we have been informed by international organizations and private voluntary organizations that Iraq is refusing to extend visas for their humanitarian assistance personnel after December 31.

The latest battle fought by Saddam uses his population as pawns. He systematically denies much needed humanitarian assistance and then blames the sanctions regime for the problem. There is a solution: rapid implementation of Security Council Resolutions 706 [and] 712, which provide an internationally agreed-upon mechanism for the equitable distribution of assistance within Iraq. At present, the issue is not one of insufficient resources but of Saddam's indifference to the needs of many sectors of the population.

We recognize that malnutrition is a problem in Iraq, but we have insufficient information on its extent. A thorough baseline assessment of humanitarian needs in Iraq is called for in Resolution 706. As far as we

know, the problems are gravest for the Kurds and the Shi'a and for the very poor in Baghdad. In fact, recent reporting from northern Iraq indicates that the government is setting up roadblocks to prevent the movement of fuel and food to the north. In the south, we continue to receive reports about people trapped in the marshes by the Iraqi army as well as the refusal by the Iraqi Government to allow the United Nations to establish humanitarian centers in the marsh area.

Nevertheless, we have not given up on eventual Iraqi acceptance of Resolutions 706 and 712. There are some recent indications that Iraq may be moving in the direction of accepting them. Prince Sadruddin will visit Iraq and will be able to explain exactly how the oil sale and food purchase mechanisms of the resolutions will work. Further, businessmen who have dealings with Iraq have approached us with questions on [Resolution] 706, indicating that the Iraqi Government does not have a complete understanding of the implementing mechanisms. These small signals give us hope that there might be a change in Saddam's position on these humanitarian resolutions. It is our understanding that Sadruddin plans to discuss with [Iraqi] officials an extension of the memorandum of understanding under which the United Nations operates in Iraq as well as the implementation of Resolutions 706 and 712.

We are saddened by reports of the suffering of the Iraqi people. But there is a limit to what we, as part of the international community, can do in the absence of Iraqi cooperation. Only Iraq stands in the way of implementing an internationally approved mechanism to deal with its humanitarian crisis.

Frozen Iraqi Assets
We are aware of the various proposals that have been put forward to make use of official Iraqi assets frozen in this country and elsewhere as a source of funding to bring humanitarian relief to the people of Iraq.

The sanctions regime does provide for this possibility under certain circumstances. The Chairman of the UN Sanctions Committee has informed all governments holding such assets that they may unfreeze them for the purposes specified in paragraph 20 of Resolution 687, i.e., for permissible humanitarian exports to Iraq. We understand that some countries have chosen to do so in limited amounts.

However, the Security Council, in Paragraph 9 of Resolution 712, also urged that any humanitarian exports to Iraq be undertaken through arrangements that assure their equitable distribution to meet humanitarian needs. The method adopted by the Security Council for this purpose is the mechanism provided under Resolutions 706 and 712—which the Council specifically made available for frozen Iraqi assets as well as the proceeds of Iraqi oil sales. This mechanism ensures that humanitarian supplies will be equitably distributed and that Iraq will not withhold supplies from the Kurds or other disfavored sectors of the civilian population. In our view, this is by far the preferable method, and at least one large holder of Iraqi assets has expressed an interest in making use of this channel. But the Iraqis have so far refused. This refusal has nothing to do with the UN terms for the sale of oil, since these funds could be used regardless of whether and when oil sales occur.

In the alternative, a state might release frozen assets to finance the shipment of humanitarian items directly to Iraq, perhaps with some sort of attempt to impose conditions on how Iraq will use and distribute those items. Based on the Iraqi track record to date, most countries are understandably reluctant to do so. In our view, it would be a serious mistake for the United States to entrust the distribution of such items to Iraq, and we have urged others who are holding Iraqi assets not to do so.

Under either alternative, the United States—like many other countries—faces an additional problem. US Government, corporate, and individual claims against Iraq currently total many billions of dollars. A large proportion of the 1,300 claims reported so far involve unpaid Iraqi debts and obligations from the pre-crisis period and certain other types of claims which are unlikely to be paid by the UN Compensation Fund. Frozen Iraqi assets in this country total just $1.2 billion. These assets offer our best hope for at least partial payment of the outstanding US claims. Clearly, every dollar of US-held Iraqi assets released today means one less dollar available in the future for the 1,300 American claimants

from all around the United States—many of whom have reported that they are already

be facing serious financial difficulties. Indeed, such a release of Iraqi assets could result in litigation against the US Government by US citizens who had counted on the use of those assets to satisfy their claims. We believe the agreed international approach represented by Resolutions 706 and 712 offers the most effective and equitable way of providing relief to the Iraqi people. We remain hopeful that this approach will be accepted by Iraq and put into effect before the humanitarian situation in Iraq reaches crisis proportions. In any event, the problem is not finding a source of funds— these funds are available for such use now, if only Iraq will agree to an effective monitoring system to ensure equitable distribution. We believe there is no need [to use]—and no point in using—the Iraqi assets held by the United States for this purpose.

Iraqi Non-Compliance with Other Humanitarian Resolutions

There have been numerous Iraqi violations of both the letter and spirit of Resolution 688, which was adopted by the Security Council last April following the brutal repression of uprisings by both the Shi'a in the south and the Kurds in the north against Saddam's regime. This resolution demands that the Government of Iraq cease attacks against civilians and that it permit unhindered UN access to the Iraqi people for the purpose of providing them assistance.

Shi'a in the South

In July, we received credible reports that a number of Shi'a, who had fled their homes following the brutal repression of their rebellion by Iraqi forces, were trapped in the vast marsh areas separating southern Iraq and Iran. What made these reports most ominous were eyewitness accounts by UN personnel that the Iraqi army had surrounded part of these marshes and appeared intent upon keeping the Shi'a pinned down in an area totally unfit for human habitation.

Prince Sadruddin, in the course of his assessment mission to Iraq in July, requested permission to visit the marshlands and to establish a base for the United Nations to monitor the situation and provide assistance to the people in that area. Following several days of stalling, the Iraqi authorities finally allowed Sadruddin to travel to the area. It was clear to Sadruddin and his team that Iraqi military had been hastily withdrawn just prior to his visit. The UN staff, which Sadruddin left to keep an eye on the situation, were, subsequently, ordered out of the area by Iraq on the grounds that they were no longer needed and, as of now, have not been permitted to return.

We are disturbed by reports indicating that there are still numbers of people, including women and children, trapped in the marshes with little food [and] only swamp water to drink who are unable to return to their homes because of the continuing large military presence in the area.

Kurds in the North

Last month, fighting again flared up between Iraqi forces and the Kurds in northern Iraq. Several days ago, we received reports of renewed fighting outside the Kurdish city of Erbil. This renewed fighting comes despite Saddam's promise to work out a plan for increased Kurdish autonomy and some degree of democracy throughout Iraq. The fighting is causing thousands of Kurdish men, women, and children to flee toward Iran once again. This most recent fighting is only the latest in a series of armed conflicts.

It is clear that failure to work out an agreement that would provide for a degree of autonomy for the Kurds, as well as allow them to exercise their right to choose their own form of government, will create further instability in northern Iraq and fuel the deplorable cycle of violence in that region. Saddam's continuing repression of the Kurds—including indiscriminate sustained artillery bombardment of residential areas—vastly complicates the UN efforts to provide adequate shelter in the north before the onset of winter.

The Government of Iraq has refused to allow the United Nations to open humanitarian centers in Kirkuk and Nasiriyah. It bases its refusal on a deliberate misinterpretation of the memorandum of understanding it signed with the United Nations in April which provides for both the Iraqis and the United Nations to agree on locations for UN humanitarian centers. The Iraqis now claim the unilateral right to designate the location of these centers, and

they have refused UN requests despite the 250,000 refugees located near these towns who have recently returned from Iran but are prevented from getting to their homes by the Iraqi authorities.

There are an estimated 300,000 people who have returned to the vicinity of their homes but are still living in tents or other temporary shelter because their homes have either been destroyed or are unsafe due to fighting or the presence of Iraqi forces. While the United Nations is providing assistance, the task is made more difficult by Iraqi refusal to permit the establishment of humanitarian centers. Saddam Hussein's continued brutality against his own people has driven many hitherto reluctant countries to concede that circumstances may, indeed, arise in which extraordinary humanitarian needs compel the international community's intervention in the internal affairs of a sovereign state. This concern lies behind the substance of Resolution 688 and also indicates why Resolutions 706 and 712 are so strict in their requirements for UN control over Iraq's future oil revenues.

Under Resolution 687, the Security Council is to consider every 60 days whether Iraq is in compliance with this cease-fire resolution so that the economic sanctions can either be modified or terminated. There have been three such reviews to date. Saddam Hussein's regime has done its utmost to evade requirements to disclose all details of its programs to develop weapons of mass destruction. It continues to make war upon Iraqi citizens who reject it. It has probed the firmness of the international community in enforcing Iraq's border with Kuwait. It has not been difficult for Security Council members to agree that, given the continued blatant disregard for the requirements of Resolution 687 by the Government of Iraq, it would be completely inappropriate to consider lifting sanctions or modifying them in any way.

In conclusion, Saddam Hussein's continuation in power will present the international community with the challenge of seeing that he remains incapable of once again posing a threat to his own people, his neighbors, and to the rest of the world. Let us be perfectly clear about one thing: This is not an issue between Saddam Hussein and the United States but between Saddam Hussein and the

United Nations. The United Nations has lived up to the daunting challenge of fulfilling the requirements of [Resolution] 687. The UN perseverance in this matter demonstrates that our faith in the United Nations has not been misplaced and bodes well for an increased UN role international problem solving as the new world order continues to evolve.

290.

Office of the Assistant Secretary/Spokesman. "Humanitarian Assistance in Iraq." *US Department of State Dispatch* 3, no. 2 (January 13, 1992): 26-29.

Following the swift defeat of his military forces in Kuwait last February, Saddam Hussein was confronted by sudden and massive uprisings by disaffected Shi'a in southern Iraq and Kurds in the north. Although these uprisings caught the Government of Iraq, as well as much of the international community, by surprise, Iraq's military was able to regroup to confront and savagely quell the uprisings. These events have triggered a large humanitarian emergency in Iraq and neighboring Turkey and Iran involving more than 1.8 million Iraqis.

The international community has responded to this emergency with both generosity and determination. The United Nations and its affiliated agencies have provided nearly $300 million in humanitarian assistance to the Gulf region since early March [1991]. The International Committee of the Red Cross has mounted its own program, providing more than $100 million in assistance. In addition, several private and voluntary agencies are operating programs to assist Iraq's vulnerable civilian population. The United States has contributed $6.9 million to these agencies and nearly $600 million in total contributions for humanitarian assistance to Iraq, including over 63,000 metric tons of food, valued at $35.9 million.

Operation Provide Comfort involved allied military forces from the United Kingdom, France, Italy, Canada, Belgium, Luxembourg, Australia, Spain, Netherlands, and Germany. During the initial phase of the operation, 425,500 refugees who had fled from their homes in northern Iraq to the border with Turkey were assisted. The allied forces provided 17,000 tons of humanitarian supplies, including food, medical supplies, and material for shelter. Eventually, in order to assist the refugees in returning to their home towns and villages, Operation Provide Comfort personnel helped reconstruct local power grids and sanitation systems and provided security so that the refugees would feel safe and be encouraged to stay in their home areas. Three temporary tent villages were set up around Zakhu in northeastern Iraq. The allied forces turned over the assistance program they had established to the UN High Commissioner for Refugees (UNHCR) on June 7, 1991. A military task force, comprised primarily of an air component with approximately 1,800 personnel, remains based in Turkey. The Government of Turkey recently agreed to extend the agreement allowing the task force to utilize its Turkish base of operations for an additional 6 months, through June 1992.

Un Security Council Resolutions
On April 5, 1991, the UN Security Council adopted Resolution 688, which, for the first time, established that a humanitarian emergency such as the mass exodus of Kurds and the other groups which fled Iraq could trigger the involvement of the Security Council as a threat to international peace and stability. Resolution 688 requires Iraq to admit UN humanitarian personnel into the country and to permit the United Nations and other agencies providing assistance to have access to all people in need. Following adoption of the resolution, the United Nations signed a memorandum of understanding with Iraqi authorities which specified modalities of the UN's operation in Iraq. Resolution 688 provides complete authority for its humanitarian operations in Iraq. The memorandum of understanding provides operational details on how the United Nations plans to carry out its mandate under Resolution 688. There have been numerous Iraqi violations of both the letter and spirit of Resolution 688 as well as the terms of the memorandum of understanding.

Approximately 375 UN humanitarian personnel are based throughout Iraq. An additional 500 UN guards also are in Iraq to protect UN personnel, assets, and operations linked with the UN humanitarian program. There are 300 Red Cross employees and 192 workers from private agencies in Baghdad and dozens of other cities in Iraq.

In northeastern Iraq, the United Nations is operating six humanitarian centers which provide relief to displaced persons and the needy and an additional four UN sub-offices from which relief supplies also are distributed.

On August 15, the Security Council adopted Resolution 706 in response to repeated Iraqi requests to be allowed to resume sales of oil for the purchase of urgently needed food and other humanitarian items and to fund other Iraqi obligations. The Security Council approved the sale of $1.6 billion of oil in order to meet the needs of Iraqi civilians before winter and other Iraqi obligations. The resolution requires the Secretary General to establish a strict system of monitoring and control that would prevent any revenues from this one-time sale of oil from reaching the coffers of the Iraqi Government and to ensure that humanitarian supplies are distributed throughout Iraq to population groups who are most in need. It should be noted that since March 22, 1991, when the Sanctions Committee lifted the embargo on food, intended shipments of some 4.2 million tons of food have been notified to the committee. This is approximately three-fourths of Iraq's annual prewar food imports. Medicines have never been included in the sanctions.

On September 28, 1991, the Security Council adopted Resolution 712 which approved the Secretary General's proposals for implementing Resolution 706. More than 3 months after passage of Resolution 706 and 2 months after passage of 712, Iraq has still neither accepted nor rejected the terms of these resolutions, although various Iraqi officials have made highly critical comments concerning their provisions.

A number of international teams have visited Iraq to assess humanitarian requirements. It is clear that certain groups in the Iraqi civilian population face serious food shortages and lack adequate medical care. These groups include, in particular, the Shi'a in southern Iraq, Kurds in the north, and poor Sunnis living in central Iraq.

There is evidence that some of these groups have experienced malnutrition and inadequate medical care for an extended time, predating the invasion of Kuwait. While Saddam Hussein cynically calculated that the misery he has inflicted on his own people might serve to sway the international community on the lifting of sanctions, Resolutions 706 and 712 have disappointed him. However, if Iraq wants to obtain food and other humanitarian items, these resolutions provide the mechanism for that to be done, and it is now up to the Iraqi Government to permit these resolutions to be implemented.

We continue to receive reports from knowledgeable sources that the Iraqi Government is blocking the distribution of needed food and medicine to vulnerable populations in the north and denying private voluntary organizations use of mosques, health clinics, and other facilities for the purpose of carrying out their work. Previously, despite Iraq's non-acceptance of Security Council Resolutions 706 and 712, many private voluntary organizations were able to use these facilities as food distribution sites. Recently, people sent by the Iraqi Government have traveled door-to-door warning residents that they will be arrested if they accept foreign food assistance. Residents who have previously accepted food have been interrogated. The Deputy Prime Minister has accused international aid workers of gathering intelligence. These events add to the evidence that Saddam's Government is not complying with Resolution 688.

The reports of the suffering of the Iraqi people are extensive, well-documented, and compelling. But there is a limit to what the international community can do in the absence of Iraqi cooperation. Only Iraq stands in the way of implementing an internationally approved mechanism to deal with its humanitarian crisis.

The sanctions regime does provide for the possibility of using Iraqi official assets frozen when economic sanctions were imposed upon Iraq in August 1990, under certain circumstances. The chairman of the UN Sanctions Committee has informed all governments holding such assets that they may unfreeze them for the purposes specified in paragraph 20 of Resolution 687, i.e., for permissible humanitarian exports to Iraq. We understand that some countries have chosen to do so in limited amounts.

Countries choosing this course of action face two broad alternatives: either they can release the frozen assets with the permission of—and in a manner prescribed by—the Iraqi Government or they can vest the assets and use them as they see fit, for example, by channeling the funds into UN humanitarian operations.

One obvious problem in releasing the assets according to the wishes of the Iraqi Government is that the Iraqis are unlikely to agree to any international control mechanism—such as that provided under Resolutions 706 and 712—to ensure that humanitarian supplies purchased with the assets are equitably distributed within Iraq. Instead, countries releasing the assets would have to trust the Iraqi Government to distribute the supplies equitably. Based on the Iraqi track record, to date, most countries are reluctant to do so.

Shi'a in the South

In July, we received credible reports that a number of Shi'a, who had fled their homes following the brutal putdown of their rebellion by Iraqi forces, were trapped in the vast marsh areas separating southern Iraq and Iran. What made these reports most ominous were eyewitness accounts by UN personnel that the Iraqi army had surrounded part of these marshes and appeared intent upon keeping the Shi'a pinned down in an area totally unfit for human habitation.

[UN High Commissioner] Sadruddin Aga Khan, in the course of his assessment mission to Iraq in July, requested permission to visit the marshlands and to establish a base for the United Nations to monitor the situation and provide assistance to the people in that area. Following several days of stalling, the Iraqi authorities finally allowed Sadruddin to travel to the area. It was clear to Saddrudin and his team that Iraqi military had been hastily withdrawn just prior to his visit. The UN staff which Sadruddin left to keep an eye on the situation were subsequently ordered out of the area by Iraq on the grounds that they were no longer needed and, as of now, have not been permitted to return.

We are very concerned with reports that indicate that there are still numbers of people, including women and children trapped in the marshes with little food, only swamp water to drink, and unable to return to their homes because of the continuing large military presence in the area.

Kurds in the North

In October, fighting again flared up between Iraqi forces and the Kurds in northern Iraq. This renewed fighting came despite Saddam's promise to work out a plan for increased Kurdish autonomy and some degree of democracy throughout Iraq. The fighting resulted in the dislocation from their villages once again of thousands of Iraqi men, women, and children. In November, ominous indications of renewed military pressure upon the Kurds have led many to flee their homes just as winter is approaching. These threats and renewed military actions are only the latest in a series. It is clear that failure to work out arrangements that would provide for a degree of autonomy for the Kurds, as well as allow them to participate in the government, will create further instability in northern Iraq and fuel the deplorable cycle of violence in that region.

Saddam's continuing repression of the Kurds—including artillery bombardment of urban and residential areas and deliberate eviction of people from their homes—vastly complicates the UN's efforts to provide adequate shelter in the north before the onset of winter and to "settle" returning refugees into their homes. Nevertheless, the United Nations has successfully completed arrangements to provide adequate protection against the harsh winter climate for 350,000 people for whom plans had been made last summer and autumn. But there remain serious problems for recently displaced persons in northern Iraq.

The United Nations has proposed that it open humanitarian centers in Kirkuk and Nasiriyah, but the Government of Iraq has refused to concur. It bases its refusal on a deliberate misinterpretation of the memorandum of understanding it signed with the United Nations last April 18 which provides for both the Iraqis and the United Nations to agree on locations for UN humanitarian centers. The Iraqis now claim the unilateral right to designate the location of these centers, and they have refused UN requests despite the 250,000 refugees located near these towns who have returned from Iran but are prevented from getting to their homes by the Iraqi authorities.

There also are an estimated 30,000 people who have returned to their former villages or to their homes but who are still living in tents or other temporary shelter because their homes have either been destroyed or are unsafe because of fighting. Resolution 688 requires that Iraqi authorities provide access for the United Nations to provide assistance to all in Iraq that require it.

Resolution 687, arguably the most far-reaching of any measure passed by the Security Council, places several stringent, but necessary, requirements upon the Iraqi Government. Among other things, Resolution 687 requires Iraq to:

• Declare and destroy or render harmless its nuclear, chemical, and biological weapons of mass destruction, as well as ballistic missiles with ranges in excess of 150 kilometers;

• Observe the demilitarized zone established between Iraq and Kuwait, by withdrawing all military forces;

• Return all stolen Kuwaiti property, financial and cultural assets, and military equipment;

• Return all captured or detained Kuwaiti citizens;

• Pay reparations to Kuwait and others who have suffered losses as a result of Iraq's invasion and the ensuing war; and

• Cooperate in the demarcation of a permanent boundary between Iraq and Kuwait.

Under the resolution, the Security Council is to consider, every 60 days, whether Iraq is in compliance so that the economic sanctions can either be modified or terminated. There have been four such reviews to date. Saddam Hussein's regime has done its utmost to evade requirements to disclose all details of its programs to develop weapons of mass destruction. It has repeatedly violated the demilitarized zone by sending Iraqi "civilians" into Kuwait to forage for weapons and munitions and by establishing border posts beyond Iraq's part of the zone. It has failed to return stolen Kuwaiti military equipment. And, most serious, Iraq has failed to provide an accounting for missing Kuwaitis believed to have been taken to Iraq or to permit the Red Cross access to places where they may be detained. It continues to make war upon Iraqi citizens who reject it. In the light of this obvious pattern of non-compliance, Security Council members have agreed that is would be completely inappropriate to consider lifting sanctions or modifying them in any way for the benefit of Iraq. Saddam Hussein's continued brutality against his own people has driven many hitherto reluctant countries to concede that there may, indeed, arise circumstances in which extraordinary humanitarian needs compel the international community's intervention in the internal affairs of a sovereign state. This concern lies behind the substance of Resolution 688 and also indicates why Resolutions 706 and 712 are so strict in their requirements for UN control over Iraq's future oil revenues.

It is not the international sanctions which starve Iraq's innocent civilian populations. It is the policies of Saddam Hussein's regime. The international community has decided that sanctions need to remain in order to secure Iraq's full compliance with the terms of the cease-fire contained in Resolution 687; most important—the destruction of all of Saddam Hussein's arsenal of nuclear, biological, and chemical weapons of mass destruction and ballistic missiles capable of delivering them against Iraq's neighbors in the Middle East. The international community witnessed and withstood earlier attempts by Saddam Hussein to use innocent nationals of other countries as human shields to protect Iraq from attack. He is now using his own population in the same manner to secure release from the constraints on his power that the continuation of sanctions have produced.

291.

Tutwiler, Margaret D. "Northern Iraq Elections." *US Department of State Dispatch* 3, no. 20 (May 18, 1992): 385.

On May 17, the people of northern Iraq will vote in free election to choose an executive leader and members of a legislative body. We hope the voting will proceed in a secure and peaceful atmosphere and help lead to a better life for all the people of northern Iraq - Turcomans, Assyrians, and Kurds. We welcome public and private assurances by the Iraqi Kurdish leadership that these elections will deal only with local administrative issues and do not represent a move toward separatism.

We and our coalition partners have made it clear to Saddam Hussein and the Iraqi regime that Iraqi forces should not engage in repressive actions against the people of Iraq, as required by UN Security Council Resolution 688. We continue to monitor developments in Iraq, and the coalition retains the capability to responds, as necessary, to Iraqi actions which threaten regional peace and security.

The US Government continues to support the sovereignty and territorial integrity of the state of Iraq and to favor replacement of the brutal Saddam Hussein regime with a new government in Baghdad which will fairly represent Iraq's pluralistic society, accept the UN Security Council resolutions, and live at peace with neighboring states. We would like to see all the people of Iraq taking part in a democratic system and enjoying the freedoms which have so long been denied to them by Saddam Hussein. As we have said many times, we do not support the emergence of an independent political entity in northern Iraq.

The US Government has provided more than $600 million in humanitarian assistance for the Iraqi people over the past year. Due in large part to the proximity and cooperation of our NATO ally Turkey, that assistance has significantly benefited northern areas where the voting will take place. Through Operation Provide Comfort, we intervened, along with our coalition partners, to rescue hundreds of thousands of refugees and help them return to their homes. US forces take part in a residual coalition military presence in the area, and we greatly value our excellent, ongoing contacts with the Iraqi Kurdish leadership.

We will not be sending official observers to the elections. US passports are not valid for travel in, to, or through Iraq without a special State Department validation. We are not approving passport validations for travel to northern Iraq during this particular period due to indications of substantial physical risk to American citizens in northern Iraq during the election period.

292.

Boucher, Richard. "Department Statements: PKK Impeding Truck Trafiic into Iraq." *US Department of State Dispatch* 3, no. 44 (November 2, 1992): 807.

[State Department Spokesperson Boucher spoke about the PKK's truck traffic into Iraq.]

We are greatly concerned by reports that the Kurdish Worker's Party (PKK) is impeding truck traffic into northern Iraq.

This truck traffic is the source of UN-sanctioned humanitarian relief supplies—including food and medicine—for the people of northern Iraq. By threatening truck drivers and their families, the PKK is jeopardizing relief efforts, just as preparations for the upcoming winter months are beginning. If winterization efforts are to be successful, supplies must begin moving into northern Iraq promptly.

We applaud the efforts of the Government of Turkey and Iraqi Kurdish groups to protect this truck traffic and Turkish efforts to restore security and block PKK blackmail.

293.

Shelly, Christine. "Annual Terrorism Report Released." *US Department of State Dispatch* 5, no. 20 (May 16, 1994): 322.

Available in the Press Office are copies of *Patterns of Global Terrorism: 1993*. The report describes the dimension of the international terrorist threat during calendar year 1993, during which we recorded 427 international terrorist attacks. This is an increase from the 361 incidents recorded the previous year. The main reason for the increase was an accelerated terror campaign perpetrated by the Kurdistan Workers Party (PKK) against Turkish interests. Most of the group's 150 attacks took place on only two days - 24 June and 4 November - and were staged throughout Western Europe. Had it not been for these two days of coordinated attacks, the level of terrorism would have continued the downward trend of recent years.

The list of states that sponsor terrorism grew by one last year. We added Sudan to the list in August 1993. The other nations that remain on the list are Cuba, Iran, Iraq, Libya, North Korea, and Syria. All seven are discussed in the report.

The bombing of the World Trade Center in New York City and the ensuing fire and smoke caused six deaths and 1,000 injuries. It was the only terrorist incident in 1993 that claimed American lives. Through the hard work of U.S. law enforcement agencies, the Administration successfully tracked down and brought to justice perpetrators of the World Trade Center bombing. The World Trade Center bombing and the FBI's discovery of the plot to blow up selected targets in New York City, including the United Nations and the Holland and Lincoln Tunnels, show that because American targets are vulnerable to terrorist threats, we cannot let down our guard.

The report also describes how the United States is countering the threat. We have been resolute in demanding justice for the families of the victims of the Pan Am 103 bombing, and we remain determined to ensure that Libya surrender the two suspects for trial in Scotland or the United States. We fought for and obtained tighter sanctions against Libya and are vigorously enforcing them. President Clinton sent Saddam Hussein a strong and unequivocal message once evidence was uncovered that his government was responsible for the plot to assassinate former President Bush. We took military action against the Iraqi intelligence headquarters that planned the attack last June, an important and appropriate response. This Administration is committed to maintaining an effective international counter-terrorism policy.

294.

Strobe Talbott. "U.S.-Turkish Leadership in the Post-Cold War World." *US Department of State Dispatch* 6, no. 17 (April 24, 1995): 358-362.

It is a pleasure to be back in Ankara. I'm particularly pleased to be here at Bilkent University. America is proud to be participating in various ways in what is happening on this splendid campus. When this institution first opened its doors to students in 1986 as modern Turkey's first private university, few would have predicted that, just nine years later, it would become one of Turkey's top centers of higher learning. In my own country, private and state universities have long coexisted and the competition for excellence between the two has significantly raised the quality of education and the quality of public discourse to the benefit of the nation as a whole. Outstanding universities, such as this one, teach good citizenship and thus serve as bulwarks of democracy.

It was fitting, therefore, that when Prime Minister Ciller spoke here last month, she spoke about democracy. She argued eloquently that the work of building a truly open society is never done; democracy is, by definition, an ongoing process. Her message is relevant not just to Turkey but to the whole world, including the United States. American democracy, too, is a work in progress. Moreover, democracy is a collaborative work. Supporters of the ideal and the process the world over reinforce and learn from each other. So we are working together on democracy not just here, but everywhere it has taken root.

There is another task on which Turkey and the United States are working together - building the institutions and habits of cooperation that promote international peace and prosperity. This challenge, too, has been the focus of Turkish-American collaboration. For nearly half a century, our two countries stood side by side in the cause of freedom. In no small measure because the United States and Turkey were allies in the Cold War, that conflict is now over. But our work is not over, there is still unfinished business. We are as much allies in the post-Cold War world as we were during the Cold War. If we continue to act together, we can seize a historic opportunity not just to combat new threats but also to shape a world that reflects our shared ideals and promotes our common interests.

This afternoon, I want to talk about how we can make the most of this opportunity. I'd like to begin - and I hope you will not find this presumptuous - by relating your national experience in the 20th century to President Clinton's vision of an international order in the 21st. Turkey's efforts to define statehood and civil society in the post-imperial phase of its own history offer valuable lessons to other countries, particularly to those who are just now emerging from the wreckage of Soviet-style communism and who, therefore, now have another chance at building civil societies of their own.

Modern Turkey and the Soviet Union were born about the same time - under similar circumstances. I thought of this earlier today as I was laying a wreath at the mausoleum of Mustafa Kemal Ataturk. Both the Turkish Republic and the Soviet Union represented great revolutionary experiments launched in the wake of World War I and the collapse of empires. The Soviet experiment lasted for over seven decades. It ended in paralysis, disintegration, and self-defeat, primarily because the political and economic system betrayed the hopes and needs of its own citizens.

The Soviet experiment failed for another reason, too. It failed because the commissars were every bit as imperialistic as the Czars had been - both both in the way they dealt with non-Russian populations within the U.S.S.R. and in their behavior toward the outside world.

Turkey's experiment was, at its core, very different. In January 1921, the Grand National Assembly declared that the new Turkish state rested "on the principle that the people personally and effectively direct their own destinies." This simple but enduring precept, which captures the essence of democracy, has produced powerful, positive, and enduring results. It has allowed Turkey to overcome difficulties and setbacks and to develop a system of free and fair elections in which men and women participate equally. Over the past two decades, Turkey has been able to move away from unresponsive and inefficient economic practices and move toward an environment in which private enterprise and free trade can flourish.

Let me say a word about Turkish foreign policy. In the way that your country first defined - then defended - its national interest, it has set an exemplary standard for the 20th century - one that is worth bearing in mind for the 21st. Under Ataturk's extraordinary leadership, the Turkish people rejected the legacy and temptation of empire and devoted themselves, instead, to the goal that Ataturk himself identi-

fied as "independence within defined national frontiers." After World War II, Turkey forged alliances with the other free peoples of the world in the fight against Soviet expansionism - not just in the West, as part of NATO, but also in the Near East, through CENTO, and in the Far East, through your contribution to the United Nations Force in Korea. Americans still remember the extraordinary bravery of the Turkish soldiers who fought at Kunu Ri and along the Imjin River and the sacrifice of the hundreds of Turks who, like so many Americans, gave their lives in that war.

Now, just as in the early 1920s, we are in another era of great transition following the collapse of an empire one that stretched from Vilnius to Vladivostock and from Murmansk to Baku - a vast territory under the hammer and sickle. The sudden implosion of communist systems has created new opportunities for freedom, prosperity, and long-term security.

Nowhere are those opportunities more apparent than in Europe. As President Clinton put it,

For the first time in history, we can have a Europe that is united by a shared commitment to democracy, free market economics, and mutual respect for borders.

Turkey, which was a front-line state in the battle against Soviet communism, now has much to gain from this process of post-Soviet integration. The emergence of stable, prosperous, democratic, and law-abiding nations along your borders can only benefit Turkey.

There are those who are skeptical about European expansion and integration. They are skeptical about whether any nations to the east of what might, be called "traditional Europe" can truly be part of a larger 21st-century Europe. To them we say: You're wrong. Europe has always defined itself not in terms of artificial geographical barriers - a river here, a mountain range there, or a strait of water somewhere else. Rather, it has defined itself as a community of nation that share values, aspirations, and ways of life - that share a sense of common interest and common destiny. Take my country, for example. The United States is in a different hemisphere from this continent, separated from Europe by the vastness of the Atlantic Ocean. Yet America has played an essential role in securing

European unity and prosperity. Your country, too, is an example of the expansiveness of the idea of Europe. Of course, Turkey has cultural ties to Central Asia and the Middle East; most of Turkey is separated from the rest of Europe by the Bosphorus and the Dardanelles. Yet it has been an important part of the European system since the 16th century.

Let me, in that regard, mention an essential European institution of which both your country and mine are members: NATO. The North Atlantic Treaty Organization has proved to be the greatest, which is to say, the most successful military alliance in history. It defended democracy and kept Europe at peace even while the continent was divided between two heavily armed, ideologically hostile camps. Now, having defended security in a divided Europe, NATO must help extend stability across an undivided Europe.

Our two nations also have important roles to play in the economic integration of the new Europe. The March 6 EU Customs Union Agreement will link Turkey more closely to the peoples of Western Europe, and it also will help to ensure that you will be a full participant in the process of integrating the nations emerging from Soviet-style communism into the European economic system. Turkish membership in the Customs Union will encourage Hungarian, Polish, Russian, and Ukrainian entrepreneurs, as they build new economic partnerships, to look toward Ankara and Istanbul, as well as toward Frankfurt, Paris, London, and New York.

Another essential aspect of building an undivided Europe is the resolution of the conflicts that currently beset individual countries. If Europe as a whole is going to evolve as a harmonious multiethnic community, its constituent states must heal their own internal wounds. An important example is Cyprus. The United States and the United Nations have been working on the problems of that troubled island for over 30 years. President Clinton believes that the time is right to seek a lasting solution that will benefit both communities on Cyprus, thus enhancing the prospects for peace in the entire region. In the past several months, the President's Special Envoy, Richard Beattie, has had constructive meetings with all of the involved parties, and we hope that direct talks under United Nations auspices

will resume soon after this Saturday's elections in north Cyprus.

Looking beyond Europe, the United States and Turkey have vital roles to play in the Middle East and Central Asia. Turkey is the European nation most closely linked to those regions by geography, history, culture, and, of course, by religion.

Let me say a word about Islam. Some have suggested that the Cold War rivalry between communism and capitalism will be replaced by a global "clash of civilizations" between Western and Muslim countries. But Turkey, today, refutes that dire prediction about tomorrow. Turkey is both a Western and a Muslim country, and its four-decade partnership with the other nations of Europe and with the United States proves how productive and enduring cooperation among "the peoples of the book" can be. It is, in this connection, significant that Turkey has contributed to the emerging peace between Israel and her Arab neighbors. That was evident yet again last week when your government hosted the most recent meeting of the Arms Control and Regional Security Working Group in Antalya. These efforts have created historic opportunities for cooperation among all of the nations of the region - I might say, among all the civilized nations of the region.

Last fall's economic summit in Casablanca, which was attended by representatives of 61 countries and over 1,100 business leaders from all regions of the world, demonstrated the potential for economic development in the Middle East. Such development will require enormous amounts of human and financial capital, and Turkey can play a leading role in supplying both. Istanbul has the potential to become a leading capital market for the Middle East, and your young, well-educated work force will be much in demand.

In addition to its human resources, Turkey has a unique advantage in its wealth of natural resources. For decades, oil has been the liquid currency of the Middle East. But with regional peace, rapid population growth, and greater economic development, water will become increasingly important, and Turkey is the only country in the region with a water surplus. Your neighbors to the south-Syria, Jordan, Lebanon, and Israel - will need access to that surplus in the decades to come.

Furthermore, Turkey is an important gateway for trade and investment in the resource-rich areas of Central Asia and the Caucasus. Most immediately, your country offers a highly promising, cost-effective route for bringing oil and gas from those regions to Western markets. A pipeline to the Mediterranean port of Ceyhan, along with other existing and potential routes, would promote economic development in Turkey, as well as in the other countries involved. That project will require cooperation on the part of all the nations in the area and, thus, could help promote greater regional stability.

As Turkey liberalizes its economy, we see trade and investment strengthening the link between our two nations. The Clinton Administration has designated Turkey as one of our 10 so-called Big Emerging Markets. That means that the Secretary of Commerce, Ron Brown, and my boss, Secretary of State Warren Christopher, have made it a top priority to improve market access, provide financing, and otherwise support U.S. companies that are seeking to trade with and invest in Turkey.

The great potential of the economic partnership between our two nations was evident two weeks ago in Washington at the U.S.-Turkey Joint Economic Commission, led by Assistant Secretary of State Richard Holbrooke, who is here at this event today, and Dr. Emre Gonensay, Senior Adviser to Prime Minister Ciller. The JEC has a full and ambitious agenda, which includes potential financing mechanisms for a pipeline to Ceyhan.

All of which is to say, there is plenty of reason for optimism about the future of U.S.-Turkish relations in the post-Cold War era. But we must temper our optimism with realism and our vision with vigilance - for every opportunity that has come with the end of the Cold War there is also a challenge; for every favorable development there seems also to be an ominous one.

While the collapse of Soviet communism created opportunities for economic integration and political freedom, it also opened the lid on a Pandora's box of ethnic conflict and civil war. The forces that threaten to tear apart individual countries and thwart our hopes for international order are concentrated in your neighborhood - on the Balkan Peninsula, in the Caucasus, in Central Asia, and in Iran and Iraq.

As a result, Turkey is yet again on the front line of the world's most important struggles just as it was during the Cold War from the late 1940s to the late 1980s and just as it was during the first major post-Cold War crisis - the repulse of Iraqi aggression and the liberation of Kuwait in 1990-91. As our Ambassador, Mare Grossman, puts it, "Turkey lives in a neighborhood that is a 360-degree challenge."

To your west, in the former Yugoslavia, the war that began with the Serbs' monstrous scheme for "ethnic cleansing" has led to over 200,000 casualties and forced over 2 million people from their homes. Continued fighting threatens to undermine stability throughout southeastern Europe and beyond.

The United States supports the sovereignty and territorial integrity of Bosnia-Herzegovina. We want to see an end to civilian casualties, human rights abuses, and the flow of refugees. We remain committed to UNPROFOR and to the NATO-enforced no-fly zone, and we stand ready to work with our allies to help implement a final peace settlement. We are pressing Serbia to improve human rights conditions for ethnic minorities throughout the country and to restore autonomy to the Albanians in Kosovo. We support Kosovar advocates of nonviolent change and have warned Slobodan Milosevic that we are prepared to take action against Serbia in response to a conflict in Kosovo caused by Serb actions. We also are determined to see that those responsible for ethnic cleansing and other war crimes are brought to justice through the international tribunal that already has begun its work.

We are mindful that many of the victims of the violence in the former Yugoslavia have ties to the people of Turkey. We are grateful for Turkey's contribution to the peacekeeping force in Bosnia and for your help in enforcing the no-fly zone. We also welcome Turkey's role as one of the founding members of the Friends of the Bosnian Croat Federation. In short, the United States and Turkey are united in their support for a multiethnic, multireligious democracy in Bosnia.

Turning eastward, we commend Turkish efforts to help end the Nagorno-Karabakh conflict. Turkey, along with the United States, has been a key member of the OSCE's Minsk Group, and has been actively involved in the ongoing negotiations to resolve the conflict peacefully. Toward that end, we applaud Turkey's move to improve its relations with Armenia. These efforts have reduced tensions in the region while giving the peoples of Azerbaijan and Armenia a real opportunity to achieve a lasting peace.

Let me now say a word about a very large country to your north - Russia, a country where I have just spent several days. The Soviet Union and before that the Russian empire used to be your neighbor, right on your frontier. Now, for the first time in over three centuries - for the first time since the year 1667 - you have no common border with Russia. But its fate and evolution are still much on your minds and on ours.

The bloody debacle in Chechnya is a reminder that the success of reform in Russia and an irreversible repudiation of rule by force are by no means guaranteed. Chechnya has literally and figuratively - broadcast to the world images that conjure up the worst memories of Russia's past and that, therefore, cloud the best visions of its future.

Chechnya stands as a warning to Russia and to the rest of the world: If any government attempts to enforce unity with brute strength, if it insists on imposing its control on people who feel disenfranchised or oppressed, the result will likely be more disintegration, more violence, and more instability. The policy of the United States in regard to Chechnya is clear. We support the sovereignty and territorial integrity of a democratic Russian Federation within its current borders. We do not countenance attempts to change international borders by armed secessionism within a state any more than we countenance. armed aggression by one state against another. We want to see Russia develop as a strong, prosperous, democratic, secure state in the 21st century, at peace with its own peoples as well as with its neighbors. But we also have made clear that we think that Russia will attain those goals only if it continues to develop a pluralistic political system, a constitutional order, and federal structures that permit all the diverse peoples of the Russian Federation to identify

themselves as citizens of a multiethnic state, not as subjects of Moscow's rule.

That same lesson should be apparent to other multiethnic states that are trying to deal with violent secessionists - force alone is not the answer; force alone can make a bad situation worse. The way to defeat outlaw groups is to deprive them of popular support by addressing legitimate needs and grievances. Inclusive democracy, in short, is the best antidote to extremism. Let me move from that general proposition to more specific observations about northern Iraq.

Cooperation between the United States and Turkey on security matters is especially vital when it comes to dealing with outlaw states such as Iraq and Iran and outlaw organizations such as the PKK and Hamas that are determined to use terror to impose their own ideologies, undermine the search for peace, and threaten the territorial integrity of their neighbors.

I already mentioned that Turkey played a stalwart role as a frontline state in the Gulf war, thus affirming its strategic importance and its reliability as an ally and friend of the U.S. Our joint efforts in Iraq have continued with Operation Provide Comfort which, for four years, has served as a deterrent against Saddam Hussein's repression of Iraq's northern population. That operation has served vital U.S. and Turkish interests in containing Saddam and has helped prevent massive refugee flows into Turkey, such as those that occurred in 1991. We look forward to Turkey's continued support of this mission that is so central to our collective interests.

The underlying problem in northern Iraq is the one identified by the United Nations Security Council - namely, that the current Iraqi Government has not been willing to respect international norms or abide by basic human rights standards. As a result, the regime in Baghdad has lost the allegiance of the majority of the Iraqi people, including the Kurds of northern Iraq. It has shown itself to be the enemy of neighboring states and the international community. For those reasons, it has, quite predictably, lost control over its borders.

Over the long run, the only way to eliminate the threat that Turkey faces along its southeastern border is to restore the rule of law to northern Iraq. That depends on the formation of a government in Baghdad that represents all of the Iraqi people and that maintains peaceful relations with all its neighbors. In the meantime, only the Iraqi Kurds can control the border and prevent the PKK from infiltrating terrorists into Turkey. Thus, the U.S. and Turkey must renew our efforts to bring to a halt the violence among Kurdish factions in northern Iraq.

It is our strong belief that the international sanctions called for by Security Council Resolution 688 must continue until the Iraqi Government forsakes terrorism; abandons its attempts to acquire and produce nuclear, biological, and chemical weapons; and ceases repression of its own citizens. Now we know that Turkey has paid a heavy price for its enforcement of these sanctions, but your country is also among those that have the most to gain from an Iraq that fulfills its obligations and responsibilities to the international community. Conversely, your country is among those that have the most to lose if Iraq remains an oppressor of its own people and an exporter of instability.

Our position on Operation Steel is clear. The United States understands Turkey's need to deal firmly with the PKK, which is a vicious terrorist organization. But we attach great importance to the assurances of the Turkish Government that the operation will be limited in scope and duration. We regard the recent withdrawal of 3,000 troops as a positive first step. President Clinton has discussed this issue with Prime Minister Ciller, and I have done the same in my meetings today.

The United States and Turkey must continue to work together, as we have for half a century, to combat threats to stability and security in this region where you live and where we have vital interests, including a vital interest in the stability and security of Turkey itself.

But as we pursue those goals together, we should draw what is perhaps the most compelling and relevant lesson from the Cold War - we should remember that we, the Western allies, did not defeat communism by military deterrence alone, nor did we win this victory by ourselves. In the end, the Berlin Wall came tumbling down and the Iron Curtain was lifted because the yearning of the people of the for-

mer Soviet Union and its satellites for human rights, political freedoms, and open societies finally triumphed over the ideology and the decrepit tyrannical apparatus of their communist rulers. The Cold War ended when peoples all across the U.S.S.R. and throughout Central and Eastern Europe - reformers and democrats and dissidents and, eventually, voters - embraced the same liberal values that unite the member states of NATO. These are the values upon which we must continue to rely - and which we must continue to advance - in the post-Cold War era.

In this sense, too, Turkey is on the front line of a global struggle between forces of reform and those of regression, between the new and the old, and between various visions of the new, some hardly more savory than the old. That struggle continues as diverse peoples seek a balance between, on the one hand, fulfillment of their religious, ethnic, and national identities and, on the other, development of inclusive, secular, democratic institutions and structures of international cooperation. It continues not just in the lands of the former Romanov empire but in the lands of former Hapsburg and Ottoman empires as well as in Central Europe and the Middle East. We want to see Turkey on the right and winning side of this struggle.

If Turkey can ensure the rights of all of its own citizens and stay on the path of economic liberalization, then it will become increasingly a model for states to the West, North, East and South - states that are just embarking on their own journeys of modernization. Your country's accomplishments in the 20th century give you the potential to be a leader in the 21st. This is just one reason among many why the United States is proud to stand with you as we work to build a safer and more prosperous future.

295.

Shelly, Christine. "Human Rights Abuses by Turkish Military and the Situation in Cyprus." *US Department of State Dispatch* 6, no. 24 (June 12 , 1995): 502.

In a statement in Washington, D.C., on June 1, 1995, Acting Department Spokesman

Christine Shelly highlights a report recently submitted to the Congress on allegations of human rights abuses by the Turkish military and on the situation in Cyprus. She notes that the report reaffirms Turkey's continuing importance as a long-standing NATO ally that is confronting a major threat to its sovereignty and territorial integrity from the terrorist Kurdistan Workers' Party. She states that the report also emphasizes that continued support for Turkey's security—both external and internal—serves major U.S. interests.

This morning, the Department submitted to the Congress a report on allegations of human rights abuses by the Turkish military and on the situation in Cyprus.

The Foreign Operations Appropriations Act for FY 1995 withheld 10% of the Foreign Military Financing (FMF) for Turkey pending submission of a report by the State Department. The report was to address alleged human rights abuses by Turkish security forces in the southeastern region of Turkey, and to address Cyprus. The 10% withholding amounted to $36.45 million of a total of $364.5 million in loans approved for FY 1995. Although the Turkish Government stated that it would not accept conditional aid and refused the 10%, Congress has nonetheless requested that the report be submitted as required in the legislation. This report was prepared by the Department in consultation with the Department of Defense.

The report reaffirms Turkey's continuing importance as a longstanding NATO ally which faces a major threat to its sovereignty and territorial integrity from the terrorist Kurdistan Workers' party (PKK). It also stresses that continued support for Turkey's security - both external and internal - serves major U.S. interests.

Among the report's conclusions is that U.S.-origin equipment, which accounts for most major items in the Turkish military inventory, has been used in operations against the PKK, during which human rights abuses have occurred. It is highly likely that such equipment was used in support of the evacuation and/or destruction of villages in southeastern Turkey. However, the report assesses that there is no evidence that verifies reports of torture or "mystery killings" involving U.S. equipment. The report notes that the Turkish

Government has recognized the need to improve its human rights situation and cites proposals which, if adopted and implemented, could lead to important and positive changes in the situation in the southeast.

The report notes further that human rights and democracy will continue to be a prominent feature of the ongoing U.S.-Turkish high-level dialogue. We ascribe great importance to the Turkish Government's democratization initiative. Enhancement of democracy for all Turkey's citizens will significantly improve the human rights situation in Turkey. We urge its rapid passage.

Note: The *Report to Congress on Human Rights Abuses by the Turkish Military and on the Situation in Cyprus* is available on the Department of State Foreign Affairs Network (DOSFAN) on the Internet and is accessible at: http://dosfan.lib.uic.edu/ERC/ bureaus/eur/releases/950601TurkeyCyprus.html.

296.

Clinton, William J. "Containing Iraqi Aggression: The U.S. Response." *US Department of State Dispatch* 7, no. 36 (September 2, 1996): 441.

Three days ago, despite clear warnings from the United States and the international community, Iraqi forces attacked and seized the Kurdish-controlled city of Irbil in northern Iraq. The limited withdrawals announced by Iraq do not change the reality: Saddam Hussein's army today controls Irbil, and Iraqi units remain deployed for further attacks.

These acts demand a strong response, and they have received one. Earlier today, I ordered American forces to strike Iraq. Our missiles sent the following message to Saddam Hussein: When you abuse your own people or threaten your neighbors, you must pay a price.

It appears that one Kurdish group which in the past opposed Saddam now has decided to cooperate with him. But that cannot justify unleashing the Iraqi army against the civilian population of Irbil. Repeatedly over the past weeks and months we have worked to secure a lasting cease-fire between the Kurdish factions. The Iraqi attack adds fuel to the factional fire and threatens to spark instability throughout the region.

Our objectives are limited but clear: to make Saddam pay a price for the latest act of brutality, reducing his ability to threaten his neighbors and America's interests.

First, we are extending the no-fly zone in southern Iraq. This will deny Saddam control of Iraqi air space from the Kuwaiti border to the southern suburbs of Baghdad, and will significantly restrict Iraq's ability to conduct offensive operations in the region.

Second, to protect the safety of our aircraft enforcing this no-fly zone, our cruise missiles struck Saddam's air defense capabilities in southern Iraq.

The United States was a co-sponsor of United Nations Security Resolution 986, which allows Iraq to sell amounts of oil to purchase food and medicine for its people, including the Kurds. Irbil, the city seized by the Iraqis, is a key distribution center for this aid. Until we are sure these humanitarian supplies can actually get to those who need them, the plan cannot go forward and the Iraqi Government will be denied the new resources it has been expecting.

Saddam Hussein's objectives may change, but his methods are always the same—violence and aggression—against the Kurds, against other ethnic minorities, against Iraq's neighbors. Our answer to that recklessness must be strong and immediate, as President Bush demonstrated in Operation Desert Storm, as we showed two years ago when Iraq massed its forces on Kuwait's border, and as we showed again today.

We must make it clear that reckless acts have consequences, or those acts will increase. We must reduce Iraq's ability to strike out at its neighbors, and we must increase America's ability to contain Iraq over the long run.

The steps we are taking today will further all those objectives. Time and again, Saddam Hussein has made clear his disdain for civilized behavior. He brutalized his own people, attacked his neighbors, supported terrorism, and sought to acquire weapons of mass destruction. Our policy is equally clear: When our interest in the security of our friends and allies is threatened, we will act with force if necessary. That is what we did this morning in Iraq.

I know the thoughts and prayers of all Americans are with our military men and women who are conducting this mission. God bless them and the nation they are serving.

MISCELLANEOUS

297.

Secretary of State Madeleine K. Albright, Jalal Talabani of the Patriotic Union of Kurdistan (PUK), and Massoud Barzani of the Kurdistan Democratic Party (KDP) Press remarks following their meeting Washington, D.C., September 17, 1998 As released by the Office of the Spokesman U.S. Department of State http://secretary.state.gov/www/statements/ 1998/980917a.html

SECRETARY ALBRIGHT: I am very pleased to welcome to the State Department today two leaders of the Iraqi Kurdish people: Mr. Barzani of the Kurdish Democratic Party, and Mr. Talabani of the Patriotic Union of Kurdistan. As they will indicate shortly, their joint meetings here this week have opened a new and hopeful chapter in their efforts to work together on behalf of their people. Our sessions here follow six months of working-level talks between the two parties in northern Iraq and recent consultations by each in Ankara and London.

We welcome today's step forward. The United States has deep concern for the safety, security and economic well being of the Iraqi Kurds—Shi'as, Sunnis, and others—who have been subject to brutal attacks by the regime in Baghdad, including the Anfal attacks in 1988 and the military campaigns in 1991. With others in the international community we have sought to protect Iraqis from the repression of Saddam Hussein and to address their humanitarian concerns. At the Security Council in New York we have reminded our colleagues that the purpose of Council Resolutions, particularly Resolution 688, is not restricted to Iraqi weapons programs, but extends as well to the safety and protection of

to the safety and protection of the Iraqi populations in both the north and the south. All this is fully consistent with our commitment to the territorial integrity and sovereign unity of Iraq.

The renewed spirit of reconciliation between Mr. Barzani and Mr. Talabani, exemplified by their joint meeting and joint statement today, will make it easier for the United States and others to help their people. They have set a timetable for resolving their differences fully consistent with the principles laid down in the 1996 Ankara Accords. We encourage them and will help where we can to see that this agenda is met. Without unity, the road ahead will remain very difficult. With unity, there is every reason for the Iraqi Kurds to look forward with hope.

As we meet, Iraq is threatening once again to end all cooperation with UN weapons inspectors, this time in response to a Council decision to suspend periodic reviews of Iraqi compliance with UN Resolutions which responded in turn to Iraq's totally unacceptable decision in August to halt cooperation with UNSCOM disarmament work. It is vital that the Security Council respond in a firm and principled way to Iraq's provocative and self-defeating acts. The Council cannot allow Iraq to gain by starting yet another cycle of defiance and threats. Its credibility and effectiveness are on the line. It, the Security Council, must insist that Iraq comply with all relevant Council Resolutions.

The United States will decide how and when to respond to Baghdad's actions based on the threat they pose to Iraq's neighbors, to regional security, to vital U.S. interests, and to the Iraqi people, including those in the north. We have not taken any option off the table. If Iraq tries to break out of its strategic box, our response will be strong and sure. But we will act on our own timetable, not Saddam Hussein's.

The United States looks forward to the day when Iraq can rejoin the family of nations as a responsible and law-abiding member. To those Iraqis inside and outside the country who want to build a democratic future for their nation, I say: the United States is on your side.

The new Radio Free Iraq is preparing to broadcast directly to the Iraqi people. We are gathering information regarding the atrocities committed by Saddam Hussein to help the Iraqi exile community in its campaign to bring him to justice. And, as today's meeting reflects, we are intensifying our efforts to help Iraqis–whether Arab or Kurd, Shiite or Sunni–to develop a deeper sense of common purpose and a more effective strategy for achieving their future in a democratic and pluralist Iraq.

Obviously, these measures are no panacea. It would not be responsible to raise false hopes or expectations. But neither can we turn our backs on the Iraqi people who have for too long been denied the freedom, security and chance for prosperity they deserve. There can be no more Anfals, no more campaigns to eradicate whole populations of innocent men, women and children.

I welcome Mr. Talabani and Mr. Barzani and congratulate them for the courageous steps they are taking; and on behalf of the United States, I look forward to working with them further to promote the humanitarian condition, human rights and safety of their people.

MR. MASSOUD BARZANI: (Through translator) First, I would like to thank Secretary Albright and the Government of the United States of America for their interest in the concerns and issues of our people and for fostering our reconciliation and for hosting us here.

We have accomplished something important in the last few days. With God's help, we must implement what we have agreed to, and we must implement those things carefully and accurately. The basis for that will be the good intentions and the support of our friends. Our people are looking forward to the results of these talks. What we have accomplished will ensure a prosperous future for our people.

Here I would like to affirm our concern and interest for the unity of Iraq. What we have done is not against the interests of any country in the region, but what we have done is to solve the existing problems.

Once again, thank you very much, Madam Secretary.

MR. JALAL TALABANI: It is a historic day. We closed a sad chapter of the history of the Kurdish people, who suffered too much in their history. It is a new day, and I hope that it will be a day that we both, Mr. Barzani and myself, and our two parties, the PUK and KDP, will do their best to implement this historic accord which we have achieved with the support of our American friends, especially Secretary Albright, whom we are very much grateful to her – to her personal contribution, to her personal encouragement and advice to us, and to our friends. Among them I want to mention the important role of our friend David Welch, who took the risk of visiting us in Iraqi Kurdistan and preparing for this meeting here, and of course for all other friends here in the State Department, in the White House, and everywhere, who supported us in achieving this historic and important achievement.

Our people are looking forward to having a united, democratic, federative Iraq. It is an opportunity for us to assure that we are not a separatist force; we are for strengthening the national unity of Iraq. We are not working with any states in the area. On the contrary, (inaudible) will have to have peace and stability in the area which help all neighbors of Iraq.

We are for better relations with the United States of America. The Kurdish people will never forget that the United States of America and the Secretary of State, friends from the State Department and from other Departments that helped us reach this important accord. We will remain as a Kurdish faithful nation grateful to them. I hope it will help to strengthen relations between American people and Iraqi people, Kurdish people included.

Again, I express my appreciation and gratitude to Madam Albright and to other friends in the State Department. Thank you very much (applause).

298.

David Welch
Deputy Assistant Secretary
Bureau of Near Eastern Affairs
Interview on Worldnet *Dialogue*
October 15, 1998
www.state.gov/www/policy_remarks/1998/
981015_welch_iraq.html

U.S. Brokered Northern Iraq Accord and
U.S.-Iraq Relations

MR. FOUCHEUX: Hello, I'm Rick Foucheux. Welcome to Worldnet's "Dialogue."

Last month Secretary of State Madeleine Albright announced a U.S.-brokered accord which has allowed a power-sharing agreement between Jalal Talabani of the Patriotic Union of Kurdistan, and Masoud Barzani of the Kurdish Democratic Party. Many are hoping that this particular agreement will lead to a general election next year. On this edition of "Dialogue" we will discuss the northern Iraq accord and the impact this agreement will have in the area, and U.S.-Iraqi relations.

Joining us to discuss these issues is David Welch, principal assistant deputy assistant secretary in the State Department's Bureau of Near Eastern Affairs. Mr. Welch, it's a pleasure to have you with us today.

MR. WELCH: Thank you, Rick.

MR. FOUCHEUX: Before we begin with our questioners overseas, can you tell us some of the highlights that have taken place since the agreement was announced?

MR. WELCH: Certainly. When this agreement was put together it marked the first time the leaders of the two principal Kurdish parties in northern Iraq had met personally in some four years. It was a landmark event in that sense. Since then they have continued their own travels through the United States and Europe on their way back to their homes in northern Iraq.

The agreement set out a calendar for its implementation, and we are in the very early stages of that. We hope that the next event will be another summit meeting of the two leaders, Mr. Barzani and Mr. Talabani, in Ankara toward the beginning of November.

MR. FOUCHEUX: Great. Well, once again, we are glad you are here, and we are looking forward to your insights in today's program.

MR. WELCH: Thank you.

MR. FOUCHEUX: Our fellow participants are standing by in Ankara and London. We begin first with Ankara. Please go ahead with your first question or comment.

Q: Good afternoon, this is—(inaudible)—from Turkish news channel and TV. My question is, you know, there's a big tension at the moment in the area between Turkey and Syria. How do you evaluate this tension?

MR. WELCH: Well, I think—first of all, I'm not in the best position to comment on the day-to-day development in the Turkish-Syrian situation, because unlike the joint statement between the Kurdish leaders in Washington, the United States does not play a mediating role in that dispute. The Government of Egypt has, as I understand it, though, the tensions have calmed somewhat in recent days, thanks to the good efforts of Egypt. Now, I believe that the parties share an interest in seeing a solution to the problems between them, and I hope that they've embarked on a way to reconcile their differences.

In terms of our own views—that is, the United States' views of the issues that divide Turkey and Syria—we have taken a position that no nation in that area should harbor terrorists, and that would include Syria. We have encouraged Egyptian mediation to resolve that matter.

Q: Despite the U.S. Government's official documents that is showing that Syria is one of the states that sponsors—countries which is supporting terrorism, why don't you clearly support Turkey while it was trying to push Syria to end terrorist support for PKK?

MR. WELCH: I'm not sure exactly what you are asking with that question. We have very different relationships with Syria and Turkey. On the one hand Syria as a U.S.-designated state sponsor of terrorism is subject to a variety of U.S. strictures and laws. On the other hand, Turkey is a long-standing ally of the United States, a member of NATO. There really isn't a comparison in that sense between the two relationships.

What we support as an outcome here is a peaceful solution. We believe that Turkey has a legitimate grievance in this case. That is, we are quite concerned about Syria's harboring of terrorists and support for groups that advocate terrorism. Otherwise we would not have listed them as a state sponsor of terrorism. In that sense I think that we do support the grievances that Turkey has in this situation, while of course we advocate a peaceful resolution of the dispute.

Q: Mr. Welch, does the U.S. administration have any idea where the PKK leader (Abdullah Ocalan ?) lives at the moment?

MR. WELCH: I'm sorry, I can't comment on that. Frankly what I know is mostly from press accounts and from my own private diplomatic contacts principally with the Government of Turkey. I would prefer not to go into detail on that. I would note some statements indicating a calming of the situation on the parts of certain members of the Turkish Government.

Q: Mr. Welch, do you believe a dialogue is a must as soon as possible between Turkey and Syria during that period unless Syria takes a positive step to clear its support for PKK?

MR. WELCH: Well, it's hard to be against dialogue almost under any circumstances. I do believe that dialogue has to be matched with results. It's been our hope that the two parties would find some process to come together to discuss these differences in a way that not only are they resolved but each can be confident that the way to resolve them is verifiable. The alternative to doing so, that is that there should be some kind of escalation of the situation between the two, I think would cause us considerable concern.

Q: Mr. Welch, as you know the Turkish Government is not really happy with the last meeting between Mr. Barzani and Talabani in Washington. What is the main disagreement between Turkey and the U.S. administration concerning northern Iraq?

MR. WELCH: Well, I am glad we have now focused on northern Iraq. Thank you for asking the question. Really I don't believe we have any significant differences between the parties who are the co-sponsors of the Ankara process—that is, Turkey, the United States and the Government of the United Kingdom. There are occasionally tactical differences or differences in interpretation, but those pale beside the fundamental agreement on the objectives.

And what are the objectives here? The objectives are to ensure peace and stability in this area of northern Iraq which for many years has been plagued by factional disputes and by the interference of outside parties, and unfortunately by terrorist activity. The Ankara process was designed to repair that situation to the best extent possible. Over the years it faltered, largely because the two leaders could not come to an understanding on how to deal with each other over the very real problems that divide them.

As I mentioned earlier, they haven't met together in four years until the event in Washington. What we were able to do here was bring them together for the first time and set out anew a process by which they could address their differences. This time it has a calendar attached, and in has in that sense a verifiable program of action by which they ought to have accomplished certain things, and the co-sponsors can monitor their doing so.

Q: Mr. Welch, Ankara still says that the agreement between Barzani and Talabani that was signed in Washington is not being presented to Ankara, or Ankara has not been informed about the agreement before it was signed. What could you say about it?

MR. WELCH: We have consulted with the Government of Turkey throughout this process. The government of Turkey has consulted with us about its own efforts to promote stability in the north. We made every effort to bring the other co-sponsors into this process. But in the end the result was basically because the United States was able to broker a summit meeting between the two leaders. We felt that that meeting was sufficiently important in order to break the ice and lend momentum to forward progress that it should be held here in Washington.

Our concern remains the same—absolutely the same objectives as before: We do believe that the security of everyone in the area is better if there is a basic understanding between the two principal Kurdish parties in northern Iraq, and that includes the security of Turkey. If these two parties are able to cooperate, then the opportunities for outside meddling and terrorism and violations of the Turkish border we believe would decrease.

Q: Mr. Welch, we have reports in Ankara that the support of the Baghdad administration to PKK rises day by day. Can you confirm it?

MR. WELCH: This is yet another one of the UN obligations on Iraq that it is regularly violating. That is, the UN Security Council resolutions declare that Iraq should cease its support for terrorism. We have credible indications that that is not the case, that it remains in support of extremist groups, including unfortunately the PKK.

Q: Mr. Welch, while they are talking about the future of Kurdish groups in the region under the agreement signed in Washington, what could you say about the future of Turkomen people in the area, in northern Iraq?

MR. WELCH: Thank you for asking this important question. I believe—and my duty in helping to mediate this process has been to achieve something better for all the people that live there. We think that the best way to do that is that they should take care of their own affairs and try and reach some understandings between them. By negotiating with the two principal armed groups there we did not mean or intend to exclude anyone. As you may know, I have myself personally visited northern Iraq twice in the last two years. That's sort of a rare trip for American officials to make. During those visits I met at length with various representatives of the Turkoman population there, and I have spoken to them in Turkey as well. We are gravely concerned for the future of all the people in that area, be they Kurds, be they Turkoman, be they Christians, Syrians—anyone, frankly. We honestly believe that that future is better if they are able to protect themselves by greater unity and stability in that area, so that they are not victim to the interference of either Baghdad or Tehran or some other outside party that has a mind to upset the situation.

The understanding that we brokered here in Washington provides for a political role for all people in the area. There are some differences as to how that would be exercised, but those differences are mainly in the area of rather basic data, such as how many people are in the population and what would be their voting apportionment within any assembly that would be elected. Those are areas which remain to be clarified in the negotiating process, probably with some help from outside so that a reliable census for example could be conducted and electoral rolls established.

Q: Mr. Welch, as you know the Turkish Government has recently decided to upgrade its political representation in Baghdad and decided to have an ambassador there. How do you evaluate this decision? Thank you.

MR. WELCH: We think this is not the time to signal any change in the relationship with Baghdad, because at this moment the Iraqi regime remains significantly estranged from the obligations it must bear under the UN Security Council resolutions. It is not cooperating, for example, with the UN Special Commission, and hasn't been since early August. Therefore at a time when there is such a division between the regime in Baghdad and the international community we frankly felt it wasn't the right signal to suggest an upgrading of relations.

Q: Mr. Welch, since the beginning of the Turkish-Syrian dispute there were some Arab countries which claimed that Israel is behind this Turkish policy by provocating Ankara. As one of the key diplomats of the State Department, how do you evaluate Turkish-Israeli ties, and also Turkish-Israeli ties are a threat for the region, changing the balances? Thank you.

MR. WELCH: I'm afraid I don't agree with that hypothesis that some have that there is some Israeli involvement behind Turkish action in this regard. My own—my government's views on this are very clear. It is quite natural for Turkey, a prominent and significant nation in that region and internationally, to have relations with whomever it wants. Israel is a good friend of the United States; so is Turkey. Naturally we would be pleased if their relationship matures and improves. We believe that's a healthy thing for the region, not a problem for the region. I don't consider it to be a threat to the region, and I certainly do not believe that Israel is in any respect behind Turkey's action vis-a-vis terrorists who threaten Turkey from the outside. The Government of Turkey takes its own decisions on matters like this, and is I think quite capable of acting independently and bearing the responsibility for that. I think it's quite wrong to suggest that there is some kind of large plot here behind these moves.

Q: I'm—(inaudible)—Los Angeles Times. Before traveling to Washington, Masoud Barzani said the reason he actually was going to Washington was because you, during your visit to northern Iraq last June, had for the first time expressed open support for the Kurds, that you had finally given the sort of guarantees that the Kurds were seeking. What sort of guarantees did you offer?

MR. WELCH: Actually I think the most important assurance that we provide to the people—all the people, not just the Kurds, but others as well—in northern Iraq is an exemplar of international engagement. It is my belief that the United States should not remain indifferent to the fate of the people in this area. We have learned from terrible lessons in the past that if we are indifferent that tragedy will only repeat itself. Let's remember that the people in northern Iraq were victims of gross human rights abuses during the 1980s and early '90s. The international community rallied in the early '90s to support them. And I think the biggest problem they have had in the period since are their own political divisions. If we could lend some help to repair that, then the security and welfare of the people there, all of the people, would have been better.

What I stressed to both leaders—not just to Mr. Barzani, but also to Mr. Talabani—and for that matter everybody else I met with there—was that international engagement is available. That is, international attention is there, including for the United States—but they have a responsibility to their own people to exercise leadership to help this situation get better, because if they don't the risks to their own people are much higher.

I didn't provide any specific assurance. Once they came to Washington we made clear to them our view that in circumstances in which the two principal Kurdish parties were divided and fighting each other, and if they were then subjected to assault from the outside or from Baghdad it would be much more difficult as a practical matter for the United States or anyone to marshal international support to help them. The Secretary of State made that explicitly clear to both Mr. Barzani and Mr. Talabani.

But the converse of that is that if they are united, and if they are embarked on a process of peaceful reconciliation, then the United States will be there to help. And if another threat comes from Baghdad, we cannot remain indifferent to that, and we will be supportive. This the Secretary of State announced publicly at the time the joint statement was put before the world.

Q: Mr. Welch, if we look at the agreement between Barzani and Talabani we see some interesting points in this agreement. We see that the agreement includes an idea of federation between the Kurdish groups in the future. This federation idea will cause or will lead to a real state in the future in the area—do you think that?

MR. WELCH: I'm glad you asked this question, because I know from talking to my friends in the government of Turkey that this has caused some concern in Turkey. Let me answer this in several ways.

First, with respect to what is stated in the agreement, it is explicitly stated in the first part of the joint statement that the aspiration of the people of Iraq is for a united, pluralistic, and democratic Iraq. In terms of what the two Kurdish parties aspire to, they would like some sort of federative solution within a united Iraq. In terms of the United States' position on that aspiration—that is, on that desire of the two Kurdish parties—we respect their desire, but we respect the desire of all the Iraqi people to have a united, pluralistic and democratic country. Frankly, they'd be a lot better off if they did. In that sense this is a statement of respect for the right of people to decide their own future within their country—something that most Americans would readily agree is part of our own national patrimony. We are, after all, a federal nation ourselves. It does not mean that the United States proposes any specific solution for that—for the nation of Iraq—that's up to the Iraqi people to decide, of whom the Kurds are a large part.

Second, what is the position of the United States with respect to an independent Kurdistan, because I know this is an area where people have asked some questions. Let me make it clear here, as I have before, the United States does not support an independent Kurdistan—be it in northern Iraq, be it any other place. We support a united Iraq. We believe that Iraq has territorial integrity as a nation in its own right, and we are not seeking to change its formation. That is our view on what should happen within Iraq.

Q: During your talks with Mr. Barzani and Mr. Talabani, did the issue of the Iraqi opposition come up? And what role, if any, did they declare themselves willing to play in such a movement? And given the failure of your previous experiment with an opposition, what new model or players if any are you looking at? And what's your reaction to Dr. Ahmed Talabi's (sp) proposal that the crowd prince of Jordan, Hassan, be the new leader of Iraq?

MR. WELCH: Well, there are several questions there. Let me try and answer the most important one—that is, what aspect of the discussions with Barzani and Talabani dealt with the opposition. I repeat what I said earlier. The purpose of the effort we launched here in September was to improve the situation in the north. We didn't set as an objective that these two leaders should declare themselves as leaders of the opposition or form any sort of united front against Baghdad. Frankly, I don't think that is necessary or appropriate under the circumstances. Let's remember, after all, that these two political leaders have a substantial experience with Saddam Hussein's regime. They don't need to be taught lessons by anybody by what it means to be victims of that regime. In that sense they are like most Iraqis: they suffer at his hands and have learned the results. We don't need to encourage them to realize that history. They are self-declared leaders of the opposition, because they do not want the authority and control of Saddam Hussein within their area. They would consider themselves to be worse off if that is the case. And it is our shared responsibility, frankly, as members of the international community to assure that that doesn't happen again.

Q: Mr. Welch, as you know Turkey sometimes carries out military operations in northern Iraq to sweep out the PKK terrorists. Those operations drew some reactions from some countries in the region or in the world. But, as you know, you support it. You have been supporting Turkey for such operations because they were against terrorism. Under changing balances in the future, will the U.S. continue to look warmly on such operations by Turkey? Thank you.

MR. WELCH: Well, let me be clear about our position. First, Turkey is a friend and ally. Second, we respect and support Turkey's right to defend itself, including against terrorism. Third, Turkey does not consult with us in advance on any such operations, and we do not support or preapprove them in advance. Fourth, when Turkey feels it necessary to conduct such operations, our reaction is that they should be limited in scope and duration, and scrupulous with respect to the effect on the human rights of the people in the area. So that is slightly different from supporting the operations per se. Other countries obviously take a different position, but then I would point out that many of those who denounce such operations are themselves responsible for the circumstances that lead to those operations or for actual support of the terrorist group the PKK involved.

Our—we have a good dialogue with the government of Turkey on these matters. It is my belief that the joint statement concluded in Washington includes some of the most important security assurances for the safety and protection of Turkey of any of these agreements so far. Am I concerned that they should be implemented? Absolutely. I will monitor this very diligently, together with my colleagues in the government of the Turkey and the United Kingdom. It's very important that that aspect of the agreement be firmly adhered to, and it is fundamental to the involvement of the United States in this process that there should be a security benefit for Turkey.

Q: Sir, I'd like to repeat my question about the Iraqi opposition and what new sort of formula you are working on for that opposition. Can we expect to see such a movement being based anew in northern Iraq?

MR. WELCH: We support the idea of an Iraqi opposition. I think we all know there is an Iraqi opposition, and it consists of most of the people of Iraq. The issue before us all is to give it a voice and a coherence so that it over time will show itself as a meaningful alternative. This is a long-term effort. It is unfortunately a characteristic of the Baghdad regime that the superlative authoritarianism of that government has been extremely successful in controlling internal dissent—not in all areas of the country, but certainly in the center. What we are suggesting from the United States' side is support for the opposition's efforts to organize itself and project its voice internationally and inside Iraq. That has several elements. First, for support of radio broadcasts that would offer a different voice and view to the Iraqi people. Second, support for efforts of the opposition to organize itself and bring various members of the Iraqi opposition together for dialogue and understanding. Third, we also support an organized and coherent effort to gather the data about Saddam Hussein's human rights violations and war crimes, so that over time this can all be put in one place, studied and analyzed, and perhaps be the basis for some further international action against him.

Q: Mr. Welch, as you know Barzani and Talabani have been planning to come to Turkey to get together again in Ankara. Will you join them during their trip to Ankara, or do you have any plan to come to Ankara to ease Turkish officials' concerns about the agreement signed in Washington?

MR. WELCH: Actually I have spent quite a bit of time with officials of the government of Turkey in recent weeks. And I hope to continue that. We suggested that the next step in the reconciliation process be a meeting at the summit level between Barzani and Talabani with Turkey, the U.K. and the U.S. in attendance in Ankara.

And let me point out with respect to that meeting its agenda could cover anything. We had suggested that it must focus on the issue of security. Why did we do that? We did that because, as I said earlier, this is the principal element of our involvement here, and a fundamental of our mediation effort. We didn't mean by suggesting that that the other issues wouldn't be on the table—of course they would be.

Now, it is up to the Government of Turkey to invite us all. I hope they will do so. If they should do so, then I personally will be very glad to attend. My boss, Secretary Albright, expects me to go there for that purpose, if such a meeting is held. In recent days I will tell you that I have spoken to Mr. Barzani and to Mr. Talabani, who are in Europe and the Persian Gulf, respectively, and they have both indicated their willingness to go if they should be welcomed there. It's up to the Government of Turkey of course to extend that welcome.

MR. FOUCHEUX: Thank you in Ankara. Now we turn to London for their questions. Please go ahead in London.

Q: Hello, this is—(inaudible)— newspaper. I have two questions. The first one: There are some reports that Mrs. Albright promised Mr. Talabani and Barzani when they were meeting in Washington that the U.S.—it will defend them in case of the Iraqi troops go to the north of Iraq, like it defends Kuwait. Can you confirm that?

My second question is that you said that the U.S. aid policy is against the disintegration of Iraq. But from the Arab world view we see that there is de facto in northern Iraq which makes the basis for a Kurdish independent state. Thank you.

MR. WELCH: With regard to your first question, Mr. Ibrahim, at the time the joint statement was agreed, Secretary Albright said publicly two things—that the United States cannot countenance a repetition of the events of the late 1980s early 1990s in northern Iraq in which many, many thousands of Iraqis, mainly Kurds, died. And, as you may recall, this was one of the first uses of chemical weapons against innocent civilians—by their own government. A second thing that she said in her statement was that the United States would include the people of Iraq, and especially those in the north, as among the concerns to which it would react were Iraq to make a move. I think this is a warning that Saddam Hussein should not ever attempt this again, because it would have a price.

With respect to the breakup of Iraq, we have declared until, as the Americans say, we are "blue in the face" that we favor a unified Iraq. As a practical matter, the Government of Iraq has not controlled certain parts of its own country for many, many years, including before the United States was actually involved in this matter. I don't know if you mean that is the breakup of Iraq. I consider that to be a failure of the regime in Baghdad; that is, a failure to its own people. We do not advocate in any respect the severance of a part of Iraq from itself, and the de facto creation of an independent state in any part of it; nor, I believe, do the two Kurdish leaders advocate such a thing. Read carefully their own statements: they want a united, pluralistic, democratic Iraq. Within that Iraq they would propose that they have a federative system. Well, that's up to all Iraqis to decide. We hope that the day will come in which the Iraqis are given such a choice.

Q: Mr. Welch, my name is— (inaudible)—newspaper. And it's well and good to say that obviously you don't set out to carve out part of Iraq and try to make it independent or federative, as the two Turkish leaders would say. But in terms of action this is precisely what is happening. A, you are starting a broadcasting station for the opposition; B, there was an attempt by CIA elements in the north not long ago when Talabani attacked Barzani in Sulaymaniyah, and all the indications are that you are heading towards that—you want a larger international involvement in the north. But you know actions are different from statements. What would you say to that?

MR. WELCH: Well, I don't agree with most of it. I mean, there are many opposition radio broadcasts. Why is it that our broadcast is singled out as the cause of the disintegration of Iraq? What we want is a different voice for the Iraqi people. We are delighted to support that, wherever it comes from. We believe that the Iraqi people deserve a different future. That's our intention here.

Again, my feeling is that there is a nation of Iraq. It has been very poorly led over the last 20 to 30 years. All you have to do is look at the comparisons in the region. Iraq has great natural resources, it has a bright and vibrant population. And what has been done with that nation? It has been ruined by one regime, and one regime is responsible for most of the history of the last 25 years. I think we all know this. Notwithstanding that fundamental challenge presented by the regime itself in Baghdad, this nation has remained unified. I believe its coherence, that is what draws it together, has a greater sense of destiny than what might draw it apart. It is not our intention to carve it up again; nor, I have to tell you quite honestly, do I think we would be able to even if we wanted to. After all, this country fought an eight-year war in which many people predicted that perhaps one part of its sectarian population—what one sectarian part of its population would break away to go to the other side. Well, that didn't happen, did it? It didn't happen because I think most

Iraqis think of themselves as Iraqis. And if an immediate neighbor couldn't carve it up, I'm not sure the United States could, even if we wanted to.

Now, I think at the end of the day, sir, I think there is probably no way I can reduce to zero the suspicions that may be out there that that is our intention. But all I can do is reaffirm once again that that is not the case. And let me put it to you this way: If tomorrow we all wake up and there is a different regime in Baghdad, and Mr. Saddam Hussein has retired, then the United States will be prepared for a different relationship with that regime. Secretary Albright declared that in a speech at the beginning of 1997, which I would ask you to go back and read, because this shows that our problem is with the regime; it is not with the people or with the country.

Q: And how would you, Mr. Welch, then interpret the move by Ankara to elevate diplomatic relations with Baghdad to an ambassadorial level immediately following the agreement in Washington? Don't you sense that the Turks are afraid that in case there is a separate entity in the north of Iraq the same example would be copied in Southeastern Turkey?

MR. WELCH: I believe I have answered and can't answer any concerns on the part of the Government of Turkey with respect to the joint statement between the two Kurdish leaders.

With regard to Turkey's decisions on relations with Baghdad, I was asked this question earlier by a Turkish journalist, and my answer is the same: this is a decision up to Turkey. It caused us some concern. We believe at a time when Baghdad is divided from the international community it frankly is not a good idea to change one's relationship with that government. I will watch to see how this decision is implemented.

Q: Hello, this is Ali Ibrahim again. In the agreement between Barzani and Mr. Talabani which the United States sponsored in Washington, there is a timetable for going to an election next June. Some critics say that the agreement is not realistic and there are lots of things about—I mean, it will be—there will be a lot of problems, like sharing the revenues and all these things, and also that the United

States has committed itself to something which it can't afford. Thank you.

MR. WELCH: Well, sir, I think this region of the world is unfortunately littered with many well-intentioned agreements that have suffered in the implementation. I am hopeful with respect to this one. I am hopeful because I think I have the personal commitment of both leaders, as expressed directly to the most senior levels of the American Government of their own leadership and responsibility in this endeavor. Obviously that alone is not good enough. It remains their obligation to try and fix their own situation. What we have shown is that we can help. We can help to bring them together, but we cannot help them or push them to a solution—they must do that themselves. We will monitor, we will cajole, we will encourage, we will push them to take those steps which are necessary to complete this process. The end result I think is a great benefit to their people. And if they don't get there they will have to ask themselves, Have they exercised their responsibility has leaders of their people to provide them for—with a better future?

Q: How do you see the Arab reaction—I mean the moderate Arab states towards the Kurdish agreement from your point of view? Did they welcome it or they are little bit critical of it?

MR. WELCH: Actually I think the reaction has been pretty good. We briefed many of our Arab friends during this negotiation and after it, and we found the reaction quite good. I think they see our purpose as clear, and that is to try and restore peace and stability in that area. The governments, the moderate American Governments who are American friends, do not have a conspiratorial view of what we are trying to achieve. They don't think that we are trying to break up Iraq.

I would point out that in the aftermath of the agreement one of the leaders has been making a trip to the Arab world. I hardly think he would be welcome in these places if they didn't like the agreement.

Q: Mr. Welch, let's presume that the agreement has advanced along the way, and many of its parts have been implemented and then Baghdad was in a position to see when there is an attempt of them to separate. And then they cracked on the Kurds. What would

then be the position of the United States? Would it send troops to be on the ground there?

MR. WELCH: Look, I'm not going to answer a hypothetical question like that. But the message here should be very clear. There is a resolution, Resolution 688, which obliges the Iraqi Government not to repress its own people. Iraq has never observed that resolution, and continues to this very day to conduct acts of repression against its own people.

As we all focus on the arms control provisions of the sanctions regime on Iraq, we should remember that one as well that is the important human rights dimension to this issue. What we have established with this joint statement and the public U.S. remarks made at the time is that there is a warning there, that the international community led by the United States will not be indifferent if Iraq tries something again like it did in the 1980s and early '90s.

Q: Do you see any connection between the accord between Mr. Talabani and Barzani in Washington and the escalation or the tension between Syria and Turkey?

MR. WELCH: I don't personally, but I mean inevitably there is some sort of connection in that I think at the root of the problem between Turkey and Syria is the issue of the PKK. But you would have to ask the Government of Turkey this question.

Q: Finally, Mr. Welch, you said that you are not seeking to see an independent Kurdish state. And I don't actually believe that this will be accepted in the area given the balance of the regional powers—Turkey on the one hand, Iraq and then Iran. But I mean you are in a sense encouraging the emergence of an entity in which the international community will be more and more involved in helping. Doesn't this sound to you like the beginning of a new state?

MR. WELCH: Well, it sounds to me like ensuring the protection and security of a group of people who want the right to determine their own future within their own country; and who in the past, because they haven't had this kind of international attention, have been victims themselves.

I don't believe, and I could not myself countenance remaining indifferent to their fate. And, yes, by their example we seek to show to all Iraqis that there is an alternative choice. But this means an alternative choice for all Iraqis—not just for those in the northern part of Iraq. Let's remember that the people in the north are not the only victims of this situation. There are as we speak ongoing counter-insurgency operations by the government against people in the south. And you know unfortunately the situation in Iraq is such that people don't pay a lot of attention to these things. There are gross human rights violations committed in the center of Iraq as we speak. Last year the special UN rapporteur for Iraq reported on hundreds of executions that have been carried out by the regime. And we should all ask ourselves, Isn't it better to show to any Iraqi who is watching that the international community knows about this and believes that there should be a better future for them? This is what we are trying to do. We are not trying to create an independent statelet in the north or in the south for that matter—or carve up this country. We are simply trying to show that there is an alternative available for people in which they'd have a better future.

Q: I have one more question. Would the Iraqi opposition use the northern Iraq again as a base, like what happened before and ended in catastrophe?

MR. WELCH: I am not sure what their intentions would be. You refer to "the" Iraqi opposition. The Iraqi opposition is somewhat divided now, and I don't know around what principles or actions they will organize themselves.

And let me say this too: there are shades of difference between the KDP and the PUK over how they will deal with the opposition. So you must ask them these questions.

But from the point of view of the United States, we are not trying by this process to encourage a platform or base for opposition activity. Quite the contrary. We thought that it was worthwhile in itself to have a process of reconciliation between the KDP and the PUK, that that would lead to a better situation in the north and protect the people there.

Now, if in the future they should decide that they want to pursue some kind of opposition activity vis-a-vis Baghdad, that's up to them. But that was not an objective of our involvement in this process, and we are not proposing that they should do so.

MR. FOUCHEUX: Mr. Welch, we've talked a lot about what the accord will mean in the Turkish and northern Iraq region. Could we broaden it a bit? Do you see this impacting in any way on the larger question of stability in the Middle East?

MR. WELCH: Well, yes I do. Let's remember that this is a very volatile area generally, and some of the most severe challenges to international peace and security in this decade have evolved around Iraq, principally caused by the Saddam Hussein regime. And at times those have involved the people of northern Iraq. For example, I referred earlier to the human rights violations that occurred in the late 1980s, including the use of chemical weapons against an innocent civilian population. I think now ten years later the international community would not tolerate such a situation again.

Second, to the extent there is greater peace and stability in the north of Iraq, the chances of a disruption there that some outside party might take advantage of, with consequences throughout the region, are lessened. And another example too is if that area is more secure and these two parties are cooperating, they have committed themselves to controlling the movement of terrorists and barring them from operating in that area—the PKK specifically. That will reduce the problems that Turkey has from border violations and terrorist operations against Turkey, and there will be less disruption as a result if they feel compelled to—they will feel less compelled to respond.

MR. FOUCHEUX: So this could be a very optimistic step forward in a very general sense?

MR. WELCH: Certainly it's an important building block. Look, there are many problems in that area—this isn't going to cure them all. But this has been one which has caused particular pain and suffering over the years, and it was important to take this step forward.

MR. FOUCHEUX: All right, Mr. Welch, let's return to Ankara once again for another question from them. Please go ahead again in Ankara.

Q: You've repeatedly expressed your concern for the rights of the Kurds in Iraq, and their right to choose the form of government they want to live under in Iraq. Can we anticipate you showing the same concern of the Kurds of Turkey?

MR. WELCH: Turkey is a democratic country. I think people there should enjoy democratic rights. That's an issue for Turkey. My concern right now is the lack of any such rights for the people of Iraq. And you will recall that whenever I was asked the question about what we support for Kurds, I made clear that we support similar rights for any Iraqi. I wish that other Iraqis were in a position to exercise such rights. I wish that other Iraqis had at least the minimum thing that the people in northern Iraq do, is some freedom from the authority and control of Saddam Hussein.

Q: John Hemming from Reuters. What is your attitude to the continued diesel trade between northern Iraq and Turkey, which is against United Nations resolutions on trade with Iraq? And secondly, this has been one of the main divisive issues between the Kurds and is being supported by the Turkish Government, which is an ally of America, and goes against the sanctions regime.

MR. WELCH: Well, I think the Turkish Government is actually trying to take some steps to control this trade. This is—there are two areas in which the Government in Baghdad is able to violate the sanctions regime. One is by the gas-oil trade across that border and the other is by gas-oil petroleum products trade out of the northern Gulf region, and that is smuggled to ports in the Gulf. We are trying to control both of these outflows. They are different in the ways in which this might happen. These are sources of revenue for the Iraqi Government—I would not exaggerate their importance. They pale in comparison for example beside the pre-war oil earnings of the Iraqi regime. But they are nonetheless important, and we believe they should be brought under control and regularized according to the sanctions regime. We have made some proposals as to how that might be accomplished to the Turkish Government, and we are in a discussion about those proposals with them right now.

MR. FOUCHEUX: Mr. Welch, again we have talked generally about some of the prob-lems with the Iraqi Government. What do you see as major current specific dangers in the region coming out of Baghdad?

MR. WELCH: Well, we believe that Iraq under Saddam Hussein remains a signifi-cant threat to peace and stability in the area. The principal problem right now is that Iraq has divorced itself from cooperation with the UN Special Commission and the IAEA in the disarmament process envisaged by the resolu-tions at the end of the Gulf War. What that has done is that it has interrupted the ability of the international community to verify that Iraq has disclosed and destroyed all these prohibited weapons. And unfortunately there are large remaining uncertainties in that process that cannot be reduced unless Iraq brings itself back into compliance. Presently the Special Commission and IAEA are operating only on a limited, truncated basis. Until they are able to restore full operation, I don't think anyone in the international community can have any confidence about the status of their weapons programs. And until they have that confidence there isn't any prospect whatsoever that Iraq can get out from under the sanctions regime. So unless they bring themselves back into compliance we are going to see that this sanc-tions regime continues.

I believe that the alternative is gravely threatening to regional peace and stability. What is that alternative? It is that we would accept that there is some potential there that Iraq might rearm itself or some practical abil-ity actually to use these weapons of mass de-struction. That is simply not going to happen. The international community decided in Reso-lution 687 that Iraq shall not have these weap-ons of mass destruction, and that is the stan-dard by which Iraq must live.

MR. FOUCHEUX: And with that our discussion comes to a close. Mr. David Welch of the U.S. State Department, thank you very much for being in our studios today. Our thanks as well to our participants in London and Ankara. In Washington, I'm Rick Foucheux for Worldnet's "Dialogue."

299.

Harold Hongju Koh
Assistant Secretary of State for Democracy, Human Rights, and Labor
Remarks to the Assembly of Turkish-American Associations
Washington, DC, October 1, 1999
www.state.gov/www/policy_remarks/1999/991001_koh_turkey.html

Thank you, Professor Lowry, for that kind introduction. First of all, let me say what a pleasure it is for me to be here at the 20th Annual Convention of the Assembly of Turkish-American Associations to discuss a topic that is tremendously important to Turkey, to the United States, and to me personally. As most of you know, I returned not long ago from a trip to Turkey, where I met many wonderful people and made very good friends. I grieved, as the world did, over the tremendous losses suffered by the people of Turkey during the catastrophic earthquake that struck only days after I had been there. As you know, American rescue teams—including a contingent from the Washington metro area—worked with Turks and other friends of Turkey to help rescue survivors. Americans also have responded generously to other relief efforts. These actions underscore the common values that unite us.

The United States has long considered Turkey a key ally. Turkey is an increasingly important partner in trade, investment, and energy. Turkey and the U.S. have a growing economic relationship, and we both strongly support the Baku-Ceyhan pipeline. But it would be a mistake to think that our mutual interests are limited to economic issues. At both the start and the end of this decade, Turkey reaffirmed its importance by the way it responded to tyranny in this region: first by supporting Operations Desert Storm and Northern Watch in Iraq, and this year, by lending critical support to NATO's effort to halt Slobodan Milosevic's brutal oppression of Kosovo's Albanian population. In that operation, Turkey demonstrated its determination and compassion, by opening its doors and extending its famous hospitality to thousands of Kosovar refugees. President Clinton and Secretary Albright personally expressed America's gratitude to Prime Minister Ecevit during their visits this week.

But I must tell you that my regard for Turkey goes even deeper than appreciating what it has done recently. Like you, I trace with pride my roots to another country. Like you, I enjoy a double blessing: I can take enormous pride in being an American and at the same time preserve a piece of my heart for the country of my parents and grandparents—in my case, Korea. I cannot tell you how much it means to me to come here to speak with all of you—whose hearts still keep a little bit of Turkey in them. As the child of immigrants, speaking to groups like yours always fills me with a mix of wonder and pride: the wonder of a child who saw his parents sacrifice so much in their quest for a better life, and the pride of a parent who can now show his American children how much their culture and heritage has enriched the United States.

When my parents left Korea 50 years ago, they watched from America while the Korean War left that country in a state painfully reminiscent of today's Kosovo. Among the troops who fought for their homeland's freedom were Turkish soldiers, far away from their homes, whose sacrifice helped begin Korea's path toward democracy. I am sure that my parents never dreamed that one day their son would be able to stand in front of a group like yours, representing the United States as its Assistant Secretary of State for Democracy, Human Rights and Labor, to thank your parents and grandparents for their sacrifice.

So the relationship between the United States and Turkey is not just multifaceted, but multilayered. I easily could spend the rest of the day talking to you if I tried to address all the issues of mutual concern. But as the Secretary's principal advisor on democracy, human rights, and labor, my primary responsibility here today is to outline some of those concerns.

During my trip 2 months ago, I traveled to Ankara, Istanbul, Sanliurfa, and Diyarbakir. I met with an extraordinary variety of individuals, asking them numerous questions in order to gain a more complete understanding of the context in which questions of human rights and democracy arise in Turkey. I was privileged to meet with a wide variety of people in all of these places, including national, provincial and local government officials, parliamentarians, human rights defenders, religious leaders, journalists, and—discussions it became increasingly clear to me that the people of the United States and the people of Turkey share important interests in and aspirations for human rights and democracy

During my travels, Turkish citizens shared their concerns about restrictions on freedom of expression, especially political, cultural and religious expression. They talked about the continued use of torture and the lack of accountability of those who commit it. They worried about the harassment of human rights defenders, including non-governmental organizations, defense lawyers, doctors, and journalists. And they provide their varying perspectives on the difficult situation in the Southeast, where terrorism by the PKK and other groups, economic underdevelopment, forced village evacuations, and the rights of Turkey's citizens of Kurdish descent remain serious concerns. Let me underscore that those who raised these issues with me were not just those who have suffered human rights abuses, but also national, provincial, and local government officials who have committed themselves to addressing these problems. I was impressed by their openness, and I pledge the United States' support for their efforts to make significant and concrete human rights improvements.

I also had the opportunity to sit down in Ankara with Prime Minister Ecevit to discuss his concerns and hear his thoughts about improving the human rights situation in Turkey. The Prime Minister reiterated to me his and his government's commitment to make human rights a top priority. In the weeks since my visit, his government has taken some important steps toward realizing that commitment. Just last Saturday, the Government released on medical grounds Akin Birdal, former President of the Human Rights Association, a noted human rights organization. The United States welcomes this and all future concrete steps to improve human rights.

Just this week in meetings with the President and Secretary of State, the Prime Minister reaffirmed his government's commitment to strengthening and enhancing human rights protections. The Prime Minister told President Clinton and Secretary Albright about some of the steps his government has taken, and they discussed where the process might head in the future. Secretary Albright took advantage of the meeting to invite State Minister for Human Rights Irtemcelik to visit the United States this fall, and the Prime Minister accepted in principle.

Since my trip, Turkey has amended anti-torture regulations to increase the punishment from 5 to 8 years for those who engage in torture or hinder torture investigations, has amended the political parties law to make it more difficult to close down such institutions, and has postponed the sentences or halted the trials of some journalists convicted or charged on speech acts. When I was in Turkey, I told Prime Minister Ecevit, Justice Minister Turk, and State Minister for Human Rights Irtemcelik that we welcomed some of the other steps that they have taken on human rights:

- removing the military judges from the State Security Courts;
- proposing legislation to ensure the accountability of civil servants and to increase the punishments for those found to have engaged in torture;
- and issuing a circular announcing no tolerance for human rights violations by law enforcement officials and outlining ways to ensure that such violations are discovered and punished.

The government's mandate is strong and signals sharper focus on these issues, and we look forward to seeing concrete improvements in human rights on the ground.

Other high-ranking Turkish officials have also recently spoken out in favor of human rights reform or taken action. President Demirel initiated a dialogue with mayors from the Southeast. In a ground-breaking speech that has spurred a national debate and intensified public calls for more democracy, Supreme Court of Appeals Chief Justice Selcuk called for revision of the Constitution to strengthen democracy and better protect the freedoms of Turkey's citizens. Constitutional Court Chief Justice Sezer has called for lifting restrictions on freedom of expression. Turkish General Staff Chairman Kivrikoglu recently stated that elected HADEP mayors should be allowed to do their job without interference and acknowledged that many Kurds want an increase in cultural rights, not autonomy. We applaud the vision of these leaders as they work to strengthen Turkey's commitment to a culture of human rights.

The challenges that face Turkey are not unique. With respect to democracy and human rights, every country in the world still has progress to make. The United States also is a work in progress; indeed, our Constitution defines our national mission as achieving "a more perfect Union." Since the United States is an open democracy, we are committed to addressing our most difficult and divisive human rights issues in public and in the courts. At times in our history, both non-governmental groups and other governments have helpfully prodded us to move faster, and to do more, to ensure justice and freedom.

It is sometimes painful when others point out our errors to us, but we Americans have welcomed the scrutiny, for such domestic and external criticism have made us stronger by pushing us to address our problems. We have learned that the promotion of human rights is not a subversive activity but an investment in democracy. I have encouraged Turkish officials to view human rights defenders as their allies as they move to make needed reforms, and to ensure that these groups— NGOs, lawyers, doctors, journalists—enjoy unfettered ability to carry out their legitimate activities. State Minister Irtemcelik's recent meeting with the chairman of the Human Rights Association of Turkey is a welcome step. We hope that such measures signal a new approach, one that will result in the reopening of closed non-governmental organizations and prevent future such closings by the government.

Currently, the Government of Turkey also is considering a number of different measures that would lift some of the restrictions on freedom of expression. This is a crucial area for reform. Full freedom of expressio— political and cultural—may feel threatening, but freedom of expression in fact enhances societal order and stability. When all elements in society have access to meaningful, peaceful political and cultural expression, emotional and contentious issues can be raised within the existing system, rather than in extremist opposition to it.

We therefore strongly support Prime Minister Ecevit's ongoing efforts to lift those arti-

cles of the Turkish Constitution, penal code and anti-terror law that restrict freedom of expression. But it is important that reforms be thorough and effective. When restrictions were lifted in the past, individuals were still prosecuted for speech acts. Here in the United States, we may not like hate speech or when Nazis parade, but if we try to block such acts we lose far more than we gain. We have learned through hard experience that the best way to respond to bad speech is with good speech, not with restrictions. In that spirit, I would like to encourage Prime Minister Ecevit to extend the limited relief offered the press under the amnesty law and to extend his reforms to all articles used to restrict freedom of expression.

We welcome and support the commitments of Prime Minister Ecevit, Foreign Minister Cem, Justice Minister Turk, and State Minister for Human Rights Irtemcelik to end the practice of torture. The government has authorized surprise inspections of detention facilities and called for initiating legal procedures against security forces accused of abuse. Only by thoroughly implementing these measures can the government begin to address this problem. Unfortunately, many of those I met in the Southeast did not know about the government's new measures or how they are to be implemented. I urged government officials at all levels to make such changes a priority and to ensure that the public, prosecutors and security forces are aware of the initiatives. As we have learned in the United States, a climate of impunity can only be ended by vigorously prosecuting, convicting, and punishing those officials who commit such acts.

Finally, let me turn to the extraordinarily difficult and sensitive challenge of the Southeast and achieving reconciliation with Turkey's Kurdish population. On my travels, many of those with whom I met told me that there is now an unprecedented opportunity for progress on this issue. I met a few mayors from the Southeast. They struck me as dedicated public servants who want to deliver quality municipal services to their citizens, but they often struggle to be accepted by Ankara and provincial authorities. We hope that other Turkish officials will follow President Demirel's lead in reaching out to political leaders in the Southeast and, as TGS Chief

Kivrikoglu stated, that the mayors will be allowed to do their jobs. The people of the Southeast, who are mainly Kurds, demonstrated their bond with the rest of the country with their prompt and generous assistance to victims of the earthquake in the Northwest.

As you all know, the United States has staunchly supported Turkey's right to defend itself against terrorism in the Southeast. But one can oppose terrorism and still support human rights. Most Kurds in Turkey do not support the use of violence. They want to remain Turkish citizens, while enjoying the basic human rights guaranteed to all people under international law, including freedom to express one's language and culture, and freedom to organize political parties that represent their interests. Far from hurting Turkey's territorial integrity, an inclusive policy that acknowledged these rights would strengthen Turkey by giving the Kurdish community a genuine stake in their country's future. The United States has long maintained that there can be no purely military solution to Kurdish issues. Any enduring solution must lie in the expansion of democracy, and in bold and imaginative political, social, and economic measures to foster full democratic political participation for all of Turkey's citizens and in the promotion of greater freedom of expression in and on the Southeast.

This November, the Organization of Security and Cooperation in Europe (OSCE) will hold its summit in Istanbul. That decision pays tribute to the respect the OSCE has for Turkey and to Turkey's own diplomatic capacities. The summit will shine a global spotlight on Turkey, and offer the entire country an opportunity to demonstrate its commitment to human rights and democracy. The United States recognizes and respects the sincerity of Prime Minister Ecevit's government, and we hope the many important reforms that it has initiated will be implemented fully in the very near future.

Fifty years ago, the people of Turkey played a crucial role in defending freedom in Korea. Five months ago, the people of Turkey helped bring to an end a brutal campaign of ethnic cleansing in Kosovo, in the process demonstrating to the world its continuing commitment to fostering human rights and democracy. It is my hope that, in the next few

years, the Ecevit Government will build on its commitment to improve human rights at home by safeguarding freedom of expression, ending torture and impunity, protecting human rights defenders, and finding a peaceful and democratic solution to the issues confronting the Southeast. As Turkey moves to implement these reforms, the United States, as a true friend and close ally, will stand with Turkey as it faces these and other challenges that will define our shared future.

Thank you very much.

300.

April 18, 2000
State's Ricciardone on Kurds in the Global Arena
At American University Center for Global Peace, April 17
http://usinfo.state.gov/regional/nea/iraq/iraq0418.htm

Francis J. Ricciardone, the Department of State's Special Coordinator for Transition in Iraq, provided his perspectives on "Kurds in the Global Arena" at American University's Center for Global Peace on April 17.

Ricciardone began his remarks with the following "take-home" points:

— First: there simply is no overarching U.S. Government policy toward "The Kurds," as such. Rather, we interact with Kurds precisely as we do with any other citizens of their various countries.

— As "globalization" inevitably turns formerly local issues into international ones, non-state players are rising in influence in the rapidly evolving business of international relations.

— Third, Iraqi Kurds are among the leaders of those free Iraqis who are breaking Baghdad's dictatorial monopoly on communications—both among Iraqis and between them and the world. In so doing they are laying the groundwork for a hopeful, modern definition of what it can mean to be an Iraqi, and what Iraq can be as a country.

Ricciardone said the United States believes the human rights of Kurds are to be protected as fully as those of their other countrymen and that a strong democracy affords the best protection for the rights of all citizens in any country.

U.S. policy toward Iraq is clear, he said: "We support the territorial integrity and unity of Iraq as necessary for regional peace and stability . . . We recognize that change in Iraq will come from within, and that who will lead the new Iraq, and how it will be organized, are questions that the Iraqi people will and must decide all together when they are free to do so.

"We look forward to the return of Iraq to the community of nations under a new government that will respect the rights of all Iraqis and of Iraq's neighbors under international law," Ricciardone said. "Iraqi Kurds are among the most committed advocates of such a new Iraq," he added.

Free Iraqi Kurds are leading their countrymen of all ethnic origins in communicating as never before and are making the most of such world access to expose the truth not only about their oppressors, but more importantly, about themselves, Ricciardone said. "In the process, they are creating a dynamic definition of who they are as Kurds and as Iraqis, for the world, for their country, and for themselves."

Following is the text of Ricciardone's remarks:

AN AMERICAN DIPLOMAT'S PERSPECTIVES ON KURDS IN THE GLOBAL ARENA REMARKS BY FRANCIS J. RICCIARDONE
American University - Center for Global Peace
April 17, 2000

Thank you, Ambassador Murphy, for your generous introduction. I commend American University's Center for Global Peace and Professors Carole O'Leary and Abdul Aziz Said for organizing this symposium. Thank you for inviting me. Secretary Albright has made clear that we in the Department of State should seize just such opportunities to converse with American and foreign publics on the issues that we manage on behalf of our citizens.

I was invited as a Foreign Service Officer with experience in Iran, Turkey, and Iraq. My job now, however, is to coordinate the United States' support for Iraqis working to promote a transition to democracy under a new government, so I will focus on our dealings with Iraqi Kurds. Obviously, my participation today does not imply that the Department of State or I endorse what others here might say.

Overview: The United States and "The Kurds"

Let me now offer you my "take-home" points:

— First: there simply is no overarching U.S. Government policy toward "The Kurds," as such. Rather, we interact with Kurds precisely as we do with any other citizens of their various countries.

To illustrate, I will recap the larger Iraq policy context underlying our relations with the Iraqi Kurds and other free Iraqis. Our approach both suits and reflects the profound changes underway in the conduct of international relations. This leads to my second point:

— As "globalization" inevitably turns formerly local issues into international ones, non-state players are rising in influence in the rapidly evolving business of international relations.

— Third, Iraqi Kurds are among the leaders of those free Iraqis who are breaking Baghdad's dictatorial monopoly on communications—both among Iraqis and between them and the world. In so doing they are laying the groundwork for a hopeful, modern definition of what it can mean to be an Iraqi, and what Iraq can be as a country.

Dealing with Kurds vs. "The Kurds"

You might reasonably have expected to hear a statement of United States policy toward "the Kurds." I am sorry to disappoint: I know of no statement of an official United States "policy" toward "the Kurds" as such. There is simply no need.

This symposium will consider questions of Kurdish identity—communal, political, or otherwise. Those are complex, sensitive, and fascinating issues for Kurdish people, their neighbors, and their governments, and for scholars anywhere to debate. But those issues certainly are beyond the United States' ability, authority, or responsibility to resolve for others. Hence, as a practical matter, we simply set aside such questions as immaterial to our ability to communicate productively and respectfully with Kurds wherever we have common interests to address.

That is, like other governments foreign to them, we deal with Kurds as citizens of their countries. Of course, we believe the human rights of Kurds are to be protected as fully as those of their other countrymen. We also believe that a strong democracy affords the best protection for the rights of all citizens in any country. I will not compare the status of Kurds in different countries. But I will briefly sketch our dealings with several sets of Kurds to show that the absence of a specific "Policy on The Kurds" does not impede useful, direct U.S. Government communications with individual Kurds and with Kurdish organizations who play important local or national roles in their countries.

Of the states blessed with large indigenous Kurdish populations, clearly Turkey, as a NATO ally, has the best and closest relations with the United States. This means that thousands of American businesspeople, scholars, journalists, politicians, tourists, diplomats and soldiers do various forms of business with Kurdish-origin Turks every day. Usually, and quite naturally, such Americans are unaware of and indifferent to the ancestry of their Turkish interlocutors. The Turkish Parliament counts many Kurdish deputies, and many Turkish municipalities routinely elect Kurdish mayors. Our diplomats meet such prominent Turkish citizens as routinely as we see Turkish politicians and officials of Balkan, Caucasian, Central Asian, or other backgrounds. We promote American exports and investment all over Turkey, including in the Southeast, where we see particular business growth opportunities.

By contrast, since the US still has no direct diplomatic relations with Iran and no official American presence there, our direct official contacts with Iranian citizens, of any description, in their own country are nil.

Iraq is, of course, a peculiar case. Few, if any, democracies have what could be called "normal," much less "good" relations with Baghdad, and of course we have no relations at all with that regime. But we do have direct and meaningful contacts with a wide range of Iraqis, either outside Iraq, or in northern Iraq—so far the only part of Iraq where its citizens can freely communicate with each other and with the outside world.

It is hard for us to imagine a future free Iraqi national parliament or government in which Kurds, and for that matter their Turcoman and Assyrian neighbors also, do not play leading roles alongside their Arab countrymen. Of course, until all Iraqis live under a national government that is accountable to them, we and many other governments will continue to deal respectfully and openly with free Iraqi Kurdish, Turcoman, Assyrian, and Arab personalities and groups as the holders of local authority, personal prestige, and wide influence. We see them in an anomalous and temporary situation, after which they will have even more impact on the strategic directions of their country and its national government. We believe that even now, such free Iraqis, far more than the Baghdad regime, best display their country's civilization and its potential.

Iraqi Kurds within US Iraq Policy

We deal with Iraqi Kurds, as with all free Iraqis, within the context of our policy toward Iraq. That policy is clear: We support the territorial integrity and unity of Iraq as necessary for regional peace and stability. We would oppose the creation of separate states or statelets either for the Kurds or for any Iraqi ethnic or sectarian community. We recognize that change in Iraq will come from within, and that who will lead the new Iraq, and how it will be organized, are questions that the Iraqi people will and must decide all together when they are free to do so. We look forward to the return of Iraq to the community of nations under a new government that will respect the rights of all Iraqis and of Iraq's neighbors under international law. We deal with Kurdish parties and individuals as important constituents and leaders of an Iraqi national movement that seeks to restore such an Iraq to all its people, and to its rightful place in the world. Iraqi Kurds are among the most committed advocates of such a new Iraq. I look forward again today to hearing some of them discuss how they want a free Iraq to work, and how to bring it about.

Let me here rebut a fallacy suggested by some opponents of the Iraqi Kurds' long struggle against tyranny. We see no comparison at all, as some have suggested, between terrorism, as practiced by the Kurdistan Workers' Party or PKK, versus the Iraqi Kurds' resistance to an outlaw regime condemned and sanctioned by the United Nations as an oppressor. There is no moral ambiguity here. We condemn PKK terrorism, period.

Shaping a New Iraq

Though Iraqis often ask our outlook, the United States Government does not and really can not prescribe how the next Baghdad government should reform the state to guarantee the rights of all its citizens and to restore and strengthen national unity. Naturally, we favor democracy, protected by the rule of law, as the best way to do this. Beyond this, it is not for us to flash "green" or "red lights" to the various plans or philosophies now discussed by free Iraqis. In general, we are most comfortable with democratic political principles that promise to strengthen national unity, stability, and prosperity, and to guarantee the full freedoms and other human rights of all Iraqis. Likewise, we are most uncomfortable with any policies that would tend to divide or to oppress Iraqis, and thus further to weaken Iraq, as the current regime continues to do. We support the universal aspiration of Iraqis to put the days of "divide-and-rule" dictatorship into the past.

The Iraqi National Congress, the umbrella grouping representing Iraqi democratic opposition parties of all ethnic, sectarian, and ideological communities including the major Kurdish parties, has described such a free Iraq as the goal of all Iraqis. As I understand the INC, they advocate a democratic Iraq with one national government, one army, one diplomatic service, one passport, one currency, and freedom of movement and commerce for all Iraqis from Zakho to Fao.

At the same time, INC thinkers, including the Kurds among them, advocate some constitutional decentralization of fiscal and political authority. I find it healthy that the INC has begun this important national debate even now, the better to develop a ready-made national consensus for the day dictatorship ends in Iraq. The Iraqis, like any other free people, will have to decide for themselves the right balance between central and decentralized authority, as also between public and private

sector responsibilities, and other difficult issues such as the role of religion in the state. And they will have to do this together. Whatever the terms of their debate, I am confident that the Iraqis will succeed in striking the right balance for them.

Iraqi Kurds as Influential Non-state Actors

Let me return now to the growing influence of Iraqi Kurds as non-state players on the global stage. It is remarkable that Iraqi Kurds, formerly among the most culturally and geographically isolated people on the planet, have embraced overt, broad engagement with the outside world with both spirit and skill. Their budding success in the world arena has been hard won, through an epic and painful learning process.

One eulogist recently has credited this engagement with the world as an enduring legacy of Mulla Mustafa Barzani. Born a simple villager into a remote province of the Ottoman Empire, Mulla Mustafa died far from his birthplace in a superpower capital. As a guerrilla leader, he had found that the force of local arms, however heroically borne, could not prevail against a modern army backed by the full resources of a then-wealthy state, no matter how poorly led. Hence, he sought and exploited secret alliances with powerful foreign states. Any advantages gained turned out to be only tactical and temporary, before alignments among states shifted without warning. From the tragic consequences, the Kurds of Iraq wisely have drawn the right lesson: not to retreat or disengage from the world stage, but rather to engage all the more fully and forthrightly, the better to ensure clarity of expectations and commitments.

How have the Iraqi Kurds—the KDP, PUK, the Islamists, the Failis, the tribal leaders—come to communicate with such impact with so many states of the world? And this, in the face of their continuing disenfranchisement and the internal embargo imposed by the regime in Baghdad? As non-state practitioners in international relations, in many respects the various Kurdish organizations now enjoy greater influence, access, credibility, and meaningful international relationships than does the regime which purports to speak for them and for all Iraqis from Iraq's seat at the United Nations. The same is slowly becoming true also for the Iraqi Kurds' as yet less well-known neighbors, the Turcoman and Assyrian parties of the Iraqi national opposition. Likewise, traditionally inward-looking Iraqi Arabs, such as tribal leaders and many Islamists, now are forging new communications channels to foreign governments and NGOs sympathetic to their human rights. Governments, international organizations, businesspeople, scholars, and NGOs care what such free Iraqis have to say, as the diverse participation here attests. And deservedly so.

Today's Symposium also aptly demonstrates that Iraqi Kurds have grasped the value of international engagement and are developing the skills both to bring home the benefits of globalization, and to manage its risks. That private Iraqi Kurdish wealth has endowed a scholarly chair in the study of conflict resolution here at American University shows a sophisticated awareness that the defeat of oppression requires far more than the force of arms. Such initiatives are indispensable to rebuild a vital Iraqi national consciousness that will sustain democratic reform by the next leaders of Iraq.

United Nations Security Council Resolutions testify to the Iraqi Kurds' growing international influence. The Kurds' impact also can be seen in their open welcome in the ministries of democratic governments. Their connectedness to the larger world likewise is evident in the presence of the many international NGOs, scholars, and journalists whom they welcome to free Iraq—without imposing official "minders." Several Iraqi Kurdish groups have permanently posted representatives abroad, who are trusted by foreign hosts for their outstanding personal abilities. Several of them are among us today. Such experienced and effective international representatives should prove invaluable assets to any future national Government of Iraq.

Professor O'Leary and Professor Said suggested to me that the Iraqi Kurds' success in dealing with powerful states lies in their dawning understanding that the key to international influence—whether for the state or non-state players—is high skill in all aspects of the use of truthful information. I concur. This is not at all the same thing as either "propaganda" or even "public relations" work. Nor is this merely "intelligence" work. Rather, I refer

to the timely and broad presentation of truth to influence international public opinion, and through it, the policies of democratic governments. For maximum punch, no medium compares to the visual.

The Iraqi Kurds' first big step on the road to international influence came as the result of televised tragedy. Images of half a million freezing and frightened Iraqi refugees moved the conscience of the world in March of 1991. Yet, only days before, for the lack of real-time video images, that same world stood silent at Baghdad's mass slaughter of innocent Iraqi Arab civilians in the south. Only three years before, the world was able to ignore the rumored but then-untelevised poison gassing of Halabja. Still earlier, the lack of televised evidence also helped shelter Saddam Hussein's criminal use of poison gas against Iranians, until the United States independently developed the evidence to lead world condemnation of this in March 1984.

The sustained international attention to Northern Iraq long after the catastrophes of 1988 and 1991, however, does not result from the one-time, one-way transmission of images of innocents' suffering, but from two-way engagement. Iraqi Kurdish leaders have opened up their part of the country far more than Baghdad has dared to reveal itself to the eyes of the world. The Iraqi Kurds do not merely purvey information to the world, but also welcome the world into Iraq. Iraqi students and teachers in Dohuk, Erbil, and Suleymania freely exchange views and information with each other and with the world via the Internet. While Baghdad bans UN-mandated human rights rapporteurs and monitors, the Kurds—and Assyrians and Turcomans—welcome all official and independent foreign visitors. While a son of the dictator controls Baghdad's mass media and bans foreign publications and broadcasts, in the north local and international broadcast channels and publications are proliferating in several languages.

In sum, while Baghdad vainly struggles to preserve an obsolete dictatorial monopoly on information, free Iraqi Kurds are leading their countrymen of all ethnic origins in communicating as never before. These free Iraqis are making the most of such world access to expose the truth not only about their oppressors, but more importantly, about themselves. In the process, they are creating a dynamic definition of who they are as Kurds and as Iraqis, for the world, for their country, and for themselves.

To me as an American diplomat, this process is stimulating to observe and a privilege to support.

Thank you again for the privilege of joining your conversation today.

(Distributed by the Office of International Information Programs, U.S. Dep't of State. Web site: usinfo.state.gov)

301.

April 18, 2000
Iraq Coordinator Riccciardone's Press Briefing in Ankara
First direct funding to Iraqi National Opposition expected soon
http://usinfo.state.gov/regional/nea/iraq/iraqa418.htm

The United States expects to provide the first tranche of direct funding to the Iraqi National Opposition very soon says Francis Ricciardone, Special Coordinator for Transition in Iraq.

"The first bit of that money is going to be about a quarter million dollars, which they plan to use to build their organization, make it more effective as a political organization that can better advocate the interests of the Iraqi people in a free future, in a country that stays together as a whole, where all Iraqis are first-class citizens, where they live in peace, not only with each other, but with their neighbors," Ricciardone said April 14 at a press briefing in Ankara, Turkey.

The U.S. has spent some money through contractors to help organize conferences and on humanitarian relief projects but has not given any money directly to the Iraqi opposition, he said.

Ricciardone also reported that the Iraqi National Opposition will be eligible for non-lethal types of training as part of the drawdown authority of the U.S. Department of Defense. That training, he said, could be useful in rebuilding the country when there is a change, and in making the Iraqi opposition

itself more effective as an organization. He added that for the moment he does not anticipate arms flowing to them.

The current government in Iraq promotes "anti-unifying tendencies . . . setting brother against brother," Ricciardone said. The U.S. approach in working with the Iraqi National Opposition is to try to bring all of the different elements of Iraq together and "stand together as Iraqis, whether they be Kurds or Turkomans or Sunni Arabs or Shiite Arabs."

Ricciardone said it is not the purpose of the United States to keep sanctions on Iraq forever. "On the contrary, it is our purpose and desire to see Saddam Hussein's government comply with what he promised to comply with (U.N. Security Council resolutions) and see the sanctions totally lifted when he totally complies." However, he said, "we don't believe he ever will, which is why we think he ultimately has to go."

Asked about Turkey's response to the PKK (Kurdistan Workers Party) in Northern Iraq, Ricciardone said the United States supports Turkey's right to defend itself against terrorism by terrorists who are harbored in neighboring states.

"We've said repeatedly that we expected the Turkish Armed Forces in defending the country will use the most limited force necessary and be scrupulous in protecting the rights of civilians. The Turkish Armed Forces have done so. So we have no complaints with the government of Turkey's national self-defense against terrorism on that score."

Following is the transcript of the press briefing:

ON-THE-RECORD PRESS BRIEFING BY FRANCIS RICCIARDONE, SPECIAL COORDINATOR FOR TRANSITION IN IRAQ
Ankara, Turkey
April 14, 2000

RICCIARDONE: It really is a pleasure for me to be here. I feel like I'm back home among friends.

Just a couple of words at the outset and then I'll be glad to respond to your questions. I'm here, because not only my government, but personally as an American diplomat who's worked in Turkey, I believe what Turkey thinks matters. I'm here to participate in the conversations that Assistant Secretary Ned Walker has come to conduct with the government of Turkey. As you probably know, we carry out consultations at that level twice a year. And it was my privilege to join this conversation, as I have in the past several times.

When I say consultations I mean that. It isn't just to brief the government of Turkey on what we're doing. That's important. We don't want there to be any surprises. But we're here also to hear the Turkish insights, points of view and advice, frankly, on how to manage some of the most difficult problems we face together. And the area that I deal with is among the most tricky and complex problems that we have to manage together. So I had particularly useful conversations today with my colleagues in the Foreign Ministry.

As you know, I deal with Iraq and, I guess the ground rules here have already been explained to you, I'd like to keep the conversation on Iraq, the future of Iraq, working with the Iraqi opposition, and so forth. The other issues, I think, Ambassador Walker addressed briefly with the press that were at the Foreign Ministry today. With that said, please go ahead and ask questions.

QUESTION: It seems that the U.S. bombing of Iraq has been increasing lately. Do you have any. . . (inaudible)?

RICCIARDONE: I'm not aware that there has been an escalation of the bombing there. On that question though, I would only say that the rules of engagement are clear and they're set with the Turkish side. We have Turkish people and Turkish military working very closely on everything that Northern Watch does. That's important to us. It's important to the government of Turkey.

Very clearly, if Saddam Hussein's forces stop shooting at our airplanes, we stop shooting back. Every time we hit a target up there it's because we have been fired at. And if Saddam Hussein stops shooting at us, or his forces stop shooting at us tomorrow, we stop hitting back tomorrow. And every day he doesn't shoot at us is a day we don't shoot at them.

QUESTION: . . . Iraqi opposition. . . (inaudible)

RICCIARDONE: As to the Turkish government's position, I wouldn't presume to

speak for the government of Turkey, of course. So it was my purpose to explain very clearly what we are about and let the government of Turkey decide for itself whether that makes sense in Turkish terms. And also again to ask for the advice of the government of Turkey on how we proceed in this very sensitive endeavor.

As to where we are with the opposition and where they are going in the next phase, they could best themselves articulate their plans and programs, but we are reaching a new point with them. Many people don't understand that we have not given one dollar to the Iraqi opposition heretofore. We have spent some money through contractors to help them organize conferences. We have spent some money on humanitarian relief projects, but we have not given any money directly to the Iraqi opposition.

We will begin doing that soon, however, as Assistant Secretary Walker informed the Senate a couple of weeks ago. Very soon we expect to provide the first tranche of direct funding in a very overt and accountable way against a program that they must specify and put in writing for us.

The first bit of that money is going to be about a quarter million dollars, which they plan to use to build their organization, make it more effective as a political organization that can better advocate the interests of the Iraqi people in a free future, in a country that stays together as a whole, where all Iraqis are first-class citizens, where they live in peace, not only with each other, but with their neighbors. We think that is important. Some Iraqis should be saying that. We don't hear that kind of thing coming from the government in Baghdad. So they'll be using the first bit of money to work on those sorts of things.

They will be eligible for training as part of the drawdown authority of the American Department of Defense. Our only plans along those lines are for non-lethal sorts of training that could be useful in rebuilding the country when there is a change, and in making the Iraqi opposition itself more effective as an organization. That's the kind of training I anticipate with them.

I do not anticipate, for the moment, that any arms will be flowing to them. That's some way down the road, at best.

QUESTION: (inaudible)

RICCIARDONE: One specific area of advice that I personally asked for from your experts was exactly on this question of what can we do now to help support the unifying tendencies among the Iraqi people against the anti-unifying tendencies which are being promoted by the current government in Iraq.

We see the current government in Iraq as setting brother against brother. And I don't mean just the Kurds against the Arabs. I mean Arabs against Arabs. Muslims against Christians. Arabs against Turkomans. We think this is very destabilizing, not just for the short run, but for the long run. And we worry about that.

Our approach in working with an Iraqi national opposition is try to bring all the different elements of Iraq together and stand together as Iraqis, whether they be Kurds or Turkomans or Sunni Arabs or Shiite Arabs. We tell them, "the United States government looks upon you first as Iraqis. You might have your own other identities as well. Many humans do multiple identities on different levels, communal levels or more national levels. That's up to you. But what matters to the United States is that you identity yourselves as Iraqis who wish to keep your country together." That's the United States approach. That's why we support an Iraqi opposition.

So we value how Turkey looks on this. It's a real problem. There really are people inside Iraq who never ever want to live under a Baghdad that drops gas on them. That's we think—a fairly normal human reaction. We want all Iraqis to feel that they are first class citizens under a future government, where they don't have to fear that that government is going to repress them, but where, instead, they will take part in the future government—in the cabinets, in the national assembly, in the national economy, in the national education system, etc. So we talked about that a lot.

QUESTION: What was the advice that they gave you?

RICCIARDONE: The advice has to be very sensitive. And we are. It's a question of problem management for now. There is no easy answer. There is no immediate solution. But we are not going to do anything in Turkey's backyard up there without staying in very close contact with the government of Turkey. And the people who live there, of course. That's why we are in touch with the free people of Iraq, whether they are living in London or in the Arab world or in the north of Iraq.

QUESTION: . . . reaction to a KDP Nevruz reception (inaudible)

RICCIARDONE: Nevruz and KDP. You know, I guess that's an issue between the government or Turkey and the KDP. There's really little I can say about that to advance the question.

QUESTION: . . . meeting in Washington, D.C. April 17-18 about Kurdish identity . . . (inaudible)

RICCIARDONE: Well, of course, I'll let the government of Turkey again speak for itself. But it goes back to the question that you raised of actions by people in Iraq that seem to suggest they want to head toward a separate solution instead of a national solution.

The reason I said yes to the invitation from this prestigious, private American institution, a leader in the conversation on foreign affairs that my government has with the American people, is to make very clear what our policy is and is not. The first thing I did before saying yes, despite their prestige and the access they would give me to important audiences, is to assure myself and the organizers that this had nothing to do with the PKK. Nothing. Nothing to do with Turkey-bashing or analyzing Turkey, putting Turkey on trial. They made that very clear.

The terms of reference are that it is a privilege for me to be able to address these academics, mostly Americans, on American policy toward Iraq, and how we deal with the Iraqi Kurds as Iraqis. It's an important opportunity for me to make clear what we are doing. People naturally have questions. People misunderstand the policy.

We start from the premise, as I will say on Monday, that we want to see an Iraq free and whole—it's national unity, it's territorial integrity preserved. And we work with the Kurds of Iraq, the Turkomans, the Assyrians, the Arabs, the Sunnis, the Shiites, all on that basis, as Iraqis who want to keep their country together and civilize it.

QUESTION: . . . status of Kurds in Turkey . . . (inaudible)

RICCIARDONE: That could be. I don't know. All I know is what I intend to speak to there. And people understand at these conferences—American diplomats speak with American academic institutions all the time—that when we speak it is to give the U.S. government position on the questions at hand. And our presence does not endorse nor does it limit what other people can say. In my country, as in yours, people are free to say what they want.

You just had a conference on minorities, I understand, down in Antalya. This is the OSCE conference, isn't it? You had Max Vander Stohl come and speak in Antalya. He is a specialist on the minorities in Iraq. It's in that sort of context—what Max said down there didn't endorse what others said.

What I will say, in my being there on Monday at American University, does not imply in any way endorsement for what others will say. I expect a lot of criticism of my government there. I'm certainly not going to endorse that by being there. But I have to respond to it. That's the way it works in a free society.

QUESTION: . . . Turkey's operation in northern Iraq . . . (inaudible)

RICCIARDONE: On terrorism, our two governments work closely together across the board, whether it's PKK or anyone else. This situation in northern Iraq and Turkey's response to it is not new. I recall that Turkey's dealing with this problem goes back to the 1980's, long before the Gulf War, long before the no-fly zones and all of that. At that time, we supported Turkey's right to defend itself. We've been consistent in supporting Turkey's right to defend itself against terrorism by terrorists who are harbored in neighboring states. I use the word "state" because that's what Iraq is, that's what it was in the '80's when Saddam Hussein was in charge of it.

So we support Turkey's right to defend itself against terrorism. We do it. Turkey does it. We are allies. No question. We've said repeatedly that we expected the Turkish Armed Forces in defending the country will use the most limited force necessary and be scrupulous in protecting the rights of civilians. The Turkish Armed Forces have done so. So we have no complaints with the government of Turkey's national self-defense against terrorism on that score.

On the question of federalism. That's an undefined term as far as the Iraqi's are concerned. So it's difficult. But I can be clear on one point. If anyone using that term implies that they mean federation or separate states, we're against it. We do not support, in fact we oppose, any breakup of Iraq into separate states. If that's what federalism means, we are certainly against it.

It's for all people to decide, however, what kind of national administrative and political organization they want to have. Some countries are more centralized in their politics and administration; some are less centralized.

My country is the United States of America. We decentralize a lot. We have 50 local assemblies, not counting the municipalities, some of which have their own assemblies. We have 50 locally elected governors. We have local taxation authority, etc.

The people of Iraq will decide all together, all of them, how they will live with each other in the future. But our consistent advice to them is, "your best future is in living together with a single Constitution that protects you all. And with you all participating in the national government. But that's just our advice to you."

For America's interests, as that of your neighbors, there is no country in the world that thinks Iraq will be better off, or that our interests will be better off, if there is no longer one Iraq but instead little pieces of Iraq. So we are very clear on that point.

QUESTION: . . . next steps in dealing with the PKK . . . (inaudible)

RICCIARDONE: I wouldn't presume to tell Turkey how to handle its internal issues, if that's what you are asking me.

On the PKK, we wish Turkey nothing but success. As far as I know, we are the only other government in the world that has in law naming the PKK as a terrorist organization. We are not romantic about them. We don't confuse the PKK for anything but what it is—a terrorist organization. We know the difference between terrorism and legitimate political advocacy. So all we can do is wish Turkey success in dealing with the terrorism problem, and then in dealing with the larger problems that are associated with it.

We are here to support Turkish democracy. That's what we want to see succeed. We won't tell you how to do it. We can't. It's not our job.

QUESTION: . . . increased ethnic schism . . . (inaudible)

RICCIARDONE: I'm not sure whether I accept your thesis about increasing racism. I have said very clearly, including to the Iraqi opposition gathered in New York last fall, that the idea of forming governments and political parties on ethnic, racial and religious grounds really bothers Americans. We think that is divisive. It doesn't bring people together. We don't support that at all.

We deal with the parties in northern Iraq as just that—political parties, a very anomalous and temporary regional administration, under a situation that no one would have designed as ideal. We encourage them to work together—not to try to advance the interests of one ethnic group over another. We would like to see the Arabs up there, the Kurds, the Turkomans, the Assyrians work on a basis that is above sectarianism. So that's why we stay in touch with all of them.

Again, we try to deal with them through the umbrella of the Iraqi National Congress, a name chosen deliberately. We don't deal with the Kurds as just Kurds. We deal with Kurds, Turkomans, Assyrians and the others as Iraqis. That's the best we think we can do to try to fight any tendencies toward separatism in northern Iraq.

QUESTION: . . . embargo issue . . . (inaudible)

RICCIARDONE: Let me take issue with your last point. We've never been keen on continuing the embargo. On the contrary, when the sanctions regime was set up in August of 1990 and codified in 687 and subsequent resolutions after the Gulf War, it was our hope and our belief, as for all members on the Security Council, I think, that Saddam Hussein would comply very quickly and the sanctions would be over. So we don't look forward to the sanctions staying forever. It is not our purpose to keep the sanctions on.

On the contrary, it is our purpose and desire to see Saddam Hussein's government comply with what he promised to comply with. And see the sanctions totally lifted when he totally complies. But we are not fools. We don't believe he ever will, which is why we think he ultimately has to go.

Now, the other part about the sanctions debate is, people often don't have a good database. They don't know the facts. We have some copies here of the web site, operated by the State Department, where we put out the facts and the figures on the amount of food, medicine, other supplies that have been delivered over the past many years under the Oil-for-Food Program. We want the Oil-for-Food Program to stay in place. On Resolution 1284, we try to make it even more clear how sanctions can be suspended, precisely because we want to get more help to the Iraqi people despite a government that is keeping relief away from them.

In the north where the government cannot interfere, all the measurements of human well-being have improved to pre-Gulf War levels. In the south, where the government gets in the way and prevents UN monitors and prevents international NGOs from overseeing the distribution of food and medicine, that's where people are suffering. The food and medicine is there in the warehouses, you can read the UN's own reporting on that.

So, we have a very different view of the sanctions, I think, than Saddam Hussein portrays to the world. We know that the sanctions regime has caused a special hardship for Turkey. And a good part of Ambassador Walker's discussions with the Foreign Ministry have been on how we can work together to try to ease the burden, not just on the Iraqi people, but to meet Turkish interests as well.

QUESTION: . . . PUK and KDP fighting each other . . . (inaudible)

RICCIARDONE: It's a consistently fluid situation, it seems to me. All we can do, through the Ankara process in fact working hand-in-glove with your government, is encourage those two parties to come to terms, live in peace not only with each other, but with all the other people who live in northern Iraq. We shouldn't be under the illusion that there's only two kinds of people in northern Iraq—KDP Kurds and PUK Kurds.

There are many others. Many other Kurds. There are Assyrians with their many parties. There are Turkomans with their many parties. There are Arabs. And through the Ankara process we are encouraging the two major Kurdish parties to come to terms with each other and live in peace. We, through working with the Iraqi opposition, are going beyond that to encourage them all to show the world and show the rest of Iraq that Arabs, Kurds, Turks, Communist, religious parties can all work together in a civilized, democratic way in the future. We think they've actually made some progress toward doing that, but it's difficult.

Thank you.

(Distributed by the Office of International Information Programs, U.S. Dep't of State. Web site: usinfo.state.gov)

WEEKLY COMPILATION OF PRESIDENTIAL DOCUMENTS

302.

[Vol. 27, no. 14 (April 8, 1991): 384–385]

The [Security Council] Resolution Is Unprecedented

Statement by President Bush, April 3, 1991

I am extremely pleased that the Security Council has voted in favor of Resolution 687. Fourteen times now the United Nations has demonstrated its determination to contribute significantly to the prospects for lasting peace and security in the Gulf region.

This latest resolution creates the basis for a formal cease–fire in the Gulf. It comes 8 months since Iraq invaded Kuwait. During these 8 months, the world community has stood up for what is right and just. It is now up to Iraq's Government to demonstrate that it is prepared to respect the will of the world community and communicate its formal acceptance of this resolution to the Security Council and the Secretary General.

The resolution is unprecedented. It creates a force to monitor the legal border between Iraq and Kuwait; it also provides a U.N. guarantee of that border. Once this observer force arrives, all remaining U.S. ground forces will be withdrawn from Iraqi territory.

The resolution establishes a fund to compensate Kuwait and other claimants for the damage caused by Iraq's aggression. The resolution also includes provisions designed to ensure that Iraq cannot rebuild its military strength to threaten anew the peace of the region. Weapons of mass destruction and the means to deliver them are to be destroyed; this is to be confirmed by onsite inspection.

Certain sanctions will remain in force until such time as Iraq is led by a government that convinces the world of its intent both to live in peace with its neighbors and to devote its resources to the welfare of the Iraqi people. The resolution thus provides the necessary latitude for the international community to adjust its relations with Iraq depending upon Iraq's leadership and behavior.

I also want to condemn in the strongest terms continued attacks by Iraqi Government forces against defenseless Kurdish and other Iraqi civilians. This sort of behavior will continue to set Iraq apart from the community of civilized nations. I call upon Iraq's leaders to halt these attacks immediately and to allow international organizations to go to work inside Iraq to alleviate the suffering and to ensure that humanitarian aid reaches needy civilians. As a result of these cruel attacks, Turkey is now faced with a mounting refugee problem. The United States is prepared to extend economic help to Turkey through multilateral channels, and we call upon others to do likewise.

303.

[Vol. 27, no. 14 (April 8, 1991): 387-391]

The President's News Conference With Prime Minister Toshiki Kaifu of Japan in Newport Beach, California
April 4, 1991

The President. Let me just say what a pleasure it's been to have Prime Minister Kaifu here in the United States. In the past year, we've resolved significant trade disputes, and we've moved to ease trade tensions. I think we've made solid progress in opening new markets to satellites and telecommunications, wood products.

We need to move ahead now in other areas—construction services, autos, auto parts, semiconductors, other areas. We need to prove that our efforts under the SII, the Structural Impediments Initiative, produce real results. I think progress has been made. It remains our best hope of fending off those who advocate managed trade between our nations.

In 1990, the U.S. trade deficit with Japan fell for the third straight year. And American exports to Japan continued to rise, up more than 75 percent since 1987. In fact, I think many Americans would be surprised to learn that Japan buys more goods from the U.S. per capita than we buy from Japan.

The Prime Minister and I both agree that we want to see a successful conclusion to the Uruguay round. And I might take this opportunity to urge the Congress of the United States to take decisive action and send a clear signal that America stands for free trade by extending the Fast Track procedures.

We had full discussions on the Gulf, and I took this occasion to thank, profoundly thank, Prime Minister Kaifu for the assistance that Japan made as a member of this coalition. Japan has provided a substantial level of financial support for Operation Desert Storm.

Just to save time, we will be putting out a more full statement here. But Mr. Prime Minister, I welcome your visit. And it's been a great pleasure having you here—all too brief a visit, but a very important one. Thank you for coming all this way.

The Prime Minister. Thank you, George, for kind remarks. You've shown yourself to be the great leader not just of this great nation, the United States, but of the entire world. Not only that, may I say, you are the private self of a countless number of people across the world who are fighting for the cause of peace and justice, for freedom and democracy.

I am most pleased to see you here in this beautiful State of California again, since we met over a year ago in a similar setting, and to be able to continue our close dialog.

I wish to take this opportunity on behalf of the entire Japanese people to pay our deep-

est respect to the great leadership you exerted as President throughout the Gulf crisis and to the dedication and sacrifice of the American soldiers, men and women, in Operations Desert Shield and Desert Storm.

The world has just overcome a great challenge in the Gulf region, and now it is time to tackle a truly historic mission, which is to build a new international order in the aftermath of the cold war. The Gulf crisis has demonstrated beyond anybody's doubt that the United States is the only superpower with the capability to play the most important role in the post-cold-war world and to do so in a responsible way.

At the same time, it has become clear that it is just as important that the like-minded countries work together and support American efforts. We deeply recognize this in Japan. Together with Americans, Europeans, Asians, and other peoples of the world, we seek to participate actively in this endeavor and cooperate for creating a new international order.

Throughout the Gulf crisis, Japan firmly supported the United States and international coalition efforts and cooperated as much as possible. And we are grateful for the appreciation expressed by the President. Nevertheless, sometimes Japan's efforts have not been properly understood and appreciated, and frankly speaking, this reception has caused disappointment among some Japanese people. Thinking about the future of Japan-U.S. relationship, which is so important to the peace and prosperity of the world, I firmly believe that we have to rectify this situation.

Japan and the United States are staunch allies, bound together with strong security ties and a close economic interdependence. I believe the world strongly desires to see friendly and cooperative bilateral relations between our two countries, in which both sides will bring their respective strengths in order to meet global challenges, and will tackle problems between our two countries.

We are with you always, standing together as firm allies and friends across the Pacific. I'm convinced that the friendship and the spirit of cooperation between our two peoples will always prevail. Thank you.

The President. What we thought we'd do is alternate questions for Prime Minister Kaifu and for me, and alternate between the Japanese journalists and the U.S. journalists. Inasmuch as we're in the United States, I'm the appointed coordinator here. [Laughter] Self-appointed.

Japan

Q. I'd like to ask a question of Prime Minister Kaifu. Because of constitutional constraints Japan was not able to send military forces during the Gulf war. However, Japan financed the $9 billion additional contribution through tax increase, and in that respect I believe it is fair to say that Japan has shed its blood in its own way. However, that contribution is not properly valued in the United States. On top of that, more recently, there seems to be a stepping up of Japan-bashing in the United States over trade issues, whereas in Japan there is dissatisfaction amongst the Japanese people. People are grumbling that Japan is not an automatic teller machine of a bank.

Now, I wonder if through your meeting today you've been able to, shall I say, lead the relations, which have been in a somewhat awkward state more recently, toward a more smoother relationship.

The Prime Minister. In the process of peace recovery, or recovery of peace in the Gulf region, Japan from the very beginning showed its basic position that Iraq is wrong. And from Japan's position, we cooperated and made contribution as much as possible. With regard to financial cooperation, we put a bill to the Diet of the Japanese Parliament. We passed a budget bill for that purpose. And for the purpose of funding that budget, we asked the Japanese people to accept an increased tax. And we were aware of the need to make this contribution, and the President has kindly appreciated that contribution that Japan made.

On the other hand, I'm certainly aware that there are divergent views in the United States. We would like to continue with our efforts so that we will be establishing a relationship of mutual confidence that is unshakable.

Iraq

Q. Mr. President, the critics are suggesting that you've abandoned the Kurds to Sad-dam Hussein's mercy; one has even likened it to your Bay of Pigs. Could you explain to us why we were willing to do so much to help liberate Kuwait and why now we are standing on the sidelines while the Kurds are struggling?

The President. Be glad to. It was never a stated objective of the coalition to intervene in the internal affairs of Iraq. Indeed, I made very clear that we did not intend to go into Iraq. I condemn Saddam Hussein's brutality against his own people. But I do not want to see United States forces, who have performed with such skill and dedication, sucked into a civil war in Iraq.

We will not have normal relations with Iraq until Saddam Hussein is out of there. But I made very, very clear from day one that it was not an objective of the coalition to get Saddam Hussein out of there by force. And I don't think there's a single parent of a single man or woman that has fought in Desert Storm that wants to see United States forces pushed into this situation—brutal, tough, deplorable as it is.

Q. If I may follow, will you offer asylum to the Kurdish refugees if Turkey keeps its borders closed?

The President. I have had a good discussion of that with Prime Minister Kaifu, and we are in agreement that we will do what we can to help the Kurdish refugees.

Japan-U.S. Relations

Q. I'd like to ask a question related to the rice issue, which I believe is on the top of the agenda between Japan and the United States. And I should like to direct this question to both the President and the Prime Minister.

The first, I should like to know, Mr. President, what your thoughts are with regard to the issue of opening up the Japanese rice market and whether you took up this matter during your meeting today.

The President. Yes, we had a full discussion of this matter. Yes, we would like to have access to the Japanese rice market. Yes, Prime Minister Kaifu explained the complications that he faces in Japan on this question. But I think the overriding point is we both realize that we must have a successful conclusion of the Uruguay round, and to do that, agriculture must be included.

The Prime Minister. Yes, let me respond to that myself, as well. The rice issue was mentioned in the context of the Uruguay round negotiations. What I said was that, regarding the Uruguay round, we recognize the importance of close cooperation between Japan and the United States to bring the round to an early and successful conclusion.

Now, I also explained that—well, there are difficult issues in the agriculture area for our countries—the United States, the European Communities, as well as for Japan. And so, I said, let us endeavor together to resolve the issue of rice together with the other issues, the difficulties for the other countries in the context of the Uruguay round.

Iraq

Q. Mr. President, in 1989 and 1990 when the talk of critics were calling on you to speak out more forcefully for the uprising in Eastern Europe and the Lithuanian aspirations for independence, you said you hesitated to do so for fear of raising expectations such as were raised in Hungary in 1956. Now, people are saying you've done just that by calling for the overthrow of Saddam Hussein, and you've let the rebels down when they moved on those expectations. Could you discuss that and give us your feelings and whether you see a parallel?

The President. I think I was right in 1989, and I think I'm right now. I made clear from the very beginning that it was not an objective of the coalition or the United States to overthrow Saddam Hussein. So, I don't think the Shiites in the south, those who are unhappy with Saddam in Baghdad, or the Kurds in the north ever felt that the United States would come to their assistance to overthrow this man.

We're not going to get sucked into this by sending precious American lives into this battle. We've fulfilled our obligations. Now, do we hurt when Kurdish people are hurt and killed and brutalized? Yes. Are we concerned at the brutal treatment of the Shiites in the south? Yes. Do we wish that the people would get rid of Saddam Hussein on their own? Absolutely. But I have not misled anybody about

the intentions of the United States of America, or has any other coalition partner, all of whom to my knowledge agree with me in this position—all of whom do.

Can we get one from the U.S. side for Prime Minister Kaifu? And then I'll take the next one from the Japanese side. Whoops. Is this one for Prime Minister—the Americans keep shooting at me. I want them to fire one at Prime Minister Kaifu. [Laughter]

Japan-U.S. Relations

Q. Mr. Prime Minister, you made note of the problem that you feel that Japan is not fully appreciated in this country, and you said that needed to be rectified. Could you tell us first, have you met and will you meet fully your pledge, your commitment, to the Desert Storm effort without any quibbling about whether it's in yen or in dollars? And what steps do you think need to be taken to rectify this image, this bad image you feel you have in the United States? And if you, Mr. President, would like to comment, I'd appreciate that, too.

The Prime Minister. With regard to the $9 billion, the Japanese budget system, the system of budgeting, is based on the Japanese yen. And I'm certainly aware that there has been some criticism rising basically out of the fluctuation—criticism arising from, shall I say, exchange rate fluctuation.

But what is important note is that that is not the only aspect where we ought to be paying our attention to. There are various roles that must be played in the Gulf region, in the interest of environmental protection and also arms control and disarmament in the region so that various countries would refrain from engaging in, say, intransparent transfer of arms and so on. So, I think there are numerous roles that can be played for the purpose of peace in that region.

I had in-depth discussions on such matters with George, and Japan wishes to play its part as actively as possible by maintaining close consultations with the United States.

Q. I should like to ask a question of Mr. President with regard to Japanese contribution related to the Gulf war. You said that you profoundly appreciated Japanese important financial contribution. Japan did not send even a medical team, not to speak of self-defense force personnel. And I wonder if you feel that it is possible to maintain a relationship of alliance with a country, Japan, which did not make a human contribution at a time of an international crisis. I would appreciate your candid remarks. And also, I wonder what you would expect of Japan to do for the purpose of preserving and further promoting this alliance.

The President. My answer is, yes, not only do I think we will preserve but I think we will strengthen this relationship. I hope most Americans understand the constitutional constraints on Japan in terms of what—I think you called them human forces, or human—human personnel.

But what I would like to emphasize to the American people and the people of Japan is, from day one—from day one, Toshiki Kaifu and the Japanese Government was in strong support of the U.N. resolutions. Japan stepped up early on to a fundamental and substantial monetary contribution. Through those months of diplomacy before force was used, Japan played a key role. And so if we have a difference now over some detail, I would simply say that this relationship is too fundamental, too important to have it on the shoals because of difficulty that I'm confident we can work out.

And to the degree that there's bashing on one side of the Pacific or another, Toshiki Kaifu and I are committed to see that that bashing doesn't go forward because it's in our interest in the United States to have this relationship strong. And I happen to think it's in Japan's interest.

I know the Prime Minister has to go, but can we take one more for each side? And we'll divide it up, one for him and one for me.

Q. Mr. President, to go back to your response to the last question and to the unanswered portion of Charles' [Charles Bierbauer, Cable News Network] question earlier, it's clear that Japan's image problem in the United States goes beyond the immediate issue of the Gulf war. What does Japan specifically need to do to overcome that problem? Given the attitudes on Capitol Hill, given the trade hawks that are circling, isn't it going to take more than just explaining some of the complications that are involved on the types of trade concession that we've been demanding in Tokyo?

The President. One, the relationship is fundamentally sound. What will it take, you asked, to make it better? The successful conclusion of the Uruguay round, to which we're both committed, would help. Working together with Japan to alleviate the suffering of these Kurdish victims of Saddam's brutality—that will help. Working with Japan to help guarantee the security and the stability of the Gulf and reconstruction of the Gulf—that will help. Moving forward in other trade areas can help, although we're closing that gap.

But, Norm [Norman Sandler, United Press International], when there are problems, it is understandable that people dwell on those specific problems and we overlook the fundamentals. And those fundamentals include the fact that the Japanese Government and the U.S. Government, as you look around the world, see eye-to-eye on almost every problem around the world.

Let me give you one more example. The answer is too long—excuse me, Toshiki—but one more example. Japan is trying to be helpful to the development and strengthening of democracy in this hemisphere. So, while we take up the difficulties, let's also remember these fundamentals that are strong as they can be.

Last one, and this is for the Prime Minister.

Soviet-Japan Relations

Q. I'd like to ask a question regarding the Soviet Union. President Gorbachev of the Soviet Union will be visiting Japan. And I wonder in relation to that, you discussed during your meeting today—well, assistance for the Soviet Union. And together with that, I should also like to know whether you had any discussions on trade in technology with the Soviet Union?

The Prime Minister. With the upcoming summit meeting with President Gorbachev's visit to Japan, I did mention in general terms that we should like to take up as a major item on our bilateral agenda the resolution of the territorial issue between Japan and the Soviet Union, so that we shall be able to sign a peace treaty which will lead us toward a genuine friendship.

However, we did not discuss specifics such as technological assistance or economic assistance. I did explain our, shall I say, diplomatic schedule ahead of us with the Soviet Government and the North Korean Government which we would like to promote for the purpose of attaining peace, stability, and prosperity in the Asia-Pacific region.

The President. Well, I think we're a little behind schedule for the—no. No, no. [Laughter] But thank you.

Never get enough. Here we go. Thank you all very much.

304.

[Vol. 27, no. 14 (April 8, 1991): 392-393]

U.S. Humanitarian Assistance to Iraqi Refugees

Statement by President Bush, April 5, 1991

The human tragedy unfolding in and around Iraq demands immediate action on a massive scale. At stake are not only the lives of hundreds of thousands of innocent men, women, and children but the peace and security of the Gulf.

Since the beginning of the Gulf war on August 2, the United States has contributed more than $35 million for refugees and displaced persons in the region. Many other countries have also contributed. It is clear, however, that the current tragedy requires a far greater effort. As a result, I have directed a major new effort be undertaken to assist Iraqi refugees. Beginning this Sunday, U.S. Air Force transport planes will fly over northern Iraq and drop supplies of food, blankets, clothing, tents, and other relief-related items for refugees and other Iraqi civilians suffering as a result of the situation there.

I want to emphasize that this effort is prompted only by humanitarian concerns. We expect the Government of Iraq to permit this effort to be carried out without any interference. I want to add that what we are planning to do is intended as a step-up in immediate aid, such as is also being provided by the British, the French, and other coalition partners. We will be consulting with the United Nations on how it can best provide for the many refugees in and around Iraq on a long term basis as necessary. We will continue consulting with our coalition partners in this and in other efforts designed to alleviate the plight of the many innocent Iraqis whose lives have been endangered by the brutal and inhumane actions of the Iraqi government.

I also want to add that this urgent air drop is but one of several steps the United States is taking to deal with this terrible situation. I will shortly be signing an order that will authorize up to $10 million from the Emergency Refugee and Migration Assistance Fund. These funds will help meet the needs of the burgeoning refugee population in the region. Our military forces in southern Iraq will continue to assist refugees and displaced persons. We are also providing considerable economic and food assistance to the Government of Turkey, to help it sustain the many refugees who have taken refuge there. We are prepared as well to deploy a U.S. military medical unit to the border area in southern Turkey to meet emergency needs.

The United States is also concerned about the welfare of those Iraqi refugees now fleeing to Iran. We will be communicating, through our established channel, to the Government of Iran our willingness to encourage and contribute to international organizations carrying out relief efforts aiding these individuals.

In an effort to help innocent people, and especially the children of Iraq, we will be donating $869,000 to UNICEF for child immunizations in Iraq. We will also be providing a further $131,000 and 1,000 tons of food to the International Committee of the Red Cross (ICRC). In all cases, funds and goods provided to international organizations will be distributed by the organizations themselves to civilian in Iraq.

Finally, I have asked Secretary Baker to travel to Turkey, en route to the Middle East, to meet with President Ozal and visit the border area to assess the refugee situation and report back to me.

305.

[Vol. 27, no. 15 (April 15, 1991): 419–420]

Remarks and an Exchange With Reporters Prior to Discussions With President Jacques Delors of the European Community Commission and President Jacques Santer of the European Council of Ministers
April 11, 1991

President Bush. You're not going to need these because this is a photo opportunity. [Laughter]

Q. Mr. President, do you support a safe haven for the Kurdish refugees?

Q. Haven't you, in effect, sir, created an enclave there by telling Iraq you will shoot down any planes that threaten the refugees?

President Bush. Photo opportunity.

I think our distinguished guests are going to have a press conference later on. I'll have a little something to say on this subject in a bit, too. But the main thing we want to do is welcome these European leaders here. The United States values its relationship with the EC — and of course, on a bilateral basis we have a wonderful relationship with Prime Minister Santer and his country, and the same for Jacques Delors when he's wearing a French hat, which is very seldom these days. We've got a great, cooperative relationship with the EC and with individual countries in Europe, and that's what this meeting is about, to put the emphasis on the EC.

Iraqi Refugees

Q. Well, you are going to discuss the Kurdish refugees?

President Bush. Absolutely. We'll be discussing that and a wide array of other questions. And I'm very pleased with the enormous cooperative refugee program now underway. It is tremendous. The suffering there is enormous. And the United States is in lockstep with Europe in terms of our approach to helping these unfortunate people that are being victimized by this brutal dictator in Baghdad.

306.

[Vol. 27, no. 15 (April 15, 1991): 421–422]

Exchange With Reporters on Aid to Iraqi Refugees
April 11, 1991

Q. Mr. President, do you agree with Prime Minister Major on the enclaves?

The President. Yes, total agreement.

Q. Iraq said you don't need to mark enclaves.

Q. What kind of enclaves?

The President. We're going to do what we need for humanitarian relief. And there is no difference between the United Kingdom and the United States, and there's no difference between the EC and the United States, and there's no difference between the United Nations Secretary-General and the United States on this question. So, I hope that you will understand that. There is no difference on this.

Q. What kind of enclave, sir?

The President. We're looking forward to give relief to these people where they are. We're going to continue to do that. And I do not expect any interference from the man in Baghdad, and he knows better than to interfere.

Q. Is the enclave a legal entity?

Q. Mr. President—

The President. Charles [Charles Bierbauer, Cable News Network], you're off on the wrong track. If you'd listen to what I said, you'd be right about this. There is no difference between these people. And it takes the United Nations action to do some formalization; that's not what we're doing. We're going to help these refugees, and please don't try to make a difference where there isn't any. If you don't believe me, do what I did yesterday: Talk to John Major, and you will see there are no differences. The United States is taking the leadership role on bringing refugees support, and we're going to continue to do it. And we're doing a magnificent job in conjunction with these allies.

And P.S., I am not going to involve any American troops in a civil war in Iraq. They are not going to be going in there to do what some of my severest critics early on now seem to want me to do. I want these kids to come home. And that's what's going to happen. And we are going to do what is right by these refugees, and I think the American people expect that, and they want that. But I don't think they want to see us bogged down in a civil war by sending in the 82d Airborne or the 101st or the 7th Cavalry. And so, I want to get that matter cleared up.

But we are together today with our European allies, just as we have been all during this magnificent operation over there.

307.

[Vol. 27, no. 16 (April 22, 1991): 444-451]

Expanded Humanitarian Assistance for the Iraqi Kurds

The President's News Conference April 16, 1991

The President. I have a brief statement here, and then I'll be glad to take a few questions. Eleven days ago, on April 5th, I announced that the United States would initiate what soon became the largest U.S. relief effort mounted in modern military history. Such an undertaking was made necessary by the terrible human tragedy unfolding in and around Iraq as a result of Saddam Hussein's brutal treatment of Iraqi citizens.

Within 48 hours, our operation was providing scores of tons of food, water, coats, tents, blankets, and medicines to the Iraqi Kurds in northern Iraq and southern Turkey. The scale of this effort is truly unprecedented. Yet the fact remains that the scale of the problem is even greater. Hundreds of thousands of Iraqi Kurds are in difficult-to-reach mountain areas in southern Turkey and along the Turkish-Iraq border.

The Government of Turkey, along with U.S., British, and French military units, and numerous international organizations, have launched a massive relief operation. But despite these efforts, hunger, malnutrition, disease, and exposure are taking their grim toll. No one can see the pictures or hear the ac-

counts of this human suffering—men, women, and most painfully of all, innocent children—and not be deeply moved.

It is for this reason that this afternoon, following consultations with Prime Minister Major, President Mitterrand, President Ozal of Turkey, Chancellor Kohl this morning, U.N. Secretary-General Perez de Cuellar, I'm announcing a greatly expanded and more ambitious relief effort. The approach is quite simple: If we cannot get adequate food, medicine, clothing, and shelter to the Kurds living in the mountains along the Turkish-Iraq border, we must encourage the Kurds to move to areas in northern Iraq where the geography facilitates rather than frustrates such a large-scale relief effort.

Consistent with United Nations Security Council Resolution 688 and working closely with the United Nations and other international relief organizations and our European partners, I have directed the U.S. military to begin immediately to establish several encampments in northern Iraq where relief supplies for these refugees will be made available in large quantities and distributed in an orderly way.

I can well appreciate that many Kurds have good reason to fear for their safety if they return to Iraq. And let me reassure them that adequate security will be provided at these temporary sites by U.S., British, and French air and ground forces, again consistent with United Nations Security Council Resolution 688. We are hopeful that others in the coalition will join this effort.

I want to underscore that all that we are doing is motivated by humanitarian concerns. We continue to expect the Government of Iraq not to interfere in any way with this latest relief effort. The prohibition against Iraqi fixed- or rotary-wing aircraft flying north of the 36th parallel thus remains in effect.

And I want to stress that this new effort, despite its scale and scope, is not intended as a permanent solution to the plight of the Iraqi Kurds. To the contrary, it is an interim measure designed to meet an immediate, penetrating humanitarian need. Our long-term objective remains the same: for Iraqi Kurds and, indeed, for all Iraqi refugees, wherever they are, to return home and to live in peace, free from repression, free to live their lives.

I also want to point out that we're acutely concerned about the problem of the Iraqi refugees now along the Iran-Iraq border and in Iran. I commend the members of the European Community for their efforts to alleviate hardship in this area. We, ourselves, have offered to contribute to international efforts designed to meet this humanitarian challenge.

As I stated earlier, the relief effort being announced here today constitutes an undertaking different in scale and approach. What is not different is basic policy. All along, I have said that the United States is not going to intervene militarily in Iraq's internal affairs and risk being drawn into a Vietnam-style quagmire. This remains the case. Nor will we become an occupying power with U.S. troops patrolling the streets of Baghdad.

We intend to turn over the administration of and security for these sites as soon as possible to the United Nations, just as we are fulfilling our commitment to withdraw our troops and hand over responsibility to U.N. forces along Iraq's southern border, the border with Kuwait.

But we must do everything in our power to save innocent life. This is the American tradition, and we will continue to live up to that tradition.

Assistance for Iraqi Refugees

Q. Mr. President, your administration estimates that up to 1,000 Kurds are dying each day. How do you respond to critics who say that you've acted too little, too late, and that you've turned your backs on the very people that you inspired to rise up against Saddam Hussein?

The President. I don't think we have responded too little, too late. It is an extraordinarily difficult logistical problem. And we have been, as I said in my statement, sending lots of humanitarian relief in there—not just the United States, incidentally, other countries as well, a lot of private relief organizations helping out. So, this has been our policy. But I think we have a better chance to facilitate the relief and to get the Kurds in more sanitary conditions by this new program I've announced here today. There's been an awful lot

of consultation with the Turks and others going into this. And in terms of the other, I simply don't accept that.

Q. How long do you think that it will be before the United Nations forces can take over from the U.S. and other allies?

The President. You mean in this new operation? We don't know that. We don't know that, but clearly the sooner the better. The United Nations forces will be coming down into the south—the Blue Helmets. And we hope and expect that to be accomplished in a very few days. But this one we're just starting, but we'll have to see what we do. And it may require for a U.N. peacekeeping force in there—or U.N. Blue Helmets—a new resolution from the Security Council. And that's a complicated problem, given the fact that some of the members who were steadfastly with us in the coalition might have problems with something of this nature.

Q. Mr. President, you keep absolving yourself of any responsibility, and yet time after time you are on the record of calling on the Iraqis to take the matter in their own hands, and you never said, not you the Kurds, not you the Shiites. So, how can you really continue to justify that in your own mind when the world's conscience—go ahead.

The President. No, go ahead, finish your question.

Q. Well, the world's conscience has been aroused by this, and we are seeing pictures of this terrible suffering.

The President. Well, I think all Americans—yes—

Q. Obviously, you were taken by surprise, and you have no long-term policy for what is going to happen eventually. Will they be refugees for the rest of their lives?

The President. I hope not. We've got enough—what looks like permanent refugees, and we're trying to do something about that in various areas. The objectives were set out very early on. And the objectives never included going into Baghdad, never included the demise and destruction of Saddam personally. You had many people that were telling me early on, let sanctions work. Let sanctions work. Don't do anything about the aggression at all. We led an international coalition of unprecedented, historic proportions and achieved objectives.

And you're asking me if I foresaw the size of the Kurdish refugee problem? The answer is: No, I did not. But do I think that the United States should bear guilt because of suggesting that the Iraqi people take matters into their own hands, with the implication being given by some that the United States would be there to support them militarily? That was not true. We never implied that. Do I think the answer is now for Saddam Hussein to be kicked out? Absolutely. Because there will not be—

Q. Is he—

The President. May I finish, please? There will not be normalized relations with the United States—and I think this is true for most coalition partners—until Saddam Hussein is out of there. And we will continue the economic sanctions.

Q. Do you concede you encouraged the revolt and the exodus?

The President. I don't concede encouraging an exodus. I did suggest—and it's well documented—what I thought would be good is if the Iraqi people would take matters into their own hands and kick Saddam Hussein out. I still feel that way, and I still hope they do.

Q. You have hundreds of thousands of refugees which will require a large number of forces. How many allied and U.S. forces will be involved inside northern Iraq?

The President. I think rather small numbers because I don't think Saddam Hussein, given the assurances he made today to the United Nations in Iraq—they had some representatives there—would venture to use force. But the problem isn't what we think about it; the problem is what do these Kurdish refugees who have been brutalized by this man think. And what they think is, look, we don't want to take his word. We need some security.

Q. Mr. President, have you actually formally notified Iraq that this is what you're going to do—set up encampments?

The President. No.

Q. Well, I mean, so this is the first word they've received of it?

The President. Well, I think they're talking with the United Nations people about en-

campments being set up. But this is the first word they know as to what the United States is going to do about it—authoritative word.

Q. Are you sure that they're not going to respond militarily to seeing force come in?

The President. They should not respond militarily. And they underestimated the United States once before on that, and they shouldn't do it again. And I don't think they will. And the United Nations people who have been talking to them in Baghdad don't think that there will be a military response. And since we said no action north of the 36th parallel, in fairness, there hasn't been any military action north of the 36th parallel.

Q. You said before that you didn't like the idea of a protected enclave within Iraq itself. But doesn't this, in effect, establish for months and the foreseeable future the United States military protecting Kurdish refugees in that area? And do you want to continue to leave it ambiguous what the U.S. would do in case there is any effort by the Iraqis against the Kurdish refugees?

The President. I hope we're not talking about a long-term effort. We're working with the French, who've taken a leadership role in a policy to encourage the Kurds to return to the cities. There's some talk about trying to get a U.N. presence along these various way stations as they go back. That would be a very useful idea, and I told Mr. Mitterrand I supported him strongly on that.

But in this one, I don't think it has to be long-term. The main thing, long-term or short-term, from the very beginning we've been trying to save the lives of these women and children and men. And now this is a logical next step to get it done much more sanitarily, get it done in a safe and sensible way.

And some might argue that this is an intervention into the internal affairs of Iraq. But I think the humanitarian concern, the refugee concern is so overwhelming that there will be a lot of understanding about this.

Q. Will the American military be militarily protecting these areas? And what will they do if there is any attack on the refugees?

The President. Well, that was the question I used to get before the war started against— what are you going to do; how are you going to respond to this? And I won't give you any details, but I will simply suggest that these people will be protected. We are not going to say to them, "Come down from the mountains; you will be protected," and then not protect them.

Q. Mr. President, given the condition of many of these refugees, how are you going to get them to these new camps? How far away or how far distance are we talking about moving them, and what role might the U.S. or the allies play in getting them there?

The President. We're going to have what you call a supply train. There will be strong— I mean, not train in the sense of railroad train, but a supply train—and there will be a lot of international support for that. The Turks will facilitate this. I can't give you—there will be maybe five or six camps in these so-called— what Ozal calls "flat areas"—but I can't give you an exact estimate on the mileage.

It's not too far in terms of long distances. But what we've got to do now is get in there and build these camps and keep our commitment to be sure that they are safe, and I think they will be. And then you ask a very good question, because how you talk these scared people into coming down, that's another question. But we will be doing our level-best, and we have very good people on the ground there now.

Q. Mr. President, how many troops do you envision being involved in this, and how certain are you of their safety?

The President. Relatively small numbers, and I'm very confident of their safety. We'll have air power around there if needed. We'll be able to protect not only our own people but we'll be able to protect the people that we're setting out to protect, which is these refugees.

Q. May I follow up on that, sir? You feel certain enough of their safety that you feel this is not inconsistent with your earlier statements about not putting one U.S. soldier's life on the line?

The President. Yes, I do. I think this is entirely different, and I just feel it's what's needed in terms of helping these people. Some may interpret it that way; I don't. I think it's purely humanitarian. And I think representations have been made as recently as today that these people would be safe, so I hope it proves that way.

Q. Mr. President, you haven't mentioned anything about the situation in the south where there are thousands of Shiites who are equally concerned about what happens when Americans withdraw.

The President. Exactly.

Q. Can we offer the same kind of assurances that they won't be attacked?

The President. The United Nations will be in there soon, and we think that will be very good assurance that they will not be attacked. People forget that the United States has been doing a wonderful job for those refugees for a long time. I've seen no credit given to our troops that are handling that with great concern and compassion. They have done a superb job.

So, what we want to do is see—in that neutral zone—see the Blue Helmets come in there, and then I will continue to keep moving our people out as rapidly as possible. I want to bring them home.

Q. But if the U.N. forces aren't enough to deter Iraqi problems down there, is there some kind of an allied coalition commitment to those people as well?

The President. I think there will be enough. I think that we're operating on the assumption that they will not be attacked with the United Nations in there. I think that would be a serious problem for Saddam Hussein if he took on the entire United Nations, having agreed to these cease-fire conditions. So, I would just stand with that.

President Saddam Hussein of Iraq

Q. Mr. President, your wife suggested yesterday—Mrs. Bush suggested that Saddam Hussein be tried for war crimes and hanged. Do you agree?

The President. I seldom differ with my wife, and I don't know that I would differ with her here. I'll tell you what's the most important thing, however, and that is to get Saddam Hussein out of there. So, if you came to me as a broker and you said, I can get him out of there, but he'd have to be able to live a happy life forevermore in some third country with all kinds of conditions never to go back and brutalize his people again, I'd have to think about it, but I might be willing to say, well, as far as our pressing charges, we'd be willing to get him out. We want him out of there so badly, and I think it's so important to the tranquility of Iraq that under that condition we might.

But his crimes—do I think he's guilty of war crimes? The environmental terror, the rape and pillage of Kuwait, what he's done to his own people? I would think there would be plenty of grounds under which he would be prosecuted for war crimes.

Q. Former President Nixon suggested a little bit earlier that maybe you should put out a contract and have Saddam Hussein assassinated. What about that?

The President. I think that's unacceptable. I'm not sure that's exactly what President Nixon said, either.

Situation in Iraq

Q. Mr. President, here you are, talking about getting rid of Saddam Hussein, putting additional U.S. forces back into Ira*Q.* How can you be sure that the U.S. is not going to get entangled in that internal situation there, that civil war that you so much want to avoid?

The President. Well, I'm positive in my own mind—put it this way—in my own mind, my judgment is—and I think it's the collective judgment of the people that figured the war out pretty well—is that he won't risk this. And Saddam Hussein is not going to want to reengage in that nature. So, we'll have to see. But certainly, any U.S. forces—and we're not talking about large numbers, I don't know exactly what the numbers are—will be protected. And they will be protected vigorously. But I don't anticipate that. I don't expect, and I don't think the French President expects that; I don't think the British Prime Minister expects it; I don't think the United Nations Secretary-General expects it; the President of Turkey—and we've got a lot of people working this problem.

It is the collective judgment—and they've been right far more than wrong on these matters—that this will not take place. But we're prepared if any force should be used against these helpless people in the refugee camps.

Q. And, Mr. President, some in Congress who voted against the war resolution to begin with now say that you didn't complete the job and have, in fact, created another Vietnam. What's your reaction on that?

The President. I've got to be careful about my reaction to some of that because— maybe you could help me by explaining which people—from what view? The ones that wanted sanctions to work, or ones that didn't want use of military force ever under any condition? Which ones are you talking about?

Q. There were some in Congress who had—well, Senator Kennedy, for example, yesterday in a public statement said that you didn't go far enough to complete the job.

The President. Well, he's entitled to his opinion. I think we completed the objectives that we spelled out; they were fulfilled. And I think the whole world knows that. Now we have another problem, a problem that's a recurring problem. This man has brutalized these people before, and now he's doing it again.

I think I would call to the attention of the critics what the objectives were, what the United Nations resolutions called for. And I think that they were admirably completed. And I am surprised at some who strongly oppose the use of force now sound to me, from some of their clarion calls, that they want to use force to solve the matters in Baghdad, and that is not what we are going to do. And if you did do it, you'd certainly want to go back through the diplomatic approach, and certainly I would not want to do that without having a lot of these people on the record in terms of support.

But I don't think that's needed. I don't believe that's what we ought to be doing. I think the American people want their sons and daughters to come home, and they're going to come home. And the only little difficulty now in terms of coming home is that we have a responsibility to do what we can to help these refugees. We've been doing it from day one. And now, as the problem gets worse and as we see the fear in these people's hearts about coming down out of the mountains, we're taking this next step.

But the fundamental policy is to bring our men and women home, and that's exactly what we're doing in the south. Gerry [Gerald Seib, Wall Street Journal] asked the right question: What guarantee? The guarantee is the agreement itself that was enacted by the

United Nations and agreed to by Iraq, and the presence of Blue Helmets of the United Nations peacekeeping force.

Q. In all fairness to Senator Kennedy, his reference was to the use of helicopter gunships against the rebels after they had apparently felt that they were encouraged by your remarks to rebel against Saddam.

The President. So, what does he want us to do? I just haven't followed what he's been saying on this subject.

Q. His criticism was that you didn't go ahead and shoot down those helicopter gunships.

The President. You know, I can understand people thinking that. I can understand their criticism. And then, how do you take care of the tanks and the riflemen and the other parts of the divisions that remained in northern Iraq? Helicopters is but a part of it.

You can say, well, if you'd have done that, maybe he'd have stopped. I don't believe that, but I don't fault him for that, if that's what his position was.

Q. Mr. President, the Kurds say that they want an independent Kurdistan. They were promised one after World War II. Why shouldn't they have that?

The President. I said early on that it was not an objective of the United States to see a fractured, destabilized Iraq. And that is the position of our Government, the position of our coalition forces. That's the answer.

Q. I'm sorry, that was after World War I they were promised one. Doesn't that bear any weight with you?

The President. A promise from World War I?

Q. Yes.

The President. No. I say, no, I believe Iraq ought to live in peace and reconciliation with the various factions in Ira*Q.* You've got the Shiites in the south, you've got the center—the Sunis and the Baathists and whoever in the center, and you have the Kurds in the north. They should reconcile their differences and keep that country, with its proud traditions, intact.

But that's a matter that we are not going to try to suggest that it be divided up, if that's what your question is. And I hope I've made that clear from the very beginning.

Q. But can they ever go back to their homes as long as Saddam Hussein is in power?

The President. Yes, I hope they can. Well, good question. They're scared to death to come down out of the mountains. But that's a very good question. But they've got to figure that out. And I think one of the things we're—I'm most hopeful about is that this plan by Francois Mitterrand bears some fruit—this way station approach so people can come back.

Now, Saddam Hussein has said for them to come back; they don't believe him. They've been betrayed by him. So, I would hope, yes, that someday they would be able to go back. A lot of them aren't country people. I've heard yesterday on some of the news of city people who were lawyers and doctors and have fled from their rather pleasant lives.

So, I would hope that there could be a reconciliation. And the easiest way for the country to be reconciled is to have a new leader. There's no question about that.

President Saddam Hussein of Iraq

Q. Mr. President, are there any behind-the-scenes negotiations going on about Saddam Hussein's future? Are there any brokers coming to you?

The President. No, not that I know of, Maureen [Maureen Santini, New York Daily News].

Q. Is he any closer today to leaving power?

The President. I would think so, but I can't prove it.

Q. And no one has even come to discuss brokering a deal?

The President. Well, there's a lot of people, a lot of resistance groups, that would like to see him out of there. They haven't come to me about it. But there's no question about a lot of people that are Iraqis that want to see him out. No question about that. But if you're asking if they've come here to the White House or proposals of that nature, I don't believe so.

Iran-U.S. Relations

Q. Mr. President, you made mention of the situation in Iran as being equally difficult.

But your plan seems to only deal with the situation in Iraq and perhaps to help your friend, President Ozal. Why is there no component here for the refugees in Iran, which are even greater in number?

The President. We've offered to help in Iran. And as you know, we have different difficult relations with the State of Iran. The Germans have stepped up to the tune of several hundred million—

Mr. Scowcroft. Two hundred and fifty million deutsche marks.

The President. Two hundred and fifty million deutsche marks to help there. The EC has taken on that in a coalition way. We've had the individual charitable organizations— Americare has been in there with medicine already. So, we want to help there. But you've got to be a realist. I mean, the Iranians still have strained relations with the United States of America. And they make that clear to various visitors that go there. But others are stepping into that breach and helping, just as we're helping with the Shiites in the south and have been to the tune of 30,000 refugees, through American compassion and American largess. Others are pitching in on the Iranian side.

Q. Is there an opportunity here to improve your relations with Iran?

The President. I would hope so. I've said over and over again I'd like to see improved relations with Iran. They know what our bottom line is, and our bottom line is those hostages. I am not going to forget those Americans that are held hostage. And I'm not suggesting Iran holds them, but I am suggesting Iran could have a great deal of influence in getting them out of there.

But yes, I hope we will have better relations. And maybe there is, Charles [Charles Bierbauer, Cable News Network], out of the plight of these refugees, maybe working together—and we are in a sense. We're helping in various areas; they're helping—that we can have common ground. And maybe that will lead to a better relationship.

You've got to remember this about Iran: Iran from day one was worried to death about a U.S. military presence in the Gulf. Their whole problem from day one, even though the military would eventually be used against

their major enemy, Saddam Hussein—they just didn't believe we'd come out. They just didn't believe we'd come out of the Gulf. And I would hope that if they see our forces, several hundred thousand of them home already, I believe, and more coming as rapidly as possible, that that fear that has separated Iran from the United States—one of the things that has separated—will be allayed. And I think it will.

Mr. Fitzwater. Final question, please.

. . .

Thank you all very much.

308.

[Vol. 27, no. 17 (April 29, 1991): 511]

Funding for Refugee Relief

Statement by the President's Press Secretary (Fitzwater), April 25, 1991[68]

The President today transmitted to Congress a request for FY 1991 supplemental appropriations for the Department of State and the Agency for International Development (AID) and language provisions for the Department of Defense. The requested funds and provisions are for humanitarian assistance efforts for refugees and displaced persons in and around Iraq as well as for peacekeeping activities.

The proposed language provisions would permit transfer from the Persian Gulf Regional Defense Fund to the Department of Defense for the incremental costs of humanitarian assistance.

In addition, the supplemental requests $123.5 million for the Department of State and $27 million for the Agency for International Development for assistance for refugees and displaced persons as well as for peacekeeping activities. The State Department and AID requests would be financed through transfers of interest earned on balances in the Defense Cooperation Account. Contributions of foreign governments would not be used.

These supplemental requests would be exempt from statutory spending limits because they are incremental costs associated with Operation Desert Shield/ Desert Storm.

309.

[Vol. 27, no. 20 (May 20, 1991): 621-622]

Postwar U.S. Military Actions in Northern Iraq

Letter from President Bush to Congressional Leaders on the Situation in the Persian Gulf
May 17, 1991

Dear Mr. Speaker: (Dear Mr. President:)
On March 19, 1991, I reported to you, consistent with the Authorization for Use of Military Force Against Iraq Resolution (Public Law 102 - 1), on the successful conduct of military operations aimed at the liberation of Kuwait. Since that time, the United Nations Security Council has adopted Resolution 687, which set forth the preconditions for a formal cease-fire. Iraq has accepted those terms, and the cease-fire and withdrawal of coalition forces from southern Iraq have been concluded. The Iraqi repression of the Kurdish people has, however, necessitated a limited introduction of U.S. forces into northern Iraq for emergency relief purposes. I am reporting these matters to you as part of our continuing effort to keep the Congress fully informed on these developments.

Resolution 687 required, as a precondition for a formal cease-fire, that Iraq officially notify the United Nations of its acceptance of the provisions of the resolution. These provisions included: (1) respect for the international boundary as agreed between Iraq and Kuwait in 1963, which the Security Council guaranteed; (2) the creation of a demilitarized zone along the Iraq-Kuwait border and the deployment of a U.N. observer unit into that zone; (3) the destruction, removal, or rendering harmless of all chemical and biological weapons, ballistic missiles with a range greater than 150 kilometers, and nuclear-weapons-usable material, together with facilities related to them, and international supervision and inspection to verify compliance; (4) the creation of a fund, drawn from future Iraqi oil revenues, to pay compensation for losses caused by the Iraqi invasion and occupation of Kuwait; (5) the continuation of the embargo of all exports of arms to Iraq; (6) the phased relaxation of certain other aspects of the U.N. sanctions against Iraq as Iraq complies with its obligations under the resolution; and (7) the renunciation by Iraq of support for international terrorism.

Iraq officially accepted those terms on April 6, and a formal cease-fire has gone into effect. Accordingly, United States Armed Forces deployed in southern Iraq began withdrawing as U.N. peacekeeping personnel deployed into the zone, and this withdrawal was completed on May 9. The United States has been assisting the U.N. Secretary General in his efforts to implement the other provisions of Resolution 687, particularly with respect to boundary demarcation, compensation, and weapons of mass destruction.

During this same period, however, Iraqi forces engaged in a campaign of brutal repression of internal opposition, with the result that many hundreds of thousands of civilians fled their homes in search of safety in the regions along the Turkish and Iranian borders. In response to this situation, on April 5 the Security Council adopted Resolution 688, which insisted that Iraq cease its repression and allow immediate access by international humanitarian organizations, and appealed to all Member States to assist in these humanitarian relief efforts.

I immediately ordered United States Armed Forces to begin air-dropping large amounts of food and other essential items to these refugees. However, it soon became clear that even this massive effort would not be enough to deal with the desperate plight of the hundreds of thousands of men, women, and children stranded and suffering in these mountainous areas. Accordingly, on April 16 I directed United States Armed Forces to begin to establish immediately several temporary encampments in northern Iraq where geographical conditions would be more suitable for relief efforts. United States, British, and French forces are providing security for these encampments.

This effort is not intended as a permanent solution to the plight of the Iraqi Kurds. It is a humanitarian measure designed to save lives, consistent with Resolution 688. It is also not an attempt to intervene militarily into the internal affairs of Iraq or to impair its territorial integrity. We intend to turn over the administration and security for these temporary sites as soon as possible to the United Nations (a process that has already begun), and to complete our total withdrawal from Iraq. Our long-term objective remains the same: for Iraqi Kurds, and indeed for all Iraqi refugees and displaced persons, to return home and to live in peace, free from repression.

I am grateful for the support that the Congress has given, and I look forward to continued cooperation in meeting these urgent humanitarian goals.

Sincerely,
George Bush

310.

[27, no. 24 (June 17, 1991): 771]

Funding for Humanitarian Relief in Iraq
Statement by President Bush on Signing
the Bill Providing Humanitarian Assistance
for Iraqi Refugees and Displaced Persons
June 13, 1991

Today I have signed H.R. 2251, an Act that provides supplemental appropriations for humanitarian assistance to refugees and displaced persons in and around Iraq and for peacekeeping activities.

I am pleased by the demonstration of bipartisan cooperation and the speed with which the Congress has worked to complete action on this legislation. This Act will enable the Departments of State and Defense and the Agency for International Development to continue their efforts on behalf of the refugees and displaced persons in and around Iraq, and to replenish those accounts which have been drawn down by the immense effort of Operation Provide Comfort. The funds provided in this Act are incremental costs of Operation Desert Shield/Desert Storm.

In the 68 days since the initiation of Operation Provide Comfort, the United States has delivered by air and land over 17,000 tons of relief supplies and provided medical assistance for thousands of Iraqi refugees and displaced persons who fled to the Turkey/Iraq border area. Countless lives were saved. Through American leadership, spearheaded so well by the military, 650,000 Iraqi refugees and displaced persons have left the inhospitable mountains and traveled to or through relief camps we built. Most are now returning to their homes. The last mountain camp has closed. The task of responding to this human tragedy is not over, but we can be grateful for what has been accomplished by the United States, the United Nations, and the international community.

George Bush
The White House,
June 13, 1991.

Note: H.R. 2251, approved June 13, was assigned Public Law No. 102 - 55.

311.

[Vol. 27, no. 24 (June 17, 1991): 966-967]
Status of Efforts to Obtain Iraqi Compliance with U.N. Resolution

Letter from President Bush to Congressional Leaders on the Situation in the Persian Gulf
July 16, 1991

Dear Mr. Speaker: (Dear Mr. President:)

Consistent with the Authorization for Use of Military Force Against Iraq Resolution (Public Law 102 - 1), and as part of my continuing effort to keep the Congress fully informed, I am again reporting on the status of efforts to obtain compliance by Iraq with the resolutions adopted by the U.N. Security Council.

As I stated in my report of May 17, 1991, U.N. Security Council Resolution 687 required as a precondition for the formal cease-fire that Iraq accept the destruction, removal or rendering harmless of all chemical and biological weapons, ballistic missiles with a range greater than 150 kilometers, and nuclear-weapons-usable material, together with related facilities and equipment; and that it accept international supervision and inspection to verify compliance with these requirements. On June 17, the Security Council approved a plan for this supervision and inspection, to be conducted by the International Atomic Energy Agency and the Special Commission created under Resolution 687.

With the strong support and encouragement of the United States, these bodies have been working actively to identify, inspect and arrange for the elimination of these weapons and related items. While some inspections of declared missiles and chemical weapons have occurred, Iraq has generally engaged in obfuscation and evasion of its obligations. In recent weeks, public attention has focused on Iraq's nuclear equipment and material, but this has also been true with respect to Iraq's undeclared chemical weapons and ballistic missiles and its continuing refusal to acknowledge any biological weapons development activities. We will not allow these Iraqi actions to succeed. We will continue to insist on the full identification and complete elimination of all relevant items as well as the imposition of a thorough and effective monitoring regime to assure Iraq's long-term compliance with Resolution 687.

In addition, the United Nations has moved forward in the implementation of other requirements of Resolution 687. The Security Council has created a U.N. Compensation Commission to consider and pay claims for losses caused by the Iraqi invasion and occupation of Kuwait, to be funded by deductions from Iraqi oil export revenues. The U.N. Iraq-Kuwait Observation Mission has deployed into the demilitarized zone created by the Security Council along the Iraq-Kuwait border, and the Iraq-Kuwait Boundary Demarcation Commission has made a substantial start toward the final demarcation of the boundary, which would eliminate one of the ostensible causes of the war. However, in light of the intransigence of Saddam Hussein and the failure of Iraq to comply with its obligations under the Resolution, the Security Council has not further relaxed the current economic sanctions.

In my last report, I described the Iraqi repression of the Kurds and other internal population groups, which necessitated the introduction of U.S. and other coalition armed forces into northern Iraq to provide relief and security for the civilian population. As I stated then, this effort was not intended as a permanent solution to the problem, nor as a military intervention in the internal affairs of Iraq. Rather, it was intended as a humanitarian measure to save lives. Having succeeded in providing safe conditions for the return of Kurdish refugees from the mountainous border areas, U.S. forces have now withdrawn from northern Iraq. However, we have informed the Iraqi Government that we will continue to monitor carefully its treatment of its citizens, and that we remain prepared to take appropriate steps if the situation requires. To this end, the coalition plans to maintain an appropriate level of forces in the region for as long as required by the situation in Iraq.

I remain grateful for Congress' support of these endeavors, and I look forward to continued cooperation toward achieving our objectives.

Sincerely,

George Bush

312.

[Vol. 31, no. 16 (April 24, 1995): 659-662]

Exchange With Reporters Prior to Discussions With Prime Minister Tansu Ciller of Turkey
April 19, 1995

The President. Let me say that, as always, it's good to have Prime Minister Ciller back in Washington. I welcome her here. Turkey is a valued, important ally of the United States, and our relationship will become even more important in the years ahead.

We're about to go into a meeting where we will discuss a number of issues, her programs for democratization and for economic reform, the Turkish operation in Northern Iraq, which obviously, the United States hopes will be limited in duration and scope. We'll talk about Cyprus and a number of other issues—whatever the Prime Minister wants to discuss. But I'm looking forward to the conversation, and I'm glad she's here.

Turkish Operations in Iraq

Q. Do you expect her to set a date for the evacuation from Iraq? And is Iraq supporting her drive against the Kurds?

The President. Why don't you ask her those questions?

Q. I will. Do you plan to set a date for withdrawal from Iraq? And is Iraq supporting this drive against the Kurds? Are there good Kurds and bad Kurds?

Prime Minister Ciller. As you know, we were together in the fight against Iraq in the Gulf crisis, and then we were together again with the United States in Provide Comfort to protect the Kurdish people in Northern Iraq against Saddam's regime. And it so happened, however, that Turkey was probably the only ally which paid—who paid very high costs because we happen to have a border with Iraq. And Northern Iraq, in time, became a no-man's land.

And this was not a decision that I enjoyed taking, but it so happened that the terrorists simply settled in Northern Iraq and planned to have operations within my country passing the borders. Any Western country in my position would have to have—would take the same kind of decision that I did. And we are there only for a limited time. We have gotten hold of the bases that we wanted to do. The majority of the job is done and over with. The withdrawal will be very soon, as I have said from the beginning.

The reason that I cannot announce a date is because it would not be fair for those people up on the mountains, 1,500 feet from the ground— meters from the ground, not feet— in the caves, in the snow, and they are approaching our borders. What they are doing is searching the caves up on the mountains for the guns and the ammunitions that would have been used to kill the innocent people in my country.

So I have to say that I'm very grateful to President Clinton for his support and for the fact that they knew about what was happening in Northern Iraq, that this became a no-man's land without authority, and it's not our mak-

ing. It is not only our responsibility either. We have to think of a way to handle this. Otherwise, Turkey always ends up being the only ally to continually pay for this operation and the end result of this operation.

Q. Are you adamantly against the establishment of a state of Kurdistan? Isn't this the motive of the rebels?

Prime Minister Ciller. We are very friendly towards the Kurdish people in Northern Iraq. We have nothing against it. In fact, the Kurdish people in Northern Iraq were quite happy to see us come in because what had happened is that the Kurdish elements had been pushed towards south and had to evacuate Northern Iraq because of the terrorists. Now that the terrorists have simply run away, there is the possibility of these Kurdish elements coming back to Northern Iraq and settling.

We had, as you know, opened up our borders to the Kurdish people in Northern Iraq. Close to a million people came over after the Gulf crisis, and we sheltered them and we fed them. And last year only, we paid $13.5 million in foodstuff to the Kurdish people living in Northern Iraq. And every year, we supply the electricity and basic needs. So this has nothing to do with the Kurdish people.

Turkey

Q. Prime Minister, today in Turkey 21 people have been arrested on allegations of trying to assassinate you. I wondered how you felt about your own security, if you were worried about the stability of your government.

Prime Minister Ciller. Well, I am not worried about the security of my country or myself. I have a mission, and that mission is a peace mission for the area. And that's what I'm going to discuss with President Clinton. And Turkey's actual acceptance into the European Community and Customs Union, I think, is a historic kind of a turnaround. And I have to thank again the President's administration and to President Clinton for the very historic support they have given on the issue, because had Turkey been separated from Europe, it would have meant that fundamentalism would have moved up to the borders of Europe. And Turkey, in the area, is the only stable ally from Korea to the Gulf crisis.

We are—look at where we are stationed. North of us is the Soviet Union, having disintegrated. The new countries that have emerged have their own problems. East to us is Middle East. We are very friendly towards Israel—and I was the first Prime Minister to go to Israel—and friendly to the Arab world at the same time. And we have good relations with the Caspian Sea—new nations that have emerged, such as Azerbaijan and Armenia . . .

Cyprus

Q. How about Greece? Cyprus?

Prime Minister Ciller. Oh, yes. The whole problem—that's why the Customs Union is so important because once—if and when Turkey is accepted as a full member into the European Union, as Greece is and as Cyprus will, together with the Turkish and the Greek side, the problem will be resolved in a very comprehensive way because then we won't have anything to fight about, such as migration or migration of labor or some of the basic problems that had continued for almost centuries now as far as I'm concerned.

The President's News Conference

Q. [*Inaudible*]

The President. I thought it was good—the press conference. There were a lot of questions. There were a broad range of questions. They were interesting questions, and I gave straightforward answers, and they were brief. So I thought it was good.

Q. Mr. President, one thing you didn't get to answer last night is that Speaker Gingrich has threatened to put all sorts of legislation that you oppose onto the debt ceiling bill and in effect threaten you to veto the bill and shut the Government down. Would you do that if there was legislation on there you didn't like?

The President. No President of the United States can ever be, in effect, blackmailed by that sort of thing. I'm going to do what I think is right for the people of this country. And again—I will say again what I said last night, the only thing that's relevant to the American people in this whole process is what we do here to affect their lives, and their future, and their children's future.

I have demonstrated my commitment to working through this process. We've already signed two good bills. We're working on this line-item veto together. We can do a lot of work. We can have a lot of good ceremonies out there in the Rose Garden, or we can have the kind of conflict that could arise unless there is a real attempt to work these things out.

And I have been very, very clear and forthright about my position about these things all along and will continue to be. But a strategy to sort of put me in a box would be an error because I will still exercise the power of the Presidency in the interest of the American people.

[*At this point, one group of reporters left the room, and another group entered.*]

The President. Nice to see you all.

Turkish Operations in Iraq

Q. Mr. President, your administration has certainly shown a certain degree of understanding of Turkey's incursion in Northern Iraq. How willing are you to cooperate in possible secret arrangements for— [*inaudible*]—incursion in this region?

The President. Well, we're going to discuss that in our meetings. And I don't think I should say anything about it until we have meetings. But you know, the United States has had a strong relationship with Turkey. And I think it's very important that we continue that relationship into the future. And in order to do it, we're going to have to understand each other's position, each other's problems, each other's potential to work together. And I've tried to do that, and I've had a good relationship with the Prime Minister. She has been very forceful in coming to the United States and stating the interest of the Turkish people. And this is one of many things that we will discuss. But I look forward to continuing to make progress on all these issues.

Turkey

Q. Will human rights and democratization be on the agenda?

The President. Sure. And the Prime Minister's talked about democratization. And I think—you know, for the Europeans, as you move toward the Customs Union and other things, these issues are quite important. And they're very important to the United States. But I have tried to also view them in the context of the imperative to fight terrorism and to promote human rights. And I think you have to do both. Preserving a democracy in which people have human freedom is a delicate operation. And it requires not only a lot of sensitivity and understanding, it requires a lot of discipline and respect for other people's rights as well. And the biggest threat to human rights all over the world today, after the—in the aftermath of the cold war when people now know that dictatorial political systems don't work, that totalitarian systems don't work, the biggest threat to human rights is the reaction caused by terrorism everywhere. And that is something we have to be sensitive to, whether it's a car bomb blowing up in the Middle East or a religious fanatic taking a vial of sarin into the subway in Japan. All these things threaten the fabric of human rights. So we have to continue to push governments all over the world to be more open to human rights and combat terrorism at the same time.

Q. Do you have any solution about—[*inaudible*]—administration?

The President. We're going to talk about it today. You know, the United States has expressed an understanding of what Turkey did, along with the hope that civilian casualties could be strictly limited, and that the operation would be limited in time and scope. But we're going to talk about it. The Prime Minister has probably got some good ideas, and we'll discuss it.

313.

[Vol. 32, no. 45 (November 11, 1996): 2339-2342]

Letter to Congressional Leaders on Iraq November 4, 1996

The White House,
Washington, November 4, 1996.
Hon. Newt Gingrich,
Speaker of the House of Representatives,
Washington, DC.
Dear Mr. Speaker: (Dear Mr. President:)
Consistent with the Authorization for Use of Military Force Against Iraq Resolution (Public Law 102-1) and as part of my effort to keep the Congress fully informed, I am report-

ing on the status of efforts to obtain Iraqi compliance with the resolutions adopted by the UN Security Council. This report covers the period from September 5 to the present. Saddam Hussein's attack on Irbil in late August and his continuing efforts to manipulate local rivalries in northern Iraq to his advantage, provide new evidence that he remains a threat to his own people, to his neighbors, and to the peace of the region. As I detailed in my last report, the United States responded to Saddam's military action in the north by expanding the Southern no-fly zone from 32 degrees to 33 degrees north latitude. The U.S. response included strikes against surface- to-air missile sites, command and control centers, and air defense control facilities south of the 33rd parallel in order to help ensure the safety of our forces enforcing the expanded no-fly zone.

Since my last report, we have further strengthened the U.S. presence in the region in order to deter Saddam. In September, we deployed two heavy battalions of the Third Brigade of the First Cavalry, one Patriot battery and eight F-117 stealth fighter aircraft to Kuwait. We also deployed 23 advanced F-16 aircraft to Bahrain and one Patriot battery to Saudi Arabia.

These forces were sent to the area, in addition to the forces that were already deployed to the region, as a tangible deterrent to any Iraqi aggression. In early September, the USS Enterprise Carrier Battle Group was deployed to the Gulf, joining the USS Carl Vinson Carrier Battle Group already there; the USS Carl Vinson Battle Group redeployed from the Gulf on October 8.

The no-fly zones over northern Iraq (Operation Provide Comfort) and southern Iraq (Southern Watch) continue to be enforced by U.S. and coalition forces. The Turkish parliament must consider renewal of Operation Provide Comfort before the end of December.

We issued strong warnings to Iraq on September 6 and 16, via our UN mission in New York, not to challenge our aircraft enforcing the extended no-fly zone or to restore damaged Iraqi earlier violent rhetoric. We will continue to monitor Iraqi action carefully and are well-positioned to respond to any future challenges.

United Nations Security Council Resolution (UNSCR) 949, adopted in October 1994, demands that Iraq not threaten its neighbors or UN operations in Iraq and that it not redeploy or enhance its military capacity in southern Iraq. In view of Saddam's reinforced record of unreliability, it is prudent to retain a significant U.S. force presence in the region in order to maintain the capability to respond rapidly to possible Iraqi aggression or threats against its neighbors.

The situation in northern Iraq remains volatile. This Administration has continued efforts to bring about and maintain a cease-fire and reconciliation between the two major Kurdish groups involved in that fighting, including maintaining an active dialogue with both. Assistant Secretary of State for Near Eastern Affairs Robert Pelletreau met with Massoud Barzani, the leader of the Kurdistan Democratic Party (KDP), in Turkey on September 18 and October 21. Assistant Secretary Pelletreau also met with Patriotic Union of Kurdistan (PUK) leader Jalal Talabani on October 22, and follow-on meetings with representatives of the KDP and the PUK took place on October 30 and 31 in Ankara. In these and other high-level meetings, this Administration has consistently warned both groups that internecine warfare in the north can only work to the advantage of Saddam Hussein.

In response to the increased uncertainty in northern Iraq, we temporarily withdrew the United States Government presence (the office of Foreign Disaster Assistance and the Military Coordination Center). In September and October, with the assistance of Turkey, we conducted a humanitarian evacuation of approximately 2,700 residents of northern Iraq whose lives were directly threatened by the Iraqi regime because of close ties to the United States Government or the Iraqi opposition. The first 2,100 of these individuals, evacuated in mid-September under Operation Quick Transit, were employees of United States Government agencies with offices in northern Iraq and their families. A second group of approximately 600 Iraqi opposition members was evacuated October 19-21. All of the evacuees are being processed on Guam under the U.S. refugee resettlement program.

We remain concerned about the safety of local employees of U.S.-funded and U.S.-based nongovernmental organizations that remain in northern Iraq. We have sought and received assurances from the KDP and PUK about their safety. We are keeping their security situation under active review and are continuing to consider all options to ensure the safety of these employees and their families.

The United States, working through the United Nations and humanitarian relief organizations, continues to provide humanitarian assistance to the people of northern Iraq. Security conditions in northern Iraq remain tenuous at best, with Iranian and PKK (Kurdistan Workers Party) activity adding to the ever-present threat from Baghdad. We see no role for Iran in the area and continue to advise all concerned not to involve themselves with Tehran.

We also continue to support the United Nations Secretary General's decision, in light of the changed circumstances on the ground, to review carefully the procedures for implementing United Nations Security Council Resolution (UNSCR) 986, which provides that Iraq may sell a certain amount of oil in order that they may use part of the proceeds to purchase food, medicine and other materials and supplies for essential civilian needs and that allocates proceeds to be used to fund vital UN activities regarding Iraq. We want to see the resolution implemented, as written and intended, in a way that ensures that humanitarian supplies to be purchased under the auspices of UNSCR 986 will actually be received by the people who need them.

On October 9, United Nations Undersecretary Gharekhan reported to the United Nations Security Council (UNSC) that the Government of Iraq is now seeking to negotiate aspects of the plan to implement UNSCR 986 related to the number of monitors and restrictions on the movement of UN personnel within Iraq. This action to renegotiate the plan—a plan that was agreed to by the Iraqis and that was memorialized in a Memorandum of Understanding between the Iraqis and the United Nations on May 20—is likely to delay implementation of UNSCR 986 even further.

The Government of Iraq has, since my last report, continued to flout its obligations under a number of Security Council resolutions in other ways. Under the terms of the Gulf War cease-fire with Iraq—outlined in UNSCR 687—Iraq must grant the United Nations Special Commission on Iraq (UNSCOM) inspectors immediate, unconditional, and unrestricted access to any location in Iraq they wish to examine and access to any Iraqi official whom they wish to interview, so that UNSCOM may fully discharge its mandate. Iraq continues, as it has for the past 5 years, to fail to live up either to the letter or the spirit of this commitment.

UNSCOM Executive Chairman Rolf Ekeus briefed the UNSC on his most recent, semiannual report on October 17. The Chairman's report outlined in comprehensive detail Iraq's past and ongoing efforts to conceal evidence of its Weapons of Mass Destruction (WMD) programs and otherwise obstruct the work of the Commission. As long as Saddam refuses to cooperate fully with UN weapons inspectors, UNSCOM will be impeded in its efforts to fulfill its mandate to ensure that Iraq's WMD program has been eliminated. We will continue to fully support the mandate and the efforts of the Special Commission to obtain Iraqi compliance with all relevant UN resolutions. We will not consider any modification of UNSC resolutions.

On October 1, implementation of the export/import monitoring mechanism approved by the Security Council in Resolution 1051 started. Resolution 1051 approved a mechanism to monitor Iraq's undertaking to reacquire proscribed weapons capabilities; it requires that countries provide timely notification of the export to Iraq of dual-use items.

Iraq also continues to stall and obfuscate rather than work in good faith toward accounting for the hundreds of Kuwaitis and third-country nationals who disappeared at the hands of Iraqi authorities during the occupation or toward the return of all of the Kuwaiti military equipment stolen during the occupation, as well as priceless Kuwaiti cultural and historical artifacts looted on instructions from Baghdad. Additionally, Iraq continues to provide refuge for known terrorists.

Iraq's repression of its Shi'a population continues with policies aimed at destroying the Marsh Arabs' way of life in southern Iraq

as well as the ecology of the southern marshes. The human rights situation throughout Iraq remains unchanged. Saddam Hussein shows no signs of complying with UNSCR 688, which demands that Iraq cease the repression of its own people.

The Multinational Interception Force (MIF) continues to enforce the sanctions regime against Iraq. In September and the first half of October, four north-bound and five south-bound vessels were diverted to various ports in the Gulf for sanctions violations. Several of these vessels contained illegal cargo hidden beneath humanitarian shipments and over 3 million gallons of illegally exported Iraqi petroleum products were intercepted.

The expeditious acceptance of these recent sanctions-violating vessels by Kuwait and the United Arab Emirates greatly contributed to our strong deterrent posture and provides further evidence that the MIF is a valuable resource in sanctions enforcement. We continue to meet one of our key foreign policy objectives by maintaining the multinational composition of the MIF. New Zealand recently sent a ship back to operate with the MIF; the United Kingdom maintains a nearly continuous presence with our forces in the northern Gulf; and we are hopeful that in early 1997, Canada, Belgium, and The Netherlands will all send ships to rejoin the MIF. We are continuing our efforts to engage the international community in maritime sanctions.

Most of the ships engaged in sanctions violations during this period were flagged in the United Arab Emirates. At our urging, the Government of the United Arab Emirates recently announced stricter penalties for sanctions violators. We remain hopeful that these actions will discourage operations from the United Arab Emirates that violate UN sanctions against Iraq.

Iran continues to contribute to sanctions violations by allowing vessels leaving Iraq to transit territorial waters in order to avoid the MIF in the northern Gulf. We have presented evidence of Iranian complicity in sanctions violations to the UN Sanctions Committee and have urged the Committee to formally denounce these actions.

Our policy with respect to sanctions enforcement remains firm; sanctions continue to send a clear message to the Government of Iraq and those who would defy UN resolutions for profit that there will be no modification or relaxation of sanctions until Iraq has fully established its peaceful intentions by complying with all UNSC resolutions.

The United Nations Compensation Commission (UNCC), established pursuant to UNSCR 687, continues to resolve claims against Iraq arising from Iraq's unlawful invasion and occupation of Kuwait. The UNCC has issued over 980,000 awards worth approximately $4.0 billion. The UNCC has authorized only limited payments for fixed awards for serious personal injury or death because Iraq refuses to comply with all relevant UN Security Council resolutions, and UN economic sanctions remain in force.

Currently, the UNCC faces a serious financial crisis in funding awards and daily operations. If Iraq eventually sells the full amount of oil authorized under the provisions of UNSCR 986, the proceeds of the sale will be transferred to the UN escrow account opened for that purpose, with 30 percent allocated to the Compensation Fund to finance awards and operations of the UNCC.

To conclude, Iraq remains a serious threat to regional peace and stability. I remain determined to see Iraq comply fully with all of its obligations under UN Security Council resolutions.

My Administration will continue to oppose any relaxation of sanctions until Iraq demonstrates its peaceful intentions through such compliance.

I appreciate the support of the Congress for our efforts and will continue to keep the Congress informed about this important matter.

Sincerely,
William J. Clinton.

314.

[Vol. 33, no. 2 (January 13, 1997): 16-19]

**Letter to Congressional Leaders on Iraq
January 7, 1997**

Dear Mr. Speaker: (Dear Mr. President)

Consistent with the Authorization for Use of Military Force Against Iraq Resolution (Public Law 102-1) and as part of my effort to keep the Congress fully informed, I am reporting on the status of efforts to obtain Iraq's compliance with the resolutions adopted by the U.N. Security Council (UNSC). This report covers the period from November 4 to the present.

Saddam Hussein remains a threat to his people and the region. The United States successfully responded to the increased threat resulting from Saddam's attack on Irbil in late August, but he continues to try to manipulate local rivalries in northern Iraq to his advantage. The United States and our coalition partners continue to enforce the no-fly zone over southern Iraq. Enforcement of the northern no-fly zone also continues uninterrupted, despite a restructuring of operations. Because of changes in its mission as a result of the closing last fall of the Military Command Center (MCC) in the city of Zakho, Iraq and the shift of humanitarian assistance in the north under UNSCR 986 to international organizations, the designation "Provide Comfort" will no longer be used to describe the operation. The United Kingdom will continue to take part in this mission; however, France has chosen not to continue to participate in this endeavor. None of these changes affect our firm commitment to ensuring that the northern no-fly zone is fully enforced.

Besides our air operations, we will continue to maintain a strong U.S. presence in the region in order to deter Saddam. U.S. force levels have returned to approximate pre-Operation Desert Strike levels, with land and carrier based aircraft, surface warships, a Marine amphibious task force, a Patriot missile battalion, and a mechanized battalion task force deployed in support of USCINCCENT operations. As an additional deterrent against Iraqi aggression, F-117 aircraft remain deployed to Kuwait. Since submission of my last report, USCINCCENT has completed the initial phases of Operation Desert Focus, with the relocation and consolidation of all combatant forces in Saudi Arabia into more secure facilities throughout Saudi Arabia. To enhance force protection throughout the region, additional military security personnel have been deployed for continuous rotation. USCINC-CENT continues to closely monitor the security situation in the region to ensure adequate force protection is provided for all deployed forces.

United Nations Security Council Resolution (UNSCR) 949, adopted in October 1994, demands that Iraq not threaten its neighbors or U.N. operations in Iraq and that it not redeploy or enhance its military capacity in southern Iraq. In view of Saddam's reinforced record of unreliability, it is prudent to retain a significant U.S. force presence in the region in order to maintain the capability to respond rapidly to possible Iraqi aggression or threats against its neighbors.

In northern Iraq, we have made some limited progress in strengthening the October 23 cease-fire and encouraging political reconciliation between the two main Iraqi Kurd groups, the Kurdistan Democratic Party (KDP) and the Patriotic Union of Kurdistan (PUK). Assistant Secretary of State for Near Eastern Affairs Robert Pelletreau co-chaired talks between the KDP and the PUK in Turkey on October 30 and November 15, alongside representatives of the Turkish and British governments. During these talks, we obtained agreement from the two parties that the neutral, indigenous Peace Monitoring Force (PMF) would demarcate and observe the cease-fire line. To support the PMF, I have directed, under the authorities of sections 552© and 614 of the Foreign Assistance Act of 1961, as amended, the drawdown of up to $4 million in Department of Defense commodities and services, and the Secretary of State has made a determination under which we will provide up to $3 million for uniforms, tents, generators and other non-lethal supplies. Issues related to PMF operations are discussed regularly by a Supervisory Peace Monitoring Group that meets in Ankara and is composed of U.S., U.K. and Turkish representatives, as well as members of the indigenous relevant parties. In these and other high level meetings, this Administration has consistently warned all concerned that internecine warfare in the north can only work to the advantage of Saddam Hussein and Iran, which we believe has no role to play in the area. In this connection,

we remain concerned about the KDP's links to Baghdad and the PUK's ties to Iran.

Despite the cease-fire and other efforts, many residents of northern Iraq continued to face threats from Baghdad due to their association with U.S.-affiliated nongovernmental organizations, who had undertaken relief work in northern Iraq over the past few years. In response, this Administration, with the assistance of Turkey, conducted a third humanitarian evacuations operation of approximately 3,780 residents of northern Iraq whose lives were directly threatened by the Iraqi regime. All of the evacuees are being processed on Guam under the U.S. refugee resettlement program, while most of the 2,700 evacuated under two previous operations are now resettled in the United States.

The United States, working through the United Nations and humanitarian relief organizations, continues to provide humanitarian assistance to the people of northern Iraq. We have contributed more than $15 million this fiscal year to programs in the north administered by the U.N. International Children's Emergency Fund (UNICEF) and the World Food Program (WFP). Security conditions in northern Iraq remain tenuous at best, with Iranian and PKK (Kurdistan Workers Party) activity adding to the ever-present threat from Baghdad.

On December 9, the U.N. Secretary General submitted his formal report to the UNSC stating that all necessary conditions for implementation of UNSCR 986 had been met. Following this action, the resolution went into effect 12:01 a.m. on December 10. UNSCR 986 authorizes Iraq to sell up to $2 billion of oil during an initial 180-day period, with the possibility of UNSC renewal for subsequent 180-day periods. Resolution 986 provides that the proceeds of this limited oil sale, all of which must be deposited in a U.N. escrow account, will be used to purchase food, medicine, and other materials and supplies for essential civilian needs for all Iraqi citizens, and to fund vital U.N. activities regarding Iraq. Critical to the success of UNSCR 986 is Iraq's willingness to follow through on its commitments under 986 to allow the U.N. to monitor the distribution of food and medical supplies to the Iraqi people.

We have already seen good evidence that the safeguards systems is working: when Saddam Hussein pushed a button in Kirkuk on December 10 to turn on the flow of oil before any oil contracts had been approved by the U.N., the U.N. made him turn it off. The oil flow began again, under proper U.N. supervision, a short time later.

The Government of Iraq has, since my last report, continued to flout its obligations under a number of Security Council resolutions in other ways. Under the terms of relevant UNSC resolutions, Iraq must grant the United Nations Special Commission on Iraq (UNSCOM) inspectors immediate, unconditional, and unrestricted access to any location in Iraq they wish to examine, and access to any Iraqi official whom they wish to interview, so that UNSCOM may fully discharge its mandate. Iraq continues, as it has for the past 5 years, to fail to live up either to the letter or the spirit of this commitment.

In his October 11 semiannual written report to the Security Council, UNSCOM Executive Chairman Rolf Ekeus outlined in comprehensive detail Iraq's past and ongoing efforts to conceal evidence of its weapons of mass destruction (WMD) programs. In his December 18 briefing to the Security Council, Ekeus urged it to take action to reverse Iraq's current blocking of UNSCOM removal of 130 SCUD motors from Iraq for analysis. As reported to the press by Security Council President Fulci that day, Ekeus informed the Council that he thought significant numbers of SCUD missiles still exist in Iraq. As long as Saddam refuses to cooperate fully with U.N. weapons inspectors, UNSCOM will be impeded in its efforts to fulfill its mandate to ensure that Iraq's WMD program has been eliminated. We will continue to fully support the mandate and the efforts of the Special Commission to obtain Iraqi compliance with all relevant U.N. resolutions.

The implementation of the export/import monitoring mechanism approved by the Security Council in Resolution 1051 began on October 1. Resolution 1051 approved a mechanism to monitor Iraq's undertaking to reacquire proscribed weapons capabilities by requiring that Iraq inform the U.N. in advance of any imports of dual-use items and that countries provide timely notification of the export to Iraq of dual-use items.

Iraq also continues to stall and obfuscate rather than work in good faith toward accounting for the hundreds of Kuwaitis and third-country nationals who disappeared at the hands of Iraqi authorities during the occupation. It has also failed to return all of the stolen Kuwaiti military equipment and the priceless Kuwaiti cultural and historical artifacts, which were looted during the occupation.

Iraq's repression of its Shi'a population continues with policies aimed at destroying the Marsh Arabs' way of life in Southern Iraq, as well as the ecology of the southern marshes. The human rights situation throughout Iraq remains unchanged. Saddam Hussein shows no signs of complying with UNSCR 688, which demands that Iraq cease the repression of its own people.

The Multinational Interception Force (MIF) remains on station in the Arabian Gulf. Our commitment to the enforcement of the sanctions regime is clearly demonstrated by the significant investment we have made with our naval forces in this area. Since my last report, 10 vessels have been intercepted and diverted for sanctions violations. Most of the vessels diverted have been engaged in illegal oil smuggling, but in recent weeks, we have begun to intercept smaller boats attempting to smuggle Iraqi dates as well. Traditionally, our naval forces encounter an increase in date smugglers as Ramadan approaches.

We continue to note suspected smugglers using the territorial waters of Iran to avoid interception by the MIF. Due to the geography of the Gulf, it is possible to transit from Iraqi ports to the UAE and the Indian Ocean without entering international waters. We believe, and have confirmed in some instances, that smugglers utilize these routes to export Iraqi petroleum products in violation of UNSCR 661. We believe that there are elements within the Iranian government who profit from charging "protection fees" for the safe passage through Iranian waters. We have presented evidence of this to the United Nations Sanctions Committee, and I am pleased to report that the Committee has decided to admonish Iran for failing to halt sanctions violators in its waters.

The recent implementation of UNSCR 986 will increase the workload of our naval forces participating in the MIF. We are prepared to meet the increased monitoring effort in the coming months. The surge in maritime traffic expected to occur with the implementation of UNSCR 986 will necessitate extreme vigilance to ensure that those who would profit from illegal trade with Iraq are not given the opportunity to succeed.

The United Nations Compensation Commission (UNCC), established pursuant to UNSCR 687, continues to resolve claims against Iraq arising from Iraq's unlawful invasion and occupation of Kuwait. The UNCC has issued over 1 million awards worth approximately $5.2 billion. At its most recent meeting, the UNCC Governing Council approved an award of $610 million on the claim by the Kuwait national oil company for the costs of extinguishing the oil well fires ignited by Iraq at the end of the Gulf War. The UNCC has authorized to date only limited payments for fixed awards for serious personal injury or death because additional funds to pay awards have been unavailable due to Iraq's refusal to comply with all relevant sanctions. With the advent of oil sales under UNSCR 986, however, 30 percent of the proceeds (which is anticipated to be as much as $100 million per month) will be allocated to the Compensation Fund. These proceeds will be used to make installment payments on awards already made and to finance the operations of the UNCC.

To conclude, Iraq remains a serious threat to regional peace and stability. I remain determined to see Iraq comply fully with all of its obligations under U.N. Security Council resolutions. My Administration will continue to oppose any relaxation of sanctions until Iraq demonstrates its peaceful intentions through such compliance.

I appreciate the support of the Congress for our efforts and shall continue to keep the Congress informed about this important issue.

Sincerely,
William J. Clinton.

315.

[Vol. 33, no. 10 (March 10, 1997): 313-316]

Letter to Congressional Leaders Reporting on Iraq
March 7, 1997

Dear Mr. Speaker: (Dear Mr. President:) Consistent with the Authorization for Use of Military Force Against Iraq Resolution (Public Law 102-1) and as part of my effort to keep the Congress fully informed, I am reporting on the status of efforts to obtain Iraq's compliance with the resolutions adopted by the United Nations Security Council (UNSC). This report covers the period from January 7 to the present.

Saddam Hussein remains a threat to his people and the region. The United States successfully responded to the increased threat resulting from Saddam's attack on Irbil in late August 1996, but he continues to try to manipulate local rivalries in northern Iraq to his advantage. The United States and our coalition partners continue uninterrupted enforcement of the no-fly zone over northern Iraq under Operation Northern Watch, the successor mission to Operation Provide Comfort. France chose not to participate in Operation Northern Watch, but the United Kingdom and Turkey remain committed to the same enforcement of the no-fly zone above the 36th parallel that existed under Operation Provide Comfort. Enforcement of the southern no-fly zone also continues, and France remains engage with our other coalition partners in conducting Operation Southern Watch.

Besides our air operations, we will continue to maintain a strong U.S. presence in the region in order to deter Saddam. U.S. force levels have returned to approximate pre-Operation Desert Strike levels, with land- and carrier-based aircraft, surface warships, a Marine amphibious task force, a Patriot missile battalion, and a mechanized battalion task force deployed in support of USCINCCENT operations. On February 20, 1997, an air expeditionary force consisting of 30 F-16s and F-15s deployed to Doha, Qatar, to further strengthen the U.S. deterrent in the region. On February 22, an F-117 squadron deployed to

Kuwait since last autumn was redeployed to the United States upon the completion of its mission. USCINCCENT has completed the initial phases of Operation Desert Focus, with the relocation and consolidation of all combatant forces in Saudi Arabia into more secure facilities throughout Saudi Arabia. To enhance force protection throughout the region, additional military security personnel have been deployed for continuous rotation. USCINCCENT continues to closely monitor the security situation in the region to ensure adequate force protection is provided for all deployed forces.

United Nations Security Council Resolution (UNSCR) 949, adopted in October 1994, demands that Iraq not utilize its military forces to threaten its neighbors or U.N. operations in Iraq and that it not redeploy troops or enhance its military capacity in southern Iraq. In view of Saddam's reinforced record of unreliability, it is prudent to retain a significant U.S. force presence in the region in order to maintain the capability to respond rapidly to possible Iraqi aggression or threats against its neighbors.

Regarding northern Iraq, we have conducted three rounds of talks, along with our British and Turkish partners, with the major Kurdish parties in northern Iraq—the Kurdistan Democratic Party (KDP) and the Patriotic Union of Kurdistan (PUK). Our immediate goal is to strengthen the U.S.—brokered cease-fire of October 23, which continues to hold, and to encourage political reconciliation between the PUK and KDP. This Administration continues to warn all concerned that internecine warfare in the north can only work to the advantage of Saddam Hussein and Iran, which we believe has no role to play in the area. In this connection, we remain concerned about Iraqi Kurd contracts with either Baghdad or Tehran.

The United States is providing political, financial, and logistical support for a neutral, indigenous Peach Monitoring Force (PMF) in northern Iraq that has demarcated the cease-fire line and will monitor the cease-fire. The PMF likely will be fully deployed in the next few weeks. Our support is being provided in the form of commodities and services in accordance with a drawdown directed by me on December 11, 1996, and in the form of funds to be used to provide other non-lethal assistance in accordance with a separate determination made by former Secretary of State Christopher on November 10, 1996.

We also are encouraging both Kurdish groups to take steps toward reconciliation. At the latest round of higher-level talks in Ankara on January 15, the Iraqi Kurds agreed to establish joint committees to cooperate in such areas as education, health, and transportation. Local representatives of the two Kurd groups, the three countries and the PNF continue to meet biweekly in Ankara and move forward on other confidence-building measures. All our efforts under the Ankara process, like all our efforts concerning Iraq, maintain support for the unity and territorial integrity of Iraq.

The United States, working through the United Nations and humanitarian relief organizations, continues to provide humanitarian assistance to the people of northern Iraq. We have contributed more than $15 million this fiscal year to programs in the north administered by the United Nations programs in the north administered by the United Nations International Children's Fund (UNICEF) and the World Food Program (WFP). Security conditions in northern Iraq remain tenuous at best, with Iranian and Kurdistan Workers Party (PKK) activity adding to the ever-present threat from Baghdad.

The oil-related provisions of UNSCR 986, which authorized Iraq to sell up to $2 billion of oil during an initial 180-day period (with the possibility of UNSC renewal of subsequent 180-day periods), went into effect on December 10, 1996. This resolution requires that the proceeds of this limited oil sale, all of which must be deposited in a U.N. escrow account, will be used to purchase food, medicine, and other materials and supplies for essential civilian needs for all Iraqi citizens and to fund vital U.N. activities regarding Iraq. Critical to the success of UNSCR 986 is Iraq's willingness to follow through on its commitments under 986 to allow the U.N. to monitor the distribution of food and medical supplies to the Iraqi people. While Iraq has already sold nearly 80 percent of the oil allowed for the first 90-day period, Iraqi efforts to impose restrictions on the access and freedom of movement of the U.N. monitors tasked with overseeing the equitable distribution of humanitarian supplies have slowed such distribution.

Since my last report, the Government of Iraq has continued to flout its obligations under UNSC resolutions in other ways. Under the terms of relevant UNSC resolutions, Iraq must grant the United Nations Special Commission on Iraq (UNSCOM) inspectors immediate, unconditional, and unrestricted access to any location in Iraq they wish to examine, and access to any Iraqi official whom they wish to interview, so that UNSCOM may fully discharge its mandate to ensure that Iraq's weapons of mass destruction program has been eliminated. Iraq continues, as it has for the past 5 years, to fail to live up either to the letter or the spirit of this commitment.

On February 23, UNSCOM Chairman Rolf Ekeus obtained permission from the Iraqi regime to remove more than 130 SCUD motors from Iraq for extensive testing in the United States and France. Iraq agreed to this action after 3 months of stalling, and only after a December 30 Security Council Presidential Statement deplored Iraq's failure to comply with its obligation to cooperate with UNSCOM. Ekeus continues to believe that Iraq maintains significant numbers of operational SCUD missiles, possibly with CBW warheads. As long as Saddam refuses to cooperate fully with U.N. weapons inspectors, UNSCOM will be impeded in its efforts to fulfill its mandate. We will continue to fully support the mandate and the efforts of UNSCOM to obtain Iraqi compliance with all relevant U.N. resolutions.

Implementation of UNSCR 1051 continues. It provides for a mechanism to monitor Iraq's efforts to reacquire proscribed weapons capabilities by requiring that Iraq notify a joint unit of UNSCOM and the International Atomic Energy Agency in advance of any imports of dual-use items. Similarly, countries must provide timely notification of exports to Iraq of dual-use items.

Iraq continues to stall and obfuscate rather than work in good faith toward accounting for the hundreds of Kuwaitis and third-country nationals who disappeared at the hands of Iraqi authorities during the occupa-tion. It has also failed to return all of the stolen Kuwaiti military equipment and the priceless Kuwaiti cultural and historical artifacts, which were looted during the occupation.

Iraq's repression of its Shi'a population continues with policies that are destroying the Marsh Arabs' way of life in southern Iraq as well as the ecology of the southern marshes. The human rights situation throughout Iraq remains unchanged. Saddam Hussein shows no sign of complying with UNSCR 688, which demands that Iraq cease the repression of its own people.

The Multinational Interception Force (MIF) has been increasingly challenged in the last few months. In the first 6 weeks of the year, 12 merchant vessels were diverted for sanctions violations. This represents the highest volume of smuggler traffic we have seen since maritime sanctions enforcement began. Most of these smugglers take gas oil illegally from Iraq via the Shatt Al Arab waterway and sell it on the spot market for enormous profit. As I have noted in previous reports, these smugglers use the territorial waters of Iran to avoid the MIF inspection in the Northern Gulf. With the help of the Iranian government, which profits from these activities by charging protection fees, these smugglers are able to export between 40,000 and 65,000 metric tons of gas oil through the Gulf each month.

To counter the efforts of those who engage in illegal trade with Iraq, we have taken a number of steps to minimize the smuggling activity. We have adjusted the positioning of our naval forces to take maximum advantage of known trade routes. We are working closely with our friends in the Gulf Cooperation Council to develop greater cooperation in border patrol and customs inspection procedures. We have publicized the involvement of the Iranian government at the United Nations and in press reports.

It is important to remember that these sanctions violations not only aid Saddam and his policy of resisting U.N. mandates, but also slow the flow of humanitarian aid to the Iraqi people who are in such great need. Committing scarce MIF assets to counter the smuggling trade results in fewer ships available to process the legal humanitarian shipments that bring food to Iraq under the provisions of

UNSCR 986 and the humanitarian exceptions to sanctions.

We continue to work closely with our maritime partners in the MIF. Recently, The Netherlands informed us that they will send a frigate and an aircraft to join the MIF in the near future. Canada will also soon be sending a ship to join the MIF. The continuing support of the international community is critical to the success of this multinational operation.

Since the implementation of UNSCR 986 in December, the MIF has not encountered any serious problems in processing the maritime traffic involved in lifting oil from the Mina Al Bakr offshore terminal. While it is still too early to tell if the inbound shipments will go as smoothly, we are hopeful that our advance planning and preparation in this area will pay off.

The United Nations Compensation Commission (UNCC), established pursuant to UNSCR 687, continues to resolve claims against Iraq arising from Iraq's unlawful invasion and occupation of Kuwait. The UNCC has issued over 1 million awards worth approximately $5.2 billion. The UNCC has authorized to date only limited payments for fixed awards for serious personal injury or death because additional funds to pay awards have been unavailable due to Iraq's refusal to comply with all relevant UNSC resolutions. With the advent of oil sales under UNSCR 986, however, 30 percent of the proceeds will be allocated to the Compensation Fund. These proceeds will be used to make installment payments on awards already made and to finance operations of the UNCC.

To conclude, Iraq remains a serious threat to regional peace and stability. I remain determined to see Iraq comply fully with all of its obligations under United Nations Security Council resolutions. My Administration will continue to pose any relaxation of sanctions until Iraq demonstrates its peaceful intentions through such compliance.

I appreciate the support of the Congress for our efforts and shall continue to keep the Congress informed about this important issue.

Sincerely,
William J. Clinton.

316.

[Vol. 33, no. 12 (May 12, 1997): 687-690]

Letter to Congressional Leaders on Iraq
May 8, 1997

Dear Mr. Speaker: (Dear Mr. President:)
Consistent with the Authorization for Use of Military Force Against Iraq Resolution (Public Law 102-1) and as part of my effort to keep the Congress fully informed, I am reporting on the status of efforts to obtain Iraq's compliance with the resolutions adopted by the United Nations Security Council (UNSC). This report covers the period from March 7 to the present.

Saddam Hussein remains a threat to his people and the region and the United States remains determined to contain the threat of Saddam's regime. Speaking on behalf of the Administration on March 26, 1997, in her first major foreign policy address, Secretary of State Madeleine Albright stated that the United States looks forward to the day when Iraq rejoins the family of nations as a responsible and law-abiding member and that, until then, containment must continue. Secretary Albright also made clear that Saddam's departure would make a difference and that, should a change in Iraq's government occur, the United States would stand ready to enter rapidly into a dialogue with the successor regime.

In terms of military operations, the United States and our coalition partners continue enforcement of the no-fly zones over northern Iraq under Operation Northern Watch, the successor mission to Operation Provide Comfort, and over southern Iraq through Operation Southern Watch. On April 22, 1997, Saddam Hussein announced that Iraqi military helicopters would be flown through the southern no-fly zone for the purpose of transporting Iraqi pilgrims from the vicinity of the Iraqi-Saudi border to various areas in Iraq, publicly disregarding the prohibition against operating Iraqi rotary and fixed wing aircraft south of the 33rd parallel. The next day, 10 helicopters crossed the southern no-fly zone and arrived at a ground staging base in western Iraq, just north of the Iraqi-Saudi border, to await the arrival of the pilgrims. Because of the possible danger to innocent Iraqi civilians, the non-threatening nature of these flights, and the religious sensitivity of the situation, the United States and our coalition partners agreed not to take military action to intercept the helicopters.

On April 25-27, the same Iraqi helicopters returned the pilgrims to their homes in various locations throughout Iraq, transiting the northern and southern no-fly zones in the process. Again, the United States and its coalition partners decided not to act against these flights for humanitarian and policy reasons. We have made clear to the Government of Iraq and to all other relevant parties, however, that the United States and its partners will continue to enforce both no-fly zones, and that we reserve the right to respond appropriately and decisively to further Iraqi provocations.

In addition to our air operations, we will continue to maintain a strong U.S. presence in the region in order to deter Saddam. United States force levels include land- and carrier-based aircraft, surface warships, a Marine amphibious task force, a Patriot missile battalion, and a mechanized battalion task force deployed in support of USCINCCENT operations. To enhance force protection throughout the region, additional military security personnel have been deployed for continuous rotation. USCINCCENT continues to closely monitor the security situation in the region to ensure adequate force protection is provided for all deployed forces.

United Nations Security Council Resolution (UNSCR) 949, adopted in October 1994, demands that Iraq not utilize its military or any other forces to threaten its neighbors or U.N. operations in Iraq and that it not redeploy troops or enhance its military capacity in southern Iraq. In view of Saddam's accumulating record of unreliability, it is prudent to retain a significant U.S. force presence in the region in order to maintain the capability to respond rapidly to possible Iraqi aggression or threats against its neighbors.

Since my last report, the Government of Iraq has continued to flout its obligations under UNSC resolutions in other ways. Under the terms of relevant UNSC resolutions, Iraq must grant the United Nations Special Commission on Iraq (UNSCOM) inspectors im-

mediate, unconditional, and unrestricted access to any location in Iraq they wish to examine, and access to any Iraqi official whom they wish to interview, so that UNSCOM may fully discharge its mandate to ensure that Iraq's weapons of mass destruction (WMD) program has been eliminated. Iraq continues, as it has for the past 6 years, to fail to live up either to the letter or the spirit of this commitment. Of particular concern is UNSCOM's report to the Security Council of serious incidents involving repeated Iraqi threats to shoot down UNSCOM aircraft, an Iraqi escort helicopter flying dangerously close to the Commission's aircraft to force it to change direction, and Iraqi personnel aboard an UNSCOM helicopter attempting to wrest control of the aircraft.

On April 11, UNSCOM Chairman Rolf Ekeus reported to the Security Council that resolution of the remaining questions about Iraq's WMD programs would require a "major political decision" on the part of Iraq's leadership to "give up, once and for all, all capabilities and ambition to retain or acquire the proscribed weapons." The UNSCOM continues to believe that Iraq instead maintains significant numbers of operational SCUD missiles, possibly with CBW warheads. In early April, UNSCOM also asked Iraq to withdraw its "full, final, and complete declaration" regarding its biological weapons programs because it contained obvious inaccuracies and fabrications, and to submit a new one. As long as the Iraqi leadership refuses to cooperate fully with U.N. weapons inspectors, UNSCOM will be impeded in its efforts to fulfill its mandate. We will continue to fully support the mandate and the efforts of UNSCOM to obtain Iraqi compliance with all relevant U.N. resolutions.

Implementation of UNSCR 1051 continues. It provides for a mechanism to monitor Iraq's effort to reacquire proscribed weapons capabilities by requiring that Iraq notify a joint unit of UNSCOM and the International Atomic Energy Agency in advance of any imports of dual-use items. Similarly, countries must provide timely notification of exports to Iraq of dual-use items.

Regarding northern Iraq, the United States continues to lead efforts to increase security and stability in the north and minimize opportunities for Baghdad or Tehran to threaten Iraqi citizens there. Acting Assistant Secretary of State for Near Eastern Affairs David Welch led a U.S. delegation to northern Iraq on April 3 and 4, the first visit to the north by a U.S. official since Saddam's attack against the region in September 1996, and the first visit at this level in several years. Welch met with leaders of the two main Iraqi Kurd groups, Massoud Barzani of the Kurdistan Democratic Party (KDP) and Jalal Talabani of the Patriotic Union of Kurdistan (PUK). Both Iraqi Kurd leaders reaffirmed their support for U.S. policy and their commitment to cooperate with us through the Ankara reconciliation process. Welch also met with Iraqi Assyrian and Turkoman political leaders, PMF personnel, and U.N. officials.

Regarding the Ankara process to help the PUK and the KDP resolve their differences, we have facilitated three rounds of higher-level talks, along with our British and Turkish partners. Our immediate goals in the process are to focus on strengthening the U.S.-brokered cease-fire of October 23, 1996, which continues to hold, and on encouraging political reconciliation between the PUK and KDP.

The United States is providing political, financial, and logistical support for a neutral, indigenous Peace Monitoring Force (PMF) in northern Iraq that has demarcated the cease-fire line and monitors the cease-fire. Our support is being provided in the form of commodities and services in accordance with a drawdown I directed on December 11, 1996, and in the form of funds to be used to provide other non-lethal assistance in accordance with a separate determination made by former Secretary of State Christopher on November 10, 1996. The PMF began full deployment in mid-April, and has already succeeded in resolving several troublesome incidents in violation of the cease-fire.

The PMF has also helped the groups move forward on several other confidence-building measures, including a mutual release on April 14 of approximately 70 detainees from each Kurd group. The two Iraqi Kurd groups also continue to work on reconciliation efforts, including an initial meeting on March

12 of a joint Higher Coordination Committee to improve cooperation on civilian services such as electricity and health. Local representatives of the two Kurd groups, the three countries, and the PMF continue to meet biweekly in Ankara and move forward on other confidence-building measures.

Security conditions in northern Iraq nonetheless remain tenuous at best, with Iranian and PKK (Kurdistan Workers Party) activity adding to the ever-present threat from Baghdad. All our efforts under the Ankara process, like all our efforts concerning Iraq, maintain support for the unity and territorial integrity of Iraq.

Implementation of UNSCR 986 is proceeding. The oil-related provisions of UNSCR 986, which authorized Iraq to sell up to $2 billion of oil during an initial 180-day period (with the possibility of UNSC renewal of subsequent 180-day periods) went into effect on December 10, 1996. The first shipments of food and humanitarian goods purchased with Iraqi oil proceeds started to arrive in Iraq on March 20.

UNSCR 986 requires that the proceeds of this limited oil sale, all of which must be deposited in a U.N. escrow account, will be used to purchase food, medicine, and other materials and supplies for essential civilian needs for all Iraqi citizens and to fund vital U.N. activities regarding Iraq. Critical to the success of UNSCR 986 is Iraq's willingness to follow through on its commitments under 986 to allow the United Nations to monitor the distribution of food and medical supplies to the Iraqi people.

During the first 90 days since implementation, Iraq sold just over $1 billion worth of oil in accordance with the terms of UNSCR 986. Significant delays in implementing distribution of humanitarian goods—caused, in part, by Iraqi efforts to impose new restrictions on the freedom of access and movement of U.N. monitors—made it impossible for the U.N. Secretary General to report on the adequacy of distribution and monitoring procedures during the first 90 days. We will continue to monitor the situation closely.

Iraq continues to stall and obfuscate rather than work in good faith toward accounting for the hundreds of Kuwaitis and third-country nationals who disappeared at the hands of Iraqi authorities during the occupation. It has also failed to return all of the stolen Kuwaiti military equipment and the priceless Kuwaiti cultural and historical artifacts that were looted during the occupation.

The human rights situation throughout Iraq remains unchanged. Iraq's repression of its Shi'a population continues with policies that are destroying the Marsh Arabs' way of life in southern Iraq, as well as the ecology of the southern marshes. Saddam Hussein shows no signs of complying with UNSCR 688, which demands that Iraq cease the repression of its own people. On April 16, the U.N. Human Rights Commission passed a resolution strongly condemning the Baghdad regime's continued human rights abuses. That same day, the Administration announced support for an effort by various Iraqi opposition groups and non-governmental organizations to document Iraqi war crimes and other violations of international humanitarian law. This effort, known as INDICT, seeks ultimately to ensure that Saddam Hussein and other members of his regime are brought to justice before an international tribunal. We are in touch with organizers of INDICT and other parties to discuss the best means to move forward.

The Multinational Interception Force (MIF) is facing an increased challenge from smugglers and Iran. As I have noted in previous reports, these smugglers use the territorial waters of Iran to avoid the MIF inspection in the Northern Gulf. With the help of the Iranian government, which profits from these activities by charging protection fees, these smugglers are able to export over 70,000 metric tons of gas oil through the Gulf each month. This represents a significant increase from the amount included in my last report. We are working closely with our allies in the Gulf and with our MIF partners to develop new strategies to curb these violations of the sanctions regime.

Although MIF exchanges with the regular Iranian naval units have been professional and courteous, Iranian Revolutionary Guard Corps naval units have been much more aggressive in confronting the MIF and are actively involved in aiding the smugglers. The MIF is acting with good judgment and caution in its encounters with Iran. Our objective is to enforce sanctions—not to engage in unproductive encounters with Iran.

We regularly provide detailed briefings regarding developments in MIF sanctions enforcement to our MIF partners and Gulf Cooperation Council allies. We also are working closely through our mission in New York with the U.N. Sanctions Committee and likeminded allies on our approach toward Iran and sanctions violators, generally.

The MIF continues to process the maritime traffic involved in lifting oil from the Mina Al Bakr offshore terminal and the delivery of much-needed humanitarian supplies to Umm Qasr in Iraq. So far, those operations are proceeding smoothly. The smuggling trade, however, continues to force the MIF to devote scarce resources to sanctions enforcement. This has resulted in fewer ships available to process the legal humanitarian shipments that bring food and other supplies to Iraq under UNSCR 986.

The United Nations Compensation Commission (UNCC), established pursuant to UNSCR 687, continues to resolve claims against Iraq arising from Iraq's unlawful invasion and occupation of Kuwait. The UNCC has issued over 1 million awards worth approximately $5.2 billion. With the advent of oil sales under UNSCR 986, 30 percent of the proceeds are being allocated to the Compensation Fund to pay awards and finance operations of the UNCC. Initial payments out of the Compensation Fund are currently being made on awards in the order in which the UNCC has approved them, in installments of $2,500.00. In January 1997, the United States Government submitted claims totaling approximately $8.8 million for expenses incurred in the efforts to assess and respond to environmental damage in the Persian Gulf region caused by Iraq's unlawful invasion and occupation of Kuwait.

To conclude, Iraq remains a serious threat to regional peace and stability. I remain determined to see Iraq comply fully with all of its obligations under U.N. Security Council resolutions. My Administration will continue to oppose any relaxation of sanctions until Iraq demonstrates its peaceful intentions through such compliance.

I appreciate the support of the Congress for our efforts and shall continue to keep the Congress informed about this important issue.

Sincerely,

William J. Clinton

317.

[Vol. 33, no. 28 (July 14, 1997): 1047-1050]

Letter to Congressional Leaders Reporting on Iraq
July 9, 1997

Dear Mr. Speaker: (Dear Mr. President:)

Consistent with the Authorization for Use of Military Force Against Iraq Resolution (Public Law 102-1) and as part of my effort to keep the Congress fully informed, I am reporting on the status of efforts to obtain Iraq's compliance with the resolutions adopted by the United Nations Security Council (UNSC). This report covers the period from May 8 to the present. Saddam Hussein remains a threat to his people and the region and the United States remains determined to contain the threat of Saddam's regime. As Secretary of State Albright stated on March 26, the United States looks forward to the day when Iraq joins the family of nations as a responsible and law-abiding member and that, until then, containment must continue. Secretary Albright made clear that Saddam's departure would make a difference and that, should a change in Iraq's government occur, the United States would stand ready to enter rapidly into a dialogue with the successor regime.

In terms of military operations, the United States and its coalition partners continue to enforce the no-fly zones over northern Iraq under Operation Northern Watch, and over southern Iraq with Operation Southern Watch. We have not detected any confirmed, intentional Iraqi violations of either no-fly zone since late April.

In addition to our air operations, we will continue to maintain a strong U.S. presence in the region in order to deter Saddam. United States force levels include land- and carrier-based aircraft, surface warships, a marine amphibious task force, a Patriot missile battalion, and a mechanized battalion task force deployed in support of USCINCCENT operations. To enhance force protection throughout the region, additional military security personnel have been deployed for continuous rotation. USCINCCENT continues to closely monitor the security situation in the region to ensure adequate force protection is provided for all deployed forces.

United Nations Security Council Resolution (UNSCR) 949, adopted in October 1994, demands that Iraq not utilize its military or any other forces to threaten its neighbors or U.N. operations in Iraq and that it not redeploy troops or enhance its military capacity in southern Iraq. In view of Saddam's accumulating record of unreliability, it is prudent to retain a significant U.S. force presence in the region in order to maintain the capability to respond rapidly to possible Iraqi aggression or threats against its neighbors.

Since my last report, the Government of Iraq has continued to flout its obligations under UNSC Resolutions. Under the terms of relevant UNSC Resolutions, Iraq must grant the U.N. Special Commission on Iraq (UNSCOM) inspectors immediate, unconditional, and unrestricted access to any location in Iraq that they wish to examine, and access to any Iraqi official whom they may wish to interview, so that UNSCOM may fully discharge its mandate to ensure that Iraq's weapons of mass destruction (WMD) program has been eliminated. Iraq continues, as it has for the past 6 years, to fail to live up to either the letter or the spirit of the commitment. Of particular concern is UNSCOM's June report to the Security Council of serious incidents involving Iraqi escort helicopters flying dangerously close to the Commission's aircraft to force it to change direction and multiple cases of Iraqi personnel aboard UNSCOM helicopters attempting to wrest control of aircraft from their pilots.

In his June report, UNSCOM Chairman Rolf Ekeus also indicated that UNSCOM had found new indications that Iraq has not fulfilled its requirement to destroy its WMD. Chairman Ekeus told the Security Council that on June 10 and 12, Iraqi officials totally blocked UNSCOM inspectors from access to three sites suspected of containing hidden information about its prohibited weapons programs. He reported that UNSCOM inspectors observed Iraqi officials shredding, burning, or hiding documents at the sites, and that senior Iraqi government officials refused to allow UNSCOM inspectors to interview officials involved in Iraq's weapons programs. Chairman Ekeus singled out Iraq's leadership as having hindered several attempts by UNSCOM inspectors to inspect areas that are suspected of being hiding places for chemical or biological weapons or technology used to manufacture those weapons.

In response to Iraqi intransigence, the U.S. sponsored and the Security Council on June 21 passed unanimously, UNSC Resolution 1115, which 1) condemns the repeated refusal of Iraqi authorities to allow access to sites designated by UNSCOM; 2) demands that Iraq cooperate fully with UNSCOM in accordance with relevant UNSC resolutions and allow UNSCOM inspection teams immediate, unconditional, and unrestricted access to any and all areas, facilities, equipment, records, and means of transportation that they wish to inspect; 3) demands that the Government of Iraq give immediate, unconditional, and unrestricted access to officials and other persons under the authority of the Iraqi Government whom UNSCOM wishes to interview; 4) provides that the periodic sanctions reviews provided for in UNSC Resolution 687 will not be conducted until after UNSCOM's next consolidated progress report—due October 11, 1997—after which time those reviews will resume; 5) expresses the firm intention to impose additional measures on those categories of Iraqi officials responsible for Iraq's noncompliance, unless advised by UNSCOM that Iraq is in substantial compliance with this resolution; and 6) reaffirms its full support for UNSCOM.

Implementation of UNSCR 1051 continues. It provides for a mechanism to monitor Iraq's effort to reacquire proscribed weapons capabilities by requiring that Iraq notify a joint unit of UNSCOM and the International Atomic Energy Agency in advance of any imports of dual-use items. Similarly, countries must provide timely notification of exports to Iraq of dual-use items.

Regarding northern Iraq, the United States continues to lead efforts to increase security and stability in the north and minimize opportunities for Baghdad or Tehran to threaten Iraqi citizens there. Following a successful trip to northern Iraq in early April, Acting Assistant Secretary of State for Near Eastern Affairs David Welch led a U.S. delegation to Turkey for a fourth round of higher-level talks on May 14 to help resolve differences between the two main Iraqi Kurd groups, Massoud Barzani of the Kurdistan Democratic Party (KDP) and Jalal Talabani of the Patriotic Union of Kurdistan (PUK).

During this latest meeting under the "Ankara Process," the U.S., British, and Turkish cosponsors of the talks obtained agreement from KDP and PUK delegations to take several steps designed to strengthen the October 23, 1996, cease-fire between the two Iraqi Kurd groups and encourage their political reconciliation.

Representatives from the Iraqi Turkoman and Iraqi Assyrian organizations participating in the neutral, indigenous Peace Monitoring Force (PMF) also attended the fourth round of talks in Ankara. The PMF participants also continue to help the Iraqi Kurd groups move forward on several other confidence-building measures, the most recent of which included several joint committee meetings on May 29 that addressed a range of civilian services and humanitarian issues affecting all residents of the north. Local representatives of the two Kurd groups, the three countries, and the PMF continue to meet biweekly in Ankara and move forward on other confidence-building measures.

As part of the Ankara process, the United States is providing political, financial, and logistical support for the PMF in northern Iraq that has demarcated the cease-fire line and monitors the cease-fire. Our support is being provided in the form of commodities and services in accordance with a drawdown directed by me on December 11, 1996, and in the form of funds to be used to provide other nonlethal assistance in accordance with a separate determination made by former Secretary of State Christopher on November 10, 1996. The PMF began full deployment in mid-April and continues to investigate and resolve reported cease-fire violations.

These steps, as with all our efforts under the Ankara process and concerning Iraq, maintain support for the unity and territorial integrity of Iraq. Security conditions in northern Iraq nevertheless remain tenuous at best, with the Iranian and PKK (Kurdistan Workers Party) activity adding to the ever-present threat from Baghdad.

The oil for food arrangement under UNSCR 986 was reauthorized under UNSCR 1111 on June 9, 1997. Under UNSCR 1111, Iraq is authorized to sell up to $2 billion of oil during a 180-day period (with the possibility of UNSC renewal for subsequent 180-day periods). Resolution 1111, like its predecessor, requires that the proceeds of this limited oil sale, all of which must be deposited in a U.N. escrow account, will be used to purchase food, medicine, and other material and supplies for essential civilian needs for all Iraqi citizens and to fund vital U.N. activities regarding Iraq. Critical to the success of UNSCR 1111 is Iraq's willingness to follow through on its commitments under the resolution to allow the U.N. to monitor the distribution of humanitarian goods to the Iraqi people. Iraq has suspended any further oil sales until a new distribution plan is approved, which will probably occur sometime in July. The Iraqi Government has prepared a new distribution plan, which is subject to the approval of the U.N. Secretary General.

Iraq continues to stall and obfuscate rather than work in good faith toward accounting for the hundreds of Kuwaitis and third-country nationals who disappeared at the hands of Iraqi authorities during the occupation. It has also failed to return all of the stolen Kuwaiti military equipment and the priceless Kuwaiti cultural and historical artifacts that were looted during the occupation.

The human rights situation throughout Iraq remains unchanged. Iraq's repression of its Shi'a population continues with policies that are destroying the Marsh Arabs' way of life in southern Iraq, as well as the ecology of the southern marshes. The U.N., in its most recent reports on implementation of UNSCR 986, recognized that the Government of Iraq continues to forcibly deport Iraqi citizens from

Kirkuk and other areas of northern Iraq still under the Iraqi Government's control. Saddam Hussein shows no signs of complying with UNSCR 688, which demands that Iraq cease the repression of its own people. The effort by various Iraqi opposition groups and nongovernmental organizations to document Iraqi war crimes and other violations of international humanitarian law, known as INDICT, continues.

The Multinational Interception Force (MIF) continues its important mission in the Arabian Gulf. The United States Navy provides the bulk of the forces involved in the maritime sanctions enforcement although we receive much-needed help from a number of close allies. In recent months, ships from the Netherlands, Canada, New Zealand, and the United Kingdom have participated in MIF operations. We continue active pursuit of broad-based international participation in these operations.

Illegal smuggling of Iraqi gasoil from the Shatt Al Arab waterway continues to increase. We estimate that over 81,000 metric tons of gasoil each month is exported from Iraq in violation of UNSCR 661. The smugglers utilize the territorial waters of Iran with the complicity of the Iranian Government, which profits from charging protection fees for these vessels, to avoid interception by the MIF in international waters. Cash raised from these illegal operations is used to purchase contraband goods, which are then smuggled back into Iraq by the same route. We continue to brief the U.N. Sanctions Committee regarding these operations and have pressed the Committee to compel Iran to give a full accounting of its involvement. We have also worked closely with our MIF partners and the Gulf Cooperation Council states to take measures to curb sanctions-breaking operations. Recent announcements by the government of the United Arab Emirates (UAE) that it intends to crack down on smugglers who operate UAE-flagged vessels is a positive step in this regard.

The United Nations Compensation Commission (UNCC), established pursuant to UNSCR 687, continues to resolve claims against Iraq arising from Iraq's unlawful invasion and occupation of Kuwait. The UNCC has issued almost 1.1 million awards worth approximately $5.9 billion. Thirty percent of the proceeds from the oil sales permitted by UNSCR 986 have been allocated to the Compensation Fund to pay awards and finance the operations of the UNCC, and these proceeds will continue to be allocated to the Fund under UNSCR 1111. Initial payments out of the Compensation Fund are currently being made on awards in the order in which UNCC has approved them, in installments of $2,500.00.

To conclude, Iraq remains a serious threat to regional peace and stability. I remain determined to see Iraq comply fully with all of its obligations under U.N. Security Council resolutions. My administration will continue to oppose any relaxation of sanctions until Iraq demonstrates its peaceful intentions through such compliance.

I appreciate the support of the Congress for our efforts and shall continue to keep the Congress informed about this important issue.
Sincerely,
William J. Clinton

318.

[Vol. 33, no. 39 (September 29, 1997): 1397-1400]

Letter to Congressional Leaders on Iraq September 23, 1997

Dear Mr. Speaker: (Dear Mr. President):
Consistent with the Authorization for Use of Military Force Against Iraq Resolution (Public Law 102-1) and as part of my effort to keep the Congress fully informed, I am reporting on the status of efforts to obtain Iraq's compliance with the resolutions adopted by the United Nations Security Council (UNSC). This report covers the period from July 9 to the present.

Saddam Hussein remains a threat to his people and the region, and the United States remains determined to contain the threat posed by his regime. Secretary of State Albright stated on March 26 that the United States looks forward to the day when Iraq rejoins the family of nations as a responsible and law-abiding member but until then, containment

must continue. Secretary Albright made clear that Saddam's departure would make a difference and that, should a change in Iraq's government occur, the United States would stand ready to enter rapidly into a dialogue with the successor regime.

In terms of military operations, the United States and its coalition partners continue to enforce the no-fly zones over northern Iraq under Operation Northern Watch and over southern Iraq through Operation Southern Watch. We have not detected any confirmed, intentional Iraqi violations of either no-fly zone during the period of this report. We have repeatedly made clear to the Government of Iraq and to all other relevant parties that the United States and its partners will continue to enforce both no-fly zones, and that we reserve the right to respond appropriately and decisively to any Iraqi provocations.

In addition to our air operations, we will continue to maintain a strong U.S. presence in the region in order to deter Iraq. United States force levels include land- and carrier-based aircraft, surface warships, a Marine amphibious task force, a Patriot missile battalion, and a mechanized battalion task force deployed in support of USCINCCENT operations. To enhance force protection throughout the region, additional military security personnel have been deployed for continuous rotation. USCINCCENT continues to monitor closely the security situation in the region to ensure adequate force protection is provided for all deployed forces.

United Nations Security Council Resolution (UNSCR) 949, adopted in October 1994, demands that Iraq not use its military or any other forces to threaten its neighbors or U.N. operations in Iraq and that it not redeploy troops or enhance its military capacity in southern Iraq. In view of Saddam's accumulating record of unreliability, it is prudent to retain a significant U.S. force presence in the region in order to maintain the capability to respond rapidly to possible Iraqi aggression or threats against its neighbors.

Since my last report, the Government of Iraq has continued to flout its obligations under UNSC resolutions. During the last 60 days, the Government of Iraq has continued to fail to fully disclose its programs for weapons of mass destruction (WMD). Without such full disclosure—mandated by Security Council Resolutions 687, 707, and 715—the U.N. Special Commission (UNSCOM) and the International Atomic Energy Agency (IAEA) cannot effectively conduct the ongoing monitoring and verification mandated by relevant UNSC resolutions. UNSCOM and the IAEA continue to provide Iraq every opportunity for full disclosure. What Iraq will not disclose, UNSCOM and IAEA will try to discover, in an effort to fill in the huge gaps in Iraq's declarations.

Iraqi threats, lying, and hiding during the past 6 years have not deterred UNSCOM and IAEA dedication to their mandates. While some nations have begun to display sanctions-fatigue, the United States remains committed to sanctions enforcement. We shall continue to oppose any suggestion that the sanctions regime should be modified or lifted before Iraq demonstrates its peaceful intentions by complying with its obligations under UNSC resolutions.

We anticipate the UNSCOM and IAEA 6-month reports to the Security Council, due October 11, which will record their conclusions regarding whether the Government of Iraq has provided the "substantial compliance" called for in UNSCR 1115 of June 21, 1997—especially regarding immediate, unconditional, and unrestricted access to facilities for inspection and to officials for interviews.

The United States is committed to providing first-class professional support to UNSCOM and the IAEA in the conduct of their highly technical work in Iraq, so that both organizations are staffed and equipped to conduct objective and accurate inspections in order to determine whether Iraq has, or has not, complied with its obligations in the field of WMD.

Implementation of UNSCR 1051 continues. It provides for a mechanism to monitor Iraq's effort to reacquire proscribed weapons capabilities by requiring that Iraq notify a joint unit of UNSCOM and the IAEA in advance of any imports of dual-use items. Similarly, U.N. members must provide timely notification of exports to Iraq of dual-use items.

Regarding northern Iraq, the United States continues to lead efforts to increase security and stability in the north and minimize opportunities for Baghdad or Tehran to threaten Iraqi citizens there. An important part of this effort has been to work toward resolving the differences between the two main Iraqi Kurd groups, the Kurdistan Democratic Party (KDP), led by Massoud Barzani, and the Patriotic Union of Kurdistan (PUK), led by Jalal Talabani. Talabani visited the United States in late July to meet with National Security Advisor Sandy Berger, Under Secretary of State Thomas Pickering, and U.N. Ambassador Bill Richardson. At these sessions, he reaffirmed his interest in the "Ankara process" of ongoing reconciliation talks jointly sponsored by the United States, the United Kingdom, and Turkey. Recently, the KDP's Barzani has also accepted our invitation to Washington.

As part of the Ankara process, the United States provides political, financial, and logistical support to the neutral, indigenous Peace Monitoring Force (PMF), comprised of Iraqi Turkomans and Assyrians. The PMF has demarcated and monitors the cease-fire line established between the two Kurdish groups in October 1996. United States support takes the form of services and commodities provided in accordance with a drawdown that I directed on December 11, 1996, and funds for other nonlethal assistance provided in accordance with a separate determination made by former Secretary of State Christopher on November 10, 1996.

The PMF also helps the Iraqi Kurds move forward on other confidence-building measures, including joint committee meetings to address a range of civilian services and humanitarian issues affecting all residents of the north. Local representatives of the two Kurdish groups, the three co-sponsors of the Ankara process and the PMF continue to meet at least biweekly in Ankara to discuss, inter alia, other confidence-building measures.

The PMF began full deployment in mid-April 1997 and its size is expected to double later this year to more than 400. The PMF continues to investigate and resolve reported cease-fire violations. Its work has become more difficult as elements of the terrorist Kurdistan Workers Party (PKK) have moved from the Turkish border toward the PUK-KDP cease-fire line. The KDP alleges that PKK elements have been operating across the cease-fire line to attack the KDP. The KDP also alleges that the PUK has joined in some of these attacks, a charge that the PUK denies. The United States, together with the United Kingdom and Turkey, continues to stress the importance of strict observance of the cease-fire.

Another important aspect of our commitment to the people of northern Iraq is in providing humanitarian relief for those in need. As part of this commitment, AID's Office of Foreign Disaster Assistance will direct an additional $4 million for relief projects to the region. These supplemental programs, announced July 31, will provide emergency health and nutritional support to 80,000 displaced women and children and improve water supplies and sanitation, particularly in the PUK-controlled province of Suleymaniyah.

The oil-for-food arrangement under UNSCR 986 was reauthorized by UNSCR 1111 on June 4, 1997, and went into effect on June 8, 1997. Under UNSCR 1111, Iraq is authorized to sell up to $1 billion worth of oil every 90 days, for a total of $2 billion during a 180-day period (with the possibility of UNSC renewal for subsequent 180-day periods). Resolution 1111, like its predecessor, requires that the proceeds of this limited oil sale, all of which must be deposited in a U.N. escrow account, will be used to purchase food, medicine, and other material and supplies for essential civilian needs for all Iraqi citizens and to fund vital U.N. activities regarding Iraq. Critical to the success of UNSCR 1111 is Iraq's willingness to follow through on its commitments under the resolution to allow the U.N. to monitor the distribution of humanitarian goods to the Iraqi people. Although UNSCR 1111 went into effect on June 8, Iraq unilaterally suspended oil sales until a new distribution plan was submitted and approved. The U.N. Secretary General approved a distribution plan on August 13 and oil sales have resumed.

Iraq continues to stall and obfuscate rather than work in good faith toward accounting for the hundreds of Kuwaitis and third-country nationals who disappeared at the hands of Iraqi authorities during the occupation. It has also failed to return all of the stolen Kuwaiti military equipment and the priceless Kuwaiti cultural and historical artifacts that were looted during the occupation.

The human rights situation throughout Iraq remains unchanged. Iraq's repression of its Shi'a population continues, with policies that are destroying the Marsh Arabs' way of life in southern Iraq and the ecology of the southern marshes. The U.N., in its most recent reports on implementation of UNSCR 986, recognized that the Government of Iraq continues forcibly to deport Iraqi citizens from Kirkuk and other areas of northern Iraq still under the Iraqi government's control. The Government of Iraq shows no signs of complying with UNSCR 688, which demands that Iraq cease the repression of its own people. The effort by various Iraqi opposition groups and non-governmental organizations to document Iraqi war crimes and other violations of international humanitarian law, known as IN-DICT, continues.

The Multinational Interception Force (MIF) continues its important mission in the Arabian Gulf. The United States Navy provides the bulk of the forces involved in the maritime sanctions enforcement authorized under UNSCR 665, although we receive much-needed help from a number of close allies. In recent months, ships from The Netherlands, Canada, New Zealand, and the United Kingdom have participated in MIF operations. We continue active pursuit of broad-based international participation in these operations.

Illegal smuggling of Iraqi gasoil from the Shatt Al Arab waterway continues to increase at an alarming rate. We now estimate that over 150,000 metric tons of gasoil each month is exported from Iraq in violation of UNSCR 661. The smugglers use the territorial waters of Iran with the complicity of the Iranian government that profits from charging protection fees for these vessels to avoid interception by the MIF in international waters. Cash raised from these illegal operations is used to purchase contraband goods that are then smuggled back into Iraq by the same route. We continue to brief the U.N. Sanctions Committee regarding these operations and have pressed the Committee to compel Iran to give a full accounting of its involvement. We have also worked closely with our MIF partners and Gulf Cooperation Council states to take measures to curb sanctions-breaking operations. A recent spill of illegal Iraqi gasoil caused the desalinization plant in Sharjah, United Arab Emirates (UAE), to suspend operation for 2 days, highlighting the environmental threat these activities pose to Gulf states. Recent announcements by the Government of the UAE that it intends to crack down on smugglers who operate UAE-flagged vessels has been backed up by strong actions against violators detained by the MIF.

The United Nations Compensation Commission (UNCC), established pursuant to UNSCR 687, continues to resolve claims against Iraq arising from Iraq's unlawful invasion and occupation of Kuwait. The UNCC has issued almost 1.1 million awards worth approximately $5.9 billion. Thirty percent of the proceeds from the oil sales permitted by UNSCR 986 have been allocated to the Compensation Fund to pay awards and to finance operations of the UNCC, and these proceeds will continue to be allocated to the Fund under UNSCR 1111. To the extent that money is available in the Compensation Fund, initial payments to each claimant are authorized for awards in the order in which the UNCC has approved them, in installments of $2,500.00.

Iraq remains a serious threat to regional peace and stability. I remain determined to see Iraq comply fully with all of its obligations under U.N. Security Council resolutions. My Administration will continue to oppose any relaxation of sanctions until Iraq demonstrates its peaceful intentions through such compliance. I appreciate the support of the Congress for our efforts and shall continue to keep the Congress informed about this important issue.

Sincerely,

William J. Clinton

319.

[Vol. 33, no. 49 (December 8, 1997): 1932-1937]

Letter to Congressional Leaders Reporting on Iraq

November 26, 1997

Dear Mr. Speaker: (Dear Mr. President:)

Consistent with the Authorization for Use of Military Force Against Iraq Resolution (Public Law 102-1) and as part of my effort to keep the Congress fully informed, I am reporting on the status of efforts to obtain Iraq's compliance with the resolutions adopted by the United Nations Security Council (UNSC). This report covers the period from September 23 to the present.

Since my last report, the Government of Iraq attempted to defy the international community by unilaterally imposing unacceptable conditions on the operations of the U.N. Special Commission (UNSCOM). On October 29, the Iraqi government announced its intention to expel all U.S. personnel working in Iraq for UNSCOM. Iraq's aim appears to have been to establish an environment under which it could restore its capacity to develop weapons of mass destruction without restriction. For 3 weeks, the Government of Iraq refused to allow American UNSCOM personnel to enter the country or to participate in site inspections, expelled UNSCOM personnel who are U.S. citizens, threatened the safety of the U.S. Air Force U-2 aircraft that flies missions for UNSCOM, tampered with UNSCOM monitoring equipment, removed UNSCOM cameras, moved and concealed significant pieces of dual-use equipment, and imposed additional unacceptable conditions on continued operations of UNSCOM. Two confrontational actions were undertaken in an atmosphere of strident, threatening Iraqi rhetoric, the dispersal of Iraqi armed forces as if in preparation for a military conflict, and the placement of innocent civilian "human shields" at military sites and at many of Saddam Hussein's palaces in violation of international norms of conduct.

On November 20, having obtained no agreement from the U.N. or the United States to alter UNSCOM or the sanctions regime—indeed, having obtained none of its stated objectives—the Iraqi government announced that it would allow UNSCOM inspectors who are U.S. citizens to return to their duties. This encouraging development, however, will be ultimately tested by Saddam Hussein's actions, not his words. It remains to be seen whether the Government of Iraq will now live up to its obligations under all applicable UNSC resolutions, including its commitment to allow UNSCOM to perform its work unhindered.

As expressed unanimously by the five permanent members (P-5) of the Security Council meeting in Geneva November 20, the will of the entire international community is for the unconditional decision of Iraq to allow the return of UNSCOM inspectors to Iraq in their previous composition. I must note that the United States was not briefed on, did not endorse, and is not bound by anything other than the terms of the P-5 statement. Neither the United States nor the U.N. are bound by any bilateral agreement between Russia and Iraq. We will carefully monitor events and will continue to be prepared for any contingency. Iraq's challenge was issued, in part, in response to U.N. Security Council Resolution (UNSCR) 1134, of October 23, in which the Security Council condemned Iraq's flagrant violations of relevant Security Council resolutions and expressed its firm intention to impose travel restrictions on the Iraqi leadership if the long-standing pattern of obstruction and harassment of UNSCOM personnel continued. In the debate of UNSCR 1134, not one nation on the Security Council questioned the need to continue sanctions. The only serious debate was over when and how to impose additional sanctions. UNSCR 1134 was based on the UNSCOM and the International Atomic Energy Agency (IAEA) 6-month reports to the UNSC that indicated that the Government of Iraq has not provided the "substantial compliance" called for in UNSCR 1115 of June 21, 1997—especially regarding immediate, unconditional and unrestricted access to facilities for inspection and to officials for interviews.

On November 12 the resolve of the international community was further demonstrated when the Security Council voted unanimously to adopt UNSCR 1137—the first new sanctions against Iraq since the Gulf War—condemning Iraq's continued violations of its obligations and imposing restrictions on the travel of all Iraqi officials and armed forces members responsible for or participating in noncompliance. The UNSC in a Presidential Statement condemned Iraq again upon the actual expulsion of the American UNSCOM personnel. The UNSC's solidarity was reflected as well in the UNSCOM Executive Chairman's and IAEA Director's decisions that all UNSCOM and IAEA personnel should depart Iraq rather than accede to the Iraqi demand that no American participate in inspection activities.

As a demonstration of our firm resolve to support the U.N., I directed the deployment of the USS GEORGE WASHINGTON, escort ships, and additional combat aircraft to the region. In this regard we take note of and welcome House Resolution 322 expressing the sense of the House that the United States should act to resolve the crisis in a manner that assures full Iraqi compliance with UNSC resolutions regarding the destruction of Iraq's capability to produce and deliver weapons of mass destruction. While the addition of these forces gives us a wide range of military options, should they be necessary, we remain firmly committed to finding a diplomatic solution.

The ongoing crisis is only one chapter in the long history of efforts by the Iraqi regime to flout its obligations under UNSC resolutions. Iraq has persistently failed to disclose fully its programs for weapons of mass destruction. It admits to moving significant pieces of dual-use equipment subject to monitoring. Without full disclosure, UNSCOM and the IAEA cannot effectively conduct the ongoing monitoring and verification mandated by UNSCR's 687, 707, 715, and other relevant resolutions.

Iraqi biological and chemical weapons are currently the most troubling issues for UNSCOM. This is due to the innate dual-use nature of the technology—how easily it can be hidden within civilian industries such as, for biological agents—the pharmaceutical industry, and for chemical agents—the pesticide industry. In both cases, Iraq continues to prevent full and immediate access to sites suspected of chemical or biological warfare activities. Until 2 months ago, for example, major aspects of Iraq's pernicious "VX" program (a powerful nerve agent) were unknown to UNSCOM due to Iraqi concealment. UNSCOM is still unable to verify that all of

Iraq's SCUD missile warheads filled with biological agents—anthrax and botulinum toxin—have been destroyed. When UNSCOM says it is making "significant progress" in these areas, it is referring to UNSCOM's progress in ferreting out Iraqi deception, not Iraqi progress in cooperating with UNSCOM.

The Iraqi regime contends that UNSCOM and the IAEA should "close the books" on nuclear and missile inspections. But there are still many uncertainties and questions that need to be resolved. Among the many problems, Iraq has:

• failed to answer critical questions on nuclear weapons design and fabrication, procurement, and centrifuge enrichment;

• failed to detail how far the theoretical and practical aspects of its clandestine nuclear efforts progressed;

• failed to explain in full the interaction between its nuclear warhead and missile design programs;

• failed to provide a written description of its post-war nuclear weapons procurement program;

• failed to account for major engine components, special warheads, missing propellants, and guidance instruments that could be used to assemble fully operational missiles; and

• failed to discuss—on the direct orders of Tariq Aziz—its actions to retain missile launchers.

In accordance with relevant UNSCR's, UNSCOM must continue to investigate the Iraqi nuclear and missile programs until it can verify with absolute certainty that all the equipment has been destroyed and that all the capabilities have been eliminated. Otherwise, Iraq will be able to strike at any city in the Middle East, delivering devastating biological, chemical, and even nuclear weapons.

UNSCOM's work must include vigorous efforts to unveil Iraq's "Concealment Mechanism." Led by elements of its special security services, Iraq has for over 6-years engaged in a massive and elaborate campaign to keep UNSCOM inspectors from finding proscribed equipment, documents, and possibly weapons themselves. Over the years, inspection teams have been prevented from doing their jobs and held—often at gunpoint—outside suspect facilities, providing enough time for evidence to be hidden or destroyed. To rout out Iraq's remaining weapons of mass destruction, UNSCOM must be granted full access to all sites, without exception.

The Iraqi regime contends that it has been forced to defy the international community in this manner out of concern for the well-being of the Iraqi people, claiming that malnutrition and inadequate medical care are the direct result of internationally imposed sanctions. To the contrary, the deep concern of the United States and the international community about the condition of the Iraqi people is evident in the fact that the international sanctions against Iraq have been carefully structured to help ensure that ordinary Iraqis need not suffer. Since their inception, the sanctions against Iraq have had exceptions for the importation into Iraq of foods and medicines. In August 1991, when Iraq claimed that it was unable to pay for its food needs, the Security Council adopted UNSCR 706 (and later 712), authorizing Iraq to sell limited amounts of petroleum on the international market, with the proceeds to be used to purchase humanitarian supplies, and to fund vital U.N. activities regarding Iraq. The Government of Iraq, however ignored the needs of its own people, by refusing to accept UNSCR's 706 and 712.

In April 1995 the Security Council proposed a new oil-for-food offer to Iraq in UNSCR 986, sponsored by the United States and others. UNSCR 986 authorized the sale of up to $1 billion of oil every 90 days for Iraq to purchase food, medicines, and other "humanitarian items" for its people. The Government of Iraq delayed implementation of UNSCR 986 for a year and a half, until December 1996.

Since December 1996, the Iraqi regime has continued to obstruct the relief plan. It has reduced the food ration for each person, even as more food was flowing into the country. In fact, there are credible reports that as food imports under UNSCR 986 increased, the regime reduced its regular food purchases, potentially freeing up money for other purposes. There are also reports that Iraq may have stockpiled food in warehouses for use by the military and regime supporters—even though the Iraqi people need the food now. Under UNSCR 1111—the 6-month renewal of UNSCR 986 passed in June 1997—the regime delayed oil sales for 2 months, even while it claimed its people were starving. In Baghdad, the regime staged threatening demonstrations against U.N. relief offices. Under both UNSCR's 986 and 1111, the U.N. Sanctions Committee has had to carefully consider each and every import contract because of the possibility that Iraq may slip orders for dual-use items that can be employed to make weapons into long lists of humanitarian goods.

Since 1990—even at the height of the Gulf War—the consistent position of the United States has been that this dispute is with Iraq's regime, not with its people. We have always been open to suggestions on how UNSCR's 986 and 1111 can be improved or expanded to better serve the needs of the people. The confrontational tactics of the Iraqi government have not altered this position.

Sanctions against Iraq were imposed as the result of Iraq's invasion of Kuwait. It has been necessary to sustain them because of Iraq's failure to comply with relevant UNSC resolutions, including those to ensure that Saddam Hussein is not allowed to resume the unrestricted development and production of weapons of mass destruction. Prior to the Gulf War, Saddam had already used chemical weapons on the Iraqi people and on Iranian troops, and he threatened to use them on coalition forces and innocent civilians in Saudi Arabia and Israel during the Gulf War. By restricting the amount of oil he can sell to a level that provides for the needs of the Iraqi people but does not allow him to pursue other, nonhumanitarian objectives, international sanctions make it virtually impossible for Saddam to gear up his weapons programs to full strength.

Saddam could end the suffering of his people tomorrow if he would cease his obstruction of the oil-for-food program and allow it to be implemented properly. He could end sanctions entirely if he would demonstrate peaceful intentions by complying fully with relevant UNSC resolutions. The United States has supported and will continue to support the sanctions against the Iraqi regime until such time as compliance is achieved.

Saddam Hussein remains a threat to his people, to the region, and to the world, and the United States remains determined to contain the threat posed by his regime. The United States looks forward to the day when Iraq rejoins the family of nations as a responsible and law-abiding member but until then, containment must continue.

Regarding military operations, the United States and its coalition partners continue to enforce the no-fly zones over Iraq under Operation Northern Watch and Operation Southern Watch. We have detected myriad intentional Iraqi violations of both no-fly zones. While these incidents (Iraqi violations of the no-fly zones) started several hours after an Iranian air raid on terrorist bases inside Iraq, it was clear that Iraq's purpose was to try and test the coalition to see how far it could go in violating the ban on flights in these regions. A maximum effort by Operation Southern Watch forces complemented by early arrival in theater of the USS NIMITZ battle group, dramatically reduced violations in the southern no-fly zone. An increase in the number of support aircraft participating in Northern Watch allowed increased operating capacity that in turn significantly reduced the number of violations in the north. We have repeatedly made clear to the Government of Iraq and to all other relevant parties that the United States and its partners will continue to enforce both no-fly zones, and that we reserve the right to respond appropriately and decisively to any Iraqi provocations.

United States force levels include land- and carrier-based aircraft, surface warships, a Marine amphibious task force, a Patriot missile battalion, a mechanized battalion task force, and a mix of special operations forces deployed in support of USCINCCENT operations. To enhance force protection throughout the region, additional military security personnel have been deployed for continuous rotation. USCINCCENT continues to monitor closely the security situation in the region to ensure adequate force protection is provided for all deployed forces.

United Nations Security Council Resolution 9491 adopted in October 1994, demands that Iraq not use its military or any other forces to threaten its neighbors or U.N. operations in Iraq and that it not redeploy troops or enhance its military capacity in southern Iraq. In view of Saddam's accumulating record of unreliability, it is prudent to retain a significant U.S. force presence in the region in order to deter Iraq and maintain the capability to respond rapidly to possible Iraqi aggression or threats against its neighbors.

Implementation of UNSCR 1051 continues. It provides for a mechanism to monitor Iraq's efforts to reacquire proscribed weapons capabilities by requiring Iraq to notify a joint unit of UNSCOM and the IAEA in advance of any imports of dual-use items. Similarly, U.N. members must provide timely notification of exports to Iraq of dual-use items.

The human rights situation throughout Iraq remains unchanged. Iraq's repression of its Shi'a population continues, with policies that are destroying the Marsh Arabs' way of life in southern Iraq and the ecology of the southern marshes. The United Nations, in its most recent reports in implementation of Resolution 986, recognized that the Government of Iraq continues forcibly to deport Iraqi citizens from Kirkuk and other areas of northern Iraq still under the Iraqi government's control. Iraq continues to stall and obfuscate rather than work in good faith toward accounting for the hundreds of Kuwaitis and third-country nationals who disappeared at the hands of Iraqi authorities during the occupation of Kuwait. The Government of Iraq shows no signs of complying with UNSC Resolution 688, which demands that Iraq cease the repression of its own people. The U.N. Human Rights Commission's special rapporteur on Iraq reported to the General Assembly of his particular concern that extrajudicial, summary or arbitrary executions and the practice of torture continue to occur in Iraq.

The INDICT campaign continues to gain momentum. Led by various independent Iraqi opposition groups and nongovernmental organizations, this effort seeks to document crimes against humanity and other violations of international humanitarian law committed by the Iraqi regime. We applaud the tenacity of the Iraqi opposition in the face of one of the most repressive regimes in history. We also take note of and welcome H.Con.Res. 137 of November 12, expressing the sense of the House of Representatives concerning the need for an international criminal tribunal to try members of the Iraqi regime for war crimes and crimes against humanity.

Regarding northern Iraq, our efforts to help resolve the differences between Massoud Barzani, leader of the Kurdistan Democratic Party (KDP) and Jalal Talabani, leader of the Patriotic Union of Kurdistan (PUK) have not yet yielded the type of permanent, stable settlement that the people of northern Iraq deserve. The Peace Monitoring Force—sponsored by the United States, Great Britain, and Turkey under the Ankara Process and comprising Iraqi Turkomans and Assyrians—was forced to withdraw from the agreed cease-fire line between the two groups, when PUK forces, joined by the terrorist Kurdish Workers Party (PKK) launched a wide-scale attack on the KDP on October 13. The KDP, supported by airstrikes and ground elements of the Turkish army, launched a counterattack on November 8. We have helped to arrange a number of temporary cease-fires and to restore humanitarian services in the course of this fighting, but the underlying causes for conflict remain. We will continue our efforts to reach a permanent settlement through mediation in order to minimize opportunities for Baghdad and/or Tehran to insert themselves into the conflict and threaten Iraqi citizens in this region.

The Multinational Interception Force (MIF) continues its important mission in the Arabian Gulf. The U.S. Navy provides the bulk of the forces involved in the maritime sanctions enforcement authorized under Resolution 665, although we receive much-needed help from a number of close allies, including during the past year: Belgium, Canada, The Netherlands, New Zealand, and the United Kingdom.

Illegal smuggling of Iraqi gasoil from the Shatt Al Arab waterway in violation of Resolution 661 has doubled since May of this year—reaching an estimated 180,000 metric tons per month—and continues to increase. The smugglers use the territorial waters of Iran with the complicity of the Iranian government that profits from charging protection fees for these vessels to avoid interception by the MIF in international waters. Cash raised from these illegal operations is used to purchase contraband goods that are then smuggled back into Iraq by the same route. We continue to brief the U.N. Sanctions Committee regarding these operations and have pressed the Committee to compel Iran to give a full accounting of its involvement. We have also worked closely with our MIF partners and Gulf Cooperation Council states to take measures to curb sanctions-breaking operations.

The United Nations Compensation Commission (UNCC), established pursuant to UNSCR 687 and 692, continues to resolve claims against Iraq arising from Iraq's unlawful invasion and occupation of Kuwait. The UNCC has issued almost 1.3 million awards worth approximately $6 billion. Thirty percent of the proceeds from the oil sales permitted by UNSCR's 986 and 1111 have been allocated to the Compensation Fund to pay awards and to finance operations of the UNCC, and these proceeds will continue to be allocated to the Fund under UNSCR 1111. To the extent that money is available in the Compensation Fund, initial payments to each claimant are authorized for awards in the order in which the UNCC has approved them, in installments of $2,500. To date, 455 U.S. claimants have received an initial installment payment, and payment is in process for an additional 487 U.S. claimants.

Iraq remains a serious threat to international peace and security. I remain determined to see Iraq comply fully with all of its obligations under U.N. Security Council resolutions. My Administration will continue to sustain and strengthen sanctions until Iraq demonstrates its peaceful intentions through such compliance.

I appreciate the support of the Congress for our efforts and shall continue to keep the Congress informed about this important issue.

Sincerely,

William J. Clinton

320.

[Vol. 34, no. 6 (February 9, 1998): 190-198]

Letter to Congressional Leaders Reporting on Iraq
February 3, 1998

Dear Mr. Speaker: (Dear Mr. President:)

Consistent with the Authorization for Use of Military Force Against Iraq Resolution (Public Law 102-1) and as part of my effort to keep the Congress fully informed, I am reporting on the status of efforts to obtain Iraq's compliance with the resolutions adopted by the United Nations Security Council (UNSC). This report covers the period from November 26, 1997, to the present.

My last report included the U.N.-Iraq stand-off which began on October 29, 1997, when the Iraqi government announced its intention to expel all U.S. personnel working in Iraq for the U.N. Special Commission (UNSCOM). Iraq's apparent aim was to force UNSCOM's withdrawal or to significantly restrict its ability to function effectively and independently, thereby establishing an environment under which Iraq could restore its capacity to develop weapons of mass destruction (WMD) without restriction. In November, the members of the U.N. Security Council thwarted this effort through joint diplomacy and the use of Secretary Council resolutions—backed by the deployment of forces in the Gulf. This resulted in the Iraqi government's explicit commitment, on November 20, 1997, to allow UNSCOM inspectors, including those who are U.S. citizens, to return unhindered to their duties.

In violation of that commitment and of U.N. Security Council Resolution (UNSCR) 687 and subsequent resolutions, including 707, 1134, and 1137, Iraq has attempted again to dictate the composition of UNSCOM inspection teams and the terms of its compliance with Council resolutions. In addition, Iraq has persisted in its efforts to defy the Council by unilaterally imposing unacceptable conditions on the operations of UNSCOM. This report covering the last 60 days reflects the failure of the Government of Iraq to live up to its obligations under all applicable UNSC resolutions and its continued hindrance of UNSCOM's work.

In December 1997, the Iraqi government reiterated its longstanding refusal to allow any access to all so-called "Presidential" sites, and said it would limit access to so-called "sensitive" sites by UNSCOM inspectors.

On January 5, 1998, an inert rocket-propelled grenade struck a building in Baghdad that houses various U.N. elements, including UNSCOM headquarters, but caused no injuries. The Iraqi government denied responsibility but has yet to arrest any suspects.

On January 12, the Government of Iraq refused to cooperate with an UNSCOM inspection team, declaring that the team was dominated by too many "Anglo-Saxons". The team had been investigating, among other things, allegations that Iraq may have used human beings as experimental subjects in chemical and biological warfare development.

On January 17, the Iraqi government declared a Jihad (holy war) against U.N. sanctions and called for 1 million Iraqi citizens to undergo military training to prepare for any consequences.

During the last 60 days, UNSCOM launched two special inspection teams that once again targeted Iraq's "Concealment Mechanism" in order to ferret out WMD programs and documents that UNSCOM—and we—believe Iraq stubbornly retains. It became clear that the Iraqis had no intention of cooperating with these inspections as specifically called for in the most recent UNSCRs on the topic—Resolutions 1134 of October 23 and 1137 of November 12. The teams were stopped en route, denied access, and prevented from video-taping equipment movement or document-destruction activity at suspect sites.

Ambassador Butler, UNSCOM's Executive Director, traveled to Baghdad on December 12, 1997, and again on January 19, 1998, to attempt to obtain Iraqi assurance that UNSCOM can resume its work unhindered, including unfettered access to "Presidential" and "sensitive" sites. Following the January 19 meetings, the Iraqis continued to defy and challenge UNSCOM by refusing to discuss access to "Presidential" sites until after Technical Meeting talks have concluded in April. As Ambassador Butler reported to the Security Council on January 22, the talks were characterized by moments "of abuse and denunciation of UNSCOM and its professional officers; an attempt to apportion literally all blame to UNSCOM, past and present, for the fact that the disarmament task has not been completed and sanctions on Iraq remained in force." Throughout, the UNSC has expressed its support for UNSCOM and its mission in

five unanimous Presidential Statements since October 1997.

This record of intransigence is only the latest chapter in the long history of efforts by the Iraqi regime to flout its obligations under relevant UNSC resolutions. Without full disclosure and free access to all sites UNSCOM and the International Atomic Energy Agency (IAEA) wish to inspect, the ongoing monitoring and verification mandated by relevant UNSC resolutions, including Resolutions 687, 707 and 715, cannot effectively be conducted. UNSCOM must be allowed to continue to investigate all of Iraq's programs until it can verify with absolute certainty that all the equipment has been destroyed and that all the capabilities have been eliminated. Otherwise, Iraq eventually will be free to develop the capacity to strike at any city in the Middle East, delivering biological, chemical and possibly even nuclear weapons.

Biological/Chemical Weapons

Iraqi biological and chemical weapons are currently the most troubling issues for UNSCOM. This is due to the innate dual-use nature of the technology: biological and chemical agents can easily be hidden within civilian sectors, such as the pharmaceutical and pesticide industries. Iraq continues to prevent full and immediate access to sites suspected of chemical or biological warfare activities. UNSCOM is still unable to verify that all of Iraq's SCUD missile warheads filled with biological agents—anthrax and botulinum toxin—have been destroyed.

Nuclear Weapons and Delivery Systems

The Iraqi regime contends that UNSCOM and the IAEA should "close the books" on nuclear and missile inspections, but there are still many uncertainties and questions that need to be resolved. Iraq has failed to answer critical questions on nuclear weapons design and fabrication, procurement, and centrifuge enrichment; to provide a written description of its post-war nuclear weapons procurement program; and to account for major engine components, special warheads, missing propellants, and guidance instruments that could be used to assemble fully operational missiles.

U.S. Force Levels

The U.S. has led international efforts to secure UNSCOM the access and cooperation it must have to do its job. As a demonstration of our resolve, the aircraft carriers USS NIMITZ, USS GEORGE WASHINGTON, their accompanying battle group combatant ships, and additional combat aircraft have remained in the region. On January 15, the Government of the United Kingdom dispatched the aircraft carrier HMS INVINCIBLE and escort ships to the Gulf via the Red Sea.

United States force levels in the region include land- and carrier-based aircraft, surface warships, a Marine amphibious task force, a Patriot missile battalion, a mechanized battalion task force, and a mix of special operations forces deployed in support of US-CINCCENT operations. To enhance force protection throughout the region, additional military security personnel have been deployed for continuous rotation. USCINC-CENT continues to monitor closely the security situation in the region to ensure adequate force protection is provided for all deployed forces.

The U.S. and its coalition partners continue to enforce the no-fly zones over Iraq under Operation Northern Watch and Operation Southern Watch. In response to a series of Iraqi no-fly zone violations in October and November 1997, we increased the number of aircraft participating in these operations. There have been no observed no-fly zone violations during the period covered by this report. We have repeatedly made clear to the Government of Iraq and to all other relevant parties that the U.S. and its partners will continue to enforce both no-fly zones.

United Nations Security Council Resolution 949, adopted in October 1994, demands that Iraq not use its military or any other forces to threaten its neighbors or U.N. operations in Iraq and that it not redeploy troops or enhance its military capacity in southern Iraq. In view of Saddam's accumulating record of brutality and unreliability, it is prudent to retain a significant U.S. force presence in the region to deter Iraq and respond rapidly to possible Iraqi aggression or threats against its neighbors.

We again take note of and welcome H. Res. 322 of November 13, 1997, expressing the sense of the House that the U.S. should act to resolve the crisis in a manner that assures full Iraqi compliance with UNSC resolutions regarding the destruction of Iraq's capability to produce and deliver WMD. While the increased forces in the region give us a wide range of military options we remain committed to exhausting all diplomatic options before resorting to other alternatives.

Sanctions

United Nations sanctions against Iraq were imposed as the result of Iraq's invasion of Kuwait. It has been necessary to maintain them because of Iraq's failure to comply with all relevant UNSC resolutions, including those ensuring the destruction, removal, or rendering harmless of Iraq's WMD.

The Iraqi regime continues to insist on the need for rapid lifting of the sanctions regime, despite its record of noncompliance with its obligations under relevant resolutions, out of alleged concern for the well-being of the Iraqi people, claiming that malnutrition and inadequate medical care are the direct result of internationally imposed sanctions.

To the contrary, since their inception, the sanctions against Iraq have exempted food and medicines—evidence of the concern of the U.S. and the international community for the welfare of the Iraqi people. In August 1991, when Iraq claimed that it was unable to pay for its food needs, the Security Council adopted UNSCR 706 (and later 712), authorizing Iraq to sell limited amounts of petroleum on the international market, with the proceeds to be used to purchase humanitarian supplies and to fund vital U.N. activities regarding Iraq. The Government of Iraq, however, ignored the needs of its own people by refusing to accept UNSCR's 706 and 712.

In April 1995 the Security Council proposed a new oil-for-food offer to Iraq in UNSCR 986, sponsored by the U.S. and others. UNSCR 986 authorized the sale of up to $1 billion of oil every 90 days for a total of $2 billion during a 180-day period for Iraq to purchase food, medicines, and other "humanitarian items" for its people, and to fund specified U.N. activities regarding Iraq. The Government of Iraq delayed implementation of UNSCR 986 for a year and a half, until December 1996.

Since December 1996, the Iraqi regime has continued to obstruct and delay the relief plan. The regime delayed oil sales for two months in June and July 1997 under the second phase of the program (UNSCR 1111), and again for over one month in December 1997 and January 1998 under the third phase (UNSCR 1143).

The United States has consistently made clear our openness to improving the oil-for-food program to better meet the essential needs of Iraq's civilian population. The Secretary General has just submitted a report to this effect to the Council. We are prepared to consider carefully and favorably the Secretary General's suggestions to improve and expand the program. Expanding 986 would serve our humanitarian and strategic interests. First, the sanctions regime is aimed at the threat Saddam poses—not the Iraqi people. We should do whatever we can to ease their plight, consistent with our interests. Second, expanding 986 will make it more difficult for Saddam to use the plight of his people as a propaganda card in the Middle East and so help us shore up the anti-Saddam coalition. Third, by expanding oil-for-food, we will broaden and strengthen the U.N.'s grip on Iraq's revenues and expenditures, tightening the leash on Saddam and making it more difficult for him to divert funds to the military and WMD.

Implementation of UNSCR 1051 continues. It provides for a mechanism to monitor Iraq's efforts to reacquire proscribed weapons capabilities by requiring Iraq to notify a joint UNSCOM/IAEA unit in advance of any imports of dual-use items. Similarly, U.N. members must provide timely notification of exports to Iraq of dual-use items.

The Multinational Interception Force (MIF), operating under the authority of UNSCR 665, is aggressively enforcing U.N. sanctions in the Gulf. The U.S. Navy is the single largest component of this international naval force, augmented by ships and aircraft from Australia, Canada, Belgium, The Netherlands, New Zealand, and the United Kingdom. Member states of the Gulf Cooperation Council support the MIF by providing logistical support and shipriders who ensure that merchant ships do not deviate from their recorded courses to legal ports and by pulling vessels caught violating sanctions into member state ports.

Since my last report, the MIF has intercepted five sanctions violators in the Gulf. Ships involved in smuggling often utilize the territorial seas of Iran to avoid MIF inspections. We have given detailed reports of these illegal activities to the U.N. Sanctions Committee in New York.

The volume of illegal smuggling of petroleum products from Iraq continues to increase. Iraq is working to improve loading facilities in the Shatt Al Arab waterway and the continuing cooperation of the smugglers with Iran frustrates the naval forces which are restricted to international waters to carry out their duties. We estimate that over 200,000 metric tons of gasoil and other petroleum cargoes leave Iraq illegally each month. Profits from this illegal trade support Saddam at the expense of the Iraqi people.

The United Nations Compensation Commission (UNCC), established pursuant to UNSCR 687 and 692, continues to resolve claims against Iraq arising from Iraq's unlawful invasion and occupation of Kuwait. The UNCC has issued almost 1.3 million awards worth approximately $6 billion. Thirty percent of the proceeds from the oil sales permitted by UNSCR's 986, 1111, and 1143 have been allocated to the Compensation Fund to pay awards and to finance operations of the UNCC. To the extent that money is available in the Compensation Fund, initial payments to each claimant are authorized for awards in the order in which the UNCC has approved them, in installments of $2,500. To date, 455 U.S. claimants have received an initial installment payment, and payment is in process for an additional 323 U.S. claimants.

Human Rights

The human rights situation throughout Iraq continues to be cause for grave concern. Reports that the Government of Iraq used humans as experimental subjects in its chemical and biological weapons programs have been noted above. Credible reports from numerous, independent sources indicate that the Government of Iraq also may have summarily executed anywhere from 800 to 1500 political detainees in November and December 1997. Opposition groups have alleged that many of those killed were serving sentences of 15-20 years for such crimes as insulting the regime or membership in an opposition political party. Max van der Stoel, Special Rapporteur for Iraq for the U.N. Human Rights Commission and Bacre Ndiaye, the Commission's Special Rapporteur for Summary Executions, are investigating these reports.

Iraq's repression of its Shi'a population continues, with policies that are destroying the Marsh Arabs' way of life in southern Iraq and the ecology of the southern marshes. Iraq continues to stall and obfuscate rather than work in good faith toward accounting for more than 600 Kuwaitis and third-country nationals who disappeared during or after the occupation of Kuwait, and nearly 5,000 Iranian prisoners of war captured by Iraq during the Iran-Iraq war. The Government of Iraq shows no sign of complying with UNSCR 688, which demands that Iraq cease the repression of its own people. The U.N. Human Rights Commission's Special Rapporteur on Iraq reported to the General Assembly his particular concern that extra-judicial, summary or arbitrary executions and the practice of torture continue to occur in Iraq.

Led by various independent Iraqi opposition groups and nongovernmental organizations, the INDICT campaign—which seeks to document crimes against humanity and other violations of international humanitarian law committed by the Iraqi regime—continues to gain momentum.

Regarding northern Iraq, the cease-fire between the Kurdish parties, established November 24, 1997, as the result of U.S. efforts, continues to hold. In recent weeks, both Massoud Barzani, leader of the Kurdistan Democratic Party (KDP) and Jalal Talabani, leader of the Patriotic Union of Kurdistan (PUK) have made positive, forward-looking statements on political reconciliation, which may signal a willingness to settle some of their differences. We will continue our efforts to reach a permanent settlement through mediation in order to help the people of northern Iraq find the permanent, stable accommodation which they

deserve, and to minimize the opportunities for Baghdad and Tehran to insert themselves into the conflict and threaten Iraqi citizens in this region. The Peace Monitoring Force—sponsored by the U.S., Great Britain and Turkey under the Ankara process and comprising Iraqi Turkomans and Assyrians—remains in garrison.

Conclusion

Iraq remains a serious threat to international peace and security. As I told the American people in my recent State of the Union address, our country is united in its view that Saddam Hussein cannot defy the will of the world. He has used weapons of mass destruction before. We are determined to deny him the capacity to use them again. I remain determined to see Iraq comply fully with all of its obligations under U.N. Security Council resolutions.

I appreciate the support of the Congress for our efforts and shall continue to keep the Congress informed about this important issue.

Sincerely,

William J. Clinton

321.

[Vol. 34, no. 26 (June 29, 1998): 1215-1220]

Letter to Congressional Leaders Reporting on Iraq's Compliance With United Nations Security Council Resolutions June 24, 1998

Dear Mr. Speaker: (Dear Mr. President:)

Consistent with the Authorization for Use of Military Force Against Iraq Resolution (Public Law 102-1) and as part of my effort to keep the Congress fully informed, I am reporting on the status of efforts to obtain Iraq's compliance with the resolutions adopted by the United Nations Security Council (UNSC). This report covers the period from April 3 to the present.

Introduction

During the 60-day period covered by this report, Iraq continued to provide access to U.N. weapons inspectors as required under the terms of the February 23 Annan-Aziz MOU and UNSC Resolution 1154. Travel restrictions on Iraq imposed under UNSC Resolution 1137 of November 12, 1997 expired by their terms after UNSCOM Executive Chairman Butler reported that Iraq was complying with access requirements. In accordance with UNSC Resolution 1134, regular sanctions reviews have resumed. However, Iraq's continued failure to meet its obligations under UNSC Resolution 687 and other relevant resolutions led the Security Council to conclude on April 27 that Iraq still had not met the conditions necessary to enable the Council to lift sanctions. Ongoing UNSCOM and IAEA inspections continue to test Iraq's long-term intentions with regard to providing full access and full disclosure to U.N. weapons inspectors.

We continue to support the international community's efforts to provide for the humanitarian needs of the Iraqi people through the "oil-for-food" program and other humanitarian efforts. Resolution 1153, which was adopted by the UNSC on February 20, expands the "oil-for-food" program considerably by raising the ceiling of permitted Iraqi oil exports to $5.2 billion every 180 days and by authorizing repairs to Iraq's degraded petroleum, health, education, and sanitation infrastructure under strict U.N. supervision in accordance with a prioritized distribution plan.

During the period covered by this report, the humanitarian needs of the Iraqi people were addressed through Phase Three of the original "oil-for-food" plan in accordance with UNSCRs 986 and 1143. The Iraqi government only recently produced an acceptable distribution plan to implement UNSCR 1153.

On May 1, I signed into law the 1998 Supplemental Appropriations and Rescissions Act. This legislation provides funding for Radio Free Europe/Radio Liberty to initiate a surrogate broadcast service for the Iraqi people. It also provides funding for efforts to support the democratic Iraqi opposition in presenting a credible alternative to the present Iraqi regime and compiling information to support the indictment of Iraqi officials for war crimes. These new programs will enable us to redouble our work with the Iraqi opposition to support their efforts to build a plural-

istic, peaceful Iraq that observes the international rule of law and respects basic human rights. Such an Iraq would have little trouble regaining it rightful place in the region and in the international community.

The United States will keep a significant military presence in the region to provide the full range of military options necessary to deter Iraqi aggression, to ensure that UNSC resolutions are enforced, and to deal with other contingencies that may arise.

U.S. and Coalition Force Levels in the Gulf Region

In view of Saddam's record of brutality and unreliability, it is prudent to retain a significant force presence in the region to deter Iraq. United States and allied forces now in the region are prepared to deal with contingencies. This gives us the capability to respond rapidly to possible Iraqi aggression or threats against its neighbors. As we make the force adjustments mentioned below, we are strengthening a rapid redeployment capability to supplement our forces in the Gulf. Our cruise missile force will be twice the pre-crisis level. In addition, we will be able to double again our cruise missile force in days. Once these moves are completed, this capability will allow for a swift, powerful strike.

The aircraft carrier USS JOHN C. STENNIS and her accompanying battle group combatant ships and combat aircraft remain in the region as United States force levels are being reduced. The aircraft carriers USS INDEPENDENCE and USS GEORGE WASHINGTON and their accompanying battle group combatant ships left the region, as scheduled. Once force level adjustments are completed, U.S. forces will include land and carrier-based aircraft, surface warships, a Marine amphibious task force, Patriot missile battalions, a mechanized battalion task force and a mix of special operations forces deployed in support of USCINCCENT operations. To enhance force protection throughout the region, additional military security personnel are also deployed. During the crisis, U.S. forces were augmented by HMS ILLUSTRIOUS and accompanying ships from the United Kingdom.

During our successful effort to compel Iraq's compliance with relevant UNSC resolutions earlier this year, the United Kingdom and a number of other nations pledged forces. Although all of the members of this international effort sought a peaceful diplomatic resolution of the crisis, all showed their resolve to achieve our common objective by military force if that becomes necessary.

Twenty nations deployed forces to the region or readied their forces for contingency deployment. Another 12 nations offered important access, basing, overflight, and other assistance essential for the multinational effort. Still others identified force contributions that were held in reserve for deployment should the need arise. For those nations with forces deployed during the crisis, most of these governments redeployed their forces back home after the crisis in keeping with our own force adjustments. These nations have made clear their willingness to repeat this deployment should Iraq again challenge the international community.

Operation Northern Watch and Operation Southern Watch

The United States and coalition partners continue to enforce the no-fly zones over Iraq under Operation Northern Watch and Operation Southern Watch. In response to a series of Iraqi no-fly zone violations in October and November 1997, we increased the number of aircraft participating in these operations. Since then, there have been no observed no-fly zone violations. In early April, we restored the preexisting level of aircraft deployed to Northern Watch. We have made clear to the Government of Iraq and to all other relevant parties that the United States and coalition partners will continue to enforce both no-fly zones.

The Maritime Interception Force

The Maritime Interception Force (MIF), operating under the authority of UNSCR 665, vigorously enforces U.N. sanctions in the Gulf. The U.S. Navy is the single largest component of this multinational force, but it is frequently augmented by ships and aircraft from Australia, Canada, Belgium, The Netherlands, New Zealand, and the United Kingdom. Today in the Gulf, ships from Canada, The Netherlands, and the United Kingdom have joined with us in maritime patrols. Member states of the Gulf Cooperation Council support the MIF by providing logistical support and shipriders and by accepting vessels diverted for violating U.N. sanctions against Iraq.

Since my last report, the MIF has intercepted several vessels involved in illegal smuggling from Iraq. Although petroleum products comprise most of the prohibited traffic, the MIF has recently diverted vessels engaged in date smuggling as well. Ships involved in smuggling have often utilized the territorial seas of Iran to avoid MIF inspections. We have provided detailed reports of these illegal activities to the U.N. Sanctions Committee in New York.

The level of petroleum smuggling from Iraq appears to be in a state of flux. For several weeks, Iran ceased allowing gasoil smugglers to use its territorial seas to avoid the MIF inspections, causing a dramatic decrease in the level of gasoil smuggling. In recent weeks, however, we have noted ships once again using Iranian waters with the apparent aid of the Iranian Revolutionary Guard forces that operate in small boats near the mouth of the Shatt Al Arab waterway. It is too early to tell what the long-term policy of Iran will be in this matter, although we are hopeful that it will take the necessary steps to curb U.N. sanctions violations occurring within its territorial seas.

Our forces continue to benefit from recent actions by the United Arab Emirates that make it difficult for sanctions violators to operate in UAE territory. We will continue to work with the Emirates to find ways to thwart the significant sanctions-busting trade which has historically been bound for UAE ports. As noted in my last report, the UAE has significantly increased its level of cooperation with the MIF. These efforts have resulted in an increase in the number of ships caught with illegal cargoes. In addition, the UAE has prohibited the use of tankers, barges, and other vessel types to transport petroleum products to UAE ports and through its waters or to store such products there. While it is still too early to determine the full effect of these measures, we are hopeful that these actions will deal a significant blow to sanctions-busting activity in the region.

Biological and Chemical Weapons

Iraqi biological and chemical weapons remain the most troubling issues for UN-SCOM. This is due to the innate dual-use nature of the technology; it can easily be hidden within civilian industries, such as the pharmaceutical industry for biological agents and the pesticide industry for chemical agents. Iraq continues to resist making a full and complete declaration of its biological weapons programs, as required by UNSCR 707.

Following its March technical evaluation meetings, UNSCOM concluded that Iraq has not provided a clear statement of the current status of the programs. Iraq's declaration still contains major mistakes, inconsistencies, and gaps. It may substantially understate Iraq's production of bulk biological weapons agents. UNSCOM is still unable to verify that all of Iraq's SCUD missile warheads filled with biological agents—anthrax, botulinum toxin, and aflatoxin—have been destroyed. UN-SCOM also suspects Iraq may be concealing additional, as-yet undisclosed, biological weapons research or development programs.

Nuclear Weapons and Delivery Systems

On May 14, the UNSC adopted a Presidential Statement on the most recent UN-SCOM and IAEA reports about Iraq's nuclear program. The Statement notes that the IAEA's investigations over the past several years have yielded a technically coherent picture of Iraq's clandestine nuclear program, but that all outstanding unanswered technical and substantive questions must be answered before the UNSC will authorize the IAEA to move from inspections to ongoing monitoring and verification in the nuclear field. While the bulk of its resources are now devoted to monitoring, the IAEA will continue to exercise its right to investigate any aspect of Iraq's nuclear program. The IAEA, in a recent report, points out that Iraq still has not provided information requested about certain sites, that concerns remain as to the completeness, accuracy, and internal consistency of Iraq's nuclear declaration and that Iraq has failed to enact laws prohibiting certain activities.

Iraq's Concealment Mechanisms

From March 26 to April 2 UNSCOM conducted inspections of the so-called "Presidential Sites." The inspectors reported that the sites appeared to have been "sanitized" prior to their visits, and, as anticipated, they discovered no materials related to Iraq's WMD programs during these inspections. In accordance with relevant UNSC resolutions, UNSCOM and the IAEA must be allowed to continue to investigate all aspects of Iraq's prohibited programs until they can verify that all relevant components have been destroyed under international supervision, and that all remaining capabilities have been eliminated. Without such verification, Iraq could develop the ability to strike at any city in the region—and beyond the region—with devastating biological, chemical, and possibly even nuclear weapons.

Dual-Use Imports

Resolution 1051 established a joint UN-SCOM/IAEA unit to monitor Iraq's imports of allowed dual-use items. Iraq must notify the unit before it imports specific items which can be used in both weapons of mass destruction and civilian applications. Similarly, U.N. members must provide timely notification of exports to Iraq of such dual-use items.

We continue to be concerned that Iraq's land borders are extremely porous. Iraq continues substantial trade with its neighbors. There is significant potential for evasion of sanctions by land routes, giving additional weight to our position that UNSCOM must have full and unconditional access to all locations, and be allowed to inspect and monitor Iraqi compliance over time.

The U.N.'s "Oil-for-Food" Program

On February 20, the Security Council adopted Resolution 1153, which raises from $2.0 billion to $5.2 billion the amount of oil Iraq is authorized to sell every 180 days. Resolution 1153 provides that the nutritional and health requirements of the Iraqi people are the top priority. My Administration's support for Resolution 1153 is fully consistent with long-standing U.S. policy. Since 1990, at the height of the Gulf War, the United States has held that the international community's dispute is with Iraq's leadership, not its people. The Security Council proposed an "oil-for-food" program in 1991 (UNSCR 706/712), which Iraq rejected. A similar program (UNSCR 986) was eventually accepted by Iraq in 1996. We supported the expansion of the "oil-for-food" program under UNSCR 1153 because it will provide additional humanitarian assistance to the Iraqi people, under strict U.N. supervision, without benefiting the regime.

Since the beginning of the "oil-for-food" program, we have consistently worked with the U.N. and other U.N. member states to find ways to improve the program's effectiveness to better meet the humanitarian needs of Iraq's civilian population. Iraq, however, has frequently failed to provide the full cooperation necessary to ensure that the program functions smoothly. For example, during calendar year 1997, the Government of Iraq refused to pump oil under UNSCR 986 for more than three months, all the while blaming the U.N. and the United States for disruptions in the flow of food and medicine which it had caused. The Iraqi government, after much prodding by the U.N. Secretary General's office, finally submitted a satisfactory distribution plan to the U.N. as called for by UNSCR 1153.

Resolution 1153 calls for an independent assessment of Iraq's oil infrastructure to determine whether it can export $5.2 billion in oil in a 180-day period, as provided for in the resolution. This report, which was submitted to the UNSC on April 15, recommended that the Sanctions Committee approve up to $300 million worth of repairs to Iraq's oil infrastructure during the period covered by UNSCR 1153. The United States has expressed its intention to support those oil infrastructure repairs needed to fund the expanded humanitarian program, provided these repairs can be carried out in a manner fully consistent with the humanitarian objectives of UNSCR 1153, and that the U.N. is able to properly monitor all aspects of the repair process. We are continuing to work with members of the Security Council to resolve these concerns.

Resolution 1153 also maintains the separate program for northern Iraq, administered directly by the U.N. in consultation with the local population. This program receives 13 to 15 percent of the funds generated under the "oil-for-food" program. The United States strongly supports this provision. The separate northern program was established because of the Baghdad regime's proven disregard for the humanitarian condition of the Kurdish, Assyrian, and Turkomen minorities of northern Iraq and its readiness to apply the most brutal forms of repression against them. The well-documented series of chemical weapons attacks a decade ago by the government against civilians in the north is only one example of this brutality. In northern Iraq, where Baghdad does not exercise control, the "oil-for-food" program has been able to operate unhindered. The Kurdish factions are seeking to set aside their differences to work together so that UNSCR 1153 is implemented as efficiently as possible. As a result, the contrast between the north and the rest of the country is striking.

The U.N. must carefully monitor implementation of Resolution 1153. The Iraqi government continues to insist on the need for rapid lifting of the sanctions regime, despite its clear record of noncompliance with its obligations under relevant U.N. resolutions—a record which was unanimously acknowledged during the Security Council's 38th sanctions review on April 27. We will continue to work with the U.N. Secretariat, the Security Council, and others in the international community to ensure that the humanitarian needs of the Iraqi people are met while denying any political or economic benefits to the Baghdad regime.

The Human Rights Situation in Iraq

The human rights situation throughout Iraq continues to be a cause for grave concern. Summary, arbitrary, and extrajudicial executions remain a primary concern. On March 10, U.N. Special Rapporteur for Iraq, Max Van der Stoel, reported that his ongoing investigation had revealed that "there is strong evidence that hundreds of prisoners have been executed in Abu Gharaib and Radwaniyah prisons since August 1997." According to credible reports, many of those killed were serving sentences of 15-20 years for such crimes as insulting the regime or being members of an opposition political party. Families in Iraq reportedly received the bodies of the executed which bore, in some cases, clear signs of torture. In April, the U.N. Human Rights Commission issued a strong condemnatory resolution describing these and other ongoing Iraqi human rights violations. The resolution extended the Special Rapporteur's mandate and condemned the "all-pervasive repression and oppression" perpetrated by the Government of Iraq.

In southern Iraq, the government continues to repress the Shi'a population, destroying the Marsh Arabs' way of life and the unique ecology of the southern marshes. In the north, outside the Kurdish-controlled areas, the government continues the forced expulsion of tens of thousands of ethnic Kurds and Turkomans from Kirkuk and other cities. The government continues to stall and obfuscate attempts to account for more than 600 Kuwaitis and third-country nationals who disappeared at the hands of Iraqi authorities during or after the occupation of Kuwait. In the course of recent prisoner exchanges brokered by the ICRC, Iraq has released more than 300 Iranian prisoners of war taken during the Iran-Iraq war in exchange for 5,600 Iraqi POWs. Yet the Government of Iraq shows no sign of complying with UNSCR 688, which demands that Iraq cease the repression of its own people.

Northern Iraq: PUK-KDP Relations

In northern Iraq, the cease-fire between the Kurdish parties, established in November 1997 as the result of U.S. efforts, continues to hold. Both Massoud Barzani, leader of the Kurdistan Democratic Party (KDP) and Jalal Talabani, leader of the Patriotic Union of Kurdistan (PUK) have made positive, forward-looking statements on political reconciliation, and talks between the two groups are now entering their sixth round. We will continue our efforts to reach a permanent reconciliation through mediation in order to help the people of northern Iraq find the permanent, stable settlement which they deserve, and to minimize the opportunities for Baghdad and Tehran to insert themselves into the conflict and threaten Iraqi citizens in this region. Baghdad continues to pressure the two groups to enter into negotiations.

The United Nations Compensation Commission

The United Nations Compensation Commission (UNCC), established pursuant to UNSCRs 687 and 692, continues to resolve claims against Iraq arising from Iraq's unlawful invasion and occupation of Kuwait. The UNCC has issued almost 1.3 million awards worth $6 billion. Thirty percent of the proceeds from the oil sales permitted by UNSCRs 986, 1111, and 1143 have been allocated to the Compensation Fund to pay awards and to finance operations of the UNCC. To the extent that money is available in the Compensation Fund, initial payments to each claimant are authorized for awards in the order in which the UNCC has approved them, in installments of $2,500. To date, 757 U.S. claimants have received an initial installment payment, and payment is still in process for approximately another 58 U.S. claimants.

Conclusion

Iraq remains a serious threat to international peace and security. I remain determined to see Iraq comply fully with all of its obligations under UNSC resolutions. The United States looks forward to the day when Iraq rejoins the family of nations as a responsible and law-abiding member.

I appreciate the support of the Congress for our efforts and shall continue to keep the Congress informed about this important issue.

Sincerely,

William J. Clinton

322.

[Vol. 34, no. 36 (September 7, 1998): 1710-1717]

Letter to Congressional Leaders Reporting on Iraq's Compliance With United Nations Security Council Resolutions September 3, 1998

Dear Mr. Speaker: (Dear Mr. President:)

Consistent with the Authorization for Use of Military Force Against Iraq Resolution (Public Law 102-1) and as part of my effort to keep the Congress fully informed, I am reporting on the status of efforts to obtain Iraq's compliance with the resolutions adopted by the United Nations Security Council (UNSC). This report covers the period from June 24 to the present.

Introduction

From June 24 until August 5, Iraq had provided site access to U.N. weapons inspectors, as required under UNSC resolutions and reaffirmed under the terms of the February 23 Secretary General/Tariq Aziz MOU and UNSC Resolution 1154. In June, UNSCOM inspectors presented a work plan to Iraq to delineate areas of concern and elements that Iraq needed to disclose. However, in June, UNSCOM revealed that it had found evidence of Iraqi weaponization of VX nerve agent and in July, Iraq refused to turn over a document accounting for use of CW during the Iran-Iraq war. On August 3-4, when Chairman Butler was in Iraq to discuss phase two of the work plan, the Iraqi Deputy Prime Minister claimed that Iraq was fully "disarmed" and demanded that this be reported to the Council; Butler refused, and subsequently departed Baghdad.

On August 5, Iraq declared that it was suspending all cooperation with UNSCOM and the IAEA, except some limited monitoring activities. On August 6, the Security Council President issued a press statement which noted that Iraq's action contravenes the February 23 MOU and relevant Security Council resolutions. On August 11/12, the IAEA and UNSCOM sent letters to the Security Council that noted that Iraq's decision to suspend cooperation with them halted "all of the disarmament activities" of UNSCOM and placed limitations on the inspection and monitoring activities of both organizations. On August 18, the Council President replied in writing to UNSCOM and IAEA on the Council's behalf reiterating full support for the full implementation of their mandates and underscoring Iraq's obligation to cooperate in the conduct of their activities, including inspections. Chairman Butler wrote to the Iraqi regime August 19 expressing his willingness to resume activity, but that offer was rebuffed.

On August 20, the Security Council met to conduct the periodic review of Iraq's compliance with relevant Security Council resolutions. It stated that "the necessary conditions do not exist for the modification of the regime established" in relevant resolutions. Moreover, the Security Council "reiterates that the decision by Iraq to suspend cooperation with UNSCOM and the IAEA (on August 5) is totally unacceptable" and that it "views with extreme concern the continuing refusal by the Government of Iraq to rescind its decision." The United States is working with other Security Council members to suspend subsequent periodic reviews until Iraq reverses course and resumes cooperation with UNSCOM and the IAEA.

The cornerstone of U.S. policy is to contain Iraq and prevent it from threatening regional peace and security. To that end, the United States has supported UNSCOM since its inception and continues to do so, as an integral part of our policy to contain Iraq and disarm it of its WMD. We have consistently worked to uphold the principle that UNSCOM must be able to do its job, free of Iraqi restrictions and impediments. That includes inspections wherever, whenever, and however the Executive Chairman of UNSCOM directs. There have been allegations recently that the United States impeded some kinds of inspections since last fall. In fact, the international effort to secure full access for UNSCOM and the IAEA last fall and winter was led by the United States. Since early August, the United States has again led the effort to reverse Iraq's decision blocking UNSCOM activities. Decisions on how UNSCOM does its job, including timing, locations and modalities for inspections, are the Chairman's to make. As Chairman Butler stated on August 14, "Consultations on policy matters take place regularly between the Executive Chairman and Council members, but all operational decisions are taken by the Executive Chairman (of UNSCOM) who has not been given and would find it invidious were any attempt made to direct his operational decisions or to micromanage the day-to-day work of the Special Commission."

Iraq's refusal to cooperate with UNSCOM and the IAEA is totally unacceptable; Iraq must meet its international obligations. In the first instance, the Council and the Secretary General must respond effectively to Iraq's flagrant challenge to their authority. We are working with Council members to ensure that there is a clear, united and forceful U.N. response to Iraq's actions. If the Council fails to persuade the Iraqi regime to resume cooperation, all other options are on the table.

We continue to support the international community's efforts to provide for the humanitarian needs of the Iraqi people through the "oil-for-food" program and other humanitarian efforts. On May 27, 1998, Iraq presented a distribution plan for the implementation of Resolution 1153, which had been adopted on February 20. Under phase three of the "oil-for-food" program, which ran from December 3, 1997, through June 2, 1998, $1.1 billion worth of humanitarian goods were approved for export to Iraq. Under the current phase, phase four, which began in June, the U.N. Sanctions Committee has approved the purchase of over $562 million worth of humanitarian goods. United States companies can participate in the "oil-for-food" program and over $165 million worth of contracts for U.S. firms have been approved since the program began.

On June 26, the Secretary of State reported to the Congress on plans to establish a program to support the democratic opposition in Iraq, as required by section 10008 of the 1998 Supplemental Appropriations and Rescissions Act (Public Law 105-174). Opposition leaders and their representatives have been generally receptive to the focus on the central themes of building a consensus on the transition from dictatorship to pluralism, conveying to the U.N. opposition views on Iraqi noncompliance with U.N. resolutions and compiling information to support the indictment of Iraqi officials for war crimes. The new Radio Free Iraq service, also funded by that Act, is preparing to broadcast directly to the Iraqi people under the direction of Radio Free Europe/Radio Liberty. These new programs will help us encourage the Iraqi people to build a pluralistic, peaceful Iraq that observes the international rule of law and respects basic human rights. Such an Iraq would have little trouble regaining its rightful place in the region and in the international community.

The United States maintains a significant military presence in the region in order to provide the full range of military options necessary to deter Iraqi aggression, to ensure that UNSC resolutions are enforced, and to deal with other contingencies that may arise.

US and Coalition Force Levels in the Gulf Region

In view of Saddam's record of aggressive behavior, it is prudent to retain a significant force presence in the region to deter Iraq and deal with any threat it might pose to its neighbors. The U.S. and allied forces now in the region are prepared to deal with all contingencies. We have the capability to respond rapidly to possible Iraqi aggression. We have restructured our in-theater force levels since my last report. We will continue to maintain a robust force posture, and moreover, have established a rapid reinforcement capability to supplement our forces in the Gulf when needed. Our cruise missile force is twice the pre-October 1997 level, a number that can be augmented significantly within days. Our contingency plans allow us the capability for a swift, powerful strike.

The aircraft carrier USS ABRAHAM LINCOLN and accompanying combatant ships and aircraft are on station in the Gulf today. Our forces in the region include land and carrier-based air-craft, surface warships, a Marine expeditionary unit, a Patriot missile battalion, a mechanized battalion task force and a mix of special operations forces deployed in support of USCINCCENT operations. To enhance force protection throughout the region, additional military security personnel are also deployed.

Operation Northern Watch and Operation Southern Watch

The United States and coalition partners continue to enforce the no-fly zones over Iraq under Operation Northern Watch and Operation Southern Watch. There have been no observed no-fly zone violations. However, on June 30, U.S. forces responded to an Iraqi "threat radar" and subsequently defended the coalition forces by firing an anti-radiation (HARM) missile. We have made clear to Iraq and to all other relevant parties that the United

States and coalition partners will continue to enforce both no-fly zones. The no-fly zones remain in effect.

The Maritime Interception Force

The Maritime Interception Force (MIF), operating under the authority of UNSC Resolution 665, vigorously enforces U.N. sanctions in the Gulf. The U.S. Navy is the single largest component of this multinational force, but it is frequently augmented by ships and aircraft from Australia, Canada, Belgium, The Netherlands, New Zealand, and the United Kingdom. Today in the Gulf, ships and aircraft from Canada and the United Kingdom are operating with us in maritime patrols. Member states of the Gulf Cooperation Council support the MIF by providing logistical support and shipriders and by accepting vessels diverted for violating U.N. sanctions against Iraq.

The MIF continues to intercept vessels involved in illegal smuggling from Iraq. In late August, we conducted stepped-up operations in the far northern Gulf in the shallow waters near the major Iraqi waterways. These operations severely disrupted smuggling operations in the region. Since the beginning of the year, over thirty vessels have been detained for violations of the embargo and sent to ports in the Gulf for enforcement actions by the GCC. Kuwait and the UAE, two countries adjacent to the smuggling routes, have also stepped up their enforcement efforts and have recently intercepted and detained vessels involved in sanctions violations. Although petroleum products comprise most of the prohibited traffic, the MIF has recently diverted vessels engaged in date smuggling as well. Smuggling into Iraq is also a target for MIF patrols. One additional difficulty remains in our effort to enforce U.N. sanctions. Ships involved in smuggling have often utilized the territorial seas of Iran to avoid MIF inspections. We have recently provided detailed reports of these illegal activities to the U.N. sanctions Committee in New York.

Chemical Weapons

Despite major progress reported by UNSCOM in accounting for SCUD CBW warheads during this period, the Iraqis have taken a giant step backward by continuing to deny the weaponization of VX nerve agent. This denial is in direct contravention of the finding for UNSCOM by the U.S. Army Edgewood Arsenal of stabilized VX nerve agent in SCUD missile warhead fragments recovered by UNSCOM in Iraq. France and Switzerland are now examining further samples taken in Iraq. They may not report results to UNSCOM until late September.

However, we, UNSCOM Executive Chairman Butler, and a team of international experts gathered by Butler are unanimously confident of the scientific accuracy of the Edgewood results—which Butler has declared publicly. Iraq is lying today about VX.

While the Iraqis provided new documents to help account for R-400 aerial bombs used for chemical weapons, they have failed to provide the needed accounting for missing 155mm mustard-filled shells.

On July 22, 1998, UNSCOM reported in a letter to the President of the Security Council that Iraq had refused to allow an UNSCOM chief inspector to take, or even copy, a document found in Iraqi air force headquarters that gave an accounting of chemical munitions used during the Iran-Iraq war. This document would be of great value in helping UNSCOM establish a true material balance for Iraqi chemical munitions—a mandatory task for UNSCOM. During Butler's aborted visit to Iraq August 3-4, the Iraqi Deputy Prime Minister told Ambassador Butler that Iraq would never give it to the Commission. This evidence directly contradicts the Iraqi claim that it has given UNSCOM all the information it has.

Biological Weapons

In July 1998, UNSCOM assembled yet another group of international experts to meet with Iraqi counterparts for review of Iraqi declarations on the biological weapons program. And again, the Iraqis presented no new material. The experts thus found, again, that Iraq's declarations are not adequate for credible verification. This conclusion covered weapons (SCUD missile BW warheads, R-400 BW bombs, drop-tanks to be filled with BW, and spray devices for BW), production of BW agents (botulinum toxin, anthrax, aflatoxin, and wheat cover smut), and BW agent growth media.

The report of this UNSCOM-250 mission of international experts recommended to the UNSCOM Executive Chairman that no further verification of Iraq's declarations be conducted until Iraq commits itself to provide new and substantive information, stating that any other approach would be counterproductive.

Long-Range Missiles

UNSCOM Executive Chairman Richard Butler reported to the Security Council on August 5 that UNSCOM and Iraq had made significant progress in the accounting of both CBW and conventional SCUD warheads, as well as the material balance of major components for SCUD engine production. However, no progress was reported in accounting for the unique SCUD propellant possessed by Iraq, and the Iraqi Deputy Prime Minister refuses to allow further discussion of Iraq's concealment program, including the hiding of SCUD warheads.

Nuclear Weapons

In an interim report to the UNSC July 29, the IAEA said that Iraq had provided no new information regarding outstanding issues and concerns. The IAEA said while it has a "technically coherent picture" of Iraq's nuclear program, Iraq has never been fully transparent and its lack of transparency compounds remaining uncertainties. The IAEA noted Iraq claims to have no further documentation on such issues as weapons design engineering drawings, experimental data, and drawings received from foreign sources in connection with Iraq's centrifuge enrichment program. The IAEA also reported that Iraq said it was "unsuccessful" in its efforts to locate verifiable documentation of the abandonment of the nuclear program. Iraq has failed to pass the measures required under UNSC Resolution 715 to implement UNSC Resolutions 687, 707 and other relevant resolutions, including the penal laws required to enforce them.

Dual-Use Imports

Resolution 1051 established a joint UNSCOM/ IAEA unit to monitor Iraq's imports of allowed dual-use items. Iraq must notify the unit before it imports specific items which can be used in both weapons of mass destruction and civilian applications. Similarly, U.N. members must provide timely notification of exports to Iraq of such dual-use items.

We continue to be concerned that Iraq's land borders are extremely porous. Iraq continues substantial trade with its neighbors. There is significant potential for evasion of sanctions by land routes, giving additional weight to our position that UNSCOM must have full and unconditional access to all locations, and be allowed to inspect and monitor Iraqi compliance over time.

Iraq's Concealment Mechanisms

In June, UNSCOM Chairman Butler presented Iraq with a proposed work plan which, had Iraq cooperated, could have moved the process of verifying the disarmament forward. However, when Butler made a return visit August 3-4, the Iraqi Deputy Prime Minister denounced UNSCOM and demanded that UNSCOM report to the Council that Iraq was "disarmed in all areas." On August 5, Iraq announced it was suspending cooperation with UNSCOM and the IAEA. The following day, the Security Council President issued a press statement declaring the Iraqi decision "totally unacceptable," noting that it "contravened" relevant Security Council resolutions.

On August 11, 1998, IAEA Director-General El Baradei wrote to the President of the Security Council that Iraq's August 5 decision to suspend its cooperation with UNSCOM and the IAEA "makes it impossible for the IAEA ... to investigate ... remaining questions and concerns ...," and that Iraq's decision will allow only "limited implementation" of monitoring that will "fall short of full implementation of the OMV plan and result in a significantly reduced level of assurance" that Iraq is not renewing its programs for weapons of mass destruction.

On August 12, 1998, UNSCOM Executive Chairman Butler sent the President of the Security Council a letter similar to the August 11 letter of the IAEA noted above, saying that "Iraq's actions bring to a halt all of the disarmament activities of the Commission and place limitations on the rights of the Commission to conduct its monitoring operations."

On August 18, the Council President replied to UNSCOM and the IAEA on behalf of the Council, reiterating the full support of the Council for IAEA and UNSCOM to fully implement their mandates and noting that Iraq is obliged to cooperate with them in their activities, including inspections. On August 19, Chairman Butler wrote to the Iraqi government seeking a resumption of the dialogue between UNSCOM and the regime and of all substantive UNSCOM work. That request was immediately rebuffed.

On August 20, the Security Council conducted its periodic review of Iraq's compliance with relevant Security Council resolutions. The Council stated that "the Sanctions Review showed that the necessary conditions do not exist for the modification of the regime" and reiterated that "the decision by Iraq to suspend cooperation with UNSCOM and the IAEA is totally unacceptable." Further, "they view with extreme concern the continuing refusal by the Government of Iraq to rescind its decision."

We continue to work with the Council in its effort to bring about full Iraqi cooperation with UNSCOM and the IAEA. We are now seeking a Council resolution that would suspend further periodic reviews until Iraq reverses course and resumes cooperation with UNSCOM and the IAEA. Iraq's refusal to cooperate is a challenge to the authority of the Security Council and to the credibility of all international weapons nonproliferation efforts, since UNSCOM and the IAEA are responsible to the Security Council for the most thorough arms control regime on earth.

The U.N.'s "Oil-for-Food" Program

We continue to support the international community's efforts to provide for the humanitarian needs of the Iraqi people through the "oil-for-food" program and other humanitarian efforts. Under the last phase of the "oil-for-food" program, which ran from December 3, 1997, through June 2, 1998, $1.1 billion worth of humanitarian goods were approved for export to Iraq. United States companies can participate in "oil-for-food" and over $165 million worth of contracts for U.S. firms have been approved.

Under the current phase of "oil-for-food" Iraq is authorized to sell up to $5.2 billion worth of oil every 180 days, up from $2.0 billion in previous phases. Although the UNSC resolution outlining this program, Resolution 1153, was adopted on February 20, Iraq did not present an acceptable distribution plan for the implementation of Resolution 1153 until May 27, 1998; it was accepted by the U.N. Secretary General on May 29.

Under the current phase of the "oil-for-food" program, 235 contracts for the purchase of humanitarian goods for the Iraqi people have been presented for approval; of these, 162 contracts worth over $562 million have been approved and 13 are on hold pending clarification of questions about the proposed contracts. With regard to oil sales, 50 contracts with a total value of $955 million have been approved so far during this phase.

The United States has supported the repair of the Iraqi oil infrastructure in order to allow sufficient oil to be exported to fund the level of humanitarian purchases the Security Council approved in UNSC Resolution 1153. Treasury is in the process of amending its regulations to allow U.S. companies to bid on oil infrastructure repair contracts just as they are permitted both to purchase Iraqi oil and sell humanitarian goods under the U.N. "oil-for-food" program.

Resolution 1153 maintains the separate program for northern Iraq, administered directly by the U.N. in consultation with the local population. This program, which the United States strongly supports, receives 13 to 15 percent of the funds generated under the "oil-for-food" program. The separate northern program was established because of the Baghdad regime's proven disregard for the humanitarian condition of the Kurdish, Assyrian, and Turkomen minorities of northern Iraq and its readiness to apply the most brutal forms of repression against them. The well-documented series of chemical weapons attacks a decade ago by the government against civilians in the north is only one example of this brutality. In northern Iraq, where Baghdad does not exercise control, the "oil-for-food" program has been able to operate relatively effectively. The

Kurdish factions are seeking to set aside their differences to work together so that UNSC Resolution 1153 is implemented as efficiently as possible.

The U.N. must carefully monitor implementation of Resolution 1153. As the current phase anticipates a doubling of goods flowing into Iraq, including equipment for infrastructure repairs in areas such as oil export capacity, generation of electricity, and water purification, the U.N. faces increasing challenges in monitoring. The Iraqi government continues to insist on the need for rapid lifting of the sanctions regime, despite its clear record of non-compliance with its obligations under relevant U.N. resolutions—a record which was unanimously acknowledged during the Security Council's 39th sanctions review on June 24. We will continue to work with the U.N. Secretariat, the Security Council, and others in the international community to ensure that the humanitarian needs of the Iraqi people are met while denying any political or economic benefits to the Baghdad regime.

The Human Rights Situation in Iraq

The human rights situation throughout Iraq continues to be a cause for grave concern. Particularly troubling are the assassinations of two distinguished Shia clerics—Ayatollah Borujerdi on April 22 and Grand Ayatollah Mirza Ali Gharavi on June 18. These killings have been widely attributed to the Baghdad regime and were followed by an increased security presence in the predominantly Shia cities of south and central Iraq, such as Najaf and Karbala. These events expose a callous disregard for human life and the free exercise of religion. Summary, arbitrary, and extra-judicial executions also remain a primary concern. Baghdad still refuses to allow independent inspections of Iraqi prisons despite the conclusion of U.N. Special Rapporteur for Iraq, Max Van der Stoel, that "there is strong evidence that hundreds of prisoners (were) executed in Abu Graraib and Radwaniyah prisons" late last year. As noted in my last report, based on these reports of summary executions and other ongoing human rights violations, the U.N. Human Rights Commission in April issued a strong condemnation of the "all-pervasive repression and oppression"

of the Iraqi government. Nevertheless, sources inside Iraq report another wave of executions in June, with about sixty people summarily killed.

In southern Iraq, the government continues to repress the Shia population, destroying the Marsh Arabs' way of life and the unique ecology of the southern marshes. In the north, outside the Kurdish-controlled areas, the government continues the forced expulsion of tens of thousands of ethnic Kurds and Turkomen from Kirkuk and other cities. The government continues to stall and obfuscate attempts to account for more than 600 Kuwaitis and third-country nationals who disappeared at the hands of Iraqi authorities during or after the occupation of Kuwait. The Government of Iraq shows no sign of complying with UNSC Resolution 688, which demands that Iraq cease the repression of its own people.

Northern Iraq: Deepening Engagement

In northern Iraq, the cease-fire between the Kurdish parties, established in November 1997 as the result of U.S. efforts, continues to hold. It is strengthened by growing and effective cooperation between the parties on humanitarian matters, particularly those related to the U.N.'s "oil-for-food" program. Working with the U.N., the Kurds have been able to resolve nutrition and medical problems and look forward to rebuilding their infrastructure as U.N. programs expand. David Welch, Principal Deputy Assistant Secretary of State for Near Eastern Affairs, led a U.S. delegation to the north, July 17-20. He encouraged the Kurds' efforts towards peace; underscored U.S. support for their human rights, physical welfare and safety; and renewed our decades-long engagement with them. During the visit, Massoud Barzani, leader of the Kurdistan Democratic Party (KDP), and Jalal Talabani, leader of the Patriotic Union of Kurdistan (PUK), made positive, forward-looking statements on political reconciliation, and they accepted separate invitations to visit the United States later this year.

The United States firmly supports the territorial integrity of Iraq. Supporting the rights and welfare of Iraqi Kurds within Iraq in no way contradicts that support. The United States is committed to ensuring that international aid continues to get through to the north, that the human rights of the Kurds and northern Iraq minority groups, such as the Turkomen, Assyrians, Yezedis and others are respected, and that the no-fly zone enforced by Operation Northern Watch is observed.

We will continue our efforts to reach a permanent reconciliation through mediation in order to help the people of northern Iraq find the permanent, stable settlement they deserve, and to minimize the influence of either Baghdad or Tehran. Baghdad continues to pressure the two groups to enter into negotiations.

The Iraqi Opposition

It is the policy of the U.S. Government to support the Iraqi opposition by establishing unifying programs on which all of the opposition can agree. Section 10008 of the 1998 Supplemental Appropriations and Rescissions Act (P.L. 105-174), earmarks $5 million in FY 98 Economic Support Funds for these programs. These programs are designed to encourage and assist political opposition groups, nonpartisan opposition groups, and unaffiliated Iraqis concerned about their nation's future in peacefully espousing democracy, pluralism, human rights, and the rule of law for their country. Based on extensive consultations with opposition leaders and representatives, we have found a deep resonance on several central themes. These are: building a consensus on the transition from dictatorship to pluralism, conveying to the U.N. opposition views on Iraqi noncompliance with U.N. resolutions and compiling information to support indictment of Iraqi officials for war crimes.

Iraq is a diverse country—ethnically, religiously, and culturally. The Iraqi opposition reflects this diversity. We emphasize themes and programs, rather than individuals and groups, in order to encourage unity and discourage the rivalries which have divided the opposition in the past. Many opposition political groups that formerly coordinated their efforts decided several years ago to work independently. We are interested in working with them towards greater unity on their own terms, not in forcing the issue by declaring that any one group must take the lead. We firmly believe they can succeed in this effort.

We anticipate that there will be a need for additional funding for these programs as the opposition becomes more active and as it grows. The funds will be administered by the Department of State working through established NGOs, Federal institutions, and comparable private organizations. To ensure transparency and accountability and to avoid creating potential rivalries among opposition groups, none of these funds will go directly to any opposition group.

The United Nations Compensation Commission

The United Nations Compensation Commission (UNCC), established pursuant to UNSC Resolutions 687 and 692, continues to resolve claims against Iraq arising from Iraq's unlawful invasion and occupation of Kuwait. The UNCC has issued over 1.3 million awards worth approximately $7 billion. Thirty percent of the proceeds from the oil sales permitted by UNSC Resolutions 986, 1111, 1143, and 1153 have been allocated to the Compensation Fund to pay awards and to finance operations of the UNCC. To the extent that money is available in the Compensation Fund, initial payments to each claimant are authorized for awards in the order in which the UNCC has approved them, in installments of $2,500. To date, 809 U.S. claimants have received an initial installment payment, and payment is still in process for another 25 U.S. claimants.

Conclusion

Iraq remains a serious threat to international peace and security. I remain determined to see Iraq comply fully with all of its obligations under UNSC resolutions. The United States looks forward to the day when Iraq rejoins the family of nations as a responsible and law-abiding member.

I appreciate the support of the Congress for our efforts and shall continue to keep the Congress informed about this important issue.

Sincerely,

William J. Clinton

323.

[Vol. 34, no. 45 (November 9, 1998): 2260-2266]

Letter to Congressional Leaders on Iraq's Compliance With United Nations Security Council Resolutions
November 5, 1998

Dear Mr. Speaker: (Dear Mr. President:)

Consistent with the Authorization for Use of Military Force Against Iraq Resolution (Public Law 102-1) and as part of my effort to keep the Congress fully informed, I am reporting on the status of efforts to obtain Iraq's compliance with the resolutions adopted by the United Nations Security Council (UNSC). This report covers the period from September 3 to the present.

Introduction

On October 31, Iraq announced that it was ceasing all cooperation with the United Nations Special Commission (UNSCOM) including monitoring activity. This announcement represents a serious escalation of Iraq's August 5 decision to suspend cooperation with UNSCOM and the International Atomic Energy Agency (IAEA). On October 31, the UNSC issued a statement condemning Iraq's decision as a "flagrant violation of relevant Council resolutions and of the Memorandum of Understanding signed between the Secretary General and the Deputy Prime Minister of Iraq" last February. Iraq's action followed its receipt of a letter from the UK (as President of the Security Council) indicating a willingness to conduct a comprehensive review, but only after Iraq returned to full compliance. Since the October 31 statement, UNSCOM has been able to conduct only very limited monitoring activity.

Earlier, on September 9, the UNSC unanimously adopted Resolution 1194, which condemns Iraq's August 5 decision as a "totally unacceptable contravention of its obligations," demands that Iraq rescind its decision and resume cooperation, and suspends bimonthly sanctions reviews until UNSCOM and IAEA report that they are satisfied that Iraq has done so.

The resolution also notes the Council's willingness to hold a comprehensive review of "Iraq's compliance with its obligations under all relevant resolutions once Iraq has rescinded its...decision [to suspend cooperation] and demonstrated that it is prepared to fulfill all its obligations, including, in particular on disarmament issues, by resuming full cooperation with the Special Commission and the IAEA..."

On September 23, the P-5 Foreign Ministers issued a statement reiterating that Iraq's actions are "totally unacceptable," and confirmed that "Iraq must respond immediately to Security Council Resolution 1194 and resume full cooperation." The statement also noted that the prerequisite for a comprehensive review was Iraq's "unconditional resumption" of cooperation with UNSCOM and the IAEA.

Tariq Aziz spent several days at the United Nations in New York at the end of September discussing the comprehensive review with Security Council members and the Secretary General. The Secretary General's Special Representative Prakash Shah is engaged in discussions in Baghdad on the subject. Despite Iraq's lobbying efforts, the Secretary General and all Council members remain united in judging Iraq's actions unacceptable; all 15 Council members supported the Council President's letter to the Secretary General that said Iraq must rescind its August 5 decision and resume cooperation with UNSCOM and the IAEA. We continue to work with the Council to convince Iraq to reverse course, but we have not ruled out any option should the Council fail to reverse Iraq's decision.

We continue to support the international community's efforts to provide for the humanitarian needs of the Iraqi people through the "oil-for-food" program. On May 27, 1998, Iraq presented a distribution plan for the implementation of Resolution 1153, which had been adopted on February 20. Under phase three of the "oil-for-food" program, which ran from December 3, 1997, through June 2, 1998, $1.2 billion worth of humanitarian goods were approved for export to Iraq. Under the current phase, phase four, which began in June, the U.N. Sanctions Committee has approved the purchase of over $1.2 billion worth of humanitarian goods. United States companies can participate in the "oil-for-food" program, and over $185 million worth of direct contracts for U.S. firms have been approved since the program began.

Recent developments in northern Iraq demonstrate once again the power of persistent diplomacy. On September 17, leaders of the two main Iraqi Kurdish parties, Massoud Barzani and Jalal Talabani, met together for the first time in over 4 years to sign a forward-looking joint statement committing their parties to reconciliation. Their talks, held at the Department of State under U.S. auspices, followed 6 months of intensive discussions and close consultation with the Kurdish parties and with our Turkish and British allies. The statesmanlike achievement of the Iraqi Kurdish leaders signals a hopeful new chapter for all the people of northern Iraq.

On October 31, I signed into law the Iraq Liberation Act of 1998. Work also continues on the existing opposition program to help opposition groups unify politically, and the new Radio Free Iraq service began broadcasting in late October. These new programs will help us encourage the Iraqi people to build a pluralistic, peaceful Iraq that observes the international rule of law and respects basic human rights. Such an Iraq would have little trouble regaining its rightful place in the region and in the international community.

U.S. and Coalition Force Levels in the Gulf Region

Saddam's record of aggressive behavior forces us to retain a highly capable force presence in the region in order to deter Iraq and deal with any threat it might pose to its neighbors. The United States and allied forces now in the theater are prepared to deal with all contingencies. We have the capability to respond rapidly to possible Iraqi aggression. We will continue to maintain a robust force posture and have established a rapid reinforcement capability to supplement our forces in the Gulf when needed. Our cruise missile force is twice the pre-October 1997 level and can be augmented significantly within days. Our contingency plans allow us the capability for swift, powerful strikes if that becomes necessary.

Our forces in the region include land and carrier-based aircraft, surface warships, a Marine expeditionary unit, a Patriot missile battalion, a mechanized battalion task force, and a mix of special operations forces deployed in support of U.S. Central Command operations. To enhance force protection throughout the region, additional military security personnel are also deployed.

Operation Northern Watch and Operation Southern Watch

The United States and coalition partners continue to enforce the no-fly zones over Iraq under Operation Northern Watch and Operation Southern Watch. There were no observed no-fly zone violations during the period covered by this report. We have made clear to Iraq and to all other relevant parties that the United States and coalition partners will continue to enforce both no-fly zones.

The Maritime Interception Force

The Maritime Interception Force (MIF), operating in accordance with Resolution 665 and other relevant resolutions, vigorously enforces UN sanctions in the Gulf. The U.S. Navy is the single largest component of this multinational force, but it is frequently augmented by ships, aircraft, and other support from Australia, Canada, Belgium, Kuwait, The Netherlands, New Zealand, the UAE, and the United Kingdom. Member states of the Gulf Cooperation Council also support the MIF by providing logistical support and shipriders and by accepting vessels diverted for violating UN sanctions against Iraq.

The MIF continues to intercept vessels involved in illegal smuggling into and out of Iraq. In late August, the MIF conducted stepped-up operations in the far northern Gulf in the shallow waters near the major Iraqi waterways. These operations severely disrupted smuggling operations in the region. A new round of stepped up activity took place in mid-October. Since the beginning of the year, over 40 vessels have been detained for violations of the embargo and sent to ports in the Gulf for enforcement actions. Kuwait and the UAE, two countries adjacent to the smuggling routes, have also stepped up their own enforcement efforts and have intercepted and detained vessels involved in sanctions violations. Although refined petroleum products leaving Iraq comprise most of the prohibited traffic, the MIF has also intercepted a growing number of ships in smuggling prohibited goods into Iraq in violation of U.N. sanctions resolutions and the "oil-for-food" program. Ships involved in smuggling frequently utilize the territorial seas of Iran to avoid MIF patrols. In September, Iran closed the Shatt Al Arab waterway to smugglers and we observed the lowest level of illegal gasoil smuggling in 2 years. Iran apparently reopened the waterway in October. Detailed reports of these smuggling activities have been provided to the UN Sanctions Committee in New York.

Chemical Weapons

Iraq continues to deny that it ever weaponized VX nerve agent or produced stabilized VX, despite UNSCOM's publicly stated confidence in the Edgewood Arsenal laboratory finding of stabilized VX components in fragments of Iraqi SCUD missile warheads. Tests by France and Switzerland on other warhead fragments have been conducted to help UNSCOM estimate the total number of warheads loaded with VX. On October 22 and 23, international experts from seven countries met to discuss all analytical results obtained in the course of UNSCOM's verification of Iraq's declarations related to VX activities. Ambassador Butler reported to the U.N. Security Council on October 26 that the international experts "unanimously concluded" that "all analytical data" provided by the United States, Swiss, and French laboratories involved were considered "conclusive and valid." Ambassador Butler continued, "the existence of VX degradation products conflicts with Iraqi declarations that the unilaterally destroyed special warheads had never been filled with CW agents." The experts recommended that UNSCOM ask Iraq to explain the origin and history of the fragments analyzed by all three laboratories and the presence of degradation products of nerve agents, and to explain the presence of a compound known as VX stabilizer and its degradation product.

Iraq still refuses to turn over to UNSCOM the Iraqi Air Force document found by UN-SCOM inspectors that details chemical weapons expended during the Iran-Iraq war. We understand that UNSCOM believes the document indicates that Iraq's official declarations to UNSCOM have greatly overstated the quantities of chemical weapons expended, which means a greater number of chemical weapons are unaccounted for than previously estimated.

Biological Weapons

Iraq has failed to provide a credible explanation for UNSCOM tests that found anthrax in fragments of seven SCUD missile warheads. Iraq has been claiming since 1995 that it put anthrax in only five such warheads, and had previously denied weaponizing anthrax at all. Iraq's explanations to date are far from satisfactory, although it now acknowledges putting both anthrax and botulinum toxin into some number of warheads. Iraq's biological weapons (BW) program, including SCUD missile BW warheads, R-400 BW bombs, drop-tanks to be filled with BW, spray devices for BW, production of BW agents (anthrax, botulinum toxin, aflatoxin, and wheat cover smut), and BW agent growth media, remains the "black hole" described by Ambassador Butler. Iraq has consistently failed to provide a credible account of its efforts to produce and weaponize its BW agents.

In response to a U.S. proposal, the Security Council agreed on October 13 to seek clarification from Iraq of statements made by Iraqi officials on October 7 concerning the existence of additional information on biological weapons still in Iraq's hands, and about Iraq's refusal to turn over the Iraqi Air Force document on chemical weapons expended in the Iran-Iraq War.

Long-Range Missiles

While Iraq continued to allow UNSCOM to witness flight tests of nonprohibited Iraqi missiles with range under 150 km (this cooperation has not been tested since the October 31 decision), there has been no change in (1) Iraq's refusal to further discuss its system for concealment of longer-range missiles and their components, (2) Iraq's refusal to provide credible evidence of its disposition of large quantities of the unique fuel required for the long-range SCUD missile, or (3) Iraq's continued test modifications to SA-2 VOLGA surface-to-air missile components, despite written objections by UNSCOM (reported to the Security Council). These areas contribute to an Iraqi capability to produce a surface-to-surface missile of range greater than its permitted range of 150 km.

While UNSCOM believes it can account for 817 of 819 imported Soviet-made SCUD missiles, Iraq has refused to give UNSCOM a credible accounting of the indigenous program that produced complete SCUD missiles that were both successfully test-flown and delivered to the Iraqi army.

Nuclear Weapons

The nuclear weapons situation remains as it was on August 11, 1998, when IAEA Director General El Baradei wrote to the President of the Security Council that Iraq's August 5 suspension of cooperation with UNSCOM and the IAEA allows only "limited implementation of its ongoing monitoring" and "makes it impossible...to investigate ...remaining questions and concerns..." In its 6-month report to the UN Security Council on October 7, the IAEA stated that it had a "technically coherent" view of the Iraqi nuclear program. There are remaining questions, but IAEA believes they can be dealt with within IAEA's ongoing monitoring and verification effort.

But the report also stated that Iraq's current suspension of cooperation with the IAEA limits the IAEA's right to full and free access. The IAEA is currently unable to investigate further aspects of Iraq's clandestine program or to ensure that prohibited activities are not being carried out in Iraq, free from the risk of detection through direct measures.

Dual-Use Imports

Resolution 1051 established a joint UNSCOM/ IAEA unit to monitor Iraq's imports of allowed dual-use items. Iraq must notify the unit before it imports specific items that can be used in both weapons of mass destruction and civilian applications. Similarly, UN members must provide timely notification of exports to Iraq of such dual-use items.

Given Iraq's current decision to suspend cooperation with UNSCOM/IAEA, we remain constantly vigilant for evidence of smuggling of items usable in weapons of mass destruction.

The UN's "Oil-for-Food" Program

We continue to support the international community's efforts to provide for the humanitarian needs of the Iraqi people through the "oil-for-food" program. Under the last phase of the "oil-for-food" program, which ran from December 3, 1997, through June 2, 1998, $1.2 billion worth of humanitarian goods were approved for export to Iraq. United States companies can participate in "oil-for-food," and $185 million worth of direct contracts for U.S. firms have been approved; millions of dollars more have been earned through subcontracts. Since the first deliveries under the "oil-for-food" program began in March 1997, 7 million tons of food worth over $2.25 billion and $336 million worth of medicine and health supplies have been delivered to Iraq.

Iraq is authorized to sell up to $5.2 billion worth of oil every 180 days, up from $2 billion in previous phases. Although Resolution 1153 was adopted on February 20, Iraq did not present an acceptable distribution plan for the implementation of Resolution 1153 until May 27, 1998; the plan was accepted by the UN Secretary General on May 29. The UN Office of the Iraq Programme (OIP) has recently released new estimates of the amount of oil revenues that will be available during this phase of the program. Citing declining world oil prices and the state of Iraq's oil industry, OIP now estimates that income for the 6-month period ending in December will be around $3.3 billion. Discussions are under way within the Sanctions Committee and OIP as to how best to meet the most immediate needs of the Iraqi people in light of this projected shortfall in income.

Under the current phase (four) of the "oil-for-food" program, 622 contracts for the purchase of humanitarian goods for the Iraqi people have been presented for approval; of these, 485 contracts worth over $1.2 billion have been approved and 80 are on hold pending clarification of questions about the proposed contracts. With regard to oil sales, 58 contracts with a total value of over $2 billion have been approved so far during this phase.

UNSC Resolution 1153 maintains a separate "oil-for-food" program for northern Iraq, administered directly by the United Nations in consultation with the local population. This program, which the United States strongly supports, receives 13 to 15 percent of the funds generated under the "oil-for-food" program. The separate northern program was established because of the Baghdad regime's proven disregard for the humanitarian needs of the Kurdish, Assyrian, and Turkomen minorities of northern Iraq and its readiness to apply the most brutal forms of repression against them. In northern Iraq, where Baghdad does not exercise control, the "oil-for-food" program has been able to operate relatively effectively. The Kurdish factions are setting aside their differences to work together so that Resolution 1153 is implemented as efficiently as possible.

The United Nations must carefully monitor implementation of Resolution 1153. As the current phase anticipates, infrastructure repairs in areas such as oil export capacity, generation of electricity, and water purification present increasing challenges to the UN monitoring regime.

The Iraqi government continues to insist on the need for rapid lifting of the sanctions regime, despite its clear record of noncompliance with its obligations under relevant UNSC resolutions. Although the Iraqi Government maintains that sanctions cause widespread suffering among the Iraqi populace, the Iraqi Government is still not prepared to comply with UNSC resolutions and thus create the conditions that would allow sanctions to be lifted. Even if sanctions were lifted and the Government of Iraq had complete control over oil revenues, it is doubtful that conditions would improve for the Iraqi people. The Iraqi government has for a number of years shown that meeting civilian needs is not among its priorities. Humanitarian programs such as "oil-for-food" have steadily improved the life of the average Iraqi (who, for example, now receives a ration basket providing 2,000 kilocalories per day; a significant improvement in nutrition since the program began) while denying Saddam Hussein control over oil reve-

nues. We will continue to work with the UN Secretariat, the Security Council, and others in the international community to ensure that the humanitarian needs of the Iraqi people are met while denying any political or economic benefits to the Baghdad regime.

Northern Iraq: Kurdish Reconciliation

On September 16 and 17, Massoud Barzani, President of the Kurdistan Democratic Party (KDP), and Jalal Talabani, Chairman of the Patriotic Union of Kurdistan (PUK), met for the first time in more than 4 years in talks held at the Department of State. Secretary Albright, welcoming the two leaders, congratulated them on the courageous step they were taking on behalf of their people. She expressed the United States deep concern for the safety, security, and economic well-being of Iraqi Kurds, Shias, Sunnis, and others who have been subject to brutal attacks by the Baghdad regime. She also made it clear that the United States will decide how and when to respond to Baghdad's actions based on the threat they pose to Iraq's neighbors, to regional security, to vital U.S. interests, and to the Iraqi people, including those in the north.

While in Washington, Mr. Barzani and Mr. Talabani signed a joint statement committing themselves to a timeline to improve the regional administration of the three northern provinces in the context of the 1996 Ankara Accords. Over the next 9 months, they will seek to unify their administrations, share revenues, define the status of their major cities, and hold elections. A key component for the success of this program will be continued meetings between the two leaders. To make this possible, both parties have condemned internal fighting, pledged to refrain from violence in settling their differences, and resolved to eliminate terrorism by establishing stronger safeguards for Iraq's borders.

The Washington talks followed 6 months of intensive diplomatic efforts including a visit to northern Iraq by Principal Deputy Assistant Secretary of State David Welch and consultations in Ankara and London by both Kurdish parties. Since the Washington talks, we have continued to work closely on these issues with the Iraqi Kurds and with Turkey and Great Britain. Both leaders met with UN officials in New York and they were together hosted by members of the House of Representatives Committee on International Relations.

The United States firmly supports the unity and territorial integrity of Iraq. Supporting the rights and welfare of Iraqi Kurds within Iraq in no way contradicts this position. In their joint statement, the Kurdish leaders clearly enunciated this principle. The United States is committed to ensuring that international aid continues to reach the north, that the human rights of the Kurds and northern Iraq minority groups, such as the Turkomen, Assyrians, Yezedis, and others are respected, and that the no-fly zone enforced by Operation Northern Watch is observed.

The Human Rights Situation in Iraq

The human rights situation throughout Iraq continues to be a cause for grave concern. As I reported September 3, the regime increased its security presence in predominantly Shia southern Iraq after the assassinations of two distinguished Shia clerics—deaths widely attributed to regime agents. Since that time, the Iraqi army has conducted a series of repressive operations against the Shia in Nasiriya and Amara Provinces. In particular, the government continues to work toward the destruction of the Marsh Arabs' way of life and the unique ecology of the southern marshes. These events expose a callous disregard for human life and the free exercise of religion.

Summary, arbitrary, and extrajudicial executions also remain a primary concern. Baghdad still refuses to allow independent inspections of Iraqi prisons despite the conclusion of UN Special Rapporteur for Iraq, Max Van der Stoel, that "there is strong evidence that hundreds of prisoners (were) executed in Abu Gharaib and Radwaniyah prisons" late last year. The UN Human Rights Commission in April issued a strong condemnation of the "all-pervasive repression and oppression" of the Iraqi government. Nevertheless, sources inside Iraq report another wave of executions in June, with about 60 people summarily killed. Preliminary reports indicate that the killings continued into July and August.

In the north, outside the Kurdish-controlled areas, the government continues the forced expulsion of tens of thousands of ethnic Kurds and Turkomen from Kirkuk and other cities. In recent months, 545 more families were reportedly expelled from Kirkuk (al-Tamim province) with 7 new Arab settlements created on land seized from the Kurds. Reports from the Kurdish-controlled areas where the displaced persons are received indicate that they are forced to leave behind almost all of their personal property. Due to a shortage of housing, they are still living in temporary shelters as winter approaches.

The government also continues to stall and obfuscate attempts to account for more than 600 Kuwaitis and third-country nationals who disappeared at the hands of Iraqi authorities during or after the occupation of Kuwait. It shows no sign of complying with Resolution 688, which demands that Iraq cease the repression of its own people.

The Iraqi Opposition

It is the policy of the United States to support the Iraqi opposition by establishing unifying programs in which all of the opposition can participate. We are working to encourage and assist political opposition groups, nonpartisan opposition groups, and unaffiliated Iraqis concerned about their nation's future in peacefully espousing democracy, pluralism, human rights, and the rule of law for their country. These committed Iraqis hope to build a consensus on the transition from dictatorship to pluralism, convey to the United Nations their views on Iraqi noncompliance with UN resolutions, and compile information to support holding Iraqi officials criminally responsible for violations of international humanitarian law.

On October 31, I signed into law the Iraq Liberation Act of 1998. It provides new discretionary authorities to assist the opposition in their struggle against the regime. This Act makes clear the sense of the Congress that the United States should support efforts to achieve a very different future for Iraq than the bitter, current reality of internal repression and external aggression.

There are, of course, other important elements of U.S. policy. These include the maintenance of UN Security Council support efforts to eliminate Iraq's prohibited weapons and missile programs and economic sanctions that continue to deny the regime the means to reconstitute those threats to international peace and security. United States support for the Iraqi opposition will be carried out consistent with those policy objectives as well. Similarly, U.S. support must be attuned to what the opposition can effectively make use of as it develops over time.

The United Nations Compensation Commission

The United Nations Compensation Commission (UNCC), established pursuant to Resolutions 687 and 692, continues to resolve claims against Iraq arising from Iraq's unlawful invasion and occupation of Kuwait. The UNCC has issued over 1.3 million awards worth approximately $7 billion. Thirty percent of the proceeds from the oil sales permitted by Resolutions 986, 1111, 1143, and 1153 have been allocated to the Compensation Fund to pay awards and to finance operations of the UNCC. To the extent that money is available in the Compensation Fund, initial payments to each claimant are authorized for awards in the order in which the UNCC has approved them, in installments of $2,500. To date, the United States Government has received funds from the UNCC for initial installment payments on approximately 1435 claims of U.S. claimants.

Conclusion

Iraq remains a serious threat to international peace and security. I remain determined to see Iraq comply fully with all of its obligations under UN Security Council resolutions. The United States looks forward to the day when Iraq rejoins the family of nations as a responsible and law-abiding member.

I appreciate the support of the Congress for our efforts and shall continue to keep the Congress informed about this important issue.

Sincerely,

William J. Clinton

324.

[Vol. 35, no. 5 (February 8, 1999): 199]

Memorandum on Assistance to Iraqi Democratic Opposition Organizations
February 4, 1999

Presidential Determination No. 99-13

Memorandum for the Secretary of State

Subject: Designations Under the Iraq Liberation Act of 1998

Pursuant to the authority vested in me as President of the United States, including under section 5 of the Iraq Liberation Act of 1998 (Public Law 105-338) (the "Act"), I hereby determine that each of the following groups is a democratic opposition organization and that each satisfies the criteria set forth in section 5(c) of the Act: the Iraqi National Accord, the Iraqi National Congress, the Islamic Movement of Iraqi Kurdistan, the Kurdistan Democratic Party, the Movement for Constitutional Monarchy, the Patriotic Union of Kurdistan, and the Supreme Council for the Islamic Revolution in Iraq. I hereby designate each of these organizations as eligible to receive assistance under section 4 of the Act.

You are authorized and directed to report this determination and designation to the Congress and arrange for its publication in the Federal Register.

William J. Clinton

Note: This message was released by the Office of the Press Secretary on February 5.

325.

[Vol. 35, no. 9 (March 8, 1999): 341-350]

Letter to Congressional Leaders Reporting on Iraq's Compliance With United Nations Security Council Resolutions
March 3, 1999

Dear Mr. Speaker: (Mr. President:)

Consistent with the Authorization for Use of Military Force Against Iraq Resolution (Public Law 102-1) and as part of my effort to keep the Congress fully informed, I am reporting on the status of efforts to obtain Iraq's compliance with the resolutions adopted by the United Nations Security Council (UNSC). My last report, consistent with Public Law 102-1, was transmitted on December 18, 1998.

Overview

As stated in my December 18 report, on December 16, United States and British forces launched military strikes on Iraq (Operation Desert Fox) to degrade Iraq's capacity to develop and deliver weapons of mass destruction (WMD) and to degrade its ability to threaten its neighbors. The decision to use force was made after U.N. Special Commission (UNSCOM) Executive Chairman Richard Butler reported to the U.N. Secretary General on December 14, that Iraq was not cooperating fully with the Commission and that it was "not able to conduct the substantive disarmament work mandated to it by the Security Council."

The build-up to the current crisis began on August 5 when the Iraqi government suspended cooperation with UNSCOM and the International Atomic Energy Agency (IAEA), except on a limited-range of monitoring activities. On October 31, Iraq announced that it was ceasing all cooperation with UNSCOM. In response to this decision, the Security Council on November 5 unanimously adopted Resolution 1205, which condemned Iraq's decision as a "flagrant violation" of the Gulf War cease-fire Resolution 687 and other relevant resolutions. Resolution 1205 also demanded that Iraq immediately rescind both its October 31 decision and its decision of August 5. This came after the passage on March 3, 1998, of Resolution 1154, warning Iraq that the "severest consequences" would result from Iraq's failure to cooperate with the implementation of Resolution 687.

Iraq ignored the Security Council's demands until November 14, when U.S. and British forces prepared to launch air strikes on Iraq. Baghdad initially tried to impose unacceptable conditions on its offer of resumption of cooperation; however, the United States and Great Britain insisted on strict compliance with all relevant Security Council resolutions.

Subsequently, Iraq agreed in writing in letters to the U.N. Secretary General to re-scind its August 5 and October 31 decisions and to resume full cooperation with UNSCOM and the IAEA in accordance with Security Council resolutions. Iraq informed the Security Council on November 14 that it was the "clear and unconditional decision of the Iraqi government to resume cooperation with UNSCOM and the IAEA."

On November 15, the Security Council issued a statement in which it stressed that Iraq's commitment "needs to be established by unconditional and sustained cooperation with the Special Commission and the IAEA in exercising the full range of their activities provided for in their mandates."

UNSCOM and the IAEA resumed their full range of activities on November 17, but Iraq repeatedly violated its commitment of cooperation. As Chairman Butler's report of December 14 details, Iraq has, over the course of the last 8 years, refused to provide the key documents and critical explanations about its prohibited weapons programs in response to UNSCOM's outstanding requests. It refused to allow removal of missile engine components, denied access to missile test data, restricted photography of bombs, and endangered the safety of inspectors by aggressively maneuvering a helicopter near them. Iraq failed to provide requested access to archives and effectively blocked UNSCOM from visiting a site on November 25.

On December 4 and again on December 11, Iraq further restricted UNSCOM's activities by asserting that certain teams could not inspect on Fridays, the Muslim sabbath, despite 7 years of doing so and the fact that other inspection teams' activities were not restricted on Fridays. Iraq blocked access to offices of the ruling Ba'ath Party on December 9, which UNSCOM held "solid evidence" contained prohibited materials. Iraq routinely removed documents from facilities prior to inspection, and initiated new forms of restrictions on UNSCOM's work. We also have information that Iraq ordered the military to destroy WMD-related documents in anticipation of the UNSCOM inspections.

Iraq's actions were a material breach of the Gulf War cease-fire resolution (UNSC Resolution 687), the February 23, 1998, Annan-Aziz Memorandum of Understanding, and Iraq's November 14 commitment to the Security Council. The threat to the region posed by Iraq's refusal to cooperate unconditionally with UNSCOM, and the consequent inability of UNSCOM to carry out the responsibilities the Security Council entrusted to it, could not be tolerated. These circumstances led the United States and the United Kingdom to use military force to degrade Iraq's capacity to threaten its neighbors through the development of WMD and long-range delivery systems. During Desert Fox, key WMD sites and the facilities of the organizations that conceal them, as well as important missile repair facilities and surface-to-air missile sites, were attacked. Operation Desert Fox degraded Saddam's ability to threaten his neighbors militarily.

UNSCOM and IAEA inspectors withdrew from Iraq on December 15 when Chairman Butler reported that inspectors were not able to conduct the substantive disarmament work required of UNSCOM by the Security Council. The United States continues to support UNSCOM and the IAEA as the agreed mechanisms for Iraq to demonstrate its compliance with UNSC resolutions concerning disarmament.

Since December 18, the Security Council has discussed next steps on Iraq. It decided on January 30 to establish three assessment panels to address disarmament issues, humanitarian issues, and Kuwait-related issues. The panels, under the chairmanship of the Brazilian Ambassador to the United Nations, are due to complete their reviews by April 15.

The United States also continues to support the international community's efforts to provide for the humanitarian needs of the Iraqi people through the "oil-for-food" program. On November 24, 1998, the Security Council unanimously adopted Resolution 1210 establishing a new 6-month phase (phase five) of the oil-for-food program (phase four ended November 25). In January, the United States announced its support for lifting the ceiling on oil sales under the oil-for-food program so that Iraqi civilian humanitarian needs can better be met.

As long as Saddam Hussein remains in power, he represents a threat to the well-being of his people, the peace of the region, and the security of the world. We will continue to contain the threat he poses, but over the long term the best way to address that threat is through a new government in Baghdad. To that end, we—working with the Congress—are deepening our engagement with the forces for change in Iraq to help make the opposition a more effective voice for the aspirations of the Iraqi people. Our efforts are discussed in more detail below.

U.S. and Coalition Force Levels in the Gulf Region

Saddam's record of aggressive behavior compels us to retain a highly capable force in the region in order to deter Iraq and deal with any threat it might pose to its neighbors, the reconstitution of its WMD program, or movement against the Kurds in northern Iraq. We demonstrated our resolve in mid-December when forces in the region carried out Operation Desert Fox to degrade Iraq's ability to develop and deliver weapons of mass destruction and its ability to threaten its neighbors. We will continue to maintain a robust posture and have established a rapid reinforcement capability to supplement our forces in the Gulf, if needed.

Our forces in the region include land and carrier based aircraft, surface warships, a Marine Expeditionary unit, a Patriot missile battalion, a mechanized battalion task force, and a mix of special operations forces deployed in support of U.S. Central Command. To enhance force protection throughout the region, additional military security personnel are also deployed. Because of the increased air-defense threat to coalition aircraft, we have also added a robust personnel recovery capability.

Operation Northern Watch and Operation Southern Watch

The United States and coalition partners continue to enforce the no-fly zones over Iraq through Operation Northern Watch and Operation Southern Watch. Since December 23, following the conclusion of Desert Fox, we have seen a significant increase in the frequency, intensity, and coordination of the Iraqi air defense system to counter enforcement of the no-fly zones. Since that date, U.S.

and coalition aircraft enforcing the no-fly zones have been subject to multiple anti-aircraft artillery (AAA) firings, radar illuminations, and over 20 surface-to-air missile attacks. Subsequent to Desert Fox, Iraq significantly increased its air defense presence in both the north and south, but it has since returned to pre-Desert Fox levels. Despite the decrease, however, Iraq has not ceased threatening coalition aircraft.

In response to Iraq's increased and repeated no-fly zone violations, and in coordination with the Secretary of Defense's advice, our aircrews have been authorized by me to respond to the increased Iraqi threat. United States and coalition forces can defend themselves against any Iraqi threat in carrying out their no-fly zone enforcement mission. On over 50 occasions since December, U.S. and coalition forces have engaged the Iraqi integrated air defense system. As a consequence, the Iraqi air defense system has been degraded substantially further since December.

The Maritime Interception Force

The multinational Maritime Interception Force (MIF), operating in accordance with Resolution 665 and other relevant resolutions, enforces U.N. sanctions in the Gulf. The U.S. Navy is the single largest component of the MIF, but it is frequently augmented by ships, aircraft, and other support from Australia, Belgium, Canada, Kuwait, The Netherlands, New Zealand, the UAE, and the United Kingdom. Member states of the Gulf Cooperation Council (GCC) provide logistical support and shipriders to the MIF and accept vessels diverted for violating U.N. sanctions against Iraq. Kuwait was especially helpful providing significant naval and coast guard assistance. Additionally, they accepted over 15 diverted sanctions violators.

Although refined petroleum products leaving Iraq comprise most of the prohibited traffic, the MIF has intercepted a growing number of ships smuggling prohibited items into Iraq in violation of U.N. sanctions and outside the parameters of the humanitarian oil-for-food program. In early December, the MIF conducted the latest in a series of periodic surge operations in the far northern Gulf near the major Iraqi waterways. These operations

disrupted smuggling in the region. Kuwait and the UAE have stepped up their own enforcement efforts. Although partially repaired and back on line, damage to the Basra refinery inflicted during Desert Fox had a significant impact on Iraq's gas and oil smuggling operations in the Gulf.

In December 1998, Iraq relocated surface-to-surface missile batteries to the coastal area of the Al Faw Peninsula. The missiles in question, with a range of nearly 60 nautical miles, could reach far into the North Arabian Gulf and posed a serious threat to the MIF. The deployment of these missiles to a position from which they could engage coalition naval forces was carried out in concert with the increased attempts to shoot down aircraft enforcing the no-fly zones and constituted an enhancement of Iraq's military capability in southern Iraq. Coalition aircraft responded with air strikes to the threat posed by these missiles and are authorized to continue to do so as necessary.

Chemical Weapons

After Iraq's November 15, 1998, pledge of unconditional cooperation with weapons inspectors, UNSCOM began to test the Iraqi promise. In a November 25 letter, Iraq continued to deny that it ever weaponized VX nerve agent or produced stabilized VX, despite UNSCOM's publicly stated confidence in the Edgewood Arsenal Laboratory finding of stabilized VX components in fragments of Iraqi SCUD missile warheads. Iraq alleges that the presence of VX was a deliberate act of tampering with the samples examined in the United States.

On November 26, Iraq agreed to cooperate with UNSCOM efforts to determine the disposition of 155mm shells filled with mustard chemical agent, and UNSCOM agreed to proceed with such an effort when logistically possible. Iraq also agreed to cooperate in verifying the tail assemblies of R-400 bombs, and in determining the precise locations of pits that had been used for the field storage of special warheads at Fallujah Forest and the Tigris Canal.

On November 30, the Iraqis failed to meet a deadline to provide various documents Chairman Butler requested pertaining to Iraq's chemical weapons program. Included in this request was the Iraqi Air Force file of documents found previously by UNSCOM inspectors that details chemical weapons expended during the Iran-Iraq war. We understand that UNSCOM believes the file indicates that Iraq's official declarations to UNSCOM have greatly overstated the quantities of chemical weapons expended, which means that at least 6,000 chemical weapons are unaccounted.

In a January 25, 1999, report to the U.N. Security Council President, UNSCOM identified as a priority chemical weapons disarmament issues: VX, the 155mm mustard shells; the Iraqi Air Force file of chemical weapons documents; R-400 bombs filled with CBW (field inspections needed); and chemical weapons production equipment (field verification is needed for 18 of 20 shipping containers UNSCOM knows were moved together). On monitoring, the report identified as priorities the ability to verify Iraqi compliance at listed facilities and to detect construction of new dual-use facilities.

Biological Weapons

Iraq has failed to provide a credible explanation for UNSCOM tests that found anthrax in fragments of seven SCUD missile warheads. Iraq has been claiming since 1995 that it put anthrax in only five such warheads, and had previously denied weaponizing anthrax at all. Iraq's explanations to date are far from satisfactory, although it now acknowledges putting both anthrax and botulinum toxin into some number of warheads.

Iraq's biological weapons (BW) program—including SCUD missile BW warheads, R-400 BW bombs, drop-tanks to be filled with BW, spray devices for BW, production of BW agents (anthrax, botulinum toxin, aflatoxin, and wheat cover smut), and BW agent growth media—remains the "black hole" described by Chairman Butler. Iraq has consistently failed to provide a credible account of its efforts to produce and weaponize its BW agents.

During the period November 17 to December 2, 1998, an undeclared Class II Biosafety Cabinet and some filter presses were discovered; these items are subject to declarations by Iraq and biological monitoring.

On November 18 and 20, Chairman Butler again asked Iraq's Deputy Prime Minister for information concerning Iraq's biological weapons programs. Iraq has supplied none of the information requested.

In the January 25, 1999, report to the U.N. Security Council President, UNSCOM identified as a priority biological weapons disarmament issue Iraq's incomplete declarations on "the whole scope of the BW program." The declarations are important because "Iraq possesses an industrial capability and knowledge base, through which biological warfare agents could be produced quickly and in volume." The report also identified the importance of monitoring dual-use biological items, equipment, facilities, research, and acquisition at 250 listed sites. The effectiveness of monitoring is "proportional to Iraq's cooperation and transparency, to the number of monitored sites, and to the number of inspectors."

Long-Range Missiles

Iraq's past practices of (1) refusing to discuss further its system for concealment of longer range missiles and their components, (2) refusing to provide credible evidence of its disposition of large quantities of the unique fuel required for the long-range SCUD missile, and (3) continuing to test modifications to SA-2 VOLGA surface-to-air missile components appear intended to enhance Iraq's capability to produce a surface-to-surface missile of range greater than its permitted range of 150 km.

While UNSCOM believes it can account for 817 of 819 imported Soviet-made SCUD missiles, Iraq has refused to give UNSCOM a credible accounting of the indigenous program that produced complete SCUD missiles that were both successfully test-flown and delivered to the Iraqi Army.

In its January 25, 1999, report to the U.N. Security Council President, UNSCOM identified the following as priority missile disarmament issues: 50 unaccounted SCUD conventional warheads; 500 tons of SCUD propellants, the destruction of which has not been verified; 7 Iraqi-produced SCUDs given to the army, the destruction of which cannot be verified; truckloads of major components for

SCUD production that are missing; the concealment of BW warheads; and the lack of accounting for VX-filled war-heads. The report identified as priorities the capability to monitor declared activities, leaps in missile technology, and changes to declared operational missiles. There are 80 listed missile sites.

Nuclear Weapons

After Iraq unconditionally rescinded its declarations of non-cooperation on November 15, the IAEA began to test the Iraqi pledge of full cooperation. The IAEA Director General Mohammed El-Baradei's December 14 report on Iraqi cooperation stated: "The Iraqi counterpart has provided the necessary level of cooperation to enable the above-enumerated activities [ongoing monitoring] to be completed efficiently and effectively." In its 6-month report to the Security Council on October 7, the IAEA stated that it had a "technically coherent" view of the Iraqi nuclear program. At that time, the IAEA also stated its remaining questions about Iraq's nuclear program can be dealt with within IAEA's ongoing monitoring and verification (OMV) effort. In the IAEA's February 8 report to the U.N. Security Council it reiterated this position.

Nonetheless, Iraq has not yet supplied information in response to the Security Council's May 14 Presidential Statement. This statement noted that the IAEA continues to have questions and concerns regarding foreign assistance, abandonment of the program, and the extent of Iraqi progress in weapons design. Iraq has also not passed penal legislation prohibiting nuclear-related activities contrary to Resolution 687.

In a February 8, 1999, report to the U.N. Secretary Council President, IAEA Director General Mohammed El-Baradei summarized previous IAEA assessments of Iraq's compliance with its nuclear disarmament and monitoring obligations. The report restates that "Iraq has not fulfilled its obligation to adopt measures and enact penal laws, to implement and enforce compliance with Iraq's obligations under Resolutions 687 and 707, other relevant Security Council resolutions and the IAEA OMV plan, as required under paragraph 34 of that plan." The IAEA states that the three areas where questions on Iraq's nuclear disarmament remain (lack of technical documentation, lack of information on external assistance to Iraq's clandestine nuclear weapons program, and lack of information on Iraq's abandonment of its nuclear weapons program) would not prevent the full implementation of its OMV plan.

The IAEA continues to plan for long-term monitoring and verification under Resolution 715. In its February 8 report, the IAEA restated that monitoring must be "intrusive" and estimated annual monitoring costs would total nearly $10 million.

Dual-Use Imports

Resolution 1051 established a joint UNSCOM/ IAEA unit to monitor Iraq's imports of allowed dual-use items. Iraq must notify the unit before it imports specific items that can be used in both weapons of mass destruction and civilian applications. Similarly, U.N. members must provide timely notification of exports to Iraq of such dual-use items. Following the withdrawal of UNSCOM and IAEA monitors, there is no monitoring of dual-use items inside Iraq. This factor has presented new challenges for the U.N. Sanctions Committee and is taken into consideration in the approval process.

The U.N.'s "Oil-for-Food" Program

We continue to support the international community's efforts to provide for the humanitarian needs of the Iraqi people through the oil-for-food program. Transition from phase four to phase five (authorized by U.N. Security Council Resolution 1210) was smooth. As in phase four, Iraq is again authorized to sell up to $5.2 billion worth of oil every 180 days. However, because of a drop in world oil prices, Iraq was only able to pump and sell approximately $3.1 billion worth of oil during phase four. Since the first deliveries under oil-for-food began in March 1997, food worth $2.75 billion, and over $497 million worth of medicine and health supplies have been delivered to Iraq.

As of January 19, under phase four of the oil-for-food program, contracts for the purchase of over $2.3 billion worth of humanitarian goods for the Iraqi people have been presented to the U.N. Office of the Iraq Program for review by the Sanctions Committee; of these, contracts worth over $1.6 billion have been approved; most of the remaining contracts are being processed by the Office of the Iraq Program. As of February 4, the United States had approved 584 contracts in phase four and had placed 28 on hold pending clarification of questions about the proposed contracts.

With regard to funds set aside for imports of parts and equipment to increase oil exports, as of February 4, 333 contracts with a total value of nearly $178 million have been approved; 94 contracts are on hold. In January, the United States released a number of holds on oil spare parts contracts. Up to $300 million had been set aside in phase four of the oil-for-food program to pay for spare parts and equipment to increase Iraqi oil exports and thus increase available humanitarian funding. The United States had requested holds on contracts that did not directly boost oil exports. As the current phase of oil-for-food again sets aside $300 million for this purpose, the United States decided to remove holds on lower priority contracts.

The Security Council met in January to discuss the humanitarian situation in Iraq. The United States supported an examination of the current situation and exploration of ways to improve the humanitarian situation, particularly with regard to vulnerable groups such as children under age five, and pregnant and nursing women. The United States has expressed its support for lifting the cap on Iraqi oil exports under the oil-for-food program, and has suggested some streamlining of approval of food and medicine contracts in the U.N. Sanctions Committee.

Three assessment panels are being formed to look at Iraqi disarmament, the humanitarian situation in Iraq, and Iraq's obligations regarding Kuwait. The panels are expected to complete their work by the middle of April.

Resolution 1210 maintains a separate oil-for-food program for northern Iraq, administered directly by the United Nations in consultation with the local population. This program, which the United States strongly supports, receives 13 to 15 percent of the funds generated under the oil-for-food program. The separate northern program was established because of the Baghdad regime's proven disregard for the humanitarian needs of the Kurdish, Assyrian, and Turkomen minorities of northern Iraq, and its readiness to apply the most brutal forms of repression against them. In northern Iraq, where Baghdad does not exercise control, the oil-for-food program has been able to operate relatively effectively. The Kurdish factions are setting aside their differences to work together so that Resolution 1210 is implemented as efficiently as possible.

The United Nations is required to monitor carefully implementation of all aspects of the oil-for-food program. The current phase marked by Resolution 1210 anticipates infrastructure repairs in areas such as oil export capacity, generation of electricity, and water purification. The U.N. monitoring regime is presented with increasing challenges, as UNSCOM monitors are no longer in Iraq.

Humanitarian programs such as oil-for-food have steadily improved the life of the average Iraqi living under sanctions (who, for example, now receives a ration basket providing over 2,000 calories per day, a significant improvement in nutrition since the program began) while denying Saddam Hussein control over oil revenues. We will continue to work with the U.N. Secretariat, the Security Council, and others in the international community to ensure that the humanitarian needs of the Iraqi people are met while denying any political or economic benefits to the Baghdad regime.

Northern Iraq: Kurdish Reconciliation
Since their ground-breaking meeting with Secretary Albright in September, Massoud Barzani, President of the Kurdistan Democratic Party (KDP), and Jalal Talabani, Chairman of the Patriotic Union of Kurdistan (PUK), have met three times to continue their work towards full reconciliation. Both parties have condemned internal fighting, pledged to refrain from violence in settling their differences, and resolved to eliminate terrorism by establishing stronger safeguards for Iraq's borders. Our deep concern for the safety, security, and economic well-being of Iraqi Kurds, Shias, Sunnis, and others who have been subject to brutal attacks by the Baghdad

regime remains a primary focus of our Iraq policy.

On November 4, the Governments of Turkey and the United Kingdom joined us in recognizing and welcoming the cooperative achievement of Mr. Barzani and Mr. Talabani. The three states reiterated the importance of preserving the unity and territorial integrity of Iraq and noted, with pleasure, the prominence the KDP and PUK have accorded this principle. We also welcomed the commitment by the KDP and PUK to deny sanctuary to the Kurdistan Workers Party (PKK), to eliminate all PKK bases from the region, and to safeguard the Turkish border. The parties believe that key decisions on Iraq's future should be made by all the Iraqi people together at an appropriate time and in a regular political process. Their work to achieve the principles embodied in the Ankara Statements are thus meant to implement a framework of regional administration until a united, pluralistic, and democratic Iraq is achieved.

On January 8, the two leaders met without recourse to U.S., U.K., or Turkish interlocutors, in Salahidin in northern Iraq. They reiterated their determination to implement the September agreement, made concrete progress on key issues of revenue sharing and closing down PKK bases, and agreed to stay in close contact.

The United States is committed to ensuring that international aid continues to reach the north, that the human rights of the Kurds and northern Iraq minority groups, such as the Turkomen, Assyrians, Yezedis, and others are respected, and that the no-fly-zone enforced by Operation Northern Watch is observed. The United States will decide how and when to respond should Baghdad's actions pose an increased threat to Iraq's neighbors, to regional security, to vital U.S. interests, and to the Iraqi people, including those in the north.

The Human Rights Situation in Iraq

The human rights situation throughout Iraq continues to be a cause for grave concern. As I reported November 5, the Iraqi army has stepped up repressive operations against the Shia in the south. In mid-November, we received unconfirmed reports from the Iraqi opposition that 150 persons had been executed

at Amara, with three bodies left hanging on the city's main bridge over the Tigris River as a warning to those who oppose the regime. An additional 172 persons, some detained since 1991, were reported to have been summarily executed in Abu Gharaib and Radwaniya prisons; as in prior waves of summary prison killings, bodies showing clear signs of torture were reportedly returned to their families. Reports reached us in December that a mass grave containing at least 25 bodies was found near the Khoraisan River in Diyala province, east of Baghdad.

The Iraqi government continues to work toward the destruction of the Marsh Arabs' way of life and the unique ecology of the southern marshes. In the past 2 months, 7 more villages were reportedly destroyed on the margins of the marshes, with irrigation water cut off and the vegetation cut down and burned. Those who could not flee to the interior of the marshes—particularly the old, infirm, women, and children—were said to have been taken hostage by regime forces.

On February 19, the Shia Grand Ayatollah Mohammed al-Sadr was murdered in Iraq along with several of his relatives. Opposition sources indicate this murder was the work of the Saddam regime. The regime also violently suppressed demonstrations that followed in Baghdad and other cities opposing the murder.

In the north, outside the Kurdish-controlled areas, the government continues the forced expulsion of ethnic Kurds and Turkomen from Kirkuk and other cities. In recent months, hundreds of families have reportedly been expelled from Kirkuk with seven new Arab settlements created on land seized from the Kurds. Reports from the Kurdish-controlled areas where the displaced persons are received indicate that they are forced to leave behind almost all of their personal property. Due to a shortage of housing, they are still living in temporary shelters.

A conference on the research and treatment of victims of chemical and biological weapons attacks in northern Iraq, organized by the Washington Kurdish Institute and sponsored by the Department of State was held on November 18-19, 1998. The conference focused on the long-range effects of the Iraqi chemical attack on the village of

Halabja, where nearly 5,000 persons were killed in 1988. According to panelists, the hideous combination of mustard gas, tabun, sarin, VX, tear gas, and possibly aflatoxin that the Iraqi military used in the attack has resulted in dramatically increased rates of cancer, respiratory problems, heart failure, infertility, miscarriages, and possibly genetic damage in the surviving population.

On December 1, the London-based IN-DICT organization announced that 12 senior Iraqi officials—including Saddam Hussein, his sons Uday and Qusay, his half-brother Barzan al-Tikriti, Vice President Taha Yasin Ramadan, and Deputy Prime Minister Tariq Aziz—would be the focus of its campaign for prosecution by an international tribunal.

The Iraqi government continues to stall and obfuscate attempts to account for more than 600 Kuwaitis and third-country nationals who disappeared at the hands of Iraqi authorities during or after the occupation of Kuwait, despite a Security Council resolution requiring it to do so. Baghdad still refuses to allow independent human rights monitors to enter Iraq, despite repeated requests by U.N. Special Rapporteur for Iraq, Max Van der Stoel. The U.N. Human Rights Commission has issued a strong condemnation of the "all-pervasive repression and oppression" of the Iraqi government.

The Iraqi Opposition

We are deepening our engagement with the forces of change in Iraq, helping Iraqis inside and outside Iraq become a more effective voice for the aspirations of the people. We will work toward the day when Iraq has a government worthy of its people—a government prepared to live in peace with its neighbors, a government that respects the rights of its citizens, rather than represses them. On October 31, I signed into law the Iraq Liberation Act of 1998. It provides significant new discretionary authorities to assist the opposition in its struggle against the regime. On January 19, I submitted to the Congress a notification of my intent to designate certain groups under the Act; I designated those groups on February 4. The assessment of additional groups that may qualify for assistance under the Act is progressing. Also on

October 31, Radio Free Iraq began operations. Its broadcasts are being heard in Iraq and its message profoundly displeases the regime.

On November 17, Assistant Secretary of State for Near Eastern Affairs, Martin Indyk, met with 17 London-based representatives of the Iraqi opposition. He heard the full range of views of the parties present, and outlined the new U.S. policy toward the opposition. Indyk urged them to work together toward the common purpose of a new government in Baghdad; the United States will help, but the opposition itself must take the lead. He urged them to do all they could to get a message to the people of Iraq that there is an alternative to Saddam Hussein, adding that the United States will support the campaign to indict Saddam as a war criminal.

Former Iraqi Foreign Minister Adnan Pachachi outlined a number of agreed points to Indyk. The group: 1) welcomed the new U.S. policy toward the opposition; 2) will work to create a democratic government in Iraq; 3) will redouble efforts to get all groups to work together; 4) wants the opposition to serve as an interlocutor for the Iraqi people with the international community; and 5) expressed thanks for the U.S. role in the recent Kurdish reconciliation.

On January 21, Secretary of State Albright announced the appointment of Frank Ricciardone as Special Representative for Transition in Iraq (SRTI). He will abbreviate his current tour as Deputy Chief of Mission in Ankara, and take up his new responsibilities in early March. He traveled with the Secretary of State to London, Riyadh, and Cairo in late January to discuss U.S. policy on this issue. He outlined U.S. intentions to help Iraq resume its rightful place in the region—a goal the United States believes can only be achieved under new Iraqi leadership. He emphasized U.S. desire to work with Iraqis—who alone can make this happen—inside Iraq and outside Iraq, as well as with Iraq's neighbors who share the same objectives.

There are, of course, other important elements of U.S. policy. These include the maintenance of Security Council support for efforts to eliminate Iraq's prohibited weapons and missile programs, and economic sanctions that continue to deny the regime the means to reconstitute those threats to international peace and security. United States support for the Iraqi opposition will be carried out consistent with those policy objectives as well. Similarly, U.S. support must be attuned to what Iraqis can effectively make use of as it develops over time.

The United Nations Compensation Commission

The United Nations Compensation Commission (UNCC), established pursuant to Resolutions 687, 692, and 1210, continues to resolve claims against Iraq arising from Iraq's unlawful invasion and occupation of Kuwait. The UNCC has issued over 1.3 million awards worth approximately $7 billion. Thirty percent of the proceeds from the oil sales permitted by Security Council resolutions have been allocated to the Compensation Fund to pay awards and to finance operations of the UNCC. Pursuant to decisions of the UNCC Governing Council, certain small claims are to receive initial payments of $2,500 toward the amounts approved on those claims before large claims of individuals and claims of corporations and governments may share in the funds available for claims payments. As money from Iraqi oil sales is deposited in the Compensation Fund the UNCC makes these initial $2,500 payments on eligible claims in the order in which those claims were approved by the UNCC. To date, the United States Government has received funds from the UNCC for initial installment payments on approximately 1435 claims of U.S. claimants.

Conclusion

Iraq remains a serious threat to international peace and security. I remain determined to see Iraq comply fully with all of its obligations under Security Council resolutions. The United States looks forward to the day when Iraq rejoins the family of nations as a responsible and law-abiding member. I appreciate the support of the Congress for our efforts and shall continue to keep the Congress informed about this important issue.

Sincerely,
William J. Clinton

326.

[Vol. 35, no. 20 (May 24, 1999): 945-951]

Letter to Congressional Leaders on Iraq's Compliance With United Nations Security Council Resolutions
May 19, 1999

Dear Mr. Speaker: (Dear Mr. President:)

Consistent with the Authorization for Use of Military Force Against Iraq Resolution (Public Law 102-1) and as part of my effort to keep the Congress fully informed, I am reporting on the status of efforts to obtain Iraq's compliance with the resolutions adopted by the United Nations Security Council (UNSC). My last report, consistent with Public Law 102-1, was transmitted on March 3, 1999.

Overview

There have been no United Nations Special Commission (UNSCOM) or International Atomic Energy Agency (IAEA) inspections in Iraq since December 15, 1998. On January 30, 1999, the UNSC established three assessment panels on Iraq to address disarmament, humanitarian, and Kuwait-related issues. Brazilian Ambassador to the United Nations Celso Amorim, who chaired the panels, presented the panels' conclusions to the Security Council on April 6.

The disarmament panel confirmed UNSCOM's earlier findings that Iraq has failed to comply with its obligations under UNSC resolutions, and that significant disarmament issues have not yet been resolved. It also confirmed the validity of the disarmament and monitoring plan endorsed by Resolution 715.

The humanitarian panel noted that, despite considerable improvements in the humanitarian situation since the oil-for-food program began, serious problems remain. The report highlighted the Government of Iraq's failure to order and distribute critical supplies, and its inequitable distribution practices. It also identified a significant shortfall in revenue for the oil-for-food program. This problem has been largely caused by low oil prices during the last year, but Iraq's limited oil production capabilities have also been a factor.

The Kuwait-issues panel cited Iraq's failure to comply with its requirement to provide information on Kuwaiti and other missing persons from the Gulf War, as well as its failure to comply with the requirement to return property stolen during the Gulf War, including Kuwait's national archives.

The 6-month reports submitted to the Security Council by Ambassador Butler and IAEA Director-General Mohammed El Baradei in April 1999 reflected the refusal by Iraq to add substantively to their ability to resolve outstanding disarmament and monitoring issues. In New York, UNSCOM continued to implement its mandate: by assessing the situation on the ground in Iraq after the military action in December, by choosing new sites for future inspection, by refining inspection protocols, by continuing a dialogue with member nations to obtain information about Iraq's past and present activities, and by continuing to improve the Export-Import Monitoring Mechanism.

The United States continues to support the international community's efforts to provide for the humanitarian needs of the Iraqi people through the oil-for-food program.

We are convinced that as long as Saddam Hussein remains in power, he will continue to threaten the well-being of his people, the peace of the region and the security of the world. We will continue to contain these threats, but over the long term the best way to address them is through a new government in Baghdad. To that end, working with the Congress, we have deepened our engagement with the forces of change in Iraq to help make the opposition a more effective voice for the aspirations of the Iraqi people.

U.S. and Coalition Force Levels in the Gulf Region

Saddam Hussein's record of aggressive behavior compels us to retain a highly capable force in the region in order to deter Iraq and respond to any threat it might pose to its neighbors, the reconstitution of its WMD program, or movement against the Kurds in northern Iraq. We demonstrated our resolve in mid-December when forces in the region carried out Operation Desert Fox to degrade Iraq's ability to develop and deliver weapons of mass destruction and its ability to threaten its neighbors. We will continue to maintain a robust posture and have established a rapid reinforcement capability to supplement our forces in the Gulf, if needed.

Our forces that deployed to the region include land- and carrier-based aircraft, surface warships, a Patriot missile battalion, a mechanized battalion task force and a mix of special operations forces deployed in support of U.S. Central Command. To enhance force protection throughout the region, additional military security personnel are also deployed. Because of the increased air-defense threat to coalition aircraft, we have also added a robust personnel recovery capability.

Operation Northern Watch and Operation Southern Watch

The United States and coalition partners enforcing the no-fly zones over Iraq under Operations Northern Watch and Southern Watch continue to be subject to multiple anti-aircraft artillery firings and radar illuminations, and have faced more than 35 surface-to-air missile attacks. Additionally, since the conclusion of Desert Fox, Iraqi aircraft have committed over 120 no-fly zone violations.

In response to Iraq's repeated no-fly-zone violations and attacks on our aircraft, I have authorized our air crews to respond directly and forcibly to the increased Iraqi threat. United States and coalition forces are fully prepared and authorized to defend themselves against any Iraqi threat while carrying out their no-fly zone enforcement mission and have, when circumstances warranted, engaged various components of the Iraqi integrated air defense system. As a consequence, the Iraqi air defense system has been degraded substantially since December 1998.

The Maritime Interception Force

The multinational Maritime Interception Force (MIF), operating in accordance with Resolution 665 and other relevant resolutions, enforces UN sanctions in the Gulf. The U.S. Navy is the single largest component of the MIF, but it is frequently augmented by ships, aircraft, and other support from Australia, Bahrain, Belgium, Canada, Kuwait, The Netherlands, New Zealand, the UAE, and the

United Kingdom. Member states of the Gulf Cooperation Council (GCC) provide logistical support and shipriders to the MIF and accept vessels diverted for violating UN sanctions against Iraq. Kuwait was especially helpful in providing significant naval and coast guard assistance. We are expanding our efforts to encourage participation in the MIF from nations in northern Europe and South America.

Although the export of refined petroleum products through the Gulf has significantly declined since Operation Desert Fox, the MIF continues to patrol the waters to prevent a resurgence of petroleum-product smuggling. Furthermore, the MIF provides a deterrent to ships smuggling prohibited items into Iraq in violation of UN sanctions and outside the parameters of the humanitarian oil-for-food program. In early April, the MIF conducted the latest in a series of periodic search operations in the far northern Gulf near the major Iraqi waterways. These operations disrupted smuggling in the region without interference from Iraq. Kuwait and the UAE have stepped up their own enforcement efforts.

In December 1998 and again in April 1999, Iraq relocated surface-to-surface missile batteries to the coastal area of the Al Faw Peninsula. The missiles in question, with a range of nearly 60 nautical miles, could reach far into the North Arabian Gulf and posed a serious threat to the MIF. The deployment of these missiles to a position from which they could engage coalition naval forces was carried out in concert with the increased attempts to shoot down aircraft enforcing the no-fly zones and constituted an enhancement of Iraq's offensive military capability in southern Iraq. On both occasions, coalition aircraft responded to the threat posed by these missiles and are authorized to continue to do so as necessary.

Chemical Weapons

April reports to the UNSC President reconfirmed January's findings that UNSCOM identified as priority chemical weapons disarmament issues: VX; 155mm mustard shells; an Iraqi Air Force file of chemical weapons documents; R-400 bombs filled with CBW (field inspections needed); and chemical weapons production equipment (field verifica-

tion is needed for 18 of 20 shipping containers UNSCOM knows were moved together). The reporters identified as key monitoring priorities the ability to verify Iraqi compliance at listed facilities and to detect construction of new dual-use facilities.

Biological Weapons

April reports to the UNSC President reconfirmed January's findings that UNSCOM identified as priority outstanding biological weapons disarmament issues Iraq's incomplete declarations on "the whole scope of the BW program." The declarations are important because "Iraq possesses an industrial capability and knowledge base, through which biological warfare agents could be produced quickly and in volume." The report also identified the importance of monitoring dual-use biological items, equipment, facilities, research and acquisition at 250 listed sites. The effectiveness of monitoring is "proportional to Iraq's cooperation and transparency, to the number of monitored sites, and to the number of inspectors."

Long-range Missiles

April reports to the UNSC President reconfirmed January's findings that UNSCOM identified as priority missile disarmament issues: 50 unaccounted for, SCUD conventional warheads; 500 tons of SCUD propellants, the destruction of which has not been verified; 7 Iraqi-produced SCUDs given to the army, the destruction of which cannot be verified; truckloads of major components for SCUD production that are missing; the concealment of BW warheads; and the lack of accounting for VX-filled warheads. The report identified the capability to monitor declared activities, leaps in missile technology, and changes to declared operational missiles. There are 80 listed missile sites.

Nuclear Weapons

In a February 8, 1999, report to the UNSC President, IAEA Director General Mohammed El-Baradei summarized previous IAEA assessments of Iraq's compliance with its nuclear disarmament and monitoring obligations. The report restates that "Iraq has not fulfilled its obligation to adopt measures and enact penal laws, to implement and enforce compliance with Iraq's obligations under resolutions 687 and 707, other relevant Security Council resolutions and the IAEA OMV plan, as required under paragraph 34 of that plan."

The IAEA continues to plan for long-term monitoring and verification under Resolution 715. In its February 8 report to the Security Council, it restated that monitoring must be "intrusive" and estimated annual monitoring costs would total nearly $10 million.

Dual-use Imports

Resolution 1051 established a joint UN-SCOM/IAEA unit to monitor Iraq's imports of allowed dual-use items. Iraq must notify the unit before it imports specific items that can be used in both weapons of mass destruction and civilian applications. Similarly, U.N. members must provide timely notification of exports to Iraq of such dual-use items. Following the withdrawal of UNSCOM and IAEA monitors, there is no monitoring by UNSCOM or IAEA inspectors of dual-use items inside Iraq, although some limited monitoring in certain sectors can be carried out by OIP inspectors. This factor has presented new challenges for the U.N. Sanctions Committee and is taken into consideration in the approval process. The United States has placed holds on a number of contracts that might otherwise have been approved as a result.

The UN's Oil-for-food Program

We continue to support the international community's efforts to provide for the humanitarian needs of the Iraqi people through the oil-for-food program. Transition from phase four to phase five (authorized by UNSC Resolution 1210) was smooth. As in phase four, Iraq is again authorized to sell up to $5.2 billion worth of oil every 180 days. However, because of a drop in world oil prices, Iraq was only able to pump and sell approximately $3.1 billion worth of oil in phase four; recent increases in world prices should provide increased revenue for this phase of oil-for-food.

As of April 5, under phase five of the oil-for-food program, 340 contracts worth nearly $1 billion have been approved. As of April 5, the United States had 145 phase four and 13 phase five contracts on hold pending clarification of questions about the proposed contracts.

Three assessment panels were formed in January to look at Iraqi disarmament, the humanitarian situation in Iraq, and Iraq's obligations regarding Kuwait. The panels presented their reports to the Security Council in April. The United States supported an examination of the current situation and exploration of ways to improve humanitarian conditions, particularly with regard to vulnerable groups such as children under age five and pregnant and nursing women. The United States has expressed its support for raising the cap on Iraqi oil exports under the oil-for-food program in order to meet humanitarian needs, and for certain other proposals made by the humanitarian assessment panel.

Resolution 1210 maintains a separate oil-for-food program for northern Iraq, administered directly by the United Nations in consultation with the local population. This program, which the United States strongly supports, receives 13 to 15 percent of the funds generated under the oil-for-food program. The separate northern program was established because of the Baghdad regime's proven disregard for the humanitarian needs of the Kurdish, Assyrian, Yezedi and Turkoman minorities of northern Iraq, and its readiness to apply the most brutal forms of repression against them. In northern Iraq areas where Baghdad does not exercise control, the oil-for-food program has been able to operate relatively effectively, as documented by the humanitarian assessment panel. The Kurdish factions have set aside their differences to work together so that Resolution 1210 is implemented as efficiently as possible.

Humanitarian programs such as oil-for-food have steadily improved the life of the average Iraqi living under sanctions (who, for example, now receives a ration basket providing over 2,000 calories per day, a significant improvement in nutrition since the program began) while denying Saddam Hussein control over oil revenues. We will continue to work with the UN Secretariat, the Security Council, and others in the international community to ensure that the humanitarian needs of the Iraqi people are met while denying any political or economic benefits to the Baghdad regime.

Northern Iraq: Kurdish Reconciliation

Since their ground-breaking meeting with Secretary Albright in September 1998, Massoud Barzani, President of the Kurdistan Democratic Party (KDP), and Jalal Talabani, Chairman of the Patriotic Union of Kurdistan (PUK), have met four times to continue their work towards full reconciliation. Both parties have condemned internal fighting, pledged to refrain from violence in settling their differences, and resolved to eliminate terrorism by establishing stronger safeguards for Iraq's borders. In particular, both parties have committed themselves to deny sanctuary to the Kurdistan Workers Party (PKK), to eliminate all PKK bases from the region and to safeguard the Turkish border. The parties believe that key decisions on Iraq's future should be made by all the Iraqi people together at an appropriate time and through a regular political process. Their work is thus meant to implement a framework of regional administration until a united, pluralistic, and democratic Iraq is achieved. A Higher Coordination Committee (HCC) made up of senior representatives from the PUK and the KDP meets regularly in northern Iraq, and officials of the State Department are in frequent contact with the parties to further the reconciliation process.

The United States is committed to ensuring that international aid continues to reach the north; that the human rights of the Kurds and northern Iraq minority groups such as the Turkomans, Assyrians, Yezedis, and others are respected; and that the no-fly zone enforced by Operation Northern Watch is observed. The United States will decide how and when to respond should Baghdad's actions pose an increased threat to Iraq's neighbors, to regional security, to vital U.S. interests, and to the Iraqi people, including those in the north.

The Human Rights Situation in Iraq

The human rights situation in Iraq continues to fall far short of international norms, in violation of Resolution 688. For over seven years, the Iraqi government has refused to allow the UN Human Rights Commission Special Rapporteur for Iraq, Max Van der Stoel, to visit Iraq. UN human rights monitors have never been allowed in. Meanwhile, increasingly disturbing reports of the most serious nature continue to emanate from Iraq. For example, 2,500 political prisoners have been summarily executed without due process of law since Fall 1997, according to detailed reports Mr. Van der Stoel received. Often, the bodies are said to have been returned to the victim's families showing clear signs of torture.

The assassination of three of Iraq's most senior Islamic clerics is of special concern. In February, Ayatollah Mohammed al-Sader—the most senior Shia cleric in Iraq—was assassinated, along with two of his sons, after attending Friday prayers in Najaf. This follows the similar killing of Sheikh Borojourdi in April 1998 and Ayatollah Ah al-Gharawi in June 1998. In each case, the killings reportedly followed months of arrests and interrogations by government security services, and have been widely attributed to agents of the regime. The deaths also come in the context of a resurgence of repression in southern Iraq, as the regime works toward the destruction of the Marsh Arabs' way of life and the unique ecology of the southern marshes. The regime also continues to ignore appeals by Mr. Van der Stoel and others for access by human rights monitors to investigate these reports.

In the north, outside the Kurdish-controlled areas, the government continues the forced expulsion of ethnic Kurds and Turkomans from Kirkuk and other cities. In recent months, hundreds of families have reportedly been expelled from Kirkuk. Reports from the Kurdish-controlled areas where the displaced persons are received indicate that they are forced to leave behind almost all of their personal property. Due to a shortage of housing, many are still living in temporary shelters.

The Iraqi Opposition

We are deepening our engagement with the forces of change in Iraq, helping Iraqis inside and outside Iraq to become a more effective voice for the aspirations of the people. We will work toward the day when Iraq has a government worthy of its people—a government prepared to live in peace with its neighbors, a government that respects the rights of its citizens.

On April 7-8, the Executive Council of the Iraqi National Congress met at Windsor, in the United Kingdom. The meeting produced three important results: it elected a seven-member interim "Presidency Committee;" it created an "outreach committee" to expand the INC's membership and build links to regional states; and it decided that a meeting of the INC National Assembly would be held no later than July 7, at a site to be determined. We applaud the Council members for this constructive, forward-looking meeting.

Senator Bob Kerrey of Nebraska attended the meeting as U.S. observer along with Special Coordinator for the Transition of Iraq, Frank Ricciardone, as well as other State Department officials and staff from the Senate Foreign Relations Committee. I believe the joint U.S. Executive-Congressional team underscores the deepening cooperation within the U.S. Government on this important issue.

The interim INC Presidency Committee met for the first time on April 10. The group reportedly established a principle of rotating leadership and discussed plans to send a delegation to the United Nations to express views on humanitarian and human rights issues.

The United Nations Compensation Commission

The United Nations Compensation Commission (UNCC), established pursuant to Resolutions 687, 692, and 1210, continues to resolve claims against Iraq arising from Iraq's unlawful invasion and occupation of Kuwait. The UNCC has issued over 1.3 million awards worth over $7 billion. Thirty percent of the proceeds from the oil sales permitted by UNSC resolutions have been allocated to the Compensation Fund to pay awards and to finance operations of the UNCC. Pursuant to decisions of the UNCC Governing Council, certain small claims are to receive initial payments of $2,500 toward the amounts approved on those claims before large claims of individuals and claims of corporations and governments may share in the funds available for claims payments. As money from Iraqi oil sales is deposited in the Compensation Fund, the UNCC makes these initial $2,500 payments on eligible claims in the order in which those claims were approved by the UNCC. To date, the U.S. Government has received funds from the UNCC for initial installment payments on approximately 1,685 claims of U.S. claimants.

Conclusion

Iraq remains a serious threat to international peace and security. I remain determined to see Iraq comply fully with all of its obligations under Security Council resolutions. The United States looks forward to the day when Iraq rejoins the family of nations as a responsible and law-abiding member. I appreciate the support of the Congress for our efforts and shall continue to keep the Congress informed about this important issue.

Sincerely,

William J. Clinton

327.

[Vol. 35, no. 31 (August 9, 1999): 1540-1544]

Letter to Congressional Leaders Reporting on Iraq's Compliance With United Nations Security Council Resolutions
August 2, 1999

Dear Mr. Speaker: (Dear Mr. President:)

Consistent with the Authorization for Use of Military Force Against Iraq Resolution (Public Law 102-1) and as part of my effort to keep the Congress fully informed, I am reporting on the status of efforts to obtain Iraq's compliance with the resolutions adopted by the United Nations Security Council (UNSC). My last report, consistent with Public Law 102-1, was transmitted on May 19, 1999.

Overview

We are convinced that as long as Saddam Hussein remains in power, he will continue to threaten the well-being of his people, the peace of the region, and vital U.S. interests. We will continue to contain these threats, but over the long term, the best way to address them is by encouraging the establishment of a new government in Baghdad. To this end, we continue to work intensively with the Iraqi opposition. In May, the Iraqi National Congress (INC) Interim Presidency Committee met with the Secretary of State, the National Security Advisor, and several Members of Congress in Washington. The Department of State has been assisting the INC in its preparations for a National Assembly meeting. Also, the Department has been working with other nongovernmental organizations to develop projects to assist the Iraqi opposition and the Iraqi people in their efforts to achieve a regime change. In June, delegations from the two main Kurdish parties traveled to Washington to discuss the next steps in implementing the reconciliation agreement they signed in Washington last year.

During the last 60 days, we have also been working with members of the UNSC to build support to adopt a resolution that would reestablish an effective disarmament and monitoring presence inside Iraq, better meet the humanitarian needs of the Iraqi people, and increase pressure on Iraq to account for those missing from the Gulf War, and return Kuwaiti property. The Security Council is currently continuing its discussions on these matters.

The United States continues to support the international community's efforts to provide for the humanitarian needs of the Iraqi people through the oil-for-food program. On May 21, the Security Council unanimously adopted Resolution 1242, extending the program for another 180 days.

U.S. and Coalition Force Levels in the Gulf Region

Saddam Hussein's record of aggressive behavior necessitates the deployment of a highly capable force in the region in order to deter Iraq from threatening its neighbors, reconstituting its WMD program, or moving against the Kurds in Northern Iraq. We will continue to maintain a robust posture and have established a rapid reinforcement capability to supplement our forces in the Gulf, if needed.

Our forces are a balanced mix of land and carrier-based aircraft, surface ships, a Patriot missile battalion, a mechanized battalion task force, and special operations units. To enhance force protection throughout the region, additional military security personnel are also deployed.

Operation Northern Watch and Operation Southern Watch

Aircraft of the United States and coalition partners enforcing the no-fly zones over Iraq under Operations Northern Watch and Southern Watch are regularly illuminated by radar and engaged by anti-aircraft artillery, and occasionally, by surface-to-air missiles.

As a result of Iraq's no-fly zone violations and attacks on our aircraft, our aircrews continue to respond with force. United States and coalition forces are fully prepared and authorized to defend themselves against Iraqi threats while carrying out their no-fly zone enforcement mission and, when circumstances warranted, have engaged various components of the Iraqi integrated air defense system. While threats to our aircraft continue, actual Iraqi aircraft violations of the no-fly zones have declined.

The Maritime Interception Force

The multinational Maritime Interception Force (MIF), operating in accordance with Resolution 665 and other relevant resolutions, continues to enforce U.N. sanctions in the Gulf. The U.S. Navy is the single largest component of the MIF, but it is frequently augmented by ships, aircraft, and other support assets from Australia, Bahrain, Belgium, Canada, Kuwait, The Netherlands, New Zealand, the UAE, and the United Kingdom. Member states of the Gulf Cooperation Council (GCC) provide logistical and personnel support to the MIF, and accept vessels diverted for violating U.N. sanctions against Iraq.

The smuggling of refined petroleum products through the Gulf has remained at a low level since Operation Desert Fox. The MIF, and our ability rapidly to augment it, will continue to serve as a critical deterrent to both the smuggling of petroleum products out of the Gulf and the smuggling of prohibited items into Iraq.

UNSCOM/IAEA: Weapons of Mass Destruction

There has been no United Nations Special Commission (UNSCOM) or International Atomic Energy Agency (IAEA) presence in Iraq since December 15, 1998. UNSCOM informed the Security Council on June 1 of the status of UNSCOM's chemical laboratory, biological room, equipment, and components in the Baghdad Monitoring and Verification Center (BMVC). The Canal Hotel houses UNSCOM offices along with those of other U.N. activities in Iraq, such as the Office of the Iraq Programme, which implements the oil-for-food program. UNSCOM has analytical equipment and materials it would like to see removed in a straightforward technical operation as a precaution. The samples include less than one kilogram of seized Iraqi mustard agent. There are no immediate safety concerns. In June, UNSCOM recommended to the Security Council that UNSCOM send a team of experts to destroy the conventional lab chemicals, chemical standards, and biological samples, and request that Iraq cooperate. In July the U.N. Secretariat, in consultation with UNSCOM, deputized a team of experts to decommission the lab. UNSCOM provided an operations plan for the mission to the Secretariat. UNSCOM and U.S. experts trained the U.N. team in Bahrain. The U.N. team consisted of an UNSCOM administrator, a biologist from a German university, and four experts from the Organization for the Prohibition of Chemical Weapons (OPCW).

Dual-Use Imports

Resolution 1051 established a joint UNSCOM/ IAEA unit to monitor Iraq's imports of allowed dual-use items. Iraq must notify the unit before it imports specific items that can be used in both weapons of mass destruction and civilian applications. Similarly, U.N. members must provide timely notification of exports to Iraq of such dual-use items. Since the withdrawal of UNSCOM and IAEA monitors, only some limited monitoring in certain sectors is being conducted by the U.N. Office of the Iraq Programme inspectors. This situation has presented new challenges for the U.N. Sanctions Committee and is a factor in the contract approval process. As a precautionary matter, the United States has placed holds on a number of dual-use contracts that might otherwise have been approved.

The U.N. Oil-for-Food Program

We continue to support the international community's efforts to provide for the humanitarian needs of the Iraqi people through the oil-for-food program. On May 21, the Security Council unanimously adopted Resolution 1242, extending the program for another 180 days. As in phase five, Iraq is again authorized to sell up to $5.2 billion worth of oil in the coming 180 days. Because of the increase in world oil prices and increased exports, Iraq may reach the ceiling during this phase. As of June 14, U.N. reporting indicates that since the start of the oil-for-food program, 5,375 contracts for humanitarian goods worth over $7 billion have been approved with 389 contracts worth $351 million on hold and approximately 1,000 contracts in various stages of processing in the United Nations.

Within the oil-for-food program, Resolution 1242 maintains a separate program for northern Iraq, administered directly by the United Nations in consultation with the local population. This program, which the United States strongly supports, ensures that when Iraq contracts for the purchase of humanitarian goods, 13 to 15 percent of the funds generated under the oil-for-food program are spent on items for northern Iraq. The separate northern program was established because of Baghdad's repression and disregard for the humanitarian needs of the Kurdish, Assyrian, Yezidi, and Turkoman minorities in northern Iraq.

Humanitarian programs such as oil-for-food have steadily improved the life of the average Iraqi living under sanctions while denying Saddam Hussein control over Iraq's oil revenues. Currently, the ration basket provides over 2,000 calories per day per Iraqi. We will continue to work with the U.N. Secretariat, the Security Council, and others in the international community to ensure that the humanitarian needs of the Iraqi people are met while denying political or economic benefits to the Baghdad regime. In addition, we are working with the United Nations and other Security Council members to mitigate the effects of the current drought in Iraq.

Northern Iraq: Kurdish Reconciliation

In June, delegations from the Kurdistan Democratic Party (KDP) and the Patriotic Union of Kurdistan (PUK) traveled to Washington to discuss the next steps in implementing the accord they signed in September 1998. Consensus was achieved on a number of confidence-building measures, including opening party offices in major cities throughout northern Iraq, eschewing negative press statements, countering the divisive influence of the Kurdistan Workers' Party (PKK), beginning the return of internally displaced persons, and creating a voter registration commission for upcoming elections. The delegations discussed other issues, such as revenue sharing, internal security, and the formation of an interim joint regional assembly and administration. They will continue these talks in northern Iraq and seek to implement steps that were agreed.

The Human Rights Situation in Iraq

The human rights situation in Iraq continues to fall far short of international norms, in violation of Resolution 688. That resolution explicitly notes that the consequences of the regime's repression of its own people constitute a threat to international peace and security in the region. It also demands immediate access by international humanitarian aid organizations to all Iraqis in need. However, for over 7 years the Iraqi government has refused to allow the U.N. Human Rights Commission Special Rapporteur for Iraq, Max Van der Stoel, to visit Iraq. U.N. human rights monitors have never been allowed into Iraq.

Severe repression continues in southern Iraq, as the regime works toward the destruction of the Marsh Arabs' way of life and the unique ecology of the southern marshes. The regime has repeatedly ignored appeals by Max Van der Stoel and others for access by human rights monitors to investigate these reports. The human rights monitors have asked to investigate the alleged assassination of three of Iraq's most senior Islamic clerics: Ayatollah Mohammed al-Sader in February 1999, Ayatollah Borujerdi in April 1998, and Ayatollah al-Gharavi in June 1998.

In the north, outside the Kurdish-controlled areas, the government continues the forced expulsion of ethnic Kurds and Turkomans from Kirkuk and other cities.

The Iraqi Opposition

We are deepening our engagement with the forces of change in Iraq, helping Iraqis both inside and outside Iraq to become a more effective voice for the aspirations of the people. We will work toward the day when Iraq has a government worthy of its people, a government prepared to live in peace with its neighbors, and respects the rights of its citizens. We believe that a change of regime in Baghdad is inevitable, and that it is urgently incumbent on the world community to support the Iraqis who are working to ensure that change is positive. These Iraqis include the resistance inside the country, and those free Iraqis now in exile or in northern Iraq, who seek to improve the chances that the next government of Iraq will truly represent, serve, and protect all the Iraqi people.

The INC has stepped up its activities since the April 7-8 meeting of the Executive Council at Windsor. The Interim Presidency Committee visited Washington from May 24 to May 28 for meetings with the Secretary of State, the National Security Advisor, and several Members of Congress. In a demonstration of the growing cohesion among the Iraqi opposition, the INC leadership was accompanied by other key Sunni opposition leaders. The INC also sent a delegation to the United Nations in May to discuss humanitarian and human rights issues.

Over the last several weeks, the INC Executive Committee met again in London and the Interim Presidency Committee has worked on preparations for their National Assembly. The Department of State assisted the INC in these efforts by funding conference planning services with Economic Support Funds. Using these same funds, the Department of State worked with other nongovernmental organizations to develop projects to assist the Iraqi opposition and the Iraqi people in their efforts to achieve regime change.

The United Nations Compensation Commission

The United Nations Compensation Commission (UNCC), established pursuant to

Resolutions 687, 692, and 1210, continues to resolve claims against Iraq arising from Iraq's unlawful invasion and occupation of Kuwait. The UNCC has issued over 1.3 million awards worth approximately $10 billion.

Thirty percent of the proceeds from authorized oil sales are allocated to the Compensation Fund to pay awards and finance UNCC operations. The UNCC Governing Council has determined that certain small claims by individuals will receive initial payments of $2,500, before paying larger claims of either individuals or businesses and government agencies. In June, the Governing Council established the rules for making payments on the remaining small claims and the larger individual, corporate, and government claims. To date, the U.S. Government has received funds from the UNCC for initial installment payments for approximately 2,288 U.S. claimants.

Conclusion

Iraq remains a serious threat to international peace and security. I remain determined to see Iraq fully comply with all of its obligations under Security Council resolutions. The United States looks forward to the day when Iraq rejoins the family of nations as a responsible and law-abiding member. I appreciate the support of the Congress for our efforts and shall continue to keep the Congress informed about this important issue.

Sincerely,

William J. Clinton

PART III

NON-FULL-TEXT ITEMS

ARTICLES, MONOGRAPHS, AND SERIES

GENERAL

328. Barkey Henri J. "Kurdish Geopolitics." *Current History* 96, no. 606 (January 1997): 1-5. Part of an issue on the Middle East. The Kurds, the largest ethnic group in the world without a state, continue to fight among themselves and with the governments of the countries occupying them. In northern Iraq, protected as a safe haven by the United States under the guise of Operation Provide Comfort, the civil war between the Kurdistan Democratic Party (KDP) and the Patriotic Union of Kurdistan (PUK) has allowed Saddam Hussein to reassert himself in the safe haven by backing the KDP. Complicating matters is the Kurdish uprising in Turkey, started in 1984 by the Kurdistan Workers Party (PKK), the effects of which have increasingly dragged Turkey's Ankara government into the politics of the Middle East. Turkish fears of the PKK and suspicions of American intentions have interfered with Operation Provide Comfort and curtailed U.S. activities in the north of Iraq.

329. Bhattacharya, Sauri P. "The Situation of the Kurds in the Post-Gulf War Period and U.S. Policy Toward it." *Asian Profile* 22 (April 1994): 151-160. This is a study of the situation of a trans-national people, but the focus is on the Kurds of Iraq who were encouraged by the Bush administration to rise in rebellion against the Iraqi regime in the aftermath of Saddam's defeat in the Gulf War. Questions about their geography, sociology, language, culture, as also a history of their movement for self-determination since the 19th century are included. The Kurds' failure in achieving self-determination in the past is not being replaced by anything really new and different. Americans, although they were ex-

pected to be of help to the Kurds in their effort to carve up a nation for themselves, seem overly cautious torn between two different directions: human rights, rule of law, and new world order on the one hand, and stability, domestic jurisdiction and the need to prove that their friendship for the Turks is real and reliable. This timid U.S. policy seems still determined by considerations of the Cold War.

330. Carley, Patricia. *U.S. Responses to Self-Determination Movements: Strategies for Nonviolent Outcomes and Alternatives to Secession*. Report from a roundtable held in conjunction with the policy planning staff of the U.S. Department of State. Washington, DC: United States Institute of Peace, 1997. viii, 30 p.: ill. Includes bibliographical references. Report on results of a U.S. Institute of Peace roundtable, held in conjunction with State Department Policy Planning Staff in March 1996 on U.S. and international policy responses to self-determination movements. Covers background on, and U.S. and/or international response to, self-determination movements of Kurds, Kashmir, Eritrea, and Tibet; self-determination, human rights, and good governance; case for secession; self-determination at the United Nations; and nonviolent alternatives to secession.

331. Central Intelligence Agency. *The World Factbook*. PRINT, WEB. Washington, DC: Central Intelligence Agency: Supt. of Docs., U.S. GPO [distributor], 1981- . Annual. The CIA *World Factbook* provides a country-by-country listing of basic statistical and factual information. Each individual entry averages a few print pages in length. Major sections of each entry include "Introduction,"

"Geography," "People," "Government," "Economy," "Communications," "Transportation," "Military," and "Transnational Issues." Information such as population, type of legal system, national holidays, number of railroads, and military strength is included. *The World Factbook* also includes an appendix listing membership in selected U.N. and international organizations and a series of reference maps of the world. *The World Factbook* is an excellent source for obtaining a quick up-to-date overview of a country. The first classified *Factbook* was published in August 1962, and the first unclassified version was published in June 1971. The 1975 *Factbook* was the first to be made available to the public with sales through the US Government Printing Office (GPO). The 1996 edition was printed by GPO, and the 1997 edition was reprinted by GPO. The year 2001 marks the 54th anniversary of the establishment of the Central Intelligence Agency and the 58th year of continuous basic intelligence support to the US Government by *The World Factbook* and its predecessor programs. The Web-based version is made available at: www.cia.gov/cia/publications/factbook/.

332. Congress. *Congressional Record: Proceedings and Debates of the ... Congress.* PRINT, WEB. Washington, DC: [Supt. of Docs., U.S. GPO, distributor], 1873- . Daily (when Congress is in session). This is a record of congressional debates and proceedings, messages to Congress, and voting records. Speeches and debates do not necessarily appear verbatim, however. Daily issues are cumulated annually into a permanent, bound, final edition for each session of Congress, creating differences in page number in and indexing between the daily and bound editions. The daily editions contain four sections: H (House proceedings), S (Senate proceedings), E (Extension of Remarks), and D (Daily Digest, a summary of daily activities). Pages in the bound volume are numbered in a single sequence. At sessions' end, the Daily Digest is issued as separate part, with a subject index and a table of bills enacted into public law. There is a separate index to the permanent, bound *Congressional Record* which includes Daily Digest volumes. In the bound annual

edition, Extension of Remarks are integrated into the body of the text. The *Congressional Record* is available in full text on the Web from the Government Printing Office's *GPO Access* Web site. Commercial online services, such as *Congressional Universe, Westlaw,* and *LEXIS-NEXIS,* also provide access to full text of the *Record.* Occasionally, the Congress, and its various committees and subcommittees, discusses the Kurdish question. The debates that originate from these discussions normally get published in the *Record.*

333. Congress. Commission on Security and Cooperation in Europe. *Situation of Kurds in Turkey, Iraq and Iran.* Washington, DC: The Commission, 1993. v, 35 p. [Implementation of the Helsinki Accords]. Congress Session: 103-1. SUDOC: Y4.SE2:H36/22. Transcript of Commission on Security and Cooperation in Europe (CSCE) briefing on the status of Kurdish minorities living in Turkey and Iraq, including human rights concerns. Mary Sue Hafner, Deputy Staff Director and General Counsel, CSCE, presents opening remarks and leads the briefing. Includes audience participation (p. 14-26). Supplementary material (p. 27-35) includes panelists' written statements. Discusses Kurdish minorities in Turkey and Iraq, status and human rights concerns. Statements and Discussion include: Background on the situation of Kurds in the Middle East; concerns about the status of Kurds living in Turkey and Iraq, emphasizing human rights issues; suggestions regarding treatment of Kurdish minorities in Turkey and Iraq, citing regional implications.

334. Congress. Commission on Security and Cooperation in Europe. *Situation of Kurds in Turkey, Iraq and Iran.* Washington, DC: The Commission, 1993. 42 p. [Implementation of the Helsinki Accords]. Congress Session: 103-2. SUDOC: Y4.SE2:P23/3. The document contains a transcript of the briefing on the Kurdish minority in the Middle East held by the Commission on Security and Cooperation in Europe (CSCE) on May 17, 1993. The Kurds constitute the fourth largest nationality in the Middle East, primarily concentrated in the states of Iran, Iraq, and Turkey, and to a lesser extent in Syria. In all countries, they lack institutional protection of human rights and individual freedoms. Includes a statement (pp. 27-32) by Dr. Mark A. Epstein on Kurdish identity and U.S. policy.

335. Congress. House. Committee on International Relations. Senate. Committee on Foreign Relations. *Country Reports on Human Rights Practices*. PRINT, WEB. Washington, DC: U.S. GPO, 1977- . Annual. (www.state.gov/g/drl/hr/c1470.htm). This report is issued as a joint committee print and submitted annually to the Congress by the Department of State. The report covers internationally recognized individual, civil, political, and worker rights, as set forth in the Universal Declaration of Human Rights. The human rights reports reflect a year of effort by hundreds of State Department and other U.S. Government employees. The U.S. embassies around the world which prepare the initial drafts of the reports, gather information throughout the year from a variety of sources, including contacts across the political spectrum, government officials, jurists, military sources, journalists, human rights monitors, academics, and labor union members. The draft reports are then reviewed by the U.S. Bureau of Human Rights and Humanitarian Affairs, in cooperation with other relevant offices in the State Department. As they corroborate, analyze, and edit the reports, Department officers draw on their own additional sources of information. These include reports and consultations with U.S. and other human rights groups, foreign government officials, representatives from the U.N. and other international and regional organizations and institutions, and experts from academia and the media. The Report covers human rights violations around the world. It describes a world where people who by right are born free and with dignity too often suffer the cruelties of authorities who deprive them of their rights in order to perpetuate their own power. It mainly covers countries that are ruled by dictators or rent by armed conflict, where bullets, torture, arbitrary detention, rape, disappearances, and other abuses are used to silence those who struggle for political freedom; to crush those whose ethnicity, gender, race or religion mark them for discrimination; or to frighten and mistreat those who

have no defenses. Documents violations, and domestic and international reaction. Full-text of reports for the years 1996-2000 on Iran, Iraq, Syria, Turkey, and other countries can be found at the following addresses:

- 1996: www.state.gov/www/global/human_rights/1996_hrp_report/96hrp_report_toc.html

- 1997: www.state.gov/www/global/human_rights/1997_hrp_report/97hrp_report_toc.html

- 1998: www.state.gov/www/global/human_rights/1998_hrp_report/98hrp_report_toc.html

- 1999: www.state.gov/g/drl/rls/hrrpt/1999/

- 2000: www.state.gov/g/drl/rls/hrrpt/2000/

- 2001: www.state.gov/g/drl/rls/hrrpt/2001/

336. Department of State. *Background Notes*. PRINT. WEB. Washington, DC: GPO, 1964- . Irregular. (www.state.gov/r/pa/bgn/). Each issue of *Background Notes* provides basic information on an individual country, including Iran, Iraq, Syria, former Soviet Union, and Turkey. A profile of the country starts each *Note*, and provides brief statistical and factual information. The *Background Notes* include a broad overview of a country and its people, history, economy, geography, and government. *Notes* also includes a discussion of U.S. relations with the country and the country's relationships with other countries. They are updated and/or revised as they are received from regional bureaus and are added to the database of the Department of State Web site.

337. Entessar, Nader. *Kurdish Ethnonationalism*. Boulder, CO: Lynne Rienner Publishers, 1992. viii, 208 p. Includes bibliographical references (p. 193-201) and index. This book's "central thesis .. is that ethnic conflict constitutes a major challenge to the contemporary nation-state system in the Middle East." Examining the "political and social dimensions of Kurdish integration into mainstream of sociopolitical life in Iran, Iraq and Turkey," the author "challenges the long-held view that assimilation is an inevitable result of modernization and the emergence of the relatively strong and centralized nation-state system in the Middle East" (p. vii). Chapter I (pp. 1-10), "Kurdish Ethnicity," addresses state and ethnicity, Kurdish identity, languages, religion, and socioeconomic marginalization. The next three chapters examine relations between the Kurds and Iran (pp. 11-48), Iraq (pp. 49-80), and Turkey (pp. 81-111). Chapter 5 (pp. 113-57) explores the "International and Regional Context of Kurdish Nationalism" and focuses on Iran-Iraq relations and the 1991 Gulf war. The last chapter, "Whither Kurdistan?" challenges the feasibility or desirability of "secessionism." At a time when more than a dozen independent states have recently formed out of the former Soviet Union, Yugoslavia, and the disintegrating Czechoslovakia, the author argues that international legal principles do not allow sovereignty for the Kurds. He recommends instead a constitutional restructuring of the existing state systems into federal structures, which will promote Kurdish integration through representation in "the decision making institutions of the national government." (abridged, Amir Hassanpour/*MEJ* 47, Winter 1993: 119)

338. Foreign Broadcast Information Service *FBIS Publications*. CD-ROM. Washington, DC: FBIS. Quarterly. The Foreign Broadcast Information Service (FBIS) operates under the aegis of the Central Intelligence Agency and oversees a worldwide network of broadcast monitoring units that are responsible for reviewing foreign media. The information selected is based on a set on intelligence requirements and is translated and disseminated to consumers. The majority of FBIS reports are currently unclassified and available to the public on CD-ROM. The FBIS was established in 1941, when the demand for information from enemy sources was pressing, as the Foreign Broadcast Monitoring Service, which recorded, translated, analyzed, and reported to other government agencies broadcasts from foreign countries. Until 1946, reports were issued by the now defunct Federal Communications Service; in that year its functions were transferred to the Central Intelligence Agency. FBIS reports are disseminated in two major categories. The more relevant one to the Kurdish question is the FBIS Daily Report series,

which covers regions of the world divided as follows: Central Eurasia, China, East Asia, East Europe, Near East/South Asia, Sub-Saharan Africa, the Americas, and West Europe. The information is obtained from full text and summaries of newspaper articles, conference proceedings, television and radio broadcasts, periodicals, and nonclassified technical reports.

339. Gunter Michael M. "United States Foreign Policy Toward the Kurds." *Orient* 40, no. 3 (1999): 427-437. This article examines three temporal periods of U.S. foreign policy toward the Kurds: the World War I period (briefly), the Kissinger period during the 1970s (briefly), and the more recent stage in the 1990s. In particular this article analyzes why U.S. foreign policy tends to treat the Iraqi Kurds as 'good' Kurds, while it considers the Turkish Kurds to be 'bad' Kurds. Support for the Iraqi Kurds is perceived as supportive of over-all U.S. foreign policy against Saddam Hussein's Iraq. Turkey, however, is seen as a valuable geostrategic NATO ally necessary to support to maintain its continuing allegiance.

340. Halperin, Morton and David J. Scheffer, with Patricia L. Small. *Self-Determination in the New World Order*. Washington, DC: Carnegie Endowment for International Peace, 1992. xiv, 178 p. Includes bibliographical references (p. 165-170) and index. Even as the world celebrates increased integration among existing states and the spread of democracy in all regions of the world, another trend is shattering the status quo: Smaller groups within states are seeking greater autonomy or independence based on their common language, culture, and tradition. This book examines these movements and the internal conflicts they often trigger. It argues for a systematic and coordinated policy response to some of the most challenging issues facing the world today. In this book, the authors review U.S. and international responses to self-determination claims during and after the Cold War. Arguing that outdated Cold War perspectives continue to influence the current policies of the United States and the international community toward self-determination movements, the authors provide a framework for evaluating the nature and legitimacy of self-determination movements around the world. Whether a movement's goal is greater protection of minority right, greater autonomy, or full independence, the authors assert that the international community should require adherence to important conditions such as democracy, international law, non-use of force, and human rights before granting support or recognition. The authors also examine a number of responses to civil wars and threats of armed conflict, ranging from monitoring and diplomatic intervention to economic sanctions and collective military intervention. They argue that self-determination is not a self-regulating process, but requires a new type of involvement by the United States and multilateral organizations.

341. Library of Congress. Federal Research Division. Irregular. *Country Studies.* PRINT, WEB. Washington, DC: The Division. These monographs are prepared by a multidisciplinary team of experts under the auspices of the Federal Research Division of the Library of Congress and sponsored by the Department of the Army. Each *Country Study* attempts to provide a comprehensive analysis of a country's economic conditions, national security situation, political structure, and social systems and institutions. A brief country profile gives basic information about the country and is followed by more lengthy chapters addressing individual topics. An appendix of statistical tables is included, along with another appendix containing an extensive bibliography. The electronic version of the *Country Studies* provides searching capabilities for the text in each *Study*, and also allows for searching across the full text of either all *Country Studies* or selected titles within the series. Reports in the *Country Studies* series rate as some of the best reference sources—governmental or nongovernmental—for providing detailed overview of a country. This series was formerly titled and widely known as *Area Handbooks*.

342. Mayall, James. "Non-intervention, Self-determination and the 'New World Order.'" *International Affairs* 67 (July 1991): 421-429. Has the Kurdish crisis changed the rules of the game on non-interference in the domestic affairs of sovereign states? No, writes the author. The Western allies were forced to intervene to protect the Kurds because Western media attention to their plight threatened the political dividends they had secured from the Gulf War. But though the New World Order rhetoric promising new support for human rights is without substance, the Kurdish situation will stand as a precedent of a kind for international protection of oppressed national minorities, if a similar situation recurs. However, the principle of self-determination is still unwelcome in the international community.

343. McDowall, David. *A Modern History of the Kurds.* 2nd rev. and updated ed. London: I.B. Tauris, 2000. xii, 515 p.: maps. Includes bibliographical references and index. McDowall examines the interplay of old and new aspects of the Kurdish struggle, the importance of local rivalries within Kurdish society, the enduring authority of certain forms of leadership and the failure of modern states to respond to the challenge of Kurdish nationalism. Extensively revised to include recent events and an updated bibliography, this book is useful for all who want a better understanding of the underlying dynamics of the Kurdish question.

344. O'Ballance, Edgar. "The Kurdish Factor in the Gulf War." *Military Review: The Professional Journal of the U.S. Army* 61 (June 1981): 13-20. Describes the roles of the Kurds of Iran, Iraq, Syria, Turkey, and U.S.S.R. in Persian Gulf affairs in the past 20 years. Long troubled by divisions within their own movement, the Kurds have fought themselves as well as several national armies. With the start of the 1980 war between Iran and Iraq, the Kurds remain divided, fighting on both sides. If the Kurds unite, however, they could tip the balance of power in the region.

345. Pelletiere, Stephen C. *The Kurds: An Unstable Element in the Gulf.* Boulder, CO: Westview Press, 1984. 220 p. Includes bibliographical references and index. A major—and often unpredictable—force in the Middle East for centuries, fragmented by the boundaries of

Iraq, Iran, Turkey, Syria, and Russia, the Kurds remain a nation that steadfastly resists assimilation (and elimination) and that frequently engages in violent revolts. In this book, the author analyzes the factors contributing to the remarkable survival of Kurdish nationalism and places the Kurds in the context of modern Middle East history. First establishing the Kurdish identity and contrasting it with that of surrounding ethnic groups, the author goes on to trace Kurdish history and to examine the configuration of the Kurdish national movement during the world wars and the period immediately following the wars, when the Kurds were temporarily supported by the Soviet Union. He also examines the Kurds' struggles against successive Middle Eastern powers and looks at the national autonomy that was forfeited because of clashes between modern and feudal forces within the Kurdish movement. The book closes with a discussion of possible future developments for the Kurds and the advantages and drawbacks of various sorts of U.S. involvement. The author destroys many myths about the Kurds and treats them not as a cultural artifact but as an important factor in the power equation of the Middle East.

346. Randal, Jonathan C. *After Such Knowledge, What Forgiveness? My Encounters with Kurdistan*. New York: Farrar, Straus and Giroux, 1997. 356 p. Includes bibliographical references (p. 343-345) and index. An American reporter who has covered the Kurds for more than a decade, Randal has interviewed many Kurdish political leaders. He provides much historical information, however, Randal's best chapters are about U.S. involvement in Kurdistan. He shows in persuasive insider detail how Nixon, Kissinger and the Shah of Iran betrayed a Kurdish uprising against Saddam Hussein in 1975; how Bush, Baker and feckless diplomats both "suckered" the Kurds into rebellion after the Gulf War and waffled on aiding them; and how the Clinton Administration might have brokered a settlement in northern Iraq in 1996 instead of allowing a civil war and then airlifting thousands of friendly Kurds to Guam. Randal's chapter on Turkey records how the United States has in recent years skirted its

own laws restricting arms sales to human rights abusers and made Turkey "the biggest single importer of American military hardware," much of it used against Kurds inside Turkey and in the so-called safe haven of northern Iraq. "After such knowledge," Randal refuses "forgiveness" to U.S. governments that have contributed to the Kurds' historical repression and present plight.

347. Wagner, J. Q. *Ethnic Conflict: The Case of the Kurds*. [Research report, August 1991-April 1992] Washington, DC: Industrial College of the Armed Forces, April, 1992. 40 p. [NTIS Accession Number: AD-A262 225/6/XAB] Report No. NDU/ICAF-92-A29. The purpose in this paper is to explore the Kurds; their history, customs, political solidarity, and their frequently frustrated quest for autonomy. Can there be an independent or autonomous Kurdistan in Iraq, Turkey, Iran, Syria, Armenia as a united Kurdistan or as a state or states within the existing political boundaries? What would Kurdish independence mean to the future stability of the Middle East? What are the United States' policy interests with regards to the Kurds? Are they vital or important policy interests? Should we attempt to influence, either overtly or covertly, events as they unfold in Kurdistan? What are our policy options?

IRAN

348. Ramazani, Rouhollah K. "The Autonomous Republic of Azerbaijan and the Kurdish People's Republic: Their Rise and Fall." *Studies on the Soviet Union* 11, no. 4 (1971): 401-427. A review of the brief histories of two Communist regimes in northern Iran. The governments were established by occupying Soviet troops. Great Britain and the United States opposed these states from the beginning. Conquest of the whole of Iran was the Soviet goal, but pressure to achieve this goal was successfully resisted. The Red Army pulled out because the United States stood firm in opposition. A year later the puppet governments fell having no further bases of support.

349. Roosevelt, Archie, Jr. "The Kurdish Republic of Mahabad." *The Middle East Journal* 1 (July 1947): 247-269. Reprinted in *A People Without a Country: The Kurds and Kurdistan* (1993), pp. 122-138. This article discusses the story of the independent Kurdish state established in Mahabad in 1946 and lasted almost one year. The author, one of a few witnesses on the scene, describes the event that led to its establishment and fall, with discussion of the U.S. role in the latter.

350. Roosevelt, Archie, Jr. *For Lust of Knowing: Memoirs of an Intelligence Officer*. Boston: Little, Brown, 1988. xiv, 500 p., [16] p. of plates: ill. Includes index. The period of World War II and its immediate aftermath was a time of discovery for many Americans of the world of Islam, of the intractable problems of the Middle East, and of the resistance of the colonial powers to the idealistic American drive for colonial independence. Archie Roosevelt's book tells the firsthand story of one man's discovery of these realities. The book is the story of political discovery, a memoir by a member of a prominent American family, succinct summaries of history, and a sophisticated travelogue. Through it run the threads of a personal romance and of the experiences of an intelligence officer. In writing the book, Roosevelt had the benefit of notes, letters, and diaries that he wrote over many years. His quotes from these contemporary sources provide vivid pictures of conditions of life and the personalities of the regions he visited, including the impressive Abdul Aziz Ibn Saud, his Syrian counselor Sheikh Yusuf Yasin, the dynamic young Habib Bourguiba, the less dynamic shah of Iran, and a host of Kurdish, Arab, and Iranian figures. Roosevelt discusses his experiences with the Kurds, particularly on Mahabad on pp. 248-288. (abridged, David D. Newsom/ *MEJ* 42, Autumn 1988: 700-701)

351. Yassin, Borhanedin A. *Vision or Reality? The Kurds in the Policy of the Great Powers, 1941-1947*. Lund, Sweden: Lund University Press, 1995. 246 p. Includes bibliographical references (p. 230-242) and index. This study traces the history of Kurdish nationalism in the crucial wartime and immediate post-war years. In particular, it looks at the creation of the short-lived People's Republic of Kurdistan in the Iranian Kurdish region during 1946. The life of the republic, together with the Kurdish question as a whole, is examined within the context of not only great power politics, but also the politics of the states in which the Kurds live, especially Iran, and developments within the Kurdish communities themselves. Historians of the early cold war typically touch briefly on the crisis resulting from the Soviet Union's refusal to withdraw from northern Iran after the war on the schedule agreed with the state's other wartime occupier, Great Britain. It was the Kurds' misfortune to find themselves and their republic at the center of this great power dispute after the War. Yassin points out that it was understandable for pragmatic reasons that the Kurds sought the protection of the Soviet Union. Soviet forces were occupying northern Iran, while the two alternative sponsors, Great Britain and the United States, were reluctant to support the Kurdish cause. Great Britain wanted to bolster central authority in Tehran in order to protect its oil interests in the country. The United States, despite its pronouncements on self-determination, showed no interest at all in the case of the Kurds. The American priority, during the final months of the war and in its aftermath, was to reinforce central authority in Iran and block Soviet influence. Yassin's point that the Kurds tried to obtain the sponsorship of the western powers but were rebuffed is a fair one. However, it must still be admitted that in opting for the backing of the Soviet Union, which had no inherent interest in their cause, and was merely engaged in a great power game, they made a historic mistake (Nigel John Ashton, *History: The Journal of the Historical Association*, 83, pp. 511-512).

IRAQ

352. Abizaid, John P. "Lessons for Peacekeepers." [Operation Provide Comfort.] *Military Review: The Professional Journal of the U.S. Army* 73 (March 1993): 11-19. The author looks at his unit's involvement in Operation Provide Comfort in northern Iraq. He offers insights as to what can be expected, the training conducted prior to deployment and operations in the theater. He also discusses some of the ways that the army might need to relook its current doctrine for conducting these types of missions.

353. Baram, Amatzia. *Between Impediment and Advantage: Saddam's Iraq.* Washington, DC: United States Institute of Peace, June 1998. 17 p. Baram, a senior fellow in the Jennings Randolph Program at the United States Institute of Peace and professor of Middle Eastern history at the University of Haifa in Israel, is considered one of the world's leading authorities on Iraq. This analysis provides a useful backdrop to the ongoing conflict with Iraq and is intended to help interested observers understand the significance of Saddam Hussein in Iraqi politics and the forces with which he grapples as he makes decisions about compliance with international demands. The report represents work in progress and summarizes the main points made during two public discussions about the nature of domestic politics in Iraq under Saddam. The Institute-sponsored meetings, November 10, 1997, and April 9, 1998, featured Baram presenting a modified version of his fellowship project that focuses on the major domestic conflicts that Saddam's regime faces and how they factor into Iraq's current and future foreign policy interests. Other participants at these events included representatives from the U.S. Department of State, the National Defense University, the Department of Defense, the Washington Institute for Near East Policy, the Middle East Institute, and other policy organizations active in U.S. foreign policy toward Iraq. C-Span covered and broadcast both events. Table of contents: Domestic tensions; Saddam's internal security objectives and concerns; Regional Strategies; Background; Part One: Chinks in Saddam's Armor (I. The Shi'is and the Kurds: Iraq's demographic predicament and its implications, II. Saddam and the Kurds after the Gulf War, III. Shi'is, Kurds, democracy, and violence in Iraq, IV. The fruits of dictatorship: Saddam's decision-making process as a source of high-risk, high-cost policies, V. Saddam and his army officers, VI. An inabil-

ity to learn: Tactical successes and a strategic bottleneck, VII. The economy: Vulnerability to inflation and its implications for foreign policy); Part Two: Domestic, Regional, and Foreign Sources of Power (VIII. Saddam's power base: the family-tribe-state symbiosis and how it can explain his survival, IX. Iraq's non-conventional arsenal: Between impediment and advantage, X. A shift in Arab attitudes). The full text of the report is available at: www.usip.org/oc/sr/baram/baram.html.

354. Barzani, Mas'ud, and Ahmed Ferhadi. *Mustafa Barzani and the Kurdish Liberation Movement.* New York: Palgrave, 2002. As a leader of the Kurdish national liberation movement for almost half a century, Mustafa Barzani witnessed many historical events that rocked the Middle East and had a strong impact on the fate of the Kurdish communities in the region. Barzani's life-long struggle began in 1907 when he was barely three years old, when he and his mother were incarcerated in the aftermath of a raid by the Ottoman Turkish forces. Barzani went on to spend most of his life fighting various governments partitioning Kurdistan. Barzani's son, Massoud, the leader of the Kurdish Democratic Party and currently the de facto ruler of much of Iraqi Kurdistan, has put together a valuable dossier of documents, stories, rare photos and has pieced them into a narrative in the first person with his reflections and analyses of historic events in the period 1931 to 1961.

355. Benjamin, Charles Michael. *Developing a Game/Decision Theoretic Approach to Comparative Foreign Policy Analysis: Some Cases in Recent American Foreign Policy.* Ph.D., University of Southern California, 1981. DAI 42 (June 1982): 5234-A. This dissertation develops a game/decision theoretic approach to comparative foreign policy analysis. Five cases in recent American foreign policy are described and analyzed: (1) Angola, 1975-76; (2) Cyprus, 1874; (3) Chile, 1962-73; (4) the Kurds, 1972-75; and (5) Cuba, 1961-62. Descriptive materials (data) are drawn principally from the published reports of Congressional committees investigating American intelligence agency activities. These reports are supplemented by participant memoirs and the accounts of academics and journalists. Metagame/options analysis is used to systematically examine the foreign policy assumptions implicit in each case. This method of analysis is superior to other decision theoretic models because it explicitly takes into account multiple actors and the interaction of their strategies to produce foreign policy outcomes. Furthermore the method requires only ordinal level measurement assumptions more appropriate to the data used in the study. Particularly highlighted is a comparison of each case study with the findings of an empirical analysis of "Pentagon Papers" documents regarding American foreign policy decision-making toward Vietnam study found that American policy makers held two simultaneous images of Vietnam, a "Regional" and a "global" image. These two images produced policy outcomes analogous to paranoid schizophrenic behavior in an individual. The concluding chapter relates findings from the examined cases to the Vietnam study. Even though the same amount of information was not available in these cases, the use of option analysis was able to locate perceptual discontinuities and multiple imaging the advantages of the metagame/options analytic method in the development of more accurate descriptive theory and more useful normative theory are also discussed and suggestions are made for further research.

356. Bennet, Barry F., and others. "Caring for Kurdish Refugees: Operation Provide Comfort." *Journal of the U.S. Army Medical Department* (November-December 1992): 37-42.

357. Bird, Catherine. "ARG Provides Comfort." [Relief operations for Kurdish refugees.] *Surface Warfare* 16 (July-August 1991): 4.

358. Bolger, Daniel P. *Savage Peace: Americans at War in the 1990s*. Novato, CA: Presidio, 1995 xi, 420 p.: ill., maps. Includes bibliographical references and index. Examines the historic role of the U.S. as the world's peacekeeper, the political and military context of contemporary peacekeeping missions, and prospects for international security; from the perspective of a battalion commander in the

U.S. Army. Case studies of American and multinational forces in the Sinai, Lebanon, Kurdistan, Somalia, and the former Yugoslavia. This thought-provoking analysis focuses on what Bolger considers the three most important "peace enforcement" missions since the Berlin Wall came down in 1989, each illustrating major aspects of this difficult form of warfare: the operations in Kurdistan, Somalia and the former Yugoslavia. At the end of the Gulf War, U.S. forces entered northern Iraq to protect the Kurds from Saddam Hussein; Bolger cites this operation as an example of the way such missions should be run. Somalia illustrates U.S. foreign policy at its worst because of policymakers who "should have known better." Bolger argues that in the former Yugoslavia, U.S. air strikes and humanitarian airlifts have served American interests even though the overall effort has been ineffective.

359. Bonner, Raymond. "Always Remember." [Iraqi campaign to exterminate the Kurds.] *The New Yorker* 68 (September 28 1992): 46-51+. Iraqi Kurds are returning to their towns in northern Iraq but are finding it nearly impossible to rebuild the lands that have been devastated by systematic, genocidal attacks under Saddam Hussein. Between 1987 and 1991, Hussein used chemical and conventional weapons in an effort seemingly designed to kill every Kurdish male between the ages of 16 and 40. Today, with a Kurdish enclave having been established in northern Iraq, the Kurds are trying to rebuild their homes and civic structures but are still hindered by Hussein's economic blockade against them and the West's embargo against Iraq. Many Kurds are accusing the United States of being reluctant to help them, and the West must realize that eventually the Kurds will seek to establish an independent state, possibly by force. The article chronicles the history of the Kurds, describes Iraqi attacks on several Kurdish villages, and discusses U.S. relations with the Kurds, Iraq, and Turkey.

360. Bozarslan, Hamit. "De la Geopolitique a l'Humanitaire: Le Cas du Kurdistan d'Irak." [From the Geopolitical to the Humanitarian: The Case of Iraqi Kurdistan.] *Cultures et*

Conflits, no. 11 (Autumn 1993): 41-64. Appears also in *L'Irak du Silence*, pp. 41-64, under the title "De l'humanitaire a la geopolitique: le cas du Kurdistan Irak," edited by Marie de Varney (Paris: L'Harmattan, 1992). Discusses the so-called humanitarian Operation Provide Comfort, which sought to provide goods and assistance to the Kurds in northern Iraq at the end of the Gulf war, arguing that it and similar operations merely serve to postpone or suspend real analyses of geopolitical relations. Provide Comfort represented a degree of intervention in the internal affairs of UN member states and disrupted Iraqi territory surrounding Kurdistan, but did not address long-term regional power relations and the struggle for Kurdish identity, which has a long history and involves several countries (e.g., Turkey, Iraq, and now the U.S.). General conclusions are drawn about the crisis of the nation-state and the amplification of ethnic conflicts.

361. Bronstone Adam. *European Union-United States Security Relations*. London: Macmillan Press Ltd., 1997. The European Union's evolution to become a global actor is examined through its relationship with the United States from the Yom Kippur war to the Gulf conflict. Case-studies of the 1973 Arab-Israeli war, martial law in Poland 1981-82 and the Kurdish crisis in Iraq 1991 (pp. 173-223) are shown to support a theoretical critique.

362. Brown, Ronald J. *Humanitarian Operations in Northern Iraq, 1991 with Marines in Operation Provide Comfort*. Washington, DC: History and Museums Division, Headquarters, U.S. Marine Corps: [U.S. GPO., Supt. of Docs., distributor], 1995. viii, 127 p.: ill., maps. This monograph tells the story of more than 3,600 U.S. Marines who supported Operation Provide Comfort, an international relief effort in northern Iraq from 7 April to 15 July 1991. This short work does not purport to tell the entire story of Operation Provide Comfort, but focuses on Marine activities and contributions. The author presents historical glimpses of the Kurds, modern Iraq, and non-Marine activities only to provide necessary background information. This monograph is not an exhaustive analysis of the op-

eration nor does it try to define Provide Comfort's place in the diplomatic history of the Middle East. The monograph relies heavily on primary sources, mostly the author's observations and the first-hand testimony of participants.

363. Bush, George. "Bush Announces Expansion of Relief Effort in Iraq." *Congressional Quarterly Weekly Report* 49, no. 16 (April 20, 1991): 1009-1011. In excerpts from a news conference, President George Bush describes the expansion of relief efforts to Kurdish refugees in Iraq.

364. Byman, Daniel. "Let Iraq Collapse." [Benefits of an Iraqi break-up.] *The National Interest*, no. 45 (Fall 1996): 48-60. Iraqi disintegration would strengthen the U.S. position in the region and provide the Kurds, the Middle East's largest ethnic group, with their own state. Despite fears of regional imbalance of power, the collapse of Iraq would end a regime hostile to U.S. interests. It would also eliminate a major threat to the Gulf states and to Israel. Finally, a Kurdish state would be dependent on the U.S. for survival and could serve as a base to control Iran.

365. Clary, D. E. *Operation Provide Comfort: A Strategic Analysis*. [Final report.] Maxwell AFB, AL: Air War College, April 1994. 37p. [NTIS Accession Number: AD-A280 675/0/XAB]. The sight of 700,000 refugees fleeing the wrath of Saddam Hussein's army into the rugged mountains of northern Iraq brought world attention to the plight of the Kurds in the aftermath of the Gulf War in April 1991. In conjunction with world leaders, President Bush established a policy to assist those refugees and return them to their homes. According to the author, President Bush's policy was fulfilled through a successful operational military strategy that evolved from that policy. An important key to the success of the strategy, was translation of policy into a clear and concise mission statement and mission objectives. These objectives then utilized coalition military, international relief organization, and private voluntary organization resources to successfully execute the mission tasks that flowed from the mission objectives.

366. Collins, John W., Jr. "Logistics Support for Operation Provide Comfort II." [Humanitarian aid for Kurds.] *Army Logistician* (May-June 1992): 22-24.

367. Congress. House. Committee on Armed Services. *Aspects of Anti-Chaos Aid to the Soviet Union*. Washington, DC: U.S. GPO, 1991. iii, 83 p. Congress Session: 102-1. SUDOC: Y4.Ar5/2a:991-92/33. Included in Legislative History of: P.L. 102-484; P.L. 102-511. Committee Serial H.A.S.C. No. 102-33. Hearings before the Defense Policy Panel to review food and medical supply problems in the Soviet Union and its newly independent republics, and to examine DOD capability to provide short-term humanitarian assistance in conjunction with private sector relief organizations. Statements and Discussion include: Capabilities of U.S. military forces to participate in humanitarian aid programs; explanation of DOD role in Operation Provide Comfort which provided protection and supplies for Kurdish refugees fleeing Iraq after the Persian Gulf war (related maps, tables, p. 5-24 passim); aspects of humanitarian assistance programs.

368. Congress. House. Committee on Armed Services. *Options for Dealing with Iraq*. Washington, DC: Washington, DC: U.S. GPO, 1992. iii, 98 p. Congress Session: 102-2. SUDOC:Y4.AR5/2A:991-92/79. Committee Serial H.A.S.C. No. 102-79. Hearings before the Defense Policy Panel to examine nonmilitary and military strategy options to obtain compliance by Iraq and Iraqi President Saddam Hussein with various UN Security Council resolutions passed in conjunction with negotiations to end the 1991 Persian Gulf War. Resolutions require the immediate end of alleged repression of the Iraqi civilian population; the destruction, removal, or dismantling of weapons of mass destruction, certain ballistic missiles, and nuclear weapons materials; and the sale of oil under UN supervision to pay for UN activities in Iraq. Supplementary material (p. 58-60) includes articles. Statements and Discussion include: Need for UN to declare Saddam Hussein in violation of resolutions and support his ouster; status of Kurdish opposition to Saddam Hussein, with review of relevant policy issues; extent and nature of Iraq violation of resolutions; recommendations for expansion of economic sanctions against Iraq; aspects of nonmilitary policy options to obtain Iraq compliance with resolutions.

369. Congress. House. Committee on Foreign Affairs. *Consideration of Miscellaneous Bills and Resolutions: Vol. III*. July 13, August 3, September 14, 22, 27, October 4, 1988. Hearing. Washington, DC: U.S. GPO, 1988. iii, 429 p. Congress Session: 100-2. SUDOC: Y4.F76/1:B49/2/v.3. Contains transcripts of Committee markup sessions as follows: August 3 session (p. 79-247) to consider: H. Res. 471 (text, p. 237-239; amended text, p. 242-246), to condemn Iraqi March 16, 1988 use of chemical weapons against the Kurdish minority in Iraq; and to urge the Administration to accelerate efforts to achieve an international chemical weapons ban. Amended bill was favorably reported.

370. Congress. House. Committee on Foreign Affairs. *Legislation to Impose Sanctions Against Iraqi Chemical Use*. Washington, DC: U.S. GPO, 1988 iii, 45 p. Congress Session: 100-2. SUDOC:Y4.F76/1:L52/16. Contains transcript of Committee markup session, with Department of State participation, on Committee draft bill (text, p. 3-9), the Sanctions Against Iraqi Chemical Weapons Use Act, to prohibit U.S. export of military and civilian goods and technology to Iraq in response to alleged Iraqi use of chemical weapons against its Kurdish minority. H.R. 5337, a clean version of the amended draft bill, was reported favorably. Supplementary material (p. 37-45) includes correspondence and: (a) H.R. 5271, the Prevention of Genocide Act of 1988, to require U.S. sanctions against Iraq for alleged use of chemical weapons in Kurdistan, and to commend Turkey for its humanitarian actions in assisting Kurdish refugees, text (p. 39-42). (b) H. Res. 471, to condemn Iraqi use of chemical weapons; and to urge the Administration to accelerate efforts to achieve an international chemical weapons ban, text (p. 43-45).

371. Congress. House. Committee on Foreign Affairs. *Emergency Relief for the Kurdish People, Communication from the President*. Washington, DC: U.S. GPO, 1991. i, 2 p. Pub. No.: H.Doc. 102-86. Congress Session: 102-1. SUDOC: Y1.1/7:102-86. Transmittal of Presidential notification, dated May 17, 1991, of the introduction of a limited number of U.S. forces into northern Iraq to provide humanitarian relief for the Kurdish people in light of continued Iraqi repression of the Kurds following the Apr. 6, 1991 cease-fire and withdrawal of U.S. forces from southern Iraq.

372. Congress. House. Committee on Foreign Affairs. *Proposed Legislation to Authorize Emergency Assistance for Refugees and Displaced Persons in and Around Iraq*. Washington, DC: U.S. GPO, 1991. iii, 107 p. Congress Session: 102-1. SUDOC: Y4.F76/1: L52/17. Hearing to examine the status and needs of Kurdish and other Iraqi refugees who fled to areas along the Iraqi-Turkish border following the Persian Gulf war, and to review related humanitarian relief activities and funding needs. Includes transcript (p. 99-107) of Committee markup session on the Emergency Supplemental Iraqi Refugee Assistance Act of 1991 (draft text, p. 104-106) to authorize FY91 supplemental appropriations for emergency humanitarian assistance to Persian Gulf war refugees in and around Iraq. Bill was favorably reported. Statements and Discussion include: Findings of House Delegation visit to Turkish-Iraqi border to assess refugee conditions and international relief efforts (rpt, p. 4-11); recommendations for U.S. humanitarian aid (related rpt, p. 40-44), extent of refugee problem in and around Iraq; role of UN in providing humanitarian assistance to displaced Iraqi civilians; review of international humanitarian relief activities along the Turkish-Iraqi border, and recommendations for assistance to Persian Gulf war refugees.

373. Congress. House. Committee on Foreign Affairs. *U.S. Policy Toward Iraq 3 Years After the Gulf War*. Washington, DC: U.S. GPO, 1994. iii, 61 p. Congress Session: 103-2. SUDOC: Y4.F76/1:IR1/15. Hearing before the Subcommittee on Europe and the Middle East to review developments in and U.S. policy options regarding Iraq, emphasizing international economic sanctions. Supplementary material (p. 41-61) includes witnesses' written statements. Statements and Discussion include: Adverse impact on Iraqi Kurds of economic sanctions. Assessment of political power of Iraqi President Saddam Hussein; review of U.S. policy options for dealing with Iraq and weakening Saddam Hussein, focusing on current economic sanctions; overview of Saddam Hussein repression of Iraqi opposition civilian populations, including the Kurds.

374. Congress. House. Committee on Hunger, Select. *Decades of Disasters: The United Nations' Response*. Washington, DC: U.S. GPO, 1991. iii, 176 p. Congress Session: 102-1. SUDOC: Y4.H89:102-10. Hearing before the Select Committee on Hunger to examine the effectiveness of and the need to improve UN disaster relief and other humanitarian emergency response mechanisms. Supplementary material (p. 44-176) includes submitted statements, witnesses' written statements, and: (a) H.R. 2258, the Freedom from Want Act, to recognize the human right to food, propose a UN Convention on the Right to Food, and require the U.S. to attempt to reform and restructure UN mechanisms for responding to international disasters and humanitarian emergencies, text (p. 115-118). (b) International Committee on the Right to Food, right to food in domestic and international law, findings and recommendations, with bibliography (p. 122-158). Statements and Discussion include: Deficiencies of UN system, with recommendations; validity of humanitarian intervention under international law, with example of UN intervention on behalf of Iraqi Kurds after the Persian Gulf war; steps toward improving UN humanitarian relief and intervention activities. Includes the following insertion: Nanda, V. P., "Humanitarian Intervention" forthcoming book excerpt, with bibliography (p. 87-107).

375. Congress. House. Committee on Hunger, Select. *Future of Humanitarian Assistance in Iraq*. Hearing. Washington, DC: U.S. GPO, 1992. iv, 130 p. Congress Session: 102-2. SUDOC: Y4.H89:102-22. Committee Serial No. 102-22. Hearing before the Select

Committee on Hunger International Task Force to examine humanitarian issues in Iraq, including status of international humanitarian relief efforts to alleviate hunger and public health problems resulting from international economic sanctions imposed against Iraq in connection with the 1991 Persian Gulf War. Supplementary material (p. 43-130) includes submitted statements, witnesses' written statements, articles, and correspondence. Statements and Discussion include: Perspectives on humanitarian conditions in Iraq; allegations regarding Iraqi human rights abuses, focusing on persecution of Kurdish minority; arguments for lifting non-military sanctions against Iraq.

376. Congress. House. Committee on International Relations. *U.S. Policy Toward Iraq*. Washington, DC: U.S. GPO, 1996. iii, 92 p. Congress Session: 104-2. SUDOC: Y4.IN8/16:IR1/3. Hearing to review developments in and U.S. policy toward Iraq. Examines Iraqi failure to comply with UN Security Council resolutions regarding Iraqi actions following the 1990-91 Persian Gulf War, and reviews international sanctions imposed on Iraq for noncompliance with UN resolutions. Supplementary material (p. 37-92) includes witnesses' written statements and written replies to Committee questions, and a submitted statement. Statements and Discussion include: Overview of conditions in Iraq; status of Iraqi efforts to acquire weapons of mass destruction; issues involved in UN resolution allowing Iraq to sell oil in order to buy humanitarian goods for Iraqi populace affected by sanctions. Recommendations for U.S. policy toward the Kurdish minority in northern Iraq; perspectives on conditions in Iraq, with suggestions concerning U.S. policy options.

377. Congress. House. Committee on Ways and Means. *Sanctions Against Iraqi Chemical Weapons Use Act*. Washington, DC: U.S. GPO, 1988. Report. 7 p. Pub. No.: H. Rpt. 100-981, pt. 1. Congress Session: 100-2. SUDOC: Y1.1/8:100-981/pt.1. Recommends passage with amendments of H.R. 5337, the Sanctions Against Iraqi Chemical Weapons Use Act, to prohibit U.S. export of certain military and civilian goods and technology to Iraq in response to Iraqi use of chemical weapons against its Kurdish minority. Committee consideration was limited to provisions authorizing the President to impose additional sanctions, including restrictions on imports of petroleum and other products from Iraq.

378. Congress. Senate. Committee on Armed Services. *Operation Desert Shield/Desert Storm*. April 24, May 8, 9, 16, 21, June 4, 12, 20, 1991. Washington, DC: U.S. GPO, 1991. Hearing. iv, 414 p. il. Pub. No.: S. Hrg. 102-326. Congress Session: 102-1. SUDOC: Y4.Ar5/3:S.hrg.102-326. Hearings to examine U.S. military forces performance in Operation Desert Shield/Desert Storm in the Persian Gulf undertaken in response to the Iraqi August 1990 invasion of Kuwait. Focuses on DOD U.S. Central Command strategy and operations. Classified material has been deleted. Statements and Discussion include: Briefing on U.S. military, Department of State, and AID assistance to Kurds fleeing Iraq after Operation Desert Storm; role of U.S. military forces in providing protection and establishing supply systems for food and goods for Kurds (related charts, pp. 11-38 passim); status of the Kurds.

379. Congress. Senate. Committee on Foreign Relations. *Chemical Weapons Use in Kurdistan: Iraq's Final Offensive*. Washington, DC: U.S. GPO, 1988. ix, 46 p. Congress Session: 100-2. SUDOC: Y4.F76/2:S.prt.100-148/corr. Staff report, based on September 11-17, 1988 study mission to Turkey along the Iraqi border by Peter W. Galbraith and Christopher Van Hollen, Jr., assessing allegations by Iraqi Kurdish refugees in Turkey that Iraq used chemical weapons in Kurdistan during a so-called final offensive to end the Kurdish insurgency following ceasefire in the Iran-Iraq war. Reviews Kurdistan political background and relationship to the Iraq republic, alleged prior use of chemical weapons by Iraq, and Kurdish eyewitness accounts of chemical attacks. Includes a summary of key findings (p. VII-VIII), photographs throughout, and: S. 2763, the Prevention of Genocide Act of 1988, to require U.S. sanctions against Iraq for use of chemical weapons in Kurdistan, and to commend Turkey for its humanitarian actions in assisting Kurdish refugees, text (p. 43-46).

380. Congress. Senate. Committee on Foreign Relations. *U.S. Policy Toward Iraq: Human Rights, Weapons Proliferation, and International Law*. Washington, DC: U.S. GPO, 1990. iii, 93 p. Congress Session: 101-2. SUDOC: Y4.F76/2:S.hrg.101-1055. Hearing to assess U.S. policy towards Iraq, focusing on the implications of Iraq's violation of international law by engaging in human rights abuses, and on Iraq's efforts to acquire missiles and chemical and nuclear weapons. Supplementary material (p. 89-93) includes witnesses' written replies to Committee questions. Statements and Discussion include: Review of Iraq human rights abuses; concern about the fate of Iraqi Kurds in Turkish refugee camps; description of Iraq persecution of Kurds, with policy recommendations; evidence of Iraq efforts to develop nuclear weapons and missiles, citing need to revise technology export controls (related list, p. 80-81).

381. Congress. Senate. Committee on Foreign Relations. *Civil War in Iraq*. Washington, DC: U.S. GPO, 1991. viii, 28 p. Congress Session: 102-1. SUDOC: Y4.F76/2:S.prt.102-27. Staff report, prepared by Peter W. Galbraith, on humanitarian and policy issues related to civil unrest in Iraq. Provides an overview of the Kurdish rebellion and describes Iraqi army suppression of the Kurds during a March 30-31, 1991 visit to Iraqi-controlled Kurdistan. Assesses and recommends U.S. humanitarian aid initiatives for the Kurds, and reviews regional implications of the conflict. Appendix (p. 23-28) includes articles.

382. Congress. Senate. Committee on Foreign Relations. *Foreign Relations Authorization Act, FY92-FY93*. Washington, DC: U.S. GPO, 1991. Report. 134 p. Pub. No.: S. Rpt. 102-98. Congress Session: 102-1. SUDOC: Y1.1/5:102-98. Recommends passage of S. 1433, the Foreign Relations Authorization Act, FY92-FY93, to amend the State Department Basic Authorities Act of 1956 and other acts to revise and authorize FY92-FY93 appropriations for Department of State and re-

lated agencies programs, in the following titles: Title I, Department of State, to: ... Title II, U.S. Informational, Educational, and Cultural Programs, to: ... c. Direct the Voice of America to establish a Kurdish language service.

383. Congress. Senate. Committee on Foreign Relations. *Kurdistan in the Time of Saddam Hussein*. Washington, DC: U.S. GPO, 1991. viii, 23 p. Congress Session: 102-1. SUDOC: Y4.F76/2:S.prt.102-56. Staff report, prepared by Peter W. Galbraith, presenting findings of September 4-11, 1991 visit to Iraqi Kurdistan to observe conditions following the 1991 uprisings by Kurdish insurgents and retaliatory attacks by the Iraqi army. Examines the need and options for international protection of the Kurds from future Iraqi attacks, and provides evidence of atrocities committed against Kurds under the rule of Saddam Hussein. Includes maps and photos throughout.

384. Congress. Senate. Committee on Foreign Relations. *Mass Killings in Iraq*. Washington, DC: U.S. GPO, 1992. iii, 51 p. Congress Session: 102-2. SUDOC: Y4.F76/2:S.hrg.102-652. Hearing to examine human rights abuses against the Kurdish minority by the Iraqi government, including allegations of mass killings. Includes: UNICEF, "UNICEF Programme Progress Report: Iraq Emergency" 1992 (p. 39-48). Statements and Discussion include: Review of alleged Iraqi human rights abuses against the Kurdish minority; evidence of mass killings of Kurds by Iraqi government; views on Kurdish refugee situation; perspectives on aid for Iraqi Kurds.

385. Congress. Senate. Committee on Foreign Relations. *Saddam's Documents*. Washington, DC: U.S. GPO, 1992. Report. vi, 10 p. Pub. No.: S. Prt. 102-111. Congress Session: 102-2. SUDOC: Y4.F76/2:S.prt.102-111. Report by Peter W. Galbraith (Committee staff), describing the acquisition and content of certain Iraqi secret police documents obtained by the author during an April 16-27, 1992 visit to the Kurdish minority area of Iraq. Focuses on evidence provided by the documents of Iraqi human rights abuses against the Kurds, including mass killings.

386. Congress. Senate. Committee on Foreign Relations. *U.S. Policy Toward Iran and Iraq*. Washington, DC: U.S. GPO, 1995. iv, 174 p. Congress Session: 104-1. SUDOC: Y4. F76/2:S.HRG.104-280. Hearings before the Subcommittee on Near Eastern and South Asian Affairs to review developments in and U.S. policy toward Iraq and Iran, focusing on U.S. dual containment policy of economic sanctions, arms controls, and political action to limit the threat to U.S. interests posed by Iran and Iraq. Supplementary material (pp. 5-8, 163-174) includes witnesses' written replies to Subcommittee questions. Statements and Discussion include: Need for U.S. action to end Iraq repression of Kurds and resolve conflict between Kurdish factions; need to present evidence of Iraq genocide against Kurds to International Court of Justice; description of alleged Iraqi atrocities against Kurds, with recommendations for U.S. policy.

387. Congress. Senate. Committee on Governmental Affairs. *Global Spread of Chemical and Biological Weapons*. Washington, DC: U.S. GPO, 1989. vi, 746 p. Congress Session: 101-1. SUDOC: Y4.G74/9:S.hrg. 101-744. Hearings before the Permanent Subcommittee on Investigations to examine concerns regarding the worldwide proliferation of chemical weapons (CW) and biological weapons (BW), and to consider measures to control CW and BW production and use. Supplementary material (pp. 221-746) includes witnesses' prepared statements, articles, and reports. Statements and Discussion include: Experiences in interviewing and treating Iraqi Kurds reportedly attacked with CW by Iraqi military; description of CW effects on victims; explanation of medical treatment and toxicological studies of Kurds (medical reports, correspondence, pp. 254-266, 630-650). Insertion: Physicians for Human Rights, "Winds of Death: Iraq's Use of Poison Gas Against Its Kurdish Population" report of medical mission to Iraqi Kurd refugee camps in Turkey, February 1989, with illustrations (pp. 657-702).

388. Congress. Senate. Committee on the Judiciary. *Aftermath of War: The Persian Gulf Refugee Crisis*. Washington, DC: U.S. GPO, 1991. ix, 37 p. Congress Session: 102-1. SUDOC: Y4.J89/2:S.prt.102-31. Staff report, prepared for the Subcommittee on Immigration and Refugee Affairs, presenting findings of Subcommittee April 15, 1991 hearing and delegation April 27-May 9 visit to Iraq evaluating the international humanitarian relief operation to assist Kurds and other ethnic and religious minorities made refugees following the war in the Persian Gulf. Also reviews the status of refugees in Iraq and other Persian Gulf areas.

389. Congress. Senate. Committee on the Judiciary. *Aftermath of War, Part II: The Plight of the Iraqi Kurds a Year Later*. Washington, DC: U.S. GPO, 1992. ix, 43 p. Congress Session: 102-2. SUDOC: Y4.J89/2:S. prt. 102-31/pt.2. Subcommittee on Immigration and Refugee Affairs staff report on the status of Iraqi Kurds following the Persian Gulf War. Report is based on staff December 10-14, 1991 visit to northern Iraq, conducted as a follow up mission to staff April 27-May 9, 1991 visit to Iraq. Evaluates the living conditions and continuing aid needs of Kurdish villagers and refugees, and assesses international security arrangements for protecting Kurds from Iraqi forces. Includes findings and recommendations (p. 1-3), and UN resolutions and related documents on humanitarian aid to civilian populations in the Persian Gulf region (p. 17-43).

390. Congress. Senate. Committee on the Judiciary. *Refugee Crisis in the Persian Gulf*. Washington, DC: U.S. GPO, 1991. iv, 245 p. Congress Session: 102-1. SUDOC: Y4.J89/2: S.hrg.102-522. Hearings before the Subcommittee on Immigration and Refugee Affairs to examine the status and needs of Kurdish and other Iraqi refugees following the 1991 Persian Gulf war, focusing on conditions in Turkey-Iraq and Iran-Iraq border areas. Also reviews related humanitarian relief activities and funding needs. Supplementary material (pp. 127-245) includes: (a) Subcommittee, "Aftermath of War: The Persian Gulf Refugee Crisis" May 20, 1991 (pp. 127-185). (b) Harvard University, "Harvard Study Team Report: Public Health in Iraq After the Gulf War" May 1991, with tables and graphs (pp. 186-245).

391. Cooley, J. K. *Payback: America's Long War in the Middle East*. Washington, DC: Brassey's, 1991. xiv, 257 p. Includes bibliographical references and index. Cooley has covered the Middle East and Africa since 1957. His theme in this book is that during the critical years from the start of the Iranian revolution to the present, the U.S. has been "paid back" for its poor judgment and often disastrous policy errors in the Middle East. Cooley puts into context the attacks on the U.S. embassy and Marine barracks in Lebanon, the hijacking of TWA Flight 847, the abductions of the CIA's William Buckley and AP bureau chief Terry Anderson, and other retaliatory acts during what he calls the Khomeini Decade. The book argues that from the end of the Iran-Iraq war in 1988 until Saddam Hussein's 1990 invasion of Kuwait, the Bush administration conducted "a strange love affair" with the Iraqi dictator, which climaxed with Desert Storm and its traumatic aftermath. The final payback, according to the author, was the terrible responsibility imposed on the Bush administration by the millions of Kurds fleeing massacre by Saddam's forces.

392. Cowan, J. W. *Operation Provide Comfort: Operational Analysis for Operations Other Than War*. [Final report.] Newport, RI: Naval War College, Joint Military Operations Dept., 16 June, 1995. 28p. [NTIS Accession Number: AD-A297 852/6/XAB]. In early February 1991 Operation Desert Storm had reached its dramatic conclusion. The United States military had displayed its incredible power and effectiveness as the world's sole remaining super power and stood ready to lead the world into the future of President Bush's New World Order. On April 5, 1991, U. S. and world attention again was sharply focused on a new and different developing human tragedy in post war Iraq. Instead of familiar footage of successful military operations, the public was now faced with the images of a half million terrorized and starving Kurdish refugees clinging to the sides of

mountains in the remote northern regions of the Iraq-Turkish border. This operation serves as a classic case in the validation of the six Principles for Operations Other than War, although it was conducted two years prior to publishing of the fundamentals in current doctrine. The peacemaking success of Operation Provide Comfort established the standard in political and public perception for the projection and use of coalition military power for the purpose of saving lives. The current world situation suggests that coalition and peacemaking operations will continue to be the most prevalent challenge facing the future employment of military forces. The experiences of Operation Provide Comfort have validated the need for continued study and development of joint doctrine for coalition and peacemaking operations.

393. Department of State. Bureau of Democracy, Human Rights, and Labor. *Annual Report on International Religious Freedom Report*. PRINT, WEB. Washington, DC: Bureau of Democracy, Human Rights, and Labor, 1999- . Annual. (www.state.gov/ g/drl/irf/rpt/). This report is issued by the Senate Committee on Foreign Relations and submitted annually to the Congress by the Department of State. The law provides that the Secretary of State shall transmit to Congress by September 1 of each year, or the first day thereafter on which the appropriate House of Congress is in session, "an Annual Report on International Religious Freedom supplementing the most recent Human Rights Reports by providing additional detailed information with respect to matters involving international religious freedom." This annual report includes 195 reports on countries worldwide. Full-text of reports for the years 1999-2002 on Iraq (the only country reportedly to persecute the Kurds on religious bases) are included in this book and can be found at the following addresses:

- 2002: www.state.gov/g/drl/rls/irf/2002/13996. htm

- 2001: www.state.gov/g/drl/rls/irf/2001/5693. htm
- 2000: www.state.gov/www/global/human_ rights/irf/irf_rpt/irf_iraq.html

- 1999: www.state.gov/www/global/human_rights/ irf/irf_rpt/1999/irf_iraq99.html

394. Department of State. Office of Humanitarian Demining Programs. *Hidden Killers, 1998: The Global Landmine Crisis.* Washington, DC: U.S. Dept. of State, Bureau of Political-Military Affairs, September 1998. 206 p. Since the Department of State's last landmine report was issued in 1994, several developments have altered significantly the status of the global humanitarian crisis caused by antipersonnel landmines. This report is designed to take account of those developments and their impact on the problem, as well as to add new information to the baseline data and update the status of 12 of the most severely mine-affected countries. Much of the background data in the 1994 report remains valid and has not been repeated in this updated edition. The section on Iraqi Kurdistan is available at: www.state.gov/www/global/arms/rpt_9809_demine_ch3k.html.

395. Doherty, Carroll J. "Prolonged Turmoil May Slow Withdrawal from Region." *Congressional Quarterly Weekly Report* 49, no. 11 (March 16, 1991): 696. Iraq's harsh crackdowns on Kurdish separatists and Iran-backed Shi'ite Muslims have raised the possibility that the US troop withdrawal from the Persian Gulf will be slow. Since the Persian Gulf war's quick end, problems, rather than opportunities, have become more apparent.

396. Doherty, Carroll J. "Bush, Congress in Agreement on Kurdish Refugee Relief." *Congressional Quarterly Weekly Report* 49, no. 17 (April 27, 1991): 1078-1079. Moved by the plight of refugees in and around Iraq, the Bush Administration and Congress agree that the US should extend all possible help to Iraqis displaced by the Persian Gulf war.

397. Doherty, Carroll J. "Panels Approve Partial Funding for Kurdish Refugee Aid." *Congressional Quarterly Weekly Report* 49, no. 18 (May 4, 1991): 1144-1145. Although Congress moved quickly to finance aid to Kurdish refugees, congressmen are still uneasy over the prospect of an open-ended US military presence in post-war Iraq.

398. Doherty, Carroll J. "Members Pass Relief Legislation for Kurds and Other Refugees." *Congressional Quarterly Weekly Report* (May 11, 1991): 1211, 1213. Congress has approved a proposal to provide more than half a billion dollars to aid displaced people in and around Iraq and to help disaster victims in other parts of the world.

399. Doherty, Carroll J. "Relief measure bogged down by disputes over details. (Disaster and starvation relief for Kurdistan and Bangladesh)." *Congressional Quarterly Weekly Report* 49, no. 20 (May 18, 1991): 1305.

400. Doherty, Carroll J. "Congress Clears Refugee Aid Bush's Signature Expected." *Congressional Quarterly Weekly Report* 49, no. 21 (May 25, 1991): 1388. Congress took the first step toward addressing the needs of Kurdish refugees in Iraq when it gave preliminary approval to HR 2251, an appropriations bill that includes $556 million in disaster and refugee aid.

401. Doherty, Caroll J. "Senate Struggles Over Response to Clinton's Attack on Iraq: Election-Year Politics Complicates Debate on Resolution of Support for Troops." *Congressional Quarterly Weekly Report* 54 (September 7, 1996): 2535-2536. Debate on U.S. Cruise missile strikes on military installations in southern Iraq, in response to Iraqi military deployment into the Kurdish "Safe Haven" in northern Iraq.

402. Downing, Linda M., and Gail McCain. "Medical Support for Kurdish Relief Effort." *U.S.A.F. Medical Service Digest* 43 (Winter 1992): 10-11.

403. Drew, Elizabeth. "Letter from Washington." [Helping the Kurds.] *The New Yorker* 67 (May 6 1991): 97-103. In taking belated responsibility for easing the plight of the Kurdish refugees in Iraq, a strained and defensive Bush administration has backed itself into a situation it had hoped to avoid. Bush's strategy in denying military aid to the Kurds and Shi'ites rebelling against Saddam Hussein was defensible but hard to explain to the public. The president apparently wanted the Iraqi military or the Baathists to force Hussein from power, but a Kurdish separatist movement threatened the preservation of an intact postwar Iraq, a goal that the administration believes is essential to maintaining the balance of power in the Persian Gulf. Moreover, Bush and his advisers feared the military consequences of getting involved in an Iraqi civil war. As a result, the administration was reluctant to give even humanitarian relief to the Kurds while the rebellion was in progress. Even now, the government fears that helping the Kurds will be the start of a long, unwelcome involvement.

404. Elmo, David S. "Distributing Food to the Kurds." *Army Logistician* (January-February 1992): 2-5.

405. Elmo, David S. "Food Distribution During Operation Provide Comfort." *Special Warfare* 5 (March 1992): 8-9.

406. Elmo, David S. "Food Distribution for Operation Provide Comfort." [Kurd relief effort.] *Military Review: The Professional Journal of the U.S. Army* 73 (September 1993): 80-81.

407. Farer, Tom J. "Human Rights and Foreign Policy: What the Kurds Learned." [A drama in one act—satire] *Human Rights Quarterly* 14 (November 1992): 62-77. The Bush administration's policy towards the Kurds in Iraq after the Persian Gulf War is satirized in a brief drama involving a national security advisor, a moderate Republican and a foreign policy expert. Casting about for language which would allow the President to engage in human rights rhetoric without committing to action, they finally settle on section 502(b) of the Foreign Assistance Act. This section's provisions on human rights abuses have been interpreted loosely by previous administrations. The stateless Kurds, with no power, may become the subject of political rhetoric but will receive no real assistance.

408. Felton, John. "Iraq Sanctions Bill Puts Administration in a Bind." *Congressional Quarterly Weekly Report* 46, no. 38 (Septem-

ber 17, 1988): 2571-2572. On Sep 9, 1988, the Senate passed a bill imposing harsh economic sanctions on Iraq as punishment for using chemical weapons against its Kurdish minority since Aug 1987. The bill, which was called premature by the State Department, is examined.

409. Felton, John. "Less Sweeping Than Senate Version: House Panels Advance Bill Imposing Sanctions on Iraq." *Congressional Quarterly Weekly Report* 46, no. 39 (September 24, 1988): 2634. House committees are moving ahead with legislation imposing sanctions on Iraq to protest its alleged use of chemical weapons against the Kurdish minority there. However, the bill is far less sweeping than a Senate-passed measure containing a broad series of economic sanctions.

410. Felton, John. "Protest of Chemical Warfare: Differences on Iraq Sanctions Complicate Foreign Aid Bill." *Congressional Quarterly Weekly Report* 46, no. 40 (October 1, 1988): 2741. Acting on the fiscal 1989 foreign aid appropriations bill, the Senate for the second time approved sanctions against Iraq for using chemical weapons against its Kurdish minority. The Senate action was an effort to force the House to accept a stronger foreign aid bill. The differences on Iraq sanctions, which complicate the foreign aid bill, are discussed.

411. Felton, John. "Hill Moving on Iraq Sanctions: Use of Chemical Weapons Against the Kurds." *Congressional Quarterly Weekly Report* 46 (October 15, 1988): 2983.

412. Ferguson, W. T. *Operation Provide Comfort: A History of JTF—A Logistical Operation.* Carlisle Barracks, PA: Army War College, May 1992. 41p. [NTIS Accession Number: AD-A295 932/8/XAB]. During Operation Desert Storm, Proven Force and Provide Comfort, I was the J-4, Special Forces Operations Command Europe, (SOCEUR) commanded by Brigadier General Richard Potter. Special Operations Command Europe deployed as part of Joint Task Force Proven Force, Incirlik, Turkey, which operated from 9 January 1991 to 22 March 1991. On 6 April

1991, Headquarters SOCEUR was alerted for participation in Operation Provide Comfort with the mission to provide humanitarian support to the Kurds in northern Iraq and southern Turkey. Other reports on Operation Provide Comfort have focused on the JTF force composition, mission, and operational concept. The objective of this personal experience monograph is to provide insight into the logistical operations and staff relationships of JTF-A during Operation Provide Comfort, 7 April 1991 through 17 June 1991. The views presented in this paper are the logistical perspective of how SOCEUR supported Operation Provide Comfort (A).

413. Fessler, Pamela. "Congress' Record on Saddam: Decade of Talk, Not Action: Before Invasion of Kuwait, Capitol Hill Politics, Inertia Undercut Objections to White House Courtship of Iraq." *Congressional Quarterly Weekly Report* 49 (April 27, 1991): 1068-1076. Highlights major foreign policy decisions since 1982. U.S. role in the Iranian-Iraqi war, including oil tanker escort, chemical weapons, sanctions, and the Kurds.

414. Freedman, L., and D. Boren. "'Safe Havens' for Kurds in Post-War Iraq." In *To Loose the Bands of Wickedness: International Intervention in Defence of Human Rights*. Edited by N. Rodley, 43-92. London: Brassey's, 1992. Since the Second World War there have been remarkable advances in the field of international humanitarian law. A major instrument in the protection of human rights has been the United Nations, whose presence is generally recognized to be non-threatening and impartial. Gross violations of human rights not only cause untold suffering for the victims, but also provoke mass flights of populations on a scale which increasingly threatens to destabilise host countries, and ultimately poses a threat to international peace and security. The international community tries to cope with the ever increasing flow of refugees, but remains reluctant to take coercive measures against the governments directly responsible for massive abuses of human rights, still sheltering behind article 2(7) of the UN Charter, which does not

"authorize the United Nations to intervene in matters which are essentially within the domestic jurisdiction of any state." Should not governments, in the light of actual events, now consider whether the price of non-intervention is too high, not only on humanitarian grounds, but also because of the escalating costs and the acute political and social problems posed by these mass exoduses? Or is the risk of power abuse for political gain too high because state sovereignty is perceived as absolute. The focus of this study is essentially a practical one. It considers what reforms and additional measures are required to strengthen the UN's capacity to intervene more effectively on humanitarian issues, particularly those traditionally excluded from UN action by article 2(7) of the Charter. Case histories are included—that of the Kurds in Iraq (pp. 43-92) and the international reaction to the civil strife in Yugoslavia.

415. Frelick, Bill. "The False Promise of Operation Provide Comfort: Protecting Refugees or Protecting State Power?" *Middle East Report* (May-June 1992): 22-27. The author, a senior policy analyst with the U.S. Committee for Refugees and associate editor of the *World Refugee Survey*, visited Kurdish refugee camps in Iran in April 1991. This article is based on a longer paper presented at the Middle East Studies Association conference in November 1991 that later appeared in *Kurdish Studies* (Spring-Fall 1992, pp. 45-53). The international regime established for refugees has been created and maintained less for their protection than to preserve the prerogatives of powerful states. Many heralded the U.S. aid to Iraqi Kurds at the end of the 1991 Gulf war as a precedent for future interventions in defense of human rights and humanitarian assistance. In retrospect, the U.S. move appears as yet another exercise designed to enhance the prerogatives of state power by a stronger against a weaker state. Britain, France and the U.S. created an occupied military zone in the name of international stability with the intent to de-stabilize the government of Iraq. This may have been a legitimate political goal, but it misrepresented the intervention under an essentially humanitarian facade.

416. Ghareeb, Edmund. *The Kurdish Question in Iraq*. Syracuse, NY: Syracuse University Press, 1981. x, 223 p.: map. Includes bibliographical references and index. Originally the author's Ph.D. dissertation (Georgetown University, 1979). In it, Ghareeb examines the history of the Kurdish issue in Iran and Turkey and then concentrates on Iraq, chronicling the Iraqi Ba'th government's attempts since 1968 to achieve a political understanding with the Kurds concerning their status in Northern Iraq. The failure of both sides to reach agreement contributed to widespread Kurdish armed rebellion which was encouraged by covert Iranian, American, and Israeli assistance. Drawing upon extensive personal interviews with pro-and anti-Ba'th Kurdish leaders, including Mulla Mustafa Barzani and members of his family, Iraqi government and Ba'th party officials, and U.S. government officials, Ghareeb discusses in detail the positions of the Ba'th and Kurdish leaders and the factors which led to the failure of negotiations between them and, ultimately, to the collapse of the Kurdish rebellion itself.

417. Goff, D. G. *Building Coalitions for Humanitarian Operations Operation Provide Comfort*. [Study project.] Carlisle Barracks, PA: Army War Coll., April 15, 1992. 38p. [NTIS Accession Number: AD-A251 202/8/XAB]. Over one million Iraqi Kurds fled the military reprisals of Saddam Hussein following their uprising in northern Iraq immediately after Desert Storm. Reports reaching the world indicated that two thousand Kurds died each day in the harsh cold mountains along the Turkish-Iraqi border. On April 5, 1991, in cooperation with other allied nations, President Bush ordered American Military forces to begin airlifting humanitarian supplies to the Kurdish refugees. This Presidential decision established the largest military coalition ever formed in support of humanitarian operations. Operation Provide Comfort was the code name used for the worldwide outpouring of humanitarian assistance provided to the Kurdish displaced persons. The coalition formed to support this

operation consisted of army, navy, marine, air force, governmental and non-governmental agencies from thirteen nations. Time was critical. The coalition had to be formed quickly to provide the necessary humanitarian assistance to stop the dying in the mountains. The process of developing a military coalition to support humanitarian operations is described in this individual study project. The conclusion presents key considerations in coalition building in the area of command relationships, rules of engagement and unit capabilities. Recommendations are made in response to the key considerations. Building coalitions to support humanitarian operations will continue into the 21st century and the United States must be prepared to lead in the formation of coalitions.

418. Goff, D. G. *Operation Provide Comfort*. Carlisle Barracks, PA: Army War College, May 1992. 58 p. [NTIS Accession Number: AD-A295 955/9]. In early 1991, as Operation Desert Storm ended, the world press reported that nearly 2,000 Kurdish men, women and children were dying each day in the harsh cold of the Turkish-Iraqi mountains. Scenes of bare feet and poorly clothed Kurdish women and children showed them walking in snow and frigid temperatures to escape Saddam Hussein's vengeance as he crushed their short-lived Kurdish nationalist uprising. Kurdish leaders reported three million Kurds had fled into the 8,000-foot mountains. World opinion and public concern for the plight of the Kurdish people forced-democratic nations to build a military coalition to provide humanitarian assistance to ease the suffering of the Kurds. The code name for this humanitarian operation was Operation Provide Comfort.

419. Gunter, Michael M. *The Kurds of Iraq: Tragedy and Hope*. New York: St. Martin's Press, 1992. x, 175 p.: map. Includes bibliographical references (p. [153]-166) and index. The end of World War I marked the collapse of Ottoman power and the decision by Britain to carve out the new, artificial state of Iraq from part of the Empire's ruins. The Kurds who found themselves within Iraq have been in an almost permanent state of revolt ever since. For its part, the Iraqi government has always feared Kurdish separatism not only for itself but because of the precedent it would set for the Shiites, some 55% of the population, and thus the very future of the Iraqi state. This book briefly reviews the background of the Kurdish national movement in Iraq, and then devotes the bulk of its analysis to the uprising which followed the 1991 Gulf War, the subsequent negotiations, UN peacekeeping operation, and creation of a *de facto* Kurdish state, as well as the vitally important policies of Turkey. The analysis concludes that, despite many remaining difficulties, there is now reason to hope that the long nightmare of the Kurds in Iraq might perhaps be nearing an end.

420. Gunter, Michael M. "Foreign Influences on the Kurdish Insurgency in Iraq." *Orient* 34, no. 1 (March 1993): 105-119. This article examines contemporary foreign influences on the Kurdish insurgency in Iraq, and focuses on the U.S. House of Representatives Pike Committee report and secret Israeli Intelligence support for the Iraqi Kurds over the years. Its central thesis is that the policies pursued by the U.S. after the 1991 Gulf War transformed the Kurdish situation inside Iraq providing an excellent opportunity for the creation of a *de facto* Kurdish state in northern Iraq.

421. Gunter, Michael M. "A Kurdish State in Northern Iraq?" *Humboldt Journal of Social Relations* 20, no. 2 (1994): 45-94. Factors that led to the May 1992 election and movement toward the creation of a de facto Kurdish state and government in northern Iraq following the Gulf war of 1991 are identified: (1) the protection of the Allied Poised Hammer forces stationed in southwestern Turkey, (2) a UN presence sanctioned by Security Council Resolution 688 (1991), and (3) Turkish cooperation and protection. The formation of the government, regional effects on surrounding states and the Kurds living in them, internal fighting, and economic problems are detailed. The nascent Kurdish state in Iraq is likely to become de facto due to continuation of neither war nor peace because of the U.S. deterrent, Turkish protection, and inability of Iraqi opposition to overthrow Saddam Hussein.

422. Gunter, Michael M. "The KDP-PUK Conflict in Northern Iraq." *The Middle East Journal* 50, no. 2 (Spring 1996): 225-241. Old rivalry over the control of population and territory between the Kurdish Democratic Party (KDP) and the Patriotic Union of Kurdistan (PUK) resulted in a civil war in the Kurdish region of Northern Iraq in May 1994. A breakaway faction of KDP emerged as the PUK in 1975, advocating Marxist ideology and has remained the main rival of KDP. The conflict between the two continued, despite the French and the U.S. effort to mediate. Although the leaders of both parties understand the ill effects of the conflict, they fail to resolve it. The civil strife threatens the future of the Kurdish Regional Government.

423. Gunter, Michael M. "Turkey and Iran Face Off in Kurdistan." *Middle East Quarterly* 5 (March 1998): 32-40. Examines the confrontation taking place in Iraqi Kurdistan among Mas'ud Barzani's Kurdistan Democratic Party (KDP), Jalal Talabani's Patriotic Union of Kurdistan (PUK), and Abdulla Ocalan's Kurdistan Workers Party (PKK), as well as U.S. involvement in the area.

424. Gunter, Michael M. *The Kurdish Predicament in Iraq: A Political Analysis*. New York: St. Martin's Press, 1999. x, 181 p. Includes bibliographical references (p. 164-175) and index. This is a well-documented, detailed account of the recent Kurdish history in Iraq. The purpose of the book is to present "a new analysis of the tragic descent into civil war and the many other events that have occurred" since 1992. In his first chapter, Gunter gives a detailed account of the divisions the Wigrams observed among the Kurds (*Cradle of Mankind: Life in Eastern Kurdistan*, by Edgar T. A. Wigrams, a British Christian missionary and his brother who lived and traveled through Kurdistan for ten years during the first decade of the 20th century). Gunter concludes that despite changes, the divisions that plagued the Kurds remain almost a century later. Presenting the past as a prologue, the author provides a background of the two main Kurdish leaders, Mas'ud Barzani of the Kurdistan Democratic Party (KDP) and Jalal Talabani of Patriotic Union of Kurdistan (PUK).

Gunter deserves credit for collecting these valuable personal details. The third chapter analyzes the Iraqi opposition, with which the Iraqi Kurds have a specific and problematic relationship. The purpose of the fourth chapter (on the KDP-PUK civil war) is "to analyze the background of the longstanding KDP-PUK rivalry and the relapse into conflict," not only to foster a better understanding of the causes of the present infra-Kurdish conflict, but also to "enable us to know how to help bring the conflict to an end and avoid similar problems in the future" (p. 68). Gunter offers a detailed description of the fighting between KDP and PUK from 1994 to 1998, as well as the failed mediation efforts by France, Turkey, the United States, and regional as well as local leaders. According to Gunter, "the inherent struggle for power between the two parties-fueled by the hostility of the regional powers-prevent the implementation of peace, and eventual fighting resumes" (p. 109). In the next chapter the author analyzes how this infra-Kurdish fighting has created a power vacuum that has forced Turkey and Iran to get involved in Iraqi Kurdistan, leading to a sharp confrontation between them, as well as prolonging the conflict between KDP and PUK through direct and indirect assistance to these organizations. The book ends with a ten-page discussion of the prospects for the Iraqi Kurds.

425. Haberman, Clyde. "The Kurds: In Flight, Once Again." *The New York Times Magazine* (May 5, 1991): 32-37+. Hope remains as elusive as ever for the long suffering Kurdish people, who faced their gravest crisis ever in their recent mass exodus from Iraq. The idea of a Kurdish homeland is a pipe dream; most of the estimated 20 million Kurds would settle for increased autonomy and improved economic development in the countries where they have sunk toward the bottom of the wage scale. In all the countries that the Kurds inhabit—Iran, Iraq, Turkey, Syria, and the Soviet Union—repression is a daily reality. In Turkey, speaking Kurdish was illegal until recently, and books and newspapers written in that language are still forbidden. In Iraq, the Kurds' repeated rebellions have led to savage suppression by Saddam Hussein's forces. Thousands have died in the Kurds'

recent flight from Iraq, and thousands more are likely to perish unless a rescue operation led by the United States succeeds quickly.

426. Harmon, Joseph M., III. "Operation Provide Comfort: A Cry for Help—The Military Role in Humanitarian Aid." *Fortitudine: Bulletin of the Marine Corps Historical Program* 21 (November-December 1992): 31-42.

427. Harriss, John (ed.). *The Politics of Humanitarian Intervention*. London: Pinter Publishers, 1995. xiii, 190 p. Includes bibliography and index. Published in association with the Save the Children Fund and the Centre for Global Governance. Amid the criticism of the UN's apparent failure to intervene in humanitarian disasters there has been little scholarly consideration of the real issues. The nature of human rights, sovereignty, UN organization and the practice of humanitarian action are some of the themes that are addressed in this volume which combines a theoretical approach with empirical analysis from those with practical experience in the field of international humanitarian assistance; some focus on UN operations in Somalia and on behalf of the Kurds in Iraq.

428. Heraclides, Alexis. "Secessionist Minorities and External Involvement." *International Organization* 44 (Summer 1990): 341-378. The author analyzes instances of involvement of a foreign state in seven postwar secessionists movements—those of Katanga, Biafra, Southern Sudan, Bangladesh, Iraqi Kurdistan, Eritrea, and the Moro Region of the Philippines in order to shed light on the possible patterns of interaction between the inter-national system and secessionist minorities. The article analyzes the constraints on, content of, and reasons for foreign involvement and tests seven assumptions of conventional wisdom to determine if they hold true in the cases studied. According to the author, although international norms are against involvement with groups that threaten territorial integrity, external state support of these groups is more extensive than would be expected, and support is given for diverse reasons rather than based solely on the prospects for tangible gain.

429. Heraclides, Alexis. *The Self-Determination of Minorities in International Politics*. London: Frank Cass, 1991. xvi, 291 p.: ill., maps. Bibliography: pp. 264-279. In International Relations, in particular, there is a dearth of knowledge on secession. Governments for their part have often reacted to communal assertiveness with contempt and coercion, a course hardly conducive to conflict resolution in a modern world of ever-rising expectations for legitimized rule, effective participation, ethnicity, group self-esteem and pride, distributive justice and new, more exacting standards for human rights and democracy. This book attempts to remedy the situation in International Relations and contribute to the further understanding of this multi-faceted problem. First, the reasons for violent separatism are being examined on the basis of the stimulating literature of communal violence and ethnicity in nearby fields of research. Then the existing international normative regime against separatism and secession is assessed and put to the task. But the main focus is on the international politics of armed separatism (that is, on the international activity of secessionist movements), and on world reaction and involvement by external parties. Seven secessionist movements—those of Katanga, Biafra, the Southern Sudan, Iraqi Kurdistan, Bangladesh, Eritrea and the Moros of the Philippines—are examined in detail to shed more light on the above questions and suggest a series of patterns of interaction between the international system and secessionist minorities. On pp. 129-146, focuses on the U.S. involvement in the 1961-1975 Iraqi Kurdish War.

430. Ignatieff, Michael. "The Seductiveness of Moral Disgust." *Social Research* 62 (Spring 1995): 77-97. The post-1989 military interventions in Somalia, Kurdish territory and Bosnia-Herzegovina are perceived as having been based on humanitarian reasons. Inspired by noble motives, such interventions are also colored by the rescuers' self perception that they are bringing decency, civility, tolerance and civilization to less rational societies. As a result, failure quickly brings moral disgust and leads to the use of imperial ruthlessness. What newly independent countries of the former

colonial empires need is the long-term rebuilding of civil society's structures and institutions rather than instant interventions with quick exit.

431. Jones, James L. "Operation Provide Comfort: Humanitarian and Security Assistance in Northern Iraq." *Marine Corps Gazette* 75 (November 1991): 98-107. In the aftermath of Desert Storm in 1991, Kurds in northern Iraq attempted to topple Saddam Hussein from power, but their villages were attacked by the Iraqi army, forcing them to flee into the mountains of southern Turkey. Operation Provide Comfort launched a multinational relief effort to protect more than one million Kurds and to provide them food, medicine, and shelter. The article highlights the involvement of U.S. marines in the relief effort.

432. Keen, David. *The Kurds in Iraq: How Safe is Their Haven Now?* London: Save the Children, 1993. 74 p.: ill. [Includes an executive summary of 11 pages.] Includes bibliographical references. Chapter 1 details how Kurdish nationalist aspirations were encouraged and then jettisoned several times in the 20th century, particularly in the 1920s, 1970s and after the Gulf War. Chapter 2 investigates the adequacy of international efforts to protect the Kurds after the collapse of their revolt in March-April 1991. It also investigates how this protection has been significantly eroded. Chapter 3 discusses the inadequacy of assistance and its implications on the Kurdish population in Iraqi Kurdistan. Chapter 4 explores the links between protecting and assisting the Kurds. There can be no lasting protection without adequate assistance, and there can be no adequate assistance and development without proper protection. Chapter 5 looks at some practical ways of improving protection and assistance in the context of ongoing conflict between the Kurds and the government of Iraq.

433. Kelley, J. M. *Tactical Implications for Peacemaking in Ethnic Conflict*. Fort Leavenworth, KS: Army Command and General Staff College, School of Advanced Military Studies, February 4, 1993. 71p. [NTIS

Accession Number: AD-A262 561/4/XAB]. Ethnic conflict is emerging as the dominant threat to world peace in the post-World War II security environment. The scope and frequency of ethnic conflict threatens world stability and could infringe on U.S. vital interests. The U.S. and the UN are involved in peace restoration operations in 13 ethnic conflicts worldwide. The U.S. Army accomplished the peacemaking mission in the past and will be challenged with peacemaking in the future. This monograph analyzes experiences from Operation Provide Comfort for tactical findings useful for formulating U.S. ground forces' peacemaking doctrine. The study begins by establishing the relevance of Operation Provide Comfort as a tool to examine peacemaking. The analysis uses 'Operations Other than War' from the emerging doctrine in Field Manual 100-5, Operations to review the Kurdish-Iraqi ethnic conflict. Three trends emerged. First, unity of command is a means to achieve unity of effort; but unity of effort is achievable without unity of command. Second, units exhibited great versatility. Third, the Army does not need dedicated forces for peacemaking in ethnic conflict. The study focuses on the emerging doctrinal principle of unity of effort and the tenet of versatility. Unity of effort and versatility are used to analyze six functional areas from Operation Provide Comfort. The six functions analyzed were: security, air operations, fire support, engineering, intelligence, and medical operations. The study found that Army forces thrived under the Operation Provide Comfort Coalition's unity of effort. The study concludes that the Army should further conventional forces versatility by adapting and modifying collateral activities already found in Special Forces doctrine.

434. Kimche, David. *The Last Option: After Nasser, Arafat & Saddam Hussein: The Quest for Peace in the Middle East*. London: Weidenfeld and Nicolson, 1991. 328 p.: maps. Includes bibliographical references and index. This book is a selective political history of the Middle East, supposedly aiming to dispel myths, but instead consolidating a partisan Israeli version of the post-1967 period. The book is divided into sections dealing with Is-

raeli-Egyptian relations, Israeli involvement in Lebanon, Kurdish-Israeli-Iranian dealing of the 1960s and 1970s, the Iran-Iraq war, Saddam's adventures in Kuwait, and, finally, the PLO and the Intifada. Kimche briefly discusses the infrequently covered Israeli links with Mustafa Barzani's Kurdish uprising in Iraq, in cooperation with Iran and the United States.

435. Kissinger, Henry. *Years of Renewal: The Concluding Volume of Memoirs*. New York: Simon & Schuster, 1999. 1151 p.: ill., maps. Includes bibliographical references (p. 1081-1120) and index. This is the concluding third volume of Henry Kissinger's series of memoirs, which began with *White House Years* and *Years of Upheaval*. In it, Kissinger assesses Richard Nixon's complex personality and peppers his explanations of China policy, Soviet policy, Middle East diplomacy, and the Kurdish tragedy with accounts of bureaucratic infighting and turf battles.

436. Korn, David A. "Iraq's Kurds: Why Two Million Fled." *Foreign Service Journal* 68 (July 1991): 20-24. Antecedents of the Kurdish rebellion following the Persian Gulf War, and U.S. response to the revolt.

437. Korn, David A. "The Last Years of Mustafa Barzani." *Middle East Quarterly* 1 (March 1994): 12-27.

438. Lyon, Alynna June. *International Contributions to the Mobilization of Ethnic Conflict: Sri Lanka, Iraq, and Rwanda*. Ph.D. University of South Carolina, 1999. DAI: 6007A: 2663. 222 p. The involvement of the international community in internal situations of ethnic conflict is becoming more common as international actors intervene to restore order after the outbreak of violent ethnic conflict. This dissertation addresses the assumption that these multilateral fig leaves will provide a "Band-Aid" and assist in ethnic conflict resolution because in many situations this has not been the case. Three examples of the failure of intervention in identity-based contention are found in Iraq, Rwanda, and Sri Lanka. The dissertation explores the historical context and content of international actor involvement (specifically outside states, international organizations, and transnational kingroups) in countries experiencing ethnic conflicts prior to the outbreak of violence. The project presents a substantive cross-national comparative analysis of foreign interference from colonialism to the contemporary political environment in three current conflicts: India and the Tamils in Sri Lanka (1987), the United States and the Kurds in Iraq (1991) and the international community involvement with the Hutus in Rwanda (1994). The dissertation presents a framework for examining what international actors bring to identity-based contention. In each case, a mobilization model is employed to illustrate how international actors contributed to the explosiveness of these ethnic situations as they advanced the factors of mobilization (the politicization of ethnic identity, resources, and political opportunity structures). The model synthesizes ethnic conflict studies with work on resource mobilization and international intervention. The dissertation offers both theoretical and practical contributions to research on international political interactions, comparative ethnic studies as well as work on transnational social movements. The project also explores changing norms of international intervention, the nature of ethnic identity, and the policy consequences of meddling in unstable contentious political environments. The study finds that there are several problems associated with international intervention in ethnic conflicts as foreign actors are often pulled into local and regional political struggles.

439. Malanczuk, Peter. "The Kurdish Crisis and Allied Intervention in the Aftermath of the Second Gulf War." *European Journal of International Law* 2, no. 2 (1991): 114-132. This article examines the legality under international law of the allied intervention in Iraq during the Kurdish Crisis in 1991. While putting the legal issues into proper perspective, the author establishes the relevant factual background of the crisis in details.

440. Maynard, Deanne E. "Iraq: United States Response to the Alleged Use of Chemical Weapons Against the Kurds." [Human Rights Issues in United States Foreign Policy].

Harvard Human Rights Yearbook 2 (Spring 1989): 179-186.

441. Meek, Philip A. "Operation Provide Comfort: A Case Study in Humanitarian Relief and Foreign Assistance." *Air Force Law Review* 37 (1994): 225-238.

442. Miles, Donna. "Helping the Kurds." [Refugee relief operation.] *Soldiers* 46 (July 1991): 13-20.

443. Miller, Judith. "Iraq Accused: A Case of Genocide." [Evidence of plan to exterminate the Kurds.] *The New York Times Magazine* (January 3, 1993): 12-17+. Researchers in the United States are going through 857 cartons of Iraqi files that could provide the legal basis for the first case of genocide ever to be brought before the World Court. The files, captured by Kurdish rebels in the uprising against Saddam Hussein immediately after the Persian Gulf war, provide the first written documentation of a campaign of terror waged for a decade against Iraq's 4 million Kurds. The material describes in chillingly bureaucratic language the "liquidations," "expulsions," and "transfers" of Kurdish victims. Researchers from the human rights group Middle East Watch, with help from the U.S. Defense Intelligence Agency, are using the documents to prepare the case.

444. Moran, C. J. *Kurdish Problem: Federalism or an Emerging State.* Carlisle Barracks, PA: Army War College, April 15, 1993. 47p. [NTIS Accession Number: AD-A264 877/2/XAB]. Whether the Kurds will successfully achieve democracy for Iraq and autonomy for Kurdistan is more a decision in the hands of US policy makers than the Kurds. Before that question can be addressed the larger issue of autonomy today, but a separate state tomorrow has to be considered. No one wants to support a separate state which would mean dissolution of the territorial integrity of Iraq and upsetting the regional balance of power. That would also run counter to respecting the concept of a nation's sovereignty which is so vital to maintaining order in the world. When the national interests of the US are considered, especially in the strategic sense or in terms of natural resources, it is difficult to make a case for supporting the Kurds beyond humanitarian assistance. The Persian Gulf War, however, presented the US a new scenario, highlighted by President Bush's call for the Kurds in northern Iraq and the Shi'a in southern Iraq to rise against Saddam Hussein. The resulting crushing of both revolts by Saddam, and ensuing flight and agony suffered by the Kurds brought them on center stage for the world to view. The US, along with coalition governments, in response to media pressure and the humanitarian needs of the fleeing Kurds, established a security zone in northern Iraq for the Kurds, and later in southern Iraq for the Shi'a. This has effectively split Iraq into three parts. The Kurds by holding elections, establishing a government, and providing political and civil administration in their area, Iraqi Kurdistan, now in essence have de facto autonomy.

445. Mortimer, Edward. "Iraq: The Road Not Taken." *The New York Review of Books* 38 (May 16, 1991): 3-4+. The United States, with its lack of support for the opposition in Iraq, actually helped Saddam Hussein maintain his grip on the country. As a result, thousands of Arabs and Kurds have been killed or wounded by Hussein's forces in Iraq's civil war, and a mass exodus of the Kurds has taken place in northern Iraq. By not supplying the insurgents with weapons or using U.S. command of Iraqi skies to help them, the Bush administration is acting on its belief that minority rule through military force is the only safe route for Iraq.

446. Nagel, Joane, and Brad Whorton. "Ethnic Conflict and the World System: International Competition in Iraq (1961-1991) and Angola (1974-1991)." *Journal of Political and Military Sociology* 20 (Summer 1992): 1-35. Most models of ethnic conflict focus on internal forces and processes that contribute to ethnic tensions. Such domestic explanations ignore an important external source of resources and support for ethnic conflict, namely international economic, geopolitical, and military competition in the world state system. World system theory has tended to overlook geopolitical and dimensions of the

international system. Just as economic competition produces economic dependency, geopolitical and military competition produce military dependency. Like economic dependency, military dependency has negative consequences for dependent states: political instability, internal and external war, and ethnic conflict. This paper explores the role of international competition in two cases, Iraq (1961-1991) and Angola (1974-1991), to reveal the results of military dependency. International competition and military dependency have several consequences for domestic ethnic conflict: (1) a militarization of conflict, (2) an escalation and lengthening of conflict, (3) an ideological transformation of conflict, (4) a strengthening of supported ethnic group boundaries, and (5) a reduction in the likelihood of negotiated solutions to ethnic conflict.

447. Nehme, Michel G., and Lokman I. Meho. "Pawns in a Deadly Game: Iraqi Kurds and the United States, 1972-1975." *International Studies* [New Delhi] 32 (January-March 1995): 41-55. The United States has failed, in two episodes, to protect the Iraqi Kurds from devastation after instigating them against Saddam Hussein. The second episode (Second Gulf War) was an overt American involvement in the Kurdish-Iraqi relations and thus received an extensive and comprehensive coverage by many scholars and reporters. The first episode (1972-1975) was a covert paramilitary intervention conducted by the CIA upon the request of the U.S. president. The literature that covered this episode is not sufficient and lacks the highlighting of the particularities of American foreign policy. This article explores this gap for it is a pass to the understanding of the Kurdish problem—a time bomb in the Middle East. The Kurds are often depicted as pawns in a deadly game subject to regional and superpower manipulation. The Kurdish leadership repeatedly immolated its people as forfeitures for the dictates of geopolitics, and twice became the sacrifice of the U.S. and its allies.

448. Nezan, Kendal. "Fragile printemps kurde en Irak." *Le Monde Diplomatique* 48, no. 569 (August 2001): 9. Examines political and economic conditions of the Kurds of Iraq, driven from their homes during the 1991 Gulf War and now in Kurdistan, a region with a limited degree of autonomy under Anglo-American air protection from the air. Discusses conflict over division of meager resources between the Democratic Party of Kurdistan, led by Massoud Barzani, and the Patriotic Union of Kurdistan, led by Jalal Talabani, ended by an agreement signed in Washington, D.C. in September 1998; assistance provided by UN agencies to finance projects in education, health, housing, and reconstruction of infrastructure.

449. Ofteringer, Ronald, and Ralf Backer. "A Republic of Statelessness: Three Years of Humanitarian Intervention in Iraqi Kurdistan." *Middle East Report (MERIP)* 24 (March-April/May-June 1994): 40-45. While it might seem that the UN Security Council Resolution 688 has afforded Iraqi Kurdistan some degree of sovereignty during the three years since the Gulf War ended, in actuality, the UN and various non-governmental organizations (NGOs) have obstructed the rehabilitation of Iraqi Kurdistan society and have compromised that society's option for self-determination. Given the deepening economic crisis and growing interference of neighboring states, moreover, the situation of the Iraqi Kurds does not differ much from that of Turkish Kurds, whose oppression continues with the knowledge and even support of the leading North Atlantic Treaty Organization member states. Recommendations are made for alternative UN and NGO courses of action. (M. Maguire/*SA*: 94-12428)

450. Pelletiere, Stephen C. *Kurds and Their AGAS: An Assessment of the Situation in Northern Iraq*. [Final report.] Carlisle Barracks, PA: Army War College Strategic Studies Institute, September 16, 1991 43p. [NTIS Accession Number: AD-A242 441/4/XAB]. In the bloody aftermath of Operation Desert Storm hundreds of thousands of Kurds left their homes in northern Iraq seeking refuge in Turkey and Iran. It fell to the U.S. military to coax them back and protect those who feared for their safety. Operation Provide Comfort has now been succeeded by Provide Comfort II, with the U.S. military still heavily in-

volved. This report documents the recent history of the Kurds, and gives a rundown on the power relations among the various groups in Kurdish society. At the same time, it warns our officers of possible dangers growing out of their mission, and suggests that the overall problem of the Kurds is much more explosive than the benign accounts appearing in the media would lead one to believe.

451. Pelletiere, Stephen C. *Managing Strains in the Coalition: What to Do About Saddam*. [Final report.] Carlisle Barracks, PA: Army War College Strategic Studies Institute, November 15, 1996. 38 p. Includes bibliographical references, pp. 20-28. [NTIS Accession Number: AD-A320 776/8/XAB]. The author examines the recent extraordinary events in Iraqi Kurdistan and in particular the behavior of America's allies. He offers a theory of why this crisis developed, why the key coalition members are divided in response to U.S. actions, what factors might guide future U.S. policy, and what it presages for the future stability of the area. The author concludes that U.S. policy needs reanchoring if interests in this vital Persian Gulf region are to be maintained.

452. Prince, James M. "A Kurdish State in Iraq?" *Current History* 92 (January 1993): 17-22. Part of an issue on the Middle East. Since April 1991, Iraqi Kurds have been maintaining a Western-supported de facto government in the safe haven north of the 36th parallel while regional powers, the United States, and Kurds in Turkey, Iran, and Syria watch to see if the dream of Kurdish autonomy will finally come true. Free elections were held in May 1992, and authority is now being slowly ceded to the elected Kurdish parliament, whose two main parties are the Patriotic Union of Kurdistan, led by Jalal al-Talabani, and the Kurdistan Democratic Party, led by Massoud Barzani. These two parties maintain a rivalry that has often degenerated into armed conflict. Nonetheless, Talabani, Barzani, and disparate opposition elements united at a preliminary Iraqi National Congress meeting in September 1992, when they voted to "respect" Kurdish aspirations regarding the creation of an independent state. The U.S. role, Kurdish tribes, and political parties in northern Iraq are discussed.

453. Ramsbotham, Oliver, and Tom Woodhouse. *Humanitarian Intervention in Contemporary Conflict: A Reconceptualization*. Cambridge, MA: Polity Press, 1996. Includes bibliographical references and index. This book is a wide-ranging assessment of the international response to devastating contemporary conflicts, such as those in Iraq, Bosnia, Somalia and Rwanda. After a thorough survey of traditional debates, the authors concentrate on an analysis of contemporary conflict, using illustrations from a wide range of post cold-war examples, one of which is humanitarian intervention in Iraq (pp. 69-85). Various options, including non-intervention, peacekeeping, and forcible humanitarian intervention, are illustrated and discussed, with profiles of the most destructive contemporary conflicts and the responses to them by the international community. The roles of governments, UN agencies, the Red Cross and non-governmental organizations are examined. From this material, the authors argue for a reconceptualization of humanitarian intervention and develop principles which should govern all of its uses.

454. Roberts, Adam. "Humanitarian War: Military Intervention and Human Rights." *International Affairs* [London] 79 (July 1993): 429-449. In 1991-1993, in northern Iraq, Somalia and former Yugoslavia, there have been major uses of foreign armed forces in the name of humanitarianism, and with some degree of authorization from the UN. These interventions have revived, but with certain new elements, perennial debates about humanitarian intervention which in its classic form is military intervention in a state, without the approval of its authorities, and with the purpose of preventing widespread suffering or death among the inhabitants. While these interventions do mark a significant turning point in international politics, it is improbable that they can remain impartial and humanitarian in all their aspects. They cannot be a substitute for tough policy choices about the future of the fractured societies involved. There is no prospect of a formal agreement among states as to the circumstances in which humanitarian considerations should prevail over state sovereignty. (*IPSA*: 44-820)

455. Rudd, Gordon William. *Operation Provide Comfort: Humanitarian Intervention in Northern Iraq, 1991 (Kurds, Military)*. Ph.D., Duke University, 1993. 485 p. DAI 55 (1994): 694-A. This dissertation studies Provide Comfort, a military operation that set out to save a half million Kurds who fled from Iraq in the spring of 1991. Unlike most military operation, Provide Comfort enjoyed no prior planning, little specific preparation, and operated beyond the range of most military doctrines. These forces had to work with civilians from the United Nations and other relief organizations with whom they were not familiar. Yet within a few months, the military operation achieved its goals of relieving the suffering and dying while returning the refugees safely to Iraq. The purpose of this dissertation is to study how the participating military organizations formed on such short notice, resolved friction and obstacles, accomplished their tasks quickly, and departed as soon as the political situation allowed. The materials used for this work include primary and secondary sources on the Kurds, Iraq, and Turkey, but the study is dominated by interviews with over a hundred participants on Provide Comfort supported by the military and civilian documentation that covered and analyzed the operation. The conclusion of this study is that even without doctrine for humanitarian assistance, the capacity of military forces to provide immediate relief on a vast scale to resolve a crisis situation significantly exceeds that of civilian organizations primarily oriented for such tasks. Specifically, military forces can neutralize a hostile environment; mobilize the necessary transportation and logistics assets to sustain the flow or resources; rebuild a civil infrastructure; and provide the command and control necessary to make the overall effort cohesive under a unified command. Finally, the manner in which the military forces were used did not degrade their wartime readiness. Provide Comfort offers new perspectives for military participation on humanitarian assistance operations.

456. Rumbaugh JR. "Operation Pacific Haven: Humanitarian Medical Support for Kurdish Evacuees." *Military Medicine* 163, no. 5 (May 1998): 269-271. This article reviews the medical aspects of the humanitarian assistance mission Joint Task Force Operation Pacific Haven from September 1996 to April 1997. It reviews the effectiveness of the deployable medical units used to support the medical screening, treatment, and processing of more than 6,600 Kurdish evacuees applying for political asylum in the United States. The distinct cultural mores and language barriers of the Kurdish population made the provision of even basic medical care a challenge. Designed for combat service support, these deployable medical units were successful in the performance of the comprehensive public health and humanitarian assistance medical support mission because of the support of two on-island military treatment facilities. In short, for military medicine to successfully conduct humanitarian assistance and/or disaster relief missions, deployable medical units need to be designed, equipped, staffed, and trained to perform these operations.

457. Sahagun, Felipe. "The New Kurdish Protectorate." *European Journal of International Affairs* 12, no. 2 (1991): 82-106. The author argues that the recent Kurdish tragedy is a direct consequence of the "Desert Storm," but Saddam Hussein and the Kurdish leaders bear responsibility as well. It is the responsibility of the Iraqi leader because he did not respect his promises of autonomy for the Kurds and had launched a terrorist assault against them leading to grave dissensions in Iraq. It is the responsibility of the Kurdish leaders because they accepted an active support from the West to revolt against the central government.

458. Salem, Naim Joseph. *The Drama of U.S.-Iraq Relations: From World War II to the Gulf War.* [United States Iraq Relations.] Ph.D. University of South Carolina, 1992. DAI: 5311A: 4077. 335 p. United States-Iraq relations are examined from the time contacts between the two countries began in the 1920s through 1992. The focus of the study is on the post-World War II period and on issue areas

that have shaped Iraq's relations with the United States during this period. These issue areas are as follows: the Palestine problem, the Kuwait question, the Kurdish minority in Iraq, and Iran and the Iran-Iraq War. Three main themes are developed. One, U.S. policy vis-a-vis Iraq represents a continuation of Britain's policy. Two, internationally dominant powers generally act to maintain the status quo in which they predominate. A fast-rising regional power, such as Iraq, frequently finds itself on a friction course with the dominant states in the international system. And three, ever since the establishment of Israel, the U.S. has predicated its policy in the Middle East on the support and sustenance of the Jewish state. The more an Arab state opposes Israel, the more that state is constrained by the United States. The research draws on State Department archives, British archives, Iraqi government documents and stated policies, in addition to a wide array of English, Arabic, and French sources.

459. Schorr, Daniel. "Ten Days That Shook the White House." [Television coverage of Kurdish refugees forces change in U.S. policy.] *Columbia Journalism Review* 30 (July-August 1991): 21-23. Television, most often manipulated in the United States to support policy, created a demand for action among Americans when footage of suffering Kurds was shown at the end of March 1991. During the first two weeks of April, President Bush was forced by the impact of what Americans and Europeans were seeing on television to reconsider his hasty withdrawal of troops from Iraq following the Persian Gulf War. Americans grew aware that their government, which had opened the floodgates of rebellion in Iraq, was attempting to evade the crisis. At first, the Bush administration operated under the belief that Americans supported getting the troops home quickly and avoiding ethnic strife. As it turned out, however, they felt some responsibility for the suffering of the Kurds and did not want to see them abandoned.

460. Schweigman, David. "Humanitarian Intervention Under International Law: The Strife for Humanity." *Leiden Journal of International Law* 6 (April 1993): 91-110. In this paper, the author investigates whether a rule of customary law exists that would allow for intervention by third states in the territory of another state on grounds of restoring respect for human rights. The main questions related to this problem are: (I) If such a rule exists, what would be the criteria to be used? (ii) What is the relation between the UN Charter, especially Articles 2(4), 2(7), and Chapter VII, and the alleged rule? Following these questions, the author focuses on the intervention on behalf of the Kurds in northern Iraq in 1991. The role of the Security Council in this intervention is examined as well as the justifications for the intervention brought forward by the actors. Finally, the legality of the intervention under customary international law is considered.

461. Sellars, Bill. "La sortie de l'impasse est-elle pour demain?" *Arabies*, no. 146 (Fall 1999): 20-23. Discusses the agreement signed in Washington, D.C. on September 17, 1998, by leaders of two Kurdish groups in northern Iraq, Massoud Barzani of the Democratic Kurdistan Party and Jalal Talabani of the Kurdistan Patriotic Union, in hope of ensuring their future cooperation in administration of areas they control. Includes interest of the US in creating a united front against the regime of President Saddam Hussein of Iraq and unfavorable view of the agreement taken by Turkey as well as by Iraq.

462. Stromseth, Jane E. "Iraqi Repression of its Civilian Population: Collective Response and Contingency Challenges." In *Enforcing Restraint: Collective Intervention in Internal Conflicts*. Edited by Lori Fisler Darmosch, 76-117. New York: Council on Foreign Relations Press, 1993. The author locates the international response to Iraq's internal conflicts in the context of a long history in which Kurdish aspirations for self-determination have consistently been subordinated to the strategic and economic interests of global and regional powers. The international community had done essentially nothing for the Kurds, even in the face of extensive evidence of a genocidal extermination campaign in the late 1980s. The turning point came in the immediate aftermath of the successful collective military action to

eject Iraq from Kuwait, when the Kurds in northern Iraq and the Shi'ites in the south mounted popular uprisings that elicited a swift and brutal response from Saddam Hussein. Thousands upon thousands fled toward and across the borders with Turkey, Iran, and Kuwait, and a humanitarian crisis of vast proportions ensued. Stromseth analyzes the debates in the UN Security Council over what became resolution 688, which condemned Iraq's repression of its civilian populations and found that the consequences of that repression threaten international peace and security. She then examines the implementation of resolution 688 through Operation Provide Comfort and the subsequent negotiations with Iraq over the terms of a UN presence on Iraqi territory for humanitarian purposes. She discusses the establishment by the allied forces of a secure zone to protect the Kurds in the north, and later a no-fly zone over the southern marshlands.

463. Swenson, R. H., and T. M. Rahe. *Water and Sanitation Efforts Among Displaced Kurdish Citizens*. Washington, DC: Agency for International Development, October, 1991. 74 p. [NTIS Accession Number: PB93-117117/XAB]. In 1991, AID cooperated with the U.S. military to provide emergency assistance to displaced Kurds in the mountains of eastern Turkey and Iran. AID assistance was channeled through the Disaster Assistance Response Team (DART). The military provided security and also transported food, water, supplies, and people. Because the eastern Turkey mountains are very remote, with few roads, helicopters were often the only means of transport, and flight coordination was difficult due to limited landing areas. U.S. policymakers thus determined that mountain settlements having insufficient water supplies would have to be relocated to an area near Zakhu, Iraq, where basic water and sanitation services could be provided. The first part of the report covers Office of Foreign Disaster Assistance (OFDA)/DART activities during the early unsettled period of Kurdish displacement. The second part focuses on the design, construction, and utility of facilities within the Zakhu camp. The second part also discusses the process of transferring management responsibility to the Private Voluntary Organization (PVO) community.

464. Towell, Pat. "Bush Warns Iraqi Government Not to Attack Fleeing Kurds." *Congressional Quarterly Weekly Report* 49, no. 1 (April 13, 1991): 933. The Bush Administration has warned Iraq to keep its armed forces away from a large section of northern Iraq where relief agencies are trying to aid hundreds of thousands of Kurdish refugees.

465. Towell, Pat. "Compassion Rules Geopolitics in Dealings With Kurds: Plight of Refugees Persuades Bush to Send Troops into Iraq and Members to Overwhelmingly Back the Move." *Congressional Quarterly Weekly Report* 49 (April 20, 1991): 998-999. The decision by President George Bush to send US troops into Iraq to aid Kurdish refugees—and the widespread congressional approval of the move—reflected how powerful compassion is in the reshaping of political wisdom.

TURKEY

466. Abramowitz, Morton (ed.). *Turkey's Transformation and American Policy*. New York: The Century Foundation Press, 2000. 298 p. Turkey has emerged during the past decade as an important player on the world scene. It is involved in many issues and areas of great interest to the United States—NATO, the Caucasus and Central Asia, the Middle East, the Balkans, and Greece—and U.S.-Turkish relations grew very close in the past decade. This book analyzes the nature of Turkey's major internal problems, such as the Kurdish question and the rise of political Islam, and the impact of these issues on U.S. policymaking. Morton Abramowitz is a senior fellow at The Century Foundation and a former president of the Carnegie Endowment for International Peace. He is a former U.S. ambassador to Turkey. Contributors include Cengiz Candar, columnist for the *Sabah* newspaper, Istanbul; Heath Lowry, author of *Ataturk*, Princeton University; Alan Makovsky, Washington Institute for Near East Policy; Ziya Onis, Koc University in Istanbul; Philip Robbins, St. Antony's College, Oxford;

M. James Wilkinson, former deputy assistant secretary of state for European affairs.

467. Barkey, Henri J., and Graham E. Fuller. *Turkey's Kurdish Question*. Lanham, MD: Rowman & Littlefield Publishers, 1998. xix, 239 p. Includes bibliographical references and index. Barkey and Fuller suggest a solution to the wrenching question of Turkey's Kurds, who now constitute an estimated 20 percent of the population. Since 1984, the leftist Kurdish Workers Party (PKK) has resisted Turkish rule in the underdeveloped southeast, the traditional heartland of Turkey's Kurds-even though the majority of them now lives in other parts of the country. Military efforts to quell the insurrection continue to drain the economy and budget, while allegations of human rights abuses aggravate Turkey's diplomatic relations, especially with Europe and, to a lesser extent, the United States. After giving succinct accounts of the history and the current situation, the authors reject the extreme options of enforced assimilation on the one hand and Kurdish independence on the other. Instead, they argue that the Turkish state and society are mature enough to move toward considerable Kurdish autonomy within a decentralized state.

468. Blank, Stephen J., Stephen C. Pelletiere, and William T. Johnsen. *Turkey's Strategic Position at the Crossroads of World Affairs*. Carlisle Barracks, PA: Strategic Studies Institute, U.S. Army War College, 1993. xi, 133 p.: maps. Includes a chapter by Pelletiere entitled: "Turkey and U.S. in the Middle East: The Kurdish Connection." This chapter discusses the origins of threat posed by the Kurdish Workers' Party (PKK), the implications of the Persian Gulf War for the PKK, Turkey's economic situation and its implications for the Kurds, possible Iran support of PKK, and U.S. policy toward the Kurds.

469. Brown, James. "The Turkish Imbroglio: Its Kurds." *Annals of the American Academy of Political and Social Science* 541 (September 1995): 116-129. The purpose of this article is to examine the current Kurdish problem in Turkey, the Turkish government's reaction to the issues raised by this problem, and the challenge the Kurdish Workers' Party (PKK) poses to Ankara through its tactics of intimidation and terrorism. This imbroglio is also detailed in both political and economic terms. The article goes on to analyze the implications of this conflict for Turkey's relations with Europe, the United States, and other regional players, such as Syria, Iraq, and Iran. The conflict could jeopardize Turkey's relations with Europe and Washington and limit Ankara's role as a stabilizing influence in the region, thereby limiting its role regionally and internationally. This linkage to the West will be very difficult to substitute. In addition, civil violence and terrorist acts by the PKK could deter foreign investments and undermine tourism, thus affecting Turkey's long-range economic plans. Finally, the future prospects and options that Turkey might consider in bringing this conflict to a manageable solution are assessed.

470. Button, Stephen H. "Turkey Struggles with Kurdish Separatism." *Military review: The Professional Journal of the U.S. Army* 75 (December 1994-January-February 1995): 70-83.

471. Chomsky, Noam. "Terrorisme, l'Aarme des Puissants." *Le Monde Diplomatique* 48, no. 573 (December 2001): 10-11. In answer to President Bush's question as to how the US has come to be feared and hated in many lands, presents examples of US support of use of armed force against dissidents by authoritarian governments, characterizing such action as terrorism by the strong against the weak. Includes use of force by Colombia and Guatemala against their own people, by Turkey against its Kurdish population, and by Israel against people in territories controlled by the Palestinian National Authority.

472. Congress. Commission on Security and Cooperation in Europe. *Human Rights in Turkey*. Washington, DC: The Commission, 1993. iii, 98 p. [Implementation of the Helsinki Accords]. Congress Session: 103-1. SUDOC: Y4.SE2:H88/3. Transcript of Commission on Security and Cooperation in Europe (CSCE) briefing on the human rights

situation in Turkey, citing improvements and continuing problems in various human rights areas during the late 1980s and since Prime Minister Suleyman Demirel became President in November 1991. Mary Sue Hafner, Deputy Staff Director and General Counsel, CSCE, presents opening remarks and leads the briefing. Includes audience participation (p. 36-42). Supplementary material (p. 43-98) includes panelists' written statements. Statements and Discussion include: Overview of human rights improvements and continuing problems in Turkey; description of and concerns about human rights abuses in Turkey, with policy recommendations; incidence of torture of suspects in police detention; issues relating to minority rights in Turkey. Briefing on alleged terrorist activities of insurgent Kurdistan Workers Party; perceived deterioration of human rights conditions since Prime Minister Demirel took office; efforts of Turkey to adopt and implement laws reflecting human rights standards of international conventions; perspectives on various human rights issues in Turkey. This report is available via the Web at: www.house.gov/csce/TurkeyUSRelations.html.

473. Congress. Commission on Security and Cooperation in Europe. *Banned Turkish Parliamentarians Discuss State of Democracy in Turkey* [Implementation of the Helsinki Accords]. Washington, DC: The Commission, 1994. iii, 20, v p. Congress Session: 103-2. SUDOC: Y4.SE2:T84. Transcript of Commission on Security and Cooperation in Europe (CSCE) briefing on Turkish Government treatment of the Kurdish minority in Turkey, focusing on human rights concerns. Briefing was held in light of recent Turkish Government actions against the Kurdish-based Democracy Party (DEP) and DEP members of the Turkish Parliament for supposed advocacy of Kurdish separatism. CSCE Staff Director Samuel G. Wise presents opening remarks (p. 1-2) and leads the briefing. Includes audience participation (p. 7-20). Statements and Discussion include: Perspectives on claimed human rights abuses against the Kurds in Turkey.

474. Congress. Commission on Security and Cooperation in Europe. *Criminalizing Parliamentary Speech in Turkey: Briefing by the International Human Rights Law Group*. Washington, DC: The Commission, 1994. iv, 49 p. [Implementation of the Helsinki Accords]. Congress Session: 103-2. SUDOC: Y4.SE2:P23/3. Transcript of Commission on Security and Cooperation in Europe (CSCE) briefing on findings by an International Human Rights Law Group (IHRLG) delegation to Turkey regarding the pending prosecution of several Kurdish minority members of the Turkish parliament for certain statements allegedly made in favor of Kurdish separatism, and the proposed dissolution of the Kurdish-based Democracy Party for supposed advocacy of Kurdish separatism. CSCE Deputy Director and General Counsel Mary Sue Hafner presents opening remarks (p. 1-2) and leads the briefing. Includes audience participation (p. 11-17). Supplementary material (p. 19-49) includes press releases, *Congressional Record* excerpts, and: IHRLG, "Criminalizing Parliamentary Speech in Turkey" May 1994 (p. 22-37).

475. Congress. Commission on Security and Cooperation in Europe. *Report on the U.S. Helsinki Commission Delegation to Bosnia-Herzegovina, Albania and Turkey*. Washington, DC: The Commission, 1994. iii, 30 p. [Implementation of the Helsinki Accords]. Congress Session: 103-2. SUDOC: Y4.SE2:B65. Commission on Security and Cooperation in Europe report on Commission delegation October 21-26, 1994 visits led by Senator Dennis DeConcini (D-Ariz) to Sarajevo, Bosnia-Herzegovina, Tirana, Albania, and Ankara and Diyarbakir, Turkey, to review military-political conditions and humanitarian concerns. Examines background and status of the conflict in Bosnia-Herzegovina; reviews economic and human rights conditions in Albania since March 1992 elections; and assesses human rights issues, the Kurdish situation, and alleged restrictions on freedom of expression in Turkey. Available via the Web at: www.house.gov/csce/deconcini94.htm.

476. Congress. Commission on Security and Cooperation in Europe. *Human Rights in Turkey*. Washington, DC: The Commission,

1995. iii, 42 p. [Implementation of the Helsinki Accords]. Congress Session: 104-1. SUDOC: Y4.SE2:H88/3/995. Transcript of Commission on Security and Cooperation in Europe (CSCE) briefing, co-sponsored by the International Human Rights Law Group, on the status of human rights in Turkey, focusing on human rights concerns relating to the continuing conflict between the Turkish Government and the separatist Kurdistan Workers Party. CSCE International Policy Director Samuel G. Wise and International Human Rights Law Group Program Director Peter Rosenblum present opening remarks (p. 1-2). Includes audience participation (p. 6-14).

477. Congress. Commission on Security and Cooperation in Europe. *Turkey-U.S. Relations: Potential and Peril*. Washington, DC: The Commission, 1995. iii, 148 p. [Implementation of the Helsinki Accords]. Congress Session: 104-1. SUDOC: Y4.SE2:104-1-8. Hearing before the Commission on Security and Cooperation in Europe to examine issues involved in U.S.-Turkey relations. Focuses on concerns regarding alleged human rights abuses in Turkey, resulting in part from the continuing conflict between the Turkish Government and Kurdish separatists. Supplementary material (p. 44-145) includes witnesses' written statements and written replies to Commission questions, submitted statements, and: Senate Foreign Relations Committee, *East or West? Turkey Checks Its Compass*, minority staff report, September 1995 (p. 104-116).

478. Congress. Commission on Security and Cooperation in Europe. *The Continued Use of Torture in Turkey*. Washington, DC: The Commission, 1997. iii, 24 p. [Implementation of the Helsinki Accords]. Congressional Session: 105-1. SUDOC: Y4.SE2:T84 /3. Transcript of Commission on Security and Cooperation in Europe (CSCE) briefing on human rights problems in Turkey, focusing on alleged use of torture by police against security detainees suspected of politically motivated crimes. Supplementary material (p. 16-24) includes press releases, and correspondence. Statements and Discussion: Overview of human rights problems in Turkey, focusing on torture of suspects in police detention; issues relating to human rights abuses and use of torture in Turkey. Available via the Web at: www.house.gov/csce/turktor.html.

479. Congress. Senate. Committee on Foreign Relations. *East or West? Turkey Checks Its Compass*. Washington, DC: U.S. GPO, 1995. v, 11 p. Congress Session: 104-1. SUDOC: Y4.F76/2:S.PRT.104-33. Report on August 17-25, 1995 staff study mission to Turkey to examine issues relating to the political situation in Turkey and Turkish foreign policy, including the treatment of the Kurdish minority, democratization and human rights, and Turkish efforts to join the European Union Customs Union.

480. Department of State. Bureau of European Affairs. *Report on Human Rights in Turkey and Situation in Cyprus*. Washington, DC: Bureau of European Affairs, 1994. Available on the Web at: dosfan.lib.uic.edu/ERC/bureaus/eur/releases/950601TurkeyCyprus.html. Report on Allegations of Human Rights Abuses by the Turkish Military and on the Situation in Cyprus. This report is submitted in compliance with the congressional requirement as set forth in public law 103-306 - August 23, 1994. It consists of two parts. The first covers allegations of human rights abuses by the Turkish security forces. The second covers Cyprus. The report provides an overview of the decade-long conflict between Turkey and the terrorist Kurdistan Workers Party (PKK), describes the types and organization of Turkish security forces combating the PKK and addresses reports of alleged human rights violations by these forces, including the possible involvement of U.S.-supplied military equipment. In preparing this report the Department of State, in coordination with the Department of Defense, has drawn on a variety of sources, including U.S. government reporting, information from NGOs, press reports, the 1994 Human Rights Report on Turkey and material provided by the Turkish government. The report reaffirms Turkey's continuing importance as a long-standing U.S. treaty ally which projects NATO and Western values into the Middle East as well as southeastern Europe. Since the end of the Cold War, Turkey has replaced Germany as the frontline European state. It confronts the most serious threats to its integrity and well-being of any Western ally. Continuing U.S. support for Turkey's security is essential. The Kurdistan Workers Party (PKK) presents a major threat to Turkey's sovereignty and territorial integrity. It is a ruthless terrorist group which receives support from Syria, Iran and some sources in Europe and has terrorized the population of southeast Turkey and destabilized the region. The Government of Turkey, in its struggle against the PKK has relied primarily on a military strategy to address this internal security matter. This strategy, which includes the evacuation and/or destruction of many villages, has resulted in human rights abuses and risks alienating the local population. A more civil-based approach by the government is required to effectively address the problem in the southeast. Turkey, as the recipient of U.S. security assistance, has the right to use U.S.-supplied weapons for legitimate self-defense and for internal security. This includes use to combat terrorism by forces such as the PKK. U.S.-origin equipment, which accounts for most major items of the Turkish military inventory, has been used in operations against the PKK during which human rights abuses have occurred. It is highly likely that such equipment was used in support of the evacuation and/or destruction of villages. However, we have no evidence that verifies reports of torture and extrajudicial killings involving U.S. equipment. The Government of Turkey has recognized the need to improve its human rights situation and has made proposals which, if adopted and implemented, could lead to important and positive changes in the situation in the southeast. These proposals include measures for the orderly phase out of the state of emergency in the southeast and constitutional amendments to broaden participation in the political process. Finally the report notes that democracy and human rights are and will continue to be a prominent feature of the ongoing U.S.-Turkish high level dialogue. The democratization measures recently introduced into the Turkish parliament, the new willingness to make public the code of conduct promulgated by the Turkish General Staff, and what appears to be the serious effort to protect civilians during the operation in northern Iraq are indications of the value of sustained discussion with the Turks on the issue of human rights. The United States can and should expect progress. (From original source)

481. Department of State. Office of the Secretary of State. Office of the Coordinator for Counterterrorism. *Patterns of Global Terrorism*. PRINT. WEB. Washington, DC: U.S. Dept. of State., 1976- . Annual. This report (www.state.gov/s/ct/rls/pgtrpt/) is submitted to the Congress by the Department of State to provide a full and complete annual report on country-by-country review and analysis of terrorist attacks; statistics on terrorism attacks and casualties; description of and background information on organizations engaging in terrorism. This source is one of the best and most complete for looking at terrorism from a U.S. foreign policy perspective. Full-text of reports for the years 1996-2001 for Europe (the region reportedly witnessing PKK terrorist activities) can be found at the following addresses:

- 2001: www.state.gov/s/ct/rls/pgtrpt/2001/html/10240.htm

- 2000: www.state.gov/s/ct/rls/pgtrpt/2000/2434.htm

- 1999: www.state.gov/www/global/terrorism/1999report/europe.html

- 1998: www.state.gov/www/global/terrorism/1998Report/europe.html

- 1997: www.state.gov/www/global/terrorism/1997Report/eurasia.html

- 1996: www.state.gov/www/global/terrorism/1996Report/europe.html

482. Doherty, Carroll J. "Pared-Back Foreign Aid Bill Heads for House Floor." *Congressional Quarterly Weekly Report* 53, no. 24 (June 17, 1995): 1760-1762. The House Appropriations Committee recently approved the FY 1996 foreign operations measure but not after rejecting an amendment which would have imposed sanctions on Turkey for its Kurdish campaign. The ease by which the measure was approved by the committee belies the heated battle political analysts expect to take place when the bill moves up to the House floor for consideration.

483. Doherty, Carroll J. "This Year, Aid is a Weapon." [US foreign aid] *Congressional Quarterly Weekly Report* 53, no. 24 (June 17, 1995): 1763. Supporters of nations receiving US aid have all but given up hope of getting increased funding for these countries. In view of the budget-cutting sentiments of most lawmakers, the best that can be hoped for is a denial of aid for the opponents of their favored governments. This is exemplified by the case of Turkey, whose lobbyists succeeded in turning back a proposal that would have imposed sanctions against it for its bloody campaign against Kurdish rebels. However, lobbyists representing groups hostile to Turkey have also succeeded in linking Turkish aid to its activities in Cyprus and Armenia.

484. Doherty, Carroll J. "House Curbs Aid to Turkey after Sharp Debate." [Foreign Operations: FY '97] *Congressional Quarterly Weekly Report* 54, no. 23 (June 8, 1996): 1610-1611. Turkey's economic aid from the US may be in jeopardy as congressional support for Turkey has significantly reduced because of its humanitarian aid blockage against Armenia and counterinsurgency efforts against the Kurds. The House has already linked the about $100 million in FY 1997 aid to removal of the blockade but the Senate is unlikely to support the House. The Turkish government and the State Dept have criticized the House's anti-Turkey provisions.

485. Esim, Sinan. "NATO's Ethnic Cleansing: The Kurdish Question in Turkey." *Monthly Review* 51, no. 2 (June 1999): 20-27. The writer discusses NATO's contrasting attitude to the ethnic cleansing in Kosovo and the Kurdish question in Turkey. The plight of the Kosovar Albanians has often been invoked to justify the NATO war against Yugoslavia. However, one need only look to one of the member countries of the alliance, Turkey, to recognize the total hypocrisy of the NATO claim of humanitarian intentions in response to ethnic cleansing and oppression. Turkish planes are participating in air operations in Yugoslavia, yet Turkey has subjected its own Kurdish population to ignominious oppression for decades and recently conducted one of the dirtiest wars ever waged against a national liberation movement. Since 1992, over 4,000 Kurdish hamlets and villages have been evacuated, and many of them torched, by Turkey's armed forces as part of a scorched earth policy and concomitant ethnic cleansing system. Turkey was supported by its NATO allies while conducting these policies, particularly by the United States.

486. Gunter, Michael M. *The Kurds in Turkey: A Political Dilemma*. Boulder, CO: Westview Press, 1990. 151 p.: ill. Includes bibliographical references (p. 129-139) and index. The book concentrates on the conditions of the Kurds in Turkey, where Kurdish identity, until very recently, had been thoroughly suppressed by the Kemalist policy of denying the Kurds a separate cultural identity from that of the majority Turks. After two brief chapters on the origin and history of the Kurds, Gunter examines Kurdish politics in Turkey and Turkish responses to Kurdish militancy in recent decades. As the author states, references to the Kurds as "mountain Turks" and a ban on the use of the Kurdish language were two weapons used by the Turkish state to suppress Kurdish demands for self-determination. Although numerous Kurdish parties and movements have emerged in recent years in Turkey, the Workers' Party of Kurdistan (PKK), has been the most radical as well as the most successful Kurdish element in Turkey. Under the tutelage of its charismatic leader, Abdullah Ocalan, the leftist PKK has had some degree of success in becoming a grassroots Kurdish organization. The author, however, contends that the PKK's violent tactics have alienated many Kurds from the party in recent years. The two chapters on the PKK describe a number of specific events occurring since the mid-1970s that have influenced the fortunes of this party. The book also describes regional and international factors that have affected the condition of the Kurdish movement in Turkey. The impact of the Iran-Iraq war on the Kurds is analyzed within the context of triangular relations between Iran,

Turkey, and Iraq. Turkey, and Iraq. The role of the Soviet Union and the United States in using the Kurds to advance their policies is also addressed (abridged, Nader Entessar/*MEJ* 45, Autumn 1991: 685-685).

487. Gunter, Michael M. "The Kurdish Factor in Turkish Foreign Policy." *Journal of Third World Studies* 11, no. 2 (Fall 1994): 440-472. The role the Kurdish factor has played in Turkish foreign policy towards the Middle East and Western Europe has largely been overlooked. The influence is expected to be more with the end of the Cold War and the disappearance of the Soviet threat to Turkey. The foreign policy towards the United States has also been affected as is apparent from the Turkey's reaction to U.S.'s criticism of its human rights records with Kurds. The growing international awareness of the Kurdish factor is likely to make it one of the dominant influences on Turkish foreign policy.

488. Gunter, Michael M. *The Kurds and the Future of Turkey*. New York: St. Martin's Press, 1997. 184 p. Includes bibliographical references (p. 167-174) and index. Gunter, a political science professor who has been a Senior Fulbright Lecturer on international relations in Turkey, provides a sequel to his *Kurds in Turkey: A Political Dilemma* (1990), focusing on Turkey's long "authoritarian tradition," Kurdish opposition groups (particularly the Kurdistan Workers Party, or PKK), the consequences of the Persian Gulf War, and how the unresolved "Kurdish question" raises obstacles to both full democracy in Turkey and sounder relations between Turkey and other countries around the world. The legitimate aspirations of 20 to 25 percent of Turkey's population must be heard, and Gunter suggests that "the preferred solution . . . is for Turkey to grant its citizens of Kurdish ethnic heritage their full cultural, social, and political rights as implied by democracy." This book is largely based on sources drawn from the Foreign Broadcast Information Service of the U.S. government.

489. Gunter Michael M. "The Continuing Kurdish Problem in Turkey after Ocalan's Capture." *Third World Quarterly* 21, no. 5

(October 2000): 849-869. Turkey's sudden and dramatic capture of Abdullah Ocalan in Nairobi, Kenya on 16 February 1999, far from ending the odyssey of the longtime leader of the Kurdistan Workers Party (PKK), has led to a process of continuing implicit bargaining between the Turkish government and the PKK that holds out the hope of a win-win result for all the parties involved. Turkey's EU candidacy, future democratization and economic success have all become involved with the stay of Ocalan's execution and the continuing Kurdish problem.

490. Hunter, Jane. "Ocalan's Odyssey." *Covert Action Quarterly*, no. 67 (Spring-Summer 1999): 31-34. Discusses U.S. and Israeli support for Turkey in its search for and arrest for treason of Abdullah Ocalan, leader of the Kurdistan Workers Party (PKK), despite Turkey's poor human rights record.

491. Jebb, C. R. *Fight for Legitimacy: Liberal Democracy Versus Terrorism*. Newport, RI: Naval War College, 2001. 139 p. [NTIS Accession Number: ADA394239/XAB]. This study uses an interdisciplinary approach to address the challenge of transnational threats, namely terrorism, to liberal democracies. Terrorism poses unique challenges to the liberal democratic state, and the transnational nature of terrorism necessitates cooperation between and among states. However, terrorism must be analyzed in a political and strategic context. The forces of globalization and fragmentation and the increasing claims of irredentism and secession, require a reexamination of state legitimacy. The best way for states to win legitimacy vis a vis terrorists is by adhering to liberal democratic values and cooperating with other such states. Such cooperation, which affects domestic and foreign policies, requires a convergence of political cultures among those cooperating states. This study analyzes three cases: the Basques in Spain, the ethnic Albanians in Macedonia, and the Kurds in Turkey. This study sheds light on how academics and policymakers ought to characterize and categorize terrorism, and it provides insights on the concepts of political legitimacy, liberal democracy, political culture, and political community. As the US assesses its

homeland defense posture, it must resist any temptation to weaken its liberal democratic values, and as a superpower, it must encourage other states to adhere to liberal democratic values as well. Liberal democracy is not just a normative concern, it is a security imperative in today's transnational security environment.

492. Kesic, Obrad. "American-Turkish Relations at Crossroads." *Mediterranean Quarterly* 6 (Winter 1995): 97-108. On September 30, 1994, United States Secretary of State Warren Christopher warned Turkey not to pursue war against Kurdish separatists at the expense of the country's commitment and responsibility to basic standards of human rights. This was the most public event in a series of ongoing incidents that have signaled a change in American-Turkish relations, pushing them into a period of uncertainty and coolness. Christopher's warning came after other, private warnings from Washington and after Ankara had shown that its patience with Washington's preaching was wearing thin. The Kurdish issue is the most immediate and visible indication that American-Turkish relations are rapidly approaching at crossroads. Both Turkish and American government officials have been expressing their frustration at a series of shared unfulfilled expectations.

493. Kirisci, Kemal and Gareth M. Winrow. *The Kurdish Question and Turkey: An Example of a Trans-State Ethnic Conflict*. London: Frank Cass, 1997. xvi, 237 p. Includes bibliographical references (p. 217-230) and index. Traces the development of the Kurdish questions in Turkey from the end of the Ottoman Empire to the present day through a close examination of events immediately before and after the founding of the republic of Turkey. Describes possible scenarios for a political solution to the Kurdish question, including secession, federal projects, the granting of various forms of autonomy, the provision of special rights, and further democratization. International reaction to developments in Turkey are also analyzed.

494. McKiernan, Kevin. "Turkey Terrorizes Its Kurds." *The Progressive* 57 (July 1993): 28-31. Much has been made of the plight of

Kurds in Iraq, but the Kurds in Turkey, virtually ignored by the world, are also in a bad way. Since 1984, when a Kurdish separatist war began in Turkey, 5,600 lives have been lost, nearly half of those within the past year. According to Amnesty International and Helsinki Watch, a widespread pattern of human-rights abuse, including the use of torture, exists in Turkey. Moreover, they say that America's military alliance with Turkey, a member of NATO that has long received U.S. military aid, is undermining Washington's ability to influence its client in Ankara. Meanwhile, the Kurds, whose overall population numbers some 25 million, remain the largest ethnic grouping in the world that lack a country to call their own. In Turkey, their very existence as a people was denied until recently. Even today, Kurdish television broadcasts are outlawed, and parents are prohibited from giving their children Kurdish names.

495. McKiernan, Kevin. "Turkey's War on the Kurds." *Bulletin of the Atomic Scientists* 55, no. 2 (March-April 1999): 26-37. Examines the use of U.S. arms against the Kurds, the obliteration and forced evacuation of 30,000 Kurdish villages, imprisonment and human rights abuses by the Turkish government, and abuses by the Kurdistan Workers Party.

496. Oztekin, Y. *Terrorism in Turkey*. Carlisle Barracks, PA: Army War College, April 2000. 32 p. [NTIS Accession Number: ADA378270/XAB]. Turkey has been fighting against the PKK (Kurdistan Worker Party) since 1985. The purpose of this study is to define what the PKK is, to explain origin of the Kurdish citizen, to define differences between the PKK and the Kurdish citizen and to try to find a solution to this problem within the frame of democratic rule. According to the author, Turkey has been the unique target of international terrorism since 1965. To understand fully Turkey's importance one must take into consideration her geographical location, social and economic potential. Turkey has always attracted international attention. It will be probably the same in the future. Turkey is the only Islamic nation in NATO. It is however; totally secular, democratic and based on

free market principles. On the other hand, Turkey was a major obstacle for the ideological and military expansion of the Soviet Union towards the Middle East. This was the main reason why Turkey had been the main target of terrorism. The author argues that the PKK has a close relationship to international terrorism and all kinds of illegal practices. Turkey has been accumulating a very costly social experience in the last three decades. International terrorism has been threatening not only Turkey, but also all democratic societies in the world. On account of this fact, the core of the solution depends on effective measures, which will have to be taken by all democratic societies, governments and institutions. The author concludes that the PKK is not a freedom fighter; it is a terrorist organization.

497. Thompson, Peter L. "United States-Turkey Military Relations: Treaties and Implications." *International Journal of Kurdish Studies* 9, nos. 1-2 (1996): 103-113. Reviews reasons for, provisions of, and outcomes of the 1980 Defense and Economic Cooperation Treaty, which commits the U.S., as a NATO leader, to support the Turkish military. Describes efforts to upgrade Turkish military forces, the role of international financial institutions and economic assistance programs, including the multilateral Turkish Defense Fund, and implications for the Kurds.

498. Tirman, John. *Spoils of War: The Human Cost of America's Arms Trade*. New York: Free Press, 1997. vii, 310 p.: map. Includes bibliographical references (p. 291-300) and index. Details the human, economic, and political dimensions of several major armaments deals brokered by the U.S. government. This tale of modern warfare is told in three interwoven stories: the world of Washington policymaking; the hot spots of the Middle East, particularly Turkey; and a key venue of American Arms manufacturing, Connecticut. These three disparate places have combined to produce one of the world's great human-rights catastrophes–the destruction of "Kurdistan," the un-sovereign homeland to 20 million people. Makes a powerful argument that the U.S. economy can break its dependency on what amounts to the sale of death. The more Blackhawks delivered to Turkey, the easier it became to kill Kurds, says Tirman, and the greater became the military's influence in Turkish society.

499. Tirman, John. "Improving Turkey's 'Bad Neighborhood': Pressing Ankara for Rights and Democracy." *World Policy Journal* 15, no. 1 (Spring 1998): 60-67. Argues that Turkey is the worst violator of human rights among all the stalwart allies of the U.S. Its persecution of Kurdish minority has lasted for decades and its curtailment of freedom of association, speech and religion has included non-Kurdish Turks as well. The U.S. has chosen to ignore these violations due to the strategic importance of Turkey and its military partnership with Israel. Although the Kurdish situation is an internal conflict, the U.S. can influence Turkey to settle its disputes with neighboring countries and change its image in Europe and in the Middle East.

500. Xulam, Kani. "Smashing the Kurds: CIA Role in Kidnapping Abdullah Ocalan." *CovertAction Quarterly*, no. 74 (Fall 2002): 34-35. Discusses the abduction of the Kurdish rebel leader Ocalan in Nairobi, Kenya by Turkish forces in February 1999, and speculates on US Central Intelligence Agency involvement.

501. Zunes, Stephen. "Continuing Storm: The U.S. Role in the Middle East." *Foreign Policy in Focus*, no. 9 (Fall 2000): 1-12. Examines US policy since the Gulf War as the dominant power in the region. Discusses importance of the oil-rich Persian Gulf states, US support for Turkey's repression of its Kurdish population, Islamic radicalism, threat of terrorism, relations between Israel and its neighbors, and regional democratization; prospects.

DECLASSIFIED NATIONAL SECURITY, CIA, AND DEPARTMENT OF STATE DOCUMENTS ON MICROFILM

GENERAL

502. John F. Kennedy Library. *The John F. Kennedy National Security Files. The Middle East National Security Files, 1963-1969*. Frederick, MD: University Publications of America, 1988. 3 microfilm reels. Microfilmed from the holdings of the John F. Kennedy Library, Boston, Massachusetts. *National Security Files, 1961-1969* are the "Country Files" of the National Security Files for White House use. The strife-torn Middle East was a major focus of the National Security Files throughout the 1960s. Early in the decade, the files show U.S. concern over President Nasser's strengthening of ties between Egypt and the Soviet Union. At the same time, the national security adviser and his staff were tracking the Yemeni civil war, the Cyprus crisis, and other trouble spots in the region, such as the Kurdish war in Iraq. A printed index, edited by Robert E. Lester and compiled by Blair D. Hydrick—containing a document-by-document listing (type of document, sender, receiver, brief description of subject matter, date of document, original classification, number of pages, and declassification date)—accompanies each collection. Each guide also contains an analytical subject index and an author index.

503. Lyndon Baines Johnson Library. *The Lyndon B. Johnson National Security Files. The Middle East National Security Files, 1963-1969*. Frederick, MD: University Publications of America, 1987. 8 microfilm reels. Microfilmed from the holdings of the Lyndon Baines Johnson Library, Austin, Texas. For complete abstract, see previous record.

504. United States. Office of Presidential Libraries. Nixon Presidential Materials Staff. *The Richard M. Nixon National Security Files. The Middle East National Security Files, 1969-1974*. Bethesda, MD: University Publications of America, 2003. Microfilmed from the holdings of The Nixon Materials Project, National Archives, College Park, Maryland, project editor Robert E. Lester. New declassified material reveals administration attempts to calm the volatile Middle East. In the National Security Council, CIA, Defense Department, and State Department material collected here, researchers will find information on the CIA and U.S. government involvment in the Kurdish war in Iraq.

505. United States. Central Intelligence Agency. *CIA Research Reports: The Middle East, 1946-1976*. Frederick, MD: University Publications of America, 1982. 3 microfilm reels; 35 mm. This collection—covering the period from 1946 through the mid-1970s—makes thousands of pages of extraordinary documentary source material available to researchers for the first time. Topics include: Developments in the Azerbaijan situation (1947); The Kurdish minority problem (1948); Faisal's attitude toward the United States (1948); The current situation in Israel (1949); The Tudeh party: Vehicle for communism in Iran (1949); Iraq: Attitudes towards foreign powers (1951); Assassination of King Abdullah ibn-Hussein (1951); Soviet arms offer to Egypt (1955); The likelihood of a British-French resort to military action against Egypt in the Suez Crisis (1956); Storm warnings up for U.S.–Arab relations (1964); Black September (1972); Report on the People's Democratic Republic of Yemen (1974). Accompanied by a printed reel guide, edited by Paul Kesaris and compiled by Robert Lester, 1983.

506. United States. Department of State. Offices of Strategic Services. *The Middle East*. Washington, DC: University Publications of America, 1977. 3 microfilms reels; 35 mm. O.S.S./State Department Intelligence and Research Reports; pt. 7. Once-secret studies from the nation's top scholars in strategic fields, parts 7 and 12 (see next record) of OSS/State Department Intelligence and Research Reports focus on the Middle East from 1941 through 1961. They cover every major political, diplomatic, economic, and military development in the region. These reports are not available in the State Department's foreign relations series, the armed forces' official histories, or any subscription service of declassified documents. Among the titles focusing on the Middle East are: Zionism: Aims and Prospects (1942); The Kurdish Revolt in Iran (1942); Illicit Arming by Arabs and Jews in Palestine (1943); Political Parties and Personalities in Egypt (1943); The Problem of Jewish Immigration into Palestine (1944); The Position of Saudi Arabia within the Arab World (1944); Iranian Oil as a Potential Source of Political Conflict (1944); Prospects for Territorial Expansion by Israel (1951); Increased Communist Threat in Iran (1951); Political Stability in Iraq (1952); Iranian Political and Economic Prospects (1953); Iran: The Shah's Anti-Corruption Campaign (1955); Saudi Arabia: A Disruptive Force in Western-Arab Relations (1956); and Iraq: The Crisis in Leadership and the Communist Advance (1959). Accompanied by a printed reel guide, edited by Paul Kesaris.

507. United States. Department of State. Offices of Strategic Services. *The Middle East: 1950-1961 Supplement*. Washington, DC: University Publications of America, 1979. 3 microfilms reels; 35 mm. O.S.S./State Department intelligence and research reports; pt. 12. For complete abstract, see previous record.

IRAN

508. United States. Department of State. *Confidential U.S. Diplomatic Post Records: Middle East, Iran, 1925-1941. Part I*. Frederick, MD: University Publications of America, 1984. 39 microfilm reels; 35 mm. This is a collection of papers from American diplomats stationed in Iran between 1925 and 1941. The papers concern the political, military, social and economic development of Iran and its relationship with other countries. The documents provide information on the evolution of United States policy in the area. The collection contains a wide range of material such as reports of political and military affairs, studies and statistics on socio-economic matters, interviews and minutes of meetings with government officials, legal documents, communications sent and received by United States diplomatic personnel, translations from the local media, translations of high level government documents, and transcripts of political meetings. Among the events documented are the founding of the Pahlevi Dynasty; Assumption of the role of hereditary Shah in 1925 by Reza Khan; Reza Shah Pahlevi's cancellation of treaties with Britain and other powers; Uprisings by Kurds; Bolshevik agitation; The Anglo-Persian oil company; Industry; Education; The occupation of Iran by British and Soviet forces in August, 1941; and The transfer of power to the Shah's son, Muhammed Reza Shah Pahlevi, in September 1941. Accompanied by a printed reel guide, edited by Paul Kesaris and compiled by Robert Lester.

509. United States. Department of State. *Confidential U.S. Diplomatic Post Records: Middle East, Iran, 1942-1944. Part II*. 15 microfilm reels; 35 mm. Frederick, MD: University Publications of America, 1984. For complete abstract, see previous record.

510. United States. Department of State. *Confidential U.S. State Department Central Files: Iran, 1945-1949 Internal Affairs, Decimal Number 891, and Foreign Affairs, Decimal Numbers 791 and 711.91*. Bethesda, MD: University Publications of America, 1985. 18 microfilm reels; 35 mm. For Iran, the years 1945 to 1954 represent a decade of tumultuous change, a period when both foreign and domestic forces battled intensely for control of the country's future. Over 60,000 pages of previously unpublished primary material offer a rich documentary resource covering every facet of modern Iranian history. The collection's comprehensive and detailed coverage of Iran's internal and foreign affairs affords scholars timely and exciting research possibilities. The diplomatic reporting of these files forms a vivid record of Iran's struggle for national identity and offers invaluable firsthand testimony on a wide range of topics, including negotiations of postwar oil concessions and their geopolitical implications; military and economic assistance from the United States; Iranian party politics; Soviet influence; unrest in Azerbaijan and Kurdistan; Iran's political direction under Ahmad Qavam; the country's economic condition; land reform; the Iranian labor movement; the volatile ministry of Mossadeq; and the Shah's emergence as the nation's central political figure. Filmed from original documents held at the National Archives, Washington, D.C. Accompanied by a printed reel guide, edited by Michael C. Davis and compiled by Blair Hydrick.

511. United States. Department of State. *Confidential U.S. State Department Central Files: Iran, 1950-1954 Internal Affairs and Foreign Affairs, Decimal Numbers 788, 888, and 988 and Foreign Affairs, Decimal Numbers 688 and 611.88*. Frederick, MD: University Publications of America, 1985. 44 microfilm reels; 35 mm. For complete abstract, see previous record.

512. United States. Department of State. *Confidential U.S. State Department Central Files. Iran, 1955-1959 Internal Affairs, Decimal Numbers 788, 888, and 988: Foreign Affairs, Decimal Numbers 688 and 611.88*. MD: University Publications of America, 1991. 27 microfilm reels; 35 mm. Here are the documents that tell what the U.S. State Department knew about the repressive nature of the Shah's rule and the degree of popular support he enjoyed. Martial law, imposed after Mohammad Mosaddeq's overthrow in 1953, was maintained until 1957. As

the collection details, the Shah continued to exercise strict political controls even after ending martial law. In 1955, Iran entered the Baghdad Pact with Britain, Iraq, Turkey, and Pakistan. In March 1959, Iran signed a bilateral defense agreement with the United States. The Central Files offer insights into the Shah's desire for close relations with the United States—which resulted in these alliances—and into his requests for U.S. military and economic aid. At the same time, he kept his options open with the Soviets, making a state visit to the USSR in 1956. The year 1955 saw the beginning of the seven-year Second Development Plan, and the Central Files cover the plan's organization, its relation to political unrest, rapid inflation, and overall economic development in Iran. Accompanied by a printed reel guide, edited by Gregory Murphy and compiled by Blair Hydrick.

513. United States. Department of State. *Confidential U.S. State Department Central Files. Iran, 1960-January 1963 Internal Affairs, Decimal Number 788, 888, and 988 and Foreign Affairs, Decimal Numbers 688 and 611.88*. MD: University Publications of America, 2002. 16 microfilm reels; 35 mm. For firsthand and in-depth reports and analysis on the many challenges faced by Iran during a trying period, scholars will find this collection a very useful source. Materials included provide insight into complex U.S. relations not only with Iran but with the entire Middle East, as Washington evaluated the area strategically as both an emerging region and a cold war battleground. Among the topics covered in this supplement are: Plight of refugees strains Iranian-Iraqi relations (9/1/60); Kurdish nationalism threatens regional stability (2/6/61); Historical perspective and present situation of Iranian tribes (10/16/62); and Land reform efforts facing stiff opposition (11/24/62). Accompanied by a printed reel guide edited by Robert Lester and compiled by Blair Hydrick.

514. United States. Department of State. *Records of the Department of State Relating to Internal Affairs of Iran, 1930-1939*. Washington, DC: National Archives and Records Service, 1981. 24 microfilm reels; 35 mm. Accompanied by a printed reel guide.

515. United States. Department of State. *Records of the Department of State Relating to Internal Affairs of Persia, 1910-1929.* Washington, DC: National Archives and Records Service, 1968. 37 microfilm reels; 35 mm. Accompanied by a printed reel guide.

IRAQ

516. United States. Department of State. *Confidential U.S. Diplomatic Post Records: Middle East, Iraq. Part I, 1925-1941.* Frederick, MD: University Publications of America, 1984. 24 microfilm reels; 35 mm. This is a collection of papers from American diplomats stationed in Iraq between 1925 and 1941. The papers concern the political, military, social, and economic development of Iraq and its relationship with other countries. The documents provide information on the evolution of United States policy in the area. The collection contains a wide range of material. Among the many important reports are: The Kurdish Situation in Iraq (1928); The Anglo-Iraq Treaty (1930); Union of Syria and Iraq under King Faisal (1931); The General Strike in Iraq (1931); Political Aspects of Anglo-Iraqi Oil Agreements (1932); Revolt of Arab Tribes on the Euphrates in Iraq (1936); Plot of Army Officers and Civilians To Overthrow King Ghazi (1939); Survey of American Interests in Iraq (1942); Anti-British Feeling in the Iraqi Parliament (1942); Iraq's Declaration of War against the Axis Powers (1943); Deterioration of the Iraqi Security Situation (1943); Soviet-Iraqi Relations (1944); and The Shiite Sect and the Position of the Shiites in Iraq (1944). Accompanied by a printed reel guide, edited by Paul Kesaris and compiled by Robert Lester.

517. United States. Department of State. *Confidential U.S. Diplomatic Post Records: Middle East, Iraq. Part II, 1942-1944.* Frederick, MD: University Publications of America, 1984. 9 microfilm reels; 35 mm. For complete abstract, see previous record.

518. United States. Department of State. *Confidential U.S. State Department Central Files. Internal Affairs, Decimal Number 890G and Foreign Affairs, Decimal Number 711.90G / Iraq, 1945-1949.* Frederick, MD: University Publications of America, 1987. 10 microfilm reels; 35 mm. The documents included in this collection illuminate Iraq's political situation and political affairs and race relations with the Kurds, the Iraqi press, and the Anglo-Iranian Oil Company. Also included are documents dealing with narcotics traffic, social manners and customs, judiciary and laws, military, finance, agriculture, natural resources, industry communications, and foreign relations with the U.S. and other countries. Accompanied by a printed reel guide, edited by Gregory Murphy and compiled by Blair D. Hydrick.

519. United States. Department of State. *Confidential U.S. State Department Central Files. Iraq, 1950-1954 Internal Affairs, Decimal Numbers 787, 887, and 987 and Foreign Affairs, Decimal Numbers, 687 and 611.87.* Frederick, MD: University Publications of America, 1987. 18 microfilm reels; 35 mm. For complete abstract, see previous record.

520. United States. Department of State. *Confidential U.S. State Department Central Files. Internal Affairs, Decimal Numbers 787, 887, and 987, and Foreign Affairs, Decimal Numbers 687 and 611.87. Iraq, 1955-1959.* 18 microfilm reels; 35 mm. Bethesda, MD: University Publications of America, 1991. The documents reproduced in this publication are among the records of the U.S. Department of State in the custody of the National Archives and Records Administration. The documents included in this collection illuminate the path to the Iraqi revolution and its aftermath as perceived by the U.S. State Department. They trace both the old and new regimes' relations with the Kurds, the Iraqi press, and the Anglo-Iranian Oil Company and follow the influence of pan-Arabist and communist elements in the population. Also included are documents dealing with narcotics traffic, social manners and customs, the judiciary and laws, the military, finance, agriculture, natural resources, industry, communications, and foreign relations with its neighbors, the United States, and other countries. For an understanding of how Iraq emerged as a military state in the second half of the 20th century, these records are invaluable. Accompanied by a printed reel guide, edited by Gregory Murphy and compiled by Blair D. Hydrick.

521. United States. Department of State. *Confidential U.S. State Department Central Files: Iraq, 1960-January 1963 Internal Affairs Decimal Numbers 787, 887, and 997 and Foreign Affairs Decimal Numbers 687 and 611.87.* Bethesda, MD: University Publications of America, 1999. 13 microfilm reels; 35 mm. Among the topics covered in this supplement are: Summary of activities of the First and Second Military Courts, including cases arising from Communist excesses following the Shawwaf revolt in Mosul and later in Kirkuk (4/4/60); An inventory of Iraqi Kurdish paramilitary capabilities (4/8/60); The farce of political parties in Iraq continues (5/12/60); Communists decry violence in Iraq's north and call for control (6/14/60); Mulla Mustafa al-Barzani defines Kurdish expectations (3/6/61); Kurds flare up in response to Al-Thawra editorial calling for "fusion" of Iraqi minorities with Arabs (3/15/61); Prime Minister Qasim accuses British and Americans of complicity in Kurdish revolt, exonerates the USSR, and dissolves the Kurdish Democratic Party (9/27/61); Echoes of the Kurdish revolt in Basra (4/9/62); French comments on the Kurdish rebellion in Iraq (8/16/62); Chronology of Iraq accusation of American backing of Kurdish revolt (8/31/62); British position should Kurdish question be brought before the UN (10/18/62); and Sheikh Ahmad Barzani calls on Kurds to accept amnesty offer (1/22/63). Accompanied by a printed reel guide, edited by Gregory Murphy and compiled by Blair D. Hydrick.

522. United States. Department of State. *Records of the Department of State Relating to Internal Affairs of Iraq, 1930-1944.* Washington, DC: National Archives and Records Service, 1974. 18 microfilm reels; 35 mm. Accompanied by a printed reel guide.

523. United States. Department of State. Office of International Information Programs.

Iraq: From Fear to Freedom. Washington, DC: U.S. Department of State, International Information Programs, 2002. Deals with Saddam Hussein since he took power in 1979, use of chemical weapons against the Kurdish village of Halabja, weapons of mass destruction, human rights violations, terrorism, corruption, and war, 1991 defeat and defiance of international sanctions and weapons inspection, and prospects for peace. Available online: usinfo.state.gov/products/pubs/iraq/ iraq.pdf.

TURKEY

524. United States. Department of State. *Records of the Department of State Relating to Internal Affairs of Turkey, 1910-29.* Washington, DC: National Archives and Records Service, 1961. 88 microfilm reels. The documents are arranged by subject according to the Department of State's decimal classification system. Documents that relate to World War I activities in Turkey dominate this Department of State decimal file. Included are correspondence, memoranda, and other documents which discuss the United States Peace Mission of 1919, conditions in Baghdad, Smyrna, and Damascus, the Lausanne Conference, the expulsion and persecution of Armenians in Turkey, and opposition to the Zionist movement. Reproduced are Turkish High Command weekly reports of war operations as well as war diaries of United States naval commanding officers. Non-war related documents are concerned with public health, concessions to United States corporations, emigration, disasters, religion, and archaeological expeditions in Asia Minor. A complete list of the documents in the collection is on reels 1-3.

525. United States. Department of State. *Records of the Department of State Relating to Internal Affairs of Turkey, 1930-1944.* 36 reels. Accompanied by a printed reel guide.

526. United States. Department of State. *Records of the Department of State Relating to Internal Affairs of Turkey, 1945-1949.* 20 reels. Accompanied by a printed reel guide.

527. United States. Department of State. *Records of the Department of State Relating to Political Relations Between the United States and Turkey, 1910-1929*. Washington, DC: National Archives and Records Service, 1961. 8 microfilm reels. The documents are arranged by subject in accordance with the Department of State's decimal classification system. The papers in this decimal file chronicle the negotiations for peace following World War I between consular and diplomatic representatives of the United States and Turkey. The majority of the documents concern the Lausanne Conference which led to the treaty ending the war between the United States and Turkey. The documents reflect the lengthy negotiations over the agenda, the treaty, and its aftermath. Modification of the terms of surrender figures prominently in the negotiations. Other agreements documented are the Treaty for the Renunciation of War (Kellogg-Briand Pact) and treaties on shipping, naturalization, extraterritoriality, and arbitration. Correspondence expressing the desire to regularize relations and resume commerce are balanced by protests against the Lausanne Treaty and the Treaty of Commerce. A list of all documents is on the first reel.

AUTHOR INDEX

TITLE INDEX

SUBJECT INDEX

CONTRIBUTORS

Michael M. Gunter is Professor in the Department of Political Science at Tennessee Technological University. He is the author of several articles and books on the Kurds, most recently, (with Mohammed M.A. Ahmed) *The Kurdish Question and International Law: An Analysis of the Legal Rights of the Kurdish People* (2000) and *The Kurdish Predicament in Iraq: A Political Analysis* (1999). His numerous articles on the Kurds appeared in such journals as *The International Journal of Kurdish Studies, The Middle East Journal, Orient*, and *Third World Quarterly*.

Lokman I. Meho is Assistant Professor, School of Information Science and Policy at University at Albany, State University of New York. He is the author of several articles and books on the Kurds and in the field of Library and Information Science, including: *Kurdish Culture and Society: An Annotated Bibliography* (2001) and *The Kurds and Kurdistan: A Selective and Annotated Bibliography* (1997). His articles appeared in such journals as *The Journal of the American Society for Information Science and Technology, Library and Information Science Research*, and *The American Archivist*.

Michel G. Nehme is Professor and Dean of the Faculty of Political Science, Public Administration and Diplomacy at Notre Dame University - Zouk Mikael, Lebanon. He is the author of several articles and books on the Kurds and the Middle East, including *Fear and Anxiety in the Arab World* (2003). His articles on the Kurds appeared in such journals as *Ethnic Forum, The Journal of Social, Political and Economic Studies,* and *Nationalism & Ethnic Politics*.